# THE FIRST AMENDMENT

## AND

# THE FOURTH ESTATE

———

## THE LAW OF MASS MEDIA

By

### T. BARTON CARTER
Associate Professor of Mass Communication
College of Communication
Boston University

### MARC A. FRANKLIN
Frederick I. Richman Professor of Law
Stanford University

### JAY B. WRIGHT
Professor of Journalism
S.I. Newhouse School of Public Communications
Syracuse University

## SIXTH EDITION

Westbury, New York
THE FOUNDATION PRESS, INC.
1994

615 Merrick Ave.
Westbury, N.Y. 11590–6607
(516) 832–6950

**Library of Congress Cataloging-in-Publication Data**

Carter, T. Barton.

   The First Amendment and the fourth estate : the law of mass media
/ by T. Barton Carter, Marc A. Franklin, Jay B. Wright. — 6th ed.

      p.    cm.

   Includes index.

   **ISBN** 1–56662–147–X

   1. Mass media—Law and legislation—United States—Cases.
2. Press law—United States—Cases.  3. Journalists—Legal status,
laws, etc.—United States—Cases.  I. Franklin, Marc A.
II. Wright, Jay B.  III. Title.

KF2750.A7F73  1994
343.7309'9—dc20
[347.30399]                        94–135

*For Richard, Ruth and Yolanda*

\*

* * *

Burke said that there were Three Estates in Parliament; but, in the Reporters' Gallery yonder, there sat a *Fourth Estate* more important far than they all. It is not a figure of speech, or witty saying; it is a literal fact,—very momentous to us in these times.

THOMAS CARLYLE in
On Heroes and Hero–Worship (1841)
(Marble edition, 1897, p. 219)

* * *

*

# PREFACE TO THE SIXTH EDITION

This Sixth Edition of *The First Amendment and the Fourth Estate: The Law of Mass Media* reflects its authors' belief that communications students are quite capable of reading Supreme Court opinions and that doing so is essential to understanding the thought processes of the justices who are making First Amendment law.

Throughout the book, the reader will find more than 30 principal cases, the decisions which help define communications law as we know it today. In between, there are references to hundreds more cases and statutes about which we think any informed professional should know something.

Since the last edition three years ago, communications law has continued its rapid change and development. Among the new principal cases in the book are *Masson v. New Yorker Magazine, Inc., U. S. v. Edge Broadcasting, Cohen v. Cowles Media, and Cincinnati v. Discovery Network, Inc.* Also new in this edition are the 1992 Cable Act, including *Turner Broadcasting System v. F.C.C.*, the FCC's Children's Television Programming policies, and expanded materials on media liability for emotional harm as well as for physical harm.

We have used earlier editions of the book in teaching both undergraduate and graduate students and have tried to incorporate what we have learned from that experience, but we welcome, of course, comments about ways of using the book or improving it.

Communications law poses some difficult dilemmas as the courts try to balance the rights of the media against the rights of those affected by the media. We hope to have captured some of the interest and excitement inherent in the courts' attempts to deal with these challenging problems.

T. BARTON CARTER
MARC A. FRANKLIN
JAY B. WRIGHT

January, 1994

*

# ACKNOWLEDGMENTS

Thanks are due the authors and copyright holders who permitted excerpts from the following works to be included in this book:

American Law Institute. Restatement (Second) of Torts, copyright 1977 by the American Law Institute; reprinted with the permission of the American Law Institute;

Blasi, Vince, "The Newsman's Privilege: An Empirical Study," Michigan Law Review, Vol. 70 (1971);

Godofsky, Stanley, "Protection of the Press from Prior Restraint and Harassment Under Libel Laws," University of Miami Law Review, Vol. 29 (1975);

Henkin, Louis, "The Right to Know and the Duty to Withhold: The Case of the Pentagon Papers," University of Pennsylvania Law Review, Vol. 120 (1971). Reprinted by permission of the publisher and Fred B. Rothman & Company;

Owen, B.M., Beebe, J.H., and Manning, W.G., Jr., Television Economics, Lexington, Mass.: Lexington Books, D.C. Heath and Company, 1974. Reprinted by permission of the publisher;

Paul, Dan, "Why a Shield Law?", University of Miami Law Review, Vol. 29 (1975).

*

# SUMMARY OF CONTENTS

*

# TABLE OF CONTENTS

## TABLE OF CONTENTS

# APPENDICES

# TABLE OF CASES

Principal cases are in italic type. Non-principal cases are in roman type.
References are to Pages.

## TABLE OF CASES

# THE FIRST AMENDMENT

## AND

# THE FOURTH ESTATE

---

## THE LAW OF MASS MEDIA

*

# Chapter I

# INTRODUCTION: THE AMERICAN LEGAL SYSTEM

For most communications students, the study of the law of freedom of expression is just one part of a full professional curriculum. Although some students in communications schools and departments may decide to go on to law school and then to practice law, the vast majority will be users or consumers of law. It is primarily for the latter that this book is intended. An intelligent professional in any aspect of communications should know enough about the law to make some on-the-spot judgments (sometimes under deadline pressure), should know enough to alert a superior when a potential legal problem is spotted, and should know—particularly after reaching management level—when to seek the advice of an attorney. With some experience, the consumer of legal advice learns how to take the attorney's advice. Some attorneys are much more cautious than others, and they will tend to give advice discouraging journalists who are clients from broadcasting or publishing materials that might lead to a law suit. Some will make constructive suggestions about editorial changes that, without diminishing the news value of a story, will minimize the likelihood of a suit. Other attorneys, particularly those who represent major media, may be much more daring and may say to a media client, "Publish or broadcast what you need to as journalists. If there's a suit, we'll worry about that then."

Newcomers are sometimes surprised to discover how uncertain the law seems to be. Many questions have never been anticipated by legislators nor been answered by the courts. Sometimes in two similar cases in different parts of the country, different courts have reached opposite conclusions. Bright attorneys disagree when they predict the outcomes of cases. Judges—even the nine justices of the Supreme Court of the United States—frequently disagree with one another and arrive at split decisions based on 5–4 or 6–3 votes. Newcomers to the law may be surprised to find, after they have read the opinion of the majority of the court and agreed with it, that they think they also agree with points made in the dissenting opinion. It should not be quite so surprising that frequently there are good arguments on *both* sides of a dispute that has reached the Supreme Court.

Textbooks like this one give heavy emphasis to opinions of the Supreme Court, because those opinions influence the application of the law in the courts below and they influence out-of-court decisions made on a much less formal basis. It should be recognized, however, that a case that reaches the Supreme Court is an unusual case rather than a typical one. If, for example, we were to examine 1,000 instances in which the media had published or broadcast something erroneous about

1

individuals, we would probably find that most of the resulting "disputes" were resolved by the media's retracting the erroneous statements or by the unhappy individuals' being advised that they did not have a libel case because they really had suffered no reputational harm as a result of the error, or by the individuals' deciding that they did not have the time, inclination or money to file a lawsuit. Even if 100 of those disputes resulted in lawsuits, the odds would still favor an out-of-court settlement or a decision by a trial court without getting into the appellate courts. If a single one of those 100 lawsuits reached the Supreme Court it would be surprising.

If Supreme Court cases are so rare, one might ask, why not study the "ordinary" cases instead? The most important answer is that the principles enunciated in the Supreme Court cases become binding on the courts below. Although there is no such thing as a perfect predictor, they can help good lawyers evaluate the chances of their clients' winning suits. The expectation of winning is one of the things that goes into a decision about whether to settle a case out of court or pursue it through a trial and appeals. A more detailed explanation of other factors which may enter into such a decision appears in Chapter III.

In this chapter we look not just at Supreme Court cases but at a variety of sources of law in America and at the way legal cases proceed.

## A. THE SOURCES OF LAW IN AMERICA

Law has always been an important force in American life—and courts have always been at the center of our legal system. All state constitutions created state court systems. The United States Constitution established the Supreme Court of the United States and empowered Congress to create lower federal courts. Many critical national questions have been addressed and resolved in court, from sedition questions after the Revolutionary War to the treatment of blacks after the Civil War, from school desegregation beginning in the 1950s to questions of Presidential behavior in office in the 1970s. Hindsight shows that not all judicial decisions over 200 years have been correct, nor have they all been popular. But the overall respect Americans have for the legal system, even when they may disagree with particular decisions or dislike particular judges, has allowed the country to solve most major problems without violent upheavals.

In general terms, the law is a system of rules of conduct that individuals and institutions are expected to follow, rules given force by a community's decision to punish those who violate them. In the United States, laws and sanctions for disobeying them come from four major sources: constitutions, statutes, administrative decisions and the judge-made law called the common law.

*Constitutions.* Although much of our legal system was borrowed from Great Britain, that country has no written constitution. This important form of law was developed in the United States. Not only is there a federal constitution, but each state has one. These documents decree governmental organization, describe the duties and responsibilities of governmental branches and officials and frequently specify certain individual rights, such as freedom of expression.

Constitutions are written to allow flexibility as social conditions change. As new questions arise courts must interpret whether the document permits or requires certain conduct. For instance, the First Amendment to the United States Constitution reads in part: "Congress shall make no law   . . .   abridging the freedom of speech, or of the press . . .." As simple as this seems, our study of mass media law will show the complexity of these words.

Note that the United States Constitution is reprinted in its entirety in Appendix A.

*Statutes.* Another source of law is the array of statutes passed by Congress and state legislatures. The law we inherited from Great Britain generally served as basic authority in the early days of the United States. After that, statutes adopted by legislative bodies began to be more important than the judicially-developed law. Today, statutes are the dominant form of lawmaking. Much judicial time is spent interpreting these laws and deciding how they apply to specific situations. Statutes are general in scope and prospective in operation.

Today all criminal laws in this country are statutory. Crimes must be described carefully so that people know precisely what is forbidden. Case law would rarely provide sufficient guidance. Obscenity is an example of an area of mass communications law where the precise wording of statutes is critical.

*Administrative Regulations and Decisions.* Today much law comes from decisions of administrative agencies. These were first developed by Congress as a way of bringing expertise to bear on areas under the legislature's responsibility. The first administrative agency was the Interstate Commerce Commission; today such agencies are numerous. The Federal Communications Commission and the Federal Trade Commission, both of which affect mass communications law, are just two of the federal agencies. Administrative agencies also exist on the state and city levels. Much more law is created by these agencies through their delegated lawmaking powers than by all the courts in the country.

*Common Law.* The term "common law" is sometimes used to distinguish the Anglo–American legal system from the "civil law" systems of continental Europe. More commonly, the term refers to those areas of law in which no statutes exist and, thus, in which courts are expected to chart their own decisional course without legislative direction. The product of this process, law based on cases alone, is called common law. It is the ever-growing result of specific but principled decisions in individual disputes rather than a written body of prospective general rules set down by a legislature.

The common law came from England, where the term first was used to distinguish law made by the King's courts from that made by ecclesiastical courts. But if the law were made by courts, not following a written statute, could not each court—each judge—decide similar cases in different ways? Not only would this cause consternation among citizens who would not know how to act, but judges might totally reconsider whole areas of law as each case arose. The concept of *stare decisis* emerged from these concerns. This is the doctrine of precedent under which judges refer to previous decisions involving basically similar legal issues and facts in order to decide the case at hand. It is then possible to look at previous cases and decisions to see how a court is likely to decide future cases. However, courts are not strictly bound by *stare decisis*. They can "distinguish" a current case from previous cases and refuse to follow the guidance of the past if they find the facts sufficiently different. Or, in an unusual situation, a court can overrule precedents and explicitly embark on a new approach to the legal area. In general, though, judges work within the boundaries of *stare decisis*.

Although the common law was dominant at the time of the Revolution, the increasing complexity of our society and other factors have brought legislation in almost all areas—and a consequent reduction in the role of the common law. It still retains importance for us, however, in the areas of defamation and privacy.

*Hierarchy.* There is a hierarchy among these four sources of law. Within a state the state constitution is dominant. If a question is not answered in the constitution, an appropriate statute, as interpreted by the courts, will be the final word. But a statute in conflict with the constitution will be struck down by the courts.

Within the spheres of their statutory authority, administrative agency rulings have the force of a statute and will be upheld by courts unless the ruling violates the constitution, the agency has violated its own rules in making the decision, or the ruling is arbitrary and capricious.

When no constitution, statute, or administrative agency ruling controls, courts will apply common law principles to decide a dispute.

*Federalism.* The hierarchy just discussed applies within a single state. But the federal structure of the United States creates a second hierarchy of legal sources that must be explored. When the United States Constitution was written, most space was devoted to creating the three branches of government—Legislature in Article I, Executive in Article II and Judiciary in Article III. Those articles dealt only with how the federal government should conduct its internal affairs. In this respect, the federal government's structure resembled that of a state government.

But the nature of federalism required that some attention be paid to the relationship between the existing state governments and the new federal government. This was addressed in Article VI, Section 2, the Supremacy Clause, which provides that

This Constitution, and the Laws of the United States which shall be made in pursuance thereof . . . shall be the supreme Law of the Land; and the Judges in every State shall be bound thereby, any Thing in the Constitution or Laws of any State to the Contrary notwithstanding.

In cases of conflict, then, the Constitution of the United States and statutes properly passed by Congress (and rulings of federal administrative agencies) are superior to conflicting laws adopted by a state. Thus, a ruling of the Federal Communications Commission has a higher place in our legal hierarchy than a conflicting provision of a state constitution.

This aspect of federalism becomes very important because many of our cases involve claims that state laws are invalid because they conflict with some federally protected right. Notice also that state court judges are obligated to declare state laws invalid if they conflict with federal provisions.

Finally, notice how important the courts are at every stage of the legal system. Although courts act only to resolve specific disputes that the parties cannot settle, the judicial power permeates every layer of the two hierarchies. When a constitutional provision is relied upon by one of the parties to the dispute, the court must interpret its meaning and its application to the dispute before it. When one party relies upon a statute, the court may have to interpret it—and may also have to decide whether it is constitutional. When an administrative ruling is involved in the dispute, the court must decide whether the agency acted constitutionally, acted within its statutory authority, followed its own rules and acted without being arbitrary or capricious. When none of these sources appears to have a bearing on the litigation, the court turns to common-law decisionmaking.

When federalism is involved, state and federal courts are obligated to assure that in cases of conflict proper scope is given to the federal provisions in resolving the case before them.

### An Introduction to Litigation

The judicial system must deal with several kinds of controversies. What they all have in common is that one party (a person, group or government) claims its rights or, in the case of government, its laws, are being violated by a second party. The controversies we consider in this book have arisen in various contexts.

One is the criminal case in which a government seeks to punish a party, perhaps a reporter, for illegal behavior. The defense may claim that the legal rule allegedly violated is invalid because it conflicts with the First Amendment. The court must decide whether the statute in question is constitutional.

The second form of litigation also arises from the passage of a statute. Here, however, those restricted by the statute do not wait to be prosecuted for a violation of the statute, but instead initiate a suit to have the statute or regulation declared unconstitutional. The court is asked to render a "declaratory judgment" that it would be unconstitutional for the government to enforce the statute against the complaining parties. Another way to test a statute's constitutionality without risking criminal prosecution is to seek an injunction to prohibit state officials from enforcing the statute—again on the ground that to do so would violate the constitutional rights of the plaintiff. Injunctions are court orders not to do something. Violations of injunctions can lead to one's being held in contempt of court.

The third type of case involves "tort" litigation between two private parties for harm that one has caused the other. Examples include auto accidents and injuries caused by defective products. A tort action is usually brought for damages for alleged violation of a common-law duty. We shall be concerned mainly with tort actions for damages for defamation and for invasion of privacy. In these cases it is possible for the defendant to argue that if the state court finds the defendant liable and orders it to pay damages to plaintiff, the action of the court would be "state action" that would infringe the defendant's constitutional right to freedom of expression.

A variety of issues arise in tort litigation. In some instances, the law imposes *strict liability* on people or businesses: regardless of the reason they harmed someone, they are responsible for the harm. In other instances, the party suing must prove that the harm resulted from the defendant's *negligence*. Sometimes an allegation is made that the defendant failed to fulfill some legal obligation to the plaintiff—a *duty*. Sometimes issues arise as to whether the defendant's actions actually *caused* the harm; there may have been a sequence of multiple events culminating in the harm.

Still other suits are based on *contract* law rather than *tort* law. One party typically alleges that another party *breached* the contract—or failed to live up to the terms of the agreement the two parties had made. Such a case arose, for example, out of the decision by two newspapers to identify publicly a man who thought he had received a promise of anonymity by the newspapers' reporters. In still other cases, people sometimes sue because material they have protected by *copyright* is used without their permission. Examples of these various kinds of cases should make them more understandable as we encounter them in various chapters of the book.

We will encounter another type of legal conflict, the administrative proceeding, when we discuss advertising and broadcasting. A party who wishes to acquire a license to broadcast, for example, must apply to the Federal Communications Commission.

The courtroom drama that comes to mind in terms of litigation actually occurs primarily in criminal cases, where facts are disputed: can the victim accurately identify the defendant or is the jury persuaded by the defendant's alibi witnesses? In conventional criminal cases, the parties agree on the legal rules but they disagree about the facts—and a trial is needed to determine the facts governed by these rules.

In most of the cases in this book, and most First Amendment cases generally, the crucial questions that will determine the outcome do not depend on disputed facts. Rather, the parties usually disagree over what legal rule applies to an accepted set of facts. Such a dispute raises legal questions to be resolved by a judge, often with no need for a trial.

The dispute will be brought in one of two court systems—state or federal. Before the United States Constitution was adopted, each state had its own court system—with trial and appellate courts. These systems survived. As a result of the adoption of the United States Constitution, and early action of Congress, a second court system—the federal system—was created.

When one party sues another party in the same state, under state libel law for example, the trial will take place in a state court. When the parties are individuals or corporations in different states, questions beyond our present concerns arise about whether the litigation will take place in a state or federal court. Regardless, the trial will provide the opportunity for the presentation of evidence, including testimony by witnesses. Usually a jury will hear the case, but in some instances the trial judge will decide the case alone.

At the conclusion of the trial, either or both of the parties may believe that errors were made in the trial—either errors in procedure or errors in substantive law. If they choose to appeal to a higher (appellate) court, they will submit a transcript of the trial proceedings and a *brief*, a document explaining the alleged errors to the appellate court. Depending on the system, the appellate court may or may not have to take the case for review; although one is entitled to one's "day in court," one is not necessarily entitled to a "second day."

Depending on the size of the state and the complexity of the state system, state verdicts might be appealed to one or more levels of appellate courts before reaching the highest court in the state—typically, but not always, called the supreme court. In the federal system, decisions from the trial court, called the U.S. District Court, are appealed to the U.S. Court of Appeals and then to the Supreme Court of the United States.

The Supreme Court performs two distinct roles. As the final appellate court for litigants who have lost cases in lower federal courts, it is at the apex of the federal system of courts. Second, states and state courts have obligations imposed upon them by the United States Constitution. Some are explicit prohibitions, such as those in Article I, Section 10, that no state may adopt an *ex post facto* law or coin its own currency. Other limitations are imposed by the Supremacy Clause of Article VI, Section 2, which declares that when federal and state law conflict, the federal law is supreme—and the judges of the state courts are required to recognize that supremacy. The Supreme Court of the United States has the power to review the actions of state courts to assure that states are complying with federal obligations.

Many of the cases we consider have come to the Supreme Court from the state courts. The losing party has usually claimed that the decision of the state courts has incorrectly interpreted the First Amendment—which applies to the states because of the Fourteenth Amendment. Although state courts may render decisions interpreting the First and Fourteenth Amendments, the Supreme Court is the *final* authority on the meaning of the United States Constitution.

In the first part of this book, our primary concern is with the First Amendment. If a case poses an important question involving the First Amendment or some other part of the United States Constitution, it can wind up in the Supreme Court whether it starts in the state courts or in the federal courts. Because broadcasting is totally the concern of federal law, the second part of the book stresses federal courts and a federal administrative agency, the Federal Communications Commission.

In most instances the Supreme Court has been given discretion by Congress to choose what cases it will hear, and of the many thousands of cases that are brought each year, the Court accepts only some 200 for hearing and decision. To seek review by the Supreme Court the litigant who lost the case in the lower court files what is called a petition for *certiorari* stating the nature of the dispute, the decision below and the reasons why the Court should review this case. Because a case usually reaches the Supreme Court only after several lower courts, state or federal, have considered it, it rarely suffices for the petitioner to allege that the judges below made a mistake—a better reason is necessary. A serious claim that a state law violates the First Amendment is such a reason.

After the petition for *certiorari* is filed, the party who won below will usually file a memorandum trying to persuade the Court that the case is not important, that there is no conflict with other decisions or that the decision is clearly correct in light of previous Supreme Court cases. In deciding whether or not to grant a petition for *certiorari*, all the justices will meet in conference and vote. The Court follows the so-called "rule of four" under which, if four justices believe the case should be heard, the petition for *certiorari* will be granted.

If the Supreme Court decides not to hear the case, it will usually not state its reasons and will issue an order that says simply "The petition for *certiorari* is denied." In this book that procedure is indicated when "certiorari denied" is part of the citation by which a case is identified. Although this outcome favors the party that won in the lower court, the legal effect is different from having the Supreme Court listen to the case on the merits and decide to affirm the decision of the lower court. When the Supreme Court denies *certiorari*, all that is clear is that the Court did not think the case worthy of full consideration. This does not mean that the Court believes that the case was correctly decided below. It may mean only that the Court does not think the issue is important enough to justify further attention. The denial of *certiorari* sets no precedent; the effect is the same as if the question had never been raised.

When the Supreme Court decides it will listen to a case, it will generally issue an order "granting" the petition for *certiorari* and directing the parties to file formal briefs arguing the merits of the controversy. The losing party below, the petitioner, prepares a brief, trying to persuade the Court to decide the case on the merits in petitioner's favor. The respondent's brief seeks to persuade the Court to affirm the result reached by the lower court.

The Court will schedule oral arguments at which the attorneys representing both parties have a limited period of time before the justices of the Court to make the best arguments they can for their clients and to answer questions posed by the justices. Because new evidence is not presented at the appellate level, and witnesses are not heard, the parties to the case need not even be present. In a sense, the discussion is about whether errors have been made in the trial court below, and it is not necessary to hear from the witnesses. The witnesses' testimony and other evidence is already reflected in the transcripts of the case filed with the Court, so the oral argument should, as the name suggests, focus on the attempts to persuade the justices as to the outcome of the case.

Following the oral arguments in the case, the justices meet privately to discuss the case and to indicate how they expect to vote. In the Supreme Court, if the Chief Justice is a member of the majority, he may assign the writing of the majority opinion to himself or to any of the other justices in the majority. Similarly, the senior justice among the dissenters may assign the dissenting opinion. When the Chief Justice is dissenting, the senior justice among the majority assigns the majority opinion. Drafts of opinions, written by the justices and their clerks, are circulated privately among the justices. Agreement is reached where possible, but each of the justices reserves the right to publish his own opinion if he chooses. In the "Pentagon Papers" case, p. 336, *infra*, to use a most unusual example, all nine justices wrote opinions.

A single opinion that has the support of a *majority* of the participating justices is denominated an "opinion of the Court." As such it becomes binding on the Court, establishing a precedent for subsequent decisions (unless later overruled by the Court itself). In other cases there is a *plurality* opinion to which several (fewer than five) justices agree. For example, six of the nine justices might vote to affirm a lower court decision, but four may do so for one reason and two may do so for a different reason. Or, there could be several individual opinions, so long as at least five justices agreed to the result in the case. A plurality opinion is entitled to substantially less precedential value than an opinion of the Court. The first line of the reported decision will indicate the nature of the opinion—a named justice either delivers the "opinion of the Court" or announces "the judgment of the Court and an opinion joined by" up to three other justices.  The "judgment of the Court" means the bare result, such as affirmance or reversal.  The reasons for the judgment are found in the opinions.  Occasionally the opinion of the Court may be unsigned—a *per curiam* opinion.

## B.  READING THE LAW

Supreme Court decisions are not, obviously, written for readers who are totally unfamiliar with legal language.  Typically, they refer to, or *cite,* earlier cases which you may or may not have read.  Not surprisingly, some of the justices are better writers than others.  The meaning of some paragraphs is perfectly clear, but some confuse even the best of lawyers and require subsequent cases to resolve the confusion.  Although reading Supreme Court decisions may seem difficult at first, it usually becomes easier as you become more familiar with the language and gradually develop some background in reading the law.

As you read the cases, note the names.  When the losing party in the lower court files a petition for *certiorari*, the petitioner's name comes first in the title of the case.  The initial plaintiff thus may later become the *respondent* and be listed second in the title in the Supreme Court.  A few other appellate courts follow the practice of putting the losing party's name first.  As you read the appellate cases in this book, do not assume that the party named first in the title was the original plaintiff.

On a related point, every title of a case is followed by a group of numbers and abbreviations called a "citation."  This tells which volumes in the law library contain the full report of the opinions in the case.  For example, the citation to Branzburg v. Hayes, 408 U.S. 665, 92 S.Ct. 2646, 33 L.Ed.2d 626, 1 Med.L.Rptr. 2617 (1972), means that the case can be found in volume 408 of the *United States Reports* (the official volumes printed by the federal government) at page 665, and similarly in volume 92 of *Supreme Court Reporter* (a series of volumes published by West Publishing Company) at page 2646, and in volume 33 of the *Lawyer's Edition, Second Series* (the second series of a set of volumes published by The Lawyers Cooperative), at page 626, and in volume 1 of *Media Law Reporter* (published by the Bureau of National Affairs, Inc., and including—as the name indicates—just media cases) at page 2617.

Current decisions of the United States Court of Appeals are found in the Federal Reporter Second Series (F.2d).  Decisions of the United States District Courts are found in the Federal Supplement (F.Supp.).  State decisions usually have two citations: one to a state reporter and one to a private service that groups state decisions in regional volumes.  Thus, in Barber v. Time, Inc., 348 Mo. 1199, 159 S.W.2d 291 (1942), the first reference is to volume 348 of the official Missouri reports at page 1199, and the second is to volume 159 of the Southwestern Reporter, Second Series, at page 291, where the Missouri case will also be found.

There are certain reporting services of special importance to electronic media regulation.  The FCC's official reports through 1986, the

*FCC Reports,* are referred to by volume number, F.C.C. or F.C.C.2d, followed by page number. Beginning with materials from October 1986, the Commission's official record, including decisions, reports, public notices and other documents, is the *FCC Record.* It is cited by volume number, F.C.C.Rcd., and the page number. When the Commission proposes rules for possible adoption, formal notice of the pending action must be given to the public. This is done through the *Federal Register* (Fed.Reg. or F.R.). The *Register* is organized chronologically and covers all federal agencies and departments. Regulations adopted by the Commission as well as its rules of organization and internal operation are reported and grouped together in another official publication called the *Code of Federal Regulations* (C.F.R.). An unofficial service reports Commission rulemaking actions and case decisions as well as court decisions relating to electronic media. The full name of this service, *Pike & Fischer's Radio Regulation,* is abbreviated as R.R. or R.R.2d, and sometimes as P & F Radio Reg. Note that the name *Radio Regulation* is deceptive: the service covers television, cable, other electronic media, telephone companies and other common carriers.

In addition to the references to reports of judicial opinions, you will note references to the *U.S. Code Annotated* (U.S.C.A.), which contains federal statutes, and to the *Code of Federal Regulations* (C.F.R.), which contains rules and regulations of federal administrative agencies.

The *U.S. Code Annotated* is, as the name suggests, a version of the *U.S. Code* (U.S.C.) that includes explanatory notes with the statutes. Other annotated publications can also be helpful. The *United States Supreme Court Reports, Lawyers' Edition,* for example, includes annotation with the opinions of the Supreme Court.

The foregoing discussion of litigation and the role of the Supreme Court, vital to an understanding of what follows, has necessarily been general and abstract. As we turn to actual cases you should review this information if some aspect of a case puzzles you. Any unusual matters will be discussed in the introduction to the case or in the notes that follow the opinions.

Some of the terms used in the text, particularly the Latin ones, may be unfamiliar to you at first. The glossary at the back of this text should help you understand new terms. As you see them used in the cases, they will become part of your legal vocabulary.

The following version of a famous case, *New York Times v. Sullivan,* is greatly abbreviated for illustration purposes here, but reading it now—along with the annotation—may help you to become familiar with legal conventions you will encounter as you read the text. A more complete version of the same opinion appears in Chapter III.

The centered heading in all capital letters indicates the name of a principal case. What you read below, unless other-

NEW YORK TIMES CO. v. SULLIVAN

wise noted, is the opinion of the court.

The original name of the case was Sullivan v. New York Times, because Sullivan was the plaintiff. In the Supreme Court and some other courts, the party that appeals the decision—in this case the *New York Times*—is listed first at the appellate level.

Note that you could have found this heading by going to the Table of Cases in the front of the book, finding the case name, and then finding the one page number that appears in italics.

Sullivan sued the Rev. Ralph David Abernathy and other black clergymen in addition to suing the *Times*. This opinion covered Rev. Abernathy's case as well as that of the *Times*.

(Together with Abernathy v. Sullivan)

Note that the correct name of the court here is Supreme Court of the United States and *not* (common practice and the Associated Press Stylebook notwithstanding) the "U.S. Supreme Court."

Supreme Court of the United States, 1964. 376 U.S. 254, 84 S.Ct. 710, 11 L.Ed.2d 686, 1 Med.L.Rptr. 1527.

See discussion at p. 10, *supra,* for explanation of citations.

The square bracket at the start of this paragraph indicates that you are reading here the words of the textbook authors—not those of the court. Sometimes it is because you are being given more background than the Court provided;

[This action was based on a full-page advertisement in *The New York Times* on behalf of several individuals and groups protesting a "wave of terror" against blacks involved in non-violent demonstrations in the South. Plaintiff, one of three elected commissioners of Montgomery, the capital of Alabama, was in charge of the police department. When he demanded a retraction, as state law required, *The Times* instead responded that it failed to sometimes it is because the authors have summarized for you.

The indenting of each line of the next two paragraphs indicates that these are directly quoted from the ad.

The indented three periods (an ellipsis) standing alone signify the omission of one or more whole paragraphs of the ad between the two paragraphs that are quoted.

The Italics used for *felony* and *ten years* were in the original ad; otherwise the notation of "emphasis added" would appear at the end of the passage.

see how he was defamed. He then filed suit against *The Times* and four clergymen whose names appeared as sponsors—although they denied having authorized this—in the ad. Plaintiff alleged that the third and the sixth paragraphs of the advertisement libelled him:

"In Montgomery, Alabama, after students sang 'My Country, 'Tis of Thee' on the State Capitol steps, their leaders were expelled from school, and truckloads of police armed with shotguns and tear-gas ringed the Alabama State College Campus. When the entire student body protested to state authorities by refusing to re-register, their dining hall was padlocked in an attempt to starve them into submission."

. . .

"Again and again the Southern violators have answered Dr. King's peaceful protests with intimidation and violence. They have bombed his home almost killing his wife and child. They have assaulted his person. They have arrested him seven times—for 'speeding,' 'loitering' and similar 'offenses.' And now they have charged him with 'perjury'—a *felony* under which they could imprison him for *ten years*. . . ."

Plaintiff claimed that he was libelled in the third paragraph by the reference to the police, because his responsibilities included supervision of the Montgomery police. He asserted that the paragraph could be read as charging the police with ringing the campus and seeking to starve the students by padlocking the dining hall. As to the sixth paragraph, he contended that the word "they" referred to his department since arrests are usually made by the police and the paragraph could be read as accusing him of committing the acts charged. Several witnesses testified that they read the statements as referring to plaintiff in his capacity as commissioner.

The defendants admitted several inaccuracies in these two paragraphs: the students sang "The Star Spangled Banner", not "My Country, 'Tis of Thee"; nine students were expelled, not for leading the demonstration, but for demanding service at a lunch counter in the county courthouse; the dining hall was never padlocked; police at no time ringed the campus though they were deployed nearby in large numbers; they were not called to the campus in connection with the demonstration; Dr. King had been arrested only four times; and officers disputed his account of the alleged assault. Plaintiff proved that he had not been commissioner when three of the four arrests occurred and that he had nothing to do with procuring the perjury indictment.

The trial judge charged that the statements were libel per se, that the jury should decide whether they were made "of and concerning" the plaintiff, and, if so, general damages were to be presumed. Although noting that punitive damages required more than carelessness, he refused to charge that they required a finding of actual intent to harm or "gross negligence and recklessness." He also refused to order the jury to separate its award of general and punitive damages. The jury returned a verdict for $500,000—the full amount demanded. The Alabama Supreme Court affirmed, holding that malice could be found in several aspects of the *Times'* conduct.]

The ending square bracket signifies the end of the textbook authors' introduction.

MR. JUSTICE BRENNAN delivered the opinion of the Court.

Here you begin reading the actual words of the official court opinion. Mr. Justice Brennan's opinion for the Court is the most important opinion, because it has the force of law.

In this case, the Court was unanimous. More commonly, you will see an opinion for a majority of the Court, as in Gertz v. Robert Welch, Inc., p. 118, *infra,* followed by one or more concurring or dissenting opinions. The opinion of the Court invariably appears first.

Again, the indented ellipsis indicates one or more paragraphs omitted

. . .

here from the official opinion. The actual opinion has 14 paragraphs before the section headed *I.* The most important material from that is what has been included in the paragraphs above inside the square brackets.

The justices commonly divide long opinions into sections identified with Roman numerals.

The square brackets with space between indicate that a citation has been omitted, because the textbook authors thought you would not need it. The words omitted here [first set of brackets] for example, are "See, *e.g.,* Alabama Code, Tit. 7, §§ 908–917." The § symbol signifies a section of a statute, so this is a reference to sections 908 through 917 in Title 7 of the Alabama Code, or set of statutes passed by the Alabama state Legislature.

The words omitted at the second set of brackets happen to be citations to cases: "See *Ex parte Virginia,* 100 U.S. 339, 346–347; *American Federa-*

I.

We may dispose at the outset of two grounds asserted to insulate the judgment of the Alabama courts from constitutional scrutiny. The first is the proposition relied on by the State Supreme Court—that "The Fourteenth Amendment is directed against State action and not private action." That proposition has no application to this case. Although this is a civil lawsuit between private parties, the Alabama courts have applied a state rule of law which petitioners claim to impose invalid restrictions on their constitutional freedoms of speech and press. It matters not that that law has been applied in a civil action and that it is common law only, though supplemented by statute. [  ] The test is not the form in which state power has been applied but, whatever the form, whether such power has in fact been exercised. [  ]

*tion of Labor v. Swing,*
312 U.S. 321."

The brackets around the words "was rejected" indicate that those words are those of the textbook authors. The actual opinion uses several hundred words to explain that the argument was rejected. If you are interested in the explanation, of course, you can refer to the full text of the opinion by using the citations at the beginning of the case.

The second contention is that the constitutional guarantees of freedom of speech and of the press are inapplicable here, at least so far as the Times is concerned, because the allegedly libelous statements were published as part of a paid, "commercial" advertisement. The argument [was rejected.]

## II.

Under Alabama law as applied in this case, a publication is "libelous per se" if the words "tend to injure a person . . . in his reputation" or to "bring [him] into public contempt"; the trial court stated that the standard was met if the words are such as to "injure him in his public office, or impute misconduct to him in his office, or want of official integrity, or want of fidelity to a public trust. . . ." The jury must find that the words were published "of and concerning" the plaintiff, but where the plaintiff is a public official his place in the governmental hierarchy is sufficient evidence to support a finding that his reputation has been affected by statements that reflect upon the agency of which he is in charge. Once "libel per se" has been established, the defendant has no defense as to stated facts unless he can persuade the jury that they were true in all their particulars. [  ] His privilege of "fair comment" for expressions of opinion depends on the truth of the facts upon which the comment is based. [  ] Unless he can discharge the burden of proving truth, general damages are presumed, and may be awarded without proof of pecuniary injury. A showing of actual malice is apparently a prerequisite to recovery of punitive damages, and the defendant may in any event forestall a punitive award by a retraction meeting the statutory requirements. Good motives and belief in truth do not negate an inference of malice, but are relevant only in mitigation of punitive damages if the jury chooses to accord them weight. [ ]

The question before us is whether this rule of liability, as applied to an action brought by a public official against critics of his official conduct, abridges the freedom of speech and of the press that is guaranteed by the First and Fourteenth Amendments.

Respondent relies heavily, as did the Alabama courts, on statements of this Court to the effect that the Constitution does not protect libelous publications. Those statements do not foreclose our inquiry here. None of the cases sustained the use of libel laws to impose sanctions upon expression critical of the official conduct of public officials. . . . In deciding the question now, we are compelled by neither precedent nor policy to give any more weight to the epithet "libel" than we have to other "mere labels" of state law. NAACP v. Button, 371 U.S. 415, 429 (1963). Like insurrection, contempt, advocacy of unlawful acts, breach of the peace, obscenity, solicitation of legal business, and the various other formulae for the repression of expression that have been challenged in this Court, libel can claim no talismanic immunity from constitutional limitations. It must be measured by standards that satisfy the First Amendment.

. . .

. . . Judge Edgerton spoke for a unanimous court which affirmed the dismissal of a Congressman's libel suit based upon a newspaper article charging him with anti-Semitism in opposing a judicial appointment. He said:

. . . "Cases which impose liability for erroneous reports of the political conduct of officials reflect the obsolete doctrine that the governed must not criticize their governors. . . . The interest of the public here outweighs the interest of appellant or any other individual. The protection of the public requires not merely discussion, but information. Political conduct and views which some respectable people approve, and others condemn, are constantly imputed to Congressmen. Er-

*The ellipsis after "public officials" indicates that text material [actually a number of sentences] was omitted within this one paragraph.*

rors of fact, particularly in regard to a man's mental states and processes, are inevitable. . . . Whatever is added to the field of libel is taken from the field of free debate." [13]

Injury to official reputation affords no more warrant for repressing speech that would otherwise be free than does factual error. Where judicial officers are involved, this Court has held that concern for the dignity and reputation of the courts does not justify the punishment as criminal contempt of criticism of the judge or his decision. Bridges v. California, 314 U.S. 252 (1941). This is true even though the utterance contains "half-truths" and "misinformation." Pennekamp v. Florida, 328 U.S. 331, 342, 343, n. 5, 345 (1946). . . . Criticism of their official conduct does not lose its constitutional protection merely because it is effective criticism and hence diminishes their official reputations.

. . .

The state rule of law is not saved by its allowance of the defense of truth. . . .

This paragraph is extremely important, because it introduces the term "actual malice" and defines it. Note that there is normally nothing in the typography to alert you to something of such importance, and you will need to develop the habit of distinguishing between the important and less important material. [You may also want to note here that "actual malice"

The constitutional guarantees require, we think, a federal rule that prohibits a public official from recovering damages for a defamatory falsehood relating to his official conduct unless he proves that the statement was made with "actual malice"—that is, with knowledge that it was false or with reckless disregard of whether it was false or not. An oft-cited statement of a like rule, which has been adopted by a number of state courts, is found in the Kansas case of Coleman v. MacLennan, 78 Kan. 711, 98 P. 281 (1908). . . .

This is correctly numbered as footnote 13. The textbook authors have decided to omit the first 12. Many of the earlier footnotes are citations that support points in the opinion.

13. See also Mill, On Liberty (Oxford: Blackwell, 1947), at 47:

". . . [T]o argue sophistically, to suppress facts or arguments, to misstate the elements of the case, or misrepresent the opposite opinion . . . all this, even to the most aggravated degree, is so continually done in perfect good faith, by persons who are not considered, and in many other respects may not deserve to be considered, ignorant or incompetent, that it is rarely possible, on adequate grounds, conscientiously to stamp the misrepresentation as morally culpable; and still less could law presume to interfere with this kind of controversial misconduct."

is a *term of art;* the Supreme Court's definition is *not* the same as an ordinary dictionary's definition of the term.]

Such a privilege for criticism of official conduct is appropriately analogous to the protection accorded a public official when *he* is sued for libel by a private citizen. In Barr v. Matteo, 360 U.S. 564, 575 (1959), this Court held the utterance of a federal official to be absolutely privileged if made "within the outer perimeter" of his duties. The States accord the same immunity to statements of their highest officers, although some differentiate their lesser officials and qualify the privilege they enjoy. But all hold that all officials are protected unless actual malice can be proved. The reason for the official privilege is said to be that the threat of damage suits would otherwise "inhibit the fearless, vigorous, and effective administration of policies of government" and "dampen the ardor of all but the most resolute, or the most irresponsible, in the unflinching discharge of their duties." Barr v. Matteo, supra, 360 U.S., at 571. Analogous considerations support the privilege for the citizen-critic of government. It is as much his duty to criticize as it is the official's duty to administer. . . .

Remember that the First Amendment forbids abridgments of freedom of the press only by *Congress.* The Fourteenth Amendment extended the protection to forbid abridgments of rights [including freedom of the press] by state governments. Thus here, where a state libel statute is the focus, the First and Fourteenth Amendments are both relevant.

We conclude that such a privilege is required by the First and Fourteenth Amendments.

The words "We hold that" alert you to the fact that you are about to read a statement of the court's *holding* or decision in the case.

## III.

We hold today that the Constitution delimits a State's power to award damages for libel in actions brought by public officials against critics of their official conduct. Since this is such an action, the rule requiring proof of actual malice is applicable. While Alabama law ap-

Any appellate court, including the Supreme Court of the United States, has the role of determining if there have been errors made at the trial court. Here the Supreme Court finds the judge's failure to instruct the jury to differentiate between general and punitive damages to be an error. Some errors are harmless—not having affected the outcome. Others, including this one, are prejudicial, and the error must be corrected.

parently requires proof of actual malice for an award of punitive damages, where general damages are concerned malice is "presumed." Such a presumption is inconsistent with the federal rule. . . . Since the trial judge did not instruct the jury to differentiate between general and punitive damages, it may be that the verdict was wholly an award of one or the other. But it is impossible to know, in view of the general verdict returned. Because of this uncertainty, the judgment must be reversed and the case remanded. [    ]

Since respondent may seek a new trial, we deem that considerations of effective judicial administration require us to review the evidence in the present record to determine whether it could constitutionally support a judgment for respondent. . . .

Applying these standards, we consider that the proof presented to show actual malice, lacks the convincing clarity which the constitutional standard demands, and hence that it would not constitutionally sustain the judgment for respondent under the proper rule of law. The case of the individual petitioners requires little discussion. Even assuming that they could constitutionally be found to have authorized the use of their names on the advertisement, there was no evidence whatever that they were aware of any erroneous statements or were in any way reckless in that regard. The judgment against them is thus without constitutional support.

As to the Times, we similarly conclude that the facts do not support a finding of actual malice. . . .

.  .  .

This is the mechanical part of the decision—a restatement of the fact that the decision by the Supreme Court of Alabama is reversed and the case is remanded to the Alabama

The judgment of the Supreme Court of Alabama is reversed and the case is remanded to that court for further proceedings not inconsistent with this opinion.

courts to correct the prejudicial error that was found.

By reversing and remanding, the court decides that Mr. Sullivan does not win, after all, and the case is sent back to the Alabama courts, should Mr. Sullivan still want to pursue the case.

Each of the nine justices may write and publish his or her own opinion, but it is extraordinary for there to be nine opinions. [It happens in the "Pentagon Papers" case, p. 336, *infra.*]

Here Justice Black, although he agreed with Justice Brennan and the rest of the court on the *outcome* of the case, wished to state his own views. Justice Douglas was the only other justice who agreed with him sufficiently to join his opinion. Justice Douglas still might have chosen to write his own concurring opinion, but he did not.

Reversed and remanded.

MR. JUSTICE BLACK, with whom MR. JUSTICE DOUGLAS joins, concurring.

I concur in reversing this half-million-dollar judgment against the New York Times Company and the four individual defendants. In reversing the Court holds that "the Constitution delimits a State's power to award damages for libel in actions brought by public officials against critics of their official conduct." I base my vote to reverse on the belief that the First and Fourteenth Amendments not merely "delimit" a State's power to award damages to "public officials against critics of their official conduct" but completely prohibit a State from exercising such a power. The Court goes on to hold that a State can subject such critics to damages if "actual malice" can be proved against them. "Malice," even as defined by the Court, is an elusive, abstract concept, hard to prove and hard to disprove. The requirement that malice be proved provides at best an evanescent protection for the right critically to discuss public affairs and certainly does not measure up to the sturdy safeguard embodied in the First Amendment. Unlike the Court, therefore, I vote to reverse exclusively on the ground that the Times and the individual defendants had an absolute unconditional constitutional right to publish in the Times advertisement their criticisms of the Montgomery agencies and officials. . . .

. . . .

The concurring opinion may add insights to the views of individual jus-

In my opinion the Federal Constitution has dealt with this deadly danger to the press in the only way possible without leaving the free

tices, but it is merely an expression of opinion and does not establish the law.

Note that Justice Douglas also agrees with Justice Goldberg.

press open to destruction—by granting the press an absolute immunity for criticism of the way public officials do their public duty. . . .

I regret that the Court has stopped short of this holding indispensable to preserve our free press from destruction.

MR. JUSTICE GOLDBERG, with whom MR. JUSTICE DOUGLAS joins, concurring in the result.

. . .

In my view, the First and Fourteenth Amendments to the Constitution afford to the citizen and to the press an absolute, unconditional privilege to criticize official conduct despite the harm which may flow from excesses and abuses. . . .

. . .

. . . It may be urged that deliberately and maliciously false statements have no conceivable value as free speech. That argument, however, is not responsive to the real issue presented by this case, which is whether that freedom of speech which all agree is constitutionally protected can be effectively safeguarded by a rule allowing the imposition of liability upon a jury's evaluation of the speaker's state of mind. If individual citizens may be held liable in damages for strong words, which a jury finds false and maliciously motivated, there can be little doubt that public debate and advocacy will be constrained. And if newspapers, publishing advertisements dealing with public issues, thereby risk liability, there can also be little doubt that the ability of minority groups to secure publication of their views on public affairs and to seek support for their causes will be greatly diminished. . . .

. . .

There were no dissenting opinions in this case, or they would be indicated here. Dissenting opinions, of course, do not establish the Law, but they may give clues to positions the court may take in the future if the dissenting justice[s] ever prevail.

After every principal case the authors include additional comment about the case—sometimes mentioning related cases and sometimes asking questions about the cases. The examples below relate to New York Times v. Sullivan and are short. Later in the text you will see that some of the notes, particularly those dealing with additional cases, are much longer.

The boldface "Notes and Questions" heading signifies the end of the official Supreme Court opinions and the beginning of the textbook authors' attempts to bring the case into focus for you.

**Notes and Questions**

1. What is the justification for the majority position?

2. The majority twice observes that deliberate falsity is used in argument. Why is such behavior not protected here?

3. Do you consider either of the concurring opinions preferable to the majority approach? Would it be desirable to enable a public official to have a jury assess the truth of charges against him—without seeking damages?

# Chapter II

# INTRODUCTION TO FREEDOM OF EXPRESSION

## A. ANTECEDENTS

### 1. THE ENGLISH BACKGROUND

In England, repression of ideas antithetical to the government was in operation by the 13th century. In 1275 and again in 1379, Parliament made it criminal to speak against the state. Later known as "seditious libel," words that questioned the crown in any way were punished by the King's Council sitting in the "starred chamber." Ecclesiastical laws forbidding heresy already existed, thus making it dangerous to say anything in opposition to the Church or the state.

With the advent of printing, around 1500, the government became even more concerned about statements that questioned the secular powers. To prevent the wider dissemination that the printing press made possible, the Crown established a system of censorship, similar to one already used by the Church, for all publications. This repression lasted until almost 1700.

The core of the censorship system was licensing. In the Elizabethan era the system was overseen by agencies of the Queen. The Stationers Company, established in 1556, gave to a select group of London printers a monopoly over all printing in the country. Its members had the exclusive right to print certain categories of books, such as Bibles and spellers, and could search other printers' offices to look for "illegal" materials. Since all printed matter was to be registered with the Stationers Company, complete prepublication review was possible.

Violators of the licensing system were tried by the infamous Court of the Star Chamber, which became notorious for its secret proceedings and severe punishments. For example, William Prynn's book, *Histrio–Mastix*, published without permission, said only whores acted in plays. The book appeared six weeks before Queen Elizabeth appeared briefly on stage, but Prynn was convicted of ridiculing the Queen. He was sentenced to a fine and life imprisonment, to be pilloried, and to have his ears docked.

Bonding was also a part of the licensing system, forcing printers not part of the Stationers Company to post a large sum of money, a bond, before being granted a license to print. Publishing anything in opposition to the Church or crown meant forfeiture of the bond.

But an unlicensed publication meant more: it could lead to charges of criminal libel. This crime was divided into four categories: (1) blasphemous libel involved heretical statements opposing the Church; (2) obscene or immoral libel dealt with unpermitted literary subject matter; (3) private libel involved offending words directed to private individuals, which also could lead to civil action (suing the publisher for monetary damages to assuage the harm to the offended person's reputation); (4) seditious libel was criticism of the crown. Frederick Siebert in *Freedom of the Press in England 1476–1776* (1952) said that "convictions for seditious libel ran into hundreds" in the 17th and 18th centuries in Great Britain.

In trials for seditious libel, the jury decided whether the defendant had published the material and whether it carried the meaning charged by the government. But judges decided whether the words were published with malice and had a "bad tendency" to damage the government, usually the two crucial points. The defendant could not plead the truth of the words as a defense; indeed, truth made the offense more severe, because truthful charges would increase the public's disrespect for the crown.

This approach to criminal libel persisted even after the licensing system disappeared in 1695, making it still unsafe to criticize the government or the Church.

Until 1688 even members of Parliament were occasionally imprisoned for discussing forbidden subjects. Parliament had long struggled with the King to assure freedom of speech for its Speaker, and this was gradually extended to all members. The privilege to initiate discussion on any subject was recognized in 1649, and later the House of Lords declared that seditious words uttered in Parliament could not be punished in court. Full freedom of speech and debate, including the right to criticize the crown, had been assured in Parliament well before the American Revolution. See F. Siebert, Freedom of the Press in England 1476–1776, 100–02, 112–16 (1952).

In addition to criminal prosecutions for libel, the English government found taxation to be an effective way to control the press. The purpose of the Stamp Act of 1711 and later laws was to reduce the circulation of newspapers. This was done by forcing publishers to raise their sale price to cover the cost of the tax, which applied not only to newspapers, but to advertisements, pamphlets and paper as well. Initially, it was effective, with half the country's newspapers going out of business in the first year of the Act. But loopholes in the law soon were found, and supporters of the government, who felt compelled not to evade the tax, became the ones most seriously hurt.

It was possible for Great Britain to have the Stamp Act, licensing, the Star Chamber and bonding and still contend that freedom of the press existed. Sir William Blackstone, the most famous compiler of the common law, wrote in the late 1760s:

> [w]here blasphemous, immoral, treasonable, schismatical, seditious, or scandalous libels are punished by the English law . . . the liberty of the press, properly understood, is by no means infringed or violated. The liberty of the press is indeed essential to the nature of

a free state; but this consists in laying no previous restraints upon publications, and not in freedom from censure for criminal matter when published. Every freeman has an undoubted right to lay what sentiments he pleases before the public: to forbid this is to destroy the freedom of the press: but if he publishes what is improper, mischievous, or illegal, he must take the consequences of his own temerity . . .. [T]o punish (as the law does at present) any dangerous or offensive writings . . . is necessary for the preservation of peace and good order, of government and religion, the only solid foundations of civil liberty. Thus the will of individuals is still left free; the abuse only of that free-will is the object of legal punishment. Neither is any restraint hereby laid upon freedom of thought or enquiry: liberty of private sentiment is still left; the disseminating, or making public, of bad sentiments, destructive of the ends of society, is the crime which society corrects.

W. Blackstone, 4 Commentaries on the Laws of England 151–52 (1765–69).

Blackstone is central to this analysis because he was a major influence on English and American legal thinking in the period when our Constitution was taking shape. His definition of freedom of the press as the absence of "previous restraints upon publications," and the distinction between liberty and licentiousness (for which punishment was considered legitimate) made clear that freedom of expression meant, as a minimum, rejection of prior restraint. Uncertainty remained as to the legitimacy of subsequent punishment for seditious libel, and as to what types of expression constituted punishable "licentiousness."

## 2.  THE COLONIAL EXPERIENCE

Those who drafted and adopted the United States Constitution and the Bill of Rights were well aware of this background of repression in Great Britain. They also knew of, and had experienced, similar restrictions on freedom of expression imposed by Britain on the colonies.

The first laws passed by Parliament levying taxes on newspapers applied only to British newspapers and were intended to be repressive. According to C. Miller in *The Supreme Court and the Uses of History*, pp.76–79 (1969), the Stamp Act of 1765 was directed specifically against the colonies and was meant to offset "the expense of defending, protecting and securing" the colonies, including the high cost of conducting the Seven Years' War just ended. In fact, the Act served more to anger colonists than to raise revenue. Many communities did not have the stamps, which were supposed to be affixed to every copy of a newspaper distributed, and many printers in other communities simply ignored the law. But the colonists saw the Act as "taxation without representation" and rebelled against it.

Prior to that, however, laws that applied to the press in England during the 17th and 18th centuries were also applied to the emerging colonial press, and the licensing of presses in the colonies closely paralleled the English practice. The colonies saw printers jailed and their books burned for publishing without permission. In 1662 Massachusetts appointed censors. When Benjamin Harris printed the first edition of *Publick Occurrences* in 1690, it became the last edition of that newspaper; he had not gained prior approval. The colonies' second newspaper, the *Boston News–Letter,* published by John Campbell beginning in 1704, clearly informed its readers that it was printed with authority.

After Parliament abolished licensing at the end of the 17th century, the colonial governors managed to retain it for several years more. Its decline in the colonies began in the early 1720s when James Franklin, Benjamin's brother, ignored an order to have his *New England Courant* licensed. He was briefly punished and once substituted his brother's name as publisher, but his refusal to obey the order brought licensing to a halt. In both England and the colonies, however, after the end of licensing, there was still the threat of punishment after the fact for matters the authorities deemed licentious. Contempt of the legislative branch was a real risk, and prosecutions for seditious libel occurred.

In 1721 the colonies first discovered the ardent views of "Cato" on Freedom of Speech in Benjamin Franklin's *Pennsylvania Gazette.* Cato was the pseudonym of two Whig journalists whose essays in London newspapers became popular and were widely reprinted in the colonies. Cato described free speech as "the Right of every Man, as far as by it he does not hurt or control the Right of another; And this is the only Check which it ought to suffer, the only Bounds it ought to know." Free speech and free government thrived together, or they failed together: "in those wretched Countries where a Man cannot call his Tongue his own he can scarce call any Thing else his own," and "Freedom of Speech is ever the Symptom as well as the Effect of good Government." In "Reflections upon Libelling," Cato favored the fullest freedom of expression but conceded that extreme libels might be punished, if they were false. These essays are reprinted in L. Levy, *Freedom of the Press from Zenger to Jefferson,* pp. 10–24 (1966).

These letters also appeared in another journal that criticized the administration. In addition to reprinting Cato's letters, the *New York Weekly Journal* published several anonymous essays that echoed these sentiments: ". . . Liberty of the Press . . . is a Curb, a Bridle, a Terror, a Shame, and Restraint to evil Ministers; and it may be the only Punishment, especially for a Time. But when did Calumnies and Lyes ever destroy the Character of one good Minister? . . . Truth will always prevail over Falsehood." Levy, *supra,* at 29.

In 1734 John Peter Zenger, who printed the *Weekly Journal,* was charged with seditious libel by the Governor General of New York, whom Zenger had criticized. Because the grand jury refused to indict, the prosecution was begun by the filing of an information—an accusation of a crime made by a public officer rather than by an indictment by a grand jury. Zenger, unable to post the high bail imposed, spent almost a year in jail awaiting trial. By the traditional common law standards he was surely guilty because he had published the articles in question and the law did not recognize truth as a defense. However, since 1670 the judge no longer had the power to coerce juries into following his instructions by imprisonment or by levying fines to ensure compliance. Jurors who decided cases "against the manifest evidence" could not be punished. This gave jurors the power to nullify disliked legal rules by refusing to follow the judge's instructions. Zenger's lawyer, Andrew Hamilton, convinced the jury that the only question in the case involved the liberty to write the truth; and the jury, despite the judge's instructions, acquitted Zenger. Although the verdict set no precedent (because a jury verdict is not a ruling on the law), it did signal a change in the political climate.

In the years preceding the Revolutionary War, freedom of expression faced another challenge—not from the government, but from rival political factions. Patriot newspapers were staunch supporters of separation from England. The Patriots argued that freedom of the press was a natural, God-given right, and they exercised it vigorously during the Partisan Press period. But they would not extend the same right to Tory newspapers, published by those who opposed revolution and separation. Tories were threatened with violence and destruction of their printing equipment by mobs who wanted only the Patriot side to be heard.

American journalism underwent changes after the Revolutionary War. Many Colonial newspapers stopped publishing, but a number of new papers were started. During the period before and after the Revolution, papers could be started with ease, though not all were able to survive financially. More than 60 new papers were started in the mid–1780s, and by the 1790s about 450 newspapers were begun. Pre-war papers were adjuncts of print shops, being amalgams of information the printer came by, including vitriolic pro- or anti-English diatribes. Since little new equipment was necessary, it was relatively simple for a print shop owner to publish a newspaper. After the war newspapers were arms of political parties rather than products of printers. They were run by editors who would slant the contents as they wished. This was one feature that remained from the pre-war period—partisanship in the press. But instead of being Patriot versus Tory, it became Federalist versus Republican.

The two major political parties had a number of supportive newspapers, but each also had a flagship. Federalists established the *Gazette of the United States* in New York City as their leading political organ, the first issue being published in 1789 and edited by John Fenno. Two years later, after the split between Hamilton and Jefferson, the Republicans established the *National Gazette* in Philadelphia under editor Philip Freneau. Freneau was passionately partisan, hitting hard at Federalists, frequently through satire and widening the Hamilton–Jefferson schism. See F. Mott, American Journalism 113–14, 122–26 (3d ed. 1962).

After the successful American revolution the governments of the former colonies sought to come together to form a nation. Their internal structures were similar, reflecting common antecedents, but no overarching government-controlled relations among these new political entities. Even before the war was ended the colonies had attempted to form a national government under the Articles of Confederation, devised in 1783. This document allowed the states to retain much power, leaving little for the central government. The Articles contained no mention of freedom of expression or conscience, but many argued such a clause was not necessary. Because the federal government had no power to interfere with citizens, there was no need to forbid it from exercising power it did not have. Additionally, most states had some form of a bill of rights in their state constitutions.

It soon became clear that a stronger national union was needed. A central government could provide security against foreign attack and could ease the movement of goods and persons among the former colonies. The new Constitution, formulated at the Constitutional Convention of 1787, created the national government with three branches.

Except for such incidental provisions as the prohibitions on *ex post facto* laws contained in Article I, Sections 9 and 10, little attention was given to protecting individual citizens against government. Some states in their own constitutions had protected citizens against state government action, but the federal Constitution was not primarily concerned with that problem. This omission led some critics to oppose ratification because the new government might itself threaten the freedom of citizens of the new country.

Although the records of the Constitutional Convention are sketchy, it is known that discussion of a bill of rights did not take place until the last few days of the meeting. That short-lived debate was inconclusive. The Constitution was promulgated without a bill of rights and sent to the states for ratification.

According to historian Leonard Levy, some of the Anti–Federalists who opposed the ratification of the Constitution "callously resorted to alarming the people. It was easier than informing them, and the provocation of an emotional climate of fear made the definition of freedom of the press, and other liberties, unnecessary. Merely to denounce the omission of freedom of the press and other liberties was superbly effective . . . . One searches in vain for a definition of any of the First Amendment freedoms in the rhetorical effusions of George Clinton, Elbridge Gerry, Patrick Henry, . . . and other advocates of a bill of rights. Nor do the newspapers, pamphlets, or debates of the state ratifying conventions offer much illumination." L. Levy, Emergence of a Free Press (1985) at 235.

Although they may not have *defined* freedom of the press, the Anti–Federalists were, according to historian Herbert J. Storing, "especially warm in their defense of a free press, because their own attempts to use the press to mobilize opinion in opposition to the Constitution and their belief that, in one way or another, attempts were being made to muzzle them. . . . But they were also concerned, more deeply, that the Federalist lack of protection for a vigorous free press signaled a basic hostility to popular enlightenment, based on a dogma that government is too important a business for the people to be involved in." H. Storing, What the Anti–Federalists Were For (1981) at 97. Levy's point about a lack of *definition* notwithstanding, there are numerous references to freedom of the press in the Anti–Federalists papers. See, for example, "A Manifesto of a Number of Gentlemen from Albany County," signed by Abraham Yates, Jr., and others, listing many objections to the proposed constitution, including the fact that it included no provision "for the liberty of the press, that grand palladium of liberty and scourge of tyrants." C. Kenyon, The Antifederalists (1966) at 363.

Even though 13 states ratified the Constitution, five expressed concern that a bill of rights had been omitted. In the words of Storing, "While the Federalists gave us the Constitution . . ., the legacy of the Anti–Federalists was the Bill of Rights." What the Anti–Federalists Were For (1981) at 65.

As a result of this dissatisfaction, James Madison introduced a set of amendments to the Constitution when the First Congress met. The House of Representatives approved an amendment that protected freedom of speech and press from infringement "by any state." The Senate struck the provision limiting the powers of the states and the final version provided that "Congress shall make no law . . . abridging the freedom of speech, or of the press. . . ." This was the third of 12 amendments submitted to the states for ratification. When the first two failed, this became the First Amendment to the United States Constitution.

Although it was later argued that the Bill of Rights was intended to protect citizens against invasions by the state as well as the federal government, this was rejected in Barron v. Baltimore, 32 U.S. (7 Pet.) 243 (1833) when the Supreme Court decided that the Bill of Rights applied solely against the federal government. Constraints on the states were those specified in Article I, Section 10 and in such other provisions as the Supremacy Clause. It was only after the Civil War, when states were placed under the additional restraints of the Thirteenth, Fourteenth and Fifteenth Amendments, that they came under a federal requirement to accord freedom of speech and press. As a result, what Congress may not do because of the First Amendment, a state may not do because of the Fourteenth Amendment. This development is discussed at p. 47, *infra*. The Constitution restrains only governments, not private individuals, from interfering with the exercise of freedom of expression.

According to Levy (at pp. 266–267):

The history of the framing and ratification of the Bill of Rights indicates slight passion on the part of anyone, except perhaps 'the people,' to enshrine personal liberties in the fundamental law of the land. . . . What import did the free speech-and-press clause possess at the time of its adoption? More complex than it appears, the clause had several meanings and did not necessarily mean what it said or say what it meant. Its meaning was surely not self-evident. The controversy in the states over the ratification of the Constitution without a bill of rights had revealed little about the substance and scope of freedom of speech-and-press, and the debates by the First Congress, which framed the First Amendment, illumined even less. Congress debated the clauses on religion, but on the remainder of the First Amendment considered only whether the right of peaceable assembly vested the people with the power to instruct their representatives how to vote. In the course of that discussion, Madison made the only recorded statement on the subject of speech or press. If by peaceable assembly, he said, "we mean nothing more than this, that the people have a right to express and communicate their sentiments and wishes, we have provided for it already. The right of freedom of speech is secured; the liberty of the press is expressly declared to be beyond the reach of this Government. . . ." Any interpretation of the meaning and compass of freedom of speech-and-press drawn from this vague statement would strain credulity. . . .

In *Free Speech in the United States* (1941), Professor Chafee, acknowledging that very little was said about the meaning of freedom of speech, reviewed some contemporary statements that suggest that in the years before the First Amendment "freedom of speech was conceived as giving a wide and genuine protection for all sorts of discussion of public matters." He argued that "such a widely recognized right must mean something," and that merely reaffirming the freedom of the press from previous censorship would have been pointless. During the 18th century, besides the narrow legal meaning of liberty of the press, there existed "a definite popular meaning: the right of unrestricted discussion of public affairs," and Chafee thought the framers were aware of basic differences between Great Britain and the former colonies.*

## B.  BASES FOR FREEDOM OF COMMUNICATION

Although Leonard Levy, in his *Emergence of a Free Press* (1985), contended that no clear understanding lay behind adoption of the First Amendment, a number of latter-day reasons have emerged to support freedom of expression. These may be seen as important to individuals and to society, and to a new concept of the purpose of the mass media.

---

* One aspect of freedom of expression that was retained was the complete parliamentary privilege for legislators. The scope of the legislator's free expression is found in Article I, Section 6 of the United States Constitution, providing that "for any Speech or Debate in either House, [Senators and Representatives] shall not be questioned in any other Place." This has been taken to mean that such speech may not form the basis for criminal or civil liability. A comparable provision is contained in virtually every state constitution to protect members of the state legislatures. These are collected in Tenney v. Brandhove, 341 U.S. 367, 375 n. 5 (1951).

## 1. FOR INDIVIDUALS

A concept of "natural law" was actively discussed for two centuries before the Constitution was adopted. In attempting to reconcile government's role with individual rights, certain personal freedoms were seen as inviolable. They were "natural rights" of individuals, rights that official persons or bodies had no power to affect. Among these rights was freedom of expression.

This concept derived in large part from the 17th century English philosopher John Locke, who contended that government's purpose was to use its power to protect life, liberty and property, natural rights to which each individual was entitled. Locke's views influenced the language of the First Amendment with the notion of free speech as a natural right, and the Fifth Amendment ("No person shall . . . be deprived of life, liberty, or property, without due process of law. . . .").

Locke discussed the origin of society in terms of a social contract. He believed the pre-social status was one of freedom. Private property was recognized, but no security existed. To achieve security, people surrendered a certain amount of freedom to establish a government. But the government rested on the consent of the governed, who would control the government rather than vice versa. A government that encroached on an individual's rights should be abolished or changed.

Several commentators believe that even with this Lockean philosophy to draw on, the framers had no clear concept of the First Amendment's purpose. Recall Levy's point that during the ratification controversy many of the advocates of a Bill of Rights had only a vague idea of what it might contain. Professor Lillian BeVier, however, in "The First Amendment and Political Speech: An Inquiry into the Substance and Limits of Principle," 30 Stan.L.Rev. 299, 307 (1978), suggested this may have been deliberate:

> If history suggests that the framers had no specific meaning in mind . . . it also permits the conclusion that no particular meanings were deliberately foreclosed, except perhaps a meaning that would permit prior licensing restraints. Thus, the framers may have intended the very vagueness of the text [of the First Amendment] to delegate to future generations the task of evolving a precise meaning.

No matter what the framers might have had in mind, however, they could not have foreseen the many changes in media technology and society generally. Thus, more expansive views of freedom of communication became necessary.

Professor Thomas I. Emerson, in *The System of Freedom of Expression,* pp. 6–9 (1970), asserted that "the system of freedom of expression in a democratic society" is based on four premises:

(1) freedom of expression facilitates self-fulfillment,

(2) it is an essential tool for advancing knowledge and discovering truth,

(3) it is a way to achieve a more stable and adaptable community, and

(4) it permits individuals to be involved in the democratic decision-making process.

Perhaps the most powerful judicial statement of the justifications for free expression is that of Justice Brandeis, concurring, in Whitney v. California, 274 U.S. 357, 375–77 (1927):

> Those who won our independence believed that the final end of the State was to make men free to develop their faculties; and that in its government the deliberative forces should prevail over the arbitrary. They valued liberty both as an end and as a means. They believed liberty to be the secret of happiness and courage to be the secret of liberty. They believed that freedom to think as you will and speak as you think are means indispensable to the discovery and spread of political truth; that without free speech and assembly discussion would be futile; that with them, discussion affords ordinarily adequate protection against the dissemination of noxious doctrine; that the greatest menace to freedom is an inert people; that public discussion is a political duty; and that this should be a fundamental principle of the American government. They recognized the risks to which all human institutions are subject. But they knew that order cannot be secured merely through fear of punishment for its infraction; that it is hazardous to discourage thought, hope and imagination; that fear breeds repression; that repression breeds hate; that hate menaces stable government; that the path of safety lies in the opportunity to discuss freely supposed grievances and proposed remedies; and that the fitting remedy for evil counsels is good ones. Believing in the power of reason as applied through public discussion, they eschewed silence coerced by law—the argument of force in its worst form. Recognizing the occasional tyrannies of governing majorities, they amended the Constitution so that free speech and assembly should be guaranteed.

Each of these explanations has been used, to a greater or lesser extent, by the Supreme Court to justify the high value placed on freedom of speech in our constitutional scheme of government. Each may justify different notions of the breadth and depth of the First Amendment freedom and each may apply with peculiar force in particular contexts.

These fundamental justifications for protecting speech tend to divide into two main groups: those that stress the values to the individual and those that stress the values to the society of freedom of speech. The emphasis on the individual, contained in what are variously called the self-fulfillment or self-realization models, is on the importance of expression as a route to individual development and fulfillment.

Large press organizations have little basis for asserting that their expressive activities contribute to their own self-fulfillment. Smaller press operations can more plausibly assert such a claim to the extent that they are the "alter-egos" of an individual publisher or editor.

The notion of self-fulfillment involves an individual's attempt to fully achieve his or her potential. Restrictions on beliefs or forms of expression inhibit this process and are "an affront to the dignity" of an individual, said Emerson. Without the individual's freedom to search for truth and to discuss questions of right or wrong, society becomes a "despotic" commander and places a person in "the arbitrary control of others." Also, a person has a right to be involved in the decisions that affect that person.

Emerson asserted that the individual's right to freedom of expression is independent of society's needs. That is, free communication may or may not enhance society's goals. Regardless, it is "a good in itself"— almost a natural right. Society's objectives must be achieved through other methods, such as counter-expression and "the regulation of conduct which is not expression."

Recall that the first point in Justice Brandeis's statement asserted the "final end of the State was to make men free to develop their faculties." In addition, from a less lofty side, it may be argued that the "safety valve" argument that both Emerson and Brandeis identify plays a role in the self-fulfillment side in the sense that "blowing off steam"— even if no other person receives the message—may help individuals to develop their potentials most fully.

The line between speech and conduct is crucially important to theorists who rely on self-fulfillment as the basis of the First Amendment, for without such a line the rationale spreads so far as to become unworkable. After all, virtually everything we do arguably contributes to our self-fulfillment. Yet no one argues that the First Amendment protects those who seek self-fulfillment by traveling at 80 miles per hour on the freeways or, more graphically, by committing murder or arson. Unfortunately, the speech-conduct line, though crucial, has proven difficult to maintain. Several theorists ask: if self-fulfillment is the rationale, what makes speech peculiarly self-fulfilling in contradistinction to all the other ways one may seek to realize that goal?

Despite these theoretical difficulties, the self-fulfillment rationale remains a powerful theme in First Amendment doctrine. Many continue to believe that there is something special about speech that justifies more protection than what we would accord to conduct. Indeed, some theorists have built their First Amendment analyses entirely from a focus on the individual. In some cases, the social goals are viewed as sub-values that may derive from the achievement of the primary goal of individual self-fulfillment. See the discussions in Baker, "Scope of First Amendment Freedom of Speech," 25 UCLA L.Rev. 964 (1978) and Redish, "The Value of Free Speech," 130 U.Pa.L.Rev. 591 (1982). Their approach is challenged in Schauer, "Must Speech Be Special?," 78

Nw.U.L.Rev. 1284 (1983), with both Baker and Redish responding in comments after that article.

## 2.  FOR SOCIETY

Just as the self-fulfillment justification is necessarily tied to individuals, the other reasons offered for protection are society-centered. Neither disputing nor relying upon the assertion that we as individuals profit from freedom of speech, these bases explain why we as a people are the better for the First Amendment freedoms. Here, categorizing the speaker as "press" or "individual" may be irrelevant. Under the social justifications, the important matter may be the role of the audience rather than the speaker. We turn now to further considerations of each social justification.

### a.  *Marketplace of Ideas*

The seminal view that freedom of expression enhances the social good came from John Milton's *Areopagitica* in 1644. Milton, an English poet and essayist, wanted a divorce and wrote an essay he hoped would lower the strict legal barriers prohibiting it. He was chastised for publishing without a license, and wrote *Areopagitica* to induce Parliament to allow unlicensed printing. Milton argued that licensing was unworkable and an affront to those who had views to express. But more, he said, it was harmful to society, since people are better able to function as citizens if they are knowledgeable and exposed to different points of view. Attempting to assuage official fears that the Crown's views would be overwhelmed if unlicensed printing were allowed, Milton wrote: "And though all the winds of doctrine were let loose to play upon the earth, so Truth be in the field, we do injuriously by licensing and prohibiting to misdoubt her strength. Let her and Falsehood grapple; who ever knew Truth put to the worse, in a free and open encounter?"

Milton, however, was not ready to give freedom of expression to everyone on every subject. As a Puritan, he would not allow free discussion of Catholicism or atheism. In the context of his time, though, Milton's view was a major shift away from the stringent censorship that prevailed.

Perhaps Milton's most enduring contribution to the philosophy of freedom of expression was his statement that unrestricted debate would lead to the discovery of truth. Writing in England some 50 years later, John Locke retained some of this faith that truth would prevail. In "A Letter Concerning Toleration" (1689), he wrote:

> [T]ruth certainly would do well enough if she were once left to shift for herself. She seldom has received, and I fear never will receive, much assistance from the power of great men, to whom she is but rarely known and more rarely welcome. She is not taught by laws, nor has she any need of force to procure her entrance into the minds

of men.  Errors indeed prevail by the assistance of foreign and
borrowed succors.  But if truth makes not her way into the understanding by her own light, she will be but the weaker for any
borrowed force violence can add to her.

Locke's regard for freedom of expression arose out of a skepticism about
the state or any individual as a source of guidance in seeking truth, and
he shared Milton's view that governmental restrictions on freedom of
inquiry would increase the likelihood of error.  He condemned those
"places where care is taken to propagate the truth without knowledge."
Like Milton, Locke opposed prior restraints, and in 1694, he joined the
opposition that finally obtained the abolition of the Licensing Order.
Yet also like Milton, Locke did not question the common law punishment
for expression after publication, and advocated the suppression of "opinions contrary to human society or to those moral rules which are
necessary to the preservation of civil society."

By 1776 the pendulum had swung still further away from government restriction of expression, on both sides of the Atlantic.  In England
Jeremy Bentham in his "Fragment on Government" was waging war
against Blackstone.  He wrote that one of the differences between a free
and a despotic government was "the security with which malcontents
may communicate their sentiments, concert their plans, and practise
every mode of opposition short of actual revolt, before the executive
power can be legally justified in disturbing them."

English philosopher and economist John Stuart Mill, who wrote 200
years after Milton, believed more in full and free discussion than did
Milton.  Mill thought that society could function well only with such
freedom.  He saw freedom of thought, discussion and investigation as
"goods in their own right" but, more importantly, society benefits from
an exchange of ideas.  People could trade their false notions for true
ones, but only if they could hear the true ones.  Such open discussion
would necessarily mean that false as well as true ideas would be
expressed.

Mill, in *On Liberty*, contended that government could not "prescribe
opinions" or "determine what doctrines or what arguments" people
should hear.  Not even if the government and the populace were at one
on an issue should coercion regarding freedom of expression be allowed:

The power itself is illegitimate.  The best government has no more
title to it than the worst.  It is as noxious, or more noxious, when
exerted in accordance with public opinion, than when in opposition
to it.  If all mankind minus one were of one opinion, and only one
person were of the contrary opinion, mankind would be no more
justified in silencing that one person, than he, if he had the power,
would be justified in silencing mankind.  .  .  .  [T]he peculiar evil
of silencing the expression of an opinion is, that it is robbing the
human race: posterity as well as the existing generation; those who
dissent from the opinion, still more than those who hold it.  If the
opinion is right, they are deprived of the opportunity of exchanging

error for truth; if wrong, they lose, what is almost as great a benefit, the clearer perception and livelier impression of truth, produced by its collision with error.

. . .

[T]he dictum that truth always triumphs over persecution is one of those pleasant falsehoods which men repeat after one another till they pass into common-places, but which all experience refutes. History teems with instances of truth put down by persecution. If not suppressed forever, it may be thrown back for centuries.  .  .  . It is a piece of idle sentimentality that truth, merely as truth, has any inherent power denied to error of prevailing against the dungeon and the stake.

The concept of the marketplace of ideas, first enunciated by Milton and later developed by Mill, was recognized in American law by Justice Oliver Wendell Holmes. In Abrams v. United States, 250 U.S. 616 (1919), Abrams and others were accused of publishing pamphlets that criticized President Wilson's sending of troops to help counter the Russian revolution. The pamphlets also advocated a strike against munitions plants. A majority of the Supreme Court ruled that publishing such pamphlets during war time was not protected by the First Amendment. In dissent, Justice Holmes, joined by Justice Louis Brandeis, argued that the pamphlets did not attack the form of the United States government, and thus did not violate the sedition statute as charged. More generally, Holmes wrote:

Persecution for the expression of opinions seems to me perfectly logical. If you have no doubt of your premises or your power and want a certain result with all your heart you naturally express your wishes in law and sweep away all opposition. To allow opposition by speech seems to indicate that you think the speech impotent, as when a man says that he has squared the circle, or that you do not care whole-heartedly for the result, or that you doubt either your power or your premises. But when men have realized that time has upset many fighting faiths, they may come to believe even more than they believe the very foundations of their own conduct that the ultimate good desired is better reached by free trade in ideas—that the best test of truth is the power of the thought to get itself accepted in the competition of the market, and that truth is the only ground upon which their wishes safely can be carried out. That at any rate is the theory of our Constitution. It is an experiment, as all life is an experiment.

A similar sentiment was voiced by Judge Learned Hand in an antitrust case in which the government was attempting to stop restrictive practices of the Associated Press. He observed that one of the most "vital of all general interests" was "the dissemination of news from as many different sources, and with as many different facets and colors as is possible. That interest is closely akin to, if indeed it is not the same as, the interest protected by the First Amendment; it presupposes that right conclusions are more likely to be gathered out of a multitude of tongues, than through any kind of authoritative selection. To many this is, and always will be, folly; but we have staked upon it our all." United States v. Associated Press, 52 F.Supp. 362 (S.D.N.Y.1943), aff'd 326 U.S. 1 (1945).

The marketplace of ideas approach has been criticized from several sides. In a Marxist attack, American philosopher Herbert Marcuse disagreed with the basic premise of the marketplace notion, that rational beings engage in a free interchange of opinions and information. People are not rational because government and mass media manipulate them— each for its own purposes, he said. In an essay entitled "Repressive Tolerance" in *A Critique of Pure Tolerance* (1965), he started from the premise that "the people must be capable of deliberating and choosing on the basis of knowledge." He was appalled by the blandness of the newspaper layout that intermingles advertisements and disasters and trivia, and the broadcaster's reporting of the momentous and the mundane in the same monotone: "It offends against humanity and truth by being calm where one should be enraged, by refraining from accusation where accusation is in the facts themselves." More than that, "in endlessly dragging debates over the media, the stupid opinion is treated with the same respect as the intelligent one, the misinformed may talk as long as the informed and propaganda rides along with education, truth with falsehood."

The "concentration of economic and political power" allows "effective dissent" to be blocked where it could freely emerge, and the "monopolistic media" prejudice "right and wrong, true and false  .  .  . wherever they affect the vital interests of the society." The situation was so dangerous that Marcuse recommended "suspension of the right of free speech and free assembly" so that "spurious objectivity" could be replaced by "intolerance against movements from the Right, and toleration of movements from the Left."

In effect, Marcuse advocated the silencing of certain views in order to achieve true freedom, a view that has been heard, in various forms, since Plato's *Republic* : "[T]he only poetry that should be allowed in a state is hymns to the gods and paeans in praise of good men; once you go beyond that and admit the sweet lyric or epic muse, pleasure and pain become your rulers instead of law and the rational principles commonly accepted as best."

Another group adopted a quite different approach. In the mid– 1940s the Commission on Freedom of the Press was organized to study the press in America. Funded primarily by Time Inc. and Encyclopedia Britannica, Inc., and chaired by Robert M. Hutchins, the Commission was composed of philosophers, historians, law professors and others. No media professionals were included on the panel, but some were called to share their views with Commission members. The Commission found that press freedom was not seriously threatened in mid–20th century America. The press had, however, despite the enforcement of antitrust laws, become increasingly concentrated in the hands of fewer individuals. Media owners, in fact, were reasonably free from government interference, but the First Amendment had little direct application to most people.

The Commission argued that publishers and broadcasters should be more socially responsible, treating each media outlet not as a personal soapbox, but as a means of disseminating a wide range of viewpoints. It suggested that the government finance new communications outlets and that an independent government agency oversee the press's performance in *A Free and Responsible Press* (1947). Such recommendations were not well received by the press, which attacked the ideas in editorials and opinion columns.

The Commission, then, encouraged altering the existing marketplace of ideas into a subsidized and more regulated one in which a number of views could be disseminated through the limited number of outlets that concentration of media ownership had caused. This social responsibility approach is explored in Siebert, et al., *Four Theories of the Press* (1956).

Philosopher and Professor William Ernest Hocking, a member of the Commission, expanded on the group's work. He noted that protecting the press when it is composed of many units protects the consumer, who will have access to a wide range of offerings. But when the number of sources shrinks, the consumer is left defenseless under traditional views of the First Amendment.

Hocking believed the public had a "right" as well as a need to have its news. Particularly since "the citizen's *political* duty is at stake, the right to have an adequate service of news becomes a *public responsibility* as well." The press thus becomes "clothed with a public interest" and must therefore be "adequate"—a term Hocking acknowledged to be "an indefinite standard." Adequacy, however, does imply giving the public a breadth of news coverage and viewpoints. To accomplish this, Hocking suggested comparing the press to privately owned public utilities or to private schools, which must meet certain government-established standards. Although government should not intrude on press activities, it should "regulate the conditions under which those activities take place, so that the public interest is better served." He defined this to mean the "best service to the most people," to be accomplished by a "continuous survey of press performance" by an independent agency, with the government supplementing the private press by issuing information on its own. W. Hocking, Freedom of the Press 161–90 (1947).

Another Commission member, Professor Zechariah Chafee, Jr., stated that the press could not play its proper part in society in the "mere absence of governmental restrictions." Rather, "affirmative action by the government or others" would be needed. Chafee started with Justice Holmes's formulation, "The best test of truth is the power of the thought to get itself accepted in the competition of the market." Abrams v. United States, 250 U.S. 616, 630 (1919). But how, Chafee asked, could views compete in a market constricted because of a lack of media outlets? He answered that "a free market requires regulation, just as a free market for goods needs law against monopoly. . . . The government can lay down the rules of the game which will promote rather than restrict free speech." Such laws might require "essential facilities accessible to all," methods to assure that communication channels remain open, and measures directed at particular communication industries "intended to promote freedom, improve content, or otherwise make them perform their proper function in a free society." Z. Chafee, 2 Government and Mass Communications 471 ff. (1947).

Later, law professor Jerome A. Barron adopted the same approach. He believes the marketplace is an antiquated concept that no longer works because of changes in the media and society since 1791. It is difficult for a person to begin a newspaper because of the prohibitive cost or to begin a broadcast service because of limits in spectrum allocation. Barron believes media censor by limiting the views they disseminate and permitting few new or unpopular ideas to be heard widely. Barron concludes that those who do not control media should be able to express their views through the mass media. "At the very minimum," Barron wrote in 1973, "the creation of two remedies is essential—(1) a nondiscriminating right to purchase editorial advertisements in daily newspapers, and (2) a right of reply for public figures and public officers defamed in newspapers." J. Barron, Freedom of the Press for Whom? 6 (1973). See also, Barron, Access to the Press—a New First Amendment Right, 80 Harv.L.Rev. 1641 (1967).

We shall consider legal responses to the Commission and to Barron later.

### b. Safety Valve

When a government permits freedom of expression it not only allows society to be exposed to a wide range of ideas, it also brings about a stable and adaptable community, according to Professor Thomas Emerson. See T. Emerson, The System of Freedom of Expression 11–14 (1970). Substituting force for logic, which is what happens when freedom of expression is suppressed, makes it impossible to come to rational decisions. In addition, coercion is ineffective in changing thoughts and beliefs. Instead, stifling expression breeds discontent that focuses not on the issues being suppressed, but on the act of suppression itself.

Thus, limiting freedom of expression leads to an inflexible and stultified society, one that cannot adapt to new circumstances because new ideas have not been allowed to flourish. Any tendency of a society to lose its vitality and become rigid is exacerbated when its members cannot exchange ideas freely. Innovative approaches to old problems and to methods of coping with new concerns will not develop unless dissent and opposition are allowed to exist. If opposition is driven underground, open confrontation may emerge between the government and the opposition, including the use of physical force.

Emerson's argument, then, is that freedom of expression will not cause society to become fragmented, to divide into opposing camps. Rather, suppression of communication will do that. Freedom of speech and press will allow dissidents to express their ideas "in a release of energy, a lessening of frustration and a channeling of resistance into courses consistent with law and order."

When people have had an opportunity to convince others of their ideas and have been rejected, the dissidents are more likely to accept the majority view. So long as they think they have not had a chance to persuade others, the minority will continue to believe their cause would be accepted if only heard. When certain they have been treated fairly, however, and have not won over others, they are less likely to use force, and others in society are less likely to view force as a legitimate alternative.

Recall Justice Brandeis's emphasis on the importance of this justification.

### c. *Self-governance*

A third reason that freedom of communication is valuable in a democratic society is that such a society is based on self-governance, on an informed citizenry that will intelligently elect representatives. James Madison believed that the people, not the government, were sovereign, and that the purpose of freedom of speech was to allow citizens to govern themselves in a free society. But in 1798, less than a decade after adoption of the First Amendment, Federalists in Congress passed the Sedition Act, which specified a fine and imprisonment for anyone who "shall write, print, utter or publish . . . any false, scandalous and malicious writing . . . against the government of the United States, or either house of the Congress . . . or the President . . . with intent to defame . . . or to excite against them . . . the hatred of the good people of the United States. . . ." Passed over Republican objections, the law prompted about 25 arrests and 10 convictions over the next three years. Thomas Jefferson and Madison objected to the legislation, Madison introducing resolutions into the Virginia legislature that called the Sedition Act unconstitutional.

In his draft of the Virginia resolutions, Madison argued that in the British form of government Parliament was omnipotent and the apparent threat was the Crown. "In the United States, the case is altogether different. The people, not the government, possess the absolute sovereignty. The legislature, no less than the executive, is under limitations of power." Thus the Constitution secures the people against invasions by both branches: "This security of the freedom of the press requires, that it should be exempt, not only from previous restraint by the executive, as in Great Britain, but from legislative restraint also; and this exemption, to be effectual, must be an exemption not only from the previous inspection of licensers, but from the subsequent penalty of laws." The Virginia Report of 1799, 225–227 (J. Randolph ed. 1850). Madison also observed that:

> Whether it has, in any case, happened that the proceedings of either, or all of those branches, evince such a violation of duty as to justify a contempt, a disrepute or hatred among the people, can only be determined by a free examination thereof, and a free communication among the people thereon.

>              .    .    .

> Let it be recollected, lastly, that the right of electing the members of the government, constitutes more particularly the essence of a free and responsible government. The value and efficacy of this right, depends on the knowledge of the comparative merits and demerits of the candidates for public trust; and on the equal freedom, consequently, of examining and discussing these merits and demerits of the candidates respectively.

Madison's rationale for freedom of expression represents a significant departure from the English thinking of that period, and is a more far-reaching conception of that freedom than Madison had expressed previously.

In the late 1940s Professor Alexander Meiklejohn agreed that self-governance is the most important concern of the First Amendment. He advocated distinguishing between two kinds of expression. Speech concerning the self-governing process was "political speech" and deserved absolute protection from government interference. Speech that was nonpolitical in character, "private speech," was protected only by the due process clause of the Fifth Amendment, which permits the government some leeway for regulation.

Meiklejohn drew this distinction between political and private speech because he believed the central purpose of the First Amendment was to give citizens the greatest opportunity to discuss and hear about society's problems, the very information one must have to function in a self-governing society.

Meiklejohn's emphasis on the self-governing focus of the First Amendment led him to reject more individualistic and subjective justifications for free speech. In *Free Speech and Its Relation to Self-Government*, pp. 65–66 (1948) he said:

> Shall we, then, as practitioners of freedom, listen to ideas which, being opposed to our own, might destroy confidence in our form of government? Shall we give a hearing to those who hate and despise freedom, to those who, if they had the power, would destroy our institutions? Certainly, yes! Our action must be guided, not by their principles, but by ours. We listen, not because they desire to speak, but because we need to hear. If there are arguments against our theory of government, our policies in war or in peace, we the citizens, the rulers, must hear and consider them for ourselves.

That is the way of public safety. It is the program of self-government.

Also, in "The First Amendment Is An Absolute," 1961 Supreme Court Review, 245, 263, he stated:

I have never been able to share the Miltonian faith that in a fair fight between truth and error, truth is sure to win.  . . . In my view, "the people need free speech" because they have decided, in adopting, maintaining, and interpreting their Constitution, to govern themselves rather than to be governed by others.

Meiklejohn's emphasis on self-government might have suggested that the First Amendment would protect only what we conventionally regard as political speech. His vagueness on this point in his 1948 edition was criticized by Chafee, who was concerned about what types of speech were being relegated to the Fifth Amendment's protection. Chafce observed that "there are public aspects to practically every subject." The citizen gains understanding from many sources: "He can get help from poems and plays and novels. No matter if Shakespeare and Whitehead do seem very far away from the issues of the next election." If Meiklejohn intended this broad view of the First Amendment, then Chafee wondered how there could be any limitations in such traditionally regulated areas as obscenity and libel. If, however, Meiklejohn were to place scholarship and the arts in the category of private speech, Chafee would regard it as "shocking to deprive these vital matters of the protection of the inspiring words of the First Amendment." Book Review, 62 Harv.L.Rev. 891, 900 (1949).

In his 1961 article Meiklejohn resolved this question in favor of the broad view of the First Amendment:

Second, there are many forms of thought and expression within the range of human communications from which the voter derives the knowledge, intelligence, sensitivity to human values: the capacity for sane and objective judgment which, so far as possible, a ballot should express. These, too, must suffer no abridgment of their freedom. I list four of them below.

1. Education, in all its phases, is the attempt to so inform and cultivate the mind and will of a citizen that he shall have the wisdom, the independence, and, therefore, the dignity of a governing citizen. Freedom of education is, thus, as we all recognize, a basic postulate in the planning of a free society.

2. The achievements of philosophy and the sciences in creating knowledge and understanding of men and their world must be made available, without abridgment, to every citizen.

3. Literature and the arts must be protected by the First Amendment. They lead the way toward sensitive and informed appreciation and response to the values out of which the riches of the general welfare are created.

4.   Public discussions of public issues, together with the spreading of information and opinion bearing on those issues, must have a freedom unabridged by our agents.   Though they govern us, we, in a deeper sense, govern them.   Over our governing, they have no power.   Over their governing we have sovereign power.

His inclusion of literature and the arts within the categorical protection of the First Amendment led Meiklejohn to rule out prosecutions even for obscenity.   He regretted that "Our dominant mood is not the courage of people who dare to think.   It is the timidity of those who fear and hate whenever conventions are questioned."   Can this breadth be reconciled with Meiklejohn's earlier view that "a merchant advertising his wares [and] a paid lobbyist fighting for the advantage of his client" are covered only by the limited protection of the Fifth Amendment?

As to libel, Meiklejohn argued that the libel of a private person "if it has no relation to the business of governing" could lead to liability, but criticism of candidates or government officials should be protected.   Yet, "vituperation which fixes attention on the defects of an opponent's character or intelligence and thereby distracts attention from the question of policy under discussion may be forbidden as a deadly enemy of peaceable assembly."

Chafee's detailed review of Meiklejohn's 1948 volume praised its political wisdom but regretted that Meiklejohn, a philosopher, had attempted to read his political ideas into the Constitution.   Chafee thought Meiklejohn's claim "of a firmly established purpose to make all political discussion immune" was negated by actions for civil and criminal libels in state courts after the Revolution, and asserted that although the framers "had no very clear idea as to what they meant" in the First Amendment, they intended the amendment to give speech "all the protection they desired, and had no idea of supplementing it by the Fifth Amendment."   Book Review, 62 Harv.L.Rev. 891, 897–98 (1949).   In his 1961 article Meiklejohn acknowledged the lack of historical support but argued that the constitutional principle of self-government was capable of development and changing consequences as its implications became understood.

Chafee also claimed that Meiklejohn's constitutional approach would be unworkable in practice because "few judges" would grant protection to certain types of inciting speech clearly within the realm of "public discussion."   Also, the line between public and private speech might well be elusive.

Others have suggested different versions of the role of political speech in terms of the First Amendment.   After reviewing several justifications for protecting speech in his "Neutral Principles and Some First Amendment Problems," 47 Indiana L.J. 1, 23–35 (1971), Robert Bork suggested that the only acceptable basis for protecting speech more than other activities is the importance of the "discovery and spread of political truth" facilitated by the unique ability of speech to deal "explicitly and specifically and directly with politics and government."   But this difference "exists only with respect to one kind of speech: explicitly and predominantly political speech. This seems to me the only form of speech that a principled judge can prefer to other claimed freedoms. All other forms of speech raise only issues of human gratification. . . ." The quotation subsequently caused Judge Bork trouble during his confirmation hearings in 1987, even though he had recanted several years earlier. See "Judge Bork Replies," 70 ABA Journal 132 (1984).

Professor Lillian BeVier agreed that the First Amendment "in principle protects only 'political' speech—speech that participates in the process of representative democracy. . . ." But she said Bork's view was too narrow, that the need to "protect political speech fully in practice may justify the Court's extending first amendment protection to categories of speech other than the strictly political." This extra tier of protection is defensible because of the difficulty in predicting how the Court will later draw the line between political and non-political speech. Rather than sacrificing some of the political to exclude all non-political, the Court should give more protection to the latter to ensure protecting the former. BeVier, The First Amendment and Political Speech: An Inquiry Into the Substance and Limits of Principle, 30 Stan.L.Rev. 299 (1978).

In commenting on the Chafee and Meiklejohn approaches to the First Amendment, Professor Alexander Bickel observed:

> Now, the interest in truth of which Chafee spoke is not inconsistent with the First Amendment's protection of demonstrable falsehood for, as I have indicated, men may be deterred from speaking what they believe to be true because they fear that it will be found to be false, or that the proof of its truth will be too expensive. Moreover, the individual interest that Chafee mentioned has its truth-seeking aspect. Yet the First Amendment does not operate solely or even chiefly to foster the quest for truth, unless we take the view that truth is entirely a product of the marketplace and is definable as the perceptions of the majority of men, and not otherwise. The social interest that the First Amendment vindicates is rather, as Alexander Meiklejohn and Robert Bork have emphasized, the interest in the successful operation of the political process, so that the country may better be able to adopt the course of action that conforms to the wishes of the greatest number, whether or not it is wise or is founded in truth.

Professor Bickel then concluded that discussion and exchange of views were "crucial to our politics. . . . It would follow, then, that the First Amendment should protect and indeed encourage speech so long as it serves to make the political process work, seeking to achieve objectives through the political process by persuading a majority of voters; but *not* when it amounts to an effort to supplant, disrupt, or coerce the process, as by overthrowing the government, by rioting, or by other forms of violence, and also *not* when it constitutes a breach of an otherwise valid law, a violation of majority decisions embodied in law." A. Bickel, The Morality of Consent 62–63 (1976).

From a different direction, Professor Vince Blasi suggested that Meiklejohn's emphasis on self-governance may be unrealistic in light of our traditionally low participation in elections and political discussions. (Blasi noted that the framers did not intend that a large majority of the population would participate in political decisions.) Rather, Blasi would stress that the press needs extensive protection because it is the only continuing and well-funded organization in the private sector that can "check" official misbehavior by extensive investigation and reporting. Government corruption is a serious problem and, as government grows, the problem gets more serious, as does the difficulty of discovering the misbehavior. The "central premise of the checking value is that abuse of government is an especially serious evil—more serious than the abuse of private power, even by institutions such as large corporations which can affect the lives of millions of people."

The checking value allows citizens to follow their private pursuits while the press serves as a "watchdog" over government. Most investigative reporting, brought to the public's attention during the Watergate affair, emphasizes the "checking value" more than the self-governance rationale. Blasi, The Checking Value in First Amendment Theory, 1977 American Bar Foundation Research Journal 521.

## C. THE FIRST AMENDMENT AND THE INSTITUTIONAL PRESS

"Congress shall make no law . . . abridging the freedom of speech, or of the press . . . .."

The lack of a broad consensus concerning the philosophical underpinnings of the majestic words of the First Amendment does not mean that the courts and legislatures of the United States are released from the obligation to obey the Amendment's dictates. To the contrary, our Nation's lawmaking bodies have clearly acknowledged that the Amendment represents a constitutional bar to government action in numerous situations.

An appreciable and important fraction of these situations involves the institution of "the press" and these specific applications of First Amendment doctrine are the core of this book. The remainder of this chapter sketches those elements of general First Amendment doctrine that apply most directly to the press. Some aspects of the First Amendment that do not primarily involve the press are presented in passing. Students interested in a more comprehensive exposition of First Amendment doctrine might consult M. Nimmer, *Nimmer on Freedom of Speech* (1984).

## 1. RESTRICTION ON GOVERNMENT POWER

Though on its face the First Amendment appears to bind only the Congress, it is well established today that the prohibitions of the First Amendment extend to all branches of both the federal and state governments by way of the "due process" clause of the Fourteenth Amendment. The First Amendment guarantees, the Supreme Court has held, are a fundamental element of the "liberty" protected by the Fourteenth Amendment. Gitlow v. New York, 268 U.S. 652 (1925).

This liberty is protected against encroachments of state governments to the exact same extent that the First Amendment itself protects the freedoms of speech and press from the federal government. Lawyers and judges have developed the shorthand expression "incorporation" to express this idea. Because the First Amendment has been "incorporated" into the Fourteenth Amendment, its prohibitions are no less specific by virtue of such incorporation. This means that branches of the state governments are bound, to the same extent as the federal government, to respect the guarantees of the First Amendment.

Despite the considerable expansion of the field of operation of the First Amendment as a result of the incorporation doctrine, it is important to remember that the First Amendment is a bar only to abridgments by government. Private parties are free to "abridge" another's exercise of the speech and press clauses at will so long as they do not violate some other valid law in the process. For example, it is established that a right to distribute printed material is part and parcel of the First Amendment freedoms and the government is prohibited from interfering with such distribution. Lovell v. Griffin, 303 U.S. 444 (1938). On the other hand, the private owner of property may prohibit such a distribution from taking place on *his* property without running afoul of the First Amendment. See PruneYard Shopping Center v. Robins, 447 U.S. 74, 6 Med.L.Rptr. 1311 (1980).

## 2. THE PROTECTED SPHERE

### a. *Speech v. Conduct*

More difficult than determining who is prohibited from interfering with protected expression is determining what forms of expressive activity fall within the protected category. Perhaps the most basic line between the protected and the unprotected is suggested by the distinction between "speech" and "conduct." Presumptively, at least, all oral and written communication falls within the protected sphere while non-verbal conduct remains outside the domain of the First Amendment. Difficulties abound when verbal and non-verbal elements are mixed into a single expressive activity, such as labor picketing, protest marches, or the wearing of armbands. See Tinker v. Des Moines Independent Community School District, 393 U.S. 503 (1969), regarding armbands.

The speech-conduct dichotomy does not, however, pose a serious problem in determining the First Amendment rights of "the institutional press." Virtually all expressive conduct by the news media is verbal in nature, either oral or written. As a first approximation, then, all mass media expression is protected as "speech."

### b. Non-protected Speech

Though speech *generally* is a protected activity, the Supreme Court has long placed certain categories of words outside the First Amendment's protection. In 1942 the Court asserted, in Chaplinsky v. New Hampshire, 315 U.S. 568 (1942), that certain classes of expression might be subject to legal sanctions. Chaplinsky had been arrested for calling a town marshal a "God-damned racketeer and a damned Fascist." The Supreme Court characterized the expression as "fighting words . . . likely to cause violence." The words were not protected expression because they invited a violent response by the person to whom they were directed. The Court then observed that other types of speech were similarly outside the protection of the First Amendment:

> There are certain well-defined and narrowly limited classes of speech, the prevention and punishment of which have never been thought to raise any Constitutional problem. These include the lewd and obscene, the profane, the libelous, and the insulting or "fighting" words—those which by their very utterance inflict injury or tend to incite an immediate breach of the peace. It has been well observed that such utterances are no essential part of any exposition of ideas, and are of such slight social value as a step to truth that any benefit that may be derived from them is clearly outweighed by the social interest in order and morality.

Libel and obscenity are matters that frequently involve the mass media. Obscenity remains a category of unprotected speech. Many libels—excluding those uttered with "actual malice" and some others—have been removed from the unprotected category by decisions since *Chaplinsky* and now receive varying degrees of First Amendment protection. We consider libel in Chapter III, and obscenity in Chapters VIII, XVII and XVIII.

In addition to the *Chaplinsky* categories, there are other kinds of speech which are treated as being outside the realm of protected speech. One is a knowing lie—knowing something is false and saying it anyway. For this reason criminal statutes punishing perjury, and the common law civil actions for fraud raise no constitutional issue under the First Amendment.

Many people presumed that "hate speech" was similarly unprotected, but the Supreme Court ruled in R.A.V. v. City of St. Paul, Minn., 112 S.Ct. 2538 (1992) that the First Amendment prohibits the government from "silencing speech on the basis of its content." A St. Paul ordinance made it a crime to engage in speech or behavior likely to arouse "anger or alarm" on the basis of "race, color, creed, religion or gender." A white teenager was accused of violating the law by burning a cross on the lawn of the house of an African–American family.  Justice Scalia, writing for a 5–member majority of the court, said, "St. Paul has not singled out an especially offensive mode of expression.  .  .  .  It has not, for example, selected for prohibition only those 'fighting words' that communicate ideas in a threatening, as opposed to merely obnoxious manner."  The view shared by Scalia and the other members of the majority was that the Minnesota ordinance unconstitutionally prohibited speech on the basis of the subjects the speech addresses.

Justice Scalia wrote,

> We have sometimes said that these categories of expression [obscenity, defamation and "fighting words"] are "not within the area of constitutionally protected speech," [  ], or that the "protection of the First Amendment does not extend" to them, [  ].  Such statements must be taken in context, however, and are no more literally true than is the occasionally repeated shorthand characterizing obscenity "as not being speech at all," [  ].  What they mean is that these areas of speech can, consistently with the First Amendment, be regulated because of their constitutionally proscribable content (obscenity, defamation, etc.)—not that they are categories of speech entirely invisible to the Constitution, so that they may be made the vehicles for content discrimination unrelated to their distinctively proscribable content.  Thus, the government may proscribe libel; but it may not make the further content discrimination of proscribing only libel critical of the government.  We recently acknowledged this distinction in [New York v.] Ferber, 458 U.S., at 763, where, in upholding New York's child pornography law, we expressly recognized that there was no "question here of censoring a particular literary theme  .  .  .." [  ]

In contrast, Justices White, Blackmun, O'Connor and Stevens, while agreeing that the St. Paul ordinance was unconstitutional, would have struck it down based on the far less sweeping ground that it was too broad and not sufficiently precisely worded.  Justice White's opinion reflected their view that it was justifiable for St. Paul to have placed hate speech on the subjects of race, religion or sex in a category separate from other speech, but that the ordinance was "fatally overbroad because it criminalizes not only unprotected expression but expression protected by the First Amendment."

### c.  Distribution

Freedom of speech and press have been held to imply more than the freedom only to speak and write.  The First Amendment guarantees include the right to disseminate the words produced after creating them.  In a milestone case, a city ordinance in Griffin, Ga., prescribed criminal penalties for distributing printed material without permission.  The Court found the ordinance was overly broad because it included all "literature," making no distinction between that which the First

Amendment does and does not protect. Also, the ordinance gave the city manager unbridled censorship powers given that he was provided no criteria for decision and was not obligated to explain why he refused permission to distribute. Lovell v. Griffin, 303 U.S. 444 (1938).

*Distribution by Mail.* Historically, one of the principal means of circulation of magazines, and to a lesser extent newspapers, has been through the United States mail. Since the creation of the Post Office, periodicals have received the benefit of rates lower than those for letters. The lower rates were designed "to encourage the dissemination of news and of current literature of educational value."

Note that the First Amendment does not enter into the question of whether to establish subsidies for media. It has not been argued that the Constitution *requires* Congress to subsidize the media. Rather, this is a question for Congress to decide—at least so long as Congress does not discriminate for or against certain periodicals because of their editorial positions or because of political favoritism.

In the Classification Act of 1879, Congress created the four classes of mail that still exist and established eligibility requirements for second-class mail that are virtually unchanged today: publication in unbound form at regular intervals at least four times a year, issued from a known office of publication and "originated and published for the dissemination of information of a public character, or devoted to literature, the sciences, arts, or some special industry."

The limitations on postal authority control over second-class mails have been developed through interpretation of these criteria. The discretion of postal officials reached its outermost limits in Milwaukee Social Democratic Publishing Co. v. Burleson, 255 U.S. 407 (1921). The Postmaster General had revoked the second-class privileges of the *Milwaukee Leader*, a left-wing newspaper critical of United States involvement in World War I. The second-class privilege was available only to "mailable" matter, and the Court found authorization for the ban in the Espionage Act of 1917, which provided that any newspaper that published false statements intended to promote the success of the enemies of the United States was "nonmailable." Furthermore, the Court reasoned that once an unspecified number of issues of a newspaper had revealed its "nonmailable" character, it was a "reasonable presumption" that future issues would be nonmailable, thus justifying the indefinite revocation.

Justice Brandeis, dissenting, argued that the nonmailability provisions gave the Postmaster General authority only to exclude from the mails specific issues that he found to be nonmailable and he could not close the mails to future issues of the same publication or future mail tendered by a particular person. To allow more would be to attribute to Congress the desire to create a "universal censor of publication" because "a denial of the use of the mail would be for most publications tantamount to a denial of the right of circulation."

Finally, in Hannegan v. Esquire, Inc., 327 U.S. 146, 1 Med.L.Rptr. 2292 (1946), the Court in effect adopted Justice Brandeis's views and drastically restricted the discretion of the Postmaster General, who had revoked the second-class privileges of *Esquire Magazine*. He had expressly stipulated that he was not finding the magazine to be obscene and thus "nonmailable" under the obscenity provisions. Instead, he argued that the "public character" eligibility requirement gave him the power to exclude publications that, though not "obscene in a technical sense," are "morally improper and not for the public welfare and the public good." The Court concluded that such a view would "grant the Postmaster General a power of censorship. Such a power is so abhorrent to our traditions that a purpose to grant it should not easily be inferred." By narrowing the sweep of the statute, the Court did not have to deal with the constitutional issue.

*Newsracks.* A different sort of distribution problem has arisen in recent years with the increase in the number of newsracks for selling newspapers. When Gannett's national newspaper, *USA Today,* was launched, the corporation counted on sales from conveniently-placed newsracks. The Gannett newsracks, as well as others, frequently became the targets of municipal ordinances. In some cases people objected to the appearance of the newsracks, prompting questions about how to balance aesthetics against First Amendment freedoms. In other instances local officials saw newsrack ordinances as a way of gaining extra revenue. Having become accustomed to receiving income from granting permissions for cable television franchises, they thought that newspapers putting up newsracks should also pay fees to the municipality—particularly if the newsracks were bolted to the sidewalks or chained to lampposts.

The city of Lakewood, Ohio, passed an ordinance requiring a rental permit before a newsrack could be placed on city property. Before the permit could be issued, a city architectural review board had to approve the newsrack, and the publisher had to indemnify the city and provide insurance naming the city as the insured. Furthermore, the mayor of Lakewood was given broad discretion to grant or refuse the permits, including the power to impose "necessary and reasonable" additional terms and conditions, providing only that he state the reasons if he denied a permit.

In 1988 the Supreme Court overturned those portions of the Lakewood newsrack ordinance "giving the Mayor unfettered discretion to deny a permit application and unbounded authority to condition the permit on any additional terms he deems 'necessary and reasonable.' " A majority of the sitting justices held that distribution of newspapers is conduct related to expression and is therefore protected by the First Amendment. The vote was 4–3. Because Chief Justice Rehnquist (whose daughter, an attorney, was involved in the case) and Justice Kennedy (who had joined the Court after the case was argued) did not vote, the decision is a fragile precedent for a First Amendment right to

locate newsracks on public property.  City of Lakewood v. Plain Dealer
Publishing Co., 486 U.S. 750, 15 Med.L.Rptr. 1481 (1988).

The Supreme Court subsequently struck down an ordinance allowing newsracks on public property for distribution of newspapers but not
commercial handbills.  City of Cincinnati v. Discovery Network, Inc.,
113 S.Ct. 1505, 21 Med.L.Rptr. 1161 (1993).  Analyzing the issue as a
commercial speech problem, the Court held that such a distinction might
be permissible under other circumstances, but commercial publications
could not be singled out to bear the entire burden of restricting the total
number of newsracks in the interests of aesthetics and safety.  The case
is discussed further in Chapter IX.

### d.  Gathering

The "right to gather" information from willing private sources
began to take shape in 1972 with two cases.  In Kleindienst v. Mandel,
408 U.S. 753 (1972), American scholars sought to invite Mandel, a
Belgian Marxist economist, to attend conferences and to speak at several
American universities.  Congress had barred visas for aliens who advocated "the economic, international, and governmental doctrines of world
communism or the establishment in the United States of a totalitarian
dictatorship."  Such an alien might be admitted temporarily if the
Attorney General approved a recommendation to that effect from the
Department of State.  A recommendation was made for Mandel but,
based on information about Mandel's behavior on a previous trip to the
United States, the Attorney General refused to approve the visa application.  Mandel and the scholars sued.  After concluding that Mandel, as
an alien, had no constitutional right of entry, the Court turned to the
rights claimed by the scholars:

> The Government  .  .  .  suggests that the First Amendment
> is inapplicable because [the scholars] have free access to Mandel's
> ideas through his books and speeches, and because "technological
> developments," such as tapes or telephone hook-ups, readily sup-
> plant his physical presence.  This argument overlooks what may be
> particular qualities inherent in sustained, face-to-face debate, discus-
> sion and questioning.  .  .  .  We are loath to hold on this record
> that existence of other alternatives extinguishes altogether any
> constitutional interest on the part of the [scholars] in this particular
> form of access.

The Court, however, concluded that this interest was overcome by the
government's longstanding power to make rules for excluding aliens.

Three dissenters argued that because the government was prevented
from encumbering the entry of books and pamphlets, there was no basis
for excluding Mandel unless it could be shown that he posed "an actual
threat to the country."  They relied on Lamont v. Postmaster General,
381 U.S. 301 (1965), in which the Court held unconstitutional a statute
permitting the government to require the addressee of unrequested

"communist political propaganda" to request in writing that the post office deliver such matter.

The second case to provide some indirect support for protection of gathering was Branzburg v. Hayes, 408 U.S. 665, 1 Med.L.Rptr. 2617 (1972). Although the Court held that the reporters had no First Amendment right to refuse to testify before a grand jury, the majority acknowledged that the Court was not suggesting "that news gathering does not qualify for First Amendment protection; without some protection for seeking out the news, freedom of the press could be eviscerated." The protection of the confidentiality of reporters' sources is considered in detail in Chapter XI.

### e.   *Refusal to Speak*

Most freedom of communication questions concern whether the government can prevent a person from, or punish a person for, speaking. The other side of that coin is whether individuals can be forced to speak against their will. The Supreme Court confronted this issue in West Virginia State Board of Education v. Barnette, 319 U.S. 624 (1943), in which it held that public school children could not be compelled to participate in a flag salute exercise. The Court said forcing someone to express a view, such as respect for the flag, was as offensive to the First Amendment as forbidding a person to do so.

The right not to speak, though infrequently asserted by mass media, continues to represent an important element of First Amendment protections. For example, in Miami Herald v. Tornillo, 418 U.S. 241, 1 Med.L.Rptr. 1898 (1974), a case we will examine in Chapter XIV, the Court held that a state statute compelling the *Herald* to print a political candidate's reply to a *Herald* attack violated the *Herald's* First Amendment right to freely exercise editorial judgment concerning the contents of its publication. The *Herald,* in effect, had a First Amendment right not to print Tornillo's reply. As the Court made clear in *Tornillo:*

> "[A] compulsion exerted by government on a newspaper to print that which it would not otherwise print . . . is unconstitutional. A responsible press is an undoubtedly desirable goal, but press responsibility is not mandated by the Constitution and like many other virtues it cannot be legislated." Id. at 284.

Despite arguments that an individual should at least be able to purchase advertising time or space in the media to disseminate a message, courts have held that a private newspaper may reject advertising for any reason, or no reason, so long as its motive or effect is not anticompetitive. See Chapter XIV.

The situation applicable to electronic media is much less clear. The courts have concluded that the airwaves represent a scarce public resource and that this permits government to require broadcasters and cable operators to grant others access to the microphone in some situations. These obligations are discussed in detail in Chapters XIV through XVIII.

### 3. ABRIDGMENT DEFINED

Determining whether the press is engaged in protected speech represents only half the question in evaluating whether a constitutional issue has been raised under the First Amendment. Courts must also determine whether an abridgment has taken place.

### a. Prior Restraints

Recall from p. 26, *supra*, that in the traditional, Blackstonian, view, prior restraints represented the quintessential, indeed exclusive, abridgments of speech. "Prior restraint" meant that rather than punishing the publisher by criminal or civil sanctions for what was published, the government barred the publication from occurring in the first place. This is, of course, the essence of censorship. In English history, the censor was an administrative official, who administered the licensing system we have already considered.

Prior restraints come in a variety of forms. Those imposed by the judiciary include *temporary restraining orders* and *injunctions*—what the press calls "gag orders." Those imposed by administrative agencies include *licensing* and *cease and desist orders*. Those imposed by the legislative branch of government in the form of statutes are sometimes called "*gag laws.*" Any of these forms of restraint may be challenged in court, because—however well intentioned they may be—they constitute censorship.

Throughout this book you will find examples of the imposition of restraints. They have been motivated by such concerns as national security (the "Pentagon Papers" case—New York Times v. United States), the fair trial rights of a defendant (Nebraska Press Association v. Stuart), sanitation and the avoidance of littering (Valentine v. Chrestensen), an individual's right of privacy (Organization for a Better Austin v. Keefe), the use of the public airwaves for the public interest, necessity and convenience (Trinity Methodist Church, South v. Federal Radio Commission), and deceptive advertising (Federal Trade Commission v. Colgate–Palmolive Co.)

Note that there is a distinction to be made between (1) not *allowing* something to be disseminated and (2) allowing it to be disseminated but imposing subsequent criminal or civil sanctions.

Although it might have been argued that only administrative or executive branch behavior could constitute a prior restraint, it has become clear in this country that judicial orders that bar publications are also analyzed as prior restraints. Nonetheless, court orders imposing prior restraints are thought somewhat less objectionable than similar administrative action because of a perception that administrators may cut procedural corners and otherwise be unfair in executing their obligations. Even so, some administrative prior restraints are permitted even today. The most obvious example is that the Supreme Court has permitted states to license motion pictures. Under such a system, it is a crime to exhibit a film that has not been approved in advance, even if the film is totally unobjectionable on any ground. This type of licensing system was upheld in Freedman v. Maryland, 380 U.S. 51, 1 Med.L.Rptr. 1126 (1965), so long as the administrative decision was subject to swift judicial review.

The deep-rooted antagonism to prior restraint is seen in the Supreme Court's decision in Near v. Minnesota, 283 U.S. 697, 1 Med. L.Rptr. 1001 (1931), the first case in which the Court invalidated a state law because it violated the First and Fourteenth Amendments to the United States Constitution. More specifically, *Near* established the Court's initial approach to the question of prior restraint. *Near* involved a Minnesota statute allowing officials to stop publication of "malicious, scandalous, and defamatory" newspapers and periodicals. Once stopped, publication could be resumed only on order of a judge, who would have to approve the content before allowing continued printing. The county attorney brought an action to stop publication of *The Saturday Press,* printed in Minneapolis. The complaint said the *Press* had accused certain government officials of being involved in bootlegging and gambling which according to the *Press,* were controlled by a "Jewish gangster."

An editorial in the last issue before the restraint demonstrates the writing in Near's newspaper. It was quoted in its entirety as Footnote 1 to Justice Butler's dissenting opinion when the Supreme Court of the United States decided the case:

. . . There have been too many men in this city and especially those in official life, who HAVE [capital letters in the original] been taking orders and suggestions from JEW GANGSTERS, therefore we HAVE Jew Gangsters, practically ruling Minneapolis.

. . .

Practically every vendor of vile hooch, every owner of a moonshine still, every snake-faced gangster and embryonic yegg in the Twin Cities is a JEW.

. . .

It is Jew, Jew, Jew, as long as one cares to comb over the records.

I am launching no attack against the Jewish people AS A RACE. I am merely calling attention to a FACT. And if the people of that race and faith wish to rid themselves of the odium and stigma THE RODENTS OF THEIR OWN RACE HAVE BROUGHT UPON THEM, they need to step to the front and help the decent citizens of Minneapolis rid the city of these criminal Jews. . . .

The state courts "perpetually enjoined" the defendants from publishing *The Saturday Press*.

The Supreme Court of the United States reversed the state court, saying the case involved "questions of grave importance." Chief Justice Charles Evans Hughes, writing for the 5–4 majority, noted that Blackstone's observation that "[t]he liberty of the press . . . consists in laying no *previous* restraints upon publications . . ." was too broad. Although prior restraint is presumed to be unconstitutional, "the protection . . . is not absolutely unlimited." The Court then suggested some areas in which such restraints might be upheld:

> No one would question but that a government might prevent actual obstruction to its recruiting service or the publication of sailing dates of transports or the number and location of troops. On similar grounds, the primary requirements of decency may be enforced against obscene publications. The security of the community life may be protected against incitements to acts of violence and the overthrow by force of orderly government. The constitutional guaranty of free speech does not "protect a man from an injunction against uttering words that may have all the effect of force." [ ] These limitations are not applicable here. Nor are we now concerned with questions as to the extent of authority to prevent publications in order to protect private rights according to the principles governing the exercise of the jurisdiction of courts of equity.

Because the defendant's charges in the Near case did not come within any of these categories, prior restraint was impermissible. Note, however, that the issue of direct government censorship of military information during wartime became an issue in the Persian Gulf in 1991. We will address the issue of wartime censorship in Chapter VII as a part of the discussion of national security.

Fred Friendly, former president of CBS News, wrote a book about the Near case 50 years later and cast new light on the personalities involved. The book details editor Jay M. Near's crusade against lawlessness in the Twin Cities of Minneapolis and St. Paul and the legal and personal troubles it brought him. Although Near's language was clearly anti–Semitic, Friendly's research indicates that Near was telling the truth about the events he reported. F. Friendly, Minnesota Rag (1981).

When judges have issued prior restraints, even though they may be impermissible, journalists have faced the difficult question of whether to obey them. The issue arose in United States v. Dickinson, 465 F.2d 496, 1 Med.L.Rptr. 1338 (5th Cir.1972). Fearing that news accounts of a preliminary hearing would be prejudicial, a federal judge ordered the press not to publish any testimony from that hearing. Two reporters violated the order. On appeal, the court of appeals held the order unconstitutional but ruled that it had to be obeyed until overturned on appeal.

The issue arose again in a case involving the *Providence Journal,*
which had lawfully obtained FBI logs of electronic surveillance of a
reputed mob leader who had recently died. The son of the reputed mob
leader sued to enjoin publication on the ground that the logs had been
wrongfully released by the FBI. A federal district court temporarily
restrained publication, but the newspaper published anyway and was
held in contempt. The newspaper was sentenced to a fine of $100,000,
and the executive editor was sentenced to 18 months' probation and 200
hours of public service.

A panel of the Court of Appeals for the First Circuit reversed,
holding that *Dickinson* and another case both recognized an exception
allowing the defendant to ignore a "transparently invalid" injunction,
which the Court of Appeals found the trial court's order to be. The case
was reheard *en banc* (all of the eligible judges sitting together), and the
full court did not vacate the panel opinion but said,

> [I]t seems to us that some finer tuning is available to minimize the
> disharmony between respect for court orders and respect for free
> speech.
>
> It is not asking much, beyond some additional expense and
> time, to require a publisher, even when it thinks it is the subject of a
> transparently unconstitutional order of prior restraint, to make a
> good faith effort to seek emergency relief from the appellate court.
> If timely access to the appellate court is not available or if timely
> decision is not forthcoming, the publisher may then proceed to
> publish and challenge the constitutionality of the order in the
> contempt proceedings.

Matter of Providence Journal Co., 820 F.2d 1354, 14 Med.L.Rptr. 1029
(1st Cir.1987) (en banc).

A petition for *certiorari* was initially granted by the Supreme Court,
then dismissed on the ground that the court-appointed special prosecutor
did not have authority to appeal on behalf of the government without
the authorization of the solicitor general. 485 U.S. 693, 15 Med.L.Rptr.
1241 (1988).

After this decision, when would a prior restraint in a federal court
*not* be "transparently invalid"? If the appellate court immediately
grants the defendant's request for review, but does not immediately
decide the case, may the defendant safely disobey the injunction on the
ground that it is being denied "timely decision"? Is proof that further
delay would have caused defendant to be "scooped" by a competitor
sufficient to show that a "timely" decision was not forthcoming?

Some states have chosen to follow a different rule that you can
violate such a restraining order at your peril: if the order is subsequently found to be constitutional, you can be punished, but if it is found to be
unconstitutional, you cannot be punished.

Among the Supreme Court cases in which prior restraints have been
held impermissible are Bantam Books, Inc. v. Sullivan, 372 U.S. 58,

1 Med.L.Rptr. 1116 (1963), and Organization for a Better Austin v. Keefe, 402 U.S. 415, 1 Med.L.Rptr. 1021 (1971). In *Bantam Books,* the Court considered a system under which a state Commission to Encourage Morality in Youth sought to limit distribution of publications deemed "objectionable" for sale to minors. Among the listed publications were *Playboy* magazine and the novel *Peyton Place.* Holding the system to be unconstitutional, the Court said, "any system of prior restraints comes to this Court bearing a heavy presumption against its constitutional validity." In *Organization for a Better Austin,* the Court considered an injunction stopping a neighborhood organization from distributing leaflets accusing a real estate broker of unethical practices. The broker had claimed the leaflets invaded his privacy. Holding the injunction to be unconstitutional, the Court said that one seeking a restraint, "carries a heavy burden of showing justification for the imposition of such a restraint." The two cases preceded the important confrontation between the press and the federal government in New York Times v. United States (the "Pentagon Papers" case), discussed in Chapter VII.

Prior restraint may present special problems when invoked against student publications in public high schools and colleges. If the high school principal were a town's mayor and the student newspaper were the local daily, prior restraint would be permissible only if one of the *Near* or similar exceptions existed. Public school officials represent the state just as a mayor does. But does the special context of a high school or college allow school officials more leeway under the First and Fourteenth Amendments than is allowed a mayor?

*Tinker,* p. 47, *supra,* a case involving the wearing of armbands as Vietnam War protest, established that public school students' First Amendment rights could be limited only if their exercise would cause material and substantial interference with school operations or if there is a "colli[sion] with the rights of others." According to the holding in *Tinker,* students do not "shed their constitutional rights to freedom of speech or expression at the schoolhouse gate."

Despite the holding in *Tinker,* students lost in a 1988 Supreme Court decision involving prior restraint on a high school newspaper. A Missouri principal had censored stories on divorce and teen pregnancy, calling them too "sensitive" to be in a student newspaper. With the help of the American Civil Liberties Union, three students had filed suit, arguing that the newspaper was a public forum and that school administrators lacked the authority to censor material that was nondefamatory or obscene. The school district argued that the students were enrolled in a journalism class that was part of the school's teaching process and that the newspaper was not a public forum. In a 5–3 decision in 1988, the Court held that First Amendment rights of students in public schools are not "automatically coextensive with the rights of adults in other settings" and that a school need not tolerate student speech that is inconsistent with its basic educational mission. Further, the court held that the school newspaper in the case could not be characterized as a forum for public expression because the newspaper's production was consistently treated as part of the curriculum and under a teacher's control, as opposed to a newspaper that might by practice be opened for "indiscriminate use" by the general public or by student organizations. Hazelwood School District v. Kuhlmeier, 484 U.S. 260, 14 Med.L.Rptr. 2081 (1988).

Several restraints were imposed in 1990, but all were short-lived. The syndicated news program "Inside Edition" was temporarily restrained from broadcasting a videotape of a physician allegedly engaged in malpractice. The order was vacated 11 days later by the court of appeals. In re King World Productions, Inc., 898 F.2d 56, 17 Med. L.Rptr. 1531 (6th Cir.1990). Lifetime Cable was briefly subjected to an order restraining it from showing "Hilary in Hiding," a British Broadcasting Corp. film about the battle between Eric Foretich and Elizabeth Morgan over custody of their child. It was vacated the same day by the U.S. Court of Appeals for the District of Columbia. In re Lifetime Cable, 17 Med.L.Rptr. 1648 (1990) (Unpublished Case). See also Broadcasting, April 16, 1990, at 73.

In another case, the government of Israel tried to stop distribution of Victor Ostrovsky's book, *By Way of Deception: A Devastating Insider's Portrait of the Mossad.* Faced with the argument that Israeli intelligence agents would be killed if the book were distributed, a judge in New York temporarily restrained publication, but the order was overturned the next day. The book had been restrained in Canada, but approximately 1,500 wholesalers and book reviewers had already received copies of the book, and 17,000 books had already been shipped to stores. State of Israel v. St. Martin's Press, Inc., 166 A.D.2d 251, 560 N.Y.S.2d 450 (1st Dept. 1990).

At a communications law seminar in November 1990, prominent attorney Floyd Abrams remarked that "The near-total ban on prior restraints we used to talk about seems secure but in a rather insecure way," noting the several prior restraint attempts during the year. "The reasons for prior restraint *always* sound pretty good," Abrams said, "and the potential for damage to First Amendment rights *always* sounds minimal, yet appellate courts have reversed consistently and quickly."

That same month the issue of a prior restraint to protect a defendant's fair trial rights arose again in the case of former Panamanian leader Manuel Noriega, and it was not so quickly reversed. Cable News Network (CNN) had obtained tape recordings of Noriega talking to members of his defense team. Normally, of course, attorney-client conversations are confidential. Fearing that Noriega's future trial could be prejudiced by CNN's playing of the tapes, the U.S. District Court for the Southern District of Florida issued a temporary restraining order barring CNN from play them. The U.S. Court of Appeals for the Eleventh Circuit affirmed the ruling, and the Supreme Court of the United States, without a written opinion, refused to overrule the lower courts or to review the order. Cable News Network v. Noriega, 498 U.S. 976 (1990). Justices Thurgood Marshall and Sandra Day O'Connor dissented. The Supreme Court's action would not necessarily have precluded their considering the prior restraint later, but the trial court subsequently lifted the restraint and essentially ended the dispute.

In *Alexander v. United States*, 113 S.Ct. 2766, 21 Med.L.Rptr. 1609 (1993), the Supreme Court considered what it is that distinguishes prior restraints from subsequent sanctions. Alexander, operator of numerous "adult entertainment" businesses in Minnesota was convicted of transporting obscene magazines and videos in interstate commerce and engaging in the business of selling obscene material. Those convictions provided the basis for a finding that he had engaged in a "pattern of racketeering" for purposes of the Racketeer Influenced and Corrupt Organizations Act (RICO), and under that act the government seized all of Alexander's 31 businesses, confiscated profits, and destroyed millions of dollars worth of books and videos, most of which had never been found to be legally obscene.

The lower court rejected Alexander's contention that the seizure and destruction was a prior restraint. Chief Justice Rehnquist, delivering the opinion of the Supreme Court, wrote that, "By lumping the forfeiture imposed in this case after a full criminal trial with an injunction enjoining future speech, petitioner stretches the term 'prior restraint' well beyond the limits established by our cases. To accept petitioner's argument would virtually obliterate the distinction, solidly grounded in our cases, between prior restraints and subsequent punishments. . . . [P]etitioner's proposed definition of the term 'prior restraint' would undermine the time-honored distinction between barring speech in the future and penalizing past speech. [The Court has struck down restraints in *Near, Organization for a Better Austin,* etc., previously as unconstitutional.] By contrast [to the restraints in those cases], the RICO forfeiture order in this case does not forbid petitioner from engaging in any expressive activities in the future, nor does it require him to obtain prior approval for any expressive activities. It only deprives him of specific assets that were found to be related to his previous racketeering violations. Assuming, of course, that he has sufficient untainted assets to open new stores, restock his inventory, and hire staff, petitioner can go back into the adult entertainment business tomorrow, and sell as many sexually explicit magazines and videotapes as he likes, without any risk of being held in contempt for violating a court order. Unlike the injunctions in Near [and] Keefe . . . the forfeiture order in this case imposes no legal impediment to—no prior restraint on—petitioner's ability to engage in any expressive activity he chooses. He is perfectly free to open an adult bookstore or otherwise engage in the production and distribution of erotic materials; he just cannot finance these enterprises with assets derived from his prior racketeering offenses. . . . In sum, we think that fidelity to our cases requires us to analyze the forfeiture here not as a prior restraint, but under normal First Amendment standards. So analyzing it, we find that petitioner's claim falls well short of the mark."

Four justices dissented.  In his dissenting opinion, Justice Kennedy wrote that, "The Court today embraces a rule that would find no affront to the First Amendment in the Government's destruction of a book and film business and its entire inventory of legitimate expression as punishment for a single past speech offense.  Until now I had thought one could browse through any book or film store in the United States without fear that the proprietor had chosen each item to avoid risk to the whole inventory and indeed to the business itself.  This ominous, onerous threat undermines free speech and press principles essential to our personal freedom."

### b.  Content–Based Burdens and Subsequent Sanctions

Though perhaps less compelling than prior restraint from a historical point of view, it is quite clear that sanctions imposed *after* publication may be like prior restraints, in that they may prevent would-be speakers and writers from publishing protected speech.  Such sanctions, whether they are penal in nature, such as imprisonment or fines, or civil damage awards, or the denial of some privilege, generally raise precisely the same issues as prior restraints on publication.

In Landmark Communications, Inc. v. Virginia, 435 U.S. 829, 3 Med.L.Rptr. 2153 (1978), the Supreme Court was faced with a statute that provided that confidential proceedings regarding investigations of judges could not be divulged.  The Court, as we will see in Chapter X, held that any threat to the administration of justice from publication of the fact that a named judge was under investigation was not sufficiently clear and present to justify such a restraint and remanded the case.

In Smith v. Daily Mail Publishing Co., 443 U.S. 97, 5 Med.L.Rptr. 1305 (1979), which we will discuss in Chapter X, the Supreme Court was faced with a statute that made it a crime for a newspaper to publish a juvenile offender's name unless the paper had obtained the prior written approval of a court.  The paper argued that the prior approval requirement acted in "operation and effect" like a licensing scheme.  As such, the paper argued that the statute carried "a 'heavy presumption' against its constitutional validity," quoting earlier cases.  The Court responded by avoiding the question:

> The resolution of this case does not turn on whether the statutory grant of authority to the juvenile judge to permit publication of the juvenile's name is, in and of itself, a prior restraint.  First Amendment protection reaches beyond prior restraints.  .  .  .

> Whether we view the statute as a prior restraint or as a penal sanction  .  .  .  is not dispositive because even the latter action requires the highest form of state interest to sustain its validity.  Prior restraints have been accorded the most exacting scrutiny in previous cases.  [ ]  However, even when a state attempts to punish publication after the event it must nevertheless demonstrate

that its punitive action was necessary to further the state interests asserted. [ ]  Since we conclude that this statute cannot satisfy the constitutional standards defined in *Landmark Communications, Inc.,* we need not decide whether, as argued by [the newspaper], it operated as a prior restraint.

This case suggests that much of the distinction traditionally drawn between prior restraints and other forms of inhibitions on the activities of the press may be vanishing.  As we shall see throughout this book, the criteria that the Court use in reviewing challenged state actions are usually quite rigorous no matter what the form of the state inhibition.

There are instances in which government may wish to disfavor certain kinds of expression in a way that stops short of imposing a prior restraint.  Such was the case when the State of New York sought to make certain that serial killer David Berkowitz, known as the "Son of Sam," and other criminals would not benefit financially from the sale of rights to their stories.  The law required "that an accused or convicted criminal's income from works describing his crime be deposited in an escrow account.  These funds are then made available to the victims of the crime and the criminal's other creditors."  The statute defined "persons convicted of a crime" to include those who, though not convicted, had "voluntarily and intelligently admitted the commission of a crime for which such person is not prosecuted."  As construed by the New York courts, however, the statute did not apply to victims of crimes. The statute, rarely used since 1977, was one of several ways in which the state sought to obtain compensation for victims of crime.  These included a statutory plan that compensated crime victims for their losses; permitting courts to order that proceeds of crime be forfeited to the state; permitting courts to order restitution at sentencing; and "prejudgment attachment procedures to ensure that wrongdoers do not dissipate their assets."

The Supreme Court considered the constitutionality of the statute in Simon & Schuster, Inc. v. Members of New York State Crime Victims Board, 502 U.S. ___, 112 S.Ct. 501, 19 Med.L.Rptr. 1609 (1991).  The case arose out of the activities of Henry Hill, an "admitted organized crime figure," whose activities are recounted in N. Pileggi's book *Wiseguy: Life in a Mafia Family*.  (The book was the basis for the movie "Goodfellas.")  Hill spent more than 300 hours in discussion with the author.  When the Victims Compensation Board learned of the book, it contacted Simon & Schuster, the publishers, to obtain the funds covered by the statute.  Some funds had already been paid to Hill's literary agent, and some were being held for later disbursement.  The publisher obeyed the orders and then sued under § 1983 for a declaration that the statute violated the First Amendment and an injunction against enforcement.  The district court upheld the statute's constitutionality, as did a divided court of appeals, but the Supreme Court decided that it was unconstitutional.

Justice O'Connor wrote for the Court:

A statute is presumptively inconsistent with the First Amendment if it imposes a financial burden on speakers because of the content of their speech.   . . .

. . .

The Son of Sam law is such a content-based statute.  It singles out income derived from expressive activity for a burden the State places on no other income, and it is directed only at works with a specified content.   Whether the First Amendment "speaker" is considered to be Henry Hill, whose income the statute places in escrow because of the story he has told, or Simon & Schuster, which can publish books about crime with the assistance of only those criminals willing to forgo remuneration for at least five years, the statute plainly imposes a financial disincentive only on speech of a particular content.

. . .

. . .  [T]he State has a compelling interest in compensating victims from the fruits of the crime, but little if any interest in limiting such compensation to the proceeds of the wrongdoer's speech about the crime.  We must therefore determine whether the Son of Sam law is narrowly tailored to advance the former, not the latter, objective.

As a means of ensuring that victims are compensated from the proceeds of crime, the Son of Sam law is significantly overinclusive.   . . .  [T]he statute applies to works on *any* subject, provided that they express the author's thoughts or recollections about his crime, however, tangentially or incidentally.  [  ]  In addition, the statute's broad definition of "person convicted of a crime" enables the Board to escrow the income of any author who admits in his work to having committed a crime, whether or not the author was ever actually accused or convicted.  [  ]

These two provisions combine to encompass a potentially very large number of works.  Had the Son of Sam law been in effect at the time and place of publication, it would have escrowed payment for such works as *The Autobiography of Malcolm X*, which describes crimes committed by the civil rights leader before he became a public figure; *Civil Disobedience*, in which Thoreau acknowledges his refusal to pay taxes and recalls his experience in jail; and even the *Confessions of Saint Augustine*, in which the author laments "my past foulness and the carnal corruptions of my soul," one instance of which involved the theft of pears from a neighboring vineyard.   . . .

. . .

. . .  We conclude simply that in the Son of Sam law, New York has singled out speech on a particular subject for a financial burden that it places on no other speech and no other income.  The State's interest in compensating victims from the fruits of crime is a compelling one, but the Son of Sam law is not narrowly tailored to advance that objective. As a result, the statute is inconsistent with the First Amendment. . . .

New York State adopted a new version of its Son of Sam law in 1992—this time placing no limits on criminals' ability to sell their stories, but making it easier for crime victims to share in the proceeds by making claims against them. "Speech is protected here," said one of the bill's sponsors, "profiting is not protected." New York Times, July 3, 1992 at 1. Variations on the problem continued to arise in 1993. Long Island teenager Amy Fisher, for example, turned over all rights to her story to KLM Productions, a production company that posted her bail prior to her conviction for shooting Mary Jo Buttafuoco. Newsday, April 7, 1993, at 23. A Massachusetts judge, in sentencing former fugitive Katherine A. Power to five years in prison for her role in a 1970 robbery and murder, prohibited her from profiting directly or indirectly from the crime and said any violation could result in a life sentence. The Boston Globe, Nov. 25, 1993 at 57. And, there was controversy when it was revealed that Guns N' Roses included a song written by mass murderer Charles Manson on a new album. The Los Angeles Times, Dec. 14, 1993 at 1.

### c.  Neutral Regulation

The great proportion of government regulation of the press has never been considered to be abridgment so long as it is *neutrally applied*—despite the considerable costs such regulation may exact from the press. Thus, for example, one may not publish a newspaper without obeying local building codes, the income tax laws and other tax statutes, the antitrust laws, the Occupational Safety and Health Act, legislation dealing with labor relations, or any of the myriad other bodies of general regulatory law administered by local, state and federal governments. (Where the rules are not neutrally applied, however, they are subject to challenge—as we will see in tax cases to be discussed in Chapter XIII.)

Because the government apparently is not attempting to suppress a particular point of view or a particular speaker with these general regulations, we might call them "non-speech" measures. If the government is attempting to prevent certain speech, we might call that an "anti-speech" regulation.

Courts have recognized that states have the power, generally called the "police power," to make and enforce regulations relating to the public health, safety, morals and general welfare. Under the police powers, municipalities have imposed restrictions on the time, place and manner of exercising freedom of expression. Generally, courts have upheld this type of regulation if it is nondiscriminatory (applying to all, not just some), not based on content, and reasonable (a regulation allowing everyone to distribute leaflets only at midnight would not be reasonable).

In Cox v. New Hampshire, 312 U.S. 569 (1941), the Supreme Court upheld an ordinance requiring licenses for parades through city streets. The licenses were granted on time, place and manner considerations. The Court said the ordinance served the community's legitimate interest in regulating traffic by, for instance, not allowing parades during rush hours and avoiding simultaneous parades. Since there was no indication that licenses were denied on a discriminatory basis, the ordinance was upheld.

Note that these categories do not involve the question of what point of view the speaker has expressed on a subject. Indeed, the Court frequently has asserted that government must not encourage or hinder speech based on whether officials like the views being expressed. For instance, a city cannot allow peaceful picketing by union members while prohibiting all other peaceful picketing. Such an ordinance in Chicago, which allowed demonstrations near school buildings only if labor matters were involved, was invalidated by the Court. Police Department of Chicago v. Mosley, 408 U.S. 92 (1972). The Court said:

> [U]nder . . . the First Amendment . . ., government may not grant the use of a forum to people whose views it finds acceptable, but deny use to those wishing to express less favored or more controversial views. And it may not select which issues are worth discussing or debating in public facilities. There is an equality of status in the field of ideas, and government must afford all points of view an equal opportunity to be heard. Once a forum is opened up to assembly or speaking by some groups, government may not prohibit others from assembling or speaking on the basis of what they intend to say. Selecting exclusions from a public forum may not be based on content alone, and may not be justified by reference to content alone.

This ringing statement has presented problems in application in certain areas, as we shall see in Chapter XVII. *Mosley* can be seen as an attempt to carefully distinguish between non-speech and anti-speech regulation. Where a non-speech regulation is challenged, it will be upheld if it is found to have a rational relationship to a legitimate state interest. But state efforts to control the content of speech must meet much more rigorous criteria, as we discuss in the next section.

## D.  APPLYING THE FIRST AMENDMENT

An "abridgment" of protected speech is not, despite the apparently unqualified language of the First Amendment, necessarily unconstitutional.

### 1.  PREFERRED POSITION

A basic tenet of constitutional law calls upon courts to presume that enactments of legislative bodies are constitutional. If the legislation has a rational basis, courts will generally hold it constitutional.  In United States v. Carolene Products Co., 304 U.S. 144 (1938), involving the validity of a federal economic regulation, Justice Stone, writing for the majority, restated this generally accepted view of deference to legislatures.  But in one of the Court's most famous footnotes, Justice Stone wrote:

> There may be narrower scope for operation of the presumption of constitutionality when legislation appears on its face to be within a specific prohibition of the Constitution, such as those of the first ten amendments, which are deemed equally specific when held to be embraced within the Fourteenth.   . . .

> It is unnecessary to consider now whether legislation which restricts those political processes which can ordinarily be expected to bring about repeal of undesirable legislation, is to be subjected to more exacting scrutiny under the general prohibitions of the Fourteenth Amendment than are most other types of legislation.   . . .

Justice Stone was suggesting that legislation that inhibits political freedoms, such as freedom of communication, must survive more "exacting judicial scrutiny" than other legislative acts.  Instead of having a presumption of constitutionality, such legislation might be presumed to inhibit a basic freedom and the government might have to show an overriding need for it, not simply a rational basis.  As a result of some cases that built on this footnote, freedom of communication became a "preferred freedom," one that courts would not allow the legislature to restrict without a compelling state interest.

Professor Nimmer, in his book *Freedom of Speech*, explained the modern method of valuing free speech and press in the balancing process:

> The First Amendment command that freedom of speech may not be abridged, although not viewed with a literal absolutism, at the very least means "that any significant restriction of First Amendment freedom carries a heavy burden of justification."  For a period Supreme Court opinions frequently referred to First Amendment freedoms as occupying "a preferred position."  Although this particular phraseology proved somewhat controversial, and has fallen into disuse, there can be no doubt that the implication it suggests for the weighing process remains an important part of First Amendment jurisprudence.  Insofar as the conflicting speech and anti-speech interests may be said to be of equal weight, the speech interest must prevail by reason of the constitutional commitment to this value.  But, of course, in the real world neither legal nor sociological calibrations are so precise as to justify the conclusion that conflicting interests are ever of exactly equal weight.  Rather, "the preference for freedom" suggests an approach, not a formula, whereby doubtful balancing questions are resolved in favor of the speech interest.  There is nevertheless a balancing, and the speech interest does not always win.

## 2. BALANCING

Most frequently, the Supreme Court has used a "balancing test" to determine the propriety of a restraint on freedom of expression. The test involves weighing two interests—the government's concern about protecting a particular interest, such as national security or individual reputation, and the individual's and society's interests in expression.

Professor Chafee, an early advocate of balancing, expressed the virtues of that approach in his *Free Speech in the United States* (1941) at 31 as follows:

> Or to put the matter another way, it is useless to define free speech by talk about rights. The agitator asserts his constitutional right to speak, the government asserts its constitutional right to wage war. The result is a deadlock. . . . To find the boundary line of any right, we must get behind rules of law to human facts. In our problem, we must regard the desires and needs of the individual human being who wants to speak and those of the great group of human beings among whom he speaks. That is, in technical language, there are individual interests and social interests, which must be balanced against each other, if they conflict, in order to determine which interest shall be sacrificed under the circumstances and which shall be protected and become the foundation of a legal right. It must never be forgotten that the balancing cannot be properly done unless all the interests involved are adequately ascertained, and the great evil of all this talk about rights is that each side is so busy denying the other's claim to rights that it entirely overlooks the human desires and needs behind that claim.

Most freedom of expression cases are decided by balancing interests. The Supreme Court, without always explaining its approach, will use one of two variations of the balancing test. Focusing on the interests at stake in the individual case is commonly characterized as "ad hoc" balancing: the specific interests applicable to the facts of the particular case are considered crucial. The court attempts to identify the state's interest in limiting or preventing the speech in question and the would-be speaker's and society's interests in having the speech permitted. Balancing on a case-by-case basis involves such case-specific factors that it is often difficult to predict what weight a resolution reached on one set of facts will be accorded in a subsequent case with somewhat different facts.

At other times, a more general process, called "definitional" or "categorical" balancing, is used. Such was the case in *Chaplinsky*, p. 48 *supra*. Here the interests analyzed transcend the merits of a particular case. Rather than asking, for example, whether the value of speech in a particular case outweighs the arguments for proscribing it, the Court might generalize and consider the values of that category of speech, or that category of speaker, and develop a more general analysis. This approach makes it easier to predict outcomes because of the explicitly generalized character of the decision.

### 3.   CLEAR AND PRESENT DANGER

Most of the remainder of this book will focus on how balancing tests between speech and anti-speech interests are applied in a wide variety of issues affecting mass media.   In defamation, for example, speech interests are balanced against the individual's interest in reputation.   In other cases, speech interests must be balanced against privacy interests, property interests, security interests, public safety and morals, and even countervailing speech interests, to name only a few.   The balance struck in each situation differs as the countervailing interests vary in weight and as the value of the speech interest itself changes in various contexts. Even in the *same* context the balancing process often yields varying results over time as the hierarchy of values and weights accorded various interests change.

One important example of the balancing process is the evolution of the "clear and present danger" test originally framed by Justice Oliver Wendell Holmes in an important series of cases arising out of the Espionage Act of 1917.   These cases represent the struggle of the courts to accommodate the federal government's interest in maintaining the integrity of its effort to wage war with dissenters' free speech rights. The Espionage Act banned attempts to cause insubordination in the armed forces or to obstruct military recruiting or to conspire to achieve these results.   Most of these cases, which confronted the Court from 1919 until the mid–1920s, involved radical speakers who opposed the war effort and criticized the political and economic structure of the country.

Based on his marketplace of ideas approach, Holmes saw the clear and present danger test as least intrusive on freedom of expression in a society in which absolute freedom was impractical.   In Schenck v. United States, 249 U.S. 47 (1919), Justice Holmes said that expression could be punished when "the words used are used in such circumstances and are of such a nature as to create a clear and present danger that they will bring about the substantive evils that Congress has a right to prevent.   It is a question of proximity and degree."

*Schenck* involved a prosecution under the Espionage Act for publishing a leaflet that interfered with recruiting by urging young men to violate the draft law.   Holmes, writing for the majority, found that the leaflet could be closely connected with violations of the Conscription Act (proximity) and that this was a serious danger to the country's security (degree).

*Abrams*, p. 37, *supra*, involved pamphlets calling for a strike of munitions workers.   The Supreme Court upheld the convictions.   This time Justices Holmes and Brandeis dissented, saying:

. . . I think that we should be eternally vigilant against attempts to check the expression of opinions that we loathe and believe to be fraught with death, unless they so imminently threaten immediate interference with the lawful and pressing purposes of the law that an immediate check is required to save the country. I wholly disagree with the argument of the Government that the First Amendment left the common law as to seditious libel in force. History seems to me against the notion. I had conceived that the United States through many years had shown its repentance for the Sedition Act of 1798, [ ], by repaying fines that it imposed. Only the emergency that makes it immediately dangerous to leave the correction of evil counsels to time warrants making any exception to the sweeping command, "Congress shall make no law . . . abridging the freedom of speech." Of course I am speaking only of expressions of opinion and exhortations, which were all that were uttered here, but I regret that I cannot put into more impressive words my belief that in their conviction upon this indictment the defendants were deprived of their rights under the Constitution of the United States.

It was uncertain what test the majority was using during this period. After some movement toward clear and present danger, the Court confronted a case involving a state statute that explicitly proscribed certain language.

The case, Gitlow v. New York, 268 U.S. 652 (1925), involved a prosecution under a New York criminal statute that barred advocating overthrow of the government by violence. The majority upheld the conviction:

By enacting the present statute the State has determined, through its legislative body, that utterances advocating the overthrow of organized government by force, violence and unlawful means, are so inimical to the general welfare and involve such danger of substantive evil that they may be penalized in the exercise of its police power. That determination must be given great weight. Every presumption is to be indulged in favor of the validity of the statute. . . . The State cannot reasonably be required to measure the danger from every such utterance in the nice balance of a jeweler's scale. A single revolutionary spark may kindle a fire that, smouldering for a time, may burst into a sweeping and destructive conflagration. It cannot be said that the State is acting arbitrarily or unreasonably when in the exercise of its judgment as to the measures necessary to protect the public peace and safety, it seeks to extinguish the spark without waiting until it has enkindled the flame or blazed into the conflagration. It cannot reasonably be required to defer the adoption of measures for its own peace and safety until the revolutionary utterances lead to actual disturbances of the public peace or imminent and immediate danger of its own destruction; but it may, in the exercise of its judgment, suppress the threatened danger in its incipiency. . . .

. . .

In other words, when the legislative body has determined generally, in the constitutional exercise of its discretion, that utterances of a certain kind involve such danger of substantive evil that they may be punished, the question whether any specific utterance coming within the prohibited class is likely, in and of itself, to bring about the substantive evil, is not open to consideration. It is sufficient that the statute itself be constitutional and that the use of the language comes within its prohibition.

. . . In such cases it has been held that the general provisions of the statute may be constitutionally applied to the specific utterance of the defendant if its natural tendency and probable effect was to bring about the substantive evil which the legislative body might prevent. . . .

Justice Holmes, with whom Justice Brandeis joined, dissented in an opinion that rejected a "natural tendency" test:

. . . I think that the criterion sanctioned by the full Court in Schenck v. United States, 249 U.S. 47, 52, applies. "The question in every case is whether the words used are used in such circumstances and are of such a nature as to create a clear and present danger that they will bring about the substantive evils that [the State] has a right to prevent." It is true that in my opinion this criterion was departed from in Abrams v. United States, 250 U.S. 616, but the convictions that I expressed in that case are too deep for it to be possible for me as yet to believe that it and Schaefer v. United States, 251 U.S. 466, have settled the law. If what I think the correct test is applied, it is manifest that there was no present danger of an attempt to overthrow the government by force on the part of the admittedly small minority who shared the defendant's views. It is said that this manifesto was more than a theory, that it was an incitement. Every idea is an incitement. It offers itself for belief and if believed it is acted on unless some other belief outweighs it or some failure of energy stifles the movement at its birth. The only difference between the expression of an opinion and an incitement in the narrower sense is the speaker's enthusiasm for the result. Eloquence may set fire to reason. But whatever may be thought of the redundant discourse before us it had no chance of starting a present conflagration. If in the long run the beliefs expressed in proletarian dictatorship are destined to be accepted by the dominant forces of the community, the only meaning of free speech is that they should be given their chance and have their way.

Justice Brandeis, in a separate opinion joined by Justice Holmes, had occasion to expand upon their thinking two years later in *Whitney* p. 33, *supra*, (another case in which the majority had rejected the clear and present danger approach):

Fear of serious injury cannot alone justify suppression of free speech and assembly. Men feared witches and burnt women. It is the function of speech to free men from the bondage of irrational fears. To justify suppression of free speech there must be reasonable ground to fear that serious evil will result if free speech is practiced. There must be reasonable ground to believe that the danger apprehended is imminent. There must be reasonable ground to believe that the evil to be prevented is a serious one. Every denunciation of existing law tends in some measure to increase the probability that there will be violation of it. . . . In order to support a finding of clear and present danger it must be shown either that immediate serious violence was to be expected or was advocated, or that the past conduct furnished reason to believe that such advocacy was then contemplated.

. . . If there be time to expose through discussion the falsehood and fallacies, to avert the evil by the processes of education, the remedy to be applied is more speech, not enforced silence. Only an emergency can justify repression. Such must be the rule if authority is to be reconciled with freedom. Such, in my opinion, is the command of the Constitution. It is therefore always open to Americans to challenge a law abridging free speech and assembly by showing that there was no emergency justifying it.

Moreover, even imminent danger cannot justify resort to prohibition of these functions essential to effective democracy, unless the evil apprehended is relatively serious. Prohibition of free speech and assembly is a measure so stringent that it would be inappropriate as the means for averting a relatively trivial harm to society. A police measure may be unconstitutional merely because the remedy, although effective as means of protection, is unduly harsh or oppressive. Thus, a State might, in the exercise of its police power, make any trespass upon the land of another a crime, regardless of the results or of the intent or purpose of the trespasser. It might, also, punish an attempt, a conspiracy, or an incitement to commit the trespass. But it is hardly conceivable that this Court would hold constitutional a statute which punished as a felony the mere voluntary assembly with a society formed to teach that pedestrians had the moral right to cross unenclosed, unposted, waste lands and to advocate their doing so, even if there was imminent danger that advocacy would lead to a trespass. The fact that speech is likely to result in some violence or in destruction of property is not enough to justify its suppression. There must be the probability of serious injury to the State. Among free men, the deterrents ordinarily to be applied to prevent crime are education and punishment for violations of the law, not abridgment of the rights of free speech and assembly.

The Court had no occasion to return to these discussions for some time. Ironically, the return occurred in a case in which the plurality of the Court recognized that the Holmes–Brandeis position had evolved to become a majority view—but the plurality then refused to apply it to its case. This curious case was Dennis v. United States, 341 U.S. 494

(1951), involving prosecution of 11 leading members of the Communist Party for conspiring to advocate the forcible overthrow of the government of the United States. The plurality observed that "Although no case subsequent to *Whitney* and *Gitlow* has expressly overruled the majority opinions in those cases, there is little doubt that subsequent opinions have inclined toward the Holmes–Brandeis rationale."

At the same time, however, the plurality noted that each case confronting Justices Holmes and Brandeis involved "a comparatively isolated event, bearing little relation in their minds to any substantial threat to the safety of the community. . . . They were not confronted with any situation comparable to the instant one—the development of an apparatus designed and dedicated to the overthrow of the Government, in the context of world crisis after crisis."

The Court adopted the test framed by Judge Learned Hand in the lower court: "In each case [courts] must ask whether the gravity of the 'evil,' discounted by its improbability, justifies such invasion of free speech as is necessary to avoid the danger." That statement "takes into consideration those factors which we deem relevant, and relates their significances. More we cannot expect from words."

The plurality found that the requisite danger existed. The formation of a "highly organized conspiracy, with rigidly disciplined members subject to call when the leaders, these petitioners, felt the time had come for action, coupled with the inflammable nature of world conditions, similar uprisings in other countries, and the touch-and-go nature of our relations with countries with whom petitioners were in the very least ideologically attuned, convince us that their convictions were justified on this score . . . .. If the ingredients of the reaction are present, we cannot bind the Government to wait until the catalyst is added."

In 1957 the Court limited the impact of the Smith Act, which had made it illegal to advocate overthrowing the government by force or violence. In Yates v. United States, 354 U.S. 298 (1957), the Court reversed five convictions under the Act and ordered new trials for the other nine defendants. Justice John M. Harlan for the Court said that *Dennis* allowed restricting only "advocacy found to be directed to 'action for the accomplishment of forcible overthrow.'" This required a direct relationship between speech and action that the government found it difficult to prove.

The status of clear and present danger after *Dennis* and *Yates* remained unclear until Brandenburg v. Ohio, 395 U.S. 444 (1969), involving prosecution of a Ku Klux Klan member for advocating racial and religious bigotry. The criminal syndicalism statute under which Ohio proceeded bore close similarities to the statute in *Whitney*. "But *Whitney* has been thoroughly discredited by later decisions. See [*Dennis*]. These later decisions have fashioned the principle that the constitutional guarantees of free speech and free press do not permit a State to forbid or proscribe advocacy of the use of force or of law violation except where such advocacy is directed to inciting or producing imminent lawless action and is likely to incite or produce such action."

Because the statute permitted punishment of advocacy with no requirement of a showing that imminent lawless action was likely to follow, the convictions could not stand. *Whitney* was overruled.

*Brandenburg* was reinforced in Hess v. Indiana, 414 U.S. 105 (1973). The defendant was arrested during an antiwar demonstration on a college campus for shouting, "We'll take the fucking street later (or again)." His subsequent conviction was overturned by the Supreme Court. "At best, [the] statement could be taken as counsel for present moderation; at worst, it amounted to nothing more than advocacy of illegal action at some indefinite future time." Because there was no showing that the words "were intended to produce, and likely to produce, *imminent* disorder, those words could not be punished by the State on the ground that they had a 'tendency to lead to violence.'"

Despite the extended period during which the clear and present danger test has been discussed in the Supreme Court, its importance and utility must not be overstated. As one observer has noted, although "it has uses in the area of seditious speech where it arose, it is not a broad-spectrum sovereign remedy for such other complaints as defamation, obscenity, and invasions of privacy, where the complex of interests at stake requires closer diagnosis and more refined treatment." Freund, The Great Disorder of Speech, 44 American Scholar 541, 544–45 (1975). Elsewhere the same observer noted that even where it is applicable, the test is not self-applying: "No matter how rapidly we utter the phrase . . . or how closely we hyphenate the words, they are not a substitute for the weighing of values." P. Freund, The Supreme Court of the United States 44 (1961).

### 4. The Literalist Interpretation of the First Amendment

Some have argued that the First Amendment allows no room for interpretation because its language is absolute: "Congress shall make no law . . . abridging the freedom of speech, or of the press . . .." They have concluded that the federal government "is without any power whatever under the Constitution to put any type of burden on speech and expression of ideas of any kind." Ginzburg v. United States, 383 U.S. 463, 476, 1 Med.L.Rptr. 1409, 1414 (1966) (Black, J., dissenting). He strongly criticized the balancing approach to First Amendment questions because the test could be used to justify a judge's predilections. But Justice Black did not believe that action should be protected to the same extent.

Justice Black's distinction between speech and action provided the escape hatch for his absolutist view. For instance, he would not have required states to allow public high school students to wear black arm bands to protest the Vietnam war. *Tinker*, p. 47, *supra*, (Black, J., dissenting). He called the behavior "action," not speech, and thus not protected by the First Amendment.

In his book, The System of Freedom of Expression 17 (1970), Professor Thomas Emerson drew a similar distinction, believing, with Justice Black, that expression should be absolutely protected by the First Amendment:

"Expression" must be freely allowed and encouraged. "Action" can be controlled, subject to other constitutional requirements, but not by controlling expression. . . . The character of the system [of freedom of expression] can flourish, and the goals of the system can be realized, only if expression receives full protection under the First Amendment. . . . The government may protect or advance other social interests through regulation of action, but not by suppressing expression.

Recall Meiklejohn, too, believed in an absolute approach to the First Amendment—but only for "political speech." As with Justice Black and Emerson, his distinction narrows the types of expression to be afforded absolute protection, leaving to the courts the problem of defining "political speech" and differentiating it from unprotected or less protected expression.

## E. "OR OF THE PRESS"

Until this point we have used the terms "freedom of speech" and "freedom of the press" interchangeably. Some have argued, however, that the speech and press guarantees have independent and distinct significance. Are there some types of activity protected under the press clause that are not protected under the speech clause? Or, are there some activities that, though they constitute protected speech, lay outside the press guarantee?

### 1. THE SPEECH CLAUSE v. THE PRESS CLAUSE?

The most prominent proponent of the theory that the press clause is of greater scope than the speech clause was Justice Potter Stewart, who contended that the press clause, in contradistinction to the speech guarantee, was a *structural* provision of the Constitution. Stewart relied heavily on the notion that the institutional press has a special role in our constitutional scheme as an additional check on the power of government officials. Because of this special role, he asserted that the institutional press in certain situations had rights of access and immunities growing out of the press clause to which the general citizenry could not lay claim.

Stewart reiterated this view in a case in which the Court overturned the conviction of a newspaper publisher for violating a statute that made it a crime to divulge information about investigations of judicial conduct being conducted by a state board. Concurring in the judgment, Stewart saw an important governmental interest in protecting the quality of its judiciary. He would have allowed the statute to be applied against individuals but would not allow the state to punish a newspaper for printing the same information. Landmark Communications, Inc. v. Virginia, 435 U.S. 829, 848–49, 3 Med.L.Rptr. 2153 (1978) (Stewart, J., concurring). We return to this case in Chapter X.

Chief Justice Burger rejected this analysis. Concurring in First National Bank of Boston v. Bellotti, 435 U.S. 765 (1978), he contended that the speech and press clauses of the First Amendment complement each other, but the latter does not give the "institutional press" a special status. First, the framers did not contemplate special privileges for the press, according to Burger. That does not mean the press clause is redundant. Rather, it is meant to focus "specifically on the liberty to disseminate expression broadly," while the speech clause is to protect "the liberty to express ideas and beliefs." The press clause, "although complementary to and a natural extension of Speech Clause liberty, merited special mention simply because it had been more often the object of official restraints." Thus, he saw "no difference between the right of those who seek to disseminate ideas by way of newspaper and those who give lectures or speeches."

Second, Burger foresaw difficulty in defining what was and was not included in the "institutional press" if it were to be accorded special status. Including some entities while excluding others would be "reminiscent of the abhorred licensing system" of England, which the First Amendment was meant, in part, to prevent. He noted that the Court had not, in related matters, allowed officials "to distinguish the protected from the unprotected on the basis of such variables as content of expression, frequency or fervor of expression, or ownership of the technological means of dissemination."

To date the issue of special protections for the press has been carefully left open by the Supreme Court in a number of areas. It remains unclear, for example, whether the constitutional rules protecting defendants in defamation actions apply equally to media and non-media defendants. In Chapter XII, the question resurfaces in the Houchins and Pell cases in connection with the press assertion of a right of access to prisons to gather information.

Regardless of how the issue of special protection is resolved, it is true as a practical matter that certain First Amendment issues arise in connection with the institutional press, while others are generally raised in the context of individual speech. Be careful to distinguish cases in which the press is asserting a special press right from cases in which the press is claiming a protection that, though it belongs to all, is unlikely to be asserted by non-media individuals and institutions. The cluster of First Amendment claims asserted primarily by the institutional press are the focus of this book.

Among the issues most frequently associated with the institutional press are gathering information, the protection of confidential sources, and question of broadcast regulation. In the chapters that follow, students should determine whether the issues raised are of particular importance to the institutionalized press and, if so, whether that fact has an impact upon how the Supreme Court balances the interests at stake.

## 2.  SPECIAL SPEECH ISSUES

Just as some aspects of First Amendment doctrine are usually associated with the press, other elements almost always involve individuals rather than the press.  Though less central to our concern with the mass media, these non-press aspects of the First Amendment are important historically and intellectually, and help complete the overall picture. Indeed, the very roots of modern First Amendment law are to be found in the cases discussed above that articulate the clear and present danger test.  Recall that these tended to involve individual, not press, defendants.  A few other areas of non-press First Amendment law deserve brief mention here before we begin our extended consideration of the issues of most concern to mass media.

### a.  *"Symbolic Speech"*

The Supreme Court has held that some limited types of nonverbal expressive conduct are entitled to protection under the First Amendment.  Examples of such "symbolic speech" include wearing an armband or displaying an American flag upside down in protest.  Because the print and broadcast media are virtually always engaged in what most consider the clearest case of verbal expression, they, unlike individuals, have had little cause to assert their claim to symbolic speech rights.

The most commonly used analysis of restrictions on symbolic speech was developed in United States v. O'Brien, 391 U.S. 367 (1968):

> This Court has held that when "speech" and "nonspeech" elements are combined in the same course of conduct, a sufficiently important governmental interest in regulating the nonspeech element can justify incidental limitations on First Amendment freedoms. . . . [W]e think it clear that a governmental regulation is sufficiently justified if it is within the constitutional power of the Government;  if it furthers an important or substantial governmental interest;  if the governmental interest is unrelated to the suppression of free expression;  and if the incidental restriction on alleged First Amendment freedoms is no greater than is essential to the furtherance of that interest.

In *O'Brien* itself the Court upheld a criminal statute punishing the deliberate mutilation of draft cards, a common form of protest against the Vietnam war in the 1960s.  For cases going the other way under this analysis, see *Tinker*, p. 47, *supra* (wearing of protest armbands in school protected);  Spence v. Washington, 418 U.S. 405 (1974) (displaying a defaced American flag as a symbol of protest against the Vietnam war protected).

Protection for symbolic speech stirred public opinion in June 1989 when the Supreme Court decided 5–4 that a Texas flag-desecration law was unconstitutional because of the First Amendment. Texas v. Johnson, 491 U.S. 397 (1989). The decision led to widespread calls for a Constitutional amendment and to the Federal Flag Protection Act of 1989, Congress's own attempt to protect the American flag from being burned or defaced. In two cases decided a year later, the Court, with the same 5–4 split, found the federal statute constitutionally flawed in the same way as the Texas statute because it suppressed expression. United States v. Eichman and United States v. Haggerty, 496 U.S. 310 (1990). Public opinion polls made clear that the First Amendment is not always popular; a New York Times/CBS News poll that year found that 83 percent of respondents thought flag burning should be against the law, and 59 percent would favor a constitutional amendment if it were the only way to make flag destruction illegal. New York Times, June 12, 1990, at p. B7. Critics said that making such an exception to the First Amendment would set a dangerous precedent.

### b.  Hostile Audience

The hostile audience issue arises when a speaker on a platform or on a street corner angers the crowd to such an extent that a breach of the peace is threatened. The question arises when the police, instead of controlling the crowd, order the speaker to stop speaking. This is sometimes said to raise the question of the "heckler's veto." Again, the issue does not involve mass media because speaker and hostile audience must confront one another for the problem to occur—and this is uniquely a speech situation. Recall *Chaplinsky*, p. 48, *supra*.

In Feiner v. New York, 340 U.S. 315 (1951), police ordered a speaker on a soap box to stop his talk because members of the audience were threatening to attack him. When the speaker refused, he was arrested. The Court said that because disorder was threatened, the policeman's order was lawful and the speaker could be punished for disobeying it. In dissent, Justice Black said those breaking the law should be arrested, not the speaker.

In subsequent cases, the Court appears to be granting greater protection to the expressive activity. See Edwards v. South Carolina, 372 U.S. 229 (1963) (187 black students in a march could not be convicted of breach of the peace for failing to obey an order to disperse, because the Court's majority found no threatened violence from the large crowd of onlookers) and Gregory v. Chicago, 394 U.S. 111 (1969) (peaceful marchers in a demonstration could not be convicted of disorderly conduct for failure to disperse when crowd became unruly). See also Village of Skokie v. National Socialist Party, 69 Ill.2d 605, 14 Ill.Dec. 890, 373 N.E.2d 21, 3 Med.L.Rptr. 1704 (1978).

### c.   The Public Forum

The media have little need to use the public forum since each publisher or broadcaster is itself a forum for expressive activity. Individuals, however, have long claimed the right to speak in places where there is a chance for them to be seen and heard, usually on public property. The Supreme Court first explicitly recognized the right to speak in a public forum in Hague v. CIO, 307 U.S. 496 (1939):

> [T]he . . . streets and parks . . . have immemorially been held in trust for the use of the public and, time out of mind, have been used for purposes of assembling, communicating thoughts between citizens, and discussing public questions. Such use of the streets and public places has, from ancient times, been a part of the privileges, immunities, rights and liberties of citizens.

But the right is not absolute. Although public streets and parks and some other public places, such as state capitol grounds and airport areas, are available for use to express ideas and opinions, the city's police powers permit certain regulations. The main consideration is that the activity not interfere with the primary purposes of the building or facility in question. Some other areas that are "public" in some senses are not public forums for expressive activities, such as jails, military bases and the reading room of the Library of Congress.

### 3.   The Captive Audience

As we have seen, the role of the audience may be relevant to arguments that implicate the First Amendment. Those justifications for freedom of expression that relied heavily upon the role of speech in the governance of the community or in the marketplace of ideas necessarily made some assumptions about the willingness of the audience to receive the message or at least messages of that type. Those justifications that are based on ideas of self-expression or self-fulfillment, with no audience implications, may nevertheless involve speech that is intended to, or does, reach an audience.

We now consider the implications for freedom of speech when the proposed audience does not wish to receive the message but lacks the freedom audiences usually have to avoid the message.

The issue may arise in media or nonmedia situations. It usually arises in the context of time, place and manner regulations that seek to reduce noise, to protect privacy or to protect audiences that are unable to avoid messages. What follows is a brief introduction to a subject that can arise in many contexts and that involves many variables. Note that some of the cases discussed below involve government efforts to protect audiences from specific kinds of speech. These attempts, as we have seen, raise much more serious questions than attempts that are not based on content. The subject of captive audiences is discussed at length in M. Nimmer, Nimmer on Freedom of Speech § 1.02[F][2] (1984).

Perhaps the most obvious case for protecting a captive audience arises when an ordinance seeks, without regard to the content of the message, to prevent sound trucks from blaring their messages in residential neighborhoods. The most apparent justification for such an ordinance would be that when persons are in their homes they should not have to endure noise that cannot be readily and easily silenced. The Supreme Court has upheld efforts to achieve this kind of result. Kovacs v. Cooper, 336 U.S. 77 (1949) (upholding ban on "loud and raucous" sound trucks). This result can be justified by stressing the special interest that persons have in the solitude of their homes or the particular difficulty of avoiding this kind of communication.

In Rowan v. U.S. Post Office, 397 U.S. 728 (1970), the Court upheld a statute allowing a homeowner who had received advertisements in the mail that the "addressee in his sole discretion believes to be erotically arousing or sexually provocative" to instruct the Post Office to order the mailer to send no more mail to the addressee. The majority relied on the sanctity of the home and rejected the claim that the homeowner had an adequate remedy in simply throwing out unwanted material. To require homeowners to receive and then discard the material would be to "license a form of trespass and would make hardly more sense than to say that a radio or television viewer may not twist the dial to cut off an offensive or boring communication and thus bar its entering his home."

There are, however, limits on the homeowners' right to avoid receiving mail. In Bolger v. Youngs Drug Products Corp., 463 U.S. 60 (1983), the Court overturned a statute that had barred the mailing of unsolicited advertisements for contraceptives. Here, the homeowner's ability to send the mail on a "short, though regular, journey from mail box to trash can . . . is an acceptable burden, at least so far as the Constitution is concerned."

Because *Rowan* and *Bolger* both involve advertisements, it may be useful to note a distinction the Supreme Court has made between restrictions on advertising of *constitutionally protected* conduct and restrictions on advertising of conduct (such as gambling) that could be legally prohibited by a state. Although he was not addressing the specific issue of homeowners' rights to avoid receiving mail, Chief Justice Rehnquist, in the majority opinion for the Supreme Court in Posadas de Puerto Rico Associates v. Tourism Company, 478 U.S. 328, 13 Med. L.Rptr. 1033 (1986), emphasized such a distinction. *Posadas* and other cases about restrictions on truthful advertising will be addressed in Chapter IX.

Outside the home, the Supreme Court has tended to protect those who would speak—at least where the audience can relatively easily avoid the communication. In Cohen v. California, 403 U.S. 15 (1971), the Court overturned a conviction for wearing, in a Los Angeles courthouse, a jacket with the message "Fuck the Draft." The words were not obscene because the message was not "erotic."

The state argued that, even so, the message could not be thrust upon unwilling or unsuspecting audiences, especially of women and children. The Court rejected the argument, 5–4. The majority asserted that government's ability to protect an audience from hearing a message was "dependent upon a showing that substantial privacy interests are being invaded in an essentially intolerable manner. Any broader view of this authority would effectively empower a majority to silence dissidents simply as a matter of personal predilections."

The state could not meet the required standard here because those who confronted the jacket "could effectively avoid further bombardment of their sensibilities simply by averting their eyes." Although the claim to a "recognizable privacy interest" was greater when "walking through a courthouse corridor than, for example, strolling through Central Park, surely it is nothing like the interest in being free from unwanted expression in the confines of one's own home."

The majority also concluded that the state had "no right to cleanse public debate to the point where it is grammatically palatable to the most squeamish among us. Yet no readily ascertainable general principle exists for stopping short of that result were we to affirm the judgment below."

The majority also recognized that "words are often chosen as much for their emotive as their cognitive force. We cannot sanction the view that the Constitution, while solicitous of the cognitive content of individual speech, has little or no regard for that emotive function which, practically speaking, may often be the more important element of the overall message sought to be communicated."

The Court reached a similar result in a case involving an ordinance forbidding the showing of nudity on screens of outdoor movie theaters that were visible from public streets. Erznoznik v. Jacksonville, 422 U.S. 205, 1 Med.L.Rptr. 1508 (1975). The screen of a drive-in movie theater "is not 'so obtrusive as to make it impossible for an unwilling individual to avoid exposure to it.'"

See Chapters VIII, XVII and XVIII for additional discussion of indecency and obscenity.

But an individual outside the home is not necessarily able to avoid undesired communications. In Public Utilities Commission v. Pollak, 343 U.S. 451 (1952), the majority upheld the right of a municipal transit company to play radio news, music and commercials over the loudspeaker systems on its buses, on the ground that the expectations of privacy were quite different when one ventured out of the house. Justice Douglas dissented: "One who tunes in on an offensive program at home can turn it off or tune in another station as he wishes. One who hears disquieting or unpleasant programs in public places, such as restaurants, can get up and leave. But the man on the streetcar has no choice but to sit and listen, or perhaps to sit and try not to listen."

In Lehman v. City of Shaker Heights, 418 U.S. 298 (1974), the Court upheld an ordinance banning political advertising in the city's transit vehicles. Five justices based their votes in whole or in part on the captive audience notion: "There is no difference when the message is visual not auricular [as was the case in *Pollak*]. In each the viewer or listener is captive." The passengers could not simply avert their eyes because "the degree of captivity makes it impractical for the unwilling viewer . . . to avoid exposure." (The case was complicated by the fact that nonpolitical advertising was permitted.)

Finally, should it matter that a large majority of the captive audience affirmatively wishes to hear the message? Professor Nimmer suggested that "there is something abhorrent in requiring even a few persons to be subjected to such a force-feeding of speech." M. Nimmer, Nimmer on Freedom of Speech § 1.02[F][2][e] (1984).

Many of these issues came together in FCC v. Pacifica Foundation, 438 U.S. 726, 3 Med.L.Rptr. 2553 (1978), in which, during the middle of a weekday, a radio station broadcast a program containing some words that might offend some listeners. The case is reprinted and the issue is discussed in detail in Chapter XVII.

# Chapter III

# DEFAMATION

In this chapter and several that follow we will consider the range of legal arguments for prohibiting certain communications because of their substantive content. In each case we will consider, among other points, the justifications offered for restriction and the value of the communication. The justifications are as diverse as the situations to which they are applied. Arguments for limiting speech and press to protect privacy are unlikely to resemble the arguments based on national security.

Even if the speech is determined to be subject to governmental control, there is the further question of what types of sanctions may be imposed. Among the array are criminal prosecutions, civil damage remedies and bans on speech imposed by administrative techniques or by court injunction. Again, particular sanctions are used for specific kinds of speech. Even when speech is found to be defamatory, for example, it is regulated after the fact and is not enjoined. On the other hand, speech held to invade privacy has been barred from publication. In sum, the sanctions available are as diverse as the justifications offered to restrict the speech in the first place.

We begin our survey of restraints on communication with a justification based on the state's interest in granting redress to persons whose reputations have been hurt by false statements. We start with defamation law in part because it is one of the earliest legal actions available against publishers and broadcasters and in part because even today it is still the most common type of legal danger that can befall publishers and broadcasters. It is certainly the most extensively litigated area of media law.

Harm to reputation is one of the earliest injuries recognized by virtually every legal system. Early societies were undoubtedly concerned that the failure to provide legal recourse to those whose reputations had been impugned would lead to breaches of the peace. Although that concern has eased as civilization has advanced, states may still be concerned about the potential for violence. Beyond that, however, traditional values emphasize the importance of an individual's good name. Whatever the justifications, the action for defamation has long had a place in the common law.

English law has redressed and punished attacks on reputation since the feudal days. After the Norman conquest, defamations were treated as a form of sin by ecclesiastical courts whose penalties were ecclesiastical in nature. During the 16th century the common law courts began to assert jurisdiction in defamation cases and to order that damages be paid to the plaintiff. As noted in Chapter II, during this period the authorities began using the law of defamation to punish political criticism of the government and its officials. These attacks were referred to as seditious libel.

Although it is doubtful that the English law of seditious libel was transplanted to this country, it seems clear that the tort law that provided damage remedies to individuals did cross the Atlantic. After independence defamation law continued to be enforced. The First Amendment's statement that "Congress shall make no law . . . abridging the freedom of speech, or of the press . . ." had no apparent impact upon defamation law until quite recently. Because defamation law was a creature of state law—the power to regulate defamation law was not delegated to Congress—the First Amendment had no immediate effect on the states' administration of that law.

Even after it became clear that the First Amendment applied to the states through the Fourteenth Amendment, these provisions were thought inapplicable to false statements that adversely affected an individual's reputation. The Supreme Court did not tie defamation and the First Amendment together until the seminal case of New York Times Co. v. Sullivan, 376 U.S. 254, 1 Med.L.Rptr. 1527 (1964). That case not only brought major changes to the law of defamation, but also provided a philosophy that has led to many other recent developments in mass media law. We shall consider the impact of this case on defamation law shortly.

## A.  THE STATE LAW OF DEFAMATION

Before we can appreciate the significance of the constitutional developments, we must understand the common-law world of defamation. The constitutional developments have not created a totally new legal area; rather they have altered some of the pre-existing state rules and left the remaining ones in place. States remain free to protect reputation in whatever manner they see fit so long as they do so in ways consistent with the First Amendment.

A second reason for inquiring into state law is that state law itself has a significant number of protections for those who are sued for defamation. It is often possible for a defendant to win a defamation case under the state's traditional rules without ever having to rely upon the protection of the First Amendment.

Why might a defendant who could win a case under First Amendment principles try to win that case under state rules? There are several practical explanations. Perhaps the major one is that, as a matter of procedure, the state defenses may permit a defendant to win the case earlier in the litigation (such as on a motion to dismiss, rather than on a motion for summary judgment or perhaps only after a trial is held). It is often faster and cheaper for a media defendant to succeed on state law grounds than to rely exclusively on the more glorious but perhaps less expeditious ground of the First and Fourteenth Amendments.

A quick example demonstrates this point.  In most states, if a statement has two possible meanings, one of which would be defamatory and one of which would not be defamatory, the jury decides how recipients of that statement understood it.  Illinois, however, has a special "innocent construction" rule providing that if a statement has one innocent meaning the defendant wins the case immediately.  The plaintiff cannot argue that the defendant "really meant" the defamatory version.  The case is simply over.  This rule has permitted defendants in Illinois to win an overwhelming percentage of their defamation cases and to win them quickly without having to rely on federal constitutional defenses.

The point is that we must understand the basic operation of traditional state defamation law as well as the Constitution.  We turn first to the state law and then to the impact of constitutional law.

## 1.  THE REPUTATION ELEMENT

### a.  *Definition*

The essence of the action for defamation is the claim that defendant has uttered a false statement that has harmed the plaintiff's reputation. Historically, some states required that the defendant's statement expose the plaintiff to hatred, ridicule, contempt, scorn, or shame, or words to that effect.  The modern view is that a statement is defamatory if it harms the plaintiff's reputation by lowering him in the estimation of the community or by deterring others from associating or dealing with him. It is easy to think of statements that will fit such a very broad definition. It obviously covers charges that plaintiff committed a crime, that he was inept in his chosen trade or profession, or that he was a member of a group or a political party that was in disrepute in the community.  It is enough that the published statement be of the sort that would lead a segment of the community to think less of the plaintiff.

That segment need not be large.  In one case, for example, the plaintiff, an expert on Palestinian art and customs, was falsely stated to have written an article for the Sunday newspaper on that subject.  The article would have impressed virtually all the newspaper's regular readers.  Unfortunately, the article had several errors that would embarrass the author among fellow experts.  The court ruled that the relevant community in that case was the small group of experts on the subject— and that a jury could find that those experts would have thought less of plaintiff as a scholar after hearing that she had written such an article. Ben–Oliel v. Press Publishing Co., 251 N.Y. 250, 167 N.E. 432 (1929).

Most cases have involved charges of volitional behavior by plaintiff, such as committing a crime or writing an article.  The broad sweep of the definition, however, extends to accusations that the plaintiff was of illegitimate birth, had been raped or was in dire financial straits.  Even though the plaintiff cannot be blamed for a condition, the courts have nonetheless bowed to reality and recognized that these kinds of charges may in fact cause others to shun, or refrain from associating with, the plaintiff. Judges "take the world as we find it" even if the segment of the community that thinks less of the plaintiff can be characterized as "wrong-thinking"—as they would be in the illegitimacy and rape examples.

At the same time, there is a limit to that principle. Consider, for example, a false charge that the mob's gunman missed his target. Were the gunman to sue and assert that his reputation had been tarnished among the underworld, it is unlikely that a court would entertain the charge. Is it appropriate to redress a claim based on an audience segment that is criminal rather than simply wrong thinking?

### b. *Corporations*

Until now, the discussion has been directed to the question of protecting the reputation of a human being. Not infrequently, however, defamatory statements are made about corporations. It is generally held that corporations also have reputations that they may vindicate through actions for defamation. Generally the corporation must be attacked in a way that affects its credit or profit-making ability if it is a corporation organized for profit. For example, in one case a corporate plaintiff's restaurant was asserted to be a good place "to meet a connection" to buy cocaine. The corporation was allowed to bring suit because such a charge might well adversely affect the restaurant's patronage. See El Meson Espanol v. NYM Corp., 521 F.2d 737 (2d Cir.1975).

A non-profit corporation may also be defamed if the charge is one that tends to interfere with its ability to obtain financial support from the public. A corporation that relies on public donations may be able to sue for defamation if the charge would interfere with its ability to obtain such funds.

Some governmental activities are undertaken by corporations specially organized for particular purposes. Such corporations are not usually permitted to bring defamation actions. The reason is that to permit such law suits would come perilously close to reviving the action for seditious libel that, as you recall, was used in England by the government against its critics. As one court has observed, "no court of last resort in this country has ever held, or even suggested, that prosecutions for libel on government have any place in the American system of jurisprudence." City of Chicago v. Tribune Co., 307 Ill. 595, 601, 139 N.E. 86, 88 (1923). This issue reemerges later in the *New York Times* case.

### c. *Ambiguity*

As noted earlier, statements are often ambiguous. In such cases the prevailing rule is to have the judge decide whether any of the statement's possible meanings can reasonably be understood to have a defamatory impact.  If the judge decides that at least one of the possible meanings would be defamatory, it then becomes a function of the jury to decide the meaning that was in fact conveyed.  In a famous example involving Horace Greeley and James Fenimore Cooper, Greeley had written in the *New York Tribune* that he was not worried about a suit that Cooper had previously filed against him because "Mr. Cooper will have to bring his action to trial somewhere.  He will not like to bring it in New York, for we are known here, nor in Otsego, for he is known there."  Cooper sued again—this time for defamation.  Greeley contended that the statement meant only "that a prophet has no honor in his own country.  The point of the article is the intimation that the plaintiff would prefer a trial where the prejudice and rivalries which assail every man at home could not reach him."  Cooper alleged that the statement meant that he was in bad repute in Otsego.  The court held that a jury should decide which of the two meanings was understood by readers of the article.  Cooper v. Greeley, 1 Denio 347 (N.Y.1845).

It should be noted here that the Supreme Court in one discussion of ambiguous statements resolved the question itself.  The case arose from a tumultuous city council meeting involving the plaintiff, who was a local real estate developer, in a negotiation with the city council.  Members of the audience characterized the plaintiff's bargaining position as "blackmail."  The defendant newspaper accurately reported the meeting and included the blackmail charges—sometimes without quotation marks.  The state courts granted plaintiff a judgment against the newspaper.

Justice Stewart, in part of a longer opinion, observed that "as a matter of constitutional law, the word 'blackmail' in these circumstances was not" defamatory:

> It is simply impossible to believe that a reader who reached the word "blackmail" in either article would not have understood exactly what was meant; it was Bresler's public and wholly legal negotiating proposals that were being criticized.  No reader could have thought that either the speakers at the meeting or the newspaper articles reporting their words were charging Bresler with the commission of a criminal offense.  On the contrary, even the most careless reader must have perceived that the word was no more than rhetorical hyperbole .  .  ..

Justice White dissented.  He could not "join the majority claim of superior insight with respect to how the word 'blackmail' would be understood by the ordinary reader in Greenbelt, Maryland."  Greenbelt Cooperative Publishing Association v. Bresler, 398 U.S. 6, 1 Med.L.Rptr. 1589 (1970).

Sometimes the words themselves may be absolutely clear but their use may present problems.  For example, former Senator George Smathers of Florida was once reported to have made the following statement to some of his rural audiences while campaigning in the Democratic primary for United States Senator against the incumbent, Claude Pepper:

"Are you aware that Claude Pepper is known all over Washington as a shameless extrovert?  Not only that, but this man is reliably reported to practice nepotism with his sister-in-law, and he has a sister, who was once a thespian in wicked New York.  Worst of all, it is an established fact that Mr. Pepper, before his marriage, practiced celibacy."  See R. Sherrill, Gothic Politics in the Deep South 150 (1968).  Smathers denies making the statement and has offered a reward to anyone who can prove he had ever made it.  See The New York Times, Feb. 24, 1983, at p. 10.  (How can one ever disprove allegations that he once made a statement?)

Had Smathers made the statement, would it be possible for a court to find a statement defamatory when the words, given their only acceptable dictionary meanings, are not likely to lower plaintiff's esteem in the community?  Would it be extremely dangerous for free speech to allow a court to decide that, even though the words themselves are not defamatory, the speaker should be punished for trying to get an uneducated audience to think that the words were defamatory?  Should the legal system be able to do something in this case?

Verbal ambiguities aside, the meaning of a statement may be altered by punctuation, paragraphing and typography.  Thus, in Wildstein v. New York Post Corp., 40 Misc.2d 586, 243 N.Y.S.2d 386 (1963), aff'd without opinion 24 A.D.2d 559, 261 N.Y.S.2d 254 (1965), the defendant wrote that the plaintiff was one of "several women described as 'associated' with" a slain executive.  The judge observed that if the word "associated" had not been in quotation marks the statement would not have been defamatory; the quotation marks implied a euphemistic use of the word, suggesting an illicit relationship between plaintiff and the deceased.  The actual paragraphing of the story may also be crucial in determining meaning.

Another problem arises when part of an article has a defamatory impact but another part of the article negates that impact.  The headline may be defamatory although the article is not;  the lead paragraph alone may be defamatory but the article as a whole may be harmless;  and one sentence may be defamatory but the whole paragraph may be harmless.  Gambuzza v. Time, Inc., 18 A.D.2d 351, 239 N.Y.S.2d 466 (1963), involved a two-page spread of 12 photographs in a magazine article, each with a three-line legend beneath it.  The story involved reports of the activities of a convicted spy.  One photograph of plaintiff was captioned "HIS ADMIRER.  Frank Gambuzza, a radio dealer who sold Abel some parts for a wireless receiver, praised the Russian for his electronic know-how."  Plaintiff alleged that the first two words suggested sympathy for Abel and his cause.  The majority noted that sometimes headlines might be read separately from the article and judged by their own words because "a person passing a newsstand . . . may be able to catch a glimpse of a headline without the opportunity or desire to read the accompanying article or may skim through the paper jumping from headline to headline."  But this was not such a case because the caption was so close to the text that they had to be read together:  "the article must be considered as a whole and its meaning gleaned not from isolated portions thereof but rather from the entire article." Two dissenters emphasized that the critical words in the caption were in bold capital type, and thus should be considered separately from the rest of the article.

In Kunst v. New York World Telegram Corp., 28 A.D.2d 662, 280 N.Y.S.2d 798 (1967), the lead paragraph and a photograph caption conveyed a defamatory implication that was negated by a statement that a "persistent and careful reader would discover near the end of the reasonably lengthy article." The majority upheld the complaint, stressing that the writing must be "construed, not with the high degree of precision expected of and used by lawyers and judges, but as it would be read and understood by an ordinary member of the public to whom it is directed." A dissenter responded, "It is true this appears near the end of the article, but the article is to be taken as a whole and read in its entirety." He relied on *Gambuzza*.

Statements may be defamatory even though the thrust of the accusations is not clear from the words used. In such indirect defamation cases, the plaintiffs' complaints must show how the statements defame them. The description of how plaintiffs do this involves the use of three technical words. If the plaintiffs themselves are not directly named they must show by "colloquium" that the statements were "of and concerning" them. If it is still not clear how the plaintiffs have been defamed, they must plead extrinsic facts that would permit a defamatory meaning to be applied to defendants' words. This allegation of extrinsic facts is called the "inducement." Finally we have "innuendo." Where a statement is not clearly defamatory on its face it is the function of the innuendo to assert the meaning that plaintiff attaches to the passage and any additions by colloquium and inducement. The innuendo is not a fact but is the plaintiff's assertion of how the passage would be understood by those who heard the defendant's words and knew the additional unstated facts.

An example may help clarify the matter. Let us assume defendant says, "The man who lives in the house two doors east of my house was the only person in the Smith home between 7 p.m. and 8 p.m. last night." If the plaintiff thinks that this statement is defamatory of him and wishes to sue, his pleading must establish how he has been defamed. For colloquium he might allege, "I am the only man who lives in the house two doors east of the speaker's house." This ties the plaintiff to the statement but does not clarify its defamatory nature. The defamation is clarified if the plaintiff alleges as inducement that the Smith house was burglarized between 7 and 8 p.m. that night. The plaintiff will then assert that the innuendo is that he is being charged by defendant with the crime of burglary.

### d.  *"Of and Concerning Plaintiff"*

In order for a defamatory statement to adversely affect the plaintiff, the reader must connect that statement with the plaintiff. The plaintiff must show that the statement objected to was "of and concerning" him. Sometimes this is a problem because of the ambiguity of the statement or because the plaintiff is only indirectly identified. In those cases our discussion about ambiguous statements will help resolve the case. If readers could plausibly believe that the plaintiff was referred to, then a jury will decide whether the statement was in fact so understood.

### e.  Groups

Another aspect of this problem involves statements that attack large groups of people. In such cases is it possible for an individual member of that group to assert that the statement hurt his personal reputation? At the extreme, an attack on all lawyers in the United States or on all clergymen would be held to be such a general broadside that no individual lawyer or clergyman could sue. The same would be true of broadside attacks on racial, religious or ethnic groups.

At the other extreme it is generally accepted that a charge made against a small group may defame all members of that group. For example, a newspaper article may assert that "the officers" of a corporation have embezzled funds. There are only four officers of the corporation. Each of them may be found to have been defamed. Even if the statement had said "one of the officers of the corporation" had embezzled funds, the group is small enough so that all four officials are put under a shadow and can sue.

As the group grows larger the impact of the statement may depend on the number within the group who accused. In one case, a defamatory charge was made against one unidentified member of a 21–member police force. All 21 sued. The court dismissed the case. It feared that allowing the action would permit a suit by an entire baseball team over a report that one member was disciplined for brawling. Such a result "would chill communication to the marrow." But suppose the charge had been against "all but one" of the members of that police force. Such a statement may reflect on each member of the force though the same charge made against only one of the 21 might not. Arcand v. Evening Call Publishing Co., 567 F.2d 1163, 3 Med.L.Rptr. 1748 (1st Cir.1977).

One case presented three aspects of this problem. Two authors, in a book about Dallas, stated that "some" department store models were "call girls . . .." The salesgirls are good, too—pretty and often much cheaper . . .." And "most of the [male] sales staff are fairies, too."

Suits were filed by all nine models, 15 of the 25 salesmen and 30 of the 382 saleswomen. The defendants did not challenge the right of the nine models to sue. (Would it have mattered if only three had sued?) The other two groups were challenged as being too large.

The case for "the salesgirls" was dismissed. The result would be the same even if the authors had explicitly referred to "all"—and even if all 382 had sued. The judge could find no case allowing a group of 382 to sue.  He cited cases rejecting suits when the statements attacked all officials of a state-wide union or all the taxicab drivers in Washington, D.C.

On the other hand, the salesmen's case was not dismissed.  It was close to others involving members of a posse, or the 12 doctors on a hospital's residential staff.  Would the result have been the same if the authors had referred to "some" or "a few" of the men?  Neiman–Marcus v. Lait, 13 F.R.D. 311 (S.D.N.Y.1952).

Is the reasoning behind these cases that attacks on a large group don't hurt any particular member of the group?  Is it that such broad accusations are not taken seriously by hearers or readers?  Is it that the legal system would find it administratively difficult to handle a damage action brought by 382 plaintiffs, even though they might deserve some compensation?

Even though all states deny damage actions to large groups, a few have attempted to use criminal statutes to prevent or punish such charges against racial or ethnic groups.  We consider this at p. 173, *infra*.

### f.  Vagueness

Some courts have found language too imprecise to form the basis of a defamation action.  An accusation that William F. Buckley, Jr. was a "fellow traveler" of fascist causes was too "loosely definable" and too "variously interpretable" to be actionable as a defamation.  The court suggested that there might be a difference between that vague charge and a more specific charge that plaintiff was a member of a particular party or group that subscribed to that type of belief.  Buckley v. Littell, 539 F.2d 882, 1 Med.L.Rptr. 1762 (2d Cir.1976), certiorari denied 429 U.S. 1062 (1977).

Similarly, a charge that a police union's collective bargaining efforts involved the "inroad of communism" was held too vague to support a suit.  National Association of Government Employees, Inc. v. Central Broadcasting Corp., 379 Mass. 220, 396 N.E.2d 996, 5 Med.L.Rptr. 2078 (1979).  The court thought it clear from the context and words used that no hearer in the community after even brief reflection would understand the speaker to be charging plaintiff with complicity in the "horrors distinctive of a totalitarian regime."

### g.  "Libel–Proof" Plaintiffs

A few libel cases have been brought by convicts.  The claims were based on errors in other stories about their actions.  The courts have developed a doctrine that "a libel-proof plaintiff is not entitled to burden a defendant with a trial in which the most favorable result the plaintiff could achieve is an award of nominal damages."  Jackson v. Longcope, 394 Mass. 577, 476 N.E.2d 617 (1985).  Despite the doctrine, the court in *Jackson* insisted that each case be investigated to be sure that the plaintiff's reputation was in fact so poor that it could have suffered no harm from errors in the defendant's article. Here, there was no question because a convicted multiple murderer was challenging a statement that he had raped and strangled all of his victims.

An effort to apply the doctrine against Ariel Sharon failed. Sharon v. Time Inc., 575 F.Supp. 1162, 10 Med.L.Rptr. 1146 (S.D.N.Y.1983). The fact that an Israeli commission had found him to have made a "grave mistake" in failing to anticipate violence at a refugee camp "cannot be said to have so severely harmed Sharon's formidable reputation as to render him libel proof to suggestions in the article that he anticipated but did not act to prevent the massacre or that he actually instigated such acts, or that he lied to the Commission, or that the Commission found that he lied but attempted to cover up his complicity in the massacre."

*Penthouse* magazine publisher Robert Guccione, however, was held to be "libel proof" with regard to charges of adultery in Guccione v. Hustler Magazine, Inc., 800 F.2d 298, 13 Med.L.Rptr. 1316 (2d Cir.1986), cert. denied 479 U.S. 1091 (1987). Guccione sued *Hustler* for a 1983 article stating that Guccione "is married and has a live-in girlfriend, Kathy Keeton," when, in fact, Guccione had been divorced four years before the article appeared. Noting that Guccione had lived with Keeton for 13 years while married, the court of appeals ruled that the statement was substantially true and that Guccione's relationship with Keeton was notorious enough to render him libel proof.

## 2. LIBEL AND SLANDER—THE DAMAGE QUESTION

So far we have been discussing the general subject of "defamation." It becomes necessary to introduce the subcategories of libel and slander. Historically, slanders were oral defamations and were handled by the common-law courts; libels were written defamations that, because of the development of printing, became a major concern of the crown. After the end of the days of the Star Chamber, oral and written defamations were redressed by the common-law courts. Those courts, however, preserved some distinctions between the two that have survived to our day.

The critical distinction relates to what types of damages a plaintiff must show in order to be allowed to bring an action for defamation. Two types of damages are central to this discussion. "Special damages" are specific provable monetary losses that the plaintiff can demonstrate that he has sustained and can trace to the defendant's defamatory statement. "General damages" are damages to reputation that the plaintiff is presumed or proved to have sustained as a result of the defendant's statement. The jury is permitted to speculate on the extent of injury based on the words used the medium used and the predicted response of the community.

The common law courts have treated libel as substantially more serious than slander. The distinction arose when relatively few people could read and the written word was awesome and thus more credible. A writing may be given more weight because it requires more thought and planning than a spontaneous oral utterance. Furthermore, the writing is more lasting and is likely to reach a larger audience than most, if not all, slanders. Thus, libels as a class were more likely to cause harm than slanders and courts declared that plaintiffs in libel cases were able to recover general damages without any showing of special damages. Therefore, plaintiffs proceeding under libel have always been at least as well off as, and often better off than, plaintiffs suing for slander for precisely the same words.

If actions are for slander, plaintiffs must prove "special damages" unless the defamatory thrusts fit into at least one of four categories. These categories are the imputation of a serious crime involving moral turpitude, imputation of an existing loathsome disease, a charge that attacks the plaintiff's competence or honesty in business, trade or profession, and a charge of unchastity in a woman. Such a spoken charge is called slander *per se* and permits an action enabling plaintiffs to claim general damages to their reputations without proving actual pecuniary harm. Here the jury may conclude that publication of the charge caused substantial harm in the community, and can measure damages according to the number and identity of those who learned of the charge, and their presumed reaction based on the seriousness and credibility of the charge. If plaintiffs can also establish special damages, these could be recovered in addition to the general damages.

Two developments have blurred the line between libel and slander. First, the courts began to distinguish between two types of libels: those clear on their face, called libel *per se,* to which courts applied the traditional general damage rules, and others, called libel *per quod,* in which the reader had to know one or more unstated facts in order to understand the defamatory thrust of the writing. Some courts began to hold that the plaintiff must prove special damages in libel *per quod* cases unless the words used, if spoken, would have fit into one of the four categories of slanders for which special damages were not required.

The second blurring has resulted from the development of new modes of communication. Until this century, a written defamation would reach more people than an oral one. But with radio and television that is not necessarily so. In analyzing new technology should we stick to the traditional oral-written line or should we develop an approach that treats all modes of mass communication as libel and other modes of communication as slander? In a few states, legislation has resolved the matter. For example, California provides that broadcasting is slander. On the other hand, an English statute calls it libel. In the states that are resolving the question by common law, the tendency has been to treat broadcasting as libel.

The resulting libel-slander rules have sometimes permitted a plaintiff to recover large amounts in general damages. At other times they have barred a plaintiff from recovering anything whatever: although serious general harm seemed likely, special damages were required but could not be proven.

In addition to the critical distinction between general and special damages, two other classifications loom large in defamation law: *nominal* damages and *punitive* damages. Although nominal damages are unimportant in most tort actions, they may be central in defamation cases. The award of a symbolic amount such as $1 usually shows that the jury found the attack to be false but also found the words not to have hurt, either because the speaker was not credible or the plaintiff's strong reputation blunted the harm (or his reputation was so low nothing could really hurt it). For an example, see the suit by Quentin Reynolds against the Hearst Corporation and one of its columnists, in which a jury award of $1 in compensatory damages and $175,000 in punitive damages against the various defendants was upheld. Reynolds v. Pegler, 223 F.2d 429 (2d Cir.), cert. denied 350 U.S. 846 (1955) (Black, J. dissenting).

A few states declare that punitive damages, which are to punish defendants for serious misbehavior, are never recoverable. Most states allow them in appropriate cases.

As we shall see shortly, the Supreme Court in Gertz v. Robert Welch, Inc., introduced some constitutional constraints on the availability of certain types of common law damages.

### 3.  THE BASIS FOR LIABILITY—THE TROUBLE SPOT

Before one person is liable in tort law for hurting another, commonly, but not universally, some "fault" must be ascribed to the actor's conduct. For example, a plaintiff cannot win an automobile accident case simply by showing that the defendant's car hit the plaintiff. Instead, plaintiff must show that the defendant driver was "at fault" in his behavior. (It is, of course, different in so-called "no-fault" states, which emphasize the harm to plaintiff rather than the fault of the defendant.) Recall the discussion of torts in Chapter I.

In defamation, the common law long took the view that fault played no part in the tort. In other words, historically, the plaintiff had only to show that the defendant's statement hurt the plaintiff's reputation and prove whatever damages were required by the libel-slander rules. It was irrelevant that the defendant did not realize that the statement could hurt plaintiff, or anyone.

Thus, a newspaper lost a case in which it published a birth announcement that was a hoax—the couple had been married only three months. Those who read the article and who knew the fact of plaintiff's recent marriage would have given the story a meaning the newspaper never intended. Even if the newspaper had tried unsuccessfully to check the story but failed to learn about the hoax, it would not have mattered.

The common law asserted that defendants in defamation cases were subject to "strict liability" or a liability that was not based on fault. The peril to free speech is readily apparent today. But the response in earlier times was that the remedy was accuracy and refusal to write about things that were not known first hand.

As we shall see, this troubling aspect of the common law has become the focus of constitutional developments.

Traditionally, the plaintiff's action for defamation has been easy to establish. The plaintiff had to prove the publication to a third person of a statement of and concerning plaintiff that injured his reputation, and then had to meet whatever damage showing was required under the relevant libel-slander rules. These elements shown, it was up to the defendant to present a defense.

### 4. COMMON LAW DEFENSES

Several common law libel defenses are typically recognized in state law. They include truth, the absolute privilege accorded participants in certain official proceedings, the qualified privilege accorded to those who quote accurately from such proceedings and the qualified privilege of criticism, sometimes called "fair comment." These defenses were used by libel defendants under strict liability prior to the New York Times v. Sullivan decision. We will discuss them first and then look at the important constitutional defense of absence of malice or absence of negligence in a separate section.

#### a. *Truth*

The most obvious defense, but one rarely used, is to prove the essential truth of the defamatory statement. Most states recognize truth as a complete defense regardless of the speaker's motives. Because the action is intended to compensate those whose reputations are damaged incorrectly, if the defendant has spoken the truth the reputational harm is deemed to provide no basis for an action. A minority of states have required the truth to have been spoken with "good motives" or for "justifiable ends" or both, but in the wake of *Sullivan* and its progeny, such requirements are not constitutional.

The defendant need not prove literal truth but must establish the "sting" of his charge. Thus, if the defendant has charged the plaintiff with stealing $25,000 from a bank, truth will be established even if the actual amount was only $12,000. If the defendant cannot prove any theft whatever but can prove that the plaintiff is a bigamist, this information will not support his defense of truth, but it may help mitigate damages to show that the plaintiff's reputation is already in low esteem for other reasons and thus he has suffered less harm than might otherwise have occurred.

Truth is little used as a defense, though it would enable a decisive confrontation, because the defense may be expensive to establish. A defendant relying on truth almost always bears the legal costs of a full-dress trial as well as the sometimes major expense of investigating the matter and gathering enough evidence to ensure the outcome.  Particularly when the charge involved is vague and does not allege specific events, the defense of truth may be costly—and risky.

The constitutional developments affect the defense of truth.  As we shall see, a private plaintiff suing a publisher or broadcaster for a statement made about a matter of public concern must bear the burden of proving that the defamatory statement is false—rather than forcing the publisher or broadcaster to prove it is true.

### b.  State Privileges

Not only are there disadvantages to the defense of truth, there are attractive alternatives.  Over the centuries the law of defamation has developed several privileges to protect those who utter defamations. Some privileges are "absolute" in the sense that if the occasion gives rise to an absolute privilege, there will be no liability even if the speaker deliberately lied about the plaintiff.  The most significant example is the federal and state constitutional privilege afforded legislators who may not be sued for defamation for any statement made during debate.  High executive officials, judges and participants in judicial proceedings also have an absolute privilege to speak freely on matters relevant to their obligations.  No matter how such a speaker abuses the privilege by lying, no tort liability will flow.  See Barr v. Matteo, 360 U.S. 564 (1959).  The only circumstance that gives absolute privilege to the media occurs when broadcasters are required to grant equal opportunity to all candidates for the same office.  If a candidate commits defamation, the broadcaster is not liable for the defamation.  See Farmers Educational & Cooperative Union of America v. WDAY, Inc., 360 U.S. 525 (1959), discussed in Chapter XVI.

The much more common type of privilege is "conditional" or "qualified."  The defendant who has such a privilege will prevail in an action for defamation unless the plaintiff can show that the speaker "abused" the privilege.  The plaintiff shows abuse by proving that the defendant did not honestly believe what he said or that defendant published more information or published it more widely than was justified by the occasion that provided the privilege.

Most common law privileges serve individuals and do not specifically affect media—with two important exceptions.  The first involves the privilege to make fair and accurate reports of governmental proceedings. Under general defamation law, one who repeats another's statement is responsible for the truth of what he repeats.  Thus, if X states that "Y told me that Z is a murderer," and Z sues X for defamation, X will be treated as the publisher who is responsible for his own statement.  In order to prevail on the defense of truth, X must prove that Z is in fact a murderer—it is not enough for X to prove that in fact Y told him that Z was a murderer. The general reason underlying this view is the reluctance to protect gossip.

It was not long, however, before the courts and the legislatures began to realize that sometimes speakers should be encouraged to repeat others' statements. The federal and state constitutions had already provided that members of the legislative branch could quote others in debate with absolute protection against legal sanctions.

The major example of the value of repetition was found in the reporting of how government was functioning and what government officials were saying. Thus, observers were to be encouraged to report what legislators said on the floor or in committee as well as events in court. It would put reporters in a hopeless situation to be able to report safely only the truthful statements of government officials or of witnesses at a trial. As a result of these considerations, a privilege developed, sometimes called the privilege of "record libel," under which reports of what occurs in governmental proceedings are privileged even if some of those quoted have spoken falsely—so long as the report is accurate or a fair summary of what transpired.

The second major common law privilege of value to the media was the privilege of fair comment upon matters of public interest.

Apparently this privilege entered English law in 1808 in Carr v. Hood, 1 Camp. 355, 170 Eng.Rep. 983. The defendant was charged with ridiculing the plaintiff author's talent so severely that sales of his book were discouraged and his reputation was destroyed. The plaintiff's attorney conceded that his client had exposed himself to literary criticism by making the book public, but insisted that the criticism should be "fair and liberal" and seek to enlighten the public about the book rather than to injure the author. The judge noted that ridicule may be an appropriate tool of criticism, but that criticism unrelated to the author as such would not be privileged. He urged that any "attempt against free and liberal criticism" should be resisted "at the threshold." The result was a rule that criticism, regardless of its merit, was privileged if it was made honestly, with honesty measured by the accuracy of the critic's descriptive observations. If a critic describing a literary, musical or artistic endeavor gave the "facts" accurately and fairly, his honest conclusions would be privileged as "fair comment" or opinion.

American law recognized this privilege, and when it was applied in cases of literary and artistic criticism it caused little confusion. Problems raised by such comment are discussed in the classic Cherry v. Des Moines Leader, 114 Iowa 298, 86 N.W. 323 (1901), in which a reviewer scathingly described a performance by the Cherry Sisters. But at the turn of the century cases arose in which the privilege of fair comment was claimed with regard to other matters of public interest, including the conduct of politicians. This was not the privilege of reporting what certain public officials were doing in their official capacity. Rather the privilege claimed would permit citizens to criticize and argue about the conduct of their officials, and these cases presented the problem of distinguishing between facts and opinion.  In the literary criticism area the application of the privilege could depend upon the accuracy of the "facts" because they were usually readily apparent.  When dealing with politics, however, the "facts" were often elusive.  This new problem created a judicial split.

Most state courts decided that in order for criticism of government officials and others to be privileged, the facts upon which the comments were based had to be true.  A minority of courts, including Coleman v. MacLennan, 78 Kan. 711, 98 P. 281 (1908), disagreed.  They decided that facts relating to matters of public interest could not form the basis for a defamation case even if the facts were incorrect, so long as the speaker honestly believed them to be true.

Confusion about "fair comment" or opinion lessened between 1974 and 1990 as a result of a passage from Gertz v. Robert Welch, Inc., 418 U.S. 323, 1 Med.L.Rptr. 1633 (1974), reprinted at p. 118, *infra* : "Under the First Amendment there is no such thing as a false idea.  However pernicious an opinion may seem, we depend for its correction not on the conscience of judges and juries but on the competition of other ideas." 418 U.S. at 339–40, 1 Med.L.Rptr. at 1640.  A number of courts began to use a four-part test from Ollman v. Evans, 713 F.2d 838, 9 Med.L.Rptr. 1969 (D.C.Cir.1983) in deciding opinion cases.  The situation changed with the Supreme Court case of Milkovich v. Lorain Journal Co., 497 U.S. 1, 17 Med.L.Rptr. 2009 (1990), p. 144, *infra*, in which the court emphasized that not all expressions of opinion are necessarily privileged.  Because that case is built on cases that recognize a Constitutional privilege we will discuss it later in this chapter.

## B.  CONSTITUTIONAL PRIVILEGE

So long as state law controlled, publishers and broadcasters could try to persuade state courts and legislatures to alter the defamation rules.  As we have seen, their success varied among the states.  Early efforts to gain further protection in defamation cases by invoking federal constitutional law to limit state power did not fare well.

In Near v. Minnesota, 283 U.S. 697, 1 Med.L.Rptr. 1001 (1931), the case that perhaps first reinforced the protection of the press in this country, the majority observed, "But it is recognized that punishment for the abuse of the liberty accorded to the press is essential to the protection of the public, and that the common-law rules that subject the libeler to responsibility for the public offense, as well as for the private injury, are not abolished by the protection extended in our Constitution."

Recall the passage in *Chaplinsky* p. 48, *supra*:

There are certain well-defined and narrowly limited classes of speech, the prevention and punishment of which have never been thought to raise any Constitutional problem.  These include the lewd and obscene, the profane, the libelous, and the insulting or

"fighting" words—those which by their very utterance inflict injury
or tend to incite an immediate breach of the peace.  It has been well
observed that such utterances are no essential part of any exposition
of ideas, and are of such slight social value as a step to truth that
any benefit that may be derived from them is clearly outweighed by
the social interest in order and morality.

This language was often quoted approvingly.  Justice Frankfurter, writing for a 5–4 majority in Beauharnais v. Illinois, 343 U.S. 250 (1952), to
sustain a state criminal libel law, relied on *Chaplinsky* for the proposition that libelous utterances were not "within the area of constitutionally protected speech."

### 1.  "ACTUAL MALICE" AND THE NEW YORK TIMES RULE

This *Chaplinsky–Beauharnais* sequence set the stage for the following case from Alabama, a state that had long followed the majority rule
that there was no privilege for incorrect facts, even in stories of public
importance.  In the decision the Supreme Court uses, for the first time,
the term "actual malice."

### NEW YORK TIMES CO. v. SULLIVAN
(Together with Abernathy v. Sullivan).

Supreme Court of the United States, 1964.
376 U.S. 254, 84 S.Ct. 710, 11 L.Ed.2d 686, 1 Med.L.Rptr. 1527.

[This action was based on a full-page advertisement in *The New
York Times* on behalf of several individuals and groups protesting a
"wave of terror" against blacks involved in non-violent demonstrations
in the South.  Plaintiff, one of three elected commissioners of Montgomery, the capital of Alabama, was in charge of the police department.
When he demanded a retraction, as state law required, the Times
instead responded that it failed to see how he was defamed.  He then
filed suit against the Times and four clergymen whose names appeared
as sponsors—although they denied having authorized this—in the ad.
Plaintiff alleged that the third and the sixth paragraphs of the advertisement libelled him:

"In Montgomery, Alabama, after students sang 'My Country, 'Tis of Thee' on the State Capitol steps, their leaders were
expelled from school, and truckloads of police armed with shotguns
and tear-gas ringed the Alabama State College Campus.  When the
entire student body protested to state authorities by refusing to re-
register, their dining hall was padlocked in an attempt to starve
them into submission."

. . .

"Again and again the Southern violators have answered Dr.
King's peaceful protests with intimidation and violence.  They have
bombed his home almost killing his wife and child.  They have

assaulted his person. They have arrested him seven times—for 'speeding,' 'loitering' and similar 'offenses.' And now they have charged him with 'perjury'—a *felony* under which they could imprison him for *ten years.* . . ."

Plaintiff claimed that he was libelled in the third paragraph by the reference to the police, because his responsibilities included supervision of the Montgomery police. He asserted that the paragraph could be read as charging the police with ringing the campus and seeking to starve the students by padlocking the dining hall. As to the sixth paragraph, he contended that the word "they" referred to his department since arrests are usually made by the police and the paragraph could be read as accusing him of committing the acts charged. Several witnesses testified that they read the statements as referring to plaintiff in his capacity as commissioner.

The defendants admitted several inaccuracies in these two paragraphs: the students sang "The Star Spangled Banner", not "My Country, 'Tis of Thee"; nine students were expelled, not for leading the demonstration, but for demanding service at a lunch counter in the county courthouse; the dining hall was never padlocked; police at no time ringed the campus though they were deployed nearby in large numbers; they were not called to the campus in connection with the demonstration; Dr. King had been arrested only four times; and officers disputed his account of the alleged assault. Plaintiff proved that he had not been commissioner when three of the four arrests occurred and that he had nothing to do with procuring the perjury indictment.

The trial judge charged that the statements were libel *per se*, that the jury should decide whether they were made "of and concerning" the plaintiff, and, if so, general damages were to be presumed. Although noting that punitive damages required more than carelessness, he refused to charge that they required a finding of actual intent to harm or "gross negligence and recklessness." He also refused to order the jury to separate its award of general and punitive damages. The jury returned a verdict for $500,000—the full amount demanded. The Alabama Supreme Court affirmed, holding that malice could be found in several aspects of the Times' conduct.]

MR. JUSTICE BRENNAN delivered the opinion of the Court.

. . .

## I.

We may dispose at the outset of two grounds asserted to insulate the judgment of the Alabama courts from constitutional scrutiny. The first is the proposition relied on by the State Supreme Court—that "The Fourteenth Amendment is directed against State action and not private action." That proposition has no application to this case. Although this is a civil lawsuit between private parties, the Alabama courts have applied a state rule of law which petitioners claim to impose invalid restrictions on their constitutional freedoms of speech and press. It matters not that that law has been applied in a civil action and that it is common law only, though supplemented by statute. [   ] The test is not the form in which state power has been applied but, whatever the form, whether such power has in fact been exercised. [   ]

The second contention is that the constitutional guarantees of freedom of speech and of the press are inapplicable here, at least so far as the Times is concerned, because the allegedly libelous statements were published as part of a paid, "commercial" advertisement. The argument [was rejected.]

## II.

Under Alabama law as applied in this case, a publication is "libelous per se" if the words "tend to injure a person  .  .  .  in his reputation" or to "bring [him] into public contempt"; the trial court stated that the standard was met if the words are such as to "injure him in his public office, or impute misconduct to him in his office, or want of official integrity, or want of fidelity to a public trust .  .  .." The jury must find that the words were published "of and concerning" the plaintiff, but where the plaintiff is a public official his place in the governmental hierarchy is sufficient evidence to support a finding that his reputation has been affected by statements that reflect upon the agency of which he is in charge. Once "libel per se" has been established, the defendant has no defense as to stated facts unless he can persuade the jury that they were true in all their particulars. [   ] His privilege of "fair comment" for expressions of opinion depends on the truth of the facts upon which the comment is based. [   ] Unless he can discharge the burden of proving truth, general damages are presumed, and may be awarded without proof of pecuniary injury. A showing of actual malice is apparently a prerequisite to recovery of punitive damages, and the defendant may in any event forestall a punitive award by a retraction meeting the statutory requirements. Good motives and belief in truth do not negate an inference of malice, but are relevant only in mitigation of punitive damages if the jury chooses to accord them weight. [   ]

The question before us is whether this rule of liability, as applied to an action brought by a public official against critics of his official conduct, abridges the freedom of speech and of the press that is guaranteed by the First and Fourteenth Amendments.

Respondent relies heavily, as did the Alabama courts, on statements of this Court to the effect that the Constitution does not protect libelous publications. Those statements do not foreclose our inquiry here. None of the cases sustained the use of libel laws to impose sanctions upon expression critical of the official conduct of public officials.  .  .  .  In deciding the question now, we are compelled by neither precedent nor policy to give any more weight to the epithet "libel" than we have to other "mere labels" of state law. NAACP v. Button, 371 U.S. 415, 429 (1963). Like insurrection, contempt, advocacy of unlawful acts, breach of the peace, obscenity, solicitation of legal business, and the various other formulae for the repression of expression that have been challenged in this Court, libel can claim no talismanic immunity from constitutional limitations. It must be measured by standards that satisfy the First Amendment.

The general proposition that freedom of expression upon public questions is secured by the First Amendment has long been settled by our decisions. . . . Mr. Justice Brandeis, in his concurring opinion in Whitney v. California, 274 U.S. 357, 375–376 (1927), gave the principle its classic formulation:

> "Those who won our independence believed . . . that public discussion is a political duty; and that this should be a fundamental principle of the American government. . . . Believing in the power of reason as applied through public discussion, they eschewed silence coerced by law—the argument of force in its worst form. Recognizing the occasional tyrannies of governing majorities, they amended the Constitution so that free speech and assembly should be guaranteed."

Thus we consider this case against the background of a profound national commitment to the principle that debate on public issues should be uninhibited, robust, and wide-open, and that it may well include vehement, caustic, and sometimes unpleasantly sharp attacks on government and public officials. See Terminiello v. Chicago, 337 U.S. 1, 4 (1949); De Jonge v. Oregon, 299 U.S. 353, 365 (1937). The present advertisement, as an expression of grievance and protest on one of the major public issues of our time, would seem clearly to qualify for the constitutional protection. The question is whether it forfeits that protection by the falsity of some of its factual statements and by its alleged defamation of respondent.

Authoritative interpretations of the First Amendment guarantees have consistently refused to recognize an exception for any test of truth—whether administered by judges, juries, or administrative officials—and especially one that puts the burden of proving truth on the speaker. Cf. Speiser v. Randall, 357 U.S. 513, 525–526 (1958). The constitutional protection does not turn upon "the truth, popularity, or social utility of the ideas and beliefs which are offered." NAACP v. Button, 371 U.S. 415, 445 (1963). As Madison said, "Some degree of abuse is inseparable from the proper use of every thing; and in no instance is this more true than in that of the press." 4 Elliot's Debates on the Federal Constitution (1876) p. 571. In Cantwell v. Connecticut, 310 U.S. 296, 310 (1940), the Court declared:

> "In the realm of religious faith, and in that of political belief, sharp differences arise. In both fields the tenets of one man may seem the rankest error to his neighbor. To persuade others to his own point of view, the pleader, as we know, at times, resorts to exaggeration, to vilification of men who have been, or are, prominent in church or state, and even to false statement. But the people of this nation have ordained in the light of history, that, in spite of the probability of excesses and abuses, these liberties are, in the long

view, essential to enlightened opinion and right conduct on the part
of the citizens of a democracy."

That erroneous statement is inevitable in free debate, and that it must
be protected if the freedoms of expression are to have the "breathing
space" that they "need . . . to survive," NAACP v. Button, 371
U.S. 415, 433 (1963), was also recognized by the Court of Appeals for the
District of Columbia Circuit in Sweeney v. Patterson, 76 U.S.App.D.C.
23, 24, 128 F.2d 457, 458, certiorari denied, 317 U.S. 678 (1942). Judge
Edgerton spoke for a unanimous court which affirmed the dismissal of a
Congressman's libel suit based upon a newspaper article charging him
with anti-Semitism in opposing a judicial appointment. He said:

> "Cases which impose liability for erroneous reports of the
> political conduct of officials reflect the obsolete doctrine that the
> governed must not criticize their governors. . . . The interest
> of the public here outweighs the interest of appellant or any other
> individual. The protection of the public requires not merely discus-
> sion, but information. Political conduct and views which some
> respectable people approve, and others condemn, are constantly
> imputed to Congressmen. Errors of fact, particularly in regard to a
> man's mental states and processes, are inevitable. . . . Whatev-
> er is added to the field of libel is taken from the field of free
> debate." [13]

Injury to official reputation affords no more warrant for repressing
speech that would otherwise be free than does factual error. Where
judicial officers are involved, this Court has held that concern for the
dignity and reputation of the courts does not justify the punishment as
criminal contempt of criticism of the judge or his decision. Bridges v.
California, 314 U.S. 252 (1941). This is true even though the utterance
contains "half-truths" and "misinformation." Pennekamp v. Florida,
328 U.S. 331, 342, 343, n. 5, 345 (1946). . . . Criticism of their
official conduct does not lose its constitutional protection merely because
it is effective criticism and hence diminishes their official reputations.

If neither factual error nor defamatory content suffices to remove
the constitutional shield from criticism of official conduct, the combination of the two elements is no less inadequate. This is the lesson to be
drawn from the great controversy over the Sedition Act of 1798, 1 Stat.
596, which first crystallized a national awareness of the central meaning
of the First Amendment. . . .

---

**13.** See also Mill, On Liberty (Oxford:
Blackwell, 1947), at 47:

". . . [T]o argue sophistically, to suppress facts or arguments, to misstate the
elements of the case, or misrepresent the
opposite opinion . . . all this, even to
the most aggravated degree, is so continually done in perfect good faith, by persons
who are not considered, and in many other
respects may not deserve to be considered,
ignorant or incompetent, that it is rarely
possible, on adequate grounds, conscientiously to stamp the misrepresentation as
morally culpable; and still less could law
presume to interfere with this kind of controversial misconduct."

Although the Sedition Act was never tested in this Court,[16] the attack upon its validity has carried the day in the court of history. Fines levied in its prosecution were repaid by Act of Congress on the ground that it was unconstitutional. . . . The invalidity of the Act has also been assumed by Justices of this Court. [ ] These views reflect a broad consensus that the Act, because of the restraint it imposed upon criticism of government and public officials, was inconsistent with the First Amendment.

There is no force in respondent's argument that the constitutional limitations implicit in the history of the Sedition Act apply only to Congress and not to the States. It is true that the First Amendment was originally addressed only to action by the Federal Government, and that Jefferson, for one, while denying the power of Congress "to control the freedom of the press," recognized such a power in the States. [ ] But this distinction was eliminated with the adoption of the Fourteenth Amendment and the application to the States of the First Amendment's restrictions. [ ]

What a State may not constitutionally bring about by means of a criminal statute is likewise beyond the reach of its civil law of libel. The fear of damage awards under a rule such as that invoked by the Alabama courts here may be markedly more inhibiting than the fear of prosecution under a criminal statute. [ ] Alabama, for example, has a criminal libel law which subjects to prosecution "any person who speaks, writes, or prints of and concerning another any accusation falsely and maliciously importing the commission by such person of a felony, or any other indictable offense involving moral turpitude," and which allows as punishment upon conviction a fine not exceeding $500 and a prison sentence of six months. [ ] Presumably a person charged with violation of this statute enjoys ordinary criminal-law safeguards such as the requirements of an indictment and of proof beyond a reasonable doubt. These safeguards are not available to the defendant in a civil action. . . . And since there is no double-jeopardy limitation applicable to civil lawsuits, this is not the only judgment that may be awarded against petitioners for the same publication.[18] Whether or not a newspaper can survive a succession of such judgments, the pall of fear and timidity imposed upon those who would give voice to public criticism is an atmosphere in which the First Amendment freedoms cannot survive. Plainly the Alabama law of civil libel is "a form of regulation that creates hazards to protected freedoms markedly greater than those that attend reliance upon the criminal law." Bantam Books, Inc. v. Sullivan, 372 U.S. 58, 70 (1963).

**16.** The Act expired by its terms in 1801.

**18.** The Times states that four other libel suits based on the advertisement have been filed against it by others who have served as Montgomery City Commissioners and by the Governor of Alabama; that another $500,000 verdict has been awarded in the only one of these cases that has yet gone to trial; and that the damages sought in the other three total $2,000,000.

The state rule of law is not saved by its allowance of the defense of truth. . . . Allowance of the defense of truth, with the burden of proving it on the defendant, does not mean that only false speech will be deterred.[19] Even courts accepting this defense as an adequate safeguard have recognized the difficulties of adducing legal proofs that the alleged libel was true in all its factual particulars. See, e.g., Post Publishing Co. v. Hallam, 59 F. 530, 540 (C.A. 6th Cir.1893); see also Noel, Defamation of Public Officers and Candidates, 49 Col.L.Rev. 875, 892 (1949). Under such a rule, would-be critics of official conduct may be deterred from voicing their criticism, even though it is believed to be true and even though it is in fact true, because of doubt whether it can be proved in court or fear of the expense of having to do so. They tend to make only statements which "steer far wider of the unlawful zone." Speiser v. Randall, supra, 357 U.S., at 526. The rule thus dampens the vigor and limits the variety of public debate. It is inconsistent with the First and Fourteenth Amendments.

The constitutional guarantees require, we think, a federal rule that prohibits a public official from recovering damages for a defamatory falsehood relating to his official conduct unless he proves that the statement was made with "actual malice"—that is, with knowledge that it was false or with reckless disregard of whether it was false or not. An oft-cited statement of a like rule, which has been adopted by a number of state courts, is found in the Kansas case of Coleman v. MacLennan, 78 Kan. 711, 98 P. 281 (1908). . . .

Such a privilege for criticism of official conduct is appropriately analogous to the protection accorded a public official when *he* is sued for libel by a private citizen. In Barr v. Matteo, 360 U.S. 564, 575 (1959), this Court held the utterance of a federal official to be absolutely privileged if made "within the outer perimeter" of his duties. The States accord the same immunity to statements of their highest officers, although some differentiate their lesser officials and qualify the privilege they enjoy. But all hold that all officials are protected unless actual malice can be proved. The reason for the official privilege is said to be that the threat of damage suits would otherwise "inhibit the fearless, vigorous, and effective administration of policies of government" and "dampen the ardor of all but the most resolute, or the most irresponsible, in the unflinching discharge of their duties." Barr v. Matteo, supra, 360 U.S., at 571. Analogous considerations support the privilege for the citizen-critic of government. It is as much his duty to criticize as it is the official's duty to administer. . . . As Madison said, [ ], "the censorial power is in the people over the Government, and not in the Government over the people." It would give public servants an unjustified preference over the public they serve, if critics of official conduct did

---

**19.** Even a false statement may be deemed to make a valuable contribution to public debate, since it brings about "the clearer perception and livelier impression of truth, produced by its collision with error." Mill, On Liberty (Oxford: Blackwell, 1947), at 15; see also Milton, Areopagitica, in Prose Works (Yale, 1959), Vol. II, at 561.

not have a fair equivalent of the immunity granted to the officials themselves.

We conclude that such a privilege is required by the First and Fourteenth Amendments.

### III.

We hold today that the Constitution delimits a State's power to award damages for libel in actions brought by public officials against critics of their official conduct. Since this is such an action, the rule requiring proof of actual malice is applicable. While Alabama law apparently requires proof of actual malice for an award of punitive damages, where general damages are concerned malice is "presumed." Such a presumption is inconsistent with the federal rule. . . . Since the trial judge did not instruct the jury to differentiate between general and punitive damages, it may be that the verdict was wholly an award of one or the other. But it is impossible to know, in view of the general verdict returned. Because of this uncertainty, the judgment must be reversed and the case remanded. [  ]

Since respondent may seek a new trial, we deem that considerations of effective judicial administration require us to review the evidence in the present record to determine whether it could constitutionally support a judgment for respondent. . . .

Applying these standards, we consider that the proof presented to show actual malice, lacks the convincing clarity which the constitutional standard demands, and hence that it would not constitutionally sustain the judgment for respondent under the proper rule of law. The case of the individual petitioners requires little discussion. Even assuming that they could constitutionally be found to have authorized the use of their names on the advertisement, there was no evidence whatever that they were aware of any erroneous statements or were in any way reckless in that regard. The judgment against them is thus without constitutional support.

As to the Times, we similarly conclude that the facts do not support a finding of actual malice. . . .

. . .

We also think the evidence was constitutionally defective in another respect: it was incapable of supporting the jury's finding that the allegedly libelous statements were made "of and concerning" respondent. Respondent relies on the words of the advertisement and the testimony of six witnesses to establish a connection between it and himself. . . . There was no reference to respondent in the advertisement, either by name or official position. A number of the allegedly libelous statements—the charges that the dining hall was padlocked and that Dr. King's home was bombed, his person assaulted, and a perjury prosecution instituted against him—did not even concern the police; despite the ingenuity of the arguments which would attach this significance to the word "They," it is plain that these statements could not reasonably be read as accusing respondent of personal involvement in the acts in question. The statements upon which respondent principally relies as referring to him are the two allegations that did concern the police or police functions: that "truckloads of police . . . ringed the Alabama State College Campus" after the demonstration on the State Capitol steps, and that Dr. King had been "arrested . . . seven times." These statements were false only in that the police had been "deployed near" the campus but had not actually "ringed" it and had not gone there in connection with the State Capitol demonstration, and in that Dr. King had been arrested only four times. The ruling that these discrepancies between what was true and what was asserted were sufficient to injure respondent's reputation may itself raise constitutional problems, but we need not consider them here. Although the statements may be taken as referring to the police, they did not on their face make even an oblique reference to respondent as an individual. Support for the asserted reference must, therefore, be sought in the testimony of respondent's witnesses. But none of them suggested any basis for the belief that respondent himself was attacked in the advertisement beyond the bare fact that he was in overall charge of the Police Department and thus bore official responsibility for police conduct; to the extent that some of the witnesses thought respondent to have been charged with ordering or approving the conduct or otherwise being personally involved in it, they based this notion not on any statements in the advertisement, and not on any evidence that he had in fact been so involved, but solely on the unsupported assumption that, because of his official position, he must have been. This reliance on the bare fact of respondent's official position was made explicit by the Supreme Court of Alabama. . . .

This proposition has disquieting implications for criticism of governmental conduct. For good reason, "no court of last resort in this country has ever held, or even suggested, that prosecutions for libel on government have any place in the American system of jurisprudence." City of Chicago v. Tribune Co., 307 Ill. 595, 601, 139 N.E. 86, 88 (1923). The present proposition would sidestep this obstacle by transmuting criticism of government, however impersonal it may seem on its face, into personal criticism, and hence potential libel, of the officials of whom the government is composed. There is no legal alchemy by which a State may thus create the cause of action that would otherwise be denied for a publication which, as respondent himself said of the advertisement, "reflects not only on me but on the other Commissioners and the community." Raising as it does the possibility that a good-faith critic of government will be penalized for his criticism, the proposition relied on by the Alabama courts strikes at the very center of the constitutionally protected area of free expression.[30] We hold that such a proposition may

30. Insofar as the proposition means only that the statements about police conduct libeled respondent by implicitly criticizing his ability to run the Police Department, recovery is also precluded in this case by the doctrine of fair comment. See American Law Institute, Restatement of Torts (1938), § 607. Since the Fourteenth Amendment requires recognition of the conditional privilege for honest misstate-

not constitutionally be utilized to establish that an otherwise impersonal attack on governmental operations was a libel of an official responsible for those operations. Since it was relied on exclusively here, and there was no other evidence to connect the statements with respondent, the evidence was constitutionally insufficient to support a finding that the statements referred to respondent.

The judgment of the Supreme Court of Alabama is reversed and the case is remanded to that court for further proceedings not inconsistent with this opinion.

Reversed and remanded.

MR. JUSTICE BLACK, with whom MR. JUSTICE DOUGLAS joins, concurring.

I concur in reversing this half-million-dollar judgment against the New York Times Company and the four individual defendants. In reversing the Court holds that "the Constitution delimits a State's power to award damages for libel in actions brought by public officials against critics of their official conduct." I base my vote to reverse on the belief that the First and Fourteenth Amendments not merely "delimit" a State's power to award damages to "public officials against critics of their official conduct" but completely prohibit a State from exercising such a power. The Court goes on to hold that a State can subject such critics to damages if "actual malice" can be proved against them. "Malice," even as defined by the Court, is an elusive, abstract concept, hard to prove and hard to disprove. The requirement that malice be proved provides at best an evanescent protection for the right critically to discuss public affairs and certainly does not measure up to the sturdy safeguard embodied in the First Amendment. Unlike the Court, therefore, I vote to reverse exclusively on the ground that the Times and the individual defendants had an absolute unconditional constitutional right to publish in the Times advertisement their criticisms of the Montgomery agencies and officials. . . .

The half-million-dollar verdict does give dramatic proof, however, that state libel laws threaten the very existence of an American press virile enough to publish unpopular views on public affairs and bold enough to criticize the conduct of public officials. . . . In fact, briefs before us show that in Alabama there are now pending eleven libel suits by local and state officials against the Times seeking $5,600,000 and five such suits against the Columbia Broadcasting System seeking $1,700,-000. Moreover, this technique for harassing and punishing a free press—now that it has been shown to be possible—is by no means limited to cases with racial overtones; it can be used in other fields where public feelings may make local as well as out-of-state newspapers easy prey for libel verdict seekers.

ments of fact, it follows that a defense of fair comment must be afforded for honest expression of opinion based upon privileged, as well as true, statements of fact. Both defenses are of course defeasible if the public official proves actual malice, as was not done here.

In my opinion the Federal Constitution has dealt with this deadly danger to the press in the only way possible without leaving the free press open to destruction—by granting the press an absolute immunity for criticism of the way public officials do their public duty.   Compare Barr v. Matteo, 360 U.S. 564 (1959).   Stopgap measures like those the Court adopts are in my judgment not enough.   This record certainly does not indicate that any different verdict would have been rendered here whatever the Court had charged the jury about "malice," "truth," "good motives," "justifiable ends," or any other legal formulas which in theory would protect the press.   Nor does the record indicate that any of these legalistic words would have caused the courts below to set aside or to reduce the half-million-dollar verdict in any amount.

. . .

We would, I think, more faithfully interpret the First Amendment by holding that at the very least it leaves the people and the press free to criticize officials and discuss public affairs with impunity.   . . .   An unconditional right to say what one pleases about public affairs is what I consider to be the minimum guarantee of the First Amendment.[6]

I regret that the Court has stopped short of this holding indispensable to preserve our free press from destruction.

MR. JUSTICE GOLDBERG, with whom MR. JUSTICE DOUGLAS joins, concurring in the result.

. . .

In my view, the First and Fourteenth Amendments to the Constitution afford to the citizen and to the press an absolute, unconditional privilege to criticize official conduct despite the harm which may flow from excesses and abuses.   . . .

. . .

. . . It may be urged that deliberately and maliciously false statements have no conceivable value as free speech.   That argument, however, is not responsive to the real issue presented by this case, which is whether that freedom of speech which all agree is constitutionally protected can be effectively safeguarded by a rule allowing the imposition of liability upon a jury's evaluation of the speaker's state of mind. If individual citizens may be held liable in damages for strong words, which a jury finds false and maliciously motivated, there can be little doubt that public debate and advocacy will be constrained.   And if newspapers, publishing advertisements dealing with public issues, thereby risk liability, there can also be little doubt that the ability of minority groups to secure publication of their views on public affairs and to seek support for their causes will be greatly diminished.   . . .

. . .

This is not to say that the Constitution protects defamatory statements directed against the private conduct of a public official or private

**6.**  Cf. Meiklejohn, Free Speech and Its
Relation to Self–Government (1948).

citizen. Freedom of press and of speech insures that government will respond to the will of the people and that changes may be obtained by peaceful means. Purely private defamation has little to do with the political ends of a self-governing society. The imposition of liability for private defamation does not abridge the freedom of public speech or any other freedom protected by the First Amendment.[4] . . .

. . .

If the government official should be immune from libel actions so that his ardor to serve the public will not be dampened and "fearless, vigorous, and effective administration of policies of government" not be inhibited, Barr v. Matteo, supra, at 571, then the citizen and the press should likewise be immune from libel actions for their criticism of official conduct. . . .

The conclusion that the Constitution affords the citizen and the press an absolute privilege for criticism of official conduct does not leave the public official without defenses against unsubstantiated opinions or deliberate misstatements. "Under our system of government, counter-argument and education are the weapons available to expose these matters, not abridgment . . . of free speech. . . ." Wood v. Georgia, 370 U.S. 375, 389 (1962). The public official certainly has equal if not greater access than most private citizens to media of communication. . . .

. . .

### Notes and Questions

1. What is the justification for the majority position?

2. The majority twice observes that deliberate falsity is used in argument. Why is such behavior not protected here?

3. Do you consider either of the concurring opinions preferable to the majority approach? Would it be desirable to enable a public official to have a jury assess the truth of charges against him—without seeking damages?

4. Commenting after *Sullivan*, Professor Kalven speculated on the case's future:

> The closing question, of course, is whether the treatment of seditious libel as the key concept for development of appropriate constitutional doctrine will prove germinal. It is not easy to predict what the Court will see in [*Sullivan*] as the years roll by. It may regard the opinion as covering simply one pocket of cases, those dealing with libel of public officials, and not destructive of the earlier notions that are inconsistent only with the larger reading of

---

**4.** In most cases, as in the case at bar, there will be little difficulty in distinguishing defamatory speech relating to private conduct from that relating to official conduct. I recognize, of course, that there will be a gray area. The difficulties of applying a public-private standard are, however, certainly of a different genre from those attending the differentiation between a malicious and nonmalicious state of mind. . . .

the Court's action. But the invitation to follow a dialectic progression from public official to government policy to public policy to matters in the public domain, like art, seems to me to be overwhelming. If the Court accepts the invitation, it will slowly work out for itself the theory of free speech that Alexander Meiklejohn has been offering us for some fifteen years now.

Kalven, The New York Times Case: A Note on "The Central Meaning of the First Amendment," 1964 Sup.Ct.Rev. 191, 221. Does his prediction seem sound? Keep it in mind as we consider the cases decided since *Sullivan*. Do not be confused by the fact that some writers and judges refer to the case as *Sullivan* and others call it the *New York Times* case.

5. Later in 1964, in Garrison v. Louisiana, 379 U.S. 64, 1 Med.L.Rptr. 1548 (1964), the Court, in an opinion by Justice Brennan, extended the principle from *Sullivan*, called the *New York Times* rule, to cases of *criminal* libel and also held that truth must be a defense in cases brought by public officials. The majority explained its refusal to protect deliberate falsity:

> Although honest utterance, even if inaccurate, may further the fruitful exercise of the right of free speech, it does not follow that the lie, knowingly and deliberately published about a public official, should enjoy a like immunity. At the time the First Amendment was adopted, as today, there were those unscrupulous enough and skillful enough to use the deliberate or reckless falsehood as an effective political tool to unseat the public servant or even topple an administration. [  ] That speech is used as a tool for political ends does not automatically bring it under the protective mantle of the Constitution. For the use of the known lie as a tool is at once at odds with the premises of democratic government and with the orderly manner in which economic, social, or political change is to be effected. Calculated falsehood falls into that class of utterances which "are no essential part of any exposition of ideas, and are of such slight social value as a step to truth that any benefit that may be derived from them is clearly outweighed by the social interest in order and morality. . . ." Chaplinsky v. New Hampshire, 315 U.S. 568, 572 (1942). Hence the knowingly false statement and the false statement made with reckless disregard of the truth, do not enjoy constitutional protection.

6. *Who must prove actual malice?* Because Sullivan was an elected public official, the Court did not address the possibility of other plaintiffs' having to prove actual malice. They had to address that issue in subsequent cases.

a. *Appointed government officials and former governmental officials— those responsible for governmental affairs.* The next major case was Rosenblatt v. Baer, 383 U.S. 75, 1 Med.L.Rptr. 1558 (1966). Plaintiff Baer had been hired by the three elected county commissioners to be Supervisor of a public recreation facility owned by Belknap County, N.H. Defendant, in his weekly newspaper column, noted that a year after plaintiff's discharge the facility was doing much better financially. The column could be understood as charging either inefficiency or dishonesty. In reversing plaintiff's state court judgment, the Supreme Court said that the vague language could be read as an attack on government— and that Baer could not sue unless he showed that he had been singled out for attack. Justice Brennan's majority opinion then held that Baer was a "public official" under the *New York Times* rule and that the trial judge's charge did not give the jury the correct "malice" standard. It said that, "It is clear . . . that the 'public official' designation applies at the very least to those among the hierarchy of government employees who have, or appear to the public to have, substantial responsibility for or control over the conduct of governmental affairs."

b. *Political Candidates.* The Court decided three cases as a group. Two of them involved false charges made about a candidate for office. The Court unanimously extended the *Sullivan* rationale to candidates because "it can hardly be doubted that the constitutional guarantee has its fullest and most urgent application precisely to the conduct of campaigns for political office." Monitor Patriot Co. v. Roy, 401 U.S. 265, 1 Med.L.Rptr. 1619 (1971) and Ocala Star–Banner Co. v. Damron, 401 U.S. 295, 1 Med.L.Rptr. 1624 (1971). In *Roy,* the charge related to criminal activity that allegedly took place many years earlier. The Court decided that the *New York Times* rule should include "anything which might touch on an official's fitness for office" when a candidate's behavior is being discussed. "The principal activity of a candidate in our political system . . . consists in putting before the voters every conceivable aspect of his public and private life that he thinks may lead the electorate to gain a good impression of him. A candidate who, for example, seeks to further his cause through the prominent display of his wife and children can hardly argue that his qualities as a husband or father remain of 'purely private' concern." The Court concluded that a "charge of criminal conduct, no matter how remote in time or place, can never be irrelevant to an official's or a candidate's fitness for office" for purposes of applying the *New York Times* rule.

In *Damron,* the candidate was said to have been charged with a crime, when in fact his brother was the one charged. Again, the *New York Times* rule applied.

In the third case, Time, Inc. v. Pape, 401 U.S. 279, 1 Med.L.Rptr. 1627 (1971), a report by the Civil Rights Commission included some unverified complaints of police brutality as examples of the types of complaints being received. *Time* reported the release of the volume and quoted one of the complaints without indicating that it had not been verified. The police named in that complaint sued *Time.* The *New York Times* rule admittedly applied and the question was whether the facts would permit a jury to find the requisite malice. The Court chose a very narrow ground that stressed the difficulties of reporting what someone has said as opposed to what someone has done. Here the Commission's own words might have been read to suggest that the complaints were probably valid and thus *Time* may have accurately captured the sense of the

Commission's report, even though it excluded the word "alleged." Even
if the story was inaccurate, the Court held as a matter of law that there
was no basis for finding deliberate or reckless falsity.

c. *Public figures.* The Supreme Court next considered two cases together, Curtis Publishing Co. v. Butts, and Associated Press v. Walker,
388 U.S. 130, 1 Med.L.Rptr. 1568 (1967). In *Butts*, the defendant
magazine had accused the plaintiff athletic director of disclosing his
game plan to an opposing coach before their game. Although he was on
the staff of a state university, Butts was paid by a private alumni
organization. In *Walker,* the defendant news service reported that the
plaintiff, a former United States Army general who resigned to engage in
political activity, had personally led students in an attack on federal
marshals who were enforcing a desegregation order at the University of
Mississippi.

In both cases, lower courts had affirmed substantial jury awards against
the defendants and had refused to apply the *New York Times* rule on the
ground that public officials were not involved. The Supreme Court
divided several ways on several issues, affirming *Butts,* 5–4, and reversing *Walker,* 9–0. Chief Justice Warren wrote the pivotal opinion in
which he concluded that both men were "public figures" and that the
standard developed in *Sullivan* should apply to "public figures" as well:

> To me, differentiation between "public figures" and "public
> officials" and adoption of separate standards of proof for each has no
> basis in law, logic, or First Amendment policy. Increasingly in this
> country, the distinctions between governmental and private sectors
> are blurred. Since the depression of the 1930's and World War II
> there has been a rapid fusion of economic and political power, a
> merging of science, industry, and government, and a high degree of
> interaction between the intellectual, governmental, and business
> worlds. Depression, war, international tensions, national and inter-
> national markets, and the surging growth of science and technology
> have precipitated national and international problems that demand
> national and international solutions. While these trends and events
> have occasioned a consolidation of governmental power, power has
> also become much more organized in what we have commonly
> considered to be the private sector. In many situations, policy
> determinations which traditionally were channeled through formal
> political institutions are now originated and implemented through a
> complex array of boards, committees, commissions, corporations,
> and associations, some only loosely connected with the Government.
> This blending of positions and power has also occurred in the case of
> individuals so that many who do not hold public office at the
> moment are nevertheless intimately involved in the resolution of
> important public questions or, by reason of their fame, shape events
> in areas of concern to society at large.
>
> Viewed in this context then, it is plain that although they are
> not subject to the restraints of the political process, "public figures,"

like "public officials," often play an influential role in ordering society. And surely as a class these "public figures" have as ready access as "public officials" to mass media of communication, both to influence policy and to counter criticism of their views and activities. Our citizenry has a legitimate and substantial interest in the conduct of such persons, and freedom of the press to engage in uninhibited debate about their involvement in public issues and events is as crucial as it is in the case of "public officials." The fact that they are not amenable to the restraints of the political process only underscores the legitimate and substantial nature of the interest, since it means that public opinion may be the only instrument by which society can attempt to influence their conduct.

He found that on the merits the standard had not been met in *Walker*. In *Butts*, he found that defendant's counsel had deliberately waived the *New York Times* rule, and he also found evidence establishing reckless behavior. He thus voted to reverse *Walker* and affirm *Butts*.

Justice Harlan, joined by Justices Clark, Stewart and Fortas, argued that the *New York Times* rule should not apply to public figures because criticism of government was not involved:

> We consider and would hold that a "public figure" who is not a public official may also recover damages for a defamatory falsehood whose substance makes substantial danger to reputation apparent, on a showing of highly unreasonable conduct constituting an extreme departure from the standards of investigation and reporting ordinarily adhered to by responsible publishers. . . .

Applying that standard Justice Harlan concluded that Walker had failed to establish a case, but that Butts had shown that the *Saturday Evening Post* ignored elementary precautions in preparing a potentially damaging story. Together with the Chief Justice's vote, there were five votes to affirm *Butts*.

Justices Brennan and White agreed with the Chief Justice in *Walker* but found no waiver in *Butts* and would have reversed both cases. They agreed with the Chief Justice that *Butts* had presented enough evidence to come within the *Times* standard but thought that errors in the charge required a new trial.

Justices Black and Douglas adhered to their position, urged that the *New York Times* rule be abandoned, and voted to reverse both cases.

7. *What exactly is "actual malice?"* Some people refer to the term "actual malice" as a "term of art," which may be a polite way of saying that the Supreme Court invented its own definition of the word *malice*. An ordinary dictionary might define *malice* as "ill will" or "evil intent," but the Supreme Court had something different in mind.

a. The Court first defined "actual malice" in *Sullivan* in terms of making a statement "with knowledge that it was false [seemingly the equivalent of a deliberate lie] or with reckless disregard of whether it was false or not." Would an unthinking or empty-headed person who made a false statement seem to fall within that definition of "actual malice"?

b. About eight months later in *Garrison*, the Court quoted its own words from *Sullivan* but said also that "[O]nly those false statements made with the high degree of awareness of their probable falsity demanded by *New York Times* may be the subject of either civil or criminal sanctions." Does that change your answer to the question posed above about an unthinking or empty-headed person?

c. *"Entertaining serious doubts."* In St. Amant v. Thompson, 390 U.S. 727, 1 Med.L.Rptr. 1586 (1968), the defendant, a candidate for public office, read on television a series of statements he had received from Mr. Albin, a member of a Teamsters' Union local. The statements, made under oath, falsely implied that the plaintiff, a deputy sheriff, had taken bribes. The defendant had not checked the facts stated by Albin, nor had he investigated Albin's reputation for veracity. The state court ruled that these failures to inquire further sufficed to meet the required standard of reckless disregard for the truth. The Supreme Court reversed and concluded that the standard of "reckless disregard" had not been met. It recognized that the term could receive no single "infallible definition" and that its outer limits would have to be developed in "case-to-case adjudication, as is true with so many legal standards for judging concrete cases, whether the standard is provided by the Constitution, statutes or case law." There "must be sufficient evidence to permit the conclusion that the defendant in fact entertained serious doubts as to the truth of his publication" in order for recklessness to be found. Anticipating the charge that this position would encourage publishers not to verify their assertions, Justice White, for the Court stated:

> The defendant in a defamation action brought by a public official cannot, however, automatically insure a favorable verdict by testifying that he published with a belief that the statements were true. The finder of fact must determine whether the publication was indeed made in good faith. Professions of good faith will be unlikely to prove persuasive, for example, where a story is fabricated by the defendant, is a product of his imagination, or is based wholly on an unverified anonymous telephone call. Nor will they be likely to prevail when the publisher's allegations are so inherently improbable that only a reckless man would have put them in circulation. Likewise, recklessness may be found where there are obvious reasons to doubt the veracity of the informant or the accuracy of his reports.

Justice Fortas dissented on the ground that the failure to make "a good-faith check" of the statement was sufficient to establish "reckless disregard." How would the Court's test apply to an extreme partisan who would readily believe anything derogatory about his opponent?

d. When, in *Butts*, the Court found that the actual malice standard was met by the behavior of *The Saturday Evening Post*, it provided us with a definition-by-example of "actual malice." In some ways, is that more helpful than the various definitions-by-words?

When you read the Supreme Court's opinion in *Gertz,* the next principal case in this chapter, be sure to watch for any clarification or change in the Court's definition of "actual malice."

8. *Procedural issues unique to "actual malice" cases.* As the Supreme Court continued to take defamation cases in the 1980s, a variety of procedural issues presented themselves.

a. *Convincing clarity.* In deciding *New York Times,* the Court had said, "[W]e consider that the proof presented to show actual malice lacks the convincing clarity which the constitutional standard demands . . .," so plaintiffs continued to need to prove actual malice with "convincing clarity."

b. *Summary judgment.* In Anderson v. Liberty Lobby, Inc., 477 U.S. 242, 12 Med.L.Rptr. 2297 (1986), the Supreme Court held, 6–3, that the standard for considering summary judgment motions must take into account the burden the plaintiff will have to meet at trial. Because the plaintiff in the case was held to be public, the Court held that on the summary judgment motion, the judge must decide "whether the evidence in the record could support a reasonable jury finding either that the plaintiff has shown actual malice by clear and convincing evidence or that the plaintiff has not."

In response to the argument that at the summary judgment stage the plaintiff need show only enough to prevail on a "preponderance of the evidence" standard, the Court responded that it "makes no sense to say that a jury could reasonably find for either party without some benchmark as to what standards govern its deliberations and within what boundaries its ultimate decision must fall, and these standards and boundaries are in fact provided by the applicable evidentiary standards."

The Court denied that its holding denigrated the role of the jury. "Credibility determinations, the weighing of the evidence, and the drawing of legitimate inferences from the facts are jury functions, not those of a judge, whether he is ruling on a motion for summary judgment or for a directed verdict."

In a footnote, the Court addressed footnote 9 in Hutchinson v. Proxmire, in which the Court had suggested that proof of actual malice "does not readily lend itself to summary disposition." That sentence "was simply an acknowledgement of our general reluctance" to grant special procedural protections to the media in addition to the substantive standards announced in cases like *Sullivan* and *Gertz.* This was not relevant here because the Court in *Liberty Lobby* was announcing a general approach to all civil cases—that the summary judgment standard was to be the same as that the plaintiff must meet at the trial itself.

Justice Brennan dissented out of concern that the majority's decision "may erode the constitutionally enshrined role of the jury, and also undermine the usefulness of summary judgment procedure." On the latter point, he was concerned that the decision would confuse the lower courts.

c. *Pretrial discovery.* Herbert v. Lando, 441 U.S. 153, 4 Med.L.Rptr. 2575 (1979), raised the issue of what types of questions the plaintiff could ask the media defendants during the pretrial effort to obtain evidence of "actual malice" for the trial. Because the case involves journalists' confidentiality, we will discuss it in Chapter XI.

d. *Independent appellate review.* In Bose Corp. v. Consumers Union, 466 U.S. 485, 10 Med.L.Rptr. 1625 (1984), the Supreme Court held in favor of the publisher of *Consumer Reports* magazine in a product disparagement suit filed by the manufacturer of loudspeakers criticized in the magazine. The magazine said that Bose 901 speakers produced sounds that "tended to wander about the room" and that a violin "appeared to be 10 feet wide and a piano stretched from wall to wall."

The federal judge who presided at the trial in Boston ruled prior to the trial that the Bose Corporation, as a "public figure" plaintiff, would have to prove actual malice to win. Also to be determined at trial was the question of whether the statements in the magazine were opinion or fact. The trial court found that the statements were indeed false statements of fact, because the sound of instruments heard through the speakers tended to wander "along the wall" between the speakers, rather than "about the room," as the magazine had stated. Finding also that the false statement was made with actual malice, the court awarded Bose $115,000 damages.

On appeal, the court did an independent review of the evidence presented at trial and reversed the trial court, saying that actual malice had not been proved after all. In seeking review by the Supreme Court, Bose argued that the appeals court had gone too far in reviewing the evidence—in effect virtually retrying the case. The Supreme Court held that appeals courts, when reviewing findings of actual malice in libel cases and other cases governed by *Sullivan*, must exercise their own judgment in determining whether actual malice was shown with convincing clarity. Thus, the court of appeals' decision in favor of Consumers Union was affirmed.

A case involving the libel of a judicial candidate in Ohio provided an opportunity for the Supreme Court to clarify the decision in *Bose* regarding independent appellate review—and simultaneously provided parallels to *Butts*. Daniel Connaughton was an unsuccessful candidate for municipal judge in Hamilton, Ohio, in 1983. A local newspaper, the *Journal News*, supported his opponent, who was the incumbent. A week prior to the election, the newspaper ran a front-page story quoting a grand jury witness as saying that Connaughton had used "dirty tricks" and offered her and her sister jobs and a trip to Florida "in appreciation" for their help in the investigation of the director of court services who had worked for the incumbent. At a libel trial in federal district court, the jury found by a preponderance of the evidence that the story in question was defamatory and false, and by clear and convincing proof that the story was published with actual malice, and awarded Connaughton $5,000 in compensatory damages and $195,000 in punitive damages.

The Court of Appeals affirmed. It separately considered the evidence supporting each of the jury's special verdicts, concluding that the findings were not clearly erroneous. It did not attempt to make an independent evaluation of the credibility of conflicting oral testimony concerning facts underlying the finding of actual malice but identified 11 subsidiary facts that the jury "could have" found and held that such findings would not have been clearly erroneous, and, based on its independent review, held that when considered cumulatively they provided clear and convincing evidence of actual malice. Harte–Hanks Communications appealed to the Supreme Court. Although the latter held that a showing of "highly unreasonable conduct constituting an extreme departure from the standards of investigation and reporting ordinarily adhered to by responsible publishers" cannot alone support a verdict in favor of a public figure plaintiff in a libel action, the rule applied by the Court of Appeals nonetheless was supportive of the court's ultimate conclusion that the *Journal News* acted with actual malice. The Court said that a reviewing court in a public figure libel case must "exercise independent judgment and determine whether the record establishes actual malice with convincing clarity" to ensure that the verdict is consistent with *New York Times* and subsequent cases. Harte–Hanks Communications, Inc. v. Connaughton, 491 U.S. 657, 16 Med.L.Rptr. 1881 (1989).

## 2. DISTINGUISHING BETWEEN PUBLIC AND PRIVATE FIGURES AFTER THE SULLIVAN CASE

It was inevitable that eventually a libel defendant would argue that the Supreme Court's emphasis on the "publicness" of the plaintiffs as individuals was misplaced, and that free, open and robust debate about *private people* involved in *public matters* is just as deserving of First Amendment protection as is debate about public figures. A plurality (fewer than five members) of the Court faced that question in Rosenbloom v. Metromedia, Inc., 403 U.S. 29, 1 Med.L.Rptr. 1597 (1971), involving a broadcaster's charge that a magazine distributor sold obscene material and was arrested in a police raid. Justice Brennan, joined by Chief Justice Burger and Justice Blackmun, held that the *New York Times* rule should be extended to "all discussion and communication involving matters of public or general concern, without regard to whether the persons involved are famous or anonymous." The arrest and the distributor's subsequent claims against the police were thought to fit this category, and the *New York Times* rule was applied. In reaching that position Justice Brennan concluded that the focus on the plaintiff's status begun in *Sullivan* bore "little relationship either to the values protected by the First Amendment or to the nature of our society. . . . Thus, the idea that certain 'public' figures have voluntarily exposed their entire lives to public inspection, while private individuals have kept theirs carefully shrouded from public view is, at best, a legal fiction." Discussion of a matter of public concern must be protected even when it involves an unknown person. If the states fear that private citizens will be unable to respond to adverse publicity, "the solution lies in the direction of ensuring their ability to respond, rather than in stifling public discussion of matters of public concern," a reference to possible use of the right of reply. 403 U.S. at 47, 1 Med.L.Rptr. at 1604.

Is this a rejection of the philosophy of *Sullivan* ? Is it persuasive?

Justice White concurred on the narrow ground that the press is privileged to report "upon the official actions of public servants in full detail." Justice Black provided the fifth vote against liability for the reasons stated in his earlier opinions. Justices Harlan, Stewart and Marshall dissented on various grounds, but they agreed that the private plaintiff should be required to prove no more than negligence in this case. Justice Douglas did not participate.

Because there was no majority opinion from the Court in *Rosenbloom*, the case provided little guidance for future defamation cases. The case is interesting historically as the "high water mark" of the extension of the New York Times rule, but the Court reconsidered the issue of what private figure plaintiffs must prove in 1974, and that case is far more important than *Rosenbloom*. The case is Gertz v. Robert Welch, Inc., considered by many to be the most important libel decision since *Sullivan*. As you will see, *Gertz* attempts to clarify the difference between public and private figure libel plaintiffs. It also holds that many private figure plaintiffs—depending on the state in which they sue and whether or not the damages are presumed—need not meet the burden of proving "actual malice" to collect compensatory damages.

## GERTZ v. ROBERT WELCH, INC.

Supreme Court of the United States, 1974.
418 U.S. 323, 94 S.Ct. 2997, 41 L.Ed.2d 789, 1 Med.L.Rptr. 1633.

[Plaintiff, an attorney, was retained to represent the family of a youth killed by Nuccio, a Chicago policeman. In that capacity, plaintiff attended the coroner's inquest and filed an action for damages but played no part in a criminal proceeding in which Nuccio was convicted of second degree murder. Respondent published *American Opinion*, a monthly outlet for the views of the John Birch Society. As part of its efforts to alert the public to an alleged nationwide conspiracy to discredit local police, the magazine's editor engaged a regular contributor to write about the Nuccio episode. The article that appeared charged a frame-up against Nuccio and portrayed plaintiff as a "major architect" of the plot. It also falsely asserted that he had a long police record, was an official of the Marxist League for Industrial Democracy, and was a "Leninist" and a "Communist-fronter." The editor made no effort to verify the story.

Gertz filed an action for libel in federal district court because of diversity of citizenship. (He lived in one state; the defendant corporation was in another state).  The trial judge first ruled that Gertz was not a public official or public figure and that under Illinois law there was no defense.  The jury awarded $50,000.  On further reflection, the judge decided that since a matter of public concern was being discussed, the *New York Times* rule should apply and he granted the defendant judgment notwithstanding the jury's verdict.  He thus anticipated the plurality's approach in *Rosenbloom.*  The court of appeals, relying on the intervening decision in *Rosenbloom,* affirmed because of the absence of "clear and convincing" evidence of "actual malice."  Gertz appealed.]

MR. JUSTICE POWELL delivered the opinion of the Court.

. . .

## II

The principal issue in this case is whether a newspaper or broadcaster that publishes defamatory falsehoods about an individual who is neither a public official nor a public figure may claim a constitutional privilege against liability for the injury inflicted by those statements. The Court considered this question on the rather different set of facts presented in [*Rosenbloom*].  Rosenbloom, a distributor of nudist magazines, was arrested for selling allegedly obscene material while making a delivery to a retail dealer.  The police obtained a warrant and seized his entire inventory of 3,000 books and magazines.  He sought and obtained an injunction prohibiting further police interference with his business. He then sued a local radio station for failing to note in two of its newscasts that the 3,000 items seized were only "reportedly" or "allegedly" obscene and for broadcasting references to "the smut literature racket" and to "girlie-book peddlers" in its coverage of the court proceeding for injunctive relief.  He obtained a judgment against the radio station, but the Court of Appeals for the Third Circuit held the *New York Times* privilege applicable to the broadcast and reversed.  415 F.2d 892 (1969).

This Court affirmed the decision below, but no majority could agree on a controlling rationale.  The eight Justices who participated in *Rosenbloom* announced their views in five separate opinions, none of which commanded more than three votes.  The several statements not only reveal disagreement about the appropriate result in that case, they also reflect divergent traditions of thought about the general problem of reconciling the law of defamation with the First Amendment.  One approach has been to extend the *New York Times* test to an expanding variety of situations.  Another has been to vary the level of constitutional privilege for defamatory falsehood with the status of the person defamed.  And a third view would grant to the press and broadcast media absolute immunity from liability for defamation.  To place our holding in the proper context, we preface our discussion of this case with a review of the several *Rosenbloom* opinions and their antecedents.

. . .

In his opinion for the plurality in [*Rosenbloom*], Mr. Justice Brennan took the *New York Times* privilege one step further.  He concluded that its protection should extend to defamatory falsehoods relating to private persons if the statements concerned matters of general or public interest.   .   .   .

.   .   .

In *Rosenbloom* Mr. Justice Harlan   .   .   .   acquiesced in the application of the privilege to defamation of public figures but argued that a different rule should obtain where defamatory falsehood harmed a private individual.  He noted that a private person has less likelihood "of securing access to channels of communication sufficient to rebut falsehoods concerning him" than do public officials and public figures, 403 U.S., at 70, and has not voluntarily placed himself in the public spotlight.  Mr. Justice Harlan concluded that the States could constitutionally allow private individuals to recover damages for defamation on the basis of any standard of care except liability without fault.

.   .   .   The principal point of disagreement among the three dissenters concerned punitive damages.  Whereas Mr. Justice Harlan thought that the States could allow punitive damages in amounts bearing "a reasonable   and   purposeful   relationship   to   the   actual   harm done   .   .   .," id., at 75, Mr. Justice Marshall concluded that the size and unpredictability of jury awards of exemplary damages unnecessarily exacerbated the problems of media self-censorship and that such damages should therefore be forbidden.

## III

We begin with the common ground.  Under the First Amendment there is no such thing as a false idea.  However pernicious an opinion may seem, we depend for its correction not on the conscience of judges and juries but on the competition of other ideas.  But there is no constitutional value in false statements of fact.  Neither the intentional lie nor the careless error materially advances society's interest in "uninhibited, robust, and wide-open" debate on public issues.   .   .   .

Although the erroneous statement of fact is not worthy of constitutional protection, it is nevertheless inevitable in free debate.   .   .   . And punishment of error runs the risk of inducing a cautious and restrictive exercise of the constitutionally guaranteed freedoms of speech and press.  Our decisions recognize that a rule of strict liability that compels a publisher or broadcaster to guarantee the accuracy of his factual assertions may lead to intolerable self-censorship.  Allowing the media to avoid liability only by proving the truth of all injurious statements does not accord adequate protection to First Amendment liberties.   .   .   .   The First Amendment requires that we protect some falsehood in order to protect speech that matters.

The need to avoid self-censorship by the news media is, however, not the only societal value at issue.  If it were, this Court would have embraced long ago the view that publishers and broadcasters enjoy an unconditional and indefeasible immunity from liability for defamation.  . . .

The legitimate state interest underlying the law of libel is the compensation of individuals for the harm inflicted on them by defamatory falsehood.  We would not lightly require the State to abandon this purpose, for, as Mr. Justice Stewart has reminded us, the individual's right to the protection of his own good name

"reflects no more than our basic concept of the essential dignity and worth of every human being—a concept at the root of any decent system of ordered liberty.  The protection of private personality, like the protection of life itself, is left primarily to the individual States under the Ninth and Tenth Amendments.  But this does not mean that the right is entitled to any less recognition by this Court as a basic of our constitutional system."  Rosenblatt v. Baer, 383 U.S. 75, 92 (1966) (concurring opinion).

Some tension necessarily exists between the need for a vigorous and uninhibited press and the legitimate interest in redressing wrongful injury.  . . .

The *New York Times* standard defines the level of constitutional protection appropriate to the context of defamation of a public person. Those who, by reason of the notoriety of their achievements or the vigor and success with which they seek the public's attention, are properly classed as public figures and those who hold governmental office may recover for injury to reputation only on clear and convincing proof that the defamatory falsehood was made with knowledge of its falsity or with reckless disregard for the truth.  This standard administers an extremely powerful antidote to the inducement to media self-censorship of the common-law rule of strict liability for libel and slander.  And it exacts a correspondingly high price from the victims of defamatory falsehood. Plainly many deserving plaintiffs, including some intentionally subjected to injury, will be unable to surmount the barrier of the *New York Times* test.  Despite this substantial abridgment of the state law right to compensation for wrongful hurt to one's reputation, the Court has concluded that the protection of the *New York Times* privilege should be available to publishers and broadcasters of defamatory falsehood concerning public officials and public figures.  [ ]  We think that these decisions are correct, but we do not find their holdings justified solely by reference to the interest of the press and broadcast media in immunity from liability.  Rather, we believe that the *New York Times* rule states an accommodation between this concern and the limited state interest present in the context of libel actions brought by public persons.  For the reasons stated below, we conclude that the state interest in compensating injury to the reputation of private individuals requires that a different rule should obtain with respect to them.

Theoretically, of course, the balance between the needs of the press and the individual's claim to compensation for wrongful injury might be struck on a case-by-case basis.  As Mr. Justice Harlan hypothesized, "it might seem, purely as an abstract matter, that the most utilitarian approach would be to scrutinize carefully every jury verdict in every libel case, in order to ascertain whether the final judgment leaves fully protected whatever First Amendment values transcend the legitimate state interest in protecting the particular plaintiff who prevailed." Rosenbloom v. Metromedia, Inc., 403 U.S., at 63 (footnote omitted). But this approach would lead to unpredictable results and uncertain expectations, and it could render our duty to supervise the lower courts unmanageable. Because an *ad hoc* resolution of the competing interests at stake in each particular case is not feasible, we must lay down broad rules of general application. Such rules necessarily treat alike various cases involving differences as well as similarities. Thus it is often true that not all of the considerations which justify adoption of a given rule will obtain in each particular case decided under its authority.

With that caveat we have no difficulty in distinguishing among defamation plaintiffs. The first remedy of any victim of defamation is self-help—using available opportunities to contradict the lie or correct the error and thereby to minimize its adverse impact on reputation. Public officials and public figures usually enjoy significantly greater access to the channels of effective communication and hence have a more realistic opportunity to counteract false statements than private individuals normally enjoy.[9] Private individuals are therefore more vulnerable to injury, and the state interest in protecting them is correspondingly greater.

More important than the likelihood that private individuals will lack effective opportunities for rebuttal, there is a compelling normative consideration underlying the distinction between public and private defamation plaintiffs. An individual who decides to seek governmental office must accept certain necessary consequences of that involvement in public affairs. He runs the risk of closer public scrutiny than might otherwise be the case. And society's interest in the officers of government is not strictly limited to the formal discharge of official duties. As the Court pointed out in Garrison v. Louisiana, 379 U.S., at 77, the public's interest extends to "anything which might touch on an official's fitness for office . . .. Few personal attributes are more germane to fitness for office than dishonesty, malfeasance, or improper motivation, even though these characteristics may also affect the official's private character."

Those classed as public figures stand in a similar position. Hypothetically, it may be possible for someone to become a public figure through no purposeful action of his own, but the instances of truly involuntary public figures must be exceedingly rare. For the most part those who attain this status have assumed roles of especial prominence in the affairs of society. Some occupy positions of such persuasive power

---

**9.** Of course, an opportunity for rebuttal seldom suffices to undo harm of defamatory falsehood. Indeed, the law of defamation is rooted in our experience that the truth rarely catches up with a lie. But the fact that the self-help remedy of rebuttal, standing alone, is inadequate to its task does not mean that it is irrelevant to our inquiry.

and influence that they are deemed public figures for all purposes. More commonly, those classed as public figures have thrust themselves to the forefront of particular public controversies in order to influence the resolution of the issues involved. In either event, they invite attention and comment.

Even if the foregoing generalities do not obtain in every instance, the communications media are entitled to act on the assumption that public officials and public figures have voluntarily exposed themselves to increased risk of injury from defamatory falsehood concerning them. No such assumption is justified with respect to a private individual. He has not accepted public office or assumed an "influential role in ordering society." Curtis Publishing Co. v. Butts, supra, at 164 (Warren, C.J., concurring in result). He has relinquished no part of his interest in the protection of his own good name, and consequently he has a more compelling call on the courts for redress of injury inflicted by defamatory falsehood. Thus, private individuals are not only more vulnerable to injury than public officials and public figures; they are also more deserving of recovery.

For these reasons we conclude that the States should retain substantial latitude in their efforts to enforce a legal remedy for defamatory falsehood injurious to the reputation of a private individual. The extension of the *New York Times* test proposed by the *Rosenbloom* plurality would abridge this legitimate state interest to a degree that we find unacceptable. And it would occasion the additional difficulty of forcing state and federal judges to decide on an *ad hoc* basis which publications address issues of "general or public interest" and which do not—to determine, in the words of Mr. Justice Marshall, "what information is relevant to self-government." Rosenbloom v. Metromedia, Inc., 403 U.S., at 79. We doubt the wisdom of committing this task to the conscience of judges. Nor does the Constitution require us to draw so thin a line between the drastic alternatives of the *New York Times* privilege and the common law of strict liability for defamatory error. The "public or general interest" test for determining the applicability of the *New York Times* standard to private defamation actions inadequately serves both of the competing values at stake. On the one hand, a private individual whose reputation is injured by defamatory falsehood that does concern an issue of public or general interest has no recourse unless he can meet the rigorous requirements of *New York Times*. This is true despite the factors that distinguish the state interest in compensating private individuals from the analogous interest involved in the context of public persons. On the other hand, a publisher or broadcaster of a defamatory error which a court deems unrelated to an issue of public or general interest may be held liable in damages even if it took every reasonable precaution to ensure the accuracy of its assertions. And liability may far exceed compensation for any actual injury to the plaintiff, for the jury may be permitted to presume damages without proof of loss and even to award punitive damages.

We hold that, so long as they do not impose liability without fault, the States may define for themselves the appropriate standard of liability for a publisher or broadcaster of defamatory falsehood injurious to a private individual. This approach provides a more equitable boundary between the competing concerns involved here. It recognizes the strength of the legitimate state interest in compensating private individuals for wrongful injury to reputation, yet shields the press and broadcast media from the rigors of strict liability for defamation. At least this conclusion obtains where, as here, the substance of the defamatory statement "makes substantial danger to reputation apparent." [11] This phrase places in perspective the conclusion we announce today. Our inquiry would involve considerations somewhat different from those discussed above if a State purported to condition civil liability on a factual misstatement whose content did not warn a reasonably prudent editor or broadcaster of its defamatory potential. Cf. Time, Inc. v. Hill, 385 U.S. 374 (1967). Such a case is not now before us, and we intimate no view as to its proper resolution.

IV

Our accommodation of the competing values at stake in defamation suits by private individuals allows the States to impose liability on the publisher or broadcaster of defamatory falsehood on a less demanding showing than that required by *New York Times.* This conclusion is not based on a belief that the considerations which prompted the adoption of the *New York Times* privilege for defamation of public officials and its extension to public figures are wholly inapplicable to the context of private individuals. Rather, we endorse this approach in recognition of the strong and legitimate state interest in compensating private individuals for injury to reputation. But this countervailing state interest extends no further than compensation for actual injury. For the reasons stated below, we hold that the States may not permit recovery of presumed or punitive damages, at least when liability is not based on a showing of knowledge of falsity or reckless disregard for the truth.

The common law of defamation is an oddity of tort law, for it allows recovery of purportedly compensatory damages without evidence of actual loss. Under the traditional rules pertaining to actions for libel, the existence of injury is presumed from the fact of publication. Juries may award substantial sums as compensation for supposed damage to reputation without any proof that such harm actually occurred. The largely uncontrolled discretion of juries to award damages where there is no loss unnecessarily compounds the potential of any system of liability for defamatory falsehood to inhibit the vigorous exercise of First Amendment freedoms. Additionally, the doctrine of presumed damages invites juries to punish unpopular opinion rather than to compensate individuals for injury sustained by the publication of a false fact. More to the point, the States have no substantial interest in securing for plaintiffs

---

**11.** Curtis Publishing Co. v. Butts, supra, at 155.

such as this petitioner gratuitous awards of money damages far in excess of any actual injury.

We would not, of course, invalidate state law simply because we doubt its wisdom, but here we are attempting to reconcile state law with a competing interest grounded in the constitutional command of the First Amendment. It is therefore appropriate to require that state remedies for defamatory falsehood reach no farther than is necessary to protect the legitimate interest involved. It is necessary to restrict defamation plaintiffs who do not prove knowledge of falsity or reckless disregard for the truth to compensation for actual injury. We need not define "actual injury," as trial courts have wide experience in framing appropriate jury instructions in tort actions. Suffice it to say that actual injury is not limited to out-of-pocket loss. Indeed, the more customary types of actual harm inflicted by defamatory falsehood include impairment of reputation and standing in the community, personal humiliation, and mental anguish and suffering. Of course, juries must be limited by appropriate instructions, and all awards must be supported by competent evidence concerning the injury, although there need be no evidence which assigns an actual dollar value to the injury.

We also find no justification for allowing awards of punitive damages against publishers and broadcasters held liable under state-defined standards of liability for defamation. In most jurisdictions jury discretion over the amounts awarded is limited only by the gentle rule that they not be excessive. Consequently, juries assess punitive damages in wholly unpredictable amounts bearing no necessary relation to the actual harm caused. And they remain free to use their discretion selectively to punish expressions of unpopular views. Like the doctrine of presumed damages, jury discretion to award punitive damages unnecessarily exacerbates the danger of media self-censorship, but, unlike the former rule, punitive damages are wholly irrelevant to the state interest that justifies a negligence standard for private defamation actions. They are not compensation for injury. Instead, they are private fines levied by civil juries to punish reprehensible conduct and to deter its future occurrence. In short, the private defamation plaintiff who establishes liability under a less demanding standard than that stated by *New York Times* may recover only such damages as are sufficient to compensate him for actual injury.

## V

Notwithstanding our refusal to extend the *New York Times* privilege to defamation of private individuals, respondent contends that we should affirm the judgment below on the ground that petitioner is either a public official or a public figure. There is little basis for the former assertion. Several years prior to the present incident, petitioner had served briefly on housing committees appointed by the mayor of Chicago, but at the time of publication he had never held any remunerative governmental position. Respondent admits this but argues that petitioner's appearance at the coroner's inquest rendered him a "de facto public official." Our cases recognize no such concept. Respondent's suggestion would sweep all lawyers under the *New York Times* rule as officers of the court and distort the plain meaning of the "public official" category beyond all recognition. We decline to follow it.

Respondent's characterization of petitioner as a public figure raises a different question. That designation may rest on either of two alternative bases. In some instances an individual may achieve such pervasive fame or notoriety that he becomes a public figure for all purposes and in all contexts. More commonly, an individual voluntarily injects himself or is drawn into a particular public controversy and thereby becomes a public figure for a limited range of issues. In either case such persons assume special prominence in the resolution of public questions.

Petitioner has long been active in community and professional affairs. He has served as an officer of local civic groups and of various professional organizations, and he has published several books and articles on legal subjects. Although petitioner was consequently well known in some circles, he had achieved no general fame or notoriety in the community. None of the prospective jurors called at the trial had ever heard of petitioner prior to this litigation, and respondent offered no proof that this response was atypical of the local population. We would not lightly assume that a citizen's participation in community and professional affairs rendered him a public figure for all purposes. Absent clear evidence of general fame or notoriety in the community, and pervasive involvement in the affairs of society, an individual should not be deemed a public personality for all aspects of his life. It is preferable to reduce the public-figure question to a more meaningful context by looking to the nature and extent of an individual's participation in the particular controversy giving rise to the defamation.

In this context it is plain that petitioner was not a public figure. He played a minimal role at the coroner's inquest, and his participation related solely to his representation of a private client. He took no part in the criminal prosecution of Officer Nuccio. Moreover, he never discussed either the criminal or civil litigation with the press and was never quoted as having done so. He plainly did not thrust himself into the vortex of this public issue, nor did he engage the public's attention in an attempt to influence its outcome. We are persuaded that the trial court did not err in refusing to characterize petitioner as a public figure for the purpose of this litigation.

We therefore conclude that the *New York Times* standard is inapplicable to this case and that the trial court erred in entering judgment for respondent. Because the jury was allowed to impose liability without fault and was permitted to presume damages without proof of injury, a new trial is necessary. We reverse and remand for further proceedings in accord with this opinion.

It is so ordered.

MR. JUSTICE BLACKMUN, concurring.

[Although I joined the *Rosenbloom* plurality opinion,] I am willing to join, and do join, the Court's opinion and its judgment for two reasons:

1.   By removing the spectors of presumed and punitive damages in the absence of *New York Times* malice, the Court eliminates significant and powerful motives for self-censorship that otherwise are present in the traditional libel action.   By so doing, the Court leaves what should prove to be sufficient and adequate breathing space for a vigorous press. What the Court has done, I believe, will have little, if any, practical effect on the functioning of responsible journalism.

2.   The Court was sadly fractionated in *Rosenbloom*.   A result of that kind inevitably leads to uncertainty.   I feel that it is of profound importance for the Court to come to rest in the defamation area and to have a clearly defined majority position that eliminates the unsureness engendered by *Rosenbloom's* diversity.   If my vote were not needed to create a majority, I would adhere to my prior view.   A definitive ruling, however, is paramount.   [  ]

For these reasons, I join the opinion and the judgment of the Court.

MR. CHIEF JUSTICE BURGER, dissenting.

The doctrines of the law of defamation have had a gradual evolution primarily in the state courts.   In [*Sullivan*], and its progeny this Court entered this field.

Agreement or disagreement with the law as it has evolved to this time does not alter the fact that it has been orderly development with a consistent basic rationale.   In today's opinion the Court abandons the traditional thread so far as the ordinary private citizen is concerned and introduces the concept that the media will be liable for negligence in publishing defamatory statements with respect to such persons.   Although I agree with much of what Mr. Justice White states, I do not read the Court's new doctrinal approach in quite the way he does.   I am frank to say I do not know the parameters of a "negligence" doctrine as applied to the news media.   Conceivably this new doctrine could inhibit some editors, as the dissents of Mr. Justice Douglas and Mr. Justice Brennan suggest.   But I would prefer to allow this area of law to continue to evolve as it has up to now with respect to private citizens rather than embark on a new doctrinal theory which has no jurisprudential ancestry.

The petitioner here was performing a professional representative role as an advocate in the highest tradition of the law, and under that tradition the advocate is not to be invidiously identified with his client. The important public policy which underlies this tradition—the right to counsel—would be gravely jeopardized if every lawyer who takes an "unpopular" case, civil or criminal, would automatically become fair game for irresponsible reporters and editors who might, for example, describe the lawyer as a "mob mouthpiece" for representing a client with a serious prior criminal record, or as an "ambulance chaser" for representing a claimant in a personal injury action.

I would reverse the judgment of the Court of Appeals and remand for reinstatement of the verdict of the jury and the entry of an appropriate judgment on that verdict.

MR. JUSTICE DOUGLAS, dissenting.

.   .   .

.   .   . The standard announced today leaves the States free to "define for themselves the appropriate standard of liability for a publisher or broadcaster" in the circumstances of this case. This of course leaves the simple negligence standard as an option with the jury free to impose damages upon a finding that the publisher failed to act as "a reasonable man." With such continued erosion of First Amendment protection, I fear that it may well be the reasonable man who refrains from speaking.

Since in my view the First and Fourteenth Amendments prohibit the imposition of damages upon respondent for this discussion of public affairs, I would affirm the judgment below.

MR. JUSTICE BRENNAN, dissenting.

I agree with the conclusion, expressed in Part V of the Court's opinion, that, at the time of publication of respondent's article, petitioner could not properly have been viewed as either a "public official" or "public figure"; instead, respondent's article, dealing with an alleged conspiracy to discredit local police forces, concerned petitioner's purported involvement in "an event of public or general interest."   .   .   .

.   .   .

Although acknowledging that First Amendment values are of no less significance when media reports concern private persons' involvement in matters of public concern, the Court refuses to provide, in such cases, the same level of constitutional protection that has been afforded the media in the context of defamation of public persons. The accommodation that this Court has established between free speech and libel laws in cases involving public officials and public figures—that defamatory falsehood be shown by clear and convincing evidence to have been published with knowledge of falsity or with reckless disregard of truth—is not apt, the Court holds, because the private individual does not have the same degree of access to the media to rebut defamatory comments as does the public person and he has not voluntarily exposed himself to public scrutiny.

While these arguments are forcefully and eloquently presented, I cannot accept them, for the reasons I stated in *Rosenbloom:*

"The *New York Times* standard was applied to libel of a public official or public figure to give effect to the [First] Amendment's function to encourage ventilation of public issues, not because the public official has any less interest in protecting his reputation than an individual in private life. While the argument that public figures need less protection because they can command media attention to counter criticism may be true for some very prominent people, even then it is the rare case where the denial overtakes the original charge.  Denials, retractions, and corrections are not 'hot' news, and rarely receive the prominence of the original story.  When the public official or public figure is a minor functionary, or has left the position that put him in the public eye . . ., the argument loses all of its force.  In the vast majority of libels involving public officials or public figures, the ability to respond through the media will depend on the same complex factor on which the ability of a private individual depends: the unpredictable event of the media's continuing interest in the story.  Thus the unproved, and highly improbable, generalization that an as yet [not fully defined] class of 'public figures' involved in matters of public concern will be better able to respond through the media than private individuals also involved in such matters seems too insubstantial a recd on which to rest a constitutional distinction." [ ]

. . .

. . . Under a reasonable-care regime, publishers and broadcasters will have to make pre-publication judgments about juror assessment of such diverse considerations as the size, operating procedures, and financial condition of the newsgathering system, as well as the relative costs and benefits of instituting less frequent and more costly reporting at a higher level of accuracy.  [ ]  Moreover, in contrast to proof by clear and convincing evidence required under the *Times* test, the burden of proof for reasonable care will doubtless be the preponderance of the evidence.  . . .

The Court does not discount altogether the danger that jurors will punish for the expression of unpopular opinions.  This probability accounts for the Court's limitation that "the States may not permit recovery of presumed or punitive damages, at least when liability is not based on a showing of knowledge of falsity or reckless disregard for the truth." [ ]  But plainly a jury's latitude to impose liability for want of due care poses a far greater threat of suppressing unpopular views than does a possible recovery of presumed or punitive damages.  Moreover, the Court's broad-ranging examples of "actual injury," including impairment of reputation and standing in the community, as well as personal humiliation, and mental anguish and suffering, inevitably allow a jury bent on punishing expression of unpopular views a formidable weapon for doing so.  Finally, even a limitation of recovery to "actual injury"— however much it reduces the size or frequency of recoveries—will not provide the necessary elbowroom for First Amendment expression.  . . .

On the other hand, the uncertainties which the media face under today's decision are largely avoided by the *Times* standard.  I reject the argument that my *Rosenbloom* view improperly commits to judges the task of determining what is and what is not an issue of "general or public interest." [3]  I noted in *Rosenbloom* that performance of this task would not always be easy. Id., at 49 n. 17.  But surely the courts, the ultimate arbiters of all disputes concerning clashes of constitutional values, would only be performing one of their traditional functions in undertaking this duty.  . . .

. . .

MR. JUSTICE WHITE, dissenting.

. . .

The impact of today's decision on the traditional law of libel is immediately obvious and indisputable.  No longer will the plaintiff be able to rest his case with proof of a libel defamatory on its face or proof of a slander historically actionable *per se*.  In addition, he must prove some further degree of culpable conduct on the part of the publisher, such as intentional or reckless falsehood or negligence.  And if he succeeds in this respect, he faces still another obstacle: recovery for loss of reputation will be conditioned upon "competent" proof of actual injury to his standing in the community.  This will be true regardless of the nature of the defamation and even though it is one of those particularly reprehensible statements that have traditionally made slanderous words actionable without proof of fault by the publisher or of the damaging impact of his publication.  The Court rejects the judgment of experience that some publications are so inherently capable of injury, and actual injury so difficult to prove, that the risk of falsehood should be borne by the publisher, not the victim.  . . .

So too, the requirement of proving special injury to reputation before general damages may be awarded will clearly eliminate the prevailing rule, worked out over a very long period of time, that, in the case of defamations not actionable *per se,* the recovery of general damages for injury to reputation may also be had if some form of material or pecuniary loss is proved.  Finally, an inflexible federal

---

**3.** The Court, taking a novel step, would not limit application of First Amendment protection to private libels involving issues of general or public interest, but would forbid the States from imposing liability without fault in any case where the substance of the defamatory statement made substantial danger to reputation apparent. As in Rosenbloom v. Metromedia, Inc., 403 U.S. 29, 44 n. 12, 48–49, n. 17 (1971), I would leave open the question of what constitutional standard, if any, applies when defamatory falsehoods are published or broadcast concerning either a private or public person's activities not within the scope of the general or public interest.

Parenthetically, my Brother White argues that the Court's view and mine will prevent a plaintiff—unable to demonstrate some degree of fault—from vindicating his reputation by securing a judgment that the publication was false.  This argument overlooks the possible enactment of statutes, not requiring proof of fault, which provide for an action for retraction or for publication of a court's determination of falsity if the plaintiff is able to demonstrate that false statements have been published concerning his activities.  Cf. Note, Vindication of the Reputation of a Public Official, 80 Harv.L.Rev. 1730, 1739–1747 (1967).  Although it may be that questions could be raised concerning the constitutionality of such statutes, certainly nothing I have said today (and, as I read the Court's opinion, nothing said there) should be read to imply that a private plaintiff, unable to prove fault, must inevitably be denied the opportunity to secure a judgment upon the truth or falsity of statements published about him. [ ]

standard is imposed for the award of punitive damages.  No longer will it be enough to prove ill will and an attempt to injure.

These are radical changes in the law and severe invasions of the prerogatives of the States.   .   .   .

.   .   .

The central meaning of [*Sullivan*], and for me the First Amendment as it relates to libel laws, is that seditious libel—criticism of government and public officials—falls beyond the police power of the State.   .   .   .

.   .   .

The Court evinces a deep-seated antipathy to "liability without fault."  But this catch-phrase has no talismanic significance and is almost meaningless in this context where the Court appears to be addressing those libels and slanders that are defamatory on their face and where the publisher is no doubt aware from the nature of the material that it would be inherently damaging to reputation.  He publishes notwithstanding, knowing that he will inflict injury.  With this knowledge, he must intend to inflict that injury, his excuse being that he is privileged to do so—that he has published the truth.  But as it turns out, what he has circulated to the public is a very damaging falsehood.  Is he nevertheless "faultless?"  Perhaps it can be said that the mistake about his defense was made in good faith, but the fact remains that it is he who launched the publication knowing that it could ruin a reputation.

In these circumstances, the law has heretofore put the risk of falsehood on the publisher where the victim is a private citizen and no grounds of special privilege are invoked.  The Court would now shift this risk to the victim, even though he has done nothing to invite the calumny, is wholly innocent of fault, and is helpless to avoid his injury.  I doubt that jurisprudential resistance to liability without fault is sufficient ground for employing the First Amendment to revolutionize the law of libel, and in my view, that body of legal rules poses no realistic threat to the press and its service to the public.  The press today is vigorous and robust.  To me, it is quite incredible to suggest that threats of libel suits from private citizens are causing the press to refrain from publishing the truth.  I know of no hard facts to support that proposition, and the Court furnishes none.

The communications industry has increasingly become concentrated in a few powerful hands operating very lucrative businesses reaching across the Nation and into almost every home.  Neither the industry as a whole nor its individual components are easily intimidated, and we are fortunate that they are not.  Requiring them to pay for the occasional damage they do to private reputation will play no substantial part in their future performance or their existence.

In any event, if the Court's principal concern is to protect the communications industry from large libel judgments, it would appear that its new requirements with respect to general and punitive damages would be ample protection.   .   .   .

It is difficult for me to understand why the ordinary citizen should himself carry the risk of damage and suffer the injury in order to vindicate First Amendment values by protecting the press and others from liability for circulating false information.  This is particularly true because such statements serve no purpose whatsoever in furthering the public interest or the search for truth but, on the contrary, may frustrate that search and at the same time inflict great injury on the defenseless individual.  The owners of the press and the stockholders of the communications enterprises can much better bear the burden.  And if they cannot, the public at large should somehow pay for what is essentially a public benefit derived at private expense.

.  .  .

.  .  .  Whether or not the course followed by the majority is wise, and I have indicated my doubts that it is, our constitutional scheme compels a proper respect for the role of the States in acquitting their duty to obey the Constitution.  Finding no evidence that they have shirked this responsibility, particularly when the law of defamation is even now in transition, I would await some demonstration of the diminution of freedom of expression before acting.

For the foregoing reasons, I would reverse the judgment of the Court of Appeals and reinstate the jury's verdict.

## Notes and Questions

1.  Why did the majority adhere to the *New York Times* rule for public officials?  Public figures?  Some have argued that Gertz was a public figure and that the case should have been analyzed along the lines of *Butts* and *Walker*.  See Pember and Teeter, Privacy and the Press Since Time, Inc. v. Hill, 50 Wash.L.Rev. 57, 75 (1974): "Gertz was a member of numerous boards and commissions in Illinois, had published several books on civil rights matters, had frequently been honored by civil rights groups and had represented some rather famous clients.  .  .  .  His publishing record belies the notion that he was a poor, helpless, private individual who could not gain access to the press."  Would that suffice to meet the standard?

2.  Why does the majority in *Gertz* prefer its approach to the plurality's approach in *Rosenbloom?*

3.  What criteria might be relevant in deciding whether a newspaper has been at fault in publishing a false statement?

4.  If a private citizen proves fault, why can he not recover traditional damages for defamation?

5.  Recall the various definitions the Court has used for the term "actual malice."  In *Gertz,* Justice Powell says that, "The [trial] court correctly noted that mere proof of failure to investigate, without more, cannot establish reckless disregard for the truth.  Rather, the publisher must act with a 'high degree of awareness of  .  .  .  probable falsity.' [  ]"  Is a "failure to investigate" or a "failure to check the facts" a

serious breach of journalistic ethics—especially when one is publishing a damaging statement about someone? Does referring to such a failure to investigate as "mere" tend to downplay too much the importance of *due care* in reporting damaging accusations?

6. The *Gertz* retrial, which did not occur for several years, produced a jury verdict for Gertz of $100,000 compensatory damages and $300,000 punitive damages. On appeal, the court affirmed. It concluded that the jury could find "actual malice" on the part of the editor of the magazine who solicited a person with a "known and unreasonable propensity to label persons or organizations as Communist, to write the article; and after the article was submitted, made virtually no effort to check the validity of statements that were defamatory *per se* of Gertz, and in fact added further defamatory material based on [the writer's] 'facts.' " Gertz v. Robert Welch, Inc., 680 F.2d 527, 8 Med.L.Rptr. 1769 (7th Cir.1982), cert. denied 459 U.S. 1226 (1983).

7. *The Firestone case.* The first significant application of *Gertz* occurred in Time, Inc. v. Firestone, 424 U.S. 448, 1 Med.L.Rptr. 1665 (1976), in which a magazine reported, perhaps incorrectly, that a member of "one of America's wealthier industrial families" had received a divorce because of his wife's adultery. The divorce decree was probably based on either "extreme cruelty" or "lack of domestication," but the judge was not explicit. The state court upheld the wife's defamation award of $100,000. *Time* argued that the "actual malice" standard should apply for two reasons. First, it asserted that the plaintiff was a public figure, but the majority disagreed: "Respondent did not assume any role of especial prominence in the affairs of society, other than perhaps Palm Beach society, and she did not thrust herself to the forefront of any particular public controversy in order to influence the resolution of the issues involved in it." The Court rejected the argument that because the case was of great public interest, the respondent must have been a public figure: "Dissolution of a marriage through judicial proceedings is not the sort of 'public controversy' referred to in *Gertz,* even though the marital difficulties of extremely wealthy individuals may be of interest to some portion of the reading public." Moreover, plaintiff was compelled to go to court to seek relief in a marital dispute and her involvement was not voluntary. The fact that she held "a few" press conferences during the case did not change her otherwise private status. She did not attempt to use them to influence the outcome of the trial or to thrust herself into an unrelated dispute.

The second claim was that negligent errors in the reporting of judicial proceedings should never lead to liability. Justice Rehnquist's opinion for the Court rejected the contention:

> It may be that all reports of judicial proceedings contain some informational value implicating the First Amendment, but recognizing this is little different from labeling all judicial proceedings matters of "public or general interest," as that phrase was used by the plurality in *Rosenbloom.* Whatever their general validity, use of

such subject matter classifications to determine the extent of consti-tutional protection afforded defamatory falsehoods may too often result in an improper balance between the competing interests in this area. It was our recognition and rejection of this weakness in the *Rosenbloom* test which led us in *Gertz* to eschew a subject matter test for one focusing upon the character of the defamation plaintiff. [  ] By confining inquiry to whether a plaintiff is a public officer or a public figure who might be assumed to "have voluntarily exposed themselves to increased risk of injury from defamatory falsehood," we sought a more appropriate accommoda-tion between the public's interest in an uninhibited press and its equally compelling need for judicial redress of libelous utterances. Cf. Chaplinsky v. New Hampshire, 315 U.S. 568 (1942).

. . .

It may be argued that there is still room for application of the *New York Times* protections to more narrowly focused reports of what actually transpires in the courtroom. But even so narrowed, the suggested privilege is simply too broad. Imposing upon the law of private defamation the rather drastic limitations worked by *New York Times* cannot be justified by generalized references to the public interest in reports of judicial proceedings. The details of many, if not most, courtroom battles would add almost nothing towards advancing the uninhibited debate on public issues thought to provide principal support for the decision in *New York Times*. [  ] And while participants in some litigation may be legitimate "public figures," either generally or for the limited purpose of that litigation, the majority will more likely resemble respondent, drawn into a public forum largely against their will in order to attempt to obtain the only redress available to them or to defend themselves against actions brought by the State or by others. There appears little reason why these individuals should substantially forfeit that degree of protection which the law of defamation would otherwise afford them simply by virtue of their being drawn into a courtroom. The public interest in accurate reports of judicial proceedings is substantially protected by [Cox Broadcasting Corp. v. Cohn, to be discussed at p. 212, *infra*.] As to inaccurate and defamatory reports of facts, matters deserving no First Amendment protection, [  ], we think *Gertz* provides an adequate safeguard for the constitutionally protected interests of the press and affords it a tolerable margin for error by requiring some type of fault.

Plaintiff had withdrawn her claim for damages to reputation before trial, but the Court held that the award could be sustained on proof of anxiety and concern over the impact of the adultery charge on her young son. The Court vacated the judgment for lack of consideration of fault by either the jury or any of the state courts. Justices Powell and Stewart, though joining the majority, asserted that the grounds of divorce were so unclear in this "bizarre case" that there was "substantial evidence" that *Time* was not negligent. Justice White, believing that the state courts had found negligence, would have affirmed the award. In addition, because the article had been written before *Rosenbloom* and *Gertz,* he saw no reason to require any showing of fault. Justice Brennan dissented on the ground that reports of judicial proceedings should not lead to liability unless the errors are deliberate or reckless. He observed that even those who would confine the central meaning of the First Amendment to "explicitly political speech" would extend protection to speech concerned with governmental behavior. He also thought the damage limits of *Gertz* had been "subverted" by the recovery allowed here with no showing of reputational harm. Justice Marshall, dissenting, thought that plaintiff was a public figure; he also doubted the existence of negligence. Justice Stevens took no part.

The Florida Supreme Court ordered a new trial but plaintiff dropped the case, saying that she had been vindicated.

Recall that under the common law "record libel" privilege, reports of governmental proceedings were privileged if they were fair and accurate reports of what had happened—even if the speaker being quoted had committed a defamation. Under the common law privilege, *Time* 's report, if incorrectly reporting the basis of the divorce decree, would not have been protected. For this reason *Time* had to assert a constitutional privilege.

8. *Are convicted people necessarily public figures?* In Wolston v. Reader's Digest Association, 443 U.S. 157, 5 Med.L.Rptr. 1273 (1979), defendant published a book in 1974 that included plaintiff's name on a list of "Soviet agents identified in the United States." A footnote said that the list consisted of agents "who were convicted of espionage or falsifying information or perjury and/or contempt charges following espionage indictments or who fled to the Soviet bloc to avoid prosecution."

Plaintiff had been convicted of contempt of court in 1958 for failing to appear before a grand jury investigating Soviet espionage. He was never indicted for any of the other offenses. At the time, plaintiff did not attempt to debate the propriety of his behavior. During the six weeks between his failure to appear and his sentencing, plaintiff's case was the subject of 15 stories in Washington and New York newspapers. "This flurry of publicity subsided" following the sentencing, and plaintiff "succeeded for the most part in returning to the private life he had led" prior to the subpoena.

When plaintiff sued for libel, the lower courts held that in both 1958 and 1974 he was a public figure and that summary judgment was properly granted against him because he had presented no evidence of actual malice. (In the Supreme Court, plaintiff abandoned the argument that even if he was a public figure in 1958, he was no longer in 1974).

The Supreme Court reversed. For the majority, Justice Rehnquist reviewed the "self-help" and the "assumption of risk" explanations developed in *Gertz* to support the public-private distinction, and concluded that the second was the more important. He then quoted the passage from *Gertz* stating that some persons may be public figures because they "occupy positions of such persuasive power and influence that they are deemed public figures for all purposes. More commonly, those classed as public figures have thrust themselves to the forefront of particular public controversies in order to influence the resolution of the issues involved."

Justice Rehnquist concluded that plaintiff had neither "voluntarily thrust" nor "injected" himself into the forefront of the controversy surrounding the investigation of Soviet espionage in the United States. (He also noted that it was difficult to determine the relevant "public controversy" into which plaintiff was alleged to have thrust himself.)

It would be more accurate to say that petitioner was dragged unwillingly into the controversy. The government pursued him in its investigation. Petitioner did fail to respond to a grand jury subpoena, and this failure, as well as his subsequent citation for contempt, did attract media attention. But the mere fact that petitioner voluntarily chose not to appear before the grand jury, knowing that his action might be attended by publicity, is not decisive on the question of public figure status. In *Gertz,* we held that an attorney was not a public figure even though he voluntarily associated himself with a case that was certain to receive extensive media exposure. 418 U.S., at 352. We emphasized that a court must focus on the "nature and extent of an individual's participation in the particular controversy giving rise to the defamation." . . .

Petitioner's failure to appear before the grand jury and citation for contempt no doubt were "newsworthy," but the simple fact that these events attracted media attention also is not conclusive of the public figure issue. A private individual is not automatically transformed into a public figure just by becoming involved in or associated with a matter that attracts public attention. To accept such reasoning would in effect reestablish the doctrine advanced by the plurality opinion in [*Rosenbloom*] which concluded that the *New York Times* standard should extend to defamatory falsehoods relating to private persons if the statements involved matters of public or general concern. We repudiated this proposition in *Gertz* and in *Firestone,* however, and we reject it again today. A libel defendant must show more than mere newsworthiness to justify application of the demanding burden of *New York Times.* [  ]

Nor do we think that petitioner engaged the attention of the public in an attempt to influence the resolution of the issues involved. . . . He did not in any way seek to arouse public sentiment in his favor and against the investigation. Thus, this is not a case where a defendant invites a citation for contempt in order to use the contempt citation as a fulcrum to create public discussion about the methods being used in connection with an investigation or prosecution. . . . In short, we find no basis whatsoever for concluding that petitioner relinquished, to any degree, his interest in the protection of his own name.

This reasoning leads us to reject the further contention of respondents that any person who engages in criminal conduct automatically becomes a public figure for purposes of comment on a limited range of issues relating to his conviction. [   ] We declined to accept a similar argument in [*Firestone*].

Here Justice Rehnquist quoted the passage from *Firestone* above about protecting those drawn into a courtroom. He concluded, "We think that these observations remain sound, and that they control the disposition of this case. To hold otherwise would create an 'open season' for all who sought to defame persons convicted of a crime."

Justice Blackmun, joined by Justice Marshall, concurred in the result. He thought that the majority "seems to hold . . . that a person becomes a limited-issue public figure only if he literally or figuratively 'mounts a rostrum' to advocate a particular view. I see no need to adopt so restrictive a definition . . . on the facts before us." He would have held that even if plaintiff had acquired public figure status in 1958, "he clearly had lost that distinction" by 1974. Although plaintiff had not pressed that argument in the Supreme Court, Justice Blackmun, noting that the lower courts had decided the point, thought it still open as a basis for decision.

He quoted the passage from *Gertz* indicating that a person may become a public figure for a limited range of issues if he "voluntarily injects himself or is drawn into a particular public controversy." (Justice Rehnquist did not refer to that passage.) Even if, in 1958, plaintiff had access to the press to rebut the charge that he was a Soviet spy, it "would strain credulity" to suggest that he could command such media interest in 1974. Also, his "conscious efforts to regain anonymity" removed any assumption of risk justification for calling him a public figure in 1974.

Justice Blackmun recognized that his view put a more difficult burden on historians than on contemporary commentators:

This analysis implies, of course, that one may be a public figure for purposes of contemporaneous reporting of a controversial event, yet not be a public figure for purposes of historical commentary on the same occurrence. Historians, consequently, may well run a greater risk of liability for defamation. Yet this result, in my view, does no violence to First Amendment values. While historical analysis is no less vital to the marketplace of ideas than reporting current events, historians work under different conditions than do their media counterparts. A reporter trying to meet a deadline may find it totally impossible to check thoroughly the accuracy of his sources. A historian writing *sub specie aeternitatis* has both the time for reflection and the opportunity to investigate the veracity of the pronouncements he makes.

Justice Brennan dissented. He thought plaintiff a public figure for the limited purpose of comment on his connection with espionage in the 1940s and 1950s. He remained a public figure in 1974 because the issue of Soviet espionage "continues to be a legitimate topic of debate to-day . . .." But he found enough evidence of "actual malice" to warrant a trial under the *New York Times* standard.

The next case was decided on the same day as *Wolston*.

9. *Are applicants for public funds public figures?* Hutchinson v. Proxmire, 443 U.S. 111, 5 Med.L.Rptr. 1279 (1979), arose from Sen. William Proxmire's awarding of one of his Golden Fleece awards—made to government agencies that he believed engaged in wasteful spending. In this case he awarded it to agencies that had funded the plaintiff-scientist's research work on aggression in animals. Proxmire had uttered the alleged defamation in several forums, including a speech prepared for delivery on the Senate floor, advance press releases, a newsletter sent to 100,000 people, and a television interview program. The Court first decided that in this case Article I, Section 6 of the Constitution—the so-called Speech or Debate Clause—protected only a speech delivered on the floor.

The Court then turned to the First Amendment issue. Chief Justice Burger began with the same *Gertz* passage that Justice Rehnquist had built upon in *Wolston*. Neither the fact that plaintiff had successfully applied for federal funds nor that he had access to media after Proxmire's charges, "demonstrates that Hutchinson was a public figure prior to the controversy . . .."

> On this record Hutchinson's activities and public profile are much like those of countless members of his profession. His published writings reach a relatively small category of professionals concerned with research in human behavior. To the extent the subject of his published writings became a matter of controversy it was a consequence of the Golden Fleece Award. Clearly those charged with defamation cannot, by their own conduct, create their own defense by making the claimant a public figure. See Wolston v. Reader's Digest, Inc., [   ].

> Hutchinson did not thrust himself or his views into public controversy to influence others. Respondents have not identified such a particular controversy; at most, they point to concern about general public expenditures. But that concern is shared by most and relates to most public expenditures; it is not sufficient to make Hutchinson a public figure. If it were, everyone who received or benefited from the myriad public grants for research could be classified as a public figure—a conclusion that our previous opinions have rejected. The "use of such subject-matter classifications to determine the extent of constitutional protection afforded defamatory falsehoods may too often result in an improper balance between the competing interests in this area." Time, Inc. v. Firestone, supra, at 456.

Moreover, Hutchinson at no time assumed any role of public prominence in the broad question of concern about expenditures. Neither his applications for federal grants nor his publications in professional journals can be said to have invited that degree of public attention and comment on his receipt of federal grants essential to meet the public figure level. The petitioner in Gertz v. Robert Welch, Inc., had published books and articles on legal issues; he had been active in local community affairs. Nevertheless, the Court concluded that his activities did not make him a public figure.

Finally, we cannot agree that Hutchinson had such access to the media that he should be classified as a public figure. Hutchinson's access was limited to responding to the announcement of the Golden Fleece Award. He did not have the regular and continuing access to the media that is one of the accoutrements of having become a public figure.

Justice Brennan was the sole dissenter. He believed that "public criticism by legislators of unnecessary governmental expenditures, whatever its form, is a legislative act shielded by the Speech or Debate Clause." He did not reach the public figure question.

Proxmire subsequently made a public retraction, before television cameras, of his comments about Hutchinson.

10. The Hutchinson case provided a pair of significant footnotes. In footnote 8, the Court noted that the district court had considered Hutchinson a public official because he served as director of research at a state mental hospital. The Chief Justice observed that "The Court has not provided precise boundaries for the category of 'public official'; it cannot be thought to include all public employees, however."

In footnote 16, the Court noted that the lower courts had not decided whether the *New York Times* standard "can apply to an individual defendant rather than to a media defendant. . . . This Court has never decided the question; our conclusion (in this case) makes it unnecessary to do so in this case."

Commonly, every state and lower federal court that has addressed the question has concluded that the *New York Times* standard does apply to all defendants. There has been some division over whether the *Gertz* standard applies to nonmedia defendants.

Notice that the Court has in fact dealt with cases involving individual defendants, such as the clergymen in the *New York Times* case itself. However, the individual was charged with some involvement in preparing or delivering a statement over some medium of mass communication.

11. *Do involuntary public figures exist?* In Dameron v. Washington Magazine, Inc., 779 F.2d 736, 12 Med.L.Rptr. 1508 (D.C.Cir.1985), cert. denied 476 U.S. 1141 (1986), plaintiff had been the only air traffic controller on duty in 1974 when a plane approaching Dulles Airport crashed into Mt. Weather. The episode received much attention: plaintiff testified in hearings and a claim under the Federal Torts Claims Act

was litigated.  In that case the court dismissed claims based on controller negligence.  In 1982 a plane crashed into the Potomac River.  Part of the story on the 1982 crash in defendant's city magazine was a sidebar on earlier plane crashes and their causes.  In that list the 1974 crash was attributed to "controller" failure.  Plaintiff sued for libel.

The court held that although plaintiff had not injected himself into any controversy, persons "can become involved in public controversies and affairs without their consent or will.  Air-controller Dameron, who had the misfortune to have a tragedy occur on his watch, is such a person.  We conclude that Dameron did become an involuntary public figure for the limited purpose of discussions of the Mt. Weather crash."

Although the Supreme Court had said that "the instances of truly involuntary public figures must be exceedingly rare," the court thought that "within the very narrow framework represented by the facts of this case, such has been Dameron's fate."

12.  *Are all businesses public figures?*  The question of whether a business is more like an individual who is a public figure or like an individual who is a private figure under the *Gertz* standard arose in Bank of Oregon v. Independent News, Inc., 298 Or. 434, 693 P.2d 35, 11 Med.L.Rptr. 1313 (1985).  An Oregon bank and its president were held to be private figures because they had not established "general fame or notoriety" in the community or exhibited "pervasive involvement in the affairs of society."

Brown & Williamson Tobacco Corp., makers of Viceroy cigarettes, was, on the other hand, treated as a public figure.  Because the plaintiff corporation won one of the biggest libel awards, we will discuss the case in a section on large verdicts later in this chapter.

13.  *Are all individuals associated with businesses public figures?*  People in business who are accused of connections with organized crime tend to be held to be public figures.  One case involved an attorney who represented persons alleged to have criminal connections and who was said to have "contributed down payments of up to $25,000 on grass transactions.  Charges against him were dismissed because he cooperated with further investigations."  Although recognizing that "mere newsworthiness" is not sufficient, the court of appeals first concluded that the issue of "drug trafficking" was "a real dispute, the outcome of which affects the general public or some segment of it."  As to plaintiff's part in it, the court noted that sometimes one can be a public figure without voluntary actions.  "For example, sports figures are generally considered public figures because of their positions as athletes or coaches.  [  ]  If a position itself is so prominent that its occupant unavoidably enters the limelight, then a person who voluntarily assumes such a position may be presumed to have accepted public figure status."  Marcone v. Penthouse International Magazine for Men, 754 F.2d 1072 (3d Cir.1985).

14.  All of the cases seen previously involve mass media of some sort. What happens when we change defendants?  Dun & Bradstreet, Inc. v. Greenmoss Builders, Inc., 472 U.S. 749, 11 Med.L.Rptr. 2417 (1985),

involved a *non-media* defendant—the Dun & Bradstreet credit reporting agency, which provides confidential information to subscribers about financial conditions of businesses. Under these agreements, the subscriber may not reveal the information to anyone else. D & B sent a report to five subscribers stating that Greenmoss Builders, a construction contractor, had filed a voluntary petition for bankruptcy. The report was incorrect. In fact, a high school student employed by D & B to review Vermont bankruptcy proceedings had inadvertently attributed to Greenmoss a bankruptcy petition filed by one of its former employees. Greenmoss' bank told Greenmoss' president that it had received the report. He immediately called D & B, explained the error, asked for a correction and asked the names of those who had received the false report. A week later, D & B wrote the five subscribers that the filing had been by a former employee and that Greenmoss "continued in business as usual." D & B refused to identify the five subscribers.

A jury in state court returned a judgment for $50,000 in compensatory damages and $300,000 in punitive damages. D & B argued that *Gertz* required a finding of "actual malice" before presumed or punitive damages could be awarded and that the trial judge had not charged the jury in those terms. The trial judge expressed doubt about whether *Gertz* applied to "non-media cases" but granted the new trial in the "interests of justice." The Vermont Supreme Court reversed. It concluded that credit agencies were not the "type of media worthy of First Amendment protection as contemplated by" the *Times* case "and its progeny." As a "matter of federal constitutional law, the media protections outlined in *Gertz* are inapplicable to nonmedia defamation actions."

The Supreme Court affirmed, but for reasons different from those relied upon by the Vermont Supreme Court. Justice Powell announced the judgment of the Court and delivered an opinion joined only by Justices Rehnquist and O'Connor. Focusing on the nature of the matter reported rather than on the medium reporting it, Powell wrote that the credit report concerned no public issue and was "speech solely in the individual interest of the speaker and its special business audience." The Court ruled that when a false defamatory statement was not a "matter of public concern," the plaintiff could win without having to prove actual malice.

In separate concurring opinions, Chief Justice Burger and Justice White called for a reexamination of the *New York Times* rule.

What if, in *Greenmoss,* a local newspaper had published the report in question? What if it had been a regional business newspaper? What if it had been a national construction industry newsletter?

15. Whether private figure plaintiffs must prove simple negligence or actual malice or something in between depends on what states they are in.

a. The "fault" required under *Gertz* is generally thought to be the sort of conduct that must be shown in automobile accident cases, when visitors slip and fall on another's premises, or when a physician is sued for harm suffered by a patient. Briefly, in each of these situations the plaintiff must show that the defendant did not behave as a hypothetical reasonable person would have behaved under similar circumstances. Thus, in an automobile accident case, the question whether the driver was at fault, or negligent, is the same as asking whether he or she behaved as a hypothetical reasonable driver confronted with the same situation would have acted.

Translating that to the press area is not so easy because it is unclear whether a reporter or editor on a small rural daily should be expected to behave in the same manner as a reporter or editor on a large urban daily or a monthly magazine. These are some of the unresolved questions that lie ahead in applying the "fault" principle of the *Gertz* rule in private plaintiff cases.

Generally, in auto accident cases and in other civil cases, the plaintiffs need only persuade the judge or jury that their version of the facts is more likely than competing versions. This is often referred to as proving your case by a "fair preponderance of the evidence" or meeting the "more likely than not" standard. Contrast this with the requirement to prove "actual malice" or with the traditional burden of proof in criminal cases, which requires the prosecution to prove its case "beyond a reasonable doubt."

b. *Variations among the states.* Remember that Justice Powell's opinion in *Gertz* provided that states might use whatever standard they wanted to use so long as they met the minimum requirements of fault and the damage rules of *Gertz*. Thus, at the extreme, nothing in the Court's opinion would prevent a state from completely abolishing all suits for defamation. Some states responded to *Gertz* by adopting the *Rosenbloom* approach. A few developed their own rules, but most appear to have chosen the *Gertz* minimum standards as their own.

c. Even though private figure plaintiffs in most states do not have to prove "actual malice" to collect compensatory damages, as a practical matter they are likely to try to prove "actual malice" with convincing clarity anyway in hopes that the court will award them punitive damages and that the award will withstand independent appellate review.

d. *The burden of proof on falsity.* Although the Court's focus was on the fault requirement, questions still lingered about who had the burden of proof on the question of truth or falsity. In Philadelphia Newspapers, Inc., v. Hepps, 475 U.S. 767, 12 Med.L.Rptr. 1977 (1986), the Court, 5–4, held that the plaintiff had the burden of proving falsity at least in cases brought by private plaintiffs where the speech was of public concern. For the majority, Justice O'Connor concluded that to "ensure that true speech on matters of public concern is not deterred, we hold that the common-law presumption that defamatory speech is false cannot stand when a plaintiff seeks damages against a media defendant for speech of public concern." (Two of the five joining the majority opinion rejected the limitation to "media" defendants.) Even though this burden would "insulate from liability some speech that is false, but unprovably so," that result is essential to avoid the "chilling" effect that would otherwise accompany true speech on matters of public concern.

The majority asserted that its conclusion added "only marginally to the burdens" on libel plaintiffs because a jury is more likely to accept a "contention that the defendant was at fault in publishing the statements at issue if convinced that the relevant statements were false. As a practical matter, then, evidence offered by plaintiffs on the publisher's fault . . . will generally encompass evidence of the falsity of the matters asserted." The majority reversed the question of the quantity of proof of falsity that a plaintiff must present.

Justice Stevens, for the dissenters, thought the majority result "pernicious." He posited a situation in which a defendant, knowing that the plaintiff could not prove the statement false, deliberately lied about the plaintiff. This situation might occur due to the passage of time, the loss of critical records, or the absence of an eyewitness. The majority's analysis was an "obvious blueprint for character assassination." In his view, as long as publishers are protected by the fault requirement, "there can be little, if any, basis for a concern that a significant amount of true speech will be deterred unless the private person victimized by a malicious libel can also carry the burden of proving falsity."

In a footnote, Justice Stevens asserted that if the issue were brought before the Court, he "would be inclined to the view that public figures should not bear the burden of disproving the veracity of accusations made against them with 'actual malice' as the *New York Times* Court used that term."

The papers of the late Supreme Court Justice Thurgood Marshall (released by the National Archives in a controversial decision in May 1993) reveal that the Supreme Court's decision in *Hepps* was initially going to be a 5–4 decision in favor of plaintiff Hepps. As revealed in Marshall's papers, Justice Sandra Day O'Connor originally favored affirming the Pennsylvania Supreme Court decision requiring a media libel defendant to prove the truth of the allegedly defamatory statement, and she had been assigned by the Chief Justice to write the majority opinion. In a subsequent memo to the Chief Justice, however, she said that her original vote had been "very tentative" and that she had come to believe that the judgment of the Pennsylvania Supreme Court should be reversed. Justice Brennan, as the senior justice on what became the new majority, then assigned Justice O'Connor to write the opinion. Media Law Reporter News Notes, Aug. 3, 1993.

### 3. SPECIFIC CONSTITUTIONAL APPLICATIONS OF THE NEW YORK TIMES RULE AND THE PRIVILEGE OF NEUTRAL REPORTAGE

#### a. *Fact vs. Opinion*

In the following 1990 case, the Supreme Court rejected previously-used opinion tests and held that not all opinion is necessarily privileged.

When unstated facts are implied, the old "fair comment" defense does not apply.

## MILKOVICH v. LORAIN JOURNAL CO.

Supreme Court of the United States, 1990.
497 U.S. 1, 110 S.Ct. 2695, 111 L.Ed.2d 1, 17 Med.L.Rptr. 2009.

[Milkovich was coach of the Maple Heights high school wrestling team, which was involved in a brawl with a competing team. The Ohio High School Athletic Association (OHSAA) censured Milkovich and placed his team on probation. Parents of some of the team members sued to enjoin OHSAA from enforcing the probation, contending OHSAA's investigation and hearing violated due process. Milkovich and the school's superintendent, Scott, testified at the hearing on the suit, both denying that Milkovich had incited the brawl through his behavior toward the crowd and a meet official. The judge granted the restraining order sought by the parents. A sports columnist who had attended both the meet and the court hearing wrote about the hearing in a column published the next day in the defendant newspaper. The headline was "Maple beat the law with the 'big lie.' " The theme of the column was that Milkovich and Scott in their testimony at the hearing misrepresented Milkovich's role in the altercation and thereby prevented the team from receiving the punishment it deserved. The concluding paragraphs of the column were as follows:

> "Anyone who attended the meet, whether he be from Maple Heights, Mentor [the opposing school] or impartial observer, knows in his heart that Milkovich and Scott lied at the hearing after each having given his solemn oath to tell the truth.

> "But they got away with it.

> "Is that the kind of lesson we want our young people learning from their high school administrators and coaches?

> "I think not."

Milkovich and Scott both sued the newspaper, alleging that the column accused them of perjury and thus was libellous *per se*. After 15 years of litigation and several appeals, the Ohio Court of Appeals held in Milkovich's case that the column was constitutionally protected opinion and granted the newspaper's motion for summary judgment. The Supreme Court reversed.]

CHIEF JUSTICE REHNQUIST delivered the opinion of the Court.

[The opinion reviewed the various constitutional limitations imposed on state libel law in the series of cases beginning with *Sullivan*. The Court also mentioned its decision in Hustler Magazine, Inc. v. Falwell, p. 251 *infra,* an emotional distress case holding that the First Amendment precluded recovery for an ad parody that "could not reasonably have been interpreted as stating actual facts about the public figure involved."]

. . .

Respondents would have us recognize, in addition to the established safeguards discussed above, still another First Amendment-based protection for defamatory statements which are categorized as "opinion" as opposed to "fact." For this proposition they rely principally on the following dictum from our opinion in *Gertz:*

"Under the First Amendment there is no such thing as a false idea. However, pernicious an opinion may seem, we depend for its correction not on the conscience of judges and juries but on the competition of other ideas. But there is no constitutional value in false statements of fact." [ ]

Judge Friendly appropriately observed that this passage "has become the opening salvo in all arguments for protection from defamation actions on the ground of opinion, even though the case did not remotely concern the question." Cianci v. New Times Publishing Co., [ ]. Read in context, though, the fair meaning of the passage is to equate the word "opinion" in the second sentence with the word "idea" in the first sentence. Under this view, the language was merely a reiteration of Justice Holmes' classic "marketplace of ideas" concept. [ ]

Thus, we do not think this passage from *Gertz* was intended to create a wholesale defamation exemption for anything that might be labeled "opinion." Not only would such an interpretation be contrary to the tenor and context of the passage, but it would also ignore the fact that expressions of "opinion" may often imply an assertion of objective fact.

If a speaker says, "In my opinion John Jones is a liar," he implies a knowledge of facts which lead to the conclusion that Jones told an untruth. Even if the speaker states the facts upon which he bases his opinion, if those facts are either incorrect or incomplete, or if his assessment of them is erroneous, the statement may still imply a false assertion of fact. Simply couching such statements in terms of opinion does not dispel these implications; and the statement, "In my opinion Jones is a liar," can cause as much damage to reputation as the statement, "Jones is a liar." As Judge Friendly aptly stated: "[It] would be destructive of the law of libel if a writer could escape liability for accusations of [defamatory conduct] simply by using, explicitly or implicitly, the words 'I think.'" [*Cianci*] It is worthy of note that at common law, even the privilege of fair comment did not extend to "a false statement of fact, whether it was expressly stated or implied from an expression of opinion." Restatement (Second) of Torts, supra, § 566 Comment a.

Apart from their reliance on the *Gertz dictum*, respondents do not really contend that a statement such as, "In my opinion John Jones is a liar," should be protected by a separate privilege for "opinion" under the First Amendment. But they do contend that in every defamation case the First Amendment mandates an inquiry into whether a statement is "opinion" or "fact," and that only the latter statements may be action-able.  They propose that a number of factors developed by the lower courts (in what we hold was a mistaken reliance on the *Gertz dictum*) be considered in deciding which is which.  But we think the " 'breathing space' " which " 'freedoms of expression require in order to survive,' " [   ], is adequately secured by existing constitutional doctrine without the creation of an artificial dichotomy between "opinion" and fact.

Foremost, we think *Hepps* stands for the proposition that a state-ment on matters of public concern must be provable as false before there can be liability under state defamation law, at least in situations, like the present where a media defendant is involved.[6]  Thus, unlike the state-ment, "In my opinion Mayor Jones is a liar," the statement, "In my opinion Mayor Jones shows his abysmal ignorance by accepting the teachings of Marx and Lenin," would not be actionable.  *Hepps* ensures that a statement of opinion relating to matters of public concern which does not contain a provably false factual connotation will receive full constitutional protection.

Next, the *Bresler–Letter Carriers–Falwell* line of cases provide pro-tection for statements that cannot "reasonably [be] interpreted as stat-ing actual facts" about an individual.  [   ]  This provides assurance that public debate will not suffer for lack of "imaginative expression" or the "rhetorical hyperbole" which has traditionally added much to the dis-course of our Nation.  [   ]

The *New York Times–Butts* and *Gertz* culpability requirements further ensure that debate on public issues remains "uninhibited, ro-bust, and wide-open."  [   ]  Thus, where a statement of "opinion" on a matter of public concern reasonably implies false and defamatory facts regarding public figures or officials, those individuals must show that such statements were made with knowledge of their false implications or with reckless disregard of their truth.  Similarly, where such a state-ment involves a private figure on a matter of public concern, a plaintiff must show that the false connotations were made with some level of fault as required by *Gertz*.  Finally, the enhanced appellate review required by *Bose Corp.*, provides assurance that the foregoing determina-tions will be made in a manner so as not to "constitute a forbidden intrusion of the field of free expression."  [   ]

We are not persuaded that in addition to these protections, an additional separate constitutional privilege for "opinion" is required to insure the freedom of expression guaranteed by the First Amendment.  The dispositive question in the present case then becomes whether or not a reasonable factfinder could conclude that the statements in the  .  .  .  column imply an assertion that petitioner Milkovich per-jured himself in a judicial proceeding.  We think this question must be

**6.** In *Hepps* the Court reserved judg-ment on cases involving non media defen-dants, [   ], and accordingly we do the same.  Prior to *Hepps* of course, where public-offi-cial or public-figure plaintiffs were involved, the *New York Times* rule already required a showing of falsity before liability could re-sult.  [   ]

answered in the affirmative.  As the Ohio Supreme Court itself observed, "the clear impact in some nine sentences and a caption is that [Milkovich] 'lied at the hearing after  .  .  .  having given his solemn oath to tell the truth.' " [   ]  This is not the sort of loose, figurative or hyperbolic language which would negate the impression that the writer was seriously maintaining petitioner committed the crime of perjury. Nor does the general tenor of the article negate this impression.

We also think the connotation that petitioner committed perjury is sufficiently factual to be susceptible of being proved true or false.  A determination of whether petitioner lied in this instance can be made on a core of objective evidence by comparing, *inter alia,* petitioner's testimony before the OHSAA board with his subsequent testimony before the trial court.  As the [Ohio Supreme Court noted in the case of the superintendent] "[w]hether or not H. Don Scott did indeed perjure himself is certainly verifiable by a perjury action with evidence adduced from the transcripts and witnesses present at the hearing.  Unlike a subjective assertion the averred defamatory language is an articulation of an objectively verifiable event."  25 Ohio St.3d, at 252, 496 N.E.2d, at 707.  So too with petitioner Milkovich.

The numerous decisions discussed above establishing First Amendment protection for defendants in defamation actions surely demonstrate the Court's recognition of the Amendment's vital guarantee of free and uninhibited discussion of public issues.  But there is another side to the equation; we have regularly acknowledged the "important social values which underlie the law of defamation," and recognize that "[s]ociety has a pervasive and strong interest in preventing and redressing attacks upon reputation."  [*Rosenblatt*].  Justice Stewart [concurring] in that case put it with his customary clarity:

"The right of a man to the protection of his own reputation from unjustified invasion and wrongful hurt reflects no more than our basic concept of the essential dignity and worth of every human being—a concept at the root of any decent system of ordered liberty.

"The destruction that defamatory falsehood can bring is, to be sure, often beyond the capacity of the law to redeem.  Yet, imperfect though it is, an action for damages is the only hope for vindication of redress the law gives to a man whose reputation has been falsely dishonored." [   ]

We believe our decision in the present case holds the balance true. The judgment of the Ohio Court of Appeals is reversed and the case remanded for further proceedings not inconsistent with this opinion.

Reversed.

[JUSTICE BRENNAN, joined by JUSTICE MARSHALL, dissented.  He said the Court addressed the opinion issue "cogently and almost entirely correctly," and agreed that the lower courts had been under a "misimpression that there is a so-called opinion privilege wholly in addition to the protections we have already found to be guaranteed by the First

Amendment. . . ." But he disagreed with the application of agreed principles to the facts. ". . . I find that the challenged statements cannot reasonably be interpreted as either stating or implying defamatory facts about petitioner. Under the rule articulated in the majority opinion, therefore, the statements are due 'full constitutional protection.'"

He characterized the columnist's assumption that Milkovich lied as "patently conjecture" and asserted that conjecture is as important to the free flow of ideas and opinions as "imaginative expression" and "rhetorical hyperbole," which the majority agreed are protected. He gave several examples:

> Did NASA officials ignore sound warnings that the Challenger Space Shuttle would explode? Did Cuban–American leaders arrange for John Fitzgerald Kennedy's assassination? Was Kurt Waldheim a Nazi officer? Such questions are matters of public concern long before all the facts are unearthed, if they ever are. Conjecture is a means of fueling a national discourse on such questions and stimulating public pressure for answers from those who know more.

The dissent argued that the language of the column itself made clear to readers that the columnist was engaging in speculation, personal judgment, emotional rhetoric, and moral outrage. "No reasonable reader could understand [the columnist] to be impliedly asserting—as fact—that Milkovich had perjured himself."]

## Notes and Questions

1. Why does the constitution require protection of rhetorical hyperbole but not opinion? Is rhetorical hyperbole less likely to damage reputation? A more valuable form of speech?

2. The majority says "the statement, 'In my opinion Mayor Jones shows his abysmal ignorance by accepting the teachings of Marx and Lenin,' would not be actionable." If the mayor does not accept the teachings of Marx and Lenin, why is the statement not actionable? Does the Court mean only that the statement that the mayor is abysmally ignorant is not actionable if the rest of the statement is true?

3. The procedural history of the Milkovich case, described at length in omitted portions of the majority opinion, illustrates the persistence and endurance that libel litigation sometimes demands of its participants. The column was published in 1974. Milkovich and Scott filed separate suits. The Milkovich case went to trial, but the judge directed a verdict for the defendants on the ground that Milkovich was required to show actual malice and had failed to do so. The Ohio Court of Appeals reversed, holding that there was sufficient evidence of actual malice. The Ohio Supreme Court and the U.S. Supreme Court denied review. On remand, the trial court granted defendants' motion for summary judgment on the ground that the column was constitutionally protected as opinion, and alternatively, that Milkovich was a public figure and had failed to make out a *prima facie* case of actual malice. The court of

appeals this time affirmed both determinations, but the Ohio Supreme Court reversed, holding that Milkovich was neither a public official nor public figure and that the column was not opinion.   The U.S. Supreme Court denied review.

Two years later, Scott's case reached the Ohio Supreme Court. Some judges had been replaced in the interval, and the court now held that the column was constitutionally protected opinion, affirming summary judgment against Scott.   Scott v. News–Herald, 25 Ohio St.3d 243, 496 N.E.2d 699 (1986).

The trial court in *Milkovich* granted summary judgment on the opinion ground, and the Ohio Court of Appeals affirmed on the authority of the *Scott* decision.   The Ohio Supreme Court denied review, but Milkovich finally won U.S. Supreme Court review 16 years after the column appeared.

4.   The decision left the Milkovich case unresolved.   In a footnote dismissing arguments that independent state grounds precluded Supreme Court review of the opinion issue, the Court recognized that the Ohio courts still might hold for the defendants on the ground that the state constitution protects opinion or on the ground that Milkovich was a public official or public figure and could not show actual malice.   The Ohio appellate court to which the case was then remanded found that the Ohio Constitution does not afford greater protection to opinion than does the federal Constitution, but it remanded the case to the trial court to determine if the column was written with some level of *Gertz* fault. 70 Ohio App.3d 480, 591 N.E.2d 394 (1990).   The case was subsequently settled out of court.

5.   In 1990, the Supreme Court vacated and remanded a lower court's decision in Immuno AG v. Moor–Jankowski, 74 N.Y.2d 548, 549 N.Y.S.2d 938, 549 N.E.2d 129, 17 Med.L.Rptr. 1161 (1989) for further reconsideration in light of *Milkovich*.   Immuno AG, an Austrian pharmaceutical company that performs tests on animals, had sued Moor–Jankowski, editor of the *Journal of Medical Primatology,* published in New York, over a letter to the editor from an animal rights activist concerned about a proposed research facility using chimpanzees for research.   When the *Journal* had published the letter, it had included an editor's note saying that Immuno's lawyers had challenged the accuracy of the letter and identifying the writer as an animal rights activist.   New York's highest court decided in 1991 that the state's constitution offers more protection for freedom of the press than does the U.S. Constitution—and dismissed the case.   Judge Judith Kaye, writing for the majority, said "We look to our state law because of the nature of the issue in controversy—liberty of the press—where this state has its own exceptional history and rich tradition."   77 N.Y.2d 906, 566 N.Y.S.2d 906, 567 N.E.2d 1270, 18 Med.L.Rptr. 1625 (1991).

6.   The *Milkovich* distinction between fact and opinion was also an issue in Unelko Corp. v. Rooney, 912 F.2d 1049, 17 Med.L.Rptr. 2317 (9th Cir.1990) cert. denied, 111 S.Ct. 1586 (1991), in which the maker of a car

windshield treatment product sued Andy Rooney of "60 Minutes" for saying the product "Rain–X" "didn't work." Although Rooney's comment was held to imply an assertion of objective fact and, under *Milkovich,* was not shielded from liability, the U.S. Court of Appeals for the Ninth Circuit upheld a grant of summary judgment for Rooney due to the manufacturer's failure to demonstrate falsity.

## b.  Altered Quotations

A 1991 case presented the Supreme Court with the question of whether a journalist's use of quotation remarks around words that are not provably the plaintiff's may be treated as reckless disregard for the truth under the actual malice standard.

### MASSON v. NEW YORKER MAGAZINE, INC.

Supreme Court of the United States, 1991.
501 U.S. ___, 111 S.Ct. 2419, 115 L.Ed.2d 447, 18 Med.L.Rptr. 2241.

JUSTICE KENNEDY delivered the opinion of the Court.

In this libel case, a public figure claims he was defamed by an author who, with full knowledge of the inaccuracy, used quotation marks to attribute to him comments he had not made.  The First Amendment protects authors and journalists who write about public figures by requiring a plaintiff to prove that the defamatory statements were made with what we have called "actual malice," a term of art denoting deliberate or reckless falsification.  We consider in this opinion whether the attributed quotations had the degree of falsity required to prove this state of mind, so that the public figure can defeat a motion for summary judgment and proceed to a trial on the merits of the defamation claim.

### I

Petitioner Jeffrey Masson trained at Harvard University as a Sanskrit scholar, and in 1970 became a professor of Sanskrit & Indian Studies at the University of Toronto.  He spent eight years in psychoanalytic training, and qualified as an analyst in 1978.  Through his professional activities, he came to know Dr. Kurt Eissler, head of the Sigmund Freud Archives, and Dr. Anna Freud, daughter of Sigmund Freud and a major psychoanalyst in her own right.  The Sigmund Freud Archives, located at Maresfield Gardens outside of London, serves as a repository for materials about Freud, including his own writings, letters, and personal library.

In 1980, Eissler and Anna Freud hired petitioner as Projects Director of the Archives.  After assuming his post, petitioner became disillusioned with Freudian psychology.  In a 1981 lecture before the Western New England Psychoanalytical Society in New Haven, Connecticut, he advanced his theories of Freud.  Soon after, the Board of the Archives terminated petitioner as Projects Director.

Respondent Janet Malcolm is an author and a contributor to respondent The New Yorker, a weekly magazine. She contacted petitioner in 1982 regarding the possibility of an article on his relationship with the Archives. He agreed, and the two met in person and spoke by telephone in a series of interviews. Based on the interviews and other sources, Malcolm wrote a lengthy article. One of Malcolm's narrative devices consists of enclosing lengthy passages in quotation marks, reporting statements of Masson, Eissler, and her other subjects.

During the editorial process, Nancy Franklin, a member of the fact-checking department at The New Yorker, called petitioner to confirm some of the facts underlying the article. According to petitioner, he expressed alarm at the number of errors in the few passages Franklin discussed with him. Petitioner contends that he asked permission to review those portions of the article which attributed quotations or information to him, but was brushed off with a never-fulfilled promise to "get back to [him]." [ ] Franklin disputes petitioner's version of their conversation. [ ]

The New Yorker published Malcolm's piece in December 1983, as a two-part series. In 1984, with knowledge of at least petitioner's general allegation that the article contained defamatory material, respondent Alfred A. Knopf, Inc., published the entire work as a book, entitled In the Freud Archives.

Malcolm's work received complimentary reviews. But this gave little joy to Masson, for the book portrays him in a most unflattering light. According to one reviewer,

"Masson the promising psychoanalytic scholar emerges gradually, as a grandiose egotist—mean-spirited, self-serving, full of braggadocio, impossibly arrogant, and in the end, a self destructive fool. But it is not Janet Malcolm who calls him such: his own words reveal this psychological profile—a self-portrait offered to us through the efforts of an observer and listener who is, surely, as wise as any in the psychoanalytic profession." Coles, Freudianism Confronts Its Malcontents, Boston Globe, May 27, 1984, pp. 58, 60.

Petitioner wrote a letter to the New York Times Book Review calling the book "distorted." In response, Malcolm stated:

"Many of [the] things Mr. Masson told me (on tape) were discreditable to him, and I felt it best not to include them. Everything I do quote Mr. Masson as saying was said by him, almost word for word. (The 'almost' refers to changes made for the sake of correct syntax.) I would be glad to play the tapes of my conversation with Mr. Masson to the editors of The Book Review whenever they have 40 or 50 short hours to spare." [ ]

Petitioner brought an action for libel under California law in the United States District Court for the Northern District of California. During extensive discovery and repeated amendments to the complaint, petitioner concentrated on various passages alleged to be defamatory, dropping some and adding others.  The tape recordings of the interviews demonstrated that petitioner had, in fact, made statements substantially identical to a number of the passages, and those passages are no longer in the case.  We discuss only the passages relied on by petitioner in his briefs to this Court.

Each passage before us purports to quote a statement made by petitioner during the interviews.  Yet in each instance no identical statement appears in the more than 40 hours of taped interviews. Petitioner complains that Malcolm fabricated all but one passage;  with respect to that passage, he claims Malcolm omitted a crucial portion, rendering the remainder misleading.

(a) *"Intellectual Gigolo."*  Malcolm quoted a description by petitioner of his relationship with Eissler and Anna Freud as follows:  " 'Then I met a rather attractive older graduate student and I had an affair with her.   One day, she took me to some art event, and she was sorry afterward.   She said, "Well, it is very nice sleeping with you in your room, but you're the kind of person who should never leave the room— you're just a social embarrassment anywhere else, though you do fine in your own room."   And you know, in their way, if not in so many words, Eissler and Anna Freud told me the same thing.   They like me well enough "in my own room."   They loved to hear from me what creeps and dolts analysts are.   I was like an intellectual gigolo—you get your pleasure from him, but you don't take him out in public.   . . .' " [  ]

The tape recordings contain the substance of petitioner's reference to his graduate student friend, [  ], but no suggestion that Eissler or Anna Freud considered him, or that he considered himself, an " 'intellectual gigolo.' " Instead, petitioner said:

"They felt, in a sense, I was a private asset but a public liability .   .  .. They liked me when I was alone in their living room, and I could talk and chat and tell them the truth about things and they would tell me. But that I was, in a sense, much too junior within the hierarchy of analysis for these important training analysts to be caught dead with me." [  ]

(b) *"Sex, Women, Fun."*  Malcolm quoted petitioner as describing his plans for Maresfield Gardens, which he had to occupy after Anna Freud's death:

" 'It was a beautiful house, but it was dark and somber and dead. Nothing ever went on there.  I was the only person who ever came. I would have renovated it, opened it up, brought it to life.  Maresfield Gardens would have been a center of scholarship, but it would also have been a place of sex, women, fun.  It would have been like the change in *The Wizard of Oz*, from black-and-white into color.' " [  ]

The tape recordings contain a similar statement, but in place of the reference to "sex, women, fun," and The Wizard of Oz, petitioner commented;

"[I]t is an incredible storehouse. I mean, the library, Freud's library alone is priceless in terms of what it contains: all his books with his annotations in them; the Schreber case annotated, that kind of thing. It's fascinating." [  ]

Petitioner did talk, earlier in the interview, of his meeting with a London analyst:

"I like him. So, and we got on very well. That was the first time we ever met and you know, it was buddy-buddy, and we were to stay with each other and [laughs] we were going to have a great time together when I lived in the Freud house. We'd have great parties there and we were [laughs]—

. . .

". . . going to really, we were going to live it up." [  ]

(c) *"It Sounded Better."* Petitioner spoke with Malcolm about the history of his family, including the reasons his grandfather changed the family from Moussaieff to Masson, and why petitioner adopted the abandoned family name as his middle name. The article contains the passage:

" 'My father is a gem merchant who doesn't like to stay in any one place too long. His father was a gem merchant, too—a Bessarabian gem merchant, named Moussaieff, who went to Paris in the twenties and adopted the name Masson. My parents named me Jeffrey Lloyd Masson, but in 1975 I decided to change my middle name to Moussaieff—it sounded better.' " [  ]

In the most similar tape recorded statement, Masson explained at considerable length that his grandfather had changed the family name from Moussaieff to Masson when living in France, "[j]ust to hide his Jewishness." Petitioner had changed his last name back to Moussaieff, but his then wife Terry objected that "nobody could pronounce it and nobody knew how to spell it, and it wasn't the name that she knew me by." Petitioner had changed his name to Moussaieff because he "just liked it." "[I]t was sort of part of analysis: a return to the roots, and your family tradition and so on." In the end, he had agreed with Terry that "it wasn't her name after all," and used Moussaieff as a middle instead of a last name. [  ]

(d) *"I Don't Know Why I Put It In."* The article recounts part of conversation between Malcolm and petitioner about the paper petitioner presented at his 1981 New Haven lecture:

"[I] asked him what had happened between the time of the lecture and the present to change him from a Freudian psychoanalyst with somewhat outré views into the bitter and belligerent anti-Freudian he had become.

"Masson sidestepped my question. 'You're right, there was nothing disrespectful of analysis in that paper,' he said. 'That remark about the sterility of psychoanalysis was something I tacked on at the last minute, and it was totally gratuitous. I don't know why I put it in.' " [   ]

The tape recordings instead contain the following discussion of the New Haven lecture:

Masson: "So they really couldn't judge the material. And, in fact, until the last sentence I they were quite fascinated. I think the last sentence was an in, [sic] possibly, gratuitously offensive way to end a paper to a group of analysts. Uh,—"

Malcolm: "What were the circumstances under which you put it [in]?   . . ."

Masson: "That it was, was true."

        . . .

". . . I really believe it. I didn't believe anybody would agree with me.

        . . .

". . . But I felt I should say something because the papers still sell within the analytic tradition in a sense.   . . .

        . . .

". . . It's really not a deep criticism of Freud. It contains all the material that would allow one to criticize Freud but I didn't really do it. And then I thought, I really must say one thing that I really believe, that's not going to appeal to anybody and that was the very last sentence. Because I really do believe psychoanalysis is entirely sterile . . .." [   ]

(e) *"Greatest Analyst Who Ever Lived."* The article contains the following self-explanatory passage:

"A few days after my return to New York, Masson, in a state of elation, telephoned me to say that Farrar, Straus & Giroux has taken The Assault on Truth [Masson's book]. 'Wait till it reaches the best seller list, and watch how the analysts will crawl,' he crowed. 'They move whichever way the wind blows. They will want me back, they will say that Masson is a great scholar, a major analyst—after Freud, he's the greatest analyst who ever lived. Suddenly they'll be calling, begging, cajoling: "Please take back what you've said about our profession; our patients are quitting." They'll try a short smear campaign, then they'll try to buy me, and ultimately they'll have to shut up. Judgment will be passed by history. There is no possible refutation of this book. It's going to cause a revolution in psychoanalysis. Analysis stands or falls with me now.' " [   ]

This material does not appear in the tape recordings. Petitioner did make the following statements on related topics in one of the taped interviews with Malcolm:

". . . I assure you when that book comes out, which I honestly believe is an honest book, there is nothing, you know, mean-minded about it. It's the honest fruit of research and intellectual toil. And there is not an analyst in the country who will say a single word in favor of it." [ ]

"Talk to enough analysts and get them right down to these concrete issues and you watch how different it is from my position. It's utterly the opposite and that's finally what I realized, that I hold a position that no other analyst holds, including, alas, Freud. At first I thought: Okay, it's me and Freud against the rest of the analytic world, or me and Freud and Anna Freud and Kur[t] Eissler and Vic Calef and Brian Bird and Sam Lipton against the rest of the world. Not so, it's me. It's me alone." [ ]

The tape of this interview also contains the following exchange between petitioner and Malcolm:

Masson: ". . . analysis stands or falls with me now."

Malcolm: "Well that's a very grandiose thing to say."

Masson: "Yeah, but it's got nothing to do with me. It's got to do with the things I discovered." [ ]

(f) *"He Had The Wrong Man."* In discussing the Archives' board meeting at which petitioner's employment was terminated, Malcolm quotes petitioner as giving the following explanations of Eissler's attempt to extract a promise of confidentiality:

"'[Eissler] was always putting moral pressure on me. "Do you want to poison Anna Freud's last days? Have you no heart? You're going to kill the poor old woman." I said to him, "What have I done? *You're* doing it. *You're* firing me. What am I supposed to do—be grateful to you?" "You could be silent about it. You could swallow it. I know it is painful for you. But you could just live with it in silence." "Why should I do that?" "Because it is the honorable thing to do." Well, he had the wrong man.'" [ ]

From the tape recordings, on the other hand, it appears that Malcolm deleted part of petitioner's explanation (italicized below), and petitioner argues that the "wrong man" sentence relates to something quite different from Eissler's entreaty that silence was "the honorable thing." In the tape recording, petitioner states:

"But it was wrong of Eissler to do that, you know. He was constantly putting various kinds of moral pressure on me and, 'Do you want to poison Anna Freud's last days? Have you no heart?' He called me: 'Have you no heart? You're going to kill the poor old woman. Have you no heart? Think of what she's done for you and you are now willing to do this to her.' I said, 'What have I, what have I done? *You* did it. You fired me. What am I supposed to do: thank you? be grateful to you?' He said, 'Well you could never talk about it. You could be silent about it. You could swallow it. I know it's painful for you but just live with it in silence.' 'Fuck you,'

I said, 'Why should I do that? Why? You know, why should one do that?' 'Because it's the honorable thing to do *and you will save face. And who knows? If you never speak about it and you quietly and humbly accept our judgment, who knows that in a few years if we don't bring you back?* ' Well, he had the wrong man." App. 215–215.

Malcolm submitted to the District Court that not all of her discussions with petitioner were recorded on tape, in particular conversations that occurred while the two of them walked together or traveled by car, while petitioner stayed at Malcolm's home in New York, or while her tape recorder was inoperable. She claimed to have taken notes of these unrecorded sessions, which she later typed, then discarding the handwritten originals. Petitioner denied that any discussion relating to the substance of the article occurred during his stay at Malcolm's home in New York, that Malcolm took notes during any of their conversations, or that Malcolm gave any indication that her tape recorder was broken.

Respondents moved for summary judgment. The parties agreed that petitioner was a public figure and so could escape summary judgment only if the evidence in the record would permit a reasonable finder of fact, by clear and convincing evidence, to conclude that respondents published a defamatory statement with actual malice as defined by our cases. [*Liberty Lobby*] The District Court analyzed each of the passages and held that the alleged inaccuracies did not raise a jury question. The court found that the allegedly fabricated quotations were either substantially true, or were " 'one of a number of possible rational interpretations' of a conversation or event that 'bristled with ambiguities,' " and thus were entitled to constitutional protection, 686 F.Supp. 1396, 1399 (1987) (quoting [*Bose*]). The court also ruled that the "he had the wrong man" passage involved an exercise of editorial judgment upon which the courts could not intrude. [ ]

The Court of Appeals affirmed, with one judge dissenting. 895 F.2d 1535 (CA9 1989). The court assumed for much of its opinion that Malcolm had deliberately altered each quotation not found on the tape recordings, but nevertheless held that petitioner failed to raise a jury question of actual malice, in large part for the reasons stated by the District Court. In its examination of the "intellectual gigolo" passage, the court agreed with the District Court that petitioner could not demonstrate actual malice because Malcolm had not altered the substantive content of petitioner's self-description, but went on to note that it did not consider the "intellectual gigolo" passage defamatory, as the quotation merely reported Kurt Eissler's and Anna Freud's opinions about petitioner. In any event, concluded the court, the statement would not be actionable under the " 'incremental harm branch' of the 'libel-proof' doctrine," id., at 1541 (quoting [*Herbert*]).

The dissent argued that any intentional or reckless alteration would prove actual malice, so long as a passage within quotation marks purports to be a verbatim rendition of what was said, contains material inaccuracies, and is defamatory 895 F.2d, at 1562–1570.  We granted certiorari, 498 U.S. ___ (1990), and now reverse.

## II

### A

Under California law, "[l]ibel is a false and unprivileged publication by writing . . . which exposes any person to hatred, contempt, ridicule, or obloquy, or which causes him to be shunned or avoided, or which has a tendency to injure him in his occupation."  Cal. Civ. Code Ann. § 45 (West 1982).  False attribution of statements to a person may constitute libel, if the falsity exposes that person to an injury comprehended by the statute.  [  ]  It matters not under California law that petitioner alleges only part of the work at issue to be false.  "[T]he test of libel is not quantitative;  a single sentence may be the basis for an action in libel even though buried in a much longer text," though the California courts recognize that "[w]hile a drop of poison may be lethal, weaker poisons are sometimes diluted to the point of impotency."  [  ]

The First Amendment limits California's libel law in various respects.  When, as here, the plaintiff is a public figure he cannot recover unless he proves by clear and convincing evidence that the defendant published the defamatory statement with actual malice, i.e., with "knowledge that it was false or with reckless disregard of whether it was false or not."  [  ].  Mere negligence does not suffice.  Rather the plaintiff must demonstrate that the author "in fact entertained serious doubts as to the truth of his publication," [*St. Amant*], or acted with a "high degree of awareness of . . . probable falsity," [*Garrison*].

Actual malice under the *New York Times* standard should not be confused with the concept of malice as an evil intent or a motive arising from spite or ill will.  See [*Greenbelt*].  We have used the term actual malice as a shorthand to describe the First Amendment protections for speech injurious to reputation and we continue to do so here.  But the term can confuse as well as enlighten.  In this respect, the phrase may be an unfortunate one.  See [*Connaughton*].  In place of the term actual malice, it is better practice that jury instructions refer to publication of a statement with knowledge of falsity or reckless disregard as to truth or falsity.  The definitional principle must be remembered in the case before us.

### B

In general, quotation marks around a passage indicate to the reader that the passage reproduces the speaker's words verbatim.  They inform the reader that he or she is reading the statement of the speaker, not a paraphrase or other indirect interpretation by an author.  By providing this information, quotations add authority to the statement and credibility to the author's work.  Quotations allow the reader to form his or her own conclusions, and to assess the conclusions of the author, instead of relying entirely upon the author's characterization of her subject.

A fabricated quotation may injure reputation in at least two senses, either giving rise to a conceivable claim of defamation. First, the quotation might injure because it attributes an untrue factual assertion to the speaker. An example would be a fabricated quotation of a public official admitting he had been convicted of a serious crime when in fact he had not.

Second, regardless of the truth or falsity of the factual matters asserted within the quoted statement, the attribution may result in injury to reputation because the manner of expression or even the fact that the statement was made indicates a negative personal trait or an attitude the speaker does not hold. John Lennon once was quoted as saying of the Beatles, "We're more popular than Jesus Christ now." [ ] Supposing the quotation had been a fabrication, it appears California law could permit recovery for defamation because, even without regard to the truth of the underlying assertion, false attribution of the statement could have injured his reputation. Here, in like manner, one need not determine whether petitioner is or is not the greatest analyst who ever lived in order to determine that it might have injured his reputation to be reported as having so proclaimed.

A self-condemnatory quotation may carry more force than criticism by another. It is against self-interest to admit one's own criminal liability, arrogance, or lack of integrity, and so all the more easy to credit when it happens. This principle underlies the elemental rule of evidence which permits the introduction of admissions, despite their hearsay character, because we assume "that persons do not make statements which are damaging to themselves unless satisfied for good reason that they are true." [ ]

Of course, quotations do not always convey that the speaker actually said or wrote the quoted material. "Punctuation marks, like words, have many uses. Writers often use quotation marks, yet no reasonable reader would assume that such punctuation automatically implies the truth of the quoted material." *Baker v. Los Angeles Examiner*, 42 Cal. 3d, at 263, 721 P.2d, at 92. In *Baker*, a television reviewer printed a hypothetical conversation between a station vice president and writer/producer, and the court found that no reasonable reader would conclude the plaintiff in fact had made the statement attributed to him. [ ] Writers often use quotations as in *Baker*, and a reader will not reasonably understand the quotation to indicate reproduction of a conversation that took place. In other instances, an acknowledgement that the work is so-called docudrama or historical fiction or that it recreates conversations from memory, not from recordings, might indicate that the quotations should not be interpreted as the actual statements of the speaker to whom they are attributed.

The work at issue here, however, as with much journalistic writing, provides the reader no clue that the quotations are being used as a rhetorical device or to paraphrase the speaker's actual statements. To the contrary, the work purports to be nonfiction, the result of numerous interviews. At least a trier of fact could so conclude. The work contains lengthy quotations attributed to petitioner, and neither Malcolm nor her publishers indicate to the reader that the quotations are anything but the reproduction of actual conversations. Further, the work was published in The New Yorker, a magazine which at the relevant time seemed to enjoy a reputation for scrupulous factual accuracy. These factors would, or at least could, lead a reader to take the quotations at face value. A defendant may be able to argue to the jury that quotations should be viewed by the reader as nonliteral or reconstructions, but we conclude that a trier of fact in this case could find that the reasonable reader would understand the quotations to be nearly verbatim reports of statements made by the subject.

## C

The constitutional question we must consider here is whether, in the framework of a summary judgment motion, the evidence suffices to show that respondents acted with the requisite knowledge of falsity or reckless disregard as to truth or falsity. This inquiry in turn requires us to consider the concept of falsity; for we cannot discuss the standards for knowledge or reckless disregard without some understanding of the acts required for liability. We must consider whether the requisite falsity inheres in the attribution of words to the petitioner which he did not speak.

In some sense, an alteration of a verbatim quotation is false. But writers and reporters by necessity alter what people say, at the very least to eliminate grammatical and syntactical infelicities. If every alteration constituted the falsity required to prove actual malice, the practice of journalism, which the First Amendment standard is designed to protect, would require a radical change, one inconsistent with our precedents and First Amendment principles. Petitioner concedes this absolute definition of falsity in the quotation context is too stringent, and acknowledges that "minor changes to correct for grammar or syntax" do not amount to falsity for purposes of proving actual malice. [ ] We agree, and must determine what, in addition to this technical falsity, proves falsity for purposes of the actual malice inquiry.

Petitioner argues that, excepting correction of grammar or syntax, publication of a quotation with knowledge that it does not contain the words the public figure used demonstrates actual malice. The author will have published the quotation with knowledge of falsity, and no more need be shown. Petitioner suggests that by invoking more forgiving standards the Court of Appeals would permit and encourage the publication of falsehoods. Petitioner believes that the intentional manufacture of quotations does not "represen[t] the sort of inaccuracy that is commonplace in the forum of robust debate to which the *New York Times* rule applies," [*Bose*], and that protection of deliberate falsehoods would hinder the First Amendment values of robust and well-informed public debate by reducing the reliability of information available to the public.

We reject the idea that any alteration beyond correction of grammar or syntax by itself proves falsity in the sense relevant to determining actual malice under the First Amendment. An interviewer who writes from notes often will engage in the task of attempting a reconstruction of the speaker's statement. That author would, we may assume, act with knowledge that at times she has attributed to her subject words other than those actually used. Under petitioner's proposed standard, an author in this situation would lack First Amendment protection if she reported as quotations the substance of a subject's derogatory statements about himself.

Even if a journalist has tape recorded the spoken statement of a public figure, the full and exact statement will be reported in only rare circumstances. The existence of both a speaker and a reporter; the translation between two media, speech and the printed word; the addition of punctuation; and the practical necessity to edit and make intelligible a speaker's perhaps rambling comments, all make it misleading to suggest that a quotation will be reconstructed with complete accuracy. The use or absence of punctuation may distort a speaker's meaning, for example, where that meaning turns upon a speaker's emphasis of a particular word. In other cases, if a speaker makes an obvious misstatement, for example by unconscious substitution of one name for another, a journalist might alter the speaker's words but preserve his intended meaning. And conversely, an exact quotation out of context can distort meaning, although the speaker did use each reported word.

In all events, technical distinctions between correcting grammar and syntax and some greater level of alteration do not appear workable for we can think of no method by which courts or juries would draw the line between cleaning up and other changes, except by reference to the meaning a statement conveys to a reasonable reader. To attempt narrow distinctions of this type would be an unnecessary departure from First Amendment principles of general applicability, and, just as important, a departure from the underlying purposes of the tort of libel as understood since the latter half of the 16th century. From then until now, the tort action for defamation has existed to redress injury to the plaintiff's reputation by a statement that is defamatory and false. See [*Milkovich*]. As we have recognized, "[t]he legitimate state interest underlying the law of libel is the compensation of individuals for the harm inflicted on them by defamatory falsehood." [*Gertz*] If an author alters a speaker's words but effects no material change in meaning, including any meaning conveyed by the manner or fact of expression, the speaker suffers no injury to reputation that is compensable as a defamation.

These essential principles of defamation law accommodate the special cases of inaccurate quotations without the necessity for a discrete body of jurisprudence directed to this subject alone. Last Term, in [*Milkovich*], we refused "to create a wholesale defamation exemption for anything that might be labeled 'opinion.'" [    ] We recognized that

"expressions of 'opinion' may often imply an assertion of objective fact."
[  ] We allowed the defamation action to go forward in that case,
holding that a reasonable trier of fact could find that the so-called
expressions of opinion could be interpreted as including false assertions
as to factual matters. So too in the case before us, we reject any special
test of falsity for quotations, including one which would draw the line at
correction of grammar or syntax. We conclude, rather, that the exceptions suggest by petitioner for grammatical or syntactical corrections
serve to illuminate a broader principle.

The common law of libel takes but one approach to the question of
falsity, regardless of the form of the communication. [  ] It overlooks
minor inaccuracies and concentrates upon substantial truth. As in other
jurisdictions, California law permits the defense of substantial truth, and
would absolve a defendant even if she cannot "justify every word of the
alleged defamatory matter; it is sufficient if the substance of the charge
be proved true, irrespective of slight inaccuracy in the details." [  ] In
this case, of course, the burden is upon petitioner to prove falsity. See
[*Hepps*]. The essence of that inquiry, however, remains the same
whether the burden rests upon plaintiff or defendant. Minor inaccuracies do not amount to falsity so long as "the substance, the gist, the
sting, of the libelous change be justified." [  ] Put another way, the
statement is not considered false unless it "would have a different effect
on the mind of the reader from that which the pleaded truth would have
produced." [  ] Our definition of actual malice relies upon this historical understanding.

We conclude that a deliberate alteration of the words uttered by a
plaintiff does not equate with knowledge of falsity for purposes of
[*Sullivan* and *Gertz*], unless the alteration results in a material change
in the meaning conveyed by statement. The use of quotations to
attribute words not in fact spoken bears in a most important way on that
inquiry, but it is not dispositive in every case.

Deliberate or reckless falsification that comprises actual malice
turns upon words and punctuation only because words and punctuation
express meaning. Meaning is the life of language. And, for the reasons
we have given, quotations may be a devastating instrument for conveying false meaning. In the case under consideration, readers of In the
Freud Archives may have found Malcolm's portrait of petitioner especially damning because so much of it appeared to be a self-portrait, told by
petitioner in his own words. And if the alterations of petitioner's words
gave a different meaning to the statements, bearing upon their defamatory character, then the device of quotations might well be critical in
finding the words actionable.

D

The Court of Appeals applied a test of substantial truth which, in
exposition if not in application, comports with much of the above
discussion. The Court of Appeals, however, went one step beyond
protection of quotations that convey the meaning of a speaker's state-

ment with substantial accuracy and concluded "that an altered quotation is protected so long as it is a 'rational interpretation' " of an actual statement drawing this standard from our decisions in Time, Inc. v. Pape, 401 U.S. 279 (1971), and [Bose]. Application of our protection for rational interpretation in this context finds no support in general principles of defamation law or in our First Amendment jurisprudence. Neither [Pape], nor [Bose], involved the fabrication of quotations, or any analogous claim, and because many of the quotations at issue might reasonably be construed to state or imply factual assertions that are both false and defamatory, we cannot accept the reasoning of the Court of Appeals on this point.

In [Pape], we reversed a libel judgment which arose out of a magazine article summarizing a report by the United States Commission on Civil Rights discussing police civil rights abuses. The article quoted the Commission's summary of facts surrounding an incident of police brutality, but failed to include the Commission's qualification that these were allegations taken from a civil complaint. The Court noted that "the attitude of the Commission toward the factual verity of the episodes recounted was anything but straightforward," and distinguished between a "direct account of events that speak for themselves," 401 U.S., at 285, 286, and an article descriptive of what the Commission had reported. [Pape] took into account the difficult choices that confront an author who departs from direct quotation and offers his own interpretation of an ambiguous source. A fair reading of our opinion is that the defendant did not publish a falsification sufficient to sustain a finding of actual malice.

In *Bose Corp.,* a Consumer Reports reviewer had attempted to describe in words the experience of listening to music through a pair of loudspeakers, and we concluded that the result was not an assessment of events that speak for themselves, but " 'one of a number of possible rational interpretations' of an event 'that bristled with ambiguities' and descriptive challenges for the writer." [ ] We refused to permit recovery for choice of language which, though perhaps reflecting a misconception, represented "the sort of inaccuracy that is commonplace in the forum of robust debate to which the *New York Times* rule applies." [ ]

The protection for rational interpretation serves First Amendment principles by allowing an author the interpretive license that is necessary when relying upon ambiguous sources. Where, however, a writer uses a quotation, and where a reasonable reader would conclude that the quotation purports to be a verbatim repetition of a statement by the speaker, the quotation marks indicate that the author is not involved in an interpretation of the speaker's ambiguous statement, but attempting to convey what the speaker said. This orthodox use of a quotation is the quintessential "direct account of events that speak for themselves." [Pape], *supra,* at 285. More accurately, the quotation allows the subject to speak for himself.

The significance of the quotations at issue, absent any qualification, is to inform us that we are reading the statement of petitioner, not Malcolm's rational interpretation of what petitioner has said or thought. Were we to assess quotations under a rational interpretation standard, we would give journalists the freedom to place statements in their subjects' mouths without fear of liability. By eliminating any method of distinguishing between the statements of the subject and the interpretation of the author, we would diminish to a great degree the trustworthiness of the printed word, and eliminate the real meaning of quotations. Not only public figures but the press doubtless would suffer under such a rule. Newsworthy figures might become more wary of journalists, knowing that any comment could be transmuted and attributed to the subject, so long as some bounds of rational interpretation were not exceeded. We would ill serve the values of the First Amendment if we were to grant near absolute, constitutional protection for such a practice. We doubt the suggestion that as a general rule readers will assume that direct quotations are but a rational interpretation of the speaker's words, and we decline to adopt any such presumption in determining the permissible interpretations of the quotations in question here.

III

A

We apply these principles to the case before us. On summary judgment, we must draw all justifiable inferences in favor of the non-moving party, including questions of credibility and of the weight to be accorded particular evidence. [*Liberty Lobby*] So we must assume, except where otherwise evidenced by the transcripts of the tape recordings, that petitioner is correct in denying that he made the statements attributed to him by Malcolm, and that Malcolm reported with knowledge or reckless disregard of the differences between what petitioner said and what was quoted.

Respondents argue that, in determining whether petitioner has shown sufficient falsification to survive summary judgment, we should consider not only the tape recorded statements but also Malcolm's typewritten notes. We must decline that suggestion. To begin with, petitioner affirms in an affidavit that he did not make the complained of statements. The record contains substantial additional evidence, moreover, evidence which, in a light most favorable to petitioner, would support a jury determination under a clear and convincing standard that Malcolm deliberately or recklessly altered the quotations.

First, many of the challenged passages resemble quotations that appear on the tapes, except for the addition or alteration of certain phrases, giving rise to a reasonable inference that the statements have been altered. Second, Malcolm had the tapes in her possession and was not working under a tight deadline. Unlike a case involving hot news, Malcolm cannot complain that she lacked the practical ability to compare the tapes with her work in progress. Third, Malcolm represented to the editor-in-chief of The New Yorker that all the quotations were from the tape recordings. Fourth, Malcolm's explanations of the time and place of unrecorded conversations during which petitioner allegedly made some of the quoted statements have not been consistent in all respects. Fifth, petitioner suggests that the progression from typewritten notes, to manuscript, then to galleys provides further evidence of intentional alteration. Malcolm contests petitioner's allegations, and only a trial on the merits will resolve the factual dispute. But at this stage, the evidence creates a jury question whether Malcolm published the statements with knowledge or reckless disregard of the alterations.

B

We must determine whether the published passages differ materially in meaning from the tape recorded statements so as to create an issue of fact for a jury as to falsity.

(a) *"Intellectual Gigolo."* We agree with the dissenting opinion in the Court of Appeals that "[f]airly read, intellectual gigolo suggests someone who forsakes intellectual integrity in exchange for pecuniary or other gain." [  ] A reasonable jury could find a material difference between the meaning of this passage and petitioner's tape-recorded statement that he was considered "much too junior within the hierarchy of analysis, for these important training analysts to be caught dead with [him]."

The Court of Appeals majority found it difficult to perceive how the "intellectual gigolo" quotation was defamatory, a determination supported not by any citation to California law, but only by the argument that the passage appears to be a report of Eissler's and Anna Freud's opinions of petitioner. [  ] We agree with the Court of Appeals that the most natural interpretation of this quotation is not an admission that petitioner considers himself an intellectual gigolo but a statement that Eissler and Anna Freud considered him so. It does not follow, though, that the statement is harmless. Petitioner is entitled to argue that the passage should be analyzed as if Malcolm had reported falsely that *Eissler* had given this assessment (with the added level of complexity that the quotation purports to represent petitioner's understanding of Eissler's view). An admission that two well-respected senior colleagues considered one an "intellectual gigolo" could be as or more damaging than a similar self-appraisal. In all events, whether the "intellectual gigolo" quotation is defamatory is a question of California law. To the extent that the Court of Appeals bases its conclusion in the First Amendment, it was mistaken.

The Court of Appeals relied upon the "incremental harm" doctrine as an alternative basis for its decision. As the court explained it, "[t]his doctrine measures the incremental reputational harm inflicted by the challenged statements beyond the harm imposed by the nonactionable remainder of the publication." [  ] The court ruled, as a matter of law, that "[g]iven the  .  .  . many provocative, bombastic statements indisputably made by Masson and quoted by Malcolm, the additional harm caused by the 'intellectual gigolo' quote was nominal or nonexistent, rendering the defamation claim as to this quote nonactionable." [   ]

This reasoning requires a court to conclude that, in fact, a plaintiff made the other quoted statements, cf. [*Liberty Lobby*]. As noted by the dissent in the Court of Appeals, the most "provocative, bombastic statements" quoted by Malcolm are those complained of by petitioner, and so this would not seem an appropriate application of the incremental harm doctrine. 895 F.2d, at 1566.

(b) *"Sex, Women, Fun."* This passage presents a closer question. The "sex, women, fun" quotation offers a very different picture of petitioner's plans for Maresfield Gardens than his remark that "Freud's library alone is priceless." [   ] Petitioner's other tape-recorded remarks did indicate that he and another analyst planned to have great parties at the Freud house and, in a context that may not even refer to Freud house activities, to "pass women on to each other." We cannot conclude as a matter of law that these remarks bear the same substantial meaning as the quoted passage's suggestion that petitioner would make the Freud house a place of "sex, women, fun."

(c) *"It Sounded Better."* We agree with the District and the Court of Appeals that any difference between petitioner's tape-recorded statement that he "just liked" the name Moussaieff, and the quotation that "it sounded better" is, in context, immaterial. Although Malcolm did not include all of petitioner's lengthy explanation of his name change, she did convey the gist of that explanation: Petitioner took his abandoned family name as his middle name. We agree with the Court of Appeals that the words attributed to petitioner did not materially alter the meaning of his statement.

(d) *"I Don't Know Why I Put It In."* Malcolm quotes petitioner as saying that he "tacked on at the last minute" a "totally gratuitous" remark about the "sterility of psychoanalysis" in an academic paper, and that he did so for no particular reason. In the tape recordings, petitioner does admit that the remark was "possibly [a] gratuitously offensive way to end a paper to a group of analysts," but when asked why he included the remark, he answered "[because] it was true . . . I really believe it." Malcolm's version contains material differences from petitioner's statement, and it is conceivable that the alteration results in a statement that could injure a scholar's reputation.

(e) *"Greatest Analyst Who Ever Lived."* While petitioner did, on numerous occasions, predict that his theories would do irreparable damage to the practice of psychoanalysis, and did suggest that no other analyst shared his views, no tape-recorded statement appears to contain the substance or the arrogant and unprofessional tone apparent in this quotation. A material difference exists between the quotation and the tape-recorded statements, and a jury could find that the difference exposed petitioner to contempt, ridicule or obloquy.

(f) *"He Had The Wrong Man."* The quoted version makes it appear as if petitioner rejected a plea to remain in stoic silence and do "the honorable thing." The tape-recorded version indicates that petitioner rejected a plea supported by far more varied motives: Eissler told petitioner that not only would silence be "the honorable thing," but petitioner would "save face." and might be rewarded for that silence with eventual reinstatement. Petitioner described himself as willing to undergo a scandal in order to shine the light of publicity upon the actions of the Freud Archives, while Malcolm would have petitioner describe himself as a person who was "the wrong man" to do "the honorable thing." This difference is material, a jury might find it defamatory, and, for the reasons we have given, there is evidence to support a finding of deliberate or reckless falsification.

C

Because of the Court of Appeals' disposition with respect to Malcolm, it did not have occasion to address petitioner's argument that the District Court erred in granting summary judgment to The New Yorker Magazine, Inc., and Alfred A. Knopf, Inc. on the basis of their respective relations with Malcolm or the lack of any independent actual malice. These questions are best addressed in the first instance on remand.

The judgment of the Court of Appeals is reversed, and the case is remanded for further proceedings consistent with this opinion.

*It is so ordered.*

JUSTICE WHITE, with whom JUSTICE SCALIA joins, concurring in part and dissenting in part.

. . .

As this case comes to us, it is to be judged on the basis that in the instances identified by the court, the reporter, Malcolm, wrote that Masson said certain things that she knew Masson did not say. By any definition of the term, this was "knowing falsehood" Malcolm asserts that Masson said these very words, knowing that he did not. The issue, as the Court recognizes, is whether Masson spoke the words attributed to him, not whether the fact, if any, asserted by the attributed words is true or false. In my view, we need to go no further to conclude that the defendants in this case were not entitled to summary judgment on the issue of malice with respect to any of the six erroneous quotations.

That there was at least an issue for the jury to decide on the question of deliberate or reckless falsehood, does not mean that plaintiffs were necessarily entitled to go to trial. If, as a matter of law, reasonable jurors could not conclude that attributing to Masson certain words that he did not say amounted to libel under California law, i.e., "expose[d] [Masson] to hatred, contempt, ridicule, or obloquy, or which causes him to be shunned or avoided, or which has a tendency to injure him in his occupation," [   ], a motion for summary judgment on this ground would be justified. I would suppose, for example, that if Malcolm wrote that Masson said that he wore contact lenses, when he said nothing about his eyes or his vision, the trial judge would grant summary judgment for the defendants and dismiss the case. The same would be true if Masson had said "I was spoiled as a child by my Mother," whereas, Malcolm reports that he said "I was spoiled as a child by my parents." But if reasonable jurors should conclude that the deliberate misquotation was libelous, the case should go to the jury.

This seems to me to be the straightforward, traditional approach to deal with this case. Instead, the Court states that deliberate misquotation does not amount to *New York Times* malice unless it results in a material change in the meaning conveyed by the statement. This ignores the fact that under *New York Times*, reporting a known falsehood—here the knowingly false attribution—is sufficient proof of malice. The falsehood, apparently, must be substantial; the reporter may lie a little, but not too much.

This standard is not only a less manageable one than the traditional approach, but it also assigns to the courts issues that are for the jury to decide. For a court to ask whether a misquotation substantially alters the meaning of spoken words in a defamatory manner is a far different inquiry than whether reasonable jurors could find that the misquotation was different enough to be libelous. In the one case, the court is measuring the difference from its own point of view; in the other it is asking how the jury would or could view the erroneous attribution.

The Court attempts to justify its holding in several ways, none of which is persuasive. First, it observes that an interviewer who takes notes of any interview will attempt to reconstruct what the speaker said and will often knowingly attribute to the subject words that were not used by the speaker. [ ] But this is nothing more than an assertion that authors may misrepresent because they cannot remember what the speaker actually said. This should be no dilemma for such authors, or they could report their story without purporting to quote when they are not sure, thereby leaving the reader to trust or doubt the author rather than believing that the subject actually said what he is claimed to have said. Moreover, this basis for the Court's rule has no application where there is a tape of the interview and the author is in no way at a loss to know what the speaker actually said. Second, the Court speculates that even with the benefit of a recording, the author will find it necessary at times to reconstruct, [ ], but again, in those cases why should the author be free to put his or her reconstruction in quotation marks, rather than report without them? Third, the Court suggests that misquotations that do not materially alter the meaning inflict no injury to reputation that is compensable as defamation. [ ] This may be true, but this is a question of defamation or not, and has nothing to do with whether the author deliberately put within quotation marks and attributed to the speaker words that the author knew the speaker did not utter.

As I see it, the defendants' motion for summary judgment based on lack of malice should not have been granted on any of the six quotations considered by the Court in Part III–B of its opinion. I therefore dissent from the result reached with respect to the "It Sounded Better" quotation dealt with in paragraph (c) of Part III–B, but agree with the Court's judgment on the other five misquotations.

**Notes and Questions**

1.  As explained in note 4, *infra*, a first Masson libel trial ended in a mistrial in June 1993.  Suppose that at a subsequent trial the jury were to find (1) that the "intellectual gigolo" quote deliberately and material- ly altered the meaning of what Masson actually said, but that the resulting misquotation was not defamatory; (2) other passages in the article were false and defamatory, but there was no evidence that Malcolm knew those were false or had serious doubts as to their truth. Would these findings meet the Court's requirement that there be a deliberate alteration that "results in a material change in the meaning conveyed by the statement"?  Why did the Court stop short of requiring a finding that the changed meaning is defamatory?  Does its analysis of specific quotations suggest that the latter is in fact the test?

2.  The district court held that even if Malcolm could be held liable, the *New Yorker* and the book publisher could not because Malcolm's actual malice, if any, could not be attributed to them.  Neither the Court of Appeals nor the Supreme Court considered that issue.  Principles of *respondeat superior* may make an employer liable for the actual malice of an employee, but Malcolm apparently was a freelancer.

3.  When *Masson* came before the U.S. Court of Appeals for the Ninth Circuit on remand from the Supreme Court, the court held that *The New Yorker* and Malcolm had to stand trial for the alleged defamation caused by the altering of the quotations.  A publisher which, in investigating a story's accuracy, learns facts casting doubt as to that accuracy, "may not ignore those doubts, even though it had no duty to conduct the investiga- tion in the first place," the court said.  In its first opinion on the case in 1989, the Ninth Circuit had applied the incremental harm doctrine, saying the "intellectual gigolo" quote was not actionable because any harm rendered by the quote was nominal or non-existent in view of the unchallenged or verifiably accurate statements made by Masson.  The Supreme Court had rejected the applicability of the incremental harm doctrine pursuant to the First Amendment but left open the possibility that the doctrine could be recognized under state law.  The Ninth Circuit declined to apply the doctrine, saying, "We believe the California Supreme Court would agree."  Masson v. The New Yorker Magazine, Inc., 960 F.2d 896, 20 Med.L.Rptr. 1009 (9th Cir.1992).

4.  Amidst much publicity, the Masson libel trial ended in a June 1993 mistrial.  Jurors had found that Janet Malcolm had fabricated five quotations and that two of them were libelous, but that *The New Yorker* did not know that Malcolm's profile of Masson contained errors and could not be held liable.  The mistrial resulted from the jurors' inability to reach a unanimous decision on damages.  The judge ordered a new trial on all issues but found that author Malcolm was an independent contractor.  Judgment in favor of the magazine was stayed pending the new trial, making it seem unlikely that there will be any verdict against

*The New Yorker.* Masson v. New Yorker Magazine, Inc., 832 F.Supp. 1350 (N.D.Cal.1993).

5. Diesen v. Hessburg, 455 N.W.2d 446, 17 Med.L.Rptr. 1849 (1990), cert. denied, 498 U.S. 1119 (1991), has been described as the "mirror image" of *Masson.* Donald Diesen, a former county attorney, claimed to have been libeled by articles in the *Duluth News–Tribune* concerning his record in prosecuting cases of domestic abuse. Diesen said that *Masson* involved the issue of allegedly defamatory statements in which the gist is right but the details wrong, but that his case involved a question of getting the details right but the gist wrong. Although a trial court had awarded Diesen a total of $785,000 in damages, the Minnesota Supreme Court reversed, holding that an allegedly false implication arising out of true statements is generally not actionable in defamation by a public official plaintiff against a media defendant.

6. In Brooks v. American Broadcasting Companies, Inc., 999 F.2d 167, 21 Med.L.Rptr. 1756 (6th Cir.1993), cert. denied, 114 S.Ct. 609 (1993), the U.S. Court of Appeals affirmed a trial court's directed verdict in favor of ABC and Geraldo Rivera related to a "20/20" segment. The plaintiff had testified that Rivera had told him, "I know you're not a hit man," several weeks before the allegedly defamatory segment, but the court ruled that, "A district court is not required to accept 'unsupported, self-serving testimony' as evidence to create a jury question as to negligence."

### c. The Privilege of Neutral Reportage

One federal case suggests the possibility of a First Amendment privilege that differs from the *Times–Gertz* variety. In the case, Edwards v. National Audubon Society, Inc., 556 F.2d 113, 2 Med.L.Rptr. 1849 (2d Cir.), cert. denied sub nom. Edwards v. New York Times Co., 434 U.S. 1002, 3 Med.L.Rptr. 1560 (1977), a *New York Times* nature reporter was following the continuing dispute between the Audubon Society and the chemical industry over the impact of various pesticides on birds. Based in part on the fact that annual bird counts conducted by the Audubon Society showed increasing numbers, some scientists retained by the industry argued that pesticides were not harmful. The Society believed that the higher numbers were due to more watchers with more skill using better observation areas.

An editorial in a Society publication asserted that whenever members heard a scientist use the bird count in an argument "you are in the presence of someone who is being paid to lie, or is parroting something he knows little about." The reporter called the Society and, the jury found, was told the names of five scientists that Society officials had in mind. The reporter then wrote a story accurately reporting the dispute and stating that a Society official had said that the scientists referred to in the editorial included five the reporter then named. In a suit by the scientists, the court held that an accurate report of this nature could not constitutionally lead to a libel judgment against the newspaper:

At stake in this case is a fundamental principle. Succinctly stated, when a responsible, prominent organization like the National Audubon Society makes serious charges against a public figure, the First Amendment protects the accurate and disinterested reporting of those charges, regardless of the reporter's private views regarding their validity. [  ] What is newsworthy about such accusations is that they were made. We do not believe that the press may be required under the First Amendment to suppress newsworthy statements merely because it has serious doubts regarding their truth. Nor must the press take up cudgels against dubious charges in order to publish them without fear of liability for defamation. [  ] The public interest in being fully informed about controversies that often rage around sensitive issues demands that the press be afforded the freedom to report such charges without assuming responsibility for them.

The contours of the press's right of neutral reportage are, of course, defined by the principle that gives life to it. Literal accuracy is not a prerequisite: if we are to enjoy the blessings of a robust and unintimidated press, we must provide immunity from defamation suits where the journalist believes, reasonably and in good faith, that his report accurately conveys the charges made. [  ] It is equally clear, however, that a publisher who in fact espouses or concurs in the charges made by others, or who deliberately distorts these statements to launch a personal attack of his own on a public figure, cannot rely on a privilege of neutral reportage. In such instances he assumes responsibility for the underlying accusations. [  ]

It is clear here, that Devlin reported Audubon's charges fairly and accurately. He did not in any way espouse the Society's accusations: indeed, Devlin published the maligned scientists' outraged reactions in the same article that contained the Society's attack. The *Times* article, in short, was the exemplar of fair and dispassionate reporting of an unfortunate but newsworthy contretemps. Accordingly, we hold that it was privileged under the First Amendment.

What are the limits of the *Edwards* principle? It was distinguished in Dixson v. Newsweek, Inc., 562 F.2d 626, 3 Med.L.Rptr. 1123 (10th Cir.1977), on the ground that *Edwards* involved public figures whereas Mr. Dixson was a private citizen. Are there times when the public should be informed of charges that are not made by a "responsible, prominent organization"? What is the test for whether a report of a particular charge is "newsworthy"? What level of error in the report, if any, should deprive the reporter of the privilege?

Some courts have rejected the neutral reportage defense as inconsistent with *St. Amant,* since *Edwards* would allow one who reports a story that he knows to be false or has serious doubts about, to be protected from liability. Dickey v. CBS, Inc., 583 F.2d 1221, 4 Med.L.Rptr. 1353 (3d Cir.1978).

One can only conjecture about whether the neutral reportage privilege retains much vitality. In the 1970s and 1980s, some courts adopted the standard and some flatly rejected it. An example of the former is Barry v. Time, Inc., 584 F.Supp. 1110, 10 Med.L.Rptr. 1809 (N.D.Cal. 1984). An example of the latter is Postill v. Booth Newspapers, Inc., 118 Mich.App. 608, 325 N.W.2d 511, 518, 8 Med.L.Rptr. 2222 (1982).

Note that the record libel privilege discussed earlier is a state privilege that can be limited by state statutes and decisions. In New York, for example, the relevant statute requires "official proceedings" before a privilege comes into play—and the New York courts have not expanded that privilege. Thus, in *Edwards,* the state statute did not apply.

## C.  REMEDIES FOR DEFAMATION

### 1.  INJUNCTIONS

Injunctions are generally unavailable for reasons discussed in Chafee's Government and Mass Communication 91–92 (1947): "One man's judgment is not to be trusted to determine what people can read. . . . So our law thinks it better to let the defamed plaintiff take his damages for what they are worth than to entrust a single judge (or even a jury) with the power to put a sharp check on the spread of possible truth." Furthermore, there are gradations of partial truth that are too subtle for a blanket injunction.

### 2.  REPLY

If the plaintiff completes the obstacle course we have described, damages are the only available remedy of any importance. The right of reply mentioned by Justice Brennan in *Rosenbloom* and *Gertz* would allow the victim of the defamation to respond in his own words in the offending publication, but states rarely require this, and such a requirement now appears to have serious constitutional problems. Miami Herald Pub. Co. v. Tornillo will be discussed in Chapter XIV. The role of reply in broadcasting, will be discussed in Chapters XIV and XVI.

### 3.  RETRACTION

The common law itself had some rules that tended to reduce the amount of damages recoverable in defamation. They were called "partial" defenses because they did not defeat liability but only reduced the size of the award. At common law if the defendant voluntarily *retracted* the statement, that fact was admissible to show that the plaintiff had not been damaged as badly as he claimed. It might also show that the defendant had not acted maliciously in the first place. Some states have enacted retraction statutes that grant further protection to mass media defendants. These apply to media only because of the requirement that the retraction be published promptly and with the same prominence as the defamation. It would be meaningless to make the retraction privilege available to media such as books and motion pictures, and the effectiveness of retraction varies even among those media that are covered in most states. It is generally thought, for example, that a retraction in the same space in a newspaper or magazine is more likely to reach the audience that read the original defamation than would most retractions over radio or television of a broadcast defamation.

The statutes vary in covering those who defame innocently, carelessly or maliciously. What they have in common is a requirement that the prospective plaintiff demand a retraction shortly after the defamation. If the publisher complies within a similar period of time, then the plaintiff may recover only his special damages, and no general damages. If the retraction is not published within the time limit, the plaintiff may recover whatever damages the common law allowed—subject now to the damage limitations of *Gertz*.

The National Conference of Commissioners on Uniform State Laws has proposed a new "Uniform Correction or Clarification of Defamation Act" designed to encourage prompt retractions. For the media, the incentive to run prompt retractions would be that plaintiffs, if the libel had been corrected, would be able to collect only for "provable economic loss"—eliminating awards for loss of reputation and awards for punitive damages. Predictably, media attorneys applauded the proposal, and plaintiffs' attorneys criticized. Attorney John J. Walsh, for example, said a damage award provides one of the few ways the public can punish the press. The New York Times, Aug. 9, 1993 at D–10. See the proposed statute in Appendix F.

## D.  CRIMINAL LIBEL AND GROUP LIBEL

### 1.  CRIMINAL LIBEL

Criminal libel is not generally available although it is part of the law in most states. California's version, which was typical, declared a libel to be "a malicious defamation" that tended to blacken the memory of the dead or of one who is alive. Malice was presumed "if no justifiable motive" was shown. Truth could be put in evidence and if the matter was "true, and was published with good motives and for justifiable ends, the party shall be acquitted." Such actions have been defended as deterring breaches of the peace—particularly when the defamed person is dead and no civil action will lie.

Criminal libel had already fallen into disuse before *Garrison*, p. 110, *supra*. The strictures placed on the action in that case diminished still further its usefulness. The role of the action is even more doubtful when it is used by prosecutors in behalf of famous or powerful persons who do not wish to bring a civil action themselves. This was the situation in 1976 when a state court declared the California criminal libel law unconstitutional because of its limitations on the defense of truth and its presumption of malice.  Because other states have taken the same path, criminal libel no longer appears to be a serious risk to publishers.

Recall *R.A.V.*, p. 48, *supra*, in which the Supreme Court in 1992 struck down as unconstitutionally overbroad a St.Paul ordinance making it a crime to engage in speech or behavior likely to arouse "anger or alarm" on the basis of "race, color, creed, religion or gender."

## 2.  GROUP LIBEL STATUTES

The main concern in the debate over group libel has been the hazards of unrestricted hate propaganda.  Curbs on group defamation have been advocated to reduce friction among racial, religious and ethnic groups.  As early as 1917 some states enacted criminal group libel laws for that purpose.  The Nazi defamation of minority groups, and conspicuous racial tensions in the United States, brought renewed attention to group libel laws in the 1940s and 1950s. David Riesman's "Democracy and Defamation: the Control of Group Libel," 42 Columbia L.Rev. 727 (1942), revived the debate as to the efficacy of group libel laws as a means of reducing group hatred and preventing the spread of socially disruptive attitudes.

The most common method of confronting group libel has been the enactment of criminal laws directed specifically at the problem.  Such laws typically prohibit communications that are abusive or offensive toward a group or that tend to arouse hatred, contempt or ridicule of the group.  Penalties have ranged from a fine of $50 or 30 days imprisonment, to $10,000 or two years in prison.

Beauharnais v. Illinois, 343 U.S. 250 (1952), is the only Supreme Court decision to review the constitutionality of group libel legislation.  The Court, 5–4, affirmed a conviction under Illinois' 1917 group libel statute.  The law prohibited publications portraying "depravity, criminality, unchastity, or lack of virtue of a class of citizens, of any race, color, creed, or religion" that subjected those described to "contempt, derision, or obloquy or which is productive of breach of the peace or riots."  Beauharnais, the president of an organization called the "White Circle League," had distributed leaflets calling on the mayor and city council to halt the "further encroachment, harassment and invasion of white people, their property, neighborhoods and persons, by the Negro."  The flyer also included an application for membership in the League and a call for a million white people to unite, adding that: "If persuasion and the need to prevent the white race from becoming mongrelized by the negro will not unite us, then the aggressions  .  .  .  rapes, robberies, knives, guns and marijuana of the negro, surely will."

Justice Frankfurter's opinion for the Court treated the statute as "a form of criminal libel law" and accepted the *dictum* of *Chaplinsky*, p. 48, *supra*, that libel was one of those "well-defined and narrowly limited classes of speech, the prevention and punishment of which has never been thought to raise any constitutional problem." He traced the history of violent and destructive racial tension in Illinois and concluded that it would "deny experience" to say that the statute was without reason. He disposed of the First Amendment question in a single paragraph near the end of his opinion:

> Libelous utterances not being within the area of constitutionally protected speech, it is unnecessary, either for us or for the State courts, to consider the issue behind the phrase "clear and present danger." Certainly no one would contend that obscene speech, for example, may be punished only upon a showing of such circumstances. Libel, as we have seen, is in the same class.

Of the four dissenters, only Justices Black and Douglas addressed the First Amendment problems that the majority had cast aside by excluding the whole area of libel from First Amendment protection. Justice Black analyzed the decision as extending the scope of the law of criminal libel from "the narrowest of areas" involving "purely private feuds" to "discussions of matters of public concern." This was an invasion of the First Amendment's absolute prohibition of laws infringing the freedom of public discussion. Justice Douglas concurred in Justice Black's opinion and wrote separately to emphasize that he would have required a demonstration that the "peril of speech" was "clear and present." He agreed with Justice Black that allowing a legislature to regulate "within reasonable limits" the right of free speech was "an ominous and alarming trend." Only a half-dozen states retain group defamation statutes. Many experts believe such statutes are unconstitutional, and they are not being enforced.

Group libel statutes also raise practical objections. Group libel prosecutions normally involve issues on which the community is sharply divided. The incidence as well as the outcome of prosecutions may thus depend on which segments of the community are represented in the office of the prosecuting attorney and on the jury. Moreover, a defendant could use the trial to promote his views and might well benefit regardless of the result: an acquittal would validate his viewpoint, while a conviction would make him a martyr whose civil liberties had been violated. These difficulties have led most commentators and many representatives of minority groups to oppose group libel legislation.

## E. PRACTICAL CONSIDERATIONS FOR MEDIA DEFENDANTS

### 1. HEADING OFF LIBEL SUITS

Recent research among libel plaintiffs suggests that many of them, unhappy though they may be when they realize that something harmful and erroneous has been published about them, are not immediately inclined to sue the media. Too frequently, people who have been defamed become angry enough to sue only after they have been treated curtly or even rudely when they tried to get the errors corrected.

Keeping this in mind, media attorneys and managers are today trying harder to prepare their employees for better handling of complaints. Such complaints should be taken seriously, and the complainer should be handled with courtesy and care. Usually that means that the complaint should be referred to a senior staff member trained in handling such complaints.

Apologies and retractions, when appropriate, can help to head off law suits before they occur. That is normally to the advantage of both the potential plaintiff and the media defendant. Defendants will, of course, have to use care in making apologies or retractions; should the potential plaintiff become an actual plaintiff, the admission may be used against the defendant in court. Publication of the correct information without embellishment is sometimes the best approach.

Professors Randall Bezanson, Gilbert Cranberg and John Soloski of the University of Iowa have contributed to the understanding of libel plaintiffs through a major study and a number of publications. See, R. Bezanson, G. Cranberg and J. Soloski, Libel Law and the Press: Myth and Reality (1987).

## 2.  MEGAVERDICTS

Much has been written in recent years about huge libel suits and jury verdicts for millions of dollars sometimes characterized as "megaverdicts" or "monster verdicts." To some extent the media play into the hands of plaintiffs seeking publicity through multi-million dollar suits, because such amounts are the stuff of which headlines are made. Much media attention was given to a $1.6 million damage verdict in 1981 in Carol Burnett's suit against the *National Enquirer*. That amount, which seemed huge at the time, was dwarfed by the $120 million for which Army General William Westmoreland sued CBS as a result of a 1982 documentary. The Westmoreland suit garnered many more newspaper headlines. By the end of the 1980's, large jury libel judgments had become more commonplace, averaging $1.5 million for the decade. Today the average is much higher. A study by the Libel Defense Resource Center showed that jury libel judgments against the media in 1990 and 1991, had jumped to an average of $9 million. San Francisco Chronicle, Sept. 3, 1993 at Al.

What press headlines usually fail to point out is how many large damage verdicts are *reversed* or *reduced* by trial and appellate courts. For many years no damage award over $500,000 was paid. Most of the damage verdicts that had been the subject of big headlines were subsequently reduced. In the Burnett case, for example, the original award was reduced to $200,000; then, with the possibility of a new trial on the damage amount, Burnett and the *National Enquirer* settled out of court for an undisclosed amount rumored to be about $400,000—still only one-fourth the amount of the original award. The Westmoreland case was settled out of court during the trial; no money changed hands between the litigants, but both sides had incurred major legal expenses.

On the other hand, some large damage awards *are* being upheld by appellate courts. In 1988 the Supreme Court denied *certiorari* in *Brown & Williamson* Tobacco Corp. v. Jacobson, 827 F.2d 1119, 14 Med.L.Rptr. 1497 (7th Cir.1987) thereby letting stand a $3.05 million damage award against CBS and television anchorman Walter Jacobson. The award was four times as large as any libel award ever upheld by the federal appellate courts previously.

Brown & Williamson manufactures Viceroy cigarettes. Walter Jacobson, an anchorman on CBS-owned station WBBM–TV, Chicago, in delivering a nightly editorial segment titled "Walter Jacobson's Perspective," commented on the cigarette industry. While discussing attempts by cigarette manufacturers to attract young people to smoking, Jacobson referred to cigarette manufacturers as "slicksters" trying to link smoking with "pot, wine, beer, and sex." He said that "Viceroy slicksters" are "not slicksters, they're liars." The court held the statement to be fact, not opinion.

Although Jacobson's remarks related to a report by the Federal Trade Commission about cigarette manufacturers' advertising strategy aimed at young people, the court held that the remarks were not protected by a privilege of fair reporting because of significant inaccuracies. Brown & Williamson attempted to prove that Jacobson's charges were false by introducing every Viceroy advertisement published between 1975 and 1982. An executive of one of their advertising agencies, Ted Bates and Company, testified that Brown & Williamson had never asked the agency to utilize a "pot," wine, beer and sex strategy in developing advertisements. The claim that Viceroy had used such strategies was false. Furthermore, Jacobson had said the Federal Trade Commission had said Viceroy had done these things, but the FTC had not. Jacobson used the term "children" to refer to the objects of the strategy rather than "young smokers" and "starters"—the terms used in the FTC report.

Acknowledging that Brown and Williamson was, for purpose of libel litigation, a public figure, the court held that the destruction of critical documents concerning the broadcast and demonstration that the reporter knew a researcher had been unable to find actual "pot, wine, beer, and sex" ads was sufficient to warrant a finding that the broadcast was made with actual malice. The court found that Jacobson's researcher had intentionally destroyed critical documents including an 18–page sample script for Jacobson's remarks and the researcher's annotated copy of the FTC report. The court said that, ". . . [H]e destroyed various documents that in all likelihood would have established that both he and Jacobson were aware that the 'tobacco industry hooks children' Perspective was false at the time that it was delivered."

The trial jury awarded the plaintiff company $3 million in compensatory damages and $2.5 million in punitive damages. That had subsequently been reduced, but the court of appeals reinstated an award of $1 million in compensatory damages, $2 million in punitive damages against CBS, and $50,000 in punitive damages against Jacobson. In doing so, the court noted that the broadcast's audience was 2.5 million, that the network's net worth exceeded $1 billion and that the reporter's net worth exceeded $5 million. The court also noted that Brown & Williamson's attorney's fees were $1,360,000 prior to post-trial motions.

Such damage awards as that in *Brown & Williamson* may encourage libel plaintiffs to file more and larger libel suits, and there may be a chilling effect on both large media organizations, who may fear that they will be the targets of such suits because of their "deep pockets," and on smaller organizations who seldom consult their legal counsel and sometimes are afraid to publish because they fear the kinds of immobilizing libel suits they read about.

More highly publicized than the *Brown & Williamson* verdict was a jury award of $19.3 million, including $5 million in punitive damages, in 1986 to entertainer Wayne Newton. Subsequent court rulings reduced the damages, and a Federal appeals court overturned the award entirely in 1990. Newton had charged that three NBC news broadcasts in 1980–81 falsely linked him to organized crime figures. A three-judge panel of the United States Court of Appeals for the Ninth Circuit found there was insufficient evidence to show that NBC had either prior knowledge of falsity or reckless disregard of the truth. Newton v. National Broadcasting Co., 930 F.2d 662 (9th Cir.1990).

Despite jury verdicts over $20 million, no award anywhere near that much money has been upheld by appellate courts. The largest upheld have been the *Brown & Williamson* verdict ($3.05 million) and $2.76 million ($200,000 actual damages plus $2 million punitive damages plus $570,000 in accrued interest) paid in 1989 by the *Pittsburgh Post–Gazette* to attorney Richard DiSalle as a result of a 1979 article repeating allegations that DiSalle had made fraudulent changes in a client's will. The *Post–Gazette* paid the money to DiSalle after the Supreme Court had declined to review the case. DiSalle v. P.G. Publishing Co., 375 Pa.Super. 510, 544 A.2d 1345, 15 Med.L.Rptr. 1873 (1988), cert. denied 492 U.S. 906 (1989).

Huge damage awards in a few media cases since *Brown & Williamson* have been highly publicized. The largest jury award was one for $58 million against WFAA–TV in Dallas; the station had been sued by former district attorney Vic Feazell in a case involving television reports alleging the taking of payments to quash drunken driving cases. Feazell and WFAA's owner, A.H. Belo Corporation, subsequently settled for an undisclosed sum. In another case, Attorney Richard A. Sprague was awarded $2.5 million in compensatory damages and $31.5 million in punitive damages by a 1990 jury in a libel suit after *The Philadelphia Inquirer* alleged improprieties in his conduct as a prosecutor; the trial judge refused to overturn or reduce the verdict. The New York Times, Sept. 20, 1992 at 1–34. As of October 1993, an appeal was pending.

A New York damage award of nearly $15.5 million was averted on a second appeal when the state's highest court overturned the verdict because of a problem with the trial judge's instructions to the jury. Restaurant owner John Prozeralik had sued the owner of Buffalo TV station WKBW after it broadcast reports linking him with organized crime. Prozeralik v. Capital Cities Communications, Inc., 188 A.D.2d 178, 593 N.Y.S.2d 662, 21 Med.L.Rptr. 1073 (1993).

*The Supreme Court enters the scene.* Concerned with high damage awards, some media organizations have joined other businesses in asking the Supreme Court for constitutional limits on such awards, thus far without success. In one of several cases in which parties have raised the question of whether the Excessive Fines Clause of the Eighth Amendment applies to awards of punitive damages in civil actions, the Supreme Court affirmed a $6 million award (more than 100 times the plaintiff's actual damages) in a case involving a trash collection business. The Court held that the Excessive Fines Clause does not apply to awards of punitive damages between private parties, although it left open the possibility of a challenge to excessive punitive awards under the Fourteenth Amendment's Due Process Clause. Browning–Ferris Industries of Vermont Inc. v. Kelco Disposal Inc., 492 U.S. 257 (1989).

In another setback to media hopes of curbing large punitive damage awards, the Supreme Court in 1991 upheld an $840,000 punitive damage award in an Alabama insurance case that had resulted from an insurance fraud that deprived the victim of $3,800 in medical coverage. A coalition of 19 media groups had filed an amicus brief arguing that "Punitive damage awards in libel cases involving matters of public concern are irreconcilable with the requirements of the First Amendment." By their 7–1 decision upholding the damage award, the members of the Court left juries broad discretion over such awards. Pacific Mutual Life Insurance Co. v. Haslip, 499 U.S. 1 (1991).

Many civil litigators had hoped the Supreme Court would revisit its decision in *Haslip* in 1993, when it decided TXO Production Corp. v. Alliance Resources Corp., 113 S.Ct. 2711 (1993), a case that arose out of TXO's suit to clear a purported cloud on Alliance's title to oil and gas rights and Alliance's subsequent counterclaim for slander of title. A jury awarded Alliance $19,000 in compensatory damages and $10 million in punitive damages—more than 500 times the compensatory damage award. The Supreme Court was deeply divided, and the six-member majority wrote three separate opinions, but they affirmed the punitive damage award. Seven justices recognized at least the existence of some substantive due process constraints on punitive damage awards, but Justices Scalia and Thomas said there are no substantive due process limits to such awards.

### 3. Non-Financial Toll

A rare glimpse of the non-financial toll on libel defendants was seen when CBS correspondent Mike Wallace said in a 1990 television interview that he was treated for depression and thought about suicide during the Westmoreland libel trial in 1985. WNYW–TV, May 15, 1990, as reported by the Associated Press.

### 4. Libel Insurance

When a court awards damages against a media defendant in a libel suit, it is legally irrelevant whether that defendant carries libel insurance. As a practical matter, of course, it is extremely important. Media employers are often reluctant to be candid about their insurance, even with their own employees. Certainly employers do not want their employees to take unnecessary risks, and media employers typically value their reputations for accuracy so they do not want to lose libel suits even if they do carry insurance. Media libel insurance policies typically provide for a deductible amount which is paid by the insured before the insurance coverage comes into play. The higher the deductible, the lower the premiums that the employer pays for the insurance. Media employers who could afford to sustain losses of $50,000 or $100,000 on each damage award against them or who can afford the legal expenses might elect to be "self-insured" for those amounts and to carry insurance policies with the $50,000 or $100,000 deductible clause to cover them for any awards or expenses greater than those amounts. The increasing size of trial court awards for libel damages has, inevitably, led to an increase in libel insurance premiums; that increase in the premiums in turn has a negative effect on virtually every insured media organization—not just those that are sued.

The *Pittsburgh Post–Gazette*'s dealings with one of its insurance companies proved difficult in the DiSalle case. The newspaper's primary insurance company paid it the full $1 million limit of its policy (of which about half was used for legal fees); but the company that carried its excess liability policy refused to honor the newspaper's insurance claim, maintaining that Pennsylvania public policy barred it from covering punitive damages. The newspaper then sued its insurance company, and the company agreed to a settlement under which it paid the newspaper $2 million but made no formal admission of liability. Editor & Publisher, Nov. 25, 1989 at 18.

### 5. Defense Costs

Even the media defendants who win their cases in trial or appellate courts may spend large sums of money defending themselves. In major cases some defendants have spent several million dollars defending themselves. While vindication in court may seem ideal, the cost of lawyers and the cost in terms of one's own employees' time may make it tempting to settle out of court with the plaintiff—even where there is substantial likelihood that the defendant would ultimately prevail should the case be decided by an appellate court. A media defendant who developed the reputation of settling out of court too easily could become a target for nuisance suits brought by plaintiffs who did not really expect to win but hoped defendants would buy them off by settling out of court without ever going to trial. Some major media organizations have adopted the position of never settling out of court for just that reason, but such a posture is difficult to maintain in an instance where the media organization really did publish a false statement, particularly where the plaintiff is a private figure who does not need to prove actual malice and who has real damages. Furthermore, the size of the verdicts of recent years makes the risk of going to trial all the greater and increases the temptation to settle out of court.

Some observers in recent years have expressed the fear that libel suits, partially because of high defense costs, could be used to harass the media. In Liberty Lobby v. Dow Jones & Co., 838 F.2d 1287, 14 Med.L.Rptr. 2249 (1988), the court of appeals upheld the dismissal of a $50 million libel suit against the publisher of the *Wall Street Journal.* For the three-judge panel, Judge Robert Bork wrote, "This suit epitomizes one of the most troubling aspects of modern libel litigation: The use of the libel complaint as a weapon to harass." The newspaper had described Liberty Lobby as an anti-Semitic group. Bork noted that Liberty Lobby had filed a number of other law suits about reports characterizing the group as racially prejudiced or anti-Semitic and that none of those suits had been successful.

### 6. STATUTE OF LIMITATIONS AND JURISDICTION

As indicated earlier, libel statutes give plaintiffs a limited period of time in which to bring suit, often one year. Beyond a year, it might become increasingly difficult for a plaintiff to prove the harm suffered, and it might also become increasingly difficult for the defendant to offer a successful defense. The Supreme Court decision in Keeton v. Hustler Magazine, 465 U.S. 770, 10 Med.L.Rptr. 1405 (1984), makes the statute of limitations a serious concern for media organizations whose publications or audiences are in more than one state. In *Keeton*, a resident of New York State brought a libel suit in New Hampshire against *Hustler Magazine*, even though the publisher was incorporated in Ohio and its principal place of business was in California. Her case had already been dismissed in Ohio as barred by the statute of limitations. New Hampshire then had a six-year limitation period. Use of New Hampshire's "long-arm statute" was unanimously upheld by the Supreme Court, because of the magazine's circulation of 10,000–15,000 copies in that state. The decision obviously has serious implications for potential media defendants, who may have to be prepared to defend themselves in libel suits long after the period for a suit has expired under the statute of limitations in the state in which they have their headquarters.

The Court in *Keeton* held that the New Hampshire courts had sufficient basis for jurisdiction even if they applied the so-called "single publication rule"—a principle under which only one legal action can be maintained for damages resulting from any single publication, all damages suffered in all jurisdictions can be recovered in the one action, and a judgment for or against the plaintiff upon the merits of any action for damages bars any other action for damages between the same parties in all jurisdictions.

In another case decided the same day, the Supreme Court faced a different issue involving jurisdiction. In Calder v. Jones, 465 U.S. 783, 10 Med.L.Rptr. 1401 (1984), the Court upheld the California courts' jurisdiction in a suit brought by actress Shirley Jones (a California resident) against a Florida corporation which publishes *The National Enquirer* and a reporter and editor for the publication. Although the reporter frequently travelled to California on business, the editor did not. The Court noted that California was the focal point of the story and that the defendants' actions were aimed at California, and that they could reasonably expect being "haled into court" in California. Merely being an employee of the magazine, however, would not be a sufficient basis for upholding jurisdiction by the California courts.

## 7. EVIDENCE AND WITNESSES

Attorneys representing media clients sometimes have a difficult choice to make: if they scare the journalists too much about possible libel suits, they may create their own chilling effect; but if they ignore the subject, the journalists may fall into traps that can make the defense of a libel suit more troubling. Plaintiffs who are public officials or public figures will, of course, be seeking evidence that the defendant published with knowledge of falsity or with a high degree of awareness of probable falsity. Internal memos or margin notes written on copy expressing doubts about the facts in a story can be just the kind of evidence the plaintiff will seek. Newsroom conversations about doubts—even doubts in one's own mind—may be discoverable; we will discuss this issue in Chapter XI. In an age in which libel litigation is common, journalists publishing material that may damage a person's reputation would be wise to think of the story subject as a potential plaintiff and to be as sure of their facts as possible. Just as such nationally-known journalists as Dan Rather and Mike Wallace have been called to discuss their stories from the witness stand, younger journalists may have to do the same and should be unafraid to do so if they have followed accepted journalistic practices. (The latter can present interesting questions, because professional standards in journalism vary. Codes of ethics—like the code of The Society of Professional Journalists (formerly Sigma Delta Chi) in Appendix C of this book—may be of some use. Principles such as getting at least two independent sources before publishing or broadcasting damaging information may be widely followed but still are not provably a part of a universally accepted code of conduct for the journalist. The behavior of the "prudent publisher," to use the term used by Justice Harlan in *Butts*, p. 112, *supra*, may vary with the individual journalist's concept of just what constitutes prudence.)

## 8. EXPERT WITNESSES

Attorneys for both plaintiffs and defendants in libel cases have in recent years sometimes put expert witnesses on the witness stands, when there is a question of negligence by the media. Plaintiffs seek witnesses who will testify that the defendant departed from professional standards; defendants counter with witnesses who will testify that mistakes may happen in even the most professional news operation and that the defendant did not depart from the standards of the profession. Some witnesses have been paid quite well for the time they spent preparing to testify and testifying. Because journalists themselves are often quite reluctant to testify against fellow journalists, some plaintiffs and defendants have sought journalism professors as witnesses. The professors are divided on the ethics of testifying in such cases—some believing that it is an appropriate way to share their expertise and others believing that it is an inappropriate role for an academic. It is far from clear that the testimony of expert witnesses on either side of the case is effective. Although trial judges and jurors may think they need the advice of doctors as expert witnesses in medical malpractice suits, judges and jurors seem to feel that they can understand journalism sufficiently well without the testimony of the expert witnesses. And, as a practical matter, some attorneys say, the contradictory testimony of the witnesses on the two sides of the case tends to negate the effectiveness of either.

# Chapter IV

# PRIVACY

Defamation and invasion of privacy are sometimes treated together in law courses as related rights to protect one's dignity. In defamation, we balance the right of freedom of expression against the right of individuals to protect their reputations. In privacy, we balance the right of freedom of expression against the right of individuals to be let alone. Although people tend to think of privacy as a basic human right and many assume that it is in the Constitution, the word privacy never appears there. Compared to defamation, privacy is a relatively new legal concept with many facets.

Concerns for privacy in the 1990s are diverse—involving such varied issues as the dissemination of personal credit information via computerized systems, electronic eavesdropping, the protection of newsrooms from police searches, release of personal information about individuals by government and a right to know what is in one's own academic records. Some of these issues we will address elsewhere in this book, because they are related to other topics. The protection of newsrooms from police searches, for example, is dealt with in Chapter XI on journalist's privilege because the "privacy" of the newsroom is directly related to the confidentiality of journalists' sources and their notes. Some of the issues, such as dissemination of personal credit information, normally do not involve the mass media and are beyond the scope of this book.

In this chapter we will be concerned primarily with invasion of privacy as a tort, or civil wrong or injury. Although the recognition of privacy torts varies from state to state, scholars generally have recognized four different torts or branches of invasion of privacy. One of these relates to the newsgathering stage of the communications process: intruding on the plaintiff's physical solitude. It is akin to the tort of trespass. The other three torts or branches of invasion of privacy relate to the publication stage of the communications process. They are publication of embarrassing private (true) facts, putting the plaintiff in a false light in the public eye and appropriation of another's name or likeness for commercial or trade purposes. Of the four branches, the "false-light" tort comes the closest to the tort of defamation, because it is the only one that involves falsity. Because of the similarities between defamation and false-light invasion of privacy, some of the traditional defenses in defamation are also applicable to this branch of invasion of privacy—including truth. However, truth will not be a successful defense if the *context* in which an otherwise true statement is made creates a false light. Also, truth is not, obviously, a defense for publication of embarrassing private facts, because the fact that an embarrassing publication is true may just make it all the more embarrassing. Because defenses that are applicable vary with the branch of invasion of privacy being discussed, we shall touch on defenses at several different points in this chapter.

## A. HISTORICAL DEVELOPMENT

The idea that a right of privacy from the media should be legally protected can be traced to a law review article by Louis D. Brandeis and his law partner, Samuel D. Warren, The Right to Privacy, 4 Harv.L.Rev. 193 (1890), often considered the most influential law review article ever published. The authors, reacting to the editorial practices of Boston newspapers, made clear their concerns:

> The press is overstepping in every direction the obvious bounds of propriety and of decency. Gossip is no longer the resource of the idle and of the vicious, but has become a trade, which is pursued with industry as well as effrontery. To satisfy a prurient taste the details of sexual relations are spread broadcast in the columns of the daily papers. To occupy the indolent, column upon column is filled with idle gossip, which can only be procured by intrusion upon the domestic circle. . . . When personal gossip attains the dignity of print, and crowds the space available for matters of real interest to the community, what wonder that the ignorant and thoughtless mistake its relative importance. Easy of comprehension, appealing to that weak side of human nature which is never wholly cast down by the misfortunes and frailties of our neighbors, no one can be surprised that it usurps the place of interest in brains capable of other things. Triviality destroys at once robustness of thought and delicacy of feelings. No enthusiasm can flourish, no generous impulse can survive under its blighting influence.

Working with a variety of rather remote precedents from other areas of law, the authors developed an argument that courts should recognize an action for invasion of privacy by media publication.

The theory was rejected in the first major case to consider it. In Roberson v. Rochester Folding Box Co., 171 N.Y. 538, 64 N.E. 442 (1902), the defendants, a flour company and a box company, obtained a good likeness of the plaintiff, a pretty girl, and reproduced it on their advertising posters. Plaintiff said she was humiliated and suffered great distress. The court, 4–3, rejected a common law privacy action on grounds that suggested concern about innovating after so many centuries; an inability to see how the doctrine, once accepted, could be judicially limited to appropriate situations; and skepticism about finding liability for behavior that might actually please some potential "victims." The Warren and Brandeis article was discussed at length, but the court concluded that the precedents relied upon were too remote to sustain the proposed rights.

The outcry was immediate. At its next session, the New York legislature created a statutory right of privacy (New York Civil Rights Law, §§ 50 and 51). The basic provision was that "a person, firm or corporation that uses for advertising purposes, or the purposes of trade, the name, portrait or picture of any living person without having first obtained the written consent of such person, or if a minor of his or her parent or guardian, is guilty of a misdemeanor." The other section provided for an injunction and created an action for compensatory and punitive damages. The meaning of "advertising purposes" was clear, but the phrase "purposes of trade" was not self-explanatory. Eventually it came to mean that an accurate story carried as editorial (non-advertising) content was not actionable.

Other states, perhaps learning from the New York experience, slowly began to develop a common law right to privacy that was not influenced by statutory language and not limited to advertising invasions. In addition to an action for commercial use of one's name, the courts also developed actions for truthful uses of plaintiff's name that were thought to be outside the areas of legitimate public concern. The action for invasion of privacy by publication of true editorial material began to take hold during the 1920s and early 1930s.

Courts in the late 1930s became more attentive to the Supreme Court's expanding protection of expression. Operating on a common law level, they tended to expand protection for the media by taking a narrow view of what were legitimately private areas.

For the embarrassing private facts tort, the courts allowed a defense of *newsworthiness* to be expanded, because they were reluctant to impose normative standards of what should be newsworthy. Instead, they leaned toward a descriptive definition of newsworthiness that protected whatever editors had decided would interest their readers. By the 1960s some doubted whether the action for invasion of privacy had any remaining vitality.

It was precisely during the last part of the 1960s and the beginning of the 1970s, however, that privacy as a general social value was perceived to be threatened in different ways by the encroachment of computers, data banks and electronic devices, as well as the media. The concept of privacy also expanded as the Supreme Court dealt with birth control, abortion and other problems in the context of a right of privacy. This was bound to have an impact on the media aspects of privacy as well.

One result of the new thinking was to broaden the area of privacy protection.

## B.  THE BRANCHES OF INVASION OF PRIVACY

Because the Supreme Court has decided many fewer privacy cases than defamation cases, we will look in this section at some state court decisions, for purposes of illustration, in addition to the Supreme Court decisions.

### 1.  PUTTING THE PLAINTIFF IN A FALSE LIGHT

As indicated earlier, the tort of *putting the plaintiff in a false light in the public eye* is the privacy tort closest to defamation, because both involve publication of falsity.  There is a critical difference between the two, however:  the publication that results in a successful defamation action is *harmful* as well as false.  The publication that results in a successful false light invasion of privacy action may not be harmful in the sense of harming the plaintiff's reputation.  It may be just the opposite—a publication that falsely portrays the plaintiff to be better than he is in real life (i.e., a hero) or simply *different* than he is in real life.

In one example, a group used the plaintiff's name without authorization on a petition to the governor to veto a bill.  Although falsely stating that plaintiff had signed the petition would not be defamatory, the court found the situation actionable because it cast plaintiff in a false light.

It may be useful to distinguish several variations of false light.  Some cases involve allegations of *embellishment:* the defendant is alleged to have added something to a news or feature story to enhance it.  Other cases involve *contextual* false light or *distortion:* a statement or photograph appears out of context, giving an erroneous (and sometimes offensive) impression.  Still other cases involve *fictionalization:* as in a television "docudrama," real people are treated fictionally (sometimes with a disclaimer which may be ignored by the audience).  As you read the cases below, note which kind of false light is involved in each.

The first two Supreme Court decisions on alleged invasions of privacy by the mass media both happen to be false light cases—but of two different kinds.  They were Time, Inc. v. Hill, 385 U.S. 374, 1 Med.L.Rptr. 1791 (1967) and Cantrell v. Forest City Publishing Co., 419 U.S. 245, 1 Med.L.Rptr. 1815 (1974).

In 1952 James Hill and his family were held hostage in their home for 19 hours by three escaped convicts who apparently treated them decently.  The incident received extensive nationwide coverage.  Thereafter the Hills moved to another state, sought seclusion and refused to make public appearances.  A novel modeled in general on the event was published the following year.  In 1955 *Life* magazine in a short article announced that a play and a motion picture were being made from the novel, which they said was "inspired" by the Hill episode.  The play, "a heartstopping account of how a family rose to heroism in a crisis," would enable the public to see the Hill story "re-enacted."  Photographs in the magazine showed actors performing scenes from the play at the house at which the original events had occurred.  The Hills claimed that the story was inaccurate because the novel and the play showed the convicts committing violence on the father and uttering a "verbal sexual insult" at the daughter.

Suit was brought under the New York statute that required plaintiff to show that the article was being used for advertising purposes or for purposes of trade. A truthful article, no matter how unpleasant for the Hills, would not have been actionable. The state courts had previously indicated that falsity would show that the article was really for the purposes of trade and not for public enlightenment. The state courts allowed recovery after lengthy litigation.

The Supreme Court, by a fragile majority, decided that the privilege to comment on matters of public interest had constitutional protection (remember that the Court extended the *New York Times* rule to matters of public interest in *Rosenbloom*, p. 117, *supra*, in 1971, and then retreated from that position in *Gertz*, p. 118, *supra*, in 1974) and could not be lost by the introduction of falsity unless actual malice could be proved. Thus, the Hill family lost.

The decision should be viewed in the context of what was happening in the court's defamation decisions in the same period. This was only three years after the Court had decided, in *Sullivan*, p. 98, *supra*, that public officials would be required to prove actual malice in defamation cases. By 1967 thinking, the members of the Hill family were public figures—having become so involuntarily as the result of having been part of a newsworthy event. And 1967 was the same year in which the Court extended the actual malice rule of *Sullivan* to public figures like Wally Butts and former Army General Edwin Walker.

One should not miss the irony that the attorney who represented the Hill family before the Supreme Court was a man with a strong sense of privacy and considerable distaste for the media: then former Vice President, not-yet-President Richard M. Nixon.

It is far from clear that the Supreme Court today would reach the same decision in the Hill case. Under the criteria for determining public figure status in *Gertz* and subsequent cases, the members of the Hill family would surely be *private* figures. Prior to the single incident that brought them unwanted attention, they certainly were not widely known people likely to be classed as all-purpose public figures. Nor had they entered any public controversy with the intention of trying to influence its outcome, so they would not be classed as "vortex" public figures. Immediately after their release by the convicts, they may have had more access to the media than private figures usually do (they reportedly turned down an opportunity to appear on the Ed Sullivan network television show), but that had undoubtedly faded by the time the article in *Life* appeared. If the Hills were private figures and we were to apply post-*Gertz* defamation thinking to the privacy area, it would seem reasonable to say that as private figure false-light plaintiffs they should not have to prove actual malice. Depending on the state in which they sued, proof of fault, simple negligence, might suffice. For the Hill family, however, this sort of speculation becomes irrelevant as a practical matter, because their case has already been decided.

The next false-light privacy case decided by the Supreme Court was Cantrell v. Forest City Publishing Co. A reporter for *The Cleveland Plain Dealer* had written a prize-winning story about a bridge collapse that had killed 44 people, including Melvin Cantrell. Some months later the reporter returned to the Cantrell home for a follow-up on how the family coped with the disaster. Although Mrs. Cantrell was not present, her children were. The reporter's story failed to make clear that Mrs. Cantrell had been absent, and a reader presumably would have concluded just the opposite from the story, which said she "will talk neither about what happened nor about how they are doing. She wears the same mask of non-expression she wore at the funeral. She is a proud woman. Her world has changed. She says that after it happened, the people in town offered to help them out with money and they refused to take it." The family sought damages on a false-light privacy theory.

The Court, in an opinion by Justice Stewart, held that the First Amendment did not protect deliberate or reckless falsity (actual malice). He also observed that because the actual malice standard was met in this case, it was not an appropriate case in which to consider the hypothetical question of whether private figure plaintiffs like the Cantrells *had* to prove actual malice or might merely be asked to prove simple negligence. As Justice Stewart put it, it was not an appropriate occasion to "consider whether a State may constitutionally apply a more relaxed standard of liability for a publisher . . . of false statements injurious to a private individual under a false-light theory of privacy, or whether the constitutional standard announced in Time, Inc. v. Hill applies to all false-light cases." The decisions in *Gertz* and subsequent private figure defamation cases would certainly suggest that the Supreme Court might not demand proof of actual malice from private figures.

Justice Douglas was the sole dissenter in *Cantrell:* "Those who write the current news seldom have the objective, dispassionate point of view—or the time—of scientific analysts. They deal in fast-moving events and the need for 'spot reporting'. . . . [I]n such matters of public import such as the present news reporting, there must be freedom from damages lest the press be frightened into playing a more ignoble role than the Framers visualized."

*Defenses.* Many of the same defenses that can be used by media defendants in defamation cases might also be argued to have application in a false-light privacy case. Truth would be a strong defense unless the words in question were literally true but were used in such a context as to put the plaintiff in a false light. One kind of qualified privilege might be offered as a defense if one had quoted accurately from a record of an official proceeding. Privileged criticism or fair comment might work as defenses if the publication alleged to put the plaintiff in a false light was actually a statement of opinion rather than a statement of fact. The statute of limitations is always relevant to a false-light case or cases brought under any of the other privacy torts, but we will mention it only here. To a large extent, the applicability of the libel defenses in privacy cases is yet to be determined in the courts.

It might be noted here that two traditionally recognized defenses for invasion of privacy—consent and newsworthiness—have little or no application in false-light cases. A plaintiff would be unlikely to have *formally* consented to being portrayed in a false light, as by a signed model release, but an argument might be made that a plaintiff *tacitly* consented to being portrayed in a false light by behaving in a way which would create an erroneous impression or by failing to protest when previously portrayed in a false light. Newsworthiness is *not* a defense in false light cases, because erroneous information is not newsworthy; there is no public purpose to be served in its dissemination. Furthermore, as we shall see in the discussion at p. 209, *infra*, courts have changed their treatment of "newsworthiness" as a consideration.

### 2.   INTRUSION ON THE PLAINTIFF'S PHYSICAL SOLITUDE

As suggested earlier, intrusion on the plaintiff's physical solitude is the only one of the four branches of privacy that comes up in the context of *newsgathering* rather than in the context of publication. In the absence of any Supreme Court decision involving such an invasion of privacy by the mass media, we will look here at some cases decided in the lower courts as examples.

The major divisions of this branch of invasion of privacy reflect the type of consent problem involved. Within each subsection we consider the types of invasions that plaintiff may complain about. The most traditional are trespass (unpermitted entry) on land and theft of personal property. The claim is that the physical zone of privacy that surrounds each of us has been intruded upon—usually in an effort to obtain information that would otherwise not be available.

#### a.   *Invasions Without Express Consent*

*Trespass.* For centuries, the act of intentionally entering the land of another without consent has made the entrant liable for trespass. The civil damages included any actual harm done to the property and some damages for the symbolic invasion of the owner's or occupier's legal interest. If accompanied by ill will or spite or a desire to harm the owner, perhaps punitive damages as well were awarded. Comparable rules applied to a person who legally enters land but then remained on it against the wishes of the owner or occupier of the land.

In one clear case, the plaintiff alleged that his wife had committed suicide during the day; that when he returned to the house that evening he discovered that the screen over the kitchen window had been cut and that a photograph of his wife that had been on a table in the living room that morning had been taken. Although the plaintiff failed to prove that the defendant's reporters had committed the trespass, the court indicated that the only problem in the case was one of identification. The trespass and theft could not be defended even if there had been great public interest in the photograph. Metter v. Los Angeles Examiner, 35 Cal.App.2d 304, 95 P.2d 491 (1939).

In a later case, plaintiff land owner sued to prevent the defendant from entering plaintiff's land in search of a fragment of a pre-Revolutionary War statue of King George III.  The court observed that even if the defendant's goal were solely to engage in historical and archeological research, "that fact will not justify his entering upon the property of another without permission.  It is unquestioned that in today's world even archeologists must obtain permission from owners of property . . . before they can conduct their explorations."  Favorite v. Miller, 176 Conn. 310, 407 A.2d 974 (1978).

Sometimes the reporter may claim that he has authority to enter the property even though the owner has not expressly consented.  Two Florida cases present examples.

In Florida Publishing Co. v. Fletcher, 340 So.2d 914, 2 Med.L.Rptr. 1088 (Fla.1976), the plaintiff alleged that after she had left town on a trip, a fire broke out in her house that killed her 17–year–old daughter; that after the daughter's body was removed from the floor a silhouette was revealed; that defendant newspaper's photographer took a photograph of the silhouette; and that plaintiff first learned of the tragedy by reading the story in a newspaper and seeing the accompanying photographs.  In her claim for trespass, the depositions revealed that police and fire officials, as was their standard practice, invited press photographers and reporters to enter the house; that the media representatives entered through an open door without objection; and that they entered quietly and did no damage to the property.  The fire marshal wanted a clear picture of the silhouette to show that the body had been on the floor before the heat of the fire damaged the room.  After the official took one picture, he ran out of film and asked the newspaper photographer to take pictures for the official investigation.  He did so and also made copies for his own paper, which published them.

The defendant moved for summary judgment on the trespass claim.  Affidavits from various government and media sources stated that entering private property and inviting the press in this type of situation was common practice.  Plaintiff filed only her own affidavit and none from media or other experts.  She conceded that it was proper for the police and fire officials to enter and also admitted that no one had objected to the entry of the press.  The trial judge granted summary judgment because the affidavits "attest to the fact that it is common usage, custom and practice for news media to enter private premises and homes to report on matters of public interest or a public event."

The Florida Supreme Court agreed that implied consent covered the case.  Research showed that implied consent by custom and usage "do not rest upon the previous nonobjection to entry by the particular owner of the property in question but rest upon custom and practice generally."  In addition to the fact that here the press entered in response to an express invitation from public officials, the court stressed that this was the first case presenting the question.  "This, in itself, tends to indicate that the practice has been accepted by the general public since it is a widespread practice of longstanding." One judge dissented on jurisdictional grounds. The Supreme Court denied *certiorari*, 431 U.S. 930 (1977). Prof. Kent Middleton, in "Journalists, Trespass and Officials: Closing the Door of Florida Publishing Co. v. Fletcher," 16 Pepperdine Law Review 259 (1989), argues against extending the custom and usage privilege.

The other Florida case is Green Valley School, Inc. v. Cowles Florida Broadcasting, Inc., 327 So.2d 810 (Fla.App.1976). State officials planned a midnight raid, under a properly issued warrant, to search the premises of a controversial local private school. The head of the party of 50 raiders invited reporters and photographers from several local media organizations to accompany the party. The defendant television station presented an extensive report of the raid on the evening news the following night, suggesting that the raid had turned up evidence of mistreatment of the students and rampant sexual misbehavior and use of drugs. The school sued the station for defamation and for trespass.

The trial judge granted summary judgment to the station on the trespass claim. The court of appeals reversed, addressing the question entirely in the following passage:

> To uphold appellees' assertion that their entry upon appellant's property at the time, manner, and circumstances as reflected by this record was as a *matter of law* sanctioned by "the request of and with the consent of the State Attorney" and with the "common usage and custom in Florida" could well bring to the citizenry of this state the hobnail boots of a Nazi stormtrooper equipped with glaring lights invading a couple's bedroom at midnight with the wife hovering in her nightgown in an attempt to shield herself from the scanning TV camera. In this jurisdiction, a law enforcement officer is not as a *matter of law* endowed with the right or authority to invite people of his choosing to invade private property and participate in a midnight raid of the premises.

On the same day that it decided *Fletcher,* the Florida Supreme Court dismissed an appeal in the Green Valley case, indicating that it found no conflict between the results in the two cases. Can they be reconciled?

As soon as we move from private residential property to premises that are usually open to the public, the questions get more difficult.

In Le Mistral v. Columbia Broadcasting System, 61 A.D.2d 491, 402 N.Y.S.2d 815, 3 Med.L.Rptr. 1913 (1978), CBS, as owner and operator of WCBS–TV in New York City, directed reporter Rich and a camera crew to visit restaurants that had been cited for health code violations. Plaintiff was on the list. The crew entered plaintiff's restaurant with cameras "rolling" and using bright lights that were necessary to get the pictures. The jury found CBS liable for trespass and awarded plaintiff $1,200 in compensatory damages and $250,000 in punitive damages. After the verdict was announced (in a passage approved on appeal), the trial judge stated:

The instructions given to the crew, whether specific to this event or as standing operating procedure, were to avoid seeking an appointment or permission to enter any of the premises where a story was sought, but to enter unannounced catching the occupants by surprise; "with cameras rolling" in the words of CBS' principal witness, Rich. From the evidence the jury was entitled to conclude that following this procedure the defendant's employees burst into plaintiff's restaurant in noisy and obtrusive fashion and following the loud commands of the reporter, Rich, to photograph the patrons dining, turned their lights and camera upon the dining room. Consternation, the jury was informed, followed. Patrons waiting to be seated left the restaurant. Others who had finished eating, left without waiting for their checks. Still others hid their faces behind napkins or table cloths or hid themselves beneath tables. (The reluctance of the plaintiff's clientele to be video taped was never explained, and need not be. Patronizing a restaurant does not carry with it an obligation to appear on television). [The] president of the plaintiff and manager of its operations, refused to be interviewed, and as the camera continued to "roll" he pushed the protesting Miss Rich and her crew from the premises. All told, the CBS personnel were in the restaurant not more than ten minutes, perhaps as little as one minute, depending on the testimony the jury chose to credit. The jury by its verdict clearly found the defendant guilty of trespass and from the admissions of CBS' own employees they were guilty of trespass. The witness Rich sought to justify her crew's entry into the restaurant by calling it, on a number of occasions, a "place of public accommodation", but, as she acknowledges, they did not seek to avail themselves of the plaintiff's "accommodation"; they had no intention of purchasing food or drink.

The trial judge upheld the determination of liability but set aside both damage awards because he had erroneously barred a defense witness from testifying as to CBS's motive and purpose in entering the premises. On appeal, the court held that its review of the record "demonstrates an adequate basis to justify the compensatory damage award rendered by the jury and, accordingly, such award must stand." As to punitive damages, the court agreed that the judge had erred in excluding the testimony because all "circumstances immediately connected with the transaction tending to exhibit or explain the motive of the defendant are admissible." One judge thought it clear that the defendants were "not motivated by actual malice or such an intentional disregard of plaintiff's rights as would justify the imposition of punitive damages. [ ] The defendant was merely pursuing a newsworthy item in the overly aggressive but good faith manner that characterizes the operation of the news media today. . . . In this sensitive and evolving First Amendment area, I would permit this precedent-setting opinion to stand as a warning to all news gatherers that future trespasses may well be met with an award of punitive damages."

The case is complicated by the disruptive presence of the television cameras. If a newspaper reporter had entered the restaurant, would the reporter have been a trespasser from the moment of entry—or only from the moment of refusing to leave? If, while leaving, the reporter continued watching the scene and making mental notes, would that be improper? If the court is suggesting that the premises were open only to those seriously considering purchasing food or drink, why should it matter whether the entry was disruptive?

Under traditional law, the owner could prevent entry by posting a notice on the front door stating that no reporters are permitted on the premises. But today it is possible that the courts of New York would develop a special rule allowing reporters to enter "newsworthy" premises—at least so long as they are not disruptive. Further, the courts might develop some First Amendment privilege to allow reporters to enter certain types of "private" premises— at least until they are explicitly asked to leave. All of this is most unclear but does serve to advise reporters of some of the lurking perils in this area. See Watkins, Private Property vs. Reporter Rights—A Problem in Newsgathering, 54 Journ.Q. 690 (1977).

In order to claim damages for trespass or theft of property, the plaintiff must own or occupy the property. If the property has been abandoned—the former owner has indicated a desire to relinquish control over it—then no civil damage action can be brought. An example of this situation may have occurred in 1975 when it was revealed that a reporter had been sifting through the garbage cans outside the house of Secretary of State Kissinger. A reporter who went on the land to reach the garbage cans would have been a trespasser. If the cans were on the public sidewalk, the only claim would be interference with personal property—the garbage. But if, as seems likely, the property has been abandoned, no civil liability would be possible. Commenting on the episode in an editorial, *Editor & Publisher* (July 19, 1975 at 6) attacked the practice: "Pawing through someone else's garbage is a revolting exercise and doing it in the name of journalism makes it none the less so." Do you agree?

*Non–Trespass Invasions.* We turn now to alleged invasions of privacy that do not fit into the trespass mold. These involve the use of cameras or high-technology equipment to obtain information about a subject, wiretapping and secretly recording conversations to which the person is a party.

Galella v. Onassis, 487 F.2d 986, 1 Med.L.Rptr. 2425 (2d Cir.1973), involved aggressive efforts by a "paparazzo" photographer to obtain photographs of the widow and children of President Kennedy. "Paparazzi make themselves as visible to the public and obnoxious to their photographic subjects as possible to aid in the advertisement and wide sale of their works." Among his actions, Galella brought his power boat close to Mrs. Onassis as she was swimming, jumped out of bushes as she was walking past, jumped into her son's path to take a photograph of him riding his bicycle and invaded the children's private schools. Those acts that reasonably put the subject in fear of personal safety would create tort liability under longstanding rules. But those that involved annoyance presented harder questions.

Mrs. Onassis claimed that when she went through the streets to go shopping or to visit a friend, or walked alone in Central Park she was engaged in private activities that should not be the subject of any unwanted photography. The court disagreed. Mrs. Onassis was "a public figure and thus subject to news coverage" although the First Amendment provided no "wall of immunity protecting newsmen" from liability for torts committed while gathering news. The court balanced Mrs. Onassis' concern about intrusion with the legitimate interests of photography by ordering Galella to stay 25 feet from Mrs. Onassis at all times, not to block her movement in public places and not to do "any act foreseeably or reasonably calculated" to place Mrs. Onassis in jeopardy or frighten her. Any further restriction on his taking and selling photographs of her would be improper.

Galella was subsequently charged with criminal contempt for violating the order, but he avoided paying a $120,000 fine for contempt by agreeing not to take any more pictures of Mrs. Onassis.

In 1979 a TV camera crew trailed a man as he was trying to pay a ransom to persons who had kidnapped his wife. Despite his pleas, the crew followed the man, apparently along public ways. The episode attracted much press discussion after the FBI said the action had "put that woman's life in danger." An editorial in *Editor & Publisher*, July 28, 1979 at 6, asserted that although the TV crew might have considered its actions "enterprising reporting . . . it was more like sheer stupidity. . . . It is this sort of arrogance and brashness that gets media in trouble with the public."

After the woman was released, the couple sued the station for endangering the woman's life. No harm actually occurred. Should the husband have been able to sue for mental anguish he suffered as a result of the crew's actions? We will address the general issue of possible media liability for emotional harm in Chapter V. Criminal liability might have been possible if it had been shown that the crew learned of the man's movements by making unauthorized interceptions of messages on a nonbroadcast frequency in violation of § 605 (now § 705) of the Communications Act. Should the law impose a sanction against reporters whose gathering efforts in fact lead to harm because kidnappers panic or get angry that their instructions apparently are not being followed?

Where solitude is invaded, the courts speak of the subject's reasonable expectations of privacy as the guide to available protection. Thus, one who leaves his curtains open, knowing that persons in the building across the street can look inside his apartment, can claim no reasonable expectation of privacy. But if the only vantage point from which the inside of the apartment can be seen is a hilltop two miles away, a court might well find that a reporter who set up a very powerful telescope on that hill and looked through the open window has invaded privacy.

Similarly, a person inside a dwelling can make no reasonable claim of invasion of privacy if he shouts at his spouse and is overheard by others outside.  But if he speaks in a normal or hushed voice—and is overheard because a highly sensitive microphone in the next apartment or across the street has picked up the communication—a court would probably find an invasion of privacy.

Wiretapping and forms of intercepting messages frequently have been involved in litigation.  The 1986 Electronic Communications Privacy Act made revisions in 18 U.S.C.A. §§ 2510–2520 (sections of the United States Code created by the Omnibus Crime Control and Safe Streets Act of 1968).  Section 2511 now provides, in part, that any person who, unless authorized, intentionally intercepts, uses or discloses any "wire, oral, or electronic communication" is subject to punishment.

In one case the court awarded damages under the original statute against a law enforcement officer who used an extension phone to intercept a conversation involving a prison inmate.  Neither participant had consented to the monitoring.  No consent was to be implied from the fact that the call was being made in a prison because no regulations informed prisoners that their calls might be monitored.  (The law enforcement exceptions in the act were held inapplicable.)  The court also found liability under the parallel Massachusetts statute that protected privacy of communications.  Campiti v. Walonis, 611 F.2d 387 (1st Cir.1979).  Recall that *Noriega*, p. 59, *supra*, also involved recording of telephone calls from prison.

Some states have statutes that are more restrictive than the federal statute.

In Ribas v. Clark, 38 Cal.3d 355, 212 Cal.Rptr. 143, 696 P.2d 637 (1985), a wife asked the defendant to listen in on an extension phone as she talked to her estranged husband.  The husband learned about the episode when the defendant testified in an arbitration hearing about matters she overheard.  He then sued for violation of a California statute that applied to any person who "intentionally taps . . . any . . . telephone wire, line, cable or instrument . . .."  The court upheld the complaint.  The statute was read broadly to bar "far more than illicit wiretapping," including the recording of a conversation without the other's consent:

> While one who imparts private information risks the betrayal of his confidence by the other party, a substantial distinction has been recognized between the secondhand repetition of the contents of a conversation and its simultaneous dissemination to an unannounced second auditor, whether that auditor be a person or mechanical device. [   ]

As one commentator has noted, such secret monitoring denies the speaker an important aspect of privacy of communication—the right to control the nature and extent of the firsthand dissemination of his statement. [   ] Partly because of this factor, the Privacy Act has been read to require the assent of all parties to a communication before another may listen.

Although the majority and the concurrers disagreed about the availability of a defense under the statute based on the content of the existing tariff, all agreed that an action lay for $3,000.

Two television cases exemplify other litigation. In one, a woman who was alleged to have traded sexual favors for a light sentence by an Ohio judge agreed to be interviewed by ABC in her home, but she refused to appear on camera. The network made surreptitious video and voice recordings, and she sued. Although the court held that there was no criminal or tortious purpose, it held that the plaintiff was entitled to try to prove in court that ABC intended to injure her. Boddie v. American Broadcasting Companies, 731 F.2d 333, 10 Med.L.Rptr. 1923 (6th Cir.1984). In the other, ABC had surreptitiously recorded a meeting between congressional investigators and a cancer insurance salesman—with the consent of the investigators. The court ruled that ABC had to show that its only purpose was to aid Congress or that it must demonstrate that it had no injurious purpose in secretly recording the encounter. Benford v. American Broadcasting Companies, 502 F.Supp. 1159, 6 Med.L.Rptr. 2489 (D.Md.1980), aff'd 661 F.2d 917 (4th Cir.), cert. denied 454 U.S. 1060 (1981). For discussion of such problems, see Spellman, "Tort Liability of the News Media for Surreptitious Recording," Journalism Quarterly, Summer 1985 at 289.

Florida has a statute that reaches participant monitoring by barring persons "not acting under color of law" from intercepting a wire or oral communication unless all parties to the communication had given their prior consent. An important lawsuit arose from a general attack on the statute by reporters who claimed that the use of concealed recording equipment was essential to investigative reporting for three reasons: it aided accuracy of reporting, persons being interviewed would not be candid if they knew they were being recorded and the recording provided corroboration in case of a suit for defamation.

The Florida Supreme Court upheld the statute's constitutionality. The statute allows "each party to a conversation to have an expectation of privacy from interception by another party to the conversation. It does not exclude any source from the press, intrude upon the activities of the news media in contacting sources, prevent the parties to the communication from consenting to the recording, or restrict the publication of any information gained from the communication. First Amendment rights do not include a constitutional right to corroborate newsgathering activities when the legislature has statutorily recognized the private rights of individuals."

In response to the argument that secret recording may be the only way to get credible information about crime, the court stated that protection against intrusion might protect even a person "reasonably suspected of committing a crime." Shevin v. Sunbeam Television Corp., 351 So.2d 723, 3 Med.L.Rptr. 1312 (Fla.1977).

Based on the briefs and without argument, the Supreme Court dismissed the appeal by the press for want of a substantial federal question, 435 U.S. 920 (1978). Justices Brennan, White and Blackmun thought the case should be given full consideration and voted to set the case for oral argument.

The Florida court had relied to some extent on the case of Dietemann v. Time, Inc., 449 F.2d 245, 1 Med.L.Rptr. 2417 (9th Cir.1971). In that case, two reporters obtained access to plaintiff's home to find out whether he was a medical quack. While plaintiff was diagnosing the alleged ailment of one reporter, the other secretly took photographs with a hidden camera. The entire conversation was transmitted to confederates outside by means of a transmitter hidden in one reporter's purse. In this part of the case, the court concluded that California would impose liability for invasion of privacy:

> [One who invites others to his home] does not and should not be required to take the risk that what is heard and seen will be transmitted by photograph or recording, or in our modern world, in full living color and hi-fi to the public at large or to any segment of it that the visitor may select. A different rule could have a most pernicious effect upon the dignity of man and it would surely lead to guarded conversations and conduct where candor is most valued, e.g., in the case of doctors and lawyers.

> The defendant claims that the First Amendment immunizes it from liability for invading plaintiff's den with a hidden camera and its concealed electronic instruments because its employees were gathering news and its instrumentalities "are indispensable tools of investigative reporting." We agree that newsgathering is an integral part of news dissemination. We strongly disagree, however, that the hidden mechanical contrivances are "indispensable tools" of newsgathering. Investigative reporting is an ancient art; its successful practice long antecedes the invention of miniature cameras and electronic devices. The First Amendment has never been construed to accord newsmen immunity from torts or crimes committed during the course of newsgathering. The First Amendment is not a license to trespass, to steal, or to intrude by electronic means into the precincts of another's home or office. It does not become such a license simply because the person subjected to the intrusion is reasonably suspected of committing a crime.

> Defendant relies upon the line of cases commencing with New York Times Co. v. Sullivan, 376 U.S. 254 (1964) . . . to sustain its contentions that (1) publication of news, however tortiously gathered, insulates defendant from liability for the antecedent tort . . ..

As we previously observed, publication is not an essential element of plaintiff's cause of action. Moreover, it is not the foundation for the invocation of a privilege. Privilege concepts developed in defamation cases and to some extent in privacy actions in which publication is an essential component are not relevant in determining liability for intrusion conduct antedating publication. [   ] Nothing in *New York Times* or its progeny suggests anything to the contrary. Indeed, the Court strongly indicates that there is no First Amendment interest in protecting news media from calculated misdeeds. [   ]

### b.  Consent Has Been Obtained

We turn now to cases in which the reporter contends that what might otherwise be a tort is not because the plaintiff consented to the conduct in question. The basic legal principle is not in doubt. Occasionally, the cases involve such neat situations as a plaintiff who signs a written consent. Usually, the cases are more complex.

In Cassidy v. American Broadcasting Companies, 60 Ill.App.3d 831, 17 Ill.Dec. 936, 377 N.E.2d 126, 3 Med.L.Rptr. 2449 (1978), an undercover policeman was sent to a massage parlor. After paying $30 he was escorted to a room to watch "de-luxe lingerie modeling." On entering the very warm room he observed camera lights. He asked, "What are we on, TV?" The model replied, "Yes, we're making a movie." As plaintiff reclined on the bed watching the model change her lingerie several times, he made suggestive remarks and advances. He then arrested the model for solicitation. The entire scene was in fact being photographed from an adjacent room by a local television station through a two-way mirror. The manager of the parlor had asked the defendant to film the episode to show that police were harassing him.

Plaintiff's suit failed because, among other reasons, the plaintiff apparently did not intend his conduct to be private because he knew that someone might be making a movie of his conduct. He testified his actions were in the line of duty as an officer and that if the model wished to sell him a completed film he would use it as evidence in his investigation. Plaintiff had no expectation of privacy.

Although plaintiff had not explicitly consented to being filmed, his conduct after being informed that a film was being made amounted to consent. But should the same rule apply if a jury could reasonably find that the model made her statement jokingly or sardonically so that a reasonable person in plaintiff's position would not have believed what she said?

The most common problems reporters face in consent cases appear to involve consents that are obtained by some type of misrepresentation. Because reporters often investigate alleged misdeeds they are unlikely to get consent to do interviews, go to certain places or record interviews if they identify themselves as reporters.  In such cases, what is the role of consent?

In *Dietemann,* the reporters posed as a couple seeking medical advice from the plaintiff, who lived a quiet life and did not advertise or even have a telephone.  They went to his gate and rang the bell.  When plaintiff appeared, the reporters falsely said that they had been sent by a certain person and wanted to see plaintiff because the female visitor had a lump in her breast that she wanted diagnosed.  Plaintiff admitted the pair to his den and made his diagnosis.  On this part of the case the court observed:

> Plaintiff's den was a sphere from which he could reasonably expect to exclude eavesdropping newsmen.  He invited two of defendant's employees to the den. One who invites another to his home or office takes a risk that the visitor may not be what he seems, and that the visitor may repeat all he hears and observes when he leaves.

Why does plaintiff take the risk that a visitor may not be who he claims to be, or that a visitor may repeat what he hears inside, but not take the risk that secret recordings and photographs are being made?  Is it that the plaintiff does in fact intend to deal with the persons who are standing before him—whatever names they give or whatever reasons they give for coming?

Courts generally rule that consent to enter one section of land does not authorize entering any other part;  and that consent to do one thing, such as reading the gas meter, does not authorize removal of the gas meter.  In these cases, it is apparent that the actor has exceeded the consent.  In *Dietemann,* however, the plaintiff gave consent to enter the land and come to the den—and that is precisely what the reporters did.  His misunderstanding about identity did not lead him to consent to one thing but to be hit with another.  (A person who wants legal protection against someone who is told a secret and then reveals it may obtain it by entering into a contract in which the recipient makes legally enforceable promises about his future behavior.)

If misrepresenting identity doesn't raise major legal problems, it does raise ethical questions that are much discussed among journalists.  The matter is reviewed at length in Zimmerman, "By Any Other Name . . .," Washington Journalism Review (Nov./Dec.1979) at 32.

The matter received much attention in 1979 when the Pulitzer Prize for local investigative reporting was denied to a newspaper that uncovered massive official corruption after it bought and ran a bar in Chicago under a false name.  At about the same time, a reporter posed as a Congressman to obtain a seat at the signing of the Egyptian–Israeli peace treaty.  The reporter said that the episode involved telling "only one lie."  *Editor & Publisher,* June 9, 1979 at 6, responded, "But *how many lies* are too many?  Are we getting back to the no-holds-barred philosophy that the story should be gotten at any cost?"  Noting that the press complains loudly when someone impersonates a newsman, the editorial continued, "We believe that newsmen's impersonations of others in order to get a story [are] equally damaging to their believability and should be scrupulously avoided." Some have suggested that if reporters will lie to get a story readers may believe that they would also lie in writing the story if they thought the matter important enough.

The argument the other way, of course, stresses that uncovering crime or other misbehavior is very hard—that it would have been virtually impossible to have demonstrated the corruption in Chicago without setting up the fake business. Another example involved a reporter who got a job as a guard at the Three Mile Island nuclear plant after the malfunctioning and then took photographs while on the job. His goal was to show how easy it was to get a job—his asserted background and references were never checked—and to show how lax security was inside the plant. Are there other ways to obtain this information? How important is it to obtain the information? Does such behavior damage the credibility of the press?

For a former *New York Times* reporter's analysis of some of these ethical issues, see T. Goldstein, *News At Any Cost: How Journalists Compromise Their Ethics to Shape the News,* 1985.

It should be noted here that although civil actions by persons deceived in these cases may not be likely, some of the cases may well involve potential criminal liability—particularly cases involving impersonation of government officials or lying to government officials.

Should different principles apply if reporters knowingly accept material improperly obtained by others? In one case, aides to a United States Senator removed numerous documents from his files, copied them, and passed the copies to columnists who knew how they had been obtained. The court held that the columnists had committed no tort:

> If we were to hold appellants liable for invasion of privacy on these facts, we would establish the proposition that one who receives information from an intruder, knowing it has been obtained by improper intrusion, is guilty of a tort. In an untried and developing area of tort law, we are not prepared to go so far. A person approached by an eavesdropper with an offer to share in the information gathered through the eavesdropping would perhaps play the nobler part should he spurn the offer and shut his ears. However, it seems to us that at this point it would place too great a strain on human weakness to hold one liable in damages who merely succumbs to temptation and listens.

Pearson v. Dodd, 410 F.2d 701, 1 Med.L.Rptr. 1809 (D.C.Cir.) cert. denied 395 U.S. 947 (1969). Should the result change if a reporter had said to the aide "I'd sure love to see your file on" a particular matter— and three days later the aide presented the file?

Ethical questions arise when reporters gain entrance to private property through a deception. After Jim Bakker was ousted in 1987 as head of the PTL ("Praise the Lord" and "People that Love") ministry, he and his wife, Tammy, put their Palm Springs house up for sale for $650,000. The real estate agent turned down scores of news organizations seeking entry to the house, but a *Los Angeles Herald Examiner* reporter posed as an affluent Florida businessman and potential buyer to gain entry.

The Bakkers were out of town at the time of the deception. A *Herald Examiner* editor defended the deception: "The press was barred. The Bakkers are news. They are in a public arena. Ordinary citizens could get into the house so why discriminate against the press? It was a sensitive story . . .. It described how they lived and there is certainly public interest in this." Editor & Publisher, Aug. 29, 1987 at 12.

Is it difficult to make meaningful distinctions among a public "need to know," "public interest" and public *curiosity?* Is an invitation to potential buyers to enter a home the same as an invitation to "ordinary citizens"?

CBS's newsmagazine "Street Stories" included an April 1992 segment in which a distraught Oakland, Calif., mother told a victim counselor and a police officer that her husband had beaten and kicked her. She subsequently sued CBS for $10 million for invasion of privacy, fraud, and intentional infliction of emotional distress, charging that members of the "Street Stories" production crew failed to identify themselves and agreed not to film her and her daughter when they accompanied a mobile crisis intervention team when they went to her house. The mother said the crew members had told her that they were shooting a story on the crisis intervention team for the San Francisco district attorney's office. In response to CBS's request for summary judgment, Judge Fern Smith said too many facts could not be resolved without further discovery and possible trial but urged that the parties attempt to work out a settlement. Broadcasting & Cable, July 5, 1993 at 14. The two sides settled shortly thereafter, with terms of the agreement not being revealed. San Francisco Chronicle, July 22, 1993 at A26.

### c. *Criminal Liability*

At several points during the foregoing discussion of civil liability, we have had occasion to touch on related criminal sanctions. In this section we draw together the likely sources of criminal liability that may confront newsgatherers.

At the outset, federal and state governments have statutes punishing such acts as the theft of government property, and the concealment or removal of official records and documents. See, e.g., 18 U.S.C.A. §§ 641, 2071. In addition, conspiracy to commit criminal acts is also a crime. Other statutes directly relate to property or information in specific areas, such as national security or nuclear energy. Knowingly receiving stolen property may also be criminal even though the recipient had nothing to do with the original theft.

In one prosecution, an editor was charged with receiving stolen property—a list of the names, home addresses and telephone numbers of

80 undercover state narcotics agents. The facts surrounding the transaction were not entirely clear and the court ruled that the state had presented insufficient proof that the defendant knew that the document had been stolen (rather than temporarily removed from the office with the intention of returning it). People v. Kunkin, 9 Cal.3d 245, 107 Cal.Rptr. 184, 507 P.2d 1392 (1973).

Other crimes involving direct harms to government may include impersonating an officer, not obeying a lawful order of a police officer or bribing a government employee. We will look at cases involving lawful orders, including State v. Laschinsky and City of Oak Creek v. Ah King, in Chapter XII, when we discuss newsgathering from public sources.

The government also uses criminal legislation to support the civil law in protecting individual property and privacy. We have seen some in operation already, such as the criminal punishment for intercepting communications whether by wiretapping or otherwise. Breaking into a home and stealing a photograph from the table would involve several criminal offenses as well as tort liability. Other protections are available. In one episode a publisher was charged with extortion by allegedly threatening to write untrue stories about people in the community unless they supplied information for forthcoming stories or agreed to advertise in the paper. Editor & Publisher, June 30, 1979 at 19.

Reporters covering a demonstration at a construction site for a nuclear plant in Oklahoma were convicted of trespassing on private property. The utility, PSO, did not want extensive coverage of the marchers—as had occurred at an early demonstration. This time, PSO warned all reporters that they would be arrested if they entered the fenced property at any point not permitted by PSO. PSO then set up a viewing area that reporters might use on its otherwise closed property. It was not clear in advance whether the demonstration or any confrontation would be visible from that point.

Several reporters used the viewing area. Others followed the demonstrators and entered the land when the demonstrators went through the fence. These reporters were the ones convicted of trespass. The judge found that they knew or should have known of PSO's intent to prosecute this conduct. He ruled that newsmen had no constitutional right of access to scenes when the general public was excluded, but he also found a First Amendment right to reasonable access to the news such as is available to the public generally. (Since the property was closed, the origin of this right is not clear.) He then decided that some balancing was required. Against the interest in gathering the news, he arrayed PSO's right to be secure in its property and the police power of the state to maintain public order and enforce criminal statutes. In making his balance the judge also threw in the fact that PSO's purpose in hampering news coverage was "an ignoble one hardly compatible with the rights of a free people." He also gave some weight to the fact that when the marchers entered the land at a point not readily visible from the "viewing area," reporters in that area demanded, and were taken to, a better spot.   (How could this have been known in time to the reporters who were with the marchers?)

The judge thought the balance favored the government because the restrictions did not deny access to "particularly significant news" since those in the viewing area could see almost everything.   When several defendants claimed that they had to enter the land to meet "their professional obligation to report the news," the judge responded that although this might have been a matter of conscience, it was also "a deliberate violation of law."   If a person commits an act of civil disobedience, he "may claim an exemption from an obligation to obey a particular law on moral or professional grounds, but that person may not claim immunity from application of sanction for committing that offense." Each was fined $25.   Stahl v. State, 665 P.2d 839, 9 Med.L.Rptr. 1945 (Okl.Crim.App.1983), cert. denied 464 U.S. 1069 (1984).

### d.   Other Civil Liability

A New York case, Ramirez v. Time, 134 A.D.2d 970, 521 N.Y.S.2d 355, 12 Med.L.Rptr. 2230 (1987), illustrates a possibility of civil liability for misconduct in newsgathering beyond the liability for intrusion on a plaintiff's physical solitude.   Dr. Janice Runkle, the veterinarian at Belmont Park raceway, mysteriously disappeared in New York on or about July 27, 1981, and her body was found a few days later in Illinois. A *Time* magazine reporter left a false message on her answering machine to the effect that he had an eyewitness who had seen her alive on July 28, 1981.

Relying on the reporter's message, representatives of Dr. Runkle's estate went to the reporter's office in the Time–Life Building in New York City and talked to him for several hours—only to discover near the end of the discussions that the message was apparently nothing but a ruse.

Dr.   Runkle's estate sued the magazine and reporter for defamation and for fraud, despite the fact that New York law permits no recovery for defamation of the dead.   Defendants moved for dismissal.   New York law requires the following elements in a cause of action for fraud: representation of a material existing fact, falsity, scienter, deception, and injury, as well as detrimental reliance by the party to whom the misrepresentation was made.   The trial judge held that there was no significant injury to the plaintiff directly springing from the misrepresentation and granted the motion to dismiss.   An intermediate appellate court affirmed without opinion, and the state's highest court dismissed an appeal as untimely.   72 N.Y.2d 829, 530 N.Y.S.2d 548, 526 N.E.2d 39 (1988).

*Ramirez* is not, of course, a privacy case, but it does illustrate the possibility of other civil actions against journalists resulting from misconduct during newsgathering.

### 3.  Publication of Embarrassing Private Facts

Publication of embarrassing private facts (which we address in this section) and appropriation of another's name or likeness for commercial or trade purposes (which we address in the next section) are the two branches of invasion of privacy that have to do with truthful publication that interferes with someone's right to be let alone.  The former is of greater importance to journalism students;  the latter is of greater importance to advertising and public relations students.  Redundant though it may seem, it may be helpful to think of the former as publication of embarrassing private *true* facts.

#### a.  Categories

The cases of publication of embarrassing private facts fall into a small number of categories—those dealing with sexual matters, commission of crime, poverty, idiosyncratic qualities and other embarrassing stories.

The important point is not whether these state cases are decided "correctly."  Cases involving this tort are so inconsistent that it is difficult to generalize except to say that plaintiffs rarely win.  The results are given in capsule form at the end of each case, without reasons, simply to satisfy curiosity—not to suggest the proper resolution.  Remember that after reviewing this catalogue of litigation, we will explore approaches to this very troublesome area.  The law aside, prospective reporters and editors should consider how the facts of each story should be handled.

*Sexual Matters.*  1.  In a study of official misconduct at a county home, a newspaper reported the involuntary sterilization of a named 18–year–old young woman seven years earlier.  Howard v. Des Moines Register and Tribune Co., 283 N.W.2d 289, 5 Med.L.Rptr. 1667 (Iowa 1979), cert. denied 445 U.S. 904 (1980) (case dismissed).

2.  A newspaper columnist included the following item: "More education stuff: The students at the College of Alameda will be surprised to learn that their student body president, Toni Diaz, is no lady, but is in fact a man whose real name is Antonio.

"Now I realize, that in these times, such a matter is no big deal, but I suspect his female classmates in P.E. 97 may wish to make other showering arrangements."  The plaintiff won a $775,000 judgment at the trial court, but it was reversed on appeal, and the parties settled the case shortly thereafter.  Diaz v. Oakland Tribune, Inc., 139 Cal.App.3d 118, 188 Cal.Rptr. 762, 9 Med.L.Rptr. 1121 (1983).

3.  During an assassination attempt on President Ford in San Francisco, Oliver Sipple knocked the arm of the assailant as she sought to aim a second shot at the President.  Sipple was the object of extensive media attention, including stories that correctly identified him as a

homosexual.  Sipple, asserting that relatives who lived in the Midwest did not know of his orientation, sued the *San Francisco Chronicle*.  The newspaper defended in part on the argument that privacy was not involved because Sipple had marched in gay parades and had acknowledged that at least 100 to 500 people in San Francisco knew he was gay. The newspaper argued that his sexual orientation was relevant to the story because, although some stereotyped gays as sissies, Sipple was an ex-marine who acted heroically.

Summary judgment for the newspaper was affirmed on appeal. First, the facts were not private.  Second, they were newsworthy.  The news coverage was prompted by "legitimate political considerations, i.e., to dispel the false public opinions that gays were timid, weak and unheroic figures and to raise the equally important political question whether the President of the United States entertained a discriminatory attitude or bias against a minority group such as homosexuals."  Sipple v. Chronicle Publishing Co., 154 Cal.App.3d 1040, 201 Cal.Rptr. 665, 10 Med.L.Rptr. 1690 (1984).

4.  Television cameras went to the scene of a report that a man was threatening harm to his housekeeper's sister.  The crew arrived and began filming as police led the stark-naked man from the house.  In a news report the following evening, plaintiff's "buttocks and genitals were visible to television viewers for a time period of approximately eight-to-nine-tenths of one second."  Taylor v. K.T.V.B., Inc., 96 Idaho 202, 525 P.2d 984 (1974) (case remanded to determine defendant's reasons for using the film; settled out of court).

5.  Plaintiff was kidnapped by her estranged husband and taken to an apartment.  He forced her to disrobe and then beat her.  Police came. Following the suicide of the husband, police hurried plaintiff from the apartment nude "save for a mere towel."  Photographers on the scene took photographs and turned them over to defendant newspaper, which ran several of them.  Cape Publications, Inc. v. Bridges, 423 So.2d 426, 8 Med.L.Rptr. 2535 (Fla.App.1982), cert. denied 464 U.S. 893 (1983) (judgment for $10,000 reversed on appeal).

6.  A group of Pittsburgh Steeler fans urged a photographer from *Sports Illustrated* to take pictures of them.  The photographer did so. From among many photographs available for use, the editors chose one that showed the plaintiff with his fly open.  Neff v. Time, Inc., 406 F.Supp. 858 (W.D.Pa.1976) (case dismissed).

7.  A television station reported the identity of a deceased rape victim.  Cox Broadcasting Corp. v. Cohn, 420 U.S. 469, 1 Med.L.Rptr. 1819 (1975) (case is reported at p. 212, *infra* ).

8.  A newspaper published a story on teenage pregnancies with a sidebar that identified the teenage father of an illegitimate child.  Most of the article focused on the teenage mother.  After the mother identified the plaintiff as the father, the reporter called the plaintiff twice to obtain comments.  The reporter first spoke with the plaintiff's mother; the second time she spoke with the reluctant plaintiff for several

minutes. In neither call did the reporter request permission to identify or quote the plaintiff. The plaintiff won a judgment of $1,500 actual and $25,000 punitive damages. Hawkins v. Multimedia, Inc., 288 S.C. 569, 344 S.E.2d 145, 12 Med.L.Rptr. 1878 cert. denied 479 U.S. 1012 (1986).

*Criminal Behavior.* 9. A magazine article about truck hijacking, to prove that it was a chancy venture, reported that 11 years earlier the plaintiff and another had hijacked a truck in Kentucky, only to find that it contained four bowling pin spotting machines. The article was published in 1967, by which time plaintiff alleged that he had served his time, had become rehabilitated, and was living in California with family and friends who did not know about his past. Briscoe v. Reader's Digest Association, 1 Med.L.Rptr. 1852 (C.D.Cal.1972) (summary judgment for defendant upheld).

10. A newspaper reproduced the front page of a 1952 edition as part of its regular feature called "Page from Our Past." The page contained an article about the cattle theft trial of three brothers who asserted that the 25–year–old matter was no longer of public concern and that they had been law-abiding and hard working citizens of the community, and had ultimately received full pardons. Roshto v. Hebert, 439 So.2d 428, 9 Med.L.Rptr. 2417 (La.1983). (Judgment for plaintiffs reversed on appeal.)

11. Plaintiff was arrested for drunk driving. At the police station, he was "hitting and banging on his cell door, hollering and cursing from the time of his arrest" until five hours later. A local broadcaster taped some of the noise and played excerpts from it on the radio. Holman v. Central Arkansas Broadcasting Co., 610 F.2d 542, 5 Med.L.Rptr. 2217 (8th Cir.1979) (case dismissed).

*Poverty.* 12. A newspaper article included a front-page photograph of the plaintiff's home. The photograph was one of a series on the newspaper's hometown and its environs. The caption read, "one of Crowley's stately homes, a bit weatherworn and unkempt, stands in the shadow of a spreading oak." Jaubert v. Crowley Post–Signal, Inc., 375 So.2d 1386, 5 Med.L.Rptr. 2084 (La.1979) (case dismissed).

*Idiosyncrasies.* 13. *The New Yorker* magazine did one of its extensive profiles on a man who, 27 years earlier, had been an 11–year–old child prodigy who had lectured to mathematicians. For the last 20 years, however, he had lived as unobtrusively as possible. The profile reported that the plaintiff was living in a hall bedroom in Boston's "shabby south end," that his room was untidy, that he had a curious laugh, that he collected street car transfers and that he was interested at the moment in the lore of the Okamakammessett Indians. The article was "merciless in its dissection of intimate details of its subject's personal life" and a "ruthless exposure of a once public character who has since sought and has now been deprived of the seclusion of private life." Sidis v. F–R Publishing Corp., 113 F.2d 806, 1 Med.L.Rptr. 1775 (2d Cir.), cert. denied 311 U.S. 711 (1940) (case dismissed). (William

James Sidis died in 1944 at age 46 of a cerebral hemorrhage, but he has continued to be a figure of interest. A biography, *The Prodigy* by Amy Wallace, was published in 1986.)

14. *Sports Illustrated* planned an article about a California beach reputed to be the world's most dangerous site for body surfing. Plaintiff, known as the most daring surfer at the site, was interviewed and was referred to in the story as one who extinguished cigarettes in his mouth, ate spiders and other insects, dove head first down a flight of stairs, had never learned to read and was perceived by other surfers as "abnormal." Virgil v. Time, Inc., 527 F.2d 1122, 1 Med.L.Rptr. 1835 (9th Cir.1975), cert. denied 425 U.S. 998 (1976) (affirming denial of summary judgment). (Although plaintiff had once consented to be interviewed, he withdrew the consent when he learned the shape the story would take. The court rejected the defense of consent.)

*Embarrassment or Ridicule.* 15. A newspaper article reported that the basketball team at the state university was in trouble because four named players, of the eight who were returning, "are on academic probation and in danger of flunking." Bilney v. Evening Star Newspaper Co., 43 Md.App. 560, 406 A.2d 652, 5 Med.L.Rptr. 1931 (1979) (case dismissed).

16. Plaintiff was a janitor who found $240,000 that had fallen from an armored car. He returned it (and received a reward of $10,000), to the scorn of his neighbors and his children's friends. When their hostile reaction was reported, he received many congratulatory letters and messages, including one from President Kennedy. The full story was reported in a periodical and reprinted in a college English textbook. Johnson v. Harcourt, Brace, Jovanovich, Inc., 43 Cal.App.3d 880, 118 Cal.Rptr. 370 (1974) (case dismissed).

17. A former employee entered a Louisville company and killed seven people with an assault rifle and then committed suicide. The widow and children of one of the victims sued after the body of their husband/father appeared, unidentified, in a newspaper photograph. Barger v. Courier Journal, 20 Med.L.Rptr. 1189 (Ky.App.1991), cert. denied, 112 S.Ct. 1763 (1992) (case dismissed).

### b. Legal Analysis

As the law has been developing, the plaintiff must show that the information made public was in fact "private" and that the disclosure would be "highly offensive to a reasonable person." We look at each element in turn.

*Private Information.* The courts have not been very attentive to this aspect of the matter—perhaps because in most cases the information is clearly something that the plaintiff has held closely and did not want bandied about. Our examples ranged from one extreme to the other. The plaintiff in the sex-change case had not publicized the surgery. On the other hand, private facts are unlikely to exist as to the exterior of a home, when someone at a football game with his fly open poses for a professional photographer or when someone at a police station shouts so loudly that others cannot help but hear what is said.

Between these extremes we have cases like that of Oliver Sipple, whose sexual orientation was not a secret among his friends and his immediate community, and who was willing to march in gay parades, but who wanted the information kept inside San Francisco. Although some cases should be eliminated on the ground that the information published had not been "private" at the time of the publication, most do seem to involve matters that most people would attempt to keep secret.

*"Highly Offensive to a Reasonable Person."* This formulation has received much more attention. Although the specific language is taken from the Restatement of Torts (Second) § 652D, similar expressions have been used in the cases during this tort's development. The single most important consideration appears to be the substance of the statement. In some cases it appears difficult to argue that the revelation would be highly offensive to a reasonable person—as in the case of the janitor who returned the money he found, even though some members of plaintiff's community criticized his behavior. It would also apply to the "weatherworn and unkempt" house. Perhaps a similar analysis would apply to the cases involving idiosyncrasies—the body surfer and the child prodigy. Even though the article about the prodigy was described as "merciless in its dissection of intimate details of its subject's personal life," perhaps what was revealed would not be highly offensive to a reasonable person. That some people may wish to keep private some of their quirks is not the same as saying that reasonable people would find the revelation of that information to be highly offensive.

It is no coincidence that the cases most commonly involve sexual topics, which are generally thought to involve the most intimate matters. Another area has involved revelations about rehabilitated criminals. Simply showing that the revelation would be highly offensive to a reasonable person does not guarantee that the defendant will be held liable for an invasion of privacy. It is, however, an essential first step. As we will see shortly in cases involving disclosure of rape victims' names, other factors may outweigh any offensiveness perceived in the disclosure.

Note that no complex damage rules, such as exist in defamation, have emerged in privacy. The plaintiff who can successfully demonstrate an invasion of privacy will recover damages measured by the emotional harm suffered. Obviously, damages here cannot rehabilitate the plaintiff in the way that damages in defamation might pay for the reputational harm caused by the false statement.

### c. *"Newsworthiness" or "Legitimate Concern" Defense*

In addition to requiring that the publicized matter be private and "highly offensive to a reasonable person," the courts demand that the matter be "not of legitimate concern to the public." Most litigation has revolved around this or similar phrases, such as claims that the article in question was "newsworthy" or that it was of "general or public concern."

There was a period in which the courts seemed to treat "newsworthy" or "of legitimate concern" as descriptive terms. Any article appearing in a newspaper would meet that requirement because if an editor chose to include it, it must be newsworthy. Such an approach, of course, would eliminate the privacy action. More recently, the courts have shifted and are now attempting to develop normative guidelines to determine when the information might be of "legitimate concern to the public."

Note that the categorization of voluntary and involuntary public figures used in post-*Gertz* libel law does not exist in privacy law. Rather than using the precise definition of public figures from *Gertz,* p. 118, *supra*, privacy law uses a more general definition equating public figures with those who are *famous* or *well-known.* Whereas in libel one generally assumes (*Dameron,* p. 139, *supra*, being a notable exception) that one must have *voluntarily* have sought attention, in privacy one can be *involuntarily* drawn into the public eye.

In privacy, it should not be surprising that those who *seek* the public limelight should be thought to have a lesser claim to privacy protection than those *brought into* the glare of publicity because they are victims of an accident or crime or are otherwise swept up in an event. But, as we have said, even involuntary subjects are not immune to public attention. As a comment to the *Restatement* puts it:

> These persons are regarded as properly subject to the public interest, and publishers are permitted to satisfy the curiosity of the public as to its heroes, leaders, villains and victims, and those who are closely associated with them. As in the case of the voluntary public figure, the authorized publicity is not limited to the event that itself arouses the public interest, and to some extent includes publicity given to facts about the individual that would otherwise be purely private.

Our examples include a variety of plaintiffs. The body surfer has voluntarily brought himself into the public eye by his prowess, his continued attendance at a particular beach, and his engaging in a particular type of activity. Sidis, who may have been a voluntary public figure at age 11 and in his teens, later sought obscurity—but the public has a legitimate concern with what happens to prodigies in later life. Is there a similar concern with criminals? Others "voluntarily" become public figures on the spur of the moment—as when Sipple knocked the arm of the President's assailant or when Johnson returned the money he found in the street.  Most of our examples, however, involved involuntary public figures—those who wished to keep their sterilization or mental retardation private, and in no other way had been voluntarily in the public spotlight.

Although courts sometimes suggest that the distinction is relevant to the decision, the difference is at most a matter of degree and more often may control the question of whether the editor will choose to name the person in the story.  As a practical matter, a voluntary public figure who is involved in an accident or other misfortune is much more likely to be named in any story that results from the episode than is a previously anonymous person.  Those who seek the limelight risk having their names used in unwanted contexts.  But this does not mean that every aspect of their lives, or that no aspects of the lives of involuntary figures, may be revealed.  The Restatement seeks to draw a line in the following comment:

> Permissible publicity to information concerning either voluntary or involuntary public figures is not limited to the particular events that arouse the interest of the public.  That interest, once aroused by the event, may legitimately extend, to some reasonable degree, to further information concerning the individual and to facts about him, which are not public and which, in the case of one who had not become a public figure, would be regarded as an invasion of his purely private life.  Thus the life history of one accused of murder, together with such heretofore private facts as may throw some light upon what kind of person he is, his possible guilt or innocence, or his reasons for committing the crime, are a matter of legitimate public interest.   .  .  .   On the same basis the home life and daily habits of a motion picture actress may be of legitimate and reasonable interest to the public that sees her on the screen.
>
> The extent of the authority to make public private facts is not, however, unlimited.  There may be some intimate details of her life, such as sexual relations, which even the actress is entitled to keep to herself.  In determining what is a matter of legitimate public interest, account must be taken of the customs and conventions of the community; and in the last analysis what is proper becomes a matter of the community mores.  The line is to be drawn when the publicity ceases to be the giving of information to which the public is entitled, and becomes a morbid and sensational prying into private lives for its own sake, with which a reasonable member of the public, with decent standards, would say that he had no concern.  The limitations, in other words, are those of common decency, having due regard to the freedom of the press and its reasonable leeway to choose what it will tell the public, but also due regard to the feelings of the individual and the harm that will be done to him by the exposure.  Some reasonable proportion is also to be maintained between the event or activity that makes the individual a public figure and the private facts to which publicity is given.  Revelations

that may properly be made concerning a murderer or the President of the United States would not be privileged if they were to be made concerning one who is merely injured in an automobile accident.

Public opinion polls sometimes suggest that people think the media too frequently invade people's privacy. A broad survey by Louis Harris & Associates, Inc., for Sentry Insurance was published in 1979 in *The Dimensions of Privacy*. Of 1,500 people interviewed for that survey, 78 percent said it would be an invasion of privacy for the media to report details of an extramarital affair that a public official was having with another person. By contrast, only 21 percent thought it would be an invasion of privacy to publish contents of confidential government papers that revealed incompetence or dishonesty by public officials.

The 1987 controversy surrounding *The Miami Herald*'s coverage of Presidential candidate Gary Hart and his relationship with Donna Rice focused attention on the extent to which journalists are willing to seek information about the private lives of public figures and on the public's view of the journalists' actions in such cases. The controversy was renewed later in the year with press revelations of candidate Pat Robertson's wedding date (shortly before the birth of his first child). Some observers argued that some people who could otherwise be good public officials would be discouraged from seeking public office because of the fear of embarrassing revelations about themselves or members of their families.

Results of a 1987 telephone survey by the Gallup Organization for the Times Mirror Co. suggested that people's attitudes were not so different from those of 1979. Of 1,501 interviewed in 1987, 68 percent said the press went too far in reporting Hart's relationship with Donna Rice, and 65 percent said the coverage of Robertson's out-of-wedlock conception of his first child went too far. Editor & Publisher, Nov. 28, 1987 at 32.

In 1987 the media reported extensively on then-Supreme Court nominees Robert Bork and Douglas Ginsburg—even going so far as to seek a list of videotapes Judge Bork had rented. Congress subsequently passed a law protecting most videotape rental records from public disclosure (see 18 U.S.C. § 2710), but the close media scrutiny of the private lives of Presidential candidates and Supreme Court nominees in recent years may lead both journalists and the public to rethink their expectations of reporting on the private lives of public figures.

### d.  Constitutional Privilege Defense

The Supreme Court of the United States has not been called upon frequently in this area because the state courts, operating at common law, have tended to protect the press. Because they have prevailed under state law, the media defendants rarely have needed recourse to the Supreme Court to assert constitutional rights. In *Cox*, the case of the naming of a deceased rape victim, however, the state court ruled that

the plaintiffs were entitled to a judgment.  The broadcaster's appeal led
to the first Supreme Court decision in this area.


## COX BROADCASTING CORP. v. COHN

Supreme Court of the United States, 1975.
420 U.S. 469, 95 S.Ct. 1029, 43 L.Ed.2d 328, 1 Med.L.Rptr. 1819.

[Mr. Cohn's 17–year–old daughter was raped in Georgia and did not
survive the occurrence.  In Georgia it was a misdemeanor for "any news
media or any other person to print and publish, broadcast, televise or
disseminate through any other medium of public dissemination  . . .
the name or identity of any female who may have been raped.   . . ."
Ga.Code Ann. § 26–9901.  Similar statutes exist in a few other states.
The girl was not identified at the time.  Eight months later, appellant's
reporter, Wassell, also an appellant, attended a hearing for the six
youths charged with the rape and murder and learned the girl's name by
inspecting the indictment in the courtroom.  His report naming the girl
was telecast.

The Georgia Supreme Court held that the complaint stated a common law action for damages for invasion of the father's own privacy.
Defendant's First Amendment argument was rejected on the ground that
the statute was an authoritative declaration that Georgia considered a
rape victim's name not to be a matter of public concern.  The court
could discern "no public interest or general concern about the identity of
the victim of such a crime as will make the right to disclose the identity
of the victim rise to the level of First Amendment protection."

On appeal, the Supreme Court first decided that the decision below
was a "final" judgment so as to give the court jurisdiction.  The Court
then turned to the First Amendment issue.]

MR. JUSTICE WHITE delivered the opinion of the Court.

    .   .   .

Georgia stoutly defends both § 26–9901 and the State's common-law
privacy action challenged here.  Her claims are not without force, for
powerful arguments can be made and have been made, that however it
may be ultimately defined, there *is* a zone of privacy surrounding every
individual, a zone within which the State may protect him from intrusion by the press, with all its attendant publicity.  Indeed, the central
thesis of the root article by Warren and Brandeis, The Right to Privacy,
4 Harv.L.Rev. 193, 196 (1890), was that the press was overstepping its
prerogatives by publishing essentially private information and that there
should be a remedy for the alleged abuses.

More compellingly, the century has experienced a strong tide running in favor of the so-called right of privacy.   . . .

    . . .  Because the gravamen of the claimed injury is the publica-
tion of information, whether true or not, the dissemination of which is
embarrassing or otherwise painful to an individual, it is here that claims

of privacy most directly confront the constitutional freedoms of speech and press.  The face-off is apparent, and the appellants urge upon us the broad holding that the press may not be made criminally or civilly liable for publishing information that is neither false nor misleading but absolutely accurate, however damaging it may be to reputation or individual sensibilities.

. . .

. . . Rather than address the broader question whether truthful publications may ever be subjected to civil or criminal liability consistently with the First and Fourteenth Amendments, or to put it another way, whether the State may ever define and protect an area of privacy free from unwanted publicity in the press, it is appropriate to focus on the narrower interface between press and privacy that this case presents, namely, whether the State may impose sanctions on the accurate publication of the name of a rape victim obtained from public records—more specifically, from judicial records which are maintained in connection with a public prosecution and which themselves are open to public inspection.  We are convinced that the State may not do so.

In the first place, in a society in which each individual has but limited time and resources with which to observe at first hand the operations of his government, he relies necessarily upon the press to bring to him in convenient form the facts of those operations.  Great responsibility is accordingly placed upon the news media to report fully and accurately the proceedings of government, and official records and documents open to the public are the basic data of governmental operations.  Without the information provided by the press most of us and many of our representatives would be unable to vote intelligently or to register opinions on the administration of government generally.  With respect to judicial proceedings in particular, the function of the press serves to guarantee the fairness of trials and to bring to bear the beneficial effects of public scrutiny upon the administration of justice.  See Sheppard v. Maxwell, 384 U.S. 333, 350 (1966).

Appellee has claimed in this litigation that the efforts of the press have infringed his right to privacy by broadcasting to the world the fact that his daughter was a rape victim.  The commission of crime, prosecutions resulting from it, and judicial proceedings arising from the prosecutions, however, are without question events of legitimate concern to the public and consequently fall within the responsibility of the press to report the operations of government.

The special protected nature of accurate reports of judicial proceedings has repeatedly been recognized.  This Court, in an opinion written by Mr. Justice Douglas, has said:

"A trial is a public event.  What transpires in the court room is public property.  If a transcript of the court proceedings had been published, we suppose none would claim that the judge could punish the publisher for contempt.  And we can see no difference though the conduct of the attorneys, of the jury, or even of the judge himself, may have reflected on the court. *Those who see and hear what transpired can report it with impunity.* There is no special perquisite of the judiciary which enables it, as distinguished from other institutions of democratic government, to suppress, edit, or censor events which transpire in proceedings before it." Craig v. Harney, 331 U.S. 367, 374 (1947) (emphasis added).

. . .

The developing law surrounding the tort of invasion of privacy recognizes a privilege in the press to report the events of judicial proceedings. The Warren and Brandeis article, supra, noted that the proposed new right would be limited in the same manner as actions for libel and slander where such a publication was a privileged communication: "the right to privacy is not invaded by any publication made in a court of justice . . . and (at least in many jurisdictions) reports of any such proceedings would in some measure be accorded a like privilege."

. . .

Thus, even the prevailing law of invasion of privacy generally recognizes that the interests in privacy fade when the information involved already appears on the public record. The conclusion is compelling when viewed in terms of the First and Fourteenth Amendments and in light of the public interest in a vigorous press. The Georgia cause of action for invasion of privacy through public disclosure of the name of a rape victim imposes sanctions on pure expression—the content of a publication—and not conduct or a combination of speech and non-speech elements that might otherwise be open to regulation or prohibition. See United States v. O'Brien, 391 U.S. 367, 376–377 (1968). The publication of truthful information available on the public record contains none of the indicia of those limited categories of expression, such as "fighting" words, which "are no essential part of any exposition of ideas, and are of such slight social value as a step to truth that any benefit that may be derived from them is clearly outweighed by the social interest in order and morality." [*Chaplinsky*]

By placing the information in the public domain on official court records, the State must be presumed to have concluded that the public interest was thereby being served. Public records by their very nature are of interest to those concerned with the administration of government, and a public benefit is performed by the reporting of the true contents of the records by the media. The freedom of the press to publish that information appears to us to be of critical importance to our type of government in which the citizenry is the final judge of the proper conduct of public business. In preserving that form of government the First and Fourteenth Amendments command nothing less than that the States may not impose sanctions on the publication of truthful information contained in official court records open to public inspection.

We are reluctant to embark on a course that would make public records generally available to the media but forbid their publication if offensive to the sensibilities of the supposed reasonable man.  Such a rule would make it very difficult for the media to inform citizens about the public business and yet stay within the law.  The rule would invite timidity and self-censorship and very likely lead to the suppression of many items that would otherwise be published and that should be made available to the public.  At the very least, the First and Fourteenth Amendments will not allow exposing the press to liability for truthfully publishing information released to the public in official court records.  If there are privacy interests to be protected in judicial proceedings, the States must respond by means which avoid public documentation or other exposure of private information.  Their political institutions must weigh the interests in privacy with the interests of the public to know and of the press to publish.[26]  Once true information is disclosed in public court documents open to public inspection, the press cannot be sanctioned for publishing it.  In this instance as in others reliance must rest upon the judgment of those who decide what to publish or broadcast.  See Miami Herald Pub. Co. v. Tornillo, 418 U.S., at 258.

Appellant Wassell based his televised report upon notes taken during the court proceedings and obtained the name of the victim from the indictments handed to him at his request during a recess in the hearing. Appellee has not contended that the name was obtained in an improper fashion or that it was not on an official court document open to public inspection.  Under these circumstances, the protection of freedom of the press provided by the First and Fourteenth Amendments bars the State of Georgia from making appellants' broadcast the basis of civil liability.[27]

Reversed.

Mr. Chief Justice Burger concurs in the judgment.

Mr. Justice Powell, concurring.

.   .   .

I am in entire accord with the Court's determination that the First Amendment proscribes imposition of civil liability in a privacy action predicated on the truthful publication of matters contained in open judicial records.  But my impression of the role of truth in defamation actions brought by private citizens differs from the Court's.   .   .   .

Mr. Justice Douglas, concurring in the judgment.

**26.** We mean to imply nothing about any constitutional questions which might arise from a state policy not allowing access by the public and press to various kinds of official records, such as records of juvenile court proceedings.

**27.** Appellants have contended that whether they derived the information in question from public records or instead through their own investigation, the First and Fourteenth Amendments bar any sanctions from being imposed by the State because of the publication.  Because appellants have prevailed on more limited grounds, we need not address this broader challenge to the validity of § 26–9901 and of Georgia's right of action for public disclosure.

I agree that the state judgment is "final," and I also agree in the reversal of the Georgia court.* On the merits, . . . there is no power on the part of government to suppress or penalize the publication of "news of the day."

MR. JUSTICE REHNQUIST, dissenting.

Because I am of the opinion that the decision which is the subject of this appeal is not a "final" judgment or decree, . . . I would dismiss this appeal for want of jurisdiction.

**Notes and Questions**

1. What issues does the majority opinion avoid deciding? Why do you think the majority took the approach it did?

2. In the Briscoe case, involving the man who hijacked the truck with the bowling pin spotters 11 years before the article was published, the Supreme Court of California observed that "Ideally, his neighbors should recognize his present worth and forget his past life of shame. But men are not so divine as to forgive the past trespasses of others, and plaintiff therefore endeavored to reveal as little as possible of his past life." That court concluded that a remand was required. If a jury should find that plaintiff had in fact been rehabilitated, it should decide whether "identifying him as a former criminal would be highly offensive and injurious to the reasonable man," and whether defendant had published the information "with a reckless disregard for its offensiveness." Could a court reach the same conclusion after *Cox*? Subsequently in *Briscoe,* the defendant was granted summary judgment in a federal court and the case was not appealed again.)

3. On the importance of the passage of time, consider this comment to Restatement, Second § 652D:

> The fact that there has been a lapse of time, even of considerable length, since the event that has made the plaintiff a public figure, does not of itself defeat the authority to give him publicity or to renew publicity when it has formerly been given. Past events and activities may still be of legitimate interest to the public, and a narrative reviving recollection of what has happened even many years ago may be both interesting and valuable for purposes of information and education. Such a lapse of time is, however, a factor to be considered, with other facts, in determining whether the publicity goes to unreasonable lengths in revealing facts about one

---

* While I join in the narrow result reached by the Court, I write separately to emphasize that I would ground that result upon a far broader proposition, namely, that the First Amendment, made applicable to the States through the Fourteenth, prohibits the use of state law "to impose damages for merely discussing public affairs . . .." [ ] In this context, of course, "public affairs" must be broadly construed—indeed, the term may be said to embrace "any matter of sufficient general interest to prompt media coverage . . .." Gertz v. Robert Welch, Inc., [ ] (Douglas, J. dissenting). By its now-familiar process of balancing and accommodating First Amendment freedoms with state or individual interests, the Court raises a specter of liability which must inevitably induce self-censorship by the media, thereby inhibiting the rough-and-tumble discourse which the First Amendment so clearly protects.

who has resumed the private, lawful and unexciting life led by the great bulk of the community . . .. Again the question is to be determined upon the basis of community standards and mores. Although lapse of time may not impair the authority to give publicity to a public record, the pointing out of the present location and identity of the individual raises a quite different problem.

Is this passage consistent with the Cox case? Does it help analyze the problem of Sidis, the child prodigy? Consider *Roshto*, p. 206, *supra*.

4. The principal opinion in *Howard*, the involuntary sterilization case, responded to the argument that plaintiff's name was unnecessary as follows:

> Here the disclosure of plaintiff's involuntary sterilization was closely related to the subject matter of the news story. It documented the article's theme of maladministration and patient abuses at the Jasper County Home. . . .

> In the sense of serving an appropriate news function, the disclosure contributed constructively to the impact of the article. It offered a personalized frame of reference to which the reader could relate, fostering perception and understanding. Moreover, it lent specificity and credibility to the report.

> In this way the disclosure served as an effective means of accomplishing the intended news function. It had positive communicative value in attracting the reader's attention to the article's subject matter and in supporting expression of the underlying theme.

> Examined in the light of the first amendment, we do not believe the disclosure could reasonably be held to be devoid of news value. [  ]

> Assuming, as plaintiff argues, the newspaper had a right to print an article that documented extrastatutory involuntary sterilizations at the Jasper County Home, the editors also had a right to buttress the force of their evidence by naming names. We do not say it was necessary for them to do so, but we are certain they had a right to treat the identity of victims of involuntary sterilizations as matters of legitimate public concern. . . .

> This is a far cry from embarrassing people by exposing their medical conditions or treatment when identity can add nothing to the probity of the account. [  ]

> The disclosure of plaintiff's identity in this case could not reasonably be viewed as the spreading of gossip solely for its own sake. . . .

> Would the same result be reached in *Cox*?

5. In Deaton v. Delta Democrat Pub. Co., 326 So.2d 471 (Miss.1976), a newspaper ran a feature about a public school class for mentally retarded children. A photograph accompanying the article showed several

members of the class and identified four children of one family. In remanding for trial, the court noted that its decision was not inconsistent with *Cox* because in its case "the information published was not taken from public records, but was by state law made unavailable to the public."

There was no suggestion in the case that the press stole the documents or in any way acquired them illegally. Apparently, the newspaper got the information from some leak. Because the data in question were in government files but were declared not available to the public, the rationale of *Cox* did not apply.

6. In Virgil v. Time, Inc., involving the body surfer, the publisher, citing *Cox,* argued in its brief that the First Amendment protected almost all true statements from liability:

> A press which must depend upon a governmental determination as to what facts are of 'public interest' in order to avoid liability for their truthful publication is not free at all.   . . .   A constitutional rule can be fashioned which protects all the interests involved. This goal is achieved by providing a privilege for truthful publications which is defeasible only when the court concludes as a matter of law that the truthful publication complained of constitutes a clear abuse of the editor's constitutional discretion to publish and discuss subjects and facts which in his judgment are matters of public interest.

The court rejected the argument and adopted the view of the Restatement (Second) of Torts, that liability may be imposed if the matter published is "not of legitimate concern to the public." Then the court relied on a passage from the Restatement that was quoted earlier in this section—that "in the last analysis what is proper becomes a matter of the community mores."

In libel and obscenity cases juries utilize community standards, and the court thought they should do so here, too, "subject to close judicial scrutiny to ensure that the jury resolutions comport with First Amendment principles." What is the difference between *Time* 's position and that adopted by the court? Is the court's view consistent with *Cox?* Over the dissents of Justices Brennan and Stewart, the Supreme Court denied certiorari in *Virgil.* 425 U.S. 998 (1976). The case was remanded for trial.

On remand, the trial judge held that the magazine was entitled to summary judgment. First, the judge concluded that the facts revealed were not "highly offensive." Even if they were, the facts were "included as a legitimate journalistic attempt to explain Virgil's extremely daring and dangerous style of body surfing at the Wedge. There is no possibility that a juror could conclude that the personal facts were included for any inherent morbid, sensational, or curiosity appeal they might have." Virgil v. Sports Illustrated, 424 F.Supp. 1286, 2 Med.L.Rptr. 1271 (S.D.Cal.1976).

7. Although the courts have tended to take this area case-by-case, editors complain that such an approach breeds intolerable uncertainty. An editor must decide today what might happen in court in several years—and the standards are said to be vague. What will be found "highly offensive to a reasonable person" or to violate "community standards and mores"? Juries given these questions may punish unpopular publishers or broadcasters.

Compare this situation with that confronting an editor in the defamation area. There the editor, with advice from lawyers, must decide whether the *New York Times* rule applies and then decide whether the publication's conduct meets that standard. And truth is always a defense. Do you see a sharp difference between the editor's position there and where the case involves privacy?

8. Sometimes government wants privacy for its proceedings and for individuals involved in those proceedings. Such may be the case when a judge is being investigated by a confidential commission, or when a juvenile is arrested, or when, as we saw in *Cox Broadcasting*, a rape has occurred. In Landmark Communications, Inc. v. Virginia, 435 U.S. 829, 3 Med.L.Rptr. 2153 (1978), for example, the Supreme Court faced the question of whether a newspaper could be fined for divulging truthful information about a confidential commission investigating judges. The Virginia constitution directed the legislature to create a commission to investigate charges against judges—and decreed that proceedings before the commission "shall be confidential." A statute creating the commission declared that the proceedings were confidential "and shall not be divulged by any person to anyone except the Commission, except that the record of any proceeding filed with the Supreme Court shall lose its confidential character." It also declared that a proceeding would be filed with the Supreme Court only when the commission finds grounds for filing a formal complaint. Landmark's newspaper, the *Virginian Pilot*, accurately reported that a named judge was under investigation by the Commission. Landmark was found guilty of a misdemeanor for divulging forbidden information and fined $500 plus costs of prosecution. The Supreme Court of Virginia affirmed.

On appeal, the Supreme Court of the United States noted that virtually every state had such a commission, and that all provided for confidentiality. The accepted reasons for confidentiality were (1) it is thought to encourage the filing of complaints and willing participation of witnesses; (2) judges are protected from injury by publication of unexamined complaints until the meritorious can be separated from the unjustified; and (3) confidence in the judiciary is maintained by avoiding premature announcement of groundless claims. In addition, when removal is justified judges are more likely to resign voluntarily or retire if publicity can be avoided.

But even accepting the value of confidentiality, the Court considered this "only the beginning of the inquiry." Landmark was not attacking the confidentiality requirement. It was objecting to making it a crime to divulge or publish the information—a step taken by only Virginia and Hawaii. Chief Justice Burger writing for the Court, said, "[N]either [Virginia]'s interest in protecting the reputation of its judges, nor its interest in maintaining the institutional integrity of its courts is sufficient to justify the subsequent punishment of speech at issue here, even on the assumption that criminal sanctions do in fact enhance the guarantee of confidentiality."

The problem with juvenile proceedings is exemplified by Smith v. Daily Mail Publishing Co., 443 U.S. 97, 5 Med.L.Rptr. 1305 (1979). In that case the Supreme Court faced questions about a state statute prohibiting publication of names from juvenile proceedings. The newspaper involved sought to avoid the imposition of sanctions by acting before any prosecution took place. A West Virginia statute made it a crime for a "newspaper" to publish the names of juveniles in connection with juvenile proceedings without a written order of the court. The respondent newspapers learned over a police radio about a killing at a junior high school. Reporters went to the scene and obtained the name of the suspect by asking witnesses, the police and a prosecuting attorney. The name was revealed thereafter in the newspapers and over several broadcast stations. After being indicted, the newspapers obtained an order from the state supreme court barring any prosecution on the ground that the statute was unconstitutional.

Chief Justice Burger's opinion for the Court, said,

Whether we view the statute as a prior restraint or as a penal sanction for publishing lawfully obtained, truthful information is not dispositive because even the latter action requires the highest form of state interest to sustain its validity. Prior restraints have been accorded the most exacting scrutiny in previous cases. [　]. However, even when a state attempts to punish publication after the event it must nevertheless demonstrate that its punitive action was necessary to further the state interests asserted. [*Landmark Communications*]. Since we conclude that this statute cannot satisfy the constitutional standards defined in *Landmark Communications, Inc.,* we need not decide whether, as argued by respondents, it operated as a prior restraint.

The Court held that the West Virginia statute was unconstitutional.

The Supreme Court of the United States decided another privacy case with parallels to *Cox* in 1989. One difference between the two cases is that where Cox Broadcasting had *intentionally* broadcast a rape victim's name, a small Florida newspaper had inadvertently violated its own internal rule against publishing rape victims' names. Some observers had hoped that the Supreme Court might use the case as a reason for a broad ruling that truthful publication by the media could not be punished under the First Amendment—thereby effectively doing away with the tort of publication of embarrassing private facts. As you will see, the Court cited *Smith* frequently in this case:

## THE FLORIDA STAR v. B.J.F.

Supreme Court of the United States, 1989.
491 U.S. 524, 109 S.Ct. 2603, 105 L.Ed.2d 443, 16 Med.L.Rptr. 1801.

JUSTICE MARSHALL delivered the opinion of the Court.

Florida Stat. § 794.03 (1987) makes it unlawful to "print, publish, or broadcast . . . in any instrument of mass communication" the name of the victim of a sexual offense. Pursuant to this statute, appellant, The Florida Star, was found civilly liable for publishing the name of a rape victim which it had obtained from a publicly released police report. The issue presented here is whether this result comports with the First Amendment. We hold that it does not.

### I

The Florida Star is a weekly newspaper which serves the community of Jacksonville, Florida, and which has an average circulation of approximately 18,000 copies. A regular feature of the newspaper is its "Police Reports" section. That section, typically two to three pages in length, contains brief articles describing local criminal incidents under police investigation.

On October 20, 1983, appellee B.J.F. reported to the Duval County, Florida, Sheriff's Department (the Department) that she had been robbed and sexually assaulted by an unknown assailant. The Department prepared a report on the incident which identified B.J.F., by her full name. The Department then placed the report in its press room. The Department does not restrict access either to the press room or to the reports made available therein.

A Florida Star reporter-trainee sent to the press room copied the police report verbatim, including B.J.F.'s full name, on a blank duplicate of the Department's forms. A Florida Star reporter then prepared a one-paragraph article about the crime, derived entirely from the trainee's copy of the police report. The article included B.J.F.'s full name. It appeared in the "Robberies" subsection of the "Police Reports" section on October 29, 1983, one of fifty-four police blotter stories in that day's edition. The article read:

> "[B.J.F.] reported on Thursday, October 20, she was crossing Brentwood Park, which is in the 500 block of Golfair Boulevard, enroute to her bus stop, when an unknown black man ran up behind the lady and placed a knife to her neck and told her not to yell. The suspect then undressed the lady and had sexual intercourse with her before fleeing the scene with her 60 cents, Timex watch and gold necklace. Patrol efforts have been suspended concerning this incident because of a lack of evidence."

In printing B.J.F.'s full name, the Florida Star violated its internal policy of not publishing the names of sexual offense victims.

On September 26, 1984, B.J.F. filed suit in the Circuit Court of
Duval County against the Department and The Florida Star, alleging
that these parties negligently violated § 794.03.  Before trial, the Department settled with B.J.F. for $2,500.  The Florida Star moved to
dismiss, claiming, *inter alia,* that imposing civil sanctions on the newspaper pursuant to § 794.03 violated the First Amendment.  The trial judge
rejected the motion.  [   ]

At the ensuing day-long trial, B.J.F. testified that she had suffered
emotional distress from the publication of her name.  She stated that
she had heard about the article from fellow workers and acquaintances;
that her mother had received several threatening phone calls from a man
who stated that he would rape B.J.F. again; and that these events had
forced B.J.F. to change her phone number and residence, to seek police
protection, and to obtain mental health counseling.  In defense, The
Florida Star put forth evidence indicating that the newspaper had
learned B.J.F.'s name from the incident report released by the Department, and that the newspaper's violation of its internal rule against
publishing the names of sexual offense victims was inadvertent.

At the close of B.J.F.'s case, and again at the close of its defense,
The Florida Star moved for a directed verdict.  On both occasions, the
trial judge denied these motions.  He ruled from the bench that § 794.03
was constitutional because it reflected a proper balance between the
First Amendment and privacy rights, as it applied only to a narrow set of
"rather sensitive  .  .  .  criminal offenses."  [   ]  At the close of the
newspaper's defense, the judge granted B.J.F.'s motion for a directed
verdict on the issue of negligence, finding the newspaper *per se* negligent
based upon its violation of § 794.03.  [   ]  This ruling left the jury to
consider only the questions of causation and damages.  The judge
instructed the jury that it could award B.J.F. punitive damages if it
found that the newspaper had "acted with reckless indifference to the
rights of others."  [   ]  The jury awarded B.J.F. $75,000 in compensato-
ry damages and $25,000 in punitive damages.  Against the actual
damage award, the judge set off B.J.F.'s settlement with the Department.

The First District Court of Appeal affirmed in a three-paragraph *per
curiam* opinion.  [   ]  In the paragraph devoted to the Florida Star's
First Amendment claim, the court stated that the directed verdict for
B.J.F. had been properly entered because, under § 794.03, a rape victim's name is "of a private nature and not to be published as a matter of
law."  [   ]  The Supreme Court of Florida denied discretionary review.

The Florida Star appealed to this court.  We noted probable jurisdiction, [   ], and now reverse.

## II

The tension between the right which the First Amendment accords
to a free press, on the one hand, and the protections which various
statutes and common-law doctrines accord to personal privacy against
the publication of truthful information, on the other, is a subject we

have addressed several times in recent years.  Our decisions in cases involving government attempts to sanction the accurate dissemination of information as invasive of privacy, have not, however, exhaustively considered this conflict.  On the contrary, although our decisions have without exception upheld the press' right to publish, we have emphasized each time that we were resolving this conflict only as it arose in a discrete factual context.

The parties to this case frame their contentions in light of a trilogy of cases which have presented, in different contexts, the conflict between truthful reporting and state-protected privacy interests.  In [Cox], we found unconstitutional a civil damages award entered against a television station for broadcasting the name of a rape-murder victim which the station had obtained from courthouse records.  In Oklahoma Publishing Co. v. District Court, 430 U.S. 308 [2 Med.L.Rptr. 1456] (1977), we found unconstitutional a state court's pretrial order enjoining the media from publishing the name or photograph of an 11–year–old boy in connection with a juvenile proceeding involving that child which reporters had attended.  Finally, in Smith v. Daily Mail Publishing Co., 443 U.S. 97 (1979), we found unconstitutional the indictment of two newspapers for violating a state statute forbidding newspapers to publish, without written approval of the juvenile court, the name of any youth charged as a juvenile offender.  The papers had learned about a shooting by monitoring a police band radio frequency, and had obtained the name of the alleged juvenile assailant from witnesses, the police, and a local prosecutor.

Appellant takes the position that this case is indistinguishable from [Cox].  [  ]  Alternatively, it urges that our decisions in the above trilogy, and in other cases in which we have held that the right of the press to publish truth overcame asserted interests other than personal privacy, can be distilled to yield a broader First Amendment principle that the press may never be punished, civilly or criminally, for publishing the truth.  [  ]  Appellee counters that the privacy trilogy is inapposite, because in each case the private information already appeared on a "public record," [  ], and because the privacy interests at stake were far less profound than in the present case.  [  ]  In the alternative, appellee urges that [Cox] be overruled and replaced with a categorical rule that publication of the name of a rape victim never enjoys constitutional protection.  [  ]

We conclude that imposing damages on appellant for publishing B.J.F.'s name violates the First Amendment, although not for either of the reasons appellant urges.  Despite the strong resemblance this case bears to [Cox], that case cannot fairly be read as controlling here.  The name of the rape victim in that case was obtained from courthouse records that were open to public inspection  .  .  .. [  ]  Significantly, one of the reasons we gave in [Cox] for invalidating the challenged damages award was the important role the press plays in subjecting trials to public scrutiny and thereby helping guarantee their fairness.  [  ]  That role is not directly compromised where, as here, the information in question comes from a police report prepared and disseminated at a time at which not only had no adversarial criminal proceedings begun, but no suspect had been identified.

Nor need we accept appellant's invitation to hold broadly that truthful publication may never be punished consistent with the First Amendment. Our cases have carefully eschewed reaching this ultimate question, mindful that the future may bring scenarios which prudence counsels our not resolving anticipatorily. [ ] Indeed, in [*Cox*], we pointedly refused to answer even the less sweeping question "whether truthful publications may ever be subjected to civil or criminal liability" for invading "an area of privacy" defined by the State. [ ] Respecting the fact that press freedom and privacy rights are both "plainly rooted in the traditions and significant concerns of our society," we instead focused on the less sweeping issue of "whether the State may impose sanctions on the accurate publication of the name of a rape victim obtained from public records—more specifically, from judicial records which are maintained in connection with a public prosecution and which themselves are open to public inspection." [ ] We continue to believe that the sensitivity and significance of the interests presented in clashes between First Amendment and privacy rights counsel relying on limited principles that sweep no more broadly than the appropriate context of the instant case.

In our view, this case is appropriately analyzed with reference to such a limited First Amendment principle. It is the one, in fact, which we articulated in *Daily Mail* in our synthesis of prior cases involving attempts to punish truthful publication: "[I]f a newspaper lawfully obtains truthful information about a matter of public significance then state officials may not constitutionally punish publication of the information, absent a need to further a state interest of the highest order." [ ] According the press the ample protection provided by that principle is supported by at least three separate considerations, in addition to, of course, the overarching " 'public interest, secured by the Constitution, in the dissemination of truth.' " [ ] The cases on which the *Daily Mail* synthesis relied demonstrate these considerations.

First, because the *Daily Mail* formulation only protects the publication of information which a newspaper has "lawfully obtain[ed]," [ ], the government retains ample means of safeguarding significant interests upon which publication may impinge, including protecting a rape victim's anonymity. To the extent sensitive information rests in private hands, the government may under some circumstances forbid its nonconsensual acquisition, thereby bringing outside of the *Daily Mail* principle the publication of any information so acquired. To the extent sensitive information is in the government's custody, it has even greater power to forestall or mitigate the injury caused by its release. The government may classify certain information, establish and enforce procedures ensuring its redacted release, and extend a damages remedy against the government or its officials where the government's mishandling of sensitive information leads to its dissemination. Where information is entrusted to the government, a less drastic means than punishing truthful publication almost always exists for guarding against the dissemination of private facts.  [  ]

A second consideration undergirding the *Daily Mail* principle is the fact that punishing the press for its dissemination of information which is already publicly available is relatively unlikely to advance the interests in the service of which the State seeks to act.  It is not, of course, always the case that information lawfully acquired by the press is known, or accessible, to others.  But where the government has made certain information publicly available, it is highly anomalous to sanction persons other than the source of its release.  We noted this anomaly in [*Cox*]: "By placing the information in the public domain on official court records, the State must be presumed to have concluded that the public interest was thereby being served."  [  ]  The *Daily Mail* formulation reflects the fact that it is a limited set of cases indeed where, despite the accessibility of the public to certain information, a meaningful public interest is served by restricting its further release by other entities, like the press.  As *Daily Mail* observed in its summary of *Oklahoma Publishing*, "once the truthful information was 'publicly revealed' or 'in the public domain' the court could not constitutionally restrain its dissemination."  [  ]

A third and final consideration is the "timidity and self-censorship" which may result from allowing the media to be punished for publishing certain truthful information.  [  ]  [*Cox*] noted this concern with over-deterrence in the context of information made public through official court records, but the fear of excessive media self-suppression is inapplicable as well to other information released, without qualification, by the government.  A contrary rule, depriving protection to those who rely on the government's implied representations of the lawfulness of dissemination, would force upon the media the onerous obligation of sifting through government press releases, reports, and pronouncements to prune out material arguably unlawful for publication.  This situation could inhere even where the newspaper's sole object was to reproduce, with no substantial change, the government's rendition of the event in question.

Applied to the instant case, the *Daily Mail* principle clearly commands reversal.  The first inquiry is whether the newspaper "lawfully obtain[ed] truthful information about a matter of public significance."  [  ]  It is undisputed that the news article describing the assault on B.J.F. was accurate.  In addition, appellant lawfully obtained B.J.F.'s name.  Appellee's argument to the contrary is based on the fact that under Florida law, police reports which reveal the identity of the victim of a sexual offense are not among the matters of "public record" which the public, by law, is entitled to inspect.  [  ]  But the fact that state officials are not required to disclose such reports does not make it unlawful for a newspaper to receive them when furnished by the government.  Nor does the fact that the Department apparently failed to fulfill its obligation under § 794.03 not to "cause or allow to be  . . .

published" the name of a sexual offense victim make the newspaper's ensuing receipt of this information unlawful.  Even assuming the Constitution permitted a State to proscribe *receipt* of information, Florida has not taken this step.  It is clear, furthermore, that the news article concerned "a matter of public significance," [   ], in the sense in which the *Daily Mail* synthesis of prior cases used that term.  That is, the article generally, as opposed to the specific identity contained within it, involved a matter of paramount public import: the commission, and investigation, of a violent crime which had been reported to authorities. [   ]

The second inquiry is whether imposing liability on appellant pursuant to § 794.03 serves "a need to further a state interest of the highest order." [   ]  Appellee argues that a rule punishing publication furthers three closely related interests: the privacy of victims of sexual offenses; the physical safety of such victims, who may be targeted for retaliation if their names become known to their assailants; and the goal of encouraging victims of such crimes to report these offenses without fear of exposure. [   ]

At a time in which we are daily reminded of the tragic reality of rape, it is undeniable that these are highly significant interests, a fact underscored by the Florida Legislature's explicit attempt to protect these interests by enacting a criminal statute prohibiting much dissemination of victim identities.  We accordingly do not rule out the possibility that, in a proper case, imposing civil sanctions for publication of the name of a rape victim might be so overwhelmingly necessary to advance these interests as to satisfy the *Daily Mail* standard.  For three independent reasons, however, imposing liability for publication under the circumstances of this case is too precipitous a means of advancing these interests to convince us that there is a "need" within the meaning of the *Daily Mail* formulation for Florida to take this extreme step. [   ]

First is the manner in which appellant obtained the identifying information in question.  As we have noted, where the government itself provides information to the media, it is most appropriate to assume that the government had, but failed to utilize, far more limited means of guarding against dissemination than the extreme step of punishing truthful speech.  That assumption is richly borne out in this case. B.J.F.'s identity would never have come to light were it not for the erroneous, if inadvertent, inclusion by the Department of her full name in an incident report made available in a press room open to the public. Florida's policy against disclosure of rape victims' identities, reflected in § 794.03, was undercut by the Department's failure to abide by this policy.  Where, as here, the government has failed to police itself in disseminating information, it is clear under [*Cox*], *Oklahoma Publishing*, and *Landmark Communications* that the imposition of damages against the press for its subsequent publication can hardly be said to be a narrowly tailored means of safeguarding anonymity. [   ]  Once the government has placed such information in the public domain, "reliance must rest upon the judgment of those who decide what to publish or broadcast," [   ], and hopes for restitution must rest upon the willingness of the government to compensate victims for their loss of privacy, and to protect them from the other consequences of its mishandling of the information which these victims provided in confidence.

That appellant gained access to the information in question through a government news release made it especially likely that, if liability were to be imposed, self-censorship would result. Reliance on a news release is a paradigmatically "routine newspaper reporting techniqu[e]." [   ] The government's issuance of such a release, without qualification, can only convey to recipients that the government considered dissemination lawful, and indeed expected the recipients to disseminate the information further. Had appellant merely reproduced the news release prepared and released by the Department, imposing civil damages would surely violate the First Amendment. The fact that appellant converted the police report into a news story by adding the linguistic connecting tissue necessary to transform the report's facts into full sentences cannot change this result.

A second problem with Florida's imposition of liability for publication is the broad sweep of the negligence *per se* standard applied under the civil cause of action implied from § 794.03. Unlike claims based on the common law tort of invasion of privacy, [   ], civil actions based on § 794.03 require no case-by-case findings that the disclosure of a fact about a person's private life was one that a reasonable person would find highly offensive. On the contrary, under the *per se* theory of negligence adopted by the courts below, liability follows automatically from publication. This is so regardless of whether the identity of the victim has otherwise become a reasonable subject of public concern—because, perhaps, questions have arisen whether the victim fabricated an assault by a particular person. Nor is there a scienter requirement of any kind under § 794.03, engendering the perverse result that truthful publications challenged pursuant to this cause of action are less protected by the First Amendment than even the least protected defamatory falsehoods: those involving purely private figures, where liability is evaluated under a standard, usually applied by a jury, or ordinary negligence. [   ] We have previously noted the impermissibility of categorical prohibitions upon media access where important First Amendment interests are at stake. [   ] More individualized adjudication is no less indispensable where the State, seeking to safeguard the anonymity of crime victims, sets its face against publication of their names.

Third, and finally, the facial underinclusiveness of § 794.03 raises serious doubts about whether Florida is, in fact, serving, with this statute, the significant interests which appellee invokes in support of affirmance. Section 794.03 prohibits the publication of identifying information only if this information appears in an "instrument of mass communication," a term the statute does not define. Section 794.03 does not prohibit the spread by other means of the identities of victims of sexual offenses. An individual who maliciously spreads word of the identity of a rape victim is thus not covered, despite the fact that the communication of such information to persons who live near, or work with, the victim may have consequences equally devastating as the exposure of her name to large numbers of strangers.  [  ]

When a State attempts the extraordinary measure of punishing truthful publication in the name of privacy, it must demonstrate its commitment to advancing this interest by applying its prohibition even-handedly, to the smalltime disseminator as well as the media giant. Where important First Amendment interests are at stake, the mass scope of disclosure is not an acceptable surrogate for injury.  A ban on disclosures effected by "instrument[s] of mass communication" simply cannot be defended on the ground that partial prohibitions may effect partial relief.  [  ]  Without more careful and inclusive precautions against alternative forms of dissemination, we cannot conclude that Florida's selective ban on publication by the mass media satisfactorily accomplishes its stated purpose.

### III

Our holding today is limited.  We do not hold that truthful publication is automatically constitutionally protected, or that there is no zone of personal privacy within which the State may protect the individual from intrusion by the press, or even that a State may never punish publication of the name of a victim of a sexual offense.  We hold only that where a newspaper publishes truthful information which it has lawfully obtained, punishment may lawfully be imposed, if at all, only when narrowly tailored to a state interest of the highest order, and that no such interest is satisfactorily served by imposing liability under § 794.03 to appellant under the facts of this case.  The decision below is therefore

Reversed.

JUSTICE SCALIA, concurring in part and concurring in the judgment.

I think it is sufficient to decide this case to rely upon the third ground set forth in the Court's opinion, [  ]: that a law cannot be regarded as protecting an interest "of the highest order," [  ], and thus as justifying a restriction upon truthful speech, when it leaves appreciable damage to that supposedly vital interest unprohibited.  In the present case, I would anticipate that the rape victim's discomfort at the dissemination of news of her misfortune among friends and acquaintances would be at least as great as her discomfort at its publication by the media to people to whom she is only a name.  . . .

This law has every appearance of a prohibition that society is prepared to impose upon the press but not upon itself.  Such a prohibition does not protect an interest "of the highest order."  For that reason, I agree that the judgment of the court below must be reversed.

JUSTICE WHITE, with whom THE CHIEF JUSTICE and JUSTICE O'CONNOR join, dissenting.

"Short of homicide, [rape] is the 'ultimate violation of self.' " [   ]
For B.J.F., however, the violation she suffered at a rapist's knifepoint
marked only the beginning of her ordeal.  A week later, while her
assailant was still at large, an account of this assault—identifying by
name B.J.F. as the victim—was published by The Florida Star.  As a
result, B.J.F. received harassing phone calls, required mental health
counseling, was forced to move from her home, and was even threatened
with being raped again.  Yet today, the Court holds that a jury award of
$75,000 to compensate B.J.F. for the harm she suffered due to the Star's
negligence is at odds with the First Amendment.  I do not accept this
result.

The Court reaches its conclusion based on an analysis of three of our
precedents and a concern with three particular aspects of the judgment
against appellant.  I consider each of these points in turn, and then
consider some of the larger issues implicated by today's decision.

I

The Court finds its result compelled, or at least supported in varying
degrees, by three of our prior cases: [Cox, Oklahoma Publishing, Daily
Mail].  I disagree.  None of these cases requires the harsh outcome
reached today.

 . . .  While there are similarities [to Cox], critical aspects of that
case make it wholly distinguishable from this one.  First, in [Cox], the
victim's name had been disclosed in the hearing where her assailants
pled guilty; and, as we recognized, judicial records have always been
considered public information in this country.  [   ]  In fact, even the
earliest notion of privacy rights exempted the information contained in
judicial records from its protections.  [   ]  Second, unlike the incident
report at issue here  . . .  the judicial proceedings at issue in [Cox]
were open as a matter of state law. . . .

These facts  . . .  were critical to our analysis in [Cox].  . . .

[Cox] stands for the proposition that the State cannot make the
press its first line of defense in withholding private information from the
public—it cannot ask the press to secrete private facts that the State
makes no effort to safeguard in the first place.  In this case, however,
the State has undertaken "means which avoid [but obviously, not
altogether prevent] public documentation or other exposure of private
information."  No doubt this is why the Court frankly admits that
"[Cox]  . . .  cannot fairly be read as controlling here."  [   ]

 . . .

 . . .  I cannot agree that [Cox, Oklahoma Publishing, Daily Mail]
require—or even substantially support—the result reached by the Court
today.

II

We are left, then, to wonder whether the three "independent reasons" the Court cites for reversing the judgment for B.J.F. support its
result.  [   ]

The first of these relied on by the Court is the fact "appellant gained access to [B.J.F.'s name] through a government news release." [   ] "The government's issuance of such a release, without qualification, can only convey to recipients that the government considered dissemination lawful," the court suggests. [   ] So described, this case begins to look like the situation in *Oklahoma Publishing,* where a judge invited reporters into his courtroom, but then tried to forbid them from reporting on the proceedings they observed. But this case is profoundly different. Here the "release" of information provided by the government was not, as the Court says, "without qualification." As the Star's own reporter conceded at trial, the crime incident report that inadvertently included B.J.F.'s name was posted in a room that contained signs making it clear that the names of rape victims were not matters of public record, and were not to be published. [   ] The Star's reporter indicated that she understood that she "[was not] allowed to take down that information" (i.e., B.J.F.'s name) and that "[was] not supposed to take the information from the police department." [   ] Thus, by her own admission the posting of the incident report did not convey to the Star's reporter the idea that "the government considered dissemination lawful" the Court's suggestion to the contrary is inapt.

Instead, Florida has done precisely what we suggested, in [*Cox*], that States wishing to protect the privacy rights of rape victims might do: "respond [to the challenge] by means which *avoid* public documentation or other exposure of private information." [   ] By amending its public records statute to exempt rape [victims'] names from disclosure, [   ], and forbidding its officials from releasing such information, [   ], the State has taken virtually every step imaginable to prevent what happened here. This case presents a far cry, then, from [*Cox*] or *Oklahoma Publishing,* where the State asked the news media not to publish information it had made generally available to the public: here, the State is not asking the media to do the State's job in the first instance. Unfortunately, as this case illustrates, mistakes happen: even when States take measures to "avoid" disclosure, sometimes rape victim's names are found out. As I see it, it is not too much to ask the press, in instances such as this, to respect simple standards of decency and refrain from publishing a victim's name, address, and/or phone number.

Second, the Court complains that appellant was judged here under too strict a liability standard. The Court contends that a newspaper might be found liable under the Florida courts' negligence *per se* theory without regard to a newspaper's scienter or degree of fault. [   ] The short answer to this complaint is that whatever merit the Court's argument might have, it is totally inapposite here, where the jury found that appellant acted with "reckless indifference towards the rights of others," [   ], a standard far higher than the *Gertz* standard the Court urges as a constitutional minimum today. [   ] B.J.F. proved the Star's negligence at trial—and, actually, far more than simple negligence; the Court's concerns about damages resting on a strict liability or mere causation basis are irrelevant to the validity of the judgment for appellee.

But even taking the Court's concerns in the abstract, they miss the mark. Permitting liability under a negligence *per se* theory does not mean that defendants will be held liable without a showing of negligence, but rather, that the standard of care has been set by the legislature, instead of the courts. The Court says that negligence *per se* permits a plaintiff to hold a defendant liable without a showing that the disclosure was "of a fact about a person's private life . . . that a reasonable person would find highly offensive." [   ] But the point here is that the legislature—reflecting popular sentiment—has determined that disclosure of the fact that a person was raped is categorically a revelation that reasonable people find offensive. And as for the Court's suggestion that the Florida courts' theory permits liability without regard for whether the victim's identity is already known, or whether she herself has made it known—these are facts that would surely enter into the calculation of damages in such a case. In any event, none of these mitigating factors was present here; whatever the force of the arguments generally, they do not justify the Court's ruling against B.J.F. in this case.

Third, the Court faults the Florida criminal statute for being underinclusive: § 794.03 covers disclosure of rape [victims'] names in "instrument[s] of mass communication," but not other means of distribution, the Court observes. [   ] But our cases which have struck down laws that limit or burden the press due to their underinclusiveness have involved situations where a legislature has singled out one segment of the news media or press for adverse treatment, [   ]. Here, the Florida law evenhandedly covers all "instrument[s] of mass communication" no matter their form, media, content, nature or purpose. It excludes neighborhood gossips, [   ], because presumably the Florida Legislature has determined that neighborhood gossips do not pose the danger and intrusion to rape victims that "instrument[s] of mass communication" do. Simply put: Florida wanted to prevent the widespread distribution of rape [victims'] names, and therefore enacted a statute tailored almost as precisely as possible to achieving that end.

Moreover, the Court's "underinclusiveness" analysis itself is "underinclusive." After all, the lawsuit against the Star which is at issue here is not an action for violating the statute which the Court deems underinclusive, but is, more accurately, for the negligent publication of appellee's name. [   ] The scheme which the Court should review, then, is not only § 794.03 (which, as noted above, merely provided the standard of care in this litigation), but rather, the whole of Florida privacy tort law. As to the latter, Florida does recognize a tort of publication of private facts. Thus, it is quite possible that the neighborhood gossip whom the Court so fears being left scott-free to spread news of a rape victim's identity would be subjected to the same (or similar) liability regime under which appellant was taxed. The Court's myopic focus on

§ 794.03 ignores the probability that Florida law is more comprehensive than the Court gives it credit for being.

Consequently, neither the State's "dissemination" of B.J.F.'s name, nor the standard of liability imposed here, nor the underinclusiveness of Florida tort law require setting aside the verdict for B.J.F. And as noted above, such a result is not compelled by our cases. I turn, therefore, to the more general principles at issue here to see if they recommend the Court's result.

### III

At issue in this case is whether there is any information about people, which—though true—may not be published in the press. By holding that only "a state interest of the highest order" permits the State to penalize the publication of truthful information, and by holding that protecting a rape victim's right to privacy is not among those state interests of the highest order, the Court accepts appellant's invitation, [  ], to obliterate one of the most note-worthy legal inventions of the 20th Century; the tort of the publication of private facts. [  ] Even if the Court's opinion does not say as much today, such obliteration will follow inevitably from the Court's conclusion here. If the First Amendment prohibits wholly private persons (such as B.J.F.) from recovering from the publication of the fact that she was raped, I doubt that there remain any "private facts" which persons may assume will not be published in the newspapers, or broadcast on television.

Of course, the right to privacy is not absolute. Even the article widely relied upon in cases vindicating privacy rights, Warren & Brandeis, The Right to Privacy, 4 Harv.L.Rev., at 193, recognized that this right inevitably conflicts with the public's right to know about matters of general concern—and that sometimes, the latter must trump the former. [  ] Resolving this conflict is a difficult matter, and I do not fault the Court for attempting to strike an appropriate balance between the two, but rather, for according too little weight to B.J.F.'s side of equation, and too much on the other.

I would strike the balance rather differently. Writing for the Ninth Circuit, Judge Merrill put this view eloquently:

> "Does the spirit of the Bill of Rights require that individuals be free to pry into the unnewsworthy private affairs of their fellowmen? In our view it does not. In our view, fairly defined areas of privacy must have the protection of law if the quality of life is to continue to be personably acceptable. The public's right to know is, then, subject to reasonable limitations so far as concerns the private facts of its individual members." [  ]

Ironically, this Court, too, had occasion to consider this same balance just a few weeks ago, in United States Department of Justice v. Reporters Committee for Freedom of the Press, 489 U.S. 749 [16 Med.L.Rptr. 1545] (1989). There, we were faced with a press request, under the Freedom of Information Act, for a "rap sheet" on a person accused of bribing a Congressman—presumably, a person whose privacy rights would be far less than B.J.F.'s. Yet this Court rejected the media's request for disclosure of the "rap sheet," saying:

> "The privacy interest in maintaining the practical obscurity of rap-sheet information will always be high. When the subject of such a rap sheet is a private citizen and when the information is in the Government's control as compilation, rather than as a record of 'what the government is up to,' the privacy interest . . . is . . . at its apex while the . . . public interest in disclosure is at its nadir." [  ]

The Court went on to conclude that disclosure of rap sheets categorical[ly] constitutes an "unwarranted" invasion of privacy. [  ] The same surely must be true—indeed, much more so—for the disclosure of a rape victim's name.

I do not suggest that the Court's decision today is radical departure from a previously charted course. The Court's ruling has been foreshadowed. In [*Hill*], we observed that—after a brief period in this century where Brandeis' view was ascendant—the trend in "modern" jurisprudence has been to eclipse an individual's right to maintain private any truthful information that the press wished to publish. More recently, in [*Cox*], we acknowledged the possibility that the First Amendment may prevent a State from ever subjecting the publication of truthful but private information to civil liability. Today, we hit the bottom of the slippery slope.

I would find a place to draw the line higher on the hillside: a spot high enough to protect B.J.F.'s desire for privacy and peace-of-mind in the wake of a horrible personal tragedy. There is no public interest in publishing the names, addresses, and phone numbers of persons who are the victims of crime—and no public interest in immunizing the press from liability in the rare cases where a State's efforts to protect a victim's privacy have failed. Consequently, I respectfully dissent.

### Notes and Questions

1. Why is the *Star*'s case not precisely covered by *Cox?*

2. Why is the *Star*'s case not precisely covered by *Daily Mail?*

3. How might the *Star*'s case have been analyzed in a state in which there was no statute?

4. How might the *Star*'s case have been analyzed if the *Star* had learned about the name from an eyewitness rather than as the result of a mistake in the sheriff's office?

5. What might change if it turned out that the *Star* got the name from a sheriff's deputy who violated a statute in revealing the name?

6. Does state law or the First Amendment protect a broadcaster that identifies a rape victim in a case in which a man arrested on a rape

charge claims that the warden beat him up?  (The alleged rape victim is the warden's daughter.)  Does *Florida Star* address this?

What would be the analysis in a case in which the rape victim is the daughter of a man who is a strong proponent of criminal rehabilitation and early paroles?  What if the rapist had been recently paroled after serving time for rape?

What would be the analysis in a case in which a statute provides that an accused rapist is not to be identified unless and until he is brought to trial?

7.  Justice White suggests that the private facts tort, in the wake of *Cox* and *Florida Star*, is dead.  Do you agree?  Will future plaintiffs have no remedy when truthful-but-embarrassing private facts are revealed about them?  Should people who commit crimes and people who are crime victims be treated alike in this regard?

8.  The decision in *Florida Star* led to a petition seeking review of an earlier case involving an alleged invasion of privacy by a television statement which disclosed the identity of a rape victim.  Ross v. Midwest Communications, Inc., 870 F.2d 271, 16 Med.L.Rptr. 1463 (5th Cir.1989).  Marla Ross was raped in 1983 by an assailant who was never apprehended.  Police assured her that her name would be held in strict confidence.  In a documentary about the possible innocence of a man accused of another rape, Minneapolis television station WCCO–TV mentioned Ross as "Marla" and showed a photograph of the house in which she lived at the time of the rape.  A federal district court granted summary judgment for the television station, holding that the details of the rape were a matter of legitimate public interest, and the U.S. Court of Appeals for the Fifth Circuit affirmed.  In his petition for review following the *Florida Star* case, Ross's attorney told the Supreme Court that its decision in *Florida Star* "shattered the fragile confidence rape survivors possessed in law enforcement promises that their identities would not be disclosed."  Med.L.Rptr. News Notes, Sept. 26, 1989.  The Supreme Court denied *certiorari*.  493 U.S. 935 (1989).

9.  The highly publicized sexual assault charges against William Kennedy Smith, along with decisions by a London tabloid, an American supermarket tabloid (*The Globe*), *The New York Times* and NBC to identify Patricia Bowman, the woman who made the allegations against him, raised anew the concerns about the proper ways of treating complainants in sexual assault cases prior to any court determination that they are, in fact, victims.  A local prosecutor in Florida filed misdemeanor charges against *The Globe*, which is published in Boca Raton.  The publication was charged with violating the criminal statute on which B.J.F.'s civil suit was based in the *Florida Star* case.  The statute provided a $500 fine and up to 60 days in jail for publishing a rape victim's name.  The trial court judge found the statute to be unconstitutional, saying, "However desirable [laws that shield rape victims' names] may be, the enforcement of such laws collides with First Amendment claims of the press to comment freely on a matter of public interest,"

and dismissed the case. His decision was affirmed. State of State v. Globe Communications Corp., 622 So.2d 1066, 21 Med.L.Rptr. 2129 (Fla.App.1993). Ethical implications of the coverage of the William Kennedy Smith coverage will be discussed later in this chapter.

### e.  Enjoining Violations of Privacy

Many commentators have observed that damages in defamation are a more adequate remedy than in truthful invasion of privacy cases. In defamation the award of damages, especially special damages, may compensate the plaintiff for a loss of reputation that has in fact injured him financially. Even a judgment for nominal damages may have a vital symbolic function. In privacy, however, once the invasion has occurred the embarrassing truth is out, and a judgment or an award of money does not undo harm caused by the publication. Counterattack and counterspeech are not useful here.

Thus, courts have looked more seriously at alternatives in privacy suits and have been somewhat more responsive to a plea for an injunction to prevent the utterance of the invasion in the first place. Often the plaintiff learns about the invasion only after actual publication, but in some situations prevention is feasible. Because the privacy action is so recent in origin, it lacks a long history like that of defamation during which the injunction came to be totally rejected in actions for private defamations.

The Supreme Court has had a curious record with regard to injunctions barring invasions of privacy by the media. Although three significant cases have presented the issue, the Court has yet to come to grips with it. In the first, a famous baseball player persuaded the New York courts to enjoin the publication of an unauthorized biography that contained false dialogue. Spahn v. Julian Messner, Inc., 21 N.Y.2d 124, 286 N.Y.S.2d 832, 233 N.E.2d 840 (1967). The defendants compromised and settled their dispute while it was being appealed to the Supreme Court.

The second chance came in a case involving a motion picture about conditions inside a Massachusetts institution for the criminally insane. The state court barred showing of the picture except to selected groups because of the producer's invasion of the privacy of the inmates, assertedly in violation of an agreement he signed in order to get permission to make the film. Commonwealth v. Wiseman, 356 Mass. 251, 249 N.E.2d 610 (1969). The Supreme Court denied *certiorari* to Wiseman, the producer, 398 U.S. 960 (1970), over the lengthy dissent of Justice Harlan, joined by Justices Douglas and Brennan:

> Petitioners seek review in this Court of a decision of the Massachusetts Supreme Judicial Court enjoining the commercial distribution to general audiences of the film "Titticut Follies." Petitioners' film is a "documentary" of life in Bridgewater State Hospital for the criminally insane. Its stark portrayal of patient-

routine and treatment of the inmates is at once a scathing indictment of the inhumane conditions that prevailed at the time of the
film and an undeniable infringement of the privacy of the inmates
filmed, who are shown nude and engaged in acts that would unquestionably embarrass an individual of normal sensitivity.  . . .

The balance between these two interests, that of the individual's privacy and the public's right to know about conditions in public
institutions, is not one that is easily struck, particularly in a case
like that before us where the importance of the issue is matched by
the extent of the invasion of privacy. . . . A further consideration is the fact that these inmates are not only the wards of the
Commonwealth of Massachusetts but are also the charges of society
as a whole.  It is important that conditions in public institutions
should not be cloaked in secrecy, lest citizens may disclaim responsibility for the treatment that their representative government affords
those in its care.  At the same time it must be recognized that the
individual's concern with privacy is the key to the dignity which is
the promise of civilized society. [  ]

. . .

I am at a loss to understand how questions of such importance
can be deemed not "certworthy."  To the extent that the Commonwealth suggests that certiorari be denied because petitioners failed
to comply with reasonable contract conditions imposed by the Commonwealth, that question in itself is one of significant constitutional
dimension, for it is an open question as to how far a government
may go in cutting off access of the media to its institutions when
such access will not hinder them in performing their functions.
[Estes v. Texas, 381 U.S. 532 (1965)].  In the case before us,
however, the only asserted interest is the State's concern for the
privacy of the inmates in its care, and the basis for the decision
below was the predominance of that interest over that of the general
public in seeing the film.

In 1988 Wiseman sought an end to the injunction, and a Massachusetts court decided in 1989 that the 22–year–old ban on the public
showing of the film could be lifted if the faces of many of the inmates
were blurred.  Wiseman said that was not technically feasible and that,
even if it were, such an action would violate his freedom of speech.
"The film would lose its meaning," Wiseman was quoted as saying, "The
whole point is that these are not faceless people.  Their faces reflect the
lives they've lived and how they've been treated."  New York Times,
Sept. 30, 1989, at 24.  In 1991 the judge revised the order to require only
that names and addresses of inmates be kept confidential.  At the
Boston Film Festival that year, the film was shown to a general audience
for the first time since its suppression in 1967.  See "Judge Lifts Bar on
'Titicut Follies' Film," News Media and the Law, Fall 1991, at 36.

A third Supreme Court case involved a claim by a former patient
trying to enjoin her analyst from publishing a book the analyst had

written about the patient's treatment. Although names and other facts were changed in the book, plaintiff alleged that she and her family were easily identifiable. The state courts granted a preliminary injunction enjoining all distribution until the litigation had concluded. The defendants, including the book's publisher, sought *certiorari*, claiming that the injunction against publishing concededly true statements of medical and scientific importance violated the First Amendment. The Court granted *certiorari*, Roe v. Doe, 417 U.S. 907 (1974), and heard oral arguments. It then decided not to decide the case by dismissing the writ of *certiorari* as having been "improvidently granted." 420 U.S. 307 (1975). The complication of the confidential relationship between the parties and the murky record caused by the use of Does and Roes might have dissuaded the Court from deciding the case.

The case then went to trial on the merits. The trial judge found that the plaintiff was entitled to a remedy because of defendant's violation of an implied agreement to treat the plaintiff in confidence. He awarded damages for the harm plaintiff suffered from the release of 220 copies of the book before the preliminary injunction was issued. He also permanently enjoined distribution of the remaining stock. Doe v. Roe, 93 Misc.2d 201, 400 N.Y.S.2d 668 (1977). By subsequent order, the remaining volumes were destroyed.

How might one analyze the competing interests in these invasion of privacy cases when the issue becomes one of a remedy for a *true* statement that is adjudged an invasion? How do these cases square with concern about prior restraint?

### f.  Ethical Considerations

In addition to considering how these matters are analyzed legally, a prospective journalist must also consider the more basic question of whether a reporter or an editor should include this type of material in a story. Even though the legal system may ultimately protect the overwhelming majority of the stories, that does not necessarily answer the question of how news media should handle them.

Most media decline to name victims of sex crimes even when the names are known, but newsroom viewpoints vary tremendously when the accused is a public figure or has a famous name. In the William Kennedy Smith case referred to earlier in this chapter, public disclosure of Patricia Bowman's history, particularly in a profile of her in the *Times*, generated a national controversy over identification of rape complainants.

The day after NBC first used Bowman's name, *The New York Times* published its profile of her, including comments by unnamed sources that she had a poor academic record and "a little wild streak" in high school, had borne a child out of wedlock and frequented expensive bars in Palm Beach. The story was accompanied by an editor's note saying that the *Times* ordinarily did not publish rape victims' names, "but editors said yesterday that NBC's broadcast took the matter out of their hands." See Butterfield and Tabor, Leap up Social Ladder for Woman in Rape Inquiry, New York Times, April 17, 1991 at A17. (In later editions the headline was changed to "Woman in Florida Rape Inquiry Fought Adversity and Sought Acceptance.")

The *Times* story set off a furor within the newspaper's own staff and around the country. A week later the *Times* ran an editor's note saying it had not intended to challenge the veracity of the woman's accusations and that the story should have included such a statement. See New York Times, April 26, 1991 at A3. The same issue of the *Times* contained a story reporting that 100 *Times* employees had signed a petition objecting to the original story about the woman and that a staff meeting of *Times* editors with 300 staffers "quickly turned confrontational." The story quoted one of the *Times* editors who approved the story as saying *Times* editors expected much of the mainstream press to follow its lead in identifying the woman, but that most news organizations did not do so. Glaverson, "Times Article Naming Rape Accuser Ignites Debate on Journalistic Values." New York Times, April 26, 1991 at A12.

After Smith's acquittal on the rape charge, Patricia Bowman appeared on the ABC News television program "Prime Time Live" without the "blue dot" that had hidden her face during most of the television coverage of the trial. Her appearance pushed the program to its highest rating ever on Thursday night. It normally finished third behind "L.A. Law" and "Knots Landing" but was in first place on the night of the Bowman appearance. New York Times, Dec. 21, 1991 at 47.

NBC similarly identified the accuser of boxer Mike Tyson. The executive producer of NBC News said that not naming her would open NBC up to criticism from people who would say, "How come you used Bowman's name, but not this one's?" USA Today, Feb. 3, 1992 at 3D. In an interview on NBC with Today co-host Katie Couric two months later, Bowman made a personal appeal to then-NBC News President Michael Gartner to stop the policy of naming rape complainants. She called the policy "frightening" and said disclosure inhibits victims from coming forward. An NBC spokesperson said the network had no plans to change the policy of making decisions on naming them on a case-by-case basis. The spokesperson said Gartner believes "the more we tell our viewers, the better informed they'll be in making up their own minds about the issues involved." USA Today, Apr. 29, 1992 at 3D.

Until the 1980s the press was often timid about revealing personal information about politicians. In an article in the April 1975 issue of *[MORE]*, Washington journalist Brit Hume condemned the reluctance of editors to publish stories about Congressmen who seem senile at Committee hearings, extramarital activities of Presidents and Congressmen, public drunkenness of Congressmen and similar matters. Are these equally deserving of disclosure? Would you distinguish between reporting actions or behavior apparent to any observer, and reporting information acquired surreptitiously?  Hume quoted an editor as saying that prying into the lives of public officials "smells of Hollywood gossip." Could you draw a line between the two?  One approach was to print such information only when the circumstance "affects their public performance."  Hume argued that this is a poor standard because it is often very difficult to tell why a Congressman is not being effective.  He cited one case in which it was thought that a Senator objected to the sexual behavior of a Congressman from his state and that the tension between them probably hurt the Congressman's effectiveness.  Hume noted other problems relating to relatives of those in public office: an official's son who gets into a minor traffic accident, or the mental health of the wife or child of a possible presidential candidate.

Electronic journalists faced a particularly difficult decision involving ethics and privacy when the Pennsylvania state treasurer, R. Budd Dwyer, shot himself during a news conference in 1987.  Several stations in Pennsylvania showed the entire suicide—Dwyer putting a .357 Magnum pistol into his mouth and pulling the trigger.  Others showed an edited version.  Enraged viewers complained that children, home from school because of a snowstorm, saw the videotape before parents could switch the channel.  Although no lawsuit was involved and the problem is how graphic a news report should be, the incident points up the difficult balance between full disclosure in news coverage and respect for the privacy of a suicide victim or his family.  See Editor & Publisher, Jan. 31, 1987 at 9.

### 4. Appropriation and Right of Publicity

The fourth branch of invasion of privacy is appropriation of another's name or likeness for commercial or trade purposes.  Its major impact is on the field of advertising, because news reports have generally been held not to be "for commercial or trade purposes."  Truth is not a defense.  A manufacturer who advertises that John Smith uses his product may not defend himself merely by proving that John Smith does use his product, although that is important for other reasons that will be discussed in Chapter IX.

What must be demonstrated to avoid a successful appropriation action is *consent*.  This usually comes in the form of a written "release" because many states require that consent to appropriation be written. Indeed, it is common for advertising agencies and even news organizations to have standard release forms available for use.  Many release forms are limited releases in that they restrict the uses that can be made of a particular name or likeness or the period of time during which the use will be permitted.  Numerous appropriation cases have been the result of using a picture in a manner not covered by the original release.

Some courts have concluded that a plaintiff who has agreed to be photographed for one purpose may complain that the photos later appeared in another magazine—one in which the plaintiff would rather not have appeared.  Douglass v. Hustler Magazine, Inc., 769 F.2d 1128

(7th Cir.1985), cert. denied 475 U.S. 1094 (1986). Compare Brewer v. Hustler Magazine, Inc., 749 F.2d 527 (9th Cir.1984) (rejecting copyright approach to issue) and Martin v. Penthouse International, Ltd., 12 Med.L.Rptr. 2058 (Cal.App.1986) (plaintiffs cannot complain that photograph documenting their public appearance at an "exotic erotic ball" constitutes appropriation even when juxtaposed with photographs of performances at the event and even if they consider the magazine "pornographic").

In another case, Stephano v. News Group Publications, Inc., 64 N.Y.2d 174, 485 N.Y.S.2d 220, 474 N.E.2d 580 (1984), a model sued for invasion of privacy under New York State's statute prohibiting appropriation for "advertising or trade purposes." The model had posed in a "bomber jacket" for a 1981 article on men's fall fashions for the *New Yorker* magazine. Contending that he had agreed to model for one article only, he sued, claiming a breach of his "right of publicity" because one of the photos was used in a "Best Bets" magazine column giving an approximate price for the jacket and listing several stores at which it would be available. The New York Court of Appeals held that the magazine's use of the photo in the "Best Bets" column was of general public interest and that it was not used for advertising or trade purposes as defined by New York law.

Determining what constitutes commercial or trade purposes has not always proved easy for the courts. A New York trial court held it was not for commercial or trade purposes when a gubernatorial candidate used a murder suspect's picture in a campaign commercial. Davis v. Duryea, 99 Misc.2d 933, 417 N.Y.S.2d 624, 5 Med.L.Rptr. 1937 (1979). On the other hand, a television station that telephoned a couple during the program, "Dialing for Dollars," and aired the ensuing conversation found itself liable for appropriation. Jeppson v. United Television, 580 P.2d 1087, 3 Med.L.Rptr. 2513 (Utah 1978). Does the following case offer any guidance?

The Zacchini case is an example of an offshoot of appropriation known as right of publicity. This particular right was once defined as follows:

> The distinctive aspect of the common-law right of publicity is that it recognizes the commercial value of the picture or representation of a prominent person or performer and protects his proprietary interest in the profitability of his public reputation or persona. Ali v. Playgirl, Inc., 447 F.Supp. 723, 3 Med.L.Rptr. 2540 (S.D.N.Y. 1978).

Unlike the traditional tort of appropriation, right of publicity is exclusively the province of well-known individuals. Also, whereas the original tort was at least partially rooted in the concept of the right to be left alone and not to be exploited for commercial or trade purposes, this new variation seems only concerned with who should reap the financial benefits. In essence it is a property right, as opposed to a personal right.

## ZACCHINI v. SCRIPPS–HOWARD BROADCASTING CO.

Supreme Court of the United States, 1977.

433 U.S. 562, 97 S.Ct. 2849, 53 L.Ed.2d 965, 2 Med.L.Rptr. 2089.

MR. JUSTICE WHITE delivered the opinion of the Court.

Petitioner, Hugo Zacchini, is an entertainer. He performs a "human cannonball" act in which he is shot from a cannon into a net some 200 feet away. Each performance occupies some 15 seconds. In August and September 1972, petitioner was engaged to perform his act on a regular basis at the Geauga County Fair in Burton, Ohio. He performed in a fenced area, surrounded by grandstands, at the fair grounds. Members of the public attending the fair were not charged a separate admission fee to observe his act.

On August 30, a freelance reporter for Scripps–Howard Broadcasting Co., the operator of a television broadcasting station and respondent in this case, attended the fair. He carried a small movie camera. Petitioner noticed the reporter and asked him not to film the performance. The reporter did not do so on that day; but on the instructions of the producer of respondent's daily newscast, he returned the following day and videotaped the entire act. This film clip, approximately 15 seconds in length, was shown on the 11 o'clock news program that night, together with favorable commentary.[1]

Petitioner then brought this action for damages, alleging that he is "engaged in the entertainment business," that the act he performs is one "invented by his father and  .  .  . performed only by his family for the last fifty years," that respondent "showed and commercialized the film of his act without his consent," and that such conduct was an "unlawful appropriation of plaintiff's professional property." App. 4–5. Respondent answered and moved for summary judgment, which was granted by the trial court.

.   .   .

.   .   . Insofar as the Ohio Supreme Court held that the First and Fourteenth Amendments of the United States Constitution required judgment for respondent, we reverse the judgment of that court.

.   .   .

Even if the judgment in favor of respondent must nevertheless be understood as ultimately resting on Ohio law, it appears that at the very least the Ohio court felt compelled by what it understood to be federal constitutional considerations to construe and apply its own law in the

---

1. The script of the commentary accompanying the film clip read as follows:

"This  .  .  . now  .  .  . is the story of a *true spectator* sport  .  .  . the sport of human cannonballing  .  .  . in fact, the great *Zacchini* is about the only human cannonball around, these days  .  .  . just happens that, *where* he is, is the Great Geauga County Fair, in Burton  .  .  . and believe me, although it's not a *long* act, it's a thriller  .  .  . and you really need to see it *in person*  .  .  . to appreciate it.  .  .  ." (Emphasis in original.)

manner it did.  In this event, we have jurisdiction and should decide the federal issue;  for if the state court erred in its understanding of our cases and of the First and Fourteenth Amendments we should so declare, leaving the state court free to decide the privilege issue solely as a matter of Ohio law.  [   ]  If the Supreme Court of Ohio "held as it did because it felt under compulsion of federal law as enunciated by this Court so to hold, it should be relieved of that compulsion.  It should be freed to decide  .  .  .  these suits according to its own local law."  [   ]

.  .  .

The Ohio Supreme Court relied heavily on Time, Inc. v. Hill, 385 U.S. 374 (1967), but that case does not mandate a media privilege to televise a performer's entire act without his consent.  Involved in Time, Inc. v. Hill was a claim under the New York "Right of Privacy" statute that Life Magazine, in the course of reviewing a new play, had connected the play with a long-past incident involving petitioner and his family and had falsely described their experience and conduct at that time.  The complaint sought damages for humiliation and suffering flowing from these nondefamatory falsehoods that allegedly invaded Hill's privacy. The Court held, however, that the opening of a new play linked to an actual incident was a matter of public interest and that Hill could not recover without showing that the Life report was knowingly false or was published with reckless disregard for the truth—the same rigorous standard that had been applied in [*Sullivan*].

Time, Inc. v. Hill, which was hotly contested and decided by a divided Court, involved an entirely different tort from the "right of publicity" recognized by the Ohio Supreme Court.  .  .  .

The differences between these two torts are important.  First, the State's interests in providing a cause of action in each instance are different.  "The interest protected" in permitting recovery for placing the plaintiff in a false light "is clearly that of reputation, with the same overtones of mental distress as in defamation."  Prosser, supra, 48 Calif.L.Rev., at 400.  By contrast, the State's interest in permitting a "right of publicity" is in protecting the proprietary interest of the individual in his act in part to encourage such entertainment.  As we later note, the State's interest is closely analogous to the goals of patent and copyright law, focusing on the right of the individual to reap the reward of his endeavors and having little to do with protecting feelings or reputation.  Second, the two torts differ in the degree to which they intrude on dissemination of information to the public.  In "false light" cases the only way to protect the interests involved is to attempt to minimize publication of the damaging matter, while in "right of publicity" cases the only question is who gets to do the publishing.  An entertainer such as petitioner usually has no objection to the widespread publication of his act as long as he gets the commercial benefit of such publication.  Indeed, in the present case petitioner did not seek to enjoin the broadcast of his act; he simply sought compensation for the broadcast in the form of damages.

. . .

Moreover, Time, Inc. v. Hill, *New York Times, Metromedia, Gertz,* and *Firestone* all involved the reporting of events; in none of them was there an attempt to broadcast or publish an entire act for which the performer ordinarily gets paid. It is evident, and there is no claim here to the contrary, that petitioner's state-law right of publicity would not serve to prevent respondent from reporting the newsworthy facts about petitioner's act. Wherever the line in particular situations is to be drawn between media reports that are protected and those that are not, we are quite sure that the First and Fourteenth Amendments do not immunize the media when they broadcast a performer's entire act without his consent. The Constitution no more prevents a State from requiring respondent to compensate petitioner for broadcasting his act on television than it would privilege respondent to film and broadcast a copyrighted dramatic work without liability to the copyright owner, [   ], or to film and broadcast a prize fight, [   ], or a baseball game, [   ], where the promoters or the participants had other plans for publicizing the event. There are ample reasons for reaching this conclusion.

The broadcast of a film of petitioner's entire act poses a substantial threat to the economic value of that performance. As the Ohio court recognized, this act is the product of petitioner's own talents and energy, the end result of much time, effort, and expense. Much of its economic value lies in the "right of exclusive control over the publicity given to his performance"; if the public can see the act free on television, it will be less willing to pay to see it at the fair.[12] The effect of a public broadcast of the performance is similar to preventing petitioner from charging an admission fee.   . . .   Moreover, the broadcast of petitioner's entire performance, unlike the unauthorized use of another's name for purposes of trade or the incidental use of a name or picture by the press, goes to the heart of petitioner's ability to earn a living as an entertainer. Thus, in this case, Ohio has recognized what may be the strongest case for a "right of publicity"—involving, not the appropriation of an entertainer's reputation to enhance the attractiveness of a commercial product, but the appropriation of the very activity by which the entertainer acquired his reputation in the first place.

Of course, Ohio's decision to protect petitioner's right of publicity here rests on more than a desire to compensate the performer for the time and effort invested in his act; the protection provides an economic incentive for him to make the investment required to produce a performance of interest to the public. This same consideration underlies the patent and copyright laws long enforced by this Court.   . . .

---

**12.** It is possible, of course, that respondent's news broadcast increased the value of petitioner's performance by stimulating the public's interest in seeing the act live. In these circumstances, petitioner would not be able to prove damages and thus would not recover. But petitioner has alleged that the broadcast injured him to the extent of $25,000, App. 5, and we think the State should be allowed to authorize compensation of this injury if proved.

There is no doubt that entertainment, as well as news, enjoys First Amendment protection. It is also true that entertainment itself can be important news. Time, Inc. v. Hill. But it is important to note that neither the public nor respondent will be deprived of the benefit of petitioner's performance as long as his commercial stake in his act is appropriately recognized. Petitioner does not seek to enjoin the broadcast of his performance; he simply wants to be paid for it. Nor do we think that a state-law damages remedy against respondent would represent a species of liability without fault contrary to the letter or spirit of [*Gertz*]. Respondent knew exactly that petitioner objected to televising his act but nevertheless displayed the entire film.

We conclude that although the State of Ohio may as a matter of its own law privilege the press in the circumstances of this case, the First and Fourteenth Amendments do not require it to do so.

Reversed.

MR. JUSTICE POWELL, with whom MR. JUSTICE BRENNAN and MR. JUSTICE MARSHALL join, dissenting.

Disclaiming any attempt to do more than decide the narrow case before us, the Court reverses the decision of the Supreme Court of Ohio based on repeated incantation of a single formula: "a performer's entire act." The holding today is summed up in one sentence:

"Wherever the line in particular situations is to be drawn between media reports that are protected and those that are not, we are quite sure that the First and Fourteenth Amendments do not immunize the media when they broadcast a performer's entire act without his consent."

I doubt that this formula provides a standard clear enough even for resolution of this case.[1] In any event, I am not persuaded that the Court's opinion is appropriately sensitive to the First Amendment values at stake, and I therefore dissent.

Although the Court would draw no distinction, I do not view respondent's action as comparable to unauthorized commercial broadcasts of sporting events, theatrical performances, and the like where the broadcaster keeps the profits. There is no suggestion here that respondent made any such use of the film. Instead, it simply reported on what petitioner concedes to be a newsworthy event, in a way hardly surprising for a television station—by means of film coverage. The report was part

---

**1.** Although the record is not explicit, it is unlikely that the "act" commenced abruptly with the explosion that launched petitioner on his way, ending with the landing in the net a few seconds later. One may assume that the actual firing was preceded by some fanfare, possibly stretching over several minutes, to heighten the audience's anticipation: introduction of the performer, description of the uniqueness and danger, last-minute checking of the apparatus, and entry into the cannon, all accompanied by suitably ominous commentary from the master of ceremonies. If this is found to be the case on remand, then respondent could not be said to have appropriated the "entire act" in its 15–second newsclip—and the Court's opinion then would afford no guidance for resolution of the case. Moreover, in future cases involving different performances, similar difficulties in determining just what constitutes the "entire act" are inevitable.

of an ordinary daily news program, consuming a total of 15 seconds. It is a routine example of the press fulfilling the informing function so vital to our system.

The Court's holding that the station's ordinary news report may give rise to substantial liability has disturbing implications, for the decision could lead to a degree of media self-censorship. [ ] Hereafter whenever a television news editor is unsure whether certain film footage received from a camera crew might be held to portray an "entire act," he may decline coverage—even of clearly newsworthy events—or confine the broadcast to watered-down verbal reporting, perhaps with an occasional still picture. The public is then the loser. This is hardly the kind of news reportage that the First Amendment is meant to foster. [ ]

In my view the First Amendment commands a different analytical starting point from the one selected by the Court. Rather than begin with a quantitative analysis of the performer's behavior—is this or is this not his entire act?—we should direct initial attention to the actions of the news media: what use did the station make of the film footage? When a film is used, as here, for a routine portion of a regular news program, I would hold that the First Amendment protects the station from a "right of publicity" or "appropriation" suit, absent a strong showing by the plaintiff that the news broadcast was a subterfuge or cover for private or commercial exploitation.[4]

. . . In a suit like the one before us, however, the plaintiff does not complain about the fact of exposure to the public, but rather about its timing or manner. He welcomes some publicity, but seeks to retain control over means and manner as a way to maximize for himself the monetary benefits that flow from such publication. But having made the matter public—having chosen, in essence, to make it newsworthy— he cannot, consistent with the First Amendment, complain of routine news reportage. Cf. Gertz v. Robert Welch, Inc., [ ], (clarifying the different liability standards appropriate in defamation suits, depending on whether or not the plaintiff is a public figure).

Since the film clip here was undeniably treated as news and since there is no claim that the use was subterfuge, respondent's actions were constitutionally privileged. I would affirm.

[MR. JUSTICE STEVENS dissented on the ground that he could not tell whether the Ohio Supreme Court had relied on federal constitutional issues in deciding the case. He would have remanded the case to that court "for clarification of its holding before deciding the federal constitutional issue."]

### Notes and Questions

1. On remand, the Ohio Supreme Court took advantage of the opportunity afforded by the majority opinion and decided that nothing in the

---

**4.** This case requires no detailed specification of the standards for identifying a subterfuge, since there is no claim here that respondent's news use was anything but bona fide. [ ] I would point out, however, that selling time during a news broadcast to advertisers in the customary fashion does not make for "commercial exploitation" in the sense intended here. [ ]

Ohio Constitution protected the behavior of the media defendant. The case was remanded for trial. Zacchini v. Scripps–Howard Broadcasting Co., 54 Ohio St.2d 286, 376 N.E.2d 582, 3 Med.L.Rptr. 2444 (1978).

2. How important is it that the majority treats the 15 seconds as the "entire act"?

3. Does this case involve an aspect of "privacy"? Does it resemble the Cox Broadcasting case in that both involved lawfully obtained information of interest or concern to the public? Can you explain why the defendant in *Cox* won while the defendant in *Zacchini* lost?

4. After *Zacchini* what would happen in a case in which a street artist who survives on contributions from passersby—a mime, an accordionist, a dancer—is photographed by the local television station and shown in a story about summer diversions on the streets of the city? Is the street artist's claim as strong as Zacchini's?

5. Johnny Carson was able to sue a manufacturer of portable toilets that were marketed under the name, "Here's Johnny." Carson v. Here's Johnny Portable Toilets, Inc., 698 F.2d 831, 9 Med.L.Rptr. 1153 (6th Cir.1983), reversing 498 F.Supp. 71 (E.D.Mich.1980). Similarly, the estate of Elvis Presley won their claim against the producers of THE BIG EL SHOW, an imitation of Presley's performances. Estate of Presley v. Russen, 513 F.Supp. 1339 (D.N.J.1981).

6. In some cases it is not even the true name or likeness of a person, but rather some character or role that is at issue. In Groucho Marx Productions v. Day and Night Co., 523 F.Supp. 485, 7 Med.L.Rptr. 2030 (S.D.N.Y.1981), rev'd on other grounds 689 F.2d 317, 8 Med.L.Rptr. 2201 (2d Cir.1982), the court held that the play, "A Day in Hollywood, a Night in the Ukraine," appropriated the Marx brothers' characters. In this context, a suit for appropriation has become a new method of protecting creative work. We will discuss other methods of protecting such work in Chapter VI.

7. Relying extensively on *Zacchini,* a California superior court decided a 1986 case against the producers of "Beatlemania," a show "consisting of Beatles look-alike, sound-alike, imitators performing live on stage twenty-nine of the more popular Lennon–McCartney songs, to a mixed-media background, and foreground of slides, and movies. . . ." The court held that "as in *Zacchini,* the defendants' taking or use amounted to virtually a complete appropriation of the Beatles' persona."

Defendants urged the court to adopt the copyright defense of fair use (discussed in Chapter VI) for right of publicity. The court indicated that such action was appropriate as a matter of California public policy but held that defendants' conduct far exceeded the limits of fair use. Apple Corps Limited v. Leber, 12 Med.L.Rptr. 2280 (Cal.Super.1986).

8. The "New Kids on the Block" sued *USA Today* and *Star* magazine for violating their right of publicity—along with trademark infringement

and misappropriation, when the "New Kids" trademark was used in articles which asked readers to participate, via a "900" telephone number, in a survey to determine the group's most popular member. A federal court held that the use of the trademark was related to newsgathering and was not merely commercial exploitation, so the First Amendment barred the claims. The appellate court affirmed, but not on constitutional grounds. Instead, it pointed out that there was nothing false or misleading about the newspapers' use of the trademarked name and that, "[I]t is often virtually impossible to refer to a particular product for purposes of comparison, criticism, point of reference or any other such purpose without using the mark.  .  .  .  Cases like these are best understood as involving a non-trademark use of a mark—a use to which the infringement laws simply do not apply.  .  .."

"[W]here the defendant uses a trademark to describe the plaintiff's product, rather than its own," Judge Kozinski wrote for the court, "we hold that a commercial user is entitled to a nominative fair use defense provided he meets the following three requirements: First, the product or service in question must be one not readily identifiable without use of the trademark; second, only so much of the mark or marks may be used as is reasonably necessary to identify the product or service; and third, the user must do nothing that would, in conjunction with the mark, suggest sponsorship or endorsement by the trademark holder." The New Kids on the Block v. News America Publishing, Inc., 971 F.2d 302, 20 Med.L.Rptr. 1468 (9th Cir.1992).

9.  In National Football League Properties v. Playoff Corporation, 808 F.Supp. 1288 (N.D.Tex.1992), a federal court in the Fifth Circuit declined to follow Judge Kozinski's test (noting that it was for the Circuit rather than the trial court to adopt or not adopt it) but nonetheless denied the National Football League's motion for a preliminary injunction to stop Playoff Corporation from selling football trading cards in which professional players are shown in game settings wearing NFL uniforms. The judge said the NFL had failed to show that failure to issue the injunction would leave the NFL irreparably harmed.

10.  Singer Bette Midler won $400,000 in compensatory damages as a result of a television commercial. When advertising agency Young & Rubicam contacted Midler's agent to ask whether she would be interested in doing a commercial for Ford, the agent declined on Midler's behalf. The agency subsequently sought out Ula Hedwig, who had been a backup singer for Midler for 10 years, to do a sound-alike rendition of Midler's recording of "Do You Want to Dance." After the commercial aired, Midler sued under both copyright law and privacy law. The Court of Appeals held that the deliberate, unconsented imitation of the distinctive voice of a professional singer in order to sell a product constitutes an unlawful appropriation of identity under California law. Midler v. Ford Motor Company, 849 F.2d 460, 15 Med.L.Rptr. 1620 (9th Cir.1988), cert. denied 112 S.Ct. 1513 (1992).

11.  Game show hostess Vanna White sued Samsung Electronics America, for using, in an advertisement, a robot dressed in a wig, gown

and jewelry reminiscent of White and posed next to a game board like the one in "Wheel of Fortune." A panel decision by the U.S. Court of Appeals for the Ninth Circuit held that the right of publicity is not limited solely to the appropriation of a name or likeness. Instead, the panel said, the right of publicity encompasses the appropriation of "identity." On March 18, 1993, the Court of Appeals refused to rehear the panel decision. Three judges dissented from the order rejecting the suggestion for rehearing *en banc*, saying that the decision "erects a property right of remarkable and dangerous breadth." "I don't see how," said Judge Alex Kozinski, one of the dissenters, "giving White the power to keep others from evoking her image in the public's mind can be squared with the First Amendment." White v. Samsung Electronics America, Inc., 989 F.2d 1512, 21 Med.L.Rptr. 1330 (9th Cir.), cert. denied 113 S.Ct. 2443 (1993).

12. In Waits (Tom) v. Frito–Lay, Inc., 20 Med.L.Rptr. 1585 (9th Cir. 1992), cert. denied, 113 S.Ct. 1047 (1993), singer Tom Waits sued the snack food manufacturer and its advertising agency for voice misappropriation and false endorsement as a result of a Doritos radio commercial featuring an imitation of Waits' distinctive singing voice. The court of appeals held that there was sufficient evidence to support the jury's findings that Frito–Lay and the advertising agency acted with malice and that consumers were likely to be misled by the commercial into believing that Waits endorsed the product. It upheld all but $100,000 of the jury verdict and award of $2.6 million.

### *Descendability*

Personal rights such as those protected by defamation and invasion of privacy law terminate at death. Thus, for example, one can publish defamatory statements about deceased individuals with impunity (unless the same statement also defames people who are still alive). Because the right of publicity is a property right, a great controversy has developed as to whether it survives the death of its creator. Currently, there seem to be three distinct approaches being taken by various courts. One is that the right terminates upon death. Under this view as soon as people die, their names, likenesses and characterizations are available for anyone to use without legal liability. At the other extreme is the position that death has no effect on the right of publicity. In jurisdictions adhering to this view, the consent of whoever owns the property in question (perhaps the individual's heirs or someone who has purchased the right) is always necessary. Finally, there is an intermediate approach that holds the right of publicity to survive death only if it was commercially exploited during the person's lifetime. *If* the right of publicity continues beyond death (either because it always does or because it was commercially exploited during the person's lifetime), the next question is how long it lasts. A state statute might stipulate a specific number of years, or the right of publicity might last as long as it continues to be exploited by the individual's heirs or forever. State statutes that provide for survivability do so for varying periods of time ranging from 50 years after death in California to 10 years after death in Tennessee.

# Chapter V

# LIABILITY FOR EMOTIONAL
# AND PHYSICAL HARM

Recently, lawsuits have begun claiming that mass media are liable for personal harm traceable in one way or another to a publication or broadcast. These cases raise some hotly disputed questions because they involve all the complexity of traditional tort law plus the special element of media involvement. The examples that follow suggest the range of situations that might give rise to this type of lawsuit. Note that some situations appear to be associated most frequently with print media, others with visual presentations, and still others with the aural aspects of music.

So many variables are arguably relevant in these cases that it is difficult to develop one overarching organizational pattern. Variables to keep in mind include the content of the speech involved (news v. fiction v. how-to-do-it), the type of audience being addressed (adults v. children), the risks inherent in the speech, and the medium being used. The first division we adopt is that between emotional distress cases and physical harm cases.

## A. NEGLIGENT AND INTENTIONAL INFLICTION OF EMOTIONAL DISTRESS

The tort of intentional *infliction of emotional distress* is separate from both defamation and privacy. When Rev. Jerry Falwell sued *Hustler* magazine publisher Larry Flynt, in a case to be discussed in this section, he sued for libel *and* invasion of privacy *and* infliction of emotional distress. The possibility that public figure libel plaintiffs, frustrated by their inability to win libel suits under *New York Times,* would sue in great numbers for infliction of emotional distress was a serious concern for the media as the Falwell case went to the Supreme Court. Some people feared that the emotional distress tort would become an attractive way for plaintiffs to circumvent the formal requirements of defamation suits.

Inflictions of emotional distress can be either *intentional* (resulting from a deliberate action of the defendant) or *negligent* (resulting from carelessness or unreasonable conduct on the part of the defendant).

The Falwell suit came about when *Hustler* magazine carried an "Ad Parody—Not to Be Taken Seriously" that included a fake interview with Rev. Jerry Falwell that implied that he was a "hypocritical incestuous drunkard." *Hustler* publisher Larry Flynt testified that he intended to cause Falwell emotional distress. The jury found that the material was so clearly parody that no reader could reasonably have taken it as fact. But the jury awarded Falwell $200,000 for emotional distress. Flynt's intention removed whatever protection the First Amendment might have offered. Falwell v. Flynt (W.D.Va.1985). The unreported case is discussed in Hustler Magazine, Inc. v. Moral Majority, Inc., 606 F.Supp. 1526 (C.D.Cal.1985) and in Note, 85 Colum.L.Rev. 1749 (1985).

The court of appeals affirmed. Falwell v. Flynt, 797 F.2d 1270, 13 Med.L.Rptr. 1145 (4th Cir.1986). The court noted that during his deposition Flynt identified himself as Christopher Columbus Cornwallis I.P.Q. Harvey H. Apache Pugh and said the parody had been written by Yoko Ono and Billy Idol. Flynt testified that he wanted to upset Falwell. When asked if he knew that his publication had portrayed Falwell as a liar, Flynt replied "A. He's a glutton. Q. How about a hypocrite? A. Yeah. . . . Q. And, wasn't one of your objectives to destroy [Falwell's] integrity, or harm it, if you could? A. To assassinate it."

Although the court agreed that the defendants were "entitled to the same level of first amendment protection in the claim for intentional infliction of emotional distress that they received in Falwell's claim for libel," this did not mean "literal application of the actual malice standard." The court held "that when the first amendment requires application of the actual malice standard, the standard is met when the jury finds that the defendant's intentional or reckless misconduct has proximately caused the injury complained of."

The court also rejected Flynt's contention that since the jury found that the parody could not be taken literally, it must be opinion and be constitutionally protected. The tort is concerned with outrageous conduct and not with "statements per se." The issue was whether the publication "was sufficiently outrageous to constitute intentional infliction of emotional distress."

The intentional element could be found from Flynt's deposition testimony. The outrageousness "is quite obvious from the language in the parody and in the fact that Flynt republished the parody after this lawsuit was filed." The final elements, showing that the conduct caused serious emotional distress, were established by Falwell's testimony that he had never had a personal experience as intense as the feeling he had when he first saw the parody. "Since I have been a Christian I don't think I have ever intentionally hurt anyone. . . . I really think that at that moment if Larry Flynt had been nearby I might have physically reacted." A colleague testified that Falwell's "enthusiasm and optimism visibly suffered" as a result of the parody; and that his "ability to concentrate on the myriad details of running his extensive ministry was diminished." That was enough to permit recovery.

A rehearing *en banc* was denied, Falwell v. Flynt, 797 F.2d 1270 (4th Cir.1986). Dissenting to the denial for rehearing, Judge Wilkinson wrote:

I share with the court a profound repugnance for the communication in this case. For all the controversy that surrounds the Reverend Falwell, the communication was an utterly unwarranted and offensive personal attack. Moreover, *Hustler* magazine, which leveled that attack, is a singularly unappealing beneficiary of First Amendment values and serves only to remind us of the costs a democracy must pay for its most precious privilege of open political debate.

The jury verdict below, however, raises serious questions under the First Amendment which this court should consider *en banc*. Foremost among them is whether those in political life should ever be able to recover damages for no other reason than hurt feelings or, to use the terminology of tort law, because critical commentary inflicted upon them a degree of emotional distress. To permit political figures to recover solely for emotional harm may in the end circumvent the careful development of the law of defamation since [*Sullivan*]. It surely will operate as a powerful inhibitor of humorous and satiric commentary and ultimately affect the health and vigor of all political debate.

## HUSTLER MAGAZINE v. FALWELL

Supreme Court of the United States, 1988.
485 U.S. 46, 108 S.Ct. 876, 99 L.Ed.2d 41, 14 Med.L.Rptr. 2281.

CHIEF JUSTICE REHNQUIST delivered the opinion of the Court.

Petitioner Hustler Magazine, Inc., is a magazine of nationwide circulation. Respondent Jerry Falwell, a nationally known minister who has been active as a commentator on politics and public affairs, sued petitioner and its publisher, petitioner Larry Flynt, to recover damages for invasion of privacy, libel, and intentional infliction of emotional distress. The District Court directed a verdict against respondent on the privacy claim, and submitted the other two claims to a jury. The jury found for petitioners on the defamation claim, but found for respondent on the claim for intentional infliction of emotional distress and awarded damages. We now consider whether this award is consistent with the First and Fourteenth Amendments of the United States Constitution.

The inside front cover of the November 1983 issue of Hustler Magazine featured a "parody" of an advertisement for Campari Liqueur that contained the name and picture of respondent and was entitled "Jerry Falwell talks about his first time." This parody was modeled after actual Campari ads that included interviews with various celebrities about their "first times." Although it was apparent by the end of each interview that this meant the first time they sampled Campari, the ads clearly played on the sexual double entendre of the general subject of "first times." Copying the form and layout of these Campari ads, Hustler's editors chose respondent as the featured celebrity and drafted an alleged "interview" with him in which he states that his "first time" was during a drunken incestuous rendezvous with his mother in an outhouse. The Hustler parody portrays respondent and his mother as drunk and immoral, and suggests that respondent is a hypocrite who preaches only when he is drunk. In small print at the bottom of the page, the ad contains the disclaimer, "ad parody—not to be taken seriously." The magazine's table of contents also lists the ad as "Fiction; Ad and Personality Parody."

Soon after the November issue of Hustler became available to the public, respondent brought this diversity action in the United States District Court for the Western District of Virginia against Hustler Magazine, Inc., Larry C. Flynt, and Flynt Distributing Co. Respondent stated in his complaint that publication of the ad parody in Hustler entitled him to recover damages for libel, invasion of privacy, and intentional infliction of emotional distress. The case proceeded to trial.[1] At the close of the evidence, the District Court granted a directed verdict for petitioners on the invasion of privacy claim. The jury then found against respondent on the libel claim, specifically finding that the ad parody could not "reasonably be understood as describing actual facts about [respondent] or actual events in which [he] participated." App. to Pet. for Cert. C1. The jury ruled for respondent on the intentional infliction of emotional distress claim, however, and stated that he should be awarded $100,000 in compensatory damages, as well as $50,000 each in punitive damages from petitioners.[2] Petitioners' motion for judgment notwithstanding the verdict was denied.

On appeal, the United States Court of Appeals for the Fourth Circuit affirmed the judgment against petitioners. Falwell v. Flynt, 797 F.2d 1270 (CA4 1986). The court rejected petitioners' argument that the "actual malice" standard of New York Times Co. v. Sullivan, 376 U.S. 254 (1964), must be met before respondent can recover for emotional distress. The court agreed that because respondent is concededly a public figure, petitioners are "entitled to the same level of first amendment protection in the claim for intentional infliction of emotional distress that they received in [respondent's] claim for libel." 797 F.2d, at 1274. But this does not mean that a literal application of the actual malice rule is appropriate in the context of an emotional distress claim. In the court's view, the New York Times decision emphasized the constitutional importance not of the falsity of the statement or the defendant's disregard for the truth, but of the heightened level of culpability embodied in the requirement of "knowing . . . or reckless" conduct. Here, the New York Times standard is satisfied by the state-law requirement, and the jury's finding, that the defendants have acted intentionally or recklessly.[3] The Court of Appeals then went on to

1. While the case was pending, the ad parody was published in Hustler magazine a second time.

2. The jury found no liability on the part of Flynt Distributing Co., Inc. It is consequently not a party to this appeal.

3. Under Virginia law, in an action for intentional infliction of emotional distress a plaintiff must show that the defendant's conduct (1) is intentional or reckless; (2) offends generally accepted standards of decency or morality; (3) is causally connected with the plaintiff's emotional distress; and (4) caused emotional distress that was se-

reject the contention that because the jury found that the ad parody did not describe actual facts about respondent, the ad was an opinion that is protected by the First Amendment. As the court put it, this was "irrelevant," as the issue is "whether [the ad's] publication was sufficiently outrageous to constitute intentional infliction of emotional distress." Id., at 1276.[4] Petitioners then filed a petition for rehearing en banc, but this was denied by a divided court. Given the importance of the constitutional issues involved, we granted certiorari.

This case presents us with a novel question involving First Amendment limitations upon a State's authority to protect its citizens from the intentional infliction of emotional distress. We must decide whether a public figure may recover damages for emotional harm caused by the publication of an ad parody offensive to him, and doubtless gross and repugnant in the eyes of most. Respondent would have us find that a State's interest in protecting public figures from emotional distress is sufficient to deny First Amendment protection to speech that is patently offensive and is intended to inflict emotional injury, even when that speech could not reasonably have been interpreted as stating actual facts about the public figure involved. This we decline to do.

At the heart of the First Amendment is the recognition of the fundamental importance of the free flow of ideas and opinions on matters of public interest and concern. "[T]he freedom to speak one's mind is not only an aspect of individual liberty—and thus a good unto itself—but also is essential to the common quest for truth and the vitality of society as a whole." Bose Corp. v. Consumers Union of United States, Inc., 466 U.S. 485, 503–504 (1984). We have therefore been particularly vigilant to ensure that individual expressions of ideas remain free from governmentally imposed sanctions. The First Amendment recognizes no such thing as a "false" idea. Gertz v. Robert Welch, Inc., 418 U.S. 323, 339 (1974). As Justice Holmes wrote, "[W]hen men have realized that time has upset many fighting faiths, they may come to believe even more than they believe the very foundations of their own conduct that the ultimate good desired is better reached by free trade in ideas—that the best test of truth is the power of the thought to get itself accepted in the competition of the market . . .." Abrams v. United States, 250 U.S. 616, 630 (1919) (dissenting opinion).

The sort of robust political debate encouraged by the First Amendment is bound to produce speech that is critical of those who hold public office or those public figures who are "intimately involved in the resolution of important public questions or, by reason of their fame, shape events in areas of concern to society at large." Associated Press v. Walker, decided with Curtis Publishing Co. v. Butts, 388 U.S. 130, 164 (1967) (Warren, C.J., concurring in result). Justice Frankfurter put it succinctly in Baumgartner v. United States, 322 U.S. 665, 673–674

vere. 797 F.2d, at 1275, n. 4 (citing Womack v. Eldridge, 215 Va. 338, 210 S.E.2d 145 (1974)).

4. The court below also rejected several other contentions that petitioners do not raise in this appeal.

(1944), when he said that "[o]ne of the prerogatives of American citizenship is the right to criticize public men and measures." Such criticism, inevitably, will not always be reasoned or moderate; public figures as well as public officials will be subject to "vehement, caustic, and sometimes unpleasantly sharp attacks." New York Times, supra, at 270. "[T]he candidate who vaunts his spotless record and sterling integrity cannot convincingly cry 'Foul!' when an opponent or an industrious reporter attempts to demonstrate the contrary." Monitor Patriot Co. v. Roy, 401 U.S. 265, 274 (1971).

Of course, this does not mean that any speech about a public figure is immune from sanction in the form of damages. Since New York Times Co. v. Sullivan, supra, we have consistently ruled that a public figure may hold a speaker liable for the damage to reputation caused by publication of a defamatory falsehood, but only if the statement was made "with knowledge that it was false or with reckless disregard of whether it was false or not." Id., at 279–280. False statements of fact are particularly valueless; they interfere with the truth-seeking function of the marketplace of ideas, and they cause damage to an individual's reputation that cannot easily be repaired by counterspeech, however persuasive or effective. See Gertz, 418 U.S., at 340, 344, n. 9. But even though falsehoods have little value in and of themselves, they are "nevertheless inevitable in free debate," id., at 340, and a rule that would impose strict liability on a publisher for false factual assertions would have an undoubted "chilling" effect on speech relating to public figures that does have constitutional value. "Freedoms of expression require 'breathing space.' " Philadelphia Newspapers, Inc. v. Hepps, 475 U.S. 767, 772 (1986) (quoting New York Times, 376 U.S., at 272). This breathing space is provided by a constitutional rule that allows public figures to recover for libel or defamation only when they can prove both that the statement was false and that the statement was made with the requisite level of culpability.

Respondent argues, however, that a different standard should apply in this case because here the State seeks to prevent not reputational damage, but the severe emotional distress suffered by the person who is the subject of an offensive publication. Cf. Zacchini v. Scripps–Howard Broadcasting Co., 433 U.S. 562 (1977) (ruling that the "actual malice" standard does not apply to the tort of appropriation of a right of publicity). In respondent's view, and in the view of the Court of Appeals, so long as the utterance was intended to inflict emotional distress, was outrageous, and did in fact inflict serious emotional distress, it is of no constitutional import whether the statement was a fact or an opinion, or whether it was true or false. It is the intent to cause injury that is the gravamen of the tort, and the State's interest in preventing emotional harm simply outweighs whatever interest a speaker may have in speech of this type.

Generally speaking the law does not regard the intent to inflict emotional distress as one which should receive much solicitude, and it is quite understandable that most if not all jurisdictions have chosen to make it civilly culpable where the conduct in question is sufficiently "outrageous." But in the world of debate about public affairs, many things done with motives that are less than admirable are protected by the First Amendment. In [*Garrison*], we held that even when a speaker or writer is motivated by hatred or ill-will his expression was protected by the First Amendment:

"Debate on public issues will not be uninhibited if the speaker must run the risk that it will be proved in court that he spoke out of hatred; even if he did speak out of hatred, utterances honestly believed contribute to the free interchange of ideas and the ascertainment of truth." Id., at 73.

Thus, while such a bad motive may be deemed controlling for purposes of tort liability in other areas of the law, we think the First Amendment prohibits such a result in the area of public debate about public figures.

Were we to hold otherwise, there can be little doubt that political cartoonists and satirists would be subjected to damages awards without any showing that their work falsely defamed its subject. Webster's defines a caricature as "the deliberately distorted picturing or imitating of a person, literary style, etc. by exaggerating features or mannerisms for satirical effect." Webster's New Unabridged Twentieth Century Dictionary of the English Language 275 (2d ed. 1979). The appeal of the political cartoon or caricature is often based on exploration of unfortunate physical traits or politically embarrassing events—an exploration often calculated to injure the feelings of the subject of the portrayal. The art of the cartoonist is often not reasoned or evenhanded, but slashing and one-sided. One cartoonist expressed the nature of the art in these words:

"The political cartoon is a weapon of attack, of scorn and ridicule and satire; it is least effective when it tries to pat some politician on the back. It is usually as welcome as a bee sting and is always controversial in some quarters." Long, The Political Cartoon: Journalism's Strongest Weapon. The Quill, 56, 57 (Nov. 1962).

Several famous examples of this type of intentionally injurious speech were drawn by Thomas Nast, probably the greatest American cartoonist to date, who was associated for many years during the post-Civil War era with Harper's Weekly. In the pages of that publication Nast conducted a graphic vendetta against William M. "Boss" Tweed and his corrupt associates in New York City's "Tweed Ring." It has been described by one historian of the subject as "a sustained attack which in its passion and effectiveness stands alone in the history of American graphic art." M. Keller, The Art and Politics of Thomas Nast 177 (1968). Another writer explains that the success of the Nast cartoon was achieved "because of the emotional impact of its presentation. It continuously goes beyond the bounds of good taste and conventional manners." C. Press, The Political Cartoon 251 (1981).

Despite their sometimes caustic nature, from the early cartoon portraying George Washington as an ass down to the present day, graphic depictions and satirical cartoons have played a prominent role in public and political debate. Nast's castigation of the Tweed Ring, Walt McDougall's characterization of presidential candidate James G. Blaine's banquet with the millionaires at Delmonico's as "The Royal Feast of Belshazzar," and numerous other efforts have undoubtedly had an effect on the course and outcome of contemporaneous debate. Lincoln's tall, gangling posture, Teddy Roosevelt's glasses and teeth, and Franklin D. Roosevelt's jutting jaw and cigarette holder have been memorialized by political cartoons with an effect that could not have been obtained by the photographer or the portrait artist. From the viewpoint of history it is clear that our political discourse would have been considerably poorer without them. Respondent contends, however, that the caricature in question here was so "outrageous" as to distinguish it from more traditional political cartoons. There is no doubt that the caricature of respondent and his mother published in Hustler is at best a distant cousin of the political cartoons described above, and a rather poor relation at that. If it were possible by laying down a principled standard to separate the one from the other, public discourse would probably suffer little or no harm. But we doubt that there is any such standard, and we are quite sure that the pejorative description "outrageous" does not supply one. "Outrageousness" in the area of political and social discourse has an inherent subjectiveness about it which would allow a jury to impose liability on the basis of the jurors' tastes or views, or perhaps on the basis of their dislike of a particular expression. An "outrageousness" standard thus runs afoul of our longstanding refusal to allow damages to be awarded because the speech in question may have an adverse emotional impact on the audience. See NAACP v. Claiborne Hardware Co., 458 U.S. 886, 910 (1982) ("Speech does not lose its protected character . . . simply because it may embarrass others or coerce them into action"). And, as we stated in FCC v. Pacifica Foundation, 438 U.S. 726 (1978):

"[T]he fact that society may find speech offensive is not a sufficient reason for suppressing it. Indeed, if it is the speaker's opinion that gives offense, that consequence is a reason for according it constitutional protection. For it is a central tenet of the First Amendment that the government must remain neutral in the marketplace of ideas." Id., at 745–746.

See also Street v. New York, 394 U.S. 576, 592 (1969) ("It is firmly settled that . . . the public expression of ideas may not be prohibited merely because the ideas are themselves offensive to some of their hearers").

Admittedly, these oft-repeated First Amendment principles, like other principles, are subject to limitations. We recognized in Pacifica Foundation, that speech that is " 'vulgar,' 'offensive,' and 'shocking' " is "not entitled to absolute constitutional protection under all circumstances." 438 U.S., at 747. In Chaplinsky v. New Hampshire, 315 U.S.

568 (1942), we held that a state could lawfully punish an individual for the use of insulting " 'fighting' words—those which by their very utterance inflict injury or tend to incite an immediate breach of the peace." Id., at 571–572.  These limitations are but recognition of the observation in Dun & Bradstreet, Inc. v. Greenmoss Builders, Inc., 472 U.S. 749, 758 (1985), that this Court has "long recognized that not all speech is of equal First Amendment importance."  But the sort of expression involved in this case does not seem to us to be governed by any exception to the general First Amendment principles stated above.

We conclude that public figures and public officials may not recover for the tort of intentional infliction of emotional distress by reason of publications such as the one here at issue without showing in addition that the publication contains a false statement of fact which was made with "actual malice," i.e., with knowledge that the statement was false or with reckless disregard as to whether or not it was true.  This is not merely a "blind application" of the New York Times standard, see Time, Inc. v. Hill, 385 U.S. 374, 390 (1967), it reflects our considered judgment that such a standard is necessary to give adequate "breathing space" to the freedoms protected by the First Amendment.

Here it is clear that respondent Falwell is a "public figure" for purposes of First Amendment law.[5]  The jury found against respondent on his libel claim when it decided that the Hustler ad parody could not "reasonably be understood as describing actual facts about [respondent] or actual events in which [he] participated."  App. to Pet. for Cert. C1. The Court of Appeals interpreted the jury's finding to be that the ad parody "was not reasonably believable."  797 F.2d, at 1278, and in accordance with our custom we accept this finding.  Respondent is thus relegated to his claim for damages awarded by the jury for the intentional infliction of emotional distress by "outrageous" conduct.  But for reasons heretofore stated this claim cannot, consistently with the First Amendment, form a basis for the award of damages when the conduct in question is the publication of a caricature such as the ad parody involved here.  The judgment of the Court of Appeals is accordingly

Reversed.

JUSTICE KENNEDY took no part in the consideration or decision of this case.

JUSTICE WHITE, concurring in the judgment.

As I see it, the decision in [*Sullivan*], has little to do with this case, for here the jury found that the ad contained no assertion of fact.  But I agree with the Court that the judgment below, which penalized the publication of the parody, cannot be squared with the First Amendment.

---

**5.**  Neither party disputes this conclusion.  Respondent is the host of a nationally syndicated television show and was the founder and president of a political organization formerly known as the Moral Majority.  He is also the founder of Liberty University in Lynchburg, Virginia, and is the author of several books and publications. Who's Who in America 849 (44th ed. 1986–1987).

**Notes and Questions**

1.   In Doe v. American Broadcasting Cos., 152 A.D.2d 482, 543 N.Y.S.2d 455, 16 Med.L.Rptr. 1958 (1989), two rape victims agreed to be interviewed on a television program if they were not identifiable. The station repeatedly assured them that neither their faces nor their voices would be recognizable. A Saturday night promotional announcement was aired for the Monday night program. On Monday morning the employer of one of the two told her that he and his wife had seen the "promo" and recognized her. On Monday night, her "outline, shape, and facial features were clear enough to identify her to those who knew her. Her voice was 'an absolute, instantaneous, positive identification.'" She was called by people who recognized her. She called to complain and was assured she would be unidentifiable in future broadcasts. The next portion of the series was shown Thursday night, and both she and the other rape victim were "recognizable to those who knew them and there appeared to be no attempt to disguise their voices. At one point during the broadcast the face of one of the plaintiffs was entirely visible. The plaintiffs, one of whom had never told her family of the rape, described the many comments from people who had recognized them on television and detailed the great distress which this had caused."

The plaintiff sued for breach of contract and for negligent and intentional infliction of emotional distress. The trial court denied defense motions for summary judgment. The majority (3–2) reversed on the intentional infliction count because the theory required a showing that the defendant's conduct "so transcends the bounds of decency as to be regarded as atrocious and intolerable in a civilized society." The defendant's actions were found not to be sufficiently "intentional, deliberate and outrageous" for her to win for intentional infliction of emotional distress, but the other two claims were left standing.

2.   A Connecticut trial court refused to dismiss claims against a radio station alleged to have defamed a woman and to have intentionally inflicted emotional distress by naming her "dog of the week" in the station's weekly "Berate the Brides" segment. Following publication of the woman's picture in a newspaper weddings section, the station's disc jockey is alleged to have said she was "too ugly to even rate" and said she had won a case of Ken–L–Ration and a dog collar. Murray v. Schlosser, 41 Conn.Sup. 362, 574 A.2d 1339, 17 Med.L.Rptr. 2069 (1990).

3.   *Communications to a Specific Audience.* So far we have been discussing publications addressed to broad audiences of which a few or several might react in a certain way. Occasionally, however, the problem is raised by a general publication that is in fact of special interest only to one recipient or to a narrow group at most. A few examples follow.

a.   In Times Mirror Co. v. Superior Court (Doe), 198 Cal.App.3d 1420, 198 Cal.App.3d 1420, 244 Cal.Rptr. 556, 15 Med.L.Rptr. 1129 (1988), stay denied 109 S.Ct. 862, cert. dism'd 489 U.S. 1094 (1989), the complaint alleged that plaintiff Doe returned home at midnight to find her roommate dead on the floor.  She looked up to confront a man.  She then fled the apartment and called the police.  The newspaper published a story that identified the plaintiff by name as having discovered the body.  After several intervening paragraphs, the article stated that "one witness" had given police a description of a man seen fleeing the apartment.

Plaintiff's suit centered on the claim that the story had told the murderer the identity of the only witness in the case and had thus subjected her to an increased risk of harm.  The trial court denied a motion for summary judgment.  On appeal, the court affirmed, 2–1.  The majority rejected an "absolute" First Amendment defense for printing the name of a witness.  (There was a dispute whether the name had come from an official source or from the reporter's work.)  Next, the newspaper argued that the fact reported was not private because plaintiff had told some friends, neighbors and relatives that she had discovered the body and confronted the murderer.  The court responded that "[t]alking to selected individuals does not render private information public. . . . On the record before us we cannot say Doe rendered otherwise private information public by cooperating in the criminal investigation and seeking solace from friends and relatives."

Next, the papers contended that the publication was newsworthy.  The court relied on privacy cases for the proposition that community mores controlled on this question and that if there was room for differing views the case was for the jury.  Jurors could find that Doe's name was not newsworthy by balancing the public benefit of knowing the name against the effect publication of her name might have on her safety and emotional well being.  The jury must also "consider the seriousness of the intrusion and the extent to which Doe voluntarily exposed herself to notoriety."

Finally, the paper relied on cases like *Smith v. Daily Mail*, discussed in Chapter X, for the proposition that absent an interest of the highest order the state may not punish a defendant for publishing lawfully obtained truthful information.  The court rejected the claim.  "The state must investigate violent crimes and protect witnesses.  Already reluctant witnesses will be more hesitant to provide information if their names will appear in the morning paper.  The state's interest is particularly strong when the criminal is still at large.  The state's interest is reflected in the regular police policy not to release the identity of witnesses. . . . The interest of the state to protect witnesses and to conduct criminal investigations is sufficient to overcome the Times' First Amendment right to publish Doe's name."

The dissenter contended that plaintiff "unhappily, became an involuntary public figure.  As a matter of law, the publication of Doe's name was newsworthy."  Nor did the mention of Doe in the story offend community notions of decency.  The majority was rejecting the reactions of the reasonable person and substituting the "subjective reaction" of the plaintiff.  "The reporter and the editor are now hostage to the paranoiac, the psychotic, the schizophrenic, whose reactions to publication now determine the scope to First Amendment media immunity."

When the defendant sought *certiorari, Florida Star* was already before the Court. Defendant contended that its case was also worthy of *certiorari* or that the state court action should be stayed until the Court decided *Florida Star.* The Court denied the stay although it had not yet decided the *Florida Star* case. Recall that *Florida Star* involved identifying the eyewitness (as well as victim), though the Court did not focus on that aspect of the case because of the statute there.

The *Times Mirror* case was settled shortly after the stay was denied. Editor & Publisher, Mar. 18, 1989, at 22. The terms were not disclosed. If the case had gone forward, how might plaintiff prove negligence? What if the newspaper did not know that the assailant knew that he had been seen by the plaintiff?

b. In Hyde v. City of Columbia, 637 S.W.2d 251 (Mo.App.1982), cert. denied 459 U.S. 1226 (1983), a newspaper report of an abduction gave the name and the address of the victim, who had escaped. The abductor was still at large. The court, using a negligence analysis, concluded that the complaint stated a cause of action:

> We determine . . . that the name and address of an abduction witness who can identify an assailant still at large before arrest is a matter of such trivial public concern compared with the high probability of risk to the victim by their publication, that a news medium owes a duty in such circumstances to use reasonable care not to give likely occasion for a third party [assailant still at large] to do injury to the plaintiff by the publication. That duty derives as an 'expression of the sum total of those considerations of policy which lead the law to say that the particular plaintiff is entitled to protection.' [  ] It derives from a balance of interests between the public right to know and the individual right to personal security—between the social value of the right the press advances and the social value of the right of the individual at risk. [  ] It derives from the social consensus that common decency considers such information of insignificant public importance compared to the injury likely to be done by the exposure. . . . To delete the name and address of the abduction victim from the news medium publication would impair no significant news function nor public interest in the reportage of crime and apprehension of criminals. To report that information when the assailant can be identified—as the news publication clearly informs—rather, encourages not only a likelihood of injury but of additional crime.

The court found no constitutional impediment to state recognition of a negligence action. The plaintiff's claim in this case "comes validly within the culminated constitutional balance struck by *Gertz* which allows a private redress against a newspaper for a negligent publication of information on a theory of fault free from the proof constraints of *New York Times.*"

Can this approach be squared with the "true-fact" privacy cases in Chapter IV? *Hyde* was settled for a payment of $6,000 from the city and nothing from the newspaper. News Media & Law, Sept.–Oct. 1983, at 41.

c. A Detroit newspaper revealed the whereabouts (and the dubious security protection) of a Colombian judge who had been targeted for death by a drug cartel. The judge sued claiming, among other things, that the article put her life in danger. The article revealed that the judge was living under her own real name in a Detroit suburb. The reporter said that he revealed the situation because of the threat the judge represented to innocent bystanders. Four months later the judge was moved out of the area. Editor & Publisher, Apr. 22, 1989, at 109; May 20, 1989, at 11.

The problems of special impact cases are discussed generally in Palmer, "When Reporting Endangers a Life," Wash.J.Rev., Oct. 1986, at 36. These problems usually involve the question of whether and when to cover a story. Palmer also discusses a situation in which a television station broadcast a false news report to help police smoke out a man who had ordered a contract killing. The man had said he would not pay unless he saw proof of the killing on television.

Although most of the special impact situations involve harm being done by an audience member, it is possible for a member of the audience to suffer the harm. In some cases a newspaper learns of something awful in the background of a respected member of the community. The paper checks with the person, who admits the truth of the story but says that if the paper publishes the story he or she will commit suicide. One paper published the revelation that the person was a former double agent, and the person committed suicide within an hour of the article's appearance. Another example of this situation occurred when local media revealed that a Seattle juvenile judge had been involved in homosexual relationships with wards of his court. His suicide occurred that day. See Brown, Seattle's Press and the Case of the Judge Who Killed Himself, Colum.J.Rev., Jan./Feb. 1989, at 3.

## B.  PHYSICAL HARM

We turn now to cases in which plaintiffs have claimed they suffered physical harm as the result of a newspaper or magazine article or broadcast show. These cases are divided between cases in which a member of the audience is alleged to have suffered the harm and cases in which an audience member is alleged to have responded to a message by hurting a third person.

This organization by plaintiff does not mean that the two groups of cases are distinct in every respect. Rather, they provide a useful grouping of cases for consideration. Indeed, as we shall see, in certain respects the two groups share common features. But in other respects each presents special problems. After considering these two main categories, we turn to cases in which the harm is said to flow from advertising.

### 1. HARM TO THE AUDIENCE

## HERCEG v. HUSTLER MAGAZINE, INC.

United States Court of Appeals, Fifth Circuit, 1987.
814 F.2d 1017, 13 Med.L.Rptr. 2345.
Cert. denied 485 U.S. 959 (1988).

Before RUBIN, JOHNSON and JONES, CIRCUIT JUDGES.

ALVIN B. RUBIN, CIRCUIT JUDGE:

An adolescent read a magazine article that prompted him to commit an act that proved fatal. The issue is whether the publisher of the magazine may be held liable for civil damages.

### I.

In its August 1981 issue, as part of a series about the pleasures— and dangers—of unusual and taboo sexual practices, Hustler Magazine printed "Orgasm of Death," an article discussing the practice of autoerotic asphyxia. This practice entails masturbation while "hanging" oneself in order to temporarily cut off the blood supply to the brain at the moment of orgasm. The article included details about how the act is performed and the kind of physical pleasure those who engage in it seek to achieve. The heading identified "Orgasm of Death" as part of a series on "Sexplay," discussions of "sexual pleasures [that] have remained hidden for too long behind the doors of fear, ignorance, inexperience and hypocrisy" and are presented "to increase [readers'] sexual knowledge, to lessen [their] inhibitions and—ultimately—to make [them] much better lover[s]."

An editor's note, positioned on the page so that it is likely to be the first text the reader will read, states: "Hustler emphasizes the often-fatal dangers of the practice of 'auto-erotic asphyxia,' and recommends that readers seeking unique forms of sexual release DO NOT ATTEMPT this method. The facts are presented here solely for an educational purpose."

The article begins by presenting a vivid description of the tragic results the practice may create. It describes the death of one victim and discusses research indicating that such deaths are alarmingly common: as many as 1,000 United States teenagers die in this manner each year. Although it describes the sexual "high" and "thrill" those who engage in the practice seek to achieve, the article repeatedly warns that the procedure is "neither healthy nor harmless," "it is a serious—and often-fatal—mistake to believe that asphyxia can be controlled" and "beyond a doubt—. . . auto-asphyxiation is one form of sex play you try only if you're anxious to wind up in cold storage, with a coroner's tag on your big toe." The two-page article warns readers at least ten different times that the practice is dangerous, self-destructive and deadly. It states that persons who successfully perform the technique can achieve intense physical pleasure, but the attendant risk is that the person may lose consciousness and die of strangulation.

Tragically, a copy of this issue of Hustler came into the possession of Troy D., a fourteen-year-old adolescent, who read the article and attempted the practice. The next morning, Troy's nude body was found, hanging by its neck in his closet, by one of Troy's closest friends, Andy V. A copy of Hustler Magazine, opened to the article about the "Orgasm of Death," was found near his feet.

Invoking the diversity jurisdiction of a federal court, Troy's mother, Diane Herceg, and Andy V. sued Hustler to recover damages for emotional and psychological harms they suffered as a result of Troy's death and for exemplary damages. Their original complaint alleged that Hustler was responsible for Troy's death on grounds of negligence, products liability, dangerous instrumentality, and attractive nuisance. In response, Hustler filed a motion to dismiss the complaint for failure to state a claim. The district court granted Hustler's motion on the basis that Texas law did not support some of the claims and others were barred by the first amendment, but it noted that the first amendment did not bar claims based on incitement and that it was "conceivable that plaintiffs could prove facts showing that Hustler's article was 'directed to inciting or producing' [Troy's death and] was 'likely to incite or produce' the death." It therefore granted leave to the plaintiffs to amend the complaint "to add an allegation of incitement." The plaintiffs subsequently filed an amended complaint reasserting the claims previously raised and adding an allegation that Troy had read the article and was incited by it to perform the act that resulted in his death. Hustler responded by filing a motion for summary judgment. The district court treated the motion as a motion to dismiss, granted the motion, and dismissed the suit insofar as it was based on any theory except incitement.

The incitement claim was then tried before a jury. Expert witnesses testified on behalf of both the plaintiffs and the defendant about the psychological implications of Troy's behavior and whether the magazine article implicitly advocated the practice it described or was likely to incite readers to attempt the procedure. The jury returned a verdict in favor of the plaintiffs awarding Diane Herceg $69,000 in actual damages and $100,000 exemplary damages and awarding Andy V. $3,000 for the pain and mental suffering he endured as the bystander who discovered Troy's body and $10,000 exemplary damages. Hustler moved for a judgment notwithstanding the verdict or for a new trial, and the plaintiffs moved to amend the judgment to provide for pre-judgment interest. The trial court denied both motions. Hustler appeals, but the plaintiffs do not cross appeal or raise any issue concerning the correctness of the district court order dismissing their other claims.

## II.

The constitutional protection accorded to the freedom of speech and of the press is not based on the naive belief that speech can do no harm but on the confidence that the benefits society reaps from the free flow and exchange of ideas outweigh the costs society endures by receiving reprehensible or dangerous ideas. Under our Constitution, as the Supreme Court has reminded us, "there is no such thing as a false idea. However pernicious an opinion may seem we depend for its correction not on the conscience of judges and juries but on the competition of other ideas." [*Gertz*] We rely on a reverse Gresham's law, trusting to good ideas to drive out bad ones and forbidding governmental intervention into the free market of ideas. One of our basic constitutional tenets, therefore, forbids the state to punish protected speech, directly or indirectly, whether by criminal penalty or civil liability.

The Supreme Court has recognized that some types of speech are excluded from, or entitled only to narrowed constitutional protection. Freedom of speech does not protect obscene materials, child pornography, fighting words, incitement to imminent lawless activity, and purposefully-made or recklessly-made false statements of fact such as libel, defamation, or fraud. Whatever the problems created in attempting to categorize speech in such fashion, the Hustler article fits none of them.

Even types of speech protected generally by the first amendment may be subject to government regulation. Freedom of speech is not an absolute. If the state interest is compelling and the means of regulation narrowly tailored to accomplish a proper state purpose, regulation of expression is not forbidden by the first amendment. The extent of the danger created by a publication therefore is not immaterial in determining the state's power to penalize that publication for harm that ensues, but first amendment protection is not eliminated simply because publication of an idea creates a potential hazard. Whether the Hustler article, therefore, placed a dangerous idea into Troy's head is but one factor in determining whether the state may impose damages for that consequence. Against the important social goal of protecting the lives of adolescents like Troy, the Constitution requires us to balance more than Hustler's right to publish the particular article, subject to the possibility of civil liability should harm ensue, but also the danger that unclear or diminished standards of first amendment protection may both inhibit the expression of protected ideas by other speakers and constrict the right of the public to receive those ideas.

While the plaintiffs alleged several different bases of liability in their original amended complaint, the issue tried was the imposition of liability on the basis of incitement, and that is the sole basis for the verdict. The question before us therefore is whether, as a matter of law, the language of "Orgasm of Death" may be defined as incitement for purposes of removing that speech from the purview of first amendment protection. If not, the judgment entered on the jury verdict cannot be affirmed even if it is conceivable that, had the case been tried on some other ground, the jury might have reached the same verdict.

### III.

Appellate review of jury findings in cases implicating first amendment rights must remain faithful both to the substantial evidence standard set forth in Rule 52(a) and the constitutional obligation of appellate courts "to 'make an independent examination of the whole record' in order to make sure 'that the judgment does not constitute a forbidden intrusion on the field of free expression.' " [*Bose*]  Although we must accept the jury's fact findings if they are fairly supported by the record, that requirement "does not inhibit an appellate court's power to correct errors of law, including those that may infect a so-called mixed finding of law and fact, or a finding of fact that is predicated on a misunderstanding of the governing rule of law."

The text of the Hustler article provides the best basis for deciding whether the article may be held to have incited Troy's behavior.  The jury was also entitled to consider evidence concerning whether Troy read the article immediately prior to attempting the autoerotic asphyxiation procedure, the psychiatric testimony about the likely effect such an article would have on normal adolescent readers, and the evidence about the probable state of his mind at the time he entered upon the experiment that resulted in his death.  Although the jury was not asked to answer special interrogatories establishing what evidence they credited or discredited, it is apparent from the verdict that the jurors believed the testimony leading to the conclusion that Troy had read the article immediately before he entered in the acts that proved fatal and that his reaction to the article was not the result of any clinical psychological abnormality.  Because these conclusions are adequately supported by evidence in the record, we accept them as true.

We are not free, however, as the Supreme Court's recent decision in [*Bose*] holds, to accept the jury's mixed finding of fact and law that the article culpably incited Troy's behavior without conducting "an independent review of the record both to be sure the speech in question actually falls within the unprotected category and to confine the perimeters of any unprotected category within acceptably narrow limits in an effort to ensure that protected expression will not be inhibited."

Although we are doubtful that a magazine article that is no more direct than "Orgasm of Death" can ever constitute an incitement in the sense in which the Supreme Court—in cases we discuss below—has employed that term to identify unprotected speech the states may punish without violating the first amendment, we first analyze the evidence on the theory that it might satisfy doctrinal tests relating to incitement, for that was the theory under which the case was tried and submitted. Substituting our judgment for the jury's, as we must, we hold that liability cannot be imposed on Hustler on the basis that the article was an incitement to attempt a potentially fatal act without impermissibly infringing upon freedom of speech.

The word incitement, like many of the words in our complex language, can carry different meanings.  It is properly used to refer to encouragement of conduct that might harm the public such as the violation of law or the use of force.  But when the word is used in that context, the state may not punish such an inducement unless the speech involved is, as the Supreme Court held in [*Brandenburg*], "directed to inciting or producing *imminent* lawless action and  . . .  *likely* to incite or produce such action."  [Id., 395 U.S. at 447 (emphasis added).]

Brandenburg, a Ku Klux Klan leader garbed in Klan regalia, had delivered a speech threatening that "if our President, our Congress, our Supreme Court, continues to suppress the white, Caucasian race, it is possible that there might have to be some revengence (sic) taken."  He challenged his conviction under an Ohio statute that punished "advocacy of the duty, necessity or propriety of crime, sabotage, violence, or unlawful methods of terrorism as a means of accomplishing industrial or political reform."  The Supreme Court reversed his conviction because neither the statute nor the state court's jury instruction distinguished between advocacy and incitement to imminent lawless action, and only the latter might constitutionally be forbidden.

Hustler argues that *Brandenburg* provides the controlling principle, and the plaintiffs assume that it may.  If that were so, it would be necessary for the plaintiffs to have proved that:

1.  Autoerotic asphyxiation is a lawless act.

2.  Hustler advocated this act.

3.  Hustler's publication went even beyond "mere advocacy" and amounted to incitement.

4.  The incitement was directed to imminent action.

The *Brandenburg* focus is repeated in subsequent Supreme Court decisions.  Thus, in *Hess v. Indiana,* the Court held provocative remarks by a demonstrator to the police could not be punished on the basis that they had a tendency to lead to violence because there was no evidence that, or rational inference from, the import of the language that "[the] words [used] were intended to produce, and likely to produce, *imminent* disorder."  [414 U.S. at 109 (emphasis in original)].  [   ]

. . .

We need not decide whether Texas law made autoerotic asphyxiation illegal or whether *Brandenburg* is restricted to the advocacy of criminal conduct.  Even if the article paints in glowing terms the pleasures supposedly achieved by the practice it describes, as the plaintiffs contend, no fair reading of it can make its content advocacy, let alone incitement to engage in the practice.

Herceg and Andy V. complain that the article provides unnecessary detail about how autoerotic asphyxiation is accomplished.  The detail is adapted from an article published by a psychiatrist in the *Journal of Child Psychiatry.*  Although it is conceivable that, in some instances, the amount of detail contained in challenged speech may be relevant in determining whether incitement exists, the detail in "Orgasm of Death" is not enough to permit breach of the first amendment.  The manner of engaging in autoerotic asphyxiation apparently is not complicated.  To understand what the term means is to know roughly how to accomplish it. Furthermore, the article is laden with detail about all facets of the practice, including the physiology of how it produces a threat to life and the seriousness of the danger of harm.

Under *Brandenburg,* therefore, the article was entitled to first amendment protection. But the parties' and, apparently, the district court's effort to apply the *Brandenburg* analysis to the type of "incitement" with which Hustler was charged appears inappropriate. Incitement cases usually concern a state effort to punish the arousal of a crowd to commit a criminal action. The root of incitement theory appears to have been grounded in concern over crowd behavior. As John Stuart Mill stated in his dissertation, *On Liberty,* "An opinion that corn-dealers are starvers of the poor, or that private property is robbery ought to be unmolested when simply circulated through the press, but may justly incur punishment when delivered orally to an excited mob assembled before the house of a corn-dealer." In *Noto v. United States* [367 U.S. 290 (1961)], the Supreme Court expressed similar views about incitement: "the mere abstract teaching . . . of the moral propriety or even moral necessity for a resort to force and violence, is not the same as preparing a group for violent action and steering it to such action." Whether written material might ever be found to create culpable incitement unprotected by the first amendment is, however, a question that we do not now reach.

## IV.

Herceg and Andy V. contend that, while the first amendment might prevent the state from punishing publication of such articles as criminal, it does not foreclose imposing civil liability for damages that result from publication. In *New York Times v. Sullivan,* the Supreme Court held, "what a State may not constitutionally bring about by means of a criminal statute is likewise beyond the reach of its civil law of libel," because the fear of civil liability might be "markedly more inhibiting than the fear of prosecution under a criminal statute." The same rationale forbids the state to impose damages for publication of "Orgasm of Death" if it could not constitutionally make the publication of that article a crime.

. . .

## V.

In the alternative, Herceg and Andy suggest that a less stringent standard than the *Brandenburg* test be applied in cases involving non-political speech that has actually produced harm. Although political speech is at "the core of the First Amendment," [N.A.A.C.P. v. Claiborne Hardware Co., 458 U.S. 886, 926–27 (1982)], the Supreme Court generally has not attempted to differentiate between different categories of protected speech for the purposes of deciding how much constitutional protection is required. Such an endeavor would not only be hopelessly complicated but would raise substantial concern that the worthiness of speech might be judged by majoritarian notions of political and social propriety and morality. If the shield of the first amendment can be eliminated by proving after publication that an article discussing a dangerous idea negligently helped bring about a real injury simply because the idea can be identified as "bad," all free speech becomes threatened. An article discussing the nature and danger of "crack" usage—or of hang-gliding—might lead to liability just as easily. As is made clear in the Supreme Court's decision in *Hess,* the "tendency to lead to violence" is not enough. Mere negligence, therefore, cannot form the basis of liability under the incitement doctrine any more than it can under libel doctrine.[38]

## VI.

Finally, even if this court were to determine that the plaintiffs may establish a cause of action under a theory of negligence, that theory could not form the basis of affirming the decision below [because the plaintiffs tried the case solely on an incitement theory after defendant won summary judgment on the various state law claims].

## VII.

Hustler's final challenge to the judgment below is to the award granted Andy V. as compensation for suffering he endured as a bystander to the tragedy. Because we have held that no liability can attach to Hustler's publication of "Orgasm of Death" under incitement theory, we need not decide whether Andy V. would have been entitled to recover damages under Texas tort law.

For the reasons stated above, the judgment of the district court is REVERSED.

EDITH H. JONES, CIRCUIT JUDGE, concurring and dissenting:

I concur in the result in this case only because I am persuaded that plaintiffs had an obligation to cross-appeal the court's dismissal of their claims based on negligence, attractive nuisance, and strict liability or dangerous instrumentality.    . . .

What disturbs me to the point of despair is the majority's broad reasoning which appears to foreclose the possibility that any state might choose to temper the excesses of the pornography business by imposing civil liability for harms it directly causes. Consonant with the first amendment, the state can protect its citizens against the moral evil of obscenity, the threat of civil disorder or injury posed by lawless mobs and fighting words, and the damage to reputation from libel or defamation, to say nothing of the myriad dangers lurking in "commercial speech." Why cannot the state then fashion a remedy to protect its children's lives when they are endangered by suicidal pornography? To deny this possibility, I believe, is to degrade the free market of ideas to a level with the black market for heroin. Despite the grand flourishes of

**38.** Accord, Walt Disney Productions, Inc. v. Shannon, 247 Ga. 402, 276 S.E.2d 580 (1981).

rhetoric in many first amendment decisions concerning the sanctity of "dangerous" ideas, no federal court has held that death is a legitimate price to pay for freedom of speech.

In less emotional terms, I believe the majority has critically erred in its analysis of this case under existing first amendment law. The majority decide at the outset that Hustler's "Orgasm of Death" does not embody child pornography, fighting words, incitement to lawless conduct, libel, defamation or fraud, or obscenity, all of which categories of speech are entirely unprotected by the first amendment. Nor do they find in the article "an effort to achieve a commercial result," which would afford it modified first amendment protection. Comforted by the inapplicability of these labels, they then accord this article full first amendment protection, holding that in the balance struck between society's interest in Troy's life and the chilling effect on the "right of the public to receive . . . ideas," Troy loses. Any effort to find a happier medium, they conclude, would not only be hopelessly complicated but would raise substantial concerns that the worthiness of speech might be judged by "majoritarian notions of political and social propriety and morality." I agree that "Orgasm of Death" does not conveniently match the current categories of speech defined for first amendment purposes. Limiting its constitutional protection does not, however, disserve any of these categories and is more appropriate to furthering the "majoritarian" notion of protecting the sanctity of human life. Finally, the "slippery slope" argument that if Hustler is held liable here, *Ladies Home Journal* or the publisher of an article on hang-gliding will next be a casualty of philistine justice simply proves too much: *This* case is not a difficult one in which to vindicate Troy's loss of life.

## I.

Proper analysis must begin with an examination of *Hustler* generally and this article in particular. *Hustler* is not a bona fide competitor in the "marketplace of ideas." It is largely pornographic, whether or not technically obscene. One need not be male to recognize that the principal function of this magazine is to create sexual arousal. Consumers of this material so partake for its known physical effects much as they would use tobacco, alcohol or drugs for their effects. By definition, pornography's appeal is therefore non-cognitive and unrelated to, in fact exactly the opposite of, the transmission of ideas.

Not only is Hustler's appeal noncognitive, but the magazine derives its profit from that fact. If Hustler stopped being pornographic, its readership would vanish.

According to the trial court record, pornography appeals to pubescent males. Moreover, although sold in the "adults only" section of newsstands, a significant portion of its readers are adolescent. Hustler knows this. Such readers are particularly vulnerable to thrillseeking, recklessness, and mimicry. Hustler should know this. Hustler should understand that to such a mentality the warnings "no" or "caution" may be treated as invitations rather than taboos.

"Orgasm of Death" provides a detailed description how to accomplish autoerotic asphyxiation. The article appears in the "Sexplay" section of the magazine which, among other things, purports to advise its readers on "how to make you a much better lover." [8]  The warnings and cautionary comments in the article could be seen by a jury to conflict with both the explicit and subliminal message of Hustler, which is to tear down custom, explode myths and banish taboos about sexual matters. The article trades on the symbiotic connection between sex and violence. In sum, as Hustler knew, the article is dangerously explicit, lethal, and likely to be distributed to those members of society who are most vulnerable to its message. "Orgasm of Death," in the circumstances of its publication and dissemination, is not unlike a dangerous nuisance or a stick of dynamite in the hands of a child. Hustler's publication of this particular article bears the seeds of tort liability although, as I shall explain, the theory on which the case was tried is incorrect.

## II.

First amendment analysis is an exercise in line-drawing between the legitimate interests of society to regulate itself and the paramount necessity of encouraging the robust and uninhibited flow of debate which is the life-blood of government by the people. That some of the lines are blurred or irregular does not, however, prove the majority's proposition that it would be hopelessly complicated to delineate between protected and unprotected speech in this case. Such a formulation in fact begs the critical question in two ways. First, a hierarchy of first amendment speech classifications has in fact developed largely in the last few years, and there is no reason to assume the hierarchy is ineluctable. Second, the essence of the judicial function is to judge. If it is impossible to judge, there is no reason for judges to pretend to perform their role, and it is a nonsequitur for them to conclude that society's or a state's judgment is "wrong." Hence, in novel cases like this one, the reasons for protecting speech under the first amendment must be closely examined to properly evaluate Hustler's claim to unlimited constitutional protection.

[Judge Jones cited the *Greenmoss* case as an example of one in which negligence was used to ground a damage recovery after the Court "evaluated the interest sought to be protected by the state against the level of first amendment interest embodied in the communication at issue."]

. . .

. . . *Hustler* is a profitable commercial enterprise trading on its prurient appeal to a small portion of the population. It deliberately

---

8. The introduction to the Sexplay section states: "Many sexual pleasures have remained hidden for too long. . . . In keeping with HUSTLER's belief that the repression of natural and healthy urges is physically and emotionally damaging, we present this series of informative articles to increase your sexual knowledge, lessen your inhibitions and—ultimately to make you a much better lover."

borders on technical obscenity, which would be wholly unprotected, to achieve its purposes, and its appeal is not based on cognitive or intellectual appreciation. Because of the solely commercial and pandering nature of the magazine neither *Hustler* nor any other pornographic publication is likely to be deterred by incidental state regulation. No sensitive first amendment genius is required to see that, as the Court concluded in *Dun & Bradstreet*, "[t]here is simply no credible argument that this type of [speech] requires special protection to insure that 'debate on public issues [will] be uninhibited, robust, and wide-open.'"
[   ]

To place *Hustler* effectively on a par with *Dun & Bradstreet's* "private speech" or with commercial speech, for purposes of permitting tort lawsuits against it hardly portends the end of participatory democracy, as some might contend. First, any given issue of *Hustler* may be found legally obscene and therefore entitled to no first amendment protection. Second, tort liability would result after-the-fact, not as a prior restraint, and would be based on harm directly caused by the publication in issue. [   ] Third, to the extent any chilling effect existed from the exposure to tort liability this would, in my view, protect society from loss of life and limb, a legitimate, indeed compelling, state interest. Fourth, obscenity has been widely regulated by prior restraints for over a century. Before *Roth v. United States*, 354 U.S. 476 (1957), there was no *Hustler* magazine and it would probably have been banned. Despite such regulation, it does not appear that the pre-*Roth* era was a political dark age. Conversely, increasing leniency on pornography in the past three decades has allowed pornography to flourish, but it does not seem to have corresponded with an increased quality of debate on "public" issues. These observations imply that pornography bears little connection to the core values of the first amendment and that political democracy has endured previously in the face of "majoritarian notions of social propriety."

. . .

The foregoing analysis immediately differentiates this case from [*Brandenburg*] which addressed prior restraints on public advocacy of controversial political ideas. Placing *Hustler* on the same analytical plane with *Brandenburg* represents an unwarranted extension of that holding, which, unlike *Dun & Bradstreet* and the commercial speech cases, rests in the core values protected by the first amendment. Even *Brandenburg*, however, recognized that the state's regulatory interest legitimately extends to protecting the lives of its citizens from violence induced by speech. . . .

### III.

Texas courts have never been called upon to assess a claim like this one. Since there is no cross-appeal, we should not speculate on the precise nature of the theory of liability a Texas court might accept, although negligence and attractive nuisance seem theoretically appropriate. [Citing *Weirum v. RKO General*, discussed at p. 281, *infra*].

. . .

**Notes and Questions**

1.  What does the majority find wrong with the plaintiffs' reliance on an incitement theory?  What does Judge Jones find wrong with it?

2.  How might the amount of detail in a news story affect the analysis of whether it is inciting behavior?  What is the relevance of the fact that the *Hustler* article is two pages long?  The court does not mention that the article is illustrated with a belt wrapped around a cross bar surrounded by half a dozen closeups of female genitalia.  Is this relevant? How about the fact that the article is in a series called "Sexplay"? Might the nature of the publication itself be relevant in that analysis?

3.  When can print media be held liable in this type of case according to the majority?

4.  Why is the majority skeptical about an action based on, say, negligence?  Who has the better of the exchange on that issue?  What is the relevance of the *Dun & Bradstreet* case?

5.  How serious is the "slippery slope" problem in this type of case?

6.  Is there a difference between (a) a pure news story about someone being killed by attempting autoerotic asphyxia, (b) a story that tells about the practice and suggests that it is erotically satisfying though very dangerous, and (c) an article that explicitly discusses the benefits and the dangers of the practice and then instructs readers step by step on how to do it if they should wish to try it?

7.  The dissent suggests that no warning of any sort could have been expected to have been effective given the expected audience and the nature of the message.  Is this correct?  If it is, what legal consequences might flow from this state of affairs?

8.  In DeFilippo v. National Broadcasting Co., Inc., 446 A.2d 1036, 8 Med.L.Rptr. 1872 (R.I.1982), plaintiff's 13–year–old son was watching the Tonight Show with Johnny Carson and his guest, a professional stuntman named Robinson.  Carson announced that after the commercial break he would attempt a stunt that involved dropping through a trapdoor with a noose around his neck.  Robinson then said "Believe me, it's not something that you want to go and try.  This is a stunt. . . ."  The audience began to laugh, producing the following dialogue:

Robinson: I've got to laugh—you know, you're all laughing.  . . .
Carson:   Explain that to me.
Robinson: I've seen people try things like this.  I really have.  I happen
          to know somebody who did something similar to it, just
          fooling around, and almost broke his neck.  . . .

The commercial break followed.  After the break, Carson did the stunt accompanied by comic dialogue.  Carson came through unscathed.  Several hours after the broadcast, plaintiffs' son was found hanging from a noose in front of the television set which was still on and tuned to the station that had presented the Tonight Show.

The plaintiffs asserted a variety of theories, including defective products, negligence, failure to warn, and intentional tort-trespass. The court upheld the trial judge's summary judgment on the ground that the First Amendment barred all actions. It identified four classes of speech that states may proscribe: obscenity, fighting words, defamation, and "words likely to produce imminent lawless action (incitement)." Only the incitement theory was possible here and that failed because the son was apparently the only person who was alleged to have "emulated the action portrayed" on the show. Moreover, the quoted dialogue indicated that those on the show tried to prevent emulation—and certainly did not invite it. To permit recovery here "on the basis of one minor's action would invariably lead to self-censorship by broadcasters in order to remove any matter that may be emulated and lead to a law suit."

Which case is stronger on its facts for the plaintiff—*Herceg* or *DeFilippo*? In her dissent in *Herceg*, Judge Jones observed that *DeFilippo* and the *Olivia N* case, *infra*, used "first amendment analysis with which I differ."

9. *Suicide.* In 1980 some 17 PBS stations chose not to show a documentary about a 62–year–old woman with breast cancer who committed suicide with the advance knowledge of her family and friends. The program manager of one of the stations explained the decision by saying that the program had the "potential for encouraging others to commit suicide." Assuming that it had that potential, might stations showing the program have incurred legal consequences? N.Y. Times, June 4, 1980, at C30. Would the case be different if the stimulus to attempting suicide had come from reading a book that presented suicide in a favorable light?

In McCollum v. CBS, Inc., 202 Cal.App.3d 989, 249 Cal.Rptr. 187, 15 Med.L.Rptr. 2001 (1988), a 19–year–old who had "had a problem with alcohol abuse as well as serious emotional problems," killed himself while lying on his bed listening to the recorded music of Ozzy Osbourne. His parents sued Osbourne and others connected with the three albums that decedent was listening to "repeatedly" that night, alleging that Osbourne's music and the album covers demonstrate a preoccupation with unusual, anti-social and even bizarre attitudes and beliefs often emphasizing such things as satanic worship or emulation, the mocking of religious beliefs and death. The message was that life is filled with nothing but despair and that "suicide is not only acceptable, but desirable."

Plaintiffs alleged a "special relationship" between Osbourne and his avid fans that was underscored by the personal manner in which the lyrics were directed and disseminated to the listeners—often using "you" so that a listener could feel that Osbourne "was talking directly to him as he listened to the music."

Among the compositions complained of was a 28–second instrumental break with "masked" lyrics sung at one and one-half times the normal rate of speech and intelligible only when the listener concentrated on the music and lyrics. Finally, plaintiff alleged generally that Osbourne knew or should have known that his music would influence the emotions and behavior of individuals with emotional instability.

The court's first response was that the First Amendment barred the action. Entertainment was protected speech. In order to prevail, plaintiff must show incitement: that "Osbourne's music was *directed and intended* toward the goal of bringing about the imminent suicide of listeners *and* (2) that it was likely *to produce such a result.*" The court found no such intent or likelihood. None of the lyrics "purport to order or command anyone to any concrete action at any specific time much less immediately. . . . Merely because art may evoke a mood of depression as it figuratively depicts the darker side of human nature does not mean that it constitutes a direct 'incitement to imminent violence.'" The court noted that such a theme was "often seen in literature and music."

Moreover, "musical lyrics and poetry cannot be construed to contain the requisite 'call to action' for the elementary reason that they simply are not intended to be and should not be read literally on their face, nor judged by a standard of prose oratory. Reasonable persons understand musical lyrics and poetic conventions as the figurative expressions which they are. No rational person would or could believe otherwise nor would they mistake musical lyrics and poetry for literal commands or directives to immediate action."

Turning to the state law questions, the court concluded that tort law would not permit recovery here. Analyzing the factors California courts consider in a duty analysis, the court concluded as a matter of law that the suicide "was not a reasonably foreseeable risk or consequence of defendants' remote artistic activities." Nor was there a "close connection" between the creation and distribution of the records and the death. "Likewise, no moral blame for that tragedy may be laid at defendants' door. . . . Finally and perhaps most significantly, it is simply not acceptable to a free and democratic society to impose a duty upon performing artists to limit and restrict their creativity in order to avoid the dissemination of ideas in artistic speech which may adversely affect emotionally troubled individuals."

Suppose it were proven that news coverage of the suicide of a famous movie star caused a "temporary increase in the number of teenagers" who took their own lives? See Eckholm, 2 Studies Link Teen–Age Suicides to TV Programs, N.Y.Times, Sept. 11, 1986 at 15, observing that such "effects have been suspected ever since Goethe's 18th–century novel 'The Sorrows of Young Werther' was blamed for a rash of suicides among European youths."

10. *Subliminal Messages.* In Vance v. Judas Priest, 104 Nev. 424, 760 P.2d 137, 15 Med.L.Rptr. 2010 (1988), the complaint alleged that music

in a Judas Priest album had subliminal lyrics that encouraged listeners to commit suicide. Two young men entered a suicide pact after extended listening to the music. CBS, Inc., producer of the records, moved for summary judgment on the ground that subliminal messages were as protected under the First Amendment as were conventional messages. The judge rejected the claim on the ground that such messages did not contribute to open robust debate or the exchange of ideas because the recipients did not know they were being exposed to ideas. The privacy rights of the audience prevailed over the speech rights of the speaker where the audience had no way to prevent the intrusion. The situation was worse than that of a captive audience because the latter at least knew they were being exposed to unwanted messages and could defend against their influence. The judge recognized that proof that subliminal messages in fact existed and that the music caused the suicides might be difficult but thought the issues warranted a trial. Subsequently, at the conclusion of the trial, a jury found for Judas Priest.

11. *Invitations to Act.* So far we have been considering situations in which the publisher or broadcaster explicitly warned the audience of the danger of replication and discouraged it, or with presentations of programs without either a warning or explicit encouragement to replicate. Sometimes, however, the publisher or broadcaster explicitly urges the audience to replicate. For example, those who offer recipes by print or broadcast media often urge (or at least expect) many in the audience to try the recipe. Other examples include advice shows in which listeners call in their problems (with cars, with mates, with neighbors) and get suggestions from "experts" or from the talk-show host.

In this type of situation when, if ever, should the media defendant be liable for harm sustained by an audience member who proceeds in reliance on the recipe or the advice? Consider the following variations on this theme:

a. In *Walt Disney Productions, Inc. v. Shannon,* cited by the majority in *Herceg,* defendant's "Mickey Mouse Club" program announced that a "special feature on today's show is all about the magic you can create with sound effects." A participant showed the audience how to reproduce the sound of a tire coming off an automobile by "putting a BB pellet inside a 'large, round balloon,' filling the balloon with air, and rotating the BB inside the balloon. Craig, who was 11 years old, undertook to repeat what he had seen on television. He put a piece of lead almost twice the size of a BB into a 'large, skinny balloon.' He blew up the balloon and the balloon burst, impelling the lead into Craig's eye and partially blinding him."

Although the court could "envision situations in which an adult could be held liable in tort solely on the ground that statements uttered by him constituted an invitation to a child to do something causing the child injury," no such liability should flow unless "what the adult invited the child to do presented a clear and present danger that injury would in fact result. Although it can be said that what the defendants allegedly

invited the child to do in this case posed a foreseeable risk of injury, it
cannot be said that it posed a clear and present danger of injury." In a
footnote, the court noted that "of an estimated 16 million children
watching this program, only the plaintiff in this case reported an
injury."

Why might "clear and present danger" be applicable here? How
might the judges in *Herceg* analyze this case? Would a negligence
standard be appropriate?

b.   In Walter v. Bauer, 109 Misc.2d 189, 439 N.Y.S.2d 821 (1981), a
fourth-grade student claimed that he had suffered an eye injury while
performing a science experiment with a ruler and rubber band. The
experiment was in a book published by defendant. Plaintiff claimed that
strict liability applied because the experiment contained an unreasonable
risk of harm for young children. The court disagreed. Strict liability
was intended "to protect the customer from defectively produced merchandise." The "plaintiff was not injured by use of the book for the
purpose for which it was designed, i.e., to be read." More important was
the chilling effect strict liability would have on publishers and authors.
"Would any author wish to be exposed to liability for writing on a topic
which might result in physical injury? E.g. How to cut trees; how to
keep bees?" This part of *Walter* was affirmed 88 A.D.2d 787, 451
N.Y.S.2d 533 (1982). What about a negligence theory?

In 1980 a jury returned a verdict holding liable a textbook publisher
for what the jury found confusing and misleading language that led to
personal injury. Two experiments in a section of a science book called
for methyl alcohol; a third, calibrating an alcohol thermometer by
heating and then cooling, did not call for methyl alcohol but did not
warn against its use either. Students used methyl alcohol for the
thermometer experiment and two were badly burned when it exploded.
The defendant argued that although 390,000 copies of the book had been
distributed, this was the first complaint. The awards totalled $825,000.
No appeal was taken. Bertrand v. Rand McNally & Co. (D.Mass.1980)
reported in National Law Journal, Sept. 22, 1980, at 3.

c.   In Alm v. Van Nostrand Reinhold Co., Inc., 134 Ill.App.3d 716,
89 Ill.Dec. 520, 480 N.E.2d 1263 (1985), plaintiff alleged that he was
injured while following instructions in a book published by defendant
entitled "The Making of Tools." The dismissal of plaintiff's action
based on a negligent failure to warn was affirmed on appeal, using state
law. If plaintiff's theory were adopted, it "would place upon publishers
the duty of scrutinizing and even testing all procedures contained in any
of their publications. The scope of liability would extend to an undeter-
minable number of potential readers."

The court adhered to an earlier case, MacKown v. Illinois Publishing
& Printing Co., 289 Ill.App. 59, 6 N.E.2d 526 (1937), which refused to
impose liability on a newspaper for physical injuries the reader suffered
from using a dandruff remedy recommended in an article. Are newspapers comparable to publishers of books?

Plaintiff in *Alm* sought to distinguish "bad advice in a 'How To' book from 'a treatise on politics, religion, philosophy, interpersonal relationships, or the like.'" The court thought such an effort would lead to impermissible content-based discriminations. "More important . . . is the chilling effect which liability would have upon publishers. . . . Even if liability could be imposed consistently with the Constitution, we believe that the adverse effect of such liability upon the public's free access to ideas would be too high a price to pay."

d. Dr. Ruth Westheimer, well-known sex therapist and talk show host, gave incorrect advice to teenagers about contraception in her 1985 book, *First Love: A Young People's Guide to Sexual Information.* In its discussion of the rhythm method of birth control, the book advised that the "safe times are the week before and the week of ovulation." In fact, these are precisely the times a woman is most likely to get pregnant. Dr. Ruth explained that she had personally proofread the book but had failed to catch the use of "safe" instead of "unsafe." The mistake was discovered by a librarian reviewing the book for possible acquisition. The librarian informed the publisher, who immediately recalled the 115,000 copies of the book. Anyone who had purchased the book was urged to return it. The book was reissued some months later with the correction and with a different cover. N.Y.Times, Jan. 1, 1986, at 24. What legal remedy might be available to a teenager who relied on the book and became pregnant? What if the teenager had not learned of the recall and had relied on the book two years after the recall?

e. Is there a difference between a physician who gives a patient incorrect diet advice during an office visit and a physician who writes that same incorrect advice in a general book advocating the diet?

f. After watching a television news broadcast about a doctor's new technique for breast enlargement, the plaintiff went to the doctor and had the procedure performed. She claimed the procedure left her with scars, severed muscles and nerves, and permanent physical and emotional pain, though the program had described the procedure as "safe and painless." In addition to suing the doctor, she sued the station claiming that it "deliberately suppressed the true facts and instead consciously and deliberately chose to broadcast a misleading and false story to the public." The trial judge had already dismissed a negligence claim. Editor & Publisher, July 9, 1988, at 20.

12. Does the "actual malice" rule of defamation provide a useful analogy for these cases? Is there any reason to protect a speaker who deliberately misstates a recipe in the hope that readers who follow it will be poisoned? On the other hand, is there a danger that the use of negligence will deter others from offering recipes or other advice? How would *Gertz* and *Dun & Bradstreet* fit into this analysis?

What criteria might be used to differentiate the conveying of information or entertainment from an invitation to act? Is the use of warnings, as in *Herceg*, controlling? Recall that the dissenting judge thought that those warnings were "invitations rather than taboos."

Recall also that the Sexplay section stated that the magazine was presenting "this series of informative articles to increase your sexual knowledge, lessen your inhibitions and—ultimately to make you a much better lover." Are there any such questions about characterizing a recipe that appears in the food section of a newspaper or magazine?

## 2. THE AUDIENCE CAUSES HARM

### OLIVIA N. v. NATIONAL BROADCASTING CO.

Court of Appeal of California, 1981.
126 Cal.App.3d 488, 178 Cal.Rptr. 888, 7 Med.L.Rptr. 2359.
Cert. denied, 458 U.S. 1108 (1982).

CHRISTIAN, J. OLIVIA N. appeals from a judgment of nonsuit terminating her action against the National Broadcasting Company and the Chronicle Broadcasting Company. Appellant sought damages for physical and emotional injury inflicted by assailants who had seen a television broadcast of a film drama.

[The case was originally dismissed before trial, but the appellate court held that improper procedure below had deprived the plaintiff of her right to a jury trial. After a jury was empaneled on the remand and plaintiff had made an opening statement, the trial judge dismissed the case on the ground that the only basis for recovery would be a showing that NBC intended that violence follow its presentation of the drama. Because plaintiff did not make that claim, the case was dismissed.]

At 8 p.m. on September 10, 1974, NBC telecast nationwide, and Chronicle Broadcasting Company broadcast locally, a film entitled "Born Innocent."

The subject matter of the television film was the harmful effect of a state-run home upon an adolescent girl who had become a ward of the state. In one scene of the film, the young girl enters the community bathroom of the facility to take a shower. She is then shown taking off her clothes and stepping into the shower, where she bathes for a few moments. Suddenly, the water stops and a look of fear comes across her face. Four adolescent girls are standing across from her in the shower room. One of the girls is carrying a "plumber's helper," waving it suggestively by her side. The four girls violently attack the younger girl, wrestling her to the floor. The young girl is shown naked from the waist up, struggling as the older girls force her legs apart. Then, the television film shows the girl with the plumber's helper making intense thrusting motions with the handle of the plunger until one of the four says, "That's enough." The young girl is left sobbing and naked on the floor.

It is alleged that on September 14, 1974, appellant, aged 9, was attacked and forcibly "artificially raped" with a bottle by minors at a San Francisco beach. [ ] The assailants had viewed and discussed the "artificial rape" scene in "Born Innocent," and the film allegedly caused the assailants to decide to commit a similar act on appellant.  Appellant offered to show that NBC had knowledge of studies on child violence and should have known that susceptible persons might imitate the crime enacted in the film.  Appellant alleged that "Born Innocent" was particularly likely to cause imitation and that NBC televised the film without proper warning in an effort to obtain the largest possible viewing audience.  Appellant alleged that as a proximate result of respondents' telecast, she suffered physical and psychological damage.

Appellant contends that where there is negligence, liability could constitutionally be imposed despite the absence of proof of incitement as defined in [Brandenburg].  Appellant argues in the alternative that a different definition of "incitement" should be applied to the present circumstances.

"Analysis of this appeal commences with recognition of the overriding constitutional principle that material communicated by the public media, including fictional material such as the television drama here at issue, is generally to be accorded protection under the First Amendment to the Constitution of the United States.  [  ]"  First Amendment rights are accorded a preferred place in our democratic society.  [  ]  First Amendment protection extends to a communication, to its source and to its recipients.  (Va. Pharmacy Bd. v. Va. Consumer Council (1976) 425 U.S. 748, 756.)  "[A]bove all else, the First Amendment means that government has no power to restrict expression because of its message, its ideas, its subject matter, or its content."  [  ]  .  .  .

.  .  .

The electronic media are also entitled to First Amendment protection.  .  .  .

Appellant does not seek to impose a prior restraint on speech; rather, she asserts civil liability premised on traditional negligence concepts.  But the chilling effect of permitting negligence actions for a television broadcast is obvious.  "The fear of damage awards  .  .  . may be markedly more inhibiting than the fear of prosecution under a criminal statute."  [Sullivan]  Realistically, television networks would become significantly more inhibited in the selection of controversial materials if liability were to be imposed on a simple negligence theory.  "[T]he pall of fear and timidity imposed upon those who would give voice to public criticism is an atmosphere in which the First Amendment freedoms cannot survive."  [Sullivan]  The deterrent effect of subjecting the television networks to negligence liability because of their programming choices would lead to self-censorship which would dampen the vigor and limit the variety of public debate.  [  ]

Although the First Amendment is not absolute, the television broadcast of "Born Innocent" does not, on the basis of the opening statement of appellant's attorney, fall within the scope of unprotected speech.  Appellant concedes that the film did not advocate or encourage violent acts and did not constitute an "incitement" within the meaning of [Brandenburg].  Notwithstanding the pervasive effect of the broadcast-

ing media (see FCC v. Pacifica Foundation (1978) 438 U.S. 726, 748;
[   ] ) and the unique access afforded children [*Pacifica*], the effect of the
imposition of liability could reduce the U.S. adult population to viewing
only what is fit for children. (See Butler v. Michigan (1957) 352 U.S.
380, 383.) Incitement is the proper test here. [   ] In areas outside of
obscenity the United States Supreme Court has "consistently held that
the fact that protected speech may be offensive to some does not justify
its suppression. See, e.g., Cohen v. California, 403 U.S. 15 (1971)."
(Carey v. Population Services International (1977) 431 U.S. 678,
701.) . . . [T]he television broadcast which is the subject of this
action concededly did not fulfill the incitement requirements of *Brandenburg*. Thus it is constitutionally protected.

Appellant would distinguish between the fictional presentation of
"Born Innocent" and news programs and documentaries. But that
distinction is too blurred to protect adequately First Amendment values.
"Everyone is familiar with instances of propaganda through fiction.
What is one man's amusement, teaches another's doctrine." [   ] If a
negligence theory is recognized, a television network or local station
could be liable when a child imitates activities portrayed in a news
program or documentary. Thus, the distinction urged by appellant
cannot be accepted. [   ] . . . "Among free men, the deterrents
ordinarily to be applied to prevent crime are education and punishment
for violations of the law, not abridgment of the rights of free speech.
. . ." [   ]. The trial court's determination that the First Amendment bars appellant's claim where no incitement is alleged must be
upheld.

. . . Appellant also relies on [*Pacifica*]. But the narrowness of
the *Pacifica* decision precludes its application here. "We simply hold
that when the Commission finds that a pig has entered the parlor, the
exercise of its *regulatory* power does not depend on proof that the pig is
obscene." ([   ]; italics added.) Furthermore, Justice Powell in his
concurrence emphasized that the court is not free "to decide on the basis
of its content which speech protected by the First Amendment is most
'valuable' and hence deserving of the most protection, and which is less
'valuable' and hence deserving of less protection." [   ] As the United
States District Court indicated in Zamora v. Columbia Broadcasting
System, 480 F.Supp. 199, 206, reliance on [*Pacifica*] "is misplaced
because of both the factual and legal bases for that decision." Other
methods of controlling violence on television must be found. *Pacifica*
deals with regulation of indecency, not the imposition of general tort
liability. Imposing liability on a simple negligence theory here would
frustrate vital freedom of speech guarantees. [*Gertz*] is also to be
distinguished: There the United States Supreme Court recognized the
power of the states to impose civil liability for defamation "so long as the
States [do] not impose liability without fault." The holding does not
extend more broadly to tort liability for speech in areas outside the law
of defamation.

The judgment is affirmed.

CALDECOTT, P.J., and POCHE, J., concurred.

[The California Supreme Court denied a hearing, 5–2.]

**Notes and Questions**

1. Is there any possible showing—short of "incitement"—that should entitle plaintiff to a judgment against NBC? What if the plaintiff can show that NBC officials had been warned by psychologists that the program was "almost certain" to provoke imitation? Is it significant that there was only one reported case of imitation? Is it significant that the show was presented at 8 p.m.?

2. Is there a difference between the "Born Innocent" program and a news story (or broadcast) that reports the details of a recent case of torture in the city—which is then imitated? What about live coverage of a hostage situation that leads to imitations?

The Food & Drug Administration has developed data suggesting that "intense publicity surrounding a dramatic tampering incident can indeed trigger a wave of tampering complaints nationwide." Grigg, Does publicity in the media cause waves of food tampering?, Editor & Publisher, Feb. 21, 1987, at 68. What are the legal consequences of news reports of tampering? Detailed reports? A drama based on a tampering episode?

3. The plaintiff in *Olivia N.* relied heavily on Weirum v. RKO General, Inc., 15 Cal.3d 40, 123 Cal.Rptr. 468, 539 P.2d 36 (1975). In that case a radio station catering to teenagers broadcast clues as to the whereabouts of a disc jockey and offered a cash prize to the first listener to reach him. Two teenagers reached the correct location but were not the first to arrive. While following the disc jockey to his next stop, the two drivers vied for position on the freeway and thereby caused a fatal accident. The court held that the station owed the decedent a duty of care and had violated it. Without relying on the fact that the contest was a boost for the station, the court easily rejected the station's First Amendment claim as "clearly without merit. The issue here is civil accountability for the foreseeable results of a broadcast which created an undue risk of harm to decedent. The First Amendment does not sanction the infliction of physical injury merely because achieved by word, rather than act." Is this sound? The court in *Olivia N.* distinguished *Weirum* on the ground that the station in that case actively encouraged the conduct leading to the accident. No such encouragement was present in "Born Innocent."

4. Some invitations to act result in harm to persons not in the audience—as when a science experiment explodes and hurts those around the experimenter, or when an inaccurate food recipe poisons all who eat the result. Is there any reason to treat these cases differently depending upon whether the person hurt is the audience member or a stranger?

5. *The Daily Pantagraph Case.* Two girls, 12 and 14, were charged in juvenile proceedings with having sexually abused three young children they were babysitting. In addition, they were alleged to have deliberate-

ly dropped one of them on the floor several times, causing a fractured skull. The juvenile court placed them in a detention center.

The girls' names and whereabouts had been released during early stages of the investigation, apparently in connection with charges being filed against an adult in another case. The girls' attorneys told Juvenile Court Judge Baner that as a result of the release, the girls had been the subject of bomb threats and there was concern for their safety. The attorneys asked the judge to order the press not to report the girls' identities or their present locations. The judge issued such an order against a group of local media, some of which sought to upset the order on appeal.

The Illinois Supreme Court, 4–3, refused requests that it hear and decide the case. The media organizations then sought to persuade the Supreme Court to stay the order while the organizations prepared to ask the full Supreme Court to review the case.

The press argued that a prior restraint could be issued only if "there were an immediate threat of irreparable harm to others which could not be alleviated by means other than a prior restraint." They also argued that since the names and original addresses were already public knowledge and could be disseminated by anyone not subject to Judge Baner's order, the order "cannot protect the juveniles from potential threats to their safety or privacy." The lawyers for the two girls argued that lifting the restraint could result in the death or serious injury of the girls.

The Court, 6–3, without opinion, denied the press organizations' motion to stay Judge Baner's order. Daily Pantagraph v. Baner, 469 U.S. 977 (1984). Justice Brennan, joined by Justices Marshall and Blackmun, dissented: "The trial court found that the names of these individuals, as well as their former location while in custody, had been lawfully released to the public. I would grant the stay with respect to that information. I would also grant the application with respect to any other information that the trial court, after a hearing, finds to have been made public." He cited *Near*, p. 55, *supra*, and his opinion in the "Pentagon Papers" case.

In *Daily Pantagraph,* it appears that on the night in question a 20–year–old man came to the house and had sexual intercourse with the 14–year–old babysitter. In an open indictment that named the 14–year–old as the victim, the man was indicted for having intercourse with a minor. Presumably it was not difficult for the press to put two and two together. Is any of this relevant? What if a juvenile judge under statutory authority to make a juvenile's name public in grievous cases, used that discretion—and then changed his mind after the juvenile, much to the judge's surprise, received death threats?

What is the significance of the fact that the information was once made public? How does this relate to the Cox Broadcasting and *Florida Star* cases involving invasions of privacy? In *Florida Star* the plaintiff's assailant was still at large but the Court did not treat the case as one involving a threat to physical security. Might that be explained by Justice Scalia's opinion, p. 228, *supra*?

No formal petition for *certiorari* was filed in the *Daily Pantagraph* case and it went back to Illinois. In In Interest of M.B., 137 Ill.App.3d 992, 92 Ill.Dec. 299, 484 N.E.2d 1154, 12 Med.L.Rptr. 1551 (1985), the court upheld the part of the order that barred the media "from revealing directly or indirectly the identity of the minor or the minor victim."

6. *The National Enquirer* published a poem by John W. Hinckley, Jr. entitled "Bloody Love," depicting Hinckley's fantasy of killing actress Jodie Foster with a knife. A front-page headline ran "Hinckley Reveals Details of His Plan to Kill Jodie Foster." Foster's lawyers told the Justice Department that the *Enquirer* had violated a federal criminal statute punishing "whoever transmits in interstate commerce any communication containing any threat to kidnap any person or any threat to injure the person of another." 18 U.S.C.A. § 875(c).

The *Enquirer*'s lawyer responded that this was not a threat because Hinckley was "fantasizing." He added that "Even if it were an outright threat, with the personalities involved and the historical context, the First Amendment protects the *Enquirer*'s right to print it." The Justice Department took no action. N.Y. Times, Aug. 25, 1982, at 15.

7. These two sections have been organized in terms of whether the recipient is harmed "directly" by relying upon or following the communication or is hurt "indirectly" by an audience member who responds to the program. In the end, how different are the two situations?

### 3. Is Advertising Different?

### EIMANN v. SOLDIER OF FORTUNE MAGAZINE, INC.

United States Court of Appeals, Fifth Circuit, 1989.
880 F.2d 830, 16 Med.L.Rptr. 2148.
Cert. denied 493 U.S. 1024 (1990).

Before Garwood, Jolly and Davis, Circuit Judges.

W. Eugene Davis, Circuit Judge:

Soldier of Fortune Magazine, Inc. appeals a $9.4 million jury verdict against it in a wrongful death action brought by the son and mother of a murder victim. The jury found that Soldier of Fortune acted with negligence and gross negligence in publishing a personal services classified advertisement through which the victim's husband hired an assassin to kill her. We reverse the judgment entered on the jury's verdict.

### I. FACTS

John Wayne Hearn shot and killed Sandra Black at the behest of her husband, Robert, who offered to pay Hearn $10,000 for doing so. Robert Black contacted Hearn through a classified advertisement that Hearn ran in Soldier of Fortune Magazine, Inc. (SOF), a publication that focuses on mercenary activities and military affairs.

The ad, which ran in the September, October and November 1984 issues of SOF, read:

EX–MARINES—67–69 'Nam Vets, Ex–DI, weapons specialist—jungle warfare, pilot, M.E., high risk assignments, U.S. or overseas. (404) 991–2684.

Hearn testified that "Ex–DI" meant ex-drill instructor; "M.E." meant multi-engine planes; and "high risk assignments" referred to work as a bodyguard or security specialist. Hearn testified that he and another former Marine placed the ad to recruit Vietnam veterans for work as bodyguards and security men for executives. Hearn's partner testified that they also hoped to train troops in South America. This partner never participated in any ad-related jobs and quit the venture shortly after the ad first ran.

Hearn and his partner testified that they did not place the ad with an intent to solicit criminal employment. However, Hearn stated that about 90 percent of the callers who responded to the ad sought his participation in illegal activities including beatings, kidnappings, jailbreaks, bombings and murders.

It also generated at least one lawful inquiry from an oil conglomerate in Lebanon seeking ten bodyguards; Hearn received a commission for placing seven men with the company.

Between early 1982 and January 1984, Black had asked at least four friends or coworkers from Bryan, Texas to kill Sandra Black or help him kill her. All four refused. Black called Hearn in October 1984 after seeing his ad in SOF.

Hearn testified that his initial conversations with Black focused on Black's inquiries about getting bodyguard work through Hearn. In later calls they discussed the sale of Black's gun collection to Hearn. Hearn testified that he traveled from his home in Atlanta to Black's home in Bryan on January 9, 1985 to look at Black's gun collection. Hearn stated that Black discussed his plans for murdering his wife during the meeting and "hinted" that he wanted Hearn to participate, but did not ask Hearn directly to kill his wife. Hearn did not act on the hint and returned to Atlanta.

Black called Hearn repeatedly after Hearn returned to Atlanta. During one call Black spoke with Hearn's girlfriend, Debbie Bannister. Hearn and Bannister met after she called him in response to his SOF ad.

Black proposed directly that Hearn kill his wife during the call to Bannister. She passed the proposal on to Hearn, who called Black and said he would consider doing it. The two talked by phone several times in the following weeks. After an aborted murder attempt about three weeks later—during which Hearn was to help Black himself kill his wife—Hearn killed Sandra Black on February 21, 1985. By that time Hearn also had killed the ex-husband of Bannister's sister on January 6, 1985 and Bannister's husband on February 2, 1985.

Neither Hearn, who was sentenced to concurrent life sentences for the murders, nor his partner had criminal records when they placed their ad in SOF. Neither had received a dishonorable discharge from the Marines. Further, Hearn included his real name and correct address in submitting the ad to SOF; the ad itself listed Hearn's correct home telephone number.

Sandra Black's son, Gary Wayne Black, and her mother, Marjorie Eimann, sued SOF and its parent, Omega Group, Ltd., for wrongful death under Texas law on the theory that SOF negligently published Hearn's classified ad.

Eimann introduced into evidence about three dozen personal service classified ads selected from the 2,000 or so classified ads that SOF had printed from its inception in 1975 until September 1984. Some ads offered services as a "Mercenary for Hire," "bounty hunter" or "mechanic"; others promised to perform "dirty work," "high risk contracts" or to "do anything, anywhere at the right price."

Eimann presented evidence that seven and perhaps as many as nine classified ads had been tied to crimes or criminal plots. Eimann introduced stories from sources including the Associated Press, United Press International, The Rocky Mountain News, The Denver Post, Time and Newsweek that reported on links between SOF classified ads and at least five of these crimes.

Eimann also presented evidence that law enforcement officials had contacted SOF staffers during investigations of two crimes linked to SOF personal service classifieds. In one case, SOF had provided correspondence from its files—along with two affidavits signed by SOF's managing editor—that were used in the 1982 criminal trial of a Houston man who was convicted of soliciting the murder of his wife; during his effort the man had tried to hire a poisons expert by placing a classified ad in the October 1981 issue of SOF. Eimann also presented testimony from a New Jersey detective, who stated that in April 1984, SOF's advertising manager had helped him to identify a man who placed a classified ad in SOF.

In addition, Eimann presented expert testimony from Dr. Park Dietz, a forensic psychiatrist who had studied SOF, its ads and readership. Dietz testified that an average SOF subscriber—a male who owns camouflage clothing and more than one gun—would understand some phrases in SOF's classified ads as solicitations for illegal activity given the "context" of those ads.

That context included other classified ads in SOF, display ads for semiautomatic rifles and books with titles such as "How to Kill," and SOF articles including "Harassing the Bear, New Afghan Tactics Stall Soviet Victory," "Pipestone Canyon, Summertime in 'Nam and the Dyin' was Easy," and "Night Raiders on Russia's Border." Dietz also described his visit to a SOF convention in summer 1987, where he photographed exhibits of weapons and tactical gear.

Based on his studies, Dietz concluded that the Hearn ad "or any other personal service ad in Soldier of Fortune in 1984 foreseeably is related to the commission of domestic crimes." He suggested that classified ads such as Hearn's would not carry such connotations if they appeared in Esquire or Vanity Fair.

Dietz conceded, however, that he had abandoned an effort to distinguish lawful SOF classified ads from criminal ones on the basis of specific code words such as "gun for hire," "mechanic" and "hunter" because some ads were too ambiguous to assign an illegal meaning to them with any certainty. He also noted that crimes had been linked to SOF classified ads that "seemed relatively innocuous." For example, one ad tied to a kidnapping and extortion plot read:

> Recovery and collection. International agents guarantee results on any type of recover[y]. Reply to Delta Enterprises, P.O. Box 5241, Rockford, Illinois 61125.

As Dietz stated, "The code system doesn't work."

SOF relied primarily on the testimony of its president, Robert K. Brown, who stated he did not know or suspect in 1984 that some of the SOF classified ads had been linked to criminal plots. Other SOF staffers and readers echoed these denials. SOF's advertising manager, Joan Steele, testified that she understood the phrase "high risk assignments" in Hearn's ad to mean "gun for hire," but in the sense of a professional bodyguard or security consultant rather than a contract killer.

The district court's first special interrogatory asked the jury whether Hearn's ad "related to" illegal activity. The court's second interrogatory asked, "Did [SOF] . . . know or should it have known from the face or the context of the Hearn advertisement that the advertisement could reasonably be interpreted as an offer to engage in illegal activity?"

The court's instructions charged SOF with knowledge that Hearn's ad reasonably could be interpreted as such an offer when (1) the relation to illegal activity appears on the ad's face; or (2) "the advertisement, embroidered by its context, would lead a reasonable publisher of ordinary prudence under the same or similar circumstances to conclude that the advertisement could reasonably be interpreted" as an offer to commit crimes. The court went on to define "context" as the magazine's (1) "nature"; (2) other advertisements; (3) articles; (4) readership; and (5) knowledge, if any, that other advertisements in the magazine could reasonably be interpreted as an offer to engage in illegal activity.

The jury answered "yes" to the first two interrogatories, and found that SOF's negligence was a proximate cause of Sandra Black's death in response to Interrogatory Three. The court then asked the jury whether SOF's negligence constituted "gross negligence," defined as "conscious indifference." The jury answered "yes" to this interrogatory as well. The jury awarded Eimann $1.9 million in compensatory damages and $7.5 million in punitive damages; the district court entered judgment on the verdict. SOF appeals.

## II.  ANALYSIS

### A.  Overview

Eimann presented this case as a straightforward negligence action revolving around one primary issue: whether SOF knew or should have known from the face or context of Hearn's ad that it represented an offer to perform illegal acts.  Based on evidence that SOF knew of links between other classified ads and other criminal plots, she contends that SOF owed a duty to recognize ads such as Hearn's that reasonably might be interpreted as criminal solicitations and refrain from publishing them.

SOF argues first that no liability can attach under these facts because the criminal activities of Hearn and Robert Black, rather than Hearn's ad, were the proximate cause of Sandra Black's murder.  SOF also argues that imposition of tort liability here contravenes first amendment protection for commercial speech because (1) the judgment below impermissibly imposed a duty on publishers to investigate its advertisers and their ads; and (2) the district court's all-encompassing definition of "context", combined with Dietz's testimony, allowed the jury to penalize SOF for the mercenary and military focus of the magazine's articles and other ads.

We need not address SOF's first amendment attacks on the judgment to resolve this appeal.[1]  Assuming without deciding that a Texas court would apply general negligence principles to this case, we conclude that no liability can attach under these principles as a matter of law.  SOF owed no duty to refrain from publishing a facially innocuous classified advertisement when the ad's context—at most—made its message ambiguous.

Under Texas law, negligence liability requires the existence of a duty, breach of that duty, and an injury proximately resulting from that breach.  [  ]  The existence of a duty presents a threshold question of law for the court; the jury determines breach and proximate cause only after the court concludes that a duty exists.  [  ]  Our resolution of this case hinges on the initial duty question.

---

1.  SOF asserts primarily that this case involves protected commercial speech; it argues further that the district court's broad definition of "context" and Eimann's emphasis on the mercenary focus of SOF's ads and articles amounted to impermissible content distinctions in violation of first amendment principles.  See, e.g., Arkansas Writers' Project, Inc. v. Ragland, 481 U.S. 221 (1987); Consolidated Edison Co. v. Public Service Comm'n, 447 U.S. 530, 536 (1980).  For their part, the Amici Curiae arguing on SOF's behalf contend that the district court erred in applying a negligence standard to a case that arguably involves commercial speech.  See Goldstein v. Gar- lick, 65 Misc.2d 538, 318 N.Y.S.2d 370, 374 (Sup.Ct.1971) (publication of false ad actionable only if published maliciously, with intent to harm, or in reckless disregard of the ad's consequences); but see South Carolina State Ports Authority v. Booz–Allen & Hamilton, Inc., 676 F.Supp. 346 (D.D.C. 1987); Norwood v. Soldier of Fortune Magazine, Inc., 651 F.Supp. 1397, 1398–1402 (W.D.Ark.1987).  We need not confront these issues given our conclusion that no liability attaches here even if the court below properly applied negligence law to a commercial speech case and properly defined the "context" used to evaluate SOF's actions.

## B.  Duty

In essence, a duty represents a legally enforceable obligation to conform to a particular standard of conduct.  [  ]  Whether the defendant in a negligence action owes a duty involves consideration of two related issues:  (1) whether the defendant owes an obligation to this particular plaintiff to act as a reasonable person would in the circumstances; and (2) the standard of conduct required to satisfy that obligation.  [  ]

. . .

Our analysis here assumes that SOF owes a duty of reasonable care to the public; we focus on the second prong of the duty issue: whether SOF's decision to print Hearn's ad violated the standard of conduct.

In answering this question we look to Judge Learned Hand's concise expression of these balancing principles in United States v. Carroll Towing, 159 F.2d 169, 173 (2d Cir.1947).  As he described it in algebraic terms, liability turns on whether the burden of adequate precautions, B, is less than the probability of harm, P, multiplied by the gravity of the resulting injury, L.  In other words, an actor falls below the standard of conduct and liability attaches when B is less than PL.  Conversely, the actor satisfies the obligation to protect against unreasonable risks when the burden of adequate precautions—examined in light of the challenged action's value—outweighs the probability and gravity of the threatened harm.  [  ]

We now turn to these individual factors.

### 1.  The Probability and Gravity of the Threatened Harm

In assessing the threatened harm we note that "nearly all human acts  .  .  .  carry some recognizable but remote possibility of harm to another."  [  ]  The SOF classified ads presented more than a remote risk.  Of the 2,000 or so personal service classified ads that SOF printed between 1975 and 1984, Eimann's evidence established that as many as nine had served as links in criminal plots.  Of these nine, the evidence revealed that SOF staffers had participated in at least two police investigations of crimes in which classified ads played a role; other crimes tied to the ads received varying amounts of media coverage.

As noted above, the gravity of the threatened harm may require precautions against even unlikely events.  [  ]  For example, the standard of care may require those who own oil storage tanks to take precautions against fires caused by an unpredictable lightning strike. [  ]  The prospect of ad-inspired crime represents a threat of serious harm.  Eimann presented evidence that SOF classified ads played a role in other crimes ranging from extortion to jailbreaks.  Sandra Black's murder illustrates one aspect of the crime linked to SOF classified advertisements.

## 2.  The Burden of Preventing the Harm

SOF contends that the standard of conduct applied by the district court impermissibly required the magazine to guard against criminal solicitation by investigating its advertisers and their ads.  It relies on a series of cases holding that newspaper publishers owe no duty in tort to investigate their advertisers for the accuracy of ads placed for publication.  See Pittman v. Dow Jones & Co., 662 F.Supp. 921, 923 (E.D.La. 1987).

However, in our view the standard of conduct against which the jury measured SOF's actions was more exacting than a duty to investigate;  it requires publishers to recognize ads that "reasonably could be interpreted as an offer to engage in illegal activity" based on their words or "context" and refrain from printing them.  Based on evidence that SOF knew other ads had been tied to crimes, Eimann's counsel contended at oral argument that SOF should have refrained from publishing Hearn's ad and all other personal service classified ads—suggestive ones and bland ones alike.  This represents an especially heavy burden given (1) the ambiguous nature of Hearn's ad;  and (2) the pervasiveness of advertising in our society.

At most, the evidence reveals that Hearn submitted a facially innocuous ad.  Standing alone, the phrase "high risk assignments" plausibly encompassed Hearn's professed goal of recruiting candidates for bodyguard jobs.  Hearn performed precisely that function for at least one client who contacted him through the ad.

Eimann's effort to portray Hearn's ad as a readily identifiable criminal solicitation falls with Dr. Dietz's repudiation of his effort to identify specific code words signalling criminal intent.  At one point in his testimony, Dr. Dietz analyzed a classified ad from the February 1980 issue of SOF.  In terms that parallel Hearn's ad, this 1980 ad recruited SOF readers for "exciting high risk undercover stateside work".  A court later convicted the individual who submitted it of mailing a threatening communication after he sent a letter instructing someone who had responded to the ad to "terminate" a person in Oklahoma City.  Dr. Dietz stated:

> In 1984, in my opinion, someone familiar with the classified ads that have been run for years in Soldier of Fortune would be able to recognize from that ad that *this is possibly someone who would be willing to be involved in criminal activity; but they might be wrong when they thought that.*  We know that sometimes there were honest advertisers, and we know that some of the readers who responded to ads were honest too (emphasis added).

Dr. Dietz's description applies with equal force to Hearn's ad.  Its bare terms reveal no identifiable offer to commit crimes, just as a locksmith's ad in the telephone directory reveals nothing about that particular advertiser's willingness to commit burglaries or steal cars.

This ambiguity persists even if we assume that SOF knew other ads had been tied to criminal plots. No evidence linked the other ads and crimes to Hearn. And as Eimann conceded, even if SOF had investigated Hearn and his partner in 1984, it would have discovered no criminal records and no false information that might have aroused suspicion.

Further, Eimann's heavy reliance on "context" cannot compensate for the fundamental ambiguity of Hearn's ad even if we assume that the district court properly defined that context. The presence in SOF of other ads and articles with violent themes provides no realistic method for gauging the likelihood that a particular ad will foster illegal activity. Do ads touting high-performance cars become solicitations for illegal activity when buyers drive them beyond the speed limit? Only when the ads run in Car and Driver magazine? Or, only when the ads run in magazines that also contain ads for radar detectors?

While we do not reach SOF's first amendment arguments, the Supreme Court's recognition of limited first amendment protection for commercial speech nonetheless highlights the important role of such communication for purposes of risk-benefit analysis. As the Court has noted, "[T]he particular consumer's interest in the free flow of commercial information . . . may be as keen, if not keener by far, than his interest in the day's most urgent political debate. . . ." [*Virginia State Board of Pharmacy*]. The Supreme Court's subsequent emphasis on the states' interest in regulating commercial speech neither erases this first amendment protection nor alters the fact that advertising is a part of daily life [citing Central Hudson Gas & Electric v. Public Service Commission of New York and Posadas de Puerto Rico v. Tourism Council of Puerto Rico, which will be discussed in Chapter IX.]

Eimann seeks to discount the importance of SOF's classified ads by stressing that (1) SOF's publisher promoted the ads because they added to the "flavor and mystique" of the magazine; and (2) the jury found that Hearn's ad "relate[d] to" illegal activity. She notes that the Supreme Court has excluded advertising of illegal activity from the scope of first amendment protection. See [*Pittsburgh Press Co.*] (newspaper's placement of help-wanted ads in sex-segregated columns violated anti-discrimination ordinance; "Any First Amendment interest which might have been served by advertising an ordinary commercial product . . . is altogether absent when the commercial activity itself is illegal. . . .") However, in the constitutional arena we have noted that the possibility of illegal results does not necessarily strip an ad of its commercial speech protection.

In Dunagin v. City of Oxford, 718 F.2d 738 (5th Cir.1983) (en banc), this court upheld the constitutionality of a Mississippi law that banned liquor advertising by local, in-state media on grounds that the ban was no broader than necessary to advance the goal of promoting prohibition in the state's dry counties. [ ] But in doing so the court rejected arguments that liquor advertising necessarily related to unlawful activity in Mississippi—even though nearly half of Mississippi's counties are dry, and even though wet counties prohibit alcohol consumption in places such as public schools and colleges. The court stated,

> The commercial speech doctrine would disappear if its protection ceased whenever the advertised product might be used illegally. Peanut butter advertising cannot be banned just because someone might someday throw a jar at the presidential motorcade. [ ]

Similarly, a standard of conduct that imposes tort liability whenever the advertised product "could reasonably be interpreted as an offer to engage in illegal activity"—or might "relate to" criminal conduct—imposes an especially heavy burden. The comments of a court faced with a duty-to-investigate claim apply here:

> For the law to permit such exposure to those in the publishing business who in good faith accept paid advertisements for a myriad of products would open the doors "to a liability in an indeterminate amount for an indeterminate time to an indeterminate class."

Yuhas v. Mudge, 129 N.J.Super. 207, 322 A.2d 824 (App.Div.1974) (citation omitted) (publisher owes no duty to investigate safety of "inherently dangerous" products advertised in its publication). Relatedly, the publication's editorial content would surely feel the economic crunch from loss of revenue that would result if publishers were required to reject all ambiguous advertisements. See Walters v. Seventeen Magazine, 195 Cal.App.3d 1119, 241 Cal.Rptr. 101, 103 (1987).

### 3. Balancing the Burdens and Risks

We conclude that the standard of conduct imposed by the district court does not strike the proper balance between the risks of harm from ambiguous advertisement and the burden of preventing harm from this source under these facts. The appreciable risk that ads such as Hearn's will cause harm, combined with the gravity of that harm, does not outweigh the onerous burden Eimann asks us to endorse.

Hearn's ad presents a risk of serious harm. But everyday activities, such as driving on high-speed, closed access roadways, also carry definite risks that we as a society choose to accept in return for the activity's usefulness and convenience. [ ] To take a more extreme example, courts have almost uniformly rejected efforts to hold handgun manufacturers liable under negligence or strict liability theories to gunshot victims injured during crimes, despite the real possibility that such products can be used for criminal purposes. [ ] Given the pervasiveness of advertising in our society and the important role it plays, we decline to impose on publishers the obligation to reject all ambiguous advertisements for products or services that might pose a threat of harm.

### III. CONCLUSION

The standard of conduct imposed by the district court against SOF is too high; it allows a jury to visit liability on a publisher for untoward consequences that flow from his decision to publish any suspicious, ambiguous ad that might cause serious harm. The burden on a publisher to avoid liability from suits of this type is too great: he must reject all such advertisements.

The range of foreseeable misuses of advertised products and services is as limitless as the forms and functions of the products themselves. Without a more specific indication of illegal intent than Hearn's ad or its context provided, we conclude that SOF did not violate the required standard of conduct by publishing an ad that later played a role in criminal activity.

The judgment of the district court is Reversed and Rendered.

## Notes and Questions

1. Given that the court says that it is deciding the case on state tort law grounds, why does it discuss the commercial speech cases?

2. What makes this a question of law for the court?

3. What changes in the facts would be needed before the court would uphold a plaintiff's judgment?

4. Could an advertisement for a high powered car trigger a publication's liability if a reader relying on the advertisement bought the car and, while driving it at 110 m.p.h. on a freeway, ran into another car?

5. In the cited *Walters,* a reader sued a magazine after she suffered injury from using a tampon that had been advertised in the magazine. The court dismissed the claim on the ground that the magazine had not sponsored the product, had not endorsed it, and had not made its advertisements so resemble its editorial text that immature readers could not tell the difference. The court distinguished Hanberry v. Hearst Corp., 276 Cal.App.2d 680, 81 Cal.Rptr. 519 (1969), in which the magazine publisher allowed certain advertisers to include the magazine's "gold seal" of approval in their advertisements.

The *Walters* court was concerned about the expense of having to check all advertisements and feared that magazines would either (a) pay for the checking staff or refuse the advertisements (either of which would raise magazine prices) or (b) run advertisements without checking and be destroyed by a large tort judgment.

6. Might one define *Weirum* as an example of an in-house promotion—a sort of self-advertising—as opposed to editorial content? If so, what difference would it make in the analysis?

7. It is generally held, often as the result of so-called Printer's Ink statutes, that publishers are not liable for harm caused readers by advertised products unless the publisher knew of the danger created by the product or of the dishonesty of the advertisement. See *Yuhas v. Mudge,* cited in *Eimann,* in which *Popular Mechanics* was held not to be liable for an injury that a reader suffered when he bought defective fireworks that had been advertised in the magazine.

8. What is the significance of the fact that Hearn's ambiguous statement appeared in an advertisement? What if it had appeared in a news story about local Vietnam veterans in which the reporter quoted Hearn as saying that he was receptive to "high risk assignments"?

9. *The Braun case.* After *Eimann,* another *Soldier of Fortune* personal services advertisement was the basis for a $12.4 million award to the sons of a murdered Atlanta businessman, Richard Braun. The ad, placed by Richard Savage, read as follows:

> GUN FOR HIRE: 37 year old professional mercenary desires job. Vietnam Veteran. Discreet and very private. Body guard, courier, and other special skills. All jobs considered. . . .

Savage was hired by one of Braun's business associates to kill him. Braun v. Soldier of Fortune Magazine, Inc., 749 F.Supp. 1083, 18 Med.L.Rptr. 1730 (M.D.Ala.1990).

The award was affirmed on appeal, 968 F.2d 1110, 20 Med.L.Rptr. 1777 (11th Cir.1992). The court first applied a risk-utility balancing test similar to that used in *Eimann.* However, in *Braun,* unlike in *Eimann,* the court found that publishing the ad was an unreasonable risk to the public. The court distinguished *Eimann* on the basis of more explicit jury instructions. The trial judge in *Eimann* had informed the jury that liability could be imposed if a "reasonable publisher would conclude 'that the advertisement *could reasonably be interpreted*' as an offer to commit crimes, 880 F.2d at 833 (emphasis added). In contrast, the trial judge in *Braun* instructed the jury that liability could be imposed only "if the ad on its face contained a 'clearly identifiable unreasonable risk' of harm to the public."

Turning to the question of whether the ad was protected by the First Amendment, the court found that "the ad on its face [made] it apparent that there was a substantial danger that Savage was soliciting illegal jobs involving the use of a gun." The court cited commercial speech cases (to be discussed in Chapter IX) for the proposition that ads concerning illegal activities. The Supreme Court denied *certiorari,* 113 S.Ct. 1028 (1993).

# Chapter VI

# COPYRIGHT AND TRADEMARK

As we discussed in Chapter IV, there are several ways to protect a creative work product. Historically, this protection was first achieved through copyright law. Although many problems in copyright law involve fiction, we will stress situations in which plaintiffs attempt to protect their efforts that have produced material in the nonfiction sector.

## A. THE NATURE OF COPYRIGHT

### 1. COPYRIGHT PROTECTION

The laws of copyright are among the most obvious but least condemned restraints on freedom of expression. Article I, § 8, of the Constitution of the United States gives Congress the power "to promote the progress of science and useful arts by securing for limited times to authors and inventors the exclusive right to their respective writings and discoveries . . . .." The first Congress utilized that authority to adopt copyright legislation and it has been with us in some form ever since.

The origins of copyright are interwoven with the licensing procedures we discussed in Chapter II. One technique for controlling the printing press was to organize printers into a group that became known as the Stationers Company. The Crown granted to that company a monopoly of all printing, with the power to seek out and suppress material published by non-members who violated the monopoly. The Crown's goal was to thwart seditious libel and other objectionable material. The printers, for their part, seized on the monopoly situation to control reproduction of whatever they printed. The result was the licensed printers' right to control copies based on the censorship of the 16th and 17th centuries. When licensing was discontinued in 1695, the rights of the printers were undermined. They petitioned Parliament to adopt protections resembling what they had under the licensing schemes. In 1709 Parliament responded with the Statute of Anne, which has set the pattern for copyright legislation both in England and in this country. The Stationers Company remained but its new role was to register printed material, which would serve to protect that material against unauthorized copying.

The first Congress adopted a similar procedure: printed matter could be protected by filing a copy with the newly established copyright office, headed by the "Register of Copyrights." The types of writings protected and the period of protection have been expanded since the 1790 statute, which protected only books, maps and charts for a period of 14 years plus renewal for a second 14–year term.

In 1976 the copyright statute enacted in 1909 was replaced with new legislation that preserved the basic philosophical strands of copyright law, including the denial of copyright for federal government documents. One major change involved the treatment of unpublished works. Under the 1909 statute, published works were protected by federal law while unpublished works were protected by state law. Under the new legislation, all protection is in a single national framework.

Additional changes were made to accommodate media that emerged after 1909 and did not easily fit within the old framework. These changes presented a number of difficult questions. For example, perhaps the most vigorous political controversy concerned the relationship between broadcasters and cable television, which will be discussed in Chapter XVIII.

## 2. SUBJECT MATTER

The copyright statute is found in title 17 of the United States Code. Section 102 of the Copyright Act of 1976 sets out the basic pattern of protection when it states that copyright protection subsists in "original works of authorship fixed in any tangible medium of expression, now known or later developed, from which they can be perceived, reproduced, or otherwise communicated, either directly or with the aid of a machine or device." The statute lists such categories as literary works, musical works, dramatic works, motion pictures and sound recordings as coming within "works of authorship." The section then states the other side of the coin: "In no case does copyright protection for an original work of authorship extend to any idea, procedure, process, system, method or operation, concept, principle, or discovery, regardless of the form in which it is described, explained, illustrated, or embodied in such work."

This issue arose in a case involving the explosion and crash of the German dirigible Hindenburg in New Jersey in 1937. The plaintiff author developed the theory that a crew member sabotaged the dirigible to please a Communist girlfriend. Plaintiff sued two others whose versions of the disaster developed a similar explanation. Hoehling v. Universal City Studios, Inc., 618 F.2d 972, 6 Med.L.Rptr. 1053 (2d Cir.), cert. denied 449 U.S. 841 (1980). The court began its discussion by placing copyright in its broader context:

> A grant of copyright in a published work secures for its author a limited monopoly over the expression it contains. The copyright provides a financial incentive to those who would add to the corpus of existing knowledge by creating original works. Nevertheless, the protection afforded the copyright holder has never extended to history, be it documented fact or explanatory hypothesis. The rationale for this doctrine is that the cause of knowledge is best served when history is the common property of all, and each generation remains free to draw upon the discoveries and insights of the past. Accordingly, the scope of copyright in historical accounts is narrow indeed, embracing no more than the author's original

expression of particular facts and theories already in the public domain. As the case before us illustrates, absent wholesale usurpation of another's expression, claims of copyright infringement where works of history are at issue are rarely successful.

The court asserted that although plaintiff had a valid copyright on his book, to prove "infringement" he had to prove that defendants had "improperly appropriated" his "expression." Although plaintiff admitted that his idea was not copyrightable, he correctly argued that "his 'expression' of *his* idea is copyrightable." The court analyzed that claim as follows:

He relies on Learned Hand's opinion in [Sheldon v. Metro–Goldwyn Pictures Corp., 81 F.2d 49 (2d Cir.), cert. denied 298 U.S. 669 (1936)] holding that *Letty Lynton* infringed *Dishonored Lady* by copying its story of a woman who poisons her lover, and Augustus Hand's analysis in Detective Comics, Inc. v. Bruns Publications, Inc., 111 F.2d 432 (2d Cir.1940), concluding that the exploits of "Wonderman" infringed the copyright held by the creators of "Superman," the original indestructible man. Moreover, Hoehling asserts that, in both these cases, the line between "ideas" and "expression" is drawn, in the first instance, by the fact finder.

*Sheldon* and *Detective Comics,* however, dealt with works of fiction, where the distinction between an idea and its expression is especially elusive. But, where, as here, the idea at issue is an interpretation of an historical event, our cases hold that such interpretations are not copyrightable as a matter of law. In Rosemont Enterprises, Inc. v. Random House, Inc., 366 F.2d 303 (2d Cir.1966), cert. denied 385 U.S. 1009 (1967), we held that the defendant's biography of Howard Hughes did not infringe an earlier biography of the reclusive alleged billionaire. Although the plots of the two works were necessarily similar, there could be no infringement because of the "public benefit in encouraging the development of historical and biographical works and their public distribution." Id. at 307; accord, Oxford Book Co. v. College Entrance Book Co., 98 F.2d 688 (2d Cir.1938). To avoid a chilling effect on authors who contemplate tackling an historical issue or event, broad latitude must be granted to subsequent authors who make use of historical subject matter, including theories or plots. Learned Hand counseled in Myers v. Mail & Express Co., 36 C.O.Bull. 478, 479 (S.D.N.Y.1919), "[t]here cannot be any such thing as copyright in the order of presentation of the facts, nor, indeed, in their selection."

The court went further, however, and asserted that even some fictitious episodes may not be protectible:

The remainder of Hoehling's claimed similarities relate to random duplications of phrases and sequences of events. For example, all three works contain a scene in a German beer hall, in which the airship's crew engages in revelry prior to the voyage. Other claimed similarities concern common German greetings of the period, such as "Heil Hitler," or songs, such as the German National anthem. These elements, however, are merely *scenes a faire,* that is, "incidents, characters or settings which are as a practical matter indispensable, or at least standard, in the treatment of a given topic." [  ] Because it is virtually impossible to write about a particular historical era or fictional theme without employing certain "stock" or standard literary devices, we have held that *scenes a faire* are not copyrightable as a matter of law. See Reyher v. Children's Television Workshop, 533 F.2d 87, 91 (2d Cir.), cert. denied 429 U.S. 980 (1976).

Finally, the court brought these several aspects of the case together and recognized that breaking the copyrighted work up into many little parts created a new danger:

All of Hoehling's allegations of copying, therefore, encompass material that is non-copyrightable as a matter of law, rendering summary judgment entirely appropriate. We are aware, however, that in distinguishing between themes, facts, and *scenes u faire* on the one hand, and copyrightable expression on the other, courts may lose sight of the forest for the trees. By factoring out similarities based on non-copyrightable elements, a court runs the risk of overlooking wholesale usurpation of a prior author's expression. A verbatim reproduction of another work, of course, even in the realm of nonfiction, is actionable as copyright infringement. See Wainwright Securities, Inc. v. Wall Street Transcript Corp., 558 F.2d 91, 2 Med.L.Rptr. 2153 (2d Cir.1977), cert. denied 434 U.S. 1014 (1978). Thus, in granting or reviewing a grant of summary judgment for defendants, courts should assure themselves that the works before them are not virtually identical. In this case, it is clear that all three authors relate the story of the Hindenburg differently.

In works devoted to historical subjects, it is our view that a second author may make significant use of prior work, so long as he does not bodily appropriate the expression of another. *Rosemont Enterprises, Inc.,* supra, 366 F.2d at 310. This principle is justified by the fundamental policy undergirding the copyright laws—the encouragement of contributions to recorded knowledge. The "financial reward guaranteed to the copyright holder is but an incident of this general objective, rather than an end in itself." Berlin v. E.C. Publications, Inc., 329 F.2d 541, 543–44 (2d Cir.), cert. denied 379 U.S. 822 (1964). Knowledge is expanded as well by granting new authors of historical works a relatively free hand to build upon the work of their predecessors.

We will return to the special problems presented by historical works in our discussion of the fair use defense.

A Supreme Court decision, Feist Publications, Inc. v. Rural Telephone Service Co., Inc., 499 U.S. 340, 18 Med.L.Rptr. 1889 (1991), illustrates the principle that facts cannot be copyrighted. Rural Telephone Service, which provides telephone service to several communities in Kansas, publishes a telephone directory.  It refused to license its white pages listings to Feist for a larger telephone directory covering 11 telephone service areas.  Feist extracted the information from Rural's directory and used it in their own, altering some of the listings and using others identical to the listings in Rural's directory.  Rural sued for copyright infringement.  The Supreme Court decided in favor of Feist.

Justice O'Connor, writing for the Court, wrote that "[t]his case concerns the interaction of two well-established propositions.  The first is that facts are not copyrightable; the other, that compilations of facts generally are.  Each of these propositions possesses an impeccable pedigree.   .  .  .   [I]t is beyond dispute that compilations of facts are within the subject matter of copyright.  Compilations were expressly mentioned in the Copyright Act of 1909, and again in the Copyright Act of 1976.   .  .  .   There is undeniable tension between these two propositions.   .  .  .   The key to resolving the tension lies in understanding why facts are not copyrightable.  The *sine qua non* of copyright is originality.  To qualify for copyright protection, a work must be original to the author."

"[T]he copyright in a factual compilation is thin," she wrote.  "Notwithstanding a valid copyright, a subsequent compiler remains free to use the facts contained in [another's] publication to aid in preparing a competing work, so long as the competing work does not feature the same selection and arrangement."  The Court has rejected, she said, "sweat of the brow" arguments that would give protection to factual compilations on the basis of hard work rather than originality.  "Rural expended sufficient effort to make the white pages directory useful," she wrote, "but insufficient creativity to make it original," concluding that the names, towns and telephone numbers copied by Feist were not original to Rural and were therefore not protected by copyright.

### 3.  Ownership

The authors of a work are the initial copyright owners unless the work is a "work made for hire."  This is defined as:

(1) a work prepared by an employee within the scope of his or her employment; or

(2) a work specially ordered or commissioned for use as a contribution to a collective work, as a part of a motion picture or other audiovisual work, as a translation, as a supplementary work, as a compilation, as an instructional text, as a test, as answer material for a test, or as an atlas, if the parties expressly agree in a written instrument signed by them that the work shall be considered a work made for hire.  17 U.S.C.A. § 101.

In the case of a "work made for hire" the original ownership belongs to the employer or person who commissioned the work.  As is the case with any property right, ownership of a copyright can be left to the owner's heirs or sold.

In Community for Creative Non–Violence v. Reid, 490 U.S. 730 (1989), the Supreme Court was asked to avoid the rigors of § 101(2) by expansively interpreting the term "employee" in section 101(1). It declined. Reid had created a sculpture for CCNV in conformance with CCNV's concept and general design ideas. The parties did not discuss copyright ownership in advance. After the sculpture was finished, each filed a competing copyright claim. The trial judge held that CCNV owned the copyright, but the Court of Appeals for the District of Columbia reversed, holding that it was not a work for hire and therefore the copyright was owned by Reid.

The Supreme Court unanimously affirmed. CCNV did not claim the sculpture was a specially commissioned work under subsection (2); there was no written agreement to that effect, and even if there had been, a sculpture is not one of the types of works to which that subsection applies. Instead, CCNV argued that Reid should be considered an "employee" for purposes of subsection (1), on the ground that CCNV had retained the right to control Reid's product and had actually exercised such control. The Court, however, held that the legislative history of the Act required the term to be understood in light of the general common law of agency, which takes into account many factors in addition to control of the work. It concluded Reid was not an employee because he was engaged in a skilled occupation, supplied his own tools, worked in his own studio, was retained for a brief time for the project in question and no others, had control of his own working hours and the employment and compensation of assistants, and was not treated as an employee for purposes of benefits, social security and payroll taxes, worker's compensation or unemployment taxes.

The Court refused to follow the interpretation given to section 101(1) by the Second Circuit, which had held that freelancers were "employees" if the hiring party had actually wielded control during the creation of the work. See Aldon Accessories Ltd. v. Spiegel, Inc., 738 F.2d 548 (2d Cir.), cert. denied 469 U.S. 982 (1984). Many publishing and communications companies headquartered in New York apparently had relied on that interpretation and therefore failed to obtain contractual assignments from their freelance contributors. As a result, some industry sources said the *CCNV* decision put in question the ownership of millions of dollars in literary and entertainment properties, and might affect 40 percent of all existing copyrights. See Scardino, "The Media Business: A Copyright Ruling Opens a Costly Can of Worms," New York Times, June 12, 1989, at D12.

The decision also generated concern among publishing, communications, and entertainment companies because of its effect on termination of copyrights. Licenses and transfers granted by authors generally may be terminated after 35 years by the authors or their survivors; companies that find themselves holding licenses rather than authorship as a result of *CCNV* now have to worry about having their interests terminated altogether.

Magazine publishers often commission freelance photographers or artists to illustrate specific articles. Sometimes they reuse the articles and/or illustrations in books, calendars, special anniversary editions, etc. After the decision in *CCNV,* how may publishers protect their interest in future use of these illustrations? What is their potential liability for past reuses that may be infringing after *CCNV?*

### 4.  RIGHTS OF COPYRIGHT OWNER(S)

Section 106 of the Copyright Act states the nature of the protection extended to the copyright owner:

Subject to sections 107 through 118, the owner of copyright under this title has the exclusive right to do and to authorize any of the following:

(1) to reproduce the copyrighted work in copies or phonorecords;

(2) to prepare derivative works based upon the copyrighted work;

(3) to distribute copies or phonorecords of the copyrighted work to the public by sale or other transfer of ownership, or by rental, lease, or lending;

(4) in the case of literary, musical, dramatic, and choreographic works, pantomimes, and motion pictures and other audiovisual works, to perform the copyrighted work publicly; and

(5) in the case of literary, musical, dramatic, choreographic works, pantomimes, and pictorial, graphic, or sculptural works, including the individual images of a motion picture or other audiovisual work, to display the copyrighted work publicly. 17 U.S.C.A. § 106.

It is possible for a copyright owner to sell some rights and retain others. A famous novelist, for example, might first sell the rights to publish excerpts of an upcoming novel to a national magazine, next sell the right to publish the hardcover first edition of the book to a publishing house, then sell the right for publication of a later paperback edition to another publishing house, and finally, sell the right to make a movie based on the book to a studio.

It is important to note that the only protections accorded copyright are statutory and are listed in § 106. An unlicensed use that does not conflict with one of the exclusive rights enumerated in § 106 is not an infringement. Beyond that, § 106 is explicitly made subject to a series of limitations listed in §§ 107–118. We will discuss the most important of these limitations, fair use, later in this chapter.

One limitation on the § 106 rights that is not mentioned in the copyright statute is the first sale doctrine. A judicially-created rule, the doctrine provides that copyright owners who sell copies of their copyrighted works have no further control over the sale or lease of those particular copies. The original copyright owners' other rights remain unimpaired.

Under the first sale doctrine, for example, a video store can buy videotapes and then rent them to the public. However, under a 1984 amendment to § 109(b)(1) of the Copyright Act, phonograph records cannot be rented (except by nonprofit libraries or nonprofit educational institutions) without the permission of the copyright holders. The rationale is that there would be little or no purpose in renting a record other than to copy it. In contrast, one can presume that customers may rent videotapes to view them without illegally copying them. For a more complete discussion of the doctrine, see United States v. Atherton, 561 F.2d 747 (9th Cir.1977).

The 1980s produced serious questions about alterations of copyrighted films—particularly the "colorizing" of classic black and white films against the wishes of the films' creators. Famous producers, directors, and actors went to Capitol Hill in 1988 to ask for a strict law forbidding such "desecration." Turner Entertainment, on the other hand, says it sells 30 percent more colored cassettes than black and white versions. Unwilling to pass a strong anti-colorizing statute, Congress enacted a compromise version, the National Film Preservation Act of 1988. National Film Registry, 2 U.S.C.A. § 179 et seq. It allows the Librarian of Congress to select 25 American films each year that are "culturally, historically or esthetically significant" and to require those films to be labeled if they are altered. In such instances a warning label, similar to the one on cigarettes, is placed on video copies of such films: "This is a colorized version of a film originally marketed and distributed to the public in black and white. It has been altered without the participation of the principal director, screenwriter and other creators of the original film." A related issue is the compression of films—"lexiconning" or speeding them up imperceptibly to shorten their showing time and thus allow more time for television commercials. Here, too, the creators argue that the film's artistic integrity is violated.

The National Film Preservation Act established the 13–member National Film Preservation Board, representing writers, directors, producers, critics and scholars, to participate in the selection of the 25 films per year.

### 5.  DURATION

Under the 1909 Act copyright protection lasted for 28 years with the opportunity for one 28–year renewal. Under the 1976 Act it lasts for the life of the author plus 50 years. With joint authors it is 50 years from the last surviving author's death. Anonymous works, pseudonymous works and works made for hire are protected for 75 years from publication or 100 years from creation, whichever comes first.  17 U.S.C.A. § 302.

### 6.  STATUTORY FORMALITIES

Under the Copyright Act of 1976, any work is protected as soon as it is "fixed in a tangible medium."  However certain formalities must be observed to prevent the work's entering the public domain—in which case no one would own it.  Until March 1, 1989, every copy had to carry notice consisting of the word copyright, copr. or © plus the name of the copyright owner.  That changed as a result of the United States' joining the Berne Union by entering into an international treaty called the Berne Convention for the Protection of Literary and Artistic Works.  To fulfill its obligations under the Berne Convention, the United States passed the Berne Convention Implementation Act of 1988.  Among other things, that statute abolished the mandatory notice of copyright.  However, copyright notices are still strongly recommended by the Copyright Office.  Another formality is that copyright owners must deposit in the Copyright Office two complete copies or phonorecords of the best edition of all works subject to copyright that are publicly distributed in the United States whether or not the work contains a notice of copyright.  Before a copyright infringement suit is brought for a work of U.S. origin, the work must be submitted to the Copyright Office for registration.  Copyright validity is presumed if the registration is made before or within five years of first publication.

### 7.  PREEMPTION OF STATE LAW

The Copyright Act of 1976 preempted all state law governing rights equivalent to copyright protection.  As previously noted, this eliminated common-law copyright protection for unpublished works.  It does not, however, mean that other state laws, such as those relating to defamation, cannot be applied to copyrighted works.

Sometimes determining what constitutes a non-equivalent right is difficult.  In *Zacchini,* p. 241, *supra,* the Supreme Court recognized a "right of publicity" for Hugo Zacchini's 15–second "human cannonball" act.  Zacchini's act was not copyrighted.  Had he "fixed" it by having it filmed or taped himself, he could have copyrighted it, but that would not have protected him from others' taking their own pictures at the event.

Notice the similarities between copyright law and this special application of privacy law in protecting one's right to control one's own creation or performance.

### 8.  INTERNATIONAL PROTECTION

For U.S. authors, the major advantage of our joining the approximately 78 other member nations of the Berne Union in 1989 is that piracy of U.S. works abroad can be fought more effectively.  Members of the Berne Union agree to treat nationals of other member countries like their own nationals for purposes of copyright.  Similarly, foreign authors who are nationals of a Berne Union country, automatically have copyright protection in the United States.

The Berne Convention includes, in Article VI, a Moral Rights Clause adopted in 1928.  It provides that, "independently of the author's copyright, and even after assignment of the said copyright, the author shall retain the right to claim authorship of the work, as well as the right to object to every deformation, mutilation, or other modification of the said work which may be prejudicial to his honor or his reputation." Under the clause, each country in which a question is raised in relation to such moral rights is responsible for enforcement of those rights.

## B.  ALLEGED OR ACTUAL INFRINGEMENTS

Infringements, real or imagined, can take a variety of forms.  In some instances permission to use all or part of the copyrighted material may have been given, but the copyright holder may allege that the user has exceeded the permission.  That may happen when the material is disseminated more widely (perhaps in another country) than originally envisioned, when the material used is more extensive than the copyright holder envisioned or when the purpose of the dissemination or the context in which the material is presented is not what the copyright holder expected.

More frequently, the problem may be that material is used with no permission having been granted at all.  In some such instances, the material has been attributed correctly to the copyright holder (which still does not give the user any right to use it without permission); in other instances the material has not been attributed.

In cases involving such literary or artistic creative work as musical or dramatic presentations, the problem may involve the question of whether the user's reproduction of the copyright holder's work actually constituted a "performance" of it.

In other cases, such as those in which two writers or two composers have created similar works, the key question will be whether one author copied the other's work.  The plaintiff in such a case attempts to prove that the defendant had access to the copyrighted work and that there is a *substantial similarity* between the copyrighted work and the defendant's work.

Two cases illustrate problems of protection of commercial rights to ideas—specifically excluded from copyright coverage under Section 102. In one of the cases, Murray v. NBC, 844 F.2d 988, 15 Med.L.Rptr. 1284 (2d Cir.1988), a plaintiff claimed that, four years before "The Cosby Show" premiered on NBC, he had proposed to the network an idea for a half-hour situation comedy starring Cosby to be titled "Father's Day." Unable to sue for copyright infringement, the plaintiff sued for misappropriation, conversion, breach of contract and violation of the Lanham

Act (on the theory that the program's origin was falsely designated). The court of appeals held that the plaintiff's idea for a program about an intact, middle-class black family was not novel and could not be protected under New York law.

A second illustration of the problem is Buchwald v. Paramount Pictures Corp., 17 Med.L.Rptr. 1257 (Cal.Super.1990). Humorist Art Buchwald sued Paramount Pictures for $5 million for breach of contract, claiming that the Eddie Murphy movie "Coming to America" was based on a screen treatment Buchwald sold to Paramount in 1983 as a vehicle for Murphy. The trial court held that evidence demonstrating similarity between Buchwald's screen treatment and the finished film, together with evidence of Paramount's unlimited access to Buchwald's idea, warranted a finding that the movie was "based upon" Buchwald's work. Buchwald was awarded damages of $250,000 plus 19 percent of the profits, but Paramount denied that there had been any profits. Additional litigation about the amounts due to Buchwald is pending.

A Chicago-area songwriter, John D. Woodbridge, also sued Paramount successfully, claiming that a song he had written 10 years earlier was used as the love theme in the 1983 ABC miniseries, "The Winds of War." He said he had written and copyrighted the song in 1965 while he was a graduate student at Michigan State University, but the miniseries credited a different composer. A jury at one trial ruled in favor of Woodbridge, but the trial judge ordered a new trial saying he had made a procedural error in the case. The second trial was averted by a settlement. Chicago Tribune, May 15, 1992 at Chicagoland, 1.

Questions about shares of profits of film and television productions continue to arise. Benjamin Melniker and Michael Uslan, executive producers of the film "Batman," sued Warner Brothers in the spring of 1992 for a share of profits in litigation based on the Buchwald case. They contend that Uslan wrote a 1980 memo showing that he "conceived of most of the aspects that made the 1989 movie such a huge success." The Washington Post, March 27, 1992 at B1.


## 1. REMEDIES

The Copyright Act of 1976 provides numerous remedies for copyright infringement. Sections 502–503 provide for an injunction against further infringement as well as destruction of all existing infringing materials. Under § 504, the copyright owner may elect to receive either the damages actually suffered plus any additional profits of the infringer or statutory damages of not less than $250 or more than $10,000. The court may also at its discretion award costs and attorney's fees.

In the case of willful infringement for commercial advantage or private financial gain, criminal sanctions are also available. Section 506 provides for fines of up to $50,000 and imprisonment for up to two years, depending on the type of work infringed and the prior record of the defendant.

2. DEFENSES

*a. Independent Creation*

Copyright protection extends only to copying the work in question. If someone independently creates a similar work, there is no copyright infringement. Thus, in any copyright suit the plaintiff must show that the defendant had access to the plaintiff's work. However, as former Beatle George Harrison learned, plaintiff does not have to prove that defendant intentionally or even consciously copied it. Bright Tunes Music Corp. v. Harrisongs Music, Ltd., 420 F.Supp. 177 (S.D.N.Y.1976).

*b. Fair Use*

As previously noted, the grant of rights to the owner of the copyright is conditioned on a series of limitations expressed in §§ 107–118. These include permitting libraries to make single photocopies of articles and permitting persons to make phonograph records of music without permission upon payment of certain royalties. Section 111 deals with the cable television problem. Probably the most important of these limitations is found in § 107, dealing with the question of fair use. Until the 1976 statute fair use had been left to develop as a judicially created exception to the rights of the copyright owner. There was great controversy over whether to recognize the defense explicitly and, if so, how to do it. The result is § 107:

> Notwithstanding the provisions of section 106, the fair use of a copyrighted work, including such use by reproduction in copies or phonorecords or by any other means specified by that section, for purposes such as criticism, comment, news reporting, teaching (including multiple copies for classroom use), scholarship, or research, is not an infringement of copyright. In determining whether the use made of a work in any particular case is a fair use the factors to be considered shall include—

> (1) the purpose and character of the use, including whether such use is of a commercial nature or is for nonprofit educational purposes;

> (2) the nature of the copyrighted work;

> (3) the amount and substantiality of the portion used in relation to the copyrighted work as a whole; and

> (4) the effect of the use upon the potential market for or value of the copyrighted work.

> The fact that a work is unpublished shall not itself bar a finding of fair use if such finding is made upon consideration of all the above factors. 17 U.S.C.A. § 107.

The following case involves two special fair use questions. One is the application of fair use to historical works. Remember our earlier discussion of historical works, p. 295, *supra.* The other question is whether fair use can be used where the copyrighted work was unpublished at the time of infringement. The case is also an excellent illustration of how courts approach fair use cases in general.

## HARPER & ROW PUBLISHERS, INC. v. NATION ENTERPRISES

Supreme Court of the United States, 1985.
471 U.S. 539, 105 S.Ct. 2218, 85 L.Ed.2d 588, 11 Med.L.Rptr. 1969.

JUSTICE O'CONNOR delivered the opinion of the Court.

This case requires us to consider to what extent the "fair use" provision of the Copyright Revision Act of 1976, 17 U.S.C. § 107 (hereinafter the Copyright Act), sanctions the unauthorized use of quotations from a public figure's unpublished manuscript. In March 1979, an undisclosed source provided The Nation magazine with the unpublished manuscript of "A Time to Heal: The Autobiography of Gerald R. Ford." Working directly from the purloined manuscript, an editor of The Nation produced a short piece entitled "The Ford Memoirs—Behind the Nixon Pardon." The piece was timed to "scoop" an article scheduled shortly to appear in Time magazine. Time had agreed to purchase the exclusive right to print prepublication excerpts from the copyright holders. . . .

I

. . . The memoirs were to contain "significant hitherto unpublished material" concerning the Watergate crisis, Mr. Ford's pardon of Former President Nixon and "Mr. Ford's reflections on this period of history, and the morality and personalities involved." . . . In addition to the right to publish the Ford memoirs in book form, the agreement gave petitioners the exclusive right to license prepublication excerpts, known in the trade as "first serial rights." . . . [A]s the memoirs were nearing completion, petitioners negotiated a prepublication licensing agreement with Time, a weekly news magazine. Time agreed to pay $25,000, $12,500 in advance and an additional $12,500 at publication, in exchange for the right to excerpt 7,500 words from Mr. Ford's account of the Nixon pardon. The issue featuring the excerpts was timed to appear approximately one week before shipment of the full length book version to bookstores. Exclusivity was an important consideration; Harper & Row instituted procedures designed to maintain the confidentiality of the manuscript, and Time retained the right to renegotiate the second payment should the material appear in print prior to its release of the excerpts.

[Mr. Navasky received a copy of the manuscript.] Mr. Navasky knew that his possession of the manuscript was not authorized and that the manuscript must be returned to his "source" to avoid discovery. [ ] He hastily put together what he believed was a "real hot news story" composed of quotes, paraphrases and facts drawn exclusively from the manuscript. [ ] Mr. Navasky attempted no independent commentary, research or criticism, in part because of the need for speed if he was to "make news" by "publish[ing] in advance of publication of the Ford book." [ ]  The 2,250 word article  . . .   appeared on April 3, 1979. As a result of The Nation's article, Time canceled its piece and refused to pay the remaining $12,500.

. . .

## II

We agree with the Court of Appeals that copyright is intended to increase and not to impede the harvest of knowledge.  But we believe the Second Circuit gave insufficient deference to the scheme established by the Copyright Act for fostering the original works that provide the seed and substance of this harvest.  The rights conferred by copyright are designed to assure contributors to the store of knowledge a fair return for their labors. [ ]

Article I, § 8, of the Constitution provides that:

> "The Congress shall have Power  . . .   to Promote the Progress of Science and useful Arts, by securing for limited Times to Authors and Inventors the exclusive Right to their respective Writings and Discoveries."

As we noted last Term, "[this] limited grant is a means by which an important public purpose may be achieved.  It is intended to motivate the creative activity of authors and inventors by the provision of a special reward, and to allow the public access to the products of their genius after the limited period of exclusive control has expired."  Sony v. Universal Studios, 464 U.S. 417 (1984).  "The monopoly created by copyright thus rewards the individual author in order to benefit the public." [ ]  This principle applies equally to works of fiction and nonfiction.  The book at issue here, for example, was two years in the making, and began with a contract giving the author's copyright to the publishers in exchange for their services in producing and marketing the work.  In preparing the book, Mr. Ford drafted essays and word portraits of hundreds of taped interviews that were later distilled to chronicle his personal viewpoint.  It is evident that the monopoly granted by copyright actively served its intended purpose of inducing the creation of new material of potential historical value.

Section 106 of the Copyright Act confers a bundle of exclusive rights to the owner of the copyright.  Under the Copyright Act, these rights— to publish, copy, and distribute the author's work—vest in the author of an original work from the time of its creation.  In practice, the author commonly sells his rights to publishers who offer royalties in exchange for their services in producing and marketing the author's work.  The copyright owner's rights, however, are subject to certain statutory exceptions.  Among these is § 107, which codifies the traditional privilege of other authors to make "fair use" of an earlier writer's work.  In addition, no author may copyright facts or ideas.  The copyright is limited to those aspects of the work—termed "expression"—that display the stamp of the author's originality.

Creation of a nonfiction work, even a compilation of pure fact, entails originality.   .  .  .   The copyright holders of "A Time to Heal" complied with the relevant statutory notice and registration procedures. Thus, there is no dispute that the unpublished manuscript of "A Time to Heal," as a whole was protected by § 106 from unauthorized reproduction. Nor do respondents dispute that verbatim copying of excerpts of the manuscript's original form of expression would constitute infringement unless excused as fair use. [ ] Yet copyright does not prevent subsequent users from copying from a prior author's work those constituent elements that are not original—for example, quotations borrowed under the rubric of fair use from other copyrighted works, facts, or materials in the public domain—as long as such use does not unfairly appropriate the author's original contributions. [ ] Perhaps the controversy between the lower courts in the case over copyrightability is more aptly a dispute over whether The Nation's appropriation of unoriginal and uncopyrightable elements encroached on the originality embodied in the work as a whole. Especially in the realm of factual narrative, the law is currently unsettled regarding the ways in which uncopyrightable elements combine with the author's original contributions to form protected expression.   .  .  .

We need not reach these issues, however, as The Nation has admitted to lifting verbatim quotes of the author's original language totalling between 300 and 400 words and constituting some 13% of The Nation article. In using generous verbatim excerpts of Mr. Ford's unpublished manuscript to lend authenticity to its account of the forthcoming memoirs, The Nation effectively arrogated to itself the right of first publication, an important marketable subsidiary right. For the reasons set forth below, we find that this use of the copyrighted manuscript, even stripped to the verbatim quotes conceded by The Nation as to be copyrightable expression, was not a fair use within the meaning of the Copyright Act.

### III

### A

Fair use was traditionally defined as "a privilege in others than the owner of the copyright to use the copyrighted material in a reasonable manner without his consent." [ ] The statutory formulation of the defense of fair use in the Copyright Act of 1976 reflects the intent of Congress to codify the common-law doctrine. Section 107 requires a case-by-case determination whether a particular use is fair, and the statute notes four nonexclusive factors to be considered. This approach was "intended to restate the [pre-existing] judicial doctrine of fair use, not to change, narrow, or enlarge it in any way." H.R.Rep. No. 94–1476, p. 66 (1976) (hereinafter House Report).

"[T]he author's consent to a reasonable use of his copyrighted works ha[d] always been implied by the courts as a necessary incident of the constitutional policy of promoting the progress of science and the useful arts, since a prohibition of such use would inhibit subsequent writers from attempting to improve upon prior works and thus . . . frustrate the very ends sought to be attained." . . .

. . .

Perhaps because the fair use doctrine was predicated on the author's implied consent to "reasonable and customary" use when he released his work for public consumption, fair use traditionally was not recognized as a defense to charges of copying from an author's as yet unpublished works. Under common-law copyright, "the property of the author . . . in his intellectual creation [was] absolute until he voluntarily part[ed] with the same." [  ] This absolute rule, however, was tempered in practice by the equitable nature of the fair use doctrine. In a given case, factors such as implied consent through *de facto* publication or performance or dissemination of a work may tip the balance of equities in favor of prepublication use. [  ] But it has never been seriously disputed that "the fact that the plaintiff's work is unpublished . . . is a factor tending to negate the defense of fair use." . . .

The Copyright Revision Act of 1976 represents the culmination of a major legislative reexamination of copyright doctrine. Among its other innovations, it eliminated publication "as a dividing line between common law and statutory protection," [  ], extending statutory protection to all works from the time of their creation. It also recognized for the first time a distinct statutory right of first publication, which had previously been an element of the common-law protections afforded unpublished works. . . .

Though the right of first publication, like the other rights enumerated in § 106, is expressly made subject to the fair use provision of § 107, fair use analysis must always be tailored to the individual case. The nature of the interest at stake is highly relevant to whether a given use is fair. From the beginning, those entrusted with the task of revision recognized the "overbalancing reasons to preserve the common law protection of undisseminated works until the author or his successor chooses to disclose them." [  ] The right of first publication implicates a threshold decision by the author whether and in what form to release his work. First publication is inherently different from other § 106 rights in that only one person can be the first publisher; as the contract with Time illustrates, the commercial value of the right lies primarily in exclusivity. Because the potential damage to the author from judicially enforced "sharing" of the first publication right with unauthorized users of his manuscript is substantial, the balance of equities in evaluating such a claim of fair use inevitably shifts.

. . .

. . . The author's control of first public distribution implicates not only his personal interest in creative control but his property interest in exploitation of prepublication rights, which are valuable in themselves and serve as a valuable adjunct to publicity and marketing. See Belushi v. Woodward, 598 F.Supp. 36 (DC 1984) (successful marketing depends on coordination of serialization and release to public); Marks, Subsidiary Rights and Permissions, in What Happens in Book Publishing, 230 (C. Grannis ed. 1967) (exploitation of subsidiary rights is necessary to financial success of new books).  Under ordinary circumstances, the author's right to control the first public appearance of his undisseminated expression will outweigh a claim of fair use.

B

Respondents, however, contend that First Amendment values require a different rule under the circumstances of this case.  The thrust of the decision below is that "[t]he scope of [fair use] is undoubtedly wider when the information conveyed relates to matters of high public concern."  . . .  Respondents explain their copying of Mr. Ford's expression as essential to reporting the news story it claims the book itself represents.  In respondents' view, not only the facts contained in Mr. Ford's memoirs, but "the precise manner in which [he] expressed himself was as newsworthy as what he had to say."  [  ]  Respondents argue that the public's interest in learning this news as fast as possible outweighs the right of the author to control its first publication.

The Second Circuit noted, correctly, that copyright's idea/expression dichotomy "strike[s] a definitional balance between the First Amendment and the Copyright Act by permitting free communication of facts while still protecting an author's expression."  [  ]  No author may copyright his ideas or the facts he narrates.  . . .  As this Court long ago observed: "[T]he news element—the information respecting current events contained in the literary production—is not the creation of the writer, but is a report of matters that ordinarily are *public juris;* it is history of the day."  International News Service v. Associated Press, [  ].  But copyright assures those who write and publish factual narratives such as "A Time to Heal" that they may at least enjoy the right to market the original expression contained therein as just compensation for their investment.

. . . The promise of copyright would be an empty one if it could be avoided merely by dubbing the infringement a fair use "news report" of the book.

Nor do respondents assert any actual necessity for circumventing the copyright scheme with respect to the types of works and users at issue here.[6]  Where an author and publisher have invested extensive

6. It bears noting that Congress in the Copyright Act recognized a public interest warranting specific exemptions in a number of areas not within traditional fair use, see, e.g., 17 U.S.C. § 115 (compulsory license for records); § 105 (no copyright in government works).  No such exemption limits copyright in personal narratives written by

resources in creating an original work and are poised to release it to the public, no legitimate aim is served by preempting the right of first publication.   . . .

In our haste to disseminate news, it should not be forgotten that the Framers intended copyright itself to be the engine of free expression.   . . .

It is fundamentally at odds with the scheme of copyright to accord lesser rights in those works that are of greatest importance to the public. Such a notion ignores the major premise of copyright and injures author and public alike.   . . .

. . .

## IV

. . . [W]hether The Nation article constitutes fair use under § 107 must be reviewed in light of the principles discussed above. The factors enumerated in the section are not meant to be exclusive: "[S]ince the doctrine is an equitable rule of reason, no generally applicable definition is possible, and each case raising the question must be decided on its own facts." [   ] The four factors identified by Congress as especially relevant in determining whether the use was fair are: (1) the purpose and character of the use; (2) the nature of the copyrighted work; (3) the substantiality of the portion used in relation to the copyrighted work as a whole; (4) the effect on the potential market for or value of the copyrighted work. We address each one separately.

*Purpose of the Use.* The Second Circuit correctly identified news reporting as the general purpose of The Nation's use. News reporting is one of the examples enumerated in § 107 to "give some idea of the sort of activities the courts might regard as fair use under the circumstances." . . . The fact that an article arguably is "news" and therefore a productive use is simply one factor in a fair use analysis.

. . . The Nation has every right to seek to be the first to publish information. But The Nation went beyond simply reporting uncopyrightable information and actively sought to exploit the headline value of its infringement, making a "news event" out of its unauthorized first publication of a noted figure's copyrighted expression.

The fact that a publication was commercial as opposed to non-profit is a separate factor that tends to weigh against a finding of fair use. "[E]very commercial use of copyrighted material is presumptively an unfair exploitation of the monopoly privilege that belongs to the owner of the copyright." [*Sony*] In arguing that the purpose of news reporting is not purely commercial, The Nation misses the point entirely. The crux of the profit/nonprofit distinction is not whether the sole motive of the use is monetary gain but whether the user stands to profit from exploitation of the copyrighted material without paying the customary price.

public servants after they leave government
service.

In evaluating character and purpose we cannot ignore The Nation's stated purpose of scooping the forthcoming hardcover and Time abstracts. The Nation's use had not merely the incidental effect but the *intended purpose* of supplanting the copyright holder's commercially valuable right of first publication. Also relevant to the "character" of the use is "the propriety of the defendant's conduct." [  ] The trial court found that The Nation knowingly exploited a purloined manuscript. Unlike the typical claim of fair use, The Nation cannot offer up even the fiction of consent as justification. Like its competitor newsweekly, it was free to bid for the right of abstracting excerpts from "A Time to Heal."   . . .

*Nature of the Copyrighted Work.*  Second, the Act directs attention to the nature of the copyrighted work. "A Time to Heal" may be characterized as an unpublished historical narrative or autobiography. The law generally recognizes a greater need to disseminate factual works than works of fiction or fantasy.   . . .   Some of the briefer quotes from the memoir are arguably necessary adequately to convey the facts: for example, Mr. Ford's characterization of the White House tapes as the "smoking gun" is perhaps so integral to the idea expressed as to be inseparable from it. But The Nation did not stop at isolated phrases and instead excerpted subjective descriptions and portraits of public figures whose power lies in the author's individualized expression. Such use, focusing on the most expressive elements of the work, exceeds that necessary to disseminate the facts.

The fact that a work is unpublished is a critical element of its "nature." Our prior discussion establishes that the scope of fair use is narrower with respect to unpublished works.   . . .

In the case of Mr. Ford's manuscript, the copyrightholders' interest in confidentiality is irrefutable; the copyrightholders had entered into a contractual undertaking to "keep the manuscript confidential" and required that all those to whom the manuscript was shown also "sign an agreement to keep the manuscript confidential." While the copyrightholders' contract with Time required Time to submit its proposed article seven days before publication, The Nation's clandestine publication afforded no such opportunity for creative or quality control. It was hastily patched together and contained "a number of inaccuracies." A use that so clearly infringes the copyrightholder's interests in confidentiality and creative control is difficult to characterize as "fair."

*Amount and Substantiality of the Portion Used.*  Next, the Act directs us to examine the amount and substantiality of the portion used in relation to the copyrighted work as a whole. In absolute terms, the words actually quoted were an insubstantial portion of "A Time to Heal." The district court, however, found that "[T]he Nation took what was essentially the heart of the book." [  ] We believe the Court of Appeals erred in overruling the district judge's evaluation of the qualitative nature of the taking. See, e.g., Roy Export Co. Establishment v. Columbia Broadcasting System, Inc., [  ] (taking of 55 seconds out of one hour and twenty-nine minute film deemed qualitatively substantial). A Time editor described the chapters on the pardon as "the most interesting and moving parts of the entire manuscript." . . .

As the statutory language indicates, a taking may not be excused merely because it is insubstantial with respect to the *infringing* work. As Judge Learned Hand cogently remarked, "[N]o plagiarist can excuse the wrong by showing how much of his work he did not pirate." [*Sheldon*] Conversely, the fact that a substantial portion of the infringing work was copied verbatim is evidence of the qualitative value of the copied material, both to the originator and to the plagiarist who seeks to profit from marketing someone else's copyrighted expression.

Stripped to the verbatim quotes, the direct takings from the unpublished manuscript constitute at least 13% of the infringing article. See [*Meeropol*] (copyrighted letters constituted less than 1% of infringing work but were prominently featured). The Nation article is structured around the quoted excerpts which serve as its dramatic focal points. In view of the expressive value of the excerpts and their key role in the infringing work, we cannot agree with the Second Circuit that the "magazine took a meager, indeed an infinitesimal amount of Ford's original language." [ ]

*Effect on the Market.* Finally, the Act focuses on "the effect of the use upon the potential market for or value of the copyrighted work." This last factor is undoubtedly the single most important element of fair use. . . . [O]nce a copyrightholder establishes with reasonable probability the existence of a causal connection between the infringement and a loss of revenue, the burden properly shifts to the infringer to show that this damage would have occurred had there been no taking of copyrighted expression. Petitioners established a prima facie case of actual damage that respondent failed to rebut. The trial court properly awarded actual damages and accounting of profits.

. . .

It is undisputed that the factual material in the balance of The Nation's article, besides the verbatim quotes at issue here, was drawn exclusively from the chapters on the pardon. The excerpts were employed as featured episodes in a story about the Nixon pardon—precisely the use petitioners had licensed to Time. The borrowing of these verbatim quotes from the unpublished manuscript lent The Nation's piece a special air of authenticity—as Navasky [*The Nation*'s editor] expressed it, the reader would know it was Ford speaking and not The Nation. Thus, it directly competed for a share of the market for prepublication excerpts. . . .

## V

. . . In sum, the traditional doctrine of fair use, as embodied in the Copyright Act, does not sanction the use made by The Nation of these copyrighted materials. Any copyright infringer may claim to benefit the public by increasing public access to the copyrighted work.

But Congress has not designed, and we see no warrant for judicially imposing, a "compulsory license" permitting unfettered access to the unpublished copyrighted expression of public figures.

The Nation conceded that its verbatim copying of some 300 words of direct quotation from the Ford manuscript would constitute an infringement unless excused as a fair use. Because we find that The Nation's use of these verbatim excerpts from the unpublished manuscript was not a fair use, the judgment of the Court of Appeals is reversed and remanded for further proceedings consistent with this opinion.

It is so ordered.

Justice Brennan, with whom Justice White and Justice Marshall join, dissenting.

The Court holds that The Nation's quotation of 300 words from the unpublished 200,000–word manuscript of President Gerald R. Ford infringed the copyright in that manuscript, even though the quotations related to a historical event of undoubted significance—the resignation and pardon of President Richard M. Nixon. Although the Court pursues the laudable goal of protecting "the economic incentive to create and disseminate ideas," this zealous defense of the copyright owner's prerogative will, I fear, stifle the broad dissemination of ideas and information copyright is intended to nurture. Protection of the copyright owner's economic interest is achieved in this case through an exceedingly narrow definition of the scope of fair use. The progress of arts and sciences and the robust public debate essential to an enlightened citizenry are ill served by this constricted reading of the fair use doctrine. [ ] I therefore respectfully dissent.

I

A

This case presents two issues. First, did The Nation's use of material from the Ford manuscript in forms other than direct quotation from that manuscript infringe Harper & Row's copyright. Second, did the quotation of approximately 300 words from the manuscript infringe the copyright because this quotation did not constitute "fair use" within the meaning of § 107 of the Copyright Act. The Court finds no need to resolve the threshold copyrightability issue. The use of 300 words of quotation was, the Court finds, beyond the scope of fair use and thus a copyright infringement. Because I disagree with the Court's fair use holding, it is necessary for me to decide the threshold copyrightability question.

.   .   .

The "originality" requirement now embodied in § 102 of the Copyright Act is crucial to maintenance of the appropriate balance between these competing interests. Properly interpreted in the light of the legislative history, this section extends copyright protection to an author's literary form but permits free use by others of the ideas and information the author communicates.  . . .

It follows that infringement of copyright must be based on a taking of literary form, as opposed to the ideas or information contained in a copyrighted work.  Deciding whether an infringing appropriation of literary form has occurred is difficult for at least two reasons.  First, the distinction between literary form and information or ideas is often elusive in practice.  Second, infringement must be based on a *substantial* appropriation of literary form.  This determination is equally challenging.  Not surprisingly, the test for infringement has defied precise formulation.  In general, though, the inquiry proceeds along two axes: *how closely* has the second author tracked the first author's particular language and structure of presentation; and *how much* of the first author's language and structure has the second author appropriated.

. . .

*The Language.*  Much of the information The Nation conveyed was not in the form of paraphrase at all, but took the form of synopsis of lengthy discussions in the Ford manuscript.  In the course of this summary presentation, The Nation did use occasional sentences that closely resembled language in the original Ford manuscript.  But these linguistic similarities are insufficient to constitute an infringement.  . . .

At most The Nation paraphrased disparate isolated sentences from the original.  A finding of infringement based on paraphrase generally requires far more close and substantial a tracking of the original language than occurred in this case.

*The Structure of Presentation.*  The article does not mimic Mr. Ford's structure.  The information The Nation presents is drawn from scattered sections of the Ford work and does not appear in the sequence in which Mr. Ford presented it.  . . .  Also, it is difficult to suggest that a 2,000–word article could bodily appropriate the structure of a 200,000–word book.  Most of what Mr. Ford created, and most of the history he recounted, was simply not represented in The Nation's article.

When The Nation was not quoting Mr. Ford, therefore, its efforts to convey the historical information in the Ford manuscript did not so closely and substantially track Mr. Ford's language and structure as to constitute an appropriation of literary form.

## II

The Nation is thus liable in copyright only if the quotation of 300 words infringed any of Harper & Row's exclusive rights under § 106 of the Act.  . . .  The question here is whether The Nation's quotation was a noninfringing fair use within the meaning of § 107.

. . .

With respect to a work of history, particularly the memoirs of a public official, the statutorily-prescribed analysis cannot properly be conducted without constant attention to copyright's crucial distinction between protected literary form and unprotected information or ideas. The question must always be: was the subsequent author's use of *literary form* a fair use within the meaning of § 107, in light of the purpose for the use, the nature of the copyrighted work, the amount of literary form used, and the effect of this use of literary form on the value of or market for the original.

Limiting the inquiry to the propriety of a subsequent author's use of the copyrighted owner's literary form is not easy in the case of a work of history. Protection against only substantial appropriation of literary form does not ensure historians a return commensurate with the full value of their labors.   . . .   Copyright thus does not protect that which is often of most value in a work of history and courts must resist the tendency to reject the fair use defense on the basis of their feeling that an author of history has been deprived of the full value of his or her labor. A subsequent author's taking of information and ideas is in no sense piratical because copyright law simply does not create any property interest in information and ideas.

The urge to compensate for subsequent use of information and ideas is perhaps understandable. An inequity seems to lurk in the idea that much of the fruit of the historian's labor may be used without compensation. This, however, is not some unforeseen by-product of a statutory scheme intended primarily to ensure a return for works of the imagination. Congress made the affirmative choice that the copyright laws should apply in this way.   . . .

. . .   Application of the statutorily prescribed analysis with attention to the distinction between information and literary form leads to a straightforward finding of fair use within the meaning of § 107.

*The Purpose of the Use.* The Nation's purpose in quoting 300 words of the Ford manuscript was, as the Court acknowledges, news reporting.   . . .

. . .

The Court concedes the validity of the news reporting purpose but then quickly offsets it against three purportedly countervailing considerations. First, the Court asserts that because The Nation publishes for profit, its publication of the Ford quotes is a presumptively unfair commercial use. Second, the Court claims that The Nation's stated desire to create a "news event" signalled an illegitimate purpose of supplanting the copyright owner's right of first publication. Third, The Nation acted in bad faith, the Court claims, because its editor "knowingly exploited a purloined manuscript."

The Court's reliance on the commercial nature of The Nation's use as "a separate factor that tends to weigh against a finding of fair use," is inappropriate in the present context. Many uses § 107 lists as paradigmatic examples of fair use, including criticism, comment and *news reporting,* are generally conducted for profit in this country, a fact of which Congress was obviously aware when it enacted § 107. To negate any argument favoring fair use based on news reporting or criticism because that reporting or criticism was published for profit is to render meaningless the congressional imprimatur placed on such uses.

Nor should The Nation's intent to create a "news event" weigh against a finding of fair use. Such a rule, like the Court's automatic presumption against news reporting for profit, would undermine the congressional validation of the news reporting purpose.  . . .  The record suggests only that The Nation sought to be the first to reveal the information in the Ford manuscript. The Nation's stated purpose of scooping the competition should under those circumstances have no negative bearing on the claim of fair use. Indeed the court's reliance on this factor would seem to amount to little more than distaste for the standard journalistic practice of seeking to be the first to publish news.

The Court's reliance on The Nation's putative bad faith is equally unwarranted. No court has found that The Nation possessed the Ford manuscript illegally or in violation of any common law interest of Harper & Row; all common law causes of action have been abandoned or dismissed in this case. Even if the manuscript had been "purloined" by someone, nothing in this record imputes culpability to The Nation. On the basis of the record in this case, the most that can be said is that The Nation made use of the contents of the manuscript knowing the copyright owner would not sanction the use.

. . .

*The Nature of the Copyrighted Work.*  . . .

The Court acknowledges that "[t]he law generally recognizes a greater need to disseminate factual works than works of fiction or fantasy," and that "some of the briefer quotations from the memoir are arguably necessary to convey the facts," ibid. But the Court discounts the force of this consideration, primarily on the ground that "the fact that a work is unpublished is a crucial element of its 'nature.' " At this point the Court introduces into analysis of this case a categorical presumption against prepublication fair use. ("Under ordinary circumstances, the author's right to control the first public appearance of his undisseminated expression will outweigh a claim of fair use.")

This categorical presumption is unwarranted on its own terms and unfaithful to congressional intent. Whether a particular prepublication use will impair any interest the Court identifies as encompassed within the right of first publication, will depend on the nature of the copyrighted work, the timing of prepublication use, the amount of expression used and the medium in which the second author communicates. Also, certain uses might be tolerable for some purposes and not others.  . . .

. . .

*The Amount and Substantiality of the Portion Used.*   More difficult questions arise with respect to judgments about the importance to this case of the amount and substantiality of the quotations used.   . . .

. . .

At least with respect to the six particular quotes of Mr. Ford's observations and reflections about President Nixon, I agree with the Court's conclusion that The Nation appropriated some literary form of substantial quality.   I do not agree, however, that the substantiality of the expression taken was clearly excessive or inappropriate to The Nation's news reporting purpose.

Had these quotations been used in the context of a critical book review of the Ford book, there is little question that such a use would be fair use within the meaning of § 107 of the Act.   The amount and substantiality of the use—in both quantitative and qualitative terms— would have certainly been appropriate to the purpose of such a use.   It is difficult to see how the use of these quoted words in a news report is less appropriate.   . . .

. . .

*The Effect on the Market.*   The Court correctly notes that the effect on the market "is undoubtedly the single most important element of fair use," and the Court properly focuses on whether The Nation's use adversely affected Harper & Row's serialization potential and not merely the market for sales of the Ford work itself.   Unfortunately, the Court's failure to distinguish between the use of information and the appropriation of literary form badly skews its analysis of this factor.

. . .

The Nation's publication indisputably precipitated Time's eventual cancellation.   But that does not mean that The Nation's use of the 300 quoted words caused this injury to Harper & Row.   Wholly apart from these quoted words, The Nation published significant information and ideas from the Ford manuscript.   If it was this publication of information, and not the publication of the few quotations, that caused Time to abrogate its serialization agreement, then whatever the negative effect on the serialization market, that effect was the product of wholly legitimate activity.

. . .

*Balancing the Interests.*   Once the distinction between information and literary form is made clear, the statutorily prescribed process of weighing the four statutory fair use factors discussed above leads naturally to a conclusion that The Nation's limited use of literary form was not an infringement.   . . .

### III

The Court's exceedingly narrow approach to fair use permits Harper & Row to monopolize information.   This holding "effect[s] an important extension of property rights and a corresponding curtailment in the free use of knowledge and of ideas." International News Service v. Associated Press, 248 U.S. at 263 (Brandeis, J. dissenting). The Court has perhaps advanced the ability of the historian—or at least the public official who has recently left office—to capture the full economic value of information in his or her possession. But the Court does so only by risking the robust debate of public issues that is the "essence of self-government." Garrison v. Louisiana, 379 U.S., at 74–75. The Nation was providing the grist for that robust debate. The Court imposes liability upon The Nation for no other reason than that The Nation succeeded in being the first to provide certain information to the public. I dissent.

## Notes and Questions

1. How would the analysis change if *The Nation's* article had appeared a week after the book was published? A week after the *Time* publication?

2. During the oral argument counsel for *The Nation* asserted that "There are two words to describe what *The Nation* was doing: news reporting." Does the majority accept that view?

3. Although most commentators have concluded that the 1976 statute does not change the prior law of fair use, it seems safer to consider cases decided since then. A sampling of post–1976 fair use cases follows.

  a. In Sony Corp. v. Universal City Studios, Inc., 464 U.S. 417 (1984), discussed in more detail later in this chapter, the Court, 5–4, held that home recording of broadcast television programs constitutes a fair use. "[A]lthough every commercial use of copyrighted material is presumptively an unfair exploitation of the monopoly privilege," a different rule applies for noncommercial uses. Here, plaintiff must show "either that the particular use is harmful, or that if it should become widespread, it would adversely affect the potential market for the copyrighted work. Actual present harm need not be shown. . . . Nor is it necessary to show with certainty that future harm will result. What is necessary is a showing by a preponderance of the evidence that *some* meaningful likelihood of future harm exists. If the intended use is for commercial gain, that likelihood may be presumed. But if it is for a noncommercial purpose, the likelihood must be demonstrated."

  Two critical findings of the trial court led the majority to deny protection. "First, Sony demonstrated a significant likelihood that substantial numbers of copyright holders who license their works for broadcast on free television would not object to having their broadcasts time-shifted by private viewers. And second, respondents failed to demonstrate that time-shifting would cause any likelihood of nonminimal harm to the potential market for, or the value of, their copyrighted works." These led the Court to conclude that time-shifting, by far the most common use of the recorders, was fair use.

  b. In Pacific and Southern Co., Inc. v. Duncan, 744 F.2d 1490, 11 Med.L.Rptr. 1135, 56 R.R.2d 1620 (11th Cir.1984), cert. denied 471 U.S.

1004 (1985), plaintiff television station WXIA–TV presented four copyrighted local news programs daily. It audiotaped and videotaped each program. It retained the audiotape and the written transcript of the program for an indefinite time; it erased the videotape after seven days. WXIA did not market clips of its own stories, though it honored requests for tapes when made.

Defendant, doing business as TV News Clips, taped the news programs of television stations and tried to sell copies of the clips to those persons or groups covered by the news reports. The copies were not copyrighted and stated "for personal use only not for rebroadcast." Defendant erased tapes after one month.

The court of appeals found a valid copyright even though the only fixed copy was defendant's. The plaintiff's tapes satisfied the requirement that the work be fixed for a period of "more than transitory duration." On the fair use question, the court turned to the four factors. The commercial nature of defendant's practices "militates quite strongly against a finding of fair use." Moreover, defendant's use "is neither productive nor creative in any way. It does not analyze the broadcast or improve it at all. . . . TV News Clips only copies and sells." Since the court treated each story on the news as a "coherent narrative," it found that the defendant had taken the entire work. The fourth factor also cut against defendant since it "uses the broadcasts for a purpose that WXIA might use for its own benefit." The potential market is undermined.

The second factor might be seen to favor defendant because of the importance to society of access to the news. "But the courts should also take care not to discourage authors from addressing important topics for fear of losing their copyright protections."

Defendant argued that every copyright must further the ends of the copyright clause and that this one did not because of WXIA's systematic destruction of videotapes. (Although the defendant treated this as a First Amendment argument, the court thought it should be addressed under fair use.) Not every copyright holder "must offer benefits to society, for the copyright is an incentive rather than a command. And, *a fortiori*, a copyright holder need not provide the most complete public access possible. WXIA provides complete access for seven days and permanent access to everything except the visual images broadcast live from within the studio. The public benefits from this creative work; therefore, enforcing the copyright statute in this case does not violate the Copyright Clause."

The court held that the district court had abused its discretion by refusing to issue an injunction after finding an infringement.

c. In Diamond v. Am–Law Publishing Corp., 745 F.2d 142 (2d Cir.1984), defendant *American Lawyer* published a story reporting that a formal grievance had been filed against plaintiff lawyer. He wrote defendant demanding an apology and a retraction. The editor invited the plaintiff to write a letter stating that no grievance had been filed.

Plaintiff then sent a long letter making that point and also attacking the reporting practices of the defendant. The letter stated that "You are authorized to publish this letter but only in its entirety." Defendant published excerpts from the letter that made the point about the grievance but omitted, without showing any deletions, the parts attacking the defendant.

Plaintiff obtained a copyright on the letter and sued for infringement. The trial court's grant of summary judgment for defendant and its award of $15,000 in attorney's fees and costs were affirmed on appeal.

Fair use was established as a matter of law. The nonuse or editing of the letter did not put the copyrighted work in an unfair or distorted light. The omissions involved an unrelated matter and did not mislead the public about the contents of the entire letter. (Even if it did, it was not clear that this made it a copyright violation.) In any event, the use here was for comment or news reporting, uses protected under § 107. The claim that too little was used differed from the usual claim and did not help the plaintiff. Finally, plaintiff could show no present or future use of the letter that had been adversely affected by defendant's use.

d.   In Salinger v. Random House, Inc., 811 F.2d 90, 13 Med.L.Rptr. 1954 (2d Cir.1987), author J.D. Salinger sought an injunction to stop publication by Random House and author Ian Hamilton of an unauthorized biography entitled *J.D. Salinger: A Writing Life.* The biography drew heavily from approximately 70 copyrighted letters written by Salinger many years ago, and Salinger alleged that their use was a copyright infringement.

The letters had been deposited by their recipients in several university libraries, where Hamilton had access to them. Reacting to Salinger's demand, Hamilton substantially revised his book after it was in galleys, rewriting or paraphrasing most of the previously quoted material from the letters so that he quoted no more than 10 percent of any one letter and, in most cases, no more than 10 words from any one letter.

The district court held that the vast majority of the material taken from the letters—the *information* in them—was not copyrightable: "For the biographer to report in his own words Salinger's ideas drawn from the letters or the fact that Salinger was depressed, elated, or angry, does not violate the copyright."

Salinger's attorneys had argued that the doctrine of fair use could not apply to unpublished works like Salinger's letters, and there was little case precedent involving unpublished works; but the district court held that "plaintiff's argument that there may be no fair use of an unpublished work is exaggerated and unreasonable." Calling Hamilton's use of Salinger's copyright material "minimal and insubstantial," the court refused to enjoin publication.

The court of appeals reversed, holding that "[t]he taking is significant not only from a quantitative standpoint but from a qualitative one as well," and enjoined distribution of the biography.

The court of appeals relied heavily on *Harper & Row* for its fair use analysis because it was "the court's first delineation of the scope of fair use as *applied to unpublished works*" (emphasis added).

In considering the application of the four fair-use factors to Hamilton's use of the Salinger letters, the court started by categorizing the purpose of the use alternatively as "criticism," "scholarship" or "research." All of these categories are viewed as appropriate to a fair use. The court went on, however, to reject specifically the district court's assertion that a biographer is entitled to an especially generous application of the defense. The district court had argued that this was necessary because of the special dilemma faced by a biographer ("to the extent he departs from the words of the letters, he distorts, sacrificing both accuracy and vividness of description"). The court of appeals, however, recognized no need to take the *expression* contained in the letters.

Although acknowledging that Salinger disavowed any intention to publish the letters during his lifetime, the court wrote that Salinger was entitled to protect his *opportunity* to sell them—an opportunity estimated by Salinger's literary agent to be worth more than $500,000. Note, however, that Salinger's interest was essentially one of privacy not profit—a situation quite different from that in *Harper & Row,* where economic gain was the plaintiff's principal concern.

In its analysis of the nature of the work, the court of appeals' opinion emphasized the insulation of unpublished works like Salinger's letters from fair use, quoting from the Supreme Court's opinion in *Harper & Row* that "the scope of fair use is narrower with respect to unpublished works." The Supreme Court denied cert. 484 U.S. 890 (1987).

e. The Second Circuit again addressed the fair use doctrine in New Era Publications International v. Henry Holt & Co., 873 F.2d 576, 16 Med.L.Rptr. 1559 (2d Cir.1989). The case involved a biography by Russell Miller entitled "Bare–Faced Messiah: The True Story of L. Ron Hubbard." The book contended that Hubbard and the Church of Scientology, which he founded, had glorified Hubbard's image over a period of 30 years through various embellished and distorted accounts of Hubbard's life and activities in Hubbard's own writings and in information put out by the church.

Miller relied in part on information from court records, official documents, interviews, and newspaper stories, but in many instances the evidence of alleged discrepancies, and distortions came from Hubbard's own unpublished works, such as letters and diaries. Copyright in these works was held by New Era under license from the Church of Scientology, to which Hubbard had bequeathed the rights upon his death.

New Era sought to enjoin publication of the biography in the United States. The case was decided by Judge Leval, who had tried the *Salinger* case. He believed *Bare–Faced Messiah* should be protected as fair use, but conceded that "given *Salinger's* strong presumption against fair use for unpublished materials, I cannot conclude that the Court of Appeals would accord fair use protection to all of Miller's quotations, or that the biography as a whole would be considered non-infringing." He concluded that the book contained 44 passages that would not qualify as fair use under *Salinger:*

Nevertheless, Leval exercised his equitable discretion to deny the injunction. He conceded that injunctive relief is common in copyright cases, but said those typically involve "piracy of artistic creations motivated exclusively by greed." This case was different:

> [A]n injunction would  . . .  suppress an interesting, well-researched, provocative study of a figure who, claiming both scientific and religious credentials, has wielded enormous influence over millions of people.  . . .  The abhorrence of the First Amendment to prior restraint is so powerful a force in shaping so many areas of our law, it would be anomalous to presume casually its appropriateness for all cases of copyright infringement.  . . .
>
> In the past, efforts to suppress critical biography through the copyright injunction have generally not succeeded because courts (sometimes straining) have found fair use. [ ] The conflict between freedom of speech and the injunctive remedy was thus avoided. Since *Salinger*, however, the issue is inescapable.

He concluded that New Era's damage remedy was adequate to protect its copyright interests with far less harm to First Amendment interests. 695 F.Supp. 1493 (S.D.N.Y.1988).

The Second Circuit affirmed, but only on the ground of laches. (Under the doctrine of laches, if without sufficient justification a plaintiff has delayed bringing an action, and that delay harms the defendant, then the action will be dismissed.) New Era had taken no steps to protect its rights until the book was in print, even though it had known for several years that it was being prepared. "The prejudice suffered by Holt as the result of New Era's unreasonable and inexcusable delay in bringing action invokes the bar of laches." Judge Miner wrote an extended opinion, however, in which the majority rejected Judge Leval's analysis on both the fair use and First Amendment points.

As to fair use, the court said Leval's analysis was too generous to Holt, and as a result the book was a more serious infringement than Leval had concluded. Leval had suggested that use of an author's words to make a point about his character ought to be viewed more favorably than use of an author's words to display the distinctiveness of his writing style. He also urged a distinction between uses to merely "enliven" the text and uses that are necessary to communicate significant points about the subject. The court of appeals rejected both of those suggestions, and also disagreed with Leval's conclusion that Miller's book would not affect the market for an authorized biography of Hubbard, which New Era said it planned to commission.

As for Leval's First Amendment concerns, the court was not persuaded "that any first amendment concerns not accommodated by the Copyright Act are implicated in this action. Our observation that the fair use doctrine encompasses all claims of first amendment in the copyright field [  ] has never been repudiated. See, e.g., [*Harper & Row*]. An author's expression of an idea, as distinguished from the idea itself, is not considered subject to the public's 'right to know.' [  ]."

Chief Judge Oakes concurred, but would have affirmed on the merits as well as on the laches ground. He believed there was no proof that *Bare-Faced Messiah* would impair the future market value of Hubbard's writings, that the public interest in encouraging biographical work justified denying the injunction, and that "a non-injunctive remedy provides the best balance between the copyright interests and the First Amendment interests at stake in this case."

Although Henry Holt Co. had prevailed on the laches ground, it took the unusual step of requesting rehearing *en banc* to challenge the panel's conclusions on the fair use issue. The request was denied, 7–5, but it provoked a heated exchange of opinions among the judges of the Second Circuit. 884 F.2d 659, 16 Med.L.Rptr. 2224 (1989).

Chief Judge Oakes (who, as a member of the panel, concurred only on the laches ground) and Judges Newman, Kearse, and Winter dissented from the denial of *en banc* consideration. In an opinion by Judge Newman, they said they feared the panel majority opinion would create "misunderstanding on the part of authors and publishers as to the copyright law of this Circuit—misunderstanding that risks deterring them from entirely lawful writings in the fields of scholarly research, biography, and journalism."

They said denial of the rehearing, "does not mean that this Circuit is committed to the language of the panel opinion. . . ." They specifically challenged the portion of the panel opinion refusing to distinguish between copying to enliven text and copying to make a point about the author's character. They also questioned the panel's suggestion that injunctive relief should normally be granted when infringement is threatened. "We do not believe that anything we have said in this opinion concerning fair use or injunctive relief is contrary to the views of a majority of the judges of this Court," the dissenters concluded.

Judge Miner, joined by Judges Meskill, Pierce, and Altimari (Miner and Altimari were the majority in the panel), wrote a separate opinion to comment on Judge Newman's opinion:

First, the panel majority opinion is consistent with settled law and leaves no room for misunderstanding. Second, a dissent from a denial of rehearing en banc lacks the authority to dispel misunderstanding in any event. Third, whether or not "this Circuit is committed to the language of the panel opinion," it surely is not committed to the language of the appended dissenting opinion.

On the merits, Judge Miner again rejected the proposed distinction between copying to enliven the copier's prose and copying where necessary to report a fact. He said those considerations were irrelevant once the court decided—as the panel did in *New Era*—that the purpose-of-use factor favored the copier anyway. "Moreover, I question whether judges, rather than literary critics, should decide whether literary material is used to enliven text or demonstrate truth. It is far too easy for one author to use another's work on the pretext that it is copied for the latter purpose rather than the former."

On the appropriateness of injunctive relief, Judge Miner said, "All now agree that injunction is not the automatic consequence of infringement and that equitable considerations always are germane to the determination of whether an injunction is appropriate." He said the panel majority proposed to amend its original opinion by prefacing the statement that "the copying of 'more than minimal amounts' of unpublished expressive material calls for an injunction barring the unauthorized use" with the words, "under ordinary circumstances."

f. A year later the Second Circuit was presented with another fair use question involving a biography of L. Ron Hubbard in New Era Publications International v. Carol Publishing Group, 904 F.2d 152, 17 Med.L.Rptr. 1913 (1990). An injunction had been issued against the publication of *A Piece of Blue Sky: Scientology, Dianetics and L. Ron Hubbard Exposed* by Jonathan Caven–Atack. New Era had argued that the book contained 121 passages drawn from 48 of Hubbard's published works. After finding that the copyright on one of the works quoted had expired, the district court analyzed the other disputed passages using the four fair use factors. According to the district court, the purpose and character of the use "strongly" favored New Era because "many of the passages lack any allowable fair use purpose." The nature of the copyrighted work also favored New Era because many of the quoted passages "are expressive rather than factual." The amount used in relation to the copyrighted work as a whole was still a third factor favoring New Era because the disputed passages constituted a "small, but significant element of" the book. The court found that the fourth factor, the effect of the use on the market for the copyrighted work did not favor either party. The court then issued a permanent injunction listing 103 infringing passages from 43 published works that had to be deleted before the biography could be published. 729 F.Supp. 992 (S.D.1990).

The court of appeals lifted the injunction finding that the disputed passages were a fair use. With regard to the purpose and character of the use the court held that critical biographies "fit 'comfortably within' [the] statutory categories 'of uses illustrative of uses that can be fair.' [*Salinger*]" Although the work was intended to be published for profit, the court distinguished it from *Harper & Row*:

However, what the Court [in *Harper & Row*] went on to consider was the infringer's knowing exploitation of the copyrighted material—obtained in an underhanded manner—for an undeserved economic profit. [  ] The present case, by contrast, does not involve "an attempt to rush to the market just ahead of the copyright holder's imminent publication, as occurred in *Harper & Row.*" *Salinger* [  ] Instead . . . the author uses Hubbard's works for the entirely legitimate purpose of making his point that Hubbard was a charlatan and the Church a dangerous cult. To be sure, the author and appellant want to make a profit in publishing the book. But the author's use of material "to enrich" his biography is protected fair use, "not-withstanding that he and his publisher anticipate profits." Id.

The nature of the copyrighted work also favored Carol because all of the works quoted were published works. Further the court of appeals found that the works were factual and "the scope of fair use is greater with respect to factual than non-factual works."

With regard to the third factor, the amount and substantiality of the portion used in relation to the copyrighted work, the court of appeals found that the quoted passages did not constitute too great a percentage of the works from which they were taken. Neither did they "take essentially the heart of Hubbard's works." Thus, the third factor favored Carol from both a quantitative and a qualitative standpoint.

Finally, in analyzing the effect of the biography on Hubbard's works as well as an authorized biography that New Era argued it intended to publish, the court of appeals first noted that:

> even assuming that the book discourages potential purchasers of the authorized biography, this is not necessarily actionable under the copyright laws. Such potential buyers might be put off because the book persuaded them (as it clearly hopes to) that Hubbard was a charlatan, but the copyright laws do not protect that sort of injury. Harm to the market for a copyrighted work or its derivatives caused by a "devastating critique" that "diminished sales by convincing the public that the original work was of poor quality" is not "within the scope of copyright protection." [  ]

In distinguishing this case from *Henry Holt*, the court again focused on the published nature of the works:

> . . . *New Era* involved the publication of previously unpublished material, "particularly from [Hubbard's] early diaries and journals." [  ] Arguably, then, the unfavorable biography in *New Era* threatened economic harm to the authorized biography, even though it fulfilled a different function, because it contained material whose market value (1) had not yet been realized by the copyright holder, and (2) might be entirely misappropriated by the infringing publication. Here, by contrast, the works quoted from are all published, and the book will not tap any sources of economic profit that would otherwise go to the authorized biography.

Having found all four fair use factors to favor Carol, the court of appeals concluded that the book's use of the quoted passages was a fair use and ordered the injunction lifted.

g.  In Wright v. Warner Books, Inc., 953 F.2d 731, 19 Med.L.Rptr. 1577 (2d Cir.1991), the U.S. Court of Appeals dealt with a dispute over publication of a biography of the late African–American author Richard Wright, about whom defendant Warner Books published a biography in 1988.  Wright's widow had brought a copyright infringement suit claiming unauthorized use of excerpts from Wright's unpublished letters and journals.  The Court of Appeals upheld the trial court's granting of summary judgment to the defendants.  The court believed that the second of the four fair use factors (nature of the copyrighted work) favored the plaintiff because of the *unpublished* nature of the materials, but that the first (purpose and character of the use), third (amount and substantiality of the portion used) and fourth (effect on the market) factors favored the defendants.

h.  The U.S. Court of Appeals for the Second Circuit ruled in 1993 that the book *Welcome to Twin Peaks* was not a fair use of the scripts for the television series "Twin Peaks."  The book told plot details of the series.  The court upheld a copyright infringement judgment but vacated a trademark infringement judgment.  The court said that any finding of confusion between the parties' use of "Twin Peaks" must be particularly compelling.  Twin Peaks Productions, Inc. v. Publications International, Ltd., 996 F.2d 1366, 21 Med.L.Rptr. 1545 (2d Cir.1993).

i.  Rapper Luther Campbell's parody of the late Roy Orbison's song "Oh, Pretty Woman" resulted in the copyright infringement case of Acuff–Rose Music Inc. v. Campbell, 972 F.2d 1429 (6th Cir.1992).  The Supreme Court has granted *certiorari*.  Performed by the rap group "2 Live Crew," the parody was entitled "Pretty Woman."  The Court of Appeals ruled that the parody was not a fair use, finding that three of the four fair use factors weighed against its being a fair use.  The court emphasized the "wholly commercial" nature of the parody, the fact that a "substantial portion of the essence" of the original song had been used, and the effect on the market for the original.  The rap group said the parodist "is an important part of American culture" and that existing precedent drew a "careful distinction between the parody of a musical work and the mere piracy of that work for commercial gain."  Home Box Office, Comedy Central, Fox, Inc., *Mad Magazine*, and NBC have filed an *amicus* brief in support of "2 Live Crew," arguing that a legitimate parody which is an "original artistic work that incorporates portions of the ideas and expressions of a recognizable, previously published work, altering or building on that previous work as a means of expressing criticism or comment" is entitled to protection under the First Amendment.  Broadcasting & Cable, June 7, 1993 at 86 and Media Law Reporter News Notes, July 13, 1993.

j.  Joe McGinniss's book about Sen. Edward Kennedy, *The Last Brother*, stirred controversy in the summer of 1993 after author William

Manchester said he had found 18 passages in the book that he claimed McGinniss had lifted from Manchester's own book, *The Death of a President*. Doris Kearns Goodwin said she had found examples in which McGinniss had used material from her book, *The Fitzgeralds and the Kennedys*, without proper credit. McGinniss strongly denied the plagiarism claims. In a five-page author's note, he said he relied extensively on the works of a number of authors, including Manchester and Goodwin, but that his biography of Kennedy is an original work based on his own interpretations. Controversy also swirled around McGinniss's concession that he fabricated quotations by Sen. Kennedy and other members of the family—echoing the controversy over Janet Malcolm's altering of quotations and then publishing the words within quotations marks [*Masson v. New Yorker*, p. 150, *supra*]. Despite the fact that the book is ostensibly a non-fiction work, McGinniss said in his "author's note" that he wrote "certain scenes and described certain events from what I have inferred to be [Sen. Kennedy's] point of view." The Boston Globe, July 28, 1993 at 21, and The Washington Post, Aug. 14, 1993 at A21.

4. U.S. District Court Judge Constance Baker Motley of Manhattan levied a $510,000 fine on Kinko's, the national chain of copying stores, for infringing the copyrights of publishers by photocopying and selling excerpts of books to college students. In Basic Books, Inc. v. Kinko's, a suit brought by eight publishers, Judge Motley said Kinko's had created a new business of publishing anthologies or "coursepacks" that usurped the copyrights and profits of the publishing industry. She said a large portion of the defendant's earnings have come from selling packets of book excerpts through their 200 stores nationwide. New York Times, Mar. 29, 1991 at D2.

5. In 1992 Congress amended Section 107 of the copyright statute, adding at the end of the list of four factors to be considered in determining if a use is a fair use: "The fact that a work is unpublished shall not itself bar a finding of fair use if such finding is made upon consideration of all the above factors."

6. Ten freelance writers filed a 1993 suit against several media defendants and the Mead Data Central Corporation (which runs the Nexis computerized data service) and University Microfilms International (which provides newspapers on microfilm) over the question of who controls the rights to reproduce the freelancers' articles in electronic media. New York Times, Dec. 13, 1993 at C–32.

### c. The First Amendment

The traditional view has been that if the defendant has extensively copied plaintiff's expression and cannot rely on the defense of fair use, the plaintiff would succeed in the infringement action. But some situations may exist in which, although the defendant's use of the copyrighted material cannot be justified as "fair use," the public's need to have the information is so great that *perhaps* the First Amendment would serve as a defense to an infringement action. Although such a situation would be rare because one can always use the facts and simply alter the form of expression, there may be situations in which the form of presentation cannot be paraphrased with the same effect as the original presentation.

The best examples of such a case may be photographs, such as the Zapruder photographs of the John Kennedy assassination or the photographs of the MyLai massacre in Vietnam. The best evidence for the public to have in debating the assassination or the massacre may be all of the actual photographs rather than another's attempted verbal description of what the photographs purport to show—even though the copier, by using all the photographs, exceeds the bounds of fair use. This problem may be unique to the visual representations. The subject is well discussed, using these examples, in Nimmer, "Does Copyright Abridge the First Amendment Guarantees of Free Speech and Press?," 17 U.C.L.A. L.Rev. 1180 (1970).

Another important question—one requiring a balancing of property rights and First Amendment rights—is to what extent a news organization can make unauthorized use of the research and labor of a competitor by either directly copying the work of its competitor or by "appropriating" the facts contained in a competitor's news release. Although the substance of news cannot be protected by copyright, the doctrine of unfair competition has been used to protect the gatherer of news from the direct, unauthorized reproduction of its material for commercial use. In International News Service v. Associated Press, 248 U.S. 215 (1918), I.N.S. was enjoined from copying news from A.P. bulletin boards and early editions of A.P. member newspapers until "the commercial value" of the news to the complainant and all of its members had passed. The Court found unfair competition in the taking of material acquired through the expenditure of skill, labor and money by A.P. for the purpose of diverting "a material portion of the profit" to I.N.S. Although the Court condemned the "habitual failure" of I.N.S. to give credit to A.P. as the source of its news, the misrepresentation was not considered essential to a finding of unfair competition: "It is something more than the advantage of celebrity of which complainant is being deprived."

This type of protection has been extended to other areas. Radio stations may not broadcast news items taken verbatim from a local newspaper, and a second publisher may not photograph an existing edition of a book in order to save the cost of setting type, whether or not the first edition was copyrighted. Where words and ideas are involved, the courts have been quite protective of the initiator, perhaps because of the fragile and ephemeral nature of the finished product.

The doctrine does not inhibit the traditional practice of getting "tips" or "leads" from any source and then going out to research and write the story. The courts in the A.P. case barred only the taking of news "either bodily or in substance, from bulletins issued by [AP] or any of its members, or from editions of their newspapers, 'until its commercial value as news to the complainant and all its members has passed away.' " The Supreme Court drew a distinction "between the utilization of tips and the bodily appropriation of news matter, either in its original form or after rewriting and without independent investigation and verification.   . . ."

## C.  PROBLEMS OF NEW TECHNOLOGIES

Perhaps the biggest problem Congress faced in drafting the Copyright Act of 1976 was providing for new technologies. As a result the courts are now having to answer difficult questions concerning the application of copyright law to these new technologies.

For example, in Sony Corp. v. Universal City Studios, Inc., p. 319, *supra*, the Court, 5–4, held that the use of videotape recorders did not infringe the copyrights of the producers of the programs that were copied. The majority began by noting that the "monopoly privileges that Congress may authorize are neither unlimited nor primarily designed to provide a special private benefit. Rather, the limited grant is a means by which an important public purpose may be achieved. It is intended to motivate the creative activity of authors and inventors by the provision of a special reward, and to allow the public access to the products of their genius after the limited period of exclusive control has expired."

The Court also observed that the clause assigned Congress the primary responsibility for defining the scope of protection. "Because the task involves a difficult balance between the interests of authors and inventors in the control and exploitation of their writings and discoveries on the one hand, and society's competing interest in the free flow of ideas, information, and commerce on the other hand, our patent and copyright statutes have been amended repeatedly."

In this case, dealing with a new technology, the majority stressed that the "judiciary's reluctance to expand the protections afforded by the copyright without explicit legislative guidance is a recurring theme. [  ] Sound policy, as well as history, supports our consistent deference to Congress when major technological innovations alter the market for copyrighted materials."

*Sony* provides but a single example of the problems related to copying. The technology of copying in the 1990s makes it easy to copy everything from book pages to audiotapes to computer software. Even where copy protection devices exist, people find ways to circumvent them. The results are enormous practical difficulties in the enforcement of copyright law. Technology is also an important part of another major copyright issue we will discuss in Chapter XVIII—cable television liability for the retransmission of broadcast television programming.

## D. TRADEMARKS

Trademarks and servicemarks, like copyright, protect intellectual property. Instead of protecting an entire movie script, an entire book or an entire magazine, as a copyright may, trademarks and servicemarks protect "identifying symbols"—words, names, symbols or even scents.

The distinction between trademarks and servicemarks is that trademarks are symbols that identify goods whereas servicemarks are symbols that identify services. Because the law governing trademarks and servicemarks is essentially the same, we will use "trademark" to represent both.

Registration of trademarks takes place under Congressional legislation. Unlike copyright and patents, trademarks are not specifically mentioned in the Constitution. The governing statute is the Federal Trademark Act of 1946, known as the Lanham Act after the late Rep. Fritz Garland Lanham. Registrations are filed with the United States Patent and Trademark Office.

Whether a term is eligible for trademark protection depends on how it is classified. For example, Miller Brewing was denied trademark protection for the term "LITE" because it was viewed as a descriptive term for a type of beer. "A term for which trademark protection is claimed will fit somewhere in the spectrum which ranges through (1) generic or common descriptive and (2) merely descriptive to (3) suggestive and (4) arbitrary or fanciful." Miller Brewing Co. v. G. Heileman Brewing Co., Inc., 561 F.2d 75, 79 (7th Cir.1977).

Generic terms can never become trademarks. They describe a kind of good or its ingredients, qualities or characteristics, and anyone can use them. For example, names like "Coco–Quinine" and "Quin–Coco" for liquid preparations of quinine in combination with chocolate and other things cannot be trademarks. William R. Warner & Co. v. Eli Lilly & Co., 265 U.S. 526 (1924).

"Merely descriptive" terms—those that describe a characteristic or ingredient—can become trademarks only by acquiring a secondary meaning "distinctive of the applicant's goods." "Suggestive" terms require the observer or listener to use imagination and perception to determine the nature of the goods. Abercrombie & Fitch Co. v. Hunting World, Inc., 537 F.2d 4 (2d Cir.1976), provides examples. Abercrombie & Fitch (A & F), a well-known store, had sued a competitor for infringing on several of the store's registered trademarks using the word "Safari." The court of appeals said that, although "safari" is a generic word, and A & F could not apply "safari" as a trademark for an expedition into the African wilderness or to the broad flat-brimmed hat known as a "Safari hat" or to the belted bush jacket with patch pockets known as a "Safari jacket," the store could retain its trademark protection for use of the word "Safari" in a "suggestive," as opposed to "merely descriptive," way. Examples of the latter include use of the term "Safari" in connection with luggage, portable grills, ice chests, and axes. The latter use was "suggestive" to A & F's customers, according to the court, of "a romantic notion of high style, coupled with an attractive foreign allusion."

The court of appeals in *Abercrombie & Fitch* said, "Having created the category [of "suggestive" terms] the courts have had great difficulty in defining it. Judge Learned Hand made the not very helpful statement: 'It is quite impossible to get any rule out of the cases beyond this: That the validity of the mark ends when suggestion ends and description begins.' "

The fourth category—those terms that are "arbitrary or fanciful"— is usually applied to words invented solely for their use as trademarks; in no way do they suggest or describe a characteristic or ingredient of the product.

Groups of letters, even an individual letter, can function as a trademark. If one uses an individual letter, the typestyle or design of the letter must be distinctive. It is also possible under the Lanham Act to protect unregistered names of performers or sports teams and to register titles, characters, names and "other distinctive features" of television programs.

Cartoon characters and literary characters can be protected under either copyright or trademark, depending on the use. For example, a "Superman" cartoon would be copyrighted, but "Superman" products would be trademarked.

Manufacturers, for obvious reasons, want to protect their exclusive rights to use names and symbols associated with their products. Sometimes, if they are not sufficiently vigilant in their protection of their trademarks, the trademarks enter the *public domain* and can be used by anyone. Aspirin, corn flakes, cubesteak, escalator, nylon, and cellophane are examples of trademarks that lost trademark protection or "went generic" because people came to use them as generic terms for the product as opposed to the name of a specific brand. The owners of the registered trademarks Xerox®, Weight Watchers®, Crayola®, Weed Eater®, and Kleenex®, knowing that people sometimes misuse their trademarks as though they were generic names, are among those that advertise in such magazines as *Editor & Publisher* and *Broadcasting,* emphasizing that their names are protected and should be capitalized.

Trademark owners particularly concerned about the problem emphasize the ® symbol next to their names or go to considerable lengths to emphasize that their names are brand names, as in broadcast commercials referring to "Sanka Brand" coffee.

Like copyright holders, trademark owners do not have unlimited exclusive rights to the use of their trademarks. Trademark owners are protected against uses that could cause confusion between their products or other similar products (trademark infringement), but that may be difficult to prove. For example, although the Boston Athletic Association registered the trademark "Boston Marathon" and licensed one television station to broadcast the race, it was unable to get an injunction prohibiting another station from also televising the event, because it failed to show sufficient evidence of relevant customer confusion. WCVB–TV v. Boston Athletic Association, 926 F.2d 42, 18 Med.L.Rptr. 1710 (1991). Trademark owners are also protected when they can prove that uses of their trademarks on dissimilar products might cause deterioration of the distinctive aspect of the trademarks (trademark dilution).

Noncommercial uses of trademarks are generally considered protected by the First Amendment. For example, an injunction prohibiting the publication of a parody of the L.L. Bean Catalogue pursuant to Maine's anti-dilution statute was found to violate the First Amendment. L.L. Bean, Inc. v. Drake Publishers, Inc., 811 F.2d 26, 13 Med.L.Rptr. 2009 (1st Cir.1987). L.L. Bean had argued that the parody, *L.L. Beam's Back–To–School–Sex–Catalog,* would tarnish its goodwill and reputation. The court responded:

> It offends the Constitution, however, to invoke the anti-dilution statute as a basis for enjoining the noncommercial use of a trademark by a defendant engaged in a protected form of expression . . . .
>
> > If the anti-dilution statute were construed as permitting a trademark owner to enjoin the use of his mark in a noncommercial context found to be negative or offensive, then a corporation could shield itself from criticism by forbidding the use of its name in commentaries critical of its conduct. The legitimate aim of the anti-dilution statute is to prohibit the unauthorized use of another's trademark in order to market incompatible products or services. The Constitution does not, however, permit the range of the anti-dilution statute to encompass the unauthorized use of a trademark in a noncommercial setting such as an editorial or artistic context.

Similarly, in Lucasfilm Ltd. v. High Frontier, 622 F.Supp. 931 (D.D.C.1985), the court rejected an infringement suit brought by the owners of the trademark "Star Wars" against public interest groups using the term in commercial advertisements discussing President Reagan's Strategic Defense Initiative.

In another case, the issue of ownership of the word "olympic" was argued in San Francisco Arts and Athletics, Inc. v. United States Olympic Committee, 479 U.S. 1052 (1987). The Olympic Committee had sought to bar a gay rights group from sponsoring an athletic competition called the Gay Olympics. In a 5–4 decision, the Court held that Congress had granted the Olympic committee exclusive commercial use of the word "olympic." The gay rights group had argued that by allowing "olympics" for handicapped children, police officers and others, but not for gays, the committee had enforced its trademark rights in a biased way, but Justice Powell, in the majority opinion, said that because the committee was not a government agency, it could not violate someone's constitutionally protected right to equal protection under the law.

The underlying purpose of the special protection given the word "olympic" appears to be more of an attempt to maintain dignity or "officialness" of the internationally sanctioned games, than to protect their commercial value.

In a major overhaul of the trademark system, Congress passed the Trademark Law Revision Act, 15 U.S.C.A. § 1051, *et seq.,* amending the Lanham Act. When it became law in 1989, the term of registration and renewal was reduced from 20 to 10 years. The amendments also permit a company to receive trademark protection for as much as three years before it actually sells a product or service with that mark. Companies formerly could register trademarks only when they had put them into use. Language in Section 43(a) of the Act includes a provision making misrepresentations about another's product or service—so-called product disparagement—actionable. United States Trademark Association, Government Affairs Bulletin, Vol. 43, No. 42, Oct. 21, 1988.

The latter provision is directed at some forms of comparative advertising in which rival advertisers have sometimes been accused of maligning their competitors' goods or services. As a result of compromise with media organizations worried about threats to free speech, it applies only to commercial advertising and promotion and not to political advertising or editorial commentary. New York Times, Oct. 21, 1988 at B6. Recall *L.L. Bean, supra.*

# Chapter VII

# NATIONAL SECURITY

Major questions arise over the possibility of government censorship in the interest of protecting national security. This is particularly true in wartime—whether it be the Vietnam War or the war in the Persian Gulf. The stakes are high, because disclosure of military and diplomatic secrets can cause irreparable harm to the interests of the United States. Balanced against the national security interests, however, are the interests of the citizens of a democratic country in knowing about their government's handling of military and diplomatic matters.

One of the most dramatic confrontations between the federal government and the press over the issue of national security occurred when *The New York Times* published excerpts from the top secret "Pentagon Papers." A relatively inconspicuous three-column headline on the front page—"Vietnam Archive: Pentagon Study Traces 3 Decades of Growing U.S. Involvement"—opened the drama on June 13, 1971. Not only was it a Sunday, but it was the day after President Richard Nixon's daughter Tricia had been married in the Rose Garden at the White House, and few government officials were in their offices. *Times* reporter Neil Sheehan wrote about a 7,000–page study commissioned by the government, and three pages of documentary material from the papers appeared elsewhere in the paper.

By Monday the Attorney General of the United States had taken the extraordinary step of sending a telegram to the publisher of the *Times* advising that publication was prohibited by the espionage law under which spies are prosecuted. *The Times* had already concluded that the espionage law did not apply to newspaper publication, and that—even if it could be demonstrated that its drafters intended for it to apply to the press—it would be an unconstitutional prior restraint.

To the attorney general's telegram (". . . I respectfully request that you publish no further information of this character."), the *Times* responded that it ". . . must respectfully decline the request . . . believing that it is in the best interest of the people of this country to be informed of the material."

The strained pleasantries out of the way, the government moved in federal district court in New York for a restraint on the *Times*. The date was June 15, and three installments had already been published. The trial judge temporarily restrained publication while he considered the case. Because the *Washington Post* also had obtained copies of the "Pentagon Papers," the government sought a restraint on the *Post* in a separate action in federal district court in the District of Columbia. The two cases moved with extraordinary speed. Both district courts ruled in favor of the newspapers. The court of appeals in the *Times* case ruled for the government, but the court of appeals in the *Post* case ruled for the newspaper. The Supreme Court handled the case on an expedited basis and handed down the opinion below on June 30—just 15 days after the imposition of the first restraint and only four days after the oral argument. Note that all nine justices wrote opinions.

Recall the discussion in Chapter II about the presumed unconstitutionality of prior restraints on the press after the 1931 decision in *Near*, p. 55, *supra*. *Near* did not involve government secrets. Nor did *Bantam Books*, p. 57, *supra*, (a case holding that a Rhode Island commission's advising against distribution of allegedly obscene and indecent publications was an unconstitutional restraint) or *Organization for a Better Austin*, p. 58, *supra*, (a case in which a Chicago real estate agent attempted to stop distribution of leaflets criticizing him, and it was held that such a restraint was an unconstitutional restraint). But all of those cases are cited in the brief *per curiam* (unsigned) opinion of the Court.

### NEW YORK TIMES CO. v. UNITED STATES

Supreme Court of the United States, 1971.
403 U.S. 713, 91 S.Ct. 2140, 29 L.Ed.2d 822, 1 Med.L.Rptr. 1031.

PER CURIAM.

We granted certiorari in these cases in which the United States seeks to enjoin the New York Times and the Washington Post from publishing the contents of a classified study entitled "History of U.S. Decision–Making Process on Viet Nam Policy." [ ]

"Any system of prior restraints of expression comes to this Court bearing a heavy presumption against its constitutional validity." [*Bantam Books*]; see also [*Near*]. The Government "thus carries a heavy burden of showing justification for the imposition of such a restraint." Organization for a Better Austin v. Keefe, 402 U.S. 415, 419 (1971). The District Court for the Southern District of New York in the *New York Times* case and the District Court for the District of Columbia and the Court of Appeals for the District of Columbia Circuit in the *Washington Post* case held that the Government had not met that burden. We agree.

The judgment of the Court of Appeals for the District of Columbia Circuit is therefore affirmed. The order of the Court of Appeals for the Second Circuit is reversed and the case is remanded with directions to enter a judgment affirming the judgment of the District Court for the Southern District of New York. The stays entered June 25, 1971, by the Court are vacated. The judgments shall issue forthwith.

So ordered.

MR. JUSTICE BLACK, with whom MR. JUSTICE DOUGLAS joins, concurring.

I adhere to the view that the Government's case against the Washington Post should have been dismissed and that the injunction against the New York Times should have been vacated without oral argument when the cases were first presented to this Court. I believe that every moment's continuance of the injunctions against these newspapers amounts to a flagrant, indefensible, and continuing violation of the First Amendment. Furthermore, after oral argument, I agree completely that we must affirm the judgment of the Court of Appeals for the District of Columbia Circuit and reverse the judgment of the Court of Appeals for the Second Circuit for the reasons stated by my Brothers Douglas and Brennan. In my view it is unfortunate that some of my Brethren are apparently willing to hold that the publication of news may sometimes be enjoined. Such a holding would make a shambles of the First Amendment.

. . .

In other words, we are asked to hold that despite the First Amendment's emphatic command, the Executive Branch, the Congress, and the Judiciary can make laws enjoining publication of current news and abridging freedom of the press in the name of "national security." The Government does not even attempt to rely on any act of Congress. Instead it makes the bold and dangerously far-reaching contention that the courts should take it upon themselves to "make" a law abridging freedom of the press in the name of equity, presidential power and national security, even when the representatives of the people in Congress have adhered to the command of the First Amendment and refused to make such a law. . . . To find that the President has "inherent power" to halt the publication of news by resort to the courts would wipe out the First Amendment and destroy the fundamental liberty and security of the very people the Government hopes to make "secure." No one can read the history of the adoption of the First Amendment without being convinced beyond any doubt that it was injunctions like those sought here that Madison and his collaborators intended to outlaw in this Nation for all time.

The word "security" is a broad, vague generality whose contours should not be invoked to abrogate the fundamental law embodied in the First Amendment. The guarding of military and diplomatic secrets at the expense of informed representative government provides no real security for our Republic. The Framers of the First Amendment, fully aware of both the need to defend a new nation and the abuses of the English and Colonial governments, sought to give this new society strength and security by providing that freedom of speech, press, religion, and assembly should not be abridged. . . .

MR. JUSTICE DOUGLAS, with whom MR. JUSTICE BLACK joins, concurring.

While I join the opinion of the Court I believe it necessary to express my views more fully.

It should be noted at the outset that the First Amendment provides that "Congress shall make no law . . . abridging the freedom of speech, or of the press." That leaves, in my view, no room for governmental restraint on the press.

There is, moreover, no statute barring the publication by the press of the material which the Times and the Post seek to use. Title 18 U.S.C. § 793(e) provides that "[w]hoever having unauthorized possession of, access to, or control over any document, writing . . . or information relating to the national defense which information the possessor has reason to believe could be used to the injury of the United States or to the advantage of any foreign nation, willfully communicates . . . the same to any person not entitled to receive it . . . [s]hall be fined not more than $10,000 or imprisoned not more than ten years, or both."

The Government suggests that the word "communicates" is broad enough to encompass publication.

There are eight sections in the chapter on espionage and censorship, §§ 792–799. In three of those eight "publish" is specifically mentioned: § 794(b) applies to "Whoever, in time of war, with intent that the same shall be communicated to the enemy, collects, records, *publishes,* or communicates . . . [the disposition of armed forces]."

Section 797 applies to whoever "reproduces, *publishes,* sells, or gives away" photographs of defense installations.

Section 798 relating to cryptography applies to whoever: "communicates, furnishes, transmits, or otherwise makes available . . . *or publishes*" the described material. (Emphasis added.)

Thus it is apparent that Congress was capable of and did distinguish between publishing and communication in the various sections of the Espionage Act.

. . .

So any power that the Government possesses must come from its "inherent power."

The power to wage war is "the power to wage war successfully." See Hirabayashi v. United States, 320 U.S. 81, 93 (1943). But the war power stems from a declaration of war. The Constitution by Art. I, § 8, gives Congress, not the President, power "[t]o declare War." Nowhere are presidential wars authorized. We need not decide therefore what leveling effect the war power of Congress might have.

These disclosures [3] may have a serious impact. But that is no basis for sanctioning a previous restraint on the press. . . .

. . .

**3.** There are numerous sets of this material in existence and they apparently are not under any controlled custody. Moreover, the President has sent a set to the Congress. We start then with a case where there already is rather wide distribution of the material that is destined for publicity, not secrecy. I have gone over the material listed in the *in camera* brief of the United States. It is all history, not future events. None of it is more recent than 1968.

The Government says that it has inherent powers to go into court and obtain an injunction to protect the national interest, which in this case is alleged to be national security. Near v. Minnesota, [ ], repudiated that expansive doctrine in no uncertain terms.

The dominant purpose of the First Amendment was to prohibit the widespread practice of governmental suppression of embarrassing information. It is common knowledge that the First Amendment was adopted against the widespread use of the common law of seditious libel to punish the dissemination of material that is embarrassing to the powers-that-be. [ ] The present cases will, I think, go down in history as the most dramatic illustration of that principle. A debate of large proportions goes on in the Nation over our posture in Vietnam. That debate antedated the disclosure of the contents of the present documents. The latter are highly relevant to the debate in progress.

Secrecy in government is fundamentally anti-democratic, perpetuating bureaucratic errors. Open debate and discussion of public issues are vital to our national health. On public questions there should be "uninhibited, robust, and wide-open" debate. [ ]

. . .

MR. JUSTICE BRENNAN, concurring.

. . .

The error that has pervaded these cases from the outset was the granting of any injunctive relief whatsoever, interim or otherwise. The entire thrust of the Government's claim throughout these cases has been that publication of the material sought to be enjoined "could," or "might," or "may" prejudice the national interest in various ways. But the First Amendment tolerates absolutely no prior judicial restraints of the press predicated upon surmise or conjecture that untoward consequences may result.* Our cases, it is true, have indicated that there is a single, extremely narrow class of cases in which the First Amendment's ban on prior judicial restraint may be overridden. Our cases have thus far indicated that such cases may arise only when the Nation "is at war," Schenck v. United States, [ ], during which times "[n]o one would question but that a government might prevent actual obstruction to its recruiting service or the publication of the sailing dates of transports or the number and location of troops." Near v. Minnesota, [ ]. Even if the present world situation were assumed to be tantamount to a time of war, or if the power of presently available armaments would justify even in peacetime the suppression of information that would set in motion a nuclear holocaust, in neither of these actions has the

---

* Freedman v. Maryland, 380 U.S. 51 (1965), and similar cases regarding temporary restraints of allegedly obscene materials are not in point. For those cases rest upon the proposition that "obscenity is not protected by the freedoms of speech and press." Roth v. United States, 354 U.S. 476, 481 (1957). Here there is no question but that the material sought to be suppressed is within the protection of the First Amendment; the only question is whether, notwithstanding that fact, its publication may be enjoined for a time because of the presence of an overwhelming national interest. . . .

Government presented or even alleged that publication of items from or based upon the material at issue would cause the happening of an event of that nature.   .   .   .

MR. JUSTICE STEWART, with whom MR. JUSTICE WHITE joins, concurring.

.   .   .

In the absence of the governmental checks and balances present in other areas of our national life, the only effective restraint upon executive policy and power in the areas of national defense and international affairs may lie in an enlightened citizenry—in an informed and critical public opinion which alone can here protect the values of democratic government.  For this reason it is perhaps here that a press that is alert, aware, and free most vitally serves the basic purpose of the First Amendment.  For without an informed and free press there cannot be an enlightened people.

Yet it is elementary that the successful conduct of international diplomacy and the maintenance of an effective national defense require both confidentiality and secrecy.   .   .   .

I think there can be but one answer to this dilemma, if dilemma it be.  The responsibility must be where the power is.  If the Constitution gives the Executive a large degree of unshared power in the conduct of foreign affairs and the maintenance of our national defense, then under the Constitution the Executive must have the largely unshared duty to determine and preserve the degree of internal security necessary to exercise that power successfully.   .   .   .

This is not to say that Congress and the courts have no role to play. Undoubtedly Congress has the power to enact specific and appropriate criminal laws to protect government property and preserve government secrets.  Congress has passed such laws, and several of them are of very colorable relevance to the apparent circumstances of these cases.  And if a criminal prosecution is instituted, it will be the responsibility of the courts to decide the applicability of the criminal law under which the charge is brought.  Moreover, if Congress should pass a specific law authorizing civil proceedings in this field, the courts would likewise have the duty to decide the constitutionality of such a law as well as its applicability to the facts proved.

But in the cases before us we are asked neither to construe specific regulations nor to apply specific laws.  We are asked, instead, to perform a function that the Constitution gave to the Executive, not the Judiciary. We are asked, quite simply, to prevent the publication by two newspapers of material that the Executive Branch insists should not, in the national interest, be published.  I am convinced that the Executive is correct with respect to some of the documents involved.  But I cannot say that disclosure of any of them will surely result in direct, immediate, and irreparable damage to our Nation or its people.  That being so, there can under the First Amendment be but one judicial resolution of the issues before us.  I join the judgments of the Court.

Mr. Justice White, with whom Mr. Justice Stewart joins, concurring.

I concur in today's judgments, but only because of the concededly extraordinary protection against prior restraints enjoyed by the press under our constitutional system. I do not say that in no circumstances would the First Amendment permit an injunction against publishing information about government plans or operations.[1] Nor, after examining the materials the Government characterizes as the most sensitive and destructive, can I deny that revelation of these documents will do substantial damage to public interests. Indeed, I am confident that their disclosure will have that result. But I nevertheless agree that the United States has not satisfied the very heavy burden that it must meet to warrant an injunction against publication in these cases, at least in the absence of express and appropriately limited congressional authorization for prior restraints in circumstances such as these.

. . .

At least in the absence of legislation by Congress, based on its own investigations and findings, I am quite unable to agree that the inherent powers of the Executive and the courts reach so far as to authorize remedies having such sweeping potential for inhibiting publications by the press. Much of the difficulty inheres in the "grave and irreparable danger" standard suggested by the United States. If the United States were to have judgment under such a standard in these cases, our decision would be of little guidance to other courts in other cases, for the material at issue here would not be available from the Court's opinion or from public records, nor would it be published by the press. . . .

It is not easy to reject the proposition urged by the United States and to deny relief on its good-faith claims in these cases that publication will work serious damage to the country. But that discomfiture is considerably dispelled by the infrequency of prior-restraint cases. Normally, publication will occur and the damage be done before the Government has either opportunity or grounds for suppression. So here, publication has already begun and a substantial part of the threatened

---

1. The Congress has authorized a strain of prior restraints against private parties in certain instances. The National Labor Relations Board routinely issues cease-and-desist orders against employers who it finds have threatened or coerced employees in the exercise of protected rights. See 29 U.S.C. § 160(c). Similarly, the Federal Trade Commission is empowered to impose cease-and-desist orders against unfair methods of competition. 15 U.S.C. § 45(b). Such orders can, and quite often do, restrict what may be spoken or written under certain circumstances. See, e.g., NLRB v. Gissel Packing Co., 395 U.S. 575, 616–620 (1969). Article I, § 8, of the Constitution authorizes Congress to secure the "exclusive right" of authors to their writings, and no one denies that a newspaper can proper-

ly be enjoined from publishing the copyrighted works of another. See Westermann Co. v. Dispatch Printing Co., 249 U.S. 100 (1919). Newspapers do themselves rely from time to time on the copyright as a means of protecting their accounts of important events. However, those enjoined under the statutes relating to the National Labor Relations Board and the Federal Trade Commission are private parties, not the press; and when the press is enjoined under the copyright laws the complainant is a private copyright holder enforcing a private right. These situations are quite distinct from the Government's request for an injunction against publishing information about the affairs of government, a request admittedly not based on any statute.

damage has already occurred.   The fact of a massive breakdown in
security is known, access to the documents by many unauthorized people
is undeniable, and the efficacy of equitable relief against these or other
newspapers to avert anticipated damage is doubtful at best.

. . . .

The Criminal Code contains numerous provisions potentially relevant to these cases.   Section 797 [5] makes it a crime to publish certain
photographs of drawings of military installations.   Section 798,[6] also in
precise language, proscribes knowing and willful publication of any
classified information concerning the cryptographic systems or communication intelligence activities of the United States as well as any information obtained from communication intelligence operations.[7]   If any of the
material here at issue is of this nature, the newspapers are presumably
now in full notice of the position of the United States and must face the
consequences if they publish.   I would have no difficulty in sustaining
convictions under these sections on facts that would not justify the
intervention of equity and the imposition of a prior restraint.

The same would be true under those sections of the Criminal Code
casting a wider net to protect the national defense.   Section 793(e)
makes it a criminal act for any unauthorized possessor of a document
"relating to the national defense" either (1) willfully to communicate or
cause to be communicated that document to any person not entitled to

**5.**   Title 18 U.S.C. § 797 provides:

"On and after thirty days from the
date upon which the President defines
any vital military or naval installation or
equipment as being within the category
contemplated under section 795 of this
title, whoever reproduces, publishes, sells,
or gives away any photograph, sketch,
picture, drawing, map, or graphical representation of the vital military or naval
installations or equipment so defined,
without first obtaining permission of the
commanding officer of the military or naval post, camp, or station concerned, or
higher authority, unless such photograph,
sketch, picture, drawing, map, or graphical representation has clearly indicated
thereon that it has been censored by the
proper military or naval authority, shall
be fined not more than $1,000 or impris-
oned not more than one year or both."

**6.**   In relevant part 18 U.S.C. § 798 provides:

"(a) Whoever knowingly and willfully
communicates, furnishes, transmits, or
otherwise makes available to an unauthorized person, or publishes, or uses in any
manner prejudicial to the safety or interest of the United States or for the benefit
of any foreign government to the detriment of the United States any classified
information—

"(1) concerning the nature, preparation, or use of any code, cipher, or
cryptographic system of the United
States or any foreign government;  or

"(2) concerning the design, construction, use, maintenance, or repair of any
device, apparatus, or appliance used or
prepared or planned for use by the
United States or any foreign government for cryptographic or communication intelligence purposes;  or

"(3) concerning the communication
intelligence activities of the United
States or any foreign government;  or

"(4) obtained by the process of communication intelligence from the communications of any foreign government, knowing the same to have been
obtained by such processes.

"Shall be fined not more than $10,000
or imprisoned not more than ten years,
or both."

**7.**   The purport of 18 U.S.C. § 798 is
clear.   . . . .

Section 798 obviously was intended to
cover publications by non-employees of the
Government and to ease the Government's
burden in obtaining convictions.

receive it or (2) willfully to retain the document and fail to deliver it to an officer of the United States entitled to receive it. The subsection was added in 1950 because pre-existing law provided no penalty for the unauthorized possessor unless demand for the documents was made. "The dangers surrounding the unauthorized possession of such items are self-evident, and it is deemed advisable to require their surrender in such a case, regardless of demand, especially since their unauthorized possession may be unknown to the authorities who would otherwise make the demand." S.Rep. No. 2369, pt. 1, 81st Cong., 2d Sess., 9 (1950). . . .[10]

It is thus clear that Congress has addressed itself to the problems of protecting the security of the country and the national defense from unauthorized disclosure of potentially damaging information. [ ] It has not, however, authorized the injunctive remedy against threatened publication. It has apparently been satisfied to rely on criminal sanctions and their deterrent effect on the responsible as well as the irresponsible press. I am not, of course, saying that either of these newspapers has yet committed a crime or that either would commit a crime if it published all the material now in its possession. That matter must await resolution in the context of a criminal proceeding if one is instituted by the United States. In that event, the issue of guilt or innocence would be determined by procedures and standards quite different from those that have purported to govern these injunctive proceedings.

MR. JUSTICE MARSHALL, concurring.

. . .

In these cases there is no problem concerning the President's power to classify information as "secret" or "top secret." Congress has specifically recognized Presidential authority, which has been formally exercised in Exec.Order 10501 (1953), to classify documents and information. See, e.g., 18 U.S.C. § 798; 50 U.S.C. § 783. Nor is there any issue here regarding the President's power as Chief Executive and Commander in Chief to protect national security by disciplining employees who disclose information and by taking precautions to prevent leaks.

. . .

It would, however, be utterly inconsistent with the concept of separation of powers for this Court to use its power of contempt to prevent behavior that Congress has specifically declined to prohibit. There would be a similar damage to the basic concept of these co-equal branches of Government if when the Executive Branch has adequate authority granted by Congress to protect "national security" it can

---

**10.** Also relevant is 18 U.S.C. § 794. Subsection (b) thereof forbids in time of war the collection or publication, with intent that it shall be communicated to the enemy, of any information with respect to the movements of military forces, "or with respect to the plans or conduct . . . of any naval or military operations . . . or any other information relating to the public defense, which might be useful to the enemy. . . ."

choose instead to invoke the contempt power of a court to enjoin the threatened conduct.   The Constitution provides that Congress shall make laws, the President execute laws, and courts interpret laws. Youngstown Sheet & Tube Co. v. Sawyer, 343 U.S. 579 (1952).   It did not provide for government by injunction in which the courts and the Executive Branch can "make law" without regard to the action of Congress.   It may be more convenient for the Executive Branch if it need only convince a judge to prohibit conduct rather than ask the Congress to pass a law, and it may be more convenient to enforce a contempt order than to seek a criminal conviction in a jury trial. Moreover, it may be considered politically wise to get a court to share the responsibility for arresting those who the Executive Branch has probable cause to believe are violating the law.   But convenience and political considerations of the moment do not justify a basic departure from the principles of our system of government.

. . .

MR. CHIEF JUSTICE BURGER, dissenting.

So clear are the constitutional limitations on prior restraint against expression, that from the time of [*Near*], until recently in [*Organization for a Better Austin*], we have had little occasion to be concerned with cases involving prior restraints against news reporting on matters of public interest.   There is, therefore, little variation among the members of the Court in terms of resistance to prior restraints against publication. Adherence to this basic constitutional principle however, does not make these cases simple.   In these cases, the imperative of a free and unfettered press comes into collision with another imperative, the effective functioning of a complex modern government and specifically the effective exercise of certain constitutional powers of the Executive.   Only those who view the First Amendment as an absolute in all circumstances—a view I respect, but reject—can find such cases as these to be simple or easy.

These cases are not simple for another and more immediate reason. We do not know the facts of the cases.   No District Judge knew all the facts.   No Court of Appeals judge knew all the facts.   No member of this Court knows all the facts.

Why are we in this posture, in which only those judges to whom the First Amendment is absolute and permits of no restraint in any circumstances or for any reason, are really in a position to act?

I suggest we are in this posture because these cases have been conducted in unseemly haste.   . . .

. . .

It is not disputed that the Times has had unauthorized possession of the documents for three to four months, during which it has had its expert analysts studying them, presumably digesting them and preparing the material for publication.   During all of this time, the Times, presumably in its capacity as trustee of the public's "right to know," has held up publication for purposes it considered proper and thus public knowledge was delayed. No doubt this was for a good reason; the analysis of 7,000 pages of complex material drawn from a vastly greater volume of material would inevitably take time and the writing of good news stories takes time. But why should the United States Government, from whom this information was illegally acquired by someone, along with all the counsel, trial judges, and appellate judges be placed under needless pressure? After these months of deferral, the alleged "right to know" has somehow and suddenly become a right that must be vindicated instanter.

. . .

The consequence of all this melancholy series of events is that we literally do not know what we are acting on. As I see it, we have been forced to deal with litigation concerning rights of great magnitude without an adequate record, and surely without time for adequate treatment either in the prior proceedings or in this Court. It is interesting to note that counsel on both sides, in oral argument before this Court, were frequently unable to respond to questions on factual points. Not surprisingly they pointed out that they had been working literally "around the clock" and simply were unable to review the documents that give rise to these cases and were not familiar with them. This Court is in no better posture. I agree generally with Mr. Justice Harlan and Mr. Justice Blackmun but I am not prepared to reach the merits.[3]

I would affirm the Court of Appeals for the Second Circuit and allow the District Court to complete the trial aborted by our grant of certiorari, meanwhile preserving the status quo in the *Post* case. I would direct that the District Court on remand give priority to the *Times* case to the exclusion of all other business of that court but I would not set arbitrary deadlines.

I should add that I am in general agreement with much of what Mr. Justice White has expressed with respect to penal sanctions concerning communication or retention of documents or information relating to the national defense.

We all crave speedier judicial processes but when judges are pressured as in these cases the result is a parody of the judicial function.

MR. JUSTICE HARLAN, with whom THE CHIEF JUSTICE and MR. JUSTICE BLACKMUN join, dissenting.

These cases forcefully call to mind the wise admonition of Mr. Justice Holmes, dissenting in Northern Securities Co. v. United States, 193 U.S. 197, 400–401 (1904):

**3.** With respect to the question of inherent power of the Executive to classify papers, records, and documents as secret, or otherwise unavailable for public exposure, and to secure aid of the courts for enforcement, there may be an analogy with respect to this Court. No statute gives this Court express power to establish and enforce the utmost security measures for the secrecy of our deliberations and records. Yet I have little doubt as to the inherent power of the Court to protect the confidentiality of its internal operations by whatever judicial measures may be required.

"Great cases like hard cases make bad law. For great cases are
called great, not by reason of their real importance in shaping the
law of the future, but because of some accident of immediate
overwhelming interest which appeals to the feelings and distorts the
judgment. These immediate interests exercise a kind of hydraulic
pressure which makes what previously was clear seem doubtful, and
before which even well settled principles of law will bend."

With all respect, I consider that the Court has been almost irresponsibly
feverish in dealing with these cases.

Both the Court of Appeals for the Second Circuit and the Court of
Appeals for the District of Columbia Circuit rendered judgment on June
23. The New York Times' petition for certiorari, its motion for accelerated consideration thereof, and its application for interim relief were
filed in this Court on June 24 at about 11 a.m. The application of the
United States for interim relief in the *Post* case was also filed here on
June 24 at about 7:15 p.m. This Court's order setting a hearing before
us on June 26 at 11 a.m., a course which I joined only to avoid the
possibility of even more peremptory action by the Court, was issued less
than 24 hours before. The record in the *Post* case was filed with the
Clerk shortly before 1 p.m. on June 25; the record in the *Times* case did
not arrive until 7 or 8 o'clock that same night. The briefs of the parties
were received less than two hours before argument on June 26.

This frenzied train of events took place in the name of the presumption against prior restraints created by the First Amendment. Due
regard for the extraordinarily important and difficult questions involved
in these litigations should have led the Court to shun such a precipitate
timetable. In order to decide the merits of these cases properly, some or
all of the following questions should have been faced:

1. Whether the Attorney General is authorized to bring these
suits in the name of the United States. . . .

2. Whether the First Amendment permits the federal courts to
enjoin publication of stories which would present a serious threat to
national security. See [*Near*], (dictum).

3. Whether the threat to publish highly secret documents is of
itself a sufficient implication of national security to justify an
injunction on the theory that regardless of the contents of the
documents harm enough results simply from the demonstration of
such a breach of secrecy.

4. Whether the unauthorized disclosure of any of these particular documents would seriously impair the national security.

5. What weight should be given to the opinion of high officers
in the Executive Branch of the Government with respect to questions 3 and 4.

6. Whether the newspapers are entitled to retain and use the
documents notwithstanding the seemingly uncontested facts that
the documents, or the originals of which they are duplicates, were

purloined from the Government's possession and that the newspapers received them with knowledge that they had been feloniously acquired. Cf. Liberty Lobby, Inc. v. Pearson, 129 U.S.App.D.C. 74, 390 F.2d 489 (1967, amended 1968).

7. Whether the threatened harm to the national security or the Government's possessory interest in the documents justifies the issuance of an injunction against publication in light of—

     a. The strong First Amendment policy against prior restraints on publication;

     b. The doctrine against enjoining conduct in violation of criminal statutes; and

     c. The extent to which the materials at issue have apparently already been otherwise disseminated.

These are difficult questions of fact, of law, and of judgment; the potential consequences of erroneous decision are enormous. The time which has been available to us, to the lower courts, and to the parties has been wholly inadequate for giving these cases the kind of consideration they deserve. It is a reflection on the stability of the judicial process that these great issues—as important as any that have arisen during my time on the Court—should have been decided under the pressures engendered by the torrent of publicity that has attended these litigations from their inception.

Forced as I am to reach the merits of these cases, I dissent from the opinion and judgments of the Court. Within the severe limitations imposed by the time constraints under which I have been required to operate, I can only state my reasons in telescoped form, even though in different circumstances I would have felt constrained to deal with the cases in the fuller sweep indicated above.

   . . .

   . . . It is plain to me that the scope of the judicial function in passing upon the activities of the Executive Branch of the Government in the field of foreign affairs is very narrowly restricted. This view is, I think, dictated by the concept of separation of powers upon which our constitutional system rests.

   . . .

The power to evaluate the "pernicious influence" of premature disclosure is not, however, lodged in the Executive alone. I agree that, in performance of its duty to protect the values of the First Amendment against political pressures, the judiciary must review the initial Executive determination to the point of satisfying itself that the subject matter of the dispute does lie within the proper compass of the President's foreign relations power. Constitutional considerations forbid "a complete abandonment of judicial control." Cf. United States v. Reynolds, 345 U.S. 1, 8 (1953). Moreover, the judiciary may properly insist that the determination that disclosure of the subject matter would irreparably impair the national security be made by the head of the Executive Department concerned—here the Secretary of State or the Secretary of Defense—after actual personal consideration by that officer. This safeguard is required in the analogous area of executive claims of privilege for secrets of state. [  ]

But in my judgment the judiciary may not properly go beyond these two inquiries and redetermine for itself the probable impact of disclosure on the national security.   . . .

Even if there is some room for the judiciary to override the executive determination, it is plain that the scope of review must be exceedingly narrow. I can see no indication in the opinions of either the District Court or the Court of Appeals in the *Post* litigation that the conclusions of the Executive were given even the deference owing to an administrative agency, much less that owing to a co-equal branch of the Government operating within the field of its constitutional prerogative.

. . .

MR. JUSTICE BLACKMUN, dissenting.

I join MR. JUSTICE HARLAN in his dissent. I also am in substantial accord with much that MR. JUSTICE WHITE says, by way of admonition, in the latter part of his opinion.

. . .

With such respect as may be due to the contrary view, this, in my opinion, is not the way to try a lawsuit of this magnitude and asserted importance.   . . .

The First Amendment, after all, is only one part of an entire Constitution. Article II of the great document vests in the Executive Branch primary power over the conduct of foreign affairs and places in that branch the responsibility for the Nation's safety. Each provision of the Constitution is important, and I cannot subscribe to a doctrine of unlimited absolutism for the First Amendment at the cost of downgrading other provisions. First Amendment absolutism has never commanded a majority of this Court. See for example, [*Near*], and [*Schenck*]. What is needed here is a weighing, upon properly developed standards, of the broad right of the press to print and of the very narrow right of the Government to prevent. Such standards are not yet developed. The parties here are in disagreement as to what those standards should be. But even the newspapers concede that there are situations where restraint is in order and is constitutional.   . . .

. . .

I strongly urge, and sincerely hope that these two newspapers will be fully aware of their ultimate responsibilities to the United States of America. Judge Wilkey, dissenting in the District of Columbia case, after a review of only the affidavits before his court (the basic papers had not then been made available by either party), concluded that there were a number of examples of documents that, if in the possession of the Post, and if published, "could clearly result in great harm to the nation," and he defined "harm" to mean "the death of soldiers, the destruction of alliances, the greatly increased difficulty of negotiation with our enemies, the inability of our diplomats to negotiate. . . ." I, for one, have now been able to give at least some cursory study not only to the affidavits, but to the material itself. I regret to say that from this examination I fear that Judge Wilkey's statements have possible foundation. I therefore share his concern. I hope that damage has not already been done. If, however, damage has been done, and if, with the Court's action today, these newspapers proceed to publish the critical documents and there results therefrom "the death of soldiers, the destruction of alliances, the greatly increased difficulty of negotiation with our enemies, the inability of our diplomats to negotiate," to which list I might add the factors of prolongation of the war and of further delay in the freeing of United States prisoners, then the Nation's people will know where the responsibility for these sad consequences rests.

## Notes and Questions

1. How many votes might have shifted had Congress enacted a statute explicitly authorizing the government to seek an injunction to bar release of information once the Attorney General determined that release would pose a "grave and immediate danger" to national security?

2. How many votes might have shifted if a criminal statute explicitly covering the behavior of the newspapers in this case rendered them subject to criminal prosecution? Would prosecution under such a statute have raised other constitutional questions?

3. Louis Henkin, in "The Right to Know and the Duty to Withhold: The Case of the Pentagon Papers," 120 U.Pa.L.Rev. 271 (1971), criticized the emphasis on the distinction between enjoining speech and punishing it after the fact because "while a criminal penalty more readily permits 'civil disobedience,' or reliance on the jury to acquit, stiff penalties will deter—and deny the right to know—almost as effectively as any injunction." In this case what are the differences between enjoining and punishing afterward?

4. Henkin had another criticism of the decision (278–80):

> More important, the upshot of the Court's apparent constitutional doctrine is unsatisfying. For, as regards governmental documents and information, the Constitution is apparently interpreted as ordaining that a branch of government can properly conceal even from other branches, surely from the public; but the Press is free to try to uncover, and if it succeeds it is free to publish. That kind of trial by battle and cleverness between the three estates and the fourth hardly seems the way best to further the various aims of a democratic society. It does not ensure that what should be concealed will not be uncovered. And, on the other hand, the rare, haphazard, fortuitous, journalistic uncovering will hardly achieve effective public knowledge of all that should be known, for almost all

that is concealed (needfully or not) will continue to be effectively withheld. (That some bits of it are sometimes selectively revealed by official "leaks" to chosen journalists only underscores the haphazard quality of what is disclosed.)

Nor does the implication that the courts will be available to adjust the competing interests promise an effective accommodation. The difficulty is not with judicial balancing in principle: that, we have accepted (*pace* Mr. Justice Black), is what the Constitution orders even as regards the "preferred freedoms" of the first amendment. But, one may ask, can courts meaningfully weigh the Government's "need" to conceal, the Press's "need" to publish, the people's "need" to know? If, on the one hand, the need for military secrecy in time of war seems obvious and paramount; if, on the other hand, as in the *Pentagon Papers* Case, many could not see why the Government should conceal documents several years old relating to an issue that had become of great national moment; who can meaningfully weigh the less obvious, less dramatic consequences of disclosure of any one of millions of documents that are the stuff of governing and of international relations? . . .

But public knowledge will not flourish even if the Court continues to insist that the Constitution requires judicial review of the Government's determination that national interest in concealment outweighs the freedom of the Press to publish. Inevitably the courts will have to legislate gross categories ("diplomatic correspondence," "internal memoranda") and even then virtually rubber stamp (and legitimate) governmental concealment. In the result, there will be few instances of Press uncovering and divulging, few cases in which the Executive will seek to bar or punish publication, few cases in which the Court will in fact reverse the Executive.

. . .

There is no happy solution, only the eternal cry and quest for better government. But surely Congress and the President could do more than they have done. The *Pentagon Papers* Case has dramatized issues, admonished bureaucrats, and created an atmosphere receptive to a major effort to increase public and scholarly knowledge even while reinforcing secrecy where it is necessary. There is need for measures to rebuild confidence in government, including confidence in its policies of disclosure and concealment. At least there ought to be provision for automatic declassification of many categories of documents, putting the burden on the bureaucracy to determine and maintain the need for reclassifying. Until Congress and Presidents turn a hard face to unnecessary classification, bureaucrats will not learn the habit of disclosure. The unhappy game of trial by cleverness between Executive and Press with an infrequent journalistic success will do little to support the people's right to know when Government abuses its responsibility to withhold.

5.   Is the Chief Justice correct in suggesting an analogy between the "Pentagon Papers" case and the Supreme Court's power to protect the confidentiality of its internal operations?

6.   Note that the pivotal opinions of Justices Stewart, White and Marshall stress the absence of Congressional authorization for the action. In non-First Amendment cases, that has not been as great a concern. Youngstown Sheet & Tube Co. v. Sawyer, 343 U.S. 579 (1952).

7.   Many who had hoped for a definitive ruling on the legitimacy of "prior restraint" were disappointed with the strategy of Alexander Bickel, who argued the case for the *New York Times*.   A lawyer who represented the *Washington Post* explained the litigation strategy in Godofsky, "Protection of the Press From Prior Restraint and Harassment Under Libel Laws," 29 U.Miami L.Rev. 462, 471–72 (1975):

> I am aware of the fact that members of academia and others have criticized those who briefed and argued this case in the Supreme Court because none of us urged adoption of a rule which would prohibit prior restraints, even in circumstances such as those suggested by Chief Justice Hughes in Near v. Minnesota.   I don't think I should attempt to explain the position of the *New York Times,* but I would like to tell you something of what went into our own thinking.

> In the first place we did not need an absolute ban on prior restraints to win the case.   The district court had found, after an evidentiary hearing, that the only danger involved in publication was the embarrassment which the United States would suffer in attempting to explain to foreign governments why the United States government could not censor its press.   We did not think that any court in this country would be prepared to support a prior restraint on this basis.

> Second, the court of appeals had also found, by a lopsided majority, that the government had failed to meet the *Near* test.   .  .  .

> Third, we knew from the Supreme Court memorandum setting the case for argument that four of the nine justices (Black, Douglas, Brennan and Marshall), would almost certainly hold that there was no basis for continuing the restraint which had been in effect during the pendency of the litigation, and we did not wish to take a position which might conceivably alienate the critical fifth vote we needed to win.   After all, unless you accept the position of Justices Black and Douglas, it's pretty hard to argue that papers can publish the sailing dates of troopships and the number and location of troop positions.

> Finally, we knew that Justices Black and Douglas had long been advocates of the absolute position with respect to the first amendment.   We also knew that these two eminent Justices had never convinced any of their brethren of the correctness of their views. We believed that Justices Black and Douglas would almost certainly

continue to urge that view on their brethren in this case. We were of the view that if Justices Black and Douglas were unable, over a period of several decades, to convince their brethren that the first amendment was absolute, we certainly would not be able to devise a series of arguments which would do so between 3:30 P.M. Friday and 5 A.M. Saturday morning.

Professor Bickel discussed the significance of the case he argued successfully in A. Bickel, *The Morality of Consent* 79–88 (1976).

8.   Although the government never sought to invoke criminal sanctions against the media in the "Pentagon Papers" episode, it did file charges against Daniel Ellsberg and Anthony Russo.  Ellsberg, a consultant to the Rand Corporation, had been authorized to possess the papers, provided he kept them on the premises of Rand and in his safe when not in use.  He was not to reproduce them, but he removed them from Rand and had them reproduced with Russo's help.  The government relied primarily on 18 U.S.C.A. § 641, charging that Ellsberg did "embezzle, steal and knowingly convert to his own use and the use of another" the documents known as the "Pentagon Papers," and on 18 U.S.C.A. § 793(d) and (e).  Subsection (e) is discussed in Justice White's opinion.  Subsection (d) involves communication and transmission of "any document, writing . . .  or note relating to the national defense . . . which . . .  the possessor has reason to believe could be used to the injury of the United States or to the advantage of any foreign nation."  The charges against Ellsberg and Russo were dismissed because of government misconduct.  The case is discussed in Nimmer, "National Security Secrets v. Free Speech: The Issues Left Undecided in the Ellsberg Case," 26 Stan.L.Rev. 311 (1974).

9.   *The Progressive's H–Bomb Case.*  In 1979 a federal district judge in Wisconsin issued a preliminary injunction, apparently the first of its kind, restraining a magazine from printing an article on national security grounds.  The article by Howard Morland, entitled "The H Bomb Secret:  How We Got It, Why We're Telling It," was to have appeared in *The Progressive*, a monthly magazine of political and social commentary with a circulation of 40,000.  See United States v. Progressive, Inc., 467 F.Supp. 990, 5 Med.L.Rptr. 2441 (W.D.Wis.1979).

The government relied on statutory authorization in the Atomic Energy Act, 42 U.S.C.A. § 2011 et seq., to seek the injunction.  Section 2274 provides in part:

> Whoever, lawfully or unlawfully, having possession of, access to, control over, or being entrusted with any document, writing, sketch, photograph, plan, model, instrument, appliance, note, or information involving or incorporating Restricted Data—
>
>    . . .
>
>      (b) communicates, transmits, or discloses the same to any individual or person, or attempts or conspires to do any of the foregoing, with reason to believe such data will be utilized to

injure the United States or to secure an advantage to any foreign nation, shall, upon conviction, be punished by a fine of not more than $10,000 or imprisonment for not more than ten years, or both.

"Restricted Data" is defined in § 2014(y) to include "all data concerning (1) design, manufacture or utilization of atomic weapons; (2) the production of special nuclear material; or (3) the use of special nuclear fuels in the production of energy . . . ." In § 2014(aa), "special nuclear material" includes "plutonium, uranium enriched in the isotope 233 or in the isotope 235," and other materials that may be designated.

The specific authority for an injunction is found in § 2280 of the Act:

> Whenever in the judgment of the Commission any person has engaged or is about to engage in any acts or practices which constitute or will constitute a violation of any provision of this chapter, or any regulation or order issued thereunder, the Attorney General on behalf of the United States may make application to the appropriate court for an order enjoining such acts or practices, or for an order enforcing compliance with such provision, and upon a showing by the Commission that such person has engaged or is about to engage in any such acts or practices, a permanent or temporary injunction, restraining order, or other order may be granted.

The judge ruled that the government had met its burden under § 2274 of the statute, which he held was not vague or overbroad. The word "communicates," which had disturbed some justices in *New York Times,* was easily resolved here: "The Court is convinced that the terms used in the statute—'communicates, transmits or discloses'—include publishing in a magazine." The judge found that the government had "met the test enunciated by two Justices in the New York Times case, namely, grave, direct, immediate and irreparable harm to the United States."

The "Pentagon Papers" case was distinguishable because the information at issue there was historical data. The only cogent national security reason for restraining its publication was embarrassment to the United States. The information in *The Progressive* article concerned "the most destructive weapon in the history of mankind, information of sufficient destructive potential to nullify the right to free speech and to endanger the right to life itself."

> The Secretary of State states that publication would increase thermonuclear proliferation and that this would "irreparably impair the national security of the United States." The Secretary of Defense says that dissemination of the Morland article will mean a substantial increase in the risk of thermonuclear proliferation and lead to use or threats that could "adversely affect the national security of the United States."

The judge recognized that a "mistake in ruling against *The Progressive* will seriously infringe cherished First Amendment rights." But "a mistake in ruling against the United States could pave the way for thermonuclear annihilation for us all. In that event, our right to life is extinguished and the right to publish becomes moot." He found the *dictum* of *Near*, p. 55, *supra*, applicable because "war by foot soldiers has been replaced in large part by war by machines and bombs." The "publication of the technical information on the hydrogen bomb contained in the article is analogous to publication of troop movements or locations in time of war and falls within the extremely narrow exception of the rule against prior restraint." The judge was also influenced by his belief that the purpose of the Morland article, to stimulate debate on nuclear non-proliferation, could be achieved without revealing the method of making such arms.

The reporter and the magazine argued that the information had been obtained from public sources, such as articles in encyclopedias. The judge responded that an affidavit from Dr. Hans Bethe asserted that "the design and operational concepts described in the manuscript are not expressed or revealed in the public literature nor do I believe they are known to scientists not associated with the government weapons program."

After study, the judge found "concepts within the article that [he did] not find in the public realm—concepts that are vital to the operation of the bomb." Although it has been asserted that the "secret" is nothing more than a few insights drawn from other scientific areas, the judge noted that sometimes what is obvious in one context may not be so obvious in another context. He cited a report that in the 1930s French scientists trying to develop a nuclear chain reaction were stymied for a year by their failure to grasp an "elementary" idea.

Although the judge recognized that it might only be a matter of time before other countries acquired their own hydrogen bombs, and that a "large, sophisticated industrial capacity" was required together with imaginative scientists, the article "could accelerate the membership of a candidate nation in the thermonuclear club." Moreover, "there are times in the course of human history when time itself may be very important." He mentioned the importance of Hitler's failure "to get his V–1 and V–2 bombs operational quickly enough to materially affect the outcome of World War II."

In prior restraint cases such as Nebraska Press Association v. Stuart, discussed in Chapter X, the Court considered among other issues, whether the restraint was likely to be effective. That matter was particularly important here because the information in question involved common sense ideas applied in unexpected ways. Writing after the decision, Morland stated that "the secret" could be said in a single sentence—and that he first heard that sentence from a student in the rear of the audience at a talk he was giving at the University of Alabama. He also said that he submitted to the court four encyclopedia articles on the subjects "Comet" and "Sun" with pertinent passages underlined. He said that government attorneys asserted that the underlinings constituted a security violation and clean copies had to be found before the articles could be released to the press. Newsweek, Apr. 9, 1979 at 14. Could Morland be restrained from telling this episode? In "national security" cases, is likely effectiveness of the restraint a relevant consideration?

*The Progressive* appealed the granting of the preliminary injunction. After refusing a government request to bar the public from the argument, the court of appeals heard oral argument on Sept. 13, 1979. The magazine asserted that the government had to prove that the publication would "surely result in direct, immediate and irreparable damage to our nation or its people," but had proven only that "in some unspecified time, some nations might acquire the capability to build a hydrogen bomb."

Just after the argument, the *Madison Press Connection* published a letter containing information that *The Progressive* had been enjoined from publishing. *The Chicago Tribune* then announced that it planned to publish the same letter. Once the information had been made public, any justification for enjoining its publication collapsed. The government then announced that it was withdrawing its complaint, and the case was dismissed. Although the government reserved its right to bring criminal charges, no such case was brought.

10. In 1980 Public Broadcasting Service broadcast a "documentary drama" portraying a love affair between a Saudi princess and a commoner, and their subsequent execution. The program also dwelt on some aspects of Saudi Arabian life that the Saudi government asserted were totally misrepresented. The program was patterned on a true story.

If the Saudi government had made a credible threat to cut off all oil shipments to the United States immediately upon the presentation of the program, and if the best evidence had been that such a cutoff would cripple the American economy, would the government have been able to obtain an injunction against the showing of the program?

Is it crucial that no "secret" was involved? Lawsuits arising from refusals to show the Saudi program are discussed in Chapter XVI.

11. After a spate of publications that named several United States covert foreign intelligence agents, presumably in an effort to undermine the U.S. intelligence activity, Congress took steps to criminalize such disclosures with the Intelligence Identities Protection Act of 1982, 50 U.S.C.A. § 401, *et seq.* Press groups, however, protested fiercely that too wide a ban would affect legitimate news accounts, based on information on the public record, of intelligence agency abuses. A critical question is whether a reporter who writes a story about the CIA violates that statute if that story contains information that identifies a covert agent. No litigation has occurred.

12. In national security cases the government has had some success when seeking to enjoin disclosures by its employees. United States v. Marchetti, 466 F.2d 1309, 1 Med.L.Rptr. 1051 (4th Cir.1972), involved an injunction obtained by the government against publication of Marchetti's book about the Central Intelligence Agency, his former employer. At the time he joined, he promised not to divulge any classified information unless specifically authorized in writing by the director. When he resigned from the CIA he signed a secrecy oath. Although recognizing that prior restraints were rarely justifiable, the court upheld this one because of the government's right to secrecy in foreign affairs. A confidential relationship inhered in the employment and "the law would probably imply a secrecy agreement had there been no formal expressed agreement." The government need not resort to ordinary criminal sanctions because of the great risk of harm from disclosure. The court recognized that by joining the CIA, Marchetti did not relinquish his rights to free speech. He might write about CIA operations and criticize the agency as any citizen might, but he could not disclose classified information obtained during his employment unless the material was already in the public domain. The court concluded that judicial review of agency objections to the text was available, but that the court could determine only whether the material was classified and if so, whether it had previously been made public. The Supreme Court denied *certiorari* 409 U.S. 1063 (1972), Justices Douglas, Brennan, and Stewart dissenting.

On remand, the judge permitted publication of all but 26 of the 168 items still in question. The director of the CIA and the Secretary of State appealed, and the judgment was reversed. Alfred A. Knopf, Inc. v. Colby, 509 F.2d 1362 (4th Cir.), cert. denied 421 U.S. 992 (1975), Justice Douglas dissenting. Apparently the trial judge could find little to explain why particular documents or parts of documents had been classified, and often the classification officer could not be identified or was unavailable. The court of appeals observed that in its earlier decision in *Marchetti* it had assumed that all information in a classified document should be held to be classified and not subject to disclosure. On this appeal the court decided that the trial judge had imposed an excessive burden on the government because he refused to recognize that there "is a presumption of regularity in the performance by a public official of his public duty. . . . That presumption leaves no room for speculation that information which the district court can recognize as proper for top secret classification was not classified at all by the official who placed the 'Top Secret' legend on the document."

13. A book by a former CIA agent was published before the CIA learned of it. The government sued the agent for breach of his employment contract, which barred publication of information learned while working at the CIA, without prepublication approval. The government did not contend that any classified information had been revealed. The judge held that the contract was enforceable and had been breached. He enjoined violation of the contract as to future works and established a

constructive trust that required Snepp to pay the CIA all royalties the book produced. United States v. Snepp, 456 F.Supp. 176, 3 Med.L.Rptr. 2585 (E.D.Va.1978).

The court of appeals agreed that a valid contract had been breached but disagreed, 2–1, on the damages question. The majority concluded that the government was entitled to try the case as a normal breach of contract case with the possibility of persuading the jury to award punitive damages, but that the constructive trust theory was not available. 595 F.2d 926, 4 Med.L.Rptr. 2313 (4th Cir.1979).

Snepp sought *certiorari* to determine whether his agreement with the CIA was enforceable and, if so, whether punitive damages were recoverable in the government's case. The government filed a conditional cross-petition seeking *certiorari* to review the constructive trust question if the court granted Snepp's petition.

The Supreme Court granted both petitions and, without oral argument, reinstated the district court's judgment permitting the constructive trust theory. The Court largely rejected Snepp's claim that the CIA contract amounted to prior restraint in a lengthy footnote:

> When Snepp accepted employment with the CIA, he voluntarily signed the agreement that expressly obligated him to submit any proposed publication for prior review. He does not claim that he executed this agreement under duress. Indeed, he voluntarily reaffirmed his obligation when he left the Agency. We agree with the Court of Appeals that Snepp's agreement is an "entirely appropriate" exercise of the CIA Director's statutory mandate to "protect intelligence sources and methods from unauthorized disclosure." [ ] Moreover, this Court's cases make clear that—even in the absence of an express agreement—the CIA could have acted to protect substantial governmental interests by imposing reasonable restrictions on employee activities that in other contexts might be protected by the First Amendment. [ ] The Government has a compelling interest in protecting both the secrecy of information important to our national security and the appearance of confidentiality so essential to the effective operation of our foreign intelligence service. [ ] The agreement that Snepp signed is a reasonable means for protecting this vital interest.

The Court's *per curiam* opinion noted that "Snepp's employment with the CIA involved an extremely high degree of trust." He published the book "on the basis of his background and exposure" to CIA activities and "deliberately and surreptitiously violated his obligation to submit all material for prepublication review." The violation of trust "does not depend upon whether his book actually contained classified information." The claim is that he should have given the CIA a chance to see whether anything he wrote "would compromise classified information or sources." 444 U.S. 507, 5 Med.L.Rptr. 2409 (1980).

Justice Stevens, joined by Justices Brennan and Marshall, dissented. They stressed that "the Government has conceded that the book contains no classified, nonpublic material. Thus, by definition, the interest in confidentiality that Snepp's contract was designed to protect has not been compromised." They argued that the remedy of constructive trust was not authorized "by any applicable law and [that] it is most inappropriate for the Court to dispose of this novel issue summarily on the Government's conditional cross-petition for certiorari." Each point was discussed at length.

See Comments, 81 Colum.L.Rev. 662 (1981) and 59 N.C.L.Rev. 417 (1981).

Snepp subsequently submitted 19 manuscripts to the CIA for approval prior to publication, and agreement was reached on 18 of them. Disagreement over the 19th led him to seek a modification of the permanent injunction requiring him to submit all writings concerning the CIA for review prior to publication. Snepp had submitted a manuscript for a potential television mini-series about his experiences in Vietnam. The CIA produced a list of 11 specific deletions as a condition to publication. While negotiations between Snepp and the CIA continued, Snepp's television deal fell through. Snepp sought damages for his lost television deal and a modification that would have put the burden on the CIA to initiate judicial proceedings if he and the CIA could not agree on what material should be deleted from a particular manuscript. After a federal district court found the CIA had acted reasonably and denied his petition, he appealed to the U.S. Court of Appeals for the Fourth Circuit, which affirmed the lower court's ruling. United States v. Snepp, 897 F.2d 138, 17 Med.L.Rptr. 1579 (4th Cir.1990).

14. Another national security problem was presented by the case of a former government employee who was not himself an author but who supplied information to journalists. Samuel L. Morison, former analyst at the Naval Intelligence Support Center, was convicted on four counts of espionage and theft of government property for his efforts to provide classified information to *Jane's Defence Weekly*. The latter is a British publication for which Morison worked part-time with the Navy's approval. The counts of espionage and theft related to classified information about an explosion at a Soviet naval base and photos of a Soviet nuclear carrier under construction. The U.S. Court of Appeals for the Fourth Circuit affirmed Morison's conviction and two-year prison sentence. United States v. Morison, 844 F.2d 1057, 15 Med.L.Rptr. 1369 (4th Cir.), cert. denied 488 U.S. 908 (1988). See also Med.L.Rptr. News Notes, Oct. 25, 1988.

15. Justice Stewart's opinion in Landmark Communications, Inc. v. Virginia, which we will discuss in Chapter X, provides a contrast. *Landmark* involves a different kind of government secret: confidential proceedings of a state commission investigating charges against judges.

16. The outbreak of war in the Persian Gulf in January 1991 inevitably led to two major issues in government-press relations in wartime. One is access by the journalists to the people they want to interview and the places they want to go to cover stories. We will discuss that issue in

Chapter XII, when we discuss public access to records, meetings and places. The other issue is direct censorship by the government of journalists' reports from the war area—something that would clearly be intolerable in peacetime and is viewed by some as equally intolerable in wartime. In addition to objecting to the practice in principle, some journalists complained that the military personnel assigned to review their stories were unqualified or simply slow. Newspaper and magazine journalists complained that, while they were required to submit written texts for review, broadcast journalists often reported live—therefore without review.

In 1991–92, the military and representatives of news media worked to develop a set of principles to give journalists greater access to military operations, but the two sides were unable to agree on whether there should be any official "security review" of news reports. The news executives argued that such review is unwarranted and unnecessary, but the Pentagon insisted that it must have the right to review stories to prevent the disclosure of information that could endanger the safety of troops or the success of a military mission. New York Times, May 22, 1992 at A–15. For criticism of the Persian Gulf censorship and of the news media's failure to protest it more effectively, see "The Other Defeat in the Gulf," New York Times, July 27, 1992 at A–17.

# Chapter VIII

# OBSCENITY

## A. THE NATURE OF OBSCENITY

Recall that in 1942 in the famous quotation from *Chaplinsky*, p. 48, *supra*, Justice Murphy stated that "lewd and obscene" words were among those "certain well-defined and narrowly limited classes of speech, the prevention and punishment of which have never been thought to raise any Constitutional problem." That may explain why, even though laws against obscenity had been in effect in this country since Colonial times, it was not until 1957 that the Supreme Court confronted the question of the impact of the First Amendment on the law of obscenity. In Roth v. United States, 354 U.S. 476 (1957), the Court held that even though it was "expression," obscenity was outside the protection of the First and Fourteenth Amendments. Yet, "sex and obscenity are not synonymous." Sex, "a great and mysterious motive force in human life, has indisputably been a subject of absorbing interest to mankind through the ages; it is one of the vital problems of human interest and public concern." Basically, the majority decided that obscenity could be determined by asking "whether to the average person, applying contemporary community standards, the dominant theme of the material taken as a whole appeals to prurient interest."

Shortly thereafter the majority consensus began to collapse as justices began groping for the line between the protected and the unprotected. For example, Justice Stewart, concurring in Jacobellis v. Ohio, 378 U.S. 184, 197 (1964), asserted that "hardcore pornography" was the only type of material that could be prohibited. He continued, "I shall not today attempt further to define the kinds of material I understand to be embraced within that shorthand description; and perhaps I could never succeed in intelligibly doing so. But I know it when I see it, and the motion picture involved in this case is not that."

In A Book Named John Cleland's Memoirs v. Attorney General of Massachusetts, 383 U.S. 413, 1 Med.L.Rptr. 1390 (1966), no majority opinion emerged as some justices began to diverge from the *Roth* approach. These developments will be discussed in Miller v. California, *infra*.

That same year Justice Stewart tried to define the term in a dissenting opinion in Ginzburg v. United States, 383 U.S. 463, 499, 1 Med.L.Rptr. 1409, 1423 (1966). He adopted a position put forward by the government that "Such materials include photographs, both still and motion picture, with no pretense of artistic value, graphically depicting acts of sexual intercourse, including various acts of sodomy and sadism, and sometimes involving several participants in scenes of orgy-like character." He also extended the class to drawings in comic-book format, and to some verbal descriptions of "such activities in a bizarre manner with no attempt whatsoever to afford portrayals of character or situation and with no pretense to literary value."

By 1967 the Court had been reduced to reversing convictions for obscenity without hearing oral argument or rendering written opinions whenever five members of the Court, using their own tests, concluded that the material in the case was not obscene. See Redrup v. New York, 386 U.S. 767 (1967).

In Kois v. Wisconsin, 408 U.S. 229 (1972), one count of defendant publisher's conviction was based on the fact that his underground newspaper ran two "relatively small pictures showing a nude man and nude woman embracing in a sitting position." The photographs accompanied an article about the arrest of one of the newspaper's photographers on a charge of possessing obscene material. The article said that the two photographs were "similar" to those taken from the photographer.

The Supreme Court summarily reversed the conviction. Relying on *Roth*, the Court concluded that it could not "fairly be said, either considering the article as it appears or the record before the state court, that the article was a mere vehicle for the publication of the pictures. A quotation from Voltaire in the flyleaf of a book will not constitutionally redeem an otherwise obscene publication," but these photographs were "rationally related to an article that itself was clearly" protected. There was no need to decide whether the dissemination of the photographs by themselves could be prohibited.

In 1973 the Supreme Court once again attempted to set up a clear definition of pornography. At the same time the Court reexamined the rationale for excluding pornography from any First Amendment protection. It is important to remember that the standard set out in the following two cases is the current standard for obscenity.

## MILLER v. CALIFORNIA

Supreme Court of the United States, 1973.

413 U.S. 15, 93 S.Ct. 2607, 37 L.Ed.2d 419, 1 Med.L.Rptr. 1441.

Mr. Chief Justice Burger delivered the opinion of the Court.

This is one of a group of "obscenity-pornography" cases being reviewed by the Court in a re-examination of standards enunciated in earlier cases involving what Mr. Justice Harlan called "the intractable obscenity problem." Interstate Circuit, Inc. v. Dallas, 390 U.S. 676, 704 (1968) (concurring and dissenting).

Appellant conducted a mass mailing campaign to advertise the sale of illustrated books, euphemistically called "adult" material. After a jury trial, he was convicted of violating California Penal Code § 311.2(a), a misdemeanor, by knowingly distributing obscene matter,[1] and the Appellate Department, Superior Court of California, County of Orange, summarily affirmed the judgment without opinion. Appellant's conviction was specifically based on his conduct in causing five unsolicited advertising brochures to be sent through the mail in an envelope addressed to a restaurant in Newport Beach, California. The envelope was opened by the manager of the restaurant and his mother. They had not requested the brochures; they complained to the police.

The brochures advertise four books entitled "Intercourse," "Man–Woman," "Sex Orgies Illustrated," and "An Illustrated History of Pornography," and a film entitled "Marital Intercourse." While the brochures contain some descriptive printed material, primarily they consist of pictures and drawings very explicitly depicting men and women in groups of two or more engaging in a variety of sexual activities, with genitals often prominently displayed.

# I

This case involves the application of a State's criminal obscenity statute to a situation in which sexually explicit materials have been thrust by aggressive sales action upon unwilling recipients who had in no way indicated any desire to receive such materials. This Court has recognized that the States have a legitimate interest in prohibiting dissemination or exhibition of obscene material[2] when the mode of

1. At the time of the commission of the alleged offense, which was prior to June 25, 1969, § 311.2(a) and § 311 of the California Penal Code read in relevant part:

"§ 311.2 Sending or bringing into state for sale or distribution; printing, exhibiting, distributing or possessing within state

"(a) Every person who knowingly: sends or causes to be sent, or brings or causes to be brought, into this state for sale or distribution, or in this state prepares, publishes, prints, exhibits, distributes, or offers to distribute, or has in his possession with intent to distribute or to exhibit or offer to distribute, any obscene matter is guilty of a misdemeanor. . . ."

"§ 311. Definitions

"As used in this chapter:

"(a) 'Obscene' means that to the average person, applying contemporary standards, the predominant appeal of the matter, taken as a whole, is to prurient interest, i.e., a shameful or morbid interest in nudity, sex, or excretion, which goes substantially beyond customary limits of candor in description or representation of such matters and is matter which is utterly without redeeming social importance.

. . .

"(e) 'Knowingly' means having knowledge that the matter is obscene."

2. This Court has defined "obscene material" as "material which deals with sex in a manner appealing to prurient interest," Roth v. United States, supra, at 487, but the Roth definition does not reflect the precise meaning of "obscene" as traditionally used in the English language. Derived from the Latin obscaenus, ob, to, plus caenum, filth, "obscene" is defined in the Webster's Third New International Dictionary (Unabridged 1969) as "1a: disgusting to the senses . . . b: grossly repugnant to the generally accepted notions of what is appropriate . . . 2: offensive or revolting as countering or violating some ideal or principle." The Oxford English Dictionary (1933 ed.) gives a similar definition, "[o]ffensive to the senses, or to taste or refinement; disgusting, repulsive, filthy, foul, abominable, loathsome."

The material we are discussing in this case is more accurately defined as "pornography" or "pornographic material." "Pornography" derives from the Greek (pornè, harlot, and graphos, writing). The word now means "1: a description of prostitutes or prostitution 2: a depiction (as in writing or painting) of licentiousness or lewdness:

dissemination carries with it a significant danger of offending the sensibilities of unwilling recipients or of exposure to juveniles. [  ] It is in this context that we are called on to define the standards which must be used to identify obscene material that a State may regulate without infringing on the First Amendment as applicable to the States through the Fourteenth Amendment.

The dissent of Mr. Justice Brennan reviews the background of the obscenity problem, but since the Court now undertakes to formulate standards more concrete than those in the past, it is useful for us to focus on two of the landmark cases in the somewhat tortured history of the Court's obscenity decisions.  In Roth v. United States, 354 U.S. 476 (1957), the Court sustained a conviction under a federal statute punishing the mailing of "obscene, lewd, lascivious or filthy . . . ." materials.  The key to that holding was the Court's rejection of the claim that obscene materials were protected by the First Amendment.  Five Justices joined in the opinion stating:

> "All ideas having even the slightest redeeming social importance --unorthodox ideas, controversial ideas, even ideas hateful to the prevailing climate of opinion—have the full protection of the [First Amendment] guaranties, unless excludable because they encroach upon the limited area of more important interests.  But implicit in the history of the First Amendment is the rejection of obscenity as utterly without redeeming social importance.  . . .

"We hold that obscenity is not within the area of constitutionally protected speech or press."  354 U.S., at 484–485 (footnotes omitted).

Nine years later, in Memoirs v. Massachusetts, 383 U.S. 413 (1966), the Court veered sharply away from the *Roth* concept and, with only three Justices in the plurality opinion, articulated a new test of obscenity.  The plurality held that under the *Roth* definition

> "as elaborated in subsequent cases, three elements must coalesce:  it must be established that (a) the dominant theme of the material taken as a whole appeals to a prurient interest in sex;  (b) the material is patently offensive because it affronts contemporary community standards relating to the description or representation of sexual matters;  and (c) the material is utterly without redeeming social value."  Id., at 418.

. . .

While *Roth* presumed "obscenity" to be "utterly without redeeming social importance," *Memoirs* required that to prove obscenity it must be affirmatively established that the material is *"utterly* without redeeming

a portrayal of erotic behavior designed to cause sexual excitement." Webster's Third New International Dictionary, supra.  Pornographic material which is obscene forms a sub-group of all "obscene" expression, but not the whole, at least as the word "obscene" is now used in our language. We note, therefore, that the words "obscene material" as used in this case, have a specific judicial meaning which derives from the *Roth* case, i.e., obscene material "which deals with sex." *Roth,* supra, at 487. See also ALI Model Penal Code § 251.4(*l*) "Obscene Defined." (Official Draft 1962.)

social value." Thus, even as they repeated the words of *Roth,* the *Memoirs* plurality produced a drastically altered test that called on the prosecution to prove a negative, i.e., that the material was *"utterly* without redeeming social value"—a burden virtually impossible to discharge under our criminal standards of proof. Such considerations caused Mr. Justice Harlan to wonder if the *"utterly* without redeeming social value" test had any meaning at all. [ ]

Apart from the initial formulation in the Roth case, no majority of the Court has at any given time been able to agree on a standard to determine what constitutes obscene, pornographic material subject to regulation under the States' police power. [ ] We have seen "a variety of views among the members of the Court unmatched in any other course of constitutional adjudication." Interstate Circuit, Inc. v. Dallas, 390 U.S., at 704–705 (Harlan, J., concurring and dissenting) (footnote omitted).[3] This is not remarkable, for in the area of freedom of speech and press the courts must always remain sensitive to any infringement on genuinely serious literary, artistic, political, or scientific expression. This is an area in which there are few eternal verities.

The case we now review was tried on the theory that the California Penal Code § 311 approximately incorporates the three-stage *Memoirs* test, supra. But now the *Memoirs* test has been abandoned as unworkable by its author,[4] and no Member of the Court today supports the *Memoirs* formulation.

## II

. . .

The basic guidelines for the trier of fact must be: (a) whether "the average person, applying contemporary community standards" would find that the work, taken as a whole, appeals to the prurient interest, [ ]; (b) whether the work depicts or describes, in a patently offensive way, sexual conduct specifically defined by the applicable state law; and (c) whether the work, taken as a whole, lacks serious literary, artistic, political, or scientific value. We do not adopt as a constitutional standard the *"utterly* without redeeming social value" test of Memoirs v. Massachusetts, 383 U.S., at 419; that concept has never commanded the adherence of more than three Justices at one time. . . .

We emphasize that it is not our function to propose regulatory schemes for the States. That must await their concrete legislative efforts. It is possible, however, to give a few plain examples of what a

**3.** In the absence of a majority view, this Court was compelled to embark on the practice of summarily reversing convictions for the dissemination of materials that at least five members of the Court, applying their separate tests, found to be protected by the First Amendment. Redrup v. New York, 386 U.S. 767 (1967). Thirty-one cases have been decided in this manner. Beyond the necessity of circumstances, however, no justification has ever been offered in support of the *Redrup* "policy." [ ] The *Redrup* procedure has cast us in the role of an unreviewable board of censorship for the 50 States, subjectively judging each piece of material brought before us.

**4.** See the dissenting opinion of Mr. Justice Brennan in Paris Adult Theatre I v. Slaton, [ ].

state statute could define for regulation under part (b) of the standard announced in this opinion, supra:

      (a) Patently offensive representations or descriptions of ultimate sexual acts, normal or perverted, actual or simulated.

      (b) Patently offensive representations or descriptions of masturbation, excretory functions, and lewd exhibition of the genitals.

Sex and nudity may not be exploited without limit by films or pictures exhibited or sold in places of public accommodation any more than live sex and nudity can be exhibited or sold without limit in such public places. At a minimum, prurient, patently offensive depiction or description of sexual conduct must have serious literary, artistic, political, or scientific value to merit First Amendment protection. [  ] For example, medical books for the education of physicians and related personnel necessarily use graphic illustrations and descriptions of human anatomy. In resolving the inevitably sensitive questions of fact and law, we must continue to rely on the jury system, accompanied by the safeguards that judges, rules of evidence, presumption of innocence, and other protective features provide, as we do with rape, murder, and a host of other offenses against society and its individual members.

Mr. Justice Brennan, [  ] [abandoning his former position], now maintains that no formulation of this Court, the Congress, or the States can adequately distinguish obscene material unprotected by the First Amendment from protected expression, [  ]. Paradoxically, Mr. Justice Brennan indicates that suppression of unprotected obscene material is permissible to avoid exposure to unconsenting adults, as in this case, and to juveniles, although he gives no indication of how the division between protected and nonprotected materials may be drawn with greater precision for these purposes than for regulation of commercial exposure to consenting adults only. Nor does he indicate where in the Constitution he finds the authority to distinguish between a willing "adult" one month past the state law age of majority and a willing "juvenile" one month younger.

Under the holdings announced today, no one will be subject to prosecution for the sale or exposure of obscene materials unless these materials depict or describe patently offensive "hard core" sexual conduct specifically defined by the regulating state law, as written or construed. We are satisfied that these specific prerequisites will provide fair notice to a dealer in such materials that his public and commercial activities may bring prosecution. . . .

    . . .

## III

Under a national Constitution, fundamental First Amendment limitations on the powers of the States do not vary from community to community, but this does not mean that there are, or should or can be, fixed, uniform national standards of precisely what appeals to the "prurient interest" or is "patently offensive." These are essentially questions of fact, and our nation is simply too big and too diverse for this Court to reasonably expect that such standards could be articulated for all 50 States in a single formulation, even assuming the prerequisite consensus exists. When triers of fact are asked to decide whether "the average person, applying contemporary community standards" would consider certain materials "prurient," it would be unrealistic to require that the answer be based on some abstract formulation. The adversary system, with lay jurors as the usual ultimate factfinders in criminal prosecutions, has historically permitted triers of fact to draw on the standards of their community, guided always by limiting instructions on the law. To require a State to structure obscenity proceedings around evidence of a *national* "community standard" would be an exercise in futility.

. . . .

It is neither realistic nor constitutionally sound to read the First Amendment as requiring that the people of Maine or Mississippi accept public depiction of conduct found tolerable in Las Vegas, or New York City. [   ] People in different States vary in their tastes and attitudes, and this diversity is not to be strangled by the absolutism of imposed uniformity. As the Court made clear in Mishkin v. New York, 383 U.S., at 508–509, the primary concern with requiring a jury to apply the standard of "the average person, applying contemporary community standards" is to be certain that, so far as material is not aimed at a deviant group, it will be judged by its impact on an average person, rather than a particularly susceptible or sensitive person—or indeed a totally insensitive one. [   ] We hold that the requirement that the jury evaluate the materials with reference to "contemporary standards of the State of California" serves this protective purpose and is constitutionally adequate.

## IV

The dissenting Justices sound the alarm of repression. But, in our view, to equate the free and robust exchange of ideas and political debate with commercial exploitation of obscene material demeans the grand conception of the First Amendment and its high purposes in the historic struggle for freedom. It is a "misuse of the great guarantees of free speech and free press. . . ." Breard v. Alexandria, 341 U.S., at 645. The First Amendment protects works which, taken as a whole, have serious literary, artistic, political, or scientific value, regardless of whether the government or a majority of the people approve of the ideas these works represent. "The protection given speech and press was fashioned to assure unfettered interchange of *ideas* for the bringing about of political and social changes desired by the people," Roth v. United States, supra, at 484 (emphasis added). [   ] But the public portrayal of hard core sexual conduct for its own sake, and for the ensuing commercial gain, is a different matter.

There is no evidence, empirical or historical, that the stern 19th century American censorship of public distribution and display of material relating to sex, [  ], in any way limited or affected expression of serious literary, artistic, political, or scientific ideas.  . . .

Mr. Justice Brennan finds "it is hard to see how state-ordered regimentation of our minds can ever be forestalled."  Paris Adult Theatre I v. Slaton (Brennan, J., dissenting).  These doleful anticipations assume that courts cannot distinguish commerce in ideas, protected by the First Amendment, from commercial exploitation of obscene material.  Moreover, state regulation of hard core pornography so as to make it unavailable to nonadults, a regulation which Mr. Justice Brennan finds constitutionally permissible, has all the elements of "censorship" for adults; indeed even more rigid enforcement techniques may be called for with such dichotomy of regulation.  . . .

In sum, we (a) reaffirm the *Roth* holding that obscene material is not protected by the First Amendment; (b) hold that such material can be regulated by the States, subject to the specific safeguards enunciated above, without a showing that the material is "*utterly* without redeeming social value"; and (c) hold that obscenity is to be determined by applying "contemporary community standards," [  ], not "national standards." The judgment of the Appellate Department of the Superior Court, Orange County, California, is vacated and the case remanded to that court for further proceedings not inconsistent with the First Amendment standards established by this opinion. [  ]

Mr. Justice Douglas, dissenting.

I.

. . .

Today the Court retreats from the earlier formulations of the constitutional test and undertakes to make new definitions.  This effort, like the earlier ones, is earnest and well intentioned.  The difficulty is that we do not deal with constitutional terms, since "obscenity" is not mentioned in the Constitution or Bill of Rights.  And the First Amendment makes no such exception from "the press" which it undertakes to protect nor, as I have said on other occasions, is an exception necessarily implied, for there was no recognized exception to the free press at the time the Bill of Rights was adopted which treated "obscene" publications differently from other types of papers, magazines, and books.  So there are no constitutional guidelines for deciding what is and what is not "obscene."  The Court is at large because we deal with tastes and standards of literature.  What shocks me may be sustenance for my neighbor.  What causes one person to boil up in rage over one pamphlet or movie may reflect only his neurosis, not shared by others.  We deal here with a regime of censorship which, if adopted, should be done by constitutional amendment after full debate by the people.

. . .

My contention is that until a civil proceeding has placed a tract beyond the pale, no criminal prosecution should be sustained.  For no more vivid illustration of vague and uncertain laws could be designed than those we have fashioned. . . .

. . .

### III.

While the right to know is the corollary of the right to speak or publish, no one can be forced by government to listen to disclosure that he finds offensive. That was the basis of my dissent in Public Utilities Comm'n v. Pollak, 343 U.S. 451, 467 (1952), where I protested against making a streetcar audience a "captive" audience. There is no "captive audience" problem in these obscenity cases. No one is being compelled to look or to listen. Those who enter news stands or bookstalls may be offended by what they see. But they are not compelled by the State to frequent those places; and it is only state or governmental action against which the First Amendment, applicable to the States by virtue of the Fourteenth, raises a ban.

. . .

MR. JUSTICE BRENNAN, with whom MR. JUSTICE STEWART and MR. JUSTICE MARSHALL join, dissenting.

In my dissent in Paris Adult Theatre I v. Slaton, decided this date, I noted that I had no occasion to consider the extent of state power to regulate the distribution of sexually oriented material to juveniles or the offensive exposure of such material to unconsenting adults. In the case before us, appellant was convicted of distributing obscene matter in violation of California Penal Code § 311.2, on the basis of evidence that he had caused to be mailed unsolicited brochures advertising various books and a movie. I need not now decide whether a statute might be drawn to impose, within the requirements of the First Amendment, criminal penalties for the precise conduct at issue here. For it is clear that under my dissent in *Paris Adult Theatre I,* the statute under which the prosecution was brought is unconstitutionally overbroad, and therefore invalid on its face. "[T]he transcendent value to all society of constitutionally protected expression is deemed to justify allowing 'attacks on overly broad statutes with no requirement that the person making the attack demonstrate that his own conduct could not be regulated by a statute drawn with the requisite narrow specificity.' " . . .

### PARIS ADULT THEATRE I v. SLATON

Supreme Court of the United States, 1973.
413 U.S. 49, 93 S.Ct. 2628, 37 L.Ed.2d 446, 1 Med.L.Rptr. 1454.

[Respondents, a district attorney and a local court solicitor, filed civil complaints seeking injunctions against petitioners, two Atlanta movie theatres, on the ground they were exhibiting obscene motion pictures. Signs outside the theaters identified them as showing "mature feature films" and stated that entrants must be "21 and able to prove it.

If viewing the nude body offends you, Please Do Not Enter." Nothing outside indicated the full nature of what was being shown. "In particular, nothing indicated that the films depicted as they did—scenes of simulated fellatio, cunnilingus, and group sex intercourse. There was no evidence that minors had ever entered the theatres." The trial court denied the injunction on the ground that the exclusion of minors and the general notice of content made the showing constitutionally permissible. The Georgia Supreme Court unanimously reversed on the grounds that the movies were "hard core pornography" and their exhibition was not protected by the First Amendment.]

MR. CHIEF JUSTICE BURGER delivered the opinion of the Court.

. . .

## II

We categorically disapprove the theory, apparently adopted by the trial judge, that obscene, pornographic films acquire constitutional immunity from state regulation simply because they are exhibited for consenting adults only. This holding was properly rejected by the Georgia Supreme Court. Although we have often pointedly recognized the high importance of the state interest in regulating the exposure of obscene materials to juveniles and unconsenting adults, [  ], this Court has never declared these to be the only legitimate state interests permitting regulation of obscene material. The States have a long-recognized legitimate interest in regulating the use of obscene material in local commerce and in all places of public accommodation, as long as these regulations do not run afoul of specific constitutional prohibitions. . . .

In particular, we hold that there are legitimate state interests at stake in stemming the tide of commercialized obscenity, even assuming it is feasible to enforce effective safeguards against exposure to juveniles and to passersby.[7] Rights and interests "other than those of the advocates are involved." Breard v. Alexandria, 341 U.S. 622, 642 (1951). These include the interest of the public in the quality of life and the total community environment, the tone of commerce in the great city centers, and, possibly, the public safety itself. The Hill–Link Minority Report of the Commission on Obscenity and Pornography indicates that there is at least an arguable correlation between obscene material and crime.

7. It is conceivable that an "adult" theater can—if it really insists—prevent the exposure of its obscene wares to juveniles. An "adult" bookstore, dealing in obscene books, magazines, and pictures, cannot realistically make this claim. The Hill–Link Minority Report of the Commission on Obscenity and Pornography emphasizes evidence (the Abelson National Survey of Youth and Adults) that, although most pornography may be bought by elders, "the heavy users and most highly exposed people to pornography are adolescent females (among women) and adolescent and young adult males (among men)." The Report of the Commission on Obscenity and Pornography 401 (1970). The legitimate interest in preventing exposure of juveniles to obscene material cannot be fully served by simply barring juveniles from the immediate physical premises of "adult" bookstores, when there is a flourishing "outside business" in these materials.

Quite apart from sex crimes, however, there remains one problem of large proportions aptly described by Professor Bickel:

> "It concerns the tone of the society, the mode, or to use terms that have perhaps greater currency, the style and quality of life, now and in the future. A man may be entitled to read an obscene book in his room, or expose himself indecently there. . . . We should protect his privacy. But if he demands a right to obtain the books and pictures he wants in the market, and to foregather in public places—discreet, if you will, but accessible to all—with others who share his tastes, *then to grant him his right is to affect the world about the rest of us, and to impinge on other privacies.* Even supposing that each of us can, if he wishes, effectively avert the eye and stop the ear (which, in truth, we cannot), what is commonly read and seen and heard and done intrudes upon us all, want it or not." 22 The Public Interest 25–26 (Winter 1971). (Emphasis added.)

. . .

But, it is argued, there are no scientific data which conclusively demonstrate that exposure to obscene material adversely affects men and women or their society. It is urged on behalf of the petitioners that, absent such a demonstration, any kind of state regulation is "impermissible." We reject this argument. It is not for us to resolve empirical uncertainties underlying state legislation, save in the exceptional case where that legislation plainly impinges upon rights protected by the Constitution itself. . . . Although there is no conclusive proof of a connection between antisocial behavior and obscene material, the legislature of Georgia could quite reasonably determine that such a connection does or might exist. . . .

From the beginning of civilized societies, legislators and judges have acted on various unprovable assumptions. Such assumptions underlie much lawful state regulation of commercial and business affairs. [ ] The same is true of the federal securities and antitrust laws and a host of federal regulations. [ ] On the basis of these assumptions both Congress and state legislatures have, for example, drastically restricted associational rights by adopting antitrust laws, and have strictly regulated public expression by issuers of and dealers in securities, profit sharing "coupons," and "trading stamps," commanding what they must and must not publish and announce. [ ] Understandably those who entertain an absolutist view of the First Amendment find it uncomfortable to explain why rights of association, speech, and press should be severely restrained in the marketplace of goods and money, but not in the marketplace of pornography.

Likewise, when legislatures and administrators act to protect the physical environment from pollution and to preserve our resources of forests, streams, and parks, they must act on such imponderables as the impact of a new highway near or through an existing park or wilderness area. . . . The fact that a congressional directive reflects unprovable assumptions about what is good for the people, including imponderable aesthetic assumptions, is not a sufficient reason to find that statute unconstitutional.

If we accept the unprovable assumption that a complete education requires certain books, see Board of Education v. Allen, 392 U.S. 236, 245 (1968) [   ], and the well nigh universal belief that good books, plays, and art lift the spirit, improve the mind, enrich the human personality, and develop character, can we then say that a state legislature may not act on the corollary assumption that commerce in obscene books, or public exhibitions focused on obscene conduct, have a tendency to exert a corrupting and debasing impact leading to antisocial behavior?   . . . The sum of experience, including that of the past two decades, affords an ample basis for legislatures to conclude that a sensitive, key relationship of human existence, central to family life, community welfare, and the development of human personality, can be debased and distorted by crass commercial exploitation of sex.   Nothing in the Constitution prohibits a State from reaching such a conclusion and acting on it legislatively simply because there is no conclusive evidence or empirical data.

It is argued that individual "free will" must govern, even in activities beyond the protection of the First Amendment and other constitutional guarantees of privacy, and that government cannot legitimately impede an individual's desire to see or acquire obscene plays, movies, and books.   We do indeed base our society on certain assumptions that people have the capacity for free choice.   Most exercises of individual free choice—those in politics, religion, and expression of ideas—are explicitly protected by the Constitution.   Totally unlimited play for free will, however, is not allowed in our or any other society.   We have just noted, for example, that neither the First Amendment nor "free will" precludes States from having "blue sky" laws to regulate what sellers of securities may write or publish about their wares.   [   ]   Such laws are to protect the weak, the uninformed, the unsuspecting, and the gullible from the exercise of their own volition.   Nor do modern societies leave disposal of garbage and sewage up to the individual "free will," but impose regulation to protect both public health and the appearance of public places.   States are told by some that they must await a "laissez faire" market solution to the obscenity-pornography problem, paradoxically "by people who have never otherwise had a kind word to say for laissez faire," particularly in solving urban, commercial, and environmental pollution problems.   [   ]

The States, of course, may follow such a "laissez faire" policy and drop all controls on commercialized obscenity, if that is what they prefer, just as they can ignore consumer protection in the marketplace, but nothing in the Constitution *compels* the States to do so with regard to matters falling within state jurisdiction.   . . .

It is asserted, however, that standards for evaluating state commercial regulations are inapposite in the present context, as state regulation of access by consenting adults to obscene material violates the constitutionally protected right to privacy enjoyed by petitioners' customers. Even assuming that petitioners have vicarious standing to assert potential customers' rights, it is unavailing to compare a theater open to the public for a fee, with the private home of Stanley v. Georgia, 394 U.S., at 568, and the marital bedroom of Griswold v. Connecticut, [381 U.S.] at 485–486. This Court, has, on numerous occasions, refused to hold that commercial ventures such as a motion-picture house are "private" for the purpose of civil rights litigation and civil rights statutes. [  ] The Civil Rights Act of 1964 specifically defines motion-picture houses and theaters as places of "public accommodation" covered by the Act as operations affecting commerce. [  ]

Our prior decisions recognizing a right to privacy guaranteed by the Fourteenth Amendment included "only personal rights that can be deemed 'fundamental' or 'implicit in the concept of ordered liberty.' [  ]." [  ] This privacy right encompasses and protects the personal intimacies of the home, the family, marriage, motherhood, procreation, and child rearing. [  ] Nothing, however, in this Court's decisions intimates that there is any "fundamental" privacy right "implicit in the concept of ordered liberty" to watch obscene movies in places of public accommodation.

If obscene material unprotected by the First Amendment in itself carried with it a "penumbra" of constitutionally protected privacy, this Court would not have found it necessary to decide *Stanley* on the narrow basis of the "privacy of the home," which was hardly more than a reaffirmation that "a man's home is his castle" Cf. Stanley v. Georgia, supra, at 564.[13] Moreover, we have declined to equate the privacy of the home relied on in *Stanley* with a "zone" of "privacy" that follows a distributor or a consumer of obscene materials wherever he goes. [  ] The idea of a "privacy" right and a place of public accommodation are, in this context, mutually exclusive. Conduct or depictions of conduct that the state police power can prohibit on a public street do not become automatically protected by the Constitution merely because the conduct is moved to a bar or a "live" theater stage, any more than a "live" performance of a man and woman locked in a sexual embrace at high noon in Times Square is protected by the Constitution because they simultaneously engage in a valid political dialogue.

. . .

Finally, petitioners argue that conduct which directly involves "consenting adults" only has for that sole reason, a special claim to constitutional protection. Our Constitution establishes a broad range of condi-

**13.** The protection afforded by Stanley v. Georgia, 394 U.S. 557 (1969), is restricted to a place, the home. In contrast, the constitutionally protected privacy of family, marriage, motherhood, procreation, and child rearing is not just concerned with a particular place, but with a protected intimate relationship. Such protected privacy extends to the doctor's office, the hospital, the hotel room, or as otherwise required to safeguard the right to intimacy involved. [  ] Obviously, there is no necessary or legitimate expectation of privacy which would extend to marital intercourse on a street corner or a theater stage.

tions on the exercise of power by the States, but for us to say that our Constitution incorporates the proposition that conduct involving consenting adults only is always beyond state regulation, is a step we are unable to take.[15]  Commercial exploitation of depictions, descriptions, or exhibitions of obscene conduct on commercial premises open to the adult public falls within a State's broad power to regulate commerce and protect the public environment.  The issue in this context goes beyond whether someone, or even the majority, considers the conduct depicted as "wrong" or "sinful."  The States have the power to make a morally neutral judgment that public exhibition of obscene material, or commerce in such material, has a tendency to injure the community as a whole, to endanger the public safety, or to jeopardize, in Mr. Chief Justice Warren's words, the States' "right  . . .  to maintain a decent society."  Jacobellis v. Ohio, 378 U.S., at 199 (dissenting opinion).

To summarize, we have today reaffirmed the basic holding of Roth v. United States, supra, that obscene material has no protection under the First Amendment.  See [Miller].  . . .  In this case we hold that the States have a legitimate interest in regulating commerce in obscene material and in regulating exhibition of obscene material in places of public accommodation, including so-called "adult" theaters from which minors are excluded.  In light of these holdings, nothing precludes the State of Georgia from the regulation of the allegedly obscene material exhibited in Paris Adult Theatre I or II, provided that the applicable Georgia law, as written or authoritatively interpreted by the Georgia courts, meets the First Amendment standards set forth in [Miller].  The judgment is vacated and the case remanded to the Georgia Supreme Court for further proceedings not inconsistent with this opinion and [Miller], supra. [ ]

Vacated and remanded.

Mr. Justice Douglas, dissenting.

My Brother Brennan is to be commended for seeking a new path through the thicket which the Court entered when it undertook to sustain the constitutionality of obscenity laws and to place limits on their application.  I have expressed on numerous occasions my disagreement with the basic decision that held that "obscenity" was not protected by the First Amendment.  I disagreed also with the definitions that evolved.  Art and literature reflect tastes; and tastes, like musical appreciation, are hardly reducible to precise definitions.  That is one reason I have always felt that "obscenity" was not an exception to the First Amendment.  . . .

**15.**  The state statute books are replete with constitutionally unchallenged laws against prostitution, suicide, voluntary self-mutilation, brutalizing "bare fist" prize fights, and duels, although these crimes may only directly involve "consenting adults."  . . .

As Professor Irving Kristol has observed: "Bearbaiting and cockfighting are prohibited only in part out of compassion for the suffering animals; the main reason they were abolished was because it was felt that they debased and brutalized the citizenry who flocked to witness such spectacles." On the Democratic Idea in America 33 (1972).

. . .

MR. JUSTICE BRENNAN, with whom MR. JUSTICE STEWART and MR. JUSTICE MARSHALL join, dissenting.

This case requires the Court to confront once again the vexing problem of reconciling state efforts to suppress sexually oriented expression with the protections of the First Amendment, as applied to the States through the Fourteenth Amendment. No other aspect of the First Amendment has, in recent years, demanded so substantial a commitment of our time, generated such disharmony of views, and remained so resistant to the formulation of stable and manageable standards. I am convinced that the approach initiated 16 years ago in [*Roth*], and culminating in the Court's decision today, cannot bring stability to this area of the law without jeopardizing fundamental First Amendment values, and I have concluded that the time has come to make a significant departure from that approach.

. . .

. . . The essence of our problem in the obscenity area is that we have been unable to provide "sensitive tools" to separate obscenity from other sexually oriented but constitutionally protected speech, so that efforts to suppress the former do not spill over into the suppression of the latter. . . .

. . .

Of course, the vagueness problem would be largely of our own creation if it stemmed primarily from our failure to reach a consensus on any one standard. But after 16 years of experimentation and debate I am reluctantly forced to the conclusion that none of the available formulas, including the one announced today, can reduce the vagueness to a tolerable level while at the same time striking an acceptable balance between the protections of the First and Fourteenth Amendments, on the one hand, and on the other the asserted state interest in regulating the dissemination of certain sexually oriented materials. Any effort to draw a constitutionally acceptable boundary on state power must resort to such indefinite concepts as "prurient interest," "patent offensiveness," "serious literary value," and the like. The meaning of these concepts necessarily varies with the experience, outlook, and even idiosyncrasies of the person defining them. Although we have assumed that obscenity does exist and that we "know it when [we] see it," Jacobellis v. Ohio, supra, at 197 (Stewart, J., concurring), we are manifestly unable to describe it in advance except by reference to concepts so elusive that they fail to distinguish clearly between protected and unprotected speech.

. . . These considerations suggest that no one definition, no matter how precisely or narrowly drawn, can possibly suffice for all situations, or carve out fully suppressible expression from all media without also creating a substantial risk of encroachment upon the guarantees of the Due Process Clause and the First Amendment.[9]

The vagueness of the standards in the obscenity area produces a number of separate problems, and any improvement must rest on an understanding that the problems are to some extent distinct. First, a vague statute fails to provide adequate notice to persons who are engaged in the type of conduct that the statute could be thought to proscribe. . . .

In addition to problems that arise when any criminal statute fails to afford fair notice of what it forbids, a vague statute in the areas of speech and press creates a second level of difficulty. We have indicated that "stricter standards of permissible statutory vagueness may be applied to a statute having a potentially inhibiting effect on speech; a man may the less be required to act at his peril here, because the free dissemination of ideas may be the loser." Smith v. California, 361 U.S. 147, 151 (1959). . . .

. . .

The problems of fair notice and chilling protected speech are very grave standing alone. But it does not detract from their importance to recognize that a vague statute in this area creates a third, although admittedly more subtle, set of problems. These problems concern the institutional stress that inevitably results where the line separating protected from unprotected speech is excessively vague. In *Roth* we conceded that "there may be marginal cases in which it is difficult to determine the side of the line on which a particular fact situation falls. . . ." 354 U.S., at 491–492. Our subsequent experience demonstrates that almost every case is "marginal." And since the "margin" marks the point of separation between protected and unprotected speech, we are left with a system in which almost every obscenity case presents a constitutional question of exceptional difficulty. . . .

. . .

. . . In addition, the uncertainty of the standards creates a continuing source of tension between state and federal courts, since the need for an independent determination by this Court seems to render superfluous even the most conscientious analysis by state tribunals. And our inability to justify our decisions with a persuasive rationale—or indeed, any rationale at all—necessarily creates the impression that we are merely second-guessing state court judges.

---

**9.** Although I did not join the opinion of the Court in Stanley v. Georgia, 394 U.S. 557 (1969), I am now inclined to agree that "the Constitution protects the right to receive information and ideas," and that "[t]his right to receive information and ideas, regardless of their social worth . . . is fundamental to our free society."

. . . Whether or not a class of "obscene" and thus entirely unprotected speech does exist, I am forced to conclude that the class is incapable of definition with sufficient clarity to withstand attack on vagueness grounds. Accordingly, it is on principles of the void-for-vagueness doctrine that this opinion exclusively relies.

The severe problems arising from the lack of fair notice, from the chill on protected expression, and from the stress imposed on the state and federal judicial machinery persuade me that a significant change in direction is urgently required. I turn, therefore, to the alternatives that are now open.

## IV

1. The approach requiring the smallest deviation from our present course would be to draw a new line between protected and unprotected speech, still permitting the States to suppress all material on the unprotected side of the line. In my view, clarity cannot be obtained pursuant to this approach except by drawing a line that resolves all doubt in favor of state power and against the guarantees of the First Amendment. We could hold, for example, that any depiction or description of human sexual organs, irrespective of the manner or purpose of the portrayal, is outside the protection of the First Amendment and therefore open to suppression by the States. That formula would, no doubt, offer much fairer notice of the reach of any state statute drawn at the boundary of the State's constitutional power. And it would also, in all likelihood, give rise to a substantial probability of regularity in most judicial determinations under the standard. But such a standard would be appallingly overbroad, permitting the suppression of a vast range of literary, scientific, and artistic masterpieces. Neither the First Amendment nor any free community could possibly tolerate such a standard. Yet short of that extreme it is hard to see how any choice of words could reduce the vagueness problem to tolerable proportions, so long as we remain committed to the view that some class of materials is subject to outright suppression by the State.

2. The alternative adopted by the Court today recognizes that a prohibition against any depiction or description of human sexual organs could not be reconciled with the guarantees of the First Amendment. But the Court does retain the view that certain sexually oriented material can be considered obscene and therefore unprotected by the First and Fourteenth Amendment. To describe that unprotected class of expression, the Court adopts a restatement of the *Roth–Memoirs* definition of obscenity. . . .

. . .

Although the Court's restatement substantially tracks the three-part test announced in Memoirs v. Massachusetts, supra, it does purport to modify the "social value" component of the test. Instead of requiring, as did *Roth* and *Memoirs,* that state suppression be limited to materials utterly lacking in social value, the Court today permits suppression if the government can prove that the materials lack "*serious* literary, artistic, political or scientific value." But the definition of "obscenity" as expression utterly lacking in social importance is the key to the conceptual basis of *Roth* and our subsequent opinions. In *Roth* we held that certain expression is obscene, and thus outside the protection of the First Amendment, precisely *because* it lacks even the slightest redeeming

social value.  [   ]  The Court's approach necessarily assumes that some
works will be deemed obscene—even though they clearly have *some*
social value—because the State was able to prove that the value, measured by some unspecified standard, was not sufficiently "serious" to
warrant constitutional protection.  That result is not merely inconsistent with our holding in *Roth;* it is nothing less than a rejection of the
fundamental First Amendment premises and rationale of the *Roth*
opinion and an invitation to widespread suppression of sexually oriented
speech.  Before today, the protections of the First Amendment have
never been thought limited to expressions of *serious* literary or political
value.  [   ]

                    . . .

    4.   Finally, I have considered the view, urged so forcefully since
1957 by our Brothers Black and Douglas, that the First Amendment bars
the suppression of any sexually oriented expression.  That position
would effect a sharp reduction, although perhaps not a total elimination,
of the uncertainty that surrounds our current approach.  Nevertheless, I
am convinced that it would achieve that desirable goal only by stripping
the States of power to an extent that cannot be justified by the commands of the Constitution, at least so long as there is available an
alternative approach that strikes a better balance between the guarantee
of free expression and the States' legitimate interests.

                              V

    Our experience since *Roth* requires us not only to abandon the effort
to pick out obscene materials on a case-by-case basis, but also to
reconsider a fundamental postulate of *Roth:*  that there exists a definable
class of sexually oriented expression that may be totally suppressed by
the Federal and State Governments.  Assuming that such a class of
expression does in fact exist, I am forced to conclude that the concept of
"obscenity" cannot be defined with sufficient specificity and clarity to
provide fair notice to persons who create and distribute sexually oriented
materials, to prevent substantial erosion of protected speech as a byproduct of the attempt to suppress unprotected speech, and to avoid very
costly institutional harms.  Given these inevitable side effects of state
efforts to suppress what is assumed to be *unprotected* speech, we must
scrutinize with care the state interest that is asserted to justify the
suppression.  For in the absence of some very substantial interest in
suppressing such speech, we can hardly condone the ill effects that seem
to flow inevitably from the effort.

    Obscenity laws have a long history in this country.   . . .

    This history caused us to conclude in *Roth* "that the unconditional
phrasing of the First Amendment [that "Congress shall make no
law  . . .  abridging the freedom of speech, or of the press  . . ."]
was not intended to protect every utterance."   . . .

    Because we assumed—incorrectly, as experience has proved—that
obscenity could be separated from other sexually oriented expression

without significant costs either to the First Amendment or to the judicial machinery charged with the task of safeguarding First Amendment freedoms, we had no occasion in *Roth* to probe the asserted state interest in curtailing unprotected, sexually oriented speech. Yet, as we have increasingly come to appreciate the vagueness of the concept of obscenity, we have begun to recognize and articulate the state interests at stake. . . .

The opinions in *Redrup* and Stanley v. Georgia reflected our emerging view that the state interest in protecting children and in protecting unconsenting adults may stand on a different footing from the other asserted state interests. . . . Similarly, if children are "not possessed of that full capacity for individual choice which is the presupposition of the First Amendment guarantees," Ginsberg v. New York, 390 U.S., at 649–650 (Stewart, J., concurring), then the State may have a substantial interest in precluding the flow of obscene materials even to consenting juveniles. [ ]

But, whatever the strength of the state interests in protecting juveniles and unconsenting adults from exposure to sexually oriented materials, those interests cannot be asserted in defense of the holding of the Georgia Supreme Court in this case. . . .

At the outset it should be noted that virtually all of the interests that might be asserted in defense of suppression, laying aside the special interests associated with distribution to juveniles and unconsenting adults, were also posited in Stanley v. Georgia, supra, where we held that the State could not make the "mere private possession of obscene material a crime." Id., at 568. That decision presages the conclusions I reach here today.

In *Stanley* we pointed out that "[t]here appears to be little empirical basis for" the assertion that "exposure to obscene materials may lead to deviant sexual behavior or crimes of sexual violence." Id., at 566 and n. 9.[26] In any event, we added that "if the State is only concerned about printed or filmed materials inducing antisocial conduct, we believe that in the context of private consumption of ideas and information we should adhere to the view that '[a]mong free men, the deterrents ordinarily to be applied to prevent crime are education and punishment for violations of the law. . . .' Whitney v. California, 274 U.S. 357, 378 (1927) (Brandeis, J., concurring)." Id., at 566–567.

---

**26.** Indeed, since *Stanley* was decided, the President's Commission on Obscenity and Pornography has concluded:

"In sum, empirical research designed to clarify the question has found no evidence to date that exposure to explicit sexual materials plays a significant role in the causation of delinquent or criminal behavior among youth or adults. The Commission cannot conclude that exposure to erotic materials is a factor in the causation of sex crime or sex delinquen-

cy." Report of the Commission on Obscenity and Pornography 27 (1970) (footnote omitted).

To the contrary, the Commission found that "[o]n the positive side, explicit sexual materials are sought as a source of entertainment and information by substantial numbers of American adults. At times, these materials also appear to serve to increase and facilitate constructive communication about sexual matters within marriage." Id., at 53.

Moreover, in *Stanley* we rejected as "wholly inconsistent with the philosophy of the First Amendment," id., at 566, the notion that there is a legitimate state concern in the "control [of] the moral content of a person's thoughts," id., at 565, and we held that a State "cannot constitutionally premise legislation on the desirability of controlling a person's private thoughts." Id., at 566. That is not to say, of course, that a State must remain utterly indifferent to—and take no action bearing on—the morality of the community.   . . .

.  .  .

If, as the Court today assumes, "a state legislature may   . . . act on the   . . . assumption that commerce in obscene books, or public exhibitions focused on obscene conduct, have a tendency to exert a corrupting and debasing impact leading to antisocial behavior," then it is hard to see how state-ordered regimentation of our minds can ever be forestalled. For if a State may, in an effort to maintain or create a particular moral tone, prescribe what its citizens cannot read or cannot see, then it would seem to follow that in pursuit of that same objective a State could decree that its citizens must read certain books or must view certain films.   .  .  .

Recognizing these principles, we have held that so-called thematic obscenity—obscenity which might persuade the viewer or reader to engage in "obscene" conduct—is not outside the protection of the First Amendment:

> "It is contended that the State's action was justified because the motion picture attractively portrays a relationship which is contrary to the moral standards, the religious precepts, and the legal code of its citizenry. This argument misconceives what it is that the Constitution protects. Its guarantee is not confined to the expression of ideas that are conventional or shared by a majority. It protects advocacy of the opinion that adultery may sometimes be proper, no less than advocacy of socialism or the single tax. And in the realm of ideas it protects expression which is eloquent no less than that which is unconvincing." Kingsley International Pictures Corp. v. Regents, 360 U.S. 684, 688–689 (1959).

Even a legitimate, sharply focused state concern for the morality of the community cannot, in other words, justify an assault on the protections of the First Amendment. [  ] Where the state interest in regulation of morality is vague and ill defined, interference with the guarantees of the First Amendment is even more difficult to justify.

In short, while I cannot say that the interests of the State—apart from the question of juveniles and unconsenting adults—are trivial or nonexistent, I am compelled to conclude that these interests cannot justify the substantial damage to constitutional rights and to this Nation's judicial machinery that inevitably results from state efforts to bar the distribution even of unprotected material to consenting adults. [  ] I would hold, therefore, that at least in the absence of distribution to juveniles or obtrusive exposure to unconsenting adults, the First and

Fourteenth Amendments prohibit the State and Federal Governments from attempting wholly to suppress sexually oriented materials on the basis of their allegedly "obscene" contents. Nothing in this approach precludes those governments from taking action to serve what may be strong and legitimate interests through regulation of the manner of distribution of sexually oriented material.

. . . Difficult questions must still be faced, notably in the areas of distribution to juveniles and offensive exposure to unconsenting adults. Whatever the extent of state power to regulate in those areas,[29] it should be clear that the view I espouse today would introduce a large measure of clarity to this troubled area, would reduce the institutional pressure on this Court and the rest of the State and Federal Judiciary, and would guarantee fuller freedom of expression while leaving room for the protection of legitimate governmental interests. . . .

**Notes and Questions**

1.  What changes are wrought by *Miller*? How are they justified?

2.  What different question is raised in *Paris*? What motivates the majority's answer to that question?

3.  What underlies Justice Douglas's argument that no prosecution for obscenity should be possible until after a particular tract has been declared "beyond the pale" in a civil proceeding?

4.  In Jenkins v. Georgia, 418 U.S. 153, 1 Med.L.Rptr. 1504 (1974), Jenkins had been convicted for showing the film "Carnal Knowledge." The state courts had relied on the jury's finding, but the Court reversed on the ground that the standards set in *Miller* did not justify the jury's verdict. Although "ultimate sexual acts" took place "the camera does not focus on the bodies of the actors at such times. There is no exhibition whatever of the actors' genitals, lewd or otherwise, during these scenes. There are occasional scenes of nudity, but nudity alone is not enough to make material legally obscene" under *Miller*. Was the Supreme Court back in the business of reviewing individual books and movies?

5.  In *Miller,* California had chosen to use a statewide community standard and the Court had observed that a national standard was "hypothetical and unascertainable." In *Jenkins,* the majority had said that a state was not required to define the phrase "contemporary community standards" in more precise geographical terms. In Hamling v. United States, 418 U.S. 87, 1 Med.L.Rptr. 1479 (1974), the Court interpreted a federal statute barring the mailing of obscene materials to make the relevant community the one from which the jury was drawn.

---

**29.** The Court erroneously states, Miller v. California, ante, [ ], that the author of this opinion "indicates that suppression of unprotected obscene material is permissible to avoid exposure to unconsenting adults . . . and to juveniles. . . ." I defer expression of my views as to the scope of state power in these areas until cases squarely presenting these questions are before the Court. See n. 9, supra; Miller v. California, supra (dissenting opinion).

6.  Further complicating the question of what is the appropriate standard, the Supreme Court subsequently decided that the shift from a national standard to community standards applies only to the first two prongs of the three-part test.  In Pope v. Illinois, 481 U.S. 497, 14 Med.L.Rptr. 1001 (1987), the Court held that the question of serious literary, artistic, political or scientific value must be decided on the basis of a reasonable person as opposed to community standard.  "Just as the ideas a work represents need not obtain majority approval to merit protection, neither, insofar as the First Amendment is concerned, does the value of the work vary from community to community based on the degree of local acceptance it has won."

Justice Scalia concurred in the Court's judgment, but raised questions concerning the need to reexamine the First Amendment treatment of obscenity:

> I join the Court's opinion with regard to an "objective" or "reasonable person" test of "serious literary, artistic, political, or scientific value," [*Miller*], because I think that the most faithful assessment of what *Miller* intended, and because we have not been asked to reconsider *Miller* in the present case.  I must note, however, that in my view it is quite impossible to come to an objective assessment of (at least) literary or artistic value, there being many accomplished people who have found literature in Dada, and art in the replication of a soup can.  Since ratiocination has little to do with esthetics, the fabled "reasonable man" is of little help in the inquiry, and would have to be replaced with, perhaps, the "man of tolerably good taste"—a description that betrays the lack of an ascertainable standard.  If evenhanded and accurate decisionmaking is not always impossible under such a regime, it is at least impossible in the cases that matter.  I think we would be better advised to adopt as a legal maxim what has long been the wisdom of mankind: *De gustibus non est disputandum*.  Just as there is no use arguing about taste, there is no use litigating about it.  For the law courts to decide "What is beauty" is a novelty even by today's standards.
>
> .  .  .
>
> All of today's opinions, I suggest, display the need for reexamination of *Miller*.

Justice Brennan and Justice Stevens (joined by Justice Marshall) wrote separate dissenting opinions arguing that, absent some connection to children or unconsenting adults, obscene materials should be protected by the First Amendment.

7.  Perhaps because motion picture censorship was permissible, states attempted to regulate more than obscenity when reviewing films.  Some attempts were struck down because the grounds other than obscenity were found too vague.  In Joseph Burstyn, Inc. v. Wilson, 343 U.S. 495, 1 Med.L.Rptr. 1357 (1952), New York had banned a film on the grounds that it was "sacrilegious," which the state defined as treating religion

with "contempt, mockery, scorn, and ridicule." The Court thought this gave the censor too much leeway, although it noted that the First Amendment did not allow freedom to exhibit "every motion picture of every kind at all times and all places."

8. The result is that although motion pictures may still be subject to administrative screening before public presentation, Times Film Corp. v. Chicago, 365 U.S. 43 (1961), they may be rejected only for those reasons that permit penalizing distributors of books and magazines after the fact: obscenity and pornography. The characteristics of different media, of course, may still lead to different results. In addition, when preliminary obligations are imposed, speedy review of adverse decisions must be assured. Freedman v. Maryland, 380 U.S. 51, 1 Med.L.Rptr. 1126 (1965).

9. Some states have attempted to attack the pornography business as a form of racketeering, using the broad-gauge weapons that have been made available to prosecutors to fight organized crime. This approach suffered a setback in Fort Wayne Books, Inc. v. Indiana, 489 U.S. 46, 16 Med.L.Rptr. 1337 (1989). Under an Indiana racketeering statute, the prosecutor attempted to seize the entire inventory of an adult bookstore on the ground that it was property used in a continuing pattern of criminal activity, namely sale of obscene material. The Supreme Court held that petitioner's obscenity convictions were crimes upon which a racketeering remedy could be predicated, but that the seizure was unconstitutional because it was tantamount to a prior restraint on materials that had to be presumed to be protected until their obscenity was properly established in an adversary proceeding.

10. In Erznoznik v. Jacksonville, 422 U.S. 205, 1 Med.L.Rptr. 1508 (1975), the Court struck down an ordinance forbidding the showing of nudity on drive-in theatre screens visible from public streets. After an unsuccessful captive audience justification, the city also asserted that the ordinance was justified as a protection of children. This also failed because the restriction was "broader than permissible. The ordinance is not directed against sexually explicit nudity, nor is it otherwise limited. Rather, it sweepingly forbids display of films containing any uncovered buttocks or breasts, irrespective of contexts or pervasiveness. Thus, it would bar a film containing a picture of a baby's buttocks, the nude body of a war victim, or scenes from a culture in which nudity is indigenous. . . . Clearly all nudity cannot be deemed obscene even as to minors."

11. An obscenity statute need not precisely describe the kinds of sexual conduct covered. In Ward v. Illinois, 431 U.S. 767, 2 Med.L.Rptr. 1929 (1977), the petitioner alleged that an Illinois obscenity statute was void for vagueness because it did not explicitly include sado-masochistic material in its ban. The Court disagreed, 5–4.

Justice White, for the majority, held that the Illinois law was sufficiently explicit in referring to the "kinds" of barred materials and that, even if it were not, the defendant had ample guidance from the state courts prior to the sale for which he was convicted. In response to an argument that sado-masochistic materials cannot be proscribed because they were not mentioned in *Miller,* Justice White asserted that the specifics in *Miller* were offered only as "examples" and "were not intended to be exhaustive."

Justice Stevens, for the dissenters, viewed the failure to require specificity in the definition of offensive material as a major and unwarranted change that would hasten the "ultimate downfall" of the *Miller* standard. "Today, the Court silently abandons one of the cornerstones of the *Miller* test." He found nothing in the statute that "specifically defines" what is prohibited. Nor had the state's supreme court "remedied this deficiency by supplying a limiting construction." To say that the statute need contain only generic references to the "kinds" of materials that are barred, "is to hold that a person can be prosecuted although the materials he sells are not specifically described in the list. Only five years ago, the Court promised that 'no one' could be so prosecuted."

12. When evaluating allegedly obscene material, the jury may look for guidance beyond the material itself to the circumstances of its sale and distribution. Citing *Hamling* and *Ginzburg,* Justice Rehnquist, for the majority, in Splawn v. California, 431 U.S. 595, 2 Med.L.Rptr. 1881 (1977), concluded that as "a matter of First Amendment law, evidence of pandering to prurient interests in the creation, promotion or dissemination of material is relevant in determining whether the material is obscene."

Justice Stevens, in a dissent joined by Justices Brennan, Stewart and Marshall, declared that the majority decision allowed non-obscene material to be classified as obscene solely because of truthful advertising that emphasized its sexually provocative nature. In a footnote, he asserted that Virginia State Board of Pharmacy v. Virginia Citizens Consumer Council, Inc., 425 U.S., 748, 1 Med.L.Rptr. 1930 (1976), which we will discuss in Chapter IX, granted constitutional protection to truthful advertisements.

13. The Eleventh Circuit reversed a declaratory judgment that 2 Live Crew's recording of "Nasty As They Wanna Be" was obscene. The district judge, as factfinder, had decided the *Miller* issues without benefit of expert testimony. The court of appeals said it was permissible for the judge to rely on his own expertise to determine whether the lyrics were patently offensive and whether they violated community standards with respect to prurient interest, but that the evidence failed to show that the judge possessed the artistic or literary knowledge needed to determine whether the work lacked "serious artistic, scientific, literary, or political value." The court rejected the state's argument that the judge could decide whether the work has such value merely by listening to it. Luke Records, Inc. v. Navarro, 960 F.2d 134 (11th Cir.1992).

14. Even though obscene materials—as defined by *Miller* —are unprotected by the U.S. Constitution, they may be protected by a state

constitution. In State v. Henry, 302 Or. 510, 732 P.2d 9, 14 Med.L.Rptr. 1011 (1987), the Oregon Supreme Court held that obscenity is protected expression under Article I, section 8, of the Oregon Constitution:

> Although the *Miller* test may pass federal constitutional muster and is recommended as a model for state legislatures by the Attorney General's Commission on Pornography, [   ], the test constitutes censorship forbidden by the Oregon Constitution. . . . [T]he problem with the Supreme Court's approach to obscene expression is that it permits government to decide what constitutes socially acceptable expression, which is precisely what Madison decried; [As Judge Tanzer stated in a previous case] "The difficulty [with the United States Supreme Court's approach] arises from the anomaly that the very purpose of the First Amendment is to protect expression which fails to conform to community standards."

> We hold that characterizing expression as "obscenity" under any definition, be it *Roth, Miller* or otherwise, does not deprive it of protection under the Oregon Constitution. Obscene speech, writing or equivalent forms of communication are "speech" nonetheless. We emphasize that the prime reason that "obscene expression cannot be restricted is that it is speech that does not fall within any historical exception to the plain wording of the Oregon Constitution that "no law shall be passed restraining the expression of [speech] freely on any subject whatsoever."

The Court did emphasize that obscenity could be regulated "in the interests of unwilling viewers, captive audiences, minors, and beleaguered neighbors."

15. The Attorney General's Commission on Pornography referred to by the Oregon Supreme Court was the Commission appointed by then Attorney General Edwin Meese. The Commission and its findings were highly controversial. Some critics charged that the Commission was predisposed to a finding that pornography was extremely harmful to society and that the selection of people to testify before the Commission was biased toward that finding.

In July 1986 the Commission submitted its final report, concluding that sexually violent materials had been shown to have negative effects. Material that showed "sexual activity without violence but with degradation, submission, domination or humiliation" was also found to have negative effects. All Commissioners found that "some" materials concerning sexual activity that did not fit either category "may be harmful." Some Commissioners "agreed that not all materials in this classification are not harmful." This third category was found to make up a "very small percentage of the total universe of pornographic materials." Finally, as to materials that featured "nudity without force, coercion, sexual activity or degradation," all Commissioners agreed that "some materials . . . may be harmful." Again, some Commissioners agreed that "not all materials in this classification are not harmful."

The Commission majority proposed a total of 92 recommendations collected at pages 433–458 of the report.

The Meese Commission became involved in additional controversy when it sent a letter to certain corporations that had been identified in testimony by the Rev. Donald Wildmon, Executive Director of the National Federation of Decency, as selling pornography, which in his opinion included *Playboy* and *Penthouse*. The letter stated that the corporation had been identified in testimony as selling pornography and asked if the corporation wished to respond. The letter further stated that the absence of a response would indicate that the corporation had no objection to being identified in the Commission's final report as a seller of pornography.

The publishers of *Playboy, Penthouse* and other magazines referred to in Wildmon's testimony obtained an injunction against the Meese Commission. The injunction prohibited the Commission from publishing a list of purported distributors of allegedly pornographic material. In addition, the Commission was required to send a new letter to all the recipients of the original advising them that the first letter was withdrawn, that no list would be published and that no response to the original letter was required. Playboy Enterprises v. Meese, 639 F.Supp. 581, 13 Med.L.Rptr. 1101 (D.D.C.1986).

16. *Pornography and Women.* In the early 1980s groups perceiving a correlation between pornography and violence toward women sought the adoption of local ordinances that defined pornography in terms of material that presented women as sexual objects or in positions of sexual subordination. Such material would then be prohibited. The focus was on specific content—the presentation of women in certain ways—and there was no room for a defense that the work taken as a whole had substantial artistic or literary value. After the city of Indianapolis adopted such an ordinance, it was challenged, and overturned, in American Booksellers Association, Inc. v. Hudnut, 771 F.2d 323, 11 Med. L.Rptr. 2465 (7th Cir.1985).

The court accepted the premises of the city that the materials barred "tend to perpetuate subordination," which in turn leads to violence against women:

> There is much to this perspective. Beliefs are also facts. People often act in accordance with the images and patterns they find around them. People raised in a religion tend to accept the tenets of that religion, often without the independent examination. . . . Words and images act at the level of the conscious. Even the truth has little chance unless a statement fits within the framework of beliefs that may never have been subjected to rational study.

Yet this simply confirmed the power of pornography as speech. "All of these unhappy effects depend on mental intermediation":

. . . Pornography affects how people see the world, their fellows, and social relations. If pornography is what pornography does, so is other speech. Hitler's orations affected how some Germans saw Jews. Communism is a world view, not simply a Manifesto by Marx and Engles or a set of speeches. Efforts to suppress communist speech in the United States were based on the belief that the public acceptability of such ideas would increase the likelihood of totalitarian government. Religions affect socialization in the most pervasive way.

Racial bigotry, anti-semitism, violence on television, reporters' biases—these and many more influence the culture and shape our socialization. None is directly answerable by more speech, unless that speech too finds its place in the popular culture. Yet all is protected as speech, however insidious. Any other answer leaves the government in control of all the institutions of our culture, the great censor and director of which thoughts are good for us.

Sexual responses often are unthinking responses, and the association of sexual arousal with the subordination of women therefore may have a substantial effect. But almost all cultural stimuli provoke unconscious responses. Religious ceremonies condition their participants. Teachers convey messages by selecting what not to cover; the implicit message about what is off limits or unthinkable may be more powerful than the messages for which they present rational argument. Television scripts contain unarticulated assumptions. People may be conditioned in subtle ways. If the fact that speech plays a role in a process of conditioning were enough to permit governmental regulation, that would be the end of freedom of speech.

. . .

Much of Indianapolis's argument rests on the belief that when speech is "unanswerable," and the metaphor that there is a "marketplace of ideas" does not apply, the First Amendment does not apply either. The metaphor is honored; Milton's *Areopagitica* and John Stuart Mill's *On Liberty* defend freedom of speech on the ground that the truth will prevail, and many of the most important cases under the First Amendment recite this position. The Framers undoubtedly believed it. As a general matter it is true. But the Constitution does not make the dominance of truth a necessary condition of freedom of speech. To say that it does would be to confuse an outcome of free speech with a necessary condition for the application of the amendment.

A power to limit speech on the ground that truth has not yet prevailed and is not likely to prevail implies the power to declare truth. At some point the government must be able to say (as Indianapolis has said): "We know what the truth is, yet a free exchange of speech has not driven out falsity, so that we must now prohibit falsity." If the government may declare the truth, why wait for the failure of speech?  Under the First Amendment, however, there is no such thing as a false idea.  Gertz v. Robert Welch, Inc., 418 U.S. 323, 339 (1974), so the government may not restrict speech on the ground that in a free exchange truth is not yet dominant.

At any time, some speech is ahead in the game; the more numerous speakers prevail.  Supporters of minority candidates may be forever "excluded" from the political process because their candidates never win, because few people believe their positions.  This does not mean that freedom of speech has failed.

The Supreme Court has rejected the position that speech must be "effectively answerable" to be protected by the Constitution.  . . .

Finally, the city argued that this was "low value" speech far from the political core, which could be regulated more readily than other speech.  The court disagreed:

> At all events, "pornography" is not low value speech within the meaning of these cases.  Indianapolis seeks to prohibit certain speech because it believes this speech influences social relations and politics on a grand scale, that it controls attitudes at home and in the legislature.  This precludes a characterization of the speech as low value.  True, pornography and obscenity have sex in common.  But Indianapolis left out of its definition any reference to literary, artistic, political, or scientific value.  The ordinance applies to graphic sexually explicit subordination in works great and small.  The Court sometimes balances the value of speech against the costs of its restriction, but it does this by category of speech and not by the content of particular works.  [ ]  Indianapolis has created an approved point of view and so loses the support of these cases.

In the absence of any element comparable to the lack of serious value in obscenity, the court was concerned that books such as Homer's *Iliad* and James Joyce's *Ulysses* might be covered by the ordinance because "both depict women as submissive objects for conquest and domination."

In response to the appellate ruling, proponents of the ordinance filed an appeal in the Supreme Court.  Based on the briefs alone, without hearing oral argument, the Court affirmed without opinion, 6–3.  475 U.S. 1001 (1986).  Chief Justice Burger and Justices Rehnquist and O'Connor voted to note probable jurisdiction of the appeal and to set the case for oral argument.

## B.  SPECIAL PROBLEMS RELATING TO CHILDREN

### 1.  PROTECTING CHILDREN FROM OBSCENE OR INDECENT MATERIALS

As Justice Brennan noted in his dissent in *Paris,* juveniles present special problems in the area of obscenity.  In *Paris* he was specifically referring to state efforts to prevent children from exposure to sexual material, obscene or otherwise, as readers, viewers and listeners. In Ginsberg v. New York, 390 U.S. 629, 1 Med.L.Rptr. 1424 (1968), the Court held that when a statute was aimed only at material "harmful to minors," the definition of obscenity could be modified to take into account its prurient appeal to minors, its offensiveness to the adult community's standards with respect to what is suitable for minors, and its redeeming value for minors. A Minneapolis ordinance, incorporating the *Ginsberg* criteria to define material "harmful to minors," required that such material be displayed only in sealed wrappers and opaque covers or in segregated areas designated "For Adults Only." The court of appeals upheld the ordinance as a valid restriction on the time, place, and manner of expression. Upper Midwest Booksellers Ass'n v. Minneapolis, 780 F.2d 1389, 12 Med.L.Rptr. 1913 (8th Cir.1985).

A Virginia statute making it a crime "to knowingly display for commercial purpose in a manner whereby juveniles may examine and peruse" material harmful to juveniles was attacked in American Booksellers Association v. Virginia, 802 F.2d 691, 12 Med.L.Rptr. 2271 (4th Cir.1986). The booksellers contended the statute would require them to restrict access to literary classics, sex education books and contemporary best-sellers.

The court of appeals, rejecting the reasoning of the *Upper Midwest* case, held the statute unconstitutional on the ground that it would limit access by adults to nonobscene material and thereby discourage exercise of First Amendment rights. The Supreme Court, however, granted the state's appeal and, through certified questions, asked the Virginia Supreme Court to construe the statute. That court interpreted it to reach only material that has no serious literary, artistic, political or scientific value even for "a legitimate minority of normal, older adolescents," and said none of the books mentioned by the booksellers would be subject to the statute. 236 Va. 168, 372 S.E.2d 618, 15 Med.L.Rptr. 2078 (1988). The U.S. Supreme Court remanded the case to the court of appeals for reconsideration in light of this construction of the statute. 488 U.S. 905 (1988).

The court of appeals held the new construction of the statute constitutional. It noted that the Virginia Supreme Court not only had narrowed the range of material covered by the statute, but also had construed the statute to require proof that the bookseller knowingly permitted juveniles to peruse "harmful" materials or failed to take reasonable steps to prevent it. 882 F.2d 125, 16 Med.L.Rptr. 2462 (4th Cir.1989), cert. denied 494 U.S. 1056 (1990).

The relationship between obscenity and offensive speech is developed in *Cohen* p. 79, *supra*, involving the words on the jacket, in which the Court rejected a captive audience rationale.

Justice Harlan concluded that the controlling point was whether "the States, acting as guardians of public morality, may properly remove this offensive word from the public vocabulary." He began consideration of that question by reemphasizing the values of free expression "in a society as diverse and populous as ours," citing Justice Brandeis's concurrence in *Whitney,* p. 33, *supra.* He then turned to the specific facts of the case:

> Against this perception of the constitutional policies involved, we discern certain more particularized considerations that peculiarly call for reversal of this conviction. First, the principle contended for by the State seems inherently boundless. How is one to distinguish this from any other offensive word? Surely the State has no right to cleanse public debate to the point where it is grammatically palatable to the most squeamish among us. Yet no readily ascertainable general principle exists for stopping short of that result were we to affirm the judgment below. For, while the particular four-letter word being litigated here is perhaps more distasteful than most others of its genre, it is nevertheless often true that one man's vulgarity is another's lyric. Indeed, we think it is largely because governmental officials cannot make principled distinctions in this area that the Constitution leaves matters of taste and style so largely to the individual.
>
> Additionally, we cannot overlook the fact, because it is well illustrated by the episode involved here, that much linguistic expression serves a dual communicative function: it conveys not only ideas capable of relatively precise, detached explication, but otherwise inexpressible emotions as well. In fact, words are often chosen as much for their emotive as their cognitive force. We cannot sanction the view that the Constitution, while solicitous of the cognitive content of individual speech, has little or no regard for that emotive function which, practically speaking, may often be the more important element of the overall message sought to be communicated. . . .

Justice Blackmun's dissent, joined by Justice Black among others, argued mainly that "Cohen's absurd and immature antic . . . was mainly conduct and little speech. [  ] Further, the case appears to me to be well within the sphere of [*Chaplinsky*]. . . . As a consequence, this Court's agonizing over First Amendment values seems misplaced and unnecessary."

Some have pressed the importance of the Cohen case as one involving political speech, emphasizing the particularly dangerous nature of limits on political expression, as well as the difficulty government would have in deciding what words to bar. In addition, the use of offensive speech often reveals important information to the rest of society— sometimes the ugliness of the speaker's cause, sometimes the deep extent of the speaker's frustration and sometimes the ugliness of the situation being challenged. On this analysis, efforts to prevent group libels and to purify political speech (except perhaps for captive audiences) would be impermissible. Compare Farber, "Civilizing Public Discourse: An Essay on Professor Bickel, Justice Harlan, and the

Enduring Significance of Cohen v. California," 1980 Duke L.J. 283 (rejecting limits on such speech) with Arkes, "Civility and the Restriction of Speech: Rediscovering the Defamation of Groups," 1974 Sup.Ct. Rev. 281 (supporting statutes proscribing certain types of attacks on racial and religious groups).

Somewhat different questions are raised when the indecent or offensive speech is available in the home, as is the case when it is broadcast on television or radio. The Federal Communications Commission regulates the broadcasting of indecent material. The Supreme Court has upheld the Commission's power to do so, although the exact limits of that power are not yet clear. We will explore that issue in more detail in Chapter XVII. Another way to access indecent material from the home is by telephone. "Dial-a-porn," prerecorded pornographic messages available to telephone callers for a small per-call fee, became a multi-million dollar industry in the 1980s.

In 1988 Congress attempted to abolish dial-a-porn by making it a crime to provide obscene or indecent commercial telephone messages in interstate commerce. The Supreme Court unanimously held the statute unconstitutional insofar as it proscribed material that was not obscene:

> Sexual expression which is indecent but not obscene is protected by the First Amendment, and the government does not submit that the sale of such materials to adults could be criminalized solely because they are indecent. The government may, however, regulate the content of constitutionally protected speech in order to promote a compelling interest if it chooses the least restrictive means to further the articulated interest. We have recognized that there is a compelling interest in protecting the physical and psychological well-being of minors. This interest extends to shielding minors from the influence of literature that is not obscene by adult standards. [*Ginsberg; New York v. Ferber,* 458 U.S. 747, 8 Med.L.Rptr. 1809 (1982)]. The government may serve this legitimate interest, but to withstand constitutional scrutiny, "it must do so by narrowly drawn regulations designed to serve those interests without unnecessarily interfering with First Amendment freedoms." [    ]

The government argued that a total ban on dial-a-porn was the only effective way to prevent it from reaching minors, because enterprising youngsters would find some way to avoid lesser restrictions such as codes, scrambling procedures, or access by credit card only. The Court refused to defer to Congress's view on that point, noting that both the FCC and the court of appeals had concluded that the lesser restrictions would be "feasible and effective" in preventing access by children.

Insofar as the statute prohibited dial-a-porn services from offering obscene material, the Court upheld the statute, even though complying with the "contemporary community standards" test of *Miller* might require the services to develop means of blocking some messages from some communities. Justices Brennan, Marshall and Stevens dissented from this portion of the decision on the ground that criminalizing distribution of obscene material to consenting adults is unconstitutional. Sable Communications of California, Inc. v. Federal Communications Commission, 492 U.S. 115, 16 Med.L.Rptr. 1961 (1989).

## 2. CHILD PORNOGRAPHY

A second major question regarding children involves legislative efforts to prevent their exploitation in the production of pornography. To what degree can the state restrict the sale of films and photographs that portray children engaged in sexual activity as a way of deterring the production of such materials? Is there more latitude for statutes aimed at child pornography than exists for general obscenity statutes? The following case is important not only for its holding on this question, but also for its discussion of the doctrine of overbreadth.

### NEW YORK v. FERBER
Supreme Court of the United States, 1982.
458 U.S. 747, 102 S.Ct. 3348, 73 L.Ed.2d 1113, 8 Med.L.Rptr. 1809.

[Ferber, the owner of a Manhattan bookstore, was arrested for selling two sexually explicit films to an undercover policeman. He was acquitted on charges of promoting an obscene sexual performance under § 263.10 of the New York Penal Law, but convicted under § 263.15 of promoting a sexual performance by a child. The conviction was overturned by the N.Y. Court of Appeals which held that § 263.15 violated the First Amendment.]

JUSTICE WHITE delivered the opinion of the Court.

At issue in this case is the constitutionality of a New York criminal statute which prohibits a person from knowingly promoting sexual performances by children under the age of 16 by distributing material which depicts such performances.

. . .

## II

The Court of Appeals proceeded on the assumption that the standard of obscenity incorporated in § 263.10, which follows the guidelines enunciated in Miller v. California, [ ], constitutes the appropriate line dividing protected from unprotected expression by which to measure a regulation directed at child pornography. . . .

The Court of Appeals' assumption was not unreasonable in light of our decisions. This case, however, constitutes our first examination of a statute directed at and limited to depictions of sexual activity involving children. We believe our inquiry should begin with the question of whether a State has somewhat more freedom in proscribing works which portray sexual acts or lewd exhibitions of genitalia by children.

## B

The *Miller* standard, like its predecessors, was an accommodation between the state's interests in protecting the "sensibilities of unwilling recipients" from exposure to pornographic material and the dangers of censorship inherent in unabashedly content-based laws. Like obscenity statutes, laws directed at the dissemination of child pornography run the risk of suppressing protected expression by allowing the hand of the censor to become unduly heavy. For the following reasons, however, we are persuaded that the States are entitled to greater leeway in the regulation of pornographic depictions of children.

*First.* It is evident beyond the need for elaboration that a state's interest in "safeguarding the physical and psychological well being of a minor" is "compelling." [ ] "A democratic society rests, for its continuance, upon the healthy well-rounded growth of young people into full maturity as citizens." Prince v. Massachusetts, 321 U.S. 158, 168 (1944). Accordingly, we have sustained legislation aimed at protecting the physical and emotional well-being of youth even when the laws have operated in the sensitive area of constitutionally protected rights. In Prince v. Massachusetts, supra, the Court held that a statute prohibiting use of a child to distribute literature on the street was valid notwithstanding the statute's effect on a First Amendment activity. In Ginsberg v. New York, [ ], we sustained a New York law protecting children from exposure to non-obscene literature. Most recently, we held that the government's interest in the "well-being of its youth" justified special treatment of indecent broadcasting received by adults as well as children. FCC v. Pacifica Foundation, 438 U.S. 726 (1978).

The prevention of sexual exploitation and abuse of children constitutes a government objective of surpassing importance. . . . The legislative judgment, as well as the judgment found in the relevant literature, is that the use of children as subjects of pornographic materials is harmful to the physiological, emotional, and mental health of the child. That judgment, we think, easily passes muster under the First Amendment.

*Second.* The distribution of photographs and films depicting sexual activity by juveniles is intrinsically related to the sexual abuse of children in at least two ways. First, the materials produced are a permanent record of the children's participation and the harm to the child is exacerbated by their circulation. Second, the distribution network for child pornography must be closed if the production of material which requires the sexual exploitation of children is to be effectively controlled.

Respondent does not contend that the State is unjustified in pursuing those who distribute child pornography. Rather, he argues that it is enough for the State to prohibit the distribution of materials that are legally obscene under the *Miller* test. While some States may find that this approach properly accommodates its interests, it does not follow that the First Amendment prohibits a State from going further. The *Miller* standard, like all general definitions of what may be banned as obscene, does not reflect the State's particular and more compelling interest in prosecuting those who promote the sexual exploitation of children.

Thus, the question under the *Miller* test of whether a work, taken as a whole, appeals to the prurient interest of the average person bears no connection to the issue of whether a child has been physically or psychologically harmed in the production of the work.  Similarly, a sexually explicit depiction need not be "patently offensive" in order to have required the sexual exploitation of a child for its production.  In addition, a work which, taken as a whole, contains serious literary, artistic, political, or scientific value may nevertheless embody the hardest core of child pornography.  "It is irrelevant to the child [who has been abused] whether or not the material  .  .  .  has a literary, artistic, political, or social value."  [  ]  We therefore cannot conclude that the *Miller* standard is a satisfactory solution to the child pornography problem.

*Third.*  The advertising and selling of child pornography provides an economic motive for and is thus an integral part of the production of such materials, an activity illegal throughout the nation.  "It rarely has been suggested that the constitutional freedom for speech and press extends its immunity to speech or writing used as an integral part of conduct in violation of a valid criminal statute."  [  ]  .  .  .

*Fourth.*  The value of permitting live performances and photographic reproductions of children engaged in lewd sexual conduct is exceedingly modest, if not *de minimis.*  We consider it unlikely that visual depictions of children performing sexual acts or lewdly exhibiting their genitals would often constitute an important and necessary part of a literary performance or scientific or educational work.  .  .  .

*Fifth.*  Recognizing and classifying child pornography as a category of material outside the protection of the First Amendment is not incompatible with our earlier decisions.  "The question whether speech is, or is not protected by the First Amendment often depends on the content of the speech."  [  ]  .  .  .  Thus, it is not rare that a content-based classification of speech has been accepted because it may be appropriately generalized that within the confines of the given classification, the evil to be restricted so overwhelmingly outweighs the expressive interests, if any, at stake, that no process of case-by-case adjudication is required.  When a definable class of material, such as that covered by § 263.15, bears so heavily and pervasively on the welfare of children engaged in its production, we think the balance of competing interests is clearly struck and that it is permissible to consider these materials as without the protection of the First Amendment.

## C

There are, of course, limits on the category of child pornography which, like obscenity, is unprotected by the First Amendment.  As with all legislation in this sensitive area, the conduct to be prohibited must be adequately defined by the applicable state law, as written or authoritatively construed.  Here the nature of the harm to be combatted requires that the state offense be limited to works that *visually* depict sexual conduct by children below a specified age.   The category of "sexual conduct" proscribed must also be suitably limited and described.

The test for child pornography is separate from the obscenity standard enunciated in *Miller,* but may be compared to it for purpose of clarity.  The *Miller* formulation is adjusted to the following respects: A trier of fact need not find that the material appeals to the prurient interest of the average person;  it is not required that sexual conduct portrayed be done so in a patently offensive manner;  and the material at issue need not be considered as a whole.  We note that the distribution of descriptions or other depictions of sexual conduct, not otherwise obscene, which do not involve live performance or photographic or other visual reproduction of live performances, retains First Amendment protection.   .  .  .

.  .  .

## III

It remains to address the claim that the New York statute is unconstitutionally overbroad because it would forbid the distribution of material with serious literary, scientific or educational value or material which does not threaten the harms sought to be combatted by the State. Respondent prevailed on that ground below, and it is to that issue we now turn.

The New York Court of Appeals recognized that overbreadth scrutiny has been limited with respect to conduct-related regulation, [  ], but it did not apply [that] test because the challenged statute, in its view, was directed at "pure speech."   The Court went on to find that § 263.15 was fatally overbroad: "[T]he statute would prohibit the showing of any play or movie in which a child portrays a defined sexual act, real or simulated, in a nonobscene manner.  It would also prohibit the sale, showing, or distributing of medical or educational materials containing photographs of such acts.  Indeed, by its terms, the statute would prohibit those who oppose such portrayals from providing illustrations of what they oppose."

## A

The traditional rule is that a person to whom a statute may constitutionally be applied may not challenge that statute on the ground that it may conceivably be applied unconstitutionally to others in situations not before the Court.  [  ]  .  .  .

What has come to be known as the First Amendment overbreadth doctrine is one of the few exceptions to this principle and must be justified by "weighty countervailing policies."  [  ]  The doctrine is predicated on the sensitive nature of protected expression: "persons whose expression is constitutionally protected may well refrain from exercising their rights for fear of criminal sanctions by a statute susceptible of application to protected expression."  [  ]  It is for this reason that we have allowed persons to attack overly broad statutes even though the conduct of the person making the attack is clearly unprotected and could be proscribed by a law drawn with the requisite specificity. [   ]

The scope of the First Amendment overbreadth doctrine, like most exceptions to established principles, must be carefully tied to the circumstances in which facial invalidation of a statute is truly warranted. Because of the wide-reaching effects of striking a statute down on its face at the request of one whose own conduct may be punished despite the First Amendment, we have recognized that the overbreadth doctrine is "strong medicine" and have employed it with hesitation, and then "only as a last resort." Broadrick v. Oklahoma, 413 U.S. 601 (1973). We have, in consequence, insisted that the overbreadth involved be "substantial" before the statute involved will be invalidated on its face.

.   .   .

*Broadrick* was a regulation involving restrictions on political campaign activity, an area not considered "pure speech," and thus it was unnecessary to consider the proper overbreadth test when a law arguably reaches traditional forms of expression such as books and films. As we intimated in *Broadrick*, the requirement of substantial overbreadth extended "at the very least," to cases involving conduct plus speech. This case, which poses the question squarely, convinces us that the rationale of *Broadrick* is sound and should be applied in the present context involving the harmful employment of children to make sexually explicit materials for distribution.

.   .   .   The requirement of substantial overbreadth is directly derived from the purpose and nature of the doctrine. While a sweeping statute, or one incapable of limitation, has the potential to repeatedly chill the exercise of expressive activity by many individuals, the extent of deterrence of protected speech can be expected to decrease with the declining reach of the regulation. This observation appears equally applicable to the publication of books and films as it is to activities, such as picketing or participation in election campaigns, which have previously been categorized as involving conduct plus speech.   .   .   .

.   .   .

## IV

Because § 263.15 is not substantially overbroad, it is unnecessary to consider its application to material that does not depict sexual conduct of a type that New York may restrict consistent with the First Amendment. As applied to Paul Ferber and to others who distribute similar material, the statute does not violate the First Amendment as applied to the States through the Fourteenth. The decision of the New York Court of Appeals is reversed and the case is remanded to that Court for further proceedings not inconsistent with this opinion.

So ordered.

JUSTICE BLACKMUN concurs in the result.

[Justice O'Connor concurred separately to emphasize the narrowness of the Court's decision. In her view the case held only that even if the New York statute made some constitutionally protected speech illegal, it was not sufficiently overbroad to justify facial invalidation. She then indicated that the compelling state interest in protecting minors might be sufficient to justify banning the works in question even if they had serious literary, artistic, political or scientific value.]

[Justice Brennan, joined by Justice Marshall, concurred in the judgment but argued that application of the statute to materials with serious literary, artistic, political or scientific value would violate the First Amendment.]

[Justice Stevens concurred in the judgment on the ground that the category of speech covered by the statute was of lower quality than other speech. Since such "marginal" speech falls near the bottom of the First Amendment hierarchy, according to Justice Stevens, the extraordinary protection of the overbreadth doctrine was not justified.]

**Notes and Questions:**

1. In what ways is *Miller* modified?

2. What is the justification for the changes?

3. After *Ferber* Congress and several states adopted similar legislation. For the Congressional version, see the Child Protection Act of 1984, 18 U.S.C.A. §§ 2251–2255, deleting the provision in 18 U.S.C.A. § 2252 that had required sexually explicit material to be obscene before child pornography could be controlled.

# Chapter IX

# ADVERTISING REGULATION

## A. WHY IS REGULATION NEEDED?

More than $100 billion is spent annually on advertising in the
United States, with about $80 billion going to buy time and space in the
mass media (the rest primarily being used for direct mail and specialty
advertising). Additional billions are spent preparing the advertisements.
When this much money is spent to promote products and services,
sometimes to millions of people at a time, there is a strong motivation to
advertise as effectively as possible. Advertisers may be tempted to
mislead or to lie in an attempt to win customers. Businesses of all sizes
have fallen prey to this, attempting to induce the greatest possible
number of people to buy what the business is selling. Some advertisements are blatantly deceptive, others simply ambiguous, some literally
true but still misleading. All of these present problems to competing
businesses, as well as to consumers who must decide what products and
services to purchase, and from whom.

Since advertising has become a major force in American commerce,
questions have emerged about how honest advertising can and should be.
Advertising is one component of an overall marketing scheme designed
to move products from manufacturers, through distributors, to retailers
where, for a variety of reasons, including the impact of advertising,
consumers purchase them. During the industrial revolution two conditions emerged that made this marketing pattern practical. First, products identified by a brand label could be moved by new transportation
systems from maker to seller throughout the country. Second, the mass
media were developing as a means to inform consumers what products
were available and, according to most advertisers, that one brand was
"better" than the others.

Among the first to exploit this new vehicle for promoting products
were patent medicine sellers. Most patent medicines contained a high
percentage of alcohol (a 94–proof compound was not unusual) and were
touted as able to cure almost every known ailment. From the Civil War
to the early 20th century, patent medicine ads ran in magazines and
newspapers and were put on posters and in brochures. Some ads
contained an early form of a now-popular advertising technique, the
testimonial. Actors, Congressmen and even clergymen were said to be
satisfied users, though there is no way of knowing whether these people
actually used or approved of the nostrums.

An example of irresponsible early advertising is one printed in a
magazine in the 1880s for Dr. Scott's Electric Corset. The corset was
said to "cure" problems of being too fat or too lean or "any bodily

ailment." It could also "ward off and cure disease" by bringing "the magnetic power" of the corset "into constant contact with all vital organs." To reassure readers, the "doctor" claimed that "professional men affirmed that there is hardly a disease that electricity and magnetism will not benefit and cure." One of the "professional men" named was a former Surgeon General of the United States.

The success of patent medicines, spurred by outlandish advertising, prompted manufacturers of other products to begin advertising. In some cases, ads for cereal, clothing and cough drops were just as deceptive as those for patent medicines.

Today the excesses may not be as blatant as they were 100 years ago, but some advertisers still attempt to deceive the public. Considerable debate exists over how to minimize unfair and misleading advertising and who should exercise these controls. For example, can advertising be controlled at all in the face of the First Amendment's protection of free expression? May advertising to certain groups (such as young children) or for certain products (such as non-prescription drugs) be regulated or even forbidden? Should certain groups (such as doctors and lawyers) not be able to advertise?

These questions and others have drawn the attention of numerous people, from consumer groups to the Federal Trade Commission (FTC), the government agency most directly involved with advertising regulation. Other federal and state agencies have addressed the problem of deceptive advertising. The advertising industry has a self-regulation process, and the media and advertising agencies have codes identifying unacceptable practices.

## B. THE FEDERAL TRADE COMMISSION

### 1. THE FTC's JURISDICTION

It was a 1906 series of articles in *Colliers* magazine on patent medicines, "The Great American Fraud," written by muckraker Samuel Hopkins Adams, along with similar pieces in other publications, that in part led to the passage of the Pure Food and Drug Act in 1906 and the Federal Trade Commission Act (FTCA) in 1914.

The FTC was established by the FTCA. The Commission was initially charged with prohibiting "unfair methods of competition in commerce." As originally conceived, this phrase had nothing to do with advertising, but was to allow the FTC to enforce antitrust laws that courts had viewed with some hostility. Soon the FTC attempted to regulate deceptive advertising as a form of "unfair competition." The Supreme Court upheld the FTC, but only as a means of eliminating unfair competition by one business against another. Protection of consumers, as such, was beyond FTC power. Federal Trade Commission v. Raladam Co., 283 U.S. 643 (1931).

Three years later the Court reversed itself and upheld the FTC's regulation of the marketing of candy to children in a way that involved "gambling" to receive a larger quantity of the product. Federal Trade Commission v. R.F. Keppel & Bro., Inc., 291 U.S. 304 (1934). In part, the Court justified the concern with customers because they were children, but this was a first step toward giving the FTC power to regulate advertising because of its effect on consumers.

Congress concurred in this extension of power by passing what are known as the Wheeler–Lea Amendments to the FTCA in 1938. One change allowed the Commission to prohibit "unfair methods of competition in commerce, and unfair or deceptive acts or practices in commerce." The omission of "competition" in the latter phrase allowed the Commission to "center its attention on the direct *protection of the consumer.*" Pep Boys—Manny, Moe & Jack v. Federal Trade Commission, 122 F.2d 158 (3d Cir.1941). False advertising of food, drugs or cosmetics also became a violation of the law. The amendments allowed the FTC to take action against deceptive advertising that affected consumers.

The Supreme Court gave effect to this Congressional intent, noting that business practices can be unfair even if they violate no antitrust laws or other statutes and affect no competitors. Federal Trade Commission v. Sperry & Hutchinson Co., 405 U.S. 233 (1972). That is, some activities might be "unfair" even though not specifically proscribed by law. The Commission can regulate "unfairness," generating a new body of law, where practices are immoral, unethical, oppressive or unscrupulous.

Another set of amendments to the FTCA was added in 1975 by the Magnuson–Moss Act, 15 U.S.C.A. § 2301. This enlarged the Commission's powers to their present reach: "Unfair methods of competition in *or affecting* commerce and unfair or deceptive acts or practices in *or affecting* commerce are hereby declared unlawful." These changes allowed the FTC to deal with unfair or deceptive practices that might be local, not directly interstate, in character, but which have an adverse impact on interstate commerce. In particular, the Commission can reach deceptive practices in large cities affecting the economically disadvantaged and poorly educated.

However, this power was later limited as a result of industry claims that the FTC was abusing its powers by using the unfairness standard to regulate truthful, nondeceptive advertising. In its 1980 FTC reauthorization bill, Congress removed the FTC's authority to use that standard to initiate any new rulemakings. In subsequent years the House and Senate have been unable to agree on an FTC authorization bill, but each year have included the unfairness prohibition in the Continuing Resolutions providing operating funds for the FTC.

Overseeing advertising is just one FTC task. The agency is composed of five commissioners, including the chairman, appointed by the President for seven-year terms and confirmed by the Senate. It has a staff of over 1,650 and an annual budget of about $70 million (compare with $100 *billion* spent on advertising annually). Its other responsibilities include laws concerning antitrust violations, warranties, granting of credit and label laws.

What is the "advertising" over which the FTC has jurisdiction? Courts view advertising as any public and deliberate effort to draw attention to a product or service, or even to a person or organization. This may include trading stamps, premiums, lotteries and labels, as well as the more common newspaper and magazine ads, television commercials and billboards.

The statute does not define "unfair" or "deceptive." Instead, the FTC has established criteria for use in determining whether an ad violates the standards, and courts usually defer to the agency's expertise in this area, overturning the Commission only when its decision is deemed arbitrary or capricious. Federal Trade Commission v. Mary Carter Paint Co., 382 U.S. 46 (1965).

Any action the FTC takes must be in the public interest. Because advertising certainly affects the public, most actions the FTC takes regarding misleading ads will meet this standard. Also, the ad must misrepresent a fact that is misleading in a material respect. 15 U.S.C.A. § 52. That is, something that would be a material factor in a consumer's decision to buy the product or service satisfies this standard. To look at it another way, is the misleading statement a material part of the ad? For example, a representative of Standard Oil Co. claimed to be standing in front of the firm's research laboratory when discussing Chevron F–310 gasoline. In fact, he was near a county court house. An FTC hearing examiner said this was not a material misleading fact, even though the ad was false in this respect.

The Commission need not prove that an advertisement actually deceived consumers, but simply that it had a tendency to do so. For example, in Charles of the Ritz v. Federal Trade Commission, 143 F.2d 676 (2d Cir.1944), a manufacturer said its skin cream could make facial skin more attractive by removing lines and rejuvenating the user's face. Although the FTC produced no witnesses who said they thought the cream could actually do all that, the court said such proof was not necessary—a "capacity to deceive" was sufficient.

Who needs to be misled? At one time the FTC and the courts said it was a "reasonable" person. Then the courts held that if even a particularly gullible person could have been misled, that was sufficient. Gelb v. Federal Trade Commission, 144 F.2d 580 (2d Cir.1944). A more recent formulation is that, "In order to establish that an act or practice is deceptive, the FTC must establish that the representations, omissions, or practices likely would mislead customers, acting reasonably, to their detriment." Federal Trade Commission v. World Travel Vacation Brokers, Inc., 861 F.2d 1020 (7th Cir.1988).

It is equally accurate to say that a literally true statement in an advertisement may be deceptive and that an absolutely untrue statement may not be deceptive.

For instance, references to Santa Claus or to a tooth fairy are not to be believed as real, but rather taken as fantasies, and are acceptable advertising techniques. Aside from fantasies, however, explicit untruths are deceptive in advertising unless they are immaterial or the FTC finds they do not affect the public interest. Falsely advertising something as an antique or as imported or saying a razor blade will shave effectively for six months, are all explicit untruths materially affecting a consumer's reaction to the ad and are adverse to the public interest.

Questions of truth and untruth are more difficult when they are implicit or subtle. Determining whether such an ad is misleading must be based on the entire advertisement, not just a portion of it. One apparently misleading statement may be clarified by another, but the latter must be as conspicuous as the first and similarly positioned.

Sometimes even an ad that is literally true may be misleading because of the way it is presented. A seller of photograph albums and family portraits was ordered to stop representing that the company sold only to selected customers and gave away the albums free. The impression given was that each family was carefully selected for the offer. In fact, the company simply chose people on a random basis or by referrals from other customers.

Also, the cost of the photographs included the "price" of the album; the portraits actually "should" have cost less by themselves. The court said that although the representations may have been true literally, the overall impression given—free gifts and special selection of customers— was misleading. Kalwajtys v. Federal Trade Commission, 237 F.2d 654 (7th Cir.1956).

Ambiguity in ads usually will be construed against the advertiser. The use of an explanatory phrase may protect the advertiser. For example, the Potato Chip Institute said a product made of dehydrated potatoes, instead of raw potatoes, should not be called "potato chips." The court held that the phrase, "fashioned from dried potato granules," on the product's label and in its advertising prevented incorrect inferences by the public. Potato Chip Institute v. General Mills, 461 F.2d 1088 (8th Cir.1972).

Finally, the advertiser need not intend to deceive, though intent may make the violation more severe. Chrysler Corp. v. Federal Trade Commission, 561 F.2d 357 (D.C.Cir.1977).

## 2. DECEPTIVE ADVERTISING TECHNIQUES

The FTC and the courts have found many advertising techniques to be misleading or deceptive. Major examples follow.

### a. Deception by Pictures

Although early concern over misleading ads stressed the words used, the FTC also has found ads deceptive because of their illustrations. It is deceptive to show an automobile with a number of options—bumper guards, striping, special wheel covers—but quote the price for a stripped-down version.  An ad showing a model wearing expensive, tailor-made clothes may be deceptive if the store sells modestly priced, factory-produced goods.  Children's toys must be able to do what the pictures show them doing.  It is considered deceptive to have special effects or film editing enhance the toys' capabilities.

One widespread violation of FTC standards involved actors dressed in white coats to give the appearance of being scientists or doctors, adding an aura of authority to the product.  See, for example, Keele Hair & Scalp Specialists, Inc. v. Federal Trade Commission, 275 F.2d 18 (5th Cir.1960).

Although anything that would be deceptive if said in words would be equally impermissible if pictured, television has aggravated the problem because of the medium's impact and its ubiquity.  For instance, the FTC considered deceptive a commercial showing a can of liquid household cleaner on a radiator, on a kitchen stove and near a candle.  The commercial did not say the product was not flammable, but the picture gave that impression.  In fact, it was highly flammable.  Adell Chemical Co., Inc., 54 F.T.C. 1801 (1958).

Television demonstrations are another source of misleading ads.  The Commission prohibited a Prestone antifreeze commercial which showed two metal strips, one coated with Prestone, the other with another antifreeze, dipped into acid.  The Prestone strip remained in one piece; the other disintegrated.  The FTC said the ad was unfair, in part, because the acid was not found in automobiles and the metal strips were not made of the metal found in automobile cooling systems.  Union Carbide Corp., 79 F.T.C. 124 (1971).

### b.  Deception Regarding Price

An effective way to lure customers to a store or to persuade them to allow salespeople into their homes is to offer something "free."  Few businesses would stay solvent if they gave away merchandise or services.  In fact, most "free" offers involve the purchasing of something first, such as a two-for-one sale.

Generally, the Commission holds that deception occurs when the cost of the "free" goods is added to other merchandise the consumer buys without the customer's knowledge.  In two-for-one offers, the merchandiser must have sold one unit of a product at the same price charged for two units when the offer was made.  Federal Trade Commission v. Mary Carter Paint Co., 382 U.S. 46 (1965).

Because customers have begun to question whether unusually low prices mean unusually low quality merchandise or services, businesses have started explaining how such a price can be charged.  For example, they may say goods are repossessed or have been bought from a merchant who needed cash or are offered at factory prices.  In these cases, the FTC has said the representation must be accurate or it constitutes deceptive advertising.  Similarly, reduced or special prices must actually be below former prices, and those earlier prices cannot have been set high in order to later lower them for a "sale."  Also, a "regular retail price" has to be that for which the item usually is sold in the retailer's trade area.

"Bait and switch" advertising is another technique based on price. The "bait" is an item advertised at a particularly attractive price, designed to persuade customers to come to the store.  Once there, customers are told the advertised item is "out of stock" or otherwise unavailable, that it had limitations anyway, and that the customer should consider a different, more expensive and available model.  The FTC considers it deceptive to advertise merchandise without a clear intention of selling it.  For instance, a sewing machine company advertised for $23.50 a model claimed to be worth $99.  The salesperson disparaged the machine to customers, showing no interest in selling it and instead praised a more expensive model.  The FTC said the company had no intention of selling the advertised model, using it only to lure customers and switch them to the more expensive machine.  This practice is forbidden by the FTC, although it must be distinguished from convincing a customer to buy a more expensive item than advertised, where the retailer has a sufficient stock of the advertised model and will sell it to customers who choose it.  World Sewing Center, Inc., 73 F.T.C. 1007 (1968).

### c.  Mockups

Among the problems presented by television is the use of mockups. A mockup is more than just a demonstration.  It is the use of an object to simulate something that is real, the technique being used because of television's technical limitations.  For instance, orange juice may look drab, almost like milk, unless a coloring agent is added to it.  Mockups are sometimes abused by advertisers, using deceptive techniques to sell a product.  The FTC has had trouble specifying what is permitted and what is not.

The Supreme Court confronted the mockup problem in FTC v. Colgate–Palmolive Co., 380 U.S. 374 (1965), when Colgate wanted to show that its Rapid Shave could shave sandpaper.  Three one-minute commercials showed the "sandpaper test," in which the announcer said that to prove the product's "super-moisturizing power, we put it right from the can onto this tough, dry sandpaper.  It was apply . . . soak  . . . and off in a stroke."  In fact, the sandpaper depicted in the commercial had to be soaked for 80 minutes before it could be shaved clean.  The substance actually used in the commercial was plexiglass to which sand had been applied.  The evidence showed that Rapid Shave could shave sandpaper, though in a longer period than the commercial showed, and that if sandpaper had been used, "the inadequacies of television transmission would have made it appear to viewers to be nothing more than plain, colored paper."

The FTC found the commercials deceptive. The Supreme Court agreed. It found three representations being made in the commercials: that Rapid Shave could shave sandpaper, that an experiment had verified that claim and that the viewer was seeing that experiment actually performed. Although Colgate argued that any deception did not relate to the product itself, the Court accepted the Commission's view that a misrepresentation of "*any* fact so long as it materially induces a purchaser's decision to buy is a deception prohibited by" the FTCA. The Court observed:

> Respondents claim that it will be impractical to inform the viewing public that it is not seeing an actual test, experiment or demonstration, but we think it inconceivable that the ingenious advertising world will be unable, if it so desires, to conform to the Commission's insistence that the public be not misinformed. If, however, it becomes impossible or impractical to show simulated demonstrations on television in a truthful manner, this indicates that television is not a medium that lends itself to this type of commercial, not that the commercial must survive at all costs. Similarly unpersuasive is respondents' objection that the Commission's decision discriminates against sellers whose product claims cannot be "verified" on television without the use of simulations. All methods of advertising do not equally favor every seller. If the inherent limitations of a method do not permit its use in the way a seller desires, the seller cannot by material misrepresentation compensate for those limitations.

The FTC also found mockups deceptive when marbles were put in the bottom of a soup bowl to push the solids in the soup closer to the surface. The advertiser claimed it was necessary because television would not show the soup to be as thick as it actually was. Campbell Soup Co., 77 F.T.C. 664 (1970). Television does have technical restraints that cause such problems. In the Rapid Shave commercial, how could an effective, but not deceptive, demonstration have been staged?

The Court in the Rapid Shave case held that demonstrations proving a product claim must not be deceptive. Using wine to represent coffee because of its deeper color is acceptable if the coffee cup is a background object in a commercial for dinner plates, but not if the commercial is for the brand of coffee. In one case, an ad for glass showed the sponsor's product to be clear and undistorted when a television camera looked through a car window. A competitor's glass created distortion. In fact, different camera angles and petroleum jelly smeared on the competitor's glass created the effect for the camera. The court held the deception impermissible, even if the two products actually performed as shown. If deception was necessary to demonstrate the difference on television, perhaps because of television's inherent technical limitations, then the difference could not be shown.   Libbey–Owens–Ford Glass Co. v. Federal Trade Commission, 352 F.2d 415 (6th Cir.1965).

In 1969 the FTC announced that advertisers would have to tell viewers that a mockup was being used to simulate reality.   Notice how this is done for simulated pictures when television sets are being advertised.

### d.   Endorsements

Sometimes it will appear that an advertiser is not extolling the product, but that someone else is—an entertainer or sports figure, or an expert or specialist in a certain field.   These testimonials or endorsements are permitted as an advertising technique if not abused.   The use of a testimonial that was never given would be deceptive because untrue. Also, it is a tort to appropriate a person's name or likeness for commercial purposes (see p. 239, *supra*).   Usually celebrities are paid for endorsing products.   This need not be revealed, since the FTC assumes the public expects such payment.   But what if a detergent manufacturer says its product is recommended by a washing machine company?   If, in fact, the soap company is paying for the recommendation, that has to be stated.   Otherwise, consumers may think the washing machine manufacturer freely chose the detergent from among a number of competing brands.

FTC guidelines say that the average consumer must be able to expect the performance claimed in an endorsement.   If an "actual consumer" claims a certain brand of television set was in the shop only once in two years, and that was for a $10 repair, this must be a fair representation of the set's quality.   Also, that "actual consumer" must really be a member of the general public, or the ad must disclose an actor is playing the part.

People who endorse products by saying they use them must actually use them, and continue to use them, as long as the ads are running. This normally applies to celebrities whose name the advertiser wants to connect to the product.   When the endorsement is by those who claim special knowledge or expertise to judge a product, the endorsers' qualifications must be pertinent to the item.   For instance, the FTC has ruled that a famous racing car driver may not endorse a toy racing car set because the skill required to drive a race car has nothing to do with judging a toy.   The decision might have been different if the driver said he and his children played with the toy and enjoyed it.   Mattel, Inc., 79 F.T.C. 667 (1971).

If special expertise is required to evaluate a product, such a judgment must not come from a lay person.   For instance, the FTC barred entertainer Pat Boone from endorsing an acne product when his knowledge of the product's effectiveness came exclusively from the advertiser's claims, not from "reliable sources independent of the advertiser."   Cooga Mooga, Inc., et al., 92 F.T.C. 310 (1978).

### e.  Tests

The testimonial can be an effective advertising technique.  Tests or surveys showing a product in its best light are equally effective.

First, tests must actually be conducted before an advertiser can imply that test results prove something about the product.  At one time *Good Housekeeping Magazine* would award its "Seal of Approval" to products not tested or inadequately tested.  The FTC would not allow this.  In the Matter of Hearst Magazine, 32 F.T.C. 1440 (1941).  Second, tests must actually have been conducted against a competing product if the ad so claims.  Third, test results must not be presented deceptively.  An advertiser cannot say a pain product was shown effective for headaches when tests were conducted on patients with toothaches.  Fourth, the test must be scientifically accurate.  Bristol–Myers randomly selected 10,000 of the 66,000 dentists in America to ask about toothpaste preferences.  Only 1,983 replied, and the company based advertisements on only a few hundred responses about the dentists' personal toothpaste and a few hundred more about the toothpaste each dentist recommended to patients.  The FTC found this number to be too small to constitute a scientifically proper survey of dentists.  Bristol–Myers Co. v. F.T.C., 185 F.2d 58 (4th Cir.1950).

Failure to disclose that more survey respondents had no preference than preferred any specific brand is considered unfair and deceptive.  In Standard Brands, Inc., 97 F.T.C. 233 (1981), the manufacturer of Fleischmann's Margarine asked a sample of physicians which brand of margarine they recommended and/or used.  Although Fleischmann's was mentioned more often than any other brand name, the largest percentage of responses indicated no preference.  Given that only 17.8 percent of the doctors actually used Fleischmann's and even fewer recommended it, the FTC found both unfair and deceptive advertisements indicating that twice as many doctors recommended Fleischmann's as any other brand and that more doctors used Fleischmann's than any other brand.

### f.  Non-disclosure

While the FTC and the courts look carefully at what advertisements say, they also look at what an ad does *not* say:  "To tell less than the truth is a well-known method of deception."  P. Lorillard Co. v. Federal Trade Commission, 186 F.2d 52 (4th Cir.1950).

For example, the *Reader's Digest* sponsored a study of the tars, nicotine and resins in leading cigarettes.  The published results noted that the differences in these elements among the various brands made little difference in the physical harm done to smokers.  The study did show Old Gold ranked lowest in these substances, though the difference was not significant.  Old Gold ran an extensive advertising campaign claiming that an "impartial test by *Reader's Digest*" showed the cigarette to be in the "best among" those tested.

The FTC said the small portion of the test referred to in the ads was misleading. The result of the test was to show that little difference existed among the various brands, not to show Old Gold was minutely "better." The Seventh Circuit upheld the Commission's decision, rejecting a defense of literal truth. The omission of the important findings of the study regarding the physical hazards of smoking was deceptive.

In another case, the FTC ordered a company to reveal that the "majority of people who are tired and run-down . . . are not so because of iron deficiency anemia," a condition the producer claimed Geritol would aid. Not disclosing this made the ads deceptive. J.B. Williams Co. v. Federal Trade Commission, 381 F.2d 884 (6th Cir.1967). Similarly, a picture of a gold-colored ring without further explanation must be made of gold. If it is gold plated or gold-colored plastic, the ad must say so. Although this may not be an explicit half-truth, consumers would readily draw an incorrect inference.

### g.  Puffery

Although most advertising is misleading if it is untrue in one form or another, some overstatement is permitted. Thus, "puffing," or "sales talk," sometimes is considered an acceptable form of extolling a product's virtues. A toothpaste can "whiten and brighten," though, in fact, it could not have such an effect on the inherent qualities of teeth. A product can be a "good bargain" or "exceptional" or "wonderful." But puffing must be used carefully.

Generally, an expression of opinion about a product or service that does not create a misleading impression in consumers' minds can be construed as puffing. It is a normal exaggeration. But when a false impression is created, the ad has gone beyond puffery to misrepresentation and is not permitted. The FTC is becoming increasingly less receptive to puffery. The Commission is wary of exaggerations because it believes that consumers do not see the exaggerated claim as "sales talk," but are instead deceived by it.

Also, the FTC discourages puffing in comparative advertising. The Commission may consider a statement that a certain felt-tip pen is "worth five of any other brand" to be too great an exaggeration. Customers may believe that one of this brand will last as long as five of the other brand. See Moretrench Corp. v. Federal Trade Commission, 127 F.2d 792 (2d Cir.1942).

### h.  Product Description

The line between puffery and misrepresentation is clearly overstepped when a rusty, dirty used car is described as "shiny and clean." But what if something is called "top quality"? This will not be permitted if a demonstrably better product exists. A television set without automatic fine tuning cannot be called "the best the industry has to offer." The FTC says only a product made from elephant tusks may be called "ivory," and "Vermont maple syrup" must come from Vermont. Such product descriptions must be truthful, not exaggerated.

In addition to the origin and quality of merchandise, its mode of manufacture must be advertised accurately. Products claimed to be handmade cannot be manufactured completely by machines in factories.

Half-truths are a problem here, as ITT Continental Baking Co. learned. In 1971 the FTC said it was deceptive to advertise that Profile Bread contained fewer calories per slice than other brands without revealing that the statement was true only because Profile was sliced thinner. In re ITT Continental Baking Co., 79 F.T.C. 248 (1971). Two years later the FTC ruled Wonder Bread did not contain more vitamins and minerals than other commercially produced bread. Commercials saying Wonder created healthy bodies "twelve ways" were deceptive if viewers were not told this. ITT Continental Baking Co., 83 F.T.C. 1105 (1973).

### i. Comparative Advertising

Not until the 1970s did advertisers go beyond the vague "Brand X" advertisement and begin comparing their own product with a specific competing brand. Initially these ads were governed by internal policies within the advertising industry and the media. Two television networks, ABC and NBC, have comparative advertising guidelines, as does the American Association of Advertising Agencies. The development of these codes shows an increasing acceptance of comparative advertising, a technique once discouraged.

The FTC has long been concerned about comparative advertising in which test results are presented inaccurately, or in which nutritional or health claims, or claims of uniqueness, are made. The Commission looks to the ad's effect on the public, and is particularly wary if children are the intended audience. Also, the FTC prefers substantiation of claims by independent testing laboratories, indicating that objective, provable claims are safest to make in comparative ads.

Another danger of this type of advertising is not stopping at comparisons, but denigrating a competitor's product or business practices. Such comments can lead to actions for disparagement or trade libel. These actions require plaintiffs to prove false disparagement, identification, publication and special damages. In addition, some states require proof of intent to injure, while others only demand proof of negligent disparagement.

Disparaging competitors or their products can also lead to unfair competition actions under section 43(a) of the Lanham Trademark Act, as the makers of Anacin discovered. In the early 1970s Anacin, an aspirin-based compound, became the best-selling pain reliever, surpassing Bayer Aspirin. In 1976 Tylenol, a non-aspirin compound, passed Anacin in sales. Shortly thereafter, Anacin initiated two advertising campaigns. The first was a 30–second television commercial beginning, "Your body knows the difference between these pain relievers . . . and Adult Strength Anacin." It claimed superiority to several non-aspirin tablets, including Tylenol and Extra–Strength Tylenol. The second advertisement, designed for magazines, read "Anacin can reduce inflammation that comes with most pain. Tylenol cannot."

Based on consumer reaction surveys, a federal district court ruled that the advertisements represented that Anacin was "a superior analgesic generally" and that it was superior because it reduced inflammation. The court held the claims to be false and ordered Anacin not to make them in future advertising. The court of appeals found the language of the ads to be ambiguous. But even if the claims were literally true, said the court, the overall impression of the ads was false. The appellate court said the lower court's use of consumer response data showed the ads had "a tendency to mislead, confuse or deceive." Because consumers could incorrectly infer that Anacin was better than Tylenol for reducing pain or inflammation, the advertised claims were deceptive. American Home Products Corp. v. Johnson & Johnson, 577 F.2d 160 (2d Cir.1978).

### 3.  FTC REMEDIES

The FTC may use a wide range of methods to stop or punish false or deceptive advertisements. The public reaction generated when the FTC simply announces it is reviewing an ad campaign may cause the company to change or stop it. But the Commission has more formal ways of approaching the problem.

#### a.  Suggestions, Orders and Penalties

On the broadest level, the FTC can issue an industry guide that suggests how businesses should act with regard to a potential problem. This guide serves as a "roadmap" through Commission regulations. Further, a particular business may request an advisory opinion about something it proposes to do. The FTC response is directed toward one firm rather than a whole industry. Industry guides and advisory opinions are informal methods, not carrying the force of law. If an advertiser violates either, the FTC can proceed only as it would against any other ad it believes to be misleading.

A trade regulation rule (TRR), however, is a formal interpretation of FTC regulations. The Commission specifically describes practices it has determined violate the FTCA. For instance, it ruled that not posting octane ratings on gasoline pumps was an unfair method of competition and a deceptive practice. National Petroleum Refiners Association v. Federal Trade Commission, 482 F.2d 672 (D.C.Cir.1973). When a firm violates a valid TRR, it has violated the FTCA. The Commission then can simply prove, for example, that the firm put out the advertisement.

It does not have to prove the advertisement was deceptive—the TRR already said that such an ad violated the FTCA.

It is possible for a company to sign a voluntary letter of compliance. The advertiser does not admit the ad was deceptive but agrees to stop the campaign and not to run similar ads in the future. This is advantageous for a firm if the campaign was about to end anyway, because it reduces the adverse publicity and legal fees involved in a formal FTC action.

A consent order is similar to voluntary compliance. This is an agreement between a firm and the Commission in which, for example, an advertiser agrees not to make certain claims or to advertise in a certain way again. However, unlike voluntary compliance, a consent order contains a "cease and desist" order, which tells the company to stop its illegal practices or face penalties. Thus, a consent order is as binding as if the dispute had gone to a full Commission hearing or to court, but the advertiser need not admit the ad was deceptive, and is saved legal costs.

Although the FTC usually uses the less formal approaches of voluntary compliance or consent orders, it also uses more formal approaches. It can issue a complaint against a company and have a hearing before an administrative law judge (ALJ), whose decision is final unless it is appealed to the full Commission or the Commission itself decides to review the case. If the decision is against the firm, the Commission will issue a cease and desist order.

Once a cease and desist order has been issued by the Commission after a hearing, no company may engage in that proscribed practice, whether the order was actually issued against it or not. That is, the FTC considers the order to be like a TRR, binding against a whole industry.

Violations of cease and desist orders can be punished by fines up to $10,000 per offense per day. The FTC can also ask a court to issue an injunction, ordering a company to stop a certain practice while the question of its deceptiveness is being decided. Finally, the Commission can bring a court action against a company to obtain relief for a consumer injured by deceptive practices.

The procedures involved in stopping or punishing an allegedly deceptive advertising campaign can be very complex and lengthy. In an unusually complex case, the FTC filed a complaint against the J.B. Williams Co. in 1962 charging that its television commercials for Geritol were misleading. The Commission's cease and desist order was issued in 1964 and upheld by the court of appeals in 1967. J.B. Williams Co., p. 407, *supra*. Two years later the FTC found the company had not yet complied with the order and gave the case to the Justice Department. A United States District Court in New York fined the company $456,000 and its advertising agency $356,000 in 1973 for not complying with the FTC's order. The company appealed and the court of appeals held J.B. Williams Co. was entitled to a jury trial to determine whether the advertisements were deceptive. United States v. J.B. Williams Co., Inc.,

498 F.2d 414 (2d Cir.1974).  The case was finally settled in 1976 when the FTC reported the company had agreed to pay $302,000 in penalties and interest.  In the 14 intervening years, the company reportedly spent $60 million on advertising Geritol.

### b.  Affirmative Disclosure

In the Geritol case, the Commission ordered J.B. Williams Co. to reveal in its commercials that iron-poor blood was rarely the cause of tiredness, which the product purported to cure.  This order was upheld in court, allowing the FTC the power to require an advertiser to disclose certain facts about a product or service necessary to correct deceptive advertisements.

Initially, affirmative disclosure orders required stating what a product would *not* do, to qualify broad claims made by advertisers.  More recently disclosure orders have required giving consumers information they would not otherwise have, including legal rights and remedies.  For instance, an order might require a firm to tell customers they do not have to return or pay for unordered merchandise.

### c.  Corrective Advertising

Another, and more controversial, form of affirmative disclosure is corrective advertising, which is meant to correct misconceptions about a product that linger from misleading advertising.  This differs from affirmative disclosure in that corrective advertising is meant to remedy past deception rather than insure that future ads are truthful.  Included as part of a cease and desist order, corrective advertising requires a firm to spend a specific amount of its advertising budget informing consumers that false information was disseminated in the past.  The order may also specify the language to be used in correcting the misconceptions.

Corrective advertising was first suggested, though not used, in the Campbell Soup case when marbles were placed in the bottom of a bowl to make the solid ingredients in vegetable soup float to the top.  Campbell Soup Co., 77 F.T.C. 664 (1970).  The Commission first successfully used corrective advertising in ordering ITT Continental Baking Co. to spend one quarter of its advertising budget over a one-year period to inform consumers that Profile Bread had only seven fewer calories per slice than ordinary bread, a difference that would not cause significant weight loss.  *ITT Continental Baking Co.*, p. 408, *supra.*

Similarly, Ocean Spray Cranberries agreed to use one quarter of its media expenditures for one year to tell consumers that the term "food energy" used in past advertising meant calories, not vitamins and minerals.  Ocean Spray Cranberries, Inc., 70 F.T.C. 975 (1972).

Since Listerine mouthwash was introduced in 1879, it had been represented as being beneficial in fighting colds, cold symptoms and sore throats.  These claims had been made in direct advertising to the consumers since 1921.  In 1975 the FTC ordered Listerine's manufacturer to stop making these claims and to state in future advertising that "Contrary to prior advertising, Listerine will not help prevent colds or sore throats or lessen their severity."  The language was to appear in every Listerine ad in type size at least as large as that of the principal text of the ad, yet be separated from that text so that it could be readily noticed.  In television commercials the disclosure was to be simultaneously presented in both audio and video portions—and during the audio portions on radio and television ads no other sounds, including music, were to occur.

In Warner–Lambert Co. v. Federal Trade Commission, 562 F.2d 749, 2 Med.L.Rptr. 2303 (D.C.Cir.1977), cert. denied 435 U.S. 950 (1978), the court upheld the FTC's power to order corrective advertising.  Section 5 of the FTCA authorized the FTC to shape remedies appropriate to the situation.  The court then rejected the claim that after Virginia State Board of Pharmacy v. Virginia Citizens Consumer Council, Inc., 425 U.S. 748, 1 Med.L.Rptr. 1930 (1976), which we will discuss later in this chapter, the First Amendment barred such an order.  The court relied on the Supreme Court's assertion that the First Amendment presented "no obstacle" to government regulation of false or misleading advertising.  Government could assure "that the stream of commercial information flow[s] cleanly as well as freely."

The court of appeals asserted that corrective advertising was not "really such an innovation.  The label may be newly coined, but the concept is well established.  It is simply that under certain circumstances an advertiser may be required to make affirmative disclosure of unfavorable facts."  Here, the court relied on cases requiring advertisers to inform the public that a baldness cure would not work in the vast majority of cases because they involve hereditary baldness; that a device to stop bedwetting would not work in cases involving organic defects or disease; and that Geritol would help only the small minority whose tiredness resulted from iron deficiency anemia.

Other support was found in cases in which past advertisements might make current ads misleading unless further explained.  In one example, a baking powder maker had advertised extensively that its product was superior to others because it was made with cream of tartar, not phosphate.  Because of increased costs, the producer replaced the cream of tartar with phosphate.  The new advertising did not mention cream of tartar, and stressed the product's low cost.  The new labels very closely resembled the old ones.  The FTC and the courts agreed that new ads can be deceptive in not advising consumers that their past reasons for buying the product were no longer valid.  Royal Baking Powder Co. v. F.T.C., 281 Fed. 744 (2d Cir.1922).

Both groups of precedents were thought to provide support for corrective advertising.

Finally, though, the court was troubled by the wording of the FTC's order.  Given the presentation requirements as to type size and absence of competing sound, as well as the obligation to continue the ads until the advertiser had spent an amount equal to one year's average ad outlay during the 1962–72 period, the court concluded that the new ads would attract much attention.

> Given these safeguards, we believe the preamble "Contrary to prior advertising" is not necessary. It can serve only two purposes: either to attract attention or to humiliate the advertiser. The Commission claims only the first purpose for it, and this we think is obviated by the other terms of the order. The second purpose, if it were intended, might be called for in an egregious case of deliberate deception, but this is not one. . . . On these facts, the confessional preamble is not warranted.

Not all Commission orders to include corrective material in ads are upheld by the courts. The Seventh Circuit allowed the FTC to stop the National Commission on Egg Nutrition, a group of egg producers, from misrepresenting scientific findings concerning the relationship among cholesterol, eggs and heart disease. But the court refused to force the egg group to include in future advertising that "many medical experts believe increased consumption of dietary cholesterol, including that in eggs, may increase the risk of heart disease." There was no long history of deception, such as in *Warner–Lambert*, requiring that false claims be erased from the public's mind. Corrective advertising in this case was too harsh a measure. National Commission on Egg Nutrition v. Federal Trade Commission, 570 F.2d 157, 3 Med.L.Rptr. 2106 (7th Cir.1977), cert. denied 439 U.S. 821 (1978).

### d.  Substantiating Advertising Claims

In 1971 the FTC began requiring certain businesses to substantiate advertising claims through tests or other documentation. This is done not only when the Commission believes an ad is misleading, but also, more generally, when the Commission asks advertisers to prove what they claim about their products. Initially entire industries from air-conditioning manufacturers to antiperspirant makers, were asked to supply substantiation. Now the Commission requires proof of claims from those whose advertisements seem most open to doubt.

The program was given impetus when Pfizer, Inc., claimed its Un–Burn product anesthetized nerve endings to stop sunburn pain. The FTC said it was an unfair trade practice to make a claim without having a reasonable basis for believing it. The proof must be available before the claim is made, not after. In the Matter of Pfizer, Inc., 81 F.T.C. 23 (1972). Testing and other forms of substantiation must precede dissemination of the ad and must be the foundation of the claims made.

One impact of the advertising substantiation approach is to replace the FTC's burden of proof to show an ad is deceptive, by forcing the company to prove it is true. If the case goes to a hearing or to court, the Commission again carries the burden, but most disputes are resolved before that time. Thus, to a point, the advertiser answers the question of an advertisement's truthfulness by supplying or not supplying substantiating evidence for the claim.

In the early 1980s the Commission made less use of advertising claim substantiation, leading to speculation that the FTC was going to abandon it altogether. However, in the mid–1980s the Commission started once again to use it more frequently. In some cases the FTC even seems to be taking a more restrictive view of what constitutes a "reasonable basis" for believing an advertising claim. In Thompson Medical Co., Inc. v. Federal Trade Commission, 791 F.2d 189 (D.C.Cir. 1986), the court of appeals affirmed a Commission decision requiring a company to provide the results of at least two "adequate, well-controlled and double-blinded clinical studies" before making claims concerning the efficacy of an over-the-counter drug.

## C. OTHER REMEDIES FOR DECEPTIVE ADVERTISING

### 1. OTHER FEDERAL AGENCIES

While the FTC is the primary federal governmental agency charged with regulating false, deceptive and misleading advertising, there are more than 30 statutes that give various other agencies some control in this area. For instance, the Federal Communications Commission can deal with advertising on radio and television, the Food and Drug Administration with food, drug and cosmetic advertising, the Securities and Exchange Commission with the advertising of stocks, bonds and securities for sale and the Postal Service with mailed advertisements. Then there are statutes forbidding the use of copies of paper currency, 18 U.S.C.A. § 504, or the United States flag in an ad 1 U.S.C.A. § 3.

### 2. STATE AND LOCAL LAWS

The FTC was created by Congress to deal with interstate commerce. When its powers were expanded to include advertising, this generally meant advertising that crossed state lines or involved products that did so. Today some local advertising also can come within its jurisdiction. But not all advertising can be dealt with by the Commission. State and local laws attempt to fill any gap.

In 1911 a New York lawyer wrote a model law making untrue, deceptive or misleading advertising a misdemeanor. The law was called the Printer's Ink Statute after the magazine that championed its passage. Eventually 37 states passed some form of the statute, and nearly all states have statutes regulating deceptive advertising or deceptive trade practices. But enforcement is spotty; few state law enforcement officials take the time or trouble to prosecute under the statutes.

Beginning in the 1960s states added other laws to protect consumers against deceptive advertising. Again, enforcement depends on the jurisdiction. Because different sets of laws enforced in different ways have proven not to be effective, the Uniform Deceptive Trade Practices Act was developed in 1964. This was intended to put the same law in force in states across the country, but only 12 states have adopted it. Another 14 states have passed statutes allowing consumers to recover without proving intent to deceive.

### 3. SELF REGULATION

Though most of this section on advertising regulation concerns how various governmental agencies oversee advertising, only a fraction of the ads that appear require scrutiny. Most advertisers are quite honest and want to abide by the law. That is, they regulate themselves, as do advertising agencies and the media carrying the ads. This is done both individually and through industry groups. Because what constitutes deceptive or misleading advertising is not always clear, self-regulatory groups aid advertisers, advertising agencies and the media by supplying guidelines interpreting policies of governmental agencies, such as the FTC, state and federal laws, and court rulings. They also attempt to regulate deceptive advertising before the government intervenes.

The National Advertising Review Board (NARB) is a major self-regulatory group created in 1971 by the Better Business Bureau, the Association of National Advertisers, the American Association of Advertising Agencies (AAAA) and the American Advertising Foundation. Initially, complaints about ads are reviewed by the National Advertising Division (NAD) of the Better Business Bureau. The NAD uses persuasion to seek changes in misleading ads. If that fails, the NAD takes the case to the NARB. Whenever the NARB finds an advertisement untruthful or inaccurate, it reports that to the media, which are unlikely to accept the ad, and to the FTC.

Several local advertising review boards have also been established.

Advertising agencies review advertisements before submitting them to the media. In order to belong to their major trade organization, agencies must subscribe to the AAAA's "Standards of Practice," which prohibit unfair, false and deceptive practices.

### 4. CONSUMER ACTION

Even if it were legally possible for consumers to sue advertisers for misleading advertisements, and generally it is not, it would be impractical. An individual consumer's damages are usually small—a cleanser that does not make a sink sparkling white does not cause much harm—and lawyers' fees would almost certainly be larger than the damages collected. For various legal reasons, it also is not practical for groups of consumers to sue in class actions. The FTC can sue on behalf of a consumer under some circumstances, but the effectiveness of this new power is untested.

Consumers can sue if a product fails to live up to its warranty, which may be indicated in an advertisement, but this is a different type of action than would be brought for false or deceptive advertising.

Some special interest groups have attempted to influence advertisers through consumer pressure. Usually, though, the target of such pressure is not an advertisement, but rather a television show being sponsored by the advertiser. Thus, various groups have organized boycotts of products manufactured by firms who sponsor shows the groups consider unacceptable because of, for example, excessive violence or sexual innuendos.

## D.  FIRST AMENDMENT PROTECTION OF ADVERTISING

### 1.  DEVELOPMENT OF THE PROTECTION

It may seem surprising to discuss advertising *regulation*. Is it not protected by the First Amendment like other expression? Recall that some categories of speech, such as obscenity, are not protected. This used to be true of advertising.

Not until 1942 did the Supreme Court consider whether advertising came within the First Amendment. That case arose when a man bought a used Navy submarine and docked it in New York City. He passed out handbills urging the people to tour the ship for a fee. Police told him that a city ordinance barred distribution of commercial handbills on the streets; only handbills containing "information or public protest" were permitted. He then printed a protest against the city's refusal to rent him a particular pier on one side of the sheet and an advertisement for his submarine tours on the other side. When police stopped him again, he obtained an injunction against the city's interfering with his distribution of the handbill. The Supreme Court ruled that commercial speech had no First Amendment protection. Although local officials could not prohibit a city's streets from being used for exercising freedom of expression, the Constitution "imposes no such restraint on government as respects purely commercial advertising." The protest on one side of the handbill was merely a ruse to evade the ordinance. Valentine v. Chrestensen, 316 U.S. 52, 1 Med.L.Rptr. 1907 (1942).

This attitude toward commercial speech may partially explain Breard v. City of Alexandria, 341 U.S. 622 (1951), in which the Court upheld an ordinance banning door-to-door solicitation for purposes of sales—as applied to solicitors of magazine subscriptions. This case followed shortly after Martin v. City of Struthers, 319 U.S. 141 (1943), in which the Court had invalidated the application of an ordinance against uninvited solicitors—as applied to members of a religious group.

For 22 years, then, courts followed the *Chrestensen* approach. But in 1964 the Court gave protection to editorial advertisements, those that promote ideas and causes rather than products or services. In *Sullivan*, p. 98, *supra*, the Court said the publication "was not a 'commercial' advertisement in the sense in which the word was used in *Chrestensen*. It communicated information, expressed opinion, recited grievances, protested claimed abuses, and sought financial support on behalf of a movement whose existence and objectives are matters of the highest public interest and concern."

Pittsburgh Press Co. v. Pittsburgh Commission on Human Relations, 413 U.S. 376, 1 Med.L.Rptr. 1908 (1973), was a step back toward *Chrestensen.* An ordinance barred employers from discriminating in employment and also barred others from aiding in such discrimination. The *Pittsburgh Press* carried Help Wanted advertisements in columns captioned "Jobs—Male Interest," "Jobs—Female Interest" and "Male—Female," according to the wishes of the advertiser. The Commission ordered the *Press* to stop using such captions except where the ordinance provided that "the employer or advertiser is free to make hiring or employment referral decisions on the basis of sex." The Supreme Court upheld the order, 5–4:

> In the crucial respects, the advertisements in the present record resemble the *Chrestensen* rather than the *Sullivan* advertisement. None expresses a position on whether, as a matter of social policy, certain positions ought to be filled by members of one or the other sex, nor does any of them criticize the Ordinance or the Commission's enforcement practices. Each is no more than a proposal of possible employment. The advertisements are thus classic examples of commercial speech.

The newspaper argued that the case involved an editorial judgment concerning the placement of such advertisements. Although the newspaper always acceded to the advertisers' requests, Justice Powell, for the majority, acknowledged that some editorial judgment was involved. He concluded, however, that in this case the newspaper was entitled to no greater protection than the advertiser itself:

> Discrimination in employment is not only commercial activity, it is *illegal* commercial activity under the Ordinance. We have no doubt that a newspaper constitutionally could be forbidden to publish a want ad proposing a sale of narcotics or soliciting prostitutes. Nor would the result be different if the nature of the transaction were indicated by placement under columns captioned "Narcotics for Sale" and "Prostitutes Wanted" rather than stated within the four corners of the advertisement.
>
> The illegality in this case may be less overt, but we see no difference in principle here. . . .

The Court emphasized that nothing in the holding allowed government to forbid the newspaper to "publish and distribute advertisements commenting on the Ordinance, the enforcement practices of the Commission, or the propriety of sex preferences in employment."

Bigelow v. Virginia, 421 U.S. 809, 1 Med.L.Rptr. 1919 (1975), involved the publication in a Virginia newspaper of a New York group's advertisement stating that abortions were legal in New York with no residency requirement and offering to provide information and to arrange abortions in accredited hospitals at low cost. An address and telephone numbers were listed. Bigelow, the managing editor of the newspaper, was prosecuted under a statute making it a misdemeanor for "any person, by publication  .  .  .  or by the sale or circulation of any publication  .  .  .  [to] encourage or prompt the procuring of" an abortion. The state courts upheld the conviction and relied on the state's interest that women come to decisions about abortions "without the commercial advertising pressure usually incidental to the sale of a box of soap powder."

The Supreme Court reversed, 7–2. In his opinion for the Court, Justice Blackmun placed the advertisement closer to that in the *New York Times* case than to those of the other cases because it conveyed "information of potential interest and value to a diverse audience." The opinion also stressed that the activities advertised were legal in New York and that, although Virginia might be concerned about the health and welfare of its citizens, it could not keep from them information about legal activities in other states.

This still left open the question of whether pure product advertisements, those simply offering X product for Y price, have any First Amendment protection. The following case answered that question.

## VIRGINIA STATE BOARD OF PHARMACY v. VIRGINIA CITIZENS CONSUMER COUNCIL, INC.

Supreme Court of the United States, 1976.
425 U.S. 748, 96 S.Ct. 1817, 48 L.Ed.2d 346, 1 Med.L.Rptr. 1930.

[A Virginia statute declared any pharmacist who "advertises  .  .  . any  .  .  .  price  .  .  .  for any drugs which may be dispensed only by prescription" guilty of "unprofessional conduct" punishable by penalties ranging from fines to revocation of license. The parties stipulated that "about 95% of all prescriptions are now filled with dosage forms prepared by the pharmaceutical manufacturer." They also stipulated that prices for the same drug in the same city varied greatly. The statute was challenged by consumer groups and an individual on the ground that the First Amendment entitled them to receive information that pharmacists wished to communicate to them. A three-judge district court agreed and invalidated the statute.]

Mr. Justice Blackmun delivered the opinion of the Court.

.  .  .

We begin with several propositions that already are settled or beyond serious dispute. It is clear, for example, that speech does not lose its First Amendment protection because money is spent to project it, as in a paid advertisement of one form or another. Buckley v. Valeo, 424 U.S. 1 (1976); [*Pittsburgh Press*; Sullivan]. Speech likewise is protected even though it is carried in a form that is "sold" for profit, [  ], and even though it may involve a solicitation to purchase or otherwise pay or contribute money.

If there is a kind of commercial speech that lacks all First Amendment protection, therefore, it must be distinguished by its content. Yet the speech whose content deprives it of protection cannot simply be speech on a commercial subject. No one would contend that our pharmacist may be prevented from being heard on the subject of whether, in general, pharmaceutical prices should be regulated, or their advertisement forbidden. Nor can it be dispositive that a commercial advertisement is uneditorial, and merely reports a fact. Purely factual matter of public interest may claim protection. [*Bigelow*].

Our question is whether speech which does "no more than propose a commercial transaction," [*Pittsburgh Press*], is so removed from any "exposition of ideas," [*Chaplinsky*], and from " 'truth, science, morality, and arts in general, in its diffusion of liberal sentiments on the administration of Government,' " [*Roth*], that it lacks all protection. Our answer is that it is not.

Focusing first on the individual parties to the transaction that is proposed in the commercial advertisement, we may assume that the advertiser's interest is a purely economic one. That hardly disqualifies him for protection under the First Amendment.   .   .   .

As to the particular consumer's interest in the free flow of commercial information, that interest may be as keen, if not keener by far, than his interest in the day's most urgent political debate. Appellees' case in this respect is a convincing one. Those whom the suppression of prescription drug price information hits the hardest are the poor, the sick, and particularly the aged. A disproportionate amount of their income tends to be spent on prescription drugs; yet they are the least able to learn, by shopping from pharmacist to pharmacist, where their scarce dollars are best spent. When drug prices vary as strikingly as they do, information as to who is charging what becomes more than a convenience. It could mean the alleviation of physical pain or the enjoyment of basic necessities.

Generalizing, society also may have a strong interest in the free flow of commercial information. Even an individual advertisement, though entirely "commercial," may be of general public interest.   .   .   . Obviously, not all commercial messages contain the same or even a very great public interest element. There are few to which such an element, however, could not be added. Our pharmacist, for example, could cast himself as a commentator on store-to-store disparities in drug prices, giving his own and those of a competitor as proof. We see little point in requiring him to do so, and little difference if he does not.

.   .   .

In concluding that commercial speech, like other varieties, is protected, we of course do not hold that it can never be regulated in any way. Some forms of commercial speech regulation are surely permissible. We mention a few only to make clear that they are not before us and therefore are not foreclosed by this case.

There is no claim, for example, that the prohibition on prescription drug price advertising is a mere time, place, and manner restriction. We have often approved restrictions of that kind provided that they are justified without reference to the content of the regulated speech, that they serve a significant governmental interest, and that in so doing they leave open ample alternative channels for communication of the information. [ ] Whatever may be the proper bounds of time, place, and manner restrictions on commercial speech, they are plainly exceeded by this Virginia statute, which singles out speech of a particular content and seeks to prevent its dissemination completely.

Nor is there any claim that prescription drug price advertisements are forbidden because they are false or misleading in any way. Untruthful speech, commercial or otherwise, has never been protected for its own sake. [ ] Obviously, much commercial speech is not provably false, or even wholly false, but only deceptive or misleading. We foresee no obstacle to a State's dealing effectively with this problem.[24] The First Amendment, as we construe it today, does not prohibit the State from insuring that the stream of commercial information flows cleanly as well as freely. [ ]

Also, there is no claim that the transactions proposed in the forbidden advertisements are themselves illegal in any way. . . .

What is at issue is whether a State may completely suppress the dissemination of concededly truthful information about entirely lawful activity, fearful of that information's effect upon its disseminators and its recipients. Reserving other questions[25] we conclude that the answer to this one is in the negative.

**24.** In concluding that commercial speech enjoys First Amendment protection, we have not held that it is wholly undifferentiable from other forms. There are commonsense differences between speech that does "no more than propose a commercial transaction," Pittsburgh Press Co. v. Pittsburgh Comm'n on Human Relations, 413 U.S., at 385, and other varieties. Even if the differences do not justify the conclusion that commercial speech is valueless, and thus subject to complete suppression by the State, they nonetheless suggest that a different degree of protection is necessary to insure that the flow of truthful and legitimate commercial information is unimpaired. The truth of commercial speech, for example, may be more easily verifiable by its disseminator than, let us say, news reporting or political commentary, in that ordinarily the advertiser seeks to disseminate information about a specific product or service that he himself provides and presumably knows more about than anyone else. Also, commercial speech may be more durable than other kinds. Since advertising is the *sine qua non* of commercial prof-

its there is little likelihood of its being chilled by proper regulation and foregone entirely.

Attributes such as these, the greater objectivity and hardiness of commercial speech, may make it less necessary to tolerate inaccurate statements for fear of silencing the speaker. [ ] They may also make it appropriate to require that a commercial message appear in such a form, or include such additional information, warnings, and disclaimers, as are necessary to prevent its being deceptive. [ ] They may also make inapplicable the prohibition against prior restraints. [ ]

**25.** We stress that we have considered in this case the regulation of commercial advertising by pharmacists. Although we express no opinion as to other professions, the distinctions, historical and functional, between professions, may require consideration of quite different factors. Physicians and lawyers, for example, do not dispense standardized products; they render professional *services* of almost infinite variety and nature with the consequent enhanced possi-

The judgment of the District Court is affirmed.

It is so ordered.

Mr. Justice Stevens took no part in the consideration or decision of this case.

[Chief Justice Burger concurred separately to emphasize that "the Court wisely leaves" the question of medical and legal services "to another day." Because 95 percent of prescriptions are already in dosage units, he thought the pharmacist "no more renders a true professional service than does a clerk who sells lawbooks." He suggested that advertising of price by professionals might be inherently misleading because "what the professional must do will vary greatly in individual cases."

Justice Stewart concurred separately to explain why the decision did not destroy the "constitutional legitimacy of every state and federal law regulating false or deceptive advertising." He emphasized that such laws generally are aimed at commercial advertisers who know the product they are advertising and can more easily verify the accuracy of representations made, than can "the press, which must often attempt to assemble the true facts from sketchy and sometimes conflicting sources under the pressure of publication deadlines." There was little likelihood of chilling accurate advertising by proscribing false advertising. "Indeed, the elimination of false and deceptive claims serves to promote the one facet of commercial price and product advertising that warrants First Amendment protection—its contribution to the flow of accurate and reliable information relevant to public and private decisionmaking."

Justice Rehnquist dissented. He disagreed on the standing issue because those interested could get the information by other means. On the merits, the Constitution did not require "the Virginia Legislature to hew to the teachings of Adam Smith." Recognizing the difficulty of drawing the line between protected speech and commercial speech in previous cases, he nevertheless thought the majority had been unwise in drawing a new line between truthful commercial speech and false and misleading commercial speech. He understood the Court's view that the First Amendment was "primarily an instrument to enlighten public decisionmaking in a democracy" to refer to "political, social, and other public issues, rather than the decision of a particular individual as to whether to purchase one or another kind of shampoo. It is undoubtedly arguable that many people in the country regard the choice of shampoo as just as important as who may be elected to local, state, or national political office, but that does not automatically bring information about competing shampoos within the protection of the First Amendment." He was also concerned that pharmacists might use this opportunity to promote the use of drugs by such advertisements as "Don't spend

bility for confusion and deception if they were to undertake certain kinds of advertising.

another sleepless night. Ask your doctor to prescribe Seconal without delay."]

**Notes and Questions**

1. Justice Blackmun responded to the dissent's standing question in a footnote observing that there was "no general principle that freedom of speech may be abridged when the speaker's listeners could come by his message by some other means, such as seeking him out and asking him what it is." To Justice Rehnquist's claim that if plaintiffs needed the information so badly they might have called the pharmacy or set up canvassing groups, Justice Blackmun responded that if "the great need for the information . . . distinguishes our prior cases at all, it makes the appellees' First Amendment claim a stronger rather than a weaker one."

2. Does the majority opinion imply some constraints other than those relating to truthful as opposed to false and misleading advertisements? In what ways might the right to engage in commercial speech be less broad than the right to engage in other types of speech?

3. After *Virginia State Board of Pharmacy* what considerations should determine the constitutionality of a statute or regulation restricting some form of advertising? How much guidance is provided by the following case?

CENTRAL HUDSON GAS & ELECTRIC CORP. v. PUBLIC
SERVICE COMMISSION OF NEW YORK

Supreme Court of the United States, 1980.
447 U.S. 557, 100 S.Ct. 2343, 65 L.Ed.2d 341, 6 Med.L.Rptr. 1497.

MR. JUSTICE POWELL delivered the opinion of the Court.

This case presents the question whether a regulation of the Public Service Commission of the State of New York violates the First and Fourteenth Amendments because it completely bans advertising by an electric utility.

. . .

II

The Commission's order restricts only commercial speech, that is, expression related solely to the economic interests of the speaker and its audience. [ ] The First Amendment, as applied to the States through the Fourteenth Amendment, protects commercial speech from unwarranted governmental regulation. [ ] Commercial expression not only serves the economic interest of the speaker, but also assists consumers and furthers the societal interest in the fullest possible dissemination of information. In applying the First Amendment to this area, we have rejected the "highly paternalistic" view that government has complete power to suppress or regulate commercial speech. "[P]eople will perceive their own best interests if only they are well enough informed, and . . . the best means to that end is to open the channels of communication, rather than to close them. . . ." Id., at 770; see Linmark Associates, Inc. v. Willingboro, 431 U.S. 85, 92 (1977). Even when advertising communicates only an incomplete version of the relevant facts, the First Amendment presumes that some accurate information is better than no information at all. Bates v. State Bar of Arizona, *supra,* at 374.

Nevertheless, our decisions have recognized "the 'commonsense' distinction between speech proposing a commercial transaction, which occurs in an area traditionally subject to government regulation, and other varieties of speech." [ ] The Constitution therefore accords a lesser protection to commercial speech than to other constitutionally guaranteed expression. [ ] The protection available for particular commercial expression turns on the nature both of the expression and of the governmental interests served by its regulation.

The First Amendment's concern for commercial speech is based on the informational function of advertising. [ ] Consequently, there can be no constitutional objection to the suppression of commercial messages that do not accurately inform the public about lawful activity. The government may ban forms of communication more likely to deceive the public than to inform it, [ ], or commercial speech related to illegal activity, [ ].

If the communication is neither misleading nor related to unlawful activity, the government's power is more circumscribed. The State must assert a substantial interest to be achieved by restrictions on commercial speech. Moreover, the regulatory technique must be in proportion to that interest. The limitation on expression must be designed carefully to achieve the State's goal. Compliance with this requirement may be measured by two criteria. First, the restriction must directly advance the state interest involved; the regulation may not be sustained if it provides only ineffective or remote support for the government's purpose. Second, if the governmental interest could be served as well by a more limited restriction on commercial speech, the excessive restrictions cannot survive.

Under the first criterion, the Court has declined to uphold regulations that only indirectly advance the state interest involved. In both *Bates* and *Virginia Pharmacy Board,* the Court concluded that an advertising ban could not be imposed to protect the ethical or performance standards of a profession. The Court noted in *Virginia Pharmacy Board* that "[t]he advertising ban does not directly affect professional standards one way or the other." In *Bates,* the Court overturned an advertising prohibition that was designed to protect the "quality" of a lawyer's work. "Restraints on advertising . . . are an ineffective way of deterring shoddy work." 433 U.S., at 378.

The second criterion recognizes that the First Amendment mandates that speech restrictions be "narrowly drawn." [ ] The regulatory technique may extend only as far as the interest it serves. The State cannot regulate speech that poses no danger to the asserted state interest, [ ], nor can it completely suppress information when narrower restrictions on expression would serve its interest as well.  For example, in *Bates* the Court explicitly did not "foreclose the possibility that some limited supplementation, by way of warning or disclaimer or the like, might be required" in promotional materials.  [ ]  And in Carey v. Population Services International, 431 U.S. 678, 701–702 (1977), we held that the State's "arguments  . . .  do not justify the total suppression of advertising concerning contraceptives."  This holding left open the possibility that the State could implement more carefully drawn restrictions.  [ ] [9]

In commercial speech cases, then, a four-part analysis has developed. At the outset, we must determine whether the expression is protected by the First Amendment.  For commercial speech to come within that provision, it at least must concern lawful activity and not be misleading. Next, we ask whether the asserted governmental interest is substantial. If both inquiries yield positive answers, we must determine whether the regulation directly advances the governmental interest asserted, and whether it is not more extensive than is necessary to serve that interest.

III

We now apply this four-step analysis for commercial speech to the Commission's arguments in support of its ban on promotional advertising.

A

The Commission does not claim that the expression at issue either is inaccurate or relates to unlawful activity.  Yet the New York Court of Appeals questioned whether Central Hudson's advertising is protected commercial speech.  Because appellant holds a monopoly over the sale of electricity in its service area, the state court suggested that the Commission's order restricts no commercial speech of any worth.  The court stated that advertising in a "noncompetitive market" could not improve the decisionmaking of consumers.  47 N.Y.2d, at 110, 390 N.E.2d, at 757.  The court saw no constitutional problem with barring commercial speech that it viewed as conveying little useful information.

This reasoning falls short of establishing that appellant's advertising is not commercial speech protected by the First Amendment.  Monopoly over the supply of a product provides no protection from competition with substitutes for that product.  Electric utilities compete with suppliers of fuel oil and natural gas in several markets, such as those for home heating and industrial power.  This Court noted the existence of interfu-

---

**9.** We review with special care regulations that entirely suppress commercial speech in order to pursue a nonspeech-related policy.  In those circumstances, a ban on speech could screen from public view the underlying governmental policy.  See *Virginia Pharmacy Board*, 425 U.S., at 780, n. 8 (Stewart, J., concurring).  Indeed, in recent years this Court has not approved a blanket ban on commercial speech unless the expression itself was flawed in some way, either because it was deceptive or related to unlawful activity.

el competition 45 years ago.  [   ]  Each energy source continues to offer peculiar advantages and disadvantages that may influence consumer choice.  For consumers in those competitive markets, advertising by utilities is just as valuable as advertising by unregulated firms.

Even in monopoly markets, the suppression of advertising reduces the information available for consumer decisions and thereby defeats the purpose of the First Amendment.  The New York court's argument appears to assume that the providers of a monopoly service or product are willing to pay for wholly ineffective advertising.  Most businesses—even regulated monopolies—are unlikely to underwrite promotional advertising that is of no interest or use to consumers.  Indeed, a monopoly enterprise legitimately may wish to inform the public that it has developed new services or terms of doing business.  A consumer may need information to aid his decision whether or not to use the monopoly service at all, or how much of the service he should purchase.  In the absence of factors that would distort the decision to advertise, we may assume that the willingness of a business to promote its products reflects a belief that consumers are interested in the advertising.  Since no such extraordinary conditions have been identified in this case, appellant's monopoly position does not alter the First Amendment's protection for its commercial speech.

### B

The Commission offers two state interests as justifications for the ban on promotional advertising.  The first concerns energy conservation.  Any increase in demand for electricity—during peak or off-peak periods—means greater consumption of energy.  The Commission argues, and the New York court agreed, that the State's interest in conserving energy is sufficient to support suppression of advertising designed to increase consumption of electricity.  In view of our country's dependence on energy resources beyond our control, no one can doubt the importance of energy conservation.  Plainly, therefore, the state interest asserted is substantial.

The Commission also argues that promotional advertising will aggravate inequities caused by the failure to base the utilities' rates on marginal cost.  The utilities argued to the Commission that if they could promote the use of electricity in periods of low demand, they would improve their utilization of generating capacity.  The Commission responded that promotion of off-peak consumption also would increase consumption during peak periods.  If peak demand were to rise, the absence of marginal cost rates would mean that the rates charged for the additional power would not reflect the true costs of expanding production.  Instead, the extra costs would be borne by all consumers through higher overall rates.  Without promotional advertising, the Commission stated, this inequitable turn of events would be less likely to occur.  The choice among rate structures involves difficult and important questions of economic supply and distributional fairness.  The State's concern that rates be fair and efficient represents a clear and substantial governmental interest.

## C

Next, we focus on the relationship between the State's interests and the advertising ban.  Under this criterion, the Commission's laudable concern over the equity and efficiency of appellant's rates does not provide a constitutionally adequate reason for restricting protected speech.  The link between the advertising prohibition and appellant's rate structure is, at most, tenuous.  The impact of promotional advertising on the equity of appellant's rates is highly speculative.  Advertising to increase off-peak usage would have to increase peak usage, while other factors that directly affect the fairness and efficiency of appellant's rates remained constant.  Such conditional and remote eventualities simply cannot justify silencing appellant's promotional advertising.

In contrast, the State's interest in energy conservation is directly advanced by the Commission order at issue here.  There is an immediate connection between advertising and demand for electricity.  Central Hudson would not contest the advertising ban unless it believed that promotion would increase its sales.  Thus, we find a direct link between the state interest in conservation and the Commission's order.

## D

We come finally to the critical inquiry in this case:  whether the Commission's complete suppression of speech ordinarily protected by the First Amendment is no more extensive than necessary to further the State's interest in energy conservation.  The Commission's order reaches all promotional advertising, regardless of the impact of the touted service on overall energy use.  But the energy conservation rationale, as important as it is, cannot justify suppressing information about electric devices or services that would cause no net increase in total energy use.  In addition, no showing has been made that a more limited restriction on the content of promotional advertising would not serve adequately the State's interests.

Appellant insists that but for the ban, it would advertise products and services that use energy efficiently.  These include the "heat pump," which both parties acknowledge to be a major improvement in electric heating, and the use of electric heat as a "backup" to solar and other heat sources.  Although the Commission has questioned the efficiency of electric heating before this Court, neither the Commission's Policy Statement nor its order denying rehearing made findings on this issue.  In the absence of authoritative findings to the contrary, we must credit as within the realm of possibility the claim that electric heat can be an efficient alternative in some circumstances.

The Commission's order prevents appellant from promoting electric services that would reduce energy use by diverting demand from less efficient sources, or that would consume roughly the same amount of energy as do alternative sources.  In neither situation would the utility's advertising endanger conservation or mislead the public. To the extent that the Commission's order suppresses speech that in no way impairs the State's interest in energy conservation, the Commission's order violates the First and Fourteenth Amendments and must be invalidated. [  ]

The Commission also has not demonstrated that its interest in conservation cannot be protected adequately by more limited regulation of appellant's commercial expression. To further its policy of conservation, the Commission could attempt to restrict the format and content of Central Hudson's advertising. It might, for example, require that the advertisements include information about the relative efficiency and expense of the offered service, both under current conditions and for the foreseeable future. [  ] In the absence of a showing that more limited speech regulation would be ineffective, we cannot approve the complete suppression of Central Hudson's advertising.

## IV

Our decision today in no way disparages the national interest in energy conservation. We accept without reservation the argument that conservation, as well as the development of alternative energy sources, is an imperative national goal. Administrative bodies empowered to regulate electric utilities have the authority—and indeed the duty—to take appropriate action to further this goal. When, however, such action involves the suppression of speech, the First and Fourteenth Amendments require that the restriction be no more extensive than is necessary to serve the state interest. In this case, the record before us fails to show that the total ban on promotional advertising meets this requirement.

Accordingly, the judgment of the New York Court of Appeals is

Reversed.

Mr. Justice Brennan, concurring in the judgment.

One of the major difficulties in this case is the proper characterization of the Commission's Policy Statement. I find it impossible to determine on the present record whether the Commission's ban on all "promotional" advertising, in contrast to "institutional and informational" advertising, is intended to encompass more than "commercial speech." I am inclined to think that Mr. Justice Stevens is correct that the Commission's order prohibits more than mere proposals to engage in certain kinds of commercial transactions, and therefore I agree with his conclusion that the ban surely violates the First and Fourteenth Amendments. But even on the assumption that the Court is correct that the Commission's order reaches only commercial speech, I agree with Mr. Justice Blackmun that "[n]o differences between commercial speech and other protected speech justify suppression of commercial speech in order to influence public conduct through manipulation of the availability of information."

Accordingly, with the qualifications implicit in the preceding paragraph, I join the opinions of Mr. Justice Blackmun and Mr. Justice Stevens concurring in the judgment.

MR. JUSTICE BLACKMUN, with whom MR. JUSTICE BRENNAN joins, concurring in the judgment.

I agree with the Court that the Public Service Commission's ban on promotional advertising of electricity by public utilities is inconsistent with the First and Fourteenth Amendments. I concur only in the Court's judgment, however, because I believe the test now evolved and applied by the Court is not consistent with our prior cases and does not provide adequate protection for truthful, nonmisleading, noncoercive commercial speech.

The Court asserts, that "a four-part analysis has developed" from our decisions concerning commercial speech. Under this four-part test a restraint on commercial "communication [that] is neither misleading nor related to unlawful activity" is subject to an intermediate level of scrutiny, and suppression is permitted whenever it "directly advances" a "substantial" governmental interest and is "not more extensive than is necessary to serve that interest." I agree with the Court that this level of intermediate scrutiny is appropriate for a restraint on commercial speech designed to protect consumers from misleading or coercive speech, or a regulation related to the time, place, or manner of commercial speech. I do not agree, however, that the Court's four-part test is the proper one to be applied when a State seeks to suppress information about a product in order to manipulate a private economic decision that the State cannot or has not regulated or outlawed directly.

. . .

I seriously doubt whether suppression of information concerning the availability and price of a legally offered product is ever a permissible way for the State to "dampen" demand for or use of the product. Even though "commercial" speech is involved, such a regulatory measure strikes at the heart of the First Amendment. This is because it is a covert attempt by the State to manipulate the choices of its citizens, not by persuasion or direct regulation, but by depriving the public of the information needed to make a free choice. As the Court recognizes, the State's policy choices are insulated from the visibility and scrutiny that direct regulation would entail and the conduct of citizens is molded by the information that government chooses to give them. [ ]

If the First Amendment guarantee means anything, it means that, absent clear and present danger, government has no power to restrict expression because of the effect its message is likely to have on the public. [ ] Our cases indicate that this guarantee applies even to commercial speech. In [*Virginia State Board of Pharmacy, supra*], we held that Virginia could not pursue its goal of encouraging the public to patronize the "professional pharmacist" (one who provided individual attention and a stable pharmacist-customer relationship) by "keeping the public in ignorance of the entirely lawful terms that competing pharmacists are offering." Id., at 770.  We noted that our decision left the State free to pursue its goal of maintaining high standards among its pharmacists by "requir[ing] whatever professional standards it wishes of its pharmacists."  Ibid.

We went on in [*Virginia State Board of Pharmacy*] to discuss the types of regulation of commercial speech that, due to the "commonsense differences" between this form of speech and other forms, are or may be constitutionally permissible.  We indicated that government may impose reasonable "time, place, and manner" restrictions, and that it can deal with false, deceptive, and misleading commercial speech.  We noted that the question of advertising of illegal transactions and the special problems of the electronic broadcast media were not presented.

Concluding with a restatement of the type of restraint that is not permitted, we said: "What is at issue is whether a State may completely suppress the dissemination of concededly truthful information about entirely lawful activity, fearful of that information's effect upon its disseminators and its recipients.   . . .   [W]e conclude that the answer to this [question] is in the negative."  Id., at 773.

.  .  .

. . .  No differences between commercial speech and other protected speech justify suppression of commercial speech in order to influence public conduct through manipulation of the availability of information.  The Court stated in Carey v. Population Services Interna tional:

> "Appellants suggest no distinction between commercial and noncommercial speech that would render these discredited arguments meritorious when offered to justify prohibitions on commercial speech.  On the contrary, such arguments are clearly directed not at any commercial aspect of the prohibited advertising but at the ideas conveyed and form of expression—*the core of First Amendment values.*"  431 U.S., at 701, n. 28 (emphasis added).

It appears that the Court would permit the State to ban all direct advertising of air conditioning, assuming that a more limited restriction on such advertising would not effectively deter the public from cooling its homes.  In my view, our cases do not support this type of suppression.  If a governmental unit believes that use or overuse of air conditioning is a serious problem, it must attack that problem directly, by prohibiting air conditioning or regulating thermostat levels.  Just as the Commonwealth of Virginia may promote professionalism of pharmacists directly, so too New York may *not* promote energy conservation "by keeping the public in ignorance."  [*Virginia State Board of Pharmacy*], 425 U.S., at 770.

Mr. Justice Stevens, with whom Mr. Justice Brennan joins, concurring in the judgment.

Because "commercial speech" is afforded less constitutional protection than other forms of speech, it is important that the commercial speech concept not be defined too broadly lest speech deserving of greater constitutional protection be inadvertently suppressed. The issue in this case is whether New York's prohibition on the promotion of the use of electricity through advertising is a ban on nothing but commercial speech.

In my judgment one of the two definitions the Court uses in addressing that issue is too broad and the other may be somewhat too narrow. The Court first describes commercial speech as "expression related solely to the economic interests of the speaker and its audience." Although it is not entirely clear whether this definition uses the subject matter of the speech or the motivation of the speaker as the limiting factor, it seems clear to me that it encompasses speech that is entitled to the maximum protection afforded by the First Amendment. Neither a labor leader's exhortation to strike, nor an economist's dissertation on the money supply, should receive any lesser protection because the subject matter concerns only the economic interests of the audience. Nor should the economic motivation of a speaker qualify his constitutional protection; even Shakespeare may have been motivated by the prospect of pecuniary reward. Thus, the Court's first definition of commercial speech is unquestionably too broad.

The Court's second definition refers to " 'speech proposing a commercial transaction.' " A salesman's solicitation, a broker's offer, and a manufacturer's publication of a price list or the terms of his standard warranty would unquestionably fit within this concept. Presumably, the definition is intended to encompass advertising that advises possible buyers of the availability of specific products at specific prices and describes the advantages of purchasing such items. Perhaps it also extends to other communications that do little more than make the name of a product or a service more familiar to the general public. Whatever the precise contours of the concept, and perhaps it is too early to enunciate an exact formulation, I am persuaded that it should not include the entire range of communication that is embraced within the term "promotional advertising."

This case involves a governmental regulation that completely bans promotional advertising by an electric utility. This ban encompasses a great deal more than mere proposals to engage in certain kinds of commercial transactions. It prohibits all advocacy of the immediate or future use of electricity. It curtails expression by an informed and interested group of persons of their point of view on questions relating to the production and consumption of electrical energy—questions frequently discussed and debated by our political leaders. For example, an electric company's advocacy of the use of electric heat for environmental reasons, as opposed to wood-burning stoves, would seem to fall squarely within New York's promotional advertising ban and also within the bounds of maximum First Amendment protection. The breadth of the ban thus exceeds the boundaries of the commercial speech concept, however that concept may be defined.

The justification for the regulation is nothing more than the expressed fear that the audience may find the utility's message persuasive. Without the aid of any coercion, deception, or misinformation, truthful communication may persuade some citizens to consume more electricity than they otherwise would. I assume that such a consequence would be undesirable and that government may therefore prohibit and punish the unnecessary or excessive use of electricity. But if the perceived harm associated with greater electrical usage is not sufficiently serious to justify direct regulation, surely it does not constitute the kind of clear and present danger that can justify the suppression of speech.

. . .

In sum, I concur in the result because I do not consider this to be a "commercial speech" case. Accordingly, I see no need to decide whether the Court's four-part analysis, adequately protects commercial speech—as properly defined—in the face of a blanket ban of the sort involved in this case.

[Justice Rehnquist dissented. He thought that a state-created monopoly, which was the subject of a comprehensive regulatory scheme, was not entitled to First Amendment protection. He further argued that the state law was an economic regulation and thus, that the speech involved occupied an extremely subordinate position in the First Amendment hierarchy. Finally, he believed that the Court, in applying the four-part test, had improperly substituted its own judgment for that of the State.]

## Notes and Questions

1. As Justice Stevens noted in his concurrence, the Court used two definitions of commercial speech. He argued that neither was adequate. Assuming he was right, is a clear definition of commercial speech possible?

2. The definition of commercial speech was the key to a decision by an FTC ALJ dismissing a complaint against the R.J. Reynolds Tobacco Company. At issue was an advertisement entitled, "Of cigarettes and science," which was alleged to be false and misleading. The ad was an editorial discussing a specific study of the possible link between smoking and heart disease. Because the advertisement did not name any brand name, list prices, discuss desirable attributes of a product, show where the product could be purchased, or contain any express promotional language, the ALJ held that the advertisement was political speech and thus beyond the FTC's jurisdiction. R.J. Reynolds Tobacco Company, Inc., 51 Antitrust & Trade Reg. Rep. 219 (1986).

The Commission reversed the decision holding that the ALJ had not considered a number of factors relevant to the determination of whether the R.J. Reynolds advertisement was commercial speech. Among these factors were whether the speaker had an economic motivation, whether the speech might promote sales of the speaker's products, whether the advertisement contained information about the attributes of a product offered for sale. The case was remanded to the ALJ with instructions to apply these factors to the facts of the case. R.J. Reynolds' petition for review was rejected on the grounds that the FTC's action was not final.

In 1987 R.J. Reynolds entered into a consent decree with the FTC. R.J. Reynolds admitted no violations but agreed not to misrepresent the study in any future advertisements. 54 Fed.Reg. 41,342 (Oct. 16, 1989).

3. If the government could bar an activity such as the sale of cigarettes, would it follow that it could bar advertising of that activity? Assuming that the government could prohibit the manufacture and sale of cigarettes, may it instead permit their continued sale but bar manufacturers from advertising (and the press from carrying the advertisements)? In fact a statute banning cigarette advertising from the electronic media was upheld. Capital Broadcasting v. Mitchell, 333 F.Supp. 582 (D.D.C. 1971), aff'd without opinion 405 U.S. 1000 (1972). However, that decision was prior to *Virginia State Board of Pharmacy* and *Central Hudson*. Furthermore, as we will discuss in Chapters XIV–XVII, broadcasting has long been treated differently than other media in terms of First Amendment protection.

4. A 1986 Supreme Court decision seems to indicate that banning advertising for lawful products does not necessarily violate the First Amendment. In 1948 Puerto Rico legalized certain forms of casino gambling in an effort to encourage tourism. Although local residents were not banned from using the casinos, the legislature provided that casinos were not to advertise to the local public. Over the years the focus of the regulation became one of identifying the primary audience of the advertisement in question. This meant that casinos might advertise within Puerto Rico if their primary audience was tourists rather than residents. In Posadas de Puerto Rico Associates v. Tourism Company of Puerto Rico, 478 U.S. 328, 13 Med.L.Rptr. 1033 (1986), the Court, 5–4, rejected a casino's facial challenge to the statute and the regulations.

For the majority, Justice Rehnquist began by noting that the case involved "pure commercial speech which does 'no more than propose a commercial transaction.'" He then applied the four-part test of *Central Hudson*. First, the regulation concerned a lawful activity and was not misleading or fraudulent. Second, the "reduction of demand for casino gambling by the residents of Puerto Rico" was a "substantial" government interest. Third, the regulation "directly advanced" the government's asserted interest:

> The Puerto Rico Legislature obviously believed . . . that advertising of casino gambling aimed at the residents of Puerto Rico would serve to increase the demand for the product advertised. We think the legislature's belief is a reasonable one. . . .

The Court rejected the casino's argument that the regulation was underinclusive because other types of gambling could be advertised to residents. The restrictions do in fact directly advance the government's interest in this case. In addition, the legislature's concern might have been casino gambling rather than horse racing, cockfighting and the lottery, which might "have been traditionally part of the Puerto Rican's roots."

Fourth, the restrictions were "no more extensive than necessary to serve the government's interest." The casino argued that the First Amendment required the government to reduce demand for casino gambling "not by suppressing commercial speech that might *encourage* such gambling, but by promulgating additional speech designed to *discourage* it." The Court disagreed:

> We think it is up to the legislature to decide whether or not such a "counterspeech" policy would be as effective in reducing the demand for casino gambling as a restriction on advertising. The legislature could conclude, as it apparently did here, that residents of Puerto Rico are already aware of the risks of casino gambling, yet would nevertheless be induced by widespread advertising to engage in such potentially harmful conduct. Cf. Capital Broadcasting Co. v. Mitchell, 333 F.Supp. 582, 585 (D.C.1971) (three-judge court) ("Congress has convincing evidence that the labelling Act of 1965 had not materially reduced the incidence of smoking") aff'd 405 U.S. 1000 (1972); Dunagin v. City of Oxford, Miss., 718 F.2d 738, 751 (5th Cir.1983) (en banc) (". . . The state's concern is not that the public is unaware of the dangers of alcohol. . . . The concern instead is that advertising will unduly promote alcohol despite known dangers"), cert. denied, 467 U.S. 1259 (1984).

This led the Court to conclude that the *Central Hudson* test had been met and that the lower courts had properly rejected the First Amendment claim.

The casino argued that cases like *Bigelow* p. 417, *supra*, dictated protection here. The Court disagreed. In *Bigelow,* the underlying activity itself was protected. Here, though, the legislature "surely could have prohibited casino gambling" by residents altogether.

Finally, the casino argued that once the government chose to legalize casino gambling for residents, the First Amendment barred it from using restrictions on advertising to reduce demand for the activity. The Court disagreed:

> In our view, [the casino] has the argument backwards. . . . [I]t is precisely *because* the government could have enacted a wholesale prohibition of the underlying conduct that it is permissible for the government to take the less intrusive step of allowing the conduct, but reducing the demand through restrictions on advertising. It would surely be a Pyrrhic victory for casino owners . . . to gain recognition of a First Amendment right . . . only to thereby force the legislature into banning casino gambling by residents altogether. It would just as surely be a strange constitutional doctrine which would concede to the legislature the authority to totally ban a product or activity, but deny to the legislature the

authority to forbid the stimulation of demand for the product or activity through advertising. . . . Legislative regulation of products or activities deemed harmful, such as cigarettes, alcoholic beverages, and prostitution, has varied from outright prohibition on the one hand, [　], to legalization of the product or activity with restrictions on stimulation of its demand on the other hand, [　]. To rule out the latter intermediate kind of response would require more than we find in the First Amendment.

Justice Brennan, joined by Justices Marshall and Blackmun, dissented. None of the differences between commercial and other speech "justify protecting commercial speech less extensively where, as here, the government seeks to manipulate behavior by depriving citizens of truthful information concerning lawful activities." Regulation of speech based on "fear that recipients will act on the information provided, . . . should be subject to strict judicial scrutiny." The majority improperly used the "relaxed standards" normally applied to commercial speech in its First Amendment analysis. It was incumbent on the government to "prove that the interests it seeks to further are real and substantial." Here there was no showing that "serious harmful effects" would result if local residents gambled in casinos.

Even if a substantial government interest had been shown, Justice Brennan found no showing that the advertising regulation would meet concerns about corruption or organized crime. Finally, he objected that Puerto Rico could "seek directly to address the specific harms" by monitoring casino operations to guard against the influences of crime, by vigorously enforcing its criminal laws to combat crime and prostitution, by putting limits on the size of the bets, or by promulgating additional speech. Contrary to the majority's view, it is not "up to the legislature" to decide whether the government's interest can be met by less intrusive means:

Rather, it is incumbent upon the government to prove that more limited means are not sufficient to protect its interests, and for a court to decide whether or not the government has sustained this burden. [　] In this case, nothing suggests that the Puerto Rico Legislature ever considered the efficacy of measures other than suppressing protected expression. More importantly, there has been no showing that alternative measures would inadequately safeguard the Commonwealth's interest in controlling the harmful effects allegedly associated with casino gambling. Under these circumstances, Puerto Rico's ban on advertising clearly violates the First Amendment.

Justice Brennan also rejected the majority's argument that banning speech was "less intrusive" than banning the activity itself. Once Puerto Rico made it legal for residents to gamble in casinos, the decision to ban truthful speech about that activity raised "serious" First Amendment questions. "I do not agree that a ban on casino advertising is 'less intrusive' than an outright prohibition of such activity. . . . [t]he 'constitutional doctrine' which bans Puerto Rico from banning advertisements concerning lawful casino gambling is not so strange a restraint—it is called the First Amendment."

Justice Stevens also dissented, joined by Justices Marshall and Blackmun. His focus was on the operation of the Puerto Rico regulatory scheme which he found to discriminate between publications and to involve aspects of prior restraint.

What does this case suggest about future efforts to limit advertising of alcoholic beverages or of cigarettes or of legal prostitution? Lower court cases upholding such bans were cited with approval in the majority opinion. What about banning advertising for motion pictures that could be banned as obscene, but which are permitted by the state? What about banning advertising for any spectator sport that charges more than $20 for a seat, on the ground that citizens should be discouraged from spending their money on such expensive events?

5. In Board of Trustees v. Fox, 492 U.S. 469 (1989), the Court held that the fourth prong of the *Central Hudson* analysis does not require that the regulation be the least restrictive means of effectively protecting the state's interest. In an opinion by Justice Scalia, the Court acknowledged that it had frequently said commercial speech restrictions could be no more extensive than "necessary" to serve the state's substantial interests, and that strictly speaking, such regulations are not "necessary" if less restrictive means are available. Indeed, in *Central Hudson* itself, the Court said "if the governmental interest could be served as well by a more limited restriction on commercial speech, the excessive restrictions cannot survive."

But Justice Scalia said "the reason of the matter requires something short of a least-restrictive-means standard." Otherwise, he said, restrictions on commercial speech would be even harder to justify than time-place-and-manner restrictions on core political speech, which need only be "tailored":

> What our decisions require is a " 'fit' between the legislature's ends and the means chosen to accomplish those ends," [ ]—a fit that is not necessarily perfect, but reasonable; that represents not necessarily the single best disposition but one whose scope is "in proportion to the interest served," [ ], that employs not necessarily the least restrictive means but, as we have put it in the other contexts discussed above, a means narrowly tailored to achieve the desired objective. Within those bounds we leave it to governmental decisionmakers to judge what manner of regulation may best be employed.
>
> We reject the contention that the test we have described is overly permissive. It is far different, of course, from the "rational basis" test used for Fourteenth Amendment equal protection analysis. [ ] There it suffices if the law could be thought to further a legitimate governmental goal, without reference to whether it does

so at inordinate cost. Here we require the government goal to be substantial, and the cost to be carefully calculated. Moreover, since the State bears the burden of justifying its restrictions, [ ], it must affirmatively establish the reasonable fit we require. By declining to impose, in addition, a least-restrictive-means requirement, we take account of the difficulty of establishing with precision the point at which restrictions become more extensive than their objective requires, and provide the legislative and executive branches needed leeway in a field (commercial speech) "traditionally subject to governmental regulation." [ ] Far from eroding the essential protections of the First Amendment, we think this disposition strengthens them. "To require a parity of constitutional protection for commercial and noncommercial speech alike could invite dilution, simply by a leveling process, of the force of the Amendment's guarantees with respect to the latter kind of speech."

The case involved a regulation of the State University of New York prohibiting commercial solicitations, such as "Tupperware parties" in dormitories. The Court remanded the case to determine whether the regulation had been applied in a manner that restricted noncommercial as well as commercial speech, and if not, whether it was overbroad nonetheless because of its potential applicability to noncommercial speech.

Justice Blackmun, joined by Justices Brennan and Marshall, dissented. They would have held the regulation overbroad on its face and therefore would not have reached the least-restrictive-means issue.

In the *Central Hudson* case the Commission "acknowledged that the ban is not a perfect vehicle for conserving energy." After *Fox* that admission obviously is not fatal to the Commission's case. Would the Court defer to the Commission's determination that the restriction was a reasonable though imperfect way of dampening unnecessary growth in energy consumption?

6. A practical consequence of the *Fox* modification of the *Central Hudson* test is evident in a case involving beer advertising. In 1935 Congress passed a statute forbidding advertising of alcohol content of malt beverages. The legislation was sought by consumer groups and much of the brewing industry to prevent brewers from engaging in "strength wars" that would increase the alcohol content of beer. In 1987 one brewing company challenged the statute on First Amendment grounds. Before *Fox* was decided, a district court granted the brewer summary judgment, holding the statute unconstitutional on the ground that the government could not show that a complete ban on advertising of alcohol content was the least restrictive means of preventing "strength wars."

The Tenth Circuit reversed, holding that the government was entitled to a trial on the third and fourth parts of the *Central Hudson* analysis. The court said advertising of alcohol content is protected by the First Amendment and would serve a significant public interest.

Nonetheless, the government might have a substantial interest in preventing "strength wars," and a ban on advertising might meet the *Fox* requirement of a reasonable fit between that goal and the means chosen by Congress to achieve it. "[W]ithout the benefit of the precedent established by [*Fox*], the district court misperceived the nature of the 'no more extensive than necessary' analysis," the court said. Adolph Coors Co. v. Brady, 944 F.2d 1543, 19 Med.L.Rptr. 1328 (10th Cir.1991).

7. *Implicit racial messages.* A group of fair housing advocates sued the *New York Times*, alleging the newspaper over a period of 20 years published real estate ads depicting "thousands of human models of whom virtually none were black," and that when black models were used it was usually in connection with housing in predominately black neighborhoods. The plaintiffs alleged that this amounted to publication of ads indicating a racial preference, in violation of the Fair Housing Act, 42 U.S.C.A. § 3604(c).

The district court refused to dismiss the suit, and the Second Circuit affirmed. The court held that the complaint stated a cause of action under the Fair Housing Act if ordinary readers would view the ads as indicating a racial preference. To the *Times*'s argument that such an interpretation would force advertisers to employ quotas in their choice of models, the court responded:

"In advertising, a conscious racial decision regarding models seems almost inevitable. All the statute requires is that in this make-up-your-own world the creator of an ad not make choices among models that create a suggestion of a racial preference. The deliberate inclusion of a black model where necessary to avoid such a message seems to us a far cry from the alleged practices that are at the core of the debate over quotas."

The court rejected the *Times*'s First Amendment argument on the ground that if the ads indicate a racial preference and thus violate the Fair Housing Act, they are not protected as commercial speech because they amount to speech advocating an illegal activity. Ragin v. New York Times Co., 923 F.2d 995, 18 Med.L.Rptr. 1666 (2d. Cir.), cert. denied 112 S.Ct. 81 (1991).

8. The Sixth Circuit upheld dismissal of a similar suit against the *Cincinnati Enquirer*. The complaint alleged that less than one percent of all the models depicted in the real estate section of the *Enquirer* over a 20–year period were black. The majority construed the complaint as alleging (1) that publication of a single ad using all white models violates the Fair Housing Act even if there is no pattern of repeated all-white ads by a single advertiser, and (2) even if no single ad violates the act, the newspaper violated the statute by a long-term pattern of advertising that in the aggregate conveyed a discriminatory message. The court held that neither theory stated a claim under the terms of the act, and that holding a publisher liable for the aggregate message of many different ads would raise serious First Amendment questions. It distinguished *Ragin* on the ground that it dealt with ads that were assumed to be

individually discriminatory. A dissenter would have allowed the complaint to go to trial on both theories, and accused the majority of misconstruing the complaint, eviscerating the statute, and misreading *Ragin*. Housing Opportunities Made Equal, Inc. v. Cincinnati Enquirer, Inc., 943 F.2d 644, 19 Med.L.Rptr. 1353 (6th Cir.1991).

9. Further clarification of what is required to show a "reasonable fit" came in a 1993 case involving racks of free magazines showing houses for sale in Cincinnati. The city said the magazines were "commercial handbills" that could not be distributed from racks on public property, even though newspapers could be distributed from such racks. Because this case involves whole magazines rather than just paid space in newspapers or magazines with more general editorial content, or commercial time on radio and television, it is different from earlier cases; but it is important to deal with it here because the Supreme Court analyzed it as it has analyzed earlier commercial speech cases.

### CINCINNATI v. DISCOVERY NETWORK, INC.

Supreme Court of the United States, 1993.
__ U.S. __, 113 S.Ct. 1505, 123 L.Ed.2d 99, 21 Med.L.Rptr. 1161.

MR. JUSTICE STEVENS delivered the opinion of the Court.

Motivated by its interest in the safety and attractive appearance of its streets and sidewalks, the city of Cincinnati has refused to allow respondents to distribute their commercial publications through freestanding newsracks located on public property. The question presented is whether this refusal is consistent with the First Amendment. In agreement with the District Court and Court of Appeals, we hold that it is not.

.  .  .

### II

There is no claim in this case that there is anything unlawful or misleading about the contents of respondents' publications. Moreover, respondents do not challenge their characterization as "commercial speech." Nor do respondents question the substantiality of the city's interest in safety and esthetics. It was, therefore, proper for the District Court and the Court of Appeals to judge the validity of the City's prohibition under the standard we set forth in *Central Hudson* and *Fox*. It was the city's burden to establish a "reasonable fit" between its legitimate interests in safety and esthetics and its choice of a limited and selective prohibition of newsracks as the means chosen to serve those interests.

There is ample support in the record for the conclusion that the city did not "establish the reasonable fit we require." *Fox*, 492 U.S., at 480. The ordinance on which it relied was an outdated prohibition against the distribution of any commercial handbills on public property. It was enacted long before any concern about newsracks developed. Its apparent purpose was to prevent the kind of visual blight caused by littering, rather than any harm associated with permanent, freestanding dispensing devices.  The fact that the city failed to address its recently developed concern about newsracks by regulating their size, shape, appearance, or number indicates that it has not "carefully calculated the costs and benefits associated with the burden on speech imposed by its prohibition.  The benefit to be derived from the removal of 62 newsracks while about 1,500–2,000 remain in place was considered "minute" by the District Court and "paltry" by the Court of Appeals.  We share their evaluation of the "fit" between the city's goal and its method of achieving it.

In seeking reversal, the city argues that it is wrong to focus attention on the relatively small number of newsracks affected by its prohibition, because the city's central concern is with the overall number of newsracks on its sidewalks, rather than with the unattractive appearance of a handful of dispensing devices.  It contends, first, that a categorical prohibition on the use of newsracks to disseminate commercial messages burdens no more speech than is necessary to further its interest in limiting the number of newsracks; and, second, that the prohibition is a valid "time, place, and manner" regulation because it is content-neutral and leaves open ample alternative channels of communication.  We consider these arguments in turn.

## III

The city argues that there is a close fit between its ban on newsracks dispensing "commercial handbills" and its interest in safety and esthetics because every decrease in the number of such dispensing devices necessarily effects an increase in safety and an improvement in the attractiveness of the cityscape.  In the city's view, the prohibition is thus *entirely* related to its legitimate interests in safety and esthetics.

We accept the validity of the city's proposition, but consider it an insufficient justification for the discrimination against respondents' use of newsracks that are no more harmful than the permitted newsracks, and have only a minimal impact on the overall number of newsracks on the city's sidewalks.  The major premise supporting the city's argument is the proposition that commercial speech has only a low value.  Based on that premise, the city contends that the fact that assertedly more valuable publications are allowed to use newsracks does not undermine its judgment that its esthetic and safety interests are stronger than the interest in allowing commercial speakers to have similar access to the reading public.

We cannot agree.  In our view, the city's argument attaches more importance to the distinction between commercial and noncommercial speech than our cases warrant and seriously underestimates the value of commercial speech.

This very case illustrates the difficulty of drawing bright lines that will clearly cabin commercial speech in a distinct category.  For respondents' publications share important characteristics with the publications that the city classifies as "newspapers." Particularly, they are "commercial handbills" within the meaning of § 714–1–C of the city's Code because they contain advertising, a feature that apparently also places ordinary newspapers within the same category. Separate provisions in the code specifically authorize the distribution of "newspapers" on the public right way, but that term is not defined. Presumably, respondents' publications do not qualify as newspapers because an examination of their content discloses a higher ratio of advertising to other text, such as news and feature stories, than is found in the exempted publications. Indeed, Cincinnati's City Manager has determined that publications that qualify as newspapers and therefore *can* be distributed by newsrack are those that are published daily and or weekly and "*primarily* presen[t] coverage of, and commentary on, current events." [   ]

The absence of a categorical definition of the difference between "newspapers" and commercial handbills" in the city's Code is also a characteristic of our opinions considering the constitutionality of regulations of commercial speech.   .   .   .

.   .   .

.   .   . [W]e have stated that speech proposing a commercial transaction is entitled to lesser protection than other constitutionally guaranteed expression, [Ohralik v. Ohio State Bar Association, 436 U.S. 447, 455–456 (1978)]. We have also suggested that such lesser protection was appropriate for a somewhat larger category of commercial speech—"that is, expression related solely to the economic interests of the speaker and its audience." [*Central Hudson*, p. 422, *supra*].   .   .   .

.   .   . In *Fox*, we described the category even more narrowly, by characterizing the proposal of a commercial transaction as "*the test* for identifying commercial speech." [   ]

Under the *Fox* test it is clear that much of the material in ordinary newspapers is commercial speech and, conversely, that the editorial content in respondents' promotional publications is not what we have described as "core" commercial speech. There is no doubt a "common sense" basis for distinguishing between the two, but under both the city's Code and our cases the difference is a matter of degree.

Nevertheless, for the purpose of deciding this case, we assume that all of the speech barred from Cincinnati's sidewalks is what we have labeled "core" commercial speech and that no such speech is found in publications that are allowed to use newsracks. We nonetheless agree with the Court of Appeals that Cincinnati's actions in this case run afoul of the First Amendment. Not only does Cincinnati's categorical ban on commercial newsracks place too much importance on the distinction between commercial and noncommercial speech, but in this case, the distinction bears no relationship *whatsoever* to the particular interests that the city has asserted. It is therefore an impermissible means of responding to the city's admittedly legitimate interests. [   ]

The city has asserted an interest in esthetics, but respondent publishers' newsracks are no greater an eyesore than the newsracks permitted to remain on Cincinnati's sidewalks. Each newsrack, whether containing "newspapers" or "commercial handbills," is equally unattractive. . . .

Cincinnati has not asserted an interest in preventing commercial harms by regulating the information distributed by respondent publishers' newsracks, which is, of course, the typical reason why commercial speech can be subject to greater governmental regulation than noncommercial speech. . . .

. . . Here, the city contends that safety concerns and visual blight may be addressed by a prohibition that distinguishes between commercial and noncommercial publications that are equally responsible for those problems. . . .

In the absence of some basis for distinguishing between "newspaper" and "commercial handbills" that is relevant to an interest asserted by the city, we are unwilling to recognize Cincinnati's bare assertion that the low "value" of commercial speech is a sufficient justification for its selective and categorical ban on newsracks dispensing "commercial handbills." Our holding, however, is narrow. As should be clear from the above discussion, we do not reach the question whether, given certain facts and under certain circumstances, a community might be able to justify differential treatment of commercial and noncommercial newsracks. We simply hold that on this record Cincinnati has failed to make such a showing. Because the distinction Cincinnati has drawn has absolutely no bearing on the interests it has asserted, we have no difficulty concluding, as did the two courts below, that the city has not established the "fit" between its goals and its chosen means that is required by our opinion in *Fox*. It remains to consider the city's argument that its prohibition is a permissible time, place, and manner regulation.

IV

The Court has held that government may impose reasonable restrictions on the time, place or manner of engaging in protected speech provided that they are adequately justified " 'without reference to the content of the regulated speech.' " . . . The city contends that its regulation of newsracks qualifies as such a restriction because the interests in safety and esthetics that it serves are entirely unrelated to the content of respondents' publications. Thus, the argument goes, the *justification* for the regulation is content neutral.

The argument is unpersuasive because the very basis for the regulation is the difference in content between ordinary newspapers and commercial speech. True, there is no evidence that the city has acted with animus toward the ideas contained within respondents' publications, but just last Term we expressly rejected the argument that "discriminatory . . . treatment is suspect under the First Amend-

ment only when the legislature intends to suppress certain ideas." [   ]
Regardless of the *mens rea* of the city, it has enacted a sweeping ban on
the use of newsracks that distribute "commercial handbills," but not
"newspapers." Under the city's newsrack policy, whether any particular newsrack falls within the ban is determined by the content of the
publication resting inside that newsrack. Thus, by any commonsense
understanding of the term, the ban in this case is "content-based."

Nor are we persuaded that our statements that the test for whether
a regulation is content-based turns on the "justification" for the regulation, [   ], compel a different conclusion. We agree with the city that its
desire to limit the total number of newsracks is "justified" by its interest
in safety and esthetics. The city has not, however, limited the number
of newsracks; it has limited (to zero) the number of newsracks *distributing commercial publications*. As we have explained, there is no justification for that particular regulation other than the city's naked assertion
that commercial speech has "low value." It is the absence of a neutral
justification for its selective ban on newsracks that prevents the city
from defending its newsrack policy as content-neutral.

. . .

In sum, the city's newsrack policy is neither content-neutral nor, as
demonstrated in Part III, *supra*, "narrowly tailored." Thus, regardless
of whether or not it leaves open ample alternative channels of communication, it cannot be justified as a legitimate time, place, or manner
restriction on protected speech.

Cincinnati has enacted a sweeping ban that bars from its sidewalks
a whole class of constitutionally protected speech. As did the District
Court and the Court of Appeals, we conclude that Cincinnati has failed
to justify that policy. The regulation is not a permissible regulation of
commercial speech, for on this record it is clear that the interests that
Cincinnati has asserted are unrelated to any distinction between "commercial handbills" and "newspapers." Moreover, because the ban is
predicated on the content of the publications distributed by the subject
newsracks, it is not a valid time, place, or manner restriction on
protected speech. For these reasons, Cincinnati's categorical ban on the
distribution, via newsrack, of "commercial handbills" cannot be squared
with dictates of the First Amendment.

The judgment of the Court of Appeals is

*Affirmed*

[JUSTICE BLACKMUN concurred separately to reiterate his belief "that
truthful, noncoercive commercial speech concerning lawful activities is
entitled to full First Amendment protection."]

CHIEF JUSTICE REHNQUIST, with whom JUSTICE WHITE and JUSTICE
THOMAS join, dissenting.

Concerned about the safety and esthetics of its streets and sidewalks, the city of Cincinnati decided to do something about the proliferation of newsracks on its street corners. Pursuant to an existing ordi-

nance prohibiting the distribution of "commercial handbills" on public property, the city ordered respondents . . . to remove their news-racks from its sidewalks within 30 days. Respondents publish and distribute free of charge magazines that consist principally of commercial speech. Together their publications account for 62 of the 1,500–2,000 newsracks that clutter Cincinnati's street corners. Because the city chose to address its newsrack problem by banning only those newsracks that disseminate commercial handbills, rather than regulating all newsracks that disseminate traditional newspapers) alike, the Court holds that its actions violate the First Amendment to the Constitution. I believe this result is inconsistent with prior precedent.

"Our jurisprudence has emphasized that 'commercial speech [enjoys] a limited measure of protection, commensurate with its subordinate position in the scale of First Amendment values,' and is subject to 'modes of regulation that might be impermissible in the realm of noncommercial expression.' " [*Fox*]; [  ] We have advanced several reasons for this treatment, among which is that commercial speech is more durable than other types of speech, since it is "the offspring of economic self-interest." [*Central Hudson*]; [*Virginia State Board of Pharmacy*]. Commercial speech is also "less central to the interests of the First Amendment" than other types of speech, such as political expression. [*Dun & Bradstreet, Inc.*, p. 140, *supra*]. Finally, there is an inherent danger that conferring equal status upon commercial speech will erode the First Amendment protection accorded noncommercial speech, "simply by a leveling process of the force of the Amendment's guarantee with respect to the latter kind of speech." [*Ohralik*].

. . . I agree with the Court that the city's prohibition against respondents' newsracks is properly analyzed under *Central Hudson* . . . but differ as to the result this analysis should produce.

. . . This case turns, then, on the application of the last part of the *Central Hudson* analysis. Although the Court does not say so, there can be no question that Cincinnati's prohibition against respondents' newsracks "directly advances" its safety and esthetic interests because, if enforced, the city's prohibition is "more extensive than necessary" to serve its interests, or, as we elaborated in *Fox*, whether there is a "reasonable fit" between the city's desired ends and the means it has chosen to accomplish those ends. [  ] Because the city's "commercial handbill" ordinance was not enacted specifically to address the problems caused by newsracks, and if enforced, the city's prohibition against respondents' newsracks would result in the removal of only 62 news-racks from its street corners, the Court finds "ample support in the record for the conclusion that the city did not establish [a] reasonable fit." [  ] I disagree.

According to the Court, the city's decision to invoke an existing ordinance "to address its recently developed concern about newsracks" indicates that "it has not 'carefully calculated' the costs and benefits associated with the burden on speech imposed by its prohibition." [  ]

The implication being that it could have accomplished its desired ends by regulating the "size, shape, appearance, or number" of all newsracks, rather than categorically banning only those newsracks that disseminate commercial speech. [   ]  Despite its protestations to the contrary, [   ]. This argument rests on the discredited notion that the availability of "less restrictive means" to accomplish the city's objectives renders its regulation of commercial speech unconstitutional.  As we observed in *Fox*, "almost all of the restrictions disallowed under *Central Hudson's* fourth prong have been substantially excessive, disregarding far less restrictive and more precise means." [   ]  That there may be other— less restrictive—means by which Cincinnati could have gone about addressing its safety and esthetic concerns, then, does not render its prohibition against respondents' newsracks unconstitutional.

Nor does the fact that, if enforced, the city's prohibition would result in the removal of only 62 newsracks from its street corners.  .  .  .  The relevant inquiry, though, is not the degree to which the locality's interests are furthered in a particular case, but rather the relation that the challenged regulation of commercial speech bears to the "overall problem" the locality is seeking to alleviate. [   ]  This follows from our test for reviewing the validity of "time, place, or manner" restrictions on noncommercial speech, which we have said is "substantially similar" to the *Central Hudson* analysis. [*Fox*]  Properly viewed, then, the city's prohibition against respondents' newsracks is directly related to its efforts to alleviate the problems caused by newsracks, since every newsrack that is removed from the city's sidewalks marginally enhances the safety of its cityscape.  This conclusion is not altered by the fact that the city has chosen to address its problem by banning only those newsracks that disseminate commercial speech, rather than regulating all newsracks alike.

.  .  .

The Court offers an alternative rationale for invalidating the city's policy: viz., the distinction Cincinnati has drawn (between commercial and noncommercial speech) in deciding which newsracks to regulate "bears no relationship *whatsoever* to the particular interests that the city has asserted."  .  .  .

Thus, despite the fact that we have consistently distinguished between commercial and noncommercial speech for the purpose of determining whether the regulation of speech is permissible, the Court holds that in attempting to alleviate its newsrack problem Cincinnati may not choose to proceed incrementally by burdening only commercial speech first.  Based on the different levels of protection we have accorded commercial and noncommercial speech, we have previously said that localities may not favor commercial over noncommercial speech in addressing similar urban problems, [   ], but before today we have never even suggested that the converse holds true.  It is not surprising, then, that the Court offers little in the way of precedent supporting its new rule.  The cases it does cite involve challenges to the restriction of noncommercial speech in which we have refused to accept distinctions drawn between restricted and nonrestricted on the ground that they bore no relationship to the interests asserted for regulating the speech in the first place.

The Court's reliance on [*Bolger*, p. 79, *supra*], is also misplaced. In that case we said that the State's interest in "shield[ing] recipients of mail from materials that they are likely to find offensive" was invalid regardless of the type of speech—commercial or noncommercial—involved. [   ] By contrast, there can be no question here that the city's safety and esthetic interests justify its prohibition against respondents' newsracks.   .   .   .

If (as I am certain) Cincinnati may regulate newsracks that disseminate commercial speech based on the interests it has asserted, I am at a loss as to why its scheme is unconstitutional because it does not also regulate newsracks that disseminate noncommercial speech.  One would have thought that the city, perhaps even following the teachings of our commercial speech jurisprudence, could have decided to place the burden of its regulatory scheme on less protected speech (*i.e.*, commercial handbills) without running afoul of the First Amendment.  Today's decision, though, places the city in the position of having to decide between restricting more speech—and allowing the proliferation of newsracks on its street corners to continue unabated.  It scarcely seems logical that the First Amendment compels such a result.  In my view, the city may order the removal of *all* newsracks from its public right-of-ways if it so chooses.  [   ]  But however it decides to address its newsrack problem, it should be allowed to proceed in the manner and scope it sees fit so long as it does not violate established First Amendment principles, such as the rule against discrimination on the basis of content.   .   .   .

Cincinnati has burdened less speech than necessary to fully accomplish its objective of alleviating the problems caused by the proliferation of newsracks on its street corners.  Because I believe the city has established a "reasonable fit" between its substantial safety and esthetic interests and its prohibition against respondents' newsracks, I would hold that the city's actions are permissible under *Central Hudson*.   .   .   .

## 2.  PROFESSIONAL ADVERTISING

For a number of years, groups regulating law and medicine did not allow their practitioners to advertise.  This was enforced through professional organizations, such as the American Bar Association and the American Medical Association, state licensing boards and sometimes by state statutes.  These barriers to professional advertising began to fall as the Supreme Court changed its view of the First Amendment protection commercial speech enjoys.  Beginning in the late 1970s, the Court began to balance the rights of professionals to convey their message to the public through advertising against the suggested needs of professional organizations to inhibit the "commercialization" of these areas.

### a.  The Legal Profession

The Supreme Court dealt with legal advertising in a case involving advertising by two lawyers who operated a "legal clinic" in which they tried to provide basic legal services to clients of moderate income.  To sustain their business, they needed a large number of clients, which they felt could be attracted only through advertising.  They placed "truthful advertisements concerning the availability and terms of routine legal services" in daily newspapers.  The state supreme court censured the attorneys for violating the state bar's code of ethics.  The Supreme Court reversed.  Bates v. State Bar of Arizona, 433 U.S. 350 (1977).

First, the Court rejected the state's three justifications for banning the ads:  that "legal clinic" was a confusing term;  that the price advertised for uncontested divorces was not in fact "very reasonable";  and that the ads did not inform the public that some legal actions, such as name changes, could be handled without an attorney.  Balancing in each case, the Court thought that the free speech interest prevailed.

The Court then noted that some ads for professional services might be found misleading in the future though the same words would not be misleading if standardized products were being offered.  The Court was particularly concerned about advertising the "quality" of legal services that are "not susceptible to measurement or verification."  Similarly, in-person solicitation might create coercive pressures that media advertising would not.

The Court relied heavily on footnote 24 of *Virginia State Board of Pharmacy,* p. 420, *supra,* in recognizing that commercial speech might well be less susceptible to chilling than non-commercial speech:

> [A]ny concern that strict requirements for truthfulness will undesirably inhibit spontaneity seems inapplicable because commercial speech generally is calculated.  Indeed, the public and private benefits from commercial speech derive from confidence in its accuracy and reliability.  Thus, the leeway for untruthful or misleading expression that has been allowed in other contexts has little force in the commercial arena.

The Supreme Court, then, allows attorneys to advertise "basic facts," such as name, telephone number, address and office hours, information concerning an attorney's educational background, and basic prices for initial consultations and "routine" legal services.  In addition, a state may not restrict the distribution of professional announcement cards to a specified audience, prohibit attorneys from listing the courts in which they are admitted to practice nor prescribe the specific wording lawyers may use to describe their areas of practice.  In re R.M.J., 455 U.S. 191 (1982).  In addition, the Court has held that attorneys have a right to list specialty certifications by private organizations such as the

National Board of Trial Advocacy. Peel v. Attorney Registration and Disciplinary Commission of Illinois, 496 U.S. 91 (1990).

In Zauderer v. Office of Disciplinary Counsel, 471 U.S. 626 (1985), the Court upheld the constitutional right of lawyers to use printed advertising to seek clients for specific cases: here, Dalkon shield litigation. The state argued that it was too difficult in these cases for regulators to distinguish accurate advertising from false or misleading ads. The Court responded that the protections "afforded commercial speech would mean little indeed if such arguments were allowed to prevail." Although the Court upheld the basic advertisement and the use of an illustration that violated state bar rules, it did find one aspect of the lawyer's ad misleading: the part in which he said that if the case was not successful "no legal fees are owed by our clients." That part was misleading because it did not reveal that clients might be liable for various court costs in case of failure.

Restrictions may still be imposed on false or deceptive ads and on the way business is solicited. Indeed, the Court did rule that in-person solicitation could still be barred because of ethical considerations that differentiate solicitation from advertising. Moreover, unlike advertising, solicitation does not promote informed decision-making by the public. Ohralik v. Ohio State Bar Association, 436 U.S. 447 (1978).

Subsequently, the Court struck down a ban on targeted direct mail solicitation. In Shapero v. Kentucky Bar Association, 486 U.S. 466 (1988), the Court found direct mail aimed at a specific audience more analogous to the newspaper advertisements held protected in *Zauderer* than the in-person solicitation held unprotected in *Ohralik*.

### b. The Medical Profession

State statutes that bar advertising by medical professionals present the additional element of the relationship between the First Amendment right to disseminate honest advertising and the state's right to protect the public's health and safety. Some contend that the latter interest is enhanced by legal and ethical bans on medical advertising.

Blanket prohibitions on ads for medical products are no longer possible after *Virginia State Board of Pharmacy*. In contrast, state bans on ads for medical services have not yet been considered by the Supreme Court.

In an optometry case, however, the Supreme Court offered some clues as to the limits of the *Bates* approach. A Texas statute banned optometrists from operating under any trade name (a fictitious company name) other than the names of the optometrists who participated in the activity. The asserted purpose was to provide information to the public about who was actually performing the work at each facility. The statute was challenged by optometrists operating under the name "Texas State Optical" on the ground that it interfered with their right of free speech. The Court disagreed and upheld the statute. Friedman v. Rogers, 440 U.S. 1 (1979).

The Court held that trade names can mislead the public because the people actually doing the work may change while the trade name does not. "The possibilities for deception are numerous." The use of trade names was different from the commercial speech involved in *Virginia State Board of Pharmacy* and *Bates*. Those "statements were self-contained and self-explanatory. Here, we are concerned with a form of commercial speech that has no intrinsic meaning." The meaning is acquired over the years from associations formed in the public mind:

> A trade name conveys no information about the price and nature of the services offered by an optometrist until it acquires meaning over a period of time by associations formed in the minds of the public between the name and some standard of price or quality. Because these ill-defined associations of trade names with price and quality information can be manipulated by the users of trade names, there is a significant possibility that trade names will be used to mislead the public.

Finally, in contrast to the earlier cases, the state restriction "has only the most incidental effect on the content of the commercial speech of Texas optometrists." The information associated with trade names, such as the kind and price of the available services, "may be communicated freely and explicitly to the public. An optometrist may advertise the type of service he offers, the prices he charges, and whether he practices as a partner, associate, or employee with other optometrists." This offers more accurate information than before the statute when "optometrists were allowed to convey the information through unstated and ambiguous associations with a trade name." The state's insistence on certain information to prevent optometrists from being deceptive was justifiable and, on balance, prevailed over the free speech claim.

The FTC issued orders prohibiting the AMA and the ADA from blanket restrictions on advertising by their members, although the Commission will allow reasonable ethical guidelines covering deceptive advertising and solicitation of especially vulnerable patients. The AMA appealed, and the order was upheld with minor modifications by the court of appeals. American Medical Association v. Federal Trade Commission, 638 F.2d 443 (2d Cir.1980). The Supreme Court subsequently affirmed without opinion. 455 U.S. 676 (1982).

### c. Other Professions

Although a ban on in-person solicitation by lawyers is constitutional, *Ohralik*, p. 447, *supra*, the same is not necessarily true for other professions. In Edenfield v. Fane, 113 S.Ct. 1792, 21 Med.L.Rptr. 1321 (1993), the Supreme Court struck down a Florida ban on in-person and telephone solicitation by Certified Public Accountants. The Court distinguished *Ohralik* on two bases. First it argued that by virtue of their training, CPAs are different than lawyers. "Unlike a lawyer, a CPA is not 'a professional trained in the art of persuasion.' A CPA's training emphasizes independence and objectivity, not advocacy."

The second distinction involved the clients that each profession serves. According to the court, prospective clients of CPA's are "sophisticated and experienced business clients." As such, they are "far less susceptible to manipulation than the young accident victim in *Ohralik*." Furthermore, the decision to hire a CPA is more likely to be made over a period of time, whereas an accident victim's hiring of an attorney may be made at the time of the initial solicitation.

### 3. CORPORATE SPEECH

Corporations are created by law. In some ways they take on lives of their own. They can sue and be sued, must pay taxes, can go bankrupt—all as individuals can. But do they have the same constitutional rights as individuals? On the one hand, the Supreme Court has said they do not have the Fifth Amendment right against self-incrimination, but that they are "persons" entitled to the protections of the Fourteenth Amendment. What about the First Amendment right of freedom of expression? The Court took a step toward answering this question in First National Bank of Boston v. Bellotti, 435 U.S. 765, 3 Med.L.Rptr. 2105 (1978).

Several corporations wanted to spend money to publicize their opposition to a referendum proposal to authorize the Massachusetts legislature to enact a graduated income tax. A state statute barred business corporations from spending money to influence votes on referenda unless the question was one "materially affecting" the corporation's business or assets. This action was brought against the state Attorney General to declare the statute unconstitutional. The state court upheld the statute on the ground that a corporation's First Amendment rights are limited to issues that "materially affect" its business, property or assets. The Supreme Court, 5–4, reversed.

For the majority, Justice Powell asserted that corporations had rights of free speech equivalent to those of individual citizens. Here the speech involved the essence of self-government and was thus protected under the First Amendment. In response to the state's argument that "communication by corporate members of the institutional press is entitled to greater constitutional protection than the same communication" by other types of corporations, Justice Powell noted that banks and other corporations might be better informed on economic issues than media corporations.

The state also argued that even though the speech was entitled to First Amendment protection, it was more important for government to sustain the active role of individual citizens in the electoral process. The argument was that "corporations are wealthy and powerful and their views may drown out other points of view." But the record

presented no such showing. Because Massachusetts allowed corporations to lobby in the legislature and they were protected in petitioning
government officials, a ban on communicating with the electorate directly could be defended only on the ground that the state lacked confidence
in the ability of the electorate to evaluate the relative merits of conflicting arguments. Such a paternalistic argument contradicted First
Amendment values.

Justice White, joined by Justices Brennan and Marshall, dissented.
He stressed that many states limit corporate political activity—and that
this was an arena in which the "expertise of legislators is at its peak and
that of judges is at its very lowest." Corporations hardly need freedom
of speech for self-fulfillment since, in the words of Professor Emerson,
such speech is not "an integral part of the development of ideas, of
mental exploration and of the affirmation of self." Justice White
concluded that the public's right to receive communications financed by
corporate expenditures is not necessarily of the same dimension as that
to hear other forms of expression. The lack of individual self-expression
is critical: "Ideas which are not a product of individual choice are
entitled to less First Amendment protection." When this raised questions about media corporations, Justice White responded in a footnote:

> [N]ewspapers and other forms of literature obviously do not lose
> their First Amendment protection simply because they are produced
> or distributed by corporations. It is, of course, impermissible to
> restrict any communication, corporate or otherwise, because of
> displeasure with its content. I need not decide whether newspapers
> have a First Amendment right to operate in a corporate form.

Justice White stressed that "the special status of corporations has placed
them in a position to control vast amounts of economic power which
may, if not regulated, dominate not only the economy but also the very
heart of our democracy, the electoral process." The state "need not
permit its own creation to consume it." Massachusetts could reasonably
have concluded that "not to impose limits upon the political activities of
corporations would have placed it in a position of departing from
neutrality and indirectly assisting the propagation of corporate views
because of the advantages its laws give to the corporate acquisition of
funds to finance such activities."

In a separate dissent, Justice Rehnquist contended that a state that
charters corporations might reasonably conclude that "those properties,
so beneficial in the economic sphere, pose special dangers in the political
sphere." He drew a sharp distinction between the corporation's right of
speech and its right to spend money for certain objects. Thus, he argued
that although "a newspaper corporation must necessarily have the
liberty to endorse a political candidate in its editorial columns, it need
have no greater right than any other corporation to contribute money to
that candidate's campaign."

Even though he concluded that the state might regulate the expenditure of corporate funds in an election campaign, he did not believe that

the free flow of information would be diminished. "All natural persons, who owe their existence to a higher sovereign than the Commonwealth, remain as free as before to engage in political activity."

However, First Amendment protection for corporate political speech is not unlimited. In Austin v. Michigan Chamber of Commerce, 494 U.S. 652 (1990), the Court upheld a Michigan statute prohibiting the use of general corporate treasury funds to support or oppose political candidates and requiring instead that separate segregated funds be used for such purposes. Media corporations were exempted from the provisions of the statute.

The majority found that the statute served a compelling government interest in eliminating "the corrosive and distorting effects of immense aggregations of wealth that are accumulated with the help of the corporate form and that have little or no correlation to the public's support for the corporation's political ideas."

The statute was found to be narrowly tailored because it allowed political expenditures through separate segregated funds. "Because persons contributing to such funds understand that their money will be used solely for political purposes, the speech generated accurately reflects contributors' support for the corporation's political views."

Justice Scalia dissented, arguing that the government had no right to attempt through censorship to assure fairness in political debate. He also contended that the government's argument was undermined by its exception for media corporations:

> But if one believes in the Court's rationale of "compelling state need" to prevent amassed corporate wealth from skewing the political debate, surely that "unique role" of the press does not give Michigan justification for *excluding* media corporations from coverage, but provides especially strong reason to *include* them. Amassed corporate wealth that regularly fits astride the ordinary channels of information is much more likely to produce the New Corruption (too much of one point of view) than amassed corporate wealth that is generally busy making money elsewhere. Such media corporations not only have vastly greater power to perpetrate the evil of overinforming, they also have vastly greater opportunity.

Justice Kennedy, joined by Justices O'Connor and Scalia, also dissented. He found the Court's decision in direct conflict with *Bellotti* because it limited First Amendment rights solely on the basis of the corporate identity. He also argued that the statute was overinclusive because it covered all corporations regardless of wealth or power and underinclusive because of the exemption for media corporations.

### 4. THE SECURITIES AND EXCHANGE COMMISSION

In the 1980s the Securities and Exchange Commission was involved in two cases raising important First Amendment questions. In Securities and Exchange Commission v. Lowe, 556 F.Supp. 1359, 9 Med.L.Rptr. 1281 (E.D.N.Y.1983), the SEC requested an injunction prohibiting Lowe and his corporations from publishing investment advisory materials. The Commission argued that publication of the materials constituted working as an investment advisor without the registration required by the Investment Advisors Act. The court refused to issue the injunction sought on the grounds it would constitute an unconstitutional prior restraint.

The Second Circuit reversed on appeal. Holding Lowe's publications to be commercial speech, the Court found no First Amendment protection from the application of the Investment Advisors Act. Because Lowe had a "history of deceptive, criminal conduct as an investment advisor, his publications [could] fairly be characterized as potentially deceptive commercial speech." The history referred to consisted of prior convictions for bad checks and misappropriating funds. Securities and Exchange Commission v. Lowe, 725 F.2d 892 (2d Cir.1984).

The Supreme Court granted *certiorari* and reversed. 472 U.S. 181 (1985). After extended analysis, the five-member majority construed the "bona fide" exception in the statute broadly and concluded that it exempted Lowe. "Bona fide" covered the publication and not the publisher. Lowe's newsletters were not "personal communications masquerading in the clothing of newspapers, news magazines, or financial publications. Moreover, there is no suggestion that they contained any false or misleading information, or that they were designed to tout any security in which the petitioners had an interest. Further, petitioners' publications are 'of general and regular circulation' ":

> The dangers of fraud, deception, or overreaching that motivated the enactment of the statute are present in personalized communications but are not replicated in publications that are advertised and sold in an open market. . . . As long as the communications between petitioners and their subscribers remain entirely impersonal and do not develop into the kind of fiduciary, person-to-person relationships that were discussed at length in the legislative history of the Act and that are characteristic of investment adviser-client relationships, we believe the publications are, at least presumptively, within the exclusion and thus not subject to registration under the Act.

Justice White, joined by the Chief Justice and Justice Rehnquist, concurred on the ground that Lowe was covered by the statute but that the First Amendment protected his right to publish. The government's justification was that it was regulating a speaking profession and that it could require that investment advisers, like lawyers, evince the qualities of truth-seeking, honor, discretion and fiduciary responsibility. Justice White responded that this principle of restricting entry to a profession had never been extended to encompass the licensing of speech *per se* or of the press. [ ] At some point, a measure is no longer a regulation of a profession but a regulation of speech or of the press; beyond that point, the statute must survive the level of scrutiny demanded by the First Amendment.

Justice White rejected the government's claim that locating that point should be left to the legislature. Quoting Marbury v. Madison, Justice White responded that "It is emphatically the province and duty of the judicial department to say what the law is." He argued that, although Congressional enactments came to the Court with a presumption in favor of their validity, Congressional "characterization of its legislation cannot be decisive of the question of its constitutionality where individual rights are at issue. [   ] Surely it cannot be said, for example, that if Congress were to declare editorial writers fiduciaries for their readers and establish a licensing scheme under which 'unqualified' writers were forbidden to publish, this Court would be powerless to hold that the legislation violated the First Amendment. It is for us, then, to find some principle by which to answer the question whether the Investment Advisers Act as applied to petitioner operated as a regulation of speech or of professional conduct."

Justice White concluded that "Where the personal nexus between professional and client does not exist, and a speaker does not purport to be exercising judgment on behalf of any particular individual with whose circumstances he is directly acquainted, government regulation ceases to function as legitimate regulation of professional practice with only incidental impact on speech; it becomes regulation of speaking or publishing as such," subject to the First Amendment.

Turning finally to what regulation might be permissible here under the First Amendment, Justice White found it unnecessary to decide whether Lowe's speech was "fully protected" or "commercial." Even if the speech was considered commercial, the means chosen to prevent investors from falling into the hands of "scoundrels and swindlers" was "extreme." It cannot "be plausibly maintained that investment advice from a person whose background indicates that he is unreliable is *inherently* misleading or deceptive," nor was he convinced that less drastic remedies than outright suppression were inadequate.

In a totally different context the SEC was involved in another case with First Amendment implications. Former *Wall Street Journal* reporter R. Foster Winans was convicted under § 10b–5 of the Securities Act of 1934, which makes it "unlawful for any person to employ any device, scheme or artifice to defraud or to engage in any act, practice or course of business which operates as fraud or deceit upon any person." Winans, one of the authors of the *Journal's* "Heard on the Street" column, took advantage of his position by passing to others information about forthcoming columns that would favorably affect the prices of the stocks mentioned. The judge held that Winans was subject to the Act because he dealt with "market-sensitive material." Winans was also convicted under mail and wire fraud statutes. United States v. Winans, 612 F.Supp. 827, 11 Med.L.Rptr. 1279 (S.D.N.Y.1985).

The conviction was affirmed on appeal. The court held that § 10b–5 applies to one who gains a competitive advantage in the stock market through "secreting, stealing, purloining or otherwise misappropriating material nonpublic information in breach of an employer-imposed fiduciary duty of confidentiality." United States v. Carpenter, 791 F.2d 1024, 12 Med.L.Rptr. 2169 (2d Cir.1986).

The Supreme Court unanimously affirmed Winans' convictions under the mail and wire fraud statute. The Court held that by secretly disclosing information contained in his column prior to publication, Winans defrauded the *Journal* of its exclusive right to that information. However, the securities fraud conviction was upheld without opinion by an evenly divided Court. Carpenter v. United States, 484 U.S. 19, 14 Med.L.Rptr. 1853 (1987).

## E.   OTHER CONSIDERATIONS

### 1.   RESPONSIBILITIES AND LIABILITIES OF ADVERTISING AGENCIES AND THE MEDIA

Advertising for products distributed nationally, and for some local businesses, is handled by advertising agencies. These firms, in consultation with the companies that have hired them, plan advertising campaigns, design the ads and contract for time and space in the media in which the ads are to run. Originally it was assumed the agency was a conduit for the manufacturer of the product or supplier of the service being advertised and that the agency was not liable for any deception in the ad.

The FTC has successfully entered orders against both the advertiser and the advertising agency. An agency is liable if it knows, or has reason to know, the advertising was false. In one case, an agency argued that it should not be a party to the case because the commercials for Sucrets lozenges were approved by the manufacturer's legal and medical departments. In finding both the agency and the manufacturer responsible for the deceptive advertisements, the court said the agency, better than anyone, should have known whether the commercials were misleading, since this "is an area in which the agency had expertise." The manufacturer's liability could not relieve the agency of responsibility for commercials that the agency had created. Merck & Co., Inc. v. Federal Trade Commission, 392 F.2d 921 (6th Cir.1968).

The FTC, then, can and usually does issue a cease and desist order against an advertising agency if it knew or should have known an advertisement was misleading. Violation of the order can be punished by a fine.

The media that carry advertisements are in a different position. For two reasons media outlets are rarely cited in FTC complaints or in legal actions taken by consumers or governmental agencies. First, media are not seen as creators of advertisements. Second, there are First Amendment concerns when media are ordered not to disseminate something, even advertisements. In spite of this, television networks, large newspapers and magazines, and other media outlets generally have elaborate procedures to review advertisements for accuracy, taste, and deception. This is probably done both to protect relations with the public and to ensure that government agencies adhere to their current attitudes on this question.

However, even when advertising agencies or media outlets are found liable for deceptive advertising, advertisers usually reimburse them for any loss they suffer. This is typically stipulated in contracts between the advertiser and the agency or outlet.

## 2.  LOTTERIES

For many years broadcasting of "any advertisement of or information concerning any lottery" was prohibited by 18 U.S.C.A. § 1304. In addition, postal regulations prohibited mailing information that publicized lotteries. 39 U.S.C.A. § 3005. Because most magazines and newspapers mail at least some of their copies, they had to comply with that restriction. Under these restrictions it was irrelevant whether the beneficiary of the lottery was a commercial enterprise or non-profit.

This was changed by the Charity Games Advertising Clarification Act of 1988, which expanded the exceptions to § 1304, effective May 7, 1990. The Commission also amended its rules to conform to these changes. Broadcasters may now advertise lotteries "if they are conducted by: (a) not-for-profit organizations; (b) governmental organizations; or (c) commercial entities, provided the lottery is clearly occasional and ancillary to the primary business of the commercial organization." Broadcast of Lottery Information (Charity Games), 67 R.R.2d 996 (1990). However, state law has not been preempted, leaving states free to restrict or prohibit lottery advertising. Thus, in many states the restrictions on broadcasters have effectively remained unchanged.

A lottery is a game of chance involving three elements: 1) a prize, something of value offered as an inducement to enter the lottery, 2) chance as the method of awarding the prize, as opposed to the entrant's skill (in solving a puzzle or writing a poem) and 3) consideration, purchasing something or otherwise offering something of value as a prerequisite to participating in the lottery. Federal Communications Commission v. American Broadcasting Co., 347 U.S. 284 (1954). For example, a cereal company offering a chance to win a television set (prize) by means of a random drawing (chance) among those sending in a box top (consideration—the box of cereal was purchased) is conducting a lottery, and the media are forbidden to publicize it in any way, including disseminating advertisements for it. (This is why companies allow an index card hand-lettered with the company's name to substitute for the box top. This eliminates the consideration, making the contest no longer a lottery.)

When states began running their own lotteries, new questions arose concerning the ban on lottery information. After an early case that somewhat limited the scope of § 1304, New York State Broadcasters Association v. United States, *supra,* the issue came to a head in New Jersey. During three consecutive news broadcasts each Thursday, the day of the drawing in the state lottery, a licensee wanted to announce: "The winning state lottery number drawn today is . . .." The Commission, in a declaratory ruling concluded that such a statement would violate § 1304, even though it was presented as a news item. A main argument was that this was "news" only to those who held tickets. Experience had shown that the lottery's telephone lines were greatly overloaded on Thursdays as people called to learn the winning number. On a typical Thursday, there were 2.75 million ticket-holders. On appeal, the court, sitting *en banc,* unanimously reversed the Commission's ban on such broadcasts. New Jersey State Lottery Commission v. United States, 491 F.2d 219 (3d Cir.1974). The court concluded that the Commission had misconstrued § 1304 by interpreting it to ban "news." Although the information here was of transitory value, the court noted that on Thursdays more people in New Jersey care about this information than care about any given stock market quotation. Thus, the size of the interested group could not be the test of news. Broadcasters should be free to decide what is news and what news will serve the public unless their decision is beyond the realm of reason. The court was also influenced by the no-censorship language of the Communications Act of 1934, 47 U.S.C.A. § 326, which reinforced its view that § 1304 should be limited to advertising and information meant to make a particular lottery more attractive to participants.

The government's petition for *certiorari* was granted to resolve the apparent conflict between the decisions of the Second and Third Circuits. After argument, but before decision, Congress passed a statute providing that § 1304 shall not apply to "an advertisement, list of prizes, or information concerning a lottery conducted by a State acting under the authority of State law . . . broadcast by a radio or television station licensed to a location in that State or an adjacent State which conducts such a lottery." 18 U.S.C.A. § 1307(a)(2). On the government's motion, the Court, over a dissent by Justice Douglas, vacated the judgment of the Third Circuit and remanded for its consideration of whether the case had become moot. United States v. New Jersey State Lottery Commission, 420 U.S. 371 (1975).

On remand, the court noted that states adjacent to New Jersey (and to intervenor New Hampshire) did not have state lotteries, so that broadcasters in those states were not permitted by § 1307 to broadcast information about the New Jersey (or New Hampshire) lottery. The concern about limited dissemination of "news" still existed, and the case was not moot. The court reaffirmed its earlier decision rejecting the Commission's interpretation of § 1304. The result is reported in New Jersey State Lottery Commission v. United States, 519 F.2d 1398 (3d Cir.1975). The opinion is reported in 34 R.R.2d 825 (1975).

Could a statute constitutionally ban the type of statement the licensee wanted to make?

There were similar exceptions for newspaper advertising for state-run lotteries. When a state-run lottery existed in the state in which a newspaper was published, 39 U.S.C.A. § 3005(d), or in an adjacent state, 18 U.S.C.A. § 1307(a), Congress allowed newspapers of general circulation containing information about the lottery to be mailed.

Under the Charity Games Advertising Clarification Act of 1988, *supra,* the adjacent state restriction was eliminated for states that have state-run lotteries. Regardless of whether a state has a state-run lottery, it does not apply to lotteries run by other government organizations or by non-profit or commercial organizations.

Shortly after the Act took effect, a district court declared the adjacent state restriction unconstitutional as applied to a North Carolina radio station. The station, located near the Virginia border, sought a declaratory judgment so that it could accept advertising for the Virginia State Lottery.

The court found that the application of the restriction to the station failed the third part of the *Central Hudson* test. Because the vast majority of the station's listeners were in Virginia and those listeners in Virginia were heavily exposed to Virginia broadcast stations—for whom the lottery advertising was legal—the court found that prohibiting the radio station from broadcasting lottery advertising failed "materially to protect North Carolina residents from the harms which may result from lottery advertising." Edge Broadcasting Co. v. United States, 732 F.Supp. 633, 17 Med.L.Rptr. 1649 (E.D.Va.1990)

The court of appeals affirmed, 2–1. 956 F.2d 263, 20 Med.L.Rptr. 1904 (4th Cir.1992). The majority accepted as substantial the government's federalism justification for the ban—the interest in permitting a non-lottery state to discourage gambling. Applying the four-prong test of *Central Hudson*, p. 422, *supra,* the majority held that the government failed the third prong—the requirement that the restriction be effective and direct. On the facts of this case, the station was so near Virginia that its North Carolina listeners got most of their news and information from Virginia media—all of which were permitted to, and did, carry lottery information: "Simply put, the North Carolina residents which the statutes purport to protect already are exposed to numerous Virginia Lottery advertisements through telecast, broadcast and print media."

The dissenter thought it a mistake to hold that simply because the 2% of North Carolinians who were exposed to the station's signal receive other information about the lottery, Congress cannot minimize the volume of that information. "Congress has the undoubted right to enact the legislation which it did. The fact that the legislation does not uniformly succeed in all instances is no reason to hold it unconstitutional." He was also concerned that since radio waves cross state lines the majority's decision if "carried to its logical conclusion, as it will be, [   ], will serve to completely invalidate the statutes involved."

The Supreme Court reversed.

## UNITED STATES  v. EDGE BROADCASTING COMPANY
Supreme Court of the United States, 1993.
___ U.S. ___, 113 S.Ct. 2696, 125 L.Ed.2d 345, 73 R.R.2d 169, 21 Med.L.Rptr. 1577.

JUSTICE WHITE delivered the opinion of the Court, except as to Part III–D.*

In this case we must decide whether federal statutes that prohibit the broadcast of lottery advertising by a broadcaster licensed to a State that does not allow lotteries, while allowing such broadcasting by a broadcaster licensed to a State that sponsors a lottery, are, as applied to respondent, consistent with the First Amendment.

.   .   .

### II

The Government argues first that gambling implicates no constitutionally protected right, but rather falls within a category of activities normally considered to be "vices," and that the greater power to prohibit gambling necessarily includes the lesser power to ban its advertisement; it argues that we therefore need not proceed with a *Central Hudson* analysis.  The Court of Appeals did not address this issue and neither do we, for the statutes are not unconstitutional under the standards of *Central Hudson* applied by the courts below.

### III

.   .   .

In *Central Hudson*, we set out the general scheme for assessing government restrictions on commercial speech. [ ]  Like the courts below, we assume that Edge, if allowed to, would air non-misleading advertisements about the Virginia lottery, a legal activity.  As to the second *Central Hudson* factor, we are quite sure that the Government has a substantial interest in supporting the policy of States that permit lotteries.  As in [*Posadas*, p. 432, *supra*], the activity underlying the relevant advertising—gambling—implicates no constitutionally protected right; rather, it falls into a category of "vice" activity that could be, and frequently has been banned altogether.  As will later be discussed, we also agree that the statutes are no broader than necessary to advance the Government's interest and hence the fourth part of the *Central Hudson* test is satisfied.

The Court of Appeals, however, affirmed the District Court's holding that the statutes were invalid because, as applied to Edge, they failed to advance directly the governmental interest supporting them.  According to the Court of Appeals, whose judgment we are reviewing, this was

---

* JUSTICE O'CONNOR joins Parts I, II, III–A,     JUSTICE KENNEDY joins Parts I, II, III–C IV of
III–B, and IV of this opinion.  JUSTICE SCALIA    this opinion.  JUSTICE SOUTER joins all but
joins all but Part III–C of this opinion.          Parts III–A, III–B and III–D of this opinion.

because the 127,000 people who reside in Edge's nine county listening area in North Carolina receive most of their radio, newspaper, and television communications from Virginia-based media. These North Carolina residents who might listen to Edge "are inundated with Virginia's lottery advertisements" and hence, the court stated, prohibiting Edge from advertising Virginia's lottery "is ineffective in shielding North Carolina residents from lottery information." This "ineffective or remote measure to support North Carolina's desire to support North Carolina's desire to discourage gambling cannot justify infringement upon commercial free speech." [   ] In our judgment, the courts below erred in that respect.

## A

The third *Central Hudson* factor asks whether the "regulation directly advances the governmental interest asserted." *Central Hudson*, [   ]. It is readily apparent that this question cannot be answered by limiting the inquiry to whether the governmental interest is directly advanced as applied to a single person or entity. Even if there were no advancement as applied in that manner—in this case, as applied to Edge—there would remain the matter of the regulation's general application to others—in this case, to all other radio and television stations in North Carolina and countrywide. The courts below thus asked the wrong question in ruling on the third *Central Hudson* factor. This is not to say that the validity of the statute's application to Edge is an irrelevant inquiry, but that issue properly should be dealt with under the fourth factor of the *Central Hudson* test. . . .

We have no doubt that the statutes directly advanced the governmental interest at stake in this case. . . . Instead of favoring either the lottery or the nonlottery State, Congress opted to support the antigambling policy of a State like North Carolina by forbidding stations in such a State from airing lottery advertising. At the same time it sought not to unduly interfere with the policy of a lottery sponsoring State such as Virginia. Virginia could advertise its lottery through radio and television stations licensed to Virginia locations, even if their signals reached deep into North Carolina. Congress surely knew that stations in one State could often be heard in another but expressly prevented each and every North Carolina station, including Edge, from carrying lottery ads. Congress plainly made the commonsense judgment that each North Carolina station would have an audience in that State, even if its signal reached elsewhere and that enforcing the statutory restriction would insulate each station's listeners from lottery ads and hence advance the governmental purpose of supporting North Carolina's laws against gambling. This congressional policy of balancing the interests of lottery and nonlottery States is the substantial governmental interest that satisfies *Central Hudson*, the interest which the courts below did not fully appreciate. It is also the interest that is directly served by applying the statutory restriction to all stations in North Carolina; and this would plainly be the case even if, as applied to Edge, there were only marginal advancement of that interest.

B

Left unresolved, of course, is the validity of applying the statutory restriction to Edge, an issue that we now address under the fourth *Central Hudson* factor, *i.e.*, whether the regulation is more extensive than is necessary to serve the governmental interest.   . . .

We have no doubt that the fit in this case was a reasonable one. Although Edge was licensed to serve the Elizabeth City area, it chose to broadcast from a more northerly position, which allowed its signal to reach into the Hampton Roads, Virginia, metropolitan area.  Allowing it to carry lottery ads reaching over 90% of its listeners, all in Virginia, would surely enhance its revenues.  But just as surely, because Edge's signals with lottery ads would be heard in the nine counties in North Carolina that its broadcasts reached, this would be in derogation of the substantial federal interest in supporting North Carolina's laws making lotteries illegal.  In this posture, to prevent Virginia's lottery policy from dictating what stations in a neighboring State may air, it is reasonable to require Edge to comply with the restriction against carrying lottery advertising.  In other words, applying the restriction to a broadcaster such as Edge directly advances the governmental interest in enforcing the restriction in nonlottery States, while not interfering with the policy of lottery States like Virginia.  We think this would be the case even if it were true, which it is not, that applying the general statutory restriction to Edge, in isolation, would no more than marginally insulate the North Carolinians in the North Carolina counties served by Edge from hearing lottery ads.

In Ward v. Rock Against Racism, 491 U.S. 781 (1989), we dealt with a time, place, or manner restriction that required the city to control the sound level of musical concerts in a city park, concerts that were fully protected by the First Amendment.  We held there that the requirement of narrow tailoring was met if "the  . . .  regulation promotes a substantial government interest that would be achieved less effectively absent the regulation," provided that it did not burden substantially more speech than necessary to further the government's legitimate interests.  *Id.*, at 799.  In the course of upholding the restriction, we went on to say that "the validity of the regulation depends on the relation it bears to the overall problem the government's interest in an individual case."  *Id.*, at 801.

The *Ward* holding is applicable here for we have observed that the validity of time, place, or manner restrictions is determined under standards very similar to those applicable in the commercial speech than is applied to fully protected speech. [*Fox*, p. 435, *supra*].  *Ward* thus teaches us that we judge the validity of the restriction in this case by the relation it bears to the general problem of accommodating the policies of both lottery and nonlottery States, not by the extent to which it furthers the Government's interest in an individual case.

This is consistent with the approach we have taken in the commercial speech context.   .   .   .

.   .   .

## C

We also believe that the courts below were wrong in holding that as applied to Edge itself, the restriction at issue was ineffective and gave only remote support to the Government's interest.

As we understand it, both the Court of Appeals and the District Court recognized that Edge's potential North Carolina audience was the 127,000 residents of nine North Carolina counties, that enough of them regularly or from time to time listen to Edge to account for 11% of all radio listening in those counties, and that while listening to Edge they heard no lottery advertisements.  It could hardly be denied, and neither court below purported to deny, that these facts, standing alone, would clearly show that applying the statutory restriction to Edge would directly serve the statutory purpose of supporting North Carolina's antigambling policy by excluding invitations to gamble from 11% of the radio listening time in the nine county area.  Without more, this result could hardly be called either "ineffective," "remote," or "conditional," [  ].   .   .   .   Otherwise, any North Carolina radio station with 127,000 or fewer potential listeners would be permitted to carry lottery ads because of its marginal significance in serving the State's interest.

Of course, both courts below pointed out, and rested their judgment on the fact, the 127,000 people in North Carolina who might listen to Edge also listened to Virginia radio stations and television stations that regularly carried lottery ads.  Virginia newspapers carrying such material also were available to them.  This exposure, the courts below thought, was sufficiently pervasive to prevent the restriction on Edge from furnishing any more than ineffective or remote support for the statutory purpose.  We disagree with conclusion because in light of the facts relied on, it represents too limited a view of what amounts to direct advancement of the governmental interest that is present in this case.

Even if all the residents of Edge's North Carolina service area listen to lottery ads from Virginia stations, it would still be true that 11% of radio listening time in that area would remain free of such material.  If Edge is allowed to advertise the Virginia lottery, the percentage of listening time carrying such material would increase from 38% to 49%. We do not think that *Central Hudson* compels us to consider this sequence to be without significance.

.   .   .

Moreover, to the extent that courts below assumed that §§ 1304 and 1307 would have to effectively shield North Carolina residents from information about lotteries to advance their purpose, they were mistaken.  As the Government asserts, the statutes were not "adopt[ed]   .   .   .   to keep North Carolina residents ignorant of the Virginia Lottery for ignorance's sake," but to accommodate nonlottery

States' interest in discouraging public participation in lotteries, even as they accommodate the countervailing interests of lottery States.   [   ] Within the bounds of the general protection provided by the Constitution to commercial speech, we allow room for legislative judgments.   [   ] Here as in [*Posadas*], the Government obviously legislated on the premise that the advertising of gambling serves to increase the demand for the advertised product.   [   ]   Congress clearly was entitled to determine that broadcast of promotional advertising of lotteries undermines North Carolina's policy against gambling, even if the North Carolina audience is not wholly unaware of the lottery's existence.   Congress has, for example, altogether banned the broadcast advertising of cigarettes, even though it could hardly have believed that this regulation would keep the public wholly ignorant of cigarettes.   .   .   .

Thus, even if it were proper to conduct a *Central Hudson* analysis of the statutes only as applied to Edge, we would not agree with the courts below that the restriction at issue here, which prevents Edge from broadcasting lottery advertising to its sizable radio audience in North Carolina, is rendered ineffective by the fact that Virginia radio and television programs can be heard in North Carolina.   In our view, the restriction, even as applied only to Edge, directly advances the governmental interest within the meaning of *Central Hudson*.

### D

Nor need we be blind to the practical effect of adopting respondent's view of the level of particularity of analysis appropriate to decide its case. Assuming for the sake of argument that Edge had a valid claim that the statutes violated *Central Hudson* only as applied to it, the piecemeal approach it advocates would act to vitiate the Government's ability generally to accommodate States with differing policies.   Edge has chosen to transmit from a location near the border between two jurisdictions with different rules, and rests its case on the spillover from the jurisdiction across the border.   Were we to adopt Edge's approach, we would treat a station that is close to the line as if it were on the other side of it effectively extending the legal regime of Virginia inside North Carolina.   One result of holding for Edge on this basis might well be that additional North Carolina communities, farther from the Virginia border, would receive broadcast lottery advertising from Edge.   Broadcasters licensed to these communities, as well as other broadcasters serving Elizabeth City, would then be able to complain that lottery advertising from Edge and other similar broadcasters renders the federal statute ineffective as applied to them.   Because the approach Edge advocates has no logical stopping point once state boundaries are ignored, this process might be repeated until the policy of supporting North Carolina's ban on lotteries would be seriously eroded.   We are unwilling to start down that road.

### IV

Because the statutes challenged here regulate commercial speech in a manner that does not violate the First Amendment, the judgment of the Court of Appeals is

*Reversed.*

JUSTICE SOUTER, with whom JUSTICE KENNEDY joins, concurring in part:

I agree with the Court that the restriction at issue here is constitutional, under our decision in [*Central Hudson*], even if that restriction is judged "as applied to Edge itself." [ ] I accordingly believe it is unnecessary to decide whether the restriction might appropriately be reviewed at a more lenient level of generality, and I take no position on that question.

JUSTICE STEVENS, with whom JUSTICE BLACKMUN joins, dissenting:

Three months ago this Court reaffirmed that the proponents of a restriction on commercial speech bear the burden of demonstrating a "reasonable fit" between the legislature's goals and the means chosen to effectuate those goals. [ ] While the " 'fit' " between means and ends need not be perfect, an infringement on constitutionally protected speech must be " 'in proportion to the interest served.' " [ ] In my opinion, the Federal Government's selective ban on lottery advertising unquestionably flunks that test; for the means chosen by the Government, a ban on speech imposed for the purpose of manipulating public behavior, is in no way proportionate to the Federal Government's asserted interest in protecting the antilottery policies of nonlottery States. Accordingly, I respectfully dissent.

As the Court acknowledges, the United States does not assert a general interest in restricting state-run lotteries. Indeed, it could not, as it has affirmatively removed restrictions on use of the airwaves and mails for the promotion of such lotteries. [ ] Rather, the federal interest in this case is entirely derivative. By tying the right to broadcast advertising regarding a state-run lottery to whether the State in which the broadcaster is located itself sponsors a lottery, Congress sought to support nonlottery States in their efforts to "discourag[e] public participation in lotteries." [ ]

Even assuming that nonlottery States desire such assistance from the Federal Government—an assumption that must be made without any supporting evidence—I would hold that suppressing truthful advertising regarding a neighboring State's lottery, an activity which is, of course, perfectly legal, is a patently unconstitutional means of effectuating the Government's asserted interest in protecting the policies of nonlottery States. Indeed, I had thought that we had so held almost two decades ago.

In [*Bigelow*, p. 417, *supra*], this Court recognized that a State had a legitimate interest in protecting the welfare of its citizens as they ventured outside the State's borders. [ ] We flatly rejected the notion, however, that a State could effectuate that interest by suppressing truthful, nonmisleading information regarding a legal activity in another State. We held that a State "may not, under the guise of exercising internal police powers, bar a citizen of another State from disseminating information about an activity that is legal in that State." [ ] To be sure, the advertising in *Bigelow* related to abortion, a constitutionally protected right, and the Court in [*Posadas*], relied on that fact in dismissing the force of our holding in that case, [ ]. But even a casual reading of *Bigelow* demonstrates that the case cannot fairly be read so narrowly. The fact that the information in the advertisement related to abortion was only one factor informing the Court's determination that there were substantial First Amendment interests at stake in the State's attempt to suppress truthful advertising about a legal activity in another State:

> Viewed in its entirety, the advertisement conveyed information of potential value to a diverse audience—not only to readers possibly in need of the services offered, but also to those with a general curiosity about, or genuine interest in, the subject matter or the law of another State and its development, and to readers seeking reform in Virginia. The mere existence of the [organization advertising abortion-related services] in New York City, with the possibility of its being typical of other organizations there, and the availability of the services offered, were not unnewsworthy. Also the activity advertised pertained to constitutional interests. [ ]

*Bigelow* is not about a woman's constitutionally protected right to terminate a pregnancy. It is about paternalism, and informational protectionism. It is about one State's interference with its citizens' fundamental constitutional right to travel in a state of enlightenment, not governmental-induced ignorance. [ ] I would reaffirm this basic First Amendment principle. In seeking to assist nonlottery States in their efforts to shield their citizens from the perceived dangers emanating from a neighboring State's lottery, the Federal Government has not regulated the content of such advertisements, to ensure that they are not misleading, nor has it provided for the distribution of more speech, such as warnings or educational information about gambling. Rather, the United States has selected the most intrusive, and dangerous, form of regulation possible—a ban on truthful information regarding a lawful activity imposed for the purpose of manipulating, through ignorance, the consumer choices of some of its citizens. Unless justified by a truly substantial governmental interest, this extreme, and extremely paternalistic, measure surely cannot withstand scrutiny under the First Amendment.

No such interest is asserted in this case. With barely a whisper of analysis, the Court concludes that a State's interest in discouraging lottery participation by its citizens is surely "substantial"—a necessary prerequisite to sustain a restriction on commercial speech, [ ]—because gambling "falls into a category of 'vice' activity that could be, and frequently has been, banned altogether," [ ].

I disagree. While a State may indeed have *an interest* in discouraging its citizens from participating in state-run lotteries, it does not necessarily follow that its interest is "substantial" enough to justify an infringement on constitutionally protected speech, especially one as draconian as the regulation at issue in this case. In my view, the sea change in public attitudes toward state-run lotteries that this country has witnessed in recent years undermines any claim that a State's interest in discouraging its citizens from participating in state-run lotteries is so substantial as to outweigh respondent's First Amendment right to distribute, and the public's right to receive, truthful, nonmisleading information about a perfectly legal activity conducted in a neighboring State.

. . . The Federal Government and the States simply do not have an overriding or "substantial" interest in seeking to discourage what virtually the entire country is embracing, and certainly not an interest that can justify a restriction on constitutionally protected speech as sweeping as the one the Court today sustains.

I respectfully dissent.

**Notes and Questions:**

1. In Valley Broadcasting Co. v. United States, 820 F.Supp. 519 (D.Nev. 1993), two radio broadcasters in Nevada sought to advertise private gambling activities over the air. The FCC concluded that they were unable to do so under § 1304 (which was interpreted to cover casino gambling as a "lottery") and accompanying rules because Utah residents made up 4 percent of the audience of one station and Californians made 19 percent of the audience of the other. Because neither state permitted private casino gambling, the FCC asserted a federalism interest in protecting the efforts of these states to stay free of such advertising. In a decision rendered before the Supreme Court decided *Edge Broadcasting*, the district judge issued a declaratory judgment that the statute and accompanying regulations were unconstitutional infringements on commercial speech. The judge found that the regulation only remotely advanced the federalism interest because it was difficult to accept the idea that the broadcasts "pose any real danger to the public policies" of the two states. Moreover, the judge concluded that the remedy was not a narrowly tailored solution, citing the state-lottery exception provided in § 1307 as an accommodation that would be appropriate for casino gambling as well as traditional state lotteries.

2. The FCC announced it would not enforce the casino ad prohibition on Nevada television stations, pending an expected appeal. Broadcasting & Cable, June 7, 1993, at 117. Given the Supreme Court's decision in *Edge Broadcasting*, what result should obtain on appeal?

### 3. CHILDREN'S ADVERTISING

The law treats children differently from adults in many ways (e.g., see variable obscenity standards, in Chapter VIII). There is considerable debate whether the same set of advertising rules should apply to both groups. Although the Supreme Court has said children must be treated with care as consumers since they are "unable to protect themselves,"

FTC v. R.F. Keppel & Bro., Inc., 291 U.S. 304 (1934), controversy exists over what, if any, protection to impose on advertising.

Nearly $600 million a year is spent on television advertising to children between the ages of 2 and 12, who are, on the average, exposed to about 20,000 commercials a year. Studies have shown that although younger children are unable to differentiate between program content and commercials, older children are skeptical about advertising claims. Studies of these and other psychological effects of television advertising are still inconclusive.

Some critics are concerned about health problems caused by commercials inducing children to eat sugared cereals, candy and other products containing large amounts of processed sugar. Others wonder whether advertising helps children learn how to be careful consumers or teaches them greed and materialism. Because younger children do not usually buy the products themselves, still other critics worry about potential conflicts between children and parents.

In the late 1960s, a number of consumer groups began advocating eliminating or severely regulating advertising directed toward children, particularly on children's television programs. The most active organization was the Boston-based Action for Children's Television (ACT), which has repeatedly petitioned both the FTC and FCC to curtail television advertising to children.

The economic impact of a ban or curtailment of advertising on children's programs is in dispute. Some argue that such an order would effectively take many children's programs off the air. The counter argument asserts that the economic burden on networks and local stations would be minimal. The impact of such a move on the sales of companies currently advertising to children is a different question.

In 1970 ACT asked the FCC to prohibit advertising on children's television shows. The Commission declined to do so but did adopt guidelines on the permissible level of commercialization in children's programming and requirements that broadcasters maintain adequate separation between program content and commercial messages. Children's Television Report and Policy Statement, 50 F.C.C.2d 1, 31 R.R.2d 1228 (1974). The Commission's decision was affirmed in Action for Children's Television v. Federal Communications Commission, 564 F.2d 458, 2 Med.L.Rptr. 2120 (D.C.Cir.1977).

In 1983, as part of a general program of deregulating commercial and program content in television, which we will discuss in Chapter XV, the Commission eliminated all quantitative commercial guidelines for television. ACT challenged the action insofar as it eliminated the guidelines for children's television contained in the *1974 Report.* ACT argued that the Commission had failed to articulate a reasoned basis for the elimination of those guidelines. The court of appeals agreed and remanded the case to the Commission with instructions to elaborate on that issue. Action for Children's Television v. Federal Communications Commission, 821 F.2d 741, 63 R.R.2d 440 (1987).

In 1983 ACT and the National Association for Better Broadcasting (NABB) filed complaints against various licensees alleging violations of the Commission's policy against "program length commercials." These complaints focused on a new marketing strategy for children's television, basing shows on toys that were already in the market. Among the shows at issue were "He–Man and the Masters of the Universe," "G.I. Joe: A Real American Hero," "Dungeons and Dragons," "Rubik the Amazing Cube," "The Shirt Tales," "Strawberry Shortcake and Care Bears Family TV Fun Festival" and "Pac–Man."

According to ACT and NABB, these shows were created for the sole purpose of selling the toys that were featured in the show. As further evidence of this allegation, ACT cited an arrangement offered by Telepictures Corporation whereby broadcasters could receive a share of the profits derived from the sale of "Thunder Cats" toys in return for carrying the "Thunder Cats" cartoon show.

The Commission rejected the complaints. "[O]nly when the program segment is 'so interwoven with, and in essence auxiliary to the sponsor's advertising . . . to the point that the entire program constitutes a single, commercial promotion for the sponsor's products or services' " will an entire program be considered a commercial. Given that the toys featured in the shows were not being advertised during those shows, the Commission did not find an interweaving of commercials and program content sufficient to constitute a program length commercial.

> The fact that programming may serve commercial goals, however, in and of itself, is not controlling. If the existence of commercial rewards from associated products were the criteria for imposing restrictions upon children's programming, then no program-related product licensing would be possible and even popular educational programs such as "Sesame Street" and critically acclaimed commercial television programs like those in the "Peanuts" series would have to be eliminated from broadcast station schedules. We see no sensible or administratively practical method of making distinctions among programs based on the subjective intentions of the program producers or on the product licensing/program production sequence. Considering that ACT's, NABB's, and the Commission's primary intention is to prevent harm to children, we must consider what, if any, possible harm might result from product-based programming. There is, however, no evidence before us to demonstrate that exposure to programming based on products harms the child audience. Action for Children's Television, 58 R.R.2d 61 (F.C.C.1985).

NABB appealed the Commission's decision as it applied to NABB's complaint against KCOP–TV in Los Angeles. NABB argued that because "He–Man and the Masters of the Universe" was provided to the station on a barter basis whereby the station furnished only two minutes of non-prime time for each show, the show was being obtained for a "token payment." According to NABB this meant that under § 317 of the Communications Act the station had to identify the show's distributors as sponsors of the program. The Commission had rejected NABB's argument by ruling that § 317 applies only when a broadcast is "so interwoven with, and in essence auxiliary to the sponsor's advertising . . . to the point that the entire program constitutes a single commercial promotion for the sponsor's products or services." The court of appeals overruled the Commission, holding that § 317 is not limited to purely commercial broadcasts. National Association for Better Broadcasting v. Federal Communications Commission, 830 F.2d 270, 63 R.R.2d 1501 (D.C.Cir.1987).

In a separate proceeding the Commission rejected ACT's petition for rulemaking pertaining to profit-sharing arrangements in the broadcasting of children's programming. ACT asserted that profit-sharing arrangements such as that offered by Telepictures for "Thunder Cats" would induce licensees to select programs for financial as opposed to public interest reasons. The Commission concluded that such a danger was extremely speculative and did not warrant a Notice of Inquiry or Notice of Proposed Rulemaking, but stressed that licensees should not allow profit sharing or product tie-ins to detract from the " 'bedrock obligation of every broadcaster to be responsive to the needs of children in that community.' " Commissioner Rivera dissented, believing that profit sharing and product tie-ins raised enough questions to justify further study. Children's Programming (Profit–Sharing Arrangements), 58 R.R.2d 90 (F.C.C.1985).

In response to these various petitions and remands, the FCC issued a combined Notice of Inquiry and Notice of Proposed Rulemaking (NOI/NPRM), Revision of Programming and Commercialization Policies, Ascertainment Requirements, and Program Log Requirements for Commercial Television Stations, 2 F.C.C.Rcd. 7463 (1987). In the NOI/NPRM the Commission asked for comments pertaining to commercialization guidelines for children's shows as well as definitions of what constitutes commercial matter. It also asked for comments on the new toys designed to interact with specific children's shows.

Although this specific NOI/NPRM did not request comments on the sponsorship identification questions raised by barter deals for children's shows, the Commission indicated in a footnote that as a result of the remand in *NABB*, it would address those issues in the near future. Subsequently, the FCC asked parties to the case to file comments.

The FTC has taken action on a case-by-case basis when it found children's advertising deceptive, ruling, for instance, that advertisers must consider the "knowledge, sophistication, maturity and experience of" young people. In the Matter of Mattel, Inc., 79 F.T.C. 667 (1971). The Commission has shown concern about commercials that make the taking of vitamins seem like eating candy, Hudson Pharmaceutical Corp., 89 F.T.C. 82 (1977), and ads showing a small child helping to make rice on a stove. Uncle Ben's, Inc., 89 F.T.C. 131 (1977).

In 1990 Congress passed the Children's Television Act of 1990. Among the provisions of the Act was a requirement that children's television programming contain no more than 10.5 minutes of advertising per hour on weekends and 12 minutes per hour on weekdays. We will return to the Children's Television Act in Chapter XVII.

The Act required the FCC to complete a proceeding implementing these requirements within 6 months. The three primary issues addressed by the proceeding were the standards to be used in setting commercial limits for children's programming, and the definition of program-length commercials and the guidelines for evaluating at renewal time broadcasters' service to children, (discussed at p. 846, *infra*).

## IN THE MATTER OF POLICIES AND RULES CONCERNING CHILDREN'S TELEVISION PROGRAMMING

## REVISION OF PROGRAMMING AND COMMERCIALIZATION POLICIES, ASCERTAINMENT REQUIREMENTS, AND PROGRAM LOG REQUIREMENTS FOR COMMERCIAL TELEVISION STATIONS

Federal Communications Commission, 1991.
68 R.R.2d 1615, ___ F.C.C.Rcd. ___.

[For the purposes of implementing the commercial limits set forth in § 102(b) of the Act, the Commission defined children's programming as "programs originally produced and broadcast primarily for an audience of children 12 years old and under." Commercial matter was defined as "air time sold for the purposes of selling a product," but the FCC added a number of clarifications:]

5. By requiring that air time be "sold," we mean that the advertiser must give some valuable consideration either directly or indirectly to the broadcaster or cablecaster as an inducement for airing the material. Without such a qualification, it would be difficult to distinguish mention of logos or brand name a writer or producer used to advance creative objectives. We also clarify that although our proposed definition only referred to air time sold "for purposes of selling a product," commercial matter also encompasses advertising for services.

6. We also find that the scope of Section 317 of the Communications Act, 47 USC § 317, which governs when the sponsors of broadcast material must be identified, is not coterminous with the scope of commercial matter. In particular we hold that material is not necessarily "commercial matter" for purposes of the Children's Television Act simply because Section 317 requires a sponsorship identification. . . . For example, nonprofit organizations purchasing air time for a public service message must identify themselves as sponsors under Section 317, even though such a message is not commercial material.

7. We accordingly find that the bare sponsorship identification announcement required under Section 317 and our implementing rules, where such material is not otherwise commercial in nature, will not be

deemed commercial matter under our definition here.  Thus, public service messages sponsored by nonprofit organizations that promote not-for-profit activities will not be considered commercial matter for purposes of applying the commercial limits.  Similarly, air time sold for purposes of presenting educational and informational material, including "spot" announcements, which the only sponsorship mention a "sponsored by," is not commercial matter.  The addition of product mentions or advertising to such an identification announcement, however, would constitute commercial matter.  Moreover, where a station or cable operator promotes one of its upcoming programs and mentions that program's sponsor, even though not required to do so under Section 317, the mention of the sponsor will constitute commercial matter for purposes of determining whether the commercial limits have been exceeded. In such a case, the mention of the sponsor is not required under the Rule and is thus clearly intended to promote the sponsor.  Thus, if such a station or cable operator's promo (1) mentions that the upcoming program is "brought to you by" a sponsor, or (2) promotes a product or service related to the program or program sponsor, or (3) mentions a prize furnished by the program sponsor, the mention of the sponsor or the sponsor's product or services, not being required under our sponsorship identification rules, will be considered commercial matter.  Promotions of upcoming programs which do not contain such sponsor-related mentions will not be deemed commercial matter.

[The Commission decided to count commercial minutes by the hour as opposed to by the program.  Where a half-hour of children's programming is both preceded and followed by adult programming, the FCC will apply the limits on a proportionate basis.  The limits will not be applied to children's programming segments less than a half hour in length.

Commercial limits will also apply to cable operators with regard to local origination channels and cable network programs.  They will not, however, apply to retransmissions of broadcast channels or access channels.  (These distinctions are discussed in more detail in Chapter XVIII).]

. . .

## V.  Program-Length Children's Commercials

*A.  Definition*

40.  We find that the definition of program-length children's commercial proposed in the *Notice*—a program associated with a product in which commercials for that product aired—strikes the best balance between the important interests involved.  This definition protects children from the confusion and deception the intermixture of related program and commercial material may inflict upon them, and still preserves the creative freedom and practical revenue sources that make children's programming possible.  For the reasons given below, we adopt this definition.

41.  ACT maintains . . . that the Commission should establish a rebuttable presumption that if there is less than a two-year time span between the introduction of a television program and a related product

or *vice versa*, this is *prima facie* evidence that the show is a program-length commercial. We do not find that this is a viable definition. We agree with numerous commenters that it would jeopardize highly acclaimed children's shows such as Sesame Street and Disney programs that have products associated with them. As CTW, the producer of Sesame Street, states, a program's relationship to products is not necessarily indicative of commercial content. According to CTW, ACT's proposal would inhibit the simultaneous introduction of any new CTW program series and associated products, such as books, magazines, games and computer software whose purpose is to extend the educational benefits of the series. We fear that such a definition would stifle creativity by restricting the sources that writers could draw upon for characters, would limit revenues from merchandising which are an important source of production funding, and would ignore the educational role toys or other related products can play in child development.

. . .

44. The definition of children's program-length commercial that we are now adopting—a program associated with a product, in which commercials for that product are aired—is clear, easy to understand and apply, and narrowly tailored. It directly addresses a fundamental regulatory concern, that children who have difficulty enough distinguishing program content from unrelated commercial matter, not be all the more confused by a show that interweaves program content and commercial matter. Removal of related commercial matter should help alleviate this confusion. Our definition also would cover programs in which a product or service is advertised within the body of the program and not separated from program content as children's commercials are required to be. Contrary to ACT's view, we find that our definition clarifies the manner in which our traditional definition of program-length commercial applies to children's programs. We have previously so held. Given the First Amendment context of this issue, our approach is a restrained one. Should abuses occur, however, we will not hesitate to revisit this issue. We also note that our definition harmonizes with, and codifies to some degree, existing policies with respect to host-selling and adequate separation of commercial from program material in children's programs.[147]

45. In addition, a program will be considered a program-length commercial if a product associated with the program appears in commercial spots not separated from the start or close of the program by at least 60 seconds of unrelated material. It is reasonably likely that a young viewer will tune in immediately before or stay tuned immediately after a program, and that in such circumstances an adjacent spot would have the same effect as if the spot were included in the program itself. We do not find record evidence justifying extending this Rule beyond 60 seconds, or further expanding our host-selling policy, as ACT requests. In

---

**147.** (*e.g.*, "And now its time for a commercial break." "And now back to the [title of the program]"). Action for Children's Television, 50 FCC2d at 14–16. . . .

light of the short attention spans of children, particularly younger children most likely to confuse program and commercial material, we believe that a 60–second separation is adequate.

. . .

**Notes and Questions**

1. In an omitted portion of *Children's Television Programming*, the FCC denied ACT's petition regarding interactive children's programs on the ground that there was no evidence that any interactive toys were currently for sale.

2. In 1993 the FCC fined three television stations $15,000 each for exceeding the commercial limit for children's programming. The stations had admitted the violations in their renewal applications. (Failure to do so is grounds for nonrenewal.) The FCC did, however, renew each station's license. Broadcasting & Cable, July 26, 1993 at 10.

3. On the question of serving the educational needs of children, Congress and the FCC have become concerned that broadcasters are seeking to meet the renewal review by listing programs as educational that do not "belong" in that category. In committee hearings, House Telecommunications Subcommittee Chairman Edward Markey (D–Mass.) relied on a private group's report showing that some stations were listing programs such as "The Jetsons," "The Flintstones" and "Yo Yogi!" as programs designed to meet children's educational needs. As to "Yo Yogi!," for example, a station reported "Snag learns that he can capture the bank-robber cockroach more successfully by using his head, rather than his muscles." For "Bucky O'Hare": "Good-doer Bucky fights off the evil toads from aboard his ship. Issues of social consciousness and responsibility are central themes of the program." Broadcasting, Oct. 5, 1992 at 40.

Subcommittee member Ron Wyden (D–Ore.) said that he was planning a bill to require stations to provide one hour of educational programming each week for pre-school children. An NAB witness responded that such a bill would be unconstitutional because it would tell stations what to air and when. There is also the issue of whether the word "educational" is impermissibly vague. Broadcasting & Cable, Mar. 15, 1993 at 49.

An editorial in that magazine notes that it had fears in 1990 about signing on to the act in the first place. What is happening in 1993 "is just the sort of 'government as schoolmaster' scenario we feared." It was also concerned about Chairman Markey's statement that "Broadcasters *can* and *will* do better than that." *Id.* at 82.

At about the same time, the FCC began taking steps to strengthen the rules by issuing a notice of inquiry (NOI) raising doubts about whether to allow 30–second and 60–second programs to count as educational and by seeking comments on whether broadcasters could count existing shows that were intended primarily as entertainment. Policies and Rules Concerning Children's Television Programming, 58 Fed.Reg. 14367, R.R.2d Curr.Serv. 53:77 (1993).

For an extensive discussion of the current state of children's television, see Broadcasting & Cable, July 26, 1993 at 37–80.

All proposals to limit advertising to children must also consider the impact of Supreme Court decisions extending First Amendment protection to commercial speech. The extent to which honest advertising can be regulated, even when directed to children, remains an open question.

# Chapter X

# PRESS COVERAGE OF THE ADMINISTRATION
# OF JUSTICE

Press coverage of the administration of justice poses special problems for the press and for the courts. It is easy to generalize about the openness of the judicial system and about Americans' distaste for secret courts, and it is easy to generalize about our proud tradition of protecting the fairness of civil and criminal trials. The generalizations too often ignore the reality: the First Amendment right to freedom of the press and the Sixth Amendment right to a fair trial sometimes appear to give rise to conflict.

Part of what we explore in this chapter relates to government-sought constraints on the press—issues we confronted in Chapters III through IX. Additional material in this chapter relates to the legal rights and responsibilities of the press as it seeks to gather news prior to publication—issues we shall confront again in other contexts in Chapters XI and XII. The special treatment in this chapter is appropriate because the problems are unique to the judicial branch of government and may involve the question of contempt of court, rather than criminal or tort liability.

That there is conflict between the press and the courts is hardly surprising. Professionals in the law and professionals in journalism are both trained to seek the truth, but they do so in quite different ways. Judges and lawyers are accustomed to seeking the truth in a courtroom where hearsay and illegally-obtained evidence have no place; speed in arriving at the truth takes second place to faith that the process will lead eventually to the truth. For journalists, on the other hand, speed is of major importance, and even hearsay and illegally-obtained evidence may be deemed newsworthy.

As journalists tell the story of a crime or arrest prior to trial, they inevitably influence opinions in the area, and it can be difficult—perhaps even impossible—to find jurors who can ignore press reports and come to a fair verdict based on evidence presented in court. On the other hand, if judges try to shape or stop the news coverage of the administration of justice, they may be interfering with the First Amendment rights of the journalists.

As long as people have talked about the problems created by pre-trial and trial news coverage, they have suggested remedies. In this chapter we will examine those remedies, and we will see that they have limited effectiveness and a variety of disadvantages. Some of the so-called remedies have to do with keeping prejudicial information from reaching the public.  They include (1) cautioning police, prosecutors and others involved with the case about the impropriety of making comments to the press, (2) shielding witnesses from the press, (3) cautioning journalists about the dangers of prejudicial news accounts and (4) encouraging the adoption of voluntary bench-bar-press guidelines.  Other so-called remedies have to do with finding unbiased jurors despite the fact that news accounts may already have revealed prejudicial information.  Among those are (5) granting a change of venue, (6) granting a change of venire, (7) relying on the effectiveness of the *voir dire,* the examination of potential jurors or (8) granting a continuance or delay.  Additional remedies have to do with keeping jurors unbiased after their selection:  (9) cautioning jurors who are allowed to leave the courtroom at the end of the day that they should not read or listen to press reports or other comment about the case or a more effective but more costly alternative, (10) sequestering the jury.  Theoretically, other more dramatic remedies might be used, but some of these are constitutionally suspect:  (11) closing the courtroom to the press and public during pretrial hearings, (12) closing the courtroom during trials, (13) imposing conditions on those allowed to enter the courtroom and (14) ordering the press not to publish certain information.  Traditionally, a way of protecting the defendant's rights has been to (15) maintain the decorum of the courtroom, and frequently judges have sought to do that by (16) keeping cameras out of the courtroom.  Serving to protect the defendant's right is the court's authority to punish those who interfere with the administration of justice by citing them for contempt of court.

## A. BACKGROUND

The judicial branch has been the object of considerable litigation as to which of its functions are to be open to public scrutiny.  A specific constitutional provision, held to be solely for the benefit of the accused and not addressed to the press, is basic to our discussion.  The Sixth Amendment to the United States Constitution provides:  "In all criminal prosecutions, the accused shall enjoy the right to a speedy and public trial, by an impartial jury of the State and district wherein the crime shall have been committed."  No directive in the Constitution affects the conduct of legislative or executive proceedings even to this extent.

The Sixth Amendment also provides for the accused to "be informed of the nature and cause of the accusation;  to be confronted with the witnesses against him;  to have compulsory process for obtaining Witnesses in his favor."  The latter poses problems for journalists who wish not to testify about secret sources, notes, documents, etc.  See, for example, Matter of Farber, 78 N.J. 259, 394 A.2d 330, 4 Med.L.Rptr. 1360 (1978), along with other cases we will discuss in Chapter XI.

The emphasis in most of this chapter will be on criminal proceedings.  The interest of the press in the judicial process, at least at the trial level, has been devoted almost exclusively to dramatic criminal cases involving either sensational crimes or prominent persons.  The press has fought hard against exclusion from these cases.  Some defendants in criminal cases have therefore sought to bar the press, and necessarily also the public, from various pretrial and trial phases of their cases lest publicity prejudice the judges or, far more likely, the juries that will ultimately hear the cases.  Thus, the role of the jury in criminal cases and the strong press (and presumably public) interest in particular criminal cases combine to create a potential conflict in criminal cases between defendants and the press.  This conflict has been called "fair trial-free press" by the bar and "free press-fair trial" by the press. Many commentators suggest that the problem is monolithic: a broad confrontation between two important segments of society.  This book regards the conflict as having several separable aspects and analyzes each one as it arises.

The major, but not the only, argument of the press is framed in terms of the public's "right to know" about the functioning of the judiciary.  In addition, the press argues that its presence may sometimes directly help the defendant.  As well as serving a "watchdog" function just by being present, deterring potential judicial or prosecutorial excesses, a reporter sometimes learns enough about a case to be moved to investigate the charges and eventually find evidence that exonerates the defendant.

Prejudicial publicity may arise in two contexts.  One involves efforts to influence judicial behavior by writing articles or editorials about pending cases.  This problem is discussed later in this chapter.  The second context centers on the institution of the jury.  In the early days jurors were likely to know of the events in question, but for several centuries, the courts have insisted that jurors be impartial.  This has not meant that they must be totally ignorant of the events in their community, but, rather, that they be willing and able to reach a verdict solely on the basis of the evidence presented at the trial.  Of course jurors' biases might come from many sources other than publicity, such as the defendant's race, religion, occupation, accent, way of walking or dressing or political affiliation.  It is sometimes difficult to determine whether a juror will be impartial.  The conventional approach has been to ask jurors questions during the preliminary screening, known as *voir dire,* that would enable the judge and the lawyers to detect bias.  Jurors who convincingly deny bias and assert an ability to be "impartial" will be seated unless extrinsic evidence indicates that they are dishonest or not psychologically able to disregard some ground for bias.  If jurors turn out to be unable or unwilling to serve impartially after being selected, the defendant can seek a new trial.

In order to understand some of the problems raised in this area, it is necessary to know that certain types of evidence must be excluded from criminal trials.  The rule of exclusion means that the information is not to be considered in determining the guilt or innocence of the defendant.

Three exclusions are most likely to cause possible problems of prejudicial publicity.  One is the rule that an accused's prior record of convictions is not generally admissible in evidence unless the defendant chooses to testify. The fear is that if jurors learn that a defendant has a prior record they may be tempted to convict even though the prosecution may have failed to establish guilt beyond a reasonable doubt in this particular situation.

The second is that confessions made by the defendant before the trial are not admissible in evidence at the trial unless they have been voluntarily made and the accused has been properly advised of his rights (the so-called "Miranda warning"). Even if other evidence shows the confession accurate, to accept a coerced confession would encourage law enforcement agencies to abuse their authority.

The third major variety of inadmissible evidence involves items seized in an unlawful search. In these cases, the evidence is almost always trustworthy—and often devastating. Nonetheless, it is excluded if the search was illegal. Again, the point is to discourage the state from engaging in offensive behavior.

In all three situations, because the evidence is inadmissible in the courtroom, the courts hope to keep jurors from gaining access to such information by other means.

Gossip, including comments about the accused by people who have no first-hand evidence of the facts, presents another problem. Hearsay evidence is not admissible in court, with certain exceptions, and it can bias potential jurors if it is disseminated by the media.

The legal community long has questioned whether a defendant can receive a fair trial in the face of pervasive publicity about the crime. Early in our history, in ruling on the trial of Aaron Burr, Chief Justice John Marshall set an early standard for juror impartiality. Marshall said a juror was impartial if free from the dominant influence of what was heard or read outside the courtroom. If jurors were able to base a decision on the testimony offered, the trial was not tainted by prejudice. United States v. Burr, 25 Fed.Cas. 49 No. 14692G (1807).

Every decade has its own sensational cases and infamous defendants. With them come revived concerns over prejudicial pretrial and trial news accounts.

The Supreme Court's first confrontations with the fair trial-free press problem in constitutional dimension were in the early 1960s. In Irvin v. Dowd, 366 U.S. 717, 1 Med.L.Rptr. 1178 (1961), the court vacated the conviction of serial-killer Leslie Irvin and remanded his case. Irvin had been widely identified as the "Mad Dog Killer" of six people in Indiana, and his confession had been widely publicized. Of 430 people examined for jury duty, the court itself excused 268 as having fixed opinions as to Irvin's guilt, and more than 90 percent of those asked had admitted to some opinion as to guilt. The Supreme Court held that a "pattern of deep and bitter prejudice" had unfairly violated Irvin's Sixth Amendment right to a fair trial. He was retried and convicted a second time.

Another troubling case occurred when Wilbert Rideau was arrested in Louisiana for bank robbery, kidnapping and murder. The sheriff invited a film crew from the local television station to film the sheriff's "interview" with Rideau. During the 20–minute interrogation, Rideau confessed to the crimes. The station showed the interview three times. After a requested change of venue was denied, Rideau was convicted and sentenced to death. The Supreme Court overturned the conviction, noting that after drawing a jury from people who could have been exposed to the confession, any "court proceedings . . . could be but a hollow formality." The Court implied that nothing could have overcome the effects of the television film and that specific proof of juror prejudice was not necessary under such circumstances. Rideau v. Louisiana, 373 U.S. 723, 1 Med.L.Rptr. 1183 (1963). Like Irvin, Rideau was convicted a second time.

Neither the Irvin case nor the Rideau case achieved quite the notoriety of the Dr. Sam Sheppard case.

SHEPPARD v. MAXWELL

Supreme Court of the United States, 1966.

384 U.S. 333, 86 S.Ct. 1507, 16 L.Ed.2d 600, 1 Med.L.Rptr. 1220.

MR. JUSTICE CLARK delivered the opinion of the Court.

[In 1954 Sheppard was charged with murdering his wife. The case attracted great public attention and extensive media coverage beginning shortly after the murder, before any arrest had been made. The publicity continued through the pretrial and trial period. Sheppard was convicted of second-degree murder. After serving several years in prison he sought *habeas corpus* in the federal courts, claiming that the state had denied him his constitutional rights during the prosecution. The district court agreed and granted the writ, but the court of appeals reversed. The Supreme Court in turn reversed, and ordered Sheppard released unless the state gave him a new trial. The Court's lengthy opinion traced the facts in great detail and placed responsibility on the trial judge for failing to give Sheppard a fair trial:

> The fact is that bedlam reigned at the courthouse during the trial and newsmen took over practically the entire courtroom, hounding most of the participants in the trial, especially Sheppard. . . .
> Having assigned almost all of the available seats in the courtroom to the news media the judge lost his ability to supervise the environment. The movement of the reporters in and out of the courtroom caused frequent confusion and disruption of the trial.

Beyond this concern with the judge's lack of control over the courtroom the Court was troubled by publicity during the trial.]

. . .

VI.

Much of the material printed or broadcast during the trial was never heard from the witness stand, such as the charges that Sheppard had purposely impeded the murder investigation and must be guilty since he had hired a prominent criminal lawyer; that Sheppard was a perjurer; that he had sexual relations with numerous women; that his slain wife had characterized him as a "Jekyll–Hyde"; that he was "a bare-faced liar" because of his testimony as to police treatment; and, finally, that a woman convict claimed Sheppard to be the father of her illegitimate child. As the trial progressed, the newspapers summarized and interpreted the evidence, devoting particular attention to the material that incriminated Sheppard, and often drew unwarranted inferences from testimony. At one point, a front-page picture of Mrs. Sheppard's bloodstained pillow was published after being "doctored" to show more clearly an alleged imprint of a surgical instrument.

Nor is there doubt that this deluge of publicity reached at least some of the jury. On the only occasion that the jury was queried, two jurors admitted in open court to hearing the highly inflammatory charge that a prison inmate claimed Sheppard as the father of her illegitimate child. Despite the extent and nature of the publicity to which the jury was exposed during trial, the judge refused defense counsel's other requests that the jurors be asked whether they had read or heard specific prejudicial comment about the case, including the incidents we have previously summarized. In these circumstances, we can assume that some of this material reached members of the jury. [  ]

## VII.

The court's fundamental error is compounded by the holding that it lacked power to control the publicity about the trial. From the very inception of the proceedings the judge announced that neither he nor anyone else could restrict prejudicial news accounts. And he reiterated this view on numerous occasions. Since he viewed the news media as his target, the judge never considered other means that are often utilized to reduce the appearance of prejudicial material and to protect the jury from outside influence. We conclude that these procedures would have been sufficient to guarantee Sheppard a fair trial and so do not consider what sanctions might be available against a recalcitrant press nor the charges of bias now made against the state trial judge.

The carnival atmosphere at trial could easily have been avoided since the courtroom and courthouse premises are subject to the control of the court. . . .

[The Court asserted that the trial judge should have "made some effort to control the release of leads, information, and gossip to the press by police officers, witnesses, and counsel for both sides."]

The fact that many of the prejudicial news items can be traced to the prosecution, as well as the defense, aggravates the judge's failure to take any action. [  ] Effective control of these sources—concededly within the court's power—might well have prevented the divulgence of inaccurate information, rumors, and accusations that made up much of the inflammatory publicity, at least after Sheppard's indictment.

More specifically, the trial court might well have proscribed extrajudicial statements by any lawyer, party, witness, or court official which divulged prejudicial matters, such as the refusal of Sheppard to submit to interrogation or take any lie detector tests; any statement made by Sheppard to officials; the identity of prospective witnesses or their probable testimony; any belief in guilt or innocence; or like statements concerning the merits of the case.   . . .   Being advised of the great public interest in the case, the mass coverage of the press, and the potential prejudicial impact of publicity, the court could also have requested the appropriate city and county officials to promulgate a regulation with respect to dissemination of information about the case by their employees.   . . .   Had the judge, the other officers of the court, and the police placed the interest of justice first, the news media would have soon learned to be content with the task of reporting the case as it unfolded in the courtroom—not pieced together from extrajudicial statements.

From the cases coming here we note that unfair and prejudicial news comment on pending trials has become increasingly prevalent. Due process requires that the accused receive a trial by an impartial jury free from outside influences.   Given the pervasiveness of modern communications and the difficulty of effacing prejudicial publicity from the minds of the jurors, the trial courts must take strong measures to ensure that the balance is never weighed against the accused.   And appellate tribunals have the duty to make an independent evaluation of the circumstances.   Of course, there is nothing that proscribes the press from reporting the events that transpire in the courtroom.   But where there is a reasonable likelihood that prejudicial news prior to trial will prevent a fair trial, the judge should continue the case until the threat abates, or transfer it to another county not so permeated with publicity. In addition, sequestration of the jury was something the judge should have raised *sua sponte* with counsel.   If publicity during the proceedings threatens the fairness of the trial, a new trial should be ordered.   But we must remember that reversals are but palliatives; the cure lies in those remedial measures that will prevent the prejudice at its inception.   The courts must take such steps by rule and regulation that will protect their processes from prejudicial outside interferences.   Neither prosecutors, counsel for defense, the accused, witnesses, court staff nor enforcement officers coming under the jurisdiction of the court should be permitted to frustrate its function.   Collaboration between counsel and the press as to information affecting the fairness of a criminal trial is not only subject to regulation, but is highly censurable and worthy of disciplinary measures.

Since the state trial judge did not fulfill his duty to protect Sheppard from the inherently prejudicial publicity which saturated the community and to control disruptive influences in the courtroom, we must reverse the denial of the habeas petition.   The case is remanded to the District Court with instructions to issue the writ and order that Sheppard be released from custody unless the State puts him to its charges again within a reasonable time.

It is so ordered.

Mr. Justice Black dissents [without opinion].

## Notes and Questions

1.   On Sheppard's retrial he was acquitted and released—after having spent 10 years in prison.   Does this necessarily mean he was innocent?

2.   Note that because the Court thinks that action by the trial judge would have met the problem, it has no need to discuss "what sanctions might be available against a recalcitrant press."

3.   Note also that the Court recognizes that nothing "proscribes the press from reporting the events that transpire in the courtroom."   This is the lesson from Craig v. Harney, discussed later in this chapter.

4.   In contrast to *Irvin* (where so many potential jurors had to be examined) and *Sheppard* (where there was other evidence of prejudice), the court found a Florida trial to have been sufficiently fair.   In Murphy v. Florida, 421 U.S. 794, 1 Med.L.Rptr. 1232 (1975), the jurors in defendant's robbery trial had learned through news stories about some or all of the defendant's earlier convictions for murder, securities theft and the 1964 theft of the Star of India sapphire from a New York museum.   The majority stated that qualified jurors need not be totally ignorant of the facts surrounding the case.   The Court found in the *voir dire* no showing of hostility to the defendant.   Four of the six jurors had volunteered that defendant's past was irrelevant.   Moreover, the defendant's attorney during *voir dire* informed several of the jurors of crimes they had not known about, leading the Court to observe "We will not readily discount the assurances of a juror insofar as his exposure to a defendant's past crimes comes from the defendant or counsel."   The indicia of impartiality "might be disregarded in a case where the general atmosphere in the community or courtroom is sufficiently inflammatory, but the circumstances surrounding petitioner's trial are not at all of that variety."   Only 20 of the 78 persons examined were excused because of an opinion of guilt.   "This may indeed be 20 more than would occur in the trial of a totally obscure person, but it by no means suggests a community with sentiment so poisoned against petitioner as to impeach the indifference of jurors who displayed no hostile animus of their own."   Only Justice Brennan dissented.

## B.   SO–CALLED REMEDIES FOR THE FAIR TRIAL–FREE PRESS PROBLEM

### 1.   The Standard Remedies

Although the judge's failure to maintain proper decorum during the trial was viewed as his major error in *Sheppard,* the Court devoted extensive consideration to the behavior of the media and suggested techniques by which the judge might have better insulated the trial. Some of those suggestions were among those listed as so-called remedies earlier in this chapter which can now be examined more thoroughly.

### a.  Cautioning, Police, Prosecutors, etc.

Cutting off information at its source is an obvious way of trying to curtail its dissemination by the news media, and police and prosecutors sometimes are the sources of news stories about confessions and probable guilt, but gags on police and attorneys may be challenged by those gagged on the ground that they interfere with the First Amendment rights of the police and attorneys to express themselves.  Furthermore, to the extent that the process of newsgathering may be protected by the First Amendment (see discussion of Richmond Newspapers v. Virginia later in this chapter), such restrictive orders may be seen as interference with that right.

### b.  Shielding Witnesses

Shielding witnesses from the press similarly may interfere with the witnesses' own First Amendment rights and may interfere with a press right to gather news.  On the other hand, of course, witnesses are under no obligation to answer questions from journalists.

### c.  Cautioning Journalists

If the court cautions journalists *prior* to publication of prejudicial information, the warning can seem to imply the threat of punishment by the contempt powers and may smack of an unconstitutional form of prior restraint on the press (see Chapter II).  If the warning is made *after* some prejudicial information has already been published, the warning is likely to be ineffective because the damage has already been done.

### d.  Encouraging the Use of Guidelines

When the Supreme Court in *Sheppard* suggested techniques for insulating trials, it also cited the *Report of the President's Commission on the Assassination of President John F. Kennedy,* in which the Commission, chaired by Chief Justice Earl Warren, expressed grave concern about whether Lee Harvey Oswald could possibly have gotten a fair trial after all the publicity that followed the assassination.  The discussion in *Sheppard* plus the observation that "reversals are still but palliatives" led the bar to begin investigating new courses of action in greater detail. The first such effort was made by the American Bar Association, which created a committee that became known as the Reardon Committee after its chairman, the late Justice Paul Reardon of Massachusetts.

Although the American Bar Association is a private organization without lawmaking powers, state courts or legislatures may be persuaded to follow its recommendations.  The report of the Reardon Committee met with mixed success but provided the basis for guidelines adopted by some state organizations.  The ABA itself has revised its fair trial-free press standards a couple of times since they were proposed by the

Reardon Committee. The most recent changes were adopted in February 1991. ABA Standards for Criminal Justice, Chapter Eight: Fair Trial–Free Press, Third Edition, 1991.

Under the ABA guidelines, lawyers should not make extrajudicial statements that will have a substantial likelihood of prejudicing a criminal proceeding, and they are specifically cautioned that there is a substantial likelihood of prejudice from release of a prior criminal record, information about the existence of a confession or admission, the performance of tests (like lie detector tests) or expected testimony. (Standard 8–1.1.)

Another section says the same standards should be applicable to the release of information to the public by law enforcement officers and agencies. (Standard 8–2.1.)

The most important of the 1991 amendments adds a new prohibition against direct restraints on the media: "Absent a clear and present danger to the fairness of a trial or other compelling interest, no rule of court or judicial order should be promulgated that prohibits representatives of the news media from broadcasting or publishing any information in their possession relating to a criminal case." (Standard 8–3.1.) The standards generally support openness of records: "In any criminal case, all judicial proceedings and related documents and exhibits, and any record made thereof, not otherwise required to remain confidential, should be acceptable to the public, except [in certain instances when fairness of the trial or another overriding interest might outweigh the usual right to a public trial]." (Standard 8–3.2.)

There has been relatively little litigation challenging a court's power to order its employees, such as clerks and marshals, or witnesses not to reveal prejudicial information about a pending case. Courts have not generally tried to issue orders to the police (in the executive branch). Rather, efforts have been made to get the executive branch to issue its own orders.

It seems clear that the court may order the prosecutor not to divulge certain potentially prejudicial information. It is not clear that a similar order could be imposed on an unwilling defendant. The defendant may argue that he is entitled to waive protections promulgated for his benefit, and he may feel compelled to speak to counter what he perceives to be prejudicial pretrial information.

Finally, attorneys, although officers subject to orders of the court, have contested orders that they not reveal information. Some have been upheld. Some have been upset on the ground that they swept beyond the needs of the case, some on the ground that they were unduly vague.

*State guidelines.* Because some journalists resented what they saw as an ABA attempt to tell them how to report news, the "Reardon Report" had more influence on those in the legal community than on the journalists. In the late 1960s and early 1970s, however, voluntary bench-bar-press-law enforcement groups were begun in many states to increase the dialogue about the problems. Some of those groups adopted guidelines that addressed many of the same problems addressed in the Reardon guidelines but reflected the input of journalists by affirming the right of the journalists to make the ultimate decisions about what they publish and by including references to the openness of the judicial system and the right of the public and press to observe it.

The effectiveness of the guidelines as a way of protecting defendants' rights, of course, is directly related to the fact that the guidelines are voluntary. Even in states in which they are followed with some regularity on criminal cases of routine interest, they tend to lose their effectiveness when sensational crimes are committed. There is also some danger that courts may use the guidelines in ways the journalists never envisioned; see Nebraska Press Association v. Stuart and Federated Publications v. Swedberg later in this chapter.

### e.  Granting Change of Venue

Where news accounts in an area may have created a situation in which it is unlikely that the accused can obtain a fair trial, a judge can transfer a trial to another area less touched by the publicity. A constitutional problem may arise in such instances, because the Sixth Amendment provides for one's trial "by an impartial jury of the State and district wherein the crime shall have been committed." Furthermore, such changes of venue are costly and bothersome to both the prosecution and the defense. If news accounts have already been statewide or national, the change is unlikely to do much to mitigate the damage. Even if the new site of the trial has been untouched by earlier news accounts, the scheduling of the trial there becomes a news event in that area, and the problem may begin anew, though with less attention because the victim(s) are not local people.

### f.  Granting Change of Venire

Rather than moving the trial, it is sometimes possible to import a panel of jurors—or veniremen—from another area where they are less likely to have formed opinions about the case. The practice is extremely rare, but it was used in the 1980 case of John Wayne Gacy, who was accused of killing 33 youths in Chicago. In his case, jurors were selected in a town 80 miles away and brought to Chicago for the trial. The practice raises questions about whether jurors from a remote area are really from, as the Sixth Amendment provides, the "State and district wherein the crime shall have been committed."

A Florida judge decided to use a jury from Palm Beach to try, in Tampa, two white men accused of setting afire an African–American New York tourist in 1993. Having tried unsuccessfully for eight days to seat a jury in Tampa, and having estimates showing that $1 million might be saved by flying in the jury instead of moving court personnel, attorneys and witnesses, the judge decided on using the Palm Beach jury. A state appellate court, however, ruled that, under the state constitution, the judge lacked authority to do that. Kohut v. Evans, 623 So.2d 569 (Fla.App.1993). Subsequently, the whole trial was moved to Palm Beach, and the defendants were convicted.

### g.  Relying on the Voir Dire

During the *voir dire,* the process under which prospective jurors are screened, attempts are made to exclude from the jury those people whose previously formed opinions will preclude their reaching a fair verdict based on the evidence presented during the trial. The *voir dire* may be successful in keeping truly biased people off a jury, but it is less successful when potential jurors have heard a specific piece of information. Also, the criticism is sometimes made that it can tend to eliminate from the jury those potential jurors who follow the news in their community most closely and who form intelligent opinions based on what they read or hear. The remaining potential jurors may be atypical of the population.

### h.  Cautioning Jurors

The Court in *Sheppard* was critical of the trial judge for failing to give the jurors sufficient instruction about not reading media accounts of the trial or listening to comment outside the courtroom. Despite the fact that judges today generally give careful instructions to jurors not to read or listen to anything about the case outside the courtroom, there is no accurate way of measuring the extent to which jurors heed the advice. Although many judges express faith in the conscientiousness of jurors in following those directions, some say that "If you believe that jurors don't read and listen to news reports of the case, you probably also believe in the Easter bunny."

### i.  Sequestering the Jury

Sequestering the jury—keeping them in a hotel during the trial—greatly reduces the risk of improper exposure to media accounts of the trial. Because the public reads about sequestration of jurors in some highly publicized cases, it seems to perceive sequestration as a more common practice than it is. Its high cost precludes its use in all but a few cases, and defense attorneys are sometimes reluctant even to suggest it because of unsureness about the effect on the jury. As some say, a juror who is unhappy about being confined for the duration of a trial cannot take out his frustrations on the judge or prosecutor and just may take them out on the accused.

### 2.  RESTRAINTS ON EXPRESSION

Because the First Amendment has traditionally been seen as a protection for the freedom to publish, restraints on the publication of

486     ADMINISTRATION OF JUSTICE          Ch. 10

information are undoubtedly the least desirable and most constitutionally suspect of the theoretically-available remedies for the fair trial-free press problem.  Two cases that illustrate the problem are *Dickinson*, p. 56, *supra*, and Nebraska Press Association v. Stuart, which we will discuss in this chapter.

The press calls them gag orders; lawyers and judges call them restrictive orders or protective orders.  By whatever name, such an order directs the press (and often others) not to disseminate information a judge thinks may prejudice jurors in a forthcoming or present trial. Violating an order can lead to a contempt citation.

### a.  Obeying Court Orders

Recall from Chapter II that two reporters who violated a federal court order not to publish testimony taken at a hearing were cited for criminal contempt and fined $300 each.  Although the court of appeals eventually held the order unconstitutional, it ruled that the order had to be obeyed until overturned on appeal.  *Dickinson*, p. 56, *supra*.

Recall also from Chapter II that a federal court held *The Providence Journal* and its executive editor in contempt of court for publishing truthful information obtained under the Freedom of Information Act while it was under a temporary restraining order (TRO) not to do so, but the U.S. Court of Appeals for the First Circuit, after a rehearing *en banc*, said "If timely access to the appellate court is not available or if timely decision is not forthcoming, the publisher may then proceed to publish and challenge the constitutionality of the order in the contempt proceedings."  *Providence Journal*, p. 57, *supra*.

States vary in their approaches to the problem of willful disobedience of orders that are subsequently determined to be invalid, and in some states, if an appellate court determines an order to be invalid, findings of contempt will be reversed.  In State v. Coe, 101 Wash.2d 364, 679 P.2d 353, 10 Med.L.Rptr. 1465 (1984), a trial judge's order holding a broadcaster in contempt for playing tapes that had been played in open court was reversed on appeal.  The judge had ordered that the tapes not be played on the air because the defendant might be suicidal.  The appellate court majority held that the state law permitted those cited for contempt to violate the order and then challenge it if the order was "patently invalid or 'void' as outside the court's power."

### b.  Validity of Restrictive or Restraining Orders

After *Sheppard* the Supreme Court did not get involved in publicity problems for several years.  Then, in the early 1970s, some courts began ordering the press not to report information it had obtained or might obtain.  Some of these cases reached the state appellate courts, but no clear pattern emerged.  A few reached individual justices of the Supreme Court when newspapers asked them to "stay" a restrictive order issued by a state court pending review by the full Supreme Court. These did not result in the Court's addressing the issue until a major case developed in 1976.

## NEBRASKA PRESS ASSOCIATION v. STUART
Supreme Court of the United States, 1976.
427 U.S. 539, 96 S.Ct. 2791, 49 L.Ed.2d 683, 1 Med.L.Rptr. 1064.

MR. CHIEF JUSTICE BURGER delivered the opinion of the Court.

The respondent State District Judge entered an order restraining the petitioners from publishing or broadcasting accounts of confessions or admissions made by the accused or facts "strongly implicative" of the accused in a widely reported murder of six persons. We granted certiorari to decide whether the entry of such an order on the showing made before the state court violated the constitutional guarantee of freedom of the press.

### I

On the evening of October 18, 1975, local police found the six members of the Henry Kellie family murdered in their home in Sutherland, Neb., a town of about 850 people. Police released the description of a suspect, Erwin Charles Simants, to the reporters who had hastened to the scene of the crime. Simants was arrested and arraigned in Lincoln County Court the following morning, ending a tense night for this small rural community.

The crime immediately attracted widespread news coverage, by local, regional, and national newspapers, radio and television stations. Three days after the crime, the County Attorney and Simants' attorney joined in asking the County Court to enter a restrictive order relating to "matters that may or may not be publicly reported or disclosed to the public," because of the "mass coverage by news media" and the "reasonable likelihood of prejudicial news which would make difficult, if not impossible, the impaneling of an impartial jury and tend to prevent a fair trial." The County Court heard oral argument but took no evidence; no attorney for members of the press appeared at this stage. The County Court granted the prosecutor's motion for a restrictive order and entered it the next day, October 22. The order prohibited everyone in attendance from "releas[ing] or authoriz[ing] for public dissemination in any form or manner whatsoever any testimony given or evidence adduced"; the order also required members of the press to observe the Nebraska Bar–Press Guidelines.[1]

1. The Nebraska Guidelines are voluntary standards adopted by members of the state bar and news media to deal with the reporting of crimes and criminal trials. They outline the matters of fact that may appropriately be reported, and also list what items are not generally appropriate for reporting, including: confessions, opinions on guilt or innocence, statements that would influence the outcome of a trial, the results of tests or examinations, comments on the credibility of witnesses, and evidence presented in the jury's absence. The publication of an accused's criminal record

. . .

Petitioners—several press and broadcast associations, publishers, and individual reporters—moved on October 23 for leave to intervene in the District Court, asking that the restrictive order imposed by the County Court be vacated.  The District Court conducted a hearing, at which the County Judge testified and newspaper articles about the Simants case were admitted in evidence.  The District Judge granted petitioners' motion to intervene and, on October 27, entered his own restrictive order.  The judge found "because of the nature of the crimes charged in the complaint that there is a clear and present danger that pretrial publicity could impinge upon the defendant's right to a fair trial."  The order applied only until the jury was impaneled and specifically prohibited petitioners from reporting five subjects: (1) the existence or contents of a confession Simants had made to law enforcement officers, which had been introduced in open court at arraignment; (2) the fact or nature of statements Simants had made to other persons; (3) the contents of a note he had written the night of the crime; (4) certain aspects of the medical testimony at the preliminary hearing; and (5) the identity of the victims of the alleged sexual assault and the nature of the assault.  It also prohibited reporting the exact nature of the restrictive order itself.  Like the County Court's order, this order incorporated the Nebraska Bar–Press Guidelines.  Finally, the order set out a plan for attendance, seating and courthouse traffic control during the trial.

. . .

The Nebraska Supreme Court rejected [the] "absolutist position," but modified the District Court's order to accommodate the defendant's right to a fair trial and the petitioners' interest in reporting pretrial events.  The order as modified prohibited reporting of only three matters: (a) the existence and nature of any confessions or admissions made by the defendant to law enforcement officers, (b) any confessions or admissions made to any third parties, except members of the press, and (c) other facts "strongly implicative" of the accused.  The Nebraska Supreme Court did not rely on the Nebraska Bar–Press Guidelines.  After construing Nebraska law to permit closure in certain circumstances, the court remanded the case to the District Judge for reconsideration of the issue whether pretrial hearings should be closed to the press and public.

We granted certiorari to address the important issues raised by the District Court order as modified by the Nebraska Supreme Court, but we denied the motion to expedite review or to stay entirely the order of the State District Court pending Simants' trial.  423 U.S. 1027 (1975).  We are informed by the parties that since we granted certiorari, Simants has been convicted of murder and sentenced to death.  His appeal is pending in the Nebraska Supreme Court.

should, under the Guidelines, be "considered very carefully."  The Guidelines also set out standards for taking and publishing photographs, and set up a joint bar-press committee to foster cooperation in resolving particular problems that emerge.

## II

[The Court concluded that the controversy was not moot because the dispute was "capable of repetition."]

## III

The problems presented by this case are almost as old as the Republic. Neither in the Constitution nor in contemporaneous writings do we find that the conflict between these two important rights was anticipated, yet it is inconceivable that the authors of the Constitution were unaware of the potential conflicts between the right to an unbiased jury and the guarantee of freedom of the press.  . . .

. . .

## IV

[The Court reviewed its cases touching this problem in which it upset convictions, including *Irvin* and *Sheppard*, and quoted the passage from *Sheppard* requiring the trial judge to take "strong measures" to protect the defendants. It then cited another group of cases, including *Murphy*, p. 481, *supra*, in which publicity did *not* lead to reversals of convictions.]

Taken together, these cases demonstrate that pretrial publicity—even pervasive, adverse publicity—does not inevitably lead to an unfair trial. The capacity of the jury eventually impaneled to decide the case fairly is influenced by the tone and extent of the publicity, which is in part and often in large part, shaped by what attorneys, police, and other officials do to precipitate news coverage. The trial judge has a major responsibility.  . . .

The state trial judge in the case before us acted responsibly, out of a legitimate concern, in an effort to protect the defendant's right to a fair trial.[4] What we must decide is not simply whether the Nebraska courts erred in seeing the possibility of real danger to the defendant's rights, but whether in the circumstances of this case the means employed were foreclosed by another provision of the Constitution.

## V

[The Court here reviewed its cases considering the imposition of a prior restraint against publishing certain material, primarily *Near* and the Pentagon Papers case, discussed at pp. 55 and 336, *supra*.]

The thread running through all these cases is that prior restraints on speech and publication are the most serious and the least tolerable infringement on First Amendment rights. A criminal penalty or a judgment in a defamation case is subject to the whole panoply of protections afforded by deferring the impact of the judgment until all avenues of appellate review have been exhausted. Only after judgment

---

**4.** The record also reveals that counsel for both sides acted responsibly in this case, and there is no suggestion that either sought to use pretrial news coverage for partisan advantage.  . . .

has become final, correct or otherwise, does the law's sanction become fully operative.

A prior restraint, by contrast and by definition, has an immediate and irreversible sanction. If it can be said that a threat of criminal or civil sanctions after publication "chills" speech, prior restraint "freezes" it at least for the time.

The damage can be particularly great when the prior restraint falls upon the communication of news and commentary on current events. Truthful reports of public judicial proceedings have been afforded special protection against subsequent punishment.   . . .

.  .  .

# VI

We turn now to the record in this case to determine whether, as Learned Hand put it, "the gravity of the 'evil,' discounted by its improbability, justifies such invasion of free speech as is necessary to avoid the danger." Dennis v. United States, 183 F.2d 201, 212 (1950), aff'd, 341 U.S. 494 (1951); see also L. Hand, The Bill of Rights 58–61 (1958). To do so, we must examine the evidence before the trial judge when the order was entered to determine (a) the nature and extent of pretrial news coverage; (b) whether other measures would be likely to mitigate the effects of unrestrained pretrial publicity; (c) how effectively a restraining order would operate to prevent the threatened danger. The precise terms of the restraining order are also important. We must then consider whether the record supports the entry of a prior restraint on publication, one of the most extraordinary remedies known to our jurisprudence.

# A

In assessing the probable extent of publicity, the trial judge had before him newspapers demonstrating that the crime had already drawn intensive news coverage, and the testimony of the County Judge, who had entered the initial restraining order based on the local and national attention the case had attracted. The District Judge was required to assess the probable publicity that would be given these shocking crimes prior to the time a jury was selected and sequestered. He then had to examine the probable nature of the publicity and determine how it would affect prospective jurors.

Our review of the pretrial record persuades us that the trial judge was justified in concluding that there would be intense and pervasive pretrial publicity concerning this case. He could also reasonably conclude, based on common human experience, that publicity might impair the defendant's right to a fair trial. He did not purport to say more, for he found only "a clear and present danger that pretrial publicity *could* impinge upon the defendant's right to a fair trial." (Emphasis added.) His conclusion as to the impact of such publicity on prospective jurors was of necessity speculative, dealing as he was with factors unknown and unknowable.

## B

We find little in the record that goes to another aspect of our task, determining whether measures short of an order restraining all publication would have insured the defendant a fair trial. Although the entry of the order might be read as a judicial determination that other measures would not suffice, the trial court made no express findings to that effect; the Nebraska Supreme Court referred to the issue only by implication. [     ]

.  .  .

We have   .  .  .   examined this record to determine the probable efficacy of the measures short of prior restraint on the press and speech. There is no finding that alternative measures would not have protected Simants' rights, and the Nebraska Supreme Court did no more than imply that such measures might not be adequate. Moreover, the record is lacking in evidence to support such a finding.

## C

We must also assess the probable efficacy of prior restraint on publication as a workable method of protecting Simants' right to a fair trial, and we cannot ignore the reality of the problems of managing and enforcing pretrial restraining orders. The territorial jurisdiction of the issuing court is limited by concepts of sovereignty, [     ]. The need for *in personam* jurisdiction also presents an obstacle to a restraining order that applies to publication at-large as distinguished from restraining publication within a given jurisdiction. [     ]

The Nebraska Supreme Court narrowed the scope of the restrictive order, and its opinion reflects awareness of the tensions between the need to protect the accused as fully as possible and the need to restrict publication as little as possible. The dilemma posed underscores how difficult it is for trial judges to predict what information will in fact undermine the impartiality of jurors, and the difficulty of drafting an order that will effectively keep prejudicial information from prospective jurors.   .  .  .

Finally, we note that the events disclosed by the record took place in a community of 850 people. It is reasonable to assume that, without any news accounts being printed or broadcast, rumors would travel swiftly by word of mouth. One can only speculate on the accuracy of such reports, given the generative propensities of rumors; they could well be more damaging than reasonably accurate news accounts. But plainly a whole community cannot be restrained from discussing a subject intimately affecting life within it.

Given these practical problems, it is far from clear that prior restraint on publication would have protected Simants' rights.

## D

Finally, another feature of this case leads us to conclude that the restrictive order entered here is not supportable. At the outset the County Court entered a very broad restrictive order, the terms of which are not before us; it then held a preliminary hearing open to the public and the press. There was testimony concerning at least two incriminating statements made by Simants to private persons; the statement— evidently a confession—that he gave to law enforcement officials was also introduced. The State District Court's later order was entered after this public hearing and, as modified by the Nebraska Supreme Court, enjoined reporting of (1) "[c]onfessions or admissions against interest made by the accused to law enforcement officials"; (2) "[c]onfessions or admissions against interest, oral or written, if any, made by the accused to third parties, excepting any statements, if any, made by the accused to representatives of the news media"; and (3) all "[o]ther information strongly implicative of the accused as the perpetrator of the slayings."

To the extent that this order prohibited the reporting of evidence adduced at the open preliminary hearing, it plainly violated settled principles: "there is nothing that proscribes the press from reporting events that transpire in the courtroom." [*Sheppard*.] See also [*Cox Broadcasting*]; Craig v. Harney, [ ]. The County Court could not know that closure of the preliminary hearing was an alternative open to it until the Nebraska Supreme Court so construed state law; but once a public hearing had been held, what transpired there could not be subject to prior restraint.

The third prohibition of the order was defective in another respect as well. As part of a final order, entered after plenary review, this prohibition regarding "implicative" information is too vague and too broad to survive the scrutiny we have given to restraints on First Amendment rights. [ ] The third phase of the order entered falls outside permissible limits.

## E

The record demonstrates, as the Nebraska courts held, that there was indeed a risk that pretrial news accounts, true or false, would have some adverse impact on the attitudes of those who might be called as jurors. But on the record now before us it is not clear that further publicity, unchecked, would so distort the views of potential jurors that 12 could not be found who would, under proper instructions, fulfill their sworn duty to render a just verdict exclusively on the evidence presented in open court. We cannot say on this record that alternatives to a prior restraint on petitioners would not have sufficiently mitigated the adverse effects of pretrial publicity so as to make prior restraint unnecessary. Nor can we conclude that the restraining order actually entered would serve its intended purpose. Reasonable minds can have few doubts about the gravity of the evil pretrial publicity can work, but the probability that it would do so here was not demonstrated with the degree of certainty our cases on prior restraint require.

Of necessity our holding is confined to the record before us.  But our conclusion is not simply a result of assessing the adequacy of the showing made in this case; it results in part from the problems inherent in meeting the heavy burden of demonstrating, in advance of trial, that without prior restraint a fair trial will be denied.  The practical problems of managing and enforcing restrictive orders will always be present.  In this sense, the record now before us is illustrative rather than exceptional.  It is significant that when this Court has reversed a state conviction because of prejudicial publicity, it has carefully noted that some course of action short of prior restraint would have made a critical difference.  [  ]  However difficult it may be, we need not rule out the possibility of showing the kind of threat to fair trial rights that would possess the requisite degree of certainty to justify restraint.  This Court has frequently denied that First Amendment rights are absolute and has consistently rejected the proposition that a prior restraint can never be employed.  [  ]

Our analysis ends as it began, with a confrontation between prior restraint imposed to protect one vital constitutional guarantee and the explicit command of another that the freedom to speak and publish shall not be abridged.  We reaffirm that the guarantees of freedom of expression are not an absolute prohibition under all circumstances, but the barriers to prior restraint remain high and the presumption against its use continues intact.  We hold that, with respect to the order entered in this case prohibiting reporting or commentary on judicial proceedings held in public, the barriers have not been overcome; to the extent that this order restrained publication of such material, it is clearly invalid.  To the extent that it prohibited publication based on information gained from other sources, we conclude that the heavy burden imposed as a condition to securing a prior restraint was not met and the judgment of the Nebraska Supreme Court is therefore

Reversed.

MR. JUSTICE BRENNAN, with whom MR. JUSTICE STEWART and MR. JUSTICE MARSHALL join, concurring in the judgment.

.   .   .   The right to a fair trial by a jury of one's peers is unquestionably one of the most precious and sacred safeguards enshrined in the Bill of Rights.  I would hold, however, that resort to prior restraints on the freedom of the press is a constitutionally impermissible method for enforcing that right; judges have at their disposal a broad spectrum of devices for ensuring that fundamental fairness is accorded the accused without necessitating so drastic an incursion on the equally fundamental and salutary constitutional mandate that discussion of public affairs in a free society cannot depend on the preliminary grade of judicial censors.

.   .   .

MR. JUSTICE WHITE, concurring.

Technically there is no need to go farther than the Court does to dispose of this case, and I join the Court's opinion.  I should add, however, that for the reasons which the Court itself canvasses there is grave doubt in my mind whether orders with respect to the press such as were entered in this case would ever be justifiable. It may be the better part of discretion, however, not to announce such a rule in the first case in which the issue has been squarely presented here. Perhaps we should go no farther than absolutely necessary until the federal courts, and ourselves, have been exposed to a broader spectrum of cases presenting similar issues. If the recurring result, however, in case after case is to be similar to our judgment today, we should at some point announce a more general rule and avoid the interminable litigation that our failure to do so would necessarily entail.

MR. JUSTICE POWELL, concurring.

Although I join the opinion of the Court, in view of the importance of the case I write to emphasize the unique burden that rests upon the party, whether it be the state or a defendant, who undertakes to show the necessity for prior restraint on pretrial publicity.

In my judgment a prior restraint properly may issue only when it is shown to be necessary to prevent the dissemination of prejudicial publicity that otherwise poses a high likelihood of preventing, directly and irreparably, the impaneling of a jury meeting the Sixth Amendment requirement of impartiality. This requires a showing that (i) there is a clear threat to the fairness of trial, (ii) such a threat is posed by the actual publicity to be restrained, and (iii) no less restrictive alternatives are available. . . .

MR. JUSTICE STEVENS, concurring in the judgment.

For the reasons eloquently stated by Mr. Justice Brennan, I agree that the judiciary is capable of protecting the defendant's right to a fair trial without enjoining the press from publishing information in the public domain, and that it may not do so. Whether the same absolute protection would apply no matter how shabby or illegal the means by which the information is obtained, no matter how serious an intrusion on privacy might be involved, no matter how demonstrably false the information might be, no matter how prejudicial it might be to the interests of innocent persons, and no matter how perverse the motivation for publishing it, is a question I would not answer without further argument. [ ] I do, however, subscribe to most of what Mr. Justice Brennan says and, if ever required to face the issue squarely, may well accept his ultimate conclusion.

## Notes and Questions

1. Is it still permissible to issue restrictive orders preventing lawyers and other court officials from making certain types of statements?

2. In 1991 the Supreme Court of the United States reversed a judgment against Attorney Dominic P. Gentile, who had held a press conference the day after his client was indicted on criminal charges. The client was acquitted by a jury six months later, and the Disciplinary Board of the State Bar of Nevada subsequently found that Gentile had violated a

Nevada Supreme Court Rule prohibiting lawyers from making extrajudicial statements to the press that they know or reasonably should know would have a "substantial likelihood of materially prejudicing" a proceeding. The Nevada Supreme Court had affirmed, rejecting Gentile's contention that the rule violated his right to free speech.

The Supreme Court of the United States reversed, holding that the "substantial likelihood of material prejudice" test applied by Nevada and most other states satisfies the First Amendment but that the Nevada rule was nonetheless void for vagueness: its grammatical structure and the absence of clarifying interpretation failed to provide fair notice to lawyers. Gentile v. State Bar of Nevada, 501 U.S. ___, 111 S.Ct. 2720 (1991).

3. As the opinions note, the press, bench and bar in Nebraska had collaborated on a set of voluntary guidelines. Such agreements exist in about half of the states, but this case was apparently the first in which a judge attempted to make the guidelines mandatory. In passing on the application for a stay, Justice Blackmun rejected this attempt out of hand, largely on the ground that the guidelines, since they were intended to be voluntary, used terms such as "consider carefully" that did not lend themselves to incorporation into a judicial order. Some members of the press had warned that guidelines might be misused in this way, and noted that guidelines had failed to deter judges from issuing restrictive orders.

4. Note that Justice Stevens suggests a possible connection between the way information is obtained and the freedom to publish that information. This is a recurring theme seen in numerous cases. Recall the Court's emphasis in *Florida Star,* p. 221, *supra,* on the fact that the rape victim's name was legally obtained.

5. When all the votes are counted in this case does the Chief Justice have more adherents than Justice Brennan?

6. Recall *Noriega,* p. 59, *supra,* in which a temporary restraint was imposed on CNN to stop the network from broadcasting taperecorded telephone calls between Noriega and members of his defense team.

7. Soon after *Nebraska Press Association* the Court had occasion to pass on a related problem. In a juvenile proceeding, an Oklahoma state judge ordered the press not to publish the name of an 11–year–old boy who was accused of firing a shot that killed a railroad switchman. His identity had been disclosed earlier during an open hearing. After the Oklahoma Supreme Court upheld the order, the press applied to the Supreme Court to stay the trial judge's order pending the filing and disposition of a petition for *certiorari.* In an unsigned order, the Supreme Court granted the stay on the ground that the name had already been made public. Citing *Nebraska Press Association* and *Cox,* p. 212, *supra,* the Court's short opinion noted that the press did not challenge the judge's order silencing counsel or public employees, or an Oklahoma statute requiring that juvenile proceedings be held in private

unless specified otherwise by the judge. Oklahoma Publishing Co. v. District Court, 429 U.S. 967, 2 Med.L.Rptr. 1008 (1976).

When the petition for *certiorari* was filed, the Court granted it and summarily reversed. The First Amendment "will not permit a state court to prohibit the publication of widely disseminated information obtained at court proceedings which were in fact open to the public." The Oklahoma court had rejected *Nebraska Press Association* and *Cox* because here there was no showing that the judge had "distinctly and expressly ordered the hearing to be public." The Supreme Court concluded that the two cases controlled nonetheless: "Whether or not the trial judge expressly made such an order, members of the press were in fact present at the hearing with the full knowledge of the presiding judge, the prosecutor, and the defense counsel. No objection was made to the presence of the press in the courtroom . . . ." Oklahoma Publishing Co. v. District Court, 430 U.S. 308, 2 Med.L.Rptr. 1456 (1977).

### c.  Gag Orders on Litigants

A special problem arises when the media are themselves parties to litigation and want to report on the case. In Seattle Times v. Rhinehart, 467 U.S. 20, 10 Med.L.Rptr. 1705 (1984), the Supreme Court held that a protective order by a trial court in the state of Washington did not violate the First Amendment even though it prohibited the *Seattle Times* newspaper from publishing certain information related to a libel case against them. The information in question had been obtained by the newspaper as part of the discovery process prior to the libel trial, and the Court reasoned that there was a sufficient showing of good cause for the order and that the rights of a litigant do not necessarily include the right to disseminate information obtained through the "legislative grace" of the discovery process. In what most journalists and attorneys representing media clients consider a disturbing trend, lower courts in other cases have also affirmed orders gagging litigants or trial participants.

### d.  Gags on Grand Jurors

In another attempt to cut off information at its source, a Florida law prohibited grand jury witnesses from disclosing their testimony. When a journalist was himself a grand jury witness, the statute effectively became a restraint on publication. In a 1990 case, the Supreme Court found the statute to violate the First Amendment. Michael Smith, a reporter for the *Charlotte Herald–News* in Charlotte County, Fla., had been called to testify before a special grand jury about information he had obtained while writing a series of newspaper stories about alleged improprieties committed by the Charlotte County state attorney's office and sheriff's department. He had been warned that any disclosure of his testimony would violate the Florida statute. Writing for a unanimous court, Chief Justice Rehnquist acknowledged various state interests in keeping grand jury testimony secret but concluded that they were insufficient "to overcome [Smith's] First Amendment right to make a truthful statement of the information he had acquired on his own." Butterworth v. Smith, 494 U.S. 624, 17 Med.L.Rptr. 1569 (1990).

### e. Gags on Counsel

A federal judge concerned about possible prejudice to the trials of individuals charged in the World Trade Center bombing case entered an order prohibiting counsel for all parties in the case from publicly discussing any aspect of the case. The U.S. Court of Appeals for the Second Circuit held that the order was not narrowly tailored, that it was entered without any finding that alternatives to such blanket prohibition would be inadequate to protect the defendants' fair trial rights, and that it violated the First Amendment. The *per curiam* opinion said, "There is no indication in the record that the court explored any alternatives or at all considered imposing any less broad proscription; indeed the court discouraged counsel from even proffering possible alternatives." United States v. Salameh, 992 F.2d 445, 21 Med.L.Rptr. 1376 (2d Cir.1993).

### 3. DENIALS OF ACCESS TO THE COURTROOM AND CONDITIONAL ACCESS

As judges faced the reality that other means of solving the fair trial-free press problems were either undesirable or ineffective, some turned to excluding the press and public from the courtroom during pretrial hearings or during trials themselves, or granted access to the courtroom only on the acceptance of conditions.

### a. Denials of Access

Journalists, of course, are also members of the public. But more, they see themselves as the eyes and ears of the public, surrogates for those who cannot attend a hearing or trial. They brought the first major challenge to closed pretrial proceedings.

Gannett Co. v. DePasquale, 443 U.S. 368, 5 Med.L.Rptr. 1337 (1979), presented the question whether members of the public are constitutionally entitled to attend a pretrial hearing. The issue arose out of a murder prosecution in upstate New York.

Wayne Clapp, a resident of a suburb of Rochester, N.Y., disappeared in 1976 after last being seen alive when he went fishing with two men. The boat they had used was found full of bullet holes, and police searched for both Clapp and his missing companions. Clapp's truck was found in Michigan, and the two missing young men and a female companion were apprehended there. Newspapers in New York State reported the arrest and police theories of the crime.

The two men moved to suppress statements they had made to the Michigan police, on the ground that they had been given involuntarily. They also moved to suppress the gun that had been obtained as the fruit of the allegedly involuntary confession. The motions came before Judge DePasquale, and defense counsel asked the judge to close the hearing because "the unabated buildup of adverse publicity had jeopardized the ability of the defendants to receive a fair trial." The prosecutor did not object. Nor did the Gannett reporter in the courtroom. The judge removed press and public from the courtroom.

On the next day the reporter complained to the judge, but the hearing had already concluded, and the judge refused to release a transcript. Three days later counsel for Gannett appeared and asked that the ruling be vacated and that a transcript of the hearing be provided. The judge held a formal hearing on these requests and denied both, concluding that an open hearing would create "a reasonable probability of prejudice to these defendants."

The New York Court of Appeals upheld the judge's action. It noted that in the interim the two defendants had pleaded guilty to lesser crimes and that the transcripts had then been released.

The Supreme Court of the United States affirmed, 5–4, in an opinion by Justice Stewart. He began by stating the dangers to a fair trial from reports about a suppression hearing. He concluded that the Sixth Amendment's provision that "the accused shall enjoy the right to a speedy and public trial by an impartial jury" extended no rights whatever to the public. "The Constitution nowhere mentions any right of access to a criminal trial on the part of the public; its guarantee, like the others enumerated [in the Sixth Amendment], is personal to the accused."

He recognized that the "strong societal interest in public trials" is based on several important considerations. The recognition of that interest "is a far cry, however, from the creation of a constitutional right on the part of the public. In an adversary system of criminal justice, the public interest in the administration of justice is protected by the participants in the litigation." If the defendant, the prosecutor and the judge agree, the public interest is fully protected.

Of the four Justices who joined Justice Stewart's opinion, three wrote separate opinions. The four dissenters joined in a lengthy opinion arguing that suppression hearings should be treated as trials with regard to the Sixth Amendment and that the Sixth Amendment guarantee of a public trial extends to the public as well as to the accused. The decision caused considerable confusion—in part because of Justice Stewart's 12 references to "trials" when the case involved "pretrial" proceedings. Several Supreme Court justices, departing from custom, spoke about the case within weeks after the decision and seemed to disagree about the meaning of their decision. Because of the Supreme Court's decisions in access-to-courtroom cases in the early 1980s, as we shall see below, concern over the confusion caused by the *Gannett* decision gradually disappeared.

Soon after *Gannett* the Court agreed to hear a case that involved related issues. Richmond Newspapers, Inc. v. Virginia, 448 U.S. 555, 6

Med.L.Rptr. 1833 (1980). Stevenson had been indicted for murder. The conviction for second degree murder was overturned on appeal because improper evidence had been admitted. The second and third trials resulted in mistrials. At the start of the fourth trial, defense counsel moved to exclude the press and public from the courtroom because he did not want witnesses to compare stories or information to leak out and be learned by the jurors (who were not sequestered). The prosecutor offered no objection, and the judge closed the courtroom. Although reporters were present, they did not object at the time. Later that afternoon, however, their attorney argued that the trial should be opened. The defendant's attorney repeated the arguments he had made earlier, including the fact that this was the defendant's fourth trial and he wanted to avoid any more mistrials. The judge observed that, apparently because the jury box faced the audience, "having people in the Courtroom is distracting to the jury. . . . When we get into our new Court Building, people can sit in the audience so the jury can't see them. The rule of the Court may be different under those circumstances."

The judge concluded that "if I feel that the rights of the defendant are infringed in any way, . . . I'm inclined to go along with the defendant's motion" when it "doesn't completely override all rights of everyone else." He refused to open the courtroom. After the state's evidence was in, the trial judge dismissed the case, found the defendant not guilty and released him. Apparently, a tape of the proceedings was made available as soon as the trial terminated.

The newspaper appealed the reporters' exclusion to the state's supreme court, which concluded that the trial judge had committed no reversible error, and affirmed. By a vote of 7–1, the Supreme Court reversed the judgment of the Virginia Supreme Court. Justice Rehnquist dissented, and Justice Powell did not participate. It is not easy to explain the reasoning that lay behind the decision because the seven justices in the majority wrote six opinions and there was no majority opinion.

Chief Justice Burger wrote the plurality opinion, joined by Justices White and Stevens. He stressed that *Gannett* had involved "pretrial" proceedings while this case involved a trial. He then traced at length the history of public criminal trials that ran back at least to the 13th century in England. (Note that no such history could be shown for pretrial proceedings because they are a recent development in criminal law.)

The reasons for this long tradition included the greater likelihood that witnesses would tell the truth and the therapeutic value of having open criminal trials that provide "an outlet for community concern, hostility, and emotion." No "community catharsis can occur if justice is" done in the dark. Public acceptance was a third reason for open trials. "People in an open society do not demand infallibility from their institutions, but it is difficult for them to accept what they are prohibited from observing. When a criminal trial is conducted in the open, there is at least an opportunity both for understanding the system in general and its workings in a particular case.   . . ."

The tradition of openness was also explained by the fact that "in earlier times, both in England and America, attendance at court was a common mode of 'passing the time.' [   ] With the press, cinema, and electronic media now supplying the representations or reality of the real life drama once available only in the courtroom, attendance at court is no longer a widespread pastime." Instead of acquiring information about courts by firsthand observation or word of mouth, people now acquire such information from the media. "In a sense this validates the media claim of functioning as surrogates for the public. While media representatives enjoy the same right of access as the public, they often are provided special seating and priority of entry so that they may report what people in attendance have seen and heard."

His review of history and modern justifications led the Chief Justice to conclude that "a presumption of openness inheres in the very nature of a criminal trial under our system of justice."

The state countered that no provision of the United States Constitution guarantees the public the right to attend criminal trials. The Chief Justice's response began with the First Amendment, whose express provisions "share a common core purpose of assuring freedom of communication on matters relating to the functioning of government." He quoted from *Bellotti*, p. 449, *supra*, that the "First Amendment goes beyond protection of the press and the self-expression of individuals to prohibit government from limiting the stock of information from which members of the public may draw." He also drew on cases that had discussed a "right to listen" or a right to "receive information and ideas." It was not crucial whether the right be called a "right of access" or a "right to gather information." The "explicit, guaranteed rights to speak and to publish concerning what takes place at a trial would lose much meaning if access to observe the trial could, as it was here, be foreclosed arbitrarily."

The Chief Justice also saw an affinity between the right to attend criminal trials and freedom of assembly:

Subject to the traditional time, place and manner restrictions, [   ], streets, sidewalks, and parks are places traditionally open, where First Amendment rights may be exercised [   ]; a trial courtroom also is a public place where the people generally—and representatives of the media—have a right to be present, and where their presence historically has been thought to enhance the integrity and quality of what takes place.

After finding support in the First Amendment, the Chief Justice asserted that the framers had worried that expressing some protections might lead to the argument that nothing else was to be protected. He concluded that efforts "culminating in the Ninth Amendment, served to allay the fears of those who were concerned that expressing certain guarantees could be read as excluding others." The Ninth Amendment provides that "The enumeration in the Constitution, of certain rights, shall not be construed to deny or disparage others retained by the people."

In a third response to the lack of an express constitutional guarantee of the public's right to attend criminal trials, the Chief Justice noted that the Court had recognized several other rights despite a similar lack of express provisions:

> Notwithstanding the appropriate caution against reading into the Constitution rights not explicitly defined, the Court has acknowledged that certain unarticulated rights are implicit in enumerated guarantees. For example, the rights of association and of privacy, the right to be presumed innocent and the right to be judged by a standard of proof beyond a reasonable doubt in a criminal trial, as well as the right to travel, appear nowhere in the Constitution or Bill of Rights. Yet these important but unarticulated rights have nonetheless been found to share constitutional protection in common with explicit guarantees. The concerns expressed by Madison and others have thus been resolved; fundamental rights, even though not expressly guaranteed, have been recognized by the Court as indispensable to the enjoyment of rights explicitly defined.

This brought the Chief Justice to the last step in the analysis— applying the principles to the record in the case:

> Despite the fact that this was the fourth trial of the accused, the trial judge made no findings to support closure; no inquiry was made as to whether alternative solutions would have met the need to ensure fairness; there was no recognition of any right under the Constitution for the public or press to attend the trial. In contrast to the pretrial proceeding dealt with in *Gannett,* supra, there exist in the context of the trial itself various tested alternatives to satisfy the constitutional demands of fairness. See, e.g., [*Nebraska Press Assn.*; *Sheppard*]. There was no suggestion that any problems with witnesses could not have been dealt with by their exclusion from the courtroom or their sequestration during the trial. See [*Sheppard*]. Nor is there anything to indicate that sequestration of the jurors would not have guarded against their being subjected to any improper information. All of the alternatives admittedly present difficulties for trial courts, but none of the factors relied on here was beyond the realm of the manageable. Absent an overriding interest articulated in findings, the trial of a criminal case must be open to the public. Accordingly, the judgment under review is reversed.

In a footnote to that passage, the Chief Justice stated that although he had "no occasion here to define the circumstances in which all or part of a criminal trial may be closed to the public, . . . our holding today does not mean that [the rights granted] are absolute." Reasonable regulations may be necessary in the interest of the "fair administration of justice" and it is "far more important that trials be conducted in a quiet and orderly setting than it is to preserve that atmosphere on city streets." He recognized that limited capacity of courtrooms may mean that all who wish to attend are not able to do so. "In such situations, reasonable restrictions on general access are traditionally imposed, including preferential seating for media representatives."

Although joining the plurality opinion, Justice White wrote separately to emphasize that if the dissenters' Sixth Amendment argument in *Gannett* had prevailed, this case would not have been necessary.

Justice Stevens, though joining the plurality opinion, also wrote separately. This was a "watershed case" because no prior case had "squarely held that the acquisition of newsworthy matter is entitled to any constitutional protection whatsoever."

He concurred in the reversal because of "the total absence of any record justification for the closure order entered in this case." (In a footnote he adhered to his view that the Sixth Amendment applied only to the accused—"the party who has the greatest interest in the right to a public trial.")

Justice Brennan, joined by Justice Marshall, concurred in an opinion that developed a "structural" view of the First Amendment. Although the First Amendment is usually "interposed to protect communication between speaker and listener," it "embodies more than a commitment to free expression and communicative interchange for their own sakes; it has a *structural* role to play in securing and fostering our republican system of government":

> Implicit in this structural role is not only "the principle that debate on public issues should be uninhibited, robust, and wide-open," [*Sullivan*], but the antecedent assumption that valuable public debate—as well as other civic behavior—must be informed. The structural model links the First Amendment to that process of communication necessary for a democracy to survive, and thus entails solicitude not only for communication itself, but for the indispensable conditions of meaningful communication.
>
> However, because "the stretch of this protection is theoretically endless," [  ], it must be invoked with discrimination and temperance. For so far as the participating citizen's need for information is concerned, "[t]here are few restrictions on action which could not be clothed by ingenious argument in the garb of decreased data flow." Zemel v. Rusk, [  ]. An assertion of the prerogative to gather information must accordingly be assayed by considering the information sought and the opposing interests invaded.
>
> This judicial task is as much a matter of sensitivity to practical necessities as it is of abstract reasoning. But at least two helpful principles may be sketched. First, the case for a right of access has special force when drawn from an enduring and vital tradition of public entry to particular proceedings or information. [  ] Such a

tradition commands respect in part because the Constitution carries the gloss of history.  More importantly, a tradition of accessibility implies the favorable judgment of experience.  Second, the value of access must be measured in specifics.  Analysis is not advanced by rhetorical statements that all information bears upon public issues; what is crucial in individual cases is whether access to a particular government process is important in terms of that very process.

To resolve the case before us, therefore, we must consult historical and current practice with respect to open trials, and weigh the importance of public access to the trial process itself.

Applying the model to this case, Justice Brennan first traced the history and tradition of public criminal trials.  For Justice Brennan the major lesson was that earlier cases had recognized that "open trials are bulwarks of our free and democratic government: public access to court proceedings is one of the numerous 'checks and balances' of our system, because 'contemporaneous review in the forum of public opinion is an effective restraint on possible abuse of judicial power.' "

In addition, Justice Brennan mentioned the fear that closed trials may "breed suspicion of prejudice and arbitrariness, which in turn spawns disrespect for law."  Also, in our system, "judges are not mere umpires, but, in their own sphere, lawmakers—a coordinate branch of government."  This gave the trial structural importance as a "genuine governmental proceeding."  Some of these factors established Justice Brennan's second point—the importance of public access to criminal trials.

Turning to the facts of the case, Justice Brennan said that whatever "countervailing interests might be sufficiently compelling to reverse" a presumption in favor of open trials "need not concern us now," for Virginia law authorized closures in the "unfettered discretion of the judge and parties."  In a footnote, he suggested that "national security concerns about confidentiality may sometimes warrant closures during sensitive portions of trial proceedings, such as testimony about state secrets."

Justice Stewart, concurring, briefly noted that whatever the First Amendment may ultimately have to say about pretrial proceedings, the question avoided in *Gannett*, the First and Fourteenth Amendments "clearly give the press and the public a right of access to trials themselves, civil as well as criminal."  He was persuaded by the history and the reasons discussed in the other opinions.  "With us, a trial is by very definition a proceeding open to the press and to the public."

Justice Blackmun, concurring, restated his preference that courts be opened under the Sixth Amendment as he had argued in his dissent in *Gannett*.  He thought that reliance in this case on various clauses in the First Amendment, the Ninth Amendment, and a "cluster of penumbral guarantees recognized in past decisions" would prove "troublesome."  Setting his losing reliance on the Sixth Amendment to one side, he concluded that "the First Amendment must provide some measure of protection for public access to the trial." But he did note that the fragmented approach here would spawn uncertainty over what must be shown before this new right may be limited in a particular case.

Justice Rehnquist, the lone dissenter, could find no public right to attend criminal trials in any provision of the Constitution. He argued that the Court's effort "over the past generation" to gather to itself "all of the ultimate decisionmaking power over how justice shall be administered, not merely in the federal system, but in each of the 50 states, is a task that no Court consisting of nine persons, however gifted, is equal to." Later: "it is basically unhealthy to have so much authority concentrated in a small group of lawyers who have been appointed to the Supreme Court and enjoy life tenure." There was no reason for the Court to "smother a healthy pluralism which would ordinarily exist in a national government embracing 50 states." Because Justice Rehnquist could find nothing in the Constitution to bar what the Virginia courts had done, he would have affirmed.

Questions about courtroom closures continued to arise after *Richmond Newspapers*. Two years later, in Globe Newspaper Co. v. Norfolk County Superior Court, 457 U.S. 596, 8 Med.L.Rptr. 1689 (1982), the Supreme Court held for *The Boston Globe* in a challenge to a Massachusetts statute that provided for automatic closure of rape and other sexual assault trials during the testimony of minors who are victims. Wrote Justice Brennan for the six-member majority, "We agree with respondent that the first interest—safe-guarding the physical and psychological well-being of a minor—is a compelling one. But as compelling as that interest is, it does not justify a mandatory-closure rule, for it is clear that the circumstances of the particular case may affect the significance of the interest. A trial court can determine on a case-by-case basis whether closure is necessary to protect the welfare of a minor victim."

In such closure decisions, the First Amendment requires that any such restriction on access to criminal trials be necessitated by compelling state interest and be narrowly tailored to serve that interest.

In Press–Enterprise Co. v. Superior Court (I), 464 U.S. 501, 10 Med.L.Rptr. 1161 (1984), the Supreme Court dealt with the issue of the closing of the *voir dire* examination of potential jurors. Holding that such proceedings in criminal trials are presumptively open to the public, the Court said that closure would be justified only where there is an overriding interest, where the closure is narrowly tailored, and where alternatives to closure have been considered. The court found no support for the trial court's conclusion that an open proceeding would have threatened the prospective jurors' interests in privacy in this case. (The problem was compounded, from the press's point of view, by the fact that the trial court had refused to release the transcript of the *voir dire* as well.)

In Waller v. Georgia, 467 U.S. 39, 10 Med.L.Rptr. 2210 (1984), the Supreme Court addressed the problem of a closure of pretrial suppression hearings over the objection of the defendant. The case involved allegations of racketeering and gambling, and a pretrial hearing was held to consider suppression of wiretaps and evidence seized during searches at the defendants' homes. The hearing was closed when the prosecution moved for closure alleging in part that the wiretap evidence would "involve" the privacy interests of some persons who were indicted but were not then on trial, and some who were not then indicted. Citing *Press–Enterprise I, supra,* the court held the closure of the suppression hearing was unjustified, noting that the entire seven-day hearing had been closed even though the tapes were played for less than 2½ hours.

## b.  *Conditional Access*

With a variety of precedents holding that trial court judges should not gag journalists and should not keep them or other members out of courtrooms during trials, it was perhaps inevitable that a trial judge would find still another way of trying to solve the fair trial free press problems. A trial court judge in the State of Washington decided to use the voluntary bench-bar-media guidelines adopted in that state as a basis for granting access to his courtroom, allowing only reporters who agreed to abide by the guidelines into the room.

The Washington Supreme Court upheld the trial judge's order in Federated Publications v. Swedberg, 96 Wash.2d 13, 633 P.2d 74, 7 Med.L.Rptr. 1865 (1981), cert. denied 456 U.S. 984 (1982). Critics of bench-bar-press guidelines said that one of the envisioned dangers of such guidelines—their misuse by the courts—had become a reality. Early predictions of a trend toward such conditions on access to courtrooms proved premature, however. Adoption of amendments to state bench-bar-press guidelines, specifically precluding their use by courts for any purpose, lessened the likelihood that the guidelines, which media representatives had adopted in good faith, might be used against them in this way.

Conditional access also arises in juvenile proceedings. In many states, hearings in juvenile cases are confidential on the ground that they are primarily to rehabilitate and are clinical rather than punitive. The Supreme Court has said that a state may "continue, if it deems it appropriate, to provide and to improve provision for the confidentiality of records of police contracts and court action relating to juveniles." In re Gault, 387 U.S. 1, 25 (1967). Judges in many states will permit reporters to attend juvenile proceedings on the condition that they agree not to reveal the names of the juveniles involved.

## 4.  Denials of Access to Court Records

Although there is a tradition of openness of court records, there are instances in which courts have withheld certain information during and sometimes after trials. Reasons offered for withholding such information include the protection of candor in the *voir dire* proceedings, the danger of prejudice from pretrial proceedings and protection of the privacy of jurors.

### a.  Transcript of Voir Dire

Recall the discussion of *Press–Enterprise I*, in which the *voir dire* was closed *and* the transcript was withheld.

### b.  Transcript of Preliminary Hearing

A second case brought by the same newspaper challenged the sealing of the transcript of a preliminary hearing.  Press–Enterprise Co. v. Superior Court (II), 478 U.S. 1, 13 Med.L.Rptr. 1001 (1986) grew out of a criminal trial in Riverside County, Calif., Municipal Court.  Robert Diaz, a nurse, had been charged with murdering 12 patients by administering a heart drug.  A preliminary hearing, closed to the public, lasted 41 days, after which the newspaper asked for a transcript of the proceedings.  The court refused and sealed the record.  The California Supreme Court had decided against the newspaper, but the Supreme Court of the United States reversed.  Chief Justice Burger's opinion for the Court held that the California Supreme Court had failed to consider the First Amendment right of access to criminal proceedings.

### c.  Jurors' Privacy

Not all limits on information about the judicial process relate to fears of the prejudicial effect of publicity.  A judge may bar release of the names of jurors in notorious cases to protect their privacy and impartiality.

For example, a trial court judge in Iowa, concerned about retaliation against jurors, ordered reporters not to print the names, addresses or phone numbers of jurors in a murder trial involving the widow of a slain motorcycle gang member.  The judge also barred photographs of the jurors entering and leaving the courthouse.  The press appealed the order, and it was overturned in light of *Nebraska Press Association*.  The Iowa Supreme Court found that no juror had expressed fear of retaliation, that other methods of preventing the suggested evil had not been tried, and that jurors' names and addresses could be published *after* the trial in any case, blunting the rationale for the order.  Also, said the court, jury lists are public information in Iowa.  Des Moines Register & Tribune Co. v. Osmundson, 248 N.W.2d 493, 2 Med.L.Rptr. 1321 (Iowa 1976).

If a judge cannot prevent the press from reporting the names of jurors that have become public, the next step might be to try to prevent the names from becoming public in a state in which jurors' names are not public property.  This was approved in a criminal prosecution of major narcotics suspects in New York City.  The trial judge gave prospective jurors numbers and never released their names or addresses.  The judge did conduct a *voir dire* based on his own questions and some submitted by counsel.  He asked jurors, among other things, the county of their residence and if they were prejudiced against African–Americans (14 defendants were African–Americans). He asked about education and group memberships, but he refused to ask the jurors about their own ethnic or religious backgrounds.

After conviction, the defendants appealed asserting, as one ground, that they had been deprived of a meaningful opportunity to use their challenges in selecting a jury. The lack of name and address meant that the defendants could not question neighbors and learn on their own about the prospective jurors.

The defendants relied in part on a 1936 statement of Clarence Darrow's that a juror's "nationality, his business, religion, politics, social standing, family ties, friends, habits of life and thought; the books and newspapers he likes and reads . . . [his] method of speech, the kind of clothes he wears, the style of haircut" were important subjects for questioning.

The court affirmed the convictions. United States v. Barnes, 604 F.2d 121 (2d Cir.1979), cert. denied 446 U.S. 907 (1980). The judge had grounds to fear threats of retaliation against the jury if it convicted. Because possible prejudice was explored, the court could see no added benefits from asking jurors about their own ethnic backgrounds. As to names and addresses, the defendants argued that "jurors must publicly disclose their identities and publicly take responsibility for the decisions they are about to make." The court disagreed. Jurors who fear retribution cannot be impartial. If an anonymous juror feels less pressure as the result of anonymity "this is as it should be—a factor contributing to his impartiality." As to religion, "our jury selection system was not designed to subject prospective jurors to a catechism of their tenets of faith."

Defendants are entitled to a fair and impartial jury and must have enough information to enable them to use their challenges sensibly. In this case the defendants had enough information to meet their needs. "Clarence Darrow's ideal has already yielded to what has been thought to be the greater necessity, *i.e.*, the need to streamline the *voir dire* process by resting the control of it in the district judge, [  ], subject to the demand that the essentials of the case should be the subject of inquiry." (The court noted that a federal statute required that the names and addresses of prospective jurors in capital cases be disclosed three days before trial.)

In 1987 New York State's highest court held that *Newsday*, the Long Island newspaper, had no right under the state's freedom of information law to the names and addresses of jurors in a murder case. The newspaper, whose reporter had missed the names when they were announced, argued that the names were already public. The commissioner of jurors refused to disclose the names to the reporter in order to protect the jurors' privacy and safety. Newsday, Inc. v. Sise, 71 N.Y.2d 146, 524 N.Y.S.2d 35, 518 N.E.2d 930, 14 Med.L.Rptr. 2140 (1987).

### d.  Cases Not Resulting in Convictions

When a court dismisses charges against a criminal defendant, or when a criminal defendant is found not guilty at a trial, there may be an interest in protecting the defendant from further attention by sealing records of the case.  In Globe Newspaper Co. v. Pokaski, 684 F.Supp. 1132 (D.Mass.1988), aff'd in part, rev'd in part 868 F.2d 497 (1st Cir.1989), the *Boston Globe* challenged the sealing of records in one case involving a Boston police officer who had first been found guilty of possession of cocaine (but the judge had subsequently reversed his finding after being informed that the officer would lose his job if found guilty) and a second case involving sexual offenses committed against juveniles (the newspaper asked for case files and docket sheets, not transcripts).  The court of appeals held that the Massachusetts statute permitting blanket or across-the-board restrictions on access to records of cases not resulting in convictions was unconstitutional, but it pointed out that the public has no constitutional right of access to records of cases in which a grand jury decides against indicting someone.  The decision clearly left open the possibility of sealing records in individual cases provided a court made specific, on the record findings that sealing was necessary:  only the *blanket* sealing was unconstitutional.

### e.  Videotape Evidence

The presumption of openness of court records does not necessarily extend to making copies of videotape evidence used at trials.  The Maryland Court of Special Appeals held that a Maryland trial court did not abuse its discretion when it refused to allow news media to copy a videotape that had been played in open court at a murder trial.  The tape shows the carjacking-murder victim, Pamela Basu, and her daughter getting into the car;  in the background are two males walking behind Mrs. Basu.  The prosecution alleged that the two males were the defendants.  The appellate court held that the presumption of access was overcome by the compelling governmental interest in preserving the fair trial rights of the two defendants, only the first of whom was being tried when the videotape was first admitted into evidence.  Group W Television, Inc. v. State, 96 Md.App. 712, 626 A.2d 1032, 21 Med.L.Rptr. 1697 (1993).

### 5.  SANCTIONS

Some special problems have caused courts to impose sanctions on the media.  Among those are efforts to influence judges to decide pending cases in a certain way, unauthorized revelations about confidential proceedings dealing with charges against judges (recall *Landmark*, p. 61, *supra*) and violations of prohibitions against the publication of names of juveniles accused of crimes (recall *Smith*, p. 61, *supra*).  The efforts-to-influence-judges problem has traditionally been handled by holding the perpetrator in contempt of court and imposing appropriate sanctions.

Contempt of court involves a variety of actions that substantially obstruct the administration of justice. These include disturbance of a judicial proceeding by shouting in the courtroom, willful refusal to obey a court order to pay alimony, and refusal to answer a grand jury question after a judge has ordered the witness to do so. If a court were to punish a member of the press for contempt, it would be more likely to be for disobeying an order of the court (recall *Dickinson* and *Providence Journal*, pp. 56–57, *supra*), for interfering with the administration of justice by publishing or broadcasting something prejudicial (the power is generally *not* used in such instances but might be), or for refusing to answer a question about a secret source, secret notes, etc. (see the discussion in Chapter XI on confidentiality in newsgathering).

*Limitations on the contempt power.* The power of federal courts to enforce contempt citations is based on a 1789 act by the first United States Congress establishing a federal judicial system. The statute allowed judges to punish "all contempts of authority." The statute stood until 1830 when federal Judge James H. Peck held an attorney in contempt for publishing an article criticizing him. Congress was so incensed by Peck's action that it impeached him and came within one vote of convicting him. Congress also passed a law in 1831 limiting the use of contempt power by federal judges to matters happening in the presence of the court "or so near thereto as to obstruct the administration of justice."

The meaning of "so near thereto" was unclear. Did it carry a geographical meaning—near to the courtroom—or a causal construction—closely related to the case before the court? Did the "contemptuous act" have to happen close to the judge or could it be far away but something the judge thought affected the administration of justice? The Supreme Court first chose the latter interpretation, allowing judges to punish for contempts happening outside the courtroom. Toledo Newspaper Co. v. United States, 247 U.S. 402 (1918).

In 1941, however, the Court reversed itself and held that the phrase was to be given a geographical meaning—summary contempt could be used only for happenings within or close to the courtroom. Nye v. United States, 313 U.S. 33 (1941).

In 1941 the Court began using the First Amendment to restrict the contempt power. Labor leader Harry Bridges had been held in contempt for threatening to have his dockworkers go on strike if the courts enforced a judicial order unfavorable to the union. In a second case decided by the Court as part of the *Bridges* decision, the *Los Angeles Times* had been held in contempt for editorials a state court believed were aimed at influencing the outcome of certain decisions it was to make. The Supreme Court ruled that the contempt power could be used against published or spoken comments made outside the courtroom only when they presented a "clear and present danger" of obstructing justice. Bridges v. California, 314 U.S. 252, 1 Med.L.Rptr. 1275 (1941).

The newspaper editorial had said that a judge would "make a serious mistake if he granted probation to" two Teamsters accused of assaulting non-union truck drivers. The majority said that given the newspaper's well-known hostility toward unions, "it is inconceivable that any judge in Los Angeles would expect anything but adverse criticism from it in the event probation were granted. Yet such criticism after final disposition of the proceedings would clearly have been privileged." The four dissenters stressed that the judge in question was facing reelection in a year and that the editorial "was hardly an exercise in futility."

The Court reiterated this stance in Pennekamp v. Florida, 328 U.S. 331, 1 Med.L.Rptr. 1294 (1946). *Miami Herald* editorials accusing the Dade County judges of coddling criminals had been based on incorrect statements. In overturning the contempt citation against the paper's editor, the Supreme Court said that the editorials did not present "a clear and present danger to the fair administration of justice in Florida." The errors were inconsequential, said the Court, in the face of a commitment to free and open discussion of the judiciary.

A year later, in Craig v. Harney, 331 U.S. 367, 1 Med.L.Rptr. 1310 (1947), the Court was confronted with another contempt citation against a paper that had criticized a judge during a trial. A lay judge was conducting a trial in which a landlord, claiming non-payment of rent, sought to regain possession of a building from a tenant who at the time was overseas in the armed forces. The judge directed the jury to find for the landlord. Twice the jury returned a verdict for the tenant, and the judge refused to accept it. The third time the jury complied but stated that it was acting against its conscience. Two days later the tenant's attorney moved for a new trial. During the jury's recalcitrance and the pendency of the motion for new trial, the newspaper published several articles and an editorial. The judge denied the motion for a new trial. He then adjudged petitioners in contempt of court for the publications and sentenced each to jail for three days. The Supreme Court reversed:

> The only substantial question raised pertains to the editorial. It called the judge's refusal to hear both sides "high handed," a "travesty on justice," and the reason that public opinion was "outraged." It said that his ruling properly "brought down the wrath of public opinion upon his head" since a serviceman "seems to be getting a raw deal." The fact that there was no appeal from his decision to a "judge who is familiar with proper procedure and able to interpret and weigh motions and arguments by opposing counsel and to make his decisions accordingly" was a "tragedy." It deplored the fact that the judge was a "layman" and not a "competent attorney." It concluded that the "first rule of justice" was to give both sides an opportunity to be heard and when that rule was "repudiated," there was "no way of knowing whether justice was done."

This was strong language, intemperate language, and, we assume, an unfair criticism. But a judge may not hold in contempt one "who ventures to publish anything that tends to make him unpopular or to belittle him . . .." [  ] The vehemence of the language used is not alone the measure of the power to punish for contempt. The fires which it kindles must constitute an imminent, not merely a likely, threat to the administration of justice. The danger must not be remote or even probable; it must immediately imperil.

. . . [T]he law of contempt is not made for the protection of judges who may be sensitive to the winds of public opinion. Judges are supposed to be men of fortitude, able to thrive in a hardy climate. . . .

. . . Judges who stand for reelection run on their records. That may be a rugged environment. Criticism is expected. Discussion of their conduct is appropriate, if not necessary. The fact that the discussion at this particular point of time was not in good taste falls far short of meeting the clear and present danger test.

## 6. RESTRICTIONS ON CAMERAS AND OTHER EQUIPMENT

When Bruno Hauptmann was brought to trial for kidnapping and slaying the son of Charles and Anne Morrow Lindbergh in 1932, journalists and photographers packed the courtroom. Hauptmann, found guilty and sentenced to death, may not have gotten a fair trial because of the adverse publicity. In response, the American Bar Association adopted Canon 35 in 1937.

Although ABA canons have no effect of their own, the Judicial Conference of the United States (an organization of the country's federal judges) and most state courts adopted similar rules, thus effectively banning broadcasting and still cameras from almost all courts for several decades. Colorado and Texas were exceptions, and a Texas case presented the Supreme Court with the issue for the first time.

In Estes v. Texas, 381 U.S. 532, 1 Med.L.Rptr. 1187 (1965), defendant had been indicted in the Texas state courts for "swindling"— inducing farmers to buy nonexistent fertilizer tanks and then to deliver to him mortgages on the properties. The nature of the charges and the large sums of money involved, attracted nationwide interest. Over defendant's objection, the trial judge permitted televising of a two-day hearing before trial.

The Supreme Court reversed, 5–4, and upset the conviction. In his majority opinion Justice Clark concluded that the use of television at the trial involved "such a probability that prejudice will result that it is deemed inherently lacking in due process" even without any showing of specific prejudices. He was concerned about the impact on jurors, judges, parties, witnesses and lawyers.

Justice Harlan, who provided the crucial fifth vote for reversal, joined the majority opinion only to the extent that it applied to televised coverage of "courtroom proceedings of a criminal trial of widespread public interest," "a criminal trial of great notoriety" and "a heavily publicized and highly sensational affair." In such cases he was worried about the impact on jurors.

In Chandler v. Florida, 449 U.S. 560, 7 Med.L.Rptr. 1041 (1981), the Court unanimously rejected the view that televising a criminal trial over the objections of the defendant automatically rendered the trial unfair. (In Florida, only the consent of the trial judge is required to allow a trial to be televised.) The defendants had argued that the impact of television on the participants introduced potentially prejudicial but unidentifiable aspects into the trial. The majority, in an opinion by Chief Justice Burger, first concluded that *Estes* did not stand for the proposition that broadcasting was barred "in all cases and under all circumstances." Because of Justice Harlan's narrow views in that case, the ruling in *Estes* should apply only to cases of widespread interest. (On this point, two Justices insisted that *Chandler* overruled *Estes* and should say so.)

Then, Chief Justice Burger continued that the risk of prejudice from press coverage of a trial was not limited to broadcasting. "The risk of juror prejudice in some cases does not justify an absolute ban on news coverage of trials by the printed media; so also the risk of such prejudice does not warrant an absolute constitutional ban on all broadcast coverage." A case attracts attention because of its intrinsic interest to the public. The "appropriate safeguard" against prejudice in such cases "is the defendant's right to demonstrate that the media's coverage of his case—be it printed or broadcast—compromised the ability of the particular jury that heard the case to adjudicate fairly." The Court also observed that the changes in technology since *Estes* supported the state's argument it now be permitted to allow television in the courtroom.

Because the defendants in *Chandler*—two former city policemen accused of burglarizing a restaurant—showed no adverse impact from the television, the convictions were upheld.

Notice that this case involved criminal defendants attacking their convictions. The case did not involve a First Amendment claim by broadcasters claiming a right to bring their equipment into the courtroom in a state that barred such entry. The Court did not discuss the impact of *Richmond Newspapers* or other First Amendment cases. As of the time *Chandler* was decided, over half the states were permitting television in the courtroom either on an experimental basis or on a permanent basis after a successful experiment had ended. In many of these states, the consent of a criminal defendant was required before entry could be allowed. Many states that barred entry or required consent of a party before entry have continued their practices after *Chandler*.

In 1987 Virginia and New York became the 44th and 45th states to permit cameras and recording equipment in trial courts, both on an experimental basis. Despite support from New York's governor and chief judge, the second phase of the New York experiment ended without agreement on permanent rules. In 1992 the legislature narrowly approved a third experimental phase to expire on Jan. 31, 1995. The third phase, viewed as "watered down" by some media observers, contains a provision under which some witnesses in criminal trials have their faces electronically obscured during testimony. The "experiment" could be extended indefinitely. New York Times, June 9, 1992 at B–4.

A three-year experiment with photographic and electronic media coverage of civil proceedings in federal courts began July 1, 1991, and is scheduled to end June 30, 1994. Approval of the experiment by the U.S. Judicial Conference was for two federal appeals courts and up to six federal district courts. The appeals courts chosen were the U.S. Circuit Courts of Appeals in New York and San Francisco. The district courts chosen were those in the Southern District of New York (New York City), the Western District of Washington (Seattle), the Eastern District of Pennsylvania (Philadelphia), the District of Massachusetts (Boston), the Eastern District of Michigan (Detroit, Ann Arbor, Bay City, Flint and Fort Huron), and the Southern District of Indiana (Indianapolis, Evansville, Muncie, New Albany and Terre Haute). Broadcasting, Dec. 31, 1990 at 70. The participating courts have the discretion to refuse, limit or terminate media coverage "in the interests of justice." As with similar state experiments, there are guidelines for behavior and equipment. When more than one media representative requests permission to cover a proceeding, pooling will be required.

The justices of the Supreme Court of the United States have made few public comments about the possibility of television in their court, despite the fact that Chief Justice Rehnquist, during the Senate hearing on his nomination as Chief Justice, said he would give "sympathetic consideration" to a request for broadcast coverage of the court. The newest Supreme Court justice, Ruth Bader Ginsburg, told the Senate Judiciary Committee during her confirmation hearings that she does not "see any problem with having [court] proceedings televised. It would be good for the public." Broadcasting & Cable, July 26, 1993 at 120.

One manifestation of the public interest in observing court trials is the success of the Courtroom Television Network, "Court TV," estimated by Nielsen Media Research now to reach 10.6 million subscribing households. The network announced in 1993 that it plans an hour-long weekly radio show featuring audio highlights of trial testimony, interviews and listener calls. The latter project is being done with WABC–FM in New York City. Broadcasting & Cable, June 7, 1993 at 92 and July 12, 1993 at 43.

*The Nixon Tapes in the Courts.* As we will see later, the saga of the Nixon tapes reached its first significant stage when the Supreme Court ordered the then President to honor a subpoena from the Watergate special prosecutor to deliver tapes of a large group of conversations for use in the so-called Watergate trial. United States v. Nixon, 418 U.S.

683 (1974). In 1974 Congress passed the Presidential Recordings and Materials Preservation Act, directing the Administrator of General Services to take custody of the former President's tapes and documents. The Administrator was directed to submit to Congress regulations governing access to Presidential materials of historical value. That act was upheld in Nixon v. Administrator of General Services, 433 U.S. 425, 2 Med.L.Rptr. 2025 (1977). That was chapter two.

The third episode took shape during the Watergate trial. The tape reels obtained from the President were played in the judge's chambers before trial. Some conversations were declared irrelevant or privileged and were not reproduced. The other conversations were rerecorded on new tapes designated Copy A for the district court and Copy B for the special prosecutor. Some but not all of the conversations on Copy A were admitted into evidence. Some but not all of these were played to the jury. Some were played in full; others only in part. "Deletions were effected not by modifying the exhibit itself, but by skipping deleted portions on the tape or by interrupting the sound transmission to the jurors' headphones." Written transcripts of the conversations being played to the jurors were provided to the jurors and others in the court—all of whom heard the tapes over headphones.

During the trial broadcasters approached Judge Sirica to obtain copies of the 22 hours of tapes played to the jury. After extensive proceedings, he denied the request for immediate access to the tapes on the ground that the convicted defendants had appeals pending and release of the tapes might prejudice their rights.

The court of appeals reversed, relying on the importance of the common law privilege of inspecting and copying judicial records. The fear of prejudice to the defendants did not outweigh the public's right to access.

The Supreme Court reversed the court of appeals. Nixon v. Warner Communications, Inc., 435 U.S. 589, 3 Med.L.Rptr. 2074 (1978). Justice Powell, writing for the majority, began by discussing the asserted common law right to inspect judicial records. Although he found some case support, the right was not absolute. "Every court has supervisory power over its own records and files and access has been denied where court files might have become a vehicle for improper purposes." Common law rights to inspect had given way in cases in which the record might be used to "gratify private spite or promote public scandal" as in divorce cases; where the record contained libelous statements; and where the record contained "business information that might harm a litigant's competitive standing." Although he thought the cases showed that the decision was "one best left to the sound discretion of the trial court," Justice Powell was willing to assume that some right to inspect the tapes existed.

The Court then reviewed Nixon's arguments against disclosure. First, he argued that he had a property interest in his voice that the broadcasters should not be allowed to exploit for commercial gain.

Second, he asserted a right of privacy. (The court of appeals had rejected that argument on the grounds that the passage of the Presidential Recordings Act contemplated release of the tapes at some time and that presidential documents are not subject to ordinary privacy claims. The broadcasters added that the privacy claim was overridden by the fact that the tapes would provide added understanding with the nuances and inflections. Nixon disagreed on the ground that out of 22 hours of tapes, broadcasters and record makers would use fractions, necessarily taken out of context.) Third, Nixon argued that United States v. Nixon authorized use of the tapes only for the trial since they were obtained from a third party. Finally, he argued that it would be unseemly for the courts to "facilitate the commercialization" of the tapes for presentation "at cocktail parties" or in "comedy acts or dramatic productions." Justice Powell continued:

> At this point, we normally would be faced with the task of weighing the interests advanced by the parties in light of the public interest and the duty of the courts.[14] On respondents' side of the scales is the incremental gain in public understanding of an immensely important historical occurrence that arguably would flow from the release of aural copies of these tapes, a gain said to be not inconsequential despite the already widespread dissemination of printed transcripts. Also on respondents' side is the presumption—however gauged—in favor of public access to judicial records. On petitioner's side are the arguments identified above, which must be assessed in the context of court custody of the tapes. Underlying each of petitioner's arguments is the crucial fact that respondents require a court's cooperation in furthering their commercial plans. The court—as custodian of tapes obtained by subpoena over the opposition of a sitting President, solely to satisfy "fundamental demands of due process of law in the fair administration of criminal justice," United States v. Nixon, 418 U.S., at 713—has a responsibility to exercise an informed discretion as to release of the tapes, with a sensitive appreciation of the circumstances that led to their production. This responsibility does not permit copying upon demand. Otherwise, there would exist a danger that the court could become a partner in the use of the subpoenaed material "to gratify private spite or promote public scandal." [  ], with no corresponding assurance of public benefit.

Having set the stage, Justice Powell announced that the Court need not decide the case because of a "unique element that was neither advanced by the parties nor given appropriate consideration by the courts below." Although the parties argued that the Presidential Recordings Act did not cover these tapes, the Court found a Congressional intent to create an administrative procedure for processing all the Nixon documents, including these recordings. (Why might each party have

---

**14.** Judge Sirica's principal reason for refusing to release the tapes—fairness to the defendants, who were appealing their convictions—is no longer a consideration. All appeals have been resolved.

argued against the Act's relevance?) "The presence of an alternative means of public access tips the scales in favor of denying release." Questions concerning the regulations prepared by the Administrator of General Services were reserved "for future consideration in appropriate proceedings."

The broadcasters argued that even the presence of the Act could not destroy their constitutional claims to inspect the documents. First, the broadcasters relied on *Cox Broadcasting*, p. 212, *supra*, which barred damage liability against a broadcaster that named a rape victim whose name was obtained from official court records. The broadcasters argued that this gave them a right to copy anything displayed in open court. Justice Powell disagreed: the case gave the press only the right to copy records "open to the public." Here, reporters heard the tapes and were given transcripts, and could comment on each. *Cox Broadcasting* did not require that copies of the tapes "to which the public has never had *physical* access" be made available for copying. "The First Amendment generally grants the press no right to information about a trial superior to that of the general public."

In their second constitutional argument, the broadcasters relied on the Sixth Amendment's guarantee of a public trial, asserting that public understanding of the trial is incomplete if the public cannot hear the tapes that the jury heard. Justice Powell thought this proved too much—because it would require recording testimony of live witnesses at trials. Also, the guarantee is to avoid the use of "courts as instruments of persecution" and confers no special benefit on the press. Finally, the right to public trial does not require that the trial be broadcast or recorded for the public. The requirement "is satisfied by the opportunity of members of the public and the press to attend the trial and to report what they have observed. [ ] That opportunity abundantly existed here."

Although the lower court decision favoring the broadcasters was reversed, the Court did not decide how the district court should dispose of the tapes. Justices White and Brennan dissented in part on the reading of the Recordings Act and would have ordered the tapes delivered immediately to the Administrator. Justices Marshall and Stevens, in separate opinions, would have affirmed the court of appeals.

The Watergate tapes continue to be the subject of litigation. In 1993, a federal judge stopped all release of Nixon's Watergate tapes until the National Archives returns recordings of strictly private conversations to Nixon. The ruling could delay release of the tapes for another five to 10 years. Of 4,000 hours of Nixon White House tapes, only 63 hours have been released to the public thus far. The New York Times, Aug. 10, 1993 at A–14.

# Chapter XI

# CONFIDENTIALITY IN NEWSGATHERING

As we saw in the last chapter, the role journalists play as *observers* of the administration of justice is of considerable concern to the courts. The judiciary must also be concerned with the role journalists may play as *participants* in the legal process when the press has, or is thought to have, evidence relevant to a legal proceeding. Constitutional guarantees of a fair trial are meant to allow the parties a complete, objective hearing on the issues. A complete hearing may require full access to all relevant evidence—including that possessed by journalists. What if a journalist refuses to divulge certain information that may be pertinent to a case? What about photographs in a newspaper's file that shed light on an incident being considered by a court? Should the paper supply the photographs so that all relevant information is before the judge and jury, or should freedom of the press also be considered? Answers to these questions, and others to be discussed in this section, will affect the completeness of the information a court has before it when it makes decisions affecting litigants' finances, freedom and even their lives.

Journalists traditionally have sought recognition of a special privilege not to have to reveal their confidential sources, even when the identity of the source is part of the evidence sought by a court, a grand jury or a legislative committee, but confidential sources are just part of a larger problem. In addition to being asked to reveal sources, journalists have been asked for their notes, for documents and other evidence which they obtained in the course of newsgathering, for unpublished materials (negatives of photos not used, outtakes of television productions, etc.), and for testimony as to their thoughts during the newsgathering and editing processes. In addition, there have been attempts to gather evidence by police searches of newsrooms or by obtaining reporters' travel records or telephone records in an attempt to deduce their sources.

## A. JOURNALIST'S PRIVILEGE

### 1. THE ROLE OF CONFIDENTIALITY

It has been generally accepted that persons thought to have relevant information may be subpoenaed to testify as witnesses at certain governmental proceedings. Nevertheless, some relationships have been held to give rise to "privileges" permitting a party to withhold information he has learned in a confidential relationship. The most venerable of these relationships have been those of physician and patient, lawyer and client, and priest and penitent. In each of these the recipient may be prevented

517

by the source from testifying as to information learned in confidence in that professional capacity.

Under common law, an assertion by journalists of a similar privilege from testifying was generally rejected.  Critics of a privilege for journalists sometimes point out that professionals in medicine and law typically must meet certain educational requirements, be certified to practice and be subject to disciplinary action if they fail to adhere to professional standards.  Journalists, on the other hand, have no minimum education requirement, require no certification or license to be journalists and are not subject to the same kinds of peer review to which doctors and lawyers are subject.  So long as freedom of the press belongs to everyone, not just to a few licensed to be journalists, professional standards are difficult to police.  Although one likes to believe that the vast majority of journalists are ethical and truthful, such incidents as that involving the Janet Cooke Pulitzer Prize-winning story on the juvenile heroin addict (who turned out not to be a real child) in the *Washington Post* attract public attention and are sometimes pointed to by critics of a privilege for journalists.

Despite the rejection of the privilege at common law, it has made headway as a statutory protection.  Since the first reporter's privilege statute was enacted in Maryland in 1896, 28 states have enacted so-called "shield" laws.  They are Alabama, Alaska, Arizona, Arkansas, California, Colorado, Delaware, Georgia, Illinois, Indiana, Kentucky, Louisiana, Maryland, Michigan, Minnesota, Montana, Nebraska, Nevada, New Jersey, New Mexico, New York, North Dakota, Ohio, Oklahoma, Oregon, Pennsylvania, Rhode Island and Tennessee.  As we shall see, these statutes may have limited utility in certain situations.

In states without privilege statutes, reporters before 1958 tried, with little success, to claim such a privilege under common law.  Then columnist Marie Torre tried a different approach.  She had reported that a CBS executive had made certain disparaging remarks about Judy Garland.  Garland sued CBS for defamation and sought by deposition to get Torre to identify the particular executive.  Torre attacked the effort as a threat to freedom of the press, refused to answer the question and asserted that the First Amendment protected her refusal.  The court, though seeing some constitutional implications, held that even if the First Amendment were to provide some protection, the reporter must testify when the information sought goes to the "heart" of the plaintiff's claim.  Garland v. Torre, 259 F.2d 545, 1 Med.L.Rptr. 2541 (2d Cir.), cert. denied 358 U.S. 910 (1958).  Torre ultimately served 10 days in jail for criminal contempt.

After *Garland* reporters continued to assert First Amendment claims, still with little success.  In the late 1960s the situation became more serious as the federal government began to serve subpoenas on reporters more frequently.  The media asserted that this made previously willing sources of information unwilling because of fear that the courts would not protect the reporter or the source and reporters would violate confidences when pressed by the government.

This raised an empirical question about the effect of subpoenas on the flow of information. Professor Vince Blasi explored this in a study that pursued three paths. First he conducted 47 interviews with reporters and editors of newspapers in seven large cities. Second, he sent a questionnaire to 67 reporters familiar with the subpoena problem. The questionnaire was designed to elicit "qualitative" rather than "quantitative" information. Finally, he sent 1,470 questionnaires to reporters on large newspapers, editors of underground papers, news magazine and broadcasting journalists. Before he could publish the results, the Supreme Court announced that it would review three cases dealing with reporters' subpoenas. Branzburg v. Hayes, p. 521, *infra*. In the following excerpts, Professor Blasi summarized his general empirical conclusions.

## THE NEWSMAN'S PRIVILEGE: AN EMPIRICAL STUDY
### Vince Blasi.
70 Michigan Law Review 229, 231–232, 284 (1971).

The three cases on the Court's docket all concern one variant of the press subpoena problem: a grand jury's effort to acquire from a reporter information about possible law violations committed by his news sources. While this is currently the most common posture in which the issue presents itself, one must take cognizance of many other manifestations of the controversy before deciding what general principles, let alone detailed standards, ought to govern press subpoena disputes. Congressional committees, such as the panel that was looking into the CBS documentary *The Selling of the Pentagon* may wish to subpoena newsmen to scrutinize the accuracy and balance of certain reporting efforts. Criminal defendants have an explicit sixth amendment right to compel the attendance of witnesses in their favor; this right may at times conflict with the reporter's interest in honoring confidences with sources, such as police officers or prosecutors, who may have given the reporter information that would be helpful to the defense. On occasion, information in the hands of newsmen might enable the police to prevent future crimes or to apprehend fugitive felons. Some journalistic endeavors border on criminal activity, such as participation in acts of demonstrative vandalism or receiving stolen documents. . . . These and other situations raise considerations that are not present in the cases that are currently before the Court, and that may call for a quite different reconciliation of the conflicting interests.

. . .

The results of a wide-ranging empirical study of the sort that I have undertaken cannot be telescoped into a tidy conclusion. Nevertheless, it may be useful for me to identify those findings and impressions that I regard as the most important and the most interesting. They are as follows: (1) good reporters use confidential source relationships mainly for the assessment and verification opportunities that such relationships afford rather than for the purpose of gaining access to highly sensitive information of a newsworthy character; (2) the adverse impact of the subpoena threat has been primarily in "poisoning the atmosphere" so as to make insightful, interpretive reporting more difficult rather than in causing sources to "dry up" completely; (3) understandings of confidentiality in reporter-source relationships are frequently unstated and imprecise; (4) press subpoenas damage source relationships primarily by compromising the reporter's independent or compatriot status in the eyes of sources rather than by forcing the revelation of sensitive information; (5) only one segment of the journalism profession, characterized by certain reporting traits (emphasis on interpretation and verification) more than type of beat, has been adversely affected by the subpoena threat; (6) reporters feel very strongly that any resolution of their conflicting ethical obligations to sources and to society should be a matter for personal rather than judicial determination, and in consonance with this belief these reporters evince a high level of asserted willingness to testify voluntarily and also a very high level of asserted willingness to go to jail if necessary to honor what they perceive to be their obligation of confidentiality; (7) newsmen prefer a flexible ad hoc qualified privilege to an inflexible per se qualified privilege; (8) newsmen regard protection for the *identity* of anonymous sources as more important than protection for the *contents* of confidential information given by known sources; (9) newsmen object most of all to the frequency with which press subpoenas have been issued in what these reporters regard as unnecessary circumstances when they have no important information to contribute; and (10) newsmen fear that an outright rejection by the Supreme Court of any sort of newsman's privilege would "poison the atmosphere" considerably and thus they regard the symbolic aspect of the current constitutional litigation to be of the utmost importance.

## 2. THE SUPREME COURT CONSIDERS THE PRIVILEGE

The first Supreme Court case to consider whether the First Amendment supports privileges claimed by reporters involved grand jury testimony. A grand jury is a group of citizens who receive evidence of alleged crimes brought to them by the prosecutor. If the grand jury believes that this evidence, uncontroverted by the accused, would justify conviction, it will return an "indictment"—a formal accusation of crime. This will set the criminal prosecution in operation. The Fifth Amendment to the United States Constitution provides that no one be brought to trial for "a capital, or otherwise infamous crime" unless first indicted by a grand jury. States need not, and some do not, use grand juries. (Where the grand jury is not used, the prosecutor instead files an "information" against the accused to get the case started.) Grand juries are able to subpoena witnesses, and all testimony before grand juries is to be kept secret. In part, this confidentiality requirement is to prevent a stigma from attaching to those whom the grand jury refuses to indict.

## BRANZBURG v. HAYES

(Together with In re Pappas and United States v. Caldwell.).

Supreme Court of the United States, 1972.

408 U.S. 665, 92 S.Ct. 2646, 33 L.Ed.2d 626, 1 Med.L.Rptr. 2617.

[This group of cases involved demands on three reporters by grand juries. In *Branzburg,* the reporter wrote a newspaper article about persons supposedly using a chemical process to change marijuana into hashish. He was called before a grand jury and directed to identify the two individuals. He refused and sought an order from the Kentucky Court of Appeals prohibiting the trial judge from insisting that he answer the questions. He based his claim on both the Kentucky privilege statute and the First Amendment. The court of appeals construed the statute to protect a reporter who refused to divulge the identity of an informant who supplied him with information but not to protect the silence of a reporter about his personal observations. Constitutional arguments were rejected.

In a second episode, Branzburg wrote a story after interviewing drug users and watching some of them smoking marijuana. He was again subpoenaed before a grand jury; but before he was due to appear, he again asked the Kentucky Court of Appeals to prevent the grand jury from forcing him to appear. Again the court denied his requested relief.

In *Pappas,* a Massachusetts television reporter recorded and photographed statements of local Black Panther Party officials during a period of racial turmoil. He was allowed to enter the Party's headquarters to cover an expected police raid in return for his promise to disclose nothing he observed within. He stayed three hours, no raid occurred, and he wrote no story. He was summoned before the county grand jury but refused to answer any questions about what had taken place while he was there. When he was recalled, he moved to quash the second summons. The motion was denied by the trial judge, who noted the absence of a statutory journalist's privilege in Massachusetts and denied the existence of a constitutional privilege. The Supreme Judicial Court of Massachusetts affirmed.

In the third case, Caldwell had been assigned by the *New York Times* to cover the Black Panther Party and other black militant groups. He was subpoenaed to appear before a federal grand jury and to bring with him notes and tape recordings of interviews given to him for publication by officers and spokesmen of the Black Panther Party concerning aims, purposes and activities of the group. The court held that in the absence of a compelling showing of need by the prosecution, Caldwell need not even appear before the grand jury, much less answer its questions.]

Opinion of the Court by MR. JUSTICE WHITE, announced by the CHIEF JUSTICE [BURGER].

. . .

## II

. . . Although the newsmen in these cases do not claim an absolute privilege against official interrogation in all circumstances, they assert that the reporter should not be forced either to appear or to testify before a grand jury or at trial until and unless sufficient grounds are shown for believing that the reporter possesses information relevant to a crime the grand jury is investigating, that the information the reporter has is unavailable from other sources, and that the need for the information is sufficiently compelling to override the claimed invasion of First Amendment interests occasioned by the disclosure. Principally relied upon are prior cases emphasizing the importance of the First Amendment guarantees to individual development and to our system of representative government, decisions requiring that official action with adverse impact on First Amendment rights be justified by a public interest that is "compelling" or "paramount," and those precedents establishing the principle that justifiable governmental goals may not be achieved by unduly broad means having an unnecessary impact on protected rights of speech, press, or association. The heart of the claim is that the burden on news gathering resulting from compelling reporters to disclose confidential information outweighs any public interest in obtaining the information.

We do not question the significance of free speech, press, or assembly to the country's welfare. Nor is it suggested that news gathering does not qualify for First Amendment protection; without some protection for seeking out the news, freedom of the press could be eviscerated. But these cases involve no intrusions upon speech or assembly, no prior restraint or restriction on what the press may publish, and no express or implied command that the press publish what it prefers to withhold. No exaction or tax for the privilege of publishing, and no penalty, civil or criminal, related to the content of published material is at issue here. The use of confidential sources by the press is not forbidden or restricted; reporters remain free to seek news from any source by means within the law. No attempt is made to require the press to publish its sources of information or indiscriminately to disclose them on request.

The sole issue before us is the obligation of reporters to respond to grand jury subpoenas as other citizens do and to answer questions relevant to an investigation into the commission of crime. Citizens generally are not constitutionally immune from grand jury subpoenas; and neither the First Amendment nor any other constitutional provision protects the average citizen from disclosing to a grand jury information that he has received in confidence. . . .

It is clear that the First Amendment does not invalidate every incidental burdening of the press that may result from the enforcement of civil or criminal statutes of general applicability. Under prior cases, otherwise valid laws serving substantial public interests may be enforced against the press as against others, despite the possible burden that may be imposed. [The Court here referred to taxation, labor and antitrust cases we will discuss in Chapter XIII.]

. . .

It has generally been held that the First Amendment does not guarantee the press a constitutional right of special access to information not available to the public generally. Zemel v. Rusk, 381 U.S. 1, 16–17 (1965); [ ]. In Zemel v. Rusk, supra, for example, the Court sustained the Government's refusal to validate passports to Cuba even though that restriction "render[ed] less than wholly free the flow of information concerning that country." Id., at 16. The ban on travel was held constitutional, for "[t]he right to speak and publish does not carry with it the unrestrained right to gather information." Id., at 17.[22]

Despite the fact that news gathering may be hampered, the press is regularly excluded from grand jury proceedings, our own conferences, the meetings of other official bodies gathered in executive session, and the meetings of private organizations. Newsmen have no constitutional right of access to the scenes of crime or disaster when the general public is excluded, and they may be prohibited from attending or publishing information about trials if such restrictions are necessary to assure a defendant a fair trial before an impartial tribunal. . . .

It is thus not surprising that the great weight of authority is that newsmen are not exempt from the normal duty of appearing before a grand jury and answering questions relevant to a criminal investigation. At common law, courts consistently refused to recognize the existence of any privilege authorizing a newsman to refuse to reveal confidential information to a grand jury. . . .

The prevailing constitutional view of the newsman's privilege is very much rooted in the ancient role of the grand jury that has the dual function of determining if there is probable cause to believe that a crime has been committed and of protecting citizens against unfounded criminal prosecutions. Grand jury proceedings are constitutionally mandated for the institution of federal criminal prosecutions for capital or other serious crimes. . . . The Fifth Amendment provides that "[n]o person shall be held to answer for a capital, or otherwise infamous crime, unless on a presentment or indictment of a Grand Jury." . . . Although state systems of criminal procedure differ greatly among themselves, the grand jury is similarly guaranteed by many state constitutions and plays an important role in fair and effective law enforcement in the overwhelming majority of the States. Because its task is to inquire into the existence of possible criminal conduct and to return only well-founded indictments, its investigative powers are necessarily broad.

. . .

22. "There are few restrictions on action which could not be clothed by ingenious argument in the garb of decreased data flow. For example, the prohibition of unauthorized entry into the White House diminishes the citizen's opportunities to gather information he might find relevant to his opinion on the way the country is being run, but that does not make entry into the White House a First Amendment right." 381 U.S., at 16–17.

A number of States have provided newsmen a statutory privilege of varying breadth, but the majority have not done so, and none has been provided by federal statute. Until now the only testimonial privilege for unofficial witnesses that is rooted in the Federal Constitution is the Fifth Amendment privilege against compelled self-incrimination. We are asked to create another by interpreting the First Amendment to grant newsmen a testimonial privilege that other citizens do not enjoy. This we decline to do.[29] Fair and effective law enforcement aimed at providing security for the person and property of the individual is a fundamental function of government, and the grand jury plays an important, constitutionally mandated role in this process. On the records now before us, we perceive no basis for holding that the public interest in law enforcement and in ensuring effective grand jury proceedings is insufficient to override the consequential, but uncertain, burden on news gathering that is said to result from insisting that reporters, like other citizens, respond to relevant questions put to them in the course of a valid grand jury investigation or criminal trial.

. . .

. . . It would be frivolous to assert—and no one does in these cases—that the First Amendment, in the interest of securing news or otherwise, confers a license on either the reporter or his news sources to violate valid criminal laws. Although stealing documents or private wiretapping could provide newsworthy information, neither reporter nor source is immune from conviction for such conduct, whatever the impact on the flow of news. Neither is immune, on First Amendment grounds, from testifying against the other, before the grand jury or at a criminal trial. . . .

Thus, we cannot seriously entertain the notion that the First Amendment protects a newsman's agreement to conceal the criminal conduct of his source, or evidence thereof, on the theory that it is better to write about crime than to do something about it. . . .

There remain those situations where a source is not engaged in criminal conduct but has information suggesting illegal conduct by others. Newsmen frequently receive information from such sources pursuant to a tacit or express agreement to withhold the source's name and suppress any information that the source wishes not published. . . .

The argument that the flow of news will be diminished by compelling reporters to aid the grand jury in a criminal investigation is not irrational, nor are the records before us silent on the matter. But we remain unclear how often and to what extent informers are actually deterred from furnishing information when newsmen are forced to testify before a grand jury. The available data indicate that some newsmen rely a great deal on confidential sources and that some informants are particularly sensitive to the threat of exposure and may

**29.** The creation of new testimonial privileges has been met with disfavor by commentators since such privileges obstruct the search for truth. . . .

be silenced if it is held by this Court that, ordinarily, newsmen must testify pursuant to subpoenas, but the evidence fails to demonstrate that there would be a significant constriction of the flow of news to the public if this Court reaffirms the prior common-law and constitutional rule regarding the testimonial obligations of newsmen. Estimates of the inhibiting effect of such subpoenas on the willingness of informants to make disclosures to newsmen are widely divergent and to a great extent speculative.[32] It would be difficult to canvass the views of the informants themselves; surveys of reporters on this topic are chiefly opinions of predicted informant behavior and must be viewed in the light of the professional self-interest of the interviewees.[33] Reliance by the press on confidential informants does not mean that all such sources will in fact dry up because of the later possible appearance of the newsman before a grand jury. The reporter may never be called and if he objects to testifying, the prosecution may not insist. . . . Moreover, grand juries characteristically conduct secret proceedings, and law enforcement officers are themselves experienced in dealing with informers, and have their own methods for protecting them without interference with the effective administration of justice. . . .

. . .

We are admonished that refusal to provide a First Amendment reporter's privilege will undermine the freedom of the press to collect and disseminate news. But this is not the lesson history teaches us. As noted previously, the common law recognized no such privilege, and the constitutional argument was not even asserted until 1958. From the beginning of our country the press has operated without constitutional protection for press informants and the press has flourished. The existing constitutional rules have not been a serious obstacle to either the development or retention of confidential news sources by the press.

It is said that currently press subpoenas have multiplied, that mutual distrust and tension between press and officialdom have increased, that reporting styles have changed, and that there is now more

---

**32.** Cf. e.g., the results of a study conducted by Guest & Stanzler, which appears as an appendix to their article, [64 Nw. U.L.Rev. 18]. A number of editors of daily newspapers of varying circulation were asked the question, "Excluding one- or two-sentence gossip items, on the average how many stories based on information received in confidence are published in your paper each year? Very rough estimate." Answers varied significantly, e.g., "Virtually innumerable," Tucson Daily Citizen (41,969 daily circ.), "Too many to remember," Los Angeles Herald–Examiner (718,221 daily circ.), "Occasionally," Denver Post (252,084 daily circ.), "Rarely," Cleveland Plain Dealer (370,499 daily circ.), "Very rare, some politics," Oregon Journal (146,403 daily circ.). This study did not purport to mea-

sure the extent of deterrence of informants caused by subpoenas to the press.

**33.** In his Press Subpoenas: An Empirical and Legal Analysis, Study Report of the Reporters' Committee on Freedom of the Press 6–12, Prof. Vince Blasi discusses these methodological problems. Prof. Blasi's survey found that slightly more than half of the 975 reporters questioned said that they relied on regular confidential sources for at least 10% of their stories. Id., at 21. Of this group of reporters, only 8% were able to say with some certainty that their professional functioning had been adversely affected by the threat of subpoena; another 11% were not certain whether or not they had been adversely affected. Id., at 53.

need for confidential sources, particularly where the press seeks news about minority cultural and political groups or dissident organizations suspicious of the law and public officials. These developments, even if true, are treacherous grounds for a far-reaching interpretation of the First Amendment fastening a nationwide rule on courts, grand juries, and prosecuting officials everywhere. . . .

. . .

The privilege claimed here is conditional, not absolute; given the suggested preliminary showings and compelling need, the reporter would be required to testify. Presumably, such a rule would reduce the instances in which reporters could be required to appear, but predicting in advance when and in what circumstances they could be compelled to do so would be difficult. Such a rule would also have implications for the issuance of compulsory process to reporters at civil and criminal trials and at legislative hearings. If newsmen's confidential sources are as sensitive as they are claimed to be, the prospect of being unmasked whenever a judge determines the situation justifies it is hardly a satisfactory solution to the problem. For them it would appear that only an absolute privilege would suffice.

We are unwilling to embark the judiciary on a long and difficult journey to such an uncertain destination. The administration of a constitutional newsman's privilege would present practical and conceptual difficulties of a high order. Sooner or later, it would be necessary to define those categories of newsmen who qualified for the privilege, a questionable procedure in light of the traditional doctrine that liberty of the press is the right of the lonely pamphleteer who uses carbon paper or a mimeograph just as much as of the large metropolitan publisher who utilizes the latest photocomposition methods. . . . The informative function asserted by representatives of the organized press in the present cases is also performed by lecturers, political pollsters, novelists, academic researchers, and dramatists. Almost any author may quite accurately assert that he is contributing to the flow of information to the public, that he relies on confidential sources of information, and that these sources will be silenced if he is forced to make disclosures before a grand jury.

. . .

Thus, in the end, by considering whether enforcement of a particular law served a "compelling" governmental interest, the courts would be inextricably involved in distinguishing between the value of enforcing different criminal laws. By requiring testimony from a reporter in investigations involving some crimes but not in others, they would be making a value judgment that a legislature had declined to make since in each case the criminal law involved would represent a considered legislative judgment, not constitutionally suspect, of what conduct is liable to criminal prosecution. The task of judges, like other officials outside the legislative branch, is not to make the law but to uphold it in accordance with their oaths.

At the federal level, Congress has freedom to determine whether a statutory newsman's privilege is necessary and desirable and to fashion standards and rules as narrow or broad as deemed necessary to deal with the evil discerned and, equally important, to refashion those rules as experience from time to time may dictate. There is also merit in leaving state legislatures free, within First Amendment limits, to fashion their own standards in light of the conditions and problems with respect to the relations between law enforcement officials and press in their own areas. It goes without saying, of course, that we are powerless to bar state courts from responding in their own way and construing their own constitutions so as to recognize a newsman's privilege, either qualified or absolute.

In addition, there is much force in the pragmatic view that the press has at its disposal powerful mechanisms of communication and is far from helpless to protect itself from harassment or substantial harm. . . .

Finally, as we have earlier indicated, news gathering is not without its First Amendment protections, and grand jury investigations if instituted or conducted other than in good faith, would pose wholly different issues for resolution under the First Amendment. Official harassment of the press undertaken not for purposes of law enforcement but to disrupt a reporter's relationship with his news sources would have no justification. Grand juries are subject to judicial control and subpoenas to motions to quash. We do not expect courts will forget that grand juries must operate within the limits of the First Amendment as well as the Fifth.

## III

We turn, therefore, to the disposition of the cases before us. From what we have said, it necessarily follows that the decision in United States v. Caldwell, must be reversed. . . .

The decisions in Branzburg v. Hayes and Branzburg v. Meigs must be affirmed. . . . In both cases, if what petitioner wrote was true, he had direct information to provide the grand jury concerning the commission of serious crimes.

The only question presented at the present time in In re Pappas is whether petitioner Pappas must appear before the grand jury to testify pursuant to subpoena. . . . We affirm the decision of the Massachusetts Supreme Judicial Court and hold that petitioner must appear before the grand jury to answer the questions put to him, subject, of course, to the supervision of the presiding judge as to "the propriety, purposes, and scope of the grand jury inquiry and the pertinence of the probable testimony." [  ]

So ordered.

Mr. Justice Powell, concurring.

I add this brief statement to emphasize what seems to me to be the limited nature of the Court's holding. The Court does not hold that newsmen, subpoenaed to testify before a grand jury, are without constitutional rights with respect to the gathering of news or in safeguarding their sources. Certainly, we do not hold, as suggested in Mr. Justice Stewart's dissenting opinion, that state and federal authorities are free to "annex" the news media as "an investigative arm of government." The solicitude repeatedly shown by this Court for First Amendment freedoms should be sufficient assurance against any such effort, even if one seriously believed that the media—properly free and untrammeled in the fullest sense of these terms—were not able to protect themselves.

As indicated in the concluding portion of the opinion, the Court states that no harassment of newsmen will be tolerated. If a newsman believes that the grand jury investigation is not being conducted in good faith he is not without remedy. Indeed, if the newsman is called upon to give information bearing only a remote and tenuous relationship to the subject of the investigation, or if he has some other reason to believe that his testimony implicates confidential source relationships without a legitimate need of law enforcement, he will have access to the court on a motion to quash and an appropriate protective order may be entered. The asserted claim to privilege should be judged on its facts by the striking of a proper balance between freedom of the press and the obligation of all citizens to give relevant testimony with respect to criminal conduct. The balance of these vital constitutional and societal interests on a case-by-case basis accords with the tried and traditional way of adjudicating such questions.*

In short, the courts will be available to newsmen under circumstances where legitimate First Amendment interests require protection.

MR. JUSTICE DOUGLAS, dissenting in United States v. Caldwell [and the other two cases].

.   .   .

It is my view that there is no "compelling need" that can be shown which qualifies the reporter's immunity from appearing or testifying before a grand jury, unless the reporter himself is implicated in a crime. His immunity in my view is therefore quite complete, for absent his

---

* It is to be remembered that Caldwell asserts a constitutional privilege not even to appear before the grand jury unless a court decides that the Government has made a showing that meets the three preconditions specified in the dissenting opinion of Mr. Justice Stewart. To be sure, this would require a "balancing" of interests by the court, but under circumstances and constraints significantly different from the balancing that will be appropriate under the court's decision. The newsman witness, like all other witnesses, will have to appear; he will not be in a position to litigate at the threshold the State's very authority to subpoena him. Moreover, absent the constitutional preconditions that Caldwell and that dissenting opinion would impose as heavy burdens of proof to be carried by the State, the court—when called upon to protect a newsman from improper or prejudicial questioning—would be free to balance the competing interests on their merits in the particular case. The new constitutional rule endorsed by that dissenting opinion would, as a practical matter, defeat such a fair balancing and the essential societal interest in the detection and prosecution of crime would be heavily subordinated.

involvement in a crime, the First Amendment protects him against an appearance before a grand jury and if he is involved in a crime, the Fifth Amendment stands as a barrier. Since in my view there is no area of inquiry not protected by a privilege, the reporter need not appear for the futile purpose of invoking one to each question. . . .

The starting point for decision pretty well marks the range within which the end result lies. The New York Times, whose reporting functions are at issue here, takes the amazing position that First Amendment rights are to be balanced against other needs or conveniences of government. My belief is that all of the "balancing" was done by those who wrote the Bill of Rights. By casting the First Amendment in absolute terms, they repudiated the timid, watered-down, emasculated versions of the First Amendment which both the Government and the New York Times advance in the case.

. . .

The press has a preferred position in our constitutional scheme, not to enable it to make money, not to set newsmen apart as a favored class, but to bring fulfillment to the public's right to know. The right to know is crucial to the governing powers of the people, to paraphrase Alexander Meiklejohn. Knowledge is essential to informed decisions.

. . .

MR. JUSTICE STEWART, with whom MR. JUSTICE BRENNAN and MR. JUSTICE MARSHALL, join, dissenting.

The Court's crabbed view of the First Amendment reflects a disturbing insensitivity to the critical role of an independent press in our society. The question whether a reporter has a constitutional right to a confidential relationship with his source is of first impression here, but the principles that should guide our decision are as basic as any to be found in the Constitution. While Mr. Justice Powell's enigmatic concurring opinion gives some hope of a more flexible view in the future, the Court in these cases holds that a newsman has no First Amendment right to protect his sources when called before a grand jury. The Court thus invites state and federal authorities to undermine the historic independence of the press by attempting to annex the journalistic profession as an investigative arm of government. Not only will this decision impair performance of the press' constitutionally protected functions, but it will, I am convinced, in the long run harm rather than help the administration of justice.

I respectfully dissent.

I

The reporter's constitutional right to a confidential relationship with his source stems from the broad societal interest in a full and free flow of information to the public. . . .

Enlightened choice by an informed citizenry is the basic ideal upon which an open society is premised,[3] and a free press is thus indispensable to a free society.   Not only does the press enhance personal self-fulfillment by providing the people with the widest possible range of fact and opinion, but it also is an incontestable precondition of self-government.   . . .   As private and public aggregations of power burgeon in size and the pressures for conformity necessarily mount, there is obviously a continuing need for an independent press to disseminate a robust variety of information and opinion through reportage, investigation, and criticism, if we are to preserve our constitutional tradition of maximizing freedom of choice by encouraging diversity of expression.

### A

In keeping with this tradition, we have held that the right to publish is central to the First Amendment and basic to the existence of constitutional democracy.   [   ]

. . .

No less important to the news dissemination process is the gathering of information.   News must not be unnecessarily cut off at its source, for without freedom to acquire information the right to publish would be impermissibly compromised.   Accordingly, a right to gather news, of some dimensions, must exist.   . . .

### B

The right to gather news implies, in turn, a right to a confidential relationship between a reporter and his source.   This proposition follows as a matter of simple logic once three factual predicates are recognized: (1) newsmen require informants to gather news;  (2) confidentiality—the promise or understanding that names or certain aspects of communications will be kept off the record—is essential to the creation and maintenance of a news-gathering relationship with informants;  and (3) an unbridled subpoena power—the absence of a constitutional right protecting, in *any* way, a confidential relationship from compulsory process—will either deter sources from divulging information or deter reporters from gathering and publishing information.

It is obvious that informants are necessary to the news-gathering process as we know it today.   If it is to perform its constitutional mission, the press must do far more than merely print public statements or publish prepared handouts.   Familiarity with the people and circumstances involved in the myriad background activities that result in the final product called "news" is vital to complete and responsible journalism, unless the press is to be a captive mouthpiece of "newsmakers."

It is equally obvious that the promise of confidentiality may be a necessary prerequisite to a productive relationship between a newsman

**3.**  See generally Z. Chafee, Free Speech in the United States (1941); A. Meiklejohn, Free Speech and Its Relation to Self-Gov-  ernment (1948);  T. Emerson, Toward a General Theory of the First Amendment (1963).

and his informants.  An officeholder may fear his superior; a member of the bureaucracy, his associates; a dissident, the scorn of majority opinion.  All may have information valuable to the public discourse, yet each may be willing to relate that information only in confidence to a reporter whom he trusts, either because of excessive caution or because of a reasonable fear of reprisals or censure for unorthodox views.  The First Amendment concern must not be with the motives of any particular news source, but rather with the conditions in which informants of all shades of the spectrum may make information available through the press to the public.  [  ]

In *Caldwell,* the District Court found that "confidential relationships . . . are commonly developed and maintained by professional journalists, and are indispensable to their work of gathering, analyzing and publishing the news."  Commentators and individual reporters have repeatedly noted the importance of confidentiality.  And surveys among reporters and editors indicate that the promise of nondisclosure is necessary for many types of news gathering.

Finally, and most important, when governmental officials possess an unchecked power to compel newsmen to disclose information received in confidence, sources will clearly be deterred from giving information, and reporters will clearly be deterred from publishing it, because uncertainty about exercise of the power will lead to "self-censorship."  [  ]  The uncertainty arises, of course, because the judiciary has traditionally imposed virtually no limitations on the grand jury's broad investigatory powers.  [  ]

After today's decision, the potential informant can never be sure that his identity or off-the-record communications will not subsequently be revealed through the compelled testimony of a newsman.  A public-spirited person inside government, who is not implicated in any crime, will now be fearful of revealing corruption or other governmental wrongdoing, because he will now know he can subsequently be identified by use of compulsory process.  The potential source must, therefore, choose between risking exposure by giving information or avoiding the risk by remaining silent.

The reporter must speculate about whether contact with a controversial source or publication of controversial material will lead to a subpoena.  In the event of a subpoena, under today's decision, the newsman will know that he must choose between being punished for contempt if he refuses to testify, or violating his profession's ethics [10] and impairing his resourcefulness as a reporter if he discloses confidential information.

.  .  .

---

10.  The American Newspaper Guild has adopted the following rule as part of the newsman's code of ethics: "[N]ewspapermen shall refuse to reveal confidences or disclose sources of confidential information in court or before other judicial or investigating bodies."  G. Bird & F. Merwin, The Press and Society 592 (1971).

The impairment of the flow of news cannot, of course, be proved with scientific precision, as the Court seems to demand. Obviously, not every news-gathering relationship requires confidentiality. And it is difficult to pinpoint precisely how many relationships do require a promise or understanding of nondisclosure. But we have never before demanded that First Amendment rights rest on elaborate empirical studies demonstrating beyond any conceivable doubt that deterrent effects exist; we have never before required proof of the exact number of people potentially affected by governmental action, who would actually be dissuaded from engaging in First Amendment activity.

. . .

To require any greater burden of proof is to shirk our duty to protect values securely embedded in the Constitution. We cannot await an unequivocal—and therefore unattainable—imprimatur from empirical studies.[19] We can and must accept the evidence developed in the record, and elsewhere, that overwhelmingly supports the premise that deterrence will occur with regularity in important types of news-gathering relationships.

Thus, we cannot escape the conclusion that when neither the reporter nor his source can rely on the shield of confidentiality against unrestrained use of the grand jury's subpoena power, valuable information will not be published and the public dialogue will inevitably be impoverished.

## II

Posed against the First Amendment's protection of the newsman's confidential relationships in these cases is society's interest in the use of the grand jury to administer justice fairly and effectively. The grand jury serves two important functions: "to examine into the commission of crimes" and "to stand between the prosecutor and the accused, and to determine whether the charge was founded upon credible testimony or was dictated by malice or personal ill will." Hale v. Henkel, 201 U.S. 43, 59. And to perform these functions the grand jury must have available to it every man's relevant evidence. [ ]

Yet the longstanding rule making every person's evidence available to the grand jury is not absolute. The rule has been limited by the Fifth Amendment, the Fourth Amendment, and the evidentiary privileges of the common law. . . . And in United States v. Bryan, 339 U.S. 323, the Court observed that any exemption from the duty to testify before

---

**19.** Empirical studies, after all, can only provide facts. It is the duty of courts to give legal significance to facts; and it is the special duty of this Court to understand the constitutional significance of facts. We must often proceed in a state of less than perfect knowledge, either because the facts are murky or the methodology used in obtaining the facts is open to question. It is then that we must look to the Constitution for the values that inform our presumptions. And the importance to our society of the full flow of information to the public has buttressed this Court's historic presumption in favor of First Amendment values.

the grand jury "presupposes a very real interest to be protected." Id., at 332.

Such an interest must surely be the First Amendment protection of a confidential relationship that I have discussed above in Part I. As noted there, this protection does not exist for the purely private interests of the newsman or his informant, nor even, at bottom, for the First Amendment interests of either partner in the news-gathering relationship. Rather, it functions to insure nothing less than democratic decisionmaking through the free flow of information to the public, and it serves, thereby, to honor the "profound national commitment to the principle that debate on public issues should be uninhibited, robust, and wide-open." New York Times Co. v. Sullivan, 376 U.S., at 270.

In striking the proper balance between the public interest in the efficient administration of justice and the First Amendment guarantee of the fullest flow of information, we must begin with the basic proposition that because of their "delicate and vulnerable" nature, NAACP v. Button, 371 U.S., at 433, and their transcendent importance for the just functioning of our society, First Amendment rights require special safeguards.

A

This Court has erected such safeguards when government, by legislative investigation or other investigative means, has attempted to pierce the shield of privacy inherent in freedom of association. In no previous case have we considered the extent to which the First Amendment limits the grand jury subpoena power. . . .

. . .

Thus, when an investigation impinges on First Amendment rights, the government must not only show that the inquiry is of "compelling and overriding importance" but it must also "convincingly" demonstrate that the investigation is "substantially related" to the information sought.

Government officials must, therefore, demonstrate that the information sought is *clearly* relevant to a *precisely* defined subject of governmental inquiry. [  ] They must demonstrate that it is reasonable to think the witness in question has that information. [  ] And they must show that there is not any means of obtaining the information less destructive of First Amendment liberties. [  ]

These requirements, which we have recognized in decisions involving legislative and executive investigations, serve established policies reflected in numerous First Amendment decisions arising in other contexts. . . .

I believe the safeguards developed in our decisions involving governmental investigations must apply to the grand jury inquiries in these cases. Surely the function of the grand jury to aid in the enforcement of the law is no more important than the function of the legislature, and its committees, to make the law.  . . .

Accordingly, when a reporter is asked to appear before a grand jury and reveal confidences, I would hold that the government must (1) show that there is probable cause to believe that the newsman has information that is clearly relevant to a specific probable violation of law;  (2) demonstrate that the information sought cannot be obtained by alternative means less destructive of First Amendment rights;  and (3) demonstrate a compelling and overriding interest in the information.

This is not to say that a grand jury could not issue a subpoena until such a showing were made, and it is not to say that a newsman would be in any way privileged to ignore any subpoena that was issued.  Obviously, before the government's burden to make such a showing were triggered, the reporter would have to move to quash the subpoena, asserting the basis on which he considered the particular relationship a confidential one.

## B

The crux of the Court's rejection of any newsman's privilege is its observation that only "where news sources themselves are implicated in crime or possess information *relevant* to the grand jury's task need they or the reporter be concerned about grand jury subpoenas."  See ante, at 691 (emphasis supplied).  But this is a most misleading construct.  For it is obviously not true that the only persons about whom reporters will be forced to testify will be those "confidential informants involved in actual criminal conduct" and those having "information suggesting illegal conduct by others."  See ante, at 691, 693.  As noted above, given the grand jury's extraordinarily broad investigative powers and the weak standards of relevance and materiality that apply during such inquiries, reporters, if they have no testimonial privilege, will be called to give information about informants who have neither committed crimes nor have information about crime.  It is to avoid deterrence of such sources and thus to prevent needless injury to First Amendment values that I think the government must be required to show probable cause that the newsman has information that is clearly relevant to a specific probable violation of criminal law.

. . .

Both the "probable cause" and "alternative means" requirements would thus serve the vital function of mediating between the public interest in the administration of justice and the constitutional protection of the full flow of information.  . . .  No doubt the courts would be required to make some delicate judgments in working out this accommodation.  But that, after all, is the function of courts of law.  Better such judgments, however difficult, than the simplistic and stultifying absolutism adopted by the Court in denying any force to the First Amendment in these cases.

The error in the Court's absolute rejection of First Amendment interests in these cases seems to me to be most profound. For in the name of advancing the administration of justice, the Court's decision, I think, will only impair the achievement of that goal. People entrusted with law enforcement responsibility, no less than private citizens, need general information relating to controversial social problems. Obviously, press reports have great value to government, even when the newsman cannot be compelled to testify before a grand jury. The sad paradox of the Court's position is that when a grand jury may exercise an unbridled subpoena power, and sources involved in sensitive matters become fearful of disclosing information, the newsman will not only cease to be a useful grand jury witness; he will cease to investigate and publish information about issues of public import. I cannot subscribe to such an anomalous result, for, in my view, the interests protected by the First Amendment are not antagonistic to the administration of justice. Rather, they can, in the long run, only be complementary, and for that reason must be given great "breathing space." NAACP v. Button, 371 U.S., at 433.

### Notes and Questions

1. Given that Justice Powell's was the vital fifth vote that made Justice White's opinion an opinion for the Court, it becomes important to understand his position. Is Justice White's opinion based on balancing? Is it the same kind of balancing that Justice Powell calls for in his concurring opinion? Recall the different types of balancing discussed at pp. 67–68, *supra*.

2. Justice Powell suggests some grounds for protecting reporters from grand jury investigations. Does Justice White's opinion suggest the same protections?

3. In what ways do Justices Powell and Stewart disagree?

4. Justice Douglas notes with obvious dismay that the reporters did not seek "absolute" privilege. What would such a privilege have meant in this case? Why do you think such an argument was not made?

5. Justice White observes that the Court would get into "practical and conceptual difficulties of a high order" if it were to develop a constitutional privilege for newsmen. Among the problems he sees is that of having to decide who is entitled to such a privilege. Could the Supreme Court rule that the privilege belongs to reporters who work for mass media but not to "the lonely pamphleteer who uses carbon paper or a mimeograph?" What about academic researchers?

6. Professor Blasi observes that the *Branzburg* group all involved the same limited question: appearance before a grand jury investigating possible crimes. How different is a demand that a reporter testify at a trial from a demand he testify before a grand jury?

7. The Supreme Court is generally skeptical about claims of privilege. In United States v. Nixon, 418 U.S. 683 (1974), the special prosecutor served a subpoena on then President Nixon seeking certain tapes and

documents that might be relevant to the Watergate cover-up trial. The President asked the courts to have the subpoena withdrawn—or quashed—on the grounds (1) that the separation of powers doctrine precluded judicial review of the President's decision that it would not be in the public interest to disclose the contents of confidential conversations between a President and his close advisers, and (2) that as a matter of constitutional law, executive privilege prevailed over the subpoena. Although granting that the need for "complete candor and objectivity from advisers calls for great deference from the courts," the Court decided that absent a claim of "need to protect military, diplomatic, or sensitive national security secrets," the Court must weigh the competing interests to determine which should prevail:

> . . . We have elected to employ an adversary system of criminal justice in which the parties contest all issues before a court of law. The need to develop all relevant facts in the adversary system is both fundamental and comprehensive. The ends of criminal justice would be defeated if judgments were to be founded on a partial or speculative presentation of the facts. The very integrity of the judicial system and public confidence in the system depend on full disclosure of all the facts, within the framework of the rules of evidence. To ensure that justice is done, it is imperative to the function of courts that compulsory process be available for the production of evidence needed either by the prosecution or by the defense.

> Only recently the Court restated the ancient proposition of law, albeit in the context of a grand jury inquiry rather than a trial,

>> "that 'the public     . . .     has a right to every man's evidence,' except for those persons protected by a constitutional, common-law, or statutory privilege, [ ] . . .." Branzburg v. Hayes, 408 U.S. 665, 688 (1972).

> . . .

> In this case we must weigh the importance of the general privilege of confidentiality of Presidential communications in performance of his responsibilities against the inroads of such a privilege on the fair administration of criminal justice. The interest in preserving confidentiality is weighty indeed and entitled to great respect. However, we cannot conclude that advisers will be moved to temper the candor of their remarks by the infrequent occasions of disclosure because of the possibility that such conversations will be called for in the context of a criminal prosecution.

> On the other hand, the allowance of the privilege to withhold evidence that is demonstrably relevant in a criminal trial would cut deeply into the guarantee of due process of law and gravely impair the basic function of the courts. A President's acknowledged need for confidentiality in the communications of his office is general in nature, whereas the constitutional need for production of relevant evidence in a criminal proceeding is specific and central to the fair

adjudication of a particular criminal case in the administration of justice. Without access to specific facts a criminal prosecution may be totally frustrated. The President's broad interest in confidentiality of communications will not be vitiated by disclosure of a limited number of conversations preliminarily shown to have some bearing on the pending criminal cases.

8. The problem of reporter's privilege arises most frequently in the context of material that has been published without attribution to a source, but sometimes they involve other problems, such as incomplete reports or efforts to get more information. The grand jury's attempt to find out what happened inside the building in *Pappas* is an example. Sometimes "outtakes" are sought. The term outtakes usually refers to parts of film or videotape that have been cut and not shown on the air. In its broadest sense it is sometimes used to refer to unused still photographs, to parts of a written manuscript that were edited out of the final printed version, or even to notes taken by a reporter relating to information that never appeared in the published story. Are government efforts to obtain this unpublished or unrecorded information different from the more conventional effort to get a reporter to identify a source of published information? Does Justice White suggest a distinction between the two situations?

Outtakes are essential when the goal is to try to judge the fairness of what was actually presented. This was the situation when a House committee sought outtakes from the CBS program, "The Selling of the Pentagon," referred to by Blasi. Sometimes information is thrust on the media and not necessarily published or broadcast—at least in its original form. In Lewis v. United States, 517 F.2d 236 (9th Cir.1975), for example, the manager of a radio station was told to produce the original of a "communique" he received from an underground group that claimed responsibility for a bombing. He refused and was held in contempt. Does this situation differ greatly from those presented in *Branzburg?* The courts are generally less sympathetic when unsolicited information has been thrust on the media or when journalists have been eyewitnesses to an event than when the media have obtained the information after-the-fact in the course of newsgathering. For example, the Florida Supreme Court held that journalists in that state have no privilege to protect them against testifying in a court proceeding as to their eyewitness observations of a relevant event. Miami Herald Publishing Co. v. Morejon, 561 So.2d 577, 17 Med.L.Rptr. 1920 (Fla.1990).

9. States sometimes find protection for confidentiality in their own state constitutions. In O'Neill v. Oakgrove Construction, Inc., 71 N.Y.2d 521, 528 N.Y.S.2d 1, 523 N.E.2d 277, 15 Med.L.Rptr. 1219 (1988), New York State's highest court held that the Gannett Newspapers in Rochester had a qualified privilege under the state constitution and the First Amendment to decline to produce unpublished photographs of a traffic accident scene. The photographs had been sought as part of a suit by a man injured when his car slid off a roadway under construction. The

newspaper photographer had taken 58 photographs, one of which was published.

10.  The Reporters Committee for Freedom of the Press reported in 1993 on a study of subpoenas served on news organizations in 1991. The study found that, although the number of subpoenas had dropped from 4,408 in 1989 to 3,281 in 1991, news organizations continued to spend large amounts of time and money fighting the subpoenas.  More than 2,200 of the 1991 subpoenas were served on television broadcasters. Houston Chronicle, Feb. 11, 1993 at A–10, and Television Digest, March 15, 1993 at 3.

11.  Punishment of reporters who refuse to disclose information varies. Texas newspaper reporter Brian Karem spent 14 days in jail after he refused to disclose the names of confidential sources who assisted him in obtaining a jail house telephone interview with an accused murderer. The state has no shield law.  Karem had been sentenced to six months in jail and fined $500 for contempt, but he was released when his source allowed her identity to be revealed.  Med.L.Rptr. News Notes, July 17, 1990.

Subsequently, Florida newspaper reporter Tim Roche wrote a story for *The Stuart News* quoting 54 words from a sealed court order in a child custody case.  Under Florida law, court officials are required to keep child custody orders secret.  A criminal inquiry by a prosecutor led to Roche's being subpoenaed, and he refused to identify his source.  He was sentenced to 30 days in jail.  The governor of Florida offered to commute the sentence to 300 hours of community service, but Roche declined.  He served 11 days before being released early because of good behavior.  New York Times, Jan. 4, 1993 at A10, and Chicago Daily Law Bulletin, April 5, 1993 at 3.  Why would a reporter refuse such an offer by the governor?  What would you do in such a situation?  (Florida's legislature subsequently passed a bill that would have provided an absolute privilege for news reporters to refuse to disclose the identities of confidential sources in court cases or governmental investigations, but the bill was vetoed by Florida Governor Lawton Chiles, who said the bill would eliminate "vital information when the judiciary is weighing the factors, potentially obstructing efforts to obtain the truth."  His veto letter suggested that he might find a qualified privilege acceptable. Media Law Reporter News Notes, June 8, 1993.)

### 3.  SHIELD LAWS

As we have seen, journalists' claims to a common law privilege not to testify, such as that enjoyed under some circumstances by doctors, lawyers and clergy, have usually been unsuccessful.  An appeal to a First Amendment privilege was not accepted by the Supreme Court in the context of the *Branzburg* facts.  In the face of such uncertainty, and perhaps responding to the suggestion in *Branzburg,* several states passed new shield laws.  Shield laws vary in detail but generally are statutory attempts to exempt journalists from divulging certain information— usually confidential sources or the information itself. The exemption can only apply to *state* proceedings, such as state grand juries or state trials.

The state laws do not always protect as fully as journalists might like. For instance, the definition of who is a journalist and therefore protected by the law can be either narrow or broad. Should a shield law include college journalists? Annette Buchanan, editor of the University of Oregon *Daily Emerald,* was subpoenaed to reveal the source of her story about the use of marijuana on the campus. She refused and was cited for contempt. The Oregon Supreme Court upheld the contempt citation, ruling that there is no constitutional privilege, but specifically refusing to rule on who is and is not a journalist. State v. Buchanan, 250 Or. 244, 436 P.2d 729, cert. denied 392 U.S. 905 (1968).

Journalists argue that, from their viewpoint, the strongest shield law would be one that protects *all* journalists, including reporters, editors, camerapersons, temporarily unemployed or former journalists, authors of non-fiction books, and free-lancers.

Among possible limits on state shield laws is the Sixth Amendment right of defendants in criminal cases to have compulsory process to obtain witnesses in their favor. Another is the limited value of state statutes, because the reporter may be called before a federal grand jury or asked to testify in a federal court or in another state without similar protection similar to what exists in his home state.

The conflict between the Sixth Amendment rights of defendants in criminal trials and First Amendment claims to testimonial privilege is well illustrated in the Farber case.

Myron Farber, a reporter for the *New York Times*, began investigating a series of mysterious deaths that had occurred several years earlier at a hospital in New Jersey. His investigations led to a series of articles and to murder indictments against a physician. During the six-month-long murder trial, the defendant's attorney had subpoenas served on the reporter and the newspaper demanding that they produce certain documents relating to interviews with witnesses at the trial. Motions to quash the subpoenas were denied, but the trial judge did order that the documents be delivered to him for *in camera* inspection. Farber and the *Times* refused. Efforts to stay the order pending appeals were denied by the state appellate courts and Justices White and Marshall.

Farber and the *Times* refused to comply and were held in civil and criminal contempt. The civil contempt involved a fine of $5,000 per day on the *Times* and a flat $1,000 on Farber, who was sentenced to jail until he complied. The criminal penalties were $100,000 on the newspaper, and $1,000 on Farber plus six months in jail. On review, the New Jersey Supreme Court affirmed, 5–2. Matter of Farber, 78 N.J. 259, 394 A.2d 330, 4 Med.L.Rptr. 1360 (1978).

The court rejected the argument that the First Amendment protected Farber's refusal because of the need to keep newsgathering and dissemination from being substantially impaired. It concluded that *Branzburg* "squarely held that no such First Amendment right exists." "Thus we do no weighing or balancing of societal interests in reaching our determination that the First Amendment does not afford appellants the privilege they claim." Moreover, "the obligation to appear at a criminal trial on behalf of a defendant who is enforcing his Sixth Amendment rights is at least as compelling as the duty to appear before a grand jury."

The court then turned to the state shield law providing that persons employed by media are privileged to refuse to disclose "in any legal . . . proceeding . . . including, but not limited to, any court, grand jury, petit jury, . . . or elsewhere" the source of information acquired or "any news or information obtained in the course of pursuing his professional activities whether or not it is disseminated." The court found a legislative desire to protect sources and information obtained by reporters "to the greatest extent permitted" by the state and federal constitutions. Because Farber was clearly covered by the statute, the court turned to the constitutional question.

The criminal defendant argued that the right to have compulsory process for obtaining witnesses in his favor prevailed over the statute if there was a conflict. The court agreed, noting that in the Nixon tapes case, the Supreme Court ordered the President to deliver materials to the special prosecutor although the President claimed an executive privilege and the prosecutor had nothing like the Sixth Amendment to support his demand.

The court concluded that the state constitution afforded a criminal defendant the right to compel witnesses to attend and to compel the production of documents "for which he may have, or may believe he has, a legitimate need in preparing or undertaking his defense." Witnesses properly summoned must testify or produce material demanded by a properly phrased subpoena. The state constitutional provision "prevails over" the shield statute, "but in recognition of the strongly expressed legislative viewpoint favoring confidentiality, we prescribe the imposition" of some procedural safeguards.

The court directed that in similar cases in the future the reporter would be "entitled to a preliminary determination before being compelled to submit the subpoenaed materials to a trial judge." The court reiterated that this result was based on its obligation to give as much effect to the shield statute as possible consistent with the conflicting constitutional provisions. The hearing was not mandated by the First Amendment.

In such a hearing, the defendant would have to show "by a fair preponderance of the evidence, including all reasonable inferences, that there was a reasonable probability or likelihood that the information sought by the subpoena was material and relevant to his defense, that it could not be secured from any less intrusive source and that the defendant had a legitimate need to see and otherwise use it."

In Farber's case, the trial judge's failure to accord such a hearing was not error because "it is perfectly clear that on the record before him a conclusion of materiality, relevancy, unavailability of another source, as well as need was quite inescapable." The judge had been trying the case for 18 weeks. "His knowledge of the factual background and of the part Farber had played was intimate and pervasive. Perhaps most significant is the trial court's thorough awareness of appellant Farber's close association with the Prosecutor's office since a time preceding the indictment." The court then listed the claims asserted by the defendant in the criminal case and considered the role of each witness and why the defendant might want Farber's files. These included some who admitted having spoken to Farber at various times, and one who refused to speak with the defense. Since there was enough to have persuaded a trial judge to order *in camera* submission of the materials had a hearing been held before such an order, and since Farber knew of all these facts, the court concluded that the requirements for an *in camera* order had been met.

The civil and criminal contempt convictions were upheld. (The majority did not mention the fact that Farber had signed a contract to write a book about the case. That issue emerged in a federal court hearing and did not enter into the state court proceeding.)

The Supreme Court denied *certiorari sub nom.* New York Times Co. v. New Jersey, 439 U.S. 997 (1978). Justice Brennan took no part in the decision.

Farber spent several days in county jail, was then released, then returned to jail. He was released again after the jury received the murder case because he could no longer effectively comply with the court's order to turn over the documents. He spent a total of 40 days in jail. The *Times* paid civil and criminal fines totalling $285,000. After the criminal trial was over—the jury having acquitted the physician— several other pending citations for contempt of court against Farber were dismissed and the sentence for criminal contempt was suspended without probation.

After *Farber* the New Jersey Legislature amended its shield law to provide more clearly that a showing of need must be made before the reporter can be required to reveal confidential information even to the trial judge in chambers, much less the litigants. The state's supreme court twice upheld the statute shortly thereafter.

In People v. Korkala, 99 A.D.2d 161, 472 N.Y.S.2d 310, 10 Med. L.Rptr. 1355 (1984), the state sought outtakes from an interview that interviewers from CBS's "60 Minutes" had held with the defendant. CBS had broadcast 22 minutes from interviews that were said to have lasted several hours. CBS argued that the New York shield law gave reporters an absolute privilege against having to turn over such information. The court disagreed on the ground that the statute covered only cases in which the source had an expectation of confidentiality. Here the defendant had spoken only with others on the subject.

On the First Amendment issue, the court balanced and concluded that although relevance was clear, it was not yet clear that the information would actually be needed in the prosecution. That depended on the tack taken by defendant at the trial. The court ordered that the outtakes be shown to the trial judge *in camera*. If the defense had taken a turn that made delivery relevant, then the judge could have ordered production of the relevant material. CBS did not appeal further. It made the outtakes available to the judge, who viewed them in a CBS screening room. CBS asserted that if the judge were to order any material to be delivered to the prosecutor, CBS might again take legal action. N.Y. Times, Apr. 6, 1984, at 25.

A danger in this procedure is suggested by an episode involving a reporter on the *Sacramento Union* whose notes were demanded by a person accused of murder. "She refused, but allowed the judge to review a copy of them. . . . As it turned out, the judge ruled that the defense attorney was the only one capable of reviewing the notes. [The reporter] was ready to face contempt charges, but the judge avoided a showdown by turning over his copy of her notes to the defense." Feed/back, Winter 1985, at 28.

New York's highest court held that outtakes from interviews with a murder suspect were not covered by the state's shield law because the suspect was a "non-confidential" source. When Donald Bent was interviewed by WTEN–TV, Albany, in 1986, his wife had been missing for several days. Bent became a suspect after his wife's body was found in the trunk of a car, and the district attorney subpoenaed "all video tapes regarding an interview" with Bent. The majority held that the state legislature had not intended that the shield law extend to non-confidential sources. In the Matter of Knight–Ridder Broadcasting, Inc. v. Greenberg, 70 N.Y.2d 151, 518 N.Y.S.2d 595, 511 N.E.2d 1116, 14 Med.L.Rptr. 1299 (1987). The shield law was subsequently amended to provide a qualified exemption from contempt charges for journalists who fail to disclose non-confidential news sources. N.Y. Civ. Rights Law § 79–h.

### 4. OTHER CONTEXTS

#### a. Civil Cases

When we turn to civil cases, the justifications change for insisting on a reporter's testimony. Because the case is not criminal, society's interest may be less direct and no one's freedom or life is at stake. The Sixth Amendment no longer applies. Instead, a private person or group is suing for injury to person, property, privacy or reputation. What happens to the *Branzburg* rationale in this situation?

Shortly after *Branzburg* an action was brought on behalf of "all Negroes in the City of Chicago who purchased homes from approximately 60 named defendants between 1952 and 1969." The claim was that the real estate brokers had engaged in "blockbusting," a discriminatory practice that involved buying homes at low prices and reselling them at high prices. To help prove their case the plaintiffs asked a reporter, Balk, to identify the source of an article he wrote in 1962 about real estate practices in Chicago, entitled "Confessions of a Block–Buster." Although sympathetic to the plaintiffs' position, Balk refused to testify because he got the story in confidence. The trial judge's refusal to order Balk to testify was affirmed on appeal. Baker v. F. & F. Investment, 470 F.2d 778, 1 Med.L.Rptr. 2551 (2d Cir.1972).

The court read *Branzburg* as offering reporters some First Amendment protection and relied heavily on Justice Powell's statement that "these vital constitutional and societal interests" should be decided on a case-by-case basis. The court observed the great weight that Justice White gave to the role of the grand jury and to the "importance of combatting crime." Because Justice Powell suggested that for him (and also the four dissenters) situations existed in criminal cases in which the First Amendment might override the interest in disclosure of information about crime, "surely in civil cases, courts must recognize that the public interest in non-disclosure of journalists' confidential sources will often be weightier than the private interest in compelled disclosure." The court found no compelling interest in disclosure in the facts of the case because the identity of the source "simply did not go to the heart of" plaintiffs' case.

A qualified privilege also was found in Democratic National Committee v. McCord, 356 F.Supp. 1394 (D.D.C.1973). The Committee for the Re-election of the President (President Nixon's reelection committee) was defending several suits arising out of the Watergate break-in. To obtain evidence for use in the trials, the committee caused subpoenas to be issued against a number of journalists. On motions to quash the subpoenas, a federal court held that because all other means had not been used to obtain the material before requesting it from reporters, and because the Committee had not shown clearly that the material was relevant to the trials, the subpoenas should not be issued. In so ruling, the court discussed "the right of the press to gather and publish, and that of the public to receive, news from . . . ofttimes confidential sources." The court also noted that the suits in question were civil, not criminal, and that the media were not parties to the suits.

The court thus adapted to civil cases the thrust of Justice Stewart's dissent in *Branzburg*, in which he contended that three conditions be met before a journalist is forced to testify or submit material: "the government must (1) show that there is probable cause to believe that the newsman has information that is clearly relevant to a specific probable violation of law; (2) demonstrate that the information sought cannot be obtained by alternative means less destructive of First Amendment rights; and (3) demonstrate a compelling and overriding interest in the information." (See p. 534, *supra*.) A number of federal cases involving subpoenas to reporters in civil suits have followed the *McCord* approach.

## b. The Press as Plaintiff

What if the reporter is a party in the case? Syndicated columnist Jack Anderson sued several officials of the Nixon administration for conspiring to harass him. The defendants asserted that the statute of limitations had run and denied the merits of the claims. As part of their defense they asked plaintiff when and how he learned about the alleged harassment and also sought information on other aspects of his claims. Several of these questions required disclosure of confidential sources but plaintiff refused to reveal them. The judge ordered Anderson to reveal the sources on the ground that they were central to the defenses being raised:

> Here the newsman is not being obliged to disclose his sources. Plaintiff's pledge of confidentiality would have remained unchallenged had he not invoked the aid of the Court seeking compensatory and punitive damages based on his claim of conspiracy. Plaintiff is attempting to use the First Amendment simultaneously as a sword and a shield. He believes he was wronged by a conspiracy that sought to retaliate against his sources and to undermine his reliability and professional standing before the public because what he said was unpopular with the conspirators. But when those he accuses seek to defend by attempting to discover who his sources were, so that they may find out what the sources knew, their version of what they told him and how they were hurt, plaintiff says this is off limits—a forbidden area of inquiry. He cannot have it both ways. Plaintiff is not a bystander in the process but a principal. He cannot ask for justice and deny it to those he accuses.

The judge rejected Anderson's claim that the conflicting claims should be "balanced." This was "most unrealistic. Having chosen to become a litigant, the newsman is not exempt from those obligations imposed by the rule of law on all litigants." The choice was plaintiff's: reveal the sources or have the case dismissed. Anderson v. Nixon, 444 F.Supp. 1195, 3 Med.L.Rptr. 1687 (D.D.C.1978). The case was subsequently dismissed.

## c. The Media as Defendants

One complex question that cuts across several areas we have discussed is whether media defendants in defamation cases are privileged to refuse to identify confidential sources who gave them the allegedly defamatory information. The philosophy of *Sullivan* counsels that debate should be open and robust—but that the press should be liable for defamations that are deliberately or recklessly false. What if the public figure plaintiff must know the source of the story to prove that the falsehood was deliberate or reckless? On the other hand, if the plaintiff can expose confidential sources simply by the expedient of suing for libel, such sources may disappear. Is *Branzburg* relevant on this aspect of reporters' privileges?

Several courts struggled with this matter in the early and mid– 1970s. (Recall that in the Judy Garland case, the newspaper was not sued.)

Herbert v. Lando, 441 U.S. 153, 4 Med.L.Rptr. 2575 (1979). The case raised the issue of what types of questions the plaintiff could ask the media defendants before the trial. The normal rule in civil cases is that any evidence that would be admissible at the trial may be obtained by "discovery" beforehand—usually either by deposition (oral testimony given by a prospective witness with only the lawyers for the sides present) or by interrogatories (written answers to written questions). This exchange of information allows the parties to know the strengths and weaknesses of their cases and avoids surprises at trial.

Lt. Col. Anthony Herbert, an admitted public figure, sued the producer and reporter of the television program "60 Minutes" and the CBS network for remarks on the program about his behavior while in military service in Vietnam. During his deposition, Lando, the producer, generally responded but he refused to answer some questions about why he made certain investigations and not others; what he concluded about the honesty of certain people he interviewed for the program; and about conversations he had with Mike Wallace, the reporter, in the preparation of the program segment. Lando contended that these thought processes and internal editorial discussions were protected from disclosure by the First Amendment. The Supreme Court disagreed.

Justice White, for the Court, began by observing that liability for defamation was "well established in the common law when the First Amendment was adopted" and the framers showed no intention of abolishing it. During the period before *New York Times,* mental processes and attitudes were often relevant on questions of conditional privilege and defendants often testified to their good faith in writing a story. "Courts have traditionally admitted any direct or indirect evidence relevant to the state of mind of the defendant and necessary to defeat a privilege" or to justify punitive damages in egregious cases.

Justice White understood the defendants to be arguing that "the defendant's reckless disregard of truth, a critical element, could not be shown by direct evidence through inquiry into the thoughts, opinions and conclusions of the publisher but could be proved only by objective evidence from which the ultimate fact could be inferred." This was a barrier of some substance "particularly when defendants themselves are prone to assert their good-faith belief in the truth of their publications, and libel plaintiffs are required to prove knowing or reckless falsehood with 'convincing clarity.' "

Justice White concluded that permitting plaintiffs "to prove their cases by direct as well as indirect evidence is consistent with the balance struck by our prior decisions." He "found it difficult to believe that error-avoiding procedures will be terminated or stifled simply because there is liability for culpable error and because the editorial process will itself be examined in the tiny percentage of instances in which error is claimed and litigation ensues."

Justice White did note that pretrial discovery techniques had led to "mushrooming litigation costs" but this was happening in all areas of litigation. Until major changes in pretrial procedures were developed for all cases, the Court would rely on "what in fact and in law are ample powers of the district judge to prevent abuse." (In this case, Lando's deposition had continued intermittently for over a year and filled nearly 3,000 pages.) Trial judges, who indirectly supervise these procedures, were reminded that discovery should be allowed only for "relevant" evidence.

These cases present two different questions. The first is when may courts order journalists to reveal confidential sources. It is highly unlikely that any court will allow a person to sue a newspaper for libel and then immediately learn all the confidential sources that were involved in the creation of the story. Much more likely, whether under state law or the First Amendment, courts will require the plaintiff to show his need for the information. The role the source played in the story's development and the article will be crucial.

The second question is what sanction should be imposed on a defendant who refuses to obey an order to disclose the identity of its confidential sources. Since *Herbert*, a few state and lower federal courts have begun to address both questions.

In Miller v. Transamerican Press, Inc., 621 F.2d 721, 6 Med.L.Rptr. 1598, reh'g denied 628 F.2d 932, 6 Med.L.Rptr. 2252 (5th Cir.1980), the court read the *Times* sequence of cases, *Branzburg* and *Herbert* to create a First Amendment privilege:

> . . . *Herbert* held that the press had no First Amendment privilege against discovery of mental processes where the discovery was for the purpose of determining whether malice existed.
>
> The policies supporting a First Amendment privilege would appear to be stronger here, where a defamation plaintiff seeks to compel disclosure of the name of a confidential informant, than they were in either *Branzburg* or *Herbert.* In *Herbert,* the Supreme Court reasoned that requiring disclosure of journalists' thought processes would have no chilling effect on the editorial process; the only effect would be to deter recklessness. However, forced disclosure of journalists' sources might deter informants from giving their stories to newsmen, except anonymously. This might cause the press to face the unwelcome alternatives of not publishing because of the inherent unreliability of anonymous tips, or publishing anonymous tips and becoming vulnerable to charges of recklessness.
>
> Similarly, there is a more apparent interest in protecting the confidentiality of journalists' sources in libel cases than in grand

jury proceedings. In *Branzburg,* the prosecutor had an interest in keeping the informant's identity secret in order to protect him from reprisal. The government and the press had a similar purpose, both were ferreting out wrongdoing and seeking to correct it. In a libel case, the plaintiff and the press are on opposite sides. And a defamed plaintiff might relish an opportunity to retaliate against the informant.

          . . .

A final First Amendment consideration, in a case involving a public figure, is that it will often be possible to establish malice or lack of malice without disclosure of the identity of the informant. A plaintiff may be able to find other evidence of malice, or a defendant may be able to come forward with sufficient evidence of prudence in printing which would carry the burden in support of a motion for summary judgment.

The privilege, however, was not absolute. The court drew on a passage in *Herbert:* "Evidentiary privileges in litigation are not favored, and even those rooted in the Constitution must give way in proper circumstances." In *Transamerican Press,* the facts indicated that (1) the identity was relevant; (2) the plaintiff had exhausted other efforts to obtain the information; and (3) on balance, after considering other fact situations, the plaintiff's need to learn the identity was compelling. The source was central to the defendant's story and plaintiff could not prove the required type of falsity without knowing the source's identity. In addition, plaintiff must present "substantial evidence" that the statement "is both factually untrue and defamatory."

After ordering the defendant to reveal the source, the court observed the judge "should protect the informant by restricting the information about the informant's identity to counsel and requiring that it be used strictly for the litigation." Is this likely to induce disclosure?

In another case, Downing v. Monitor Publishing Co., 120 N.H. 383, 415 A.2d 683, 6 Med.L.Rptr. 1193 (1980), the court refused to require the plaintiff to prove the statement false before the defendant had to disclose the source. Plaintiff need only "satisfy the trial court that he has evidence to establish that there is a genuine issue of fact regarding" falsity. Then the court anticipated the question of what should happen if the defendant refused to disclose the source:

We come to the question of enforcement of the court's order. Of course, the trial court is free to exercise its contempt power to enforce its order. We are aware, however, that most media personnel have refused to obey court orders to disclose, electing to go to jail instead. Confining newsmen to jail in no way aids the plaintiff in proving his case. Although we do not say that the contempt power should not be exercised, we do say that something more is required to protect the rights of a libel plaintiff. Therefore, we hold that when a defendant in a libel action, brought by a plaintiff who is required to prove actual malice under *New York Times,* refuses to declare his sources of information upon a valid order of the court, there shall arise a presumption that the defendant had no source. This presumption may be removed by a disclosure of the sources a reasonable time before trial. Because such a disclosure may, for the press, be similar to the disclosure of a "trade secret," there may be circumstances under which an appropriate order limiting outside access to the informant's name when disclosed would not be improper.

In one highly publicized case a trial judge, to punish the defendant for refusal to reveal the source, ordered all of the defendant's defenses to be struck—and awarded judgment for plaintiff. On appeal, the state's highest court reversed. First, it doubted the need for the identity of the source, which apparently only told the newspaper where the relevant information could be found. But even if the order to disclose was valid, the appropriate remedy for disobedience was to tailor the sanction to those aspects of the case in which plaintiff was hampered by the defendant's refusal to disclose the essential information. Sierra Life Insurance Co. v. Magic Valley Newspapers, 101 Idaho 795, 623 P.2d 103, 6 Med.L.Rptr. 1769 (1980).

The results in these cases appear to permit the defendant who refuses to obey an order still to prevail on the truth-falsity issue, or to prove that the damages claimed were not caused by the defamation.

State shield laws may affect this question if they directly create a testimonial privilege for reporters that extends to cases where the reporter is a party. Otherwise, even the most elaborate shield statutes will not be used in libel cases. California's version states: "A . . . reporter . . . cannot be adjudged in contempt by a judicial . . . body . . . for refusing to disclose . . . the source of any information procured . . .."

### d. Identifying Violators of Judicial Orders

Another issue of privilege arises when a judge or a grand jury wants to learn who told a reporter information that was supposed to be secret. The problem is illustrated by the case of the late William Farr, a newspaper reporter who covered the Charles Manson trial in Los Angeles. To reduce potentially prejudicial publicity in that case, the trial judge ordered the attorneys and certain others not to speak about specific phases of the case. Farr reported certain facts that he could only have learned from a person covered by the judge's order. The judge demanded that Farr identify his source despite the California privilege statute: "A publisher, editor, reporter . . . cannot be adjudged in contempt by a court . . . for refusing to disclose the source of any information procured for publication and published in a newspaper . . .." Farr stated that the information had come from forbidden sources including two of the six attorneys. Each attorney denied having been a source. The judge again asked Farr to identify the individuals. Farr refused and was held in contempt.

The statute was held inapplicable because the legislature had no power to prohibit the court from seeking to preserve the integrity of its own operations. The legislature's efforts to immunize persons from punishment for violation of court orders, violated the separation of powers. To immunize Farr "would severely impair the trial court's discharge of a constitutionally compelled duty to control its own officers. The trial court was enjoined by controlling precedent of the United States Supreme Court to take reasonable action to protect the defendants in the Manson case from the effects of prejudicial publicity." Farr v. Superior Court, 22 Cal.App.3d 60, 99 Cal.Rptr. 342, 1 Med.L.Rptr. 2545 (1971). The Supreme Court of California denied a hearing, and the Supreme Court of the United States denied *certiorari* 409 U.S. 1011 (1972).

In a later proceeding Farr argued that a contempt citation upon him was essentially a sentence of imprisonment for life because he clearly would not comply. The court noted that an order committing a person until he complies with a court order is "coercive and not penal in nature." The purpose of this sanction is not to punish but to obtain compliance with the order. Where an individual demonstrates conclusively that the coercion will fail, the contempt power becomes penal and comes within a five-day maximum sentence set by California statute. The case was remanded to determine whether coercion could be justified. In re Farr, 36 Cal.App.3d 577, 111 Cal.Rptr. 649 (1974).

*Farr* was followed by Rosato v. Superior Court, 51 Cal.App.3d 190, 124 Cal.Rptr. 427, 1 Med.L.Rptr. 2560 (1975), in which four employees of the *Fresno Bee* were ordered to testify about how they obtained a copy of a grand jury report that had been ordered sealed. The reporters' privilege did not apply to questions directed at learning whether persons under the court's sealing order had violated it. A hearing was denied in the state supreme court, and a petition for *certiorari* was denied 427 U.S. 912 (1976). Two reporters and two editors served 15 days in jail. The judge then held a hearing and concluded that they would not testify. They were found in criminal contempt, sentenced to five-day terms, given credit for time served and released.

### e. Disclosing Information to Other Bodies

Not only do courts ask journalists for information, so do legislatures and administrative agencies. In 1971 the House of Representatives Commerce Committee subpoenaed then-CBS president Frank Stanton, ordering him to produce portions of film shot for, but not shown on, the documentary "The Selling of the Pentagon." When Stanton refused to give the "outtakes" to the Committee, it voted 25–13 to recommend that Congress issue a contempt citation. The House refused to do so.

Later, Daniel Schorr, a former CBS journalist, obtained a copy of a "secret" report of the House Intelligence Committee concerning the Central Intelligence Agency. He gave the report to the *Village Voice*, which published it in 1976.  When asked by the House Ethics Committee to name the person from whom he received the report, Schorr declined. The Committee did not vote to ask for a contempt citation.

In Massachusetts a television reporter prepared a story on alleged misconduct by a state judge.  The state Commission on Judicial Conduct allowed the judge to prepare a defense by asking the reporter to identify those to whom he spoke.  Upon his refusal, he was held in contempt. Justice Brennan of the Supreme Court of the United States, acting as Circuit Justice, stayed the imposition of the contempt citation.  He pointed to the four dissents and Justice Powell's concurrence in *Branzburg* to suggest "at least a limited First Amendment right to resist intrusion into newsgatherers' confidences."  He believed that at least four Justices would vote to hear the case on appeal.  In re Roche, 448 U.S. 1312, 6 Med.L.Rptr. 1551 (1980).  The Massachusetts Supreme Judicial Court, however, citing *Branzburg*, subsequently affirmed the contempt order.  In re Roche, 381 Mass. 624, 411 N.E.2d 466, 6 Med.L.Rptr. 2121 (1980).

The potential for a press-Congress confrontation was created when *Newsday*'s Timothy Phelps and National Public Radio's Nina Totenberg reported Professor Anita Hill's previously-confidential allegations about then-Supreme-Court-nominee Clarence Thomas in October 1991.  A nearly five-month investigation to try to determine who leaked the accusation of sexual harassment failed to identify the person(s) who made the unauthorized disclosures.  Special Counsel Peter E. Fleming subpoenaed Phelps and Totenberg, both of whom refused to answer questions.  He sought the support of leaders of the Senate Rules Committee, but they declined to take any action—such as a contempt citation—to try to force the reporters to testify.  New York Times, May 6, 1992 at A18.

### f.  The Breach of Contract Problem

A Minnesota case presents a different problem.  Thus far we have been primarily concerned with protecting the rights of journalists, but sources may also want to be protected.  In Cohen v. Cowles Media Company, a source who had been promised confidentiality sued two newspapers after he was publicly identified.

### COHEN v. COWLES MEDIA COMPANY
Supreme Court of the United States, 1991.
501 U.S. ___, 111 S.Ct. 2513, 115 L.Ed.2d 586,
18 Med.L.Rptr. 2273.

JUSTICE WHITE delivered the opinion of the Court.

The question before us is whether the First Amendment prohibits a plaintiff from recovering damages, under state promissory estoppel law, for a newspaper's breach of a promise of confidentiality given to the plaintiff in exchange for information.  We hold that it does not.

During the closing days of the 1982 Minnesota gubernatorial race, Dan Cohen, an active Republican associated with Wheelock Whitney's Independent–Republican gubernatorial campaign, approached reporters from the St. Paul Pioneer Press Dispatch (Pioneer Press) and the Minneapolis Star and Tribune (Star Tribune) and offered to provide documents relating to a candidate in the upcoming election. Cohen made clear to the reporters that he would provide the information only if he was given a promise of confidentiality. Reporters from both papers promised to keep Cohen's identity anonymous and Cohen turned over copies of two public court records concerning Marlene Johnson, the Democratic–Farmer–Labor candidate for Lieutenant Governor. The first record indicated that Johnson had been charged in 1969 with three counts of unlawful assembly, and the second that she had been convicted in 1970 of petit theft. Both newspapers interviewed Johnson for her explanation and one reporter tracked down the person who had found the records for Cohen. As it turned out, the unlawful assembly charges arose out of Johnson's participation in a protest of an alleged failure to hire minority workers on municipal construction projects and the charges were eventually dismissed. The petit theft conviction was for leaving a store without paying for $6.00 worth of sewing materials. The incident apparently occurred at a time during which Johnson was emotionally distraught, and the conviction was later vacated.

After consultation and debate, the editorial staffs of the two newspapers independently decided to publish Cohen's name as part of their stories concerning Johnson. In their stories, both papers identified Cohen as the source of the court records, indicated his connection to the Whitney campaign, and included denials by Whitney campaign officials of any role in the matter. The same day the stories appeared, Cohen was fired by his employer.

Cohen sued respondents, the publishers of the Pioneer Press and Star Tribune, in Minnesota state court, alleging fraudulent misrepresentation and breach of contract. The trial court rejected respondents' argument that the First Amendment barred Cohen's lawsuit. A jury returned a verdict in Cohen's favor, awarding him $200,000 in compensatory damages and $500,000 in punitive damages. The Minnesota Court of Appeals, in a split decision, reversed the award of punitive damages after concluding that Cohen had failed to establish a fraud claim, the only claim which would support such an award. 445 N.W.2d 248, 260 (Minn.App.1989). However, the court upheld the finding of liability for breach of contract and the $200,000 compensatory damage award. Id., at 262.

A divided Minnesota Supreme Court reversed the compensatory damages award. [ ] After affirming the Court of Appeals' determination that Cohen had not established a claim for fraudulent misrepresentation, the court considered his breach of contract claim and concluded that "a contract cause of action is inappropriate for these particular circumstances." [ ] The court then went on to address the question whether Cohen could establish a cause of action under Minnesota law on a promissory estoppel theory. Apparently, a promissory estoppel theory was never tried to the jury, nor briefed, nor argued by the parties; it first arose during oral argument in the Minnesota Supreme Court when one of the justices asked a question about equitable estoppel. [  ]

In addressing the promissory estoppel question, the court decided that the most problematic element in establishing such a cause of action here was whether injustice could be avoided only by enforcing the promise of confidentiality made to Cohen. The court stated the "[u]nder a promissory estoppel analysis there can be no neutrality towards the First Amendment. In deciding whether it would be unjust not to enforce the promise, the court must necessarily weigh the same considerations that are weighed for whether the First Amendment has been violated. The court must balance the interest in protecting a promise of anonymity." [  ] After a brief discussion, the court concluded that "in this case enforcement of the promise of confidentiality under a promissory estoppel theory would violate defendants' First Amendment rights." [  ]

We granted certiorari to consider the First Amendment implications of this case. [  ]

Respondents initially contend that the Court should dismiss this case without reaching the merits because the promissory estoppel theory was not argued or presented in the courts below and because the Minnesota Supreme Court's decision rests entirely on the interpretation of state law. These contentions do not merit extended discussion. It is irrelevant to this Court's jurisdiction whether a party raised below and argued a federal-law issue that the state supreme court actually considered and decided. [  ] Moreover, that the Minnesota Supreme Court rested its holding on federal law could not be made more clear than by its conclusion that "in this case enforcement of the promise of confidentiality under a promissory estoppel theory would violate defendants' First Amendment rights." [  ] It can hardly be said that there is no First Amendment issue present in the case when respondents have defended against this suit all along by arguing that the First Amendment barred the enforcement of the reporters' promises to Cohen. We proceed to consider whether that Amendment bars a promissory estoppel cause of action against respondents.

The initial question we face is whether a private cause of action for promissory estoppel involves "state action" within the meaning of the Fourteenth Amendment such that the protections of the First Amendment are triggered. For if it does not, then the First Amendment has no bearing on this case. The rationale of our decision in [*Sullivan*, p. 98, *supra*] and subsequent cases compels the conclusion that there is state action here. Our cases teach that the application of state rules of law in state courts in a manner alleged to restrict First Amendment freedoms constitutes "state action" under the Fourteenth Amendment. [  ] In this case, the Minnesota Supreme Court held that if Cohen could recover at all it would be on the theory of promissory estoppel, a state-law doctrine which, in the absence of a contract, creates obligations never explicitly assumed by the parties. These legal obligations would be enforced through the official power of the Minnesota courts. Under our cases, that is enough to constitute "state action" for purposes of the Fourteenth Amendment.

Respondents rely on the proposition that "if a newspaper lawfully obtains truthful information about a matter of public significance then state officials may not constitutionally punish publication of the information, absent a need to further a state interest of the highest order." [*Smith v. Daily Mail Publishing Co.*, p. 61, *supra*]. That proposition is unexceptionable, and it has been applied in various cases that have found insufficient the asserted state interests in preventing publication of truthful, lawfully obtained information. [ ].

This case however, is not controlled by this line of cases but rather by the equally well-established line of decisions holding that generally applicable laws do not offend the First Amendment simply because their enforcement against the press has incidental effects on its ability to gather and report the news. As the cases relied on by respondents recognize, the truthful information sought to be published must have been lawfully acquired. The press may not with impunity break and enter an office or dwelling to gather news. Neither does the First Amendment relieve a newspaper reporter of the obligation shared by all citizens to respond to a grand jury subpoena and answer questions relevant to a criminal investigation, even though the reporter might be required to reveal a confidential source. [*Branzburg*, p. 521, *supra*]. The press, like others interested in publishing, may not publish copyrighted material without obeying the copyright laws. See [*Zacchini*, p. 241, *supra*]. Similarly, the media must obey the National Labor Relations Act, [ ], and the Fair Labor Standards Act, [ ]; may not restrain trade in violation of the antitrust laws, [ ]; and must pay nondiscriminatory taxes. [ ] It is therefore beyond dispute that "[t]he publisher of a newspaper has no special immunity from the application of general laws. He has no special privilege to invade the rights and liberties of others." [ ] Accordingly, enforcement of such general laws against the press is not subject to stricter scrutiny than would be applied to enforcement against other persons or organizations.

There can be little doubt that the Minnesota doctrine of promissory estoppel is a law of general applicability. It does not target or single out the press. Rather, in so far as we are advised, the doctrine is generally applicable to the daily transactions of all the citizens of Minnesota.

Justice Blackmun suggests that applying Minnesota promissory estoppel doctrine in this case will "punish" Respondents for publishing truthful information that was lawfully obtained. [ ] This is not strictly accurate because compensatory damages are not a form of punishment, as were the criminal sanctions at issue in Smith. If the contract between the parties in this case had contained a liquidated damages provision, it would be perfectly clear that the payment to petitioner would represent a cost of acquiring newsworthy material to be published at a profit, rather than a punishment imposed by the State. The payment of compensatory damages in this case is constitutionally indistinguishable from a generous bonus paid to a confidential news source. In any event, as indicated above, the characterization of the payment makes no difference for First Amendment purposes when the law being applied is a general law and does not single out the press. Moreover, Justice Blackmun's reliance on cases like [*Florida Star* and *Smith*] is misplaced. In those cases, the State itself defined the content of publications that would trigger liability. Here, by contrast, Minnesota law simply requires those making promises to keep them. The parties themselves, as in this case, determine the scope of their legal obligations and any restrictions which may be placed on the publication of truthful information are self-imposed.

Also, it is not at all clear that Respondents obtained Cohen's name "lawfully" in this case, at least for purposes of publishing it. Unlike the situation in *The Florida Star*, where the rape victim's name was obtained through lawful access to a police report, respondents obtained Cohen's name only by making a promise which they did not honor. The dissenting opinions suggest that the press should not be subject to any law, including copyright law for example, which in any fashion or to any degree limits or restricts the press' right to report truthful information. The First Amendment does not grant the press such limitless protection.

Nor is Cohen attempting to use a promissory estoppel cause of action to avoid the strict requirements for establishing a libel or defamation claim. As the Minnesota Supreme Court observed here, "Cohen could not sue for defamation because the information disclosed [his name] was true." [ ] Cohen is not seeking damages for injury to his reputation or his state of mind. He sought damages in excess of $50,000 for breach of a promise that caused him to lose his job and lowered his earning capacity. Thus this is not a case like [*Hustler*, p. 251, *supra*], where we held that the constitutional libel standards apply to a claim alleging that the publication of a parody was a state-law tort of intentional infliction of emotional distress.

Respondents and *amici* argue that permitting Cohen to maintain a cause of action for promissory estoppel will inhibit truthful reporting because news organizations will have legal incentives not to disclose a confidential source's identity even when that person's identity is itself newsworthy. Justice Souter makes a similar argument. But if this is the case, it is no more than the incidental, and constitutionally insignificant, consequence of applying to the press a generally applicable law that requires those who make certain kinds of promises to keep them. Although we conclude that the First Amendment does not confer on the press a constitutional right to disregard promises that would otherwise be enforced under state law, we reject Cohen's request that in reversing the Minnesota Supreme Court's judgment we reinstate the jury verdict awarding him $200,000 in compensatory damages. [ ] The Minnesota Supreme Court's incorrect conclusion that the First Amendment barred

Cohen's claim may well have truncated its consideration of whether a promissory estoppel claim had otherwise been established under Minnesota law and whether Cohen's jury verdict could be upheld on a promissory estoppel basis.   Or perhaps the State Constitution may be construed to shield the press from a promissory estoppel cause of action such as this one.   These are matters for the Minnesota Supreme Court to address and resolve in the first instance on remand.   Accordingly, the judgment of the Minnesota Supreme Court is reversed, and the case is remanded for further proceedings not inconsistent with this opinion.

*So ordered.*

JUSTICE BLACKMUN, with whom JUSTICE MARSHALL and JUSTICE SOUTER join, dissenting.

.  .  .

Contrary to the majority, I regard our decision in [*Hustler*] to be precisely on point.   There, we found that the use of a claim of intentional infliction of emotional distress to impose liability for the publication of a satirical critique violated the First Amendment.   There was no doubt that Virginia's tort of intentional infliction of emotional distress was "a law of general applicability" unrelated to the suppression of speech.   Nonetheless, a unanimous Court found that, when used to penalize the expression of opinion, the law was subject to the strictures of the First Amendment.   In applying that principle, we concluded, [   ], that "public figures and public officials may not recover for the tort of intentional infliction of emotional distress by reason of publications such as the one here at issue without showing in addition that the publication contains a false statement of fact which was made with 'actual malice.' " as defined by [*Sullivan*].   In so doing, we rejected the argument that Virginia's interest in protecting its citizens from emotional distress was sufficient to remove from First Amendment protection a "patently offensive" expression of opinion.   [   ][3]

As in *Hustler*, the operation of Minnesota's doctrine of promissory estoppel in this case cannot be said to have a merely "incidental" burden on speech; the publication of important political speech is the claimed violation.   Thus, as in *Hustler*, the law may not be enforced to punish the expression of truthful information or opinion.[4]   In the instant case, it is undisputed that the publication at issue was true.

**3.** The majority attempts to distinguish *Hustler* on the ground that there the plaintiff sought damages for injury to his state of mind whereas the petitioner here sought damages "for a breach of a promise that caused him to lose his job and lowered his earning capacity." [   ] I perceive no meaningful distinction between a statute that penalizes published speech in order to protect the individual's psychological well being or reputational interest, and one that exacts the same penalty in order to compensate the loss of employment or earning po-

tential.   Certainly, our decision in *Hustler* recognized no such distinction.

**4.** The majority argues that, unlike the criminal sanctions we considered in [*Smith*], the liability at issue here will not "punish" respondents in the strict sense of that word. [   ] While this may be true, we have long held that the imposition of civil liability based on protected expression constitutes "punishment" of speech for First Amendment purposes.   See, e.g., [*Pittsburgh Press, Gertz*].   Though they be civil, the sanctions we review in this case

To the extent that truthful speech may ever be sanctioned consistent with the First Amendment, it must be in furtherance of a state interest "of the highest order." [*Smith*] Because the Minnesota Supreme Court's opinion makes clear that the State's interest in enforcing its promissory estoppel doctrine in this case was far from compelling, [ ], I would affirm that court's decision.

I respectfully dissent.

JUSTICE SOUTER, with whom JUSTICE MARSHALL, JUSTICE BLACKMUN and JUSTICE O'CONNOR join, dissenting.

I agree with Justice Blackmun that this case does not fall within the line of authority holding the press to laws of general applicability where commercial activities and relationships, not the content of publication, are at issue. . . . "There is nothing talismanic about natural laws of general applicability," [ ], for such laws may restrict First Amendment rights just as effectively as those directed specifically at speech itself. Because I do not believe the fact of general applicability to be dispositive, I find it necessary to articulate, measure, and compare the competing interests involved in any given case to determine the legitimacy of burdening constitutional interests, and such has been the Court's recent practice in publication cases. [ ]

Nor can I accept the majority's position that we may dispense with balancing because the burden on publication is in a sense "self-imposed" by the newspaper's voluntary promise of confidentiality. [ ] This suggests both the possibility of waiver, the requirements for which have not been met here [see *Curtis Publishing Co.*], as well as a conception of First Amendment rights as those of the speaker alone, with a value that may be measured without reference to the importance of the information to public discourse. But freedom of the press is ultimately founded on the value of enhancing such discourse for the sake of a citizenry better informed and thus more prudently self-governed." . . .

The importance of this public interest is integral to the balance that should be struck in this case. There can be no doubt that the fact of Cohen's identity expanded the universe of information relevant to the choice faced by Minnesota voters in that State's 1982 gubernatorial election, the publication of which was thus of the sort quintessentially subject to strict First Amendment protection. [ ] The propriety of his leak to respondents could be taken to reflect on his character, which in turn could be taken to reflect on the character of the candidate who had retained him as an adviser. An election could turn on just such a factor; if it should, I am ready to assume that it would be to the greater public good, at least over the long run.

This is not to say that the breach of such a promise of confidentiality could never give rise to liability. One can conceive of situations in

are no more justifiable as "a cost of acquiring newsworthy material," [ ], than were the libel damages at issue in *New York* *Times* a permissible cost of disseminating newsworthy material.

which the injured party is a private individual, whose identity is of less public concern than that of the petitioner; liability there might not be constitutionally prohibited. Nor do I mean to imply that the circumstances of acquisition are irrelevant to the balance, see, e.g., [*Florida Star*], although they may go only to what balances against, and not to diminish, the First Amendment value of any particular piece of information.

Because I believe the State's interest in enforcing a newspaper's promise of confidentiality insufficient to outweigh the interest in unfettered publication of the information revealed in this case, I respectfully dissent.

### Notes and Questions

1. Note that the decision left the Minnesota Supreme Court free to decide that the potential interference with editorial autonomy, which it mistakenly thought would violate the First Amendment, does violate state policies underlying the equitable remedy of promissory estoppel. Should the state court have decided the case on that basis in the first instance?

The newspapers argued that the state court decision in fact rested on such a ground, and that the Supreme Court therefore lacked jurisdiction. The Supreme Court rejected the argument, noting that the state court had concluded that "in this case enforcement of the promise of confidentiality under a promissory estoppel theory would violate defendants' First Amendment rights." If the state court had substituted "free speech rights" for the last three words, would its decision have been reviewable by the Supreme Court?

2. The majority opinion does not respond to Justice Blackmun's argument that the burden on speech arising from liability for breach of a promise is no more "incidental" than the burden arising from libel or intentional infliction of emotional distress. Is there a satisfactory answer to that argument? If all civil liability for publication were treated as imposing similar burdens on speech, what constitutional limitations on contract liability might be suggested by the libel analogy?

3. In the reporter's privilege cases, media argue that unless they are allowed to honor promises of confidentiality, sources will not be willing to rely on those promises and will stop communicating to reporters, thereby chilling the flow of information to the public. Would a similar chilling effect occur if courts held that promises of confidentiality were not enforceable?

4. On remand, the Minnesota Supreme Court held that Cohen was entitled to $200,000 in damages. It rejected the newspapers' argument that the state free speech clause should be construed to preclude liability but left open the possibility of doing so in some other case. "The enforceability of promises of confidentiality given a news source is a question of first impression, and this case presents only one variation of such promises. The full First Amendment implications of this new issue

CONFIDENTIALITY IN NEWSGATHERING

may not yet have surfaced." Cohen v. Cowles Media Co., 479 N.W.2d 387, 19 Med.L.Rptr. 1858 (Minn.1992).

5. In another breach of promise case, a Minnesota resident alleged that she had agreed to be interviewed by *Glamour* magazine concerning her sexual abuse by a therapist only on the condition that she not be identified. The magazine changed her last name, but she contended that the use of her actual first name, profession and other details made her identifiable. The U.S. Court of Appeals for the 8th Circuit ruled that the plaintiff can proceed with her lawsuit: "When the promise was made not to identify plaintiff, the plain meaning of the promise was that [the freelance writer who wrote the article] would mask the identity of the plaintiff in such a way that a reasonable reader could not identify Jill Ruzicka by factual description . . .. There is nothing vague or ambiguous about such a promise." Ruzicka v. Conde Nast Publications, Inc., 999 F.2d 1319, 21 Med.L.Rptr. 1821 (8th Cir.1993).

### g. *The Future of Shield Laws*

Following the Court's decision in *Branzburg* there was substantial disagreement about whether a statutory privilege was desirable, and, if so, the extent and nature of the privilege. The disagreement has never been resolved. As noted earlier, scholars of the law of evidence tend to oppose all privileges as obstacles to the search for truth. The legal profession has accepted some privileges but has refused to endorse a privilege for reporters. At its February 1974 meeting, the House of Delegates of the American Bar Association voted 157–122 to reject the proposition that a reporter's privilege is essential "to protect the public interest . . . in the free dissemination of news and information to the American people on matters of public importance."

Privilege legislation has also been opposed by a few representatives of the press: in 1974 the *Washington Post* argued in an editorial that the "best shield is the First Amendment, without the supposed reinforcement of even the purest form of shield law." Editor & Publisher, Mar. 30, 1974 at 15. The justification for this position is the belief that Congress has no business legislating about the press, whether protectively or otherwise. If Congress is conceded power to help the press now it may later be assumed to have power to enact legislation hostile to the press. This concern was also raised during the debate over the Newspaper Preservation Act. Those holding this view would prefer to litigate each case in the courts solely in terms of the First Amendment.

This view is likely to produce more litigation than would a statute that provides protection—even if limited to certain types of cases. Some media representatives, particularly those from smaller newspapers and broadcasters, believe a limited statute would help avoid expensive litigation without creating new dangers.

Congress considered federal shield laws since *Branzburg*. None has been enacted because of the lack of consensus similar to that we have just considered among lawyers, scholars and journalists.

## B.  SEARCH WARRANTS AND SUBPOENAS

Basically, law enforcement officials may choose from among three methods for obtaining relevant evidence.  The first is simply to ask the person who probably has it to turn it over.  The lack of formality simplifies and expedites the process.  The drawback is that if the possessor of the information decides not to cooperate he may legally destroy or transfer possession of the material after learning that the police want it.

The second procedure is the subpoena, discussed in *Branzburg* and *Farber*.  Prosecutorial officials ask either the court or grand jury for authority to issue a subpoena for evidence sought in connection with an investigation, or act under delegated authority.  The recipient may not legally destroy the material after being served with the subpoena.  A recipient who thinks the subpoena asks something illegal may challenge it.  If the recipient claims not to have the material or information being sought, he makes a statement to that effect under oath.  It may be difficult to prove whether the person illegally destroyed the material after receiving the subpoena.

The third method, the search warrant, played the central role in a case involving *The Stanford Daily*, the campus newspaper at Stanford University.  A magistrate must decide whether a police request for a search warrant establishes probable cause to believe that the material sought is at the named location.  If the magistrate is persuaded, the police may execute the warrant by appearing at the specified location without prior notice and may search the premises until they find the identified material.

Police believed that *Stanford Daily* photographers had taken photographs that would aid in identifying persons who had assaulted policemen during a violent demonstration.  The police obtained a search warrant and served it on the *Daily*.  After the search, the *Daily* brought an action against the chief of police and other local officials, and the case, Zurcher v. Stanford Daily, 436 U.S. 547, 3 Med.L.Rptr. 2377 (1978), eventually reached the Supreme Court.  Justice White wrote for the majority that valid warrants may be issued to search *any* property, and that even though the Fourth Amendment may protect the materials sought to be seized, nothing in the First Amendment bars searches of newspaper offices.

After the decision a few states enacted bans on the issuance of search warrants against media, and Congress passed the Privacy Protection Act of 1980, which makes it unlawful for an official of any government to search or seize "any work product material possessed by a person reasonably believed to have a purpose to disseminate to the public a newspaper, book, broadcast, or other similar form of public communication, in or affecting interstate or foreign commerce."  This provision usually does not apply where there is probable cause to believe that the person possessing the materials has committed or is committing the offense to which the materials relate.

A second ground for searching for work products is "reason to believe that the immediate seizure of such materials is necessary to prevent the death of, or serious bodily injury to, a human being."

"Work product" is defined to mean materials other than contraband prepared in anticipation of communication to the public, no matter who authored them, and may include "mental impressions, conclusions, opinions, or theories of the person who prepared, produced, or created such material."

A second major provision deals with "documentary materials," which are defined as materials "upon which information is recorded, and includes, but is not limited to," written or printed materials, photographs, films, tapes, discs and punch cards. The same two exceptions to the ban on searches and seizures that applied to work products apply to documentary materials possessed by "a person reasonably believed to have a purpose to disseminate.    . . ." In addition, government officials may search for documentary materials (1) where there is reason to believe that giving notice of a subpoena would lead to destruction or concealment; and (2) where the material has not been delivered in response to an earlier subpoena and all appellate remedies have been exhausted.

*Telephone Records.* The government may learn about reporters' sources and activities in ways that do not involve search warrants or subpoenas. Reporters Committee for Freedom of the Press v. American Telephone & Telegraph Co., 593 F.2d 1030, 4 Med.L.Rptr. 1177 (D.C.Cir. 1978), involved government requests for records of long distance calls charged to (but perhaps not made to or from) certain telephone numbers. Reporters charged that the First and Fourth Amendments required that subscribers be given notice before AT & T honored the government's request for toll-call records. The court, 2–1, concluded that balancing was not appropriate because "Government access to third-party evidence in the course of a good faith felony investigation in no sense 'abridges' plaintiffs' information-gathering activities." The possibility of bad-faith investigations (to harass reporters) did not warrant prior judicial intervention unless the reporter could establish "a clear and imminent threat of such future misconduct." The dissenter would have afforded reporters the opportunity to have prior judicial decisions made on such requests on a case-by-case basis. *Certiorari* was denied. 440 U.S. 949, 4 Med.L.Rptr. 2536 (1979), Brennan, Marshall and Stewart, JJ., dissenting.

Sometimes the problem can go beyond a record of the numbers to which journalists place calls to the content of those calls. A federal district court judge in 1987 ordered the U.S. government to expunge its records resulting from an illegal wiretap on the phone of *New York Times* reporter Hedrick Smith. The wiretap in 1969 was carried out by the FBI at the request of then-Secretary-of-State Henry Kissinger, who had apparently been trying to determine Smith's confidential source for stories on Nixon administration activities. The court ordered the government to destroy logs of the 138 conversations that had been monitored. See Editor & Publisher, Aug. 8, 1987 at 29.

*Department of Justice Guidelines.* In 1979, after the Department of Justice obtained records of a reporter's toll calls from the local telephone company, the press urged government attention to the problem. The result was the promulgation, in 1980, of amendments to the subpoena guidelines to provide that discussions with the reporter should precede any subpoena to the telephone company where the appropriate Assistant Attorney General concludes that such disclosure would not jeopardize the investigation. Before any subpoena is issued, the "express authorization of the Attorney General" is required. Such authorization should not be requested from the Attorney General unless there is reason to believe a crime has been committed, the need is clear, and alternative investigation steps have been unsuccessfully explored. The reporter should be informed within 45 days (though that may be delayed another 45 days) and the information obtained shall be closely held to prevent unauthorized persons from learning what the records reveal. The amended guidelines, which may be altered by any successor Attorney General, are in 45 Federal Register 76436 (Nov. 19, 1980), are codified in 28 Code of Federal Regulations 50.10, and are reprinted in 6 Med.L.Rptr. 2153 (1980).

## C.  IMPLICATIONS FOR JOURNALISTS

Journalists would not want to go through their careers in constant fear of subpoenas or jail terms; that sort of "chill" would seriously damage the newsgathering process and the free flow of information to the public. On the other hand, journalists handling sensitive material or dealing with confidences would be foolish not to make themselves aware of the shield law protection or lack thereof in the state(s) in which they work. Journalists sometimes will find that their sources, particularly those in official positions who are experienced at dealing with the press, are themselves familiar with the state shield laws.

Legalities aside, identifiable sources and attributable quotes strengthen good news stories. That is enough reason not to promise confidentiality to every source who asks for such a promise. Even in those instances in which reporters believe that pledges of confidentiality are the only way they can get information from sources, they should be certain they have authorization from their employers before making such promises. As we have seen from the cases, reporters and their employer publications or stations are often "in it together" when a court seeks evidence in their hands. News organizations are well advised to be sure that editors, news directors, reporters and others are all aware of the organization's policy on confidential sources and information before pledges are made or subpoenas are served.

Although journalists can reasonably expect their employers to be supportive when subpoena problems arise, legal problems can create stress. When reporters' notes are subpoenaed, who owns the notes—the reporters or their employers? Absent any formal understanding to the contrary, employers may assert that they have "bought" them as part of the reporters' work product when the reporters endorsed their pay checks, even though the employers do not normally ask for the notes. Journalists may be more likely to feel that they have "sold" only their finished stories and that the notes are still their personal property. Should it make any difference whether reporters take notes in notebooks from their employers' supply rooms or in notebooks they buy themselves?

Obviously, where sensitive material is concerned, journalists should be careful about what materials they create and where they store them. Generating photocopies of confidential materials or writing memos within the news organization which might reveal or tend to reveal confidential information are examples of creating additional pieces of paper which could be subject to subpoena and should therefore not be done unnecessarily. Despite the protection against newsroom searches afforded by the Privacy Protection Act of 1980, p. 559, *supra*, journalists may prefer to keep their most confidential notes or documents away from their offices—even away from their homes in safe deposit boxes, for instance. This is not to suggest that paranoia should be the order of the day, and most reporters will never face such problems, but caution is in order for those handling the most sensitive information.

Computers also raise questions. If the confidential information is stored in the computer, can the journalist be compelled to create a printout? In the event of a newsroom search, could the journalist be compelled to give law enforcement agents the password?

Even where there is no subpoena or search, journalists will sometimes find themselves having to make difficult decisions about the release of unpublished (not necessarily confidential) information. Suppose, for example, a newspaper photographer arriving at the scene of a fatal auto accident shoots a 36–exposure roll of film. Only one of the photos is published in the newspaper. An insurance company, involved in subsequent litigation, asks the newspaper if it can buy prints of the other photographs, because they are believed to show some details of the accident better than the police photos. Should the newspaper turn over the unpublished photos? Would doing so be a harmless extension of the newspaper's usual role of disseminating the truth about events? Would the fact that the newspaper last week turned over unpublished photos of a children's Halloween party to the children play any part in the decision? Would accident victims or other news subjects be less cooperative with press photographers if they thought the latter might give or sell the photographs for non-journalistic purposes, including use in litigation?

These questions and others relating to the confidentiality problems are difficult to answer.  Although it may at first be easy for journalists to say they would go to jail rather than to reveal a source or break a confidence, that becomes more difficult when relatives, neighbors and friends outside of journalism ask how journalists think they are "above the law" and not subject to the same obligations that other citizens have. Although a few journalists have briefly become famous by going to jail and writing about the experience, the fact is that the experience is inconvenient and disruptive at the least and quite difficult at the worst.

# Chapter XII

# NEWSGATHERING FROM NON–JUDICIAL PUBLIC SOURCES

Journalists obtain news from government sources and government-controlled places the same way they obtain news of other kinds—by cultivating sources, making phone calls, asking questions or observing. Sometimes government and the people in it are reluctant sources, and the journalist can use legal help in obtaining access to the information. The recognition by the Supreme Court in Richmond Newspapers v. Virginia (see Chapter X) of a First Amendment right of the public to attend trials is still an unusual recognition of a constitutional protection for newsgathering; more typically, the First Amendment has been recognized only as a right to publish news that one already possesses. Because a constitutional right of newsgathering was far from clearly established, journalists and others interested in observing the workings of government lobbied successfully in the 1960s and later for legislation at both the federal and state levels to provide access to government information.

In this chapter we consider access to non-judicial public records, access to public meetings, and access to public places. Refer to the related discussion in Chapter X of access to judicial records and courtrooms and to Chapter IV for discussion of access to private places.

## A. ACCESS TO PUBLIC RECORDS

### 1. Freedom of Information Act

As long as legislatures were the preeminent lawmakers in the country, persons concerned with government actions could follow the process. With the New Deal, however, vast numbers of administrative agencies and organizations emerged. (We discussed one administrative agency, the Federal Trade Commission, in Chapter IX and will discuss another, the Federal Communications Commission, in XV–XVIII.) Congress empowered most to promulgate their own internal rules, to issue substantive regulations, to enforce laws, to adjudicate some controversies and take other action of great importance to citizens. The sheer number of regulations and orders being promulgated made it difficult to keep track of the process. In addition, some of the agencies were not open about their operations.

In 1946 Congress passed the Administrative Procedure Act to require all administrative agencies to follow certain procedures in the adoption of regulations and in their adjudicative hearings. Congress also sought to make the internal rules and procedures of agencies more readily available to the public.

For a variety of reasons, this first effort at openness was not notably successful. In 1967 Congress responded to growing criticism by adopting the first version of the Freedom of Information Act. The FOIA was amended in 1974 to expand its scope. 5 U.S.C.A. § 552. Continuing the process of revising the FOIA, Congress passed the Freedom of Information Reform Act in 1986—adopting a number of changes the media had sought for years. The amendments were inserted by the Senate in an anti-drug bill and subsequently accepted by the House of Representatives. The changes reflected a compromise: Senate Republicans led by Sen. Orrin Hatch (R.–Utah) wanted amendments curtailing public access to law enforcement records and informant files, while Senate Democrats successfully negotiated changes in the act's fee structure as part of the package. [H.R. 5484, 99th Cong., 2nd Sess., 132 Cong.Rec. S14033 (daily ed. Sept. 27, 1986)].

See How to Use the Federal FOI Act, 6th Edition, published by the FOI Service Center, a project of The Reporters Committee for Freedom of the Press, at 6–7, 30–32.

The FOIA applies to all federal government agencies except Congress, the courts, the government of the District of Columbia, and courts martial or the military during wartime. The Act requires each agency to publish in the *Federal Register* a description of its organization and a list of its personnel through whom the public can obtain information. Each agency must also explain the procedures by which it will furnish information. Each agency must make available to the public staff manuals and internal instructions that affect members of the public, final opinions in adjudicated cases and current indexes.

Agencies must respond quickly to requests for information. Should an agency not comply with the FOIA, a member of the public may ask a federal district court to enforce the act. The court may review in private the material the agency wishes to withhold, but it is the agency that bears the burden of showing that the material may be withheld under one of the exemptions to the Act discussed below. If the court decides the information should be released, it can order the government to pay all costs associated with the court action. Additionally, the agency employee who authorized the improper withholding of the information may be punished.

The FOIA contains nine exemptions—categories of material that need not be made available to the public. The exemptions are:

(b) This section does not apply to matters that are—

(1)(A) specifically authorized under criteria established by an Executive order to be kept secret in the interest of national defense or foreign policy and (B) are in fact properly classified pursuant to such Executive order;

(2) related solely to the internal personnel rules and practices of an agency;

(3) specifically exempted from disclosure by statute (other than [the Privacy Act] ), provided that such statute (A) requires that the matters be withheld from the public in such a manner as to leave no discretion on the issue, or (B) establishes particular criteria for withholding or refers to particular types of matters to be withheld;

(4) trade secrets and commercial or financial information obtained from a person and privileged or confidential;

(5) inter-agency or intra-agency memorandums or letters which would not be available by law to a party other than an agency in litigation with the agency;

(6) personnel and medical files and similar files the disclosure of which would constitute a clearly unwarranted invasion of personal privacy;

(7) records or information compiled for law enforcement purposes, but only to the extent that the production of such law enforcement records or information (A) could reasonably be expected to interfere with enforcement proceedings, (B) would deprive a person of a right to a fair trial or an impartial adjudication, (C) could reasonably be expected to constitute an unwarranted invasion of personal privacy, (D) could reasonably be expected to disclose the identity of a confidential source, including a State, local, or foreign agency or authority or any private institution which furnished information on a confidential basis, and, in the case of a record or information compiled by criminal law enforcement authority in the course of a criminal investigation or by an agency conducting a lawful national security intelligence investigation, information furnished by a confidential source, (E) would disclose techniques and procedures for law enforcement investigations or prosecutions, or would disclose guidelines for law enforcement investigations or prosecutions if such disclosure could reasonably be expected to risk circumvention of the law, or (F) could reasonably be expected to endanger the life or physical safety of any individual;

(8) contained in or related to examination, operating, or condition reports prepared by, on behalf of, or for the use of an agency responsible for the regulation or supervision of financial institutions; or

(9) geological and geophysical information and data, including maps, concerning wells.

[Any reasonably segregable portion of a record must be provided to any person requesting such record after deletion of the portions that are exempt under this subsection.]

The Freedom of Information Act may be used by anyone. Businesses—not just media businesses—often use it to get information about customers, competitors, suppliers, regulators and markets. Public interest groups and trade associations also use it. There are thousands of requests and hundreds of lawsuits brought under FOIA each year. Although there are too many media cases to discuss them all here, some examples may be useful.

The Reporters Committee for Freedom of the Press sued the Justice Department for refusing to disclose criminal identification records, commonly known as "rap sheets." The FBI maintains such records on more than 24 million persons. They normally contain a history of the arrests, charges, convictions and incarcerations of the subject. Sometimes they are incorrect or incomplete, and sometimes they contain information about other people with the same or similar names. Although the information about specific individual arrests, convictions, etc., are usually available in public records in the local area in which they happened, the compilations are generally unavailable except in Florida, Wisconsin and Oklahoma. The Reporters Committee's case reached the Supreme Court, which held in 1989 that a third party request for law enforcement records or information about a private citizen (even one charged with or convicted of a crime) "can reasonably be expected to invade that citizen's privacy," and that the FBI's rap sheets are therefore exempt from disclosure under the Freedom of Information Act. United States Department of Justice v. Reporters Committee For Freedom of the Press, 489 U.S. 749, 16 Med.L.Rptr. 1545 (1989).

The Court held in another case that records that were not originally created for, but were later collected for law enforcement purposes, could be withheld under the Freedom of Information Act—thus adding to materials that can be withheld under the seventh exemption. John Doe Agency v. John Doe Corp., 493 U.S. 146, 17 Med.L.Rptr. 1225 (1989). (The case was so titled because the appellate court had sealed the records, but the government later allowed the agencies to be named. The Supreme Court justices did not name the Grumman Corp. as the requestor of the records, but *The New York Times* reported that one of Grumman's lawyers accidentally let the name slip after the Supreme Court accepted the case. Editor & Publisher, Dec. 16, 1989 at 37.)

Some litigation is initiated by requestors of records; other litigation consists of so-called "reverse FOIA" suits. In the latter, some plaintiffs have brought actions in federal courts to try to stop the government from releasing information the plaintiffs think should not be released. In Chrysler Corporation v. Brown, 441 U.S. 281, 4 Med.L.Rptr. 2441 (1979), the automaker sought to enjoin disclosure of affirmative action information it had submitted to the government. The Supreme Court decided against Chrysler, however, holding that the FOIA is a disclosure statute and that the exemptions allow, but do not require, agencies to withhold particular information.

Agencies may set reasonable fees for finding and copying material requested by the public. These fees are to be waived when the information will be of primary benefit to the general public. The structure for fees and fee waivers included in the 1986 amendments provides that "news media," educational and scientific institutions are to be charged duplication fees for FOI Act requests only when the requests exceed 100 pages. These "non-commercial" requestors will also be exempt from charges for the first two hours of search time. Commercial requestors will normally be charged for both search time and duplication charges, but they can request fee waivers if they can demonstrate that disclosure is in the public interest and will "contribute significantly to public understanding of the operations or activities of the government."

Under orders from Congress, the Office of Management and Budget (OMB) issued guidelines in 1987 to help federal agencies develop fee schedules in accordance with the 1986 amendments.

Congress had not defined the term "news media," but OMB defined "Representatives of the News Media" to include persons gathering information for organizations that publish or broadcast news (defining "news" as information about current events). Examples of news media cited in the guidelines include "television or radio stations and publishers of periodicals (but only in those instances when they can qualify as disseminators of 'news') who make their products available for purchase or subscription by the general public."

Press representatives hailed the fee waiver as a significant step, but the Justice Department soon issued a memorandum suggesting the "safeguarding [of] federal funds by granting waivers or reductions only where it is determined that the statutory standard is satisfied." The News Media & The Law, Spring 1987 at 31–32.

How to Use the Federal FOI Act, 6th Edition, a publication of the FOI Service Center, offers this tip:

> Experience shows that requestors seeking relatively modest numbers of documents are more likely to be granted fee waivers than those whose requests encompass several thousand pages. In this regard, you may want to show that you have narrowed your request as much as possible and therefore are not unduly burdening the agency.

The computer technology of the 1990s presents quite different problems for requestors of information than existed when the Freedom of Information Act was passed. Receiving a computer tape of government data will do requestors little good if they do not have the computer program necessary to access the data. Government sometimes argues, on the other hand, that the purchase agreements they made when they purchased computer software do not permit it to give free copies of the software to parties who are requesting the data. It has also been alleged that there are instances in which government has switched from one computer program to another, archived the old records, and then failed to save the software necessary to access the data in its own archives— essentially rendering that data useless for government as well as for requestors. The Reporters Committee for Freedom of the Press issued a 30–page booklet about access to electronic records in 1990.

In November 1993 a bill (S 1782) was introduced in the Senate to amend the Freedom of Information Act to ensure public access to information in an electronic format. The Electronic Freedom of Information Act, if enacted, would require that "An agency shall provide records in any form in which such records are maintained by that agency as requested by any person," and that "An agency shall make reasonable efforts to provide records in an electronic form requested by any person, even where such records are not usually maintained in such form." There is also now discussion at several levels about the possibilities of providing on-line access to government records by the public.

The Supreme Court has had occasion to pass on several cases interpreting the Act. These are often technical in nature and not particularly useful for our purposes. Most recently, the Supreme Court held that names and other identifying information could be deleted from State Department documents, sought under the Freedom of Information Act, concerning Haitian nationals who had attempted to emigrate illegally to the U.S. The documents had been requested under the FOIA by a Florida lawyer, but the State Department had cited exemption 6, which applies to privacy interests. U.S. Dept. of State v. Ray, 502 U.S. ___, 112 S.Ct. 541, 19 Med.L.Rptr. 1641 (1991).

The Supreme Court held in 1993 that the federal government is not entitled to presume that confidentiality—and exemption 7(d) of the Freedom of Information Act—applies to *all* sources supplying information to the FBI during a criminal investigation, but the Court said the FBI may rely on an inference of confidentiality from more narrowly defined circumstances. The Court said that a source should be deemed "confidential" if the source furnished information with the understanding that the FBI would not divulge it except to the extent it thought necessary for law enforcement purposes. Justice Department v. Landano, 508 U.S. ___, 113 S.Ct. 2014, 21 Med.L.Rptr. 1513 (1993).

## 2. THE PRIVACY ACT

The movement toward openness in government has been tempered by growing concern about the dangers to individual privacy resulting from the growing number of records and federal agencies keeping records. In response to these concerns, Congress passed the Privacy Act of 1974. 5 U.S.C.A. § 552a. One major part of the Act permits subjects of records to see their files, obtain copies and to correct inaccuracies. The individual is not required to give the agency any reason for wanting to see his file. Civil actions may be brought for improper refusals to provide the file and for improper refusals to make corrections.

The part of the Act of most interest to the press, however, is the part that restricts disclosure of the contents of records unless certain conditions are met:

**(b) Conditions of disclosure.**—No agency shall disclose any record which is contained in a system of records by any means of communication to any person, or to another agency, except pursuant to a written request by, or with the prior written consent of, the individual to whom the record pertains, unless disclosure of the record would be—

(1) to those officers and employees of the agency which maintains the record who have a need for the record in the performance of their duties;

(2) required under section 552 of this title [FOIA];

(3) for a routine use as defined  . . .;

(4) to the Bureau of the Census for purposes of planning or carrying out a census or survey or related activity . . .;

(5) to a recipient who has provided the agency with advance adequate written assurance that the record will be used solely as a statistical research or reporting record, and the record is to be transferred in a form that is not individually identifiable;

(6) to the National Archives of the United States as a record which has sufficient historical or other value to warrant its continued preservation by the United States Government, or for evaluation by the Administrator of General Services or his designee to determine whether the record has such value;

(7) to another agency or to an instrumentality of any governmental jurisdiction within or under the control of the United States for a civil or criminal law enforcement activity if the activity is authorized by law, and if the head of the agency or instrumentality has made a written request to the agency which maintains the record specifying the particular portion desired and the law enforcement activity for which the record is sought;

(8) to a person pursuant to a showing of compelling circumstances affecting the health or safety of an individual if upon such disclosure notification is transmitted to the last known address of such individual;

(9) to either House of Congress, or, to the extent of matter within its jurisdiction, any committee or subcommittee thereof, any joint committee of Congress or subcommittee of any such joint committee;

(10) to the Comptroller General, or any of his authorized representatives, in the course of the performance of the duties of the General Accounting Office; or

(11) pursuant to the order of a court of competent jurisdiction.

Attempts by the Reagan administration in the 1980s to reduce disclosure of information by the federal government under the Freedom of Information Act also had an impact on use of the Privacy Act as a reason for non-disclosure.

### 3.  STATE OPEN RECORDS STATUTES

Although they vary a great deal, state access to records statutes exist in every state, and they are frequently parallel to the federal statute by beginning with a premise that all government records should be publicly available and then listing a series of exceptions or exemptions.  These statutes are generally still new enough that they are subject to frequent amendment, and journalists are well advised to obtain copies of the open records statute for their states to see what is available.

### 4.  USING THE STATUTES

Freedom of information legislation can sometimes be helpful to a journalist—or, for that matter, any other member of the public seeking information—but that is not to say that it is frequently relied upon by the average journalist covering government.  Establishing a good relationship with friendly sources inside government is a much more common way of obtaining information than using the statutes.  When, however, the information would otherwise be unavailable, the reporter needs to know how to use the statute.

Requestors of information are advised to:  (1) make requests as simple as possible, (2) make requests as specific as possible, (3) cite the freedom of information statute, (4) ask to whom an appeal should be addressed if the initial request is denied and (5) either put dollar limits on the amounts they are willing to pay for the information or ask to be advised of the cost before the request is filled.

Even with attempts to strengthen the federal statute in 1974 and the state statutes in other years, a number of problems remain.  Among those most frequently cited are (1) charging excessive fees for the records, (2) taking delays in filling requests, (3) demanding unreasonable specificity in identifying the records sought, (4) contaminating otherwise releasable records by filing them with classified information and (5) applying the exemptions too broadly.

Regrettable though it may be, it is a fact of life that the level of compliance with the state statutes is sometimes a factor of the level of government from which information is sought.  Small town officials are still heard to deny access to information and to respond to mentions of their states' freedom of information laws by saying, "That's just some law passed in the state capital.  What are they going to do to me about it?"  With few penalties built into the state laws for non-compliance and little enforcement, the freedom of information legislation still has a long way to go before it becomes very helpful from the journalists' point of view.

## B.  ACCESS TO PUBLIC MEETINGS

Guidelines for access to meetings of Congress or its committees and access to information about Congressional proceedings are prescribed initially in the Constitution.  (Art. I, § 5):

Each House may determine the Rules of its Proceedings.    . . .
Each House shall keep a Journal of its Proceedings, and from time to time publish the same, excepting such Parts as may in their Judgment require Secrecy;  and the Yeas and Nays of the Members of either House on any question shall, at the Desire of one fifth of those Present, be entered on the Journal.

From the earliest days, sessions of the full House or Senate have usually been open to the public.  Senate sessions were occasionally closed for discussion of treaties or nominations, and in the 30 years between 1945 and 1975, the Senate held 17 closed sessions, devoted usually to foreign relations or defense questions.  Guide to the Congress of the United States 73 (2d ed. 1976).

Although most sessions of the full House and Senate have been open, most committee meetings were closed unless hearings were being held.  After 1970 there was a sharp increase in open committee meetings, extending first to mark-up sessions (in which a pending bill may be approved, amended or rewritten), and later to conference committee meetings in which representatives of the two houses try to reconcile two different versions of proposed legislation.  In 1975 the House and Senate voted to require open conferences unless a majority of conferees from either chamber vote in public to close a session.  Can such negotiations be conducted effectively in open sessions?  Should all meetings of all committees and subcommittees be open?

A different problem arises out of the conduct of Congressional investigations.  The power to legislate implies the power to inquire into subjects that may require legislation and allows Congress to conduct investigations and hold hearings.  Congress may compel the attendance of witnesses and the production of documents at these hearings under threat of citation for contempt.  The arguments against open hearings do not involve national security or the inhibiting effect of publicity on legislative compromise.  Rather they reflect a concern for the privacy of witnesses and those whose behavior is under scrutiny.  The advent of television coverage of some Congressional hearings has made this concern more significant and has led to some restrictions on coverage.

### 1.  THE "SUNSHINE" ACT

At the urging of Congressmen and Senators from Florida, which had had good experience with its "Sunshine" Law, Congress, in 1976, passed a federal "Government in the Sunshine Act."  5 U.S.C.A. § 552b.  The statement of purpose accompanying the Act declares that "the public is entitled to the fullest practicable information regarding the decisionmaking processes of the Federal Government." The Act sought to "provide the public with such information while protecting the rights of individuals and the ability of the Government to carry out its responsibilities."

Essentially, the Act provides that all federal agencies headed by boards of two or more persons appointed by the President—approximately 50 agencies—must hold "every portion of every meeting" open to the public. Adequate advance notice must be given of each meeting. Even if a meeting is closed because it falls within one of the ten exemptions to be noted, the agency must make public a transcript or minutes of all parts of the meeting that do not contain exempt material. Meetings may be closed only after a publicly recorded vote of a majority of the full membership of the agency.

The exemptions apply where the agency "properly determines" that a portion of its meeting "is likely to" result in the disclosure of specified information. The exemptions include verbatim copies of several FOIA exemptions—(1) involving national defense or foreign policy; (2) involving internal rules and practices of the agency; (3) matters specifically exempted from disclosure by another statute; (4) trade secrets; (7) law enforcement investigatory records; and (8) involving financial institutions. In addition, another exemption tracks very closely the "clearly unwarranted invasion of personal privacy" language of the sixth exemption of the FOIA. Given the similar goals of the two statutes, it is not surprising that they contain similar exemptions.

In addition, the Sunshine Act contains the following summarized exemptions not found in the FOIA:

 (5) disclosures that "involve accusing any person of a crime, or formally censuring any person;"

 (9) "premature disclosures" involving agencies that regulate currencies, securities, commodities, or financial institutions, where the disclosure would be likely to (i) lead to "significant financial speculation" in these items or (ii) "significantly endanger the financial stability of any financial institution" or where the disclosure would be likely to "significantly frustrate implementation of a proposed agency action."

 (10) information concerning an agency's issuance of a subpoena or its participation in a civil action or proceeding.

## 2. State Open Meetings Statutes

Clearly, less governmental business is conducted by the state legislature than by the multitude of agencies created by the legislature or by the executive branch under legislative authorization. In an effort to bring these agencies and their decision-making processes under public scrutiny many state legislatures have adopted "open meeting" or "sunshine" laws.

Enforcement provisions of the state laws vary. Some statutes provide that actions improperly taken in closed meetings can be declared null and void. Journalists generally favor fines or other penalties for public officials who disregard the open meetings statutes.

## C.  ACCESS TO PUBLIC PLACES

In addition to keeping records and holding meetings, governments also control access to their owned or leased buildings and grounds. No general legislation covers these situations. Instead, each has been handled under regulations issued by the person in control or by specific departments of the government. These vary greatly.

### 1.  ACCESS AND TERRORISM

Terrorist activity has shown the tension between the efforts of the press to gather news and the desire of law enforcement officials to isolate the terrorists and to prevent them from learning in advance what action the police are planning to take. The problem is, of course, aggravated if the terrorists have taken hostages whose lives are now in danger. Some have suggested that reporters covering such events receive training in psychology so that they understand the impact their coverage may have on the situation itself. Some police officials have proposed guidelines for handling future episodes, such as requiring that broadcast journalists be kept farther from the scene than are print reporters so that officials could brief the print press without risking the possibility that important information might reach the terrorists prematurely.

Many reporters have objected to plans that keep reporters from the scene. They urge that the matter be left to the sense of responsibility of the reporters. One journalist has said that "suppressing news of terrorism would be a denial of democracy that could take more lives than it saves. It is unworkable and philosophically unthinkable." The Quill (Dec. 1977) at 23.

Much discussion followed the seizure by Hanafi Muslims of B'nai B'rith headquarters in Washington, D.C. in 1977. Among the hostages taken was a reporter. His views are expressed in Fenyvesi, Looking Into the Muzzle of Terrorists, The Quill (July–Aug. 1977) at 16. In discussing the tension between newsgathering and the safety of hostages, he cited three "egregious examples" of press behavior during the siege. One involved a group of persons who had eluded the terrorists and had hidden, undiscovered, on a lower floor. A reporter saw a basket of supplies being lifted to a floor not known to be inhabited. The reporter's story to that effect was heard by supporters of the terrorists who informed those in the building, who then sought—but failed—to capture the group.

The second example involved a reporter who asked the leader whether he had set a deadline for compliance with his demands—at a time when the police and "all the other experts had thought that the absence of a deadline was one encouraging sign." In the third example, a reporter suggested over the telephone to the leader that the police were trying "to trick" him and "pulling a fast one" while pretending to negotiate in good faith. The leader "flew into a rage" and selected 10 older male hostages for execution if the police tried to fool him. Several additional articles in the same issue of *The Quill* discuss other aspects of covering terrorism.

Although the wisdom of police action in these episodes is much debated, there has been little legal challenge to police decisions that prevent reporters from entering the building in question or getting too close to the building. Almost all states have statutes that authorize police to bar access and provide that failure to obey an order to remain outside is punishable as failing to obey lawful police orders.

## 2. ACCESS TO PRISONS

As we saw at p. 498, *supra*, a series of Supreme Court cases have suggested a possible right to receive information separate from the interest of the speaker or supplier of that information. In 1974 the Supreme Court decided two companion cases involving efforts to obtain information from inmates confined in prisons. Pell v. Procunier, 417 U.S. 817, 1 Med.L.Rptr. 2379 (1974), involved a ban on press interviews with named inmates in the California prison system. The Court concluded in *Pell* that the security and penological considerations of incarceration were sufficient to justify rejection of the inmates' claims that the interview ban violated their First Amendment rights. Saxbe v. Washington Post Co., 417 U.S. 843, 1 Med.L.Rptr. 2314 (1974), involved a similar ban in the federal prison system.

Justice Stewart, writing for the Court in *Pell* and in *Saxbe,* addressed the claims raised by the press. He noted that "this regulation is not part of an attempt by the State to conceal the conditions in its prisons or to frustrate the press' investigation and reporting of those conditions." Reporters could visit the institutions and "speak about any subject to any inmates whom they might encounter." Interviews with inmates selected at random were also permitted and both the press and the public could take tours through the prisons. "In short, members of the press enjoy access to California prisons that is not available to other members of the public." Indeed, the only apparent restriction was the one being challenged.

The majority placed great weight on *Branzburg*, p. 521, *supra*, involving the question of a reporter's privilege not to disclose confidential information to grand juries. We considered this case at length in Chapter XI. *Branzburg* contained a passage that said:

> It has generally been held that the First Amendment does not guarantee the press a constitutional right of special access to information not available to the public generally . . .. Despite the fact that newsgathering may be hampered, the press is regularly

excluded from grand jury proceedings, our own conferences, the meetings of other official bodies in executive session, and the meetings of private organizations. Newsmen have no constitutional right of access to the scenes of crime or disaster when the general public is excluded.

This passage led Justice Stewart to add: "Similarly, newsmen have no constitutional right of access to prisons or their inmates beyond that afforded the general public." He reached this conclusion even though another part of *Branzburg* had observed that "without some protection for seeking out the news, freedom of the press could be eviscerated." Justice Stewart continued:

> The First and Fourteenth Amendments bar government from interfering in any way with a free press. The Constitution does not, however, require government to accord the press special access to information not shared by members of the public generally. It is one thing to say that a journalist is free to seek out sources of information not available to members of the general public, that he is entitled to some constitutional protection of the confidentiality of such sources, cf. Branzburg v. Hayes, supra, and that government cannot restrain the publication of news emanating from such sources. Cf. N.Y. Times v. United States, supra. It is quite another thing to suggest that the Constitution imposes upon government the affirmative duty to make available to journalists sources of information not available to members of the public generally. That proposition finds no support in the words of the Constitution or in any decision of this Court. Accordingly, since § 415.071 does not deny the press access to sources of information available to members of the general public, we hold that it does not abridge the protections that the First and Fourteenth Amendments guarantee.

Four Justices dissented on the press question. Justice Powell (writing in dissent in *Saxbe*) asserted:

> The specific issue here is whether the Bureau's prohibition of prisoner-press interviews gives rise to a claim of constitutional dimensions. The interview ban is categorical in nature. Its consequence is to preclude accurate and effective reporting on prison conditions and inmate grievances. These subjects are not privileged or confidential. The Government has no legitimate interest in preventing newsmen from obtaining the information that they may learn through personal interviews or from reporting their findings to the public. Quite to the contrary, federal prisons are public institutions. The administration of these institutions, the effectiveness of their rehabilitative programs, the conditions of confinement that they maintain, and the experiences of the individuals incarcerated therein are all matters of legitimate societal interest and concern. . . .

.  .  .  An informed public depends on accurate and effective reporting by the news media.  No individual can obtain for himself the information needed for the intelligent discharge of his political responsibilities.  For most citizens the prospect of personal familiarity with newsworthy events is hopelessly unrealistic.  In seeking out the news the press therefore acts as an agent of the public at large. It is the means by which the people receive that free flow of information and ideas essential to intelligent self-government.  By enabling the public to assert meaningful control over the political process, the press performs a crucial function in effecting the societal purpose of the First Amendment.  .  .  .

This constitutionally established role of the news media is directly implicated here.  For good reasons, unrestrained public access is not permitted.  The people must therefore depend on the press for information concerning public institutions.  The Bureau's absolute prohibition of prisoner-press interviews negates the ability of the press to discharge that function and thereby substantially impairs the right of the people to a free flow of information and ideas on the conduct of their Government.  The underlying right is the right of the public generally.  The press is the necessary representative of the public's interest in this context and the instrumentality which effects the public's right.  I therefore conclude that the Bureau's ban against personal interviews must be put to the test of First Amendment review.

There seems to be little question that "big wheels" do exist and that their capacity to influence their fellow inmates may have a negative impact on the correctional environment of penal institutions.  .  .  .

Justice Powell concluded, however, that prison authorities could handle that situation by narrow rules barring interviews with inmates under disciplinary suspension and limiting the number of interviews with any given inmate within a specified time period.

The Bureau of Prisons also argued that a case-by-case assessment of each interview request would be administratively burdensome and correctionally unsound.  Justice Powell responded that the Bureau could meet its obligations by promulgating rules setting up reasonable restrictions on the time, place and manner of conducting interviews much as it was already doing in the case of interviews with family, friends, attorneys and clergy.  Finally, the Bureau objected that it was difficult to tell "who constitutes the press."  Justice Powell responded that although the concept was vague and many might claim to be included, the Bureau could define the term in a rule like the one it was already using for another purpose: "A newspaper entitled to second class mailing privileges; a magazine or periodical of general distribution; a national or international news service; a radio or television network or station."  If too many qualified persons wanted interviews, Justice Powell suggested that media representatives might form pools as they do for news events when press access is limited.

Justices Brennan and Marshall joined Justice Powell's dissent. They also joined a dissent by Justice Douglas that emphasized the absolute nature of the ban and the importance of the information.

As emerged in later cases, the majority opinions in *Pell* and *Saxbe* contained a serious ambiguity. If the First Amendment did not authorize a right of access in these cases, why did it matter that the prisons had generally operated quite openly? In other words, was the majority decision based on the fact that the prisons in these cases already were fairly generous in allowing outsiders to visit, or on the view that no right of access could be found in the Constitution? Subsequent cases revealed a second ambiguity—does the press lose these cases because it is asking for a special privilege that members of the general public do not have? If members of the public had sought entry to interview a specific named and willing prisoner, and the prison authorities had responded in the same fashion, would the Supreme Court majority have written its opinion any differently?

A few years later, the Supreme Court returned to the prison question in a slightly different context.

## HOUCHINS v. KQED, INC.

Supreme Court of the United States, 1978.
438 U.S. 1, 98 S.Ct. 2588, 57 L.Ed.2d 553, 3 Med.L.Rptr. 2521.

[A suicide occurred at the Alameda County Jail at Santa Rita, California. KQED, licensee of a television station in nearby San Francisco, reported the story and quoted a psychiatrist as saying that conditions at the Little Greystone building were responsible for the illnesses of his patient-prisoners at the jail. In an earlier proceeding, a federal judge had ruled that the conditions at Greystone constituted cruel and unusual punishment. Houchins, the county sheriff, refused to admit a camera crew KQED sent to get the story and to photograph the facilities, including Greystone. At the time, no public tours of the jail were permitted.

KQED and the NAACP filed suit under 42 U.S.C.A. § 1983 claiming violation of their First Amendment rights. The NAACP claimed that information about the jail was essential to permit public debate on jail conditions in Alameda County. The complaint requested preliminary and permanent injunctions to prevent the sheriff from "excluding KQED news personnel from the Greystone cells and Santa Rita facilities and generally preventing full and accurate news coverage of the conditions prevailing therein."

Shortly after the suit was filed, the sheriff announced a program of monthly tours. The press received advance notice, and several reporters, including one from KQED, went on the first tour. Each tour was limited to 25 persons and did not include Little Greystone. Cameras and tape recorders were barred, though the sheriff did supply photographs of some parts of the jail. Tour members "were not permitted to interview inmates and inmates were generally removed from view."

KQED argued that the tours were unsatisfactory because advance scheduling prevented timely access and because photography and interviewing were barred. The sheriff defended his policy on grounds of "inmate privacy," the danger of creating "jail celebrities" who would "undermine jail security," and the concern that unscheduled tours would "disrupt jail operations."

The district judge issued a preliminary injunction barring the sheriff from denying access to "responsible representatives" of the news media "at reasonable times and hours" and "from preventing KQED news personnel and responsible representatives of the news media from utilizing photographic and sound equipment or from utilizing inmate interviews in providing full and accurate coverage of the Santa Rita facilities." He found that a more flexible policy was "both desirable and attainable" without danger to prison discipline. The court of appeals, in three separate opinions, rejected the sheriff's argument that *Pell* and *Saxbe* controlled, and affirmed the injunction.]

MR. CHIEF JUSTICE BURGER announced the judgment of the Court and delivered an opinion, in which MR. JUSTICE WHITE and MR. JUSTICE REHNQUIST joined.

The question presented is whether the news media have a constitutional right of access to a county jail, over and above that of other persons, to interview inmates and make sound recordings, films, and photographs for publication and broadcasting by newspapers, radio and television.

. . .

### III

We can agree with many of the respondents' generalized assertions; conditions in jails and prisons are clearly matters "of great public importance." Pell v. Procunier, supra, at 830 n. 7. Penal facilities are public institutions which require large amounts of public funds, and their mission is crucial in our criminal justice system. Each person placed in prison becomes in effect, a ward of the state for whom society assumes broad responsibility. It is equally true that with greater information, the public can more intelligently form opinions about prison conditions. Beyond question, the role of the media is important; acting as the "eyes and ears" of the public, they can be a powerful and constructive force, contributing to remedial action in the conduct of public business. They have served that function since the beginning of the Republic, but like all other components of our society media representatives are subject to limits.

The media are not a substitute for or an adjunct of government, and like the courts, they are "ill-equipped" to deal with problems of prison administration. Cf. Procunier v. Martinez, [   ]. We must not confuse the role of the media with that of government; each has special, crucial functions each complementing—and, sometimes conflicting with—the other.

The public importance of conditions in penal facilities and the media's role of providing information afford no basis for reading into the Constitution a right of the public or the media to enter these institutions, with camera equipment, and take moving and still pictures of inmates for broadcast purposes. This Court has never intimated a First Amendment guarantee of a right of access to all sources of information within government control. Nor does the rationale of the decisions upon which respondents rely lead to the implication of such a right.

. . .

The right to *receive* ideas and information is not the issue in this case. [   ] The issue is a claimed special privilege of access which the Court rejected in *Pell* and *Saxbe,* a right which is not essential to guarantee the freedom to communicate or publish.

### IV

. . .

Unarticulated but implicit in the assertion that media access to the jail is essential for informed public debate on jail conditions is the assumption that media personnel are the best qualified persons for the task of discovering malfeasance in public institutions. But that assumption finds no support in the decisions of this Court or the First Amendment. Editors and newsmen who inspect a jail may decide to publish or not to publish what information they acquire. [   ] Public bodies and public officers, on the other hand, may be coerced by public opinion to disclose what they might prefer to conceal. No comparable pressures are available to anyone to compel publication by the media of what they might prefer not to make known.

There is no discernible basis for a constitutional duty to disclose, or for standards governing disclosure of or access to information. Because the Constitution affords no guidelines, absent statutory standards, hundreds of judges would, under the Court of Appeals' approach, be at large to fashion ad hoc standards, in individual cases, according to their own ideas of what seems "desirable" or "expedient." We, therefore, reject the Court of Appeals' conclusory assertion that the public and the media have a First Amendment right to government information regarding the conditions of jails and their inmates and presumably all other public facilities such as hospitals and mental institutions.

"There is no constitutional right to have access to particular government information, or to require openness from the bureaucracy. [Citing Pell v. Procunier, *supra.*] The public's interest in knowing about its government is protected by the guarantee of a Free Press, but the protection is indirect. The Constitution itself is neither a Freedom of Information Act nor an Official Secrets Act.

"The Constitution, in other words, establishes the contest, not its resolution. Congress may provide a resolution, at least in some instances, through carefully drawn legislation. For the rest, we must rely, as so often in our system we must, on the tug and pull of the political forces in American society." Stewart, "Or of the Press," 26 Hastings L.J. 631, 636 (1975).

Petitioner cannot prevent respondents from learning about jail conditions in a variety of ways, albeit not as conveniently as they might prefer. Respondents have a First Amendment right to receive letters from inmates criticizing jail officials and reporting on conditions. See Procunier v. Martinez, [   ]. Respondents are free to interview those who render the legal assistance to which inmates are entitled. See id., at 419. They are also free to seek out former inmates, visitors to the prison, public officials, and institutional personnel, as they sought out the complaining psychiatrist here.

Moreover, California statutes currently provide for a prison Board of Corrections that has the authority to inspect jails and prisons and *must* provide a public report at regular intervals.  . . .

Neither the First Amendment nor the Fourteenth Amendment mandates a right of access to government information or sources of information within the government's control. Under our holdings in *Pell* [and *Saxbe*], until the political branches decree otherwise, as they are free to do, the media have no special right of access to the Alameda County Jail different from or greater than that accorded the public generally.

The judgment of the Court of Appeals is reversed and the case is remanded for further proceedings.

Reversed.

MR. JUSTICE MARSHALL and MR. JUSTICE BLACKMUN took no part in the consideration or decision of this case.

MR. JUSTICE STEWART, concurring in the judgment.

I agree that the preliminary injunction issued against the petitioner was unwarranted, and therefore concur in the judgment. In my view, however, KQED was entitled to injunctive relief of more limited scope.

The First and Fourteenth Amendments do not guarantee the public a right of access to information generated or controlled by government, nor do they guarantee the press any basic right of access superior to that of the public generally. The Constitution does no more than assure the public and the press equal access once government has opened its doors. Accordingly, I agree substantially with what the opinion of The Chief Justice has to say on that score.

We part company, however, in applying these abstractions to the facts of this case. Whereas he appears to view "equal access" as meaning access that is identical in all respects, I believe that the concept of equal access must be accorded more flexibility in order to accommodate the practical distinctions between the press and the general public.

When on assignment, a journalist does not tour a jail simply for his own edification. He is there to gather information to be passed on to others, and his mission is protected by the Constitution for very specific reasons. "Enlightened choice by an informed citizenry is the basic ideal upon which an open society is premised . . .." Branzburg v. Hayes, 408 U.S. 665, 726 (dissenting opinion). Our society depends heavily on the press for that enlightenment. . . .

That the First Amendment speaks separately of freedom of speech and freedom of the press is no constitutional accident, but an acknowledgment of the critical role played by the press in American society. The Constitution requires sensitivity to that role, and to the special needs of the press in performing it effectively. A person touring Santa Rita Jail can grasp its reality with his own eyes and ears. But if a television reporter is to convey the jail's sights and sounds to those who cannot personally visit the place, he must use cameras and sound equipment. In short, terms of access that are reasonably imposed on individual members of the public may, if they impede effective reporting without sufficient justification, be unreasonable as applied to journalists who are there to convey to the general public what the visitors see.

Under these principles, KQED was clearly entitled to some form of preliminary injunctive relief. At the time of the District Court's decision, members of the public were permitted to visit most parts of the Santa Rita Jail, and the First and Fourteenth Amendments required the Sheriff to give members of the press *effective* access to the same areas. The Sheriff evidently assumed that he could fulfill this obligation simply by allowing reporters to sign up for tours on the same terms as the public. I think he was mistaken in this assumption, as a matter of constitutional law.

The District Court found that the press required access to the jail on a more flexible and frequent basis than scheduled monthly tours if it was to keep the public informed. By leaving the "specific methods of implementing such a policy . . . [to] Sheriff Houchins," the Court concluded that the press could be allowed access to the jail "at reasonable times and hours" without causing undue disruption. The District Court also found that the media required cameras and recording equipment for effective presentation to the viewing public of the conditions at the jail seen by individual visitors, and that their use could be kept consistent with institutional needs. These elements of the Court's order were both sanctioned by the Constitution and amply supported by the record.

In two respects, however, the District Court's preliminary injunction was overbroad. It ordered the Sheriff to permit reporters into the Little Greystone facility and it required him to let them interview randomly encountered inmates. In both these respects, the injunction gave the press access to areas and sources of information from which persons on the public tours had been excluded, and thus enlarged the scope of what the Sheriff and Supervisors had opened to public view.  The District Court erred in concluding that the First and Fourteenth Amendments compelled this broader access for the press.

Because the preliminary injunction exceeded the requirements of the Constitution in these respects, I agree that the judgment of the Court of Appeals affirming the District Court's order must be reversed. But I would not foreclose the possibility of further relief for KQED on remand.  In my view, the availability and scope of future permanent injunctive relief must depend upon the extent of access then permitted the public, and the decree must be framed to accommodate equitably the constitutional role of the press and the institutional requirements of the jail.

MR. JUSTICE STEVENS, with whom MR. JUSTICE BRENNAN and MR. JUSTICE POWELL join, dissenting.

The Court holds that the scope of press access to the Santa Rita jail required by the preliminary injunction issued against petitioner is inconsistent with the holding in Pell v. Procunier, [   ], that "newsmen have no constitutional right of access to prisons or their inmates beyond that afforded the general public" and therefore the injunction was an abuse of the District Court's discretion.  I respectfully disagree.

. . .

For two reasons, which shall be discussed separately, the decisions in *Pell* and *Saxbe* do not control the propriety of the District Court's preliminary injunction.  First, the unconstitutionality of petitioner's policies which gave rise to this litigation does not rest on the premise that the press has a greater right of access to information regarding prison conditions than do other members of the public.  Second, relief tailored to the needs of the press may properly be awarded to a representative of the press which is successful in proving that it has been harmed by a constitutional violation and need not await the grant of relief to members of the general public who may also have been injured by petitioner's unconstitutional access policy but have not yet sought to vindicate their rights.

. . .

It is well settled that a defendant's corrective action in anticipation of litigation or following commencement of suit does not deprive the court of power to decide whether the previous course of conduct was unlawful.  . . .

In Pell v. Procunier, [   ], the Court stated that "newsmen have no constitutional right of access to prisons or their inmates beyond that afforded the general public."  But the Court has never intimated that a nondiscriminatory policy of excluding entirely both the public and the press from access to information about prison conditions would avoid constitutional scrutiny.  Indeed, *Pell* itself strongly suggests the contrary.

. . .

The decision in *Pell*, therefore, does not imply that a state policy of concealing prison conditions from the press, or a policy denying the press any opportunity to observe those conditions, could have been justified simply by pointing to like concealment from, and denial to, the general public.   If that were not true, there would have been no need to emphasize the substantial press and public access reflected in the record of that case.   What *Pell* does indicate is that the question whether respondents established a probability of prevailing on their constitutional claim is inseparable from the question whether petitioner's policies unduly restricted the opportunities of the general public to learn about the conditions of confinement in Santa Rita jail.   As in *Pell*, in assessing its adequacy, the total access of the public and the press must be considered.

Here, the broad restraints on access to information regarding operation of the jail that prevailed on the date this suit was instituted are plainly disclosed by the record.   . . .   Petitioner's no-access policy, modified only in the wake of respondents' resort to the courts, could survive constitutional scrutiny only if the Constitution affords no protection to the public's right to be informed about conditions within those public institutions where some of its members are confined because they have been charged with or found guilty of criminal offenses.

## II

The preservation of a full and free flow of information to the general public has long been recognized as a core objective of the First Amendment to the Constitution.   It is for this reason that the First Amendment protects not only the dissemination but also the receipt of information and ideas.   . . .

In addition to safeguarding the right of one individual to receive what another elects to communicate, the First Amendment serves an essential societal function.   Our system of self-government assumes the existence of an informed citizenry.[21]   . . .   It is not sufficient, therefore, that the channels of communication be free of governmental restraints.   Without some protection for the acquisition of information about the operation of public institutions such as prisons by the public at large, the process of self-governance contemplated by the Framers would be stripped of its substance.[22]

---

**21.**   See A. Meiklejohn   . . ..

**22.**   Admittedly, the right to receive or acquire information is not specifically mentioned in the Constitution.   But "the protection of the Bill of Rights goes beyond the specific guarantees to protect from   . . . abridgment those equally fundamental personal rights necessary to make the express guarantees fully meaningful.   . . .   The dissemination of ideas can accomplish noth-

ing if otherwise willing adherents are not free to receive and consider them.   It would be a barren marketplace of ideas that had only sellers and no buyers."   Lamont v. Postmaster General, 381 U.S., at 308 (Brennan, J., concurring).   It would be an even more barren marketplace that had willing buyers and sellers and no meaningful information to exchange.

For that reason information-gathering is entitled to some measure of constitutional protection.  See, e.g., Branzburg v. Hayes, [  ]; Pell v. Procunier, [  ].  As this Court's decisions clearly indicate, however, this protection is not for the private benefit of those who might qualify as representatives of the "press" but to insure that the citizens are fully informed regarding matters of public interest and importance.

A recognition that the "underlying right is the right of the public generally" is also implicit in the doctrine that "newsmen have no constitutional right of access to prisons or their inmates beyond that afforded the general public."  Pell v. Procunier, [  ].  In *Pell* it was unnecessary to consider the extent of the public's right of access to information regarding the prison and its inmates in order to adjudicate the press claim to a particular form of access, since the record demonstrated that the flow of information to the public, both directly and through the press, was adequate to survive constitutional challenge; institutional considerations justified denying the single, additional mode of access sought by the press in that case.

Here, in contrast, the restrictions on access to the inner portions of the Santa Rita jail that existed on the date this litigation commenced concealed from the general public the conditions of confinement within the facility.  The question is whether petitioner's policies, which cut off the flow of information at its source, abridged the public's right to be informed about those conditions.

The answer to that question does not depend upon the degree of public disclosure which should attend the operation of most governmental activity.  Such matters involve questions of policy which generally must be resolved by the political branches of government.[25]  Moreover, there are unquestionably occasions when governmental activity may properly be carried on in complete secrecy.  For example, the public and the press are commonly excluded from "grand jury proceedings, our own conferences, [and] the meetings of other official bodies gathering in executive session  .  .  .."  Branzburg v. Hayes  .  .  ..

In this case, however, "[r]espondents do not assert a right to force disclosure of confidential information or to invade in any way the decisionmaking processes of governmental officials." [28]  They simply seek an end to petitioner's policy of concealing prison conditions from the public.  Those conditions are wholly without claim to confidentiality.  While prison officials have an interest in the time and manner of public acquisition of information about the institutions they administer, there is no legitimate, penological justification for concealing from citizens the conditions in which their fellow citizens are being confined.

The reasons which militate in favor of providing special protection to the flow of information to the public about prisons relate to the

25. In United States v. Nixon, 418 U.S. 683, 705 n. 15, we pointed out that the Founders themselves followed a policy of confidentiality  .  .  ..

28. Saxbe v. Washington Post Co. [  ] (Powell, J. dissenting).

unique function they perform in a democratic society. Not only are they public institutions, financed with public funds and administered by public servants; they are an integral component of the criminal justice system. . . .

. . .

In this case, the record demonstrates that both the public and the press had been consistently denied any access to the inner portions of the Santa Rita jail, that there had been excessive censorship of inmate correspondence, and that there was no valid justification for these broad restraints on the flow of information. An affirmative answer to the question whether respondent established a likelihood of prevailing on the merits did not depend, in final analysis, on any right of the press to special treatment beyond that accorded the public at large. Rather, the probable existence of a constitutional violation rested upon the special importance of allowing a democratic community access to knowledge about how its servants were treating some of its members who have been committed to their custody. An official prison policy of concealing such knowledge from the public by arbitrarily cutting off the flow of information at its source abridges the freedom of speech and of the press protected by the First and Fourteenth Amendments to the Constitution.

. . .

I would affirm the judgment of the Court of Appeals.

**Notes and Questions**

1.  What part of the majority opinion in *Pell* does Chief Justice Burger utilize? What part does Justice Stewart utilize? What part does Justice Stevens utilize?

2.  To what extent does Justice Stewart agree with Chief Justice Burger? With Justice Stevens?

3.  Under Justice Stewart's view, why can't the KQED crew go into Little Greystone?

4.  Would any of the three opinions treat the NAACP differently from KQED, if it had asked to send a small group into the jail to investigate conditions?

5.  What opinions would have been affected if the sheriff had decided to discontinue the public tours before the Supreme Court decided the case? What if the sheriff discontinues the tours after the decision?

6.  How many other types of government facilities come within Justice Stevens's analysis? Could the sheriff have asserted any legitimate need for secrecy in running the jail?

3.   ACCESS TO MILITARY OPERATIONS

When the United States began a military operation on the island nation of Grenada in the Caribbean Sea in 1983, the press was excluded from entry to the island until two days after the operation began. Then only a limited number of reporters were brought to the island by U.S. military aircraft. All travel restrictions were lifted within two weeks of the beginning of the operation, but Larry Flynt, publisher of *Hustler* magazine, sued the Secretary of Defense and others for declaratory and injunctive relief. No damages were sought. Flynt's suit failed because the issue was moot: the operation was over, and there was no "reasonable expectation" that the Grenada controversy would recur. Judge Edwards, in a concurring opinion for the court of appeals, asserted that the court had no occasion to consider "whether it is unconstitutional for the government to ban the press from covering military actions where the sole or principal justification offered by the government is the safety of the press (and especially where an allegation is made that the government's actual motivation is to prevent press coverage which might influence public opinion)." That issue was encompassed in Flynt's complaint. Flynt v. Weinberger, 762 F.2d 134, 11 Med.L.Rptr. 2118 (D.C.Cir.1985).

The press outcry over being denied immediate access to the military operation on Grenada led to a Department of Defense (DOD) panel under the direction of Maj. Gen. Winant Sidle to consider alternatives. That panel proposed, and DOD put into effect, a plan for a limited pool to cover the early stages of surprise military operations. Under the plan, DOD picks organizations to participate in the pool, and the organizations pick the specific reporters. The media were asked to adopt voluntary guidelines to maintain security in such cases. The media pool arrangement came under fire from journalists when they were kept waiting in a hotel while the U.S. attacked Iranian oil platforms in 1987. The journalists said the pool arrangement was a good concept but was not working well in practice. Editor & Publisher, Nov. 7, 1987 at 9.

Similar complaints were heard after the U.S. invasion of Panama in 1989. A media pool was sent from Washington to Panama four hours after the invasion began, but journalists complained that they were kept away from the action. A report commissioned by the Pentagon's chief public affairs officer detailed "instance after instance of foul-ups" beginning with Secretary of Defense Richard Cheney's "excessive concern for secrecy." See "DOD criticizes U.S. handling of Panama coverage," Broadcasting, March 26, 1990 at 100, and "Panning the Pentagon," Editor & Publisher, March 31, 1990 at 11.

When U.S. troops were sent to Saudi Arabia in 1990 following Iraq's invasion of Kuwait, the complaints about the pool arrangements surfaced again. Two pools were called nearly a week after the first U.S. troops arrived. One went to Saudi Arabia and the other pool members were sent to U.S. Navy ships in the area. DOD attributed the delay in sending the pools to Saudi objections to the media presence. Editor & Publisher, Aug. 18, 1990 at 11.

In the months leading up to the start of the air war against Iraq, the Pentagon came up with new regulations for combat pool reporters, including a requirement that the reporters pass a physical fitness test involving push-ups, sit-ups and a mile-and-a-half run.  Requirements were adjusted according to age and sex, and reportedly few journalists had trouble with them.  Editor & Publisher, Jan. 12, 1991 at 8.  During the air war in January and February there were numerous press complaints about required "security review" of their stories and about allegations that their military escorts took them to unnewsworthy locations and sometimes picked the soldiers to be interviewed.  There were also complaints that pool reports—particularly reports by print media reporters—sometimes took hours to be reviewed, even though broadcast journalists sometimes were able to send live transmissions with little or no interference from their military escorts.  Even before the outbreak of hostilities, nine publications and four journalists brought suit against the Department of Defense charging unfair practices and seeking an injunction against implementing the press policies.  The suit was filed by the New York-based Center for Constitutional Rights.  Broadcasting, "Journalists in a War of Strict Press Rules," Jan. 28, 1991 at 22.

The suit against the Department of Defense was dismissed by a federal court.  Judge Leonard Sand held that the plaintiffs' claims asking for injunctive relief to prevent the government's limiting of reporters' access to the battlefield in future conflicts were moot.  Despite his finding that the problem was capable of repetition because of the U.S. military's relatively brief combat actions in recent years, he held that,

> "Since the regulations have been lifted and the press is no longer constrained from travelling throughout the Middle East, there is no longer any presently operative practice for this Court to enjoin.  Furthermore, there is no threat of irreparable harm since [Agence France–Presse, the plaintiff in a similar case decided simultaneously] and the NATION [the first-named of the publications suing] plaintiffs are able to gather and report news freely.  Since injunctive relief is not appropriate for past injuries, this Court holds that all of plaintiffs' claims requesting injunctive relief are moot."

Nation Magazine v. U.S. Department of Defense, 762 F.Supp. 1558, 19 Med.L.Rptr. 1257 (S.D.N.Y.1991).

Press concerns over problems in war coverage continued long after the war ended.  After eight months of talks with news organizations, the Pentagon issued a set of principles to give journalists greater access to future military operations than they had in the Persian Gulf war.  The guidelines say journalists "will be provided access to all major military units."  The news organizations and the Pentagon could not agree on the critical issue of the military's "security review" of articles and broadcasts.  New York Times, May 22, 1992 at A–15.

## 4. ACCESS TO ACCIDENT SCENES

The same principles would appear to apply when a reporter has lawfully entered an area—and is then asked to leave because of danger or for some other reason. The issue is analyzed in State v. Lashinsky, 81 N.J. 1, 404 A.2d 1121, 5 Med.L.Rptr. 1418 (1979). In a fatal freeway accident, a car left the road, ran down an embankment and overturned. Lashinsky, a news photographer, came upon the scene and, believing that the event was worthy of news coverage, parked 150 feet away, put his press card in his windshield, walked toward the wreckage and began taking several photographs. Fifteen or 20 minutes later a state trooper arrived. By this time 40 or 50 people had gathered. A member of a local first aid squad that had reached the scene before the trooper reported that there were casualties. A seriously injured girl, who was going into shock, was pinned inside the automobile against the corpse of her mother who had been decapitated.

The trooper returned to his car and radioed for an ambulance and more police. On returning to the scene he noticed gas and oil were leaking from the car and that the battery had cracked open. In addition, much personal property was strewn around the site. Fearing a fire and wanting to protect the property and preserve the area for investigation, the trooper ordered everyone not involved in first aid to leave the area. Lashinsky and some others refused. The trooper asked Lashinsky individually to leave. He retreated five feet but refused to move further. When he showed his press pass issued by the state police, the trooper said "I don't care at this point" and again asked him to leave. There was evidence that the reporter then engaged the trooper in a heated argument lasting three or more minutes telling the trooper to "do his own job and let Lashinsky do his."

Lashinsky was arrested and convicted of violating a statute providing that "Any person who in any place, public or private . . . obstructs, molests or interferes with any person lawfully therein . . . is a disorderly person." The conviction was affirmed, 4–3. Although not directly addressing the situation of a policeman's orders, the statute was broad enough to cover the "interference" involved in this case. The photographer's failure to obey prevented the first aid team from getting the trooper's assistance in their work and kept the trooper from helping. The court held that the statute had been violated. In passing it noted that an officer could not make someone a criminal simply by issuing an order. In each case there must be "an assessment of defendant's actions in light of *all* the surrounding circumstances—the activity giving rise to a policeman's order, the reasonableness of that order itself and the defendant's reaction to it." The conditions were met in this case because of the fire danger, property strewn around, the need to preserve the area for investigation and the crowd control problem faced by a single officer.

The reporter then argued that the statute did not apply to him because he was a member of the press. The majority said that an officer who is made aware that a member of the press is gathering news should "be mindful that such an individual has a legitimate and proper reason to be where he is and, if possible, this important interest should be accommodated." But here, the officer "virtually working alone, could not, in his professional judgment, have permitted defendant to remain, even as a member of the press, and still discharged his own paramount responsibilities for the safety and welfare of those who were his immediate concern." Under these circumstances the reporter was obligated to retreat. Although under state law a right to gather news is protected, "the liberty which the press seeks to assure our people can be meaningfully enjoyed only in a society where there is an adequate measure or order."

Finally, the majority held the statute was not unconstitutionally vague.

Justice Pashman agreed with the standard being used but dissented from its application to this case. He found no "interference" or "obstruction" by the reporter. "Defendant's actions . . . constitute the precise type of conduct in which any media photographer must engage if he is to adequately report a news event." The justice concluded that although the order was reasonable as to non-media bystanders his request to the defendant "although given in good faith, was clearly unreasonable." Since the original order to withdraw was unreasonable as to the defendant, he could not be punished for standing up for his rights against it.

A major disagreement between the majority and Justice Pashman involved the role of the bystanders. The trooper testified that when he asked people to clear the scene 15 or 20 bystanders stayed with defendant. Apparently, the trooper was concerned that if Lashinsky stayed some bystanders would stay and perhaps others would return. The dissenter argued that in such a case the trooper may properly arrest the bystanders. But it "would be absurd to rule that a media representative forfeits this special access right merely because others over whose actions he has no control refuse to abide by a reasonable police request."

Finally, because the trooper knew defendant was a member of the press, the trooper should have realized that defendant was "sufficiently mature to evaluate the safety risks posed by the overturned vehicle and to position himself so as to minimize those risks. This is not to say that newsmen must be allowed access to any site, no matter what the risk of harm might be. Where, however, as in the present case, the risk is not substantial, a media representative should be allowed to situate himself" near the vehicle, according to Justice Pashman.

The other two dissenters agreed with the majority that the defendant's conduct "hardly brings credit or distinction to the press." Nonetheless, his "arrogant behavior" did not violate the criminal statute under which he was charged because that requires a "physical interference." They argued that the state could punish Lashinsky's behavior but had not passed an appropriate statute prior to this case.

After this case arose, but before the decision, the legislature did pass a statute providing: "A person in a gathering commits a petty disorderly persons offense if he refuses to obey a reasonable official request or order to move: (1) To prevent obstruction of a highway or other public passage; or (2) To maintain public safety by dispersing those gathered in dangerous proximity to a fire or other hazard . . .."

Of course, a state may, if it wishes, provide special access rights for reporters. Under California Penal Code, § 409(a), for example, whenever "a menace to the public health or safety is created by a calamity such as flood, storm, fire, earthquake, explosion, accident or other disaster, [a law enforcement officer] may close the area where the menace exists for the duration thereof by means of ropes, markers or guards to any and all persons not authorized by such officer to enter or remain within the closed area."

Subsection (b) provides for closing areas around any "emergency field command post" established as the result of a calamity "or any riot or other civil disturbance."

Subsection (d), however, provides that "nothing in this section shall prevent a duly authorized representative of any news service . . . from entering the areas closed pursuant to this section."

A more recent case involving access to accident scenes is City of Oak Creek v. Ah King, 148 Wis.2d 532, 436 N.W.2d 285, 16 Med.L.Rptr. 1273 (1989). An airliner crashed into what the court called a "non-public area" of a publicly owned airport in Wisconsin. The airport's media guide for airport emergencies provided that "no representatives of the media will be permitted to enter non-public/restricted areas of the airport without an authorized escort." Following a crash at the airport, law enforcement authorities ordered the crash site secured and stationed officers on streets leading to the site with instructions to keep out all unauthorized persons.

Ah King, a television cameraman, followed an emergency vehicle through a police roadblock. He and others in his car were ordered to leave, but, as they were walking back to the car, Ah King jumped over a fence, ran to the top of the hill, and began taking pictures of the crash site. He was again ordered to leave and said he would not do so unless he was arrested, which he was. There were "No Trespassing" signs on the fence he jumped over. He was convicted of disorderly conduct. The Supreme Court of Wisconsin upheld his conviction, pointing out that "the United States Supreme Court has not recognized a constitutional protection for news gatherers' access to an accident scene" and that "the needs and rights of the injured and dying should be recognized . . . as having preference over . . . 'rights' that the dissenting justices would give to a 'news gatherer' who is simply concentrating on trying to beat out his competition and make his employer's deadline."

Recall from Chapter IV the possibility that trespassing can also be considered an invasion of privacy, and Prof. Kent Middleton's article, cited on p. 191, *supra*.

### 5.   ACCESS TO POLLING PLACES

In recent years it has become commonplace for the media to interview voters as they leave polling places—raising concerns that projections of voting patterns and expected results will affect the behavior of those who have not yet voted.  Time zones compound the problems, so that projections from the East may affect votes in the West.

The leading case is Daily Herald Co. v. Munro, 838 F.2d 380, 14 Med.L.Rptr. 2332 (9th Cir.1988).  A Washington statute passed in 1983 prohibited the conduct of any exit poll or public opinion poll within 300 feet of a polling place.  Several newspapers and broadcasting networks challenged the statute, contending that the 300-foot boundary precluded accurate exit polling and thereby violated the First Amendment.  Both the district court and the Court of Appeals for the Ninth Circuit agreed, holding the statute unconstitutional on its face.

The court of appeals held that it was a restriction on speech, not merely a restriction on access to news sources, because it restricted both the dissemination of information gathered by the polling and communication between the pollster and the voter.  It was content-based, because it restricted only discussion about the voter's choices.  The statute therefore was unconstitutional unless it was narrowly tailored to accomplish a compelling governmental interest by the least restrictive means available.  The interest advanced by the state was to prevent disruption at the polling place, but the statute banned nondisruptive polling as well.  It was not the least restrictive means, because disruption could be prevented by excluding pollsters from a smaller area, or perhaps by requiring them to inform voters that participation was voluntary.  It was not a permissible time, place and manner restriction because its effect was to preclude exit polling altogether.

More fundamentally, insofar as the purpose of the statute was to protect the integrity of elections, it was unconstitutional because that purpose was not a constitutionally permissible reason for regulating speech.  There was some evidence in the record suggesting that the legislature's true concern was not disruption, but a belief that early projection of results tended to discourage voter participation.  Without deciding which was the true motive, the court said "[T]he general interest of protecting voters from outside influences is not sufficient to justify speech regulation."

After the *Daily Herald* case, similar statutes were held unconstitutional in Minnesota, Florida and Montana.  In Georgia, a 250-foot exclusion was held unconstitutional, but the judge engaged in a "narrowing construction" of the statute, reducing the limit to 25 feet and holding that constitutional. National Broadcasting Co. v. Cleland, 697 F.Supp. 1204, 15 Med.L.Rptr. 2265 (N.D.Ga.1988).

The perceived evil of early projection of winners is that those who have not yet voted will either decide not to vote, or will be influenced to vote for the projected "winner." One solution would be to delay projections until the polls have closed. In recent elections, the major networks have adhered to a policy of not projecting results for a particular state until polls have closed in that state. That does not solve the problem for the western states or others with late poll closing times, however; their voters might still be influenced in presidential elections by projections from other states. One solution might be a uniform national hour for poll closing. One proposal that has received some support in Congress is to close all polls in presidential elections (except those in Hawaii and Alaska) at 9 p.m. E.S.T.

Despite the fact that federal courts in some jurisdictions have blocked the enforcement of exit polling laws, Lyle Denniston points out that the Supreme Court's decision in Burson v. Freeman, 504 U.S. ___, 112 S.Ct. 1846, 20 Med.L.Rptr. 1137 (1992), upholding a Tennessee law barring *campaigning* within 100 feet of the entrance to any polling place could lead to laws banning others in the same area. Says Denniston, "Politicians would invite constitutional trouble if they persuaded legislatures to put limits on press activity near polling places. But the Supreme Court's ruling in the Tennessee case suggests an alternative: passing laws to ban *everyone* but voters from the 'free zone' around the polls." "Are Exit Polls an Endangered Species?," Washington Journalism Review, Sept. 1992 at 50.

## D. DISCRIMINATORY ACCESS

Our focus has been on the question whether any statute or constitutional provision requires unwilling government officials to reveal information or to permit the press or public to gather information from government files, meetings or areas under government control. (Occasionally, a statute like the Privacy Act bars willing officials from supplying information.) The situation was one in which government officials wanted nobody to learn certain information.

A quite different question arises when government officials are willing to part with information that they are not required to divulge—but want to discriminate among the prospective gatherers. The government's interest in this situation is no longer that the material should remain confidential or that secrecy is needed, because the official is quite prepared to divulge the information. The claim of government secrecy has been replaced by the desire of a government official to play favorites in the disclosure process either for personal or political reasons.

Reporters have no right to force an unwilling private person to reveal information. If the private source does decide to speak, there is no reason why he cannot decide to sell the story to the highest bidder or to give it first to a reporter who is a close friend.

But government traditionally must behave in a non-discriminatory fashion. Even though government officials may not be required by statute or constitution to reveal certain information, they do not have unlimited control over the method of dissemination.

The starting point in general is that unless an official can demonstrate some reason for treating two apparently similar persons differently, the one who is being treated less well is not receiving equal protection of the laws. Notice that this constitutional protection in the Fourteenth Amendment applies broadly to all government action. If a government welfare program were arbitrarily to pay more money to redheads than to other recipients, the others would be able to claim a denial of equal protection.

We have already seen situations in which this rule of law might operate. If, in the Lashinsky case, two press photographers had been taking photographs and the state trooper had ordered Lashinsky to leave the scene while allowing his competitor to stay, the case would have been very different. Unless Lashinsky's behavior justified that different treatment, the trooper's actions would have amounted to unacceptable discrimination against Lashinsky. The trooper's action could not be justified on his or the state's disapproval of the editorial policy of Lashinsky's newspaper or on official disapproval of the gory photos that Lashinsky might have been attempting to obtain.

But all distinctions may not be invidious. Where press cards must be limited for some reasons, some government agencies may prefer media organizations that regularly cover the situations in which the cards will be needed. For example, if media representatives need press cards to get through police lines at emergencies, the police might give several cards to media that cover fires, police emergencies and disasters before granting any press cards to a newspaper that stressed political or fashion news and did not regularly cover emergencies. Drawing these lines may be quite difficult. This situation is explored in Los Angeles Free Press, Inc. v. City of Los Angeles, 9 Cal.App.3d 448, 88 Cal.Rptr. 605 (1970), cert. denied 401 U.S. 982 (1971), Justices Black, Douglas and Brennan dissenting.

Sometimes gender differences between reporters have been asserted to justify unequal treatment. The question of admitting women sports reporters to locker rooms went to court when the New York Yankees refused to allow them in after games. (This is not a case of private discrimination because Yankee Stadium was located on property owned by the city and thus involved governmental action.) The judge ordered that the women be admitted when the men were admitted. The players' privacy could be protected in less restrictive ways than by totally excluding women reporters. "The other two interests asserted by defendants, maintaining the status of baseball as a family sport and conforming to traditional notions of decency and propriety, are clearly too insubstantial to merit serious consideration." Ludtke v. Kuhn, 461 F.Supp. 86, 4 Med.L.Rptr. 1625 (S.D.N.Y.1978).

Twelve years later the subject of women in men's locker rooms generated controversy again after *Boston Herald* sports reporter Lisa Olson complained that several members of the New England Patriots "positioned themselves inches away from my face and dared me to touch their private parts" while she attempted to conduct an interview. Several players were fined by the league. In the uproar that followed, Cincinnati Bengals coach Sam Wyche barred a woman reporter from his team's locker room and was fined $30,000 for violating National Football League rules about access. To suggestions that there be a separate interview room, sportswriter Ailene Voisin said, "Anyone who says we don't need access to the locker room is naive and hasn't been around professional sports reporting." Editor & Publisher, Oct. 13, 1990 at 11.

The issue of discriminatory access may arise in a variety of contexts. For example, a public official may not like the way a particular newspaper has been treating him, and he may respond by holding a press conference and ordering guards not to admit anyone from that newspaper. Or, an official may decide to reveal information in a private talk with one reporter in his office, even though reporters seek entry to the meeting. Is there a critical difference between holding a public meeting and excluding one person and holding a private meeting and excluding all others?

Sometimes the different treatment may be based on characteristics of the individual. For example, in Sherrill v. Knight, 569 F.2d 124, 3 Med.L.Rptr. 1514 (D.C.Cir.1977), Sherrill, Washington correspondent for *The Nation,* had credentials for the House and Senate press galleries but was denied a White House press pass because of Secret Service objections. He was said to be a security risk because he had assaulted the press secretary to the governor of Florida and also faced assault charges in Texas.

The Secret Service had been ordered by the trial court to formulate "narrow and specific" standards for deciding who posed a sufficient danger to the President to be denied a press card. Security officials were the appellants in the court of appeals. That court began by discussing the claim and distinguishing several matters that were not involved in this case:

> These considerations can perhaps be best understood by first recognizing what this case does *not* involve. It is not contended that standards relating to the security of the President are the sole basis upon which members of the general public may be refused entry to the White House, or that members of the public must be afforded notice and hearing concerning such refusal. The first amendment's protection of a citizen's right to obtain information concerning "the way the country is being run" does not extend to every conceivable avenue a citizen may wish to employ in pursuing this right. Nor is the discretion of the President to grant interviews or briefings with

selected journalists challenged.   It would certainly be unreasonable
to suggest that because the President allows interviews with some
bona fide journalists, he must give this opportunity to all.   Finally,
appellee's first amendment claim is not premised upon the assertion
that the White House must open its doors to the press, conduct
press conferences, or operate press facilities.

Rather, we are presented with a situation where the White
House has voluntarily decided to establish press facilities for corre-
spondents who need to report therefrom.   These press facilities are
perceived as being open to all bona fide Washington-based journalists, whereas most of the White House itself, and press facilities in
particular, have not been made available to the general public.
White House press facilities having been made publicly available as
a source of information for newsmen, the protection afforded newsgathering under the first amendment guarantee of freedom of the
press, see [Branzburg and Pell], requires that this access not be
denied arbitrarily or for less than compelling reasons.   [  ]   Not
only newsmen and the publications for which they write, but also
the public at large have an interest protected by the first amendment in assuring that restrictions on newsgathering be no more
arduous than necessary, and that individual newsmen not be arbitrarily excluded from sources of information.

The court recognized that the safety of the President was a compelling, indeed overwhelming, interest that would justify restrictions on a
reporter's access to the White House.   But simply telling the reporter
that he was barred "for reasons of security" did not meet the procedural
safeguards that were required in this case.   The court ordered the Secret
Service to "publish or otherwise make publicly known the actual standard employed in determining whether an otherwise eligible journalist
will obtain a White House pass."   This did not lend itself to the narrow
specifications required by the trial judge.   It is enough if the Service is
guided by the standard of whether the applicant "presents a potential
source of physical danger   .   .   .   so serious as to justify his exclusion."
In addition, a reporter who is barred must get notice of the facts the
Service is relying on and have a chance to rebut them.

Occasionally, the basis for the different treatment is to be found in
the nature of the media involved.   Some states have barred journalists
with tape recorders from legislative chambers, though they have allowed
reporters to use pencil and pad.   These limits, which have rarely been
challenged, have usually been upheld.

Television has presented special problems.   In Chapter X, we considered the question of television cameras in the courtroom.   Television has
also raised questions in connection with the coverage of executions.   In
Garrett v. Estelle, 556 F.2d 1274, 2 Med.L.Rptr. 2265 (5th Cir.1977),
cert. denied 438 U.S. 914 (1978), the court upheld Texas' refusal to allow
cameras or tape recorders into the execution chamber.   The state was
willing to allow press pool reporters into the chamber and to permit

other reporters to view the events over simultaneous closed circuit television.  The court held, following *Pell* and *Saxbe,* that "the first amendment does not accompany the press where the public may not go." There was no public right to entry or to film the event.

The reporter then argued that he was being denied equal protection of the law because "other members of the press are allowed free use of their usual reporting tools."  The court disagreed because the regulation also denied "the print reporter use of his camera and the radio reporter use of his tape recorder.  Garrett is free to make his report by means of anchor desk or stand-up delivery on the TV screen, or even by simulation."

The final argument was that Texas had already chosen to make executions public by televising them over a closed circuit.  Texas responded that legislation closing executions had already been upheld, Holden v. Minnesota, 137 U.S. 483 (1890), and that the limited televising of the execution should not be equated with making the event public. The court agreed that the closed circuit television was for those allowed to be present and should not be used to justify opening the event to the public.

In KQED Inc. v. Vasquez, 18 Med.L.Rptr. 2323 (N.D.Cal.1991), a federal district court held that a prison warden may not exclude all media representatives from witnessing an execution, in view of long custom and practice, but excluding cameras was held to be constitutionally acceptable.  The court said, "It's well settled that the press has a right of access to whatever the public has a right to, but it has no special right of access and no right that's not available to the public generally."

## Chapter XIII

# OWNERSHIP OF THE MEDIA AND RELATED PROBLEMS

Although the press is the only industry mentioned by name in the U.S. Constitution, and the First Amendment gives it a unique protection from a great deal of government intrusion, the media are still businesses and as such are subject to antitrust laws, certain tax laws and some other laws affecting business. Although there is, of course, no "Federal Print Commission" regulating the print media, there is a Federal Communications Commission (FCC) regulating the electronic media. In this chapter we will look at some of these ownership/business concerns.

## A. NEWSPAPER ECONOMICS AND ANTITRUST LAW

In the next chapter we will address the issue presented in Miami Herald Publishing Co. v. Tornillo, 418 U.S. 241 (1974): can one successfully assert a legal right to use print media owned by another? The problem of limited access to the print media is more often a local, rather than regional or national, concern. The reason, simply, is that the United States has increasingly become a country of one newspaper cities—in all but the largest cities. Even in many cities with two newspapers, both are owned by the same company and often speak with the same editorial voice. Although persons who want access to media can sometimes find a measure of relief through local electronic media, many still think the problem is serious. It is worthwhile to consider how the economic structure of the newspaper industry has produced a situation that antitrust laws could not avoid.

The goals of American antitrust law were set in 1890, with the enactment of the Sherman Antitrust Act, 15 U.S.C.A. §§ 1 and 2. Section 1 states a desire to "protect trade and commerce against unlawful restraints and monopolies," and then declares illegal "every contract, combination in the form of trust or otherwise, or conspiracy, in restraint of trade, or commerce." Section 2 provides that "Every person who shall monopolize, or attempt to monopolize, or combine or conspire with any other person or persons, to monopolize any part of the trade or commerce . . . shall be guilty of a misdemeanor."

During the early 1800s, more dailies appeared. The period up to the Civil War was one in which "the newspaper was still basically individualistic and political—the creature of an individual editor/publisher, devoted to his personal views and those of his friends." B. Owen, Economics and Freedom of Expression 45 (1975). Changes began around 1880 that continued well into this century. Economies of scale in printing and distribution favored newspapers with large circulations and competition in the cities intensified.   By 1920 newspaper circulation was at a saturation point, and there was no further opportunity to produce a specialized product for a specific untapped audience.

Ben Bagdikian and others have expressed concern over the concentration of ownership of American newspapers and their decreasing numbers.   Between 1900 and 1980, for instance, the number of daily newspapers declined from 2,042 to 1,730, but in those same eight decades the number of newspaper *owners* declined from 2,023 to 760. Bagdikian, The Media Monopoly (1983) at 9.

The quoted provisions of the Sherman Act have been applied against business enterprises engaged in manufacturing or marketing tangible products.   Whether they can as readily be invoked against organizations involved in gathering and disseminating news was first considered in the early 1940s when the Associated Press was charged with violating both sections by creating a system of by-laws that prohibited local AP members from selling "spontaneous" news (as opposed to researched news) to non-members, and granted to its one member in each city the effective power to block all non-member local competitors from membership in AP.   Among other findings, the lower court determined that because of these restrictions 1,179 English language dailies with a circulation of 42 million were obligated not to supply AP news or their own "spontaneous" news to any nonmembers of AP.   The lower court (Learned Hand, J.) concluded that the AP By–Laws "unlawfully restricted admission to AP membership, and violated the Sherman Act insofar as the By–Laws' provisions clothed a member with powers to impose or dispense with conditions upon the admission of his business competitor."   Over three dissents, the Supreme Court affirmed.   Associated Press v. United States, 326 U.S. 1 (1945).   In doing so, the majority had to respond to the wire service's First Amendment argument:

> That Amendment rests on the assumption that the widest possible dissemination of information from diverse and antagonistic sources is essential to the welfare of the public, that a free press is a condition of a free society.   Surely a command that the government itself shall not impede the free flow of ideas does not afford non-governmental combinations a refuge if they impose restraints upon that constitutionally guaranteed freedom.   Freedom to publish means freedom for all and not for some.   Freedom to publish is guaranteed by the Constitution, but freedom to combine to keep others from publishing is not.

In a concurring opinion, Justice Frankfurter observed:

> To be sure, the Associated Press is a cooperative organization of members who are "engaged in a commercial business for profit." [  ]   But in addition to being a commercial enterprise, it has a relation to the public interest unlike that of any other enterprise pursued for profit.   A free press is indispensable to the workings of our democratic society.   The business of the press, and therefore the

business of the Associated Press, is the promotion of truth regarding public matters by furnishing the basis for an understanding of them. Truth and understanding are not wares like peanuts or potatoes. And so, the incidence of restraints upon the promotion of truth through denial of access to the basis for understanding calls into play considerations very different from comparable restraints in a cooperative enterprise having merely a commercial aspect.  I find myself entirely in agreement with Judge Learned Hand that "neither exclusively, nor even primarily, are the interests of the newspaper industry conclusive;  for that industry serves one of the most vital of all general interests:  the dissemination of news from as many different sources, and with as many different facets and colors as is possible.  That interest is closely akin to, if indeed it is not the same as, the interest protected by the First Amendment;  it presupposes that right conclusions are more likely to be gathered out of a multitude of tongues, than through any kind of authoritative selection.  To many this is, and always will be, folly;  but we have staked upon it our all."  52 F.Supp. 362, 372.

The Supreme Court has decided a variety of newspaper antitrust cases since Associated Press v. United States.

One type is suggested by Lorain Journal v. United States, 342 U.S. 143 (1951), in which the Justice Department charged that the *Lorain* (Ohio) *Journal*'s conduct constituted an attempt to monopolize interstate commerce in violation of the Sherman Act.  From 1933 to 1948 the *Journal* had a substantial monopoly of the mass dissemination of news and advertising in Lorain.  In 1948, however, the FCC licensed the Elyria–Lorain Broadcasting Company to operate WEOL radio in Elyria, Ohio, eight miles south of Lorain.  In an effort to preserve its monopoly, the *Lorain Journal* attempted to prevent WEOL from selling any advertising, by refusing to accept advertising from any Lorain County advertiser who advertised or whom the newspaper believed to be about to advertise over WEOL.  The trial court found that "the purpose and intent of this procedure was to destroy the broadcasting company" and issued an injunction enjoining such behavior.  The Supreme Court affirmed, noting that the *Journal*'s coverage of 99 percent of Lorain families made it a critical medium of advertising for Lorain businesses, and that the publisher's refusals to print advertising of those also using WEOL, if unchecked, would cut off WEOL's revenues and destroy it as a competitor.

In Times–Picayune Publishing Co. v. United States, 345 U.S. 594 (1953), the publisher of a morning and an afternoon paper in New Orleans set a unit rate that required an advertiser to place his ads in both papers or in neither but did not bar those who also chose to advertise in the one afternoon competitor.  The Department of Justice claimed that unit rates were really "tying agreements" that violated the Sherman Act.  The district court agreed that the power of the unopposed morning paper was forcing advertisers to place ads in the related afternoon paper, hurting the other afternoon paper because some advertisers who wanted the morning space would not also be able to afford both afternoon papers. On appeal, the Supreme Court, 5–4, reversed and held that the government had failed to establish its case. The majority viewed the "market" as including all three dailies, which meant that the morning paper did not hold a dominant position in the market, and therefore that the fairly strong afternoon partner was not being forced on unwilling advertisers. The dissenters thought the morning and afternoon markets were separate and agreed with the government's and the district court's view of the case.

In certain circumstances, refusal to accept advertising may violate the antitrust laws.

In Homefinders of America, Inc. v. Providence Journal Company, 621 F.2d 441, 6 Med.L.Rptr. 1018 (1st Cir.1980), a federal court of appeals held that the Sherman Act was *not* violated by the *Providence Journal*'s refusal to publish *false and misleading* advertisements submitted by a rental referral firm that charged fees to prospective tenants. (The newspaper had received numerous complaints about "bait and switch" practices by the advertiser before it refused the advertising.)

That case can be distinguished from Home Placement Service, Inc. v. Providence Journal Co., 682 F.2d 274, 8 Med.L.Rptr. 1881 (1st Cir.1982), which held that the refusal of the newspaper to accept *nonmisleading* classified advertising from a rental referral service which charged a fee *did* violate antitrust laws. The rental referral service was in competition with the newspaper. The court of appeals remanded the case for a determination of whether injunctive relief was appropriate and for an award of damages. This resulted in an award of $1 in nominal damages, trebled to $3, against the newspaper publisher. Although the court found the refusal to be a violation of the Sherman Act, it found the harm "immeasurable"—partially because the plaintiff had gone out of business without establishing an earnings history.

Another type of problem is suggested by United States v. Times Mirror Co., 274 F.Supp. 606 (C.D.Cal.1967), aff'd without opinion 390 U.S. 712 (1968). The Justice Department sought to prevent the Times Mirror Company, publisher of the *Los Angeles Times*, the largest daily newspaper in southern California, from acquiring the Sun Company, publisher of the largest "independent" daily newspaper in southern California. The Justice Department charged that the effect of the acquisition would be to "substantially lessen competition" in violation of Section 7 of the Clayton Act, 15 U.S.C. § 18, a major addition to the antitrust arsenal. The district court focused on the elements of the acquisition relevant to the effects on competition: whether the *Times* and the *Sun* were in the same product and geographical markets so as to be in competition for the consumer's dollar, the existing concentration in the southern California newspaper industry and the degree of control exercised by Times Mirror over the *Sun*'s policies. The district court concluded that the acquisition would substantially lessen competition in violation of the Clayton Act.

## The Newspaper Preservation Act

A significant antitrust confrontation between the Justice Department and the newspaper industry occurred in Citizen Publishing Co. v. United States, 394 U.S. 131 (1969). In 1940 the only two daily newspapers in Tucson, Ariz., the *Citizen*, an evening paper, and the *Star*, a daily and Sunday paper, negotiated a 25–year joint operating agreement. The agreement provided that each paper would retain its own editorial and news departments and its corporate identity, but that business operations would be integrated "to end any business or commercial competition between the two papers." The agreement was implemented in three ways. One was price fixing. Newspapers were sold and distributed by a single circulation department and advertising placed in either paper was sold through a single advertising department. Second, all profits realized were pooled and distributed to the *Star* and *Citizen* pursuant to an agreed ratio. Third, the *Star* and the *Citizen* agreed that neither paper nor any person affiliated with either would engage in any business in the metropolitan area of Tucson in conflict with the agreement. Prior to 1940 the two papers competed vigorously with each other. Though their circulations were about equal, the *Star* sold 50 percent more advertising than the *Citizen* and operated at an annual profit of about $26,000, while the *Citizen* 's annual losses averaged about $23,550. Following the agreement, all commercial rivalry between the papers ceased. Combined profits rose from $27,531 in 1940 to $1,727,-217 in 1964.

The government charged violations of the Sherman and Clayton Acts. The district court found that the agreement violated the antitrust laws and the Supreme Court affirmed. Its opinion focused on the applicability to the defendants of the "failing company doctrine." This judicially created doctrine held that the acquisition of one company by another did not violate the antitrust laws when "the resources of the one company were so depleted and the prospect of rehabilitation so remote that 'it faced the grave probability of a business failure,' " and there was "no other prospective purchaser." But the district court had found that at the time the *Star* and *Citizen* entered into the operating agreement, there was no serious probability that the *Citizen* was on the verge of going out of business or that, even had the *Citizen* been contemplating liquidation, the *Star* was the only available purchaser. The Supreme Court rejected the defense and affirmed the lower court's decree.

Congressional reaction was swift, largely because the decision raised doubt about the validity of similar agreements in 22 other cities. The result was the passage, in 1970, of the Newspaper Preservation Act, 15 U.S.C.A. § 1801 et seq. Congress declared its purpose to maintain "a newspaper press editorially and reportorially independent and competitive in all parts of the United States." Joint newspaper operating agreements were authorized to link virtually all mechanical and commercial aspects of the newspaper but there was to be no combination of editorial or reportorial staffs. A "failing newspaper" was defined as one that "regardless of its ownership or affiliation, is in probable danger of financial failure." The Act provided that joint agreements previously entered into are valid if when started, "not more than one of the newspaper publications involved . . . was likely to remain or become a financially sound publication." Future joint operating agreements required the approval of the Attorney General, who must first "determine that not more than one of the newspaper publications involved in the arrangement is a publication other than a failing newspaper" and that approval of the agreement would advance the policy of the Act. Predatory practices that would be unlawful if engaged in by a single entity may not be engaged in by the members of the joint operating agreement.

This Act is an exception to the general hostility between press and government. Here, the press actively sought Congressional intervention, whereas the press is usually protesting against government action and relying upon the First Amendment for protection. Apart from the obvious political pressures, why might Congress have passed such legislation? The Act has had its most important role in preserving the 22 joint operating agreements that were in existence at the time of *Citizen Publishing*. Only a handful of new agreements have been proposed and approved since the Act went into effect.

Examination of requests for new joint operating agreements can be a complicated and time-consuming process requiring detailed financial information about the newspapers involved. Even though a newspaper may seem to be endangered by financial losses, it may be owned by a chain large enough to absorb those losses. Market conditions that have adversely affected a money-losing newspaper may be only temporary. Predicting the effect of a JOA on advertisers and potential competitors is at best difficult.

A few figures will show the effect of JOA agreements on advertisers and potential competitors. Studies have shown that advertising provides 75 to 80 percent of the income of most newspapers. Joint operators and monopolists are asserted to charge about the same advertising rates— rates significantly higher than duopolists. Owen, Newspaper and Television Station Joint Ownership, 18 Antitrust Bull. 787 (1973). The situation in San Francisco is illustrative. The basic display rate of the *Chronicle* rose from $1.20 a line to $2.32 per line ten months after the agreement. The *Chronicle*'s increase may well have been due to the fact that as part of the agreement a third paper ceased publication and the *Chronicle* obtained a monopoly in the morning. The afternoon paper's rate rose from $1.03 to $1.55 during the same period. More significantly, an advertiser could buy space in both papers for $2.50 per line after the agreement. This is the common result of such agreements and presents obvious problems to prospective competitors.

The first major challenge to the Act came in San Francisco. A small paper that had hoped to move into competition with the large papers filed an antitrust action claiming that their agreement made it virtually impossible for another paper to break in. Advertisers whose rates had been increased by the agreement joined the challenge. The defendants asserted that the Act validated their agreement. Plaintiffs moved to dismiss the defense on the ground that the Act was unconstitutional. Bay Guardian Co. v. Chronicle Publishing Co., 344 F.Supp. 1155 (N.D.Cal.1972). A First Amendment challenge to the Act was rejected:

> Plaintiffs contend that the Act is unconstitutional because it permits the defendant newspapers to combine so as to prevent the plaintiffs' newspaper from publishing. This effect of the Act, they contend, causes it to be in violation of the freedom of the press guarantee of the First Amendment.

> The simple answer to the plaintiffs' contention is that the Act does not authorize any conduct. It is a narrow exception to the antitrust laws for newspapers in danger of failing. Thus it is in many respects merely a codification of the judicially created "failing company" doctrine. See, 83 Harv.L.R. 673 (1970).

> . . .

> Here the Act was designed to preserve independent editorial voices. Regardless of the economic or social wisdom of such a course, it does not violate the freedom of the press. Rather it is merely a selective repeal of the antitrust laws. It merely looses the same shady market forces which existed before the passage of the Sherman, Clayton and other antitrust laws.

> Such a repeal, even when applicable only to the newspaper industry, does not violate the First Amendment.

The assistant general in charge of the antitrust division once commented upon the limited power of antitrust law to prevent the decline of newspaper competition:

> In some instances, this decline can be attributed to the higher average costs imposed on a smaller paper as a result of the existence of economies of scale and the disposition of many large advertisers to place a disproportionately large portion of their advertising dollars with the newspaper having the larger circulation. In addition, the decline may be in part a result of increased competition from the broadcasting media and from weekly or free-distribution newspapers, the latter being particularly a phenomenon of suburban areas. There is, however, some reasons to hope that new, more efficient printing technology will ease the economies of scale problem and, in the long run, lead to a rebirth of competing daily newspapers.

Shenefield, Ownership Concentration in Newspapers, 65 A.B.A.J. 1332 (1979). He noted that his division was trying to preserve the opportunity for such a development by closely scrutinizing mergers and joint operating agreements; by making sure that dominant daily newspapers do not use their power to erect barriers to entry by newcomers; and to reduce and limit joint ownership of newspaper and broadcast facilities in the same market. This latter concern is explored shortly.

To suggest the potential for revival within the industry, Shenefield noted that the circulation of weekly newspapers increased from 21.3 million to 37.9 million between 1960 and 1977. During that same period, the circulation of daily newspapers rose only from 58.9 million to 61.7 million. A 1986 estimate places the number sold at 62.8 million, up just more than a million in nine years. A. Wells, Mass Media and Society at 77 (1987).

Considerable controversy arose over the 1981 application by the Seattle Times Company and the *Seattle Post–Intelligencer* for approval of a joint operating agreement for the two metropolitan daily newspapers in Seattle. The Committee for an Independent P–I, made up of the newspaper's employees and advertisers, and the publishers of smaller newspapers, challenged the joint operating agreement on the ground that the owners had not made a good faith effort to sell the *Post–Intelligencer*. The U.S. Court of Appeals for the Ninth Circuit held in 1983 that the Attorney General's finding that one of the newspapers was "failing" was justified by the showing that the newspaper would probably fail, even without evidence of greater effort to sell the paper. Committee for an Independent P–I v. Hearst Corp., 704 F.2d 467, 9 Med.L.Rptr. 1489 (9th Cir.), cert. denied 464 U.S. 892 (1983).

A 1987 application for a joint operating agreement by the *Detroit News* and *Detroit Free Press* was approved by the attorney general in 1988—after much media attention and extensive court proceedings. Each of the newspapers is owned by a major media corporation—the *Free Press* by Knight–Ridder, Inc., and the *News* by Gannett. The *Free Press* described itself as a failing newspaper and reported that it had been losing money since 1959.

The attorney general approved the JOA despite the recommendation of the administrative law judge. The attorney general concluded that the *News* had the power to outlast the *Free Press* by continuing a price war and that the *Free Press* had no way to extricate itself unilaterally from this predicament.

Various public interest groups sued to prevent implementation of the agreement, alleging that the two parent groups were using their extensive financial resources (what lawyers call "deep pockets") to depress prices artificially, thereby creating losses to justify approval of a JOA that would produce large profits for both in the future. The district court upheld the JOA, and the court of appeals affirmed. Michigan Citizens for an Independent Press v. Thornburgh, 868 F.2d 1285, 16 Med.L.Rptr. 1065 (D.C.Cir.1989). The majority said:

> The real difficulty with this case . . . is the effect that the prospect of a JOA has on the behavior of competing newspapers. [ ] It is feared that a statute authorizing a JOA creates a self-fulfilling prophecy. Newspapers in two newspaper towns will compete recklessly because of a recognition that the loser will be assured a soft landing.

. . . [But] the record of years of fierce competition and consequent losses to both papers led the Attorney General reasonably to conclude that both papers were principally pursuing market domination and that their strategies had been followed before any mutual discussion of a JOA. Nevertheless, the Attorney General implicitly recognized that it would be impossible completely to preclude competing newspapers from factoring into their business strategy the prospect of a JOA. As he laconically put it, "newspapers cannot be faulted for considering and acting upon an alternative that Congress has created."

We can envision a perfectly rational different policy, one that would require a showing that the weaker paper was more bloodied before approving a JOA and therefore might discourage the sort of competition we saw in Detroit. Congress, however, delegated to the Attorney General, and not to us, the delicate and troubling responsibility of putting content into the ambiguous phrase "probable danger of financial failure." . . .

Judge Ruth Bader Ginsburg, dissenting, said the attorney general's interpretation "allows parties situated as Gannett and Knight–Ridder are artificially to generate and maintain the conditions that will yield them a passing JOA. I remain unpersuaded that, with passage of the Newspaper Preservation Act, Congress opened the door to this sort of self-serving, competition-quieting arrangement." She urged that the case be remanded to the attorney general to give him an opportunity to show why his approval should not be deferred until "the results of the current competition afford a firmer basis for predicting whether the Free Press, profitably for itself, for readers, and for advertisers, can survive."

Rehearing en banc was denied by a 5–4 vote. 868 F.2d 1300, 16 Med.L.Rptr. 1315. The Supreme Court, by a 4–4 vote (Justice White abstaining for unexplained "personal reasons"), affirmed without opinion. 493 U.S. 38, 16 Med.L.Rptr. 2496 (1989).

The ruling ended a 42–month legal and public relations battle, clearing the way for implementation of the JOA in late November. Within weeks, the two newspapers had an editorial disagreement over a police corruption story both had been pursuing vigorously. See "Debate in Detroit," Editor & Publisher, Dec. 30, 1989 at 9.

During the summer of 1989, while the decision on the Detroit JOA was still pending, the House Economic and Commercial Law Subcommittee heard testimony on whether the Newspaper Preservation Act should be repealed, amended, or left alone. A preponderance of witnesses criticized the NPA, in part calling for an end to loopholes permitting newspapers to generate losses intentionally to qualify. Editor & Publisher, August 12, 1989 at 26. Among groups advocating repeal of the JOA were the Association of Alternative Newsweeklies (a group of 60 member newspapers headed by long-time JOA-opponent Bruce B. Brugmann) and the groups that unsuccessfully opposed the Detroit JOA and one in York, Pa.

Attorney General Richard Thornburgh approved the JOA for the *York Daily Record* and the *York Dispatch* in February 1990, just 18 days before the *Record* planned to close because of steady losses by the newspaper's parent company since 1980.  The attorney general's decision cleared the way for the 20th JOA under the Newspaper Preservation Act.  Editor & Publisher, March 3 at 13.  A federal district court denied a York citizens' groups request to block the JOA, and it went into effect in March.  Editor & Publisher, March 17, 1990 at 13.

## B.  NEWSPAPER TAXATION PROBLEMS

Special problems arise with taxation of the press—particularly in instances in which the tax appears discriminatory.  The first significant case involving taxation of the press arose from the efforts of Gov. Huey Long of Louisiana to silence criticism of his actions by the state's larger newspapers.  The Louisiana legislature enacted a gross receipts tax that was to apply to those newspapers, magazines and other periodicals having a circulation of more than 20,000 copies per week.  The result was a tax limited to major newspapers.  The Supreme Court unanimously rejected it.  Grosjean v. American Press Co., 297 U.S. 233, 1 Med. L.Rptr. 2685 (1936).  Justice Sutherland's opinion did not rely on the political background, nor did it focus on equal protection.  Instead it reviewed the history of press regulation and concluded that the tax operated as a prior restraint on publishing because it led publishers to reduce press runs to avoid the tax, thus limiting the public's access to information.  Because the First Amendment was meant at least to avoid most types of prior restraint the Court had little difficulty in rejecting the tax.  The Supreme Court's opinion was criticized in C. Miller, The Supreme Court and the Uses of History, 78 (1969):

> It is evident that the Court's chief historical supports in this case, that early Americans valued their press as a vehicle for criticism of British policies and that the colonists were furious at the stamp tax (which included fees on newspapers), have no historical relationship to each other.  Although these two cherished uprights were used in constructing the story of American freedom, it was the Court, not history, that built a crossbeam between them.

The next year the Supreme Court made clear that *Grosjean* was not to be read as a general barrier to taxation of the media.  Arizona had levied a tax on the sales or gross income of "practically every person or concern engaged in selling merchandise or services in the state."  A newspaper publisher, relying on *Grosjean,* challenged the tax, but the Supreme Court of Arizona rejected the challenge and distinguished *Grosjean* on the ground that newspapers there had been singled out for special treatment.  As a concurring justice observed, in *Grosjean* "a situation existed in the state of Louisiana which was unparalleled in American history.  A single individual had obtained a control over the entire executive, legislative, and judicial machinery of that state as absolute as that exercised by any modern European dictatorship."  Giragi v. Moore,

49 Ariz. 74, 64 P.2d 819 (1937). The publisher appealed to the Supreme Court of the United States, claiming a conflict with *Grosjean*. The appeal was dismissed by the Supreme Court for "want of a substantial federal question." 301 U.S. 670 (1937).

The following year the Supreme Court held that taxes levied by states and municipalities on gross advertising receipts of media having interstate circulation did not unconstitutionally burden interstate commerce. Western Live Stock v. Bureau of Revenue, 303 U.S. 250 (1938). See also, Matter of New Yorker Magazine, Inc. v. Gerosa, 3 N.Y.2d 362, 165 N.Y.S.2d 469, 144 N.E.2d 367 (1957), appeal dism'd for want of a substantial federal question 356 U.S. 339 (1958). Fairly apportioned taxes that do not unfairly burden interstate enterprises are permissible, and media receive no special protection.

In Minneapolis Star and Tribune Co. v. Minnesota Commissioner of Revenue, 460 U.S. 575 (1983), the Supreme Court held that a Minnesota tax violated the First Amendment. The tax was imposed on publications' use of paper and ink exceeding $100,000 annually. After the enactment of the tax, 11 publishers, producing 14 of the 388 paid circulation newspapers in the state, incurred a tax liability in 1974. The Star and Tribune Co. was only one of the 11 publishers, but the company paid approximately two-thirds of the revenue raised by the tax. In holding the tax unconstitutional, the Supreme Court noted that the press had been singled out for special treatment, that no adequate justification had been offered for the special treatment of newspapers and that the tax targeted a small group of newspapers.

In Arkansas Writers' Project, Inc. v. Ragland, 481 U.S. 221, 13 Med.L.Rptr. 2313 (1987), the Supreme Court held unconstitutional a state sales tax statute that exempted newspapers and "religious, professional, trade and sports . . . publications printed and published within this State . . . when sold through regular subscriptions," but did not exempt general-interest magazines like that published by the Arkansas Writers' Project. The tax was found to discriminate against a small group of publications (as in *Minneapolis Star and Tribune*) and was found not to serve a compelling state interest.

In Texas Monthly, Inc. v. Bullock, 489 U.S. 1, 16 Med.L.Rptr. 1177 (1989), an attack on a sales tax scheme that exempted religious periodicals but not general interest magazines succeeded on freedom of religion grounds. The Court held that the exemption violated the establishment clause because it benefitted religious organizations as such, rather than nonprofit or philosophical organizations generally, and its primary purpose and effect were not secular.

*Texas Monthly* also argued that the exemption violated the press clause, but only Justice White accepted that argument. The other members of the majority did not address it. Justice Scalia, in a dissent in which Chief Justice Rehnquist and Justice Kennedy joined, said neither the establishment clause nor the press clause should preclude the state from favoring religion with a tax exemption. "Just as the

Constitution sometimes *requires* accommodation of religious expression despite not only the Establishment Clause but also the Speech and Press Clauses, so it sometimes permits accommodation despite all those clauses.   Such accommodation is unavoidably content-based because the Freedom of Religion Clause is content-based."

In Leathers v. Medlock, 499 U.S. 439, 18 Med.L.Rptr. 1953 (1991), the Supreme Court considered an Arkansas sales tax extending to the sale of cable television service but exempting the sale of newspapers and magazines.   The Arkansas Supreme Court had held that the tax violated the First Amendment prior to being amended to include the sale of services that unscramble television signals.   Cable television operators asserted the tax was discriminatory because of the newspaper exemption;   the state argued that enough difference exists between cable television and the service of unscrambling satellite signals to justify their differential tax treatment.   The Supreme Court made it clear that differential taxation of the media is not unconstitutional *per se*.   The Supreme Court held that the state's application of the tax "to cable television services alone, or to cable and satellite services, while exempting the print media, does not violate the First Amendment."   In an opinion by Justice O'Connor, the majority read *Grosjean, Minneapolis Star* and *Arkansas Writers'* as forbidding differential taxation of the press only if "the tax is directed at, or presents the danger of suppressing, particular ideas."   In further proceedings, the Supreme Court of Arkansas held that the tax did not violate the Equal Protection Clause of the Fourteenth Amendment because it was rationally related to the state's interest in making satellite transmissions available in rural areas where cable was not feasible.   Medlock v. Leathers, 311 Ark. 175, 842 S.W.2d 428 (1992), cert. denied 113 S.Ct. 2929 (1993).

## C.  FCC OWNERSHIP LIMITATIONS

Our discussion so far has dealt with print media rather than with users of the broadcast spectrum, to the extent that legal controls for the two differ.   At the heart of this distinction is the requirement that all broadcast facilities be licensed by the Federal Communications Commission.   Under the Communications Act of 1934, the Commission has sole power to allocate the broadcast spectrum, to establish general standards of operation and to license persons to use designated parts of the spectrum.   Although the details of broadcast regulation are covered in Chapters XIV–XVII, it is appropriate to examine now the Commission's efforts to maximize diversity of ownership of broadcast facilities.

### 1.  LOCAL CONCENTRATION

*Duopoly*.  Local concentration of control of mass media facilities has been a problem for the Commission at least since 1938, when it received an application for a standard broadcasting station in Flint, Mich., from applicants who already controlled another corporation that operated a standard broadcasting station in the same area. Although there were no rival applicants, the Commission refused to grant the second facility without a compelling showing that the public interest would be served in such a situation.

This was the beginning of the so-called "duopoly" rule, which the Commission formalized in a general rule that it would not grant a license to any applicant who already held a similar facility or license so located that the service areas of the two would overlap.

In the 1960s the Commission returned to this subject and recognized that the dwindling number of American newspapers made the impact of individual broadcasting stations "significantly greater." This reinforced the need for diversity in the broadcast media and led the Commission to announce that it would probably never again grant a duopoly.

During this period, however, the Commission was granting to the same applicant one AM, one FM and one television station in the same locality because this was not a duplication of facilities in the same service area. In 1970 the Commission moved the next step and adopted the so-called "one-to-a-customer" rule. This meant that in the future the Commission would not grant a television license to the owner of an AM station in the community, or vice versa. The Commission rejected an argument "that the good profit position of a multiple owner in the same market results in more in-depth informational programs being broadcast and, thus, in more meaningful diversity. We do not doubt that some multiple owners may have a greater capacity to so program, but the record does not demonstrate that they generally do so. The citations and honors for exceptional programming appear to be continually awarded to a very few licensees—perhaps a dozen or so multiple owners out of a total of hundreds of such owners." Amendment of §§ 73.35, 73.240 and 73.636 of the Commission Rules Relating to Multiple Ownership of Standard, FM and Television Broadcast Stations, 22 F.C.C.2d 306 (1970).

When an AM licensee sought to add an FM station, that presented a special problem because traditionally FM had been weak as a competitive force, and indeed the Commission during the 1950s had encouraged AM stations to acquire FM stations. But by 1970 FM stations were becoming more powerful competitors and were becoming increasingly profitable. For this reason, the rules as initially adopted would have banned not only VHF-radio combinations, but also AM–FM combinations. However, concerned that AM–FM combinations might still be "economically and/or technically interdependent," and that the rules would hinder development of FM service, the Commission subsequently modified the rules to permit the formation of new AM–FM combinations. Multiple Ownership of Standard, FM and TV Broadcast Stations, 28 F.C.C.2d 662, 21 R.R.2d 1551 (1971).

As for UHF stations, the Commission acknowledged that they were still weak competitively and that few would go on the air unless affiliated with an established radio station. Therefore, the Commission refused to adopt a firm rule against radio-UHF combinations but indicated that it would review those on a case-by-case basis. Finally, the Commission announced that its ban on VHF-radio combinations would apply only in the future and no divestitures would be required, due to the large number of existing combinations and a sense that ordering divestiture for such a large group might very well create instability.

In late 1988 the Commission modified the duopoly rule to allow greater overlap between commonly-owned AM or commonly-owned FM stations. The change reduced the minimum spacing required between such stations. The FCC also announced that it would be inclined to grant waivers of the one-to-a-market rule in those top 25 markets that have at least 30 broadcast voices.

A few years later, the FCC announced a further relaxation of the duopoly rules for radio. Arguing that the marked increase in competition had produced an extremely fragmented radio marketplace in which radio licensees would experience increasingly severe economic and financial stress, the Commission concluded that increased economies of scale were necessary for these licensees. The FCC decided to allow owners to own more stations in any single market. The exact number depended on the total number of stations in the market. The Commission also imposed a cap of 25 percent on the combined audience share of all stations owned by the one licensee as of the filing date of the application to acquire a new station. Radio Multiple Ownership Rules, 7 F.C.C.Rcd. 2755, 70 R.R.2d 903 (1992).

The relaxation of the duopoly rules, as well as changes in the multiple ownership rules, discussed later in this chapter, produced an extremely negative reaction by Congress. In response to this, the Commission modified its new duopoly rules. Licensees in markets with fewer than 15 radio stations are permitted to own up to three stations as long as the number owned is less than 50 percent of the total number of stations in the market. In markets with 15 or more stations, licensees are permitted to own up to four stations. No more than two can be in the same service. In addition, the Commission reaffirmed the audience share cap of 25 percent. Radio Multiple Ownership Rules, Recon., 7 F.C.C.Rcd. 6387, 71 R.R.2d. 227 (1992).

The FCC has also issued a notice of proposed rulemaking (NPRM) proposing various ways to relax the duopoly rules for television. Among the alternatives proposed are allowing common ownership of one AM, one FM and one TV station, allowing only TV–AM combinations, or deleting the one-to-a-market rule. Review of the Commission's Regulations Governing Television Broadcasting, 7 F.C.C.Rcd. 4111 (1992).

*Cross-ownership.* When the Commission adopted its one-to-a-customer rules, it also proposed the adoption of another set of rules that would proscribe common ownership of newspapers and broadcast facilities serving the same area, and require divestiture of prohibited combinations. Although the Commission had flirted with such a regulation in the early 1940s, it abandoned the attempt. The basis for the Commission movement in 1970 was an awareness that 94 television stations were affiliated through common control with newspapers in the same city. In addition, of course, "some newspapers own television stations in other cities, which also serve the city in which the newspaper is located." The Commission thought this situation was very similar to the joint ownership of two television stations in the same community, something the Commission has never permitted. "The functions of newspapers and television stations as journalists are so similar that their joint ownership is, in this respect, essentially the same as the joint ownership of two television stations." After extensive consideration the Commission adopted rules in 1975 that prohibit granting a license for a television or radio station to any applicant who already controls, owns or operates a daily newspaper serving part of the same area.

The rule was to apply retroactively only to a few small communities where the sole newspaper owned the sole television station. Common ownership of the only newspaper and the only radio station was to be dissolved unless the community had an independently owned television station. Multiple Ownership Rules, Second Report and Order, 50 F.C.C.2d 1046, 32 R.R.2d 954, reconsidered, 53 F.C.C.2d 589, 33 R.R.2d 1603 (1975). The Commission rejected widespread divestiture as too "harsh" without a clear showing of need. Some appealed the prospective ban itself, others the refusal to order more divestitures.

The Supreme Court unanimously upheld the Commission's three-part rules on whether a newspaper should be permitted to hold a broadcasting license in the same community in which the newspaper is located. Federal Communications Commission v. National Citizens Committee for Broadcasting, 436 U.S. 775, 43 R.R.2d 152, 3 Med.L.Rptr. 2409 (1978). In an opinion by Justice Marshall, the Court first held that the Commission had acted within its statutory and constitutional authority in promulgating a rule that prospectively barred newspaper owners from holding broadcast licenses in the same community. The statutory authority came from § 303(r) of the 1934 Act, which permitted the Commission to promulgate rules and regulations to give effect to the provisions of the Act. "It was not inconsistent with the statutory scheme . . . for the Commission to conclude that the maximum benefit to the 'public interest' would follow from allocation of broadcast licenses so as to promote diversification of the mass media as a whole." Even though the record was not conclusive on the point, the Commission "acted rationally in finding that diversification of ownership would enhance the possibility of achieving greater diversity of viewpoints." It was also permissible for the Commission to make diversification the controlling factor in selecting new applicants.

The Commission's constitutional power to exclude a class of applicants from holding licenses was upheld on the scarcity rationale of Red Lion Broadcasting Co. v. Federal Communications Commission, 395 U.S. 367, 16 R.R.2d 2029, 1 Med.L.Rptr. 2053 (1969), (discussed at length in Chapter XIV), which rejected the claim of an "unabridgeable First

Amendment right to broadcast comparable to the right of every individual to speak, write, or publish":

> The physical limitations of the broadcast spectrum are well known. Because of problems of interference between broadcast signals, a finite number of frequencies can be used productively; this number is far exceeded by the number of persons wishing to broadcast to the public. In light of this physical scarcity, Government allocation and regulation of broadcast frequencies are essential, as we have often recognized. [ ] No one here questions the need for such allocation and regulation, and, given that need, we see nothing in the First Amendment to prevent the Commission from allocating licenses so as to promote the "public interest" in diversification of the mass communications media.

Efforts to affect the coverage of public issues in broadcasting "may be permissible where similar efforts to regulate the print media would not be." The basic thrust of the opinion was that since the Commission was being forced to choose among applicants for limited facilities, it was free to "enhance the diversity of information heard by the public without ongoing government surveillance of the content of speech."

Second, the Court upheld the Commission's decision to order divestiture in 16 "egregious" cases of small communities, in each of which a single company owned the only newspaper and the only television station or, if there was no television station, the only radio station. The danger in these situations was sufficient to warrant divestiture. Third, the Supreme Court found that the Commission had adequately explained that diversification was not its only concern:

> The Order identified several specific respects in which the public interest would or might be harmed if a sweeping divestiture requirement were imposed: the stability and continuity of meritorious service provided by the newspaper owners as a group would be lost; owners who had provided meritorious service would unfairly be denied the opportunity to continue in operation; "economic dislocations" might prevent new owners from obtaining sufficient working capital to maintain the quality of local programming; and local ownership of broadcast stations would probably decrease. [ ] We cannot say that the Commission acted irrationally in concluding that these public interest harms outweighed the potential gains that would follow from increasing diversification of ownership.

The result, then, was to permit continuation of all but 16 existing combinations, but to bar future newspaper-broadcast co-located combinations.

The Court noted that the Commission's study of "existing co-located newspaper-television combinations showed that in terms of percentage of time devoted to several categories of local programming, these stations had displayed 'an undramatic but nonetheless statistically significant superiority' over other television stations."

The Court observed that remaining combinations still could be challenged on an individual basis. Diversification "will be a relevant but somewhat secondary factor." A challenger might also show that a common owner has "engaged in specific economic or programming abuses" attributable to the existence of its combination.

When Rupert Murdoch's News America Corp. purchased six television stations from Metromedia, the FCC granted a two-year waiver of the cross-ownership rules as applied to his properties in New York and Chicago.

The two-year waiver was upheld on appeal. Health and Medicine Policy Research Group v. Federal Communications Commission, 807 F.2d 1038, 61 R.R.2d 1450 (D.C.Cir.1986). The Commission granted a similar waiver when News America bought channel 25 in Boston. Twentieth Holdings Corp., 1 F.C.C.Rcd. 1201, 61 R.R.2d 1484 (1986). As of December 1987 News America had sold only the Chicago newspaper and for months there had been stories circulating that he planned to ask for a permanent waiver for the New York and Boston newspapers. Boston Business Journal, June 22, 1987 at 1. However, in December 1987 Congress included a provision in the FCC's budget authorization prohibiting the Commission from either altering the cross-ownership rules or extending temporary waivers. (The only two existing waivers were held by News America.)

News America appealed the FCC's subsequent denial of its petition for an extension of the temporary waivers. Noting that the continuing budget resolution struck at "Murdoch with the precision of a laser beam," the court of appeals found it fatally underinclusive. News America Publishing v. Federal Communications Commission, 844 F.2d 800, 64 R.R.2d 1309, 15 Med.L.Rptr. 1161 (D.C.Cir.1988).

In the meantime News America had sold the *New York Post.* Although the court decision gave News America the option of seeking an extension of the waiver for the Boston newspaper and television station, the company decided instead to sell the television station. It was purchased by the Boston Celtics.

Ironically, in 1993 News America reacquired the *New York Post.* At the time, no other parties were interested in acquiring the paper, which would have ceased publishing if it could not be sold. The FCC granted News America a waiver of the cross-ownership rules apparently reasoning that even a cross-owned paper would provide more diversity than no paper at all.

*Television–Cable cross-ownership.* In 1970 the Commission prospectively barred cross-ownership of a local cable system by a local television licensee.

After years of debate over whether or not to require divestiture of the existing combinations, the Commission finally decided to grandfather all cases in which a television station owned a cable system in an overlapping area—so long as the station was not the only commercial broadcast station serving the cable community. The Commission's cable cross-ownership rules were codified in the Cable Communications Policy Act of 1984 (discussed at length in Chapter XVIII).

## 2. NATIONAL CONCENTRATION

The Commission has also demonstrated a continuing concern that a few nationwide entities might dominate broadcasting.

Beginning in 1940 the Commission adopted rules limiting the number of stations that might be held by a single owner. In 1953 the Commission resolved that the rules should prohibit the ownership or control, directly or indirectly, by any party of more than seven AM stations, seven FM stations and seven television stations of which not more than five could be VHF. The Commission explained its position as follows:

> The vitality of our system of broadcasting depends in large part on the introduction into this field of licensees who are prepared and qualified to serve the varied and divergent needs of the public for radio service. Simply stated, the fundamental purpose of this facet of the multiple ownership rules is to promote diversification of ownership in order to maximize diversification of program and service viewpoints as well as to prevent any undue concentration of economic power contrary to the public interest. In this connection, we wish to emphasize that by such rules diversification of program services is furthered without any governmental encroachment on what we recognize to be the prime responsibility of the broadcast licensee. (See Section 326 of the Communications Act.)  . . .

The Commission chose an equal number of AM and FM stations because at that time 538 of the 600 FM stations were owned by AM licensees, the result of a conscious Commission policy to encourage AM stations to put FM stations on the air because most of those operating FM stations alone were finding it extremely unprofitable. The number seven was chosen "in order that present holdings of such stations be not unduly disrupted." Very few owners had holdings in excess of seven, and the Commission planned to hold a divestiture hearing for each of them. Rules and Regulations Relating to Multiple Ownership, 18 F.C.C. 288 (1953).

This limitation rule was challenged immediately by a group owner who claimed that the Commission was illegally using the rule procedure to foreclose the right of an applicant to a hearing as to whether the license would be in the public interest, by making a categorical judgment linking the public interest with a given maximum concentration of holdings. The Supreme Court rejected the challenge in United States v. Storer Broadcasting Co., 351 U.S. 192, 1 Med.L.Rptr. 1983 (1956). The Court viewed the Commission's action as "but a rule that announces the Commission's attitude on public protection against such concentration." The opinion did state, however, that the Commission's responsibility to behave in the public interest required it to grant a hearing to an applicant who had already reached the maximum number of stations but nonetheless asserted sufficient reasons why the rule should be waived in its particular case.

In 1984 the Commission voted to expand the limits on multiple ownership from 7–7–7 to 12–12–12. The new rule made no distinction between VHF and UHF television. Faced with mounting criticism of the new rule and threatened Congressional action, the Commission revised the television portion of the order. One entity may now own 12 television stations provided the total reach of these stations is less than 25 percent of the television households in the country. For the purposes of this rule, a UHF is counted as covering only 50 percent of the television households in its market. In an attempt to encourage minority ownership, the Commission also decided to allow those who purchase interests in minority-controlled broadcast outlets to own 14 stations in any service and to reach up to 30 percent of the television households in the country as long as at least two of the stations in each service are more than half-owned by minorities. Multiple Ownership (12–12–12 Reconsideration), 100 F.C.C.2d 74, 57 R.R.2d 967 (1985).

At the same time the FCC relaxed the duopoly rules for radio, it also relaxed the multiple ownership rules. In Radio Multiple Ownership Rules, p. 611, *supra,* the Commission decided to permit licensees to own up to 30 AM and 30 FM stations nationwide. This was modified on reconsideration to 18 AM and 18 FM stations. This is scheduled to be raised to 20 AM and 20 FM after two years. Licensees may acquire an attributable interest in an additional three AM and three FM stations as long as they are controlled by either minorities or small business (total revenues of less than $500,000 and total assets of less than $1,000,000.) *Radio Multiple Ownership Rules, Recon.,* p. 611, *supra.* The Commission has also proposed relaxing the multiple ownership rules for television. *Review of the Commission's Regulations Governing Television Broadcasting,* p. 611, *supra.*

### 3.  CONGLOMERATES IN BROADCASTING

Occasionally the problem has been raised, not in terms of multiple ownership of competing media, but concern about other businesses in which a prospective licensee is engaged. The prime example is a merger that was proposed between ABC, which in its capacity as group owner, owned 17 broadcasting stations, and International Telephone and Telegraph, a vast conglomerate with manufacturing facilities, telecommunication operations and other activities in 66 countries throughout the world.

Critics were concerned that ITT would use the broadcasting facilities to further the interests of the parent corporation in ways that might include distorting the news and making editorial decisions on grounds other than professional journalistic criteria. The Commission rejected these concerns on the ground that "it is too late in the day to argue that such outside business interests are disqualifying. . . . We cannot in this case adopt standards which when applied to other cases would require us to restructure the industry unless we are prepared to undertake that task. We could not, in good conscience, forbid ABC to merge with ITT without instituting proceedings to separate NBC from RCA, both of which are bigger than the respective principals in this case." The Commission granted the application for transferring of the 17 licenses by a 4–3 vote. Memorandum Opinion and Order 7 F.C.C.2d 245, 9 R.R.2d 12 (1966).

While an appeal by the Justice Department on antitrust grounds was pending, the parties abandoned their proposed merger. Would there be any problem if, for example, General Motors sought to acquire a television station in Detroit? Are different questions raised if a book publisher or motion picture producer seeks a television license?

*The Gannett–Combined Communications Merger.* In 1979 the FCC approved what was at that time the largest deal in broadcasting history. The parties were Gannett, which at the time published 77 daily and 32 weekly newspapers and owned WHEC–TV in Rochester, N.Y., and Combined Communications Corp., which at the time owned newspapers in Cincinnati and Oakland (Cal.) plus five VHF, two UHF, six AM and six FM stations. In addition, Gannett owned Louis Harris and Associates, the polling firm, and Combined was a major supplier of outdoor advertising. The deal called for $370 million in Gannett stock to go to Combined. After spin-offs to meet the FCC's cross-ownership policies, Gannett had 79 daily newspapers, seven television stations and 12 radio stations.

The final result, because of the spin-offs, violated no concentration rule. Nonetheless, the Commission considered whether granting the applications to transfer ownership of the stations would be in the "public interest." The majority concluded that the deal was not likely to adversely affect competition or raise antitrust concerns.

The First Amendment issue, however, raised harder questions. The FCC noted that Gannett had represented that "local autonomy will be the touchstone for the operation of each newspaper and broadcast property" and that the newspapers would operate separately from the broadcast properties. For example, Gannett asserted that in 1976, of its 35 papers that made endorsements, 22 endorsed Gerald Ford and 13 endorsed Jimmy Carter. Decentralized operation was the goal, although everyone recognized that under § 310 of the 1934 Act, Gannett had to retain ultimate control of its stations.

Some were concerned about the possibility that the size of the combination would lead advertisers and stock market investors to exercise more control over management than would occur with less centralized control. They feared that a large communications entity might "harm diversity of information and opinion through its institutional pressures rather than by any intentional acts of its corporate leadership."

The FCC stressed countervailing considerations: "Media chains may have more freedom and might be inclined to take more risks in their reporting of news and opinion because their financial health allows a degree of independence from the political views of their major advertisers." The size of the organization might permit more coverage of national news in competition with the wire services, the television networks and the largest newspapers and magazines.

Because all of these newspapers and stations face "substantial local mixed-media competition," even if a "Gannett" view entered a new market it was not eliminating other views available in that market. Affirmatively, the Commission noted that the deal had resulted in the break-up of cross-ownership interests in Phoenix and St. Louis, as well as sale of WHEC–TV to a buyer controlled by a minority group. This made WHEC–TV the first network-affiliated major market television station controlled by a minority group. The merger was approved, 5–1.

The dissenter was greatly concerned by the "trend" toward placing "organs of information and news and opinion in this country in fewer and fewer hands. This is an unhealthy thing for a democracy: absentee ownership, on a vast scale, of newspapers and broadcasting stations. . . . Where are the William Allen Whites of 1979? Too many of them have been bought out, one by one, by the chains. They've been made offers they could not refuse."

*The Capital Cities Communications–American Broadcasting Companies Merger.* In early 1985 Capital Cities Communications (CCC) announced plans to acquire American Broadcasting Companies, Inc. (ABC) for $3.5 billion. This transaction, larger by far than any previous broadcast sale or merger, resulted in the formation of a new company, Capital Cities/ABC, Inc. (CC/ABC).

To meet the various FCC ownership rules, CC/ABC sold more than $1 billion worth of broadcast, cable and newspaper holdings. The Commission approved the merger in late 1985, granting a waiver of the duopoly rule to allow CC/ABC to retain TV stations in both New York and Philadelphia. Soon after the 1988 modifications in the duopoly rule, p. 611, *supra,* were announced, the Commission ruled on an additional waiver request. The CC/ABC merger had produced ownership of TV–AM–FM combinations in New York City, Chicago, and Los Angeles and of an AM–FM combination in San Francisco. The FCC granted permanent waivers in all four cases because all four cities were in the top 25 television markets and each had over 30 separately owned and operated broadcast stations after the proposed waivers. The FCC found 94 separate licensees in New York, 105 in Chicago, 79 in Los Angeles, and 57 in San Francisco. The Commission did not scrutinize each proposal for economic efficiencies because it had already concluded that such efficiencies generally exist. Allowing the combinations would not undermine the benefits that flow from the "Commission's traditional pro-competitive and diversity policies."

Commissioner Dennis concurred separately. She had suggested a two-tier approach in lieu of the 25 market–30 licensee approach. She would have restricted waivers to markets with at least 10 television stations, 45 separate owners and 65 broadcast stations. "In all other markets, we should not only retain the rule, but enforce it strictly." Because the four markets involved here met even her tighter requirements, she concurred. Capital Cities/ABC, Inc., 66 R.R.2d 1146 (1989).

*The General Electric Purchase of RCA.* In 1985 General Electric announced the purchase of RCA for more than $6 billion. Among RCA's various subsidiaries is NBC. The purchase did not require waivers of specific FCC rules or divestiture of any broadcast properties because GE did not have any separate media holdings. In both the CC/ABC and the GE/RCA cases there was little concern for the more general media concentration issues addressed in the Gannett case.

# Chapter XIV

# ACCESS TO THE MEDIA

As we noted in our discussion of the philosophical justifications for the First Amendment, many people believe that the intended beneficiary of the First Amendment was the public not the press. Traditionally, protecting the press was seen as benefitting the public. However, some have come to question this latter idea. According to Professor Jerome Barron and other scholars, the development of mass media has reduced the "marketplace of ideas" to nothing more than a romantic fantasy. Reasoning that increased concentration in media ownership had resulted in a marketplace failure, Barron contends that a government-created right of access to the media is not just allowed, but indeed required by the First Amendment. See Chapter II. In 1973 Barron had the chance to argue this point before the Supreme Court on behalf of Pat Tornillo.

## A. ACCESS TO PRINT MEDIA

### MIAMI HERALD PUBLISHING CO. v. TORNILLO

Supreme Court of the United States, 1974.
418 U.S. 241, 94 S.Ct. 2831, 41 L.Ed.2d 730, 1 Med.L.Rptr. 1898.

MR. CHIEF JUSTICE BURGER delivered the opinion of the Court.

The issue in this case is whether a state statute granting a political candidate a right to equal space to reply to criticism and attacks on his record by a newspaper, violates the guarantees of a free press.

I

In the fall of 1972, appellee, Executive Director of the Classroom Teachers Association, apparently a teachers' collective-bargaining agent, was a candidate for the Florida House of Representatives. On September 20, 1972, and again on September 29, 1972, appellant printed editorials critical of appellee's candidacy.* In response to these editorials appellee demanded that appellant print verbatim his replies, defending the role of the Classroom Teachers Association and the organization's accomplishments for the citizens of Dade County. Appellant declined to print the appellee's replies, and appellee brought suit in Circuit Court, Dade County, seeking declaratory and injunctive relief and actual and punitive damages in excess of $5,000. The action was premised on Florida Statute § 104.38 (1973), a "right of reply" statute which provides that if a candidate for nomination or election is assailed

---

* [The editorials are reprinted in the opinion. The proposed replies are printed in Lange, The Role of the Access Doctrine in the Regulation of the Mass Media: A Critical Review and Assessment, 52 N.C.L.Rev. 1, 60 n. 272 (1973)—ed.]

regarding his personal character or official record by any newspaper, the candidate has the right to demand that the newspaper print, free of cost to the candidate, any reply the candidate may make to the newspaper's charges. The reply must appear in as conspicuous a place and in the same kind of type as the charges which prompted the reply, provided it does not take up more space than the charges. Failure to comply with the statute constitutes a first-degree misdemeanor.[2]

Appellant sought a declaration that § 104.38 was unconstitutional. After an emergency hearing requested by appellee, the Circuit Court denied injunctive relief because, absent special circumstances, no injunction could properly issue against the commission of a crime, and held that § 104.38 was unconstitutional as an infringement on the freedom of the press under the First and Fourteenth Amendments to the Constitution. 38 Fla.Supp. 80 (1972). The Circuit Court concluded that dictating what a newspaper must print was no different from dictating what it must not print. The Circuit Judge viewed the statute's vagueness as serving "to restrict and stifle protected expression." Id., at 83. Appellee's cause was dismissed with prejudice.

On direct appeal, the Florida Supreme Court reversed, holding that § 104.38 did not violate constitutional guarantees. 287 So.2d 78 (1973). It held that free speech was enhanced and not abridged by the Florida right-of-reply statute, which in that court's view, furthered the "broad societal interest in the free flow of information to the public." Id., at 82. It also held that the statute is not impermissibly vague; the statute informs "those who are subject to it as to what conduct on their part will render them liable to its penalties." Id., at 85.[4] Civil remedies, including damages, were held to be available under this statute; the case was remanded to the trial court for further proceedings not inconsistent with the Florida Supreme Court's opinion.

. . .

# III
## A

The challenged statute creates a right to reply to press criticism of a candidate for nomination or election. The statute was enacted in 1913 and this is only the second recorded case decided under its provisions.

**2.** "104.38 *Newspaper assailing candidate in an election; space for reply*—If any newspaper in its columns assails the personal character of any candidate for nomination or for election in any election, or charges said candidate with malfeasance or misfeasance in office, or otherwise attacks his official record, or gives to another free space for such purpose, such newspaper shall upon request of such candidate immediately publish free of cost any reply he may make thereto in as conspicuous a place and in the same kind of type as the matter that calls for such reply, provided such reply does not take up more space than the matter replied to. Any person or firm failing to comply with the provisions of this section shall be guilty of a misdemeanor of the first degree, punishable as provided in § 775.082 or § 775.083."

**4.** The Supreme Court placed the following limiting construction on the statute:

"[W]e hold that the mandate of the statute refers to 'any reply' which is wholly responsive to the charge made in the editorial or other article in a newspaper being replied to and further that such reply will be neither libelous nor slanderous of the publication nor anyone else, nor vulgar nor profane." Id., at 86.

Appellant contends the statute is void on its face because it purports to regulate the content of a newspaper in violation of the First Amendment. Alternatively it is urged that the statute is void for vagueness since no editor could know exactly what words would call the statute into operation. It is also contended that the statute fails to distinguish between critical comment which is and which is not defamatory.

## B

The appellee and supporting advocates of an enforceable right of access to the press vigorously argue that government has an obligation to ensure that a wide variety of views reach the public.[8] The contentions of access proponents will be set out in some detail.[9] It is urged that at the time the First Amendment to the Constitution was enacted in 1791 as part of our Bill of Rights the press was broadly representative of the people it was serving. While many of the newspapers were intensely partisan and narrow in their views, the press collectively presented a broad range of opinions to readers. Entry into publishing was inexpensive; pamphlets and books provided meaningful alternatives to the organized press for the expression of unpopular ideas and often treated events and expressed views not covered by conventional newspapers. A true marketplace of ideas existed in which there was relatively easy access to the channels of communication.

Access advocates submit that although newspapers of the present are superficially similar to those of 1791 the press of today is in reality very different from that known in the early years of our national existence. In the past half century a communications revolution has seen the introduction of radio and television into our lives, the promise of a global community through the use of communications satellites, and the specter of a "wired" nation by means of an expanding cable television network with two-way capabilities. The printed press, it is said, has not escaped the effects of this revolution. Newspapers have become big business and there are far fewer of them to serve a larger literate population. Chains of newspapers, national newspapers, national wire and news services, and one-newspaper towns,[13] are the dominant features of a press that has become noncompetitive and enormously powerful and influential in its capacity to manipulate popular opinion and change the course of events. Major metropolitan newspapers have collaborated to establish news services national in scope. Such national news organizations provide syndicated "interpretive reporting" as well

8. See generally Barron, Access to the Press—A New First Amendment Right, 80 Harv.L.Rev. 1641 (1967).

9. For a good overview of the position of access advocates see Lange, The Role of the Access Doctrine in the Regulation of the Mass Media: A Critical Review and Assessment, 52 N.C.L.Rev. 1, 8–9 (1973) (hereinafter Lange).

13. "Nearly half of U.S. daily newspapers, representing some three-fifths of daily and Sunday circulation, are owned by newspaper groups and chains, including diversified business conglomerates. One-newspaper towns have become the rule with effective competition operating in only 4 percent of our large cities." Background Paper by Alfred Balk in Twentieth Century Fund Task Force Report for a National News Council, A Free and Responsive Press 18 (1973).

as syndicated features and commentary, all of which can serve as part of the new school of "advocacy journalism."

The elimination of competing newspapers in most of our large cities, and the concentration of control of media that results from the only newspaper's being owned by the same interests which own a television station and a radio station, are important components of this trend toward concentration of control of outlets to inform the public.

The result of these vast changes has been to place in a few hands the power to inform the American people and shape public opinion.[15] Much of the editorial opinion and commentary that is printed is that of syndicated columnists distributed nationwide and, as a result, we are told, on national and world issues there tends to be a homogeneity of editorial opinion, commentary, and interpretive analysis. The abuses of bias and manipulative reportage are, likewise, said to be the result of the vast accumulations of unreviewable power in the modern media empires. In effect, it is claimed, the public has lost any ability to respond or to contribute in a meaningful way to the debate on issues. The monopoly of the means of communication allows for little or no critical analysis of the media except in professional journals of very limited readership. . . .

The obvious solution, which was available to dissidents at an earlier time when entry into publishing was relatively inexpensive, today would be to have additional newspapers. But the same economic factors which have caused the disappearance of vast numbers of metropolitan newspapers,[16] have made entry into the marketplace of ideas served by the print media almost impossible. It is urged that the claim of newspapers to be "surrogates for the public" carries with it a concomitant fiduciary obligation to account for that stewardship. From this premise it is reasoned that the only effective way to insure fairness and accuracy and to provide for some accountability is for government to take affirmative action. The First Amendment interest of the public in being informed is said to be in peril because the "marketplace of ideas" is today a monopoly controlled by the owners of the market.

Proponents of enforced access to the press take comfort from language in several of this Court's decisions which suggests that the First Amendment acts as a sword as well as a shield, that it imposes obligations on the owners of the press in addition to protecting the press from government regulation. In Associated Press v. United States, [ ], the Court, in rejecting the argument that the press is immune from the antitrust laws by virtue of the First Amendment, stated:

**15.** "Local monopoly in printed news raises serious questions of diversity of information and opinion. What a local newspaper does not print about local affairs does not see general print at all. And, having the power to take initiative in reporting and enunciation of opinions, it has extraordinary power to set the atmosphere and determine the terms of local consideration of public issues." B. Bagdikian, The Information Machines 127 (1971).

**16.** The newspapers have persuaded Congress to grant them immunity from the antitrust laws in the case of "failing" newspapers for joint operations. 84 Stat. 466, 15 U.S.C. § 1801 et seq.

"The First Amendment, far from providing an argument against application of the Sherman Act, here provides powerful reasons to the contrary. That Amendment rests on the assumption that the widest possible dissemination of information from diverse and antagonistic sources is essential to the welfare of the public, that a free press is a condition of a free society. Surely a command that the government itself shall not impede the free flow of ideas does not afford non-governmental combinations a refuge if they impose restraints upon that constitutionally guaranteed freedom. Freedom to publish means freedom for all and not for some. Freedom to publish is guaranteed by the Constitution, but freedom to combine to keep others from publishing is not. Freedom of the press from governmental interference under the First Amendment does not sanction repression of that freedom by private interests." (Footnote omitted.)

In New York Times Co. v. Sullivan, [  ], the Court spoke of "a profound national commitment to the principle that debate on public issues should be uninhibited, robust and wide-open." It is argued that the "uninhibited, robust" debate is not "wide-open" but open only to a monopoly in control of the press. Appellee cites the plurality opinion in Rosenbloom v. Metromedia, Inc., 403 U.S. 29, 47, and n. 15 (1971), which he suggests seemed to invite experimentation by the States in right-to-access regulation of the press.[18]

Access advocates note that Mr. Justice Douglas a decade ago expressed his deep concern regarding the effects of newspaper monopolies:

"Where one paper has a monopoly in an area, it seldom presents two sides of an issue. It too often hammers away on one ideological or political line using its monopoly position not to educate people, not to promote debate, but to inculcate in its readers one philosophy, one attitude—and to make money." "The newspapers that give a variety of views and news that is not slanted or contrived are few indeed. And the problem promises to get worse . . .." The Great Rights 124–125, 127 (E. Cahn ed. 1963).

They also claim the qualified support of Professor Thomas I. Emerson, who has written that "[a] limited right of access to the press can be safely enforced," although he believes that "[g]overnment measures to encourage a multiplicity of outlets, rather than compelling a few outlets

---

**18.** "If the States fear that private citizens will not be able to respond adequately to publicity involving them, the solution lies in the direction of ensuring their ability to respond, rather than in stifling public discussion of matters of public concern.*

"[*] Some states have adopted retraction statutes or right-of-reply statutes . . ..

"One writer, in arguing that the First Amendment itself should be read to guarantee a right of access to the media not limited to a right to respond to defamatory falsehoods, has suggested several ways the law might encourage public discussion. Barron, Access to the

Press—A New First Amendment Right, 80 Harv.L.Rev. 1641, 1666–1678 (1967). It is important to recognize that the private individual often desires press exposure either for himself, his ideas, or his causes. Constitutional adjudication must take into account the individual's interest in access to the press as well as the individual's interest in preserving his reputation, even though libel actions by their nature encourage a narrow view of the individual's interest since they focus only on situations where the individual has been harmed by undesired press attention. A constitutional rule that deters the press from covering the ideas or activities of the private individual thus conceives the individual's interest too narrowly."

to represent everybody, seems a preferable course of action." T. Emerson, The System of Freedom of Expression 671 (1970).

## IV

However much validity may be found in these arguments, at each point the implementation of a remedy such as an enforceable right of access necessarily calls for some mechanism, either governmental or consensual. If it is governmental coercion, this at once brings about a confrontation with the express provisions of the First Amendment and the judicial gloss on that Amendment developed over the years.[20]

The Court foresaw the problems relating to government-enforced access as early as its decision in Associated Press v. United States, supra. There it carefully contrasted the private "compulsion to print" called for by the Association's bylaws with the provisions of the District Court decree against appellants which "does not compel AP or its members to permit publication of anything which their 'reason' tells them should not be published." 326 U.S., at 20 n. 18. In Branzburg v. Hayes, [ ], we emphasized that the cases then before us "involve no intrusions upon speech or assembly, no prior restraint or restriction on what the press may publish, and no express or implied command that the press publish what it prefers to withhold." In Columbia Broadcasting System, Inc. v. Democratic National Committee, 412 U.S. 94, 117 (1973), the plurality opinion as to Part III noted:

> "The power of a privately owned newspaper to advance its own political, social, and economic views is bounded by only two factors: first, the acceptance of a sufficient number of readers—and hence advertisers—to assure financial success; and, second, the journalistic integrity of its editors and publishers."

An attitude strongly adverse to any attempt to extend a right of access to newspapers was echoed by several Members of this Court in their separate opinions in that case. Id., at 145 (Stewart, J., concurring); id., at 182 n. 12 (Brennan, J., dissenting). Recently, while approving a bar against employment advertising specifying "male" or "female" preference, the Court's opinion in Pittsburgh Press Co. v. Human Relations Comm'n, 413 U.S. 376, 391 (1973), took pains to limit its holding within narrow bounds:

> "Nor, *a fortiori*, does our decision authorize any restriction whatever, whether of content or layout, on stories or commentary originated by Pittsburgh Press, its columnists, or its contributors. On the contrary, we reaffirm unequivocally the protection afforded to editorial judgment and to the free expression of views on these and other issues, however controversial."

Dissenting in *Pittsburgh Press*, Mr. Justice Stewart, joined by Mr. Justice Douglas, expressed the view that no "government agency—local,

---

**20.** Because we hold that § 104.38 violates the First Amendment's guarantee of a free press we have no occasion to consider appellant's further argument that the statute is unconstitutionally vague.

state, or federal—can tell a newspaper in advance what it can print and what it cannot." [   ]

We see that beginning with *Associated Press,* supra, the Court has expressed sensitivity as to whether a restriction or requirement constituted the compulsion exerted by government on a newspaper to print that which it would not otherwise print. The clear implication has been that any such a compulsion to publish that which " 'reason' tells them should not be published" is unconstitutional. A responsible press is an undoubtedly desirable goal, but press responsibility is not mandated by the Constitution and like many other virtues it cannot be legislated.

Appellee's argument that the Florida statute does not amount to a restriction of appellant's right to speak because "the statute in question here has not prevented the *Miami Herald* from saying anything it wished" begs the core question. Compelling editors or publishers to publish that which " 'reason' tells them should not be published" is what is at issue in this case. The Florida statute operates as a command in the same sense as a statute or regulation forbidding appellant to publish specified matter. Governmental restraint on publishing need not fall into familiar or traditional patterns to be subject to constitutional limitations on governmental powers. Grosjean v. American Press Co., [   ]. The Florida statute exacts a penalty on the basis of the content of a newspaper. The first phase of the penalty resulting from the compelled printing of a reply is exacted in terms of the cost in printing and composing time and materials and in taking up space that could be devoted to other material the newspaper may have preferred to print. It is correct, as appellee contends, that a newspaper is not subject to the finite technological limitations of time that confront a broadcaster but it is not correct to say that, as an economic reality, a newspaper can proceed to infinite expansion of its column space to accommodate the replies that a government agency determines or a statute commands the readers should have available.[22]

Faced with the penalties that would accrue to any newspaper that published news or commentary arguably within the reach of the right-of-access statute, editors might well conclude that the safe course is to avoid controversy. Therefore, under the operation of the Florida statute, political and electoral coverage would be blunted or reduced. Government-enforced right of access inescapably "dampens the vigor and limits the variety of public debate," New York Times Co. v. Sullivan, [   ]. The Court, in Mills v. Alabama, 384 U.S. 214, 218 (1966), stated:

---

**22.** "However since the amount of space a newspaper can devote to 'live news' is finite,* if a newspaper is forced to publish a particular item, it must as a practical matter, omit something else.

"[*] The number of column inches available for news is predetermined by a number of financial and physical factors, including circulation, the amount of advertising, and increasingly, the availability of newsprint. . . ."

Note, 48 Tulane L.Rev. 433, 438 (1974) (one footnote omitted).

Another factor operating against the "solution" of adding more pages to accommodate the access matter is that "increasingly subscribers complain of bulky, unwieldly papers." Bagdikian, Fat Newspapers and Slim Coverage, Columbia Journalism Review 19 (Sept./Oct.1973).

"[T]here is practically universal agreement that a major purpose of [the First] Amendment was to protect the free discussion of governmental affairs.    This of course includes discussions of candidates . . .."

Even if a newspaper would face no additional costs to comply with a compulsory access law and would not be forced to forego publication of news or opinion by the inclusion of a reply, the Florida statute fails to clear the barriers of the First Amendment because of its intrusion into the function of editors.   A newspaper is more than a passive receptacle or conduit for news, comment, and advertising.   The choice of material to go into a newspaper, and the decisions made as to limitations on the size and content of the paper, and treatment of public issues and public officials—whether fair or unfair—constitute the exercise of editorial control and judgment.   It has yet to be demonstrated how governmental regulation of this crucial process can be exercised consistent with First Amendment guarantees of a free press as they have evolved to this time. Accordingly, the judgment of the Supreme Court of Florida is reversed.

It is so ordered.

MR. JUSTICE BRENNAN, with whom MR. JUSTICE REHNQUIST joins, concurring.

I join the Court's opinion which, as I understand it, addresses only "right of reply" statutes and implies no view upon the constitutionality of "retraction" statutes affording plaintiffs able to prove defamatory falsehoods a statutory action to require publication of a retraction.   See generally Note, Vindication of the Reputation of a Public Official, 80 Harv.L.Rev. 1730, 1739–1747 (1967).

MR. JUSTICE WHITE, concurring.

The Court today holds that the First Amendment bars a State from requiring a newspaper to print the reply of a candidate for public office whose personal character has been criticized by that newspaper's editorials.   According to our accepted jurisprudence, the First Amendment erects a virtually insurmountable barrier between government and the print media so far as government tampering, in advance of publication, with news and editorial content is concerned.   New York Times Co. v. United States, 403 U.S. 713 (1971).   A newspaper or magazine is not a public utility subject to "reasonable" governmental regulation in matters affecting the exercise of journalistic judgment as to what shall be printed.   Cf. Mills v. Alabama, 384 U.S. 214, 220 (1966).   We have learned, and continue to learn, from what we view as the unhappy experiences of other nations where government has been allowed to meddle in the internal editorial affairs of newspapers.   Regardless of how beneficent-sounding the purposes of controlling the press might be, we prefer "the power of reason as applied through public discussion" and remain intensely skeptical about those measures that would allow government to insinuate itself into the editorial rooms of this Nation's press.   .  .  .

.   .   .

To justify this statute, Florida advances a concededly important interest of ensuring free and fair elections by means of an electorate informed about the issues.  But prior compulsion by government in matters going to the very nerve center of a newspaper—the decision as to what copy will or will not be included in any given edition—collides with the First Amendment.  Woven into the fabric of the First Amendment is the unexceptionable, but nonetheless timeless, sentiment that "liberty of the press is in peril as soon as the government tries to compel what is to go into a newspaper."  2 Z. Chafee, Government and Mass Communications 633 (1947).

The constitutionally obnoxious feature of § 104.38 is not that the Florida Legislature may also have placed a high premium on the protection of individual reputational interests;  for government certainly has "a pervasive and strong interest in preventing and redressing attacks upon reputation."  Rosenblatt v. Baer, 383 U.S. 75, 86 (1966).  Quite the contrary, this law runs afoul of the elementary First Amendment proposition that government may not force a newspaper to print copy which, in its journalistic discretion, it chooses to leave on the newsroom floor.   .   .   .

.   .   .

Reaffirming the rule that the press cannot be forced to print an answer to a personal attack made by it, however, throws into stark relief the consequences of the new balance forged by the Court in the companion case also announced today.  Gertz v. Robert Welch, Inc., [  ], goes far toward eviscerating the effectiveness of the ordinary libel action, which has long been the only potent response available to the private citizen libeled by the press.  Under *Gertz,* the burden of proving liability is immeasurably increased, proving damages is made exceedingly more difficult, and vindicating reputation by merely proving falsehood and winning a judgment to that effect are wholly foreclosed.  Needlessly, in my view, the Court trivializes and denigrates the interest in reputation by removing virtually all the protection the law has always afforded.

Of course, these two decisions do not mean that because government may not dictate what the press is to print, neither can it afford a remedy for libel in any form.  *Gertz* itself leaves a putative remedy for libel intact, albeit in severely emaciated form;  and the press certainly remains liable for knowing or reckless falsehoods under New York Times Co. v. Sullivan, [  ], and its progeny, however improper an injunction against publication might be.

One need not think less of the First Amendment to sustain reasonable methods for allowing the average citizen to redeem a falsely tarnished reputation.   .   .   .   To me it is a near absurdity to so deprecate individual dignity, as the Court does in *Gertz,* and to leave the people at the complete mercy of the press, at least in this stage of our history when the press, as the majority in this case so well documents, is steadily becoming more powerful and much less likely to be deterred by threats of libel suits.

**Notes and Questions**

1.   Although the statute was limited to attacks on candidates in election campaigns, the majority treated the case as involving a general right of access to the press.  Should it have mattered that the law was designed to assure the free flow of information to the public only in the political area and only at a specific point in the political process?  The Florida Supreme Court had emphasized this aspect of the state's objective in upholding the statute (287 So.2d 78, 80–81, 86 (Fla.1973)):

> The election of leaders of our government by a majority of the qualified electors is the fundamental precept upon which our system of government is based, and is an integral part of our nation's history.  Recognizing that there is a right to publish without prior governmental restraint, we also emphasize that there is a correlative responsibility that the public be fully informed.

> The entire concept of freedom of expression as seen by our founding fathers rests upon the necessity for a fully informed electorate.  James Madison wrote that, "A popular government without popular information or the means of acquiring it is but a prologue to a farce or tragedy; or, perhaps both.  Knowledge will forever govern ignorance; and a people who mean to be their own governors, must arm themselves with the power which knowledge gives" (to W.T. Barry, August 4, 1822).

> The public *"need to know"* is most critical during an election campaign.  By enactment of the first comprehensive corrupt practices act relating to primary elections in 1909 our legislature responded to the need for insuring free and fair elections.  . . . The statutory provision . . . was enacted not to punish, coerce or censor the press but rather as a part of a centuries old legislative task of *maintaining conditions conducive to free and fair elections.* The Legislature in 1913 decided that owners of the printing press had already achieved such political clout that when they engaged in character assailings, the victim's electoral chances were unduly and improperly diminished.  To assure fairness in campaigns, the assailed candidate had to be provided an equivalent opportunity to respond; otherwise not only the candidate would be hurt *but also* the people would be deprived of both sides of the controversy.

> What some segments of the press seem to lose sight of is that the First Amendment guarantee is "not for the benefit of the press so much as for the benefit of us all." [10]  Speech concerning public affairs is more than self expression.  It is the essence of self government. [11]

.   .   .

10.   Time, Inc. v. Hill, 385 U.S. 374, 389 (1967).

11.   Garrison v. Louisiana, 379 U.S. 64, 74–75 (1964).

In conclusion, we do not find that the operation of the statute would interfere with freedom of the press as guaranteed by the Florida Constitution and the Constitution of the United States. Indeed it strengthens the concept in that it presents both views leaving the reader the freedom to reach his own conclusion. This decision will encourage rather than impede the wide open and robust dissemination of ideas and counterthought which the concept of free press both fosters and protects and which is essential to intelligent self government.

Is the justification for an access statute strongest—or weakest—when limited to election campaigns rather than being categorical? For the legislative history of the statute, including the odd fact that it was sponsored by an editor and that seven of the eight newspapermen in the legislature supported it, see Hoffer and Butterfield, "The Right to Reply: A Florida First Amendment Aberration," 53 Journ.Q. 111 (1976).

2. In Mills v. Alabama, 384 U.S. 214, 1 Med.L.Rptr. 1334 (1966), cited in *Tornillo,* the Court unanimously reversed the conviction of a newspaper editor for writing an editorial in violation of a statute prohibiting "electioneering" or solicitation of votes on election day:

Suppression of the right of the press to praise or criticize governmental agents and to clamor and contend for or against change, which is all that this editorial did, muzzles one of the very agencies the Framers of our Constitution thoughtfully and deliberately selected to improve our society and keep it free. The Alabama Corrupt Practices Act by providing criminal penalties for publishing editorials such as the one here silences the press at a time when it can be most effective. It is difficult to conceive of a more obvious and flagrant abridgment of the constitutionally guaranteed freedom of the press.

The state claimed to be protecting the public from confusing "last minute charges" that could not be answered, but the Court noted that such charges could still be made on the day before the election. No "test of reasonableness can save" such a statute.

3. *Access in Electoral Campaigns.* Can a special case be made for requiring access to the media in election campaigns? On balance, is the right of reply likely to expand or contract the breadth of political debate?

4. The West Virginia Supreme Court relied on the last paragraph of Chief Justice Burger's opinion to reverse an injunction compelling a weekly newspaper to publish a political advertisement. In furtherance of a policy of not publishing political ads in the last issue before an election, the newspaper declined an ad from a political action committee opposing a local bond issue. Holding the injunction unconstitutional, the court read *Tornillo* for the proposition that "government can never compel a private newspaper to publish anything, without violating the First Amendment's guarantee of a free press." Citizen Awareness Regarding Education v. Calhoun County Publishing Inc., 185 W.Va. 168, 406 S.E.2d 65, 19 Med.L.Rptr. 1061 (1991).

5.  How did the Florida court and the Supreme Court analyze the issue of "compulsion" to print in terms of the traditional First Amendment framework of prior restraints and subsequent punishment?  Is an affirmative obligation to print something any more or less onerous than a negative ban on certain kinds of publication?  From a philosophical standpoint, can *Tornillo* be seen as a conflict between "freedom from" and "freedom to?"  Or a conflict between "press" and "speech?"

6.  Might the statute in *Tornillo* have withstood attack if it had required a demonstration of "falsity"—or deliberate falsity—in the newspaper coverage before making access available?

7.  Is there a basis for Justice Brennan's assertion that the Court's opinion does not bring into question a statute that would give defamation plaintiffs who prove falsity the right to a mandatory retraction?  Consider the differences among statutes that required the paper to say "We were wrong" or "A court has ordered us to state that it has found that we were in error" or "A court has ordered us to retract our statement."

What about a statute that gave the publisher a choice between paying damages and issuing a retraction?

8.  In a book devoted almost exclusively to the access question, it is claimed that the *Tornillo* ruling is "almost devoid of reasoned support, its use of precedent is disingenuous, and the constitutional principle announced is not consistent with other rules grounded in the First Amendment."  B. Schmidt, Jr., Freedom of the Press vs. Public Access 13 (1976).  Because unreasoned opinions are fragile, "the sweeping and conclusive fashion in which the Court rejected the constitutionality of access statutes may prove less durable than less categorical arguments against broad access requirements."  Later, at p. 234, the author suggested that the Court may have written sweepingly to counter the broad claims of the Florida opinions and the academic supporters of access.  Although the case does recognize "autonomy of the press" as a "guarantee of constitutional dimension," later cases may impose some limit on the broad proposition, as in other First Amendment areas.

9.  One response to the *Tornillo* problem was more discussion of unofficial "press councils" to pass upon complaints brought against media by members of the public.  The subject was explored in Ritter and Leibowitz, "Press Councils:  The Answer to Our First Amendment Dilemma," 1974 Duke L.J. 845.  Published reports by the National News Council, including those published in the 1970s in *Columbia Journalism Review*, demonstrate the results of the council's efforts.  With the demise of the National News Council in the 1980s due to lack of interest and inadequate funding, hopes that press councils would solve access problems died too.

10.  A public opinion survey undertaken by Public Agenda Foundation suggested that many respondents disagreed with the results in *Tornillo*.  By overwhelming votes, the respondents rejected any kind of censorship or prohibition on what newspapers or television might report.  But, by

even larger margins, they wanted their media to be "fair." Thus, the following laws were supported: requiring newspapers to give major party candidates equal coverage (82 percent to 12 percent); requiring newspapers to give opponents of a controversial policy as much coverage as proponents (73 percent to 17 percent); requiring newspapers to cover activities of "major" third party candidates (63 percent in favor). Respondents expressed similar feelings about broadcasters' obligations. As we shall see, for many years broadcasters were under obligations similar to those that respondents would impose on newspapers.

On the other hand, "Most Americans have not worked through the complexities involved in government regulation of the media, and many of the respondents found questions about the problems of enforcing fairness to be frustrating and confusing." The Speaker and the Listener: A Public Perspective on Freedom of Expression 28–31 (1980).

One editorial response asserted that "[t]he foundation's findings reveal what we consider a tremendous ignorance, or, more politely, misunderstanding, on the part of the public as to what freedom of the press is all about." San Francisco Chronicle, Oct. 28, 1980 at 48.

The respondents also found newspapers "not usually fair" (54 percent) and "not usually accurate" (52 percent). The comparable figures for television were 46 percent and 37 percent.

11. *Access to Public Utility Newsletters.* In Pacific Gas & Electric Co. v. Public Utilities Commission of California, 475 U.S. 1 (1986), PG & E had for years included a newsletter that had the appearance of a small newspaper in its billing envelopes. The PUC ordered PG & E to transmit messages for a consumer interest organization (TURN) in its billing envelopes four times a year for the next two years. TURN was chosen because it disagreed with PG & E on many issues.

The Court, 5–3, held the PUC's order unconstitutional. For the four-vote plurality, Justice Powell began by citing *Bellotti,* p. 75, *supra,* for the proposition that the identity of the speaker was not decisive in determining whether speech was protected. Further, there was "no doubt" that PG & E's newsletter "receives the full protection of the First Amendment. [ ] In appearance no different from a small newspaper, [the newsletter's] contents range from energy-saving tips to stories about wild-life conservation, and from billing information to recipes." It "includes the kind of discussion of 'matters of public concern' that the First Amendment both fully protects and implicitly encourages."

The PUC's order discriminated on the basis of the viewpoint of the selected speaker—and thus was not content-neutral. Although the trigger here was not particular speech, as it was in *Tornillo,* the PUC's order raised the possibility that PG & E might "be forced—at TURN's discretion—to help disseminate hostile views." This might have led PG & E to conclude that the safe course was to avoid controversy. Although PG & E has no right to be free from attack, "it *does* have the right to be free from government restrictions that abridge its own rights in order to 'enhance the relative voice' of its opponents." [citing Buckley v. Valeo, 424 U.S. 1 (1976)]. The PUC order required PG & E "to assist in disseminating TURN's views; it does not equally constrain both sides of the debate about utility regulation."

The order also "impermissibly requires [PG & E] to associate with speech with which [it] may disagree." If TURN were to use the space to urge readers to vote for a certain slate of legislative candidates or to argue in favor of legislation, PG & E "may be forced either to appear to agree with TURN's views or to respond." This raised concerns that some of the justices raised in *PruneYard,* p. 47, *supra.* None of these points depended on who "owned" the "extra space" in the billing envelope:

> Nothing in *Tornillo* suggests that the result would have been different had the Florida Supreme Court decided that the newspaper space needed to print candidates' replies was the property of the newspaper readers, or had the court ordered the *Miami Herald* to distribute inserts owned and prepared by the candidates together with its newspapers. The constitutional difficulty with the right-of-reply statute was that it required the newspaper to disseminate a message with which the newspaper disagreed. This difficulty did not depend on whether the particular paper on which the replies were printed belonged to the newspaper or to the candidate.

Finally, the plurality concluded that although the state's interest in fair and effective utility regulation may be compelling, the state could meet that interest by means that did not violate the First Amendment, such as by awarding costs and fees. Nor could a state interest in making a variety of views available to PG & E's customers justify the order. This interest could not be advanced on by means that were not content-neutral.

Justice Marshall's concurring vote was devoted largely to explaining why this case differed from *PruneYard.* He rejected the view that "corporations' First Amendment rights are coextensive with those of individuals."

12. *Paid Advertisements.* The statute in question in *Tornillo* applied to newspaper "columns" generally. Would a different question of access have been raised if Tornillo had wanted to purchase space for political advertising? With the exception of one lower court case in 1919, courts have uniformly held that a private newspaper may reject advertising for any reason, or no reason, so long as its motive or effect is not anti-competitive, and most state action claims have been denied. When a litigant relied on the "access argument" to contend that a private paper that has established itself as a forum for advertising has an obligation to accept advertisements expressing opinions on matters of public concern, the court rejected it in a single paragraph: "We do not understand this to be the concept of freedom of the press recognized in the First Amendment." Chicago Joint Board, Amalgamated Clothing Workers of

America v. Chicago Tribune Co., 435 F.2d 470 (7th Cir.1970), cert. denied 402 U.S. 973 (1971).

13.  A separate but related problem is presented when the government itself wishes to place official notices in local newspapers—often required by statute to do so.  Though there are few cases, it appears that the courts uniformly hold that newspapers may reject such advertising if they desire.

14.  The rates that a newspaper may charge (if it does accept editorial advertising) are frequently regulated.  A number of states as well as the federal government (Federal Election Campaign Act Amendments of 1974, § 205(a), 2 U.S.C.A. § 435) require that a periodical charge political advertisers no more than it charges others who make "comparable use" of the same space for other purposes.  Constitutional attacks on these statutes have been rejected in both Massachusetts, Opinion of the Justices to the Senate, 363 Mass. 909, 298 N.E.2d 829, 835 (1973), and New Hampshire, Chronicle & Gazette Publishing Co., Inc. v. Attorney General, 94 N.H. 148, 48 A.2d 478 (1946), appeal dism'd 329 U.S. 690 (1947), on the ground that the regulation dealt exclusively with commercial aspects of the operation of the periodical.  Compare Gore Newspapers Co. v. Shevin, 397 F.Supp. 1253 (S.D.Fla.1975), invalidating Florida's statute requiring newspapers when they sold space to candidates to charge a rate that did not exceed "the lowest local rate available to advertisers otherwise qualifying for maximum frequency discounts, bulk discounts, and advertising packages."  The court assumed that the "cheapest rate is not an unprofitable rate."  Nonetheless, it declared the statute unconstitutional because it restrained the content of the publication.  The judge relied on the *Tornillo* rationale that the access statute imposed a penalty on the press for printing certain types of material.  Here, the restraint was aimed at revenue rather than content, but the judge thought the same principle applicable.

## B.  ACCESS TO BROADCAST MEDIA

Miami Herald v. Tornillo was not the first case to consider a forced right of access to the media.  In 1969 the Court decided a similar case involving the broadcast media.  The case, Red Lion Broadcasting v. FCC, involved a challenge to the personal attack part of the broader fairness doctrine.  The case also refers to the "equal opportunities" rule (sometimes incorrectly called the "equal time" rule), which applies during election campaigns.  Although we look at each of these doctrines in detail in Chapter XVI, including the FCC's 1987 decision eliminating the fairness doctrine, we must introduce each one now so that *Red Lion* can be fully understood.

As part of the first Communications Act, Congress passed what is now § 315, which requires any broadcaster who sells or gives time for a candidate's use to treat all other candidates for the same office equally.  This means that a broadcaster who sells a candidate for Congress 15 minutes of prime time, must be prepared to sell each opponent of that candidate the same amount of prime time at equivalent prices.

The fairness doctrine, on the other hand, was not imposed by Congress. Developed by the Commission on its own in the 1940s, the doctrine had two separate parts. One part required the broadcaster to air issues that "are so critical or of such great public importance that it would be unreasonable for a licensee to ignore them completely." Much more attention has been paid to the second part of the doctrine—that if a broadcaster did cover a "controversial issue of public importance" it had to take steps to assure that important contrasting views were also presented. These views could be presented by the licensee itself or by speakers chosen by the licensee.

The personal attack aspect of the fairness doctrine emerged in decisions in which the FCC ordered stations that had broadcast programs attacking a person's character during a discussion of a controversial issue of public importance to inform the person and offer him time to present his side. The Red Lion case arose from such a situation.

As the Red Lion case was being litigated, the FCC decided to promulgate a formal rule to make the personal attack doctrine more precise and more readily enforceable. The personal attack rule applied when "during the presentation of views on a controversial issue of public importance, an attack is made upon the honesty, character, integrity, or like personal qualities of an identified person or group." Notice and an opportunity to respond were required.

At the same time the FCC decided to promulgate a formal political editorial rule providing that when a licensee editorially endorsed a candidate for political office, other candidates for the same office were to be advised of the endorsement and offered a reasonable opportunity to respond. The same opportunity was to be extended to any candidate who was attacked in an editorial.

As soon as these two formal rules were announced, the Radio Television News Directors Association (RTNDA) sued to declare the rules unconstitutional. The court of appeals agreed and held that the rules violated the First Amendment. The Supreme Court heard both cases together and decided them in the same opinion.

### RED LION BROADCASTING CO. v. FEDERAL COMMUNICATIONS COMMISSION

Supreme Court of the United States, 1969.
395 U.S. 367, 89 S.Ct. 1794, 23 L.Ed.2d 371, 16 R.R.2d 2029, 1 Med.L.Rptr. 2053.

Mr. Justice White delivered the opinion of the Court.

The Federal Communications Commission has for many years imposed on radio and television broadcasters the requirement that discussion of public issues be presented on broadcast stations, and that each side of those issues must be given fair coverage. This is known as the fairness doctrine, which originated very early in the history of broadcasting and has maintained its present outlines for some time.   It is an obligation whose content has been defined in a long series of FCC rulings in particular cases, and which is distinct from the statutory requirement of § 315 of the Communications Act that equal time be allotted all qualified candidates for public office.   Two aspects of the fairness doctrine, relating to personal attacks in the context of controversial public issues and to political editorializing, were codified more precisely in the form of FCC regulations in 1967.   The two cases before us now, which were decided separately below, challenge the constitutional and statutory bases of the doctrine and component rules.   *Red Lion* involves the application of the fairness doctrine to a particular broadcast, and *RTNDA* arises as an action to review the FCC's 1967 promulgation of the personal attack and political editorializing regulations, which were laid down after the *Red Lion* litigation had begun.

I.

A.

The Red Lion Broadcasting Company is licensed to operate a Pennsylvania radio station, WGCB.   On November 27, 1964, WGCB carried a 15–minute broadcast by the Reverend Billy James Hargis as part of a "Christian Crusade" series.   A book by Fred J. Cook entitled "Goldwater—Extremist on the Right" was discussed by Hargis, who said that Cook had been fired by a newspaper for making false charges against city officials; that Cook had then worked for a Communist-affiliated publication; that he had defended Alger Hiss and attacked J. Edgar Hoover and the Central Intelligence Agency; and that he had now written a "book to smear and destroy Barry Goldwater."   When Cook heard of the broadcast he concluded that he had been personally attacked and demanded free reply time, which the station refused.   After an exchange of letters among Cook, Red Lion, and the FCC, the FCC declared that the Hargis broadcast constituted a personal attack on Cook; that Red Lion had failed to meet its obligation under the fairness doctrine as expressed in Times–Mirror Broadcasting Co., 24 P & F Radio Reg. 404 (1962), to send a tape, transcript, or summary of the broadcast to Cook and offer him reply time; and that the station must provide reply time whether or not Cook would pay for it.   On review in the Court of Appeals for the District of Columbia Circuit, the FCC's position was upheld as constitutional and otherwise proper.   [   ]

. . .

C.

Believing that the specific application of the fairness doctrine in *Red Lion,* and the promulgation of the regulations in *RTNDA,* are both authorized by Congress and enhance rather than abridge the freedoms of speech and press protected by the First Amendment, we hold them valid and constitutional, reversing the judgment below in *RTNDA* and affirming the judgment below in *Red Lion.*

## II.

The history of the emergence of the fairness doctrine and of the related legislation shows that the Commission's action in the *Red Lion* case did not exceed its authority, and that in adopting the new regulations the Commission was implementing congressional policy rather than embarking on a frolic of its own.

## A.

Before 1927, the allocation of frequencies was left entirely to the private sector, and the result was chaos. It quickly became apparent that broadcast frequencies constituted a scarce resource whose use could be regulated and rationalized only by the Government. Without government control, the medium would be of little use because of the cacaphony of competing voices, none of which could be clearly and predictably heard. Consequently, the Federal Radio Commission was established to allocate frequencies among competing applicants in a manner responsive to the public "convenience, interest, or necessity."

Very shortly thereafter the Commission expressed its view that the "public interest requires ample play for the free and fair competition of opposing views, and the commission believes that the principle applies . . . to all discussions of issues of importance to the public." . . . After an extended period during which the licensee was obliged not only to cover and to cover fairly the views of others, but also to refrain from expressing his own personal views, Mayflower Broadcasting Corp., 8 F.C.C. 333 (1940), the latter limitation on the licensee was abandoned and the doctrine developed into its present form.

There is a twofold duty laid down by the FCC's decisions and described by the 1949 Report on Editorializing by Broadcast Licensees, 13 F.C.C. 1246 (1949). The broadcaster must give adequate coverage to public issues, [ ], and coverage must be fair in that it accurately reflects the opposing views. [ ] This must be done at the broadcaster's own expense if sponsorship is unavailable. [ ] Moreover, the duty must be met by programming obtained at the licensee's own initiative if available from no other source. . . .

When a personal attack has been made on a figure involved in a public issue, both the doctrine of cases such as *Red Lion* and *Times Mirror Broadcasting Co.*, 24 P & F Radio Reg. 404 (1962), and also the 1967 regulations at issue in *RTNDA* require that the individual attacked himself be offered an opportunity to respond. Likewise, where one candidate is endorsed in a political editorial, the other candidates must themselves be offered reply time to use personally or through a spokesman. These obligations differ from the general fairness requirement that issues be presented, and presented with coverage of competing views, in that the broadcaster does not have the option of presenting the attacked party's side himself or choosing a third party to represent that side. But insofar as there is an obligation of the broadcaster to see that both sides are presented, and insofar as that is an affirmative obligation, the personal attack doctrine and regulations do not differ from the preceding fairness doctrine. The simple fact that the attacked men or unendorsed candidates may respond themselves or through agents is not a critical distinction, and indeed, it is not unreasonable for the FCC to conclude that the objective of adequate presentation of all sides may best be served by allowing those most closely affected to make the response, rather than leaving the response in the hands of the station which has attacked their candidacies, endorsed their opponents, or carried a personal attack upon them.

## B.

[The Court concluded that the Commission's mandate to "from time to time, as public convenience, interest, or necessity requires" promulgate "such rules and regulations and prescribe such restrictions and conditions . . . as may be necessary to carry out the provisions of this chapter" (47 U.S.C.A. § 303 and § 303(r)) gave it the statutory authority to promulgate the regulations. Further reinforcing this view was the 1959 amendment to § 315 stating that the exemptions from § 315 for certain news programs did not exempt licensees "from the obligation imposed upon them under this Act to operate in the public interest and to afford reasonable opportunity for the discussion of conflicting views on issues of public importance." That amendment was interpreted by the Court as express acceptance by Congress of the Commission's position that the fairness doctrine inhered in the public interest standard.]

## III.

The broadcasters challenge the fairness doctrine and its specific manifestations in the personal attack and political editorial rules on conventional First Amendment grounds, alleging that the rules abridge their freedom of speech and press. Their contention is that the First Amendment protects their desire to use their allotted frequencies continuously to broadcast whatever they choose, and to exclude whomever they choose from ever using that frequency. No man may be prevented from saying or publishing what he thinks, or from refusing in his speech or other utterances to give equal weight to the views of his opponents. This right, they say, applies equally to broadcasters.

## A.

Although broadcasting is clearly a medium affected by a First Amendment interest, United States v. Paramount Pictures, Inc., 334 U.S. 131, 166 (1948), differences in the characteristics of new media justify differences in the First Amendment standards applied to them. [ ] For example, the ability of new technology to produce sounds more raucous than those of the human voice justifies restrictions on the sound level, and on the hours and places of use, of sound trucks so long as the restrictions are reasonable and applied without discrimination. [ ]

Just as the Government may limit the use of sound-amplifying equipment potentially so noisy that it drowns out civilized private speech, so may the Government limit the use of broadcast equipment. The right of free speech of a broadcaster, the user of a sound truck, or any other individual does not embrace a right to snuff out the free speech of others. Associated Press v. United States, 326 U.S. 1, 20 (1945).

When two people converse face to face, both should not speak at once if either is to be clearly understood. But the range of the human voice is so limited that there could be meaningful communications if half the people in the United States were talking and the other half listening. Just as clearly, half the people might publish and the other half read. But the reach of radio signals is incomparably greater than the range of the human voice and the problem of interference is a massive reality. The lack of know-how and equipment may keep many from the air but only a tiny fraction of those with resources and intelligence can hope to communicate by radio at the same time if intelligible communication is to be had, even if the entire radio spectrum is utilized in the present state of commercially acceptable technology.

It was this fact, and the chaos which ensued from permitting anyone to use any frequency at whatever power level he wished, which made necessary the enactment of the Radio Act of 1927 and the Communications Act of 1934, as the Court has noted at length before. National Broadcasting Co. v. United States, 319 U.S. 190, 210–214 (1943). It was this reality which at the very least necessitated first the division of the radio spectrum into portions reserved respectively for public broadcasting and for other important radio uses such as amateur operation, aircraft, police, defense, and navigation; and then the subdivision of each portion, and assignment of specific frequencies to individual users or groups of users. Beyond this, however, because the frequencies reserved for public broadcasting were limited in number, it was essential for the Government to tell some applicants that they could not broadcast at all because there was room for only a few.

Where there are substantially more individuals who want to broadcast than there are frequencies to allocate, it is idle to posit an unabridgeable First Amendment right to broadcast comparable to the right of every individual to speak, write, or publish. If 100 persons want broadcast licenses but there are only 10 frequencies to allocate, all of them may have the same "right" to a license; but if there is to be any effective communication by radio, only a few can be licensed and the rest must be barred from the airwaves. It would be strange if the First Amendment, aimed at protecting and furthering communications, prevented the Government from making radio communication possible by requiring licenses to broadcast and by limiting the number of licenses so as not to overcrowd the spectrum.

This has been the consistent view of the Court. Congress unquestionably has the power to grant and deny licenses and to eliminate existing stations. FRC v. Nelson Bros. Bond & Mortgage Co., 289 U.S. 266 (1933). No one has a First Amendment right to a license or to monopolize a radio frequency; to deny a station license because "the public interest" requires it "is not a denial of free speech." National Broadcasting Co. v. United States, 319 U.S. 190, 227 (1943).

By the same token, as far as the First Amendment is concerned those who are licensed stand no better than those to whom licenses are refused. A license permits broadcasting, but the licensee has no constitutional right to be the one who holds the license or to monopolize a radio frequency to the exclusion of his fellow citizens. There is nothing in the First Amendment which prevents the Government from requiring a licensee to share his frequency with others and to conduct himself as a proxy or fiduciary with obligations to present those views and voices which are representative of his community and which would otherwise, by necessity, be barred from the airwaves.

This is not to say that the First Amendment is irrelevant to public broadcasting. On the contrary, it has a major role to play as the Congress itself recognized in § 326, which forbids FCC interference with "the right of free speech by means of radio communication." Because of the scarcity of radio frequencies, the Government is permitted to put restraints on licensees in favor of others whose views should be expressed on this unique medium. But the people as a whole retain their interest in free speech by radio and their collective right to have the medium function consistently with the ends and purposes of the First Amendment. It is the right of the viewers and listeners, not the right of the broadcasters, which is paramount. See FCC v. Sanders Bros. Radio Station, 309 U.S. 470, 475 (1940); FCC v. Allentown Broadcasting Corp., 349 U.S. 358, 361–362 (1955); 2 Z. Chafee, Government and Mass Communications 546 (1947). It is the purpose of the First Amendment to preserve an uninhibited marketplace of ideas in which truth will ultimately prevail, rather than to countenance monopolization of that market, whether it be by the Government itself or a private licensee. Associated Press v. United States, 326 U.S. 1, 20 (1945); New York Times Co. v. Sullivan, 376 U.S. 254, 270 (1964); Abrams v. United States, 250 U.S. 616, 630 (1919) (Holmes, J., dissenting). "[S]peech concerning public affairs is more than self-expression; it is the essence of self-government." Garrison v. Louisiana, 379 U.S. 64, 74–75 (1964). See Brennan, The Supreme Court and the Meiklejohn Interpretation of the First Amendment, 79 Harv.L.Rev. 1 (1965). It is the right of the public to receive suitable access to social, political, esthetic, moral, and other ideas and experiences which is crucial here. That right may not constitutionally be abridged either by Congress or by the FCC.

## B.

Rather than confer frequency monopolies on a relatively small number of licensees, in a Nation of 200,000,000, the Government could surely have decreed that each frequency should be shared among all or some of those who wish to use it, each being assigned a portion of the broadcast day or the broadcast week. The ruling and regulations at issue here do not go quite so far. They assert that under specified circumstances, a licensee must offer to make available a reasonable amount of broadcast time to those who have a view different from that which has already been expressed on his station. The expression of a political endorsement, or of a personal attack while dealing with a controversial public issue, simply triggers this time sharing. As we have said, the First Amendment confers no right on licensees to prevent others from broadcasting on "their" frequencies and no right to an unconditional monopoly of a scarce resource which the Government has denied others the right to use.

In terms of constitutional principle, and as enforced sharing of a scarce resource, the personal attack and political editorial rules are indistinguishable from the equal-time provision of § 315, a specific enactment of Congress requiring stations to set aside reply time under specified circumstances and to which the fairness doctrine and these constituent regulations are important complements. That provision, which has been part of the law since 1927, Radio Act of 1927, § 18, 44 Stat. 1170, has been held valid by this Court as an obligation of the licensee relieving him of any power in any way to prevent or censor the broadcast, and thus insulating him from liability for defamation. The constitutionality of the statute under the First Amendment was unquestioned. Farmers Educ. & Coop. Union v. WDAY, 360 U.S. 525 (1959).

Nor can we say that it is inconsistent with the First Amendment goal of producing an informed public capable of conducting its own affairs to require a broadcaster to permit answers to personal attacks occurring in the course of discussing controversial issues, or to require that the political opponents of those endorsed by the station be given a chance to communicate with the public.[18] Otherwise, station owners and a few networks would have unfettered power to make time available only to the highest bidders, to communicate only their own views on public issues, people and candidates, and to permit on the air only those with whom they agreed. There is no sanctuary in the First Amendment for unlimited private censorship operating in a medium not open to all. "Freedom of the press from governmental interference under the First Amendment does not sanction repression of that freedom by private interests." Associated Press v. United States, 326 U.S. 1, 20 (1945).

## C.

It is strenuously argued, however, that if political editorials or personal attacks will trigger an obligation in broadcasters to afford the

---

**18.** The expression of views opposing those which broadcasters permit to be aired in the first place need not be confined solely to the broadcasters themselves as proxies. "Nor is it enough that he should hear the arguments of adversaries from his own teachers, presented as they state them, and accompanied by what they offer as refuta- tions. That is not the way to do justice to the arguments, or bring them into real contact with his own mind. He must be able to hear them from persons who actually believe them; who defend them in earnest, and do their very utmost for them." J. Mill, On Liberty 32 (R. McCallum ed. 1947).

opportunity for expression to speakers who need not pay for time and whose views are unpalatable to the licensees, then broadcasters will be irresistibly forced to self-censorship and their coverage of controversial public issues will be eliminated or at least rendered wholly ineffective. Such a result would indeed be a serious matter, for should licensees actually eliminate their coverage of controversial issues, the purposes of the doctrine would be stifled.

At this point, however, as the Federal Communications Commission has indicated, that possibility is at best speculative. The communications industry, and in particular the networks, have taken pains to present controversial issues in the past, and even now they do not assert that they intend to abandon their efforts in this regard. It would be better if the FCC's encouragement were never necessary to induce the broadcasters to meet their responsibility. And if experience with the administration of these doctrines indicates that they have the net effect of reducing rather than enhancing the volume and quality of coverage, there will be time enough to reconsider the constitutional implications. The fairness doctrine in the past has had no such overall effect.

That this will occur now seems unlikely, however, since if present licensees should suddenly prove timorous, the Commission is not powerless to insist that they give adequate and fair attention to public issues. It does not violate the First Amendment to treat licensees given the privilege of using scarce radio frequencies as proxies for the entire community, obligated to give suitable time and attention to matters of great public concern. To condition the granting or renewal of licenses on a willingness to present representative community views on controversial issues is consistent with the ends and purposes of those constitutional provisions forbidding the abridgment of freedom of speech and freedom of the press. Congress need not stand idly by and permit those with licenses to ignore the problems which beset the people or to exclude from the airways anything but their own views of fundamental questions. The statute, long administrative practice, and cases are to this effect.

Licenses to broadcast do not confer ownership of designated frequencies, but only the temporary privilege of using them. 47 U.S.C. § 301. Unless renewed, they expire within three years. 47 U.S.C. § 307(d). The statute mandates the issuance of licenses if the "public convenience, interest, or necessity will be served thereby." 47 U.S.C. § 307(a). In applying this standard the Commission for 40 years has been choosing licensees based in part on their program proposals. In FRC v. Nelson Bros. Bond & Mortgage Co., 289 U.S. 266, 279 (1933), the Court noted that in "view of the limited number of available broadcasting frequencies the Congress has authorized allocation and licenses." In determining how best to allocate frequencies, the Federal Radio Commission considered the needs of competing communities and the programs offered by competing stations to meet those needs; moreover, if needs or programs shifted the Commission could alter its allocations to reflect those shifts. Id., at 285.　．．．

## D.

The litigants embellish their First Amendment arguments with the contention that the regulations are so vague that their duties are impossible to discern. Of this point it is enough to say that, judging the validity of the regulations on their face as they are presented here, we cannot conclude that the FCC has been left a free hand to vindicate its own idiosyncratic conception of the public interest or of the requirements of free speech. . . .

We need not and do not now ratify every past and future decision by the FCC with regard to programming. There is no question here of the Commission's refusal to permit the broadcaster to carry a particular program or to publish his own views; of a discriminatory refusal to require the licensee to broadcast certain views which have been denied access to the airwaves; of government censorship of a particular program contrary to § 326; or of the official government view dominating public broadcasting. Such questions would raise more serious First Amendment issues. But we do hold that the Congress and the Commission do not violate the First Amendment when they require a radio or television station to give reply time to answer personal attacks and political editorials.

## E.

It is argued that even if at one time the lack of available frequencies for all who wished to use them justified the Government's choice of those who would best serve the public interest by acting as proxy for those who would present differing views, or by giving the latter access directly to broadcast facilities, this condition no longer prevails so that continuing control is not justified. To this there are several answers.

Scarcity is not entirely a thing of the past. Advances in technology, such as microwave transmission, have led to more efficient utilization of the frequency spectrum, but uses for that spectrum have also grown apace. Portions of the spectrum must be reserved for vital uses unconnected with human communication, such as radio-navigational aids used by aircraft and vessels. Conflicts have even emerged between such vital functions as defense preparedness and experimentation in methods of averting midair collisions through radio warning devices. "Land mobile services" such as police, ambulance, fire department, public utility, and other communications systems have been occupying an increasingly crowded portion of the frequency spectrum and there are, apart from licensed amateur radio operators' equipment, 5,000,000 transmitters operated on the "citizens' band" which is also increasingly congested. Among the various uses for radio frequency space, including marine, aviation, amateur, military, and common carrier users, there are easily enough claimants to permit use of the whole with an even smaller allocation to broadcast radio and television uses than now exists.

Comparative hearings between competing applicants for broadcast spectrum space are by no means a thing of the past. The radio spectrum has become so congested that at times it has been necessary to suspend new applications. The very high frequency television spectrum is, in the country's major markets, almost entirely occupied, although space reserved for ultra high frequency television transmission, which is a relatively recent development as a commercially viable alternative, has not yet been completely filled.[25]

The rapidity with which technological advances succeed one another to create more efficient use of spectrum space on the one hand, and to create new uses for that space by ever growing numbers of people on the other, makes it unwise to speculate on the future allocation of that space. It is enough to say that the resource is one of considerable and growing importance whose scarcity impelled its regulation by an agency authorized by Congress. Nothing in this record, or in our own researches, convinces us that the resource is no longer one for which there are more immediate and potential uses than can be accommodated, and for which wise planning is essential. This does not mean, of course, that every possible wavelength must be occupied at every hour by some vital use in order to sustain the congressional judgment. The substantial capital investment required for many uses, in addition to the potentiality for confusion and interference inherent in any scheme for continuous kaleidoscopic reallocation of all available space may make this unfeasible. The allocation need not be made at such a breakneck pace that the objectives of the allocation are themselves imperiled.

Even where there are gaps in spectrum utilization, the fact remains that existing broadcasters have often attained their present position because of their initial government selection in competition with others

**25.** In a table prepared by the FCC on the basis of statistics current as of August 31, 1968, VHF and UHF channels allocated to and those available in the top 100 market areas for television are set forth:

**Commercial**

| Market Areas | Channels Allocated | | Channels On the Air, Authorized, or Applied for | | Available Channels | |
|---|---|---|---|---|---|---|
| | VHF | UHF | VHF | UHF | VHF | UHF |
| Top 10 | 40 | 45 | 40 | 44 | 0 | 1 |
| Top 50 | 157 | 163 | 157 | 136 | 0 | 27 |
| Top 100 | 264 | 297 | 264 | 213 | 0 | 84 |

**Noncommercial**

| Market Areas | Channels Reserved | | Channels On the Air, Authorized, or Applied for | | Available Channels | |
|---|---|---|---|---|---|---|
| | VHF | UHF | VHF | UHF | VHF | UHF |
| Top 10 | 7 | 17 | 7 | 16 | 0 | 1 |
| Top 50 | 21 | 79 | 20 | 47 | 1 | 32 |
| Top 100 | 35 | 138 | 34 | 69 | 1 | 69 |

1968 FCC Annual Report 132–135.

before new technological advances opened new opportunities for further uses.  Long experience in broadcasting, confirmed habits of listeners and viewers, network affiliation, and other advantages in program procurement give existing broadcasters a substantial advantage over new entrants, even where new entry is technologically possible.  These advantages are the fruit of a preferred position conferred by the Government. Some present possibility for new entry by competing stations is not enough, in itself, to render unconstitutional the Government's effort to assure that a broadcaster's programming ranges widely enough to serve the public interest.

In view of the scarcity of broadcast frequencies, the Government's role in allocating those frequencies, and the legitimate claims of those unable without governmental assistance to gain access to those frequencies for expression of their views, we hold the regulations and ruling at issue here are both authorized by statute and constitutional.[28]  The judgment of the Court of Appeals in *Red Lion* is affirmed and that in *RTNDA* reversed and the causes remanded for proceedings consistent with this opinion.

It is so ordered.

Not having heard oral argument in these cases, Mr. Justice Douglas took no part in the Court's decision.

### Notes and Questions

1.  The Court states that the differences among the technical aspects of media warrant different regulatory treatment.  Compare Jackson, J., concurring, in Kovacs v. Cooper, 336 U.S. 77, 97 (1949): "The moving picture screen, the radio, the newspaper, the handbill, the sound truck and the street corner orator have differing natures, values, abuses and dangers.  Each, in my view, is a law unto itself."

2.  The Court states that only a tiny fraction of those who want to broadcast are able to do so "even if the entire radio spectrum is utilized."  Who decided how much of the spectrum to allocate to radio? Could a niggardly or inefficient allocation of radio space justify government exercise of its regulatory power?  The notion of "scarcity" plays a major role in the Court's analysis.  What does the term appear to mean in the opinion?

---

**28.**  We need not deal with the argument that even if there is no longer a technological scarcity of frequencies limiting the number of broadcasters, there nevertheless is an economic scarcity in the sense that the Commission could or does limit entry to the broadcasting market on economic grounds and license no more stations than the market will support.  Hence, it is said, the fairness doctrine or its equivalent is essential to satisfy the claims of those excluded and of the public generally.  A related argument, which we also put aside, is that quite apart from scarcity of frequencies, technological or economic, Congress does not abridge freedom of speech or press by legislation directly or indirectly multiplying the voices and views presented to the public through time sharing, fairness doctrines, or other devices which limit or dissipate the power of those who sit astride the channels of communication with the general public. Cf. Citizen Pub. Co. v. United States, 394 U.S. 131 (1969).

Consider whether scarcity is present in the following contexts: (a) all three radio outlets allocated to a community are being used; (b) of the five radio outlets allocated three are being used; (c) all 40 radio outlets allocated to an urban area are being used; (d) seven of the 40 outlets are vacant.

3.  Does Justice White's next-to-last paragraph suggest that the reality of scarcity in the past will be enough to justify continuing regulation even if it were determined that no scarcity exists today?

4.  Accepting limits on the part of the spectrum allocated to radio, does it follow that government must be involved in assigning space to specific applicants?   Even if government is involved in the individual assignments, might the channels be assigned by other devices, such as auctioning them off in perpetuity?   Or for a period of years?

5.  Justice White says that "It is the right of the viewers and listeners, not the right of the broadcasters, which is paramount. [   ] It is the purpose of the First Amendment to preserve an uninhibited marketplace of ideas in which truth will ultimately prevail, rather than to countenance monopolization of that market, whether it be by the Government itself or a private licensee."   What philosophical strands are being brought together here?

6.  When Justice White says that the "right" involved in the case belongs to "the public" and that this "right may not constitutionally be abridged either by Congress or by the FCC," is he suggesting that the absence of government control of broadcasters' programming would deny the public's constitutional right to "receive suitable access to social, political, esthetic, moral and other ideas and experiences?"

7.  Is the Court's concern about licensees' refusing to air controversial material if they must provide response time consistent with the Court's analysis in *Tornillo* ?   Is it surprising that the Court did not cite *Red Lion* in its decision in *Tornillo* ?   Is there a difference between technological and economic scarcity?   For a strong rejection of the scarcity rationale, see Telecommunications Research and Action Center v. Federal Communications Commission, 801 F.2d 501, 61 R.R.2d 330, 13 Med. L.Rptr. 1881, reh'g denied 806 F.2d 1115, 61 R.R.2d 1342, 13 Med. L.Rptr. 1896 (D.C.Cir.1986), cert. denied 482 U.S. 919 (1987), which will be discussed in Chapter XV.

8.  There is reason to believe that Fred Cook's demand for reply time was part of a broader effort to use the fairness doctrine to soften attacks on the Kennedy administration by right-wing political commentators. The plan was to monitor right-wing programs and then to demand reply time for personal attacks or to demand balance under the general fairness doctrine.   F. Friendly, The Good Guys, The Bad Guys and the First Amendment (1976).   If the result was that licensees cancelled several right-wing commentators would that affect your reaction to the *Red Lion* decision?   Did Cook misuse the doctrine?

9. Aside from the spectrum scarcity arguments there are intrinsic differences between print and broadcast media. There is a physical limit to the number of words that can be uttered intelligibly over a broadcasting facility during a 24–hour day. Based on an estimate of about 200,000 words, using normal speaking patterns, one author suggests that a newspaper is the equivalent of between one and three 24–hour programs. But the reader of a newspaper can at any time go directly to what interests him and skim or ignore the rest. In broadcasting, the choice is made for the listener by the broadcaster; the speed, content, and sequence are fixed. Baxter, Regulation and Diversity in Communications Media, 64 Am.Econ.Rev. 392 (1974). Might such differences justify greater regulation of broadcasting?

10. Other differences between the print and electronic media emphasize the greater impact of broadcasting in conveying certain types of information. The vivid telecasts during the Vietnam War are thought to have been a strong factor in the shift of public attitude against that war, beyond the potential of any verbal journalism. Another major difference is the role of sound in broadcasting, which makes it possible to use songs and jingles effectively in advertising. During the discussion of the broadcast advertising of cigarettes, one court observed:

> Written messages are not communicated unless they are read, and reading requires an affirmative act. Broadcast messages, in contrast, are "in the air." In an age of omnipresent radio, there scarcely breathes a citizen who does not know some part of a leading cigarette jingle by heart. Similarly, an ordinary habitual television watcher can *avoid* these commercials only by frequently leaving the room, changing the channel, or doing some other such affirmative act. It is difficult to calculate the subliminal impact of this pervasive propaganda, which may be heard even if not listened to, but it may reasonably be thought greater than the impact of the written word.

Banzhaf v. Federal Communications Commission, 405 F.2d 1082, 1100–01, 14 R.R.2d 2061, 1 Med.L.Rptr. 2037 (D.C.Cir.1968), cert. denied 396 U.S. 842 (1969). Does this suggest an additional basis for regulating some aspects of broadcasting?

In considering this, recall the refusal of the Supreme Court to declare unconstitutional all motion picture censorship. In Times Film Corp. v. Chicago, 365 U.S. 43 (1961), the Court, 5–4, refused to hold "that the public exhibition of motion pictures must be allowed under any circumstances" and that the state may punish only after the fact. As the "Pentagon Papers" case, p. 336, *supra*, suggests, prior restraints may be permissible in some exceptional circumstances. Given that the film producers were presumably not claiming greater protection than what was given print media, might the motion picture decision be simply an anticipation of that development? Or might the Court be concerned about the explicit and vivid depiction of sexual episodes—and fear the impact of the medium on viewers more than it fears the printed page in such circumstances?  Might such a concern with motion pictures apply to television?  Note that 47 U.S.C.A. § 326 bans the Commission from "censorship" of programming.

Does the *Banzhaf* view of broadcasting imply a "captive audience" comparable to the addresses of sound trucks in residential neighborhoods, or political advertisements in mass transit vehicles?  Is turning off the program like averting your eyes from offensive wording on someone's jacket?  Is it relevant to this aspect of the discussion that most television sets and radios are in private homes?  We will discuss this question in Chapter XVII.

11.  The Supreme Court returned to these questions once again in Columbia Broadcasting System, Inc. v. Democratic National Committee, 412 U.S. 94, 27 R.R.2d 907, 1 Med.L.Rptr. 1855 (1973).  The Court decided that broadcasters were not obligated to accept paid advertisements from "responsible" individuals and groups.  The majority relied upon *Red Lion.*

Justice Stewart in a separate concurring opinion stated "I agreed with the Court in *Red Lion,* although with considerable doubt, because I thought that that much Government regulation of program content was within the outer limits of First Amendment tolerability."

In another concurring opinion, Justice Douglas stated of *Red Lion:* "I did not participate in that decision and, with all respect, would not support it.  The Fairness Doctrine has no place in our First Amendment regime."  He argued that the uniqueness of the spectrum was "due to engineering and technical problems.  But the press in a realistic sense is likewise not available to all.  Small or 'underground' papers appear and disappear; and the weekly is an established institution.  But the daily papers now established are unique in the sense that it would be virtually impossible for a competitor to enter the field due to the financial exigencies of this era.  The result is that in practical terms the newspapers and magazines, like TV and radio, are available only to a selected few."

12.  Cable has its own access questions.  They will be addressed in Chapter XVIII.

# Chapter XV

# INTRODUCTION TO BROADCASTING

As *Red Lion* makes clear, legal controls for broadcasters differ significantly from those for print media. In this chapter we consider how broadcasting operates and why this has led to legal regulation quite unlike that of the print sector. Major sections of the Communications Act of 1934 are reprinted in Appendix B. An organizational chart of the FCC is reprinted in Appendix D.

## A. THE SPECTRUM AND ITS UTILIZATION

### 1. THE NATURE OF THE SPECTRUM

The electromagnetic spectrum is a unique natural resource. Utilization does not use it up or wear it out. It does not require continual maintenance to remain usable. It is subject to pollution (interference), but once the interference is removed the pollution totally disappears. The value of the spectrum lies primarily in its use for conveying a wide variety of information at varying speeds over varying distances: in other words, for communications.

All electromagnetic radiation is a form of radiant energy, similar in many respects to heat, light or X-radiation. All of these types of radiation are considered by physicists to be waves resulting from the periodic oscillations of charged subatomic particles. All radiation has a measurable frequency, or rate of oscillation, which is measured in cycles per second, or hertz. One thousand cycles per second equals one kilocycle per second (1 kHz); 1,000 kilocycles per second equals one Megacycle per second (1 MHz); and 1,000 Megacycles per second equals one Gigacycle per second (1 GHz). The frequencies of electromagnetic radiation that comprise the radio spectrum span a wide range, from 10 kHz to 3,000,000,000,000 cycles per second (3,000 GHz), all of which are nearly incomprehensibly rapid. Present technology allows use of the spectrum only up to around 40 GHz.

The radio spectrum resource itself has three dimensions: space, time and frequency. Two spectrum users can transmit on the same frequency at the same time if they are sufficiently separate physically; the physical separation necessary will depend on the power at which each signal is transmitted. They then occupy different parts of the spectrum in the spatial sense. Similarly, the spectrum can be divided in terms of frequency, dependent on the construction of the transmitting and receiving equipment; or time, dependent largely on the hours of use.

The spectrum is subject to the phenomenon of interference. One radio signal interferes with another to the extent that both have the same dimensions. That is, two signals of the same frequency that occupy the same physical space at the same time will interfere with each other (co-channel interference). Signals on adjacent channels may also interfere with each other. Interference usually obscures or destroys any information that either signal is carrying. The degree to which two signals occupy the same physical space depends on the intensity of the radiated power at a given point, which in turn depends on the construction of the transmitting equipment and antenna.

The spectrum is divided into numbered bands, extending from Very Low Frequencies (VLF) to Very, Ultra, Super and Extremely High Frequencies (EHF) and beyond. The lower frequencies of the radio spectrum are used for "point-to-point" communications and for navigational aids. AM radio is located in the range between 300 and 3,000 kHz, known as the Medium Frequency band (MF). FM radio and VHF television (channels 2–13) are in the Very High Frequency band (VHF), from 30 to 300 MHz. The Ultra High Frequency band (UHF), from 300 to 3,000 MHz, is the location of UHF television (channels 14–69). Still higher frequencies are used for microwave relays and communication satellites.

The effective limitations on use of the radio spectrum are defined by (1) the propagation characteristics of the various frequencies and (2) the level of interference. Low frequency radio waves are best suited to long distance communications. In the lowest frequency bands the radio waves propagate primarily along the ground or water and follow the curvature of the earth. The attenuation of these "ground waves" generally increases with frequency; VLF waves may be propagated for thousands of miles, which explains their value for point-to-point communication. Ground waves in the HF band below VHF can propagate no more than a few hundred miles, and above that band they become unimportant. Sky wave propagation is important up to the start of the VHF band. These radio waves tend to depart from the earth's surface and are reflected by the ionosphere, an electrically charged region of the atmosphere 35 to 250 miles above the earth. The amount of reflection depends on the level of daily solar activity, the time of day, the season and geographical location, as well as the length of the signal path and the angle at which the waves strike the ionosphere. The reflection of sky waves is much greater at night when they may be transmitted over great distances. Above 30 MHz, radio waves tend to pierce the ionosphere rather than to be reflected, and line of sight transmission becomes increasingly necessary. As the frequency increases above 30 MHz, surface objects absorb radiation at an increasing rate until a clear unobstructed line of sight becomes necessary at 1 GHz. In the very highest frequencies, the waves are subject to substantial absorption by water vapor and oxygen in the atmosphere and cannot be used for communication.

Interference constitutes the second major limitation on the use of the electromagnetic spectrum. As noted above, interference results when two signals attempt to occupy the same spectrum in all of its three dimensions. Even if two users wish to transmit on the same frequency, interference can be avoided by sufficient geographical separation between transmitters, limitations on the power radiated by each transmitter, limitations on antenna height or separation of the signals in time. The first three techniques cause spatial differentiation; the last affects the temporal dimension.

Standard (AM) broadcasting propagates its waves by "amplitude modulation." The sound waves vary in power, producing variations in the height of the waves that are transmitted. The receiving unit decodes these height variations, reproducing the original sounds. AM transmissions occur in the MF band and thus have a long range primary service through ground waves, particularly near the lower end of the band. AM also can utilize sky waves to provide a secondary service at night.

FM broadcasting utilizes "frequency modulation" rather than "amplitude modulation." In this system the height of the wave is held constant but the frequency of the waves transmitted is varied. This type of broadcasting provides higher quality service with less interference than does AM, but it serves smaller areas, because the waves of the VHF band do not follow the surface of the earth and are not reflected by the ionosphere. This also means that FM service is unaffected by skywave interference at night.

Television utilizes separate signals for the visual and the sound components. The picture is transmitted by amplitude modulation and the sound by frequency modulation. Since the transmissions are either in the VHF or UHF bands, the range of the signal is short, and television cannot utilize either long ground waves or sky waves.

### 2. ALLOCATION OF THE SPECTRUM

The method of dividing the spectrum resource among prospective users is enormously complex and highly controversial. The general term "allocation policy" comprehends three separate but not always distinct processes, each of which involves both technical and nontechnical considerations. The allocation process is the division of the spectrum into blocks of frequencies to be used by specified services or users. Thus, the television service is allocated certain frequencies in the VHF and UHF bands, microwave users are allocated frequencies in the UHF and SHF bands, and so on. The second process, allotment, involves the distribution of spectrum rights within allocated bands to users in various geographical areas. Assignment, the third process, denotes the choice among potential individual users of allocated and allotted channels or frequency bands. We usually refer to all three processes under the general label of "allocation policy."

Perhaps the most important objective consideration in formulating an allocation policy is the technical usability of the spectrum itself. Technical usability is dependent primarily on three factors: the propagation characteristics of each frequency range, interference problems and their resolution, and limitations imposed by the communications system itself, especially the transmitting and receiving equipment. In other words, it is dependent on the physics of radio waves, other users of the spectrum and the technical state of the electronics industry. Frequency characteristics themselves seldom pose significant problems, for, although there are optimal frequency ranges for various services, these tend to be broad ranges. Consequently, there is usually considerable flexibility in the initial choice of a frequency for a given service except for whatever priority is given to those already utilizing the space.

Several forms of interference may present problems since interference can be caused by an overcrowded frequency, insufficient geographical separation or unduly strong power levels.

The third constraint on spectrum allocation involves the technology of the communications system used, especially the antenna system and the transmitting and receiving equipment. Any major change in receivers might create economic problems for the public and thus for the industry as a whole.

The problem of crowding in the broadcasting industry began early in the 1920s. The episode is recounted by Justice Frankfurter in his opinion for the Court in National Broadcasting Co. v. United States, 319 U.S. 190, 1 Med.L.Rptr. 1965 (1943), a case to which we return later:

Federal regulation of radio begins with the Wireless Ship Act of June 24, 1910, 36 Stat. 629, which forbade any steamer carrying or licensed to carry fifty or more persons to leave any American port unless equipped with efficient apparatus for radio communication, in charge of a skilled operator. The enforcement of this legislation was entrusted to the Secretary of Commerce and Labor, who was in charge of the administration of the marine navigation laws. But it was not until 1912 when the United States ratified the first international radio treaty, 37 Stat. 1565, that the need for general regulation of radio communication became urgent. In order to fulfill our obligations under the treaty, Congress enacted the Radio Act of August 13, 1912, 37 Stat. 302. This statute forbade the operation of radio apparatus without a license from the Secretary of Commerce and Labor; it also allocated certain frequencies for the use of the Government, and imposed restrictions upon the character of wave emissions, the transmission of distress signals and the like.

The enforcement of the Radio Act of 1912 presented no serious problems prior to the World War. Questions of interference arose only rarely because there were more than enough frequencies for all the stations then in existence. The war accelerated the development of the art, however, and in 1921 the first standard broadcast stations were established. They grew rapidly in number, and by 1923 there were several hundred such stations throughout the country. The Act of 1912 had not set aside any particular frequencies for the use of private broadcast stations; consequently, the

Secretary of Commerce selected two frequencies, 750 and 833 kilocycles, and licensed all stations to operate upon one or the other of these channels. The number of stations increased so rapidly however, and the situation became so chaotic, that the Secretary, upon the recommendation of the National Radio Conferences which met in Washington in 1923 and 1924, established a policy of assigning specified frequencies to particular stations. The entire radio spectrum was divided into numerous bands, each allocated to a particular kind of service. The frequencies ranging from 550 to 1500 kilocycles (96 channels in all, since the channels were separated from each other by 10 kilocycles) were assigned to the standard broadcast stations. But the problems created by the enormously rapid development of radio were far from solved. The increase in the number of channels was not enough to take care of the constantly growing number of stations. Since there were more stations than available frequencies, the Secretary of Commerce attempted to find room for everybody by limiting the power and hours of operation of stations in order that several stations might use the same channel. The number of stations multiplied so rapidly, however, that by November, 1925, there were almost 600 stations in the country, and there were 175 applications for new stations. Every channel in the standard broadcast band was, by that time, already occupied by at least one station, and many by several. The new stations could be accommodated only by extending the standard broadcast band, at the expense of the other types of services, or by imposing still greater limitations upon time and power. The National Radio Conference which met in November, 1925, opposed both of these methods and called upon Congress to remedy the situation through legislation.

[During 1926 courts held that the Secretary of Commerce lacked the power to stem the tide, and his pleas for self-regulation went unheeded by the burgeoning new industry.]

From July, 1926, to February 23, 1927, when Congress enacted the Radio Act of 1927, 44 Stat. 1162, almost 200 new stations went on the air. These new stations used any frequencies they desired, regardless of the interference thereby caused to others. Existing stations changed to other frequencies and increased their power and hours of operation at will. The result was confusion and chaos. With everybody on the air, nobody could be heard. . . .

### a. The Federal Communications Commission

Congress usually creates administrative agencies when the task at hand requires continuing supervision, extensive technical considerations, the development of expert skills or all of these. The thought is that a group devoting full attention to such a problem may do a better job than Congress might do in sporadic legislative forays into an area. In 1927 Congress had no ability or time or desire to unravel the mess that had developed on the airwaves. The basic decision for Congress, in retrospect, was whether to decree a system of private ownership for the airwaves and to allow the courts to unravel the matters through lawsuits invoking property law, to opt for outright public ownership, or to create an administrative body to develop and enforce an allocation system that would bring order from the chaos. Congress chose the last of these.

All agencies must function within the direction that the legislature gives them by statute. Here, Congress had no specific idea how the FCC should proceed. Instead, Congress provided in § 303 that "Except as otherwise provided in this Act, the Commission from time to time, as public convenience, interest, or necessity requires shall . . .." The list that followed included powers to: assign bands of frequencies to the various classes of radio stations and assign individual frequencies; decide the times each station may operate; establish areas to be served by any station; regulate the apparatus used with respect to the sharpness of the transmissions; take steps to prevent interference; suspend licenses upon a showing that the licensee violated any statute or regulation or transmitted obscene communications; make rules and regulations that are necessary to carry out the other provisions of the statute; and require licensees to keep records the FCC may deem desirable.

Notice that all these powers are conditioned on a showing that "public convenience, interest, or necessity requires" the regulation. This is a vague standard, and, as we shall see, the FCC has rarely been barred from acting on the ground that Congress did not authorize the particular regulation.

An administrative agency such as the FCC usually functions in a variety of ways. Within its statutory authorization it may issue rules or regulations that have the virtual effect of statutes. At other times, it may have to choose between two applicants for a broadcasting license in what resembles a judicial proceeding. Still other times, it performs executive branch functions, as when it seeks out broadcasters or ham operators who are violating their licenses by using excessive power or using unauthorized frequencies.

This variety of regulatory patterns may not comport with traditional understandings about the separation of powers, but these multi-function agencies have been with us for so long that little concern remains about their structure. As we shall see, however, questions are continually raised about whether the agency followed the statutory requirements in performing its functions, whether it followed its own rules, and whether its processes comport with constitutional requirements.

An administrative agency like the FCC makes public announcements of possible changes in rules, through published Notices of Proposed Rulemaking (NPRMs), and similar announcements of inquiries, through Notices of Inquiry (NOIs). The public in general—and in particular those affected by the rules or inquiries—then have opportunity to voice their opinions for or against the proposed changes. In this way, such an agency is behaving as a quasi-legislature, providing room for debate before acting.

The rules or regulations adopted by the agency are, of course, binding on the people or businesses under its regulatory jurisdiction, but Congress always has the authority to create or change statutes, thus in effect overruling the administrative agencies.

In 1927 Congress created the five-member Federal Radio Commission to rationalize the radio spectrum and make allocations. In 1934 the agency was expanded to seven members, given jurisdiction over telephone and telegraph communication as well, and renamed the Federal Communications Commission. In 1982 Congress voted to return to a five-member commission. See 47 U.S.C.A. §§ 154, 155. Each member is appointed by the President for a five-year term subject to Senate confirmation. No more than three members may be from the same political party. The terms are staggered so that no more than one expires in any year. If a member resigns in the middle of a term, the new appointment is for only the unexpired portion of that term. One consequence is that many of those appointed do not have the independence of beginning with a five-year term. The Chairman, chosen by the President, is the chief executive officer and has major administrative responsibilities including the setting of the agenda.

Of the agency's several offices and bureaus for its various functions, the most important for our purposes is the Mass Media Bureau—formed by the 1982 merger of the Broadcast Bureau and the Cable Bureau—which receives all applications for licenses, renewals and transfers. (A new Cable Services Bureau was created in late 1993. Broadcasting & Cable, Dec. 20, 1993 at 55.) Under delegated authority from the Commission, the Mass Media Bureau's staff is authorized to issue some licenses and renew others. In cases in which it has no such power, it may still recommend to the Commissioners which applications to grant and which to deny, thus assuming the position of an advocate within the agency. In addition, complaints of violations of the equal opportunities provision of § 315 or the other political access rules discussed in Chapter XVI are processed through the Mass Media Bureau.

When an adjudicatory hearing is required, usually in a licensing case, it is conducted by an Administrative Law Judge (ALJ), formerly called a hearing examiner, who is an independent employee of the Commission. The Mass Media Bureau may also appear before the ALJ to argue in favor of or against an applicant. The judge renders an initial decision that will become effective unless appealed. The appeal will be either to the Commission itself or to the Review Board. This Board, composed of senior employees of the Commission, sits in panels of three and reviews the initial decisions. The Commission chooses whether or not to accept appeals from the Review Board.

Within the Commission the Mass Media Bureau takes positions and makes recommendations. Any applicant who is unhappy with the Commission's decision may then appeal to the courts—usually to the United

States Court of Appeals for the District of Columbia. But once the Commission renders a decision, the Bureau's role ceases. The General Counsel then takes over to represent the Commission in any litigation that results from the Commission's decision. The General Counsel may also advise the Commission as it prepares to promulgate rules. Sometimes one part of the agency may disagree with another. For example, during reconsideration of the *1974 Fairness Report*, discussed in Chapter XVI, *infra*, the General Counsel's office proposed that complaints that a licensee had not sufficiently covered issues of public importance should be considered only at renewal time. The Bureau opposed the proposal, and the Commissioners agreed with the Bureau.

The Radio Act of 1927 and the Communications Act of 1934 rejected the idea of a market system of spectrum allocation and of any property rights in the spectrum resource. The Federal Communications Commission has the sole power to allocate the radio spectrum, to establish general standards of operation and to license persons to use designated parts of the spectrum.

Many services must be placed, but some critics of Commission policies charge undue reliance on the bloc allocation concept, which calls for allocating discrete frequency bands to classes of users essentially without regard to geographical location, and maintaining a relatively strict segregation among allocations. This can lead to such anomalous results as marine bands in Nebraska and forestry bands in New York City. These problems are exacerbated by the general administrative difficulty of changing an allocation once made: the start-up costs are so great and the capital investment is usually so heavy that there is a strong economic incentive not to move users from one frequency band to another. Thus, as new uses develop, they are allocated higher and higher frequencies, with little consideration of which frequencies are technically best suited for which services. For example, location of radio broadcasting in the AM band (535–1605 kHz) may be inefficient. Local broadcasting might be moved to the current FM band (88–108 MHz), which is much better suited technically to local radio, and long distance broadcasting might be moved to frequencies below 500 kHz to take advantage of the long distance ground wave propagation characteristics at those frequencies.

Another claim is that area coverage by broadcasting stations would require less spectrum if the Commission were to drop its so-called "local station goal." High-powered stations in major urban centers could serve the entire country in only one-third the spectrum space presently used. Yet local stations are important; they are outlets for local news and forums for local citizens to express their views, they serve local advertisers, and they provide such local services as weather reports (which might be critical in areas subject to flash flooding or sudden tornadoes or storms).

## b.  AM Allocation

AM broadcasting occupies slightly more than 1 MHz of spectrum in the Medium Frequency band between 535 kHz and 1605 kHz. This is divided into 107 assignable channels each with a bandwidth of 10 kHz. AM stations are divided into four major classes: Class I "clear channel" stations are high-powered stations designed to provide primary (ground-wave) service to a metropolitan area and its environs and secondary nighttime (skywave) service to an extended rural area. Class II stations also operate on clear channels with primary service areas limited by interference from Class I stations. A Class II station must usually avoid causing interference within the normally protected service areas of Class I or other Class II stations. Class III stations are medium powered and are designed to provide service primarily to larger cities and contiguous rural areas. Class IV stations are low powered and operate on local channels to provide service to a city or town and contiguous areas.

The 1927 Act creating the Federal Radio Commission had charged the Commission to provide "fair, efficient, and equitable radio service" to all areas of the country. The Commission then proceeded by establishing general engineering constraints such as maximum interference standards, and by allocating each of the 107 frequencies to a class of stations. Within these general constraints, the Commission adopted a first-come-first-served approach. An applicant who can find a promising community can apply for a license to serve that community if it can find a channel that will satisfy the various general constraints. An applicant must show that it will not interfere excessively with the signals of existing stations nor expose too many of its new listeners to interference beyond certain acceptable limits.

*Clear Channels.* As noted earlier, because of the skywave phenomenon, powerful AM stations can be received at great distances at night. In the 1940s, with an estimated 20 million persons uncovered by local radio service at night, the FCC created a group of 25 powerful stations operating at 50 kw. Each station shared its daytime channel frequency with other stations around the country. But at sundown all the others left the air so that the channel was clear except for the powerful station, which could reach distant and remote areas of the country.

With the development of FM radio and a surge in interest in AM radio, some argued that the clear channel stations should have their protections reduced to allow more diversity. In response, the clear channel stations argued that their power should be increased to 750 kw so that they could provide additional service. The FCC faced the issue in 1961 but reached no conclusion. In a compromise, it ordered that 13 of the 25 frequencies be shared with one or two other stations, but left the remainder fully protected, while it continued to consider the problem.

In 1980 the Commission acted decisively. The number of persons unserved by nighttime local radio was down to four million, and applicants were clamoring for space on the AM spectrum. The Commission decided to end the clear channel concept, but to protect those stations from interference for a radius of 750 miles. This would still permit them to reach larger areas than ordinary stations but it would permit an additional 125 stations to broadcast at night.

*Expanding the Band.* A second way to increase the number of AM stations is to expand the part of the spectrum available for such broadcasting. This occurred in 1979, when the World Administrative Radio Conference (WARC) at its meeting (held once every 20 years) decided to increase the AM band in the Western Hemisphere so that it will run from 525 to 1705 kHz.

Agreements reached at subsequent Regional Administrative Radio Conferences (RARC) limit stations in the new section of the band to 10 kw. The Commission has decided to use the expanded band to reduce congestion in the existing AM band. By allowing existing AM licensees to operate new stations in the expanded band, and then, after a transition period, shut down their old stations, the Commission hopes to reduce interference and improve signal quality. The FCC will limit the entire expanded band to these migrating AM stations. AM Improvement, 6 F.C.C.Rcd. 6273, 69 R.R.2d 1395 (1991).

### c. FM Allocation

FM broadcasting, which began around 1940, is located in the VHF band. It occupies the frequencies between 88 and 108 MHz, which are excellent for aural broadcast service and allow an effective range of 30 to 75 miles. That spectrum space is divided into 100 assignable channels, each 200 kHz wide. The lowest 20 channels are reserved for noncommercial educational stations; the remaining 80 are given over to commercial use. Commercial FM channels are divided into several classes, ranging from those serving small towns to those powerful enough to serve cities and large surrounding areas. Commercial FM assignments are based on a Table of Assignments, in which communities are assigned a specific number of FM stations of specified power and on specific channels. Licenses are given only for stations within the communities listed in the Table of Assignments or within a 15 mile radius—unless an application to change the table is granted.

In the late 1970s the demand for FM licenses increased dramatically as FM outlets started to overcome the traditional dominance of AM stations. The superior quality of the FM signal and the availability of stereo were the keys to this change. In an effort to meet the increased demand for FM stations, the FCC began to add ("drop in") FM stations where they would not interfere with existing broadcasters.

### d.  Television Allocation

The first licensing of television stations in this country occurred in 1941 and involved 18 channels.  The first assignment plan was developed in 1945, based solely on the VHF channels.  It involved the assignment of about 400 stations to 140 major market centers.  Early comers quickly preempted the 100 choice assignments.  In 1948, because of unexpected problems with tropospheric interference and concern that the 1945 assignment plan could cause problems, the Commission ordered a freeze on channel assignments.  The freeze ended with the issuance of the Sixth Report and Order on Television Allocations, 17 Fed.Reg. 3905, 1 R.R. 91:601 (1952), creating the Table of Assignments.  The Commission rejected the idea of moving all television to the UHF band.  Instead, the 12 VHF channels were retained, and 70 new UHF channels were added, so that the Table provided for about 620 VHF and 1400 UHF stations.  Television uses an enormous amount of spectrum compared to radio.  One VHF channel uses six MHz—six times more than the entire AM band.

The Commission generated the Table of Assignments from its hierarchy of priorities:  (1) to provide at least one television service to every part of the United States;  (2) to provide each community with at least one television station;  (3) to provide a choice of at least two television services to all parts of the U.S.;  (4) to provide each community with at least two television stations;  and (5) to assign remaining channels to communities on the basis of population, geographic location and the number of television services already available to that community.  Note the emphasis on "local" outlets.  Is this a sound hierarchy?

In making these assignments, the Commission decided to "intermix" VHF and UHF channels as a single service in the same markets.  Many observers warned that the newer UHF channels could not survive but the Commission apparently believed that the demand for VHF would overflow into the UHF band and it also feared that failure to intermix would relegate UHF stations to markets overshadowed by VHF outlets in nearby metropolitan areas, or to remote rural areas.  In any event, the Table of Assignments called for combined VHF and UHF channels in the following pattern:  6–10 for cities with population over 1,000,000;  4–6 for cities with 250,000 to 1,000,000;  2–4 for those with populations between 50,000 and 250,000;  and 1–2 for communities under 50,000.

Because the Table tended to allot three VHF stations to most markets with only a few getting more than three, the three major networks could now program almost entirely through VHF affiliates.  This gave them strong audience and advertiser support.  (In 1971, for example, 108 of the nation's 207 television markets, covering 58 percent of the nation's television households, could receive the three networks but no VHF independent stations.  R. Noll, M. Peck, and J. McGowan, Economic Aspects of Television Regulation 168 (1973)).  Without adequate set penetration, UHF stations found it difficult if not impossible to secure advertising revenues and network affiliation. By 1957 there were 395 VHF stations and 96 UHF stations on the air. Almost 300 VHF stations had joined the 108 that already existed and 161 UHF stations had gone on the air; in that period, however, 65 UHFs were forced out of business, while only four VHFs left the air. By this time Dumont, a fourth network, had collapsed. By 1960 only 75 (15 percent) of the 575 commercial stations on the air were UHF, even though 70 percent of the total channel assignments were UHF.

The Commission recognized that intermixture was not working. In 1956, while considering broader solutions such as the transfer of all television to the UHF band, the Commission adopted deintermixture as an "interim" measure in several communities, making them all-UHF. In 1961 the Commission planned to deintermix eight more communities. This time, however, the opposition from established VHF stations was formidable. After a fierce battle, Congress entered the fray and enacted a compromise: the All Channel Receiver Act of 1962. The Act, which became § 303(s) of the Communications Act, authorized the Commission to order that all sets shipped in interstate commerce be capable of receiving both VHF and UHF signals. The VHF interests gave their support for the proposal in exchange for the Commission's indefinite suspension of deintermixture proposals. The Commission did require "all-channel" receivers and declared a moratorium on most pending deintermixture proposals. The Commission's regulation came too late for many of the UHF pioneers of the 1950s.

The continued underutilization of UHF spots led the FCC to begin to reallocate frequencies to competing uses of the airwaves. Channels 70–83 have been reassigned for land mobile use. In some cities Channels 14 to 20 are being used by land mobile operators and are being shared elsewhere.

In addition to the intermixture problem, UHF stations are also more expensive to operate because it takes 10 times as much power for a UHF transmitter to reach the same area as a VHF transmitter. Because of the inferior wave-propagation qualities of UHF signals compared to VHF signals, UHF stations are permitted to operate at a power of 5,000 kw compared to 100 or 316 kw for VHF stations. But the energy costs are so high that few UHF stations operate at maximum permitted power.

A few UHF stations have become profitable as the result of developments in cable television. Because of changes in FCC rules governing cable systems, it became possible for a single television station, in effect, to become a network by supplying its programs by satellite to cable systems throughout the country. The operation of these "superstations" is described more extensively in the discussion of cable television in Chapter XVIII.

Arguing that the UHF spectrum is underutilized, representatives of the land mobile radio industry petitioned the FCC to reallocate portions of the UHF spectrum for their use. In response the Commission issued a NPRM proposing allocation of up to six additional UHF channels (some were previously reallocated in 1972) in eight major metropolitan areas to land mobile. The proposal was vigorously opposed by members of the broadcast industry who contended that UHF television is in a period of tremendous growth and that, due in part to FCC-mandated improvements in television receivers, this growth and a concomitant increase in demand for UHF spectrum space are likely to continue.

In addition, broadcasters argued that the development of a new television service, high definition television (HDTV), discussed *infra,* made it necessary to retain the currently unused UHF spectrum. The Commission delayed any further action on the land-mobile petition pending decisions on HDTV.

*New Television Outlets.* In 1982 the FCC approved the start of a new television service of perhaps as many as 4,000 low-power television (LPTV) stations throughout the country. These stations operate at a power sufficient to reach viewers within a radius of 10–15 miles. It is up to the applicant to find spots on the VHF and UHF bands in which such stations will not interfere with existing stations.

LPTV operators are permitted to join together by satellite to set up networks. Neither the duopoly or one-to-a-market rules discussed in Chapter XIII apply to LPTV. There is no limit set on the number of LPTV licenses one entity can have. Programming restrictions are also minimal. Section 315 applies only to licensee-originated programming.

*High Definition Television.* HDTV is television with approximately twice as many scan lines as the current United States standard of 525 lines. Coupled with a change in the aspect ratio (the ratio between the width and height of the picture) HDTV delivers vastly superior picture quality. Proponents of the new service claim that it is equivalent in quality to 35 mm. film.

A major problem with HDTV, however, was that early systems required a bandwidth greater than 6 MHz. Initially two methods of getting around that problem were proposed. One used two adjacent UHF channels to deliver a single HDTV signal. In 1986 an experimental broadcast using this system was transmitted over channels 58 and 59 in Washington. Another proposed system used non-adjacent channels. This would have allowed a current VHF station to transmit HDTV by transmitting the remainder of the signal over a UHF channel in the same market.

The possibility of HDTV service indicated a potential need for future UHF spectrum. On the other hand, HDTV was only a possibility. Standards had yet to be established, and no current method of delivery to homes had been agreed upon. Thus, as noted above, the Commission had to balance a current need claimed by the land mobile industry and a potential need claimed by broadcasters.

The suggestion that the Commission set an HDTV standard points out another problem faced by the Commission in allocating spectrum for new services. Should the Commission determine the technical standards for such a service or leave it to the marketplace to decide? In the past the Commission has tried both approaches. For example, in 1953 the Commission chose the NTSC standard for color television.

In contrast, in 1982 the FCC authorized AM radio stations to broadcast in stereo but refused to choose from among five incompatible systems. Licensees were free to use any of the five systems. AM Stereophonic Broadcasting, 51 R.R.2d 1 (1982). Six years later the FCC again refused to choose among the two remaining systems or to mandate that all AM stereo receivers be capable of decoding the signals produced by both systems. AM Stereophonic Broadcasting, 64 R.R.2d 516 (1988).

Finally, in 1993, the Commission chose Motorola's C–Quam system as the national standard. An appeal by the manufacturer of the only remaining competing system is expected. Broadcasting & Cable, Nov. 1, 1993 at 14.

What factors should influence the Commission's decision on setting a standard for a new service? In the case of AM stereo, is it relevant that after 10 years less than 20 percent of AM stations broadcast in stereo?

By 1990, improved HDTV systems requiring only 6 MHz per channel were developed. Based on these developments, the Commission decided to restrict proposed HDTV systems to those requiring a maximum of 6 MHz. These systems would not have to be compatible with the existing NTSC standard. Instead, the Commission will require programming to be simulcast in both NTSC and the selected HDTV format. Advanced Television Systems, 5 F.C.C.Rcd. 5627, 68 R.R.2d 163 (1990).

In 1992 the Commission decided a number of additional issues. These included limiting initial eligibility for HDTV licenses to existing TV licensees and adopting an initial two-year deadline for broadcasters to apply for HDTV licenses (to be paired with their original licenses) and a three-year deadline for construction of HDTV facilities, once assigned. In addition, once HDTV becomes the prevalent medium, broadcasters will be forced to convert to HDTV by surrendering one of each of their paired broadcast channels and ceasing to broadcast in NTSC. The Commission also announced its intention to adopt a 100 percent simulcasting requirement at the earliest appropriate date. Advanced Television Systems, 57 Fed.Reg. 21,744 (May 8, 1992).

In its order, the Commission suggested that the date for conversion to HDTV should be "15 years from either selection of an HDTV system or the date a Table of [HDTV] Allotments is effective, whichever is later." The FCC also proposed that the 100 percent simulcasting requirement go into effect no later than four years after the application/construction period has passed. Meanwhile, the six proposed HDTV systems were tested in 1992.

Broadcasters have indicated some concern over the FCC's plan. The same digital technology that allows HDTV to be compressed into 6 MHz may allow an improved NTSC signal. Even if it doesn't equal the quality of HDTV, it may be good enough to deter consumers from investing in more expensive HDTV sets. At the same time digital NTSC will permit compressing several NTSC signals into a single 6 MHz channel (multichannel NTSC). If broadcasters are locked into HDTV and consumers choose digital NTSC, the broadcasters will be at a serious competitive disadvantage with cable and other media that have the capability of transmitting both. Broadcasting, Aug. 24, 1992 at 3.

Before the FCC could choose an HDTV standard, the proponents of the remaining proposed standards, decided to merge and develop a single HDTV standard. This will delay the initial choice of a standard. However, because it reduces the likelihood of a court challenge to the FCC's choice, it may result in HDTV reaching the market sooner than previously expected. Broadcasting & Cable, May 31, 1993, at 59.

The merged HDTV group, dubbed the "grand alliance" has agreed with the FCC's high-definition television advisory committee on a time-table that calls for the delivery of a finished prototype for testing by mid-May, 1994. Meanwhile, the FCC has dropped consideration of the systems that had been proposed by the various members of the grand alliance prior to the merger agreement. Broadcasting & Cable, July 12, 1993, at 69.

## B. JUSTIFICATIONS FOR GOVERNMENT REGULATION

### 1. "PUBLIC INTEREST" AND GOVERNMENT REGULATION

We have just been considering the special nature of the spectrum and various actions that the FCC has taken to regulate the behavior of those who use part of the spectrum. We turn now to the legal question of what justifies the Commission in undertaking these forms of regulation, plus other types of regulation that we consider later. Although a few cases challenged this power early in the life of the FCC, the first major case to address the problem was National Broadcasting Co. v. United States, 319 U.S. 190 (1943).

After conducting a study of business practices and ownership patterns of radio networks in 1941, the Federal Communications Commission concluded that the major networks (NBC and CBS) exerted too much control over the broadcast industry through control over local station programming. To correct this situation, the Commission issued the Chain Broadcasting Regulations, which defined permissible relationships between networks and stations in terms of affiliation, network programming of affiliates' time and network ownership of stations. These regulations were aimed at dissuading individual licensees from entering contracts that gave the networks the power to exert such control over licensees. NBC challenged the Commission's authority to adopt regulations controlling licensee behavior not related to technical and engineering matters.

The first claim was that Congress had not authorized the FCC to adopt these regulations. Section 303 of the Act provided that the

Commission "as public interest, convenience, or necessity requires, shall . . . have authority to make special regulations applicable to radio stations engaged in chain broadcasting." NBC argued that the "public interest" language was to be read as limited to technical and engineering aspects of broadcasting—and that these were not the basis for the FCC's regulations in this case.

The Court noted that several sections of the Act authorized the FCC in furtherance of the "public interest, convenience, or necessity" to do such things as "study new uses for radio, . . . and generally encourage the larger and more effective use of radio in the public interest" and to provide a "fair, efficient and equitable distribution [of licenses] among the states." Building from these several grants of power, the Court rejected NBC's claim:

> The Act itself establishes that the Commission's powers are not limited to the engineering and technical aspects of regulation of radio communication. Yet we are asked to regard the Commission as a kind of traffic officer, policing the wave lengths to prevent stations from interfering with each other. But the Act does not restrict the Commission merely to supervision of the traffic. It puts upon the Commission the burden of determining the composition of that traffic. The facilities of radio are not large enough to accommodate all who wish to use them. Methods must be devised for choosing from among the many who apply. And since Congress itself could not do this, it committed the task to the Commission.
>
>    .  .  .
>
>    .  .  . The Commission's licensing function cannot be discharged, therefore, merely by finding that there are no technological objections to the granting of a license. If the criterion of "public interest" were limited to such matters, how could the Commission choose between two applicants for the same facilities, each of whom is financially and technically qualified to operate a station? Since the very inception of federal regulation by radio, comparative considerations as to the services to be rendered have governed the application of the standard of "public interest, convenience, or necessity."
> [ ]
>
>    .  .  .
>
> These provisions, individually and in the aggregate, preclude the notion that the Commission is empowered to deal only with technical and engineering impediments to the "larger and more effective use of radio in the public interest." We cannot find in the Act any such restriction of the Commission's authority. Suppose, for example, that a community can, because of physical limitations, be assigned only two stations. That community might be deprived of effective service in any one of several ways. More powerful stations in nearby cities might blanket out the signals of the local stations so that they could not be heard at all. The stations might interfere with each other so that neither could be clearly heard.

One station might dominate the other with the power of its signal. But the community could be deprived of good radio service in ways less crude.   One man, financially and technically qualified, might apply for and obtain the licenses of both stations and present a single service over the two stations, thus wasting a frequency otherwise available to the area.   The language of the Act does not withdraw such a situation from the licensing and regulatory powers of the Commission, and there is no evidence that Congress did not mean its broad language to carry the authority it expresses.

The Court then considered NBC's claims that if Congress did authorize the FCC to do this, the statute was unconstitutional.   The first argument was that the phrase "public interest" was too vague a standard for delegating functions to the FCC.   The Court disagreed and relied on an earlier broadcasting case in which it had said that the phrase "is as concrete as the complicated factors for judgment in such a field of delegated authority permit."   The phrase is not to be interpreted as giving the FCC "unlimited power."

Next, the Court rejected NBC's First Amendment claim:

We come, finally, to an appeal to the First Amendment.   The Regulations, even if valid in all other respects, must fall because they abridge, say the appellants, their right of free speech.   If that be so, it would follow that every person whose application for a license to operate a station is denied by the Commission is thereby denied his constitutional right of free speech.   Freedom of utterance is abridged to many who wish to use the limited facilities of radio. Unlike other modes of expression, radio inherently is not available to all.   That is its unique characteristic, and that is why, unlike other modes of expression, it is subject to governmental regulation. Because it cannot be used by all, some who wish to use it must be denied.   But Congress did not authorize the Commission to choose among applicants upon the basis of their political, economic or social views, or upon any other capricious basis.   If it did, or if the Commission by these Regulations proposed a choice among applicants upon some such basis, the issue before us would be wholly different.   The question here is simply whether the Commission, by announcing that it will refuse licenses to persons who engage in specified network practices (a basis for choice, which we hold is comprehended within the statutory criterion of "public interest"), is thereby denying such persons the constitutional right of free speech. The right of free speech does not include, however, the right to use the facilities of radio without a license.   The licensing system established by Congress in the Communications Act of 1934 was a proper exercise of its power over commerce.   The standard it provided for the licensing of stations was the "public interest, convenience, or necessity."   Denial of a station license on that ground, if valid under the Act, is not a denial of free speech.

**Notes and Questions**

1. The origin of the phrase, "public interest, convenience and necessity," § 309(a), or "public convenience, interest or necessity," § 307(a), is unclear from legislative documents. A former chairman of the Commission, Newton Minow, suggests the origin in Equal Time 8–9 (1964): Sen. Clarence C. Dill, who had played a major part in the early legislation, told Minow that the drafters had reached an impasse in attempting to define a regulatory standard for this new, uncharted activity. A young lawyer who had been loaned to the Senate by the Interstate Commerce Commission proposed the words because they were used in other federal statutes.

Judge Henry Friendly, in The Federal Administrative Agencies 54–55 (1962), comments on the standard:

> The only guideline supplied by Congress in the Communications Act of 1934 was "public convenience, interest, or necessity." The standard of public convenience and necessity introduced into the federal statute book by the Transportation Act, 1920, conveyed a fair degree of meaning when the issue was whether new or duplicating railroad construction should be authorized or an existing line abandoned. It was to convey less when, as under the Motor Carrier Act of 1935, or the Civil Aeronautics Act of 1938, there would be the added issue of selecting the applicant to render a service found to be needed; but under those statutes there would usually be some demonstrable factors, such as, in air route cases, ability to render superior one-plane or one-carrier service because of junction of the new route with existing ones, lower costs due to other operations, or historical connection with the traffic, that ought to have enabled the agency to develop intelligible criteria for selection. The standard was almost drained of meaning under section 307 of the Communications Act, where the issue was almost never the need for broadcasting service but rather who should render it.

2. The Federal Radio Commission's first obligation was to clear the airwaves to avoid destructive interference. It decided in 1928 that "as between two broadcasting stations with otherwise equal claims for privileges, the station which has the longest record of continuous service has the superior right." Great Lakes Broadcasting Co., 3 F.R.C.Ann. Rep. 32 (1929), modified on other grounds 37 F.2d 993 (D.C.Cir.), cert. dism'd 281 U.S. 706 (1930). In that case, involving three competing stations, the Commission also stated, however, that if there was a "substantial disparity" in the services being offered by the stations, "the claim of priority must give way to the superior service." The Commission was soon evaluating service in terms of program content. In *Great Lakes,* the Commission contented itself with noting that stations using formats that appeal to only a "small portion" of the public were not serving the public interest because each member of the listening public is entitled to service from each station in the community.

3.  In its early years the Radio Commission showed no hesitation in denying renewal of licenses because of the content of the speech uttered over the station.   Section 29 of the 1927 Act, reenacted as § 326 of the 1934 Act, provided in relevant part:

> Nothing in this Act shall be understood or construed to give the licensing authority the power of censorship over the radio communications or signals transmitted by any radio station, and no regulation or condition shall be promulgated or fixed by the licensing authority which shall interfere with the right of free speech by means of radio communication.   .   .   .

In 1930 the Commission denied renewal of a license to KFKB on the ground that the station was being controlled and used by Dr. J.R. Brinkley to further his personal interest.   Dr. Brinkley had three half-hour programs daily in which he answered anonymous inquiries on health and medicine and usually recommended several of his own tonics and prescriptions that were known to the public only by numerical designations.   Druggists paid a fee to Dr. Brinkley for each sale they made.

In affirming the denial of renewal, KFKB Broadcasting Association v. Federal Radio Commission, 47 F.2d 670 (D.C.Cir.1931), the court rejected the station's argument that the Commission had censored in violation of § 29:

> This contention is without merit.   There has been no attempt on the part of the commission to subject any part of appellant's broadcasting matter to scrutiny prior to its release.   In considering the question whether the public interest, convenience, or necessity will be served by a renewal of appellant's license, the commission has merely exercised its undoubted right to take note of appellant's past conduct, which is not censorship.

In Trinity Methodist Church, South v. Federal Radio Commission, 62 F.2d 850 (D.C.Cir.1932), cert. denied 288 U.S. 599 (1933), the controlling figure was the minister of the church, Dr. Shuler, who regularly defamed government institutions and officials, and attacked labor groups and various religions.   The Commission's denial of renewal was affirmed.   The court concluded that the broadcasts "without facts to sustain or to justify them" might fairly be found not to be within the public interest:

> If it be considered that one in possession of a permit to broadcast in interstate commerce may, without let or hindrance from any source, use these facilities, reaching out, as they do, from one corner of the country to the other, to obstruct the administration of justice, offend the religious susceptibilities of thousands, inspire political distrust and civic discord, or offend youth and innocence by the free use of words suggestive of sexual immorality, and be answerable for slander only at the instance of the one offended, then this great science, instead of a boon, will become a scourge and the nation a

theater for the display of individual passions and the collision of personal interests.  This is neither censorship nor previous restraint, nor is it a whittling away of the rights guaranteed by the First Amendment, or an impairment of their free exercise.  Appellant may continue to indulge his strictures upon the characters of men in public office.  He may just as freely as ever criticize religious practices of which he does not approve.  He may even indulge private malice or personal slander—subject, of course, to being required to answer for the abuse thereof—but he may not, as we think, demand, of right, the continued use of an instrumentality of commerce for such purposes, or any other, except in subordination to all reasonable rules and regulations Congress, acting through the Commission, may prescribe.

4.   The Supreme Court did not again consider the FCC's power until 26 years after *NBC*.  Many scholars view that case, *Red Lion,* as the most important broadcast regulation case ever decided.  We discussed *Red Lion* in Chapter XIV, *supra*, but it is worth revisiting.  Examine again the Notes and Questions following *Red Lion.*

5.   Consistent with the First Amendment, is there any justification other than the scarcity rationale for regulating broadcasting differently than other media?  See Federal Communications Commission v. Pacifica, reprinted in Chapter XVII.

6.   The Supreme Court's most recent extended discussion of the bases for regulating broadcasting occurred in Federal Communications Commission v. League of Women Voters of California.  The three plaintiffs were the League, which wished to persuade public noncommercial educational broadcasters to take editorial positions;  a listener who wished to hear such editorials;  and a noncommercial broadcaster that wished to take editorial stands.  The impediment was § 399 of the Public Broadcasting Act of 1967, as amended in 1981:

> No noncommercial educational broadcasting station which receives a grant from the Corporation for Public Broadcasting under subpart C of this part may engage in editorializing.  No noncommercial educational broadcasting station may support or oppose any candidate for public office.

The case in fact centered on the first sentence of the section, which most of the justices thought severable from the second sentence.  The core of the decision, centering on the nature of "public broadcasting," is reprinted in Chapter XVI.  Here we focus on the majority's background discussion of the bases for regulating broadcasting.

The issue arose in the context of determining the "appropriate standard of review."  The trial court, whose judgment of unconstitutionality was on direct review, had held that § 399 could survive constitutional scrutiny only if it served a "compelling" governmental interest.  The FCC argued that a less demanding standard was appropriate.  It based this argument in part on the "special characteristic" of spectrum scarcity and in part on the unique role of noncommercial broadcasting in this country.

The response of the five-member majority follows.

## FEDERAL COMMUNICATIONS COMMISSION v. LEAGUE OF WOMEN VOTERS OF CALIFORNIA

Supreme Court of the United States, 1984.
468 U.S. 364, 104 S.Ct. 3106, 82 L.Ed.2d 278, 10 Med.L.Rptr. 1937.

[After setting forth the facts discussed in the introduction to this case, *supra*, and reviewing the history of noncommercial broadcasting, Justice Brennan addressed the appropriate standard of review in the following passage:]

JUSTICE BRENNAN delivered the opinion of the Court.

. . .

At first glance, of course, it would appear that the District Court applied the correct standard. Section 399 plainly operates to restrict the expression of editorial opinion on matters of public importance, and, as we have repeatedly explained, communication of this kind is entitled to the most exacting degree of First Amendment protection. [ ] Were a similar ban on editorializing applied to newspapers and magazines, we would not hesitate to strike it down as violative of the First Amendment. E.g., Mills v. Alabama, 384 U.S. 214 (1966). But, as the Government correctly notes, because broadcast regulation involves unique considerations, our cases have not followed precisely the same approach that we have applied to other media and have never gone so far as to demand that such regulations serve "compelling" governmental interests. At the same time, we think the Government's argument loses sight of concerns that are important in this area and thus misapprehends the essential meaning of our prior decisions concerning the reach of Congress' authority to regulate broadcast communication.

The fundamental principles that guide our evaluation of broadcast regulation are by now well established. First, we have long recognized that Congress, acting pursuant to the Commerce Clause, has power to regulate the use of this scarce and valuable national resource. The distinctive feature of Congress' efforts in this area has been to ensure through the regulatory oversight of the FCC that only those who satisfy the "public interest, convenience and necessity" are granted a license to use radio and television broadcast frequencies. 47 U.S.C.A. § 309(a).[11]

---

**11.** [ ].

The prevailing rationale for broadcast regulation based on spectrum scarcity has come under increasing criticism in recent years. Critics, including the incumbent Chairman of the FCC, charge that with the advent of cable and satellite television technology, communities now have access to such a wide variety of stations that the scarcity doctrine is obsolete. See, e.g., Fowler & Brenner, A Marketplace Approach to Broadcast Regulation, 60 Tex. L.Rev. 207, 221–226 (1982). We are not prepared, however, to reconsider our long-standing approach without some signal from Congress or the FCC that technological developments have advanced so far that

Second, Congress may, in the exercise of this power, seek to assure that the public receives through this medium a balanced presentation of information on issues of public importance that otherwise might not be addressed if control of the medium were left entirely in the hands of those who own and operate broadcasting stations. Although such governmental regulation has never been allowed with respect to the print media, *Miami Herald Publishing Co. v. Tornillo,* 418 U.S. 241 (1974), we have recognized that "differences in the characteristics of new media justify differences in the First Amendment standards applied to them." *Red Lion Broadcasting Co. v. FCC,* 395 U.S. 367, 386 (1969). The fundamental distinguishing characteristic of the new medium of broadcasting that, in our view, has required some adjustment in First Amendment analysis is that "[b]roadcasting frequencies are a scarce resource [that] must be portioned out among applicants." *Columbia Broadcasting System, Inc. v. Democratic National Committee,* 412 U.S. 94, 101 (1973). Thus, our cases have taught that, given spectrum scarcity, those who are granted a license to broadcast must serve in a sense as fiduciaries for the public by presenting "those views and voices which are representative of his community and which would otherwise, by necessity, be barred from the airwaves." *Red Lion,* supra, at 389. As we observed in that case, because "[i]t is the purpose of the First Amendment to preserve an uninhibited marketplace of ideas in which truth will ultimately prevail, . . . the right of the public to receive suitable access to social, political, esthetic, moral and other ideas and experiences [through the medium of broadcasting] is crucial here [and it] may not constitutionally be abridged either by the Congress or the FCC." Id., at 390.

Finally, although the government's interest in ensuring balanced coverage of public issues is plainly both important and substantial, we have, at the same time, made clear that broadcasters are engaged in a vital and independent form of communicative activity. As a result, the First Amendment must inform and give shape to the manner in which Congress exercises its regulatory power in this area. Unlike common carriers, broadcasters are "entitled under the First Amendment to exercise 'the widest journalistic freedom consistent with their public [duties].'" *Columbia Broadcasting System, Inc. v. FCC,* 453 U.S. 367, 395 (1981) (quoting *Columbia Broadcasting System, Inc. v. Democratic National Committee,* supra, at 110). See also *FCC v. Midwest Video Corp.,* 440 U.S. 689, 703 (1979). Indeed, if the public's interest in receiving a balanced presentation of views is to be fully served, we must necessarily rely in large part upon the editorial initiative and judgment of the broadcasters who bear the public trust. See *Columbia Broadcasting System, Inc. v. Democratic National Committee,* supra, at 124–127.

Our prior cases illustrate these principles. In *Red Lion,* for example, we upheld the FCC's "fairness doctrine"—which requires broadcasters to provide adequate coverage of public issues and to ensure that this

some revision of the system of broadcast regulation may be required.

coverage fairly and accurately reflects the opposing views—because the doctrine advanced the substantial governmental interest in ensuring balanced presentations of views in this limited medium and yet posed no threat that a "broadcaster [would be denied permission] to carry a particular program or to publish his own views." Id., at 396.[12] Similarly, in Columbia Broadcasting System, Inc. v. FCC, supra, the Court upheld the right of access for federal candidates imposed by § 312(a)(7) of the Communications Act both because that provision "makes a significant contribution to freedom of expression by enhancing the ability of candidates to present, and the public to receive, information necessary for the effective operation of the democratic process," id., at 396, and because it defined a sufficiently *"limited* right of 'reasonable' access" so that "the discretion of broadcasters to present their views on any issue or to carry any particular type of programming" was not impaired. Id., at 396–397 (emphasis in original). Finally, in Columbia Broadcasting System, Inc. v. Democratic National Committee, supra, the Court affirmed the FCC's refusal to require broadcast licensees to accept all paid political advertisements. Although it was argued that such a requirement would serve the public's First Amendment interest in receiving additional views on public issues, the Court rejected this approach, finding that such a requirement would tend to transform broadcasters into common carriers and would intrude unnecessarily upon the editorial discretion of broadcasters. 412 U.S., at 123–125. The FCC's ruling, therefore, helped to advance the important purposes of the Communications Act, grounded in the First Amendment, of preserving the right of broadcasters to exercise "the widest journalistic freedom consistent with [their] public obligations," and of guarding against "the risk of an enlargement of Government control over the content of broadcast discussion of public issues." 412 U.S., at 110, 127.[13]

**12.** We note that the FCC, observing that "[i]f any substantial possibility exists that the [fairness doctrine] rules have impeded, rather than furthered, First Amendment objectives, repeal may be warranted on that ground alone," has tentatively concluded that the rules, by effectively chilling speech, do not serve the public interest, and has therefore proposed to repeal them. Notice of Proposed Rulemaking In re Repeal or Modification of the Personal Attack and Political Editorial Rules, 48 Fed.Reg. 28295, 28298, 28301 (June 21, 1983). Of course, the Commission may, in the exercise of its discretion, decide to modify or abandon these rules, and we express no view on the legality of either course. As we recognized in *Red Lion,* however, were it to be shown by the Commission that the fairness doctrine "has the effect of reducing rather than enhancing" speech, we would then be forced to reconsider the constitutional basis of our decision in that case. 395 U.S., at 393.

**13.** This Court's decision in FCC v. Pacifica Foundation, 438 U.S. 726 (1978), upholding an exercise of the Commission's authority to regulate broadcasts containing "indecent" language as applied to a particular afternoon broadcast of a George Carlin monologue, is consistent with the approach taken in our other broadcast cases. There, the Court focused on certain physical characteristics of broadcasting—specifically, that the medium's uniquely pervasive presence renders impossible any prior warning for those listeners who may be offended by indecent language, and, second, that the ease with which children may gain access to the medium, especially during daytime hours, creates a substantial risk that they may be exposed to such offensive expression without parental supervision. Id., at 748–749. The governmental interest in reduction of those risks through Commission regulation of the timing and character of such "indecent broadcasting" was thought suffi-

Thus, although the broadcasting industry plainly operates under restraints not imposed upon other media, the thrust of these restrictions has generally been to secure the public's First Amendment interest in receiving a balanced presentation of views on diverse matters of public concern. As a result of these restrictions, of course, the absolute freedom to advocate one's own positions without also presenting opposing viewpoints—a freedom enjoyed, for example, by newspaper publishers and soapbox orators—is denied to broadcasters. But, as our cases attest, these restrictions have been upheld only when we were satisfied that the restriction is narrowly tailored to further a substantial governmental interest, such as ensuring adequate and balanced coverage of public issues. [ ] Making that judgment requires a critical examination of the interests of the public and broadcasters in light of the particular circumstances of each case. E.g., FCC v. Pacifica Foundation, supra.

[Justice Brennan then turned to a consideration of the specifics of this case. His discussion of this issue, and those of the dissenting justices are reprinted in Chapter XVII.]

## Notes and Questions

1. Opponents of content regulation of broadcasting took footnotes 11 and 12 as a sign that the Court was willing to reconsider the First Amendment status of broadcasters. According to the Commission, the *1985 Fairness Report,* discussed in Chapter XVI, *infra,* was a specific response to these footnotes.

2. The scarcity rationale was attacked by the court of appeals in *TRAC,* p. 646, *supra.* The case was an appeal of the Commission's refusal to apply the political broadcast rules to teletext and is discussed in greater detail in Chapter XVIII. The court acknowledged that it was bound by *Red Lion,* but sharply criticized the Supreme Court's reliance on scarcity as a rationale distinguishing between the broadcast and print media:

> . . . The basic difficulty in this entire area is that the line drawn between the print media and the broadcast media, resting as it does on the physical scarcity of the latter, is a distinction without a difference. Employing the scarcity concept as an analytic tool, particularly with respect of new and unforeseen technologies, inevitably leads to strained reasoning and artificial results.

> It is certainly true that broadcast frequencies are scarce but it is unclear why that fact justifies content regulation of broadcasting in a way that would be intolerable if applied to the editorial process of the print media. All economic goods are scarce, not least the newsprint, ink, delivery trucks, computers, and other resources that

ciently substantial to outweigh the broadcaster's First Amendment interest in controlling the presentation of its programming. Id., at 750. In this case, by contrast, we are faced not with indecent expression, but rather with expression that is at the core of First Amendment protections, and no claim is made by the Government that the expression of editorial opinion by noncommercial stations will create a substantial "nuisance" of the kind addressed in FCC v. Pacifica Foundation.

go into the production and dissemination of print journalism. Not everyone who wishes to publish a newspaper, or even a pamphlet, may do so. Since scarcity is a universal fact, it can hardly explain regulation in one context and not another. The attempt to use a universal fact as a distinguishing principle necessarily leads to analytical confusion.

Neither is content regulation explained by the fact that broadcasters face the problem of interference, so that the government must define usable frequencies and protect those frequencies from encroachment. This governmental definition of frequencies is another instance of a universal fact that does not offer an explanatory principle for differing treatment. A publisher can deliver his newspapers only because government provides streets and regulates traffic on the streets by allocating rights of way. Yet no one would contend that the necessity for these governmental functions, which are certainly analogous to the government's function in allocating broadcast frequencies, could justify regulation of the content of a newspaper to ensure that it serves the needs of citizens.

There may be ways to reconcile *Red Lion* and *Tornillo* but the "scarcity" of broadcast frequencies does not appear capable of doing so. Perhaps the Supreme Court will one day revisit this area of the law and either eliminate the distinction between print and broadcast media, surely by pronouncing *Tornillo* applicable to both, or announce a constitutional distinction that is more usable than the present one.

How convincing is the court's critique? What constitutional distinction might it find more usable than the scarcity rationale?

### 2.   IS BROADCASTING "GOVERNMENT ACTION"?

The issues raised in *Red Lion* revolve around the broadcaster's claim that the First Amendment protects it from government regulation. Sometimes claims in the name of the First Amendment are made by private citizens against the media. In *Tornillo,* the citizen's claim failed. But when such a claim is made against broadcast media a new element enters the picture. When government undertakes to provide a forum for discussion, or a street for parades, it must not discriminate among prospective users according to their views. Government must be neutral in such situations. If too many want to parade or use the forum, government might develop a lottery system or a queuing system; but it could not prefer those those views it liked. Some have argued that this analysis applies to broadcasters—that they are so closely related to, and regulated by, government that their actions are government action, and, thus, bound by the neutrality principle.

The Supreme Court avoided this question in *Columbia Broadcasting System, Inc.*, p. 670, *supra*. The Democratic National Committee wanted to buy commercial time to urge financial support for the party.

Another group (BEM) sought to buy time to oppose the war in Vietnam. The broadcasters refused to sell time to either group because the proposed commercials did not fit into the type of programming the broadcasters wanted to present.  The DNC and BEM asked the FCC to order the broadcasters to take their commercials—at least as long as they were taking commercials from other sources.  The FCC refused. The Supreme Court upheld the FCC's refusal.

The Court was badly fragmented by the DNC–BEM claim that the broadcasters should be treated as government.  Three justices met it head on and rejected it.  They were concerned that the "concept of journalistic independence could not co-exist with a reading of the challenged conduct of the licensee as government action" because a government medium could not exercise editorial judgment as to what content should be carried or excluded.

The three observed, however, that even if the First Amendment applied to this case, the groups were not entitled to access.  Here, they relied on Meiklejohn's theme that the essential point was "not that everyone shall speak, but that everything worth saying shall be said." Congress and the Commission might reasonably conclude that "the allocation of journalistic priorities should be concentrated on the licensee rather than diffused among many.  This policy gives the public some assurance that the broadcaster will be answerable if he fails to meet its legitimate needs.  No such accountability attaches to the private individual."

Three other justices agreed that even if government action were involved in the case, there was no violation of the groups' rights under the First Amendment.  They therefore refused to pass on the question of government involvement.

Justice Douglas, concurring, did not decide the question.  He noted that if a licensee were to be considered a federal agency it would "within limits of its time be bound to disseminate all views."  If a licensee was not considered a federal agency "I fail to see how constitutionally we can treat TV and radio differently than we treat newspapers."  He agreed that "The Commission has a duty to encourage a multitude of voices but only in a limited way, viz., by preventing monopolistic practices and by promoting technological developments that will open up new channels. But censorship or editing or the screening by Government of what licensees may broadcast goes against the grain of the First Amendment."

In dissent Justice Brennan, with whom Justice Marshall concurred, disagreed:

> Thus, given the confluence of these various indicia of "governmental action"—including the public nature of the airwaves, the governmentally created preferred status of broadcasters, the extensive Government regulation of broadcast programming, and the specific governmental approval of the challenged policy—I can only conclude that the Government "has so far insinuated itself into a position" of participation in this policy that the absolute refusal of

broadcast licensees to sell air time to groups or individuals wishing to speak out on controversial issues of public importance must be subjected to the restraints of the First Amendment.

The dissenters then concluded that the absolute refusal did violate the First Amendment. "The retention of such *absolute* control in the hands of a few Government licensees is inimical to the First Amendment, for vigorous, free debate can be attained only when members of the public have *some* opportunity to take the initiative and editorial control into their own hands." The emergence of broadcasting as "the public's prime source of information," has "made the soapbox orator and the leafleteer virtually obsolete."

The case, however, indicates only that the Constitution does not create a right of access to broadcasting. It does not address the question whether Congress might enact a statute requiring broadcasters as a condition of their licenses to give a certain period of time per day or week to members of the public. How might those who wish to speak be selected? Would such a statute be valid? Might the Commission issue a rule to the same effect? Even if such a statute or rule would be constitutional, would it be sound? What does this controversy say about the "agenda-setting" role of media?

In the DNC–BEM case much of the majority's approach was based on the power to enforce the broadcaster's responsibility to program in the public interest because of the two prongs of the fairness doctrine. It is ironic that the fairness doctrine, resisted by the broadcasters in *Red Lion,* also shielded them from having to give unlimited access to their broadcasting facilities. As a broadcaster, which would you find a greater interference with your freedom—the fairness doctrine or a rule requiring you to give some persons or groups access to your facilities?

## C. INITIAL LICENSING

### 1. The Administrative Process at Work

In this section we consider the process by which the Commission grants licenses to applicants. To seek a license for a broadcast frequency, an applicant first asks the Commission for a construction permit to build the facility. If the construction permit is granted, the license will then follow almost automatically if the facility is constructed on schedule. The process for such applications was discussed at p. 655, *supra.*

As noted earlier, anyone whose application for a construction permit or license is rejected may appeal to the courts.

An indication of how the United States Court of Appeals for the District of Columbia (which hears most of these appeals) views its role in reviewing broadcast licensing is found in Greater Boston Television Corp. v. Federal Communications Commission, 444 F.2d 841, 850–53, 20 R.R.2d 2052, 1 Med.L.Rptr. 2003 (D.C.Cir.1970), cert. denied 403 U.S. 923 (1971), (footnotes citing a wealth of authorities have been excluded):

Assuming consistency with law and the legislative mandate, the agency has latitude not merely to find facts and make judgments, but also to select the policies deemed in the public interest. The function of the court is to assure that the agency has given reasoned consideration to all the material facts and issues. This calls for insistence that the agency articulate with reasonable clarity its reasons for decision, and identify the significance of the crucial facts, a course that tends to assure that the agency's policies effectuate general standards, applied without unreasonable discrimination. . . .

Its supervisory function calls on the court to intervene not merely in case of procedural inadequacies or bypassing of the mandate in the legislative charter, but more broadly if the court becomes aware, especially from a combination of danger signals, that the agency has not really taken a "hard look" at the salient problems, and has not genuinely engaged in reasoned decision-making. If the agency has not shirked this fundamental task, however, the court exercises restraint and affirms the agency's action even though the court would on its own account have made different findings or adopted different standards. Nor will the court upset a decision because of errors that are not material, there being room for the doctrine of harmless error. . . .

This posture of self-restraint would apply to administrative agencies generally.

But the most complex cases before the Commission are those in which more than one applicant seeks a single vacant frequency or channel. These are called "mutually exclusive" applications because only one can be granted. These cases almost always raise serious fact questions that must be resolved in a hearing. These hearings can be very time-consuming because each of two or more parties not only attempts to present arguments why it should get the spot, but also may present evidence attacking each of the other applicants.

In these cases there may be specific questions, such as whether one of the applicants is an alien, or whether another is inadequately financed or proposes to use inadequate engineering equipment. But even if all the applicants meet every basic qualification, a hearing would still be needed to determine which qualified applicant should get the award.

We might note now that the same hearing process may be required at other stages in the licensing process. If a licensee applies for a renewal, if claims are made that the licensee has misbehaved in some way or should not get the license renewed, any fact questions that need to be resolved will be explored at a similar hearing conducted by an ALJ.

In the interests of simplicity, the foregoing description of the administrative process assumed that when the FCC decided to grant or renew a license to an applicant who had no competitors that was the end of the process. If the applicant had beaten out challengers they could carry the fight into the courts. But if the applicant had no challenger and the

Commission decided in its favor, the Bureau—even if it had disagreed with that result—could not attack the decision of its agency. For many years the Commission firmly rejected all efforts of listeners or citizen groups to take a formal part in the licensing process. Formally stated, the FCC denied outsiders "standing" to participate.

In 1966, however, the court of appeals ordered that citizen groups be allowed to participate in these proceedings. In Office of Communications of United Church of Christ v. Federal Communications Commission, 359 F.2d 994, 7 R.R.2d 2001, 1 Med.L.Rptr. 1993 (D.C.Cir.1966), the opinion by then Circuit Judge Burger said in part:

> The argument that a broadcaster is not a public utility is beside the point. True it is not a public utility in the same sense as strictly regulated common carriers or purveyors of power, but neither is it a purely private enterprise like a newspaper or an automobile agency. A broadcaster has much in common with a newspaper publisher, but he is not in the same category in terms of public obligations imposed by law. A broadcaster seeks and is granted the free and exclusive use of a limited and valuable part of the public domain; when he accepts that franchise it is burdened by enforceable public obligations. A newspaper can be operated at the whim or caprice of its owners; a broadcast station cannot. After nearly five decades of operation the broadcast industry does not seem to have grasped the simple fact that a broadcast license is a public trust subject to termination for breach of duty.

> . . .

> Public participation is especially important in a renewal proceeding, since the public will have been exposed for at least three years to the licensee's performance, as cannot be the case when the Commission considers an initial grant, unless the applicant has a prior record as a licensee. In a renewal proceeding, furthermore, public spokesmen, such as Appellants here, may be the only objectors. In a community served by only one outlet, the public interest focus is perhaps sharper and the need for airing complaints often greater than where, for example, several channels exist. Yet if there is only one outlet, there are no rivals at hand to assert the public interest, and reliance on opposing applicants to challenge the existing licensee for the channel would be fortuitous at best. Even when there are multiple competing stations in a locality, various factors may operate to inhibit the other broadcasters from opposing a renewal application. An imperfect rival may be thought a desirable rival, or there may be a "gentleman's agreement" of deference to a fellow broadcaster in the hope he will reciprocate on a propitious occasion.

He also noted that the fears of regulatory agencies that they will be flooded with applications are rarely borne out.

Since this case, the feared flood has not developed, though citizen groups are playing a much more active part in the regulatory processes of the Commission than ever before. The role of citizen groups is extensively discussed in D. Guimary, *Citizens' Groups and Broadcasting* (1975). Their most common legal action is the filing of a petition to deny a renewal application on the ground that the applicant has failed to meet the required level of public service.

*Negotiation and Agreement.* Another possibility is to negotiate. In order to avoid the expense of defending against petitions to deny renewals, broadcasters have begun entering into agreements with citizen groups that challenge their license applications or renewals. In return for withdrawal of the challenge, a broadcaster typically undertakes to make certain changes in its station's operation. The broadcaster may promise to change its employment policies, to support local production of broadcast programming or to attempt to expand certain types of programming.

The Commission has generally allowed broadcasters to enter into the agreements if they maintain responsibility at all times for determining how best to serve the public interest. However, as part of a series of rule changes aimed at curbing abuses of the licensing process (discussed later in this chapter), the Commission has indicated it will scrutinize these arguments more closely. Does recognition of these private agreements serve the public interest? Does it allow broadcasters to "buy off" citizen groups who may be in the best position to point out programming deficiencies or offensive overcommercialization?

## 2.  INTRODUCTION TO BASIC QUALIFICATIONS

In the 1934 Act, Congress empowered the Federal Communications Commission to grant licenses to applicants for radio stations for periods of up to three years "if public convenience, interest, or necessity will be served thereby." § 307(a). In 1981 license terms were changed to five years for television and seven years for radio. Section 307(b) requires the Commission to make "such distribution of licenses, frequencies, hours of operation, and of power among the several states and communities as to provide a fair, efficient, and equitable distribution of radio service to each of the same."

As we have seen, the Commission responded by allocating a portion of the spectrum for standard (AM) radio service and then subdividing that space further by requiring very powerful stations to use certain frequencies and weaker stations to utilize others and some stations to leave the air at sundown. The Commission used its rule-making powers to develop these allocations and then set engineering standards of separation and interference. The 1934 Act empowered the Commission to promulgate "such rules and regulations and prescribe such restrictions and conditions, not inconsistent with law, as may be necessary to carry out the provisions of this chapter." § 303(r).

In addition to requiring proof that a grant will serve the "public convenience, interest, or necessity," § 307(a), the Act also requires that each applicant demonstrate that it meets basic "citizenship, character, and financial, technical, and other qualifications," § 308(b). An applicant that fails to satisfy any one of the following "basic qualifications" is ineligible to receive a license.

a. *Legal Qualifications.* An applicant for a license must comply with the specific requirements of the Communications Act and the Commission's rules. For example, there are restrictions on permitting aliens to hold radio and broadcast licenses. § 310(b). Prior revocation of an applicant's license by a federal court for an antitrust violation precludes grant of a new application. § 313. An application will be denied if its grant would result in violation of the Commission's multiple ownership rules or chain broadcasting regulations.

b. *Technical Qualifications.* An applicant for a broadcast station must also comply with the Commission's standards for transmission. These standards include such issues as interference with existing or allocated stations and efficiency of operation, gains or losses of service to affected populations, structure, power and location of the antenna, coverage and quality of the signal in the areas to be served, and studio location and operating equipment utilized.

c. *Financial Qualifications.* Although the applicant must show that it has an adequate financial base to commence operations, it need not demonstrate that it can sustain operations indefinitely. The test applied by the Commission is that the applicant must have sufficient funds to operate a broadcast station for three months without advertising revenue. The Commission may also inquire into the applicant's estimates of the amounts that will be actually required to operate the station and the reliability of its proposed sources of funds, such as estimated advertising revenues.

d. *Character Qualifications.* For many years character issues considered by the Commission included past criminal convictions of the applicant, trafficking in broadcast licenses, failure to keep the Commission informed of changes in the applicant's status and other situations that raised questions as to the integrity or reliability of the applicant in the broadcasting function. In 1985 in keeping with the move toward deregulation, the Commission narrowed the scope of character examinations. The Commission decided to confine its interest to three areas: misconduct involving violations of the Act or Commission rules; misrepresentations or lack of candor before the Commission; and fraudulent programming.

Other than those issues, the Commission considered as relevant only criminal fraud convictions, adjudicated cases of broadcast-related antitrust or anticompetitive misconduct and felony convictions substantially related to operating as a broadcaster in a manner consistent with Commission rules and policies. Character Qualifications in Broadcast Licensing, 102 F.C.C.2d 1179, 59 R.R.2d 801 (1986). The policy statement was upheld on appeal. National Association for Better Broadcasting v. Federal Communications Commission, 830 F.2d 270 (D.C.Cir. 1987).

Several years later the Commission expanded the scope of character examinations to include any felony conviction, regardless of whether it was broadcast related or not. The FCC's rationale for this expansion was that "[b]ecause all felonies are serious crimes, any conviction provides an indication of an applicant's or licensee's propensity to obey the law." The FCC also expanded consideration of antitrust violations to cover all mass-media-related violations instead of just broadcast-related ones.

On reconsideration, the FCC clarified its position with regard to misdemeanor convictions. They do not have to be reported to the Commission, but in appropriate cases serious misdemeanor convictions may be considered in evaluating the character qualifications of an applicant. Character Qualifications Policy, 69 R.R.2d 279 (1991).

With regard to both felony convictions and antitrust violations the Commission will, however, continue to take into consideration mitigating factors such as "the willfulness of the misconduct, the frequency of the misconduct, the currentness of the misconduct, the seriousness of the misconduct, the nature of the participation (if any) of managers or owners, efforts made to remedy the wrong, overall record of compliance with FCC rules and policies, and rehabilitation." The Commission also reiterated its willingness to condition license grants on the outcome of allegations being adjudicated in courts or other agencies. Character Qualifications Policy, 67 R.R.2d 1107 (1990).

e. The final category of basic qualifications, "other," has been interpreted to refer primarily to character issues, but it may also overlap with public interest considerations.

### 3. Substantive Considerations

Assuming an applicant has met the basic qualifications such as citizenship and financial security, how does the Commission decide if granting the application will serve the "public interest, convenience and necessity"? In this section we will take an extensive look at the substantive considerations in the process, starting with the single applicant for the single vacancy.

As noted earlier, that applicant may not get the license. Given that the FCC was created in large part to reduce crowding and eliminate chaos, what role may it play when only one applicant seeks an available spot? A first answer may be found in *NBC*, where the Court recognized that the FCC may act beyond its policeman's role and may consider the public interest. Sometimes the public interest might be better served by leaving a vacancy that a good applicant might later fill rather than taking the first comer.

But this, of course, requires that the FCC be able to distinguish a "good" applicant from a lesser one. From the beginning the Commission has confronted the tension between using criteria that directly address programming considerations and the concern that too close a look at proposed programming may amount to government control.

The Commission believed that the "entire listening public within the service area of a station, or a group of stations in one community, is entitled to service from that station or stations." Specialized stations were entitled to little or no consideration. In the Commission's opinion, "the tastes, needs, and desires of all substantial groups among the listening public should be met, in some fair proportion by a well-rounded program, in which entertainment, consisting of music of both classical and lighter grades, religion, education and instruction, important public events, discussions of public questions, weather, market reports and news, and matters of interest to all members of the family find a place." Recognizing that communities differed and that other variables were relevant, the Commission did not erect a "rigid schedule."

Over the years the Commission has taken different positions on what constitutes serving the public interest. The current position is that licensees are obligated to determine the needs and interests of their community and then present programs that meet those needs and interests. During the '70s the Commission also prescribed a specific methodology for determining the needs and interests of their community. The Primer on Ascertainment of Community Problems by Broadcast Applicants, 27 F.C.C.2d 650, 21 R.R.2d 1507 (1971). Amendment of the Primers on Ascertainment of Community Problems, 76 F.C.C.2d 401, 47 R.R.2d 189 (1980). These ascertainment requirements were eliminated for commercial broadcasting in two separate proceedings.

In those proceedings the Commission emphasized that they were only eliminating formal ascertainment requirements, not the licensee's obligation to determine and serve the needs and interests of its community. Deregulation of Radio, 84 F.C.C.2d 968, 49 R.R.2d 1, reconsideration denied, 87 F.C.C.2d 797, 50 R.R.2d 93 (1981); Revision of Programming and Commercialization Policies, Ascertainment Requirements and Program Log Requirements for Commercial Television Stations, 98 F.C.C.2d 1076, 56 R.R.2d 1005 (1984). Radio deregulation was upheld in Office of Communication of the United Church of Christ v. F.C.C., 707 F.2d 1413, 53 R.R.2d 1371 (D.C.Cir.1983). With the exception of the elimination of children's television commercialization guidelines, discussed at p. 468, *supra*, TV deregulation was also affirmed on appeal. Action for Children's Television v. Federal Communications Commission, 821 F.2d 741, 63 R.R.2d 440 (D.C.Cir.1987).

*Equal Employment Opportunity.* In addition to the general public interest issues of employment discrimination by licensees, the Commission's rules generally require that each applicant for a broadcast license, for assignment or transfer of control of a license, and renewal applicants who have not previously done so "file with the Commission programs designed to provide equal employment opportunities for Blacks (not of

Hispanic origin), Asians or Pacific Islanders, American Indians or Alaskan Natives, Hispanics, and women."

4. THE COMPARATIVE PROCEEDING

If two or more applicants file for use of the same or interfering facilities, the Commission must proceed by way of comparative hearing among all qualified applicants to determine which will best serve the public interest. An applicant in a comparative proceeding must not only meet minimum qualifications but must also prevail when judged on the Commission's comparative criteria. These criteria, which involve considerations other than those applied in the non-comparative proceeding, evolved through adjudication rather than rulemaking.

POLICY STATEMENT ON COMPARATIVE
BROADCAST HEARINGS
Federal Communications Commission, 1965.
1 F.C.C.2d 393, 5 R.R.2d 1901.

By the Commission: COMMISSIONERS HYDE and BARTLEY dissenting and issuing statements; COMMISSIONER LEE concurring and issuing a statement.

[The Commission noted that choosing one from among several qualified applicants for a facility was one of its primary responsibilities. The process involved an extended hearing in which the various applicants were compared on a variety of subjects. The "subject does not lend itself to precise categorization or to the clear making of precedent. The various factors cannot be assigned absolute values." Moreover, the membership of the Commission is continually changing and each member has his or her own idea of what factors are important. Thus, the statement is not binding and the Commission is not obligated to deal with all cases "as it has dealt in the past with some that seem comparable." Nonetheless, it is "important to have a high degree of consistency of decision and of clarity in our basic policies." The statement was to "serve the purpose of clarity and consistency of decision, and the further purpose of eliminating from the hearing process time-consuming elements not substantially related to the public interest." The Commission declared that this statement "does not attempt to deal with the somewhat different problems raised where an applicant is contesting with a licensee seeking renewal of license." The Commission then turned to the merits and identified "two primary objectives:" "best practicable service to the public" and "maximum diffusion of control of the media of mass communications."]

Several factors are significant in the two areas of comparison mentioned above, and it is important to make clear the manner in which each will be treated.

1. *Diversification of control of the media of mass communications.*—Diversification is a factor of primary significance since, as set forth above, it constitutes a primary objective in the licensing scheme.

2. *Full-time participation in station operation by owners.*—We consider this factor to be of substantial importance.  It is inherently desirable that legal responsibility and day-to-day performance be closely associated.  In addition, there is a likelihood of greater sensitivity to an area's changing needs, and of programming designed to serve these needs, to the extent that the station's proprietors actively participate in the day-to-day operation of the station.  This factor is thus important in securing the best practicable service.  It also frequently complements the objective of diversification, since concentrations of control are necessarily achieved at the expense of integrated ownership.

We are primarily interested in full-time participation.   .   .   .

Attributes of participating owners, such as their experience and local residence, will also be considered in weighing integration of ownership and management.  While, for the reasons given above, integration of ownership and management is important per se, its value is increased if the participating owners are local residents and if they have experience in the field.  Participation in station affairs on the basis described above by a local resident indicates a likelihood of continuing knowledge of changing local interests and needs.   .   .   .

.   .   .

3. *Proposed program service.*—.   .   .   The importance of program service is obvious.  The feasibility of making a comparative evaluation is not so obvious.  Hearings take considerable time and precisely formulated program plans may have to be changed not only in details but in substance, to take account of new conditions obtaining at the time a successful applicant commences operation.  Thus, minor differences among applicants are apt to prove to be of no significance.

.   .   .

Decisional significance will be accorded only to material and substantial differences between applicants' proposed program plans.  [   ] Minor differences in the proportions of time allocated to different types of programs will not be considered.  Substantial differences will be considered to the extent that they go beyond ordinary differences in judgment and show a superior devotion to public service.   .   .   .

In light of the considerations set forth above, and our experience with the similarity of the program plans of competing applicants, taken with the desirability of keeping hearing records free of immaterial clutter, no comparative issue will ordinarily be designated on program plans and policies, or on staffing plans or other program planning elements, and evidence on these matters will not be taken under the standard issues.  The Commission will designate an issue where examination of the applications and other information before it makes such action appropriate, and applicants who believe they can demonstrate significant differences upon which the reception of evidence will be useful may petition to amend the issues.

No independent factor of likelihood of effectuation of proposals will be utilized. The Commission expects every licensee to carry out its proposals, subject to factors beyond its control, and subject to reasonable judgment that the public's needs and interests require a departure from original plans. If there is a substantial indication that any party will not be able to carry out its proposals to a significant degree, the proposals themselves will be considered deficient.

4. *Past broadcast record.*—This factor includes past ownership interest and significant participation in a broadcast station by one with an ownership interest in the applicant. It is a factor of substantial importance upon the terms set forth below.

A past record within the bounds of average performance will be disregarded, since average future performance is expected. Thus, we are not interested in the fact of past ownership per se, and will not give a preference because one applicant has owned stations in the past and another has not.

We are interested in records which, because either unusually good or unusually poor, give some indication of unusual performance in the future. . . .

. . .

5. *Efficient use of frequency.*—In comparative cases where one of two or more competing applicants proposes an operation which, for one or more engineering reasons, would be more efficient, this fact can and should be considered in determining which of the applicants should be preferred. . . .

6. *Character.*—The Communications Act makes character a relevant consideration in the issuance of a license. See section 308(b), 47 U.S.C. 308(b). Significant character deficiencies may warrant disqualification, and an issue will be designated where appropriate. Since substantial demerits may be appropriate in some cases where disqualification is not warranted, petitions to add an issue on conduct relating to character will be entertained. In the absence of a designated issue, character evidence will not be taken. Our intention here is not only to avoid unduly prolonging the hearing process, but also to avoid those situations where an applicant converts the hearing into a search for his opponents' minor blemishes, no matter how remote in the past or how insignificant.

7. *Other factors.*—As we stated at the outset, our interest in the consistency and clarity of decision and in expedition of the hearing process is not intended to preclude the full examination of any relevant and substantial factor. We will thus favorably consider petitions to add issues when, but only when, they demonstrate that significant evidence will be adduced.[13]

---

**13.** Where a narrow question is raised, for example on one aspect of financial qualification, a narrowly drawn issue will be appropriate. In other circumstances, a broader inquiry may be required. This is a matter for ad hoc determination.

. . .

## Notes and Questions

1. At the same time the Commission narrowed its use of character as a threshold qualification, Character Qualifications in Broadcast Licensing, p. 679, *supra,* it eliminated character as a comparative criterion.

2. How well do these comparative criteria predict which applicant will best serve the public interest? Are each of these criteria equal, or should more weight be given to certain ones? If so, which ones?

3. Although the Commission has emphasized localism, there has always been an undercurrent of doubt. In the early 1960s when the Commission appeared to favor not only local programs but also live presentations, Judge Friendly observed, "I wonder also whether the Commission is really wise enough to determine that live telecasts, so much stressed in the decisions, e.g., of local cooking lessons, are always 'better' than a tape of Shakespeare's Histories." Friendly, The Federal Administrative Agencies: The Need for Better Definition of Standards, 75 Harv.L.Rev. 1055, 1071 (1962). This concern was restated in a different context by a former chairman of the Commission:

> [T]he automatic preference accorded local applicants disregards the possibility that, depending on the facts of a particular case, a competitor's proposed use of a professional employee-manager from outside the community might very well bring imagination, an appreciation of the role of journalism, and sensitivity to social issues far exceeding that of a particular local owner-manager.

Hyde, FCC Policies and Procedures Relating to Hearings on Broadcast Applications, 1975 Duke L.J. 253, 277 (1975).

The Chairman of the House Communications Subcommittee once estimated that local television averaged 80 percent nonlocal programming and "maybe that's the way the viewers want it." He was suggesting that Congress might reconsider the desirability of localism. See Broadcasting, Nov. 22, 1976 at 20.

4. Although the following is technically a renewal case, it is appropriately considered here because, for reasons to be seen at p. 708, *infra,* the court of appeals remanded an earlier decision in this matter to the Commission. On this remand, the Commission is treating the incumbent as though he were competing for a new station. Discussion of Geller's past record at WVCA–FM might be treated as though it was addressed to his performance at some other station he owned—and used for whatever predictive value it might have on his qualifications for this new license. The case is useful here as a short checklist of the current status of the comparative factors. The competitors are Simon Geller and Grandbanke Corp.

## APPLICATION OF SIMON GELLER

Federal Communications Commission, 1985.
102 F.C.C.2d 1443, 59 R.R.2d 579.

By the Commission:

. . .

11. The Court of Appeals affirmed the Commission's denial of a renewal expectancy to Geller. Accordingly, that finding will not be revisited on remand, and Geller will receive no renewal expectancy in the overall comparative analysis.

### PROPOSED PROGRAMMING

12. Geller proposes to continue his present format, broadcasting 99.52% symphonic music, no news, 0.24% public affairs, and 0.24% other nonentertainment programming. Grandbanke proposes to devote 16.9% of its broadcast time to news, 5.9% to public affairs, and 5.9% to other nonentertainment programming, with 55% of its news to be local and regional. Unlike Geller, Grandbanke proposes that its informational programming will be directly related to ascertained community needs and interests. Whereas Geller proposed a 44–hour 27–minute–a–week program schedule, Grandbanke proposes to broadcast 136 hours of programming a week.

13. The Commission concluded that Grandbanke deserved a substantial preference for proposed programming for its demonstrated superior devotion to public service. This preference arose from Grandbanke's superior attention to presenting informational programming responsive to ascertained community needs and interests and was enhanced by the significant discrepancy between the applicants' proposed hours of operation and the relative restrictiveness of Geller's programming.

14. As it did with respect to the renewal expectancy, the court affirmed the award of a substantial preference to Grandbanke for its proposed programming.

### EFFICIENT USE OF FREQUENCY

15. Because of differences between their engineering proposals, Grandbanke's facilities will have greater coverage than Geller's. Grandbanke's 1 mV/m contour will cover more than 300 square miles, providing a signal to nearly 360,000 people, as opposed to Geller's 73 square miles and 43,000 people. All relevant areas are served by at least five other aural signals.

16. The Commission awarded Grandbanke a slight preference based on the superiority of its coverage. Only a slight preference was warranted since the areas in question are already well served by at least five other aural signals.

17. The court did not specifically address this issue. Grandbanke will therefore continue to receive a slight preference.

## INTEGRATION OF OWNERSHIP INTO MANAGEMENT

18. Geller is WVCA–FM's sole owner and employee and will devote full time to the operation of the station. He has been a resident of Gloucester for 13 years. Grandbanke proposes that its 66% owner Edward Mattar will serve as the station's general manager. Mattar has had 3 years of broadcast experience and proposes to move to Gloucester in the event Grandbanke's application is granted.

19. The Commission previously held that despite Geller's technical advantages under the integration criterion, Geller merited only a slight preference over Grandbanke. The Commission reasoned that the rationale of the integration proposal was that an integrated owner would tend to be more sensitive to an area's changing needs and that Geller's poor past broadcast record detracted from these assurances.

20. The Court criticized the Commission's conclusions in this regard. In the court's view, the Commission had failed to reconcile its integration analysis in this case with past precedent. . . . The court noted that the Commission did not make, as it usually does, an explicit analysis of the quantitative and qualitative aspects of integration. Moreover, the court noted that the Commission does not customarily reduce the merit accorded for a quantitative integration advantage unless the applicant has committed misconduct. The court speculated that the Commission may have engaged in the type of "functional analysis" of the essentially structural characteristic of integration, which was previously disapproved by the court. . . .

. . .

22. Having reexamined the integration aspect of this case pursuant to the court's remand, we conclude that our prior treatment of this issue constituted the type of functional analysis previously criticized by the court.[27] We will therefore reevaluate the integration criterion using our ordinary analytical approach. This approach encompasses a weighing of the customary quantitative and qualitative factors, without attempting to factor in other considerations. . . .

23. Turning first to the quantitative aspect of integration, we agree with Grandbanke that, consistent with precedent, an applicant proposing 100% integration deserves a moderate preference over an applicant proposing 66% integration. Qualitatively, Geller's integration is enhanced by his long term local residence, which outweighs Grandbanke's proposal that Mattar will move to Gloucester prospectively and Mattar's limited broadcast experience. Geller will therefore receive a qualitatively enhanced moderate integration preference to be taken into account in the overall comparative analysis.

**27.** Central Florida Enterprises, Inc. v. FCC, 598 F.2d 37, 56 (D.C.Cir.1978), cert. dismissed, 441 U.S. 957 (1979).

## DIVERSIFICATION OF MEDIA OWNERSHIP

24.   Geller owns no media interests other than WVCA.   On the other hand, Grandbanke's principals have interests in other broadcast stations.   Edward Mattar, Grandbanke's 66% owner, has a 100% interest in station WINQ–FM, Winchendon, Massachusetts.   Stockholders with a 34% interest in Grandbanke have a 100% interest in Station WNCS–FM, Montpelier, Vermont.

25.   The Commission awarded Geller a moderate preference for diversification.   In the Commission's view, based on the degree of media ownership alone, Geller would have been entitled to a substantial preference.   However, the Commission believed that Geller's preference should be diminished because of his failure to present substantial amounts of informational programming.   The Commission reasoned that the rationale of diversification was to present the public with diverse and antagonistic points of view.   Since Geller had virtually abandoned his role as an information source, the Commission concluded that he did not qualify as a diverse and antagonistic voice or deserve full credit for diversification.

26.   The court rejected the Commission's analysis.   The court held that the crux of the diversification issue is ownership, based on the probability that diverse ownership will lead to a diversity of views. Moreover, the court held that a direct evaluation of the content of a broadcaster's views would be questionable under the First Amendment. In this vein, the court indicated that there was no basis for inferring that the amount of informational programming presented necessarily represented the broadcaster's as a diverse voice.   On remand, the court required, at minimum, that the Commission adequately explain its apparent departure from established principles.

.   .   .

28.   Having reexamined our diversification analysis pursuant to the court's mandate, we conclude that it must be revised.   As in the case of integration, we believe that our prior discussion relied on an improper functional analysis.   In accordance with the court's ruling, we will not look behind the presumption that underlies the diversification criterion. Our prior conclusion that, based on considerations of media ownership alone, Geller deserves a substantial preference stands unabridged.   In line with the court's views, no other considerations are relevant in this assessment.   Accordingly, Geller will receive a substantial preference for diversification.

## OVERALL COMPARATIVE ANALYSIS

.   .   .

30.   In his comments, Geller maintains that once his integration and diversification preferences are given their proper weights, undiminished by "multiple counting" of his past broadcast record, these advantages are decisive.   Grandbanke, which considers Geller's integration and diversification advantages to be moderate, submits on the other hand that its advantages for proposed programming and efficient use of

frequency are dispositive. Grandbanke continues to assert that Geller's failure to provide substantial amounts of informational programming responsive to local needs and interests should weigh heavily in the comparative balancing.

31. The framework for the comparative evaluation of broadcast applicants is provided by the Commission's 1965 Policy Statement on Comparative Broadcast Hearings. There, the Commission enunciated two primary objectives: (1) best practicable service to the public, and (2) diversification of control of the media of mass communications. The former objective encompasses several factors of which those relevant here are: (1) integration of ownership into management, (2) proposed programming, and (3) efficient use of frequency. Under the best practicable service criterion, we have concluded that Grandbanke deserves a substantial preference for proposed programming and a slight preference for efficient use of frequency, while Geller deserves an enhanced moderate preference for integration. On balance, we believe Grandbanke should receive a moderate preference for best practicable service. As to diversification, the other primary criterion, Geller receives a substantial preference. Thus, we are faced with a situation in which each applicant is superior to the other with respect to one of the primary objectives of the comparative process. However, the substantial preference awarded to Geller for diversification clearly outweighs the moderate preference awarded to Grandbanke for best practicable service. For this reason, we believe that Geller is ultimately the preferred applicant.

. . .

**Notes and Questions**

1. How are the various pluses compared?

2. In 1988 Simon Geller sold his station for $1 million. Does this change your opinion as to the correctness of the FCC's decision? Should it?

3. The bribery episode noted earlier raises the question of whether there are better ways to decide comparative cases than through the approach developed in the Policy Statement. Is it that Congress gave the FCC a difficult, if not impossible, task?

Some critics have suggested that the Commission emphasize one or two factors, such as diversity, and use these as the major bases for decision. Others have suggested using more factors but giving each a preannounced weight, so that the result would be more predictable than it is now.

Still another suggestion is to award the license to the winner of a lottery among equally qualified applicants. The theory of this approach is that sometimes there is simply no superior applicant and it is unrealistic, if not dishonest, to announce a single winner on the merits. The lottery idea might be applied to all applicants who met the basic tests and also had offered maximum diversification or some other added criteria.

In 1980 the FCC voted, 4–3, to order its staff to prepare a decision that would award the license by lottery to one of two applicants who were both judged superior to a third but equal to each other. Two dissenters complained that one applicant should win on the merits. The third dissenter argued that the action was "an impermissible abdication of the Commission's statutory responsibilities and an improper denial of the hearing rights of the applicants." The FCC had an obligation to make "public-interest judgments" rather than use lotteries. In early 1981 the FCC abandoned the idea of a lottery, but shortly thereafter Congress amended § 309 of the Communications Act to authorize the use of lotteries.

In response to that amendment, the Commission developed lottery procedures for some licensing proceedings including LPTV. These procedures gave preferences (additional chances) for minority ownership and diversity. Then, in 1984, the Commission decided that even though the lottery statute did not authorize the use of lotteries to resolve ties in comparative proceedings, the general public interest standard gave the FCC the authority to adopt such a system. Thus, where the Commission finds applicants who "are in true equipoise on comparative factors" it will use a lottery to decide which applicant will be awarded the license. Lottery Selection Among Applicants, 57 R.R.2d 427 (1984). The system was never used.

In 1989 the Commission voted to propose replacing the comparative hearing process with a random lottery for all new radio and television licenses. How should such a system operate? Should all applicants who meet basic qualifications be eligible? Some of the Commissioners indicated that they would be receptive to suggestions for improvements in the current system short of abandonment of the comparative process. Random Selection Procedures for Selecting Among Competing Broadcast Applicants, 4 F.C.C.Rcd. 2256 (1989). In a speech, the FCC's general counsel asserted that under a lottery the FCC would still insist on certain basic qualifications and would maintain preferences for minority ownership and media diversifications by giving applicants with those characteristics better odds in the lottery. She also noted that most licensees acquired their licenses without meeting the stringent comparative criteria—either in uncontested cases or by purchases or by settlements of comparative cases. In these cases "nobody accuses us of abdicating our responsibility to license in the public interest, even though the comparative criteria are never used in these cases." Broadcasting, Mar. 27, 1989, at 64.

However, the vast majority of comments filed in response to the NPRM opposed the use of a lottery. The Commission then voted to terminate the proceeding. Random Selection of Broadcast Applicants, 67 R.R.2d 1514 (1990).

4. Still another approach would be to auction airwave licenses. This would also serve to increase government revenue. Most proposals so far deal with new services or with those already being assigned by lottery.

See, e.g., Auctions Urged for Airwaves, N.Y. Times (Natl), Mar. 18, 1993 at C1. There is some early indication that the Clinton Administration may want to apply an auction approach to existing broadcast assignments when they come up for renewal—a position that would raise enormous political problems for any auction proposal. One reason for giving serious consideration to auctions is an increasing concern that the lottery approach has simply produced entities that specialize in making massive numbers of applications for a new service—and then sell the assignments that they have won in the lottery.

Generally, see Auctioning Radio Spectrum Licenses (study of the Congressional Budget Office, March 1992).

5. The 1965 Policy Statement which has controlled comparative licensing since 1965 is suddenly in doubt. The process began in Bechtel v. Federal Communications Commission, 957 F.2d 873, 70 R.R.2d 397 (D.C.Cir.1992), in which three parties were seeking a license. Bechtel was eliminated on the ground that the other two were proposing integration of ownership and management whereas Bechtel was proposing to hire a full-time manager. This overcame whatever advantages Bechtel might have had over the others.

On Bechtel's appeal from the grant to one of the other parties, the court vacated and remanded on the ground that the FCC had never come to grips with Bechtel's challenge to the significance being given to the integration factor. The Commission had simply followed its past practices without explanation. In passing, the court noted that Bechtel had challenged the other parties and the Commission to show a single case in the last ten years "in which a licensee prevailed in a comparative hearing based upon its integration proposal and then actually constructed and operated the station in conformity with that proposal for a period substantially exceeding one year." According to the court, no example was produced.

In addition, the court cited one episode alleged by Bechtel in which an integrated applicant won a license and then within five months had contracted to sell it for $4,000,000 to a group broadcaster.

On reconsideration, the Commission ultimately adhered to its earlier approach, and vigorously defended the integration criterion on three grounds. First, integrated owners have shown an active interest in broadcasting. Second, an integrated operator was likelier to learn quickly about community concerns and complaints, without having to wait for them to filter up through management. Third, it was more likely that whatever changes an integrated owner wanted to put into operation would actually be made without having to be delegated to layers of employees and management. Anchor Broadcasting Limited Partnership, 72 R.R.2d 98 (1993).

The Commission also responded to the remand in *Bechtel* by issuing a notice of proposed rule making aimed at reconsidering the entire 1965 statement. Reexamination of the Policy Statement on Comparative Broadcast Hearings, 7 F.C.C.Rcd. 2664 (1992). The Commission has asked for comments on whether to retain each of the factors set out in that statement. It has also suggested awarding a "finder's preference" for applicants who persuade the Commission to allot a new frequency, and for a "service continuity preference" designed "to enhance the public interest in the comparative process by encouraging comparative applicants to retain the stations they are attempting to secure through the comparative hearing for a certain period of time."

The Commission is also considering whether to accord definite weights or points for each factor used in the process; whether to define precisely when such points are awarded; and whether to provide a "tie breaker" procedure to resolve cases in which no applicant "receives a dispositive preference under the comparative criteria."

The Commission also expressed the belief that any proposed action here would be fully consistent with preferences given to minority applicants.

6. *Minority Ownership.* As the foregoing discussion of the lottery indicates, the FCC has developed a variety of policies aimed at increasing the role of minorities in broadcasting. Although the Commission has changed its views from time to time, it has generally enforced such policies. In 1989, however, two cases raised questions about the role of race in licensing proceedings. In Shurberg Broadcasting of Hartford, Inc. v. Federal Communications Commission, 876 F.2d 902 (D.C.Cir. 1989), the court of appeals held unconstitutional the FCC's practice permitting licensees whose renewals are being challenged to sell the stations at "distress" prices to minority applicants. However, in Winter Park Communications, Inc. v. Federal Communications Commission, 873 F.2d 347 (D.C.Cir.1989), a different panel of the same court upheld the Commission's policy of granting minorities some preference in comparative cases.

The Supreme Court heard both cases together and, in an opinion written by Justice Brennan, decided, 5–4, that both policies were constitutional. The Court held that "benign race-conscious measures mandated by Congress—even if those measures are not 'remedial' in the sense of being designed to compensate victims of past governmental or societal discrimination—are constitutionally permissible to the extent that they serve important governmental objectives within the power of Congress and are substantially related to achievement of those objectives."

Applying this standard, the Court found "that they serve the important governmental objective of broadcast diversity." In finding that broadcast diversity was an important governmental objective, Brennan quoted with approval Justice White's statement in *Red Lion* that "[i]t is the right of the viewers and listeners, not the right of the broadcasters, which is paramount." He went on to argue that not only minorities, but all listeners and viewers benefit from enhanced broadcast diversity.

The Court then concluded "that they are substantially related to the achievement of that objective." For this finding Brennan relied heavily on the expertise of the Commission and Congress. He rejected the contention that the Commission's linking of broadcast diversity and minority ownership constituted impermissible stereotyping:

> Rather, both Congress and the FCC maintain simply that expanded minority ownership of broadcast outlets will, in the aggregate, result in greater broadcast diversity. A broadcasting industry with representative minority participation will produce more variation and diversity than will one whose ownership is drawn from a single racially and ethnically homogenous group.   . . .

Justice O'Connor wrote a lengthy dissent, joined by Chief Justice Rehnquist and Justices Scalia and Kennedy, in which she attacked almost every aspect of Brennan's opinion. O'Connor argued that the Court had incorrectly applied a less rigorous standard than was required by the equal protection clause and that even under that more relaxed standard the FCC's policies were still unconstitutional.

Justice O'Connor questioned why the particular viewpoints that might come from the specific minorities favored under the FCC policies, assuming such viewpoints could be identified, should be given special status compared to other "underrepresented" viewpoints. She also argued that the policies did not assure a direct fit between the means and the ends, as required by the equal protection clause:

> . . . The policy is overinclusive: many members of a particular racial or ethnic group will have no interest in advancing the views the FCC believes to be underrepresented, or will find them utterly foreign. The policy is underinclusive: it awards no preference to disfavored individuals who may be particularly well versed in and committed to presenting those views. The FCC has failed to implement a case-by-case determination, and that failure is particularly unjustified when individualized hearings already occur, as in the comparative licensing process. [ ]   . . .

Justice Kennedy, joined by Justice Scalia, wrote a separate dissent in which he compared the Court's decision to Plessy v. Ferguson, the case upholding the "separate but equal doctrine" later overturned in Brown v. Board of Education. He argued that the Court was in effect "welcoming the return of racial classification to our Nation's laws." He argued that the FCC policies at issue operated to exclude all those racial and ethnic minorities not covered by the policies. He concluded by noting his regret "that after a century of judicial opinions we interpret the Constitution to do no more than move us from 'separate but equal' to 'unequal but benign.'" Metro Broadcasting, Inc. v. Federal Communications Commission, 497 U.S. 547 (1990).

7. *Women's Ownership.* The *Metro Broadcasting* decision had stated that the FCC's "gender preference policy is not before us today." That issue was decided by the court of appeals in Lamprecht v. Federal Communications Commission, 958 F.2d 382, 70 R.R.2d 658 (D.C.Cir. 1992). The court, 2–1, in an opinion by Thomas, Circuit Justice, recognized that Congress had ordered the Commission to continue

granting gender preferences. Since it was impossible to find the Commission's action beyond statutory authorization, the court turned to constitutional questions—and concluded that the practice was unconstitutional on equal protection grounds. The government's methods were held not to be "substantially related" to the goal it hoped to achieve—more diverse programming if women were granted a preference in the licensing process.

The court understood that the Supreme Court had used a standard of "intermediate scrutiny" in situations such as *Metro*. This meant that "not only [must] sex-based generalizations be 'supported,' but [the support must] be strong enough to advance 'substantially' the legitimating government interest." Under that standard, the court could not find sufficient evidence in the FCC record to show that preferring women would have anything like the effect that the evidence in *Metro* suggested would occur if racial minority groups were granted preferences. There was no strong showing that women owners would program differently from men. The court concluded:

> When a government treats people differently because of their sex, equal-protection principles at the very least require that there be a meaningful factual predicate supporting a link between the government's means and its ends. In this case, the government has failed to show that its sex-preference policy is substantially related to achieving diversity on the airwaves. We therefore hold that the policy violated the Constitution.

The Commission decided not to seek further review, and ended preferences for women applicants.

8. In a related matter, the Commission refused to grant preferences to women applicants in the lotteries being held to award LPTV licenses. Lottery Selection (Preference for Women), 102 F.C.C.2d 1401, 58 R.R.2d 1077 (1985), aff'd sub nom. Pappas v. Federal Communications Commission, 807 F.2d 1019, 61 R.R.2d 1398 (D.C.Cir.1986).

## D. RENEWAL OF LICENSES

### 1. INTRODUCTION

Section 307(d) authorizes renewals only on the same terms as initial grants—when the public interest, convenience and necessity will be served. At the outset, as it sought to unclutter the AM spectrum, the Commission frequently denied renewals, but after the initial flurry, denials were rare unless the broadcaster's behavior fell far below par. A study of denials and reasons for them is discussed at p. 696, *infra*. Due to the large volume of renewal applications now filed annually, the FCC staff cannot fully investigate the performance of each applicant. Instead, the Commission has relied increasingly on informal complaints from citizens or citizen groups, and on petitions to deny renewal that became possible after the United Church of Christ case, p. 677, *supra*. Section 307(d) authorizes renewals only on the same terms as initial grants—public interest, convenience and necessity.

The FCC has been generally reluctant to deny renewals except in egregious cases. The reason is the size of the penalty that denial of renewal inflicts on the licensee in a world in which VHF stations may be worth $500 million and more, and even radio stations are often worth tens of millions of dollars.

*Penalties and Short Renewals.* Before 1960 the Commission had few weapons for dealing with misbehavior, because Congress assumed that denial of renewal would suffice in most cases, with revocation during the term to handle the most serious violations. But the Commission came to view denial of renewal as too harsh for all but the most serious violations of rules or other misbehavior. In the 1960 amendments to the Communications Act, Congress explicitly authorized shorter renewals by amending § 307(d), but this could not be utilized until the end of the license period. To fill this gap, Congress responded with §§ 503(b) et seq. to provide the Commission with "an effective tool in dealing with violations in situations where revocation or suspension does not appear to be appropriate." Under § 503(b), the Commission could impose a fine, called a forfeiture, against a licensee who had violated a specific rule. The maximum penalty is now $25,000 for each violation. Each day of a continuing violation constitutes a separate offense, but the total penalty shall not exceed $250,000 for licensees or cable operators.

The added array of sanctions reduced the likelihood that the denial of renewal would be used for what the Commission perceived to be lesser transgressions of the rules. The Commission has resorted extensively to the short-term renewal. The expectation is that if the licensee performs properly during that period it will then return to the regular renewal cycle. In addition to its probationary impact, a short renewal imposes burdens of legal expenses and administrative effort in preparing and defending the application.

Single instances of fraudulent behavior toward advertisers or conducting rigged contests were among the violations that traditionally led to forfeitures or short-term renewals. Among the most common types of fraud are billing advertisers for commercials that were never actually broadcast and the practice of "double-billing." The latter involves cooperative advertising in which a national manufacturer promises to share advertising expenses with its local retailers. The retailer gets a discount for volume, but the station sends it two bills—one for the actual discounted amount due and a second based on a higher non-discounted rate to be forwarded to the national manufacturer as the basis for the sharing.

After many years of warning against the practice and punishing violators with forfeitures and other minor penalties, the Commission, in the 1970s, began to deny license renewals to violators. The courts upheld the FCC. See White Mountain Broadcasting Co. v. Federal Communications Commission, 598 F.2d 274, 45 R.R.2d 681 (D.C.Cir. 1979) (upholding denial of renewal where the practice had continued for

5½ years with full knowledge of the president and sole shareholder of licensee).

In the 1980s, however, the Commission again changed its attitude toward enforcing these regulations. In 1986, as part of an ongoing attempt to reduce overly restrictive regulations as well as those that duplicate other federal or state law, the Commission eliminated the rules on fraudulent billing. Elimination of Unnecessary Broadcast Regulation (Business Practices), 59 R.R.2d 1500 (1986). The court of appeals rejected a petition for review of the Commission's order. Telecommunications Research and Action Center v. Federal Communications Commission, 800 F.2d 1181, 61 R.R.2d 61 (D.C.Cir.1986).

## 2. SUBSTANTIVE GROUNDS FOR NONRENEWAL

### a. *Non–speech Considerations*

Just as the Commission may deny an uncontested application for a vacant channel, it may deny renewal when no other applicant seeks the spot and even when no complaint has been made. The Mass Media Bureau may argue against renewals when it believes that they would not serve the public interest.

Lying to the FCC may be the clearest basis for denying renewal. In its early years the FCC did not treat dishonesty toward the Commission with heavy sanctions. This led to more examples of such behavior. Finally, the Commission denied the renewal of a station whose general manager for 12 years had concealed from the Commission the fact that a vice-president of a network secretly owned 24 percent of the station's stock. The station appealed on the grounds, among others, that the harsh treatment came without warning and that there was no indication that the FCC would not have renewed the station's application even if it had known the truth.

The Supreme Court upheld the denial of renewal. The fact that the FCC had previously dealt more mildly with similar cases did not prevent it from changing course without warning. Also, the "fact of concealment may be more significant than the facts concealed. The willingness to deceive a regulatory body may be disclosed by immaterial and useless deceptions as well as by material and persuasive ones." The fact that stockholders of a majority of the shares had no knowledge of the dishonesty did not bar the FCC from acting—"the fact that there are innocent stockholders can not immunize the corporation from the consequences of such deception." Stockholders often suffer from the misdeeds of their chosen officers. Federal Communications Commission v. WOKO, Inc., 329 U.S. 223 (1946).

Sometimes the Commission has held that the manager's deceit is the licensee's responsibility because of its failure to exercise adequate control and supervision consistent with its responsibilities as a licensee. Renewal was denied and the court affirmed in such a case. Continental

Broadcasting, Inc. v. Federal Communications Commission, 439 F.2d 580, 20 R.R.2d 2126 (D.C.Cir.), cert. denied 403 U.S. 905 (1971).

Because the license is issued to the licensee, the licensee must meet the standards of the Communications Act and the FCC. Misbehavior of the officers may show either that the licensee knew of the misbehavior or a serious failure to control the station. In an appropriate situation, either may justify denial of renewal.

### b. Speech Considerations

As you will recall, p. 694, *supra*, in its early days the Commission was not hesitant about denying license renewals when it disapproved of the speech being uttered. The potential implications of that practice were not tested because the situation eased after the famous Mayflower Broadcasting Corp. case, 8 F.C.C. 333 (1940), in which the Commission renewed a license but appeared to criticize the licensee for editorializing: "A truly free radio cannot be used to advocate the causes of the licensee. . . . In brief, the broadcaster cannot be an advocate." The case apparently deterred controversial discussion and therefore reduced the need for the Commission to judge speech directly. The situation changed after the Commission's Report on Editorializing by Broadcast Licensees, 13 F.C.C. 1246, 1 R.R. pt. 3, ¶ 91.21 (1949), which directed licensees to devote a reasonable portion of their broadcast time to the discussion of controversial issues of public importance and to encourage the presentation of various views on these questions. This has also affected renewal cases.

One study indicates that 64 radio and television licenses were revoked or not renewed between 1970 and 1978, compared with 78 during the years from 1934 to 1969. Weiss, Ostroff & Clift, Station License Revocations and Denials of Renewal, 1970–78, 24 J. Broadcasting 69 (1980). The authors analyzed the grounds for revocation or nonrenewal in the 64 cases. Since multiple grounds were common, 110 reasons were listed. The most common were misrepresentations to the FCC (18), failure to pursue the renewal procedure (16), fraudulent billing practices (11), departure from promised programming (11) and unauthorized transfer of control by the licensee (10).

Few of the 64 involved speech grounds. Even those that did were commonly combined with other derelictions because the Commission has been reluctant to single out a speech basis for nonrenewal. For example, although the study showed that four licenses were lost for "news slanting," all four of these stations were also listed under "misrepresentations to the Commission," three were listed under character qualifications, and the fourth was also listed under failure to prosecute renewal. Similarly, although three cases listed "fairness" violation as grounds for nonrenewal, one of these was also one of the group of four listed above and had four separate reasons for nonrenewal. A second was also listed for misrepresentation. The third, the Brandywine case, is discussed shortly.

This situation is not surprising. First, a station that senses that it may be doing something wrong may seek to hide the matter without realizing that misrepresentation to the Commission may be much more serious that its substantive misbehavior. Recall the WOKO case. Second, misbehavior sometimes occurs because the licensee has not exerted sufficient control over management or employees. In such a case, the FCC combines the misbehavior with inadequate supervision as grounds for the denial of renewal. Third, the posture of the courts has not encouraged the FCC to deny renewals on pure speech grounds—as a few examples will make clear.

In one case, the FCC found that a disc jockey had been using vulgar and suggestive language. When the FCC began to investigate, the licensee denied all knowledge of the offending conduct. Because of the history of complaints, the Commission found that denial incredible, which raised a question about the licensee's character qualifications. After renewal was denied the court affirmed but did so explicitly on the character ground, refusing to pass on whether the speech alone would have justified non-renewal. Robinson v. Federal Communications Commission, 334 F.2d 534, 2 R.R.2d 2001 (D.C.Cir.), cert. denied 379 U.S. 843 (1964).

In Walton Broadcasting, Inc., 78 F.C.C.2d 857, 47 R.R.2d 1233 (1980), the Commission denied renewal to a station that had tried to build upon the popularity of a new disc jockey by having him disappear and reporting that he had been kidnapped. Listeners jammed telephone lines to the police and the radio station. The licensee was an absentee owner who took no steps to rectify the matter until after the FCC began investigating. The renewal was denied because the licensee failed to exercise adequate control over the station's operations:

> The misconduct in this case, the hoax broadcast of news and the false announcement about the kidnapping or disappearance in a non-news context over a 4–day period, was designed to shock and alarm KIKX's listening public. The misconduct can be traced directly to the licensee's failure to require promotion formats be approved, its failure to transmit and to emphasize the substance of its policies to its station manager, its failure to insure that the manager understood its policies, its failure to check to see if he transmitted the information to on-the-air personnel, and its failure to understand and inculcate the most elementary principle of public trusteeship.

The licensee was also found responsible for six technical violations of the logging rules and 12 engineering violations. Since the control was inadequate and the resulting misconduct was quite serious, the penalty of nonrenewal was justified.

Another kind of deception was attempted by a minister whose initial efforts to acquire a station for his seminary were challenged by groups who believed that his past record showed that he would not honor the fairness doctrine or his other obligations. The prospective licensee responded by promising to provide balance. Within 10 days of obtaining the license, the licensee began drastically altering its format, and groups complained that the licensee was not living up to its obligations. The Commission denied renewal on two grounds: alleged violations of the fairness doctrine and deception practiced on the Commission in obtaining the license. On appeal, the court affirmed, 2–1. Two judges agreed on the deception ground, while the dissenter found that ground "too narrow a ledge" for decision. He thought that the Commission had really denied renewal because of speech uttered on the station, and he concluded that this was impermissible. Brandywine–Main Line Radio, Inc. v. Federal Communications Commission, 473 F.2d 16, 25 R.R.2d 2010, 1 Med.L.Rptr. 2067 (D.C.Cir.1972), cert. denied 412 U.S. 922 (1973), Douglas, J., dissenting.

The most dramatic nonrenewal on speech grounds involved the station in Jackson, Miss., that was the subject of the United Church of Christ case discussed at p. 677, *supra*. Strangely, the case did *not* involve a Commission decision not to renew. Groups claimed that the station had violated the fairness doctrine, had failed to air contrasting viewpoints on racial matters, had given blacks inadequate exposure, had generally been disrespectful to blacks, had discriminated against local Catholics and had given inadequate time to public affairs. Blacks constituted 45 percent of the population of the station's primary service area. The FCC gave the licensee a short renewal and ordered it to honor its obligations.

After the FCC had been ordered to allow the citizen groups to participate and to reconsider the case, it decided that the station deserved renewal because the allegations had not been proven.

On a second appeal, the court reversed on the ground that the FCC's decision was not supported by substantial evidence. The FCC's errors included placing the burden of proof on the citizen groups rather than on the renewal applicant and failing to accept uncontradicted testimony about the station's practices, including cutting off national programs that showed blacks in a favorable light or that discussed racial issues. Sometimes the licensee falsely blamed technical difficulties for the interruptions in service. Office of Communication, United Church of Christ v. Federal Communications Commission, 425 F.2d 543, 16 R.R.2d 2095 (D.C.Cir.1969).

Rather than remand again, the court itself vacated the license and ordered the FCC to invite applications for the now vacant channel—and to provide for interim operation of the facility. Finally, the station was taken over by a different licensee.

Generally, however, a licensee runs no risk of losing its license because of what it broadcasts so long as the content is not obscene or otherwise proscribed, as discussed in Chapter XVII. The clearest judicial exposition of this view occurred when a petition to deny renewal was filed against a radio station that had broadcast several programs that "made offensive comments concerning persons of the Jewish faith, equating Judaism with Socialism and Socialism with Communism." The Commission granted renewal without a hearing. The court of appeals affirmed. Anti–Defamation League of B'nai B'rith v. Federal Communications Commission, 403 F.2d 169, 14 R.R.2d 2051 (D.C.Cir. 1968), cert. denied 394 U.S. 930 (1969).

The court approvingly quoted from the Commission's opinion in the case:

> The Commission has long held that its function is not to judge the merit, wisdom or accuracy of any broadcast discussion or commentary but to insure that all viewpoints are given fair and equal opportunity for expression and that controverted allegations are balanced by the presentation of opposing viewpoints. Any other position would stifle discussion and destroy broadcasting as a medium of free speech. To require every licensee to defend his decision to present any controversial program that has been complained of in a license renewal hearing would cause most—if not all—licensees to refuse to broadcast any program that was potentially controversial or offensive to any substantial group. More often than not this would operate to deprive the public of the opportunity to hear unpopular or unorthodox views.

The court rejected the petitioner's main contention that "recurrent bigoted appeals to anti-Semitic prejudice" was a basis for denial of renewal. Here it quoted extensively from the opinion of a concurring Commissioner:

> It is not only impractical—and impossible in any ultimate sense—to separate an appeal to prejudice from an appeal to reason in this field, it is equally beyond the power or ability of authority to say what is religious or racial. There are centuries of bloody strife to prove that man cannot agree on what is or is not "religion."
>
> . . .
>
> Nevertheless these subjects will and must be discussed. But they cannot be freely discussed if there is to be an official ban on the utterance of "falsehood" or an "appeal to prejudice" as officially defined. All that the government can properly do, consistently with the right of free speech, is to demand that the opportunity be kept open for the presentation of all viewpoints. Yet this would be impossible under the rule espoused by the ADL. . . . If what the ADL calls "appeals to racial or religious prejudice" is to be classed with hard-core obscenity, then it has no right to be heard on the air, and the only views which are entitled to be broadcast on matters of concern to the ADL are those which the ADL holds or finds acceptable. This is irreconcilable with either the Fairness Doctrine or the right of free speech.
>
> Talk of "responsibility" of a broadcaster in this connection is simply a euphemism for self-censorship. It is an attempt to shift the onus of action against speech from the Commission to the

broadcaster, but it seeks the same result—suppression of certain views and arguments. . . . Attempts to impose such schemes of self-censorship have been found as unconstitutional as more direct censorship efforts by government. [  ]

### 3.  COMPARATIVE RENEWAL PROCEEDINGS

In the early years of regulation of each medium, except perhaps for AM, so many vacant frequencies existed that few applicants tried to oust incumbents. When such a challenge did occur, the Commission undertook the difficult comparison of the incumbent's actual performance and the challenger's proposed operation. In a major case involving renewal of the license of a Baltimore AM station, the Commission's analysis showed some reasons favoring the incumbent and others favoring the challenger. Hearst Radio, Inc. (WBAL), 15 F.C.C. 1149, 6 R.R. 994 (1951). Although the incumbent had not integrated ownership and management, this did not matter because its actual performance was now available for review. Similarly, although the incumbent also controlled an FM station, a television station and a newspaper in Baltimore, it had not abused its power, so this was not a serious problem. The Commission found little difference in programming, despite the challenger's strong assertions to the contrary, and concluded:

> We have found that both of the applicants are legally, technically, and financially qualified and must therefore choose between them as their applications are mutually exclusive. We have discussed at some length why the criteria which we may sometimes consider as determining factors when one of the applicants is not operating the facilities sought and where the applicants have not proved their abilities, are not controlling factors in the light of the record of operation of WBAL. The determining factor in our decision is the clear advantage of continuing the established and excellent service now furnished by WBAL and which we find to be in the public interest, when compared to the risks attendant on the execution of the proposed programming of Public Service Radio Corporation, excellent though the proposal may be.

This decision was thought to give renewal applicants such an advantage that prospective challengers sought entry by other means, such as buying an existing facility or seeking available, though less desirable, vacant frequencies. In its 1965 Policy Statement on Comparative Broadcast Hearings, p. 682, *supra*, the Commission noted that it was not attempting to deal with "the somewhat different problems raised where an applicant is contesting with a licensee seeking renewal of license." Yet, later that year, in a case in which two applicants were challenging the incumbent, the Commission stated that, on further consideration, it had "concluded that the policy statement should govern the introduction of evidence in this and similar proceedings where a renewal application is contested. . . . However, we wish to make it clear that the parties will be free to urge any arguments they may deem applicable concerning the relative weights to be afforded the evidence bearing on the various comparative factors." Seven (7) League Productions, Inc., 1 F.C.C.2d 1597 (1965).

Although the Commission might have developed a special set of standards governing renewal cases, it has found it quite difficult to do so. This was not a serious problem so long as few applicants challenged renewal applicants. But, in the 1960s and early 1970s, those who wished to get into broadcasting were faced with virtually no vacancies on the spectrum (except UHF) and greatly increasing prices for existing stations. Despite the warning of *Hearst,* applicants began increasingly to challenge incumbents. Whether because the incumbents were superior—or at least equal—or because the denial of renewal imposed a serious financial penalty, the Commission continued to favor renewal applicants.

Although everyone seemed to agree that giving some preference or "renewal expectancy" to the incumbent was reasonable, neither the Commission nor the courts could set up clear guidelines as to what level of performance entitled a licensee to renewal expectancy or how much weight to give renewal expectancy. In 1970 the FCC announced a policy statement stating that in any hearing between an incumbent and a challenger, the incumbent would obtain a controlling preference by demonstrating substantial past performance without serious deficiencies. If the incumbent's record met that non-comparative renewal standard, the Commission would not even consider the challenger's application.

The policy statement was challenged in the courts and overturned. Citizen's Communications Center v. Federal Communications Commission, 447 F.2d 1201, 22 R.R.2d 2001 (D.C.Cir.1971). The Court ruled that the policy statement was inconsistent with the 1934 Act's requirement of a "full hearing" under § 309(e). This, together with a Supreme Court case, was understood to require that where "two or more applications for permits or licenses are mutually exclusive, the Commission must conduct one full comparative hearing of the applications." The hearing proposed in the policy statement was not "comparative" because it looked in the first instance only at the record of the incumbent.

Although establishing that renewal expectancy should never reach the level of a controlling preference, the case did not state how much weight it could have in relation to the other comparative criteria. In subsequent decisions the FCC did little, if anything, to clarify the situation, but appeared nonetheless to be giving substantial weight to renewal expectancy. Finally, in a case where the incumbent was renewed despite a number of factors seemingly favoring the challenger, the court ordered the Commission to articulate and justify its comparative renewal policy. Central Florida Enterprises, Inc. v. Federal Communications Commission, 598 F.2d 37, 44 R.R.2d 345 (D.C.Cir.1978). On remand the FCC again awarded the license to the incumbent. The challenger appealed once more.

CENTRAL FLORIDA ENTERPRISES, INC. v. FEDERAL
COMMUNICATIONS COMMISSION

United States Court of Appeals, District of Columbia Circuit, 1982.
683 F.2d 503.
Cert. denied 460 U.S. 1084 (1983).

Before ROBINSON, CHIEF JUDGE, WILKEY, CIRCUIT JUDGE, and FLANNERY,
DISTRICT JUDGE for the District of Columbia.

WILKEY, CIRCUIT JUDGE:

. . .

In its decision appealed in *Central Florida I* the FCC concluded that
the reasons undercutting Cowles' bid for renewal did "not outweigh the
substantial service Cowles rendered to the public during the last license
period." Accordingly, the license was renewed. Our reversal was rooted
in a twofold finding. First, the Commission had inadequately investigated and analyzed the four factors weighing against Cowles' renewal.
Second, the process by which the FCC weighed these four factors against
Cowles' past record was never "even vaguely described" and, indeed,
"the Commission's handling of the facts of this case [made] embarrass-
ingly clear that the FCC [had] practically erected a presumption of
renewal that is inconsistent with the full hearing requirement" of the
Communications Act. We remand[ed] with instructions to the FCC to
cure these deficiencies.

On remand the Commission has followed our directives and corrected, point by point, the inadequate investigation and analysis of the four
factors cutting against Cowles' requested renewal. The Commission
concluded that, indeed, three of the four merited an advantage for
Central Florida, and on only one (the mail fraud issue) did it conclude
that nothing needed to be added on the scale to Central's plan or
removed from Cowles'. We cannot fault the Commission's actions here.

We are left, then, with evaluating the way in which the FCC
weighed Cowles' main studio move violation and Central's superior
diversification and integration, on the one hand, against Cowles' substantial record of performance on the other. This is the most difficult
and important issue in this case, for the new weighing process which the
FCC has adopted will presumably be employed in its renewal proceedings
elsewhere. We therefore feel that it is necessary to scrutinize carefully
the FCC's new approach, and discuss what we understand and expect it
to entail.

For some time now the FCC has had to wrestle with the problem of
how it can factor in some degree of "renewal expectancy" for a broadcaster's meritorious past record, while at the same time undertaking the
required comparative evaluation of the incumbent's probable future
performance versus the challenger's. As we stated in *Central Florida I*,
"the incumbent's past performance is some evidence, and perhaps the
best evidence, of what its future performance would be." And it has

been intimated—by the Supreme Court in FCC v. National Citizens Committee for Broadcasting (NCCB) and by this court in Citizens Communications Center v. FCC and *Central Florida I*—that some degree of renewal expectancy is permissible. But *Citizens and Central Florida I* also indicated that the FCC has in the past impermissibly raised renewal expectancy to an irrebuttable presumption in favor of the incumbent.

We believe that the formulation by the FCC in its latest decision, however, is a permissible way to incorporate some renewal expectancy while still undertaking the required comparative hearing. *The new policy, as we understand it, is simply this: renewal expectancy is to be a factor weighed with all the other factors, and the better the past record, the greater the renewal expectancy "weight."*

> In our view [states the FCC], the strength of the expectancy depends on the merit of the past record. Where, as in this case, the incumbent rendered substantial but not superior service, the "expectancy" takes the form of a comparative preference weighed against [the] other factors . . .. An incumbent performing in a superior manner would receive an even stronger preference. An incumbent rendering minimal service would receive no preference.

This is to be contrasted with Commission's *1965 Policy Statement on Comparative Broadcast Hearings,* where "[o]nly unusually good or unusually poor records have relevance."

If a stricter standard is desired by Congress, it must enact it. We cannot: the new standard is within the statute.

The reasons given by the Commission for factoring in some degree of renewal expectancy are rooted in a concern that failure to do so would hurt broadcast *consumers.*

> The justification for a renewal expectancy is three-fold. (1) There is no guarantee that a challenger's paper proposals will, in fact, match the incumbent's proven performance. Thus, not only might replacing an incumbent be entirely gratuitous, but *it might even deprive the community of an acceptable service and replace it with an inferior one.* (2) Licensees should be encouraged through the likelihood of renewal to make investments *to ensure quality service. Comparative renewal proceedings cannot function as a "competitive spur" to licensees if their dedication to the community is not rewarded.* (3) Comparing incumbents and challengers as if they were both new applicants could lead to a haphazard restructuring of the broadcast industry especially considering the large number of group owners. *We cannot readily conclude that such a restructuring could serve the public interest.*

*We are relying, then, on the FCC's commitment that renewal expectancy will be factored in for the benefit of the public, not for incumbent broadcasters.* . . . As we concluded in *Central Florida I,* "[t]he only legitimate fear which should move [incumbent] licensees is the fear of their own substandard performance, and that would be all to the public good."

There is a danger, of course, that the FCC's new approach could still degenerate into precisely the sort of irrebuttable presumption in favor of renewal that we have warned against. But this did not happen in the case before us today, and our reading of the Commission's decision gives us hope that if the FCC applies the standard in the same way in future cases, it will not happen in them either. The standard is new, however, and much will depend on how the Commission applies it and fleshes it out. Of particular importance will be the definition and level of service it assigns to "substantial"—and whether that definition is ever found to be "opaque to judicial review," "wholly unintelligible," or based purely on "administrative 'feel.' " [27]

In this case, however, the Commission was painstaking and explicit in its balancing. The Commission discussed in quite specific terms, for instance, the items it found impressive in Cowles' past record. It stressed and listed numerous programs demonstrating Cowles' "local community orientation" and "responsive[ness] to community needs," discussed the percentage of Cowles' programming devoted to news, public affairs, and local topics, and said it was "impressed by [Cowles'] reputation in the community. Seven community leaders and three public officials testified that [Cowles] had made outstanding contributions to the local community. Moreover, the record shows no complaints . . .." The Commission concluded that "Cowles' record [was] more than minimal," was in fact " 'substantial,' i.e., 'sound, favorable and substantially above a level of mediocre service which might just minimally warrant renewal.' "

The Commission's inquiry in this case did not end with Cowles' record, but continued with a particularized analysis of what factors weighed against Cowles' record, and how much. The FCC investigated fully the mail fraud issue. It discussed the integration and diversification disadvantages of Cowles and conceded that Central had an edge on these issues—"slight" for integration, "clear" for diversification. But it reasoned that "structural factors such as [these]—of primary importance in a new license proceeding—should have lesser weight compared with

---

**27.** Id. at 50 (quoting earlier proceeding, 60 F.C.C.2d 372, 422 (1976)). We think it would be helpful if at some point the Commission defined and explained the distinctions, if any, among: substantial, meritorious, average, above average, not above average, not far above average, above mediocre, more than minimal, solid, sound, favorable, not superior, not exceptional, and unexceptional—all terms used by the parties to describe what the FCC found Cowles' level of performance to have been. We are especially interested to know what the standard of comparison is in each case. "Average" compared to all applicants? "Mediocre" compared to all incumbents? "Favorable" with respect to the FCC's expectations? We realize that the FCC's task is a subjective one, but the use of imprecise terms needlessly compounds our difficulty in evaluating what the Commission has done. We think we can discern enough to review intelligently the Commission's actions today, but if the air is not cleared or, worse, becomes foggier, the FCC's decisionmaking may again be adjudged "opaque to judicial review."

the preference arising from substantial past service." [31] Finally, with respect to the illegal main studio move, the FCC found that "licensee misconduct" in general "may provide a more meaningful basis for preferring an untested challenger over a proven incumbent." The Commission found, however, that here the "comparative significance of the violation" was diminished by the underlying facts . . .. The FCC concluded that "the risk to the public interest posed by the violation seems small when compared to the actuality of depriving Daytona Beach of Cowles' tested and acceptable performance."

Having listed the relevant factors and assigned them weights, the Commission concluded that Cowles' license should be renewed. We note, however, that despite the finding that Cowles' performance was " 'substantial,' i.e., 'sound, favorable and substantially above a level of mediocre service,' " the combination of Cowles' main studio rule violation and Central's diversification and integration advantages made this a "close and difficult case." Again, we trust that this is more evidence that the Commission's weighing did not, and will not, amount to automatic renewal for incumbents.

We are somewhat reassured by a recent FCC decision granting, for the first time since at least 1961, on *comparative* grounds the application of the challenger for a radio station license and denying the renewal application of the incumbent licensee.[38] In that decision the Commission found that the *incumbent deserved no renewal expectancy* for his past program record and that his application was inferior to the challenger's on comparative grounds. Indeed, it was the *incumbent's* preferences on the diversification and integration factors which were overcome (there, by the challenger's superior programming proposals and longer broadcast week). The Commission found that the incumbent's "inadequate [past performance] reflects poorly on the *likelihood of future service in the public interest.*" Further, it found that the incumbent had no "legitimate renewal expectancy" because his past performance was neither "meritorious" nor "substantial."

**31.** . . .

Here we have a caveat. We do not read the Commission's new policy as *ignoring* integration and diversification considerations in comparative renewal hearings. In its brief at page 6 the Commission states that "an incumbent's meritorious record should outweigh in the comparative renewal context a challenging applicant's advantages under the structural factors of integration and diversification." Ceteris paribus, this may be so—depending in part, of course, on how "meritorious" is defined. But where there are weights on the scales other than a meritorious record on the one hand, and integration and diversification on the other, the Commission must afford the latter two *some* weight, since while they alone may not outweigh a meritorious rec-

ord they may tip the balance if weighed with something else. See *Citizens*, 447 F.2d at 1208–09 n. 23.

That, of course, is precisely the situation here, since the main studio move violation must also be balanced against the meritorious record. The Commission may not weigh the antirenewal factors separately against the incumbent's record, eliminating them as it goes along. It must weigh them all simultaneously. . . .

**38.** In re Applications of Simon Geller and Grandbanke Corp., FCC Docket Nos. 21104–05 (Released 15 June 1982). We intimate no view at this time, of course, on the soundness of the Commission's decision there; we cite it only as demonstrating that the Commission's new approach may prove to be more than a paper tiger.

We have, however, an important caveat.   In the Commission's
weighing of factors the scale mid-mark must be neither the factors
themselves, nor the interests of the broadcasting industry, nor some
other secondary and artificial construct, but rather the intent of Congress, which is to say the interests of the listening public.   All other
doctrine is merely a means to this end, and it should not become more.
If in a given case, for instance, the factual situation is such that the
denial of a license renewal would not undermine renewal expectancy *in a
way harmful to the public interest,* then renewal expectancy should not
be invoked.[40]

Finally, we must note that we are still troubled by the fact that the
record remains that an incumbent *television* licensee has *never* been
denied renewal in a comparative challenge.   American television viewers
will be reassured, although a trifle baffled, to learn that even the worst
television stations—those which are, presumably, the ones picked out as
vulnerable to a challenge [42]—are so good that they never need replacing.
We suspect that somewhere, sometime, somehow, some television licensee *should* fail in a comparative renewal challenge, but the FCC has
never discovered such a licensee yet.   As a court we cannot say that it
must be Cowles here.

We hope that the standard now embraced by the FCC will result in
the protection of the public, not just incumbent licensees.   And in
today's case we believe the FCC's application of the new standard was
not inconsistent with the Commission's mandate.   Accordingly the Commission's decision is

Affirmed.

## Notes and Questions

1.   Ironically, less than a year later, when the court was presented with
the case where the Commission awarded a radio license to a new
applicant rather than the incumbent, the court did not approve.   Simon
Geller had operated a one-man classical music FM station in Gloucester,
Mass., since the early 1960s.   In 1981 Grandebanke Corporation filed a
competing application.   The Commission held that because less than one
percent of the station's programming was of a nonentertainment nature
and the station broadcast no news, editorials or locally produced programming, Geller was not entitled to the benefit of renewal expectancy.
Simon Geller, 91 F.C.C.2d 1253, 52 R.R.2d 709 (1982).

---

**40.**  Thus, the three justifications given
by the Commission for renewal expectancy,
[   ], should be remembered by the FCC in
future renewal proceedings and, where
these justifications are in a particular case
attenuated, the Commission ought not to
chant "renewal expectancy" and grant the
license.

**42.**  Counsel for the FCC conceded at
oral argument, "I grant you, [competitors]
wouldn't challenge the [incumbent] they
thought was exceptional or far above average."   The dissent from the Commission's
decision declared it a "readily apparent fact
that competing applicants file against only
the ne'er-do-wells of the industry."   86
F.C.C.2d at 1055 n. 99.

On appeal the FCC's action was vacated and the case remanded. The court began by characterizing it as "yet another meandering effort by the [FCC] to develop a paradigm for its license renewal hearings."

> For years this court has urged the FCC to put some bite into its comparative hearings. [*Central Florida I*] Indeed, we have too long hungered for just one instance in which the FCC properly denied an incumbent's renewal expectancy. Unfortunately, in the process of seeking to respond to this court's signals with regard to renewal expectancy, the FCC ignored its own precedents as to the other factors that must be considered in conducting a comparative analysis.

The court of appeals agreed that Geller was entitled to no renewal expectancy because his programming did not even attempt to respond to ascertained community needs and problems. The FCC then properly turned to the comparative criteria. Here, however, the court concluded that the FCC had improperly diminished the value of Geller's obvious advantages of diversification and integration of ownership and management because it tied each to its view of Geller's programming. The FCC thus failed to accord to Geller the importance it had usually attached to diversification and integration in prior cases. The case was remanded for further consideration. Geller v. F.C.C., 737 F.2d 74, 56 R.R.2d 435 (D.C.Cir.1984). As discussed previously, p. 686, *supra,* the Commission granted Geller's application for renewal.

2. Is the latest Commission explanation of its comparative renewal standards clear? Exactly how much renewal expectancy is there? Has the Commission adequately justified the need for a strong renewal expectancy? Some would argue that it is impossible to devise an adequate system of comparing incumbents and new applicants and that comparative renewals should be eliminated. Would this eliminate the incentive for licensees to serve the public interest?

3. In Monroe Communications Corp. v. Federal Communications Commission, 900 F.2d 351, 17 Med.L.Rptr. 1703 (D.C.Cir.1990), the court concluded that the Commission

> arbitrarily and capriciously awarded a renewal expectancy to Video 44 in light of record evidence of Video 44's marked and apparently permanent cutback in non-entertainment programming through the latter part of its prior license period. Further, we conclude that the Commission arbitrarily failed to consider in the license renewal proceeding allegations of obscene broadcasts by Video 44.

Judge Silberman, concurring in the opinion of the court, added:

> It appears to me that virtually all the factors upon which the FCC relies in awarding or renewing broadcast licenses are in a sense fictitious; they are not really predictive of programming substance. Nor is it apparent to me that it is possible to articulate a public interest in any particular kind of programming (such as "nonentertainment"). When I sit on these cases, therefore, I feel somewhat

like Alice in Wonderland. We have no alternative as a reviewing court, however, but to treat the FCC's elaboration of the public interest as if it made sense and therefore to insist on a consistent application of what we may really think are fanciful factors.

Quite obviously the FCC shrinks from the prospect of taking the license away from the incumbent, but in the absence of a system whereby a license holder pays the public for the license (as in an auction) it is hard to see how the FCC can justify the weight it places on incumbency in this case. The Commission appears to act as if incumbency and the renewal expectancy were a property interest—which it is not.

4. The extension of license terms, p. 678, *supra*, meant that there were no renewal applications for two years. With a new round of applications came renewed criticism of the comparative criteria as well as complaints that challengers were abusing the system. The most frequent claim was that challengers were using the system to extort money from existing broadcasters. In response, the Commission issued an NOI/NPRM aimed at reforming the comparative renewal process. Among the proposed changes were limits on the amount of money that challengers can receive in return for withdrawing applications and/or petitions to deny and stricter ownership and financial disclosure requirements. The Commission also proposed to clarify the comparative licensing criteria, questioned the heavy weight given diversification of media as a criterion, and requested comments on both the weight that should be accorded renewal expectancy and the bases for awarding it. Formulation of Policies and Rules Relating to Broadcast Renewal Applicants, Competing Applicants, and Other Participants to the Comparative Renewal Process and to the Prevention of Abuses of the Renewal Process, 3 F.C.C.Rcd. 6019 (1988).

In 1989 the FCC took some initial steps towards curbing abuse of the license renewal process. First, the Commission adopted a prohibition on "all payments to competing applicants (other than the incumbent licensee) for the withdrawal of an application prior to the Initial Decision stage of a comparative hearing. Thereafter, we will approve settlements that do not exceed the withdrawing party's legitimate and prudent expenses for filing and litigating the competing application."

The Commission reasoned that this would weed out weak applications filed for the purpose of extracting settlement payments. The cost of staying in until an initial decision would be too great for a non *bona fide* applicant. Further, an applicant that lost in the initial decision stage would have very little leverage, especially if the initial decision was in the incumbent's favor.

At the same time allowing recovery of legitimate and prudent expenses after the initial decision provides "an efficient way to resolve comparative licensing proceedings, preserve funds for service to the public, and allow us to conserve our limited administrative resources."

The Commission also placed a legitimate and prudent expense limitation on settlements of petitions to deny:

41. We believe that a legitimate and prudent expense limitation on settlement payments of petitions to deny strikes the appropriate balance between deterring abuse and not discouraging the filing of such petitions. By prohibiting payments in excess of legitimate and prudent expenses we are removing the profit motive for filing petitions to deny. This should help ensure that petitions are filed for legitimate public interest purposes. By permitting recovery of legitimate and prudent expenses, we are preserving the petition to deny process as a monitoring and regulatory tool. It is more likely that individuals or public interest groups will perform their function of informing us of licensee deficiencies if they can maintain hope of recovery of the expenses they incur. To preserve the private attorney general function of petitions to deny, we believe we should provide for the possibility that a petitioner can be made economically whole.

The FCC also announced that it would review all future citizens' agreements—contracts in which licensees agree to "implement a nonfinancial reform such as a programming or an employment initiative" in return for the dismissal of a petition to deny. In determining whether an agreement furthers the public interest the Commission:

. . . will presume that any agreement with a petitioner that calls for the *petitioner*, or any person or organization related to the petitioner, to carry out for a fee, any programming, employment or other "nonfinancial" initiative does not further the public interest and hence will be disapproved. As discussed above, this type of arrangement is particularly susceptible to abuse. In contrast, a licensee's agreement with a petitioner to make changes in operations or programming, either *by itself* or through *disinterested third parties* without further participation by the petitioner, will likely be approved. For example, we will regard an agreement to increase minority employment by using, for a fee, the services of *petitioner* or any person or organization related to petitioner, as presumptively contrary to the public interest, and it will likely be disapproved. In contrast, we will regard an agreement to increase the pool of minority applicants for employment by contracting with a third party, completely independent from petitioner, as consistent with the public interest, and it will likely be approved.

The Commission will allow these presumptions to be rebutted by clear and convincing evidence that they are incorrect as applied to a specific citizens' agreement. Broadcast Renewal Applicants (Abuses of Comparative Renewal Process), 66 R.R.2d 708 (1989).

Various petitions for reconsideration were denied, 67 R.R.2d 1515 (1990). At the same time, the Commission adopted similar rules governing petitions to deny and citizens' agreements for new stations, license modification, and transfer applications. Abuses of the Broadcast Licensing and Allotment Processes, 67 R.R.2d 1526 (1990).

## E. TRANSFER OF LICENSES

In part because of the Commission's renewal policies, radio and television licenses have acquired substantial value. When a licensee decides to leave broadcasting altogether or to switch services or locations at the end of a license period, the licensee has no opportunity to reap profit. To make a profit, the licensee must seek renewal and, during the term, sell the facilities and goodwill and assign the license to a prospective buyer. In some ways this "transfer" procedure resembles the sale of any business, but the Commission's rules substantially affect the transaction.

Section 310(d) of the Communications Act requires the Commission to pass on all transfers and find that "the public interest, convenience, and necessity will be served thereby." But it also provides that in deciding whether the public interest would be served by the transfer the Commission "may not consider whether the public interest . . . might be served by the transfer . . . to a person other than the proposed transferee or assignee." Why might Congress have imposed this limitation?

When a transferee applies for its first full term, should it be judged as an original applicant who must compete in a comparative hearing without any advantage of incumbency or as a renewal applicant? What are the justifications for each view?

Despite the possible objections to transfer applications, most are granted, usually with little or no delay. This kind of turnover suggests a problem for the Commission. If licenses acquire substantial value a tendency may develop to build up stations and then sell them at a profit. This might be viewed as undermining the "public interest" philosophy of the licensing process. On the other hand, the public may benefit from someone's building up a station, even though that person's motive is to sell it for a profit.

# Chapter XVI

# LEGAL CONTROL OF BROADCAST PROGRAMMING: POLITICAL SPEECH

In this chapter and the next we will consider direct regulation of content, but not necessarily prohibitions on speech. In this chapter we will focus on political speech, including news. The next chapter will cover content regulation of other types of speech, which the FCC and courts have tended to treat as lower in the hierarchy of First Amendment values.

We begin this chapter with Congressional legislation to provide access and fairness in the electoral process. No speech is prohibited. Rather, broadcasters are told that they must allow certain candidates to use the station's facilities. In addition, if a candidate for an office is allowed to use the facilities his opponents must be allowed equal opportunities.

We then turn to doctrines developed by the Commission itself that require a broadcaster who has allowed certain types of comments to be made over his facilities to expose his listeners to contrasting viewpoints on that subject.

In each case consider whether the regulations, although not prohibitory, may nonetheless indirectly influence broadcasters to air or not to air certain types of content.

## A. EQUAL OPPORTUNITIES AND ACCESS IN POLITICAL CAMPAIGNS

### 1. EQUAL OPPORTUNITIES—SECTION 315

In the Radio Act of 1927, § 18 provided:

> If any licensee shall permit any person who is a legally qualified candidate for any public office to use a broadcasting station, he shall afford equal opportunities to all other such candidates for that office in the use of such broadcasting station; . . . *Provided,* That such licensee shall have no power of censorship over the material broadcast under the provisions of this paragraph. No obligation is hereby imposed upon any licensee to allow the use of its station by any such candidate.

This became § 315 of the 1934 Act. Although the Commission has explicit rulemaking power to carry out the provisions of § 315(a), few rules have been promulgated. Most of the problems involve requests in the heat of an election campaign and for this reason few decisions were reviewed by the courts until the 1980s.

### a.  General Application

One major limitation on the applicability of § 315 was defined in 1951, when it was held that the section did not apply to uses of a broadcast facility on behalf of a candidate unless the candidate appeared personally during the program.  This meant that friends and campaign committees could purchase time without triggering § 315.  Felix v. Westinghouse Broadcasting Co., 186 F.2d 1 (3d Cir.1950).  This raised a separate set of problems discussed at p. 742, *infra*.

Section 315 applies only to "legally qualified" candidates for public office.  According to § 73.1940(a) of the Commission's rules, a legally qualified candidate is one who:

> (i) has publicly announced his or her intention to run for nomination or office;

> (ii) is qualified under the applicable local, state or federal law to hold the office for which he or she is a candidate;  and

> (iii) has met the qualifications set forth in either paragraphs (a)(2), (3), or (4) below.

In essence, these other subparagraphs require the candidate either to have qualified for a place on the ballot or to have made a public commitment to seeking election by the write-in method as well as a substantial showing of being a bona-fide candidate for the office.

Another basic question was resolved in Farmers Educational & Cooperative Union v. WDAY, Inc., 360 U.S. 525 (1959), when the Court unanimously held that a licensee was barred from censoring the comments of a speaker exercising rights under § 315.  The Court also held, 5–4, that the section preempted state defamation law and created an absolute privilege that protected the licensee from liability for statements made by such a candidate.  Are these rulings sound?  Because of the way the litigation arose, neither party challenged the constitutionality of § 315.  Note, however, that although the station is protected from liability for defamation, the person who utters the statements is subject to liability under the general rules of defamation considered earlier.

Content problems under § 315 are rare, but do arise.  Among the candidates running in 1972 for the Democratic nomination for Senator from Georgia, one was broadcasting the following spot announcement:

> I am J.B. Stoner.  I am the only candidate for U.S. Senator who is for the white people.  I am the only candidate who is against integration.  All of the other candidates are race mixers to one degree or another.  I say we must repeal Gambrell's civil rights law. Gambrell's law takes jobs from us whites and gives those jobs to the niggers.  The main reason why niggers want integration is because the niggers want our white women.  I am for law and order with the

knowledge that you cannot have law and order and niggers too. Vote white. This time vote your convictions by voting white racist J.B. Stoner into the run-off election for U.S. Senator. Thank you.

Several groups asked the Commission to rule that a licensee may, and has the responsibility to, withhold announcements under § 315 if they "pose an imminent and immediate threat to the safety and security of the public it serves." The groups alleged that the spot had created racial tension and that the Mayor of Atlanta had urged broadcasters not to air the advertisement. Letter to Lonnie King, 36 F.C.C.2d 635, 25 R.R.2d 54 (1972). The Commission refused to issue the requested order:

> The relief requested in your letter would amount to an advance approval by the Commission of licensee censorship of a candidate's remarks. By way of background, we note that Constitutional guarantees do not permit the proscription of even the advocacy of force or of law violation "except where such advocacy is directed to inciting or producing imminent lawless action and is likely to incite or produce such action." Brandenburg v. Ohio, 395 U.S. 444, 447 (1969). And a prior restraint bears a heavy presumption against its constitutional validity. Carroll v. President and Commissioners of Princess Anne, 393 U.S. 175, 181 (1968). While there may be situations where speech is "so interlaced with burgeoning violence that it is not protected," Carroll v. President and Commissioners of Princess Anne, 393 U.S. at 180 and while a similar approach might warrant overriding the no-censorship command of Section 315, we need not resolve that difficult issue here, for we conclude on the basis of the information before us that there is no factual basis for the relief you request. Despite your report of threats of bombing and violence, there does not appear to be that clear and present danger of imminent violence which might warrant interfering with speech which does not contain any direct incitement to violence. A contrary conclusion here would permit anyone to prevent a candidate from exercising his rights under Section 315 by threatening a violent reaction. In view of the precise commands of Sections 315 and 326, we are constrained to deny your requests.

The FCC has also received occasional complaints about political announcements that contain indecent language. The problem of indecent and obscene political announcements will be discussed in Chapter XVII.

### b. Exemptions

During its early years the statute apparently caused few serious problems. The advent of television, however, changed matters dramatically. In 1956 the Commission issued two major rulings during the presidential campaign. In one it ruled that stations carrying President Eisenhower's appearance in a two-to-three minute appeal on behalf of the annual drive of the United Community Funds would be a "use" of the facility by a candidate that would trigger the equal opportunities provision. The section carried no exception for "public service," nor did it require the appearance to be "political." Columbia Broadcasting System (United Fund), 14 R.R. 524 (F.C.C.1956). One week before the election, President Eisenhower requested and received 15 minutes of free time from the three networks to discuss the sudden eruption of war in the Middle East. The Democrats' request for equal time was granted by the networks, although the FCC later indicated that § 315 did not apply. Columbia Broadcasting System (Suez Crisis), 14 R.R. 720 (F.C.C.1956).

This response to an incumbent's speaking as President rather than as candidate was unusual for the Commission, which had interpreted "use" very broadly. It did so again in 1959 when a third-party candidate for mayor of Chicago, Lar Daly, asked equal time on the basis of two series of television clips of his opponents, incumbent Mayor Richard Daley and the Republican challenger. One group of clips showed the two major candidates filing their papers (46 seconds), Mayor Daley accepting the nomination (22 seconds) and a one-minute clip asking the Republican why he was running. A second group of clips included "nonpolitical" activities such as a 29–second clip of Mayor Daley on a March of Dimes appeal and 21 seconds of his greeting President Frondizi of Argentina at a Chicago airport. The Commission, in a long opinion, ruled that both groups required equal time. Columbia Broadcasting System, Inc. (Lar Daly), 26 F.C.C. 715 (1959). It relied on the words "use" and "all" in the statute and thought the issue of who initiated the appearance (such as the March of Dimes asking the Mayor to appear) to be irrelevant. Although formal campaigning was the most obvious way of putting forward a candidacy, "of no less importance is the candidate's appearance as a public servant, as an incumbent office holder, or as a private citizen in a nonpolitical role." Such "appearances and uses of a nonpolitical nature may confer substantial benefits on a candidate who is favored."

Congressional response was swift—and negative. Hearings began within days after the decision, and the result was an amended version of § 315:

> Sec. 315. (a) If any licensee shall permit any person who is a legally qualified candidate for any public office to use a broadcasting station, he shall afford equal opportunities to all other such candidates for that office in the use of such broadcasting station: *Provided,* That such licensee shall have no power of censorship over the material broadcast under the provisions of this section. No obligation is hereby imposed upon any licensee to allow the use of its station by any such candidate.* Appearance by a legally qualified candidate on any—
>
> (1) bona fide newscast,

---

* In 1971 Congress amended this sentence by adding "under this subsection" after the word "imposed." The reason for this is explained when we consider § 312(a)(7) shortly.

(2) bona fide news interview,

(3) bona fide news documentary (if the appearance of the candidate is incidental to the presentation of the subject or subjects covered by the news documentary), or

(4) on-the-spot coverage of bona fide news events (including but not limited to political conventions and activities incidental thereto),

shall not be deemed to be use of a broadcasting station within the meaning of this subsection. Nothing in the foregoing sentence shall be construed as relieving broadcasters, in connection with the presentation of newscasts, news interviews, news documentaries, and on-the-spot coverage of news events, from the obligation imposed upon them under this chapter to operate in the public interest and to afford reasonable opportunity for the discussion of conflicting views on issues of public importance.

Recall the significance of this episode to the Court in *Red Lion*, p. 635, *supra*.

*Broadcast Coverage of Candidate Press Conferences and Debates.* Through the 1960s and 1970s, various proposals were made in Congress to amend or repeal § 315. Nothing came of any of them. But in 1975 the Commission responded dramatically to two petitions. It overruled its 1962 decisions that coverage of a debate did not come within the exemption for on-the-spot coverage of bona fide news events. The Commission said that it had misinterpreted legislative history when it required the appearance of the candidate to be "incidental" to the coverage of a separate news event. The Commission now concluded that, in 1959, Congress intended to run the risks of political favoritism among broadcasters in an effort to allow broadcasters to "cover the political news to the fullest degree." Debates were exempt if controlled by someone other than the candidates or the broadcaster, as with the Economic Club and UPI convention, and if judged to be bona fide news events under § 315(a)(4).

In a companion ruling, the Commission decided that full coverage of a press conference by any incumbent or candidate would come within the exemption for on-the-spot coverage of a bona fide news event if it "may be considered newsworthy and subject to on-the-spot coverage." But the Commission refused to bring a press conference within the exemption for bona fide news interviews because the licensee did not "control" the format and the event was not "regularly scheduled." Petitions of Aspen Institute and CBS, Inc., 55 F.C.C.2d 697, 35 R.R.2d 49 (1975).

Appeals were taken against both parts of the Commission's 1975 rulings. The main contentions were that the Commission had not followed the Congressional mandate when it permitted the candidate to "become the event" under the (a)(4) exemption, and that the statute did not allow the Commission to uphold licensee decisions if only they are in "good faith"—that it is for the Commission to make these judgments. By a vote of 2–1, the court affirmed both rulings, Chisholm v. Federal

Communications Commission, 538 F.2d 349, 1 Med.L.Rptr. 2207 (D.C.Cir.1976). The opinions disagreed over the significance of the complex legislative history, with the majority concluding that the Commission's interpretation was "reasonable." Rehearing *en banc* was denied. A petition for certiorari was denied 429 U.S. 890 (1976) White, J., dissenting.

Seizing on the Commission's rulings, the League of Women Voters set up "debates" between the two major Presidential candidates in 1976. They were held in auditoriums before invited audiences. The candidates were questioned by panelists selected by the League after consultation with the participants. Television was allowed to cover the events—but the League imposed restrictions against showing the audience or any audience reactions. Although the networks complained about the restrictions and about the way the panelists were selected, they did carry the programs live and in full.

In 1980, just before the primaries began, President Carter, seeking renomination as Democratic candidate for President in a contest against Sen. Edward M. Kennedy, held a press conference that was carried live in prime time by the three commercial networks and the Public Broadcasting Service. Senator Kennedy, claiming that President Carter had used more than five minutes on that occasion to attack him and to misstate several of his positions, sought relief from the FCC.

In Kennedy for President Committee v. Federal Communications Commission, 636 F.2d 432, 47 R.R.2d 1537, 6 Med.L.Rptr. 1705 (D.C.Cir. 1980) (*Kennedy I*), the Senator asked for equal opportunities under § 315 to respond to the "calculated and damaging statements" and to "provide contrasting viewpoints." The FCC denied the request. On appeal, the court affirmed.

The press conference was exempt under § 315(a)(4) so long as the broadcasters reasonably believed that the conference was a "bona fide news event." The Commission said, in a passage approved by the court, that an incumbent President "may well have an advantage over his opponent in attracting media coverage" but "absent strong evidence that broadcasters were not exercising their bona fide news judgment, the Commission will not interfere with such judgments." The Senator was free to hold a press conference the next day to rebut the charges. Indeed, generally, Senator Kennedy was getting substantial media coverage.

The court traced the history of the exemptions to § 315 and adhered to its decision in *Chisholm* upholding the Commission's new approach to § 315. "The only inquiry now in order is whether there was anything so peculiar about the February 13 presidential press conference as to remove it from the ambit of *Aspen* and *Chisholm*." The court found no reason to doubt the broadcasters' good faith. It also concluded that the actual content of the event could not control the question of exemption. In addition to the difficult judgments about content, context and impact of particular statements that the Commission and the courts would have to make, the goal of the exemptions would be defeated if broadcasters could not know until after an event whether it was exempt.

Senator Kennedy then argued that the First Amendment required that he be granted time to respond, even if the statute did not. The court rejected the contention on the basis of *CBS*, p. 670, *supra*:

> From its inception more than a half-century ago, federal regulation of broadcasting has largely entrusted protection of that public right to short-term station licensees functioning under Commission supervision, and with liberty as well as responsibility to determine who may get on the air and when. The history of this era portrays Congress' consistent refusal to mandate access to the air waves on a non-selective basis and, contrariwise, its decision "to permit private broadcasting to develop with the widest journalistic experience consistent with its public obligations." *CBS* The Commission has honored that policy in a series of rulings establishing that a private right to utilize the broadcaster's facilities exists only when specially conferred. The net of these many years of legislative and administrative oversight of broadcasting is that "[o]nly when the interests of the public are found to outweigh the private journalistic interests of the broadcasters will government power be asserted within the framework of the Act."

The First Amendment permits Congress to enforce the public's primary interests by using broadcasters as public trustees, and *CBS* shows that no one has a constitutional right to broadcast his own views on any matter.

Again in 1980 the League took steps to sponsor debates among the major candidates. It decided that John Anderson's showing in public opinion polls was sufficiently strong to warrant his inclusion in a three-way debate. When President Jimmy Carter refused to participate in a debate with Anderson, the League went ahead anyway and staged an Anderson–Reagan debate. If networks decided to cover the event, as CBS and NBC did, the coverage would be exempt under (a)(4) because the networks and licensees were making the judgment it was a bona fide news event even without the President.

After Anderson's ratings fell to around 10 percent, the League invited Carter and Reagan to debate. Both accepted the invitation and held a single head-to-head debate a week before the election.

In Petitions of Henry Geller et al., 95 F.C.C.2d 1236, 54 R.R.2d 1246 (1983), the FCC reversed long-standing administrative decisions by permitting broadcasters themselves to sponsor debates between political candidates without having to provide uninvited candidates with equal broadcasting opportunities. Such debates may still fall within the § 315(a)(4) exemption. The Commission concluded that its previous interpretations neither represented the outer bounds of its legislated authority under the statute nor met the overriding Congressional mandate to encourage broadcast coverage of electoral issues. Third-party sponsorship was not the *sine qua non* of impartiality.  For example, the risks of favoritism in the news interview format (§ 315(a)(2)) were thought to be no different than in the debate format and therefore disparate treatment was not justified.  The League of Women Voters' argument that this approach creates too great a risk of favoritism was rejected.  The risks inherent in broadcaster-sponsored debates were no greater than the *Chisholm* court had understood the 1959 amendments to be willing to accept.

The Commission also noted that in many cases a broadcaster may be "the ideal, and perhaps the only, entity interested in promoting a debate between candidates for a particular office, especially at the state or local level."  Exempting broadcaster-sponsored debates would therefore increase the number of debates and ultimately benefit the public.  Finally, a debate's exempt status "should not be contingent upon whether a broadcaster is the sponsoring or controlling entity—for such control generally would not affect the program's news value."  The Commission also made clear that this new interpretation of § 315(a)(4) did not authorize licensees to favor or disfavor any candidate.  The League's expedited appeal was rejected without opinion.  League of Women Voters v. FCC, 731 F.2d 995 (D.C.Cir.1984).

A more recent First Amendment attack on the application of (a)(4) to candidate debates was rejected in Johnson v. Federal Communications Commission, 829 F.2d 157, 63 R.R.2d 1492, 14 Med.L.Rptr. 1711 (D.C.Cir.1987).  Sonia Johnson, who was running for President in 1984 as the nominee of the Citizens Party, and her running mate, Richard Walton, argued that "by 1984 the televised presidential and vice-presidential debates had become so institutionalized as to be a prerequisite for election."  Thus, "their exclusion from the 1984 debates [restricted] their access to the ballot and impinge[d] upon associational choices protected by the First Amendment."  Treating the claim as a demand for broadcast access, the court of appeals found *Kennedy I* and *CBS v. DNC* controlling.  "In the present case, we find the First Amendment interests of candidates, broadcasters and the public adequately served by the adjustments made in the Communications Act, and perceive no basis for disturbing the Commission's denial of petitioners' complaint."

A 1987 debate between Gov.  Michael Dukakis of Massachusetts and Rep.  Richard Gephardt (D.–Mo.) presented the Commission with a slightly different question.  Could a candidate-sponsored as opposed to broadcast-sponsored debate be considered exempt under § 315(a)(4)?  In extending the exemption to candidate-sponsored debates, the Commission reemphasized its position that the identity of the sponsor is not a factor in determining if an event is newsworthy.  As long as the broadcaster retains ultimate control over the amount and type of coverage, an event can qualify for exemption (a)(4).  WCVB–TV, 63 R.R.2d 665 (M.Med.Bur.1987).

*"On the spot" Defined.*  The "on the spot" language of § 315(a)(4) also has produced litigation.  Groups afraid that an exempt program,

such as a debate, might be recorded and played over several times to the detriment of excluded candidates, have argued that the statute permits only one showing—and that it must be live.  The FCC rejected this and allowed the broadcaster to tape the live event and to present it once during the next 24 hours.  When that ruling was challenged, the court affirmed the Commission.  The agency had authority to develop a balance between rigidly equal opportunities and the new freedom provided by the 1959 exemptions.  There was no showing that the FCC had misconstrued the law, and it had fully explained what it was doing.  Office of Communication of the United Church of Christ v. Federal Communications Commission, 590 F.2d 1062, 44 R.R.2d 261, 4 Med. L.Rptr. 1410 (D.C.Cir.1978).

The one-day rule was eliminated in *Henry Geller, supra.*  The reasonableness of a delayed broadcast would now be left to the broadcaster's good faith determination that the delay of more than one day after the occurrence of the exempt debate would better serve the community.  Such delay, however, must be motivated by concerns of informing the public, and not in order to favor or disfavor any candidate.

*Other Exemptions.*  The other subdivisions, (a)(1), (a)(2) and (a)(3), have given rise to fewer problems.  In 1976 supporters of Ronald Reagan complained when a Miami television station broadcast six-minute interviews with President Gerald Ford on five consecutive evening newscasts. The complaint asserted that the segments were from a single half-hour interview that had been broken up into five parts.  The Commission held that even if the 30–minute interview would not have been exempt under § 315, inclusion of the segments within newscasts would not preclude "exempt status pursuant to § 315(a)(1) unless it has been shown that such a decision is clearly unreasonable or in bad faith." Even though this was broadcast during the last week of a primary campaign and might benefit President Ford, the complainants "have not shown that the licensee in deciding to air them, considered anything other than their newsworthiness."  Citizens for Reagan, 58 F.C.C.2d 925, 36 R.R.2d 885 (1976).  Does the statute's use of "bona fide" support the Commission's decision to leave the decision in the first instance with the licensee?

The use of the term "bona fide" was one of the factors cited by the court of appeals in denying a newscaster's appeal of a Commission ruling that § 315(a)(1) did not exempt his appearances from equal opportunity obligations.  Even though the plain language seemed to exempt all appearances on a bona fide newscast, the court refused to overturn the Commission's interpretation that it applied only to "coverage of the candidate that is presented to the public as news."  In the court's view, by limiting the exemption to "bona fide newscasts" Congress was making it clear that the underlying basis of the exemption was newsworthiness.  Relying on *Red Lion,* the court also rejected the newscaster's contention that applying the statute to him violated the First Amendment.  Branch v. Federal Communications Commission, 824 F.2d 37, 63

R.R.2d 826, 14 Med.L.Rptr. 1465 (D.C.Cir.1987). *Certiorari* was denied 485 U.S. 959 (1988).

The FCC has granted general exemptions under (a)(2) to such programs as "Today," "Donahue" and "Good Morning America." In determining whether a show falls under the (a)(2) exemption "the Commission considers the following factors: (1) whether it is regularly scheduled; (2) how long it has been broadcast; (3) whether the broadcaster produces and controls the program; (4) whether the broadcaster's decisions on the format, content and participants are based on its reasonable, good faith journalistic judgment rather than on an intention to advance the candidacy of a particular person; and (5) whether the selection of persons to be interviewed and topics to be discussed are based on their newsworthiness." CBS Inc., 63 R.R.2d 483 (M.Med.Bur. 1987).

## c. *Nonpolitical Appearances*

For many years the Commission defined "use" as "any positive appearance by a candidate by voice or picture." Thus, in United Way of America, 35 R.R.2d 137 (F.C.C.1975), which was decided at about the same time as the Aspen–CBS petitions, the Commission, 4–3, adhered to its earlier rulings that an appearance by candidate Ford opening an annual charity fund drive came within § 315. Similarly, the Commission consistently held that appearances by television personalities or film stars after they had announced their candidacy for office constituted "uses" under § 315. In Adrian Weiss, 58 F.C.C.2d 342, 36 R.R.2d 292 (1976), the Broadcast Bureau ruled that the showing of old Ronald Reagan films on television would require the offering of equal opportunities to other Republican presidential aspirants. The Bureau relied heavily on the claim that non-political uses can be very effective. The Commission refused to review the Bureau's decision, with two Commissioners concurring separately and two dissenting. These four all thought that common sense dictated exempting movies made before Reagan actively entered politics, but the two concurring Commissioners thought that any change should be made by Congress.

In 1991, as part of an extensive review of its political broadcasting rules, the Commission narrowed its definition to "non-exempt candidate appearances that are controlled, approved, or sponsored by the candidate (or the candidate's authorized committee) after the candidate becomes legally qualified." This effectively overrules Adrian Weiss but not United Way of America. Codification of the Commission's Political Programming Policies, 7 F.C.C.Rcd. 678, 70 R.R.2d 239 (1991).

In Pat Paulsen, 33 F.C.C.2d 297, aff'd 33 F.C.C.2d 835, 23 R.R.2d 861 (1972), aff'd 491 F.2d 887, 29 R.R.2d 854 (9th Cir.1974), the Commission rejected a comedian's argument that applying § 315 would deprive him of due process and equal protection by forcing him to give up his livelihood in order to run for public office. Their interpretation was held permissible "to achieve the important and legitimate objectives of encouraging political discussion and preventing unfair and unequal use of the broadcast media." The Commission applied this same interpretation in Branch, p. 720, *supra*.

### d.  Lowest Unit Rate

In 1971 Congress amended § 315 to require that candidates using broadcast facilities during the 45 days before a primary and the 60 days before a general election be charged rates not to exceed "the lowest unit charge of the station for the same class and amount of time for the same period."

At all other times, the rates charged candidates are not to exceed "the charges made for comparable use of such station by other users thereof." 47 U.S.C.A. § 315(b). The major difference between the two quoted passages is that during the 45– and 60–day periods, the candidate pays the rate that the highest-volume advertiser would pay for that time. At other times the candidate pays the rates charged to those who advertise as little or as much as the candidate does.

In July 1990 the Mass Media Bureau conducted an audit of 30 television and radio stations to determine the level of compliance with the political programming rules, particularly the lowest unit rate requirement. In September 1990 it issued a preliminary report on the results of its audit. The Bureau found that, "at sixteen of the twenty audited television stations (80%), candidates paid more for broadcast time than commercial advertisers in virtually every daypart or program time period analyzed. Indeed, candidates sometimes paid more than every commercial advertiser aired in the same dayparts. Candidates fared better on radio, paying more than commercial advertisers at only four of the eight audited stations that sold time to candidates."

The primary cause of the disparity was the fact that candidates tended to buy non-preemptible, fixed-time commercials. This assured that the candidates' commercials would not only run, but would do so at the exact times they wanted. In contrast, commercial advertisers tended to buy preemptible commercials. Because they were willing to take the risk that their commercials might be preempted if enough non-preemptible commercials were sold, they paid a lower rate. Technically, preemptible commercials are a different class of time, and thus, selling them at a lower rate is not a violation of the lowest unit rate requirement. However, the Bureau indicated a concern that candidates were not being given adequate information regarding the likelihood that a preemptible commercial would in fact be preempted and the availability of "make-good" commercials in the event that preemption did occur.

Based on its preliminary findings the Bureau urged broadcasters to "disclose to candidates all rates and the availability of package options available to commercial advertisers. . . . This disclosure should specify all discount privileges, including every level of preemptibility, the approximate clearance potential of time purchased at current effective selling levels, and special package plans. The disclosure should also indicate the station's policies with respect to make goods and the availability of negotiating for time if that is the practice with commercial advertisers." Political Programming Audit, 68 R.R.2d 113 (M.M.Bur. 1990).

The audit resulted in further questions from both candidates and broadcasters still seemingly confused over the exact requirements of the lowest unit rate provision of the Act. In mid–1991 the FCC issued an NPRM aimed at clearing up the confusion. Among the questions addressed in the NPRM are what constitutes a distinct class of time, how to "calculate the lowest unit charge when using a variety of different option privileges and discounts," and how much disclosure of the various option privileges and discounts should be made to political candidates.

The audit also proposed a stricter sponsorship identification requirement as a prerequisite for candidates availing themselves of the lowest unit rate. Under the proposal, sponsoring candidates' pictures would have to fill a minimum of 20 percent of the screen for at least six seconds. Broadcasting, June 17, 1991 at 21.

In *Codification of Commission's Political Programming Policies*, p. 721, *supra*, the FCC imposed a full disclosure requirement on licensees with regard to advertising rates. At a minimum this disclosure must include:

a) A description and definition of each class [of time] available to commercial advertisers which is complete enough to allow candidates to identify and understand what specific attributes differentiate each class;

b) A complete description of the lowest unit charge and related privileges (such as priorities against preemption and make goods prior to specific deadlines) for each class of time offered to commercial advertisers;

c) A description of the station's method of selling preemptible time based upon advertiser demand, commonly known as the "current selling level," with the stipulation that candidates will be able to purchase at these demand-generated rates in the same manner as commercial advertisers;

d) An approximation of the likelihood of preemption for each kind of preemptible time; and

e) An explanation of the station's sales practices, if any, that are based on audience delivery.

In the same proceeding, the Commission made several other decisions regarding lowest unit rate. Licensees are required to treat political candidates the same as their most-favored commercial advertiser, not only with regard to advertising rates but also to other sales practices including "make goods, preemption priorities and any other factors that enhance the value of a spot."

Licensees are now permitted to create more than one class of preemptible time, as long as the classes are distinguished by some demonstrable benefit to the advertiser, e.g. different levels of protection against preemption. Similarly, licensees can now have separate non-preemptible and fixed position classes of time. (Fixed position guarantees an exact time for the spot, non-preemptible only guarantees that the spot will run sometime during a particular day or time period.) Stations may not, however, create special classes of time for candidates only.

Stations that offer timely make goods to commercial advertisers for a specific class of time must offer similar make goods to political candidates. These make goods "must air before the election 'where the licensee would so treat its most-favored commercial advertiser where time is of the essence.'" Make goods must also be included in the calculation of lowest unit charge. Thus, where a make good is placed in a more valuable program or daypart, the cost of the make good must be included in the calculation of lowest unit charge for that program or daypart.

Another question raised during the 1990 elections involved jurisdiction over lowest-unit-rate disputes. Various Alabama and Georgia television stations had been sued for alleged violations of the lowest-unit-rate requirement. The cases had produced conflicting district court rulings on the question of whether the FCC has exclusive jurisdiction over lowest-unit-rate violations. The candidates had also filed complaints with the FCC.

The FCC issued a declaratory ruling preempting any state cause of action involving § 315(b). At the same time it outlined the procedures for bringing a lowest-unit-rate complaint. Complainants are required to file a short, plain statement of the claim sufficient to show that the complainant is entitled to the relief requested. The complaint must served on the station. The station will then be given ten days to answer. If the Mass Media Bureau determines that a *prima facie* case has been made, the parties will be given the choice of either mediation or evaluation and disposition by the Bureau. Lowest Unit Charge Requirements (Preemption of State Jurisdiction), 6 F.C.C.Rcd. 7511, 70 R.R.2d 1 (1991). Two petitions for reconsideration were denied. 7 F.C.C.Rcd. 4123, 70 R.R.2d 1355 (1992).

### 2. REASONABLE ACCESS—SECTION 312(a)(7)

In 1971 Congress also adopted § 312(a)(7), providing that the Commission may revoke a license:

(7) for willful or repeated failure to allow reasonable access to or to permit purchase of reasonable amounts of time for the use of a broadcasting station by a legally qualified candidate for Federal elective office on behalf of his candidacy.

The legislative history indicates that one purpose of the overall legislation was to "give candidates for public office greater access to the media so that they may better explain their stand on the issues and thereby more fully and completely inform the voters."

It was not until 1980 that cases involving the section began to reach the courts.

The first case raised the questions of when the campaign had begun and how requests should be treated. The Carter–Mondale Committee asked each major network to sell it 30 minutes of prime time in December 1979 (just after the formal announcement that President Carter was seeking renomination), in order to show a documentary on President Carter's first term. CBS offered two five-minute segments, one of which would be in prime time. ABC indicated that it would make time available beginning in January 1980. NBC said that it was "too early in the political season for nationwide broadcast time to be made available for paid political purposes." The Committee complained to the FCC, which found the stations in violation of § 312(a)(7), by a vote of 4–3.

The Supreme Court upheld the FCC decision. CBS, Inc. v. Federal Communications Commission, 453 U.S. 367, 49 R.R.2d 1191, 7 Med. L.Rptr. 1563 (1981). Chief Justice Burger, for the majority, agreed with the FCC that the section had "created an affirmative, promptly enforceable right of reasonable access to the use of broadcast stations for individual candidates seeking federal elective office" rather than simply codifying prior policies that the FCC had developed under the general public interest standard. The Court relied on the specific language of the statute itself, the legislative history and what the Court found to be the FCC's consistent administrative interpretation of the language since the statute's enactment. Perhaps the "most telling evidence" of Congressional intent was the contemporaneous change in § 315 from a statement that "No obligation is imposed upon any licensee to allow the use of its station by" a candidate to the statement that no such obligation "is imposed under this subsection [§ 315(a)]."

Next the Court rejected the contention that the FCC's interpretation under the statute, particularly its emphasis on case-by-case individualized analysis, intruded on editorial discretion and judgment to an extent not intended by Congress. The Court summarized the state of affairs under various FCC edicts as follows:

> Broadcasters are free to deny the sale of air time prior to the commencement of a campaign, but once a campaign has begun, they must give reasonable and good faith attention to access requests from "legally qualified" candidates for federal elective office. Such requests must be considered on an individualized basis, and broadcasters are required to tailor their responses to accommodate, as much as reasonably possible, a candidate's stated purposes in seeking air time. In responding to access requests, however, broadcasters may also give weight to such factors as the amount of time previously sold to the candidate, the disruptive impact on regular programming, and the likelihood of requests for time by rival

candidates under the equal opportunities provision of § 315(a).
These considerations may not be invoked as pretexts for denying
access; to justify a negative response, broadcasters must cite a
realistic danger of substantial program disruption—perhaps caused
by insufficient notice to allow adjustments in the schedule—or of an
excessive number of equal time requests.  Further, in order to
facilitate review by the Commission, broadcasters must explain their
reasons for refusing time or making a more limited counteroffer.  If
broadcasters take the appropriate factors into account and act
reasonably and in good faith, their decisions will be entitled to
deference even if the Commission's analysis would have differed in
the first instance.  But if broadcasters adopt "across-the-board
policies" and do not attempt to respond to the individualized situation of a particular candidate, the Commission is not compelled to
sustain their denial of access.

The Court upheld the process by which the FCC decides whether an
election campaign has, in fact, started.  Such a decision "is not, and
cannot be, purely one of editorial judgment."  Moreover, by limiting
access to the period after a campaign starts the FCC "has limited its
impact on broadcasters and given substance to [the statute's] command
of reasonable access."

Next the Court upheld the FCC's insistence that broadcasters respond to each request individually.  The Court understood the FCC to be
mandating "careful consideration of, not blind assent to, candidates'
desires for air time."  It quoted from FCC statements that although the
broadcaster was not to "second guess" the "political wisdom" of a
candidate's request, that request was "by no means conclusive of the
question of how much time, if any, is appropriate.  Other . . .
factors, such as disruption or displacement of regular programming . . . must be considered in the balance."  Although "the
adoption of uniform policies might well prove more convenient for
broadcasters, such an approach would allow personal campaign strategies and the exigencies of the political process to be ignored."  Thus, a
policy allowing program lengths of a single fixed duration might be
"unreasonable" as to a candidate who wanted a different length.

The Court concluded that the Commission's actions were a "reasoned attempt to effectuate the statute's access requirement, giving
broadcasters room to exercise their discretion but demanding that they
act in good faith."  These ground rules were sufficiently clear in late
1979 to permit the FCC to rule that the networks had violated the
statute by failing to grant "reasonable access."

Finally, the Court rejected the network's assertion that § 312(a)(7)
was unconstitutional:

The First Amendment interests of candidates and voters, as
well as broadcasters, are implicated by § 312(a)(7).  We have recognized that "it is of particular importance that candidates have
the . . . opportunity to make their views known so that the

electorate may intelligently evaluate the candidates' personal qualities and their positions on vital public issues before choosing among
them on election day." [*Buckley*]. [   ] Indeed, "speech concerning public affairs is . . . the essence of self-government."
[*Garrison*]. The First Amendment "has its fullest and most urgent
application precisely to the conduct of campaigns for public office."
[*Monitor Patriot Co.*]. Section 312(a)(7) thus makes a significant
contribution to freedom of expression by enhancing the ability of
candidates to present, and the public to receive, information necessary for the effective operation of the democratic process.

Petitioners are correct that the Court has never approved a
*general* right of access to the media. [   ] Nor do we do so today.
Section 312(a)(7) creates a *limited* right to "reasonable" access that
pertains only to legally qualified federal candidates and may be
invoked by them only for the purpose of advancing their candidacies
once a campaign has commenced. The Commission has stated that,
in enforcing the statute, it will "provide leeway to broadcasters and
not merely attempt *de novo* to determine the reasonableness of their
judgments . . .." If broadcasters have considered the relevant
factors in good faith, the Commission will uphold their decisions.
See 629 F.2d, at 25. Further, § 312(a)(7) does not impair the
discretion of broadcasters to present their views on any issue or to
carry any particular type of programming.

Section 312(a)(7) represents an effort by Congress to assure
that an important resource—the airwaves—will be used in the
public interest. We hold that the statutory right of access, as
defined by the Commission and applied in these cases, properly
balances the First Amendment rights of federal candidates, the
public, and broadcasters.

After *CBS*, the general rule for federal candidates is that broadcasters cannot establish across-the-board policies, but rather must consider
the particular needs of each individual candidate. There is one exception to that, however. Stations may establish a policy of not selling any
political advertisements during news programming. Commission Policy
in Enforcing Section 312(a)(7), 68 F.C.C.2d 1079, 43 R.R.2d 1079 (1978).

The relation between § 312(a)(7) and § 315 was central to Kennedy
for President Committee v. Federal Communications Commission, 636
F.2d 417, 47 R.R.2d 1521, 6 Med.L.Rptr. 1722 (D.C.Cir.1980) (*Kennedy
II*). On March 14, 1980, President Carter made a 30–minute speech in
the afternoon and held a press conference from 9 to 9:30 p.m. The three
major commercial networks carried both programs live, except that ABC
delayed the press conference for three hours. Senator Kennedy charged
that these programs saturated the public with the President's views on
the economy only four days before the Illinois primary. He asked for
free time to reply under § 312(a)(7). The networks denied the request,
the Commission refused to order that time be granted, and the court
affirmed.

The court began by noting that Congress, in 1971, enacted § 312(a)(7) and § 315(b)(1), requiring lowest charges to candidates using broadcast facilities, because Congress was concerned about the rising cost of candidates' televised appearances:

It was believed that the informational and educational aspects of political broadcasting could greatly be enhanced by ensuring that more time would be made available to candidates at lower rates. This expectably would encourage less dependence on thirty- to sixty-second "spots" necessarily little more than slogans—in favor of longer, more illuminating presentations; it would also enable more candidates to afford the television appearances so instrumental to present-day electioneering.

The court concluded that the "most straightforward reading" of § 312(a)(7) "is that broadcasters may fulfill their obligation thereunder either by allotting free time to a candidate *or* by selling the candidate time at the rates prescribed by Section 315(b)." Considering the legislative history, the FCC's consistent administrative interpretations and the apparent statutory scheme of the various provisions, the court concluded that § 312(a)(7), although seeking to assure federal candidates access to broadcasting, did not "confer the privilege of using the broadcaster's facilities without charge." The choice of giving or selling time is for the broadcaster:

Should Section 312(a)(7) be construed as automatically entitling a candidate to responsive broadcast access whenever and for whatever reason his opponent has appeared on the air, Section 315(a)'s exemptions would soon become meaningless. Statutes are to be interpreted, if possible, to give operation to all of their parts, and to maintain them in harmonious working relationship.

Because Kennedy never claimed that he had not been given an opportunity to buy time, he could not invoke § 312(a)(7). Nor had he sought relief under § 315.

## B.  THE FAIRNESS DOCTRINE

Beginning in Chapter XIV with *Red Lion,* and at several points during the licensing discussion, we have had occasion to note the existence of, and to consider aspects of, the Commission-created fairness doctrine. Although, as we will discuss later in this chapter, the general fairness doctrine is no longer in force, it played an important part in the development of the rules covering broadcasting, and Congress is considering reviving the doctrine.

### 1.  IN GENERAL

The Commission was concerned with fairness and the exposure of varying views since its earliest days. The Federal Radio Commission in 1928 indicated as much in a discussion of the implications of the limited spectrum. It observed that there was not room "for every school of thought, religious, political, social, and economic, each to have its separate broadcasting station, its mouthpiece in the ether." Such ideas "must find their way into the market of ideas by the existing public-service stations, and if they are of sufficient importance to the listening public the microphone will undoubtedly be available. If it is not, a well-founded complaint will receive the careful consideration of the commission in its future action with reference to the station complained of." Great Lakes Broadcasting Co., 3 F.R.C.Ann.Rep. 32 (1929), modified on other grounds 37 F.2d 993 (D.C.Cir.), cert. dism'd 281 U.S. 706 (1930). The doctrine evolved through case law until it became the subject of a major report in 1949.

In 1959, when § 315 was amended, p. 715, *supra*, many people interpreted the phrase, "nothing in the foregoing sentence shall be construed as relieving broadcasters . . . from the obligation under this chapter to operate in the public interest and to afford reasonable opportunity for the discussion of conflicting views on issues of public importance" as codifying the fairness doctrine in the Communications Act. This interpretation was the majority view until 1986, when the court of appeals held that the fairness doctrine was not codified in the Communications Act. *TRAC*, p. 672, *supra*. We will discuss the substance of this case—an appeal of the Commission's refusal to apply the fairness doctrine, as well as § 315 and § 312(a)(7) to teletext—in Chapter XVIII.

## IN THE MATTER OF THE HANDLING OF PUBLIC ISSUES UNDER THE FAIRNESS DOCTRINE AND THE PUBLIC INTEREST STANDARDS OF THE COMMUNICATIONS ACT
### (1974 FAIRNESS REPORT)
Federal Communications Commission, 1974.
48 F.C.C.2d 1, 30 R.R.2d 1261.

By the Commission: COMMISSIONER HOOKS concurring in part and dissenting in part and issuing a separate statement; COMMISSIONER QUELLO concurring and issuing a separate statement.

[The Commission first restated its commitment to the goal of "uninhibited, robust, wide open" debate on public issues and the need to recognize that achievement of this goal must be compatible with the public interest in "the larger and more effective use of radio" § 303(g). This included the fact that "ours is a commercially-based broadcast system" and that the Commission's policies "should be consistent with the maintenance and growth of that system." The Commission then quoted a critical passage from its Report on Editorializing, 13 F.C.C. 1246, 1249 (1949), in which the fairness doctrine was formally announced:

     It is axiomatic that one of the most vital questions of mass communication in a democracy is the development of an informed public opinion through the public dissemination of news and ideas concerning the vital public issues of the day.  .  .  .  The Commission has consequently recognized the necessity for licensees to devote a reasonable percentage of their broadcast time to the presentation of news and programs devoted to the consideration and discussion of public issues of interest in the community served by the particular station.  And we have recognized, with respect to such programs, the paramount right of the public in a free society to be informed and to have presented to it for acceptance or rejection the different attitudes and viewpoints concerning these vital and often controversial issues which are held by the various groups which make up the community.  It is this right of the public to be informed, rather than any right on the part of the Government, any broadcast licensee or any individual member of the public to broadcast his own particular views on any matter, which is the foundation stone of the American system of broadcasting.

The *1974 Fairness Report* stressed that two basic duties were involved: "(1) the broadcaster must devote a reasonable percentage of time to the coverage of public issues;  and (2) his coverage of these issues must be fair in the sense that it provides an opportunity for the presentation of contrasting points of view."  The Commission also noted that in 1970 it had described the two parts of the fairness doctrine "as the single most important requirement of operation in the public interest—the *sine qua non* for grant of a renewal of license."  The Commission denied that imposition of these two duties could be inhibiting:

18.   In evaluating the possible inhibitory effect of the fairness doctrine, it is appropriate to consider the specifics of the doctrine and the procedures employed by the Commission in implementing it. When a licensee presents one side of a controversial issue, he is not required to provide a forum for opposing views on that same program or series of programs.  He is simply expected to make provision for the opposing views in his *overall programming*.  Further, there is no requirement that any precisely equal balance of views be achieved, and all matters concerning the particular opposing views to be presented and the appropriate spokesmen and format for their presentation are left to the licensee's discretion subject only to a standard of reasonableness and good faith.

19.   As a matter of general procedure, we do not monitor broadcasts for possible violations, but act on the basis of complaints received from interested citizens.  These complaints are not forwarded to the licensee for his comments unless they present *prima facie* evidence of a violation.  Allen C. Phelps, 21 FCC2d 12 (1969). Thus, broadcasters are not burdened with the task of answering idle or capricious complaints.  By way of illustration, the Commission received some 2,400 fairness complaints in fiscal 1973, only 94 of which were forwarded to licensees for their comments.

20. While there may be occasional exceptions, we find it difficult to believe that these policies add significantly to the overall
administrative burdens involved in operating a broadcast station. . . . The Supreme Court has made it clear and it should
be reemphasized here that "if present licensees should suddenly
prove timorous, the Commission is not powerless to insist that they
give adequate and fair attention to public issues." Red Lion Broadcasting Co. v. FCC, 395 U.S. at 393.

As to the first duty imposed, the Commission noted:

We have, in the past, indicated that some issues are so critical or of
such great public importance that it would be unreasonable for a
licensee to ignore them completely. [  ] But such statements on
our part are the rare exception, not the rule, and we have no
intention of becoming involved in the selection of issues to be
discussed, nor do we expect a broadcaster to cover each and every
important issue which may arise in his community.

26. We wish to emphasize that the responsibility for the selection of program material is that of the individual licensee. That
responsibility "can neither be delegated by the licensee to any
network or other person or group, or be unduly fettered by contractual arrangements restricting the licensee in his free exercise of his
independent judgments." Report on Editorializing, 13 FCC at 1248.
We believe that stations, in carrying out this responsibility, should
be alert to the opportunity to complement network offerings with
local programming on these issues, or with syndicated programming.

The Commission then turned to the second, and more frequently litigated, aspect of the fairness doctrine.]

2. *A Reasonable Opportunity for Opposing Viewpoints*

. . .

28. It has frequently been suggested that individual stations should
not be expected to present opposing points of view and that it should be
sufficient for the licensee to demonstrate that the opposing viewpoint
has been adequately presented on another station in the market or in
the print media. See WSOC Broadcasting Co., 17 P & F Radio Reg. 548,
550 (1958). While we recognize that citizens receive information on
public issues from a variety of sources, other considerations require the
rejection of this suggestion. First, in amending section 315(a) of the
Communications Act in 1959, Congress gave statutory approval to the
fairness doctrine, including the requirement that broadcasters themselves provide an opportunity for opposing viewpoints. See BEM, 412
U.S. at 110, note 8. Second, it would be an administrative nightmare for
this Commission to attempt to review the overall coverage of an issue in
all of the broadcast stations and publications in a given market. Third,
and perhaps most importantly, we believe that the requirement that
*each* station provide for contrasting views greatly increases the likeli-

hood that individual members of the public will be exposed to varying points of view.    . . .

### a.  What is a "controversial issue of public importance"?

29.   It has frequently been suggested that the Commission set forth comprehensive guidelines to aid interested parties in recognizing whether an issue is "controversial" and of "public importance."   However, given the limitless number of potential controversial issues and the varying circumstances in which they might arise, we have not been able to develop detailed criteria which would be appropriate in all cases.   For this very practical reason, and for the reason that our role must and should be limited to one of review, we will continue to rely heavily on the reasonable, good faith judgments of our licensees in this area.

30.   Some general observations, however, are in order.   First of all, it is obvious that an issue is not necessarily a matter of significant "public importance" merely because it has received broadcast or newspaper coverage.   "Our daily papers and television broadcasts alike are filled with news items which good journalistic judgment would classify as newsworthy, but which the same editors would not characterize as containing important controversial public issues."   Healey v. FCC, 460 F.2d 917,. 922 (D.C.Cir.1972).   Nevertheless, the degree of media coverage is one factor which clearly should be taken into account in determining an issue's importance.   It is also appropriate to consider the degree of attention the issue has received from government officials and other community leaders.   The principal test of public importance, however, is not the extent of media or governmental attention, but rather a subjective evaluation of the impact that the issue is likely to have on the community at large.   If the issue involves a social or political choice, the licensee might well ask himself whether the outcome of that choice will have a significant impact on society or its institutions.   It appears to us that these judgments can be made only on a case-by-case basis.

31.   The question of whether an issue is "controversial" may be determined in a somewhat more objective manner.   Here, it is highly relevant to measure the degree of attention paid to an issue by government officials, community leaders, and the media.   The licensee should be able to tell, with a reasonable degree of objectivity, whether an issue is the subject of vigorous debate with substantial elements of the community in opposition to one another.   It is possible, of course, that "programs initiated with no thought on the part of the licensee of their possible controversial nature will subsequently arouse controversy and opposition of a substantial nature which will merit presentation of opposing views."   Report on Editorializing, 13 FCC at 1251.   In such circumstances, it would be appropriate to make provision for opposing views when the opposition becomes manifest.

### b. What specific issue has been raised?

32.  One of the most difficult problems involved in the administration of the fairness doctrine is the determination of the *specific* issue or issues raised by a particular program.  This would seem to be a simple task, but in many cases it is not.  . . .

. . .

### c. What is a "reasonable opportunity" for contrasting viewpoints?

. . .

37.  The first point to be made with regard to the obligation to present contrasting views is that it cannot be met "merely through the adoption of a general policy of not refusing to broadcast opposing views where a demand is made of the station for broadcast time."  Report on Editorializing, 13 FCC at 1251.  The licensee has a duty to play a conscious and positive role in encouraging the presentation of opposing viewpoints.[13]  . . .

38.  In making provision for the airing of contrasting viewpoints, the broadcaster should be alert to the possibility that a particular issue may involve more than two opposing viewpoints.  Indeed, there may be several important viewpoints or shades of opinion which warrant broadcast coverage.

. . .

41.  In providing for the coverage of opposing points of view, we believe that the licensee must make a reasonable allowance for presentations by genuine partisans who actually believe in what they are saying. The fairness doctrine does not permit the broadcaster "to preside over a 'paternalistic' regime," BEM, 412 U.S. at 130, and it would clearly not be acceptable for the licensee to adopt a "policy of excluding partisan voices and always itself presenting views in a bland, inoffensive manner. . . ."  . . .

42.  This does not mean, however, that the Commission intends to dictate the selection of a particular spokesman or a particular format, or indeed that partisan spokesmen must be presented in every instance. We do not believe that it is either appropriate or feasible for a governmental agency to make decisions as to what is desirable in each situation.  In cases involving personal attacks and political campaigns, the natural opposing spokesmen are relatively easy to identify.  This is not

---

**13.**  This duty includes the obligation defined in Cullman Broadcasting Co., 40 FCC 576, 577 (1963) . . ..

We do not believe that the passage of time since *Cullman* was decided has in any way diminished the importance and necessity of this principle.  If the public's right to be informed of the contrasting views on controversial issues is to be truly honored, broadcasters must provide the forum for the expression of those viewpoints at their own expense if paid sponsorship is unavailable.

the case, however, with the majority of public controversies. Ordinarily, there are a variety of spokesmen and formats which could reasonably be deemed to be appropriate. We believe that the public is best served by a system which allows individual broadcasters considerable discretion in selecting the manner of coverage, the appropriate spokesmen, and the techniques of production and presentation.

43.    Frequently, the question of the reasonableness of the opportunity provided for contrasting viewpoints comes down to weighing the *time* allocated to each side. Aside from the field of political broadcasting, the licensee is not required to provide equal time for the various opposing points of view. Indeed, we have long felt that the basic goal of creating an informed citizenry would be frustrated if for every controversial item or presentation on a newscast or other broadcast the licensee had to offer equal time to the other side.    .  .  .    Similarly, we do not believe that it would be appropriate for this Commission to establish any other mathematical ratio, such as 3 to 1 or 4 to 1, to be applied in all cases. We believe that such an approach is much too mechanical in nature and that in many cases our pre-conceived ratios would prove to be far from reasonable. In the case of a 10–second personal attack, for example, fairness may dictate that more time be afforded to answer the attack than was given the attack itself.

.  .  .

### E.    Fairness and Accurate News Reporting

58.    In our 1949 Report on Editorializing, we alluded to a licensee's obligation to present the news in an accurate manner:

> It must be recognized, however, that the licensee's opportunity to express his own views  .  .  .   does not justify or empower any licensee to exercise his authority over the selection of program material to distort or suppress the basic factual information upon which any truly fair and free discussion of public issues must necessarily depend.   .  .  .   A licensee would be abusing his position as public trustee of these important means of mass communication were he to withhold from expression over his facilities relevant news or facts concerning a controversy or to slant or distort the presentation of such news. No discussion of the issues involved in any controversy can be fair or in the public interest where such discussion must take place in a climate of false or misleading information concerning the basic facts of the controversy, 13 FCC at 1254–55.

It is a matter of critical importance to the public that the basic facts or elements of a controversy should not be deliberately suppressed or misstated by a licensee. But, we must recognize that such distortions are "so continually done in perfect good faith, by persons who are not considered  .  .  .  ignorant or incompetent, that it is rarely possible, on adequate grounds, conscientiously to stamp the misrepresentations as morally culpable.   .  .  ." J.S. Mill, On Liberty 31 (People's ed. 1921).

Accordingly, we do not believe that it would be either useful or appropriate for us to investigate charges of news misrepresentations in the absence of substantial extrinsic evidence or documents that on their face reflect deliberate distortion. See The Selling of the Pentagon, 30 F.C.C.2d 150 (1971).

## Notes and Questions

1. In 1976 the Commission denied reconsideration of the *1974 Fairness Report*. 58 F.C.C.2d 691, 36 R.R.2d 1021 (1976). Commissioner Robinson dissented because he doubted the value of the efforts involved and was concerned about the intrusion into editorial decisions. He noted that in 1973 and 1974, of 4,280 formal fairness complaints, only 19 resulted in findings adverse to the licensee. These included seven in the political editorial area, seven cases of personal attack and five general fairness complaints. Of the 19 violations, only eight resulted in tangible penalty to the licensee—seven political editorializing cases and one personal attack case involved forfeitures under § 503. Because this sanction is available only for violations of formal rules, it was not available for violations of the uncodified general doctrine.

2. *The Affirmative Duty to Raise Issues.* The Commission referred to the fairness doctrine as having two parts. Virtually all the litigation and discussion have involved the second part: the requirement that a licensee who presented one side of a controversial issue of public importance had to present contrasting views.

In 1976, for the first time, the Commission applied the first part. A Congresswoman sent an 11–minute tape opposing strip mining to West Virginia radio stations to counter a presentation in favor of strip mining that had been distributed to many stations by the U.S. Chamber of Commerce. One station, WHAR, refused to play the tape because it had not presented the first program. Indeed, it had presented nothing on the issue except items on regular newscasts taken from the AP news service. Several persons and groups complained to the Commission contending that in this part of West Virginia at this time the question of strip mining was of primary importance. In its renewal application WHAR had cited "development of new industry" and "air and water pollution" as issues of great concern to its listeners. In addition, bills on the subject were pending in Congress at the time and local newspapers were extensively discussing the question. (Presentation of a five-minute tape by an outspoken foe of strip mining was not relevant because he did not discuss the economic or ecological aspects of strip mining or the pending legislation.)

The Commission asserted that although a violation of the first part "would be an exceptional situation and would not counter our intention to stay out of decisions concerning the selection of specific programming matter," this was such a case and demonstrated an "unreasonable exercise" of discretion. The Commission quoted the passage from *Red Lion* that "if the present licensees should suddenly prove timorous, the Commission is not powerless to insist that they give adequate and fair attention to public issues." The lack of any prior request to program on this subject was irrelevant because "it is the station's obligation to make an affirmative effort to program on issues of concern to its community." The role of the AP news items was minimal because it was not even clear which ones were aired. "Where, as in the present case, an issue has significant and possibly unique impact on the licensee's service area, it will not be sufficient for the licensee as an indication of compliance with the fairness doctrine to show that it may have broadcast an unknown amount of news touching on a general topic related to the issue cited in a complaint." The station was ordered to tell the Commission within 20 days how it intended to meet its fairness obligations. Rep. Patsy Mink, 59 F.C.C.2d 987, 37 R.R.2d 744 (1976).

What is the difference between saying (1) a station has an obligation to present programs on the need for good dental hygiene, even though the subject may not be controversial and (2) a station must present programs on a controversial issue in the community? Are both covered by the fairness doctrine?

What is the justification for requiring each station in a community to present a range of views on controversial issues of public importance? Why is it not enough if the spectrum as a whole provides contrasting viewpoints? Is there more—or less—reason to require a station to raise important subjects when other stations in the community are doing so? Thus, in the strip mining case, should it matter that other broadcasters are devoting extensive coverage to the subject? What has this obligation to do with "fairness"?

3. *Defining the "Issue."* In American Security Council Educational Foundation v. Federal Communications Commission, 607 F.2d 438, 45 R.R.2d 1433, 5 Med.L.Rptr. 1193 (D.C.Cir.1979), the ASCEF analyzed a full year's news programming of CBS. It transcribed all CBS news reports, broke them into sentences, and then determined whether each was relevant to four topics: "United States military and foreign affairs; Soviet Union military and foreign affairs; China military and foreign affairs; and Vietnam affairs." Each relevant sentence was put into one of three categories: Viewpoint A was that the "threat to U.S. security is more serious than perceived by the government or that the United States ought to *increase* its national security efforts." Viewpoint B was that the government's perception is essentially correct and viewpoint C was that the threat is less serious than perceived and national security efforts should be decreased. The ASCEF analysis put 3.54 percent of the content into viewpoint A; 34.63 percent into viewpoint B, and 61.83 percent into viewpoint C. Based on these results and claimed similar disparities for later years, ASCEF filed a fairness complaint with the FCC asking that CBS be ordered to provide a reasonable opportunity for the expression of "A viewpoints."

The FCC dismissed the complaint without calling for any response from CBS on the ground that the complaint did not identify "the particular issue of a controversial nature" that was involved.   The court, 6–3, affirmed:

> We affirm the Commission's decision that ASCEF failed to base its complaint on a particular well-defined issue because (1) the indirect relationships among the issues aggregated by ASCEF under the umbrella of "national security" do not provide a basis for determining whether the public received a reasonable balance of conflicting views, and (2) a contrary result would unduly burden broadcasters without a countervailing benefit to the public's right to be informed.

Since the fairness doctrine was issue-oriented, it was essential that the "issue" be clearly identified.   Here "national security" was an umbrella that held within it too many issues that were only tangentially related, such as detente with China, America's commitment to NATO, SALT, and response to the Soviet Union's role in the Middle East.

The court suggested that a fairness complaint could be based on an issue that consisted of separately identifiable subissues only if the main issue was well defined.   If ASCEF had used single issues it could have analyzed actual views "instead of superimposing artificial A, B, and C viewpoints on the broadcasts studied."   Then the FCC could have determined the question of balance and, if necessary, framed a specific remedy.

Acceptance of ASCEF's approach would also have burdened broadcasters.   "CBS could have had to review all of its news programming relevant to national security over at least a year's time.   . . .   It would have been virtually impossible to know which broadcasts should be included as relevant to national security, or how views discussed   . . .   should be tallied to measure 'balance' under the fairness doctrine."

Further burdens would have fallen on editors: "An editor preparing an evening newscast would be required to decide whether any of the day's newsworthy events is tied, even tangentially, to events covered in the past, and whether a report on today's lead story, in some remote way, balances yesterday's, last week's or last year's." *Certiorari* was denied 444 U.S. 1013 (1980).

4.   What constitutes balance?   In paragraph 43 of the *1974 Fairness Report*, p. 729, *supra*, the Commission rejected any strict mathematical determination of balance.   Instead, in each case the Commission decided whether in its judgment the licensee acted reasonably in concluding that the coverage was balanced.   The factors considered included the total amount of time devoted to each side, the frequency with which each side was presented and the size of audience for each presentation.   For an extensive discussion of this process see Public Media Center v. Federal Communications Commission, 587 F.2d 1322, 44 R.R.2d 721 (D.C.Cir. 1978).

5.   *Commercials.*   In the 1960s the Commission decided that advertisements for cigarettes required stations to present some programming on

the dangers of smoking.   This ruling was upheld in Banzhaf v. Federal
Communications Commission, 405 F.2d 1082, 14 R.R.2d 2061, 1 Med.
L.Rptr. 2037 (D.C.Cir.1968), cert. denied 396 U.S. 842 (1969).   Although
the licensee could decide how to meet this requirement, most licensees
presented material that had been prepared by the American Cancer
Society and similar organizations.   We trace subsequent developments in
cigarette advertising in the next note.

The Commission attempted to treat the cigarette case as unique.
Thus, when opponents of high-powered automobiles wanted the FCC to
require licensees to present contrasting views on the value of such cars,
the FCC refused.   On appeal, the court of appeals could not distinguish
the cigarette situation from the high-powered car situation and ordered
the FCC to be consistent.   Friends of the Earth v. Federal Communications Commission, 449 F.2d 1164, 22 R.R.2d 2145 (D.C.Cir.1971).

The Commission, in an omitted portion of the *1974 Fairness Report*,
rethought the question of applying the fairness doctrine to commercials.
It finally decided to divide commercials into those that simply try to sell
products and those that present a "meaningful statement which obviously addresses, and advocates a point of view on, a controversial issue of
public importance."   The latter, also called "editorial advertisements,"
gave rise to obligations under the fairness doctrine.   If an advertisement
is false or misleading, it might give rise to some action by the Federal
Trade Commission or by competitors, but the fairness doctrine was not
the appropriate way to handle commercials that did not address public
issues.

This position was quickly challenged in the courts in a case involving a commercial for snowmobiles.   Environmental groups complained
that the commercials showed only one side of the controversial issue of
the desirability of snowmobiles.   The FCC rejected the complaint on the
ground that, although the environmental effects of snowmobiles might
involve a controversial issue of public importance, the commercials
themselves were not devoted to an obvious or meaningful discussion of
that issue.

The court of appeals affirmed.   Public Interest Research Group v.
Federal Communications Commission, 522 F.2d 1060, 34 R.R.2d 1375
(1st Cir.1975), cert. denied 424 U.S. 965 (1976).   The appellants argued
that the FCC had no authority to retreat from its earlier rulings that
selling commercials might invoke the fairness doctrine.   The court
disagreed.   "In the absence of statutory or constitutional barriers, an
agency may abandon earlier precedents and frame new policies."   Congress had not frozen the fairness doctrine in any particular form.   Nor
was there any reason to require the FCC to apply the doctrine to all
commercials or to none.

Finally, the appellants argued that the First Amendment itself
required that the fairness doctrine be rigorously enforced so that the
airwaves would be true public forums for the presentation of divergent
views.   The court rejected this argument.   Although the *Red Lion*

approach might be furthered by extending the fairness doctrine to all advertising, the court did "not view that question, in the short and long run, as so free from doubt that courts should impose an inflexible response as a matter of constitutional law. We believe that the first amendment permitted the Commission not only to experiment with full-scale application of the fairness doctrine to advertising but also to retreat from its experiment when it determined from experience that the extension was unworkable."

6. *Cigarettes.* After the *Banzhaf* decision, Congress moved into the picture. In 1969 it adopted 15 U.S.C.A. § 1335: "After January 1, 1971, it shall be unlawful to advertise cigarettes on any medium of electronic communication subject to the jurisdiction of the Federal Communications Commission."

The statute was challenged by broadcasters—but not by cigarette manufacturers. It was upheld by a three-judge court in Capital Broadcasting Co. v. Mitchell, 333 F.Supp. 582 (D.D.C.1971), aff'd without opinion 415 U.S. 1000 (1972). The dissenting opinion in the lower court suggested that the cigarette manufacturers were not at all unhappy to be ordered to stop advertising on radio and television because it had become unprofitable.

The court rejected the argument that this amounted to censorship in violation of § 326 because licensees were still free to present pro-smoking messages—except to the extent that Congress had forbidden commercial messages. The Commission was leaving that decision to the licensees. Moreover, some aspects of anti-smoking messages might still be found to invoke the fairness doctrine—but health danger was not one of them. Also, it was permissible to consider at renewal time whether a licensee carried programs on the dangers of smoking—not because it was a controversial issue, but because one aspect of meeting the public interest is to warn about dangers to health and safety, even if they are obvious and non-controversial. What might the Commission do at renewal time if it found that a licensee had presented several debates on cigarette smoking in which half the speakers argued that there was no health hazard in smoking? Is there a tension between saying that licensees are free to program pro-smoking material if they wish and that they will be judged at renewal time on how they have programmed on matters of health and safety?

## 2. PERSONAL ATTACK RULES

As we saw in *Red Lion,* p. 635, *supra,* the personal attack part of the general fairness doctrine was crystallized into a rule, 47 C.F.R. § 73.123:

(a) When, during the presentation of views on a controversial issue of public importance, an attack is made upon the honesty, character, integrity or like personal qualities of an identified person or group, the licensee shall, within a reasonable time and in no event later than 1 week after the attack, transmit to the person or group attacked (1) notification of the date, time and identification of the broadcast; (2) a script or tape (or an accurate summary if a script or tape is not available) of the attack; and (3) an offer of a reasonable opportunity to respond over the licensee's facilities.

(b) The provisions of paragraph (a) of this section shall not be applicable (1) to attacks on foreign groups or foreign public figures; (2) to personal attacks which are made by legally qualified candidates, their authorized spokesmen, or those associated with them in the campaign, on other such candidates, their authorized spokesmen, or persons associated with the candidates in the campaign; and (3) to bona fide newscasts, bona fide news interviews, and on-the-spot coverage of a bona fide news event (including commentary or analysis contained in the foregoing programs, but the provisions of paragraph (a) of this section shall be applicable to editorials of the licensee).

The first point to note is that the episode must occur "during the presentation of views on a controversial issue of public importance." This limitation means that personal attacks unrelated to such a discussion do not invoke the rule—and presumably are left exclusively to defamation suits. Why is this distinction drawn?

Sometimes it is difficult to determine what constitutes "during the presentation of views on a controversial issue of public importance." In Straus Communications, Inc. v. Federal Communications Commission, 530 F.2d 1001, 35 R.R.2d 1649 (D.C.Cir.1976), a licensee's argument that time for reply was not justified because the attack did not take place during such a discussion was rejected by the Commission. On appeal, the court ruled that the Commission had used the wrong standard when stating that it "believed" that the comment was sufficiently related to an earlier discussion of a meat boycott to justify the conclusion that the personal attack occurred during a continuation of that discussion. The court concluded that the proper approach was for the Commission to judge "the objective reasonableness of the licensee's determination" that the meat boycott discussion had long since ended.

See also Polish American Congress v. Federal Communications Commission, 520 F.2d 1248, 34 R.R.2d 1359 (7th Cir.1975), cert. denied 424 U.S. 927 (1976), in which the complainants had claimed that a skit of Polish jokes on television violated the personal attack part of the fairness doctrine. The Commission rejected the complaint. On appeal, the court stated that the order had to be upheld "if the Commission properly determined that ABC's conclusion that the broadcast did not involve a controversial issue of public importance was not unreasonable nor in bad faith." The court concluded that "the Commission was correct in ruling that ABC did not overstep its discretion in failing to find a controversial issue of public importance." This was true whether the issue was stated to be (1) whether "Polish Americans are inferior to other human beings in terms of intelligence, personal hygiene, etc." or (2) whether "promulgating" Polish jokes by broadcasting them is desirable. If the former, ABC could reasonably conclude that even if some people felt that way they had not generated enough support to raise a controversial issue of public importance. Even if they had, ABC could conclude that the skit presented did not constitute a "discussion" of this issue. If the issue was the latter, no controversy was shown.

Another issue raised in *Polish American Congress* (although it was not addressed due to the lack of a controversial issue of public importance) was the size of the group attacked. Remember from the discussion of group libel, p. 89, *supra*, that once the group gets too large there is no identification—the individual plaintiff would have difficulty showing that his own personal reputation was harmed. Should the same apply to the personal attack rule when the attack is on a large group rather than on an individual or on a small group? In Diocese of Rockville Centre, 50 F.C.C.2d 330, 32 R.R.2d 376 (1973), a licensee had broadcast a statement that perhaps an earlier writer was correct when he stated "The Roman Church is filled with men who were led into it merely by ambition, who though they might have been useful and respectful as laymen, are hypocritical and immoral." The Commission ruled that the group is not sufficiently "identified" unless the licensee "could reasonably be expected to know exactly who or what finite group" is best able to inform the public of the contrasting viewpoint. The reference to "men" who fill the "Roman Church" was found too vague.

The Commission has made clear that attacks during discussion of controversial issues of public importance are not misbehavior—and wide-open debate is encouraged—so long as the rules are followed.

### 3. FAIRNESS IN POLITICAL CAMPAIGNS

The fairness doctrine entered into political issues in two ways. The first involved the use of broadcasting by the party in power, particularly the President, between political campaigns. The courts took the view that when the President spoke on an issue of national concern, the party out of power had no automatic right to reply. The only exception occurred when the President delivered five uninterrupted speeches during a seven-month period about the war in Indochina. Because broadcast coverage of that dispute had otherwise been roughly in balance, the FCC decided that the networks were obligated to provide free time for a spokesman from the other side of the issue.

But that instance aside, the courts considered the speeches of a President just one factor to weigh in deciding whether the required rough balance in the presentation of contrasting views had been achieved. As usual, the FCC would generally defer to the views of the licensees, and the courts would generally defer to the views of the FCC. The subject is explored extensively in Democratic National Committee v. Federal Communications Commission, 481 F.2d 543, 27 R.R.2d 168 (D.C.Cir.1973) (unsuccessful Democratic attempt to obtain free reply time to counter President's speeches on economic policy.)

The second role of the fairness doctrine in politics involves the campaign itself. Because § 315 was construed not to cover appearances by anyone other than candidates, and because the section also does not cover ballot propositions, many important political campaign broadcasts must be regulated, if at all, under provisions much less precise than § 315. Not surprisingly, as television has become increasingly important in election campaigns, questions not covered by § 315 have arisen more frequently.

### a. Uses by Supporters

Turning first to a close parallel situation, what are the controlling principles when Candidate A's friends or campaign committee purchase time to further his candidacy or to attack B, his opponent? In its Letter to Nicholas Zapple, 23 F.C.C.2d 707, 19 R.R.2d 421 (1970), the Commission stated that the 1959 amendment to § 315 had explicitly recognized the operation of the fairness doctrine when the candidate's own appearance was exempted from § 315. The doctrine was thought equally applicable here. Moreover, when a candidate is supported or his opponent attacked, although the licensee has the responsibility of identifying suitable speakers for opposing views, "barring unusual circumstances, it would not be reasonable for a licensee to refuse to sell time to spokesmen for or supporters of candidate B comparable to that previously bought on behalf of candidate A." But there was no obligation to provide B's supporters with free time. Although usually requiring that time be given away, if necessary, to get contrasting views before the public, the Commission thought this unsound in the political arena. To hold otherwise would require licensees, or other advertisers, to subsidize B's campaign. The rejection of subsidization meant that even if A's friends mounted a personal attack on B, B would not get free time. The Commission has adhered closely to the *Zapple* ruling, which is sometimes referred to as the "quasi equal opportunities" or "political party" corollary to the fairness doctrine.

In 1979 the Commission decided that Congress intended that "uses" under § 315 and *Zapple* were to be mutually exclusive of the fairness doctrine. The Commission concluded that licensees should not be responsible for "uses" since they have no control over them. As a result, the personal attack rule was rewritten to provide that it did not apply to personal attacks occurring during uses under § 315 or those occurring under *Zapple* situations.

More generally, the fairness doctrine was declared not to apply to issues raised during "uses." The Commission believed that issues raised during "uses" were likely to be of such public interest that other views would be aired in due course without the goad of the fairness doctrine. Personal Attacks and Applicability of the Fairness Doctrine to Section 315 "Uses," 78 F.C.C.2d 457, 45 R.R.2d 1635 (1979).

A new problem emerged in 1980 involving groups organized by friends of Ronald Reagan but not controlled by the candidate. These groups are not bound by spending limits that may bind the candidates themselves. When these groups began to buy time on broadcast stations, the Carter campaign committee complained to the FCC that the stations selling time to these "independent expenditure groups" should be required to make equal, and free, opportunities available to the Carter campaign (and presumably to all other campaigns). These should be free, the Carter committee asserted, because it and the Reagan campaign were each limited to $29.4 million for campaigning because they agreed to accept federal funds. As a result, they could not match both the money Reagan was spending and that being spent by the independent groups.

The FCC rejected the claim on the ground that friends of Carter could start comparable groups to match the expenditures being made by the Reagan groups. To allow the Carter campaign free time would put the Commission in the position of benefitting one of the candidates at the expense of the other, whose friends had been required to pay for his time.

In *Kennedy II,* p. 727, *supra,* after rejecting the candidate's claims under § 312 and § 315, the court turned to the role of the fairness doctrine in political campaigns. The Broadcast Bureau and the Commission had found three fatal flaws in Kennedy's reliance on the fairness doctrine in this case—and the court agreed. First, he had failed to define the particular controversial issue involved with sufficient specificity. Second, there was no showing that the networks had failed to present contrasting viewpoints on the national economy in their overall programming. The fairness doctrine "does not operate with the dissective focus of" § 315(a). "Intelligent assessment of the nature and caliber of a broadcaster's overall programming obviously cannot be confined to one program, or even to one day's presentations, so a failure to show some fairness deficiency on the whole is necessarily fatal."

Even if imbalance were established, the third flaw was that Senator Kennedy had no "individual right to broadcast his views on the current economic crisis." Kennedy did not show that he was "uniquely and singularly qualified to represent those who dispute the President's economic leadership or strategies."

Finally, the fairness doctrine extended to political campaigns because the question of which candidate should be elected might be considered a "controversial issue of public importance." This means that even if no requests for time were made under § 315 or § 312, a broadcaster might be required to introduce the issue under the first part of the fairness doctrine. If some views had been expressed about the campaign during non-uses, the licensee would have been obligated under the second part of the doctrine to provide coverage of contrasting views.

The Commission's dismissal of a fairness complaint alleging unbalanced coverage of economic matters was upheld in Democratic National Committee v. Federal Communications Commission, 717 F.2d 1471, 54 R.R.2d 941 (1983). Disparities approximating 3 to 1 and 4 to 1 in favor of the pro-Administration economic view occurred on the networks. Compliance with fairness doctrine obligations was to be measured by a standard of good faith and reasonableness, not by reference to "rough approximations of equality." Because the disparities were not "glaring," and the audiences were not shown to be very different in size, the Commission's dismissal of the complaint was reasonable. Although the court cited data showing that fairness complainants prevailed in roughly 1 in 1,000 cases, the court rejected Commission statements that fairness complaints would inevitably be futile.

### b. Political Editorials

In a section of the personal attack rules, 47 C.F.R. § 73.123(c), the Commission covered political editorials:

> (c) Where a licensee, in an editorial (i) endorses or (ii) opposes a legally qualified candidate or candidates, the licensee shall, within 24 hours after the editorial, transmit to respectively (i) the other qualified candidate or candidates for the same office or (ii) the candidate opposed in the editorial (1) notification of the date and the time of the editorial; (2) a script or tape of the editorial; and (3) an offer of a reasonable opportunity for a candidate or a spokesman of the candidate to respond over the licensee's facilities: *Provided, however,* That where such editorials are broadcast within 72 hours prior to the day of the election, the licensee shall comply with the provisions of this paragraph sufficiently far in advance of the broadcast to enable the candidate or candidates to have a reasonable opportunity to prepare a response and to present it in a timely fashion.

Be sure to note that a single editorial on behalf of one candidate creates an opportunity to respond for *each* opposing candidate. This is true regardless of the number of opposing candidates. Friends of Howard Miller, 72 F.C.C.2d 508, 45 R.R.2d 1142 (1979).

### c. Ballot Propositions

In an omitted part of the *1974 Fairness Report*, the Commission reached the conclusion that such matters as referenda, initiative and recall propositions, bond proposals and constitutional amendments were to be regulated under the general fairness doctrine. The area was thought closer to general political discussion not involving elections than it was to the election of individuals to office. Thus, the *Cullman* doctrine requiring the licensee to present contrasting views, by the use of free time if necessary, was applicable. One argument against the *Cullman* doctrine was that some groups might spend their available money on non-broadcast media, wait for the other side to buy broadcast time, and then insist on free time under *Cullman* to counter their adversary. The Commission was not persuaded. First, this concern could always be raised against *Cullman* but the Commission thought it most important that the public have access to contrasting views. On the tactical level, the Commission noted that the fairness doctrine did not guarantee equality of exposure of views nor who would be chosen as speakers. Those who relied solely on *Cullman* "have no assurance of obtaining equality by such means." Fairness Report, 48 F.C.C.2d 1, 33, 30 R.R.2d 1261, 1302 (1974).

### 4.　THE ELIMINATION OF THE FAIRNESS DOCTRINE

As noted earlier, in 1987 the Commission eliminated the fairness doctrine. We now turn to the sequence of events that led to that decision, beginning with the *1985 Fairness Report.* Inquiry Into Section 73.1910 of the Commission's Rules and Regulations Concerning the General Fairness Doctrine Obligations of Broadcast Licensees, 102 F.C.C.2d 143, 58 R.R.2d 1137 (1985). In the report the Commission concluded that the doctrine was no longer justified. Although it did not question "the interest of the listening and viewing public in obtaining access to diverse and antagonistic sources of information," the FCC thought that the doctrine was neither a "necessary or appropriate means by which to effectuate this interest." The interest in "viewpoint diversity is fully served by the multiplicity of voices in the marketplace today." Moreover, "the intrusion by government into the content of programming occasioned by the enforcement of the doctrine unnecessarily restricts the journalistic freedom of broadcasters" and "actually inhibits the presentation of controversial issues of public importance to the detriment of the public and in degradation of the editorial prerogatives of broadcast journalists."

On the scarcity point, the FCC asserted that since *Red Lion* there had been a 48 percent increase in radio outlets and a 44 percent increase in television outlets. By 1984, 96 percent of television households received five or more signals. During that period the networks' share of the market had declined from 90 percent to 76 percent and the number of independent television stations had risen from 90 to 214. Other electronic distribution systems, such as cable and multichannel multipoint distribution systems, had exploded. Finally, the FCC pointed to the continued availability of over 1,700 daily newspapers and the increase in the number of periodicals from 6,960 in 1950 to 10,688 in 1982. The Commission concluded that "the dynamics of the information services marketplace overall insures that the public will be sufficiently exposed to controversial issues of public importance."

On the inhibition point, the Commission stressed that the fairness doctrine reduced the number of diverse views and the amount of controversial programming reaching the public. The reasoning began with the fact that enforcement of the first prong of the doctrine was virtually nonexistent. But the responsive programming requirement of the second prong came into play whenever a licensee undertook to present controversial programs even if beyond what was required under the first prong. The result was that broadcasters were being encouraged "to air only the minimal amount of controversial issue programming sufficient to comply with the first prong. By restricting the amount and type of controversial programming aired, a broadcaster minimizes the potentially substantial burdens associated with the second prong of the doctrine."

Broadcasters were burdened by being found in violation of the second prong because of the risks of being ordered to present programs without compensation or of having to defend against the charges and incurring legal expenses. The Commission cited the Spokane station that spent $20,000 in legal fees in successfully defending a fairness charge and NBC's expense of more than $100,000 in an earlier case. The more remote risk of nonrenewal was an additional burden listed by the Commission.

The answer was not to enforce the first prong more rigorously because that "would increase the government's intrusion into the editorial decisionmaking process of broadcast journalists. It would enlarge the opportunity for governmental officials to abuse the doctrine for partisan political purposes."

The FCC also noted that it was inextricably involved in the "dangerous task of evaluating the merits of particular viewpoints" as it tried to distinguish statements that are "significant enough to warrant broadcast coverage" and those that "do not rise to the level of a major viewpoint of sufficient public importance that triggers responsive programming obligations."

If a responsive obligation was imposed, the Commission had to then consider the content offered by the licensee to show that it had met its obligation. In addition, the Commission noted how much of its staff time was needed to deal with inquiries and complaints related to the doctrine—6,787 in 1984. Finally, the Commission cited examples in which the fairness doctrine was misused by White House administrations intent upon gaining political advantage.

All of these costs were said to be unnecessary because of the recent increase in available information sources. To the argument that the doctrine was useful to provide broadcasters with a protection against outside pressures, the Commission responded that broadcasters were not asking for such protection and that print journalists did not need such protection.

Despite all the negative points made in the report, the Commission did not eliminate the doctrine. Instead, because of the "intense Congressional interest in the Fairness Doctrine" and uncertainty as to whether the doctrine was codified in § 315 of the Communications Act, the FCC deferred action until Congress had an opportunity to review the report—and announced that it would continue to enforce the doctrine.

However, during the 1980s a fairness complaint against Meredith Corporation's WTVH in Syracuse, N.Y., was working its way through the Commission and the court of appeals. Initially, the Commission found the station had violated the fairness doctrine. The court of appeals reversed and remanded. The Commission then decided that the doctrine was unconstitutional and that it disserved the public interest. The Commission's decision was appealed by the public interest group that had brought the original fairness complaint.

## SYRACUSE PEACE COUNCIL v. FEDERAL COMMUNICATIONS COMMISSION

United States Court of Appeals, District of Columbia Circuit, 1989.
867 F.2d 654, 65 R.R.2d 1759, 16 Med.L.Rptr. 1225.

Before WALD, CHIEF JUDGE, and STARR and WILLIAMS, CIRCUIT JUDGES.

WILLIAMS, CIRCUIT JUDGE.

Under the "fairness doctrine," the Federal Communications Commission has, as its 1985 Fairness Report explains, required broadcast media licensees (i) "to provide coverage of vitally important controversial issues of interest in the community served by the licensees," and (2) "to provide a reasonable opportunity for the presentation of contrasting viewpoints on such issues." [  ] In adjudication of a complaint against Meredith Corporation, licensee of station WTVH in Syracuse, New York, the Commission concluded that the doctrine did not serve the public interest and was unconstitutional. Accordingly it refused to enforce the doctrine against Meredith. Although the Commission somewhat entangled its public interest and constitutional findings, we find that the Commission's public interest determination was an independent basis for its decision and was supported by the record. We uphold that determination without reaching the constitutional issue.

### I.

In the summer of 1982 Meredith ran a series of advertisements over WTVH arguing that the Nine Mile II nuclear power plant was a "sound investment for New York." Syracuse Peace Council complained to the Commission that Meredith had failed to give viewers conflicting perspectives on the plant and had thereby violated the second of the fairness doctrine's two requirements.

In its initial decision the Commission agreed with Syracuse that Meredith had failed to fulfill its obligations under the doctrine and demanded that the station within 20 days give notice of how it planned to meet those obligations. [  ]

Meredith filed a petition for reconsideration in which it argued that the fairness doctrine was unconstitutional. [  ] Before ruling on Meredith's petition, the Commission completed its 1985 Fairness Report, the culmination of a separate inquiry into both the wisdom and constitutionality of the fairness doctrine. [  ]

On the issue of whether the doctrine continued to promote the public interest, the 1985 Report said that the Commission was "firmly convinced that the fairness doctrine, as a matter of policy, disserves the public interest . . ." [  ] In reaching that conclusion the Commis-

sion invoked essentially the same grounds as it has in the present
action—chiefly, that growth in the number of broadcast outlets reduced
any need for the doctrine, that the doctrine often worked to dissuade
broadcasters from presenting *any* treatment of controversial viewpoints,
that it put the government in the doubtful position of evaluating
program content, and that it created an opportunity for incumbents to
abuse it for partisan purposes.  Despite all this, it declined to eliminate
the doctrine, expressing concern that it might be statutorily mandated.
[   ]

The 1985 Report also raised serious doubts about the continuing
constitutionality of the fairness doctrine, but, saying that it was "the
province of the federal judiciary—and not this Commission—to interpret
the Constitution," [   ], the Commission refused to make a constitutional
ruling.

After issuing the 1985 Report, the FCC in due course considered
Meredith's petition for reconsideration.  In that context it again refused
to address the constitutional issue—not on the ground that Meredith
had raised the defense belatedly but solely on the theory that that issue
should be left to Congress and the courts.  It invoked its 1985 Report in
support of this view.  [   ]

On appeal, this court reversed and remanded the case to the
Commission.  [   ]  We noted the principle that regulatory agencies
cannot invalidate an act of Congress, [   ], but said that an agency could
not blind itself to a constitutional defense to a "self-generated" policy.
[   ]  In the meantime, we observed, this court had in another decision
found that the fairness doctrine was *not* mandated by statute.  [*TRAC*]
Thus on remand the Commission would have to resolve Meredith's
constitutional defense, *unless* it determined in light of the 1985 Report
that enforcement of the doctrine was contrary to the public interest.
[   ]  We explicitly noted that the 1985 Report had concluded that indeed
the doctrine no longer served the public interest standard of the Communications Act, [   ], and that in the Report the Commission had "largely
undermined the legitimacy of its own rule" and "eviscerate[d] the
rationale" for the doctrine.

On remand, the Commission expanded the scope of the Meredith
proceedings by soliciting comments from the public on the general
questions whether "in light of the 1985 Fairness Report, enforcement of
the fairness doctrine is constitutional and whether enforcement of the
doctrine is contrary to the public interest."  [   ]  In its Memorandum
Order and Opinion [   ], the Commission ruled in favor of Meredith.

The FCC relied heavily on the conclusions drawn in the 1985
Fairness Report, and in fact incorporated that Report into the record and
"reaffirm[ed] [its] findings and conclusions."  [   ]  After reciting and
endorsing the 1985 Fairness Report's conclusions, the Commission declared that "the fairness doctrine chills speech and is not narrowly
tailored to achieve a substantial government interest."  [   ]  Consequently, the FCC concluded "under existing Supreme Court precedent,

as set forth in *Red Lion* and its progeny, that the fairness doctrine contravenes the First Amendment and thereby disserves the public interest." [  ]

## II.

At no time during the long and intricate proceedings in this case has any party suggested that the fairness doctrine is constitutionally compelled. Nor can it be claimed here, in view of this court's TRAC decision, that the doctrine is statutorily mandated. Accordingly, the Commission has the authority to reject the doctrine if it concludes, without being arbitrary or capricious, that it no longer serves the public interest.

The Commission has slightly complicated the issue, however, by asserting that "the policy and constitutional considerations in this matter are inextricably intertwined." [  ] If that were true, we could resolve the case only by addressing the constitutional issue.

But it is an elementary canon that American courts are not to "pass upon a constitutional question . . . if there is also present some other ground upon which the case may be disposed of." See Ashwander v. Tennessee Valley Authority, 297 U.S. 288, 345–48 (1936) (Brandeis, J., concurring). . . .

Thus, if we are persuaded that the Commission would have found that the fairness doctrine did not serve the public interest even if it had forgone its ruminations on the constitutional issue, we must end our inquiry without reaching that issue. In fact, as we explain in part III, we have no doubt that even in the absence of constitutional problems the Commission would have reached the same outcome. We then turn in part IV to petitioners' objections to the Commission's policy decision, and in part V to issues relating to the Commission's withdrawal of the doctrine's "first prong," the requirement of coverage of controversial issues.

## III.

It is quite true that the Commission at the outset of its opinion here asserted that the constitutional and policy issues were "inextricably intertwined," [  ], and at the end suggested that its policy conclusion was a mere consequence of its constitutional one, [  ] ("the fairness doctrine contravenes the First Amendment and *thereby* disserves the public interest") (emphasis added). Those who would have us grasp the constitutional nettle call our attention to these references. [  ]

But the Commission's reasoning behind its "intertwining" assertion belies any inference that its policy judgment *depends* upon its constitutional view. . . .

. . .

Happily the Commission's opinion is not written in exclusively constitutional terms. . . .

. . . The Commission's incorporation of the [1985] Report's reasoning here confirms our conclusion that the Commission would have made the same public interest finding if it had approached the issue free of "intertwining."

## IV.

The FCC's decision that the fairness doctrine no longer serves the public interest is a policy judgment. There is no real dispute that fostering fair, balanced and diverse coverage of controversial issues is a good thing. Nor, so far as we can tell from the record or briefs, is there any question that discouraging any coverage at all, having government officials second-guess editorial judgments, or allowing incumbents an opportunity for abuse of power are things to be avoided, all other things being equal. The Commission's problem was to make predictive and normative judgments about the tendency of the fairness doctrine to produce each of these things, about how bad the bad effects were and how good the good ones, and ultimately about whether bad effects outweighed good.

In this situation, we owe great deference to the Commission's judgment. . . .

The Commission's factual judgments here are almost entirely predictive—statements about the overall effects of a policy on licensees and others. The Supreme Court has observed that "[I]n such cases complete factual support for the Commission's ultimate conclusions is not required since 'a forecast of the direction in which the future public interest lies necessarily involves deductions based on the expert knowledge of the agency.' " FCC v. WNCN Listeners Guild, [ ]. . . .

Of course, an agency can act arbitrarily or capriciously in the exercise of a policy judgment, and we must assure ourselves that that did not happen here. . . .

Before addressing those specific attacks, we must describe two core findings of the 1985 Report—that the fairness doctrine often operated to chill broadcaster speech on controversial issues and that recent increases in broadcasting outlets undercut the need for the doctrine—on which the Commission relied heavily in the present decision. It found that the doctrine produced chilling effects by placing burdens on stations which chose to air numerous programs on controversial issues—including the fear of denial of license renewal due to fairness doctrine violations, the cost of defending fairness doctrine attacks and of providing free air time to opposing views if a fairness violation is found, and the reputational harm resulting from even a frivolous fairness challenge. While the FCC recognized that to a degree the first prong of the fairness doctrine offset this effect by requiring broadcasters to present some controversial issues, it nonetheless found that broadcasters were encouraged[:]

to air only the minimal amount of controversial issue programming sufficient to comply with the first prong. By restricting the amount and type of controversial programming aired, a broadcaster minimizes the potentially substantial burdens associated with the strict letter of its regulatory obligations. Therefore, despite the first prong obligation, in net effect the fairness doctrine often discourages the presentation of controversial issue programming.

102 F.C.C.2d at 161.

The 1985 Fairness Report also noted that paradoxically the chilling effect often fell on the expression of unorthodox or "fringe" views on controversial issues. [　] Since the doctrine compelled coverage only of "major" or "significant" opinions, the FCC claimed that in assessing fairness doctrine compliance, the Commission was called upon to evaluate broadcasters' decisions concerning the importance of given viewpoints. The Report expressed its fear that the fairness doctrine thus had the potential "to interject the government, even unintentionally, into the position of favoring one type of opinion over another." [　]

In assessing whether any need for the doctrine persisted, the 1985 Report found a dramatic increase in broadcasting outlets since the 1974 Fairness Report, [　]. This expansion in broadcasting capacity was found to have been spread widely across American society. The FCC found that by 1984 96% of television households received five or more over-the-air (non-cable) television signals, compared with 83% in 1972. [　] Those receiving nine or more signals had tripled, from 21% of TV households in 1972 to 64% in 1984. [　] Of course some signals may for one reason or another be unable to function as serious alternative sources. But the new signals are plainly not trivial in the aggregate, as they have driven the networks' audience share down from 90% in [1969] to 76% in 1984. [　]

The Commission also found significant growth in radio outlets since the 1974 Fairness Report. The number of radio stations grew by 30% between 1974 and 1985. The subset of FM service increased during the same period by 60%, leading the FCC to proclaim that "there has also been a fundamental change in the structure of the radio market. Once predominantly an AM only service, radio is now composed of two very competitive services." [　] The Commission noted that radio expansion impacted smaller communities as well as larger urban areas; "the number of radio voices available in each local market has grown." [　]

Looking at substitute electronic media such as low power television, video cassette recorders, satellite master antenna systems, and so forth, the Commission found that the gains in radio and television accessibility and diversity actually understated the true development of broadcast media available to the viewing public. [　] The Report also noted that print media coverage of controversial issues offered Americans exposure to the type of information which the fairness doctrine was designed to foster.

We now turn to the specific objections to the Commission's conclusions.

## INSUFFICIENCY OF EVIDENCE TO SUPPORT FCC POSITION

Although there is some criticism of the 1985 Report's findings as to the growth of access to media signals, that commentary focuses largely on the point that some of the figures used by the Commission may exaggerate the significance of the alternative sources. But the Commission has included the figures on changes in audience shares, clearly reflecting its recognition that not all sources are equal. Some parties also assert that the FCC was overly concerned with aggregate or national figures at the expense of local data. Yet in looking at the Commission's finding concerning the number of households which receive five or more non-cable television signals—a whopping 96%—it seems to us that only a diminutive share of the population has been unaffected by the growth the Commission has recounted. Accordingly, we view these attacks as peripheral.

Several parties, however, have attacked the evidence of broadcaster chill and what they contend is the Commission's failure to respond adequately to the attacks. . . .

. . . It appears that numerically the main body of evidence comes from the comments submitted to the Commission by the National Association of Broadcasters ("NAB"), which presented 45 broadcaster accounts of the fairness doctrine on their industry and policies. It is clear, however, that the FCC also relied on important additional sources, including submissions by some *proponents* of the fairness doctrine. For example, it pointed to evidence from Public Media Center that after it had warned broadcasters that it would demand free response time from stations that accepted advertising on a specific controversy, more than two-thirds of those contacted had refused to sell advertising on the subject at all. [ ]

The 1985 Report responded substantially to the . . . attacks made on the NAB study. . . . We are persuaded that the self-interested character of the broadcasters' evidence did not bar the Commission from giving it substantial weight.

. . .

Third, the Commission made specific rebuttals of some . . . criticisms of NAB examples. . . . For example, one of the criticisms, twice invoked, was that the particular broadcaster need not have been deterred, since in the view of the critics the station's ordinary news coverage would have satisfied its obligations under the doctrine. In rebuttal, the Commission found the critic's observations highly speculative. [ ] Surely the FCC is right. The fairness doctrine applies to ordinary mortals who adjust their affairs on the basis of estimates of risk. The estimating process costs time and effort. It hardly disproves an alleged deterrent effect to suggest that by more careful research or analysis, or by greater brilliance, the deterred party might have come out the other way. This is typical of this line of critiques, and to avoid repetition we pass on the remaining attacks.

. . .

Finally, [the United Church of Christ] attacks any reliance on the NAB study on the ground that it was "not based on a statistically valid sample of broadcasters' experiences, but rather, was merely a series of anecdotal accounts." [ ] The comment is quite valid, but in the absence of either any statistically valid evidence on the other side, or even a suggestion of how the Commission could have constructed a statistically valid study, we are perplexed as to what the Commission was supposed to have done. Editorial decisions are obviously driven by many factors. Isolation of causes in any scientific way seems virtually impossible. The fairness doctrine has been applicable in one form or another from 1949 until the present decision, so the Commission could not compare stations' practices under the rule with their conduct free of the rule. (Comparison to practice in other nations would encounter the usual cross-cultural difficulties.)

We note that when speaking of a state-enforced "right-of-reply" applicable to newspapers, the Supreme Court has taken it as self-evident that such a duty *"inescapably* 'dampens the vigor and limits the variety of public debate.'" Miami Herald Publishing Co. v. Tornillo, [ ] (emphasis added). [ ] Of course we recognize that the fairness doctrine differs from the right-of-reply at issue in *Tornillo* and that *Red Lion* applies different constitutional standards to the broadcast media. But we think the Court's approach suggests that where a rule imposes potentially onerous and at least irksome consequences on the exercise of speech, there is nothing very startling about an inference that the rule will often deter speech. We think the Commission could properly find that effect from the evidence before it here.

## FAILURE TO CONSIDER EVIDENCE OF DOCTRINE'S BENEFICENT EFFECTS

UCC also charges that the Commission ignored or discounted evidence of the benefits derived from the fairness doctrine. [ ] We think part of the problem here arises out of UCC's apparent assumption that the Commission believed that the fairness doctrine rarely (or never) increased diversity of expression. Indeed, the Commission only purported to find that "the overall NET effect of the doctrine is to reduce the coverage of controversial issues of public importance," [ ], a finding clearly consistent with a belief that the doctrine frequently produced its intended effects. We do not read the Commission's focus on the negative aspects as manifesting a blindness to unwelcome evidence but rather as a focus on what it viewed as novel or surprising. To say that a rule has often produced its intended effects is to tell a dog-bites-man story— not front-page stuff. The Commission was naturally more struck by evidence of unintended consequences—hardly in the man-bites-dog class, but closer.

. . .

We must confess, however, some perplexity at the Commission's insistence that the doctrine's overall "net effect [was] to reduce the coverage of controversial issues." [The court noted that *Red Lion* had said that if such a situation occurred "there will be time enough to reconsider the constitutional implications."] The Court then proceeded to declare, "[T]he fairness doctrine in the past has had no such overall effect." [ ] The Court did not explicate the basis for that finding.

We are frankly uncertain how anyone could be sure either way. The definitional problems alone are staggering. How could a court or agency persuasively define standards by which to evaluate the "quality" of coverage? Once it had done so, by what yardstick could it balance quality increments due to broadcasters' responding as intended against quality decrements due to the deterrent effects? The Commission does not explain. Nor do the challengers, who evidently are happy to weigh these unweighables but read the scales differently.

Despite this confusion, we believe we can "discern the path" followed by the Commission. [ ] It found itself confronted with evidence that it read as establishing that the doctrine has very substantial deterrent effects (and, as we have said, we believe that finding was permissible). It also quite plainly made the normative judgment that government decisions on program content and government forced expressions of ideas, together with the associated risks of partisan abuse, were anathema. . . . It was persuaded that the doctrine's deterrent effects were on the same scale as its expression-generating ones, and it plainly discounted the *value* of the latter as "governmentally-coerced speech." [ ] Accordingly, it rejected the doctrine as a matter of policy. That policy judgment seems to us by no means arbitrary or capricious. . . .

## FAILURE TO CONSIDER ALTERNATIVES

Petitioners Geller and Lampert contest the FCC's refusal to adopt their proposed alternative to the elimination of the fairness doctrine. The two have repeatedly urged the Commission to review fairness matters only at license renewal, and to adopt a malice standard for this review.

The FCC has twice declined to return to its pre–1962 practice of resolving fairness doctrine complaints at renewal, first in its 1974 Fairness Report, [ ], affirmed by this court, [ ], and then in its 1987 Alternatives Report, [ ]. The 1987 Report found . . . several specific defects . . . in the renewal review plan. First, by linking fairness evaluations with the renewal process, broadcasters would view the potential sanctions as being more threatening than those currently in effect, as loss of license or suspension would be seen as more likely. [ ] Second, the renewal plan deprives the broadcaster of a contemporaneous ruling on its behavior and chance to quickly rectify any imbalance in its programming. The FCC believed this could make broadcasters more conservative in coverage of controversial issues. [ ] Finally, it would only delay rather than diminish the government's meddling in the editorial process. [  ]

Geller and Lampert coupled their renewal-only suggestion with the idea that review would proceed under a "malice" standard such as that of [*Sullivan*], and with an alternative suggestion that the Commission continue to act case-by-case but under a malice standard. As to the first, the Commission agreed that such a standard would reduce the chilling effect, but judged that reduction inadequate to offset what it believed would be the increased chill from postponement to renewal. [  ] As to the second, the Commission in its reconsideration order in the present case expressed doubt whether a malice standard would substantially reduce the chilling effect when compared with the Commission's practice of deferring to broadcasters' reasonable judgments, [  ], and said that the difference in impact on licensees would be a matter of degree rather than of kind, [  ]. Although its discussion of the subject is more than usually framed in constitutional terms, we read it as concluding that the proposals only mildly mitigated the ill effects that drove the Commission to reject the fairness doctrine as previously enforced. That judgment seems well within its discretion, especially as the proposals would also appear to materially diminish the positive effects of the doctrine.

## DEPARTURE FROM 1985 DECISION

Some parties complain that the present decision represents an unexplained abandonment of the Commission's 1985 decision to persist in enforcement of the doctrine.   . . .

The 1985 Fairness Report had found that the doctrine disserved the public interest, but had refrained from dropping the doctrine on policy grounds only because of concern that perhaps it was statutorily mandated, [  ], and because of the intense congressional interest then brewing over the fairness doctrine, [  ]. This court's *TRAC* decision removed the first obstacle (except insofar as the Supreme Court might find otherwise); a successful presidential veto of Congress's attempt to mandate the fairness doctrine clearly diminished the second. Though we find no explicit reference to these reasons in the decision under review, they appear so obvious and compelling that a remand to extract the magic words from the Commission would be pure waste. [  ]

## V.

Several parties attack the Commission's repeal of the so-called "first prong" of the fairness doctrine—the requirement that broadcasters provide coverage of important controversial issues of interest to the community they serve. First, they contend that they were not adequately notified of the Commission's intent to reconsider the first prong in this proceeding. Second, petitioners argue that the FCC's abandonment of the first prong was arbitrary and capricious.

## NOTICE

[The court held the notice adequate.]

## WHETHER RESCISSION OF THE FIRST PRONG
## WAS ARBITRARY AND CAPRICIOUS

[The court held inadequate the Commission's suggestion that the doctrine was a unified whole—so that if one part fell so did the other. The Commission had not explained why the parts were not severable.]

In other portions of its decision, however, the Commission went on to supply reasons for terminating the first prong. . . .

First, removal of the fairness doctrine's second requirement would reduce the need for the coverage requirement. With the chilling effects of the second requirement ended, the Commission expected that "coverage of controversial issues will be forthcoming naturally, without the need for continued enforcement of the first prong." . . .

Second, it viewed the coverage requirement as in significant part duplicative of its independent requirement that broadcasters cover issues "of importance" to their communities. [ ] While the FCC acknowledged on reconsideration that the two programming requirements were not identical, it saw sufficient similarity to believe that the community issues rule would fill any material regulatory gap. [ ]

Third, in its discussion of the fairness doctrine as a whole the Commission relied heavily on its view that government involvement in the editorial process was offensive. [ ] That judgment of course applies to the editorial decisions required for enforcement of the first prong, and the Commission made the point expressly: "[T]he doctrine requires the government to second-guess broadcasters' judgment on such sensitive and subjective matters as to the 'controversiality' and 'public importance' of a particular issue. . . ." [ ] It also alluded to the offensive character of government first-prong decisions in distinguishing that part of the doctrine from the community issues requirement. . . .

> While enforcement of the doctrine's first prong requires the government to judge, on a case-by-case basis, whether a specific issue is both controversial and of vital importance to mandate coverage by the broadcaster, enforcement of the issue responsive obligation requires a different level of government intervention in determining, at renewal time, whether broadcasters' *overall* programming covered the needs and interests of its community.

[ ] (emphasis in original). [ ]

We believe that these reasons, particularly in light of the Commission's background findings on the increased diversity of outlets and programming, adequately support its removal of the first prong.

## CONCLUSION

We conclude that the FCC's decision that the fairness doctrine no longer served the public interest was neither arbitrary, capricious nor an abuse of discretion, and are convinced that it would have acted on that finding to terminate the doctrine even in the absence of its belief that the doctrine was no longer constitutional. Accordingly we uphold the Commission without reaching the constitutional issues. The petition for review is denied.

WALD, CHIEF JUDGE, concurring in part and dissenting in part.

I concur in Parts I–IV of Judge Williams' opinion, which uphold the FCC's decision to abrogate the second prong of the fairness doctrine as an exercise of its statutory authority to regulate in the public interest. I dissent, however, from Part V, which sustains the Commission's decision to eliminate the fairness doctrine's first prong. . . . I believe that this aspect of the Commission's decision is not supported by the record and was not adopted in compliance with the Administrative Procedure Act, that it proposed to eliminate the first as well as the second prong of the doctrine. . . .

. . .

Neither can the Commission's action be justified by reference to the overlap between first prong obligations and the duty to cover issues of importance to the community. While a substantial overlap does exist, the requirements are by no means duplicative. The community issues requirement obliges broadcasters to devote reasonable air time to the coverage of issues important to the local community. The first prong of the fairness doctrine focuses on the broadcaster's obligation to cover *controversial* issues. It seems entirely foreseeable that some broadcasters might provide abundant coverage of community issues generally but might—perhaps from fear of incurring the displeasure of the public or of advertisers—steer clear of issues of a controversial nature. . . .

[Chief Judge Wald rejected the argument that the first prong could be repealed solely because it might no longer be a necessary spur for most broadcasters. There was no claim that it would be "counterproductive."]

Moreover, I do not believe that the FCC's obligation to identify the costs of an unwanted regulation could be satisfied by a bare showing that the rule would impinge on broadcasters' editorial freedom. I believe it is still the law that, in the regulation of electronic media, "[i]t is the right of the viewers and listeners, not the right of the broadcasters, which is paramount." [*Red Lion*]. . . .

. . . [T]he Commission has made no effort whatsoever to explain how continued enforcement of the doctrine's first prong could induce broadcasters to alter their programming decisions in ways which would ultimately disserve the public interest.

. . . In eliminating prong one along with prong two of the fairness doctrine, the FCC appears to have been motivated primarily by a morbid fear that it might be accused of doing things halfway.  This is deregulation running riot.

STARR, CIRCUIT JUDGE, concurring.

.  .  .

.  .  .  With all respect to the court's view annunciated today, I am convinced that the record in this case simply will not, fairly read, yield the conclusion that the agency has based the specific decision before us independently on non-constitutional grounds.  There is, therefore, no proper basis for skirting the Commission's constitutional analysis (unless we were to conclude, as I do not, that the Commission erred in even considering that issue);  in short, the constitutional justifications for the Commission's action must, alas, be considered.

.  .  .

.  .  .  There is no escaping this hard, cold fact:  in the wake of the generously worded *Meredith* remand, the Commission has rendered a *Red Lion* decision.  It has switched gears from three years ago and gone beyond the less heroic, public-interest reach of the 1985 Report.

.  .  .

.  .  .  *Meredith* has unleashed *Red Lion,* and it will not do to pretend, with cheery *bravado,* that *Red Lion* is still secure in its pre-*Meredith* cage.  *Red Lion* is now out on the streets, released by a deliberate and careful FCC decision.

For its part, the court airily treats this as just another case coming out of yet another agency here in town charged with making yet another broad public interest determination.  This will not do.  .  .  .

.  .  .

.  .  .  Where, as here, the agency's policy judgment is wholly driven by its constitutional analysis, reasoning and conclusions, the reviewing court is obliged to analyze the case in those terms.  .  .  .

.  .  .  Indeed, the Supreme Court has expressly invited the FCC to examine whether the constitutional underpinnings of the doctrine remain viable.  FCC v. League of Women Voters, 468 U.S. 364, 377 n. 11 (1984).  In view of the fairness doctrine's unique, constitutionally-charged history, it is hardly unreasonable for the FCC to view the public interest through First Amendment lenses.

.  .  .

In sum, as the FCC's decision is adequate in all respects and singularly unlikely to be altered on remand, I think the court is obliged to examine the FCC's decision—grounded in the Constitution—as it comes to us.  It is to that issue, avoided by my colleagues, but pressed exclusively by all parties before this court, that I must now turn.

## II

### A

The question before us—that is, the legality of the FCC's action—is somewhat of a hybrid, exhibiting both constitutional and administrative law characteristics. As I see it, judicial review of the FCC's Order is most correctly viewed as involving two distinct tasks. First, the court is called upon to scrutinize the Commission's interpretation of the constitutional principles enunciated in *Red Lion* and its progeny. This task involves measuring the FCC's articulation of constitutional principles, as distinguished from its application of those principles to the facts. Our scope of review in this particular is plenary. [ ] Second, we are called upon to review the Commission's factual determinations. . . .

The parties have assumed that the Commission's findings of fact are subject to review under the "arbitrary and capricious" standard laid down in the APA, 5 U.S.C. section 706 (1985); [ ]. However, where, as here, factual determinations are intimately connected with the evaluation of constitutionality under the First Amendment, the Supreme Court has held (outside the agency context) that those findings should be reviewed independently. Bose Corp. v. Consumers Union of U.S., Inc., [ ] (and cases cited therein). On reflection, I believe that in this instance the parties' assumption is well-founded; the administrative law model of review indeed applies notwithstanding the presence of important First Amendment questions. Although the FCC's factual findings are closely intermingled with its ultimate conclusion as to the constitutionality vel non of the fairness doctrine, independent review by the judiciary seems inappropriate for several reasons.

First, the FCC's Order does not deny a constitutional claim. No one has urged that the fairness doctrine is constitutionally compelled. Rather, the FCC has determined, pursuant to its obligation to uphold the Constitution, that the First Amendment requires elimination of the fairness doctrine. That point is of pivotal importance because the decisional law of the Supreme Court indicates that independent appellate review of facts is appropriate only where the decision under review *denies* a constitutional claim. [ ]

This conclusion flows from the principle that independent review, where applicable, derives from the Constitution itself. Bose v. Consumers Union, 466 U.S. at 510 ("The requirement of independent review . . . is a rule of federal constitutional law"). Thus, where no constitutional rights are threatened by the findings at issue, the reason undergirding the unusual tack of independent appellate review of facts does not exist. . . .

Independent review of the Commission's findings also seems inappropriate because we have before us the predictive judgments of a federal agency concerning the (perceived) effects of its own policy. The Supreme Court has recognized that the FCC is possessed of substantial expertise with respect to the impact of the fairness doctrine on the communications marketplace. [ ] Indeed, the Court has accorded weight to factual findings underlying an FCC decision that broadcast regulation was inconsistent with the First Amendment. [CBS v. DNC] The present case is thus readily distinguishable from instances in which the Supreme Court has independently reviewed the case-specific findings of juries or trial judges. See e.g., Miller v. California, 413 U.S. 15 (1973) (independent review of jury determination that a specific publication or film is "patently offensive" and appeals to the "prurient interest"). . . . In view of the FCC's obvious expertise, we would be unwise (and unfaithful to the APA) to disregard the Commission's ultimate conclusions of fact with respect to the fairness doctrine's chilling effect; its interference with broadcasters' editorial discretion; and the explosive growth of media outlets.

Under these principles, the Commission's Order should be upheld. It is based on reasonable factual findings and embodies a correct statement of applicable constitutional principles. . . .

. . . To reiterate: I would hold only that the FCC's decision to eliminate the fairness doctrine correctly interprets *Red Lion* and is based, as the court's opinion effectively demonstrates, on an adequate factual record. Such a decision would therefore not automatically foreclose a future FCC (or Congress) from reestablishing the fairness doctrine in its present (or some modified) form. The fate of any future attempt to resurrect (or refashion) the fairness doctrine would depend, obviously, on the Supreme Court's articulation of applicable constitutional doctrine (e.g., *Red Lion*); but it would also be affected by the scope of review applied to the facts upon which the "new" fairness doctrine was sought to be justified. Of course, as we have just seen, the line of cases culminating in *Bose Corp.* indicates that factual findings underlying the *denial* of a First Amendment challenge would be subject to independent review. Although this situation is, again, not before us today, it bears mentioning that this additional burden imposed on proponents of allegedly unconstitutional government action (i.e., a "new" or "resurrected" fairness doctrine) represents the inevitable result of our system of constitutional supremacy.

I should hasten to add that this burden, while substantial, appears to be by no means hopelessly insurmountable. To the contrary, under the *Red Lion* framework (assuming, as I do, continued High Court allegiance to its teachings), the constitutionality of the fairness doctrine is linked in part to technological developments (and behavior) in the communications marketplace. Those developments obviously continue to unfold, with impacts that can only foggily be predicted. What is more, we have precious little experience in a *sans*–fairness doctrine regulatory environment. It remains to be seen whether the necessarily predictive judgments embodied in the Order will withstand the hard, true test of time. [  ]

In short, it is not at all inconceivable that detailed reconsideration by a future FCC or carefully considered Congressional findings, [  ], could persuade a future court that, notwithstanding the FCC's contrary findings vindicated by today's decision, some in futuro version of the fairness doctrine could be implemented consistent with First Amendment strictures.

C

As to the constitutional principles applicable to this case, the parties are congenially in accord (1) that *Red Lion* principles govern; and (2) that, under the *Red Lion* framework, government restrictions on broadcasters' speech are valid only if "narrowly tailored to further a substantial government interest, such as ensuring adequate and balanced coverage of public issues." Order at 5049 (quoting FCC v. League of Women Voters, 468 U.S. at 380). It is also by now well recognized that this standard affords broadcasters somewhat less First Amendment protection than that enjoyed by their print media counterparts. [ ]

But there consensus abruptly stops. Although the parties agree that *Red Lion* is king, they strenuously disagree over the proper interpretation of that seminal decision. For its part, the FCC argues that the constitutional question turns on whether enforcement of the fairness doctrine

(1) chills speech and results in the net reduction of the presentation of controversial issues of public importance and

(2) excessively infringes on the editorial discretion of broadcast journalists and involves unnecessary government intervention to the extent that it is no longer narrowly tailored to meet its objective.

[ ] The FCC believes that regulatory intervention through the vehicle of the fairness doctrine is not "narrowly tailored" if the number (and distribution) of media outlets ensures public access to diverse viewpoints. [ ] That is, if access to diverse viewpoints can be achieved without the fairness doctrine, then the doctrine is not "narrowly tailored" because it unnecessarily interferes with editorial decisions. Finally, the FCC interprets *Red Lion* to render the fairness doctrine unconstitutional if either of these tests (net reduction or not "narrowly tailored") is satisfied. [ ]

Petitioners' most vigorous attack is aimed at the proposition that the numerosity of media outlets and intrusive impact of the fairness doctrine may, without more, render the fairness doctrine unconstitutional. Petitioners contend that the relevant concern is the number of media outlets relative to the demand of broadcasters (expressed through license applications) for such outlets. More pertinently, petitioners direct our attention to the unique characteristic of broadcast regulation, namely the potential for interference occasioned by the fact that the broadcast spectrum can physically accommodate only a finite number of users. The potential for signal interference among competing broadcasters, it is argued, necessitates an allocation system whereby regulatory authority assures to broadcasters exclusive use of their portions of the spectrum. As this system by its nature excludes some who wish to broadcast, the readmission of excluded speakers via the fairness doctrine is constitutionally permissible, petitioners maintain, as an adjunct to the licensing system.

To recap: as petitioners see it, the fairness doctrine is constitutionally permissible so long as *allocational scarcity* exists, namely, that demand for broadcast frequencies exceeds supply. [  ]  The FCC, in contrast, asserts that the constitutionality of the doctrine depends on *numerical scarcity* in the sense that, without government intervention, the public is not provided with access to diverse viewpoints.

There is thus a rather pivotal difference in the perspectives vying for judicial approbation.  As I see it, the FCC's position is much better founded; indeed, in my view, petitioners have fallen badly into error by misreading *Red Lion*.  There is, to be sure, language in *Red Lion* with respect to the scarcity of the broadcast spectrum and the consequent tendency toward unrequited demand for frequencies.  [  ]  Under *Red Lion*, however, that sort of scarcity seems to constitute a necessary (rather than sufficient) condition of the fairness doctrine's legitimacy. That is, allocational scarcity accounts for the fundamental difference in First Amendment treatment of print and broadcast media.  [  ]  However, spectrum scarcity, without more, does not necessarily justify regulatory schemes which intrude into First Amendment territory.  This point is made clear by the familiar cases in which the Court has upheld broadcast regulation on the ground that the regulation *furthered* substantial First Amendment interests, see *Red Lion,* [  ]; Columbia Broadcasting Co. v. FCC, 453 U.S. 367, 396 (1981); and by [CBS v. DNC], where the Court held that the FCC need not require licensees to accept all paid political advertisements because such a requirement unduly impinged upon broadcasters' rights and produced little public benefit. In short, petitioners conflate the Supreme Court's choice of a standard for evaluating broadcast regulation with the Court's application of its chosen standard to the interests assertedly advanced by a particular regulatory regime.

Petitioners' reliance on the concept of allocational scarcity is logically flawed as well.  As part of their attack on numerical scarcity, petitioners contend that "[t]he *Red Lion* Court did not speak in terms of satisfaction, or hypothesize a point at which 'enough' diversity is present. . . .  Only when supply and demand [for licenses] reach equipoise does the governmental interest change."  [  ]  The argument is an intriguing one; but I think, with all respect, that it focuses with undue exclusivity on the market for broadcast licenses, whereas the central concern of *Red Lion* is that the fairness doctrine "preserve an uninhibited marketplace of ideas."  [  ]  Indeed, a reading of *Red Lion* yields no evidence that the mere presence of excluded *broadcasters* is to be regarded as dispositive of the *public's* need for programming of a particular type.  Especially since individual members of the listening or viewing public, such as disappointed broadcast license applicants, may express their viewpoints on controversial issues in any number of ways that do not involve applying for and receiving a broadcasting license, it seems odd (and inaccurate) to equate scarcity in licenses with scarcity in the marketplace of ideas.  Indeed, petitioners' argument ultimately flies in the teeth of *Red Lion's* admonition that "it is the right of viewers and listeners and not that of broadcasters, which is paramount."  [  ]

In contrast, the FCC has correctly discerned that, under *Red Lion,* the constitutionality of the fairness doctrine is closely related to the incapacity of the communications marketplace to give expression to diverse voices.   .   .   .

The governing constitutional doctrine therefore recognizes that the communications marketplace may be sufficiently responsive to the public's need for controversial issue programming so that government regulation is unnecessary.   Cf. *Red Lion,* 395 U.S. at 397 (fairness doctrine constitutional in light of the fact that the increased carrying capacity of the broadcast spectrum has been devoted largely to uses unrelated to debate on controversial issues).   As a corollary of that principle, the FCC also recognized that, where the communications marketplace itself provides a plethora of voices, the fairness doctrine is not only superfluous, it is positively harmful.   This is of singular importance in the analysis.   As the Court has stated time and again, regulatory schemes that tread unnecessarily on the editorial discretion of broadcasters contravene the First Amendment.   [   ]   Columbia Broadcasting System, Inc. v. FCC, 453 U.S. at 395.   ("[T]he broadcasting industry is entitled under the First Amendment to exercise 'the widest journalistic freedom consistent with its public [duties].' ") quoting [CBS v. DNC].

The Commission is also correct in interpreting the Supreme Court's holdings as rendering the fairness doctrine constitutionally problematic where the "net effect" of the doctrine is a reduction in coverage of controversial public issues.   .   .   .   Obviously, as the fairness doctrine exists to *promote speech* on controversial issues, it seems manifest that the doctrine should not readily enjoy constitutional approbation if it ceases to promote and secure bedrock constitutional interests.

## D

As the court's opinion ably demonstrates, the Commission's factual determinations (1) that the growth of broadcast outlets ensures the public's access to viewpoint diversity, and (2) that the fairness doctrine ultimately operates to reduce coverage of controversial issues, find reasonable support in the record.   Rather than rehearse the salient points of the record in detail, it suffices for present purposes to highlight several points.

Significantly, petitioners do not dispute that, since the late '60s when *Red Lion* was handed down, the number of media sources has expanded dramatically.   The number of full power TV stations has increased 54 percent, [   ], with the result that nearly 96 percent of U.S. households with television received 5 or more signals.   Nearly two thirds of U.S. households received 9 or more signals.   [   ]   Similarly, the number of radio stations has increased 57 percent since the first year of the Nixon Administration, when *Red Lion* was first introduced to the world of constitutional law.   [   ]   As of 1987, listeners had access to an average of 6 radio stations in the smallest markets and a whopping 25 stations in the largest markets.   [   ]   As commuters and Walkman aficionados know, all news-all talk stations (or some variation thereof) abound in large markets.

The Commission also took account of the growth of various non-broadcast media, the most important of which is cable television. More than half of the nation's TV households currently subscribe to cable. [  ] But, as Judge Williams' opinion for the court persuasively indicates, the data offered by petitioners in this respect fall short of drawing into question the impressive statistics marshalled by the FCC. No more need be said in these already overlong pages on that score.

Petitioners also contend that the increase in media sources has not resulted in significant increases in controversial issue programming. They point in particular to FM radio and UHF TV as examples of media sources that have grown rapidly without contributing significantly to viewpoint diversity. The FCC responds that petitioners offer little to back up their opinion-laden allegations. [  ] But, even assuming that UHF TV and FM radio programs are not particularly intensive in their coverage of controversial issues, I am satisfied that the FCC did not put all of its eggs in one part of the large communications-market basket. Rather, as we just saw, the Order points to growth in broadcast media and non-broadcast technologies such as cable and satellite television. [  ] The Commission has also indicated that these technologies are contributing to viewpoint diversity. For example, one well-known cable channel . . . is devoted solely to news; two cable channels are given over to coverage of Congress and related issues. [  ] We are told that the media stand ready and able to enter (and in some instances are entering) the courthouses of this blessed land, if the least dangerous branch decides to opt in favor of glasnost in its own house. In short, inasmuch as the Commission has relied on credible evidence concerning the growth and programming in many types of media, I cannot, in conscience, condemn as arbitrary and capricious its ultimate finding that the communications market as a whole provides "reasonable assurance" of public access to viewpoint diversity.

As to the FCC's finding that the fairness doctrine so chilled speech as to result in a net reduction in the coverage of controversial issues, the court quite correctly notes that, where government regulation imposes substantial (and, to a certain extent, unpredictable) consequences on speech, drawing an inference of some chilling effect hardly represents an heroic step in our First Amendment tradition. [  ] Of greater difficulty is the FCC's finding of a net reduction in controversial issue programming. Petitioners' main argument in this particular is that the Commission gave undue weight to testimony of chilling effect and insufficient weight to evidence that the doctrine stimulated speech.

. . .

. . . In view of the attention given by the Supreme Court to the net reduction issue, FCC v. League of Women Voters, 468 U.S. at 379 n. 12 (a finding that the fairness doctrine has the net effect of reducing speech would require reconsideration of *Red Lion*), and the principle that the interests of broadcasters, while important, are ultimately secondary to those of the viewing and listening public, our review should focus on the evidence adduced by the Commission in favor of its conclusion of a net reduction.

In this respect, my reading of the Order suggests that the Commission, based on its regulatory experience and testimony before the agency concerning chilling effects, reasonably determined that the fairness doctrine's predominant effect on speech was inhibitory. [ ] Specifically, the Commission found that the fairness doctrine chilled individual program decisions *and* induced broadcasters to adopt categorical policies against carrying editorials, political advertisements or nationally-produced public affairs programs. [ ] The Commission further noted that, by virtue of the fairness doctrine, many broadcasters were encouraged not to air controversial issue programming above that minimal amount required by the first part of the doctrine. [ ] The Commission was also entitled to take into account the fact that the doctrine, by requiring coverage only of "major" contrasting viewpoints, fell with particular severity on broadcasters who express unorthodox views, thus tending to deprive the public of "uninhibited, robust and wide-open" debate. [ ] Finally, the Commission pointed to the fact that "no broadcaster indicated to us that its station's coverage of controversial issues has increased as a result of the fairness doctrine." [ ]

These findings, taken together, reasonably support the Commission's ultimate conclusion that elimination of the fairness doctrine would unleash a substantial amount of controversial issue programming. . . .

## E

A final criticism directed at the Order concerns the Commission's decision to eliminate the first part of the fairness doctrine. . . .

[Judge Starr rejected the FCC's severability analysis.] More plausible is the Commission's contention that, as the first part of the fairness doctrine is "largely duplicative" of the requirement that broadcasters cover issues responsive to the needs of their community, retention of Part One would produce "no added public benefit." [ ] This point is rather unilluminating, however, in light of the Commission's emphasis elsewhere on the distinctions between Part One of the fairness doctrine and the requirement of community issue programming. [ ] Indeed, petitioners point out that the FCC loosened the issue-responsive obligation in part because of a distinct obligation imposed under Part One. [ ] In light of the admitted difference between the two regulatory standards, I am of the view that the Commission's "largely duplicative" rationale is inadequate.

Despite these deficiencies, I nonetheless agree that the Commission reasonably eliminated Part One in light of the FCC's findings that the explosive growth in media outlets, combined with the removal of the deterrent to controversial public issue programming imposed by Part

Two of the doctrine, will adequately ensure availability of such programs.  [   ]  The reasonableness of the Commission's decision to eliminate Part One is reinforced by the (inevitably) predictive quality of the FCC's reasoning.  It is in this sense that I agree with Judge Williams that the Commission is entitled to conclude that elimination of Part One would not create an impermissible regulatory gap.   . . .

## Notes and Questions

1.  The reference to the presidential veto is to an episode occurring when Congress passed the Fairness in Broadcasting Act of 1987 (S. 742). The Act read as follows:

> To clarify the congressional intent concerning, and to codify, certain requirements of the Communications Act of 1934 that ensure that broadcasters afford reasonable opportunity for the discussion of conflicting views on issues of public importance.

> *Be it enacted by the Senate and House of Representatives of the United States of America in Congress assembled,* That this Act may be cited as the "Fairness in Broadcasting Act of 1987".

SEC.  2 FINDINGS

The Congress finds that—

(1) despite technological advances, the electromagnetic spectrum remains a scarce and valuable public resource;

(2) there are still substantially more people who want to broadcast than there are frequencies to allocate;

(3) a broadcast license confers the right to use a valuable public resource and a broadcaster is therefore required to utilize that resource as a trustee for the American people;

(4) there is a substantial governmental interest in conditioning the award or renewal of a broadcast license on the requirement that the licensee ensure the widest possible dissemination of information from diverse and antagonistic sources by presenting a reasonable opportunity for the discussion of conflicting views on issues of public importance;

(5) while new video and audio services have been proposed and introduced, many have not succeeded, and even those that are operating reach a far smaller audience than broadcast stations;

(6) even when and where new video and audio services are available, they do not provide meaningful alternatives to broadcast stations for the dissemination of news and public affairs;

(7) for more than thirty years, the Fairness Doctrine and its corollaries, as developed by the Federal Communications Commission on the basis of the provisions of the Communications Act of 1934, have enhanced free speech by securing the paramount right of the broadcast audience to robust debate on issues of public importance; and

(8) the Fairness Doctrine (A) fairly reflects the statutory obligations of broadcasters under that Act to operate in the public interest, (B) was given statutory approval by the Congress in making certain amendments to that Act in 1959, and (C) strikes a reasonable balance among the First Amendment rights of the public, broadcast licensees, and speakers other than owners of broadcast facilities.

## SEC. 3 AMENDMENT TO THE COMMUNICATIONS ACT OF 1934

(a) Section 315 of the Communications Act of 1934 (47 U.S.C. 315) is amended—

(1) by redesignating subsections (a) through (d) as subsections (b) through (e), respectively; and

(2) by inserting before subsection (b) the following new subsection:

"(a)(1) A broadcast licensee shall afford reasonable opportunity for the discussion of conflicting views on issues of public importance.

"(2) The enforcement and application of the requirement imposed by this subsection shall be consistent with the rules and policies of the Commission in effect on January 1, 1987."

## SEC. 4 EFFECTIVE DATE

This Act and the amendment to the Communications Act of 1934 added by this Act shall take effect upon the date of enactment.

President Reagan vetoed the bill and issued the following statement explaining his veto:

I am returning herewith without my approval S. 742, the "Fairness in Broadcasting Act of 1987," which would codify the so-called "fairness doctrine." This doctrine, which has evolved through the decisional process of the Federal Communications Commission (FCC), requires Federal Officials to supervise the editorial practices of broadcasters in an effort to ensure that they provide coverage of controversial issues and a reasonable opportunity for the airing of contrasting viewpoints on those issues. This type of content-based regulation by the Federal Government is, in my judgment, antagonistic to the freedom of expression guaranteed by the First Amendment.

In any other medium besides broadcasting, such Federal policing of the editorial judgment of journalists would be unthinkable. The framers of the First Amendment, confident that public debate would be freer and healthier without the kind of interference represented by the "fairness doctrine," chose to forbid such regulations in the clearest terms: "Congress shall make no law . . .

abridging the freedom of speech, or the press." More recently, the United States Supreme Court, in striking down a right-of-access statute that applied to newspapers, spoke of the statute's intrusion into the function of the editorial process and concluded that "[i]t has yet to be demonstrated how governmental regulation of this crucial process can be exercised consistent with First Amendment guarantees of a free press as they have evolved to this time." [*Tornillo*].

I recognize that 18 years ago the Supreme Court indicated that the fairness doctrine as then applied to a far less technologically advanced broadcast industry did not contravene the First Amendment. [*Red Lion Broadcasting Co.*]. The *Red Lion* decision was based on the theory that usable broadcast frequencies were then so inherently scarce that government regulation of broadcasters was inevitable and the FCC's "fairness doctrine" seemed to be a reasonable means of promoting diverse and vigorous debate of controversial issues.

The Supreme Court indicated in *Red Lion* a willingness to reconsider the appropriateness of the fairness doctrine if it reduced rather than enhanced broadcast coverage. In a later case, the Court acknowledged the changes in the technological and economic environment in which broadcasters operate. It may now be fairly concluded that the growth in the number of available media outlets does indeed outweigh whatever justifications may have seemed to exist at the period during which the doctrine was developed. The FCC itself has concluded that the doctrine is an unnecessary and detrimental regulatory mechanism. After a massive study of the effects of its own rule, the FCC found in 1985 that the recent explosion in the number of new information sources such as cable television has clearly made the "fairness doctrine" unnecessary. Furthermore, the FCC found that the doctrine in fact inhibits broadcasters from presenting controversial issues of public importance, and thus defeats its own purpose.

Quite apart from these technological advances, we must not ignore the obvious intent of the First Amendment, which is to promote vigorous public debate and a diversity of viewpoints in the public forum as a whole, not in any particular medium, let alone in any particular journalistic outlet. History has shown that the dangers of an overly timid or biased press cannot be averted through bureaucratic regulation, but only through the freedom and competition that the First Amendment sought to guarantee.

S. 742 simply cannot be reconciled with the freedom of speech and the press secured by our Constitution. It is, in my judgment, unconstitutional. Well-intentioned as S. 742 may be, it would be inconsistent with the First Amendment and with the American tradition of independent journalism. Accordingly, I am compelled to disapprove this measure.

Was President Reagan's veto justified? There was no attempt to override because proponents of the bill were convinced that they did not have enough votes in the Senate for an override. The underlying constitutional questions may well return to center stage. It now appears that there is sentiment on the FCC (depending on two new appointments) to revive the doctrine as a rule. There is also interest in Congress in enacting the Fairness Doctrine as legislation—the past support appears to be holding firm and there is now the expectation that President Clinton would not veto it. Broadcasting & Cable, Aug. 2, 1993 at 39.

2. Under the majority's view, how might a new fairness doctrine come into being? Under Judge Starr's view, what would it take to bring a new fairness doctrine into being?

3. On the constitutional side, what does Judge Starr's discussion of "scarcity" add to the discussion in *Red Lion* ?

4. If something like S. 742 should be enacted, how should a court treat its findings in a case challenging its constitutionality? Do the Congressional "findings" make the FCC's "findings" irrelevant?

5. After the Commission eliminated the fairness doctrine, several groups filed petitions asking the Commission to eliminate the personal attack and political editorial rules. These groups argued that the same logic that required the elimination of the fairness doctrine impelled the elimination of these rules, both of which originated as corollaries of the fairness doctrine. The Commission issued a Notice of Inquiry on the question.

6. Responding to Congressional concern that *Syracuse Peace Council* had already eliminated those rules, then–FCC Chairman Dennis Patrick sent a letter to Rep. John Dingell (D.–Mich.) indicating that *Syracuse Peace Council* was limited to the facts of that case. Thus, technically, the Commission had not yet made a decision concerning enforcement of the personal attack and political editorial rules, the Zapple doctrine or the application of the fairness doctrine to political campaigns and ballot issues. Patrick noted, however, that anyone charged with violating one of these rules would be free to cite *Syracuse Peace Council*, "arguing that because of the similarities between the general fairness doctrine and the particular rule at issue . . ., [*Syracuse Peace Council*] serves as precedent for the conclusion that the particular rule is unconstitutional."

7. In 1992 the Commission decided that broadcast criticism of a television news anchor's decision to conceive a second child after her first was born with the mother's congenitally deformed hands and feet (a 50 percent chance), did not involve attacks on the mother's honesty, character or integrity and thus, did not involve personal attacks. The condition was ectrodactylism. The decision addressed the issue on the merits and did not address whether the rule should be retained. Bree Walker Lampley, 70 R.R.2d 993 (Staff Ruling DA 92–179 adopted Feb. 10, 1992 by Chief, Fairness/Political Programming Branch, Mass Media Bureau).

8. In 1992 the Commission decided, 3–2, that the obligation to provide balanced coverage of ballot issues had not survived the demise of the general doctrine since the ballot proposition jurisprudence was "derived entirely from" the general doctrine—and had fallen with it. Arkansas AFL–CIO v. KARK–TV, 7 F.C.C.Rcd. 541, 70 R.R.2d 369 (1992).

On appeal the panel majority agreed with the result of the D. C. Circuit in the *TRAC* case, p. 672, that the 1959 amendment to § 315 had not enacted the fairness doctrine into statute. It rejected the literal analysis of the *TRAC* court, but reached the same result on the basis of legislative history. It then agreed with *Syracuse Peace Council*, p. 747, that the FCC was free to repeal its own creation if it wanted to do so. The dissenter thought the legislative history supported the view that the Congress had indeed affirmatively enacted the fairness doctrine—and that the FCC was without power to abandon it.

In a rehearing *en banc,* the Eighth Circuit affirmed the panel's holding, 7–5. Arkansas AFL–CIO v. Federal Communications Commission, 11 F.3d 1430 (8th Cir.1993).

## C. NONCOMMERCIAL BROADCASTING AND POLITICAL SPEECH

Virtually all of our attention so far has been devoted to commercial broadcasting. Most of the litigation and regulation has involved commercial broadcasters and, in terms of viewers, commercial broadcasting is the preeminent part of the picture. But it is not the only part. AM broadcasting developed too early for the Commission to be able to consider reserving spots for noncommercial educational stations. In allocating FM and television, however, the Commission was able to plan in advance and reserved certain spots for educational broadcasters. These are usually operated by academic institutions, by governmental groups or by groups organized by private citizens. A station run by a sectarian academic institution may be eligible for a reserved educational spot in the community in which the school is located. If an organization's central purpose is religious, it is not eligible for a reserved channel.

The development of public broadcasting and several questions it raises, are considered in the following case.

### ACCURACY IN MEDIA, INC. v. FEDERAL COMMUNICATIONS COMMISSION
United States Court of Appeals, District of Columbia Circuit, 1975.
521 F.2d 288.
Cert. denied 425 U.S. 934, 35 R.R.2d 241 (1976).

Before BAZELON, CHIEF JUDGE, LEVENTHAL, CIRCUIT JUDGE and WEIGEL, UNITED STATES DISTRICT JUDGE for the Northern District of California.

BAZELON, CHIEF JUDGE.

Accuracy in Media, Inc. (AIM) filed two complaints with the FCC against the Public Broadcasting Service (PBS) concerning two programs distributed by PBS to its member stations. AIM alleged that the programs, dealing with sex education and the American system of criminal justice, were not a balanced or objective presentation of each subject and requested the FCC to order PBS to rectify the situation. The legal basis for AIM's complaints was the Fairness Doctrine and 47 U.S.C. § 396(g)(1)(A) (1970). On its initial hearing of the matter, the FCC concluded that the PBS had not violated the Fairness Doctrine and invited comments from interested parties on its authority to enforce whatever standard of program regulation was contained in § 396(g)(1)(A). AIM does not seek review of the Commission's decision on the Fairness Doctrine issue.

Section 396(g)(1)(A) is part of the Public Broadcasting Act of 1967, an act which created the Corporation for Public Broadcasting (CPB) and authorized it to fund various programming activities of local, noncommercial broadcasting licensees. Section 396(g)(1)(A) qualifies that authorization in the following language:

> In order to achieve the objectives and to carry out the purposes of this subpart, as set out in subsection (a) of this section, the Corporation is authorized to—
>
> > (A) facilitate the full development of educational broadcasting in which programs of high quality, obtained from diverse sources, will be made available to noncommercial educational television or radio broadcast stations, with strict adherence to objectivity and balance in all programs or series of programs of a controversial nature. . . .

AIM contends that since the above-mentioned PBS programs were funded by the CPB, pursuant to this authorization, the programs must contain "strict adherence to objectivity and balance", a requirement AIM contends is more stringent than the standard of balance and fairness in overall programming contained in the Fairness Doctrine. AIM alleges that the two relevant programs did not meet this more stringent standard of objectivity and balance.

After consideration of the comments received on the matter, invited in its preliminary decision discussed above, the Commission concluded that it had no jurisdiction to enforce the mandate of § 396(g)(1)(A) against CPB. . . .

## I. THE ORGANIZATION OF PUBLIC BROADCASTING IN THE UNITED STATES

Resolution of the issues raised by AIM's petition requires an understanding of the operation of the public broadcasting system. There are three tiers to this operation, each reflecting a different scheme of governmental regulation. The basic level is comprised of the local, noncommercial broadcasting stations that are licensed by the FCC and, with a few exceptions, subject to the same regulations as commercial licenses. Through the efforts of former Commissioner Frieda Hennock, the FCC has reserved exclusive space in its allocation of frequencies for such noncommercial broadcasters. Other than this specific reservation, noncommercial licenses are still subject to the same renewal process and potential challenges as their commercial counterparts.

Such was the state of the public broadcasting system until the passage of the Educational Television Facilities Act in 1962. The Act added the element of government funding to public broadcasting by establishing a capital grant program for noncommercial facilities. This second level of the system was reorganized and expanded by the Public Broadcasting Act of 1967 which created the Corporation for Public Broadcasting (CPB). The Corporation, the product of a study made by the Carnegie Commission on Educational Television, was established as a funding mechanism for virtually all activities of noncommercial broadcasting. In setting up this nonprofit, private corporation, the Act specifically prohibited CPB from engaging in any form of "communication by wire or radio."

The third level of the public broadcasting system was added in 1970 when CPB and a group of noncommercial licensees formed the Public Broadcasting Service (PBS) and National Public Radio. The Public Broadcasting Service operates as the distributive arm of the public television system. As a nonprofit membership corporation, it distributes national programming to approximately 150 educational licensees via common carrier facilities. This interconnection service is funded by the Corporation (CPB) under a contract with PBS; in addition, much of the programming carried by PBS is either wholly or partially funded by CPB. National Public Radio provides similar services for noncommercial radio. In 1974, CPB and the member licensees of PBS agreed upon a station program cooperative plan [14] to insure local control and origination of noncommercial programming funded by CPB. Though PBS is the national coordinator under this scheme, it is not a "network" in the commercial broadcasting sense, and does not engage in "communication by wire or radio," except to the extent that it contracts for interconnection services.

## II.   FCC JURISDICTION OVER THE CORPORATION FOR PUBLIC BROADCASTING

With the structure of the public broadcasting system in view, we turn to AIM's contention that the FCC should enforce the mandate of § 396(g)(1)(A) against the CPB. Since the Section is clearly directed to the Corporation and its programming activities, we have no doubt that

---

**14.** The Station Program Cooperative (SPC) is a unique concept in program selection and financing for public television stations. Though the idea of public television as a "fourth network" had been proposed at various times, the 1974 plan reversed this trend toward centralization. Under the SPC, certain programming will be produced only if the individual local stations decide together to fund the production. The local licensees will be financed through the CPB and other sources; the funding of specific programs will be by a 4 to 5 ratio (station funds to national cooperative funds). The aim of this cooperative is to reinforce the existing licensee responsibility for programming discretion. Through this plan the local stations will eventually assume the responsibility for support of the cooperative and the Corporation will concentrate on new programming development. [   ]

the Corporation must respect the mandate of the Section. However, we conclude that nothing in the language and legislative history of the Federal Communications Act or the Public Broadcasting Act of 1967 authorizes the FCC to enforce that mandate against the CPB.

Section 398 of the Communications Act expresses the clear intent of Congress that there shall be no direct jurisdiction of the FCC over the Corporation. That section states that nothing in the 1962 or 1967 Acts "shall be deemed (1) to amend any other provision of, or requirement under this Act; or (2) to authorize any department, agency, officer, or employee of the United States to exercise any direction, supervision or control over educational television or radio broadcasting, or over the Corporation or any of its grantees or contractors . . .." Since the FCC is obviously an "agency . . . of the United States" and since any enforcement of § 396(g)(1)(A) would necessarily entail "supervision" of the Corporation, the plain words of subsection (2) preclude FCC jurisdiction. . . .

Congress desired to establish a program funding agency which would be free from governmental influence or control in its operations. Yet, the lawmakers feared that such complete autonomy might lead to biases and abuses of its own. The unique position of the Corporation is the synthesis of these competing influences. Reference to the legislative history of the 1967 Act shows a deep concern that governmental regulation or control over the Corporation might turn the CPB into a Government spokesman. Congress thus sought to insulate CPB by removing its "programming activity from governmental supervision." . . .

. . .

AIM maintains that this view of FCC jurisdiction to enforce § 396(g)(1)(A) renders the Section nugatory and hence ignores the Congressional sentiment that biases and abuses within the public broadcasting system should be controlled. We do not view our holding on the FCC's jurisdiction as having that effect. Rather, we take notice of the carefully balanced framework designed by Congress for the control of CPB activities.

The Corporation was established as nonprofit and non-political in nature and is prohibited from owning or operating "any television or radio broadcast station, system or network, community antenna system, or interconnection, or production facility." Numerous statutory safeguards were created to insure against partisan abuses.[28] Ultimately, Congress may show its disapproval of any activity of the Corporation

---

**28.** Other statutory checks on the Corporation include: restricting the Board membership to no more than eight out of fifteen members from the same political party, § 396(c)(1). The composition of the Board was an important issue during debate and the decision to make the Board bipartisan was a significant addition to the original Carnegie Commission proposal. The Act also requires that the CPB's accounts be audited annually by an independent accountant, § 396(*l*)(1)(A), and *may* be audited by the General Accounting Office, § 396(*l*)(2)(A).

through the appropriation process.[29]   This supervision of CPB through
its funding is buttressed by an annual reporting requirement.[30]
Through these statutory requirements and control over the "purse-
strings," Congress reserved for itself the oversight responsibility for the
Corporation.

A further element of this carefully balanced framework of regulation
is the accountability of the local noncommercial licensees under established FCC practice, including the Fairness Doctrine in particular.   This
existing system of accountability was clearly recognized in the 1967
legislative debates as a crucial check on the power of the CPB.    .  .  .

.  .  .

The framework of regulation of the Corporation for Public Broadcasting we have described—maximum freedom from interference with
programming coupled with existing public accountability requirements—
is sensitive to the delicate constitutional balance between the First
Amendment rights of the broadcast journalist and the concerns of the
viewing public struck in Columbia Broadcasting System, Inc. v. Democratic National Committee, 412 U.S. 94 (1973).   There the Supreme
Court warned that "only when the interests of the public are found to
outweigh the private journalistic interests of the broadcasters" will
governmental interference with broadcast journalism be allowed.   The
Court on the basis of this rule rejected a right of access to broadcast air
time greater than that mandated by the Fairness Doctrine as constituting too great a "risk of an enlargement of Government control over the
content of broadcast discussion of public issues."

It is certainly arguable that FCC application of the standard—
whatever that standard may be—of § 396(g)(1)(A) could "risk [an]
enlargement of Government control over the content of broadcast discussion of public issues" in the following two ways:  whereas the existing
Fairness Doctrine requires only that the presentation of a controversial
issue of public importance be balanced in *overall* programming,
§ 396(g)(1)(A) might be argued to require balance of controversial issues
within each individual program.   Administration of such a standard
would certainly require a more active role by the FCC in oversight of
programming.   Furthermore, whereas the FCC has at present carefully
avoided anything but the most limited inquiry into the factual accuracy
of programming, § 396(g)(1)(A) by use of the term "objective" could be
read to expand that inquiry and thereby expand FCC oversight of
programming.   Both of these potential enlargements of government
control of programming, whether directed against the CPB, PBS or
individual noncommercial licensees, threaten to upset the constitutional
balance struck in *CBS*.   We will not presume that Congress meant to
thrust upon us the substantial constitutional questions such a result

**29.**  Section 396(k) assures that most of
the CPB's operating budget be derived
through the Congressional appropriation
process.

**30.**  47 U.S.C. § 396(i) (1970).

would raise. We thus construe § 396(g)(1)(A) and the scheme of regulation for public broadcasting as a whole to avoid such questions.

. . . We hold today only that the FCC has no function in this scheme of accountability established by § 396(g)(1)(A) and the 1967 Act in general other than that assigned to it by the Fairness Doctrine. Therefore, we deny the petition for review and affirm the Commission's decision rejecting jurisdiction over the Corporation for Public Broadcasting.

So Ordered.

### Notes and Questions

1.  What was the difference between the fairness doctrine and AIM's reading of § 396(g)(1)(A)? Why does the court think that one would call for more Commission intervention in programming than the other?

2.  The court suggests that, although thought of by many as a "fourth network," PBS does not properly fit such a description. Why not?

3.  Since many of these stations are run by state and local governments, which also provide some of the financing, an additional set of problems has emerged with regard to the power of the state to impose restrictions more stringent than those imposed by Congress. In State of Maine v. University of Maine, 266 A.2d 863 (Me.1970), the state-run educational television system was partially financed from state funds. A statute ordered that no facilities "supported in whole or in part by state funds shall be used directly or indirectly for the promotion, advertisement or advancement of any political candidate . . . or for the purpose of advocating or opposing any specific program, existing or proposed, of governmental action which shall include, but shall not be limited to, constitutional amendments, tax referendums or bond issues."

The court concluded that the limitations ran counter to federal demands that a licensee operating in the public interest may not flatly ban all such programming. The role of state funding gave the state no added power in this area. Although the state "has a valid surviving power to protect its citizens in matters involving their health and safety or to protect them from fraud and deception, it has no such valid interest in protecting them from the dissemination of ideas as to which they may be called upon to make an informed choice."

4.  Despite the ruling in the AIM case, the Commission retains several controls over public noncommercial broadcasters. The primary power is to be found in the licensing process. A fundamental dispute over the proper role of educational stations emerged when WNET in New York was challenged on its application for renewal: Commissioner Hooks dissented from the approval on the ground that the station was programming for a very small elite minority and essentially neglecting the needs of larger groups in the community who would benefit from language, vocational and remedial programs. Elite programming is defended on the ground that the noncommercial stations do not get enough money from public sources and must solicit funds from their communities. It is

thought that a station that presents culturally high-level programs for the wealthier segments of the community will have better success at raising the funds necessary to keep the station going. Is this a problem? How might the situation be changed?

5. Concern about adequate funding for public broadcasting has increased during the past decade because of decreases in federal funding. In 1981 Congress created the Temporary Commission on Alternative Financing for Public Telecommunications (TCAF). Chaired by Commissioner Quello of the FCC, TCAF was directed as part of its investigation of alternative funding to oversee an 18–month experiment allowing some public broadcasters to sell advertising. Nine public television stations participated in the experiment. Although the advertising experiment generated significant income for the participants, it was not extended.

TCAF recommended to Congress that advertising not be allowed but that enhanced underwriting (allowing identification of contributors to include product identifications and slogans) be given explicit approval. What are the risks of allowing advertising on noncommercial stations? What other funding mechanisms should be considered?

6. In keeping with these recommendations and the Public Broadcasting Amendments Act of 1981, the Commission reconsidered its 1982 ruling prohibiting the inclusion of brand names in donor acknowledgements. Under the new rules "donor acknowledgements utilized by public broadcasters may include (1) logograms or slogans which identify and do *not* promote, (2) location, (3) value neutral descriptions of a product line or service, (4) brand and trade names and product or service listings." Noncommercial Educational Broadcasting Stations, 55 R.R.2d 1190 (1984).

7. Section 399(b) required public broadcasters to make and retain for 60 days (to allow inspection by government or public) audio tapes for all programs "in which any issue of public importance is discussed." It was declared unconstitutional in an *en banc* decision, 5–4. Community–Service Broadcasting of Mid–America, Inc. v. Federal Communications Commission, 593 F.2d 1102, 43 R.R.2d 1675, 4 Med.L.Rptr. 1257 (D.C.Cir.1978). The majority relied on equal protection grounds—that no similar burden was imposed on commercial broadcasters. Several members of the majority also expressed varying degrees of certainty that such a provision imposed on all broadcasters would violate the First Amendment. The dissenters thought that the statutory requirement of "objectivity and balance" justified the special obligation of § 399(b).

8. Another troublesome question in the 1967 Act involves § 399: "No noncommercial educational broadcast station may engage in editorializing or may support or oppose any candidate for political office." What arguments might be made against such a provision? What arguments to sustain it?

In 1982 a district judge declared unconstitutional the ban on editorializing by stations accepting CPB grants. The Supreme Court, 5–4, affirmed.

### FEDERAL COMMUNICATIONS COMMISSION v. LEAGUE OF WOMEN VOTERS OF CALIFORNIA

Supreme Court of the United States, 1984.
468 U.S. 364, 104 S.Ct. 3106, 82 L.Ed.2d 278, 10 Med.L.Rptr. 1937.

JUSTICE BRENNAN delivered the opinion of the Court.

[The background of the case and an excerpt from an earlier part of Justice Brennan's opinion appear at p. 669, *supra.*]

### III

We turn now to consider whether the restraint imposed by § 399 satisfies the requirements established by our prior cases for permissible broadcast regulation. Before assessing the government's proffered justifications for the statute, however, two central features of the ban against editorializing must be examined, since they help to illuminate the importance of the First Amendment interests at stake in this case.

### A

First, the restriction imposed by § 399 is specifically directed at a form of speech—namely, the expression of editorial opinion—that lies at the heart of First Amendment protection. In construing the reach of the statute, the FCC has explained that "although the use of noncommercial educational broadcast facilities by licensees, their management or those speaking on their behalf for the propagation of the licensee's own views on public issues is not permitted, such prohibition should not be construed to inhibit any *other* presentations on controversial issues of public importance." In re Complaint of Accuracy in Media, Inc., 45 F.C.C.2d 297, 302 (1973) (emphasis added). The Commission's interpretation of § 399 simply highlights the fact that what the statute forecloses is the expression of editorial opinion on "controversial issues of public importance." As we recently reiterated in NAACP v. Claiborne Hardware Co., 458 U.S. 886 (1982), "expression on public issues 'has always rested on the highest rung of the hierarchy of First Amendment values.' " Id., at 913 (quoting Carey v. Brown, 447 U.S. 455, 467 (1980)). And we have emphasized that:

> "The freedom of speech and of the press guaranteed by the Constitution embraces at least the liberty to discuss publicly and truthfully all matters of public concern without previous restraint or fear of subsequent punishment. . . . Freedom of discussion, if it would fulfill its historic function in this nation, must embrace all issues about which information is needed or appropriate to enable the members of society to cope with the exigencies of their period." Thornhill v. Alabama, 310 U.S. 88, 101–102 (1940).

The editorial has traditionally played precisely this role by informing and arousing the public, and by criticizing and cajoling those who hold government office in order to help launch new solutions to the problems of the time. Preserving the free expression of editorial opinion, therefore, is part and parcel of "our profound national commitment . . . that debate on public issues should be uninhibited, robust, and wide-open." [*Sullivan*]. As we recognized in [*Mills*], the special place of the editorial in our First Amendment jurisprudence simply reflects the fact that the press, of which the broadcasting industry is indisputably a part, United States v. Paramount Pictures, Inc., 334 U.S. 131, 166 (1948), carries out a historic, dual responsibility in our society of reporting information and of bringing critical judgment to bear on public affairs. Indeed, the pivotal importance of editorializing as a means of satisfying the public's interest in receiving a wide variety of ideas and views through the medium of broadcasting has long been recognized by the FCC; the Commission has for the past 35 years actively encouraged commercial broadcast licensees to include editorials on public affairs in their programming. Because § 399 appears to restrict precisely that form of speech which the Framers of the Bill of Rights were most anxious to protect—speech that is "indispensable to the discovery and spread of political truth"—we must be especially careful in weighing the interests that are asserted in support of this restriction and in assessing the precision with which the ban is crafted. [*Whitney*] (Brandeis, J., concurring).

Second, the scope of § 399's ban is defined solely on the basis of the content of the suppressed speech. A wide variety of non-editorial speech "by licensees, their management or those speaking on their behalf," In re Complaint of Accuracy in Media, Inc., supra, 45 F.C.C.2d, at 302, is plainly not prohibited by § 399. Examples of such permissible forms of speech include daily announcements of the station's program schedule or over-the-air appeals for contributions from listeners. Consequently, in order to determine whether a particular statement by station management constitutes an "editorial" proscribed by § 399, enforcement authorities must necessarily examine the content of the message that is conveyed to determine whether the views expressed concern "controversial issues of public importance." Ibid.

As Justice Stevens observed in Consolidated Edison Co. v. Public Service Commission, 447 U.S. 530 (1980), however, "[a] regulation of speech that is motivated by nothing more than a desire to curtail expression of a particular point of view on controversial issues of general interest is the purest example of a 'law . . . abridging the freedom of speech, or of the press.' A regulation that denies one group of persons the right to address a selected audience on 'controversial issues of public policy' is plainly such a regulation." Id., at 546 (concurring opinion); accord id., at 537–540 (majority opinion). Section 399 is just such a regulation, for it singles out noncommercial broadcasters and denies them the right to address their chosen audience on matters of public importance. . . .

### B

In seeking to defend the prohibition on editorializing imposed by § 399, the Government urges that the statute was aimed at preventing two principal threats to the overall success of the Public Broadcasting Act of 1967. According to this argument, the ban was necessary, first, to protect noncommercial educational broadcasting stations from being coerced, as a result of federal financing, into becoming vehicles for government propagandizing or the objects of governmental influence; and, second, to keep these stations from becoming convenient targets for capture by private interest groups wishing to express their own partisan viewpoints.[16] By seeking to safeguard the public's right to a balanced presentation of public issues through the prevention of either governmental or private bias, these objectives are, of course, broadly consistent with the goals identified in our earlier broadcast regulation cases. But, in sharp contrast to the restrictions upheld in *Red Lion* or in *Columbia Broadcasting System, Inc. v. FCC,* which left room for editorial discretion and simply required broadcast editors to grant others access to the microphone, § 399 directly prohibits the broadcaster from speaking out on public issues even in a balanced and fair manner. The Government insists, however, that the hazards posed in the "special" circumstances of noncommercial educational broadcasting are so great that § 399 is an indispensable means of preserving the public's First Amendment interests. We disagree.

### (1)

When Congress first decided to provide financial support for the expansion and development of noncommercial educational stations, all concerned agreed that this step posed some risk that these traditionally independent stations might be pressured into becoming forums devoted solely to programming and views that were acceptable to the Federal government. That Congress was alert to these dangers cannot be doubted. It sought through the Public Broadcasting Act to fashion a system that would provide local stations with sufficient funds to foster their growth and development while preserving their tradition of autonomy and community-orientation. . . .

The intended role of § 399 in achieving these purposes, however, is not as clear. The provision finds no antecedent in the Carnegie Report, which generally provided the model for most other aspects of the Act. It was not part of the Administration's original legislative proposal. And it was not included in the original version of the Act passed by the Senate. The provision found its way into the Act only as a result of an amendment in the House. Indeed, it appears that, as the House Committee Report frankly admits, § 399 was added not because Congress thought it was essential to preserving the autonomy and vitality of local

---

**16.** The Government also contends that § 399 is intended to prevent the use of taxpayer monies to promote private views with which taxpayers may disagree. This argument is readily answered by our decision in *Buckley v. Valeo,* 424 U.S. 1, 90–93 (1976) (per curiam). As we explained in that case, virtually every congressional appropriation will to some extent involve a use of public money as to which some taxpayers may object. Id., at 91–92. Nevertheless, this does not mean that those taxpayers have a constitutionally protected right to enjoin such expenditures. Nor can this interest be invoked to justify a congressional decision to suppress speech. . . .

stations, but rather "out of an abundance of caution." H.R.Rep. No. 572, 90th Cong., 1st Sess. 20 (1967). [ ] [18]

More importantly, an examination of both the overall legislative scheme established by the 1967 Act and the character of public broadcasting demonstrates that the interest asserted by the Government is not substantially advanced by § 399. First, to the extent that federal financial support creates a risk that stations will lose their independence through the bewitching power of governmental largesse, the elaborate structure established by the Public Broadcasting Act already operates to insulate local stations from governmental interference. Congress not only mandated that the new Corporation for Public Broadcasting would have a private, bipartisan structure, see §§ 396(c)–(f), but also imposed a variety of important limitations on its powers. The Corporation was prohibited from owning or operating any station, § 396(g)(3), it was required to adhere strictly to a standard of "objectivity and balance" in disbursing federal funds to local stations, § 396(g)(1)(A), and it was prohibited from contributing to or otherwise supporting any candidate for office, § 396(f)(3).

The Act also established a second layer of protections which serve to protect the stations from governmental coercion and interference. Thus, in addition to requiring the Corporation to operate so as to "assure the maximum freedom [of local stations] from interference with or control of program content or other activities," § 396(g)(1)(D), the Act expressly forbids "any department, agency, officer, or employee of the United States [from] exercis[ing] any direction, supervision, or control over educational television or radio broadcasting, or over the Corporation or any of its grantees or contractors . . .," § 398(a). . . . The principal thrust of the amendments, therefore, has been to assure long-term appropriations for the Corporation and, more importantly, to insist that it pass specified portions of these funds directly through to local stations to give them greater autonomy in defining the uses to which those funds should be put. Thus, in sharp contrast to § 399, the unifying theme of these various statutory provisions is that they substantially reduce the risk of governmental interference with the editorial judgments of local stations without restricting those stations' ability to speak on matters of public concern.[19]

---

**18.** . . .

Of course, as the Government points out, Congress has consistently retained the basic proscription on editorializing in § 399, despite periodic reconsiderations and modifications of the Act in 1973, 1978, and 1981. Brief for the United States 25–27; see also n. 7, supra. A reviewing court may not easily set aside such a considered congressional judgment. At the same time, "[d]eference to a legislative finding cannot limit judicial inquiry when First Amendment rights are at stake. . . . Were it otherwise, the scope of freedom of speech and of

the press would be subject to legislative definition and the function of the First Amendment as a check on legislative power would be nullified." Landmark Communications, Inc. v. Virginia, 435 U.S. 829, 843–844 (1978).

**19.** Furthermore, the risk that federal coercion or influence will be brought to bear against local stations as a result of federal financing is considerably attenuated by the fact that CPB grants account for only a portion of total public broadcasting income. CPB, Public Broadcasting Income: Fiscal Year 1982, at Table 2 (Final Report,

Even if these statutory protections were thought insufficient to the task, however, suppressing the particular category of speech restricted by § 399 is simply not likely, given the character of the public broadcasting system, to reduce substantially the risk that the Federal Government will seek to influence or put pressure on local stations. An underlying supposition of the Government's argument in this regard is that individual noncommercial stations are likely to speak so forcefully on particular issues that Congress, the ultimate source of the stations' Federal funding, will be tempted to retaliate against these individual stations by restricting appropriations for all of public broadcasting. But, as the District Court recognized, the character of public broadcasting suggests that such a risk is speculative at best. There are literally hundreds of public radio and television stations in communities scattered throughout the United States and its territories, see CPB, 1983–84 Public Broadcasting Directory 20–50, 66–86 (Sept. 1983). Given that central fact, it seems reasonable to infer that the editorial voices of these stations will prove to be as distinctive, varied, and idiosyncratic as the various communities they represent. More importantly, the editorial focus of any particular station can fairly be expected to focus largely on issues affecting only its community.[20] Accordingly, absent some showing by the Government to the contrary, the risk that local editorializing will place all of public broadcasting in jeopardy is not sufficiently pressing to warrant § 399's broad suppression of speech.

Indeed, what is far more likely than local station editorials to pose the kinds of dangers hypothesized by the Government are the wide variety of programs addressing controversial issues produced, often with substantial CPB funding, for national distribution to local stations. . . .

Furthermore, the manifest imprecision of the ban imposed by § 399 reveals that its proscription is not sufficiently tailored to the harms it seeks to prevent to justify its substantial interference with broadcasters' speech. Section 399 includes within its grip a potentially infinite variety of speech, most of which would not be related in any way to governmental affairs, political candidacies or elections. Indeed, the breadth of editorial commentary is as wide as human imagination permits. But the Government never explains how, say, an editorial by local station management urging improvements in a town's parks or museums will so

Dec. 1983) (noting that federal funds account for 23.4% of total income for all public broadcasting stations). The vast majority of financial support comes instead from state and local governments, as well as a wide variety of private sources, including foundations, businesses, and individual contributions; indeed, as the CPB recently noted, "[t]he diversity of support in America for public broadcasting is remarkable," CPB, 1982 Annual Report 2 (1982). Given this diversity of funding sources and the decentralized manner in which funds are

secured, the threat that improper federal influence will be exerted over local stations is not so pressing as to require the total suppression of editorial speech by these stations.

**20.** This likelihood is enhanced with respect to public stations because they are required to establish community advisory boards which must reasonably reflect the "diverse needs and interests of the communities served by such station[s]." § 396(k)(9)(A). . . .

infuriate Congress or other Federal officials that the future of public broadcasting will be imperiled unless such editorials are suppressed. Nor is it explained how the suppression of editorials alone serves to reduce the risk of governmental retaliation and interference when it is clear that station management is fully able to broadcast controversial views so long as such views are not labelled as its own.  [    ]

The Government appears to recognize these flaws in § 399, because it focuses instead on the suggestion that the source of governmental influence may well be state and local governments, many of which have established public broadcasting commissions that own and operate local noncommercial educational stations.[22]  The ban on editorializing is all the more necessary with respect to these stations, the argument runs, because the management of such stations will be especially likely to broadcast only editorials that are favorable to the state or local authorities that hold the purse strings.  The Government's argument, however, proves too much.  First, § 399's ban applies to the many private noncommercial community organizations that own and operate stations that are not controlled in any way by state or local government.  Second, the legislative history of the Public Broadcasting Act clearly indicates that Congress was concerned with "assur[ing] complete freedom from any *Federal Government influence.*"  [    ]  Consistently with this concern, Congress refused to create any federally owned stations and it expressly forbid the CPB to own or operate any television or radio stations, § 396(g)(3).  By contrast, although Congress was clearly aware in 1967 that many noncommercial educational stations were owned by state and local governments, it did not hesitate to extend Federal assistance to such stations, it imposed no special requirements to restrict state or local control over these stations, and, indeed, it ensured through the structure of the Act that these stations would be as insulated from Federal interference as the wholly private stations.

Finally, although the Government certainly has a substantial interest in ensuring that the audiences of noncommercial stations will not be led to think that the broadcaster's editorials reflect the official view of the government, this interest can be fully satisfied by less restrictive means that are readily available.  To address this important concern, Congress could simply require public broadcasting stations to broadcast a disclaimer every time they editorialize which would state that the editorial represents only the view of the station's management and does not in any way represent the views of the Federal Government or any of the station's other sources of funding.  Such a disclaimer—similar to those often used in commercial and noncommercial programming of a controversial nature—would effectively and directly communicate to the

---

**22.** As the Government points out in its Brief, at least two-thirds of the public television broadcasting stations in operation are licensed to (a) state public broadcasting authorities or commissions, in which commission members are often appointed by the governor with the advice and consent of the state legislature, (b) state universities or educational commissions, or (c) local school boards or municipal authorities. [    ]

audience that the editorial reflected only the views of the station rather than those of the government.   . . .

In sum, § 399's broad ban on all editorializing by every station that receives CPB funds far exceeds what is necessary to protect against the risk of governmental interference or to prevent the public from assuming that editorials by public broadcasting stations represent the official view of government. The regulation impermissibly sweeps within its prohibition a wide range of speech by wholly private stations on topics that do not take a directly partisan stand or that have nothing whatever to do with federal, state or local government.

(2)

Assuming that the Government's second asserted interest in preventing noncommercial stations from becoming a "privileged outlet for the political and ideological opinions of station owners and management," Brief at 34, is legitimate, the substantiality of this asserted interest is dubious. The patent over- and underinclusiveness of § 399's ban "undermines the likelihood of a genuine [governmental] interest" in preventing private groups from propagating their own views via public broadcasting. [*Bellotti*] If it is true, as the government contends, that noncommercial stations remain free, despite § 399, to broadcast a wide variety of controversial views through their power to control program selection, to select which persons will be interviewed, and to determine how news reports will be presented, Brief at 41, then it seems doubtful that § 399 can fairly be said to advance any genuinely substantial governmental interest in keeping controversial or partisan opinions from being aired by noncommercial stations.   . . .

In short, § 399 does not prevent the use of noncommercial stations for the presentation of partisan views on controversial matters; instead, it merely bars a station from specifically communicating such views on its own behalf or on behalf of its management. If the vigorous expression of controversial opinions is, as the Government assures us, affirmatively encouraged by the Act, and if local licensees are permitted under the Act to exercise editorial control over the selection of programs, controversial or otherwise, that are aired on their stations, then § 399 accomplishes only one thing—the suppression of editorial speech by station management. It does virtually nothing, however, to reduce the risk that public stations will serve solely as outlets for expression of narrow partisan views. What we said in [CBS v. DNC], supra, applies, therefore, with equal force here: the "sacrifice [of] First Amendment protections for so speculative a gain is not warranted.   . . ." 412 U.S., at 127.

Finally, the public's interest in preventing public broadcasting stations from becoming forums for lopsided presentations of narrow partisan positions is already secured by a variety of other regulatory means that intrude far less drastically upon the "journalistic freedom" of noncommercial broadcasters. [   ]

The requirements of the FCC's fairness doctrine, for instance, which apply to commercial and noncommercial stations alike, ensure that such editorializing would maintain a reasonably balanced and fair presentation of controversial issues. Thus, even if the management of a noncommercial educational station were inclined to seek to further only its own partisan views when editorializing, it simply could not do so.  . . . Since the breadth of § 399 extends so far beyond what is necessary to accomplish the goals identified by the Government, it fails to satisfy the First Amendment standards that we have applied in this area.

We therefore hold that even if some of the hazards at which § 399 was aimed are sufficiently substantial, the restriction is not crafted with sufficient precision to remedy those dangers that may exist to justify the significant abridgement of speech worked by the provision's broad ban on editorializing. The statute is not narrowly tailored to address any of the government's suggested goals. Moreover, the public's "paramount right" to be fully and broadly informed on matters of public importance through the medium of noncommercial educational broadcasting is not well served by the restriction, for its effect is plainly to diminish rather than augment "the volume and quality of coverage" of controversial issues. *Red Lion,* supra, at 393. Nor do we see any reason to deny noncommercial broadcasters the right to address matters of public concern on the basis of merely speculative fears of adverse public or governmental reactions to such speech.

## IV

Although the Government did not present the argument in any form to the District Court, it now seeks belatedly to justify § 399 on the basis of Congress' Spending Power. Relying upon our recent decision in Regan v. Taxation With Representation, 461 U.S. 540 (1983), the Government argues that by prohibiting noncommercial educational stations that receive CPB grants from editorializing, Congress has, in the proper exercise of its Spending Power, simply determined that it "will not subsidize public broadcasting station editorials." Brief of the United States 42. In *Taxation With Representation,* the Court found that Congress could, in the exercise of its Spending Power, reasonably refuse to subsidize the lobbying activities of tax-exempt charitable organizations by prohibiting such organizations from using tax-deductible contributions to support their lobbying efforts.  . . .

Of course, if Congress were to adopt a revised version of § 399 that permitted noncommercial educational broadcasting stations to establish "affiliate" organizations which could then use the station's facilities to editorialize with non-federal funds, such a statutory mechanism would plainly be valid under the reasoning of *Taxation With Representation.* Under such a statute, public broadcasting stations would be free, in the same way that the charitable organization in *Taxation With Representation* was free, to make known its views on matters of public importance through its non-federally funded, editorializing affiliate without losing federal grants for its non-editorializing broadcast activities. [  ] But in the absence of such authority, we must reject the Government's contention that our decision in *Taxation With Representation* is controlling here.

## V

In conclusion, we emphasize that our disposition of this case rests upon a narrow proposition. We do not hold that the Congress or the FCC are without power to regulate the content, timing, or character of speech by noncommercial educational broadcasting stations. Rather, we hold only that the specific interests sought to be advanced by § 399's ban on editorializing are either not sufficiently substantial or are not served in a sufficiently limited manner to justify the substantial abridgment of important journalistic freedoms which the First Amendment jealously protects. Accordingly, the judgment of the District Court is affirmed.

JUSTICE REHNQUIST, with whom THE CHIEF JUSTICE and JUSTICE WHITE join, dissenting.

All but three paragraphs of the Court's lengthy opinion in this case are devoted to the development of a scenario in which the government appears as the "Big Bad Wolf," and appellee Pacifica as "Little Red Riding Hood." In the Court's scenario the Big Bad Wolf cruelly forbids Little Red Riding Hood from taking to her grandmother some of the food that she is carrying in her basket. Only three paragraphs are used to delineate a truer picture of the litigants, wherein it appears that some of the food in the basket was given to Little Red Riding Hood by the Big Bad Wolf himself, and that the Big Bad Wolf had told Little Red Riding Hood in advance that if she accepted his food she would have to abide by his conditions. Congress in enacting § 399 of the Public Broadcasting Act, 47 U.S.C. (Supp. V) § 399, has simply determined that public funds shall not be used to subsidize noncommercial, educational broadcasting stations which engage in "editorializing" or which support or oppose any political candidate. I do not believe that anything in the First Amendment to the United States Constitution prevents Congress from choosing to spend public monies in that manner. Perhaps a more appropriate analogy than that of Little Red Riding Hood and the Big Bad Wolf is that of Faust and Mephistopheles; Pacifica, well aware of § 399's condition on its receipt of public money, nonetheless accepted the public money and now seeks to avoid the conditions which Congress legitimately has attached to receipt of that funding.

. . .

The Court's three-paragraph discussion of why § 399, repeatedly reexamined and retained by Congress, violates the First Amendment is to me utterly unpersuasive. Congress has rationally determined that the bulk of the taxpayers whose monies provide the funds for grants by the CPB would prefer not to see the management of local educational stations promulgate its own private views on the air at taxpayer expense.

Accordingly Congress simply has decided not to subsidize stations which engage in that activity.

.   .   .

This is not to say that the government may attach *any* condition to its largess; it is only to say that when the government is simply exercising its power to allocate its own public funds, we need only find that the condition imposed has a rational relationship to Congress' purpose in providing the subsidy and that it is not primarily "aimed at the suppression of dangerous ideas." Cammarano v. United States, 358 U.S. 498, 513 (1959), quoting Speiser v. Randall, 357 U.S. 513, 519 (1958). In this case Congress' prohibition is directly related to its purpose in providing subsidies for public broadcasting, and it is plainly rational for Congress to have determined that taxpayer monies should not be used to subsidize management's views or to pay for management's exercise of partisan politics. Indeed, it is entirely rational for Congress to have wished to avoid the appearance of government sponsorship of a particular view or a particular political candidate. Furthermore, Congress' prohibition is strictly neutral. In no sense can it be said that Congress has prohibited only editorial views of one particular ideological bent. Nor has it prevented public stations from airing programs, documentaries, interviews, etc. dealing with controversial subjects, so long as management itself does not expressly endorse a particular viewpoint. And Congress has not prevented station management from communicating its own views on those subjects through any medium other than subsidized public broadcasting.

For the foregoing reasons I find this case entirely different from the so-called "unconstitutional condition" cases, wherein the Court has stated that the government "may not deny a benefit to a person on a basis that infringes his constitutionally protected interests—especially his interest in freedom of speech." Perry v. Sindermann, 408 U.S. 593, 597 (1972). In those cases the suppressed speech was not content-neutral in the same sense as here, and in those cases, there is at best only a strained argument that the legislative purpose of the condition imposed was to avoid *subsidizing* the prohibited speech. Speiser v. Randall, supra, is illustrative of the difference. In that case California's decision to deny its property tax exemption to veterans who would not declare that they would not work to overthrow the government was plainly directed at suppressing what California regarded as speech of a dangerous content. And the condition imposed was so unrelated to the benefit to be conferred that it is difficult to argue that California's property tax exemption actually subsidized the dangerous speech.

Here, in my view, Congress has rationally concluded that the bulk of taxpayers whose monies provide the funds for grants by the CPB would prefer not to see the management of public stations engage in editorializing or the endorsing or opposing of political candidates. Because Congress' decision to enact § 399 is a rational exercise of its spending powers and strictly neutral, I would hold that nothing in the First

Amendment makes it unconstitutional.  Accordingly, I would reverse the judgment of the District Court.

JUSTICE WHITE:

Believing that the editorializing and candidate endorsement proscription stand or fall together and being confident that Congress may condition use of its funds on abstaining from political endorsements, I join JUSTICE REHNQUIST's dissenting opinion.

JUSTICE STEVENS, dissenting.

The court jester who mocks the King must choose his words with great care.  An artist is likely to paint a flattering portrait of his patron.  The child who wants a new toy does not preface his request with a comment on how fat his mother is.  Newspaper publishers have been known to listen to their advertising managers.  Elected officials may remember how their elections were financed.  By enacting the statutory provision that the Court invalidates today, a sophisticated group of legislators expressed a concern about the potential impact of government funds on pervasive and powerful organs of mass communication.  One need not have heard the raucous voice of Adolph Hitler over Radio Berlin to appreciate the importance of that concern.

As Justice White correctly notes, the statutory prohibitions against editorializing and candidate endorsements rest on the same foundation.  In my opinion that foundation is far stronger than merely "a rational basis" and it is not weakened by the fact that it is buttressed by other provisions that are also designed to avoid the insidious evils of government propaganda favoring particular points of view.  The quality of the interest in maintaining government neutrality in the free market of ideas—of avoiding subtle forms of censorship and propaganda—outweigh the impact on expression that results from this statute.  Indeed, by simply terminating or reducing funding, Congress could curtail much more expression with no risk whatever of a constitutional transgression.

. . .

Although appellees originally challenged the validity of the entire statute, in their amended complaint they limited their attack to the prohibition against editorializing.  In its analysis of the case, the Court assumes that the ban on political endorsements is severable from the first section and that it may be constitutional.[3]  In view of the fact that the major difference between the ban on political endorsements is based on the content of the speech, it is apparent that the entire rationale of the Court's opinion rests on the premise that it may be permissible to predicate a statutory restriction on candidate endorsements on the difference between the content of that kind of speech and the content of other expressions of editorial opinion.

---

**3.**  The Court actually raises the wrong severability issue.  The serious question in this regard is whether the entire public funding scheme is severable from the prohibition on editorializing and political en- dorsements.  The legislative history of the statute indicates the strength of the congressional aversion to these practices. . . .

The Court does not tell us whether speech that endorses political candidates is more or less worthy of protection than other forms of editorializing, but it does iterate and reiterate the point that "the expression of editorial opinion" is a special kind of communication that "is entitled to the most exacting degree of First Amendment protection." [  ].[4]

Neither the fact that the statute regulates only one kind of speech, nor the fact that editorial opinion has traditionally been an important kind of speech, is sufficient to identify the character or the significance of the statute's impact on speech. Three additional points are relevant. First, the statute does not prohibit Pacifica from expressing its opinion through any avenue except the radio stations for which it receives federal financial support. It eliminates the subsidized channel of communication as a forum for Pacifica itself, and thereby deprives Pacifica of an advantage it would otherwise have over other speakers, but it does not exclude Pacifica from the marketplace for ideas. Second, the statute does not curtail the expression of opinion by individual commentators who participate in Pacifica's programs. The only comment that is prohibited is a statement that Pacifica agrees or disagrees with the opinions that others may express on its programs. Third, and of greatest significance for me, the statutory restriction is completely neutral in its operation—it prohibits all editorials without any distinction being drawn concerning the subject matter or the point of view that might be expressed.[5]

## II

The statute does not violate the fundamental principle that the citizen's right to speak may not be conditioned upon the sovereign's

**4.** Thus, once again the Court embraces the obvious proposition that some speech is more worthy of protection than other speech—that the right to express editorial opinion may be worth fighting to preserve even though the right to hear less worthy speech may not—a proposition that several members of today's majority could only interpret "as an aberration" in Young v. American Mini Theaters, 427 U.S. 50, 87 (1976) (dissenting opinion) ("The fact that the 'offensive' speech here may not address 'important' topics—'ideas of social and political significance,' in the Court's terminology, does not mean that it is less worthy of constitutional protection." Ibid.).

**5.** Section 399's ban on editorializing is a content based restriction on speech, but not in the sense that the majority implies. The majority speaks of "editorial opinion" as if it were some sort of special species of opinion, limited to issues of public importance. The majority confuses the typical content of editorials with the meaning of editorial itself. An editorial is, of course, a statement of the *management's* opinion on

any topic imaginable. The Court asserts that what the statute "forecloses is the expression of editorial opinion on 'controversial issues of public importance.'" The statute is not so limited. The content which is prohibited is that the station is not permitted to state its opinion with respect to any matter. In short, it may not be an on-the-air advocate if it accepts government funds for its broadcasts. The prohibition on editorializing is not directed at any particular message a station might wish to convey, [  ]. . . .

Paradoxically, section 399 is later attacked by the majority as essentially being underinclusive because it does not prohibit "controversial" national programming that is often aired with substantial federal funding. . . . Next, § 399's ban on editorializing is attacked by the majority on overinclusive grounds—because it is content-neutral—since it prohibits a "potentially infinite variety of speech, most of which would not be related in any way to governmental affairs, political candidacies or elections." . . . .

agreement with what the speaker intends to say. On the contrary, the statute was enacted in order to protect that very principle—to avoid the risk that some speakers will be rewarded or penalized for saying things that appeal to—or are offensive to—the sovereign.[7] The interests the statute is designed to protect are interests that underlie the First Amendment itself.

In my judgment the interest in keeping the Federal Government out of the propaganda arena is of overriding importance. That interest is of special importance in the field of electronic communication, not only because that medium is so powerful and persuasive, but also because it is the one form of communication that is licensed by the Federal Government.[8] When the Government already has great potential power over the electronic media, it is surely legitimate to enact statutory safeguards to make sure that it does not cross the threshold that separates neutral regulation from the subsidy of partisan opinion.

The Court does not question the validity of the basic interests served by § 399. Instead, it suggests that the statute does not substantially serve those interests because the Public Broadcasting Act operates in many other respects to insulate local stations from governmental interference. In my view, that is an indication of nothing more than the strength of the governmental interest involved here—Congress enacted many safeguards because the evil to be avoided was so grave. Organs of official propaganda are antithetical to this nation's heritage and Congress understandably acted with great caution in this area. It is no answer to say that the other statutory provisions "substantially reduce the risk of government interference with the editorial judgments of the local stations without restricting the stations' ability to speak out on matters of public concern." [ ] The other safeguards protect the stations from interference with judgments that they will necessarily make in selecting programming, but those judgments are relatively amorphous. No safeguard is foolproof; and the fact that funds are dispensed according to largely "objective" criteria certainly is no guarantee. Individuals must always make judgments in allocating funds, and pressure can be exerted in subtle ways as well as through outright fund-cutoffs.

Members of Congress, not members of the Judiciary, live in the world of politics. When they conclude that there is a real danger of political considerations influencing the dispensing of this money and that

---

**7.** . . . Moreover, the statute will also protect the listener's interest in not having his tax payments used to finance the advocacy of causes he opposes. The majority gives extremely short shrift to the Government's interest in minimizing the use of taxpayer monies to promote private views with which the taxpayers may disagree. The Court briefly observes that the taxpayers do not have a constitutionally protected right to enjoin such expenditures and then leaps to the conclusion that given the fact that the funding scheme itself is not unconstitutional, this interest cannot be used to support the statute at issue here. The conclusion manifestly does not follow from the premise, and this interest is plainly legitimate and significant.

**8.** We have consistently adhered to the following guiding principles applicable to First Amendment claims in the area of broadcasting, and they bear repeating at some length: [quoting from *Red Lion*].

this provision is necessary to insulate grantees from political pressures in addition to the other safeguards, that judgment is entitled to our respect.

The magnitude of the present danger that the statute is designed to avoid is admittedly a matter about which reasonable judges may disagree.[10]  Moreover, I would agree that the risk would be greater if other statutory safeguards were removed.  It remains true, however, that Congress has the power to prevent the use of public funds to subsidize the expression of partisan points of view, or to suppress the propagation of dissenting opinions.  No matter how great or how small the immediate risk may be, there surely is more than a theoretical possibility that future grantees might be influenced by the ever present tie of the political purse strings, even if those strings are never actually pulled.

. . . .

### III

The Court describes the scope of § 399's ban as being "defined solely on the basis of the content of the suppressed speech," ante, at 18, and analogizes this case to the regulation of speech we condemned in Consolidated Edison Co. v. Public Serv. Comm'n, 447 U.S. 530 (1980). This description reveals how the Court manipulates labels without perceiving the critical differences behind the two cases.

In *Consolidated Edison* the class of speakers that was affected by New York's prohibition consisted of regulated public utilities that had been expressing their opinion on the issue of nuclear power by means of written statements inserted in their customers' monthly bills.  Although the scope of the prohibition was phrased in general terms and applied to a selected group of speakers, it was obviously directed at spokesmen for a particular point of view.  The justification for the restriction was phrased in terms of the potential offensiveness of the utilities' messages to their audiences.  It was a classic case of a viewpoint-based prohibition.

In this case, however, although the regulation applies only to a defined class of noncommercial broadcast licensees, it is common ground that these licensees represent heterogenous points of view.[12]  There is simply no sensible basis for considering this regulation a viewpoint restriction—or, to use the Court's favorite phrase, to condemn it as

**10.** The majority argues that the Government's concededly substantial interest in ensuring that audiences of educational stations will not perceive the station to be a government propaganda organ can be fully satisfied by requiring such stations to broadcast a disclaimer each time they editorialize stating that the editorial "does not in any way represent the views of the Federal Government. . . ." [ ] This solution would be laughable were it not so Orwellian: the answer to the fact that there is a real danger that the editorials are really government propaganda is for the government to require the station to tell the audience that it is not propaganda at all!

**12.** That does not necessarily mean, however, "that the editorial voices of these stations will prove to be as distinctive, varied, and idiosyncratic as the various communities they represent," [ ] at 25, given the potential effects of government funding, [ ].

"content-based"—because it applies equally to station owners of all shades of opinion.  Moreover, the justification for the prohibition is not based on the "offensiveness" of the messages in the sense that that term was used in *Consolidated Edison*.  Here, it is true that taxpayers might find it offensive if their tax monies were being used to subsidize the expression of editorial opinion with which they disagree, but it is the fact of the subsidy—not just the expression of the opinion—that legitimates this justification.  Furthermore, and of greater importance, the principal justification for this prohibition is the overriding interest in forestalling the creation of propaganda organs for the Government.

I respectfully dissent.

## Notes and Questions

1.  How realistic are the fears of the dissenting justices?  President Nixon once vetoed the CPB budget because of dissatisfaction with CPB programming.  Are noncommercial licensees likely to be influenced by the "power of the purse?"  If, indeed, prohibitions on specific forms of speech are unconstitutional, how can noncommercial licensees be insulated from government control?

2.  In response to a complaint by Sen. James F. Buckley (R.–N.Y.), the Commission held that § 312(a)(7) was equally applicable to commercial and noncommercial stations.  However, only those noncommercial stations using channels specifically reserved for noncommercial broadcasting are prohibited from charging for the time they must make available.  Senator James F. Buckley, 63 F.C.C.2d 952, 38 R.R.2d 1255 (1976).

3.  The crucial difference between commercial and non-commercial broadcasting involves the question of the licensee's ability to control content and to reject programming.  In *League of Women Voters* the Court was faced with the problem of indirect control of PBS stations through the CPB funding mechanism.  Consider, however, that more than 140 PBS stations are under some form of government ownership.  What effect should that have on the ability of those licensees to control content and reject programming?  The issue was posed dramatically in 1980, when several PBS stations decided to cancel a previously scheduled showing of "Death of a Princess," a dramatization of the circumstances surrounding the 1977 execution for adultery of a Saudi Arabian princess and her commoner lover.  Strong objections to the program had been voiced by the Saudi Arabian government.

Two separate actions requesting injunctions requiring the airing of the program were filed by viewers against PBS licensees, the Alabama Educational Television Commission (AETC) and the University of Houston.  The denial of an injunction against AETC was upheld on appeal while a separate panel reversed the granting of an injunction against the University of Houston.  The two cases were then consolidated for rehearing *en banc*.  The issue arose in Muir v. Alabama Educational Television Commission, 688 F.2d 1033, 52 R.R.2d 935, (5th Cir.1982), 8 Med.L.Rptr. 2305, cert. denied 460 U.S. 1023 (1983).

The 22 judges who participated in the rehearing produced a total of six separate opinions. Judge Hill, whose opinion was referred to by all as the majority opinion, declared the central issue in the case to be "whether the First Amendment rights of viewers impose limits on the programming discretion of public television stations licensed to state instrumentalities." In an opinion written by Judge Hill, they determined that no such limits were imposed despite plaintiffs' argument that public television stations are public forums.

> A facility is a public forum only if it is designed to provide a general public right of access to its use, or if such public access has historically existed and is not incompatible with the facility's primary activity.
>
> . . .
>
> . . . The pattern of usual activity for public television stations is the statutorily mandated practice of the broadcast licensee exercising sole programming authority. The general invitation extended to the public is not to schedule programs, but to watch or decline to watch what is offered. It is thus clear that the public television stations involved in the cases before us are not public forums.

Plaintiffs also tried to argue that cancelling a previously scheduled show constituted "censorship" in violation of the First Amendment. Again, the court was not persuaded.

> We conclude that the defendants' editorial decisions to cancel "Death of a Princess" cannot be properly characterized as "censorship." Had the states of Alabama and Texas sought to prohibit the exhibition of the film by another party then indeed a question of censorship would have arisen. Such is not the case before us. The states have not sought to forbid or curtail the right of any person to show or view the film. . . . The state officials in charge of AETC and KUHT–TV have simply exercised their statutorily mandated discretion and decided not to show a particular program at a particular time. There is a clear distinction between a state's exercise of editorial discretion over its own expression, and a state's prohibition or suppression of the speech of another.

However, subsequent cases have held that Judge Rubin's opinion is the majority opinion. See, e.g., Schneider v. Indian River Community College Foundation, Inc., 875 F.2d 1537 (11th Cir.1989). He viewed the issue to be

> whether an individual viewer has a right to compel a television station operated by a state agency to broadcast a single program previously scheduled by an employee of the agency that a higher-ranking state official has decided, because of its content, to cancel.

He concluded that no such authority existed:

> Judicial reassessment of the propriety of a programming decision
> made in operating a television station involves not only interference
> with station management but also reevaluation of all the content-
> quality-audience reaction factors that enter into a decision to use or
> not to use a program by a medium that cannot possibly, by its very
> nature, accommodate everything that every viewer might desire.
> With deference to the dicta observations made in the *Pico* plurality
> opinion, our reexamination of such a decision cannot logically be
> confined to occasions when higher officials overrule subordinates. If
> it is forbidden censorship for the higher official to cancel a program,
> it is equally censorship for the lower officials to decide initially to
> reject a program.

Other judges also viewed the case as presenting a much narrower
issue. In his concurrence, Judge Garwood stated:

> First, plaintiffs are not attacking governmental "public" broad-
> casting as such. Nor do they seek to require its operation to be on a
> pure "open forum" basis—like an empty stage available to all
> comers—where each citizen can cause the broadcast of his or her
> program of choice, with the inevitable selectivity determined by
> completely content neutral factors such as lot, or first come first
> served or the like. Rather, plaintiffs seek to become a part of
> governmental "public" broadcasting essentially as it is, except they
> want it to broadcast this particular program of their choice. Howev-
> er, there is simply no way for them—together with all others who
> might wish to assert similar rights for their favorite "dramatiza-
> tion"—to become a part of *such* "conventional" (as distinguished
> from pure "open forum") governmental broadcasting *except* on the
> basis of governmental selection of the individual programs.

The three dissenting opinions, for the seven dissenters, all focused
on the state's ability to censor ideas. As Judge Johnson stated:

> The clearly defined issue in these appeals is whether the execu-
> tive officers of a state operated public television station may cancel a
> previously scheduled program because it presents a point of view
> disagreeable to the religious and political regime of a foreign coun-
> try. The majority opinion permitting cancellation on these grounds
> flies completely in the face of the First Amendment and our tradi-
> tion of vigilance against governmental censorship of political and
> religious expression.

The dissenting judges argued that the majority's reliance on the
editorial discretion conferred by the Communications Act on broadcast
licensees elevated the Act above the Constitution. Although disagreeing
among themselves as to the exact standards for judging the programming decisions of state licensees, they all agreed that the editorial
discretion of state broadcasters should be limited by the First Amendment.

# Chapter XVII

# LEGAL CONTROL OF BROADCAST PROGRAMMING: NONPOLITICAL SPEECH

In Chapter XVI we examined legal controls on broadcast programming that were primarily concerned with political speech. We now turn to other content regulation of broadcasting. Here, the restrictions often take the form of direct bans on speech. As we examine these cases ask yourself whether these restrictions are more, or less, justifiable than those covered in the previous chapter.

## A. DRUGS

### YALE BROADCASTING CO. v. FEDERAL COMMUNICATIONS COMMISSION

United States Court of Appeals, District of Columbia Circuit, 1973.
478 F.2d 594, 26 R.R.2d 383, cert. denied 414 U.S. 914 (1973).

Before DANAHER, SENIOR CIRCUIT JUDGE, and ROBINSON AND WILKEY, CIRCUIT JUDGES.

WILKEY, CIRCUIT JUDGE:

The source of this controversy is a Notice issued by the Federal Communications Commission regarding "drug oriented" music allegedly played by some radio stations. This Notice and a subsequent Order, the stated purposes of which were to remind broadcasters of a pre-existing duty, required licensees to have knowledge of the content of their programming and on the basis of this knowledge to evaluate the desirability of broadcasting music dealing with drug use. Appellant, a radio station licensee, argues first that the Notice and the Order are an unconstitutional infringement of its First Amendment right to free speech. . . .

. . .

Despite all its attempts to assuage broadcasters' fears, the Commission realized that if an Order can be misunderstood, it will be misunderstood—at least by some licensees. To remove any excuse for misunderstanding, the Commission specified examples of how a broadcaster could obtain the requisite knowledge. A licensee could fulfill its obligation through (1) pre-screening by a responsible station employee, (2) monitoring selections while they were being played, or (3) considering and responding to complaints made by members of the public. The Order made clear that these procedures were merely suggestions, and were not

794

to be regarded as either absolute requirements or the exclusive means for fulfilling a station's public interest obligation.

Having made clear our understanding of what the Commission has done, we now take up appellant's arguments seriatim.

### III.  AN UNCONSTITUTIONAL BURDEN ON FREEDOM OF SPEECH

Appellant's first argument is that the Commission's action imposes an unconstitutional burden on a broadcaster's freedom of speech. This contention rests primarily on the Supreme Court's opinion in Smith v. California,[12] in which a bookseller was convicted of possession and selling obscene literature. The Supreme Court reversed the conviction. Although the State had a legitimate purpose in seeking to ban the distribution of obscene materials, it could not accomplish this goal by placing on the bookseller the procedural burden of examining every book in his store. To make a bookseller criminally liable for all the books sold would necessarily "tend to restrict the books he sells to those he has inspected; and thus the State will have imposed a restriction upon the distribution of constitutionally protected as well as obscene literature . . .."

Appellant compares its own situation to that of the bookseller in *Smith* and argues that the Order imposes an unconstitutional burden on a broadcaster's freedom of speech. The two situations are easily distinguishable.

Most obviously, a radio station can only broadcast for a finite period of twenty-four hours each day; at any one time a bookstore may contain thousands of hours' worth of readable material. Even if the Commission had ordered that stations pre-screen all materials broadcast, the burden would not be nearly so great as the burden imposed on the bookseller in *Smith*. As it is, broadcasters are not even required to pre-screen their maximum of twenty-four hours of daily programming. Broadcasters have specifically been told that they may gain "knowledge" of what they broadcast in other ways.

A more subtle but no less compelling answer to appellant's argument rests upon *why* knowledge of drug oriented music is required by the Commission. In *Smith*, knowledge was imputed to the purveyor in order that a criminal sanction might be imposed and the dissemination halted. Here the goal is to assure the broadcaster has adequate knowledge.   . . .

We say that the licensee must have *knowledge* of what it is broadcasting; the precise *understanding* which may be required of the licensee is only that which is reasonable. No radio licensee faces any realistic possibility of a penalty for misinterpreting the lyrics it has chosen or permitted to be broadcast. If the lyrics are completely obscure, the station is not put on notice that it is in fact broadcasting material which

12.  361 U.S. 147 (1959).

would encourage drug abuse.  If the lyrics are meaningless, incoherent, the same conclusion follows.  The argument of the appellant licensee, that so many of these lyrics are obscure and ambiguous, really is a circumstance available to some degree in his defense for permitting their broadcast, at least until their meaning is clarified.  Some lyrics or sounds are virtually unintelligible.  To the extent they are completely meaningless gibberish and approach the equivalent of machinery operating or the din of traffic, they, of course, do not communicate with respect to drugs or anything else, and are not within the ambit of the Commission's order.  Speech is an expression of sound or visual symbols which is intelligible to some other human beings.  At some point along the scale of human intelligibility the sounds produced may slide over from characteristics of free speech, which should be protected, to those of noise pollution, which the Commission has ample authority to abate.[15]

We not only think appellant's argument invalid, we express our astonishment that the licensee would argue that before the broadcast it has no knowledge, and cannot be required to have any knowledge, of material it puts out over the airwaves.  We can understand that the individual radio licensees would not be expected to know in advance the content or the quality of a network program, or a free flowing panel discussion of public issues, or other audience participation program, and certainly not a political broadcast.  But with reference to the broadcast of that which is frequently termed "canned music," we think the Commission may require that the purveyors of this to the public make a reasonable effort to know what is in the "can."  No producer of pork and beans is allowed to put out on a grocery shelf a can without knowing what is in it and standing back of both its content and quality.  The Commission is not required to allow radio licensees, being freely granted the use of limited air channels, to spew out to the listening public canned music, whose content and quality before broadcast is totally unknown.

Supposedly a radio licensee is performing a public service—that is the raison d'etre of the license.  If the licensee does not have specific knowledge of what it is broadcasting, how can it claim to be operating in the public interest?  Far from constituting any threat to freedom of speech of the licensee, we conclude that for the Commission to have been less insistent on licensees discharging their obligations would have verged on an evasion of the Commission's own responsibilities.

By the expression of the above views we have no desire whatsoever to express a value judgment on different types of music, poetry, sound, instrumentation, etc., which may appeal to different classes of our most diverse public.  "De gustibus non est disputandum."  But what we are saying is that whatever the style, whatever the expression put out over the air by the radio station, for the licensee to claim that it has no responsibility to evaluate its product is for the radio station to abnegate completely what we had always considered its responsibility as a licensee.  All in all, and quite unintentionally, the appellant-licensee in its

**15.**  Cf. Noise Control Act of 1972, Pub.L. No. 92–574, 86 Stat. 1234 (1972).

free speech argument here has told us a great deal about quality in this particular medium of our culture.

. . .

For the reasons given above, the action of the Federal Communications Commission is

Affirmed.

## Notes and Questions

1. A motion for a rehearing *en banc* was denied over the objection of Chief Judge Bazelon, who commented that

> . . . the Order restated its basic threat: "the broadcaster could jeopardize his license by failing to exercise licensee responsibility in this area." As we have recognized, "licensee responsibility" is a nebulous concept. It could be taken to mean—as the panel opinion takes it—only that "a broadcaster must 'know' what it is broadcasting." On the other hand, in light of the earlier Notice, and in light of the renewed warnings in the Order about the dangers of "drug-oriented" popular songs, broadcasters might have concluded that "responsibility" meant "prohibition."

> . . .

> This case presents several other questions of considerable significance: Is the popular song a constitutionally protected form of speech? [23] Do the particular songs at which these directives were aimed have a demonstrable connection with illegal activities? If so, is the proper remedy to "discourage or eliminate" the playing of such songs? Can the FCC assert regulatory authority over material that could not constitutionally be regulated in the printed media? [25]

> Clearly, the impact of the Commission's order is ripe for judicial review. And, on that review, it would be well to heed Lord Devlin's recent warning:

> > If freedom of the press . . . [or freedom of speech] perishes, it will not be by sudden death. . . . It will be a long time dying from a debilitating disease caused by a series of erosive measures, each of which, if examined singly, would have a good deal to be said for it.

**23.** Popular songs might be considered mere entertainment, or even noise pollution. Yale Broadcasting Co. v. FCC, at 598, 599. On the other hand, historians and sociologists have noted that the popular song has been an important medium of political, moral, and aesthetic expression in American life. [  ]

**25.** See Brandywine–Main Line Radio, Inc. v. FCC, 473 F.2d 16 (1972) (Chief Judge Bazelon, dissenting) (application of the Fairness Doctrine). Unlike the "Fairness Doctrine" cases, there can be no assertion here that the chilling effect is incidental to providing access to the media for viewpoints that would contribute to a fuller debate on public issues. The question is thus presented whether the rationale of the "Fairness Doctrine", or any other realities of the electronic media, warrant intrusion on broadcasters' free speech rights in this case.

2.　The Supreme Court denied *certiorari* 414 U.S. 914 (1973).　Justice Brennan would have granted the writ and set the case for argument. Justice Douglas dissented along the lines sketched by Chief Judge Bazelon.　He noted that the Commission majority apparently had intended to ban drug-related lyrics from the air and that at a Congressional hearing the Chairman testified that if a licensee were playing songs that the Commission thought promoted the use of "hard drugs," "I know what I would do, I would probably vote to take the license away." Even though drug lyrics might not cause great concern if banned, "next year it may apply to comedy programs, and the following year to news broadcasts."　He concluded that

> The Government cannot, consistent with the First Amendment, require a broadcaster to censor its music any more than it can require a newspaper to censor the stories of its reporters.　Under our system the Government is not to decide what messages, spoken or in music, are of the proper "social value" to reach the people.

3.　Could Congress ban pro-drug broadcasts—whether of songs or of normal speech?　Are your views here consistent with your views about Congressional power to ban cigarette commercials?

4.　Could Congress ban pro-drug messages in the print media?　What about pro-cigarette messages?　In 1985 the American Medical Association recommended extending the ban on cigarette advertisements to all media.　Recall our discussion of the constitutionality of banning nondeceptive advertising for lawful products, p. 432, *supra*.

5.　In 1985 the Parents Music Resource Center proposed that record companies place warning labels on records with lyrics that contain "explicit sexual language, profanity, violence, the occult and the glorification of drugs and alcohol."　Broadcasting, Sept. 26, 1985 at 28.　Some record companies subsequently agreed to a voluntary system of warning labels.　What if the Commission were to ban the playing of records with warning labels?　What if the Commission merely indicated a belief that playing records with those labels is against the public interest?

## B.　OBSCENITY AND INDECENCY

The subject of obscenity did not become a problem on radio and television until the 1960s.　In the earlier years of these media, the licensees apparently had no practical reason to want to test the limits of permissible communication and were unsure what the Commission might legally do to licensees who stepped over the line.

In the 1934 Act, § 326, the prohibition on censorship, also contained a passage forbidding the use of obscene or indecent speech in broadcasting.　In 1948 that ban was removed from § 326 and added to the general criminal law in 18 U.S.C.A. § 1464:

> Whoever utters any obscene, indecent, or profane language by means of radio communication shall be fined not more than $10,000 or imprisoned not more than two years, or both.

Several other sections empower the Commission to impose sanctions for violation of § 1464.

In 1964 the Commission considered renewal of stations belonging to the Pacifica Foundation. Complaints had been filed regarding five programs: two poets' reading their own works; one author's reading from his novel; a recording of Edward Albee's "Zoo Story"; and a program "in which eight homosexuals discussed their attitudes and problems." All were late at night except one of the poetry readings. The Commission indicated that it was "not concerned with individual programs" but with whether there had been a pattern of programming inconsistent with the public interest. Although it found nothing to bar renewal, the Commission discussed the five programs because it would be "useful" to the "industry and the public."

The Commission found three of the programs were well within the licensee's judgment under the public interest standard. The Commission recognized that provocative programming might offend some listeners. To rule such programs off the air, however, would mean that "only the wholly inoffensive, the bland, could gain access to the radio microphone or TV camera." The remedy for offended listeners was to turn off the program. The two poetry readings raised different questions. One did not measure up to the licensee's standards for presentation but it had not been carefully screened because it had come from a reputable source. The other reading, broadcast at 7:15 p.m., involving 28 poems, was aired because the station's editor admitted he had been lulled by the poet's "rather flat, monotonous voice" and did not catch unidentified "offensive words" in the 19th poem. The errors were isolated and thus caused no renewal problem. Pacifica Foundation, 36 F.C.C. 147, 1 R.R.2d 747 (1964). For a history of Pacifica's struggle in 1964, including the fact that no broadcaster came to its defense, see Barton, "The Lingering Legacy of Pacifica: Broadcasters' Freedom of Silence," 53 Journ.Q. 429 (1976).

Another episode involved a taped interview on a noncommercial FM station with Jerry Garcia, leader of a musical group known as the Grateful Dead. Garcia apparently used "various patently offensive words as adjectives, introductory expletives, and as substitutes for 'et cetera.'" The opinion gave no examples. The Commission imposed a forfeiture of $100 for "indecency" and apparently hoped for a court test of its powers. Eastern Educational Radio (WUHY–FM), 24 F.C.C.2d 408, 18 R.R.2d 860 (1970). The licensee paid the fine, and the case was over.

Next came charges of obscenity leveled at "topless radio," midday programs consisting of "call-in talk shows in which masters of ceremonies discuss intimate sexual topics with listeners, usually women." The format quickly became popular. The Commission responded to complaints by ordering its staff to tape several of the shows and to present a condensed tape of some of the most offensive comments. The next day Chairman Burch spoke to the National Association of Broadcasters condemning the format. Two weeks later the Commission issued a Notice of Apparent Liability proposing a forfeiture of $2,000 against one licensee. Sonderling Broadcasting Corp. (WGLD–FM), 27 R.R.2d 285 (F.C.C.1973). The most troublesome language was apparently:

> Female Listener:    . . .    of course I had a few hangups at first about—in regard to this, but you know what we did—I have a craving for peanut butter all that [sic] time so I used to spread this on my husband's privates and after a while, I mean, I didn't even need the peanut butter anymore.

> Announcer: (Laughs) Peanut butter, huh?

> Listener: Right. Oh, we can try anything—you know—any, any of these women that have called and they have, you know, hangups about this, I mean they should try their favorite—you know like—uh.    . . .

> Announcer: Whipped cream, marshmallow . . ..

In addition, the host's conversation with a complaining listener was thought to be suffused with "leering innuendo." The Commission thought this program ran afoul of both the "indecency" and "obscenity" standards of § 1464. On the other hand, the Commission disclaimed any intention to ban the discussion of sex entirely:

> We are emphatically not saying that sex *per se* is a forbidden subject on the broadcast medium. We are well aware that sex is a vital human relationship which has concerned humanity over the centuries, and that sex and obscenity are not the same thing. In this area as in others, we recognize the licensee's right to present provocative or unpopular programming which may offend some listeners, Pacifica Foundation, 36 FCC 147, 149 (1964). Second, we note that we are not dealing with works of dramatic or literary art as we were in *Pacifica*. We are rather confronted with the talk or interview show where clearly the interviewer can readily moderate his handling of the subject matter so as to conform to the basic statutory standards—standards which, as we point out, allow much leeway for provocative material.    . . .    The standards here are strictly defined by the law: The broadcaster must eschew the "obscene or indecent."

Again the Commission sought a test: "we welcome and urge judicial consideration of our action." Commissioner Johnson dissented on several grounds, including the view that the Commission had no duty to act in these cases and should leave the matter to possible prosecution by Justice Department. Sonderling denied liability but paid the fine. Two citizen groups asked the Commission to reconsider on the grounds that listeners' rights to hear such programs had been disregarded by the Commission's action. The Commission reaffirmed its action. 41 F.C.C.2d 777, 27 R.R.2d 1508 (1973). It indicated that it had based its order "on the pervasive and intrusive nature of broadcast radio, even if children were left completely out of the picture." It went on, however, to point out that children were in the audience during these afternoon programs and there was some evidence that the program was not intended solely for adults. "The obvious intent of this reference to children was to convey the conclusion that this material was unlawful, and that it was even more clearly unlawful when presented to an audience which included children."

The citizen groups appealed but lost. Illinois Citizens Committee for Broadcasting v. Federal Communications Commission, 515 F.2d 397 (D.C.Cir.1974). The court refused to allow the petitioners to make certain procedural arguments that it thought were open only to the licensee itself. On the merits:

> The excerpts cited by the Commission contain repeated and explicit descriptions of the techniques of oral sex. And these are presented, not for educational and scientific purposes, but in a context that was fairly described by the FCC as "titillating and pandering." The principles of Ginzburg v. United States, 383 U.S. 463 (1966) are applicable, for commercial exploitation of interests in titillation is the broadcaster's sole end. It is not a material difference that here the tone is set by the continuity provided by the announcer rather than, as in *Ginzburg,* by the presentation of the material in advertising and sale to solicit an audience. We cannot ignore what the Commission took into account—that the announcer's response to a complaint by an offended listener and his presentation of advertising for auto insurance are suffused with leering innuendo. Moreover, and significantly, "Femme Forum" is broadcast from 10 a.m. to 3 p.m. during daytime hours when the radio audience may include children—perhaps home from school for lunch, or because of staggered school hours or illness. Given this combination of factors, we do not think that the FCC's evaluation of this material infringes upon rights protected by the First Amendment.

> The FCC found Sonderling's broadcasts obscene . . . ..

> . . .

> Petitioners object that the Commission's determination was based on a brief condensation of offensive material and did not take into account the broadcast as a whole, as would seem to be required by certain elements of both the *Memoirs* and the *Miller* tests. The Commission's approach is not inappropriate in evaluating a broadcasting program that is episodic in nature—a cluster of individual and typically disconnected commentaries, rather than an integrated presentation. It is commonplace for members of the radio audience to listen only to short snatches of a broadcast, and programs like "Femme Forum" are designed to attract such listeners. . . .

> We conclude that, where a radio call-in show during daytime hours broadcasts explicit discussions of ultimate sexual acts in a titillating context, the Commission does not unconstitutionally in-

fringe upon the public's right to listening alternatives when it determines that the broadcast is obscene.

The court explicitly did not rely upon the Commission's argument that it had latitude to hold things "indecent" that are not obscene.

A motion for rehearing *en banc* was denied over the lengthy dissent of Chief Judge Bazelon. He was much concerned about the ability of the Commission, by "raised eyebrow" and the Chairman's speech, virtually to end a popular format. He saw this as "flagrant and illegal censorship." He also found four areas of error committed by the panel.

## INTRODUCTION TO THE PACIFICA CASE

Two points are required to introduce the following case. The first involves the notion of "nuisance" in law. Activities that may be socially desirable are often called nuisances if located in the wrong place. This might include a factory that emits smoke in an amount that would be acceptable in a factory district, but is unacceptable in a residential district. The legal goal is to encourage the factory either to conform to the needs of its surroundings or to relocate to a factory area.

The second point involves a conflict within the Court about the legitimacy of regulations based on the content of the communication. In Police Department of Chicago v. Mosley, 408 U.S. 92 (1972), the Court invalidated an ordinance that barred picketing outside schools unless the picketing was related to a labor-management dispute concerning the school. "Once a forum is opened up to assembly or speaking by some groups, government may not prohibit others from assembling or speaking on the basis of what they intend to say."

In Young v. American Mini Theatres, Inc., 427 U.S. 50, 1 Med. L.Rptr. 1151 (1976), Detroit adopted a zoning ordinance requiring that theaters that specialized in showing sexually explicit movies had to be separated from one another by a minimum distance. The Court upheld the ordinance, 5–4, but there was no majority opinion. Justice Stevens, for the plurality of four, said that the *Mosley* statement must be kept in context. Even though the First Amendment did not permit "total suppression of erotic materials that have some arguably artistic value, it is manifest that society's interest in protecting this type of expression is of a wholly different, and lesser, magnitude than the interest in untrammeled political debate . . .. [F]ew of us would march our sons and daughters off to war to preserve the citizen's right to see 'Specified Sexual Activities' exhibited in the theaters of our choice."

The plurality then concluded that the record supported the city council's conclusions that unfortunate effects followed from the clustering of such enterprises in one area.

Justice Powell provided the crucial fifth vote on the ground that this case involved "an example of innovative land-use regulation, implicating First Amendment concerns only incidentally and to a limited extent." The ordinance did not "restrict in any significant way the viewing of these movies by those who desire to see them."

The four dissenters considered the decision "a drastic departure from established principles of First Amendment law." These principles require that regulations concerning the time, place and manner of communicating "be content-neutral except in the limited context of a captive or juvenile audience."

As we will see, this conflict reappears in *Pacifica*.

## FEDERAL COMMUNICATIONS COMMISSION v. PACIFICA FOUNDATION

Supreme Court of the United States, 1978.

438 U.S. 726, 98 S.Ct. 3026, 57 L.Ed.2d 1073, 43 R.R.2d 493, 3 Med.L.Rptr. 2553.

[George Carlin, a "satiric humorist," recorded a 12–minute monologue entitled "Filthy Words" before a live audience in a California theater. The theme was "the words you couldn't say on the public, ah, airwaves. . . ." Carlin then proposed a basic list: "The original seven words were shit, piss, fuck, cunt, cocksucker, mother-fucker, and tits. Those are the ones that will curve your spine, grow hair on your hands and (laughter) maybe, even bring us, God help us, peace without honor (laughter) um, and a bourbon." Carlin then discussed "shit" and "fuck" at length, including the various phrases that use each word. The following passage gives some idea of the format:

> Now the word shit is okay for the man. At work you can say it like crazy. Mostly figuratively. Get that shit out of here, will ya? I don't want to see that shit anymore. I can't *cut* that shit, buddy. I've had that shit up to here. I think you're full of shit myself. (laughter) He don't know shit from Shinola. (laughter) You know that? (laughter) Always wondered how the Shinola people felt about that. (laughter) Hi, I'm the new man from Shinola. (laughter) Hi, how are ya? Nice to see ya. (laughter) How are ya? (laughter) Boy, I don't know whether to shit or wind my watch. (laughter) Guess, I'll shit on my watch. (laughter) Oh, *the* shit is going to hit *de* fan. (laughter) Built like a brick shit-house. (laughter) Up, he's up shit's creek. (laughter) He's had it. (laughter) He hit me, I'm sorry. (laughter) Hot shit, holy shit, tough shit, eat shit. (laughter) Shit-eating grin. Uh, whoever thought of that was ill. (murmur laughter) He had a shit-eating grin! He had a what? (laughter) Shit on a stick. (laughter) Shit in a handbag. I always like that.

One Tuesday afternoon at 2 p.m., Pacifica's FM radio station in New York City played the monologue during a discussion about society's attitude toward language. The station warned that the monologue included language that might offend some listeners. A man who apparently did not hear the warning heard the broadcast while driving with his young son and complained to the Commission. In response to an inquiry from the Commission, Pacifica responded that Carlin was a "significant social satirist" who "like Twain and Sahl before him, examines the language of ordinary people." Apparently, no one else complained about the broadcast.

The Commission ruled that Pacifica's action was subject to administrative sanction. Instead of imposing a formal sanction, it put the order in the file for possible use if subsequent complaints were received. The Commission asserted four reasons for treating broadcasting differently from other media: access by unsupervised children; since radio receivers are in the home, privacy interests are entitled to extra deference; unconsenting adults may tune in without a warning that offensive language is being used; and scarcity of spectrum space requires government to license in the public interest. Further facts are stated in the opinions.]

MR. JUSTICE STEVENS delivered the opinion of the Court (Parts I, II, III, and IV–C) and an opinion in which THE CHIEF JUSTICE and MR. JUSTICE REHNQUIST joined (Parts IV–A and IV–B).

This case requires that we decide whether the Federal Communications Commission has any power to regulate a radio broadcast that is indecent but not obscene.

. . .

. . . [T]he Commission found a power to regulate indecent broadcasting in two statutes: 18 U.S.C. § 1464, which forbids the use of "any obscene, indecent, or profane language by means of radio communications," and 47 U.S.C. § 303(g), which requires the Commission to "encourage the larger and more effective use of radio in the public interest."

The Commission characterized the language used in the Carlin monologue as "patently offensive," though not necessarily obscene, and expressed the opinion that it should be regulated by principles analogous to those found in the law of nuisance where the "law generally speaks to *channeling* behavior more than actually prohibiting it. . . . [T]he concept of 'indecent' is intimately connected with the exposure of children to language that describes, in terms patently offensive as measured by contemporary community standards for the broadcast medium, sexual or excretory activities and organs, at times of the day when there is a reasonable risk that children may be in the audience." 56 F.C.C.2d, at 98.[5]

. . . In summary, the Commission stated: "We therefore hold that the language as broadcast was indecent and prohibited by 18 U.S.C. 1464."

After the order issued, the Commission was asked to clarify its opinion by ruling that the broadcast of indecent words as part of a live newscast would not be prohibited. . . . The Commission noted that its "declaratory order was issued in a specific factual context," and

5. Thus, the Commission suggested, if an offensive broadcast had literary, artistic, political or scientific value, and were preceded by warnings, it might not be indecent in the late evening, but would be so during the day, when children are in the audience.

declined to comment on various hypothetical situations presented by the petition.[7] . . .

The United States Court of Appeals for the District of Columbia reversed, with each of the three judges on the panel writing separately. . . .

Having granted the Commission's petition for certiorari, 434 U.S. 1008, we must decide: (1) whether the scope of judicial review encompasses more than the Commission's determination that the monologue was indecent "as broadcast"; (2) whether the Commission's order was a form of censorship forbidden by § 326; (3) whether the broadcast was indecent within the meaning of § 1464; and (4) whether the order violates the First Amendment of the United States Constitution.

## I

The general statements in the Commission's memorandum opinion do not change the character of its order. Its action was an adjudication. . . . The specific holding was carefully confined to the monologue "as broadcast."

. . . Accordingly, the focus of our review must be on the Commission's determination that the Carlin monologue was indecent as broadcast.

## II

The relevant statutory questions are whether the Commission's action is forbidden "censorship" within the meaning of 47 U.S.C. § 326 and whether speech that concededly is not obscene may be restricted as "indecent" under the authority of 18 U.S.C. § 1464. The questions are not unrelated, for the two statutory provisions have a common origin. . . .

The prohibition against censorship unequivocally denies the Commission any power to edit proposed broadcasts in advance and to excise material considered inappropriate for the airwaves. The prohibition, however, has never been construed to deny the Commission the power to review the content of completed broadcasts in the performance of its regulatory duties.[9]

---

**7.** The Commission did, however, comment that:

" '[I]n some cases, public events likely to produce offensive speech are covered live, and there is no opportunity for journalistic editing.' Under these circumstances we believe that it would be inequitable for us to hold a licensee responsible for indecent language. . . . We trust that under such circumstances a licensee will exercise judgment, responsibility, and sensitivity to the community's needs, interests and tastes."

[ ]

**9.** Zechariah Chafee, defending the Commission's authority to take into account program service in granting licenses, interpreted the restriction on "censorship" narrowly: "This means, I feel sure, the sort of censorship which went on in the seventeenth century in England—the deletion of specific items and dictation as to what should go into particular programs." 2 Z. Chafee, Government and Mass Communications 641 (1947).

During the period between the original enactment of the provision in 1927 and its re-enactment in the Communications Act of 1934, the courts and the Federal Radio Commission held that the section deprived the Commission of the power to subject "broadcasting matter to scrutiny prior to its release," but they concluded that the Commission's "undoubted right" to take note of past program content when considering a licensee's renewal application "is not censorship."

Not only did the Federal Radio Commission so construe the statute prior to 1934; its successor, the Federal Communications Commission, has consistently interpreted the provision in the same way ever since. [ ] And, until this case, the Court of Appeals for the District of Columbia has consistently agreed with this construction. . . .

Entirely apart from the fact that the subsequent review of program content is not the sort of censorship at which the statute was directed, its history makes it perfectly clear that it was not intended to limit the Commission's power to regulate the broadcast of obscene, indecent, or profane language. . . .

There is nothing in the legislative history to contradict this conclusion. . . .

We conclude, therefore, that § 326 does not limit the Commission's authority to impose sanctions on licensees who engage in obscene, indecent, or profane broadcasting.

### III

The only other statutory question presented by this case is whether the afternoon broadcast of the "Filthy Words" monologue was indecent within the meaning of § 1464.[13] Even that question is narrowly confined by the arguments of the parties.

The Commission identified several words that referred to excretory or sexual activities or organs, stated that the repetitive, deliberate use of those words in an afternoon broadcast when children are in the audience was patently offensive, and held that the broadcast was indecent. Pacifica takes issue with the Commission's definition of indecency, but does not dispute the Commission's preliminary determination that each of the components of its definition was present. Specifically, Pacifica does not quarrel with the conclusion that this afternoon broadcast was patently offensive. Pacifica's claim that the broadcast was not indecent within the meaning of the statute rests entirely on the absence of prurient appeal.

---

**13.** In addition to § 1464, the Commission also relied on its power to regulate in the public interest under 47 U.S.C. § 303(g). We do not need to consider whether § 303 may have independent significance in a case such as this. The statutes authorizing civil penalties incorporate § 1464, a criminal statute. See 47 U.S.C. §§ 312(a)(6), 312(b)(2), and 503(b)(1)(E). But the validity of the civil sanctions is not linked to the validity of the criminal penalty. The legislative history of the provisions establishes their independence. . . .

The plain language of the statute does not support Pacifica's argument. The words "obscene, indecent, or profane" are written in the disjunctive, implying that each has a separate meaning. Prurient appeal is an element of the obscene, but the normal definition of "indecent" merely refers to nonconformance with accepted standards of morality.

Pacifica argues, however, that this Court has construed the term "indecent" in related statutes to mean "obscene" as that term was defined in [*Miller*]. Pacifica relies most heavily on the construction this Court gave to 18 U.S.C. § 1461 in Hamling v. United States, 418 U.S. 87. See also United States v. Twelve 200-foot Reels of Film, 413 U.S. 123, 130 n. 7 (18 U.S.C. § 1462) (dicta). . . .

The reasons supporting *Hamling's* construction of § 1461 do not apply to § 1464. Although the history of the former revealed a primary concern with the prurient, the Commission has long interpreted § 1464 as encompassing more than the obscene. The former statute deals primarily with printed matter enclosed in sealed envelopes mailed from one individual to another; the latter deals with the content of public broadcasts. It is unrealistic to assume that Congress intended to impose precisely the same limitations on the dissemination of patently offensive matter by such different means.[17]

Because neither our prior decisions nor the language or history of § 1464 supports the conclusion that prurient appeal is an essential component of indecent language, we reject Pacifica's construction of the statute. When that construction is put to one side, there is no basis for disagreeing with the Commission's conclusion that indecent language was used in this broadcast.

## IV

Pacifica makes two constitutional attacks on the Commission's order. First, it argues that the Commission's construction of the statutory language broadly encompasses so much constitutionally protected speech that reversal is required even if Pacifica's broadcast of the "Filthy Words" monologue is not itself protected by the First Amendment. Second, Pacifica argues that inasmuch as the recording is not obscene, the Constitution forbids any abridgment of the right to broadcast it on the radio.

## A

The first argument fails because our review is limited to the question whether the Commission has the authority to proscribe this particu-

**17.** This conclusion is re-enforced by noting the different constitutional limits on Congress' power to regulate the two different subjects. Use of the postal power to regulate material that is not fraudulent or obscene raises "grave constitutional questions." Hannegan v. Esquire, Inc., 327 U.S. 146, 156. But it is well settled that the First Amendment has a special meaning in the broadcasting context. See, e.g., FCC v. National Citizens Committee for Broadcasting, 436 U.S. 775; Red Lion Broadcasting Co., Inc. v. FCC, 395 U.S. 367; Columbia Broadcasting System, Inc. v. Democratic National Committee, 412 U.S. 94. For this reason, the presumption that Congress never intends to exceed constitutional limits, which supported Hamling's narrow reading of § 1461, does not support a comparable reading of § 1464.

lar broadcast. As the Commission itself emphasized, its order was "issued in a specific factual context." 59 F.C.C.2d, at 893. That approach is appropriate for courts as well as the Commission when regulation of indecency is at stake, for indecency is largely a function of context—it cannot be adequately judged in the abstract.

The approach is also consistent with [*Red Lion*].  . . .

It is true that the Commission's order may lead some broadcasters to censor themselves. At most, however, the Commission's definition of indecency will deter only the broadcasting of patently offensive references to excretory and sexual organs and activities.[18] While some of these references may be protected, they surely lie at the periphery of First Amendment concern. Cf. [*Bates*]. [*Young*]. The danger dismissed so summarily in *Red Lion*, in contrast, was that broadcasters would respond to the vagueness of the regulations by refusing to present programs dealing with important social and political controversies. Invalidating any rule on the basis of its hypothetical application to situations not before the Court is "strong medicine" to be applied "sparingly and only as a last resort." Broadrick v. Oklahoma, 413 U.S. 601, 613. We decline to administer that medicine to preserve the vigor of patently offensive sexual and excretory speech.

## B

When the issue is narrowed to the facts of this case, the question is whether the First Amendment denies government any power to restrict the public broadcast of indecent language in any circumstances.[19] For if the government has any such power, this was an appropriate occasion for its exercise.

The words of the Carlin monologue are unquestionably "speech" within the meaning of the First Amendment. It is equally clear that the Commission's objections to the broadcast were based in part on its content. The order must therefore fall if, as Pacifica argues, the First Amendment prohibits all governmental regulation that depends on the content of speech. Our past cases demonstrate, however, that no such absolute rule is mandated by the Constitution.

The classic exposition of the proposition that both the content and the context of speech are critical elements of First Amendment analysis is Mr. Justice Holmes' statement for the Court in [*Schenck*]:

**18.** A requirement that indecent language be avoided will have its primary effect on the form, rather than the content, of serious communication. There are few, if any, thoughts that cannot be expressed by the use of less offensive language.

**19.** Pacifica's position would of course deprive the Commission of any power to regulate erotic telecasts unless they were obscene under Miller v. California, 413 U.S. 15. Anything that could be sold at a newsstand for private examination could be publicly displayed on television.

We are assured by Pacifica that the free play of market forces will discourage indecent programming. "Smut may," as Judge Leventhal put it, "drive itself from the market and confound Gresham," 556 F.2d at 35; the prosperity of those who traffic in pornographic literature and films would appear to justify his skepticism.

"We admit that in many places and in ordinary times the defendants in saying all that was said in the circular would have been within their constitutional rights. But the character of every act depends upon the circumstances in which it is done. . . . The most stringent protection of free speech would not protect a man in falsely shouting fire in a theatre and causing a panic. It does not even protect a man from an injunction against uttering words that may have all the effect of force. . . . The question in every case is whether the words used are used in such circumstances and are of such a nature as to create a clear and present danger that they will bring about the substantive evils that Congress has a right to prevent." 249 U.S. 47, 52.

Other distinctions based on content have been approved in the years since *Schenck*. The government may forbid speech calculated to provoke a fight. See [*Chaplinsky*]. It may pay heed to the " 'commonsense differences' between commercial speech and other varieties." [*Bates*] It may treat libels against private citizens more severely than libels against public officials. See [*Gertz*]. Obscenity may be wholly prohibited. [*Miller*] And only two Terms ago we refused to hold that a "statutory classification is unconstitutional because it is based on the content of communication protected by the First Amendment." [*Young*]

The question in this case is whether a broadcast of patently offensive words dealing with sex and excretion may be regulated because of its content. Obscene materials have been denied the protection of the First Amendment because their content is so offensive to contemporary moral standards. [*Roth*] But the fact that society may find speech offensive is not a sufficient reason for suppressing it. Indeed, if it is the speaker's opinion that gives offense, that consequence is a reason for according it constitutional protection. For it is a central tenet of the First Amendment that the government must remain neutral in the marketplace of ideas. If there were any reason to believe that the Commission's characterization of the Carlin monologue as offensive could be traced to its political content—or even to the fact that it satirized contemporary attitudes about four-letter words [22]—First Amendment protection might be required. But that is simply not this case. These words offend for the same reasons that obscenity offends.[23] Their place in the hierarchy of First Amendment values was aptly

---

**22.** The monologue does present a point of view; it attempts to show that the words it uses are "harmless" and that our attitudes toward them are "essentially silly." [  ] The Commission objects, not to this point of view, but to the way in which it is expressed. The belief that these words are harmless does not necessarily confer a First Amendment privilege to use them while proselytizing, just as the conviction that obscenity is harmless does not license one to communicate that conviction by the indiscriminate distribution of an obscene leaflet.

**23.** The Commission stated: "Obnoxious, gutter language describing these matters has the effect of debasing and brutalizing human beings by reducing them to their mere bodily functions . . . ." 56 F.C.C.2d, at 98. Our society has a tradition of performing certain bodily functions in private, and of severely limiting the public exposure or discussion of such matters. Verbal or physical acts exposing those intimacies are offensive irrespective of any message that may accompany the exposure.

sketched by Mr. Justice Murphy when he said, "such utterances are no essential part of any exposition of ideas, and are of such slight social value as a step to truth that any benefit that may be derived from them is clearly outweighed by the social interest in order and morality." [*Chaplinsky*]

Although these words ordinarily lack literary, political, or scientific value, they are not entirely outside the protection of the First Amendment. Some uses of even the most offensive words are unquestionably protected. See, e.g., Hess v. Indiana, 414 U.S. 105. Indeed, we may assume, *arguendo,* that this monologue would be protected in other contexts. Nonetheless, the constitutional protection accorded to a communication containing such patently offensive sexual and excretory language need not be the same in every context. It is a characteristic of speech such as this that both its capacity to offend and its "social value," to use Mr. Justice Murphy's term, vary with the circumstances. Words that are commonplace in one setting are shocking in another. To paraphrase Mr. Justice Harlan, one occasion's lyric is another's vulgarity. Cf. [*Cohen*].

In this case it is undisputed that the content of Pacifica's broadcast was "vulgar," "offensive," and "shocking." Because content of that character is not entitled to absolute constitutional protection under all circumstances, we must consider its context in order to determine whether the Commission's action was constitutionally permissible.

## C

We have long recognized that each medium of expression presents special First Amendment problems. Joseph Burstyn, Inc. v. Wilson, 343 U.S. 495, 502–503. And of all forms of communication, it is broadcasting that has received the most limited First Amendment protection. Thus, although other speakers cannot be licensed except under laws that carefully define and narrow official discretion, a broadcaster may be deprived of his license and his forum if the Commission decides that such an action would serve "the public interest, convenience, and necessity." Similarly, although the First Amendment protects newspaper publishers from being required to print the replies of those whom they criticize, [*Tornillo*], it affords no such protection to broadcasters; on the contrary, they must give free time to the victims of their criticism. [*Red Lion*]

The reasons for these distinctions are complex, but two have relevance to the present case. First, the broadcast media have established a uniquely pervasive presence in the lives of all Americans. Patently offensive, indecent material presented over the airwaves confronts the citizen, not only in public, but also in the privacy of the home, where the individual's right to be let alone plainly outweighs the First Amendment rights of an intruder. [*Rowan*] Because the broadcast audience is constantly tuning in and out, prior warnings cannot completely protect the listener or viewer from unexpected program content. To say that one may avoid further offense by turning off the radio when he hears indecent language is like saying that the remedy for an assault is to run away after the first blow. One may hang up on an indecent phone call, but that option does not give the caller a constitutional immunity or avoid a harm that has already taken place.[27]

Second, broadcasting is uniquely accessible to children, even those too young to read. Although Cohen's written message might have been incomprehensible to a first grader, Pacifica's broadcast could have enlarged a child's vocabulary in an instant. Other forms of offensive expression may be withheld from the young without restricting the expression at its source. Bookstores and motion picture theaters, for example, may be prohibited from making indecent material available to children. We held in [*Ginsberg*], that the government's interest in the "well being of its youth" and in supporting "parents' claim to authority in their own household" justified the regulation of otherwise protected expression. Id., at 640 and 639.[28] The ease with which children may obtain access to broadcast material, coupled with the concerns recognized in *Ginsberg*, amply justify special treatment of indecent broadcasting.

It is appropriate, in conclusion, to emphasize the narrowness of our holding. This case does not involve a two-way radio conversation between a cab driver and a dispatcher, or a telecast of an Elizabethan comedy. We have not decided that an occasional expletive in either setting would justify any sanction or, indeed, that this broadcast would justify a criminal prosecution. The Commission's decision rested entirely on a nuisance rationale under which context is all-important. The concept requires consideration of a host of variables. The time of day was emphasized by the Commission. The content of the program in which the language is used will also affect the composition of the audience,[29] and differences between radio, television, and perhaps closed-circuit transmissions, may also be relevant. As Mr. Justice Sutherland wrote, a "nuisance may be merely a right thing in the wrong place—like a pig in the parlor instead of the barnyard." Euclid v. Ambler Realty Co., 272 U.S. 365, 388. We simply hold that when the Commission finds that a pig has entered the parlor, the exercise of its regulatory power does not depend on proof that the pig is obscene.

The judgment of the Court of Appeals is reversed.

**27.** Outside the home, the balance between the offensive speaker and the unwilling audience may sometimes tip in favor of the speaker, requiring the offended listener to turn away. See Erznoznik v. Jacksonville, 422 U.S. 205.

**28.** The Commission's action does not by any means reduce adults to hearing only what is fit for children. Cf. Butler v. Michigan, 352 U.S. 380, 383. Adults who feel the need may purchase tapes and records or go to theatres and nightclubs to hear these words. In fact, the Commission has not unequivocally closed even broadcasting to speech of this sort; whether broadcast audiences in the late evening contain so few children that playing this monologue would be permissible is an issue neither the Commission nor this Court has decided.

**29.** Even a prime-time recitation of Chaucer's Miller's Tale would not be likely to command the attention of many children who are both old enough to understand and young enough to be adversely affected by passages such as, "And prively he caughte hire by the queynte." G. Chaucer, *The Miller's Tale* 1.3276 (c. 1386).

Mr. Justice Powell, with whom Mr. Justice Blackmun joins, concurring.

I join Parts I, II, III, and IV(C) of Mr. Justice Stevens' opinion. The Court today reviews only the Commission's holding that Carlin's monologue was indecent "as broadcast" at two o'clock in the afternoon, and not the broad sweep of the Commission's opinion. . . .

I also agree with much that is said in Part IV of Mr. Justice Stevens' opinion, and with its conclusion that the Commission's holding in this case does not violate the First Amendment. Because I do not subscribe to all that is said in Part IV, however, I state my views separately.

I

It is conceded that the monologue at issue here is not obscene in the constitutional sense. See 56 F.C.C.2d 94, 98 (1975); Brief for Petitioner 18. Nor, in this context, does its language constitute "fighting words" within the meaning of [*Chaplinsky*]. Some of the words used have been held protected by the First Amendment in other cases and contexts. [ ] I do not think Carlin, consistently with the First Amendment, could be punished for delivering the same monologue to a live audience composed of adults who, knowing what to expect, chose to attend his performance. See Brown v. Oklahoma, 408 U.S. 914 (1972) (Powell, J., concurring in result). And I would assume that an adult could not constitutionally be prohibited from purchasing a recording or transcript of the monologue and playing or reading it in the privacy of his own home. [*Stanley*]

But it also is true that the language employed is, to most people, vulgar and offensive. It was chosen specifically for this quality, and it was repeated over and over as a sort of verbal shock treatment. The Commission did not err in characterizing the narrow category of language used here as "patently offensive" to most people regardless of age.

The issue, however, is whether the Commission may impose civil sanctions on a licensee radio station for broadcasting the monologue at two o'clock in the afternoon. The Commission's primary concern was to prevent the broadcast from reaching the ears of unsupervised children who were likely to be in the audience at that hour. In essence, the Commission sought to "channel" the monologue to hours when the fewest unsupervised children would be exposed to it. See 56 F.C.C.2d at 98. In my view, this consideration provides strong support for the Commission's holding.

The Court has recognized society's right to "adopt more stringent controls on communicative materials available to youths than on those available to adults." [*Erznoznik*] This recognition stems in large part from the fact that "a child . . . is not possessed of that full capacity for individual choice which is the presupposition of First Amendment guarantees." [*Ginsberg*] (Stewart, J., concurring in result). Thus, children may not be able to protect themselves from speech which, although shocking to most adults, generally may be avoided by the unwilling through the exercise of choice. At the same time, such speech may have a deeper and more lasting negative effect on a child than an adult. For these reasons, society may prevent the general dissemination of such speech to children, leaving to parents the decision as to what speech of this kind their children shall hear and repeat:

> "[C]onstitutional interpretation has consistently recognized that the parents' claim to authority in their own household to direct the rearing of their children is basic in the structure of our society. 'It is cardinal with us that the custody, care and nurture of the child reside first in the parents, whose primary function and freedom include preparation for obligations the state can neither supply nor hinder.' Prince v. Massachusetts, [321 U.S. 158, 166 (1944) ]. The legislature could properly conclude that parents and others, teachers for example, who have this primary responsibility for children's well-being are entitled to the support of laws designed to aid discharge of that responsibility." [*Ginsberg*]

The Commission properly held that the speech from which society may attempt to shield its children is not limited to that which appeals to the youthful prurient interest. The language involved in this case is as potentially degrading and harmful to children as representations of many erotic acts.

In most instances, the dissemination of this kind of speech to children may be limited without also limiting willing adults' access to it. Sellers of printed and recorded matter and exhibitors of motion pictures and live performances may be required to shut their doors to children, but such a requirement has no effect on adults' access. See [*Ginsberg*]. The difficulty is that such a physical separation of the audience cannot be accomplished in the broadcast media. During most of the broadcast hours, both adults and unsupervised children are likely to be in the broadcast audience, and the broadcaster cannot reach willing adults without also reaching children. This, as the Court emphasizes, is one of the distinctions between the broadcast and other media to which we often have adverted as justifying a different treatment of the broadcast media for First Amendment purposes. [ ] In my view, the Commission was entitled to give substantial weight to this difference in reaching its decision in this case.

A second difference, not without relevance, is that broadcasting—unlike most other forms of communication—comes directly into the home, the one place where people ordinarily have the right not to be assaulted by uninvited and offensive sights and sounds. . . . The Commission also was entitled to give this factor appropriate weight in the circumstances of the instant case. This is not to say, however, that the Commission has an unrestricted license to decide what speech, protected in other media, may be banned from the airwaves in order to protect unwilling adults from momentary exposure to it in their homes.[2]

---

**2.** It is true that the radio listener quickly may tune out speech that is offen- sive to him. In addition, broadcasters may preface potentially offensive programs with

Making the sensitive judgments required in these cases is not easy. But this responsibility has been reposed initially in the Commission, and its judgment is entitled to respect.

## II

As the foregoing demonstrates, my views are generally in accord with what is said in Part IV(C) of Mr. Justice Stevens' opinion. I therefore join that portion of his opinion. I do not join Part IV(B), however, because I do not subscribe to the theory that the Justices of this Court are free generally to decide on the basis of its content which speech protected by the First Amendment is most "valuable" and hence deserving of the most protection, and which is less "valuable" and hence deserving of less protection. Compare ante, at 15–19; [*Young*], (opinion of Stevens, J.), with id., at 73 n. 1 (Powell, J., concurring).[3] In my view, the result in this case does not turn on whether Carlin's monologue, viewed as a whole, or the words that comprise it, have more or less "value" than a candidate's campaign speech. This is a judgment for each person to make, not one for the judges to impose upon him.[4]

The result turns instead on the unique characteristics of the broadcast media, combined with society's right to protect its children from speech generally agreed to be inappropriate for their years, and with the interest of unwilling adults in not being assaulted by such offensive speech in their homes. Moreover, I doubt whether today's decision will prevent any adult who wishes to receive Carlin's message in Carlin's own words from doing so, and from making for himself a value judgment as to the merit of the message and words. . . .

MR. JUSTICE BRENNAN, with whom MR. JUSTICE MARSHALL joins, dissenting.

I agree with Mr. Justice Stewart that, under Hamling v. United States, 418 U.S. 87 (1974), and United States v. 12 200–ft. Reels of Film, 413 U.S. 123 (1973), the word "indecent" in 18 U.S.C. § 1464 must be construed to prohibit only obscene speech. . . .

## I

For the second time in two years, see [*Young*], the Court refuses to embrace the notion, completely antithetical to basic First Amendment values, that the degree of protection the First Amendment affords protected speech varies with the social value ascribed to that speech by

warnings. But such warnings do not help the unsuspecting listener who tunes in at the middle of the program. In this respect, too, broadcasting appears to differ from books and records, which may carry warnings on their faces, and from motion pictures and live performances, which may carry warnings on their marquees.

**3.** The Court has, however, created a limited exception to this rule in order to bring commercial speech within the protection of the First Amendment. See [*Ohralik*].

**4.** For much the same reason, I also do not join Part IV(A). I had not thought that the application *vel non* of overbreadth analysis should depend on the Court's judgment as to the value of the protected speech that might be deterred. . . .

five Members of this Court.  See opinion of Mr. Justice Powell  .  .  ..
Yet despite the Court's refusal to create a sliding scale of First Amendment protection calibrated to this Court's perception of the worth of a
communication's content, and despite our unanimous agreement that
the Carlin monologue is protected speech, a majority of the Court
nevertheless finds that, on the facts of this case, the FCC is not
constitutionally barred from imposing sanctions on Pacifica for its airing
of the Carlin monologue.  This majority apparently believes that the
FCC's disapproval of Pacifica's afternoon broadcast of Carlin's "Dirty
Words" recording is a permissible time, place, and manner regulation.  .  .  .

## A

Without question, the privacy interests of an individual in his home
are substantial and deserving of significant protection.  In finding these
interests sufficient to justify the content regulation of protected speech,
however, the Court commits two errors.  First, it misconceives the
nature of the privacy interests involved where an individual voluntarily
chooses to admit radio communications into his home.  Second, it
ignores the constitutionally protected interests of both those who wish to
transmit and those who desire to receive broadcasts that many—including the FCC and this Court—might find offensive.

.  .  .     I believe that an individual's actions in switching on and
listening to communications transmitted over the public airways and
directed to the public at-large do not implicate fundamental privacy
interests, even when engaged in within the home.  Instead, because the
radio is undeniably a public medium, these actions are more properly
viewed as a decision to take part, if only as a listener, in an ongoing
public discourse.  See Note, Filthy Words, the FCC, and the First
Amendment: Regulating Broadcast Obscenity, 61 Va.L.Rev. 579, 618
(1975).  Although an individual's decision to allow public radio communications into his home undoubtedly does not abrogate all of his privacy
interests, the residual privacy interests he retains vis-á-vis the communication he voluntarily admits into his home are surely no greater than
those of the people present in the corridor of the Los Angeles courthouse
in *Cohen* who bore witness to the words "Fuck the Draft" emblazoned
across Cohen's jacket.  Their privacy interests were held insufficient to
justify punishing Cohen for his offensive communication.

Even if an individual who voluntarily opens his home to radio
communications retains privacy interests of sufficient moment to justify
a ban on protected speech if those interests are "invaded in an essentially intolerable manner," [*Cohen*], at 21, the very fact that those interests
are threatened only by a radio broadcast precludes any intolerable
invasion of privacy; for unlike other intrusive modes of communication,
such as sound trucks, "[t]he radio can be turned off," Lehman v. City of
Shaker Heights, 418 U.S. 298, 302 (1974)—and with a minimum of
effort.  .  .  .  Whatever the minimal discomfort suffered by a listener
who inadvertently tunes into a program he finds offensive during the

brief interval before he can simply extend his arm and switch stations or flick the "off" button, it is surely worth the candle to preserve the broadcaster's right to send, and the right of those interested to receive, a message entitled to full First Amendment protection. . . .

The Court's balance, of necessity, fails to accord proper weight to the interests of listeners who wish to hear broadcasts the FCC deems offensive. It permits majoritarian tastes completely to preclude a protected message from entering the homes of a receptive, unoffended minority. No decision of this Court supports such a result. Where the individuals comprising the offended majority may freely choose to reject the material being offered, we have never found their privacy interests of such moment to warrant the suppression of speech on privacy grounds. . . .

### B

Most parents will undoubtedly find understandable as well as commendable the Court's sympathy with the FCC's desire to prevent offensive broadcasts from reaching the ears of unsupervised children. Unfortunately, the facial appeal of this justification for radio censorship masks its constitutional insufficiency. . . .

Because the Carlin monologue is obviously not an erotic appeal to the prurient interests of children, the Court, for the first time, allows the government to prevent minors from gaining access to materials that are not obscene, and are therefore protected, as to them. It thus ignores our recent admonition that "[s]peech that is neither obscene as to youths nor subject to some other legitimate proscription cannot be suppressed solely to protect the young from ideas or images that a legislative body thinks unsuitable for them." [*Erznoznik*] [3] The Court's refusal to follow its own pronouncements is especially lamentable since it has the anomalous subsidiary effect, at least in the radio context at issue here, of making completely unavailable to adults material which may not constitutionally be kept even from children. . . .

In concluding that the presence of children in the listening audience provides an adequate basis for the FCC to impose sanctions for Pacifica's broadcast of the Carlin monologue, the opinions of my Brother Powell and my Brother Stevens both stress the time-honored right of a parent to raise his child as he sees fit—a right this Court has consistently been vigilant to protect. See Wisconsin v. Yoder, 406 U.S. 205 (1972); Pierce

---

**3.** It may be that a narrowly drawn regulation prohibiting the use of offensive language on broadcasts directed specifically at younger children constitutes one of the "other legitimate proscription[s]" alluded to in *Erznoznik*. This is so both because of the difficulties inherent in adapting the *Miller* formulation to communications received by young children, and because such children are "not possessed of that full capacity for individual choice which is the presupposition of the First Amendment guarantees." [*Ginsberg*] (Stewart, J., concurring). I doubt, as my Brother Stevens suggests, ante, at 17 n. 20, that such a limited regulation amounts to a regulation of speech based on its content, since, by hypothesis, the only persons at whom the regulated communication is directed are incapable of evaluating its content. To the extent that such a regulation is viewed as a regulation based on content, it marks the outermost limits to which content regulation is permissible.

v. Society of Sisters, 268 U.S. 510 (1925). Yet this principle supports a result directly contrary to that reached by the Court. *Yoder* and *Pierce* hold that parents, *not* the government, have the right to make certain decisions regarding the upbringing of their children. As surprising as it may be to individual Members of this Court, some parents may actually find Mr. Carlin's unabashed attitude towards the seven "dirty words" healthy, and deem it desirable to expose their children to the manner in which Mr. Carlin defuses the taboo surrounding the words. Such parents may constitute a minority of the American public, but the absence of great numbers willing to exercise the right to raise their children in this fashion does not alter the right's nature or its existence. Only the Court's regrettable decision does that.[4]

## C

As demonstrated above, neither of the factors relied on by both the opinion of my Brother Powell and the opinion of my Brother Stevens—the intrusive nature of radio and the presence of children in the listening audience—can, when taken on its own terms, support the FCC's disapproval of the Carlin monologue. These two asserted justifications are further plagued by a common failing: the lack of principled limits on their use as a basis for FCC censorship. No such limits come readily to mind, and neither of the opinions constituting the Court serve to clarify the extent to which the FCC may assert the privacy and children-in-the-audience rationales as justification for expunging from the airways protected communications the Commission finds offensive. . . .

. . . The opinions of both my Brother Powell and my Brother Stevens take the FCC at its word, and consequently do no more than permit the Commission to censor the afternoon broadcast of the "sort of verbal shock treatment," opinion of Mr. Justice Powell, *ante*, at 2, involved here. To insure that the FCC's regulation of protected speech does not exceed these bounds, my Brother Powell is content to rely upon the judgment of the Commission while my Brother Stevens deems it prudent to rely on this Court's ability accurately to assess the worth of various kinds of speech.[6] For my own part, even accepting that this case is limited to its facts, I would place the responsibility and the right to weed worthless and offensive communications from the public airways where it belongs and where, until today, it resided: in a public free to

**4.** The opinions of my Brothers Powell and Stevens rightly refrain from relying on the notion of "spectrum scarcity" to support their result. As Chief Judge Bazelon noted below, "although scarcity has justified *increasing* the diversity of speakers and speech, it has never been held to justify censorship." 556 F.2d, at 29 (emphasis in original). See [*Red Lion*].

**6.** Although ultimately dependent upon the outcome of review in this Court, the approach taken by my Brother Stevens would not appear to tolerate the FCC's suppression of any speech, such as political speech, falling within the core area of First Amendment concern. The same, however, cannot be said of the approach taken by my Brother Powell, which, on its face, permits the Commission to censor even political speech if it is sufficiently offensive to community standards. A result more contrary to rudimentary First Amendment principles is difficult to imagine.

choose those communications worthy of its attention from a marketplace unsullied by the censor's hand.

## II

. . .

   . . . The idea that the content of a message and its potential impact on any who might receive it can be divorced from the words that are the vehicle for its expression is transparently fallacious. A given word may have a unique capacity to capsule an idea, evoke an emotion, or conjure up an image. Indeed, for those of us who place an appropriately high value on our cherished First Amendment rights, the word "censor" is such a word. Mr. Justice Harlan, speaking for the Court, recognized the truism that a speaker's choice of words cannot surgically be separated from the ideas he desires to express when he warned that "we cannot indulge the facile assumption that one can forbid particular words without also running a substantial risk of suppressing ideas in the process." [*Cohen*] Moreover, even if an alternative phrasing may communicate a speaker's abstract ideas as effectively as those words he is forbidden to use, it is doubtful that the sterilized message will convey the emotion that is an essential part of so many communications.

   . . .

   The Court apparently believes that the FCC's actions here can be analogized to the zoning ordinances upheld in [*Young*]. For two reasons, it is wrong. First, the zoning ordinances found to pass constitutional muster in *Young* had valid goals other than the channeling of protected speech. [ ] No such goals are present here. Second, . . . the ordinances do not restrict the access of distributors or exhibitors to the market or impair the viewing public's access to the regulated material. [ ] Again, this is not the situation here. Both those desiring to receive Carlin's message over the radio and those wishing to send it to them are prevented from doing so by the Commission's actions. Although, as my Brethren point out, Carlin's message may be disseminated or received by other means, this is of little consolation to those broadcasters and listeners who, for a host of reasons, not least among them financial, do not have access to, or cannot take advantage of, these other means.

   . . .

## III

   It is quite evident that I find the Court's attempt to unstitch the warp and woof of First Amendment law in an effort to reshape its fabric to cover the patently wrong result the Court reaches in this case dangerous as well as lamentable. Yet there runs throughout the opinions of my Brothers Powell and Stevens another vein I find equally disturbing: a depressing inability to appreciate that in our land of cultural pluralism, there are many who think, act, and talk differently from the Members of this Court, and who do not share their fragile sensibilities. It is only an acute ethnocentric myopia that enables the Court to approve the censorship of communications solely because of the words they contain.

. . . The words that the Court and the Commission find so unpalatable may be the stuff of everyday conversations in some, if not many, of the innumerable subcultures that comprise this Nation. Academic research indicates that this is indeed the case. [ ] As one researcher concluded, "[w]ords generally considered obscene like 'bullshit' and 'fuck' are considered neither obscene nor derogatory in the [black] vernacular except in particular contextual situations and when used with certain intonations." [ ] Cf. Keefe v. Geanakos, 418 F.2d 359, 361 (C.A.1, 1969) (finding the use of the word "motherfucker" commonplace among young radicals and protestors).

Today's decision will thus have its greatest impact on broadcasters desiring to reach, and listening audiences comprised of, persons who do not share the Court's view as to which words or expressions are acceptable and who, for a variety of reasons, including a conscious desire to flout majoritarian conventions, express themselves using words that may be regarded as offensive by those from different socio-economic backgrounds.[8] . . .

. . .

MR. JUSTICE STEWART, with whom MR. JUSTICE BRENNAN, MR. JUSTICE WHITE, and MR. JUSTICE MARSHALL join, dissenting.

. . .

The statute pursuant to which the Commission acted, 18 U.S.C. § 1464, makes it a federal offense to utter "any obscene, indecent, or profane language by means of radio communication." The Commission held, and the Court today agrees, that "indecent" is a broader concept than "obscene" as the latter term was defined in [Miller], because language can be "indecent" although it has social, political or artistic value and lacks prurient appeal. 56 F.C.C.2d, at 97–98. But this construction of § 1464, while perhaps plausible, is by no means compelled. To the contrary, I think that "indecent" should properly be read as meaning no more than "obscene." Since the Carlin monologue concededly was not "obscene," I believe that the Commission lacked statutory authority to ban it. Under this construction of the statute, it is unnecessary to address the difficult and important issue of the Commission's constitutional power to prohibit speech that would be constitutionally protected outside the context of electronic broadcasting.

. . .

**8.** Under the approach taken by my Brother Powell, the availability of broadcasts *about* groups whose members comprise such audiences might also be affected. Both news broadcasts about activities involving these groups and public affairs broadcasts about their concerns are apt to contain interviews, statements, or remarks by group leaders and members which may contain offensive language to an extent my Brother Powell finds unacceptable.

**Notes and Questions**

1. There are now products available to control what programs can be seen on a television set. Using a weekly schedule, a parent can enter the day, time, channel number and duration of time of each program the parent wishes a child to be able to see. If the set is turned to a channel that is not cleared for that day and time, no picture or sound will appear. A key permits changes to be made. If this were standard equipment on all television sets (and radios) might it meet some of the concerns in *Pacifica*?

2. Is the "risk" of tuning in an offensive program on radio or television any greater than the risk of encountering offensive language on a person's clothing on the streets, as in *Cohen*, p. 79, *supra*? Or offensive films visible from the street while being shown at an outdoor movie theater, *Erznoznik*, p. 382, *supra*? If averting your eyes is an adequate remedy in these cases, why is turning off the radio or television set not adequate here? Is the fact that one may occur in the home relevant?

3. It is easier to warn viewers that an adult, or possibly offensive, program is being presented when television is involved. In some countries such programs carry a white dot in a corner of the picture so that a viewer can know the nature of the programming instantly. Would this solve our problems so far as television is concerned? Is there a similar technique that can be used for radio? Is it enough that certain stations become known as likely to present certain kinds of material offensive to some? What more could the licensee have done here to warn adult listeners? See Glasser and Jassem, "Indecent Broadcasts and the Listener's Right of Privacy," 24 J. Broadcasting 285 (1980).

4. It has long been agreed that Congress has preempted the matter of obscenity on radio and television—both of which are within "radio communication." Thus, a state may not impose its movie censorship scheme on films shown on television.

5. Shortly after the 1978 *Pacifica* decision, a primary election for governor was held in Georgia. J.B. Stoner, a legally qualified candidate, speaking under § 315, made broadcast messages using the word "nigger." Black groups asked the Commission to bar such language as indecent under the *Pacifica* principle. The Broadcast Bureau rejected the request. First, it ruled that the word was not "language that describes in terms patently offensive by contemporary community standards for the broadcast medium, sexual or excretory activities and organs, at times of the day when there is reasonable risk that children may be in the audience," quoting the Commission's language in *Pacifica*. Also, the Commission had already announced that "we intend strictly to observe the narrowness of the Pacifica holding." Even if the Commission were to find the word obscene or indecent, under § 315 the candidate could not be prevented from using the word during his "use" of the licensee's facilities. Julian Bond, 69 F.C.C.2d 943, 43 R.R.2d 1015 (Bd.Bur.1978).

6.   During the 1980 Presidential campaign, one radio commercial began as follows: A man says "Bullshit!"   After a woman says "What?," the man's voice replies: "Carter, Reagan and Anderson.  It's all bullshit! Bullshit!"   Then the party's candidate says "Too bad people have to use such strong language, but isn't that what you think too?  That's why we started an entirely new political party, the Citizens Party."   The FCC, which received many complaints and inquiries, responded that the precedents were quite clear that no censorship was possible—at least unless a candidate created a clear and present danger of riot or violence.

The campaign director said that for six months the media had been covering only the three major candidates "despite the fact that they have little to say of substance about the problems of the nation."   He observed that "It's a sad commentary on the media that we received more attention as a result of using that word than we've received in the last six months combined."

7.   In 1983 *Hustler* magazine publisher Larry Flynt was reported to be intending to use clips from X-rated films in television ads supporting his presidential candidacy.  This caused Sen. Jeremiah Denton (R–Ala.) to introduce legislation to allow broadcasters to refuse to air pornographic political announcements despite the non-censorship provision of § 315. Subsequently, the FCC indicated that it would not apply the no-censorship provision to obscene or indecent political announcements.   The issue never arose as Flynt chose not to run.

8.   During the election campaign of 1992, some federal candidates sought to present advertisements purporting to depict dead fetuses. Broadcasters sought to channel them to later evening hours on the ground of indecency or at least to disassociate the station from the advertisement.   The technical claim of indecency was based on the assertion that the advertisements presented excretory functions.

In the summer of 1992, the Chief of the Mass Media Bureau responded to broadcaster inquiries about these ads by rejecting the channeling idea in the abstract.   See discussion in Letter to Daniel Becker, 7 F.C.C.Rcd. 7282 (Mass Med.Bur. 1992).  The chief declined to rule that all depictions of dead fetuses were indecent because the process required case-by-case adjudication.   Moreover, the Commission had refused to issue declaratory rulings in indecency cases so as to "avoid imposing prior restraints on protected speech."

Nor could the requirements of § 312(a)(7) be met by channeling programs that the broadcaster might think were unsuitable for children. The candidate's access rights were paramount.

One of the requesters had sent along a tape of a proposed advertisement, contending that it showed "six shots of aborted fetuses   .   .   . badly discolored in whole or in part, [some of which] appear covered with a wet, dark shiny substance."   The Bureau rejected the claim that this involved excretory functions within the indecency definition.   "Neither the expulsion of fetal tissue nor fetuses themselves constitutes 'excrement.'"

Nonetheless, the chief observed that broadcasters were not

> without recourse in providing their viewers with appropriate warn-
> ings where, in the licensees' good faith judgment, the material
> presented in a political use program could be disturbing to child
> viewers.  In the circumstances presented here we would not regard
> such an advisory, presented in a non-editorializing and neutral
> fashion, to either violate the non-discrimination rules  . . .  or
> to invoke the political editorializing rule.

In some situations the Commission had concluded that selective use of
disclaimers or viewer advisories might amount to endorsing one candidate over another and invoke the political editorializing rule.  But in
this the case of photographs of fetuses a broadcaster who used a
disclaimer or advisory on these programs was not required to use similar
advisories for programs presented by opponents of this candidate (unless
they independently called for such advisories).

In October, 1992, Daniel Becker, a Congressional candidate presented an 30–minute ad to Atlanta television station WAGA–TV for broadcast the Sunday afternoon before the general election immediately after
its telecast of a football game involving the Atlanta Falcons.  The ad
included graphic depictions of fetuses.  The FCC staff refused to rule
definitely on the station's request for permission to channel it to a later
time, in part because the FCC had not viewed it.  But it stated that in
the past FCC staff had "informally" concluded that the ban in 18
U.S.C.A. § 1464 against broadcasting indecent speech was an "exception" to § 315.  Under these circumstances it "would not be unreasonable" for a licensee to channel material that it "reasonably and in good
faith" believed to be indecent.  Letter to Daniel Becker, 7 F.C.C.Rcd.
7282, 71 R.R.2d 995 (M.Med.Bur. 1992).

At the same time, the FCC stated that it was issuing a public notice
to begin the process of confronting the issue in a more orderly fashion by
seeking comments on how such cases should be handled in the future
and whether a rule might be appropriate.

While awaiting the FCC ruling, the station involved in the Becker
dispute, WAGA–TV, sued in federal district court for a declaratory ruling
that it could channel the program and for an injunction against the
efforts of Becker and his campaign to force the station to present the
program on Sunday afternoon.  The judge viewed the proposed program
and found that a four minute segment "contain[ed] graphic depictions
and descriptions of female genitalia, the uterus, excreted uterine fluid,
dismembered fetal body parts and aborted fetuses.  This portion of the
videotape depicts the activities and materials in a manner which is
patently offensive according to contemporary community standards."
After concluding that the statutory ban on indecent programming constituted an exception to the requirements of §§ 315 and 312(a)(7), the
judge granted the declaratory judgment and the injunction.  Gillett
Communications of Atlanta, Inc. v. Becker, 807 F.Supp., 757, 20 Med.
L.Rptr. 1947 (N.D.Ga.1992).

Efforts by Becker and his campaign to stay the judge's ruling in the court of appeals failed, as did efforts to get Justice Anthony Kennedy, sitting as Circuit Justice for the 11th Circuit, to grant a stay.

9. Following *Pacifica* the Commission's enforcement of the indecency provisions of § 1464 was essentially nonexistent. In the mid–1980s, citizen groups put increasing pressure on the Commission actively to enforce § 1464.

In 1987 the Commission took action against three broadcast stations and one amateur radio operator. One station had broadcast excerpts from the play, "Jerker." The play was running in Los Angeles and had previously run in New York. Much of the play consists of telephone conversations between two homosexuals dying of AIDS in which they share their sexual fantasies. In an interview with the play's director that preceded the excerpts, the play was characterized as "blazingly erotic." The Commission rejected arguments by Pacifica that the excerpts should be considered in the context of the play's message—"the need to affirm life in the face of death." "Notwithstanding the licensee's assertion, we do not believe the context dilutes or ameliorates the patently offensive manner in which the sexual activity was described." Pacifica Foundation, Inc., 2 F.C.C.Rcd. 2698, 62 R.R.2d 1191 (1987).

A second station had aired a song that in the Commission's view "contained a number of patently offensive references to sexual organs and activities as measured by contemporary community standards for the broadcast medium." The Regents of the University of California, 2 F.C.C.Rcd. 2703, 62 R.R.2d 1199 (1987)

The complaint against the third station centered on "The Howard Stern Show." The show is an example of a radio format that is often referred to as "shock radio." Characterized by humor that is full of sexual innuendo and ridicule, it is considered offensive and tasteless by its opponents. At the same time, it is successful in the ratings. For example, Stern's show had moved from number 16 to three in the Philadelphia market. The following excerpts were cited by the Commission as examples of the programming they found indecent:

*Excerpt 1*

Howard Stern: "God, my testicles are like down to the floor. Boy, Susan, you could really have a party with these. I'm telling you, honey."

Ray: "Use them like Bocci balls."

*Excerpt 2*

Howard Stern: "Let me tell you something, honey. These homos you are with are all limp."

Ray: "Yeah. You've never even had a real man."

Howard Stern: "You've probably never been with a man with a full erection."

*Excerpt 3*

Susan: "No, I was in a park in New Rochelle, N.Y."

Howard Stern:    "In a park in New Rochelle?   On your knees?"

Susan:           "No, no."

Ray:             "And squeezing someone's testicles, probably."

*Excerpt 5*
As part of a discussion of lesbians

Howard Stern:    "I mean to go around porking other girls with vibrating rubber products and they want the whole world to come to a standstill."

*Excerpt 6*
Howard Stern:    "Have you ever had sex with an animal?"

Caller:          "No."

Howard Stern:    "Well, don't knock it.   I was sodomized by Lamb-chop, you know that puppet Sherri Lewis holds?"

Howard Stern:    "Baaaaah.   That's where I was thinking that Sherri Lewis, instead of like sodomizing all the people at the Academy to get that shot on the Emmys she could've had Lambchop do it."

Infinity Broadcasting Corp. of Pennsylvania, 2 F.C.C.Rcd. 2705, 62 R.R.2d 1202 (1987).   Several stations toned down "shock radio" shows as a result of the Commission's actions.

Because the application of the indecency provisions of § 1464 in these cases represented a departure from previous Commission Policy, the stations were warned, but no further action was taken.   At the same time, in a public notice, the Commission announced its intent to expand its enforcement of § 1464.   New Indecency Enforcement Standards to be Applied to All Broadcast and Amateur Radio Licensees, 2 F.C.C.Rcd. 2726, 62 R.R.2d 1218 (1987).

Rather than limiting enforcement of § 1464 to the seven "dirty words" contained in the Carlin dialogue, the Commission announced it would "apply the *generic* definition of broadcast indecency advanced in *Pacifica,* which is: 'Language or material that depicts or describes, in terms patently offensive as measured by contemporary community standards for the broadcast medium, sexual or excretory activities or organs.' "

The Commission also announced a change in the times during which programming would be subject to the indecency provisions of § 1464. ". . . [I]ndecency will be actionable when there is a reasonable risk that children may be in the audience, but   . . .   this benchmark is not susceptible to a uniform standard.   . . .   [D]espite prior assumptions that children were not in the broadcasting audience at 10:00 p.m., recent evidence for the markets involved indicates that there is still a reasonable risk that children may be in the listening audience at [those] hours.   . . ."   Thus, as was the case in both the new Pacifica case and the Regents of the University of California case, programs after 10 p.m. could still be subject to the indecency provisions of § 1464 if there was evidence that children were in the audience.

In response to various Petitions for Clarification and Petitions for Reconsideration, including ones from the three broadcast licensees involved in the original decision, the Commission issued a further opinion and order on indecency. Infinity Broadcasting Corporation of Pennsylvania (Indecency Policy Reconsideration), 64 R.R.2d 211 (1987). The FCC began by rejecting a request by Morality in Media that some "sexually explicit, yet non-obscene material" be absolutely prohibited. Such a prohibition would in the Commission's opinion be unconstitutional because the Supreme Court decision in *Pacifica* authorized only "the imposition of reasonable time, place and manner restrictions on the broadcast of indecent material in order to advance the government's interest in protecting children." In a footnote the Commission indicated that it would rely on parents to supervise their children after midnight, thus creating a "safe harbor" for broadcasts of indecent—but not obscene—programs. Although the footnote did not indicate when the "safe harbor" would end, the FCC's general counsel suggested at a press conference that 6 a.m. was the appropriate time. In a concurrence, Commissioner Dennis suggested that the "safe harbor" start at the conclusion of prime time.

Next the Commission declined to define "patently offensive" or exempt material with "serious literary, artistic, political or scientific value."

14. "Patently offensive" is a phrase that must, of necessity, be construed with reference to specific facts. We cannot and will not attempt to provide petitioners with a comprehensive index or thesaurus of indecent words or pictorial depictions that will be considered patently offensive. There is no way to construct a definitive list that would be both comprehensive and not over-inclusive in the abstract, without reference to the specific context. All we hold here, therefore, is that, in the three cases before us, we properly found the material identified as indecent to be patently offensive.

15. Our approach here is consistent with that of the courts, which have likewise never attempted to identify with the degree of certainty requested by petitioners the complete and definitive range of material that falls within the generic, legal definitions of certain categories of speech. [The Commission cited obscenity law as a specific example where the term "patently offensive" had passed constitutional muster.]

.  .  .

17. The merit of a work is also one of the many variables that make up a work's "context," as the Court implicitly recognized in *Pacifica* when it contrasted the Carlin monologue to Elizabethan comedies and works of Chaucer. But merit is simply one of many variables, and it would give this particular variable undue importance if we were to single it out for greater weight or attention than we give other variables. We decline to do so in deciding the three cases before us. We must, therefore, reject an approach that would

hold that if a work has merit, it is *per se* not indecent.  At the same time, we must reject the notion that a work's "context" can be reviewed in a manner that artificially excludes merit from the host of variables that ordinarily comprise context.  The ultimate determinative factor in our analysis, however, is whether the material, when examined in context, is patently offensive.   .  ..

After reviewing the three specific cases and concluding that the broadcasts in each case were indecent, the Commission did clarify the definition of the phrase, "contemporary community standards," as used in the definition of indecency.  The standard is that of "an average broadcast viewer."  Thus, the Commission will use a national standard for indecency as opposed to the local standard for obscenity prescribed by *Miller*.

Finally, the FCC turned to a request that it defer to the reasonable, good faith judgment of a licensees when determining whether they have violated § 1464:

.  .  .  Although we acknowledge that the statute requires a broadcaster to make judgments as to whether certain material would violate the statute, the fact that the decision may not be an easy one cannot excuse the broadcaster from having to exercise its judgment, any more than it can excuse the Commission from exercising its enforcement responsibilities.  We note, however, that it is standard procedure for the Commission, in deciding whether to impose a sanction for violation of the law and, if so, what those sanctions should be, to give weight to the reasonable determinations of licensees endeavoring to comply with the law.  Because licensees demonstrating reasonable judgment have no cause to fear the imposition of unjustified sanctions, we reject the petitioners' contentions that the editorial decisions of broadcasters will be inappropriately chilled by continuation of this approach.

The Commission's decision was appealed by various trade organizations and public interest groups.

### ACTION FOR CHILDREN'S TELEVISION v. FEDERAL COMMUNICATIONS COMMISSION

United States Court of Appeals, District of Columbia Circuit, 1988.
852 F.2d 1332, 65 R.R.2d 45, 15 Med.L.Rptr. 1907.

Before ROBINSON, RUTH B. GINSBURG, and SENTELLE, CIRCUIT JUDGES.

GINSBURG, CIRCUIT JUDGE.

.  .  .

### IV.

The FCC acknowledges a change of regulatory course: The Commission now measures broadcast material against the generic definition of indecency, while formerly "no action was taken unless material involved the repeated use, for shock value, of words similar or identical to those satirized in the Carlin 'Filthy Words' monologue." [*Indecency Policy Reconsideration*] Petitioners charge that the Commission has failed to supply an adequate explanation for the change. [ ] Specifically, petitioners say that the Commission deliberately narrowed the former standard to make it reasonably certain and to afford broadcasters ample breathing space. [ ] The new standard, they contend, is "inherently vague" and was installed without any evidence of a problem justifying a thickened regulatory response. [ ]

The explanation offered by the Commission, in its *Reconsideration Order,* is that it found the deliberately-repeated-use-of-dirty-words policy "unduly narrow as a matter of law" and inconsistent with its obligation responsibly to enforce Section 1464. [ ] The former approach permitted the unregulated broadcast of any material that did not contain Carlin's "filthy words," no matter how the material might affect children exposed to it. It made no legal or policy sense, the FCC said, to regulate the Carlin monologue but not "material that portrayed sexual or excretory activities or organs in as patently offensive a manner . . . simply because it avoided certain words." [ ]

We find the FCC's explanation adequate. Short of the thesis that *only* the seven words are properly designated indecent—an argument petitioners disavow—some more expansive definition must be attempted. The FCC rationally determined that its former policy could yield anomalous, even arbitrary, results. No reasonable formulation tighter than the one the Commission has announced has been suggested in this review proceeding. The difficulty, or "abiding discomfort," we conclude, is not the absence of "reasoned analysis" on the Commission's part, but the "[v]agueness . . . inherent in the subject matter." [ ] We turn next to that issue.

## V.

Petitioners charge that the term "indecent" is inherently unclear, and that the FCC's generic definition of indecency adds nothing significant in the way of clarification. The Commission's definition, petitioners therefore contend, provides broadcasters no meaningful guide identifying the category of material subject to regulation; accordingly, petitioners urge, the definition should be ruled unconstitutionally vague. In our view the Supreme Court's disposition of *Pacifica* stops "what the Constitution calls an 'inferior court' " from addressing this question on the merits. [ ]

The generic definition of indecency now employed by the FCC is virtually the same definition the Commission articulated in the order reviewed by the Supreme Court in [*Pacifica*]. However, the Court did not address, specifically, whether the FCC's definition was on its face unconstitutionally vague. The Court did hold the Carlin monologue indecent within the meaning of Section 1464. 438 U.S. at 741. We infer from this holding that the Court did not regard the term "indecent" as so vague that persons "of common intelligence must necessarily guess at its meaning and differ as to its application." . . .

. . . [I]f acceptance of the FCC's generic definition of "indecent" as capable of surviving a vagueness challenge is not implicit in *Pacifica,* we have misunderstood Higher Authority and welcome correction.

## VI.

Intervenors ACLU *et al.* argue that the FCC's generic definition of indecency is substantially overbroad. As we read *Pacifica,* only two members of the five-member majority thought it in order to rule on overbreadth, so we proceed to address that issue on the merits. The ACLU's challenge is predicated on the absence of redemption from indecency status for material that has "serious merit." We hold that "serious merit" need not, in every instance, immunize indecent material from FCC channeling authority.

. . . According to intervenors, a proper definition of indecency would include the requirement that the "work, taken as a whole, lacks serious literary, artistic, political, or scientific value." [ACLU Brief, quoting *Miller*] . . . .

. . .

Indecent but not obscene material, we reiterate, qualifies for First Amendment protection whether or not it has serious merit. Children's access to indecent material, however, may be regulated, because "even where there is an invasion of protected freedoms 'the power of the state to control the conduct of children reaches beyond the scope of its authority over adults. . . .' " [ ] Channeling is designed to protect unsupervised children. [ ] Some material that has significant social value may contain language and descriptions as offensive, from the perspective of parental control over children's exposure, as material lacking such value.[13] Since the overall value of a work will not necessarily alter the impact of certain words or phrases on children, the FCC's approach is permissible under controlling case law: merit is properly treated as a factor in determining whether material is patently offensive, but it does not render such material *per se* not indecent. [ ] The FCC's definition, therefore, is not vulnerable to the charge that it is substantially overbroad.

## VII.

We have upheld the FCC's generic definition of indecency in light of the sole purpose of that definition: to permit the channeling of indecent material, in order to shelter children from exposure to words and phrases their parents regard as inappropriate for them to hear. [ ]

**13.** The Carlin monologue itself may be an example of indecent material possessing significant social value. . . .

Other examples that come readily to mind include descriptions of the doings of Gargantuan and Pantagruel in Rabelais' classic, certain passages in the works of Joyce, words and phrases found in the writings of D.H. Lawrence, James Baldwin, and Frank Harris.

Petitioners press two linked objections to the FCC's "current thinking" that 12:00 midnight is the hour after which indecent material may be broadcast without sanctions.[15] The FCC's channeling decision is arbitrary and capricious, petitioners contend, because it is not based on adequate factual or analytic foundation. [ ] Tied to and coloring that contention, petitioners charge that the Commission's action regarding channeling violates the First Amendment because it reduces adults to seeing and hearing material fit only for children.

We agree that, in view of the curtailment of broadcaster freedom and adult listener choice that channeling entails, the Commission failed to consider fairly and fully what time lines should be drawn. We therefore vacate, in the *Pacifica Foundation* and *Regents of the University of California* cases, the FCC's ruling that the broadcast under review was actionable, and we remand those cases to the agency for thoroughgoing reconsideration of the times at which indecent material may be aired.

[The court affirmed the FCC's ruling in *Infinity* because the programming at issue was broadcast between 6 and 10 a.m. The court could find no rational distinction between those early morning programs and the Carlin broadcast in the earlier Pacifica case, which was aired in the early afternoon.]

Each of the April 29, 1987, rulings reported an FCC finding that the broadcast occurred at a time of day when there was a reasonable risk that children may have been in the audience. In *Pacifica Foundation,* involving a 10:00–11:00 p.m. broadcast, the Commission relied on ratings data indicating that "approximately 112,200 children age 12–17 are in the Los Angeles metro survey area radio audience per average quarter hour between 7 p.m. and midnight on Sunday night." [ ] In *Regents of the University of California,* involving a program aired after 10:00 p.m., available data indicated that approximately 1,200 children between 12 and 17 years of age are still in the radio audience per average quarter hour in the Santa Barbara area between 7 p.m. and midnight on Saturday evenings. There are approximately 4,900 children within this age group within the City of Santa Barbara itself and 27,800 in the county. [ ]

Even were we to treat each of the two rulings solely as an *ad hoc* adjudication, we would regard the evidence on which the Commission rested its channeling decisions as insubstantial, and its findings more ritual than real. It is familiar law that an agency treads an arbitrary course when it fails to "articulate any rational connection between the facts found and the choice made." [ ] We conclude the Commission followed such a course here.

In each instance under inspection the cited population figures appear to estimate the number of teens in the *total* radio audience. There is no indication of the size of the predicted audience for the specific radio stations in question. [ ] More troubling, the FCC ventures no explanation why it takes teens 12–17 to be the relevant age group for channeling purposes. In the Commission's 1976 legislative proposal, cited to the Supreme Court in the FCC's *Pacifica* brief, the Commission would have required broadcasters to minimize the risk of exposing to indecent material children *under* age 12. The FCC reasoned: "Age 12 was selected since it is the accepted upper limit for children's programming in the industry and at the Commission. . . ." [ ] We cannot tell from the record before us whether the Commission is now spreading the focus of its concern to children over 12. [ ] If it is thus widening its sights, that apparent change in policy warrants explanation. If, on the other hand, the FCC continues to consider children under 12 as the age group of concern, it should either supply information on the listening habits of children in that age range, or explain how it extrapolates relevant data for that population from the available ratings information.

[Noting that in the Santa Barbara case only four percent of the teens living in that area were estimated to be in the radio listening audience, the court questioned whether that "amounts to a 'reasonable risk' for channeling purposes."]

We do not, however, remand solely for reconsideration of the individual rulings. In the *Reconsideration Order* the FCC offered some advice to broadcasters:

> [W]hereas previously we indicated that 10:00 p.m. was a reasonable delineation point, we now indicate that 12:00 midnight is our current thinking as to when it is reasonable to expect that it is late enough to ensure that the risk of children in the audience is minimized and to rely on parents to exercise increased supervision over whatever children remain in the viewing and listening audience.

64 R.R.2d at 219 n. 47. The Commission next listed several competing interests, . . ., and said that its approach accommodated them. As noted by Commissioner Dennis, however, "the arguments the majority gives in support of midnight as the critical hour may well be equally true if applied to an earlier hour." [ ] We agree that the FCC's midnight advice, indeed its entire position on channeling, was not adequately thought through.

At oral argument . . . General Counsel for the FCC suggested that if this Court found the midnight safe harbor problematic, we could disregard it and permit the Commission to make future channeling decisions on a case-by-case basis. However, the FCC itself has recognized that "the effect of that approach may well be to cause broadcasters to forego the broadcast of certain protected speech altogether, rather than to channel it to late night hours." [ ] In common with the Commission, we are constrained to agree with that assessment. Facing the uncertainty generated by a less than precise definition of indecency *plus* the lack of a safe harbor for the broadcast of (possibly) indecent material, broadcasters surely would be more likely to avoid such programming altogether than would be the case were one area of uncertainty eliminated.  We conclude that, in view of the constitutionally protected expression interests at stake, the FCC must afford broadcasters clear notice of reasonably determined times at which indecent material safely may be aired.

It is within our authority to instruct the FCC to establish a safe harbor by means of a rulemaking proceeding.  [  ]  We call attention, however, to the clear statement made by one Commissioner: "The fact is the Commission has no scientific body of information that conclusively establishes one time as more appropriate than another as the critical hour after which to permit broadcast of indecent speech.  What is necessary is a notice of proposed rulemaking to establish a record."  [  ] The inadequate record relevant to channeling made in the cases the Commission adjudicated lends support to that Commissioner's view.

The FCC noted that a channeling decision must accommodate these competing interests:

> (1) the government, which has a compelling interest in protecting children from indecent material;  (2) parents, who are entitled to decide whether their children are exposed to such material if it is aired;  (3) broadcasters, who are entitled to air such material at times of day when there is not a reasonable risk that children may be in the audience;  and (4) adult listeners, who have a right to see and hear programming that is inappropriate for children but not obscene.

[  ]  .  .  .  [T]he first two interests identified by the FCC coalesce;  the government's role is to facilitate parental supervision of children's listening.  .  .  .  Thus, the FCC must endeavor to determine what channeling rule will most effectively promote parental—as distinguished from government—control.

A securely-grounded channeling rule would give effect to the government's interest in promoting parental supervision of children's listening, without intruding excessively upon the licensee's range of discretion or the fare available for mature audiences and even children whose parents do not wish them sheltered from indecent speech.  Such a rule would present a clearly-stated position enabling broadcasters to comprehend what is expected of them and to conform their conduct to the legal requirement.

## Conclusion

Broadcast material that is indecent but not obscene is protected by the First Amendment;  the FCC may regulate such material only with due respect for the high value our Constitution places on freedom and choice in what people say and hear.  We have concluded that, under governing precedent, the FCC's definition of indecent broadcast material, though vagueness is inherent in it, is not constitutionally defective, and that the Commission's declaratory order in [*Infinity*] must be affirmed.  But we have also found that the FCC has not implemented its authority to channel such material in a reasonable manner. We therefore vacate in part the reconsideration order under review and return [*Pacifica*] and [*Regents of the University of California*] to the Commission for redetermination, after a full and fair hearing, of the times at which indecent material may be broadcast.

*It is so ordered.*

## Notes and Questions

1. Prior to the circuit court's decision, in April 1988, the Commission had issued its first indecency decisions since the new policy was announced. It dismissed five indecency complaints including one involving the reading of selections from James Joyce's *Ulysses* over Pacifica's New York station.

2. In October, 1988, however, Congress passed a requirement that the FCC enforce its anti-indecency policy 24 hours a day. The FCC complied with the requirement and passed the 24–hour–a–day ban. The ban's January 27, 1989, effective date was then stayed by the court of appeals.

3. Both proponents and opponents of the 24–hour–a–day ban had hoped that the Supreme Court might provide support for their position in *Sable,* p. 390, *supra.*

The Court in *Sable* did not make any specific reference to the pending dispute over broadcast indecency. In August 1989, 17 media groups, relying heavily on *Sable* and the earlier decision of the court of appeals, filed briefs challenging the constitutionality of the 24–hour ban on indecent broadcast speech.

The Commission then asked the court of appeals to remand the case involving the 24–hour ban to the Commission to give it a chance to build a record justifying the ban. In September 1989, over the opposition of the media challengers, the court of appeals remanded the case to the Commission for a "full and fair" inquiry on the ban.

Shortly thereafter, the Commission issued an NOI soliciting public comment on the validity of a total ban on broadcast indecency. The FCC asserted two government interests served by indecency regulation: "protecting children from exposure to indecent material" and "assisting parents in supervising their children." The Commission asked for comments as to whether the 24–hour ban would advance these interests.

17. The more difficult issue is whether a record can be developed to demonstrate that a 24–hour ban is a sufficiently limited means of restricting children's access to indecent broadcasts. In order to develop such a record, we need to compile information on many interrelated subjects, such as: (1) children's access to the broadcast media as well as their actual viewing and listening habits; (2) the feasibility of alternative means of restricting children's access to broadcasts, including time channeling alone or in conjunction with parental supervision, ratings or warning devices or alternative

broadcast technologies; and (3) the availability of indecent material for adults through non-broadcast means.

Noting the court's criticism in *ACT I* of the reliance on data regarding children ages 12 to 17 even though the Commission's 1976 legislative proposal defined children as 12 or younger, the Commission started the NOI by adopting a definition of children as ages 17 and younger. The Commission then asked for information on both children's access to the broadcast media as well as their actual listening and viewing habits. Included in this was information regarding VCR use, specifically: "(1) the availability of VCR equipment to children; (2) the ability of children to use VCR equipment; and (3) children's actual use of the equipment for delayed viewing."

The Commission then asked for comments on alternatives to a 24-hour ban, "including: (1) channeling indecent broadcasts to a time of day when children most likely will not be exposed to them, including reliance on parental supervision to protect children; (2) program rating codes or pre-broadcast warning devices; and (3) feasible technologies that can be used to keep indecent broadcasts from children."

Finally, the Commission asked for comments on whether a 24-hour ban would impermissibly infringe an adult's First Amendment rights:

> . . . [W]e seek comment on whether non-broadcast alternatives, including cable with a lock-box capacity, videocassettes, audiocassettes, records, motion pictures, theatres and nightclubs, provide adults with sufficient access to visual and audio indecency. Do the costs associated with each alternative reduce its practical availability to adults? Are there differences in the types of alternatives available for video versus audio indecency?

Enforcement of Prohibitions Against Broadcast Indecency in 18 U.S.C. § 1464, R.R. Current Service 53:475 (1989).

In mid-1990 the Commission issued a report supporting the 24-hour ban. First, the Commission found that there was a compelling government interest "in protecting children from broadcast indecency, both to facilitate parental supervision and to promote the well-being of children who may be exposed to indecent material." Second, the FCC concluded that no alternative to the 24-hour ban would be effective.

> 68. In sum, the evidence establishes that, given the pervasiveness and accessibility of radio and television, unsupervised children in pursuit of entertainment need be neither "enterprising" nor "disobedient" to turn on a television or radio, or to record a program on a VCR, at any time of day or night. Accordingly, we conclude that there exists a reasonable risk that a sufficient number of children are in the broadcast audience at all times to warrant narrowly-tailored government regulation of indecent broadcasting. . . .

Finally, the Commission concluded that indecent programming is available to adults in a variety of other media including cable, wireless cable,

SMATV and, in the near future, DBS. Enforcement of Prohibitions Against Broadcast Indecency in 18 U.S.C. 1464, 5 F.C.C.Rcd. 5297, 67 R.R.2d 1714 (1990).

The Commission's action was reversed on appeal. Action for Children's Television v. Federal Communications Commission, 932 F.2d 1504, 69 R.R.2d 179, 18 Med.L.Rptr. 2153 (D.C.Cir.1991). The court found the reversal mandated by *ACT I*:

> Our holding in *ACT I* that the Commission must identify some reasonable period of time during which indecent material may be broadcast necessarily means that the Commission may not ban such broadcasts entirely. The fact that Congress itself mandated the total ban on broadcast indecency does not alter our view that, under *ACT I*, such a prohibition cannot withstand constitutional scrutiny. While "we do not ignore" Congress' apparent belief that a total ban on broadcast indecency is constitutional, it is ultimately the judiciary's task, particularly in the First Amendment context, to decide whether Congress has violated the constitution. [ ] . . .

> Nothing else in the intervening thirty-four months has reduced the precedential force *ACT I*. Indeed, the Supreme Court's decision in *Sable*, striking down a total ban on indecent commercial telephone messages, affirmed the protected status of indecent speech and reiterated the strict constitutional standard that government efforts to regulate the content of speech must satisfy. [ ]

The court's decision essentially placed the Commission in the position it had been in after *ACT I*, but prior to the appropriations rider. In other words the Commission was once again directed to initiate a proceeding to determine "'the times at which indecent material may be broadcast,' to carefully review and address the specific concerns we raised in *ACT I*": among them, the appropriate definitions of "children" and "reasonable risk" for channeling purposes, the paucity of station- or program-specific audience data expressed as a percentage of the relevant age group population, and the scope of the government's interest in regulating indecent broadcasts.

The government's petition for *certiorari*, based largely on an argument that such broadcasts invaded the privacy of the home, was denied, Federal Communications Commission v. Action for Children's Television, 112 S.Ct. 1282 (1992) (White and O'Connor, JJ., dissenting).

Following these events, Infinity Broadcasting petitioned the FCC to declare that the Howard Stern Show, p. 823, *supra*, could be presented during morning drive time because its surveys showed that children do not listen to radio during that period. How should the Commission determine the appropriate hours for a safe harbor for indecent speech? What evidence will it need to support its decision?

4.  The Public Telecommunications Act of 1992, Pub.Law 102–356, § 16(a), 106 Stat. 949, 954, included provisions requiring the FCC to promulgate regulations prohibiting the broadcasting of indecent pro-

gramming between the hours of 6 a.m. and 12 midnight. Public radio and television stations that go off the air before or at midnight will be allowed to broadcast indecency between 10 p.m. and midnight.

In promulgating these rules the Commission set forth its reasons for limiting indecent programming to the hours specified in the Public Telecommunications Act. Once again, for the purpose of channeling indecency away from children, the Commission defined children as anyone seventeen years and under. This was important because the ratings data for radio available to the Commission was for children 12–17.

Both the television and radio data showed substantial numbers of children in the audience at all hours, although the numbers for late night and early morning were lower than the rest of the day. Based on this data the Commission concluded that the safe harbor time set out in the Public Telecommunications Act "reasonably balances the compelling interest of protecting children from exposure to indecent broadcast material at all times against the interests of broadcasters and adults."

Under these rules broadcasters would be permitted to defend themselves by submitting "market-wide data demonstrating that there is no appreciable child audience during the relevant time period would raise a viable defense to a charge of indecency outside of the safe harbor." However, data demonstrating that few or no children were listening to that station at the time when the indecent material was aired, would not be considered. The FCC's reason for refusing to consider station-specific data is that it "does not account for children's grazing. Grazing is the practice of rapidly tuning through the entire channel menu in a short period of time. This tuning may not be reflected in a station's ratings. Broadcast Indecency, 71 R.R.2d 1116 (1992).

Within a week, broadcasters sought to upset the new rules in the United States Court of Appeals for the District of Columbia. The complainants relied on the earlier decisions of the court and argued that nothing in this record met the fatal flaws that upset the earlier rules. The court agreed, holding that the new rules violated the First Amendment. ___ F.3d ___, 1993 WL 479512 (D.C.Cir.1993).

5. During these developments, the FCC was addressing individual complaints about indecency, with most attention being paid to the broadcasts of radio personality Howard Stern. In late 1992 and early 1993, the Commission issued several notices of apparent liability (NAL) for Stern programs from 1988 through 1991 totalling $600,000. One case involved a licensee that had bought local rights to Stern's broadcasts involving remarks made during 12 programs in 1991. (Forfeitures up to $25,000 per violation may be imposed under § 503(b) of the Act.) Letter to Greater Los Angeles Radio, Inc., 7 F.C.C. Rcd. 7321, 71 R.R.2d 979 (1992) By early 1993, the notices of apparent liability involving Howard Stern totalled an additional $600,000—in part because of fines assessed according to the number of markets in which a particular

broadcast was heard.  Sagittarius Broadcasting Corporation, 71 R.R.2d 989 (1992).

The FCC identified a list of excerpts from the shows that suggest its concern.  The following samples are direct quotes from the FCC record and are quoted in full:

—"The closest I came to making love to a black woman was, I masturbated to a picture of Aunt Jemima."

—[Concerning a criminal trial in which the television personality Pee Wee Herman was found to have masturbated twice within 10 minutes in a movie theater]: "I, who am the head of the masturbator club, I run a masturbation society.  I am someone totally devoted to masturbation.  I must tell you, to do that twice in 10 minutes is unbelievable."

—"First I want to just strip and rape [rival Los Angeles disc jockeys] Mark and Brian.  I want my two bitches laying there in the cold, naked.  . . .  I want them bleeding from the buttocks."

—"Hey FCC, penis.  . . .  I do draw the line at vagina.  Whoa, I can't believe I just said that word."

—Concerning actress Michelle Pfeiffer: "I would not even need a vibrator.  . . .  Boy, her rump would be more black and blue than a Harlem cub scout."

See Broadcasting, Nov. 2, 1992 at 55.  For a list of indecency fines levied on other broadcasters, see Broadcasting, Aug, 31, 1992 at 25.

Infinity Broadcasting has challenged the Commission's determinations.  Among other points it notes that the FCC did not find indecent a Stern song parody that refers to masturbation, rape, erections and homosexuality.  Since some references to masturbation, for example, are being held indecent and others are not the FCC is obligated to explain clearly where the line is being drawn.  Broadcasting & Cable, March 1, 1993 at 44.

Because the FCC can only issue NALs and has no authority to impose fines, when a licensee refuses to accept the notice and contests the issue, the government attempts to enforce the liability in the district court.  This step has been reached in a 1987 indecency case against Evergreen Media involving WLUP(AM) in Chicago.  Evergreen is seeking a ruling that the indecency provision is unconstitutionally vague.

6.   On the same day that the Commission issued the NAL to Infinity for $600,000, it approved Infinity's purchase of three FM stations from Cook Inlet Radio License Partnership, L.P.  The transfer had been opposed by Americans for Responsible Television, the American Family Association, the Family Research Council, Focus on the Family and several individuals.  The objections were based on the FCC's indecency findings involving the Howard Stern.  Cook Inlet Radio License Partnership, L.P., 71 R.R.2d 992 (1992).

The majority argued that the enforcement proceedings against Infinity were the proper forum for addressing the indecency complaints. In addition, Commissioners Quello and Barrett, in separate concurrences, argued that denying the transfer application would punish Cook Inlet. Commissioner Duggan voiced similar sentiments in his concurrence in *Sagittarius*.

Chairman Sykes dissented in *Cook Inlet*. Noting the "apparent pattern of noncompliance with the indecency laws," he argued that he could not make the affirmative finding that Infinity was fit to be a licensee. Thus, he could not find that the transfer would serve the public interest.

7. In *Video 44*, p. 708, *supra*, the Review Board had designated the question of obscene programming as an issue. The Commission in turn eliminated it as an issue, holding that initial determinations on obscenity should be left to local officials. The Commission indicated that it would take appropriate action in cases where a licensee was convicted of violating an obscenity statute.

Acting on a Petition for Reconsideration, the Commission reversed itself on the obscenity issue:

> 11. Although it may be preferable, in most cases, to deal with questions of obscenity in the context of a previously adjudicated prosecution in a local judicial district, we are persuaded, on reflection, that we should retain the ability to pursue a range of options when allegations of a violation of Section 1464 are raised against a licensee. Those options include not only referring complaints against licensees to the U.S. Department of Justice for a possible criminal prosecution for obscenity under Section 1464, *e.g.*, *Pacifica Foundation, Inc.*, 2 F.C.C.Rcd. at 2701 para. 26, but also undertaking our own action and exercising one of the many administrative sanctions available to us. *E.g.*, 47 U.S.C. §§ 303(m) (suspension of license), 312(a) (revocation of license), 312(b) (cease and desist order) & 503(b) (forfeiture). . . .

However, the Commission still refused to examine the specific obscenity allegations against Video 44 because they were first presented in the context of a renewal proceeding. Such allegations must be presented shortly after the broadcast in question and may not be held until the end of the license term. Video 44, 3 F.C.C.Rcd. 757, 64 R.R.2d 378 (1988).

In *Monroe Communications*, p. 708, *supra*, the court of appeals held that the Commission had not adequately justified its contemporaneous complaint requirement. The FCC had argued that the rule "would guarantee the Commission flexibility in responding to the obscenity allegations in a responsible manner; would enable the Commission to put the licensee on notice that its broadcasts were unacceptable, thus minimizing the chilling effect on a broadcaster's disposition to air protected speech that might result from allowing allegations of obscenity to be raised for the first time in the context of comparative renewal hearings, and would ensure that allegations of obscenity are judged by contemporary community standards, as required by [*Miller*], rather than the standards of a later period."

The court dismissed the first argument because allegations of obscene broadcasts were clearly relevant to the public interest and no other factor bearing on the public interest was subject to a contemporaneous complaint requirement. The chilling effect argument was rejected because the court did not see how the threat of eventual nonrenewal was any more chilling than the threat of an immediate forfeiture or license revocation. Finally, the court found the argument that the requirement would ensure adherence to *Miller* to "make[ ] no sense whatsoever." Adjudications of obscenity, whether by the courts or the FCC, always require a determination at a later date of what the standards were at the time of the allegedly obscene broadcast. The court instructed the FCC either to consider the obscenity complaints against Video 44 or to better justify its refusal to do so.

In *Video 44*, p. 708, *supra*, the Commission found it unnecessary to address the obscenity complaints because it had already decided to award the license to a competing applicant.

8. As the Commission indicated in *Video 44*, it had referred the Pacifica broadcast of "Jerker" to the Justice Department for a possible obscenity prosecution. The Justice Department declined to take any action.

## C.  SAFETY—VIOLENCE AND PANIC

Although the Surgeon General has issued reports on the relationship between violence and television, and other academic studies have addressed the same issue primarily in connection with children, the Commission has never attempted to regulate the area in any substantive way. It has been asked several times but each time has refused.

In 1972, for example, the Commission was asked to analogize the area to cigarette smoking because of the actions of the Surgeon General in the two areas. George Corey, 37 F.C.C.2d 641, 25 R.R.2d 437 (1972). The complainant sought to have three Boston stations carry a public service notice at appropriate times: "Warning: Viewing of violent television programming by children can be hazardous to their mental health and well being." The Commission rejected the request on two grounds. First, it stated any action should come by rulemaking rather than moving against a few stations. Second, the Commission rejected the contention that the fairness doctrine was applicable to violent programming. The cigarette episode was discussed:

> However, it could not reasonably or logically be concluded that the mere viewing of a person smoking a cigarette during a movie being broadcast on television constitutes a discussion of a controversial issue of public importance thus raising a fairness doctrine obligation. Similarly, we cannot agree that the broadcast of violent

episodes during entertainment programs necessarily constitutes the presentation of one side of a controversial issue of public importance. It is simply not an appropriate application of the fairness doctrine to say that an entertainment program—whether it be Shakespeare or an action-adventure show—raises a controversial issue if it contains a violent scene and has a significant audience of children. Were we to adopt your construction that the depiction of a violent scene is a discussion of one side of a controversial issue of public importance, the number of controversial issues presented on entertainment shows would be virtually endless (e.g., a scene with a high-powered car; or one showing a person taking an alcoholic drink or cigarette; depicting women in a soft, feminine or light romantic role). Finally, we note that there are marked differences in the conclusiveness of the hazard established in this area as against cigarette smoking. [ ]

The real thrust of your complaint would appear to be not fairness in the discussion of controversial issues but the elimination of violent TV children's programming because of its effect on children. That issue is being considered particularly by appropriate Congressional committees and agencies such as [the Department of Health, Education and Welfare—now the Department of Health and Human Services]. [ ] It is a difficult, complex, and sensitive matter. But whatever its resolution, there is no basis for the action along the lines proposed by you.

In its Report on the Broadcast of Violent, Indecent, and Obscene Material, 51 F.C.C.2d 418, 32 R.R.2d 1367 (1975), the Commission explained to Congress that the violence area was unlike the obscenity area because of the totally different statutory framework involved. In the absence of any prohibitions on violence in programming, "industry self-regulation is preferable to the adoption of rigid governmental standards." The Commission took this position for two reasons. First, it feared the constitutional questions that would emerge from such an intrusion into program content. Second the judgments concerning the suitability of certain programming for children are "highly subjective." A speech by Chairman Wiley was quoted to the effect that slapstick comedy, an episode in "Peter Pan" when Captain Hook is eaten by a crocodile, and the poisoning of Snow White by the witch, all raise judgmental questions for which there is no objective standard.

*Mass Hysteria.* Another substantive problem involves programs that frighten the listening public. At 11 p.m. on Oct. 30, 1974, a radio station in Rhode Island presented a contemporary version of the famous H.G. Wells' "War of the Worlds," that had been presented on that same night in 1938. A meteorite was reported to have fallen in a sparsely populated community killing several people; later "black-eyed, V-shaped mouthed, glistening creatures dripping saliva" were reported to have emerged from what turned out to be a capsule, and other landings were reported. What steps would you expect the licensee to take before presenting such a program—or is it inappropriate to present such material at any time? Telephone calls from frightened, and later from angry, listeners flooded the station, police and other public service departments.

The licensee had taken several steps before the program to inform state public safety officials in the listening area of the station. The state police in turn sent notices to all their stations in the area alerting them to the program. Approximately once an hour from noon until 10 p.m. the licensee broadcast the following promotional announcement: "Tonight at 11 p.m., WPRO invites you to listen to a spoof of the 1930s a special Hallowe'en classic presentation. . . ." The last was made about an hour before the program. Three announcements were made during the program—after 47, 48, and 56 minutes. The reason for the timing was said to be that the first 30 to 35 minutes of the show involved what appeared to be a meteor crashing in a remote spot and the arrival of creatures was not reported until 30 minutes into the program.

The Commission told the licensee that it had not met its responsibility to operate in a manner consistent with the public interest. The warnings were inadequate because "it is a well known fact that the radio audience is constantly changing. The only way to assure adequately that the public would not be alarmed in this case would be an introductory statement repeated at frequent intervals throughout the program." One Commissioner dissented because intrusion into presentations of drama should be made with "utmost caution" and the licensee's precautions "were not in my opinion unreasonable." Capital Cities Communications, Inc., 54 F.C.C.2d 1035, 34 R.R.2d 1016 (1975).

Would the Commission's suggestions impinge on the dramatic effect sought by the licensee? Is that relevant? Can you think of other ways to meet the Commission's concern? Recall the greater ease of warning an unwilling audience about possibly offensive programs over television as opposed to radio. Is that distinction applicable here?

A St. Louis radio station's broadcast that the United States was under nuclear attack led the Commission to impose a fine of $25,000. The station was found in violation of § 325(a) of the Communications Act, which makes it a crime to "knowingly transmit a false or fraudulent signal of distress." The program included the sound of the Emergency Broadcast System tone followed by the sound of exploding bombs. The station blamed the program on an employee who thought that the public took the threat of nuclear warfare too lightly. Emmis Broadcasting Co., KSHE–FM, 6 F.C.C.Rcd. 2289, 69 R.R.2d 195 (1991).

9. After the St. Louis incident, as well as incidents in Pasadena and Providence the Commission issued an NPRM seeking comments on a new hoax rule. The Pasadena case involved a radio station airing a call from a man who supposedly had killed his girlfriend. A police investigation of the "murder" ensued and the hoax was only exposed when viewers of a "Unsolved Mysteries" (NBC) story on the "crime" notified police of the similarities between the caller and a disc jockey who had subsequently been hired by the station.

In the Providence hoax, a station's news director announced that the station's morning man had been shot just outside the station. The news director then refused to disclose the hoax even when ordered to by the station's general manager. The news director and morning man were both fired. Broadcasting, July 29, 1991 at 68.

In 1992, after receiving comments, the Commission decided to issue a rule rather than rely on a policy. In part the rule approach was chosen because it permitted the Commission to use the forfeiture provisions of § 503(b) rather than simply the non-monetary sanctions available under a policy approach. The Commission issued the following rule:

> No licensee or permittee of any broadcast station shall broadcast false information concerning a crime or a catastrophe if (a) the licensee knows this information is false, (b) it is foreseeable that broadcast of the information will cause substantial public harm, and (c) broadcast of the information does in fact directly cause substantial public harm. Any programming accompanied by a disclaimer will be presumed not to pose foreseeable harm if the disclaimer clearly characterizes the program as a fiction and is presented in a way that is reasonable under the circumstances.
>
> FOOTNOTE 1. For purposes of this rule, "public harm" must begin immediately, and cause direct and actual damage to property or to the health or safety of the general public, or diversion of law enforcement or other public health and safety authorities from their duties. The public harm will be deemed foreseeable if the licensee could expect with a significant degree of certainty that public harm would occur. A "crime" is any act or omission that makes the offender subject to criminal punishment by law. A "catastrophe" is a disaster or imminent disaster involving a violent or sudden event affecting the public.

The disclaimer feature was prompted by concern over broadcasts of acknowledged fiction. In comments, the Commission observed that a disclaimer would be presumptively reasonable if it came at the beginning and at the end of the program and at intervals during the program no longer than 15 minutes apart. Broadcast Hoaxes, 7 FCC Rcd 4106, 70 R.R.2d 1383 (1992).

According to *The New York Times*, on April 1, 1993, more than 1,000 people in the San Diego area "swarmed to a small airport to see a supposed landing of the space shuttle Discovery. . . . The hoax by KGB–FM tied up traffic for hours" at the airport. N.Y.Times, Apr. 3, 1993 at 6 (nat'l ed.). What action might the FCC take?

## D.　CHILDREN'S PROGRAMMING

Over the years groups have expressed special concern about programs aimed at children. Some, as we discussed, p. 465, *supra*, have been concerned primarily with commercials. Others have been concerned about the content of the programs themselves or that there is too little children's programming. All of these concerns and conflicts became more heated in the late 1970s and continue today. As we consider each situation, note the different approaches being considered. Sometimes it is prohibiting certain content; sometimes it involves mandatory programming; and sometimes it is conditional in the sense that if a broadcaster presents one kind of content it may be obligated to present other types of programs. Also note that occasionally the FCC invokes the aid of private groups, such as the National Association of Broadcasters (NAB) to alter a practice within the industry.

### 1.  PROGRAM CONTENT

Most of the concern about the impact of television on children has stressed the use of violence and sexual innuendo. Although some groups have been concerned about these matters so far as adults are concerned, more seem concerned about their impact on children. Under Butler v. Michigan, 352 U.S. 380 (1957), it is unlawful for government to impose a complete ban on printed matter that is legally protected as to adults, simply to keep the material from children. Might that rule be different with television or radio? Does *Pacifica* suggest differences?

The NAB is a private voluntary organization whose membership includes the three major networks, well over half the television stations in the country and some 3,000 radio broadcasters. The NAB promulgated codes and standards that members had to follow if they wished to retain membership. The codes addressed such matters as how many minutes of commercials were appropriate in an hour; what types of commercials should not be accepted; what material should not be shown on the screen; and how subjects, such as suicide or astrology or religion should be developed. In 1982, as the result of an antitrust action brought by the Justice Department, the NAB cancelled the advertising standards of the Codes and dissolved the Code Boards of Directors.

A broadcaster that adhered to the code could display the NAB seal. The NAB maintained a staff that advised members about the propriety of their behavior under the codes.

In 1975 the result of the interaction of the network officials, the FCC chairman and the NAB was the promulgation of the "family viewing policy" as an amendment to the NAB's Television Code. Under the policy, programs of a violent or sexually-oriented nature were wholly barred from the time slots before 9 p.m. (8 p.m. Central Time). This required moving some programs that had been popular in earlier prime-time slots and also involved decisions about which programs were affected in the first place. The entire story of the development and early enforcement of the family viewing policy is traced at length in G. Cowan, *See No Evil: The Backstage Battle over Sex and Violence on Television* (1979). See Writers Guild of America v. Federal Communications Commission, 609 F.2d 355, 46 R.R.2d 813 (9th Cir.1979), cert. denied 449 U.S. 824 (1980).

In 1990 Congress passed an exemption to the antitrust laws for "any joint discussion, consideration, review, action, or agreement by or among persons in the television industry for the purpose of, and limited to, developing and disseminating voluntary guidelines designed to alleviate the negative impact of violence in telecast material." 104 Stat. 5089. The exemption was scheduled to sunset Dec. 1, 1993, but Attorney General Janet Reno extended it indefinitely. Broadcasting & Cable, Dec. 6, 1993 at 90.

In May 1993 the House Telecommunication Subcommittee held a hearing on violent television programming. Subcommittee Chairman Edward Markey (D–Mass.) called for a television rating system similar to that used by the motion picture industry. He also suggested "requiring sets sold in the U.S. to incorporate technology to block channels or programs that parents deem too violent for their children." This would be accomplished by including a computer chip—the "V chip"—in each set. Broadcasting & Cable, May 17, 1993 at 41. For the V chip to function, shows would have to be rated (either by broadcasters or by some government agency). Each broadcast of a show rated "violent" would have to carry a signal that would activate the V chip. Broadcasting & Cable, Aug. 23, 1993 at 64.

Shortly thereafter the broadcast networks and 15 major cable networks agreed to run violence warning labels. In addition, ABC announced that starting in August 1993, it would offer a recorded message, accessible through a toll free number, listing the ABC shows containing a violence warning. Broadcasting & Cable, Aug. 2, 1993 at 16, 20.

CBS, however, announced that none of its fall series merited the violence warning, but that specific episodes would carry the warning if it is warranted. Broadcasting & Cable, July 26, 1993 at 20.

In August 1993, the National Council for Families & Television sponsored an industry-wide summit conference on TV violence. Attendees included broadcast and cable executives, program producers, public interest groups, academics and government officials. At the conference Sen. Paul Simon (D–Ill.) warned that if the industry didn't do something about television violence, Congress would. Sen. Simon offered a seven-point plan to reduce television violence.

Form industry advisory committee on TV violence.

Exercise self-restraint when it comes to violence.

Involve the entire industry: broadcasters, cable, independents, syndicators and the movies.

Glamorized violence should be avoided, harsh realities of violence must be portrayed and non-violent problem-solving should be encouraged.

Violent promos should be eliminated or reduced, and certainly avoided when children are most likely to be watching.

The medium must be used to help educate the nation about the harmful effects of television violence.

Recognize more clearly the international dimensions of your product.

Broadcasting & Cable, Aug. 9, 1993 at 18–26.

Within a few days after the conference, three bills aimed at curbing television violence had been filed. One filed by House Telecommunications Subcommittee Chairman Edward Markey (D–Mass) would require TV sets to contain the V chip. Senate Commerce Chairman Ernest Hollings (D–S.C.) filed a bill to channel violence to hours when few children are watching, in essence treating broadcast violence the same as broadcast indecency. The bill filed by House Telecommunications Subcommittee member John Bryant (D–Tex.) would require the Commission to "consider stations' efforts to reduce violent programming at license renewal time." The other major feature of the bill is a proposal to allow the FCC to set violence standards and fine stations for violation of these standards. Broadcasting & Cable, Aug. 9, 1993 at 10.

## 2.  Too Few Programs for Children

There has long been concern that too few programs are written expressly for children. Following a petition in 1970 from Action for Children's Television (ACT) to require children's programming, the FCC spent much of the 1970s trying to decide how to react. In 1974 it issued a Policy Statement asking licensees to "make a meaningful effort" to increase overall programming for children; to air "a reasonable amount" of programming designed to educate and inform children, not simply to entertain them; to address the needs of both preschool and school-age children; and to air these programs on weekdays as well as weekends.

The Commission, in 1979, concluded that over a five-year period, the amount of children's programming per station had increased less than one hour per week (from 10.5 to 11.3 hours) and that this was totally accounted for by new programming from independent stations. Network affiliates had not increased their programming at all. No significant increase in education or informational programs was detected. Few licensees sought to develop age-specific programs for children. Finally, although only 8 percent of children's television viewing occurs on weekends, almost half the programs for children are presented on weekends.

The staff concluded that "the small numbers of children and their limited appeal to advertisers, combined with the small number of outlets in most markets, create incentives for the commercial television system to neglect the specific needs of the child audience." Age-specific programming would be even less attractive to broadcasters because of the further splitting of an already small market.

In Children's Television Programming and Advertising Practices, 75 F.C.C.2d 138 (1979), the FCC announced a proposed rulemaking in which it listed five options. These were to rescind the 1974 Policy Statement and rely on program sources other than commercial broadcasting; to maintain or modify the policy statement; to institute mandatory programming requirements; to develop renewal guidelines; or to increase the number of video outlets.

The Commission completed the proceeding in 1983. Mandatory children's programming obligations for television stations were rejected. The FCC found that the amount and variety of children's programming available was substantial and diverse. It noted that the establishment of quotas might be impermissible content-based regulation and would create difficult definitional problems. Such quotas would also preclude the establishment of experimental children's services and efforts at specialization. Although no quotas were created, each licensee has the obligation to consider the needs of all significant elements of the community. A licensee at renewal time must demonstrate the attention devoted to the needs of children in its viewing audience, but may consider the alternative program sources available to children in their area. Children's Television Programming, 55 R.R.2d 199 (1984). On appeal, the D.C. Circuit affirmed the Commission's position that alternatives such as public broadcasting and cable could be considered in assessing the need for children's programming. Action for Children's Television v. Federal Communications Commission, 756 F.2d 899, 57 R.R.2d 1406 (D.C.Cir. 1985).

An effort by citizen groups to deny license renewals to television stations that had no regularly scheduled children's programming failed in Washington Association for Television and Children v. Federal Communications Commission, 712 F.2d 677, 54 R.R.2d 293 (D.C.Cir.1983). The Commission's policy statement did not require regular scheduling, and the Commission did not have to prefer a station that presented regularly scheduled cartoons to one that presented educational specials.

Section 103 of the Children's Television Act of 1990, p. 469, *supra*, requires the Commission, when reviewing an application for renewal of a broadcast license, to consider whether the licensee "has served the educational and informational needs of children through the licensee's overall programming, including programming specifically designed to serve such needs." Pursuant to the Act, the FCC adopted the following guidelines for assessing how well licensees have met these requirements.

## IN THE MATTER OF POLICIES AND RULES CONCERNING CHILDREN'S TELEVISION PROGRAMMING

## REVISION OF PROGRAMMING AND COMMERCIALIZATION POLICIES, ASCERTAINMENT REQUIREMENTS, AND PROGRAM LOG REQUIREMENTS FOR COMMERCIAL TELEVISION STATIONS

Federal Communications Commission, 1991.
6 F.C.C.Rcd. 2111, 68 R.R.2d 1615.

. . .

14.   The Children's Television Act requires that, in reviewing television license renewal applications, we consider whether the licensee has served "the educational and informational needs of children through the licensee's overall programming, including programming specifically designed to serve such needs."   . . .   In light of the legislative intent, we will implement this programming provision by reviewing a licensee's renewal application to determine whether, over the course of its license term, it has served the educational and informational needs of children in its overall programming, including programming specifically designed to serve such needs.

### A.   Age Range of "Children"

15.   The Act does not define "children" for purposes of the educational and informational programming renewal review requirement.   . . . After reviewing the variety of positions taken in the record, we find that the different policies underlying the Act's programming provision necessitate a broader conception of "children" than we used for commercial limits.   While it is primarily younger children who need protection from commercial matter that they do not fully comprehend, older as well as younger children have unique needs and can benefit from programming directed to them.   Teenagers are undergoing a transition to adulthood. They are still very influenced by adult role models and peers, including those portrayed on television.   They are generally inexperienced and yet face many crucial decisions concerning sex, drugs, and their own identities.   To fully comply with the Act's directive that licensees demonstrate responsiveness to the needs of the child audience, we believe that we must interpret the programming renewal review requirement to apply to programs originally produced and broadcast for an audience of children 16 years of age and under.

. . .

18.   The *Notice* asked whether the Act requires broadcasters to target particular segments of the child audience.   The legislative history, we find, permits but does not require such targeting to satisfy our renewal review.   Imposing such a requirement would contravene the legislative intent to afford broadcasters maximum flexibility in determining the "mix" of programming they will present to meet children's special needs.   Requiring each broadcaster to serve all age groups in order to

pass our renewal review would probably result in less expensive and lower quality programming, possibly engendering what INTV describes as "sameness and mediocrity." We thus decline to adopt suggestions that broadcasters program to all ages or to each subset of children within the under 16 range. Stations may select the age groups they can most effectively serve.

B.  *Standard*

   1.  *Programming*

19.  Although we stated the desire to avoid any *de facto* system of "precensorship" and to leave it to licensees to interpret the meaning of educational and informational programming, the *Notice* asked those commenters desiring a delineation of the Act's programming renewal review requirement to address what definition of "educational and informational" programming we might use. The *Notice* specifically referred to a description by Senator Inouye, as programming which furthers a child's intellectual, emotional and social development. After further reflection, we believe that a general definition of "educational and informational" programming for children would provide needed guidance to the industry as well as to Commission staff administering the statute, and would give licensees sufficient flexibility to exercise their discretion in serving children's needs. We also encourage licensees to use the assessment criteria proposed in the *Notice* in determining how to meet the educational and informational needs of children in their communities.

   . . .

21.  We believe that a definition based on Senator Inouye's view, described above, or based on McGannon's formulation—content that serves children's cognitive/intellectual or social/emotional needs—is closer to the spirit of the Act and to our desire to stimulate, and not dictate, programming responsive to children's needs. Thus, programming that furthers the positive development of the child in any respect, including the child's cognitive/intellectual or emotional/social needs, can contribute to satisfying the licensee's obligation to serve the educational and informational needs of children.

22.  The *Notice* proposed to require each licensee to assess the needs of children given (1) the circumstances within the community, (2) other programming on the station, (3) programming aired on other broadcast stations within the community, and (4) other programs for children available in the broadcaster's community of license. Licensees would then air programs intended to meet "the educational and informational needs of children" responding to this assessment. In order to avoid unnecessary burdens, we are not requiring use of the proposed assessment criteria. We do, however, adopt them as permissive guidelines for exercise of licensee discretion in applying this definition. These factors can serve to make licensees' decisionmaking process more objective and may make it easier for licensees to justify programming decisions that

are questioned. We therefore encourage their use. We are concerned with licensee responsiveness to children's needs, not with the precise methodology they use to assess those needs. We thus do not adopt proposals for structured assessment procedures. Licensees will retain reasonable discretion to determine the manner in which they assess the educational and informational needs of children in their communities, provided that they are able to demonstrate the methodology they have used.

. . .

24. The Act imposes no quantitative standards and the legislative history suggests that Congress meant that no minimum amount criterion be imposed. Given this strong legislative directive direction, and the latitude afforded broadcasters in fulfilling the programming requirement, we believe that the amount of "specifically designed" programming necessary to comply with the Act's requirement is likely to vary according to other circumstances, including but not limited to, type of programming aired and other nonbroadcast efforts made by the station. We thus decline to establish any minimum programming requirement for licensees for renewal review independent of that established in the Act.

25. At the request of numerous parties, we clarify that short segment programming, including vignettes and PSAs, may qualify as specifically designed educational and informational programming for children. Such material is well suited to children's short attention spans and can often be locally produced with acceptable production quality. It thus may be a particularly appropriate way for a local broadcaster to respond to specific children's concerns. Whether or not short segment programming fully satisfies the requirement to air programming "specifically designed" to meet children's needs depends on the entire context of the licensee's programming and nonbroadcast efforts directed at children. We also clarify that qualifying programming need not be locally produced and need not be live action, as opposed to animation. We can see no reason in the statute's purpose or legislative history for these restrictions. As the legislative history also indicates, general audience programming can contribute, as part of the licensee's overall programming, to serving children's needs pursuant to the Act. It does not by definition, however, satisfy the additional requirement that licensees air some programming "specifically designed" to serve the educational and informational needs of children.

. . .

### 2. Nonbroadcast efforts

27. Section 103(b) of the Act permits the Commission, in evaluating compliance with the broadcaster's obligation to demonstrate at renewal time that it served the educational and informational needs of children, to consider "in addition" to its programming (1) "any special nonbroadcast efforts . . . which enhance the educational and informational value" of programming meeting such needs and (2) any "special efforts"

to produce or support programming broadcast by another station in the licensee's market that is specifically designed to meet such needs.
. . .

28.  For nonbroadcast efforts to contribute to satisfying the Act's programming renewal review requirement, they must enhance the "educational and informational value" to children of television programming broadcast either by the licensee or by another station in the community. Thus, however, praiseworthy, community outreach efforts unrelated to television programming will not qualify.  Similarly, we do not believe that support for children's radio programming, as some urge, although a very laudable objective, qualifies under Section 103(b)(2) as support for another licensee's programming.  . . .   For efforts to be credited toward satisfying the Act's programming renewal review requirements, they must somehow enhance or support educational and informational television programming for children.

26.  If a station produces or buys children's programs broadcast on another station, so as to qualify under Section 103(b)(2) of the Act, we hold that both stations may rely on such programming in their renewal applications.  The extent of support, measured in both time and money, given to another station's programming will determine the weight afforded it.  . . .

. . .

### Notes and Questions

1.  In 1992 the FCC audited 141 television stations and 27 cable systems.  Eight televisions and three cable systems were cited for running too much commercial matter during children's programming. Broadcasting, July 13, 1992 at 38.

2.  The November 1993 television ratings for children showed that educational "FCC-friendly" shows attracted far fewer viewers than cartoons and other entertainment programs.  Broadcasting & Cable, Jan. 17, 1994 at 24.

cartoons and other entertainment programs. Broadcasting & Cable, Jan. 17, 1994 at 24.

## Chapter XVIII

# CABLE AND NEW TECHNOLOGIES

Until this point our discussion of the electronic media has been addressed solely to broadcasting. Some programs reached the public through radios and others through television sets. We turn now to other forms of communication that do not necessarily involve broadcasting—though the end product does emerge through the television set. It is important to recognize at the outset that although broadcasting and the television set have been joined, new technology permits the television set to be used for communications that have not been broadcast. The most obvious example is the use of video cassette players and recorders, which permit the owners of television sets to buy video cassettes at stores and play them on their television sets at home—all without any use of the spectrum. That activity much more closely resembles the showing of movies at home than anything else.

## A. CABLE TELEVISION

Cable television involves the transmission of electrical signals over wires to television sets in homes or elsewhere. The technique involves a studio, called the "head-end," and coaxial and/or fiber optic cables that physically connect the head-end with the television set of every user of the system. The cable is capable of carrying such a wide range of electrical signals that it can simultaneously carry signals sufficient for 55 or more television channels. (As the signals are carried along the cable they become weaker and must be amplified along the way.)

It is possible to transmit certain signals in scrambled form that require decoders, while others can be received by all users. It is also possible to run a system in which the users are able to send signals back to the head-end: voting on a question asked on a program, ordering merchandise or telling a quarterback what plays to call in a semiprofessional football game.

The programming sent out from the head-end can come from many sources. System owners might send out a variety of motion pictures they have bought or rented; they might send camera crews to cover local high school football games; they might present live programs from their own studios; they might carry programs prepared by others specially for cable that they receive by wire or by satellite; or they might seek to transmit over their systems the signals and programs broadcast by television stations. This last source of programming raises serious questions regarding the relationship between cable and over-the-air television. So long as the cable system carries only programming from other sources, cable television is simply another competitor of broadcasting, along with movies, phonograph records, books and other communications media. In fact, however, cable has been intimately involved with broadcasting since its inception—and that has produced substantial conflict.

## 1. DEVELOPMENT

Cable transmission was first used in the 1950s to provide television reception to remote locations that otherwise would have received none. For example, a community located in the mountains of West Virginia could construct an antenna on high ground to receive the signals of nearby television stations and transmit them through cable to households in the community. Such systems were called CATV for "community antenna television." Since cable was the only means of bringing television service to these remote areas, television broadcasters welcomed the additional viewers.

It was soon realized, however, that cable could do more than merely provide television service to remote areas. In 1961 a cable operator began serving San Diego, a city already served by three VHF network affiliates. The cable operator erected an antenna capable of picking up signals from Los Angeles, 100 miles away. In addition to the three networks received locally, cable offered four independent stations that served Los Angeles with sports, old motion pictures and reruns of network shows. The San Diego experience demonstrated that the three channels offered by over-the-air signals were not enough to satisfy an ordinary audience and that viewers were willing to pay for more diversified programming through importation of distant signals. In effect, cable television service filled in the uneven pattern of FCC station allocation. Because cable offered a service alternative to that offered by local, over-the-air stations, television broadcasters began to view cable transmission as a competitive threat.

The spread of color television also provided a new impetus to cable development. VHF signals tend to bounce off large obstacles rather than bend around them. Hence a tall building can act like a weak transmitter, rebroadcasting the television signal at the same frequency as the station from which the signal originates. The result is interference, barely noticeable on a black-and-white set, but more pronounced on a color set. Cable provided the residents of large cities something that an over-the-air television signal could not—a high quality color picture. Hence, cable television invaded large cities, despite the presence of a full complement of VHF signals.

Finally, cable began to originate programming not available to viewers of network or independent television. Cable systems offered entertainment programming, sports events and special programs designed to meet the interests of discrete groups. The discovery that viewers were willing to pay a few dollars more per month for programming not available on over-the-air television led to the development of pay cable service.

Pay cable involves the cable distribution of non-broadcast programming for which the subscriber is charged an additional program or channel fee beyond the regular monthly fee for the system's television signal reception service. The systems for distributing pay cable vary technically. The simplest method is to distribute the programming on one or more channels of a cable television system in garbled form. System subscribers who wish to receive the additional programming are supplied with a device that converts the programming transmission so that it can be understood. It is technically possible, but expensive, to use systems that permit a separate charge to be made for each program viewed. These either require the subscriber to purchase a ticket for each program in advance, which when inserted into a decoding device in the subscriber's home, provides access to the programming, or to utilize the return communications capacity of a cable system or a telephone connection to activate a central computer facility that releases the programming through the subscriber's decoding device (an addressable converter) and performs the billing functions.

Most cable systems utilize a fee structure known as "tiering." A relatively low monthly fee gives the subscriber access to the local over-the-air television stations as well as any community access or local origination channels. Access channels carry programming produced by citizens or community groups, and local origination consists of local news, sports and public affairs programming produced by the cable operator. Sometimes advertiser-supported services such as the Entertainment and Sports Programming Network (ESPN), the Cable News Network (CNN) and over-the-air signals imported from other parts of the country are included.

An additional monthly fee gives the subscriber access to other specialized programming services ranging from children's programs to adult entertainment. These services are usually bundled together in groups called "tiers." Thus, the subscriber must sometimes take several unwanted program services to obtain one desired service. Usually a higher tier includes all the programming available in lower tiers.

The range of programming available via cable has grown greatly. Among the services now available are programming directed to racial and religious groups, all-news and all-sports channels, live coverage of Congress, children's programming, "superstations" (discussed *infra*), movie and entertainment channels, adult movies and cultural programming.

In the late 1970s and early 1980s, new programming services were constantly beginning. Then a shakeout in the industry began to take place. CBS shut down CBS Cable after its operation lost $30 million in its first year. The RCA and Rockefeller Center entry, The Entertainment Channel, was discontinued after posting a $35 million loss in nine months.

In 1983 Ted Turner agreed to pay ABC and Westinghouse $12.5 million each to shut down Satellite News Channel, which was the main competitor to Turner's Cable News Network, and CNN Headline News. Group W and ABC promised not to compete in the cable news business for at least three years.

The late 1980s and early 1990s have brought another wave of new cable channels. Many of these are new services produced by existing cable programmers. For example, TNT and the Cartoon Network belong to Turner Broadcasting, while the Sci-Fi Channel belongs to USA Network.

Thus, cable has provided a variety of services. It began as a way of bringing to a community programming that would have been available but for geographical barriers. Then it imported programs from communities beyond the reach of normal reception. Later it became a service for those who wished to improve reception of their local signals. These features have been combined with each other as well as with the origination of new programming on cable. Now it is possible to obtain the origination without any of the other features—and this origination may be local or part of a network that programs specially for cable subscribers.

By 1993 cable systems had been installed in 55 million (62.4 percent) of the nation's 92.1 million television homes. Systems varied in size from a few hundred homes to some in larger cities with hundreds of thousands of subscribers. The largest multiple system operators (MSOs) owned hundreds of systems. Pay cable reached 43.5 million of these subscribers. The pay systems ranged from Home Box Office, with 16 million subscribers, to specialized services with only a few thousand subscribers.

## 2. JURISDICTION

### a. *FCC Jurisdiction*

When the first CATV systems emerged in the late 1950s, rural television stations became concerned about their local dominance. Their requests that the FCC assume jurisdiction over the activities of these new enterprises were rejected on the ground that the problem was trivial and no different from a request for protection against motion picture theaters or publishers who also compete with broadcasting.

In 1962, however, the FCC changed direction and began to deny cable systems permission to carry broadcast signals that might adversely affect local television. The Commission had two main concerns. First, it believed that if cable systems were allowed to import distant signals this would fragment the audience available to local stations, erode their revenue bases, affect their programming, and perhaps cause the stations to leave the air—to the public's detriment.

The second concern was that a cable system's use of retransmitted broadcast programming, for which the cable system had paid nothing, gave it an unfair competitive advantage over local television stations because the latter had to pay considerable sums to those who held the copyrights on particular programs.*

These two concerns—for fragmentation and program costs—led the FCC to embark on a series of regulations designed to keep cable systems subservient to over-the-air broadcasting. This attitude persisted from the mid–1960s to the mid–1970s. Recall that this was the period of weak UHF stations, for whom audience fragmentation might well have been fatal.

One of the restrictions imposed during this period was a ban on importing distant signals (those from outside the market area) into a top–100 market unless the cable system could prove that the importation would not hurt UHF development in that market. Although the regulation was challenged on the ground that the FCC had no statutory authority to issue it, the Supreme Court ruled that the regulation was "reasonably ancillary to the effective performance of [the FCC's] responsibilities for the regulation of television broadcasting." United States v. Southwestern Cable Co., 392 U.S. 157 (1968).

Although *Southwestern Cable* established that the Commission did have jurisdiction over cable, it left unanswered the boundaries of that jurisdiction. The next challenge arose from the promulgation in the late 1960s of rules requiring larger cable systems to originate a certain amount of programming from their own resources. This requirement was upheld, 5–4, by the Supreme Court in United States v. Midwest Video Corp., 406 U.S. 649 (1972), on the ground that the regulation was "reasonably ancillary" to the FCC's obligations to regulate over-the-air television. Because cable operators had become enmeshed with television broadcasting, the FCC could require them to engage in the functional equivalent of broadcasting. In 1974, however, after this victory, the FCC eliminated the origination requirement because it concluded that quality local programming could not be obtained by government mandate.

Instead, the Commission issued rules requiring new cable systems to allocate four channels to public, educational, local government and leased access. The systems had to make equipment available for studio use by the public and could not control who might use the facilities or what they might say. Charges for use of the facilities were controlled. This time, a legal challenge succeeded. In Federal Communications Commission v. Midwest Video Corp., 440 U.S. 689, 45 R.R.2d 58, 4 Med.L.Rptr. 2345 (1979) (*Midwest II*), the Court, 6–3, held that the rules violated a provision of the 1934 Communications Act that "a person engaged in . . . broadcasting shall not . . . be deemed a common carrier" who must accept business from anyone who wished to

---

* The copyright issue was sharpened when the Supreme Court held that cable retransmission of broadcast signals without consent did not constitute a "performance" within the 1909 Copyright Act and thus created no liability for copyright infringement. Fortnightly Corp. v. United Artists Television, 392 U.S. 390 (1968) and Teleprompter Corp. v. Columbia Broadcasting System, 415 U.S. 394 (1974).

patronize it. The Court considered the same limitation applicable to cable systems.

The mandatory access rules had also been challenged on First Amendment grounds. The Court chose not to address that issue at that time. As we will discuss later in this chapter, the Cable Communications Policy Act of 1984 authorizes the imposition of access channel requirements and for larger systems mandates leased access. However, as we will see in the notes following Preferred Communications, Inc. v. City of Los Angeles, p. 860, *infra,* in two separate district court decisions access channel requirements instituted pursuant to these provisions have been declared unconstitutional.

In the early 1980s there were no serious challenges to the Commission's jurisdiction over cable, perhaps because the Commission changed its regulatory posture towards cable. As we will discuss later in this chapter, the Commission had begun to eliminate its regulations governing cable in the late 1970s.

#### b. Preemption

Cable, unlike broadcasting, is regulated by both state and federal government. State and local jurisdiction was originally based primarily on the cable operator's use of the city streets and other rights of way. As we have seen, federal jurisdiction grew out of the FCC's jurisdiction over broadcasting. Gradually a conflict arose over where the line between state and federal jurisdiction should be drawn.

The majority of cable operators preferred to have state and local jurisdiction restricted as much as possible. They believed that some cities were making impossible demands in return for their franchises and imposing heavy burdens on the cable operators once the franchises were awarded. There were also serious fears that franchise renewal in cable would not carry the same renewal expectancy that is present in broadcasting (discussed in Chapter XV).

At the same time the FCC was gradually asserting the right to preempt more and more state and local regulation. As these issues reached the courts, the Commission's position was generally being upheld. In 1984 the Commission received strong support for its asserted right to preempt in Capital Cities Cable, Inc. v. Crisp, 467 U.S. 691, 56 R.R. 263, 10 Med.L.Rptr. 1873 (1984) even though ironically the FCC was not directly involved in the case.

The case centered on an Oklahoma statute banning the advertising of alcoholic beverages, except by the use of certain on-premises signs. In 1980 the state Attorney General concluded that retransmission of an out-of state commercial over cable television would violate the statute. Cable operators sued for declaratory and injunctive relief.

Although the lower courts focused on whether the advertising in question was protected by the commercial speech doctrine as discussed in Chapter IX, the Supreme Court chose to decide the case on federal preemption grounds. Noting that the FCC had already preempted "signal carriage, pay cable, leased channel regulations, technical standards, access, and several areas of franchisee responsibility," the Court concluded that "to the extent it has been invoked to control the distant broadcast and nonbroadcast signals imported by cable operators, the Oklahoma advertising ban plainly . . . trespasses into the exclusive domain of the FCC."

### c. Cable Communications Policy Act of 1984

The FCC's increasingly aggressive policy of preemption had already led the National League of Cities (NLC) to pursue legislative relief. However, lengthy negotiations between the NLC and the National Cable Television Association (NCTA) had not produced a compromise satisfactory to both constituencies. Perhaps given new impetus by court decisions such as *Crisp,* a compromise bill was drafted and presented to Congress with the backing of both parties. This bill was enacted into law as the Cable Communications Policy Act of 1984.

One of the provisions of the Cable Act amended § 2 of the Communications Act of 1934 to include within the FCC's jurisdiction "cable service to all persons engaged within the United States in providing such service, and to the facilities of cable operators which relate to such service, as provided in Title VI." 47 U.S.C.A. § 152. In addition, Title VI, Cable Communications was added to the Communications Act of 1934. 47 U.S.C.A. §§ 521–559. Thus, the Commission no longer has to derive its jurisdiction over cable from its jurisdiction over broadcasting, and courts will no longer have to determine whether a Commission rule is reasonably ancillary to its jurisdiction over broadcasting.

Even with the enactment of the 1984 Cable Act, some questions remained concerning the degree to which the Commission can preempt state and local regulation of cable. In City of New York v. Federal Communications Commission, 814 F.2d 720, 62 R.R.2d 914 (D.C.Cir. 1987), the court held that the FCC's refusal to set technical standards for certain classes of cable channels, while at the same time preempting franchising authorities from setting such standards, was arbitrary and capricious. At the same time the court upheld the FCC's preemption of local and state standards for those channels for which the Commission had established its own standards. The Supreme Court affirmed the ruling relying heavily on § 624 of the Cable Act. City of New York v. Federal Communications Commission, 486 U.S. 57, 64 R.R.2d 1423 (1988).

Subsequently, the Commission adopted new technical standards for all NTSC signals on all channel classes. The Commission also preempted all inconsistent state and local technical standards, other than those for rural systems or systems serving fewer than 100 subscribers. Cable Television Technical Requirements. 70 R.R.2d 679 (1992).

As part of the 1984 Act, the FCC was required to conduct a study of the cable industry's operation under the Act and to submit a report to Congress based on that report. In accordance with that requirement, the FCC issued an NOI in 1989 seeking comment on the validity of various allegations that the industry was abusing its market power:

> There are increasing consumer complaints about high and rising basic cable rates, poor service quality, and the dropping or repositioning of broadcast signals. Television broadcasters echo the last complaint and have also voiced concern about cable operators' ability to offer their own basic channels that compete unfairly with broadcasters for local advertising revenue. Other video service competitors—such as multichannel multipoint distribution service ("MMDS") companies and distributors of programming to home satellite dish ("HSD") owners—allege that large, vertically integrated cable operators are denying them access to programs. Some program suppliers assert that they cannot gain access to the cable systems of operators that also produce their own programming. Some program suppliers also complain that rising national concentration in cable system ownership has led to their inability to gain access to large cable systems. Operators of small, independent cable systems and non-cable multichannel video services alike claim that they pay discriminatorily high rates to certain program sources which are under the control or strong influence of large multiple system operators ("MSOs"). The common thread running through all these complaints is that, with the advent of large, multisystem cable owners and their growing control over sources of programming, the cable industry has become so concentrated that it is no longer responsive to the public and can now unfairly impede competitors from offering alternative service to viewers.

Competition, Rate Regulation and the Commission's Policies Relating to the Provision of Cable Television Service, 55 Fed.Reg. 1484, December 29, 1989.

Continuing complaints about excessive cable rates and insufficient services finally led to the passage of the Cable Television Consumer Protection and Competition Act of 1992. The 1992 Cable Act required the FCC to conduct numerous rulemaking proceedings by October 5, 1993.

### 3. FRANCHISING

Cable systems operate under franchise authority granted by a municipality, though state agencies also may grant permission to operate. See, e.g., Clear Television Cable Corp. v. Board of Public Utility Commissioners, 85 N.J. 30, 424 A.2d 1151 (1981). A franchise gives the cable operator access to city streets and other rights-of-way within a defined area for specific periods of time. Franchises usually are awarded after competitive bidding by several companies and are almost always exclusive. Franchise agreements specify services the system must provide, construction schedules and franchise fees.

For a while the competition among cable operators for city franchises was incredibly intense. At the height of the franchising process operators were willing to promise almost anything to obtain a franchise. For example, in 1981, Denver attracted bids from three firms, one offering a 215–channel system including a 107–channel home network. The three offered basic home services for monthly fees ranging from nothing to $3.95.

Unfortunately, once they had obtained the franchises, some operators discovered that cable was not necessarily the goldmine they had anticipated. These operators began asking cities to renegotiate the franchise agreements and eliminate some of the promised services, or selling the franchises to other operators. One company that found itself in that position, Warner Amex Cable Communications, built a 56–channel system in Milwaukee in lieu of the 108–channel system originally agreed upon.

From the 1970s into the early 1980s, when franchising competition was at its peak, cities were able to demand far more than large numbers of channels. Access channels, studios, mobile vans, financial contributions to access foundations and free wiring of public buildings were commonly sought and offered. In many cities, cable companies ended up providing benefits totally unrelated to cable service. These benefits ranged from building new libraries to planting trees along the roads.

The 1984 Cable Act left franchising the province of state and local governments with only a few restrictions. Most important of these is the prohibition on regulating cable service as a common carrier. 47 U.S.C.A. § 541. The 1992 Cable Act did nothing to change this.

One of the great fears of cable operators was non-renewal. The 1984 Cable Act set out specific guidelines for franchise renewal in great detail in § 626 of the Communications Act. 47 U.S.C.A. § 546. It appears to create a strong renewal expectancy.

The 1992 Cable Act clarified some of these requirements. Franchisees are now required to submit a specific written notice to invoke renewal proceedings. Franchising authorities must commence renewal proceedings within six months of receiving this written notice. Submission of a renewal notice does not preclude the right of a franchise authority from revoking a franchise for cause during the renewal process. 47 U.S.C.A. § 546.

The 1992 Act prohibits transfers of cable systems within 36 months of acquisition or initial construction. The Commission is permitted to waive this requirement "in the cases of default, foreclosure, or other financial distress." 47 U.S.C.A. § 537.

The 1992 Act also limits law suits against franchising authorities or other governmental bodies arising out of the regulation of cable service to injunctive or declaratory relief. Essentially this provision protects franchising authorities and other governmental bodies from any liability for monetary damages. 47 U.S.C.A. § 555.

For many years, there were no serious challenges to the cities' authority to extract everything possible from the cable companies by running what was, in essence, an auction, with the franchise going to the highest bidder. Probably, most companies were loath to start fights with the cities for fear of being denied the franchises. As a result, serious questions remained unanswered. What is the connection between a city's control of public rights of way and authority over cable programming? Is awarding a franchise based in part on programming promises a violation of the First Amendment? If there is room for more than one company's cables, does awarding an exclusive franchise violate the First Amendment?

These issues were raised in a suit against the city of Los Angeles. The case arose when Preferred Communications requested a cable franchise after refusing to participate in the city's competitive franchising process. When denied the franchise, Preferred sued, alleging the franchising process violated the First Amendment. The suit was dismissed for failure to state a claim upon which relief could be granted and Preferred appealed. [Note: When a suit is dismissed for failure to state a claim upon which relief can be granted, it means that even if every fact in dispute is assumed to be in the plaintiff's favor, the plaintiff would still lose the case. Thus, the issue on appeal is not should the plaintiff have won the case, but rather, has the plaintiff at least indicated a chance of winning the case. If the plaintiff wins the appeal, the case will then proceed further.]

The court of appeals framed the issue in the case as follows:

Can the City, consistent with the First Amendment, limit access by means of an auction process to a given region of the City to a single cable television company, when the public utility facilities and other public property in that region necessary to the installation and operation of a cable television system are physically capable of accommodating more than one system?

The court, in a sweeping opinion, concluded that the city could not. Preferred Communications, Inc. v. City of Los Angeles, 754 F.2d 1396, 57 R.R.2d 1396 (9th Cir.1985).

The Supreme Court affirmed, but on narrower grounds.

## CITY OF LOS ANGELES v. PREFERRED COMMUNICATIONS, INC.

Supreme Court of the United States, 1986.
476 U.S. 488, 106 S.Ct. 2034, 80 L.Ed.2d 480, 60 R.R.2d 792, 12 Med.L.Rptr. 2244.

JUSTICE REHNQUIST delivered the opinion of the Court.

Respondent Preferred Communications, Inc., sued petitioners City of Los Angeles (City) and the Department of Water and Power (DWP) in the United States Court for the Central District of California. The complaint alleged a violation of respondent's rights under the First and Fourteenth Amendments, and under §§ 1 and 2 of the Sherman Act, by reason of the City's refusal to grant access to DWP's poles or underground conduits used for power lines. The Court of Appeals for the Ninth Circuit affirmed with respect to the Sherman Act, but reversed as to the First Amendment claim. [  ] We granted certiorari with respect to the latter issue, [  ].

Respondent's complaint against the City and DWP alleged, *inter alia,* the following facts: Respondent asked Pacific Telephone and Telegraph (PT & T) and DWP for permission to lease space on their utility poles in order to provide cable television service in the South Central area of Los Angeles. [  ] These utilities responded that they would not lease the space unless respondent first obtained a cable television franchise from the City. [  ] Respondent asked the City for a franchise, but the City refused to grant it one, stating that respondent had failed to participate in an auction that was to award a single franchise in the area. [  ]¹

The complaint further alleged that cable operators are First Amendment speakers, [  ], that there is sufficient excess physical capacity and

1. California authorizes municipalities to limit the number of cable television operators in an area by means of a "franchise or license" system, and to prescribe "rules and regulations" to protect customers of such operators. [  ] Congress has recently endorsed such franchise systems. [  ] Pursuant to the authority granted by the State, the City has adopted a provision forbidding the construction or operation of a cable television system within city limits unless a franchise is first obtained. [  ] A City ordinance provides that franchises are to be allotted by auction to the bidder offering "the highest percentage of gross annual receipts" derived from the franchise and "such other compensation or consideration . . . as may be prescribed by the Council in the advertisement for bids and notice of sale." [  ]

In October 1982, the City published an advertisement soliciting bids for a cable franchise in the South Central area of Los Angeles. The advertisement indicated that only one franchise would be awarded, and it established a deadline for the submission of bids. [  ] It also set forth certain nonfinancial criteria to be considered in the selection process, including the degree of local participation in management or ownership reflecting the ethnic and economic diversity of the franchise area, the capacity to provide 52 channels and two-way communication, the willingness to set aside channels for various public purposes and to provide public access facilities, the willingness to develop other services in the public interest, the criminal and civil enforcement record of the company and its principals, the degree of business experience in cable television or other activities, and the willingness to engage in creative and aggressive affirmative action. [  ] Respondent did not submit a bid in response to this solicitation, and the franchise was eventually awarded to another cable operator.

economic demand in the south central area of Los Angeles to accommodate more than one cable company, [ ], and that the City's auction process allowed it to discriminate among franchise applicants based on which one it deemed to be the "best." [ ] Based on these and other factual allegations, the complaint alleged that the City and DWP had violated the Free Speech Clause of the First and Fourteenth Amendments, §§ 1 and 2 of the Sherman Act, the California Constitution, and certain provisions of state law. [ ]

The City did not deny that there was excess physical capacity to accommodate more than one cable television system. But it argued that the physical scarcity of available space on public utility structures, the limits of economic demand for the cable medium, and the practical and esthetic disruptive effect that installing and maintaining a cable system has on the public right-of-way justified its decision to restrict access to its facilities to a single cable television company. [ ]

. . .

. . . [The Court of Appeals] held that, taking the allegations in the complaint as true, [ ], the City violated the First Amendment by refusing to issue a franchise to more than one cable television company when there was sufficient excess physical and economic capacity to accommodate more than one. [ ] The Court of Appeals expressed the view that the facts alleged in the complaint brought respondent into the ambit of cases such as [*Tornillo*], rather than of cases such as [*Red Lion*] and [*Taxpayers for Vincent*]. [ ]

We agree with the Court of Appeals that respondent's complaint should not have been dismissed, and we therefore affirm the judgment of that court; but we do so on a narrower ground than the one taken by it. The well-pleaded facts in the complaint include allegations of sufficient excess physical capacity and economic demand for cable television operators in the area which respondent sought to serve.[2] The City, while admitting the existence of excess physical capacity on the utility poles, the rights-of-way and the like, justifies the limit on franchises in terms of minimizing the demand that cable systems make for the use of public property. The City characterizes these uses as the stringing of "nearly 700 miles of hanging and buried wire and other appliances necessary for the operation of its system." [ ] The City also characterizes them as "a permanent visual blight," [ ], and adds that the process of installation and repair of such a system in effect subjects City facilities designed for other purposes to a servitude which will cause traffic delays and hazards and esthetic unsightliness. Respondent in its turn replies that the City does not "provide anything more than speculations and assumptions," and that the City's "legitimate concerns are easily satisfied without the need to limit the right to a single speaker." [ ]

2. They also include allegations that the City imposes numerous other conditions upon a successful applicant for a franchise. It is claimed that, entirely apart from the limitation of franchises to one in each area, these conditions violate respondent's First Amendment rights. The Court of Appeals did not reach these contentions, and neither do we.

We of course take the well-pleaded allegations of the complaint as true for the purpose of a motion to dismiss, [  ]. Ordinarily such a motion frames a legal issue such as the one which the Court of Appeals undertook to decide in this case. But this case is different from a case between private litigants for two reasons: first, it is an action of a municipal corporation taken pursuant to a city ordinance that is challenged here, and, second, the ordinance is challenged on colorable First Amendment grounds. The City has adduced essentially factual arguments to justify the restrictions on cable franchising imposed by its ordinance, but the factual assertions of the City are disputed at least in part by the respondent. We are unwilling to decide the legal questions posed by the parties without a more thoroughly developed record of proceedings in which the parties have an opportunity to prove those disputed factual assertions upon which they rely.

We do think that the activities in which respondent allegedly seeks to engage plainly implicate First Amendment interests. Respondent alleges:

"The business of cable television, like that of newspapers and magazines, is to provide its subscribers with a mixture of news, information and entertainment. As do newspapers, cable companies use a portion of their available space to reprint (or retransmit) the communications of others, while at the same time providing some original content." [  ]

Thus, through original programming or by exercising editorial discretion over which stations or programs to include in its repertoire, respondent seeks to communicate messages on a wide variety of topics and in a wide variety of formats. We recently noted that cable operators exercise "a significant amount of editorial discretion regarding what their programming will include." [*Midwest Video II*] Cable television partakes of some of the aspects of speech and the communication of ideas as do the traditional enterprises of newspaper and book publishers, public speakers and pamphleteers. Respondent's proposed activities would seem to implicate First Amendment interests as do the activities of wireless broadcasters, which were found to fall within the ambit of the First Amendment in [*Red Lion*], even though the free speech aspects of the wireless broadcasters' claim were found to be outweighed by the government interests in regulating by reason of the scarcity of available frequencies.

Of course, the conclusion that respondent's factual allegations implicate protected speech does not end the inquiry. "Even protected speech is not equally permissible in all places and at all times." [  ] Moreover, where speech and conduct are joined in a single course of action, the First Amendment values must be balanced against competing societal interests. See, *e.g., [Vincent; O'Brien]*. We do not think, however, that it is desirable to express any more detailed views on the proper resolution of the First Amendment question raised by the respondent's complaint and the City's responses to it without a fuller development of the disputed issues in this case. We think that we may know more than we know now about how the constitutional issues should be resolved when we know more about the present uses of the public utility poles and rights-of-way and how respondent proposes to install and maintain its facilities on them.

. . .

We affirm the judgment of the Court of Appeals reversing the dismissal of respondent's complaint by the District Court, and remand the case to the District Court so that petitioners may file an answer and the material factual disputes between the parties may be resolved.

*It is so ordered.*

JUSTICE BLACKMUN, with whom JUSTICE MARSHALL and JUSTICE O'CON-NOR join, concurring.

I join the Court's opinion on the understanding that it leaves open the question of the proper standard for judging First Amendment challenges to a municipality's restriction of access to cable facilities. Different communications media are treated differently for First Amendment purposes. [ ] In assessing First Amendment claims concerning cable access, the Court must determine whether the characteristics require a new analysis. As this case arises out of a motion to dismiss, we lack factual information about the nature of cable television. Recognizing these considerations, [ ], the Court does not attempt to choose or justify any particular standard. It simply concludes that, in challenging Los Angeles' policy of exclusivity in cable franchising, respondent alleges a cognizable First Amendment claim.

## Notes and Questions

1. When the district court judge later applied the *O'Brien* test to the city's franchise regulations, she held several of the key provisions unconstitutional. The exclusivity provision was invalid because it was an unnecessarily restrictive means of protecting the city's admittedly substantial interest in safe and efficient use of utility poles and conduits. A provision allowing the city to deny a franchise on the basis of the applicant's character was not narrowly tailored to serve the city's substantial interest in assuring that applicants were honest, because the city was also allowed to consider whether the applicant had been involved in litigation over other cable franchises. Requirements that the franchisee offer state-of-the-art service failed to serve any compelling governmental interest, as did a provision limiting the duration of the franchise.

The court said that the city had a compelling interest in requiring a franchisee to provide access channels, but that the city had failed to show the necessity of requiring a 52–channel system to set aside six free channels for the public, government, and educational access and two for leased access.

The court upheld provisions favoring local franchise applicants over those who had no local owners or managers. Such a preference was a sufficiently narrow means of advancing the city's compelling interest in "promoting cultural pride, diversity of self-expression and enhancing the economic welfare of the residents." Preferred Communications, Inc. v. City of Los Angeles, 67 R.R.2d 36 (C.D.Cal.1990). The case is on appeal in the Ninth Circuit.

2. Might some standard between the current newspaper standard and the current broadcasting standard be a useful resolution of the issue? If so, what should that standard be? In considering this question, look at the Cable Communications Policy Act of 1984. Which provisions, if any, should be declared unconstitutional?

3. *Preferred* had been expected to resolve a number of cases involving constitutional challenges to the cable franchising process. The Supreme Court's refusal to set a specific First Amendment standard for cable meant that the lower courts had to proceed with little guidance. The results have been inconsistent as can be seen from the cases in the following notes.

4. In Central Telecommunications v. TCI Cablevision, Inc., 800 F.2d 711 (8th Cir.1986) the court held:

> [t]he evidence reveals that the City's cable television market is currently a natural monopoly which, under present technology, offers room for only one operator at a time. Thus, we hold that the City could properly offer a de facto exclusive franchise in order to create competition for its cable television market.

TCI had asserted a First Amendment defense to allegations that it had engaged in illegal monopolistic practices aimed at keeping exclusive control of the local cable market. In essence, TCI argued that exclusive franchises were unconstitutional and therefore Central Telecommunications had not been deprived of any protectable interest when TCI's conduct prevented Central Communications from being awarded the exclusive franchise instead of TCI. The Supreme Court denied *certiorari,* 480 U.S. 910 (1987).

5. Similarly, a district court judge rejected Erie Telecommunications, Inc.'s First Amendment attack on the franchise-fee and access-channel provisions of its franchise agreement with the City of Erie. According to the judge, "In its effort to preserve an uninhibited marketplace of ideas, government is entrusted with protecting the First Amendment rights of cable television viewers." Erie Telecommunications, Inc. v. City of Erie, 659 F.Supp. 580, 62 R.R.2d 1467 (W.D.Pa.1987).

On appeal, the court never reached the First Amendment issue. As part of the franchise agreement, Erie Telecommunications had executed a Mutual Release and Covenant in which it had agreed to release the city from any and all claims related to the franchise agreement. The court held that this precluded the cable company's raising any challenges to the agreement. Erie Telecommunications, Inc. v. City of Erie, Pennsylvania, 853 F.2d 1084, 65 R.R.2d 1 (3d Cir.1988).

6. In Chicago Cable Communications v. Chicago Cable Commission, 879 F.2d 1540, 66 R.R.2d 1222 (7th Cir.1989), cert. denied 493 U.S. 1044 (1990), the Commission fined a group of three cable franchisees for failing to honor the local origination clause of the franchises. That clause required 4½ hours per week of local programming geared to Chicago. The violation was said to have occurred when the group presented local programming that had been prepared by a suburban affiliate even though the group said that it selected programs that it believed would be interesting to its Chicago customers.

Among other defenses, the group contended that the First Amendment prevented the content control inherent in the clause and its enforcement. The district court enforced the fine, and the court of appeals affirmed. The court adhered to an earlier cable decision in which it said that "there are enough differences between cable television and the non-television media to allow more government regulation of the former." In deciding to adopt the *O'Brien* analysis, the court said that it was not abandoning First Amendment scrutiny because of the natural monopoly characteristics of cable. "Rather, each medium of expression must be assessed by standards properly suited to it."

The court concluded that the government had met its burdens of establishing the elements of the *O'Brien* test. Promotion of "community self-expression can increase direct communications between residents by featuring topics of local concern. Encouragement of 'localism' certainly qualifies as an important or substantial interest." The court approvingly quoted the district court's statement that the "important qualities of localism (community pride, cultural diversity, *etc.*) may not be furthered enough simply by the availability of local broadcast television stations for retransmission over cable systems, but may require original cable programming specifically concerning the locality and directed at that locality's residents." An additional interest fostered by the requirement was providing jobs for residents: "Production of programming in the City provides career opportunities as well as potential internships for students studying communications at local schools." These were enough to satisfy *O'Brien's* second prong.

As to the congruence between means and ends, the court relied on Supreme Court language to the effect that "so long as the neutral regulation promotes a substantial government interest that would be achieved less effectively absent the regulation," an incidental burden on speech is permissible. Here on the one hand was a requirement of only 4½ hours per week with no requirement of any specific kind of programming. "As long as the particular episode is geared to Chicago—be it sports, politics, news, weather, entertainment, *etc.*—[the group] has full discretion over what it may desire to transmit. This restriction on [the group's] control in meeting the minimal [local origination] requirements does not divest it of discretion, for, as in *Midwest Video,* the cable operator here still retains the ultimate decision" over which programs to present.

On the other hand, cable "is an economically scarce medium. Unlike the traditional forms of print media, a cable programmer enjoys a virtual monopoly over its area, without the threat of an alternative provider. As a result the government, which serves as the representative of the cable customers, is duty-bound to recognize the effects of 'medium scarcity' by ensuring that the few programmers who are granted a franchise make optimum use of it. [   ] With this in mind, it is within the City's rights, arguably its responsibilities, to proffer some requirements guaranteeing that the cable customers are, to the extent possible, accorded a range of programming from the franchisee, since the cable viewing public has no other channel to which to turn." The Supreme Court denied *certiorari,* 493 U.S. 1044 (1990).

7.  However, in Century Federal, Inc. v. City of Palo Alto, California, 648 F.Supp. 1465, 61 R.R.2d 1348 (N.D.Cal.1986), the court, applying the *O'Brien* test, ruled that a franchising process under which the cities of Palo Alto, Menlo Park and Atherton intended to grant only one franchise was unconstitutional on its face. The court found that four of the five "substantial" interests asserted by the cities to support their grant of a *de facto* exclusive franchise were based on the idea that cable is a natural monopoly. "Essentially, the Cities argue that if there is a reasonable probability that their service area will economically support only one CTV operator, then they should be able to choose, at the outset, that operator who will provide the highest quality service and use the offer of an exclusive franchise as a plum to bargain for certain concessions, e.g., access channels, that they might not be able to acquire if an operator knew that it would have to compete with other cable providers." The court found that rationale unacceptable as an asserted government interest under *O'Brien.* "The paternalistic role in the First Amendment that the Cities envision for government is simply inconsistent with the purpose and goals of the First Amendment."

The cities' final asserted interest, minimizing disruption of the public domain, was found not to be furthered by the franchising process. The court reasoned that if multiple cable systems were installed simultaneously, there would be no more disruption of the public domain than if a single system were installed.

The court took care to point out that it was not holding that cities "necessarily have to open their cable facilities to all comers regardless of size, shape, quality or qualifications." It was only holding that the cities had not offered evidence of a substantial government interest that justified granting a *de facto* exclusive franchise.

8.  Later, in further proceedings in the same case, the court also held that the cities' access channel, universal service and state-of-the-art technology requirements were unconstitutional. Citing *Tornillo* and *Pacific Gas,* the court found the access channels to be an impermissible intrusion into the editorial functions of the cable operator. Freedom of

speech necessarily implies " 'a concomitant freedom *not* to speak publicly, one which serves the same ultimate end as freedom of speech in its
affirmative aspect.' [*Pacific Gas*]." Requiring service to an entire community as a prerequisite to serving any part of the community infringed
that right not to speak.

Finally, turning to the cities' requirement for state-of-the-art technology, the court applied the *O'Brien* test. The cities' assertion that the
important government interest served by the regulation was preventing
disruption of the public domain for system improvements was dismissed
as overly speculative. Century Federal, Inc. v. City of Palo Alto, 63
R.R.2d 1736 (N.D.Cal.1987).

9. In still a third proceeding in the case, the court also struck down the
franchise fee, performance bond requirement and security fund requirement mandated by the franchising process. The court emphasized that
other similar users of the public rights of way such as Pacific Bell and
Pacific Gas and Electric were not subject to the same fees and requirements. Thus, under [*Minneapolis Star*, p. 608, *supra*] (a case involving
a state tax on newsprint and ink used in publications of a certain
circulation value), "the government had an unusually heavy burden of
justification." The court found that the city had not met that burden.
Century Federal, Inc. v. City of Palo Alto, 710 F.Supp. 1559, 65 R.R.2d
875 (N.D.Cal.1988).

10. Similarly, in Group W Cable, Inc. v. Santa Cruz, 669 F.Supp. 954,
63 R.R.2d 1656, 14 Med.L.Rptr. 1769 (N.D.Cal.1987), Group W successfully challenged Santa Cruz's refusal to renew its franchise. Applying
*O'Brien* the court held that the city's grant of an exclusive franchise to a
competing company violated the First Amendment. Relying on *Miami
Herald*, the court also struck down franchising provisions requiring
public access channels and state-of-the-art-technology.

11. One problem raised by holdings such as *Century Federal* and *Santa
Cruz* is the effect on existing franchisees who have complied with access
channel, universal service and state-of-the-art technology requirements
in return for exclusive franchises. Suddenly, a second company is
allowed to cable only the most lucrative sections of a city without the
expense of access channels and state-of-the-art technology. Not only is
the first company deprived of the exclusive franchise it bargained for,
but the second company has a major competitive edge. In Sacramento,
after a district court decision prohibiting an exclusive franchise, the city
granted additional franchises, which do not contain universal service
requirements. The original franchisee then filed suit claiming that the
grant of these additional franchises violates its franchise agreement.
The case was settled out of court.

#### 4. RATE REGULATION

The 1984 Act only allowed regulation of rates of basic cable service,
and even that was only allowed in the absence of effective competition.

47 U.S.C.A. § 543. This provision was viewed as a major victory for cable operators, who had long argued that rate regulation was unnecessary due to competition from other communication technologies. Opponents of the provision contended that cable is effectively a monopoly and, thus, cable rates are not subject to adequate pressure from competition.

The Commission initially defined effective competition as the availability of three or more off-the-air television signals in the market. The Commission rejected the suggestion of some parties that the availability of the three major networks be part of the definition. Cable Communications Act Rules, 58 R.R.2d 1 (1985).

The court of appeals held that the standard for measuring signal availability was insufficiently justified and remanded that issue for further proceedings. American Civil Liberties Union v. Federal Communications Commission, 823 F.2d 1554, 63 R.R.2d 729 (D.C.Cir.1987), cert. denied 485 U.S. 959 (1988).

On remand, the Commission modified the definition of effective competition. A cable system was subject to effective competition only if three or more off-air signals were available in all geographic areas served by that system. The three signals did not have to be the same ones for all parts of the cable system's service area. A presumption of availability was created if the station's predicted coverage met a certain minimum standard or the station was "significantly viewed" in that community. However, the presumption could be rebutted by actual engineering data. Cable Communications Policy Act Rules (Signal Availability Standard), 3 F.C.C.Rcd. 2617, 64 R.R.2d 1276 (1988).

Three years later, the Commission revisited this area and concluded that in at least some cases cable rates had increased unreasonably. Under the three-signal definition of effective competition, less than four percent of all cable systems were subject to rate regulation. The FCC decided, therefore, to change the definition once again. Under the new definition a cable system was subject to effective competition if (1) six unduplicated over-the air broadcast signals were available in the entire cable community or (2) an independently owned, competing multichannel video service was available to at least 50 percent of the homes and subscribed to by at least 10 percent of the homes passed by the cable system. Effective Competition, 6 F.C.C.Rcd. 4545 (1991).

Despite these changes rates continued to rise. In response, Congress made rate regulation one of the cornerstones of the 1992 Cable Act making several major changes in this area. As was the case prior to the 1992 Act, rate regulation is precluded for cable systems subject to effective competition, p. 867, *supra*. However, the 1992 Act sets out the following requirements for effective competition. Either "fewer than 30 percent of the households in the franchise area subscribe to the cable service of a cable system," or the franchise area must be served by at least two "unaffiliated multichannel video programmers" offering comparable video programming to at least half of the households in that area and at least 15 percent of the households in the franchise area must subscribe to programming services offered by "multichannel video programming distributors other than the largest multichannel video programming distributors," or at least 50 percent of the households in the area must be served by a multichannel video programming distributor operated by the franchising authority for that area.

In April 1993 the FCC issued its first *Report and Order* on rate regulation. Cable Rate Regulation, 72 R.R.2d 733 (1993). The *R & O,* more than 500 pages long, started with a finding that, on average, cable systems subject to effective competition had rates 10 percent lower than those not subject to effective competition. The Commission concluded, therefore, that rates for systems not subject to effective competition should be rolled back 10 percent as a result of its rate regulation rules.

To determine whether a specific rate is reasonable, it will be compared to a table of benchmarks "based on the average September 30, 1992, rates of systems subject to effective competition." The applicable benchmark for a given system will be determined by certain characteristics such as "number of channels, subscribers, and satellite signals."

When the new rates went into effect, many cable customers found themselves paying more than before. As a first step in determining why the law did not have its intended effect, the FCC sent letters of inquiry to at least 51 cable companies in 21 states.

The Act also places severe restrictions on the practice of tiering, p. 852, *supra.* Cable systems must offer a separate basic service, subscription to which is required for access to any other programming tier. At a minimum this tier must include all must-carry stations, any PEG channels required by the franchise agreement, and any other television station carried by the cable system except for stations retransmitted by a "satellite carrier beyond the local service area of such station." Requiring subscribers to subscribe to any channel or tier other than the basic tier as a prerequisite to purchasing video programming offered on a per channel or per programming basis is prohibited. Systems that cannot comply with this provision due to technological limitations are exempted until the technological limitation is eliminated as a result of equipment upgrades. This exemption expires 10 years after the enactment of the 1992 Cable Act. 47 U.S.C.A. § 543.

### 5. SIGNAL CARRIAGE RULES AND COPYRIGHT

All of the major challenges to the Commission's jurisdiction over cable resulted from the Commission's various signal carriage rules. Each of these rules was designed to protect local broadcasting from cable competition.

### a. *Leapfrogging and Superstations*

One of the earliest restrictions, called the anti-leapfrogging rule, provided that when it was permissible to import distant signals, the system had to select from among those nearest to the city in which the system was operating. The FCC deleted this rule in 1976. One result was the emergence of the so-called "superstation"—a VHF or UHF independent station that makes its programs available to cable systems throughout the country, via satellite transmission.

The most famous superstation is Ted Turner's Channel 17 in Atlanta, which has access to 200 live sporting events each year. By late 1990 the station was distributing its programs nationwide to 55.5 million subscribers. The satellite company was charging the cable systems 10 cents per subscriber per month. The cable systems was making the programs available as part of their basic monthly charge to attract subscribers.

Channel 17 prospered by increased charges for advertising on its programs that were now reaching up to 45 million more viewers than previously. As a result, Channel 17's local advertisers were replaced by those marketing national products when the superstation emerged. Program suppliers have increased charges to Channel 17 because the program is reaching a much larger audience than it did before and cable distribution may preclude sales to local stations in cities receiving the cable program.

### b.   *Copyright Problems*

The removal of FCC restrictions has made the role of copyright law crucially important. In the 1976 copyright statute, in § 111, a complex compromise provides, in effect, that cablecasters need pay no royalties for programs on "local" (or "must carry") stations that they are required to carry. Cablecasters are permitted to carry the copyrighted programs of "distant" (or "may carry") stations without the owner's consent in return for the payment of a compulsory royalty fee. This fee is fixed by statute and depends on the size of the cable system and whether the distant station is commercial or educational.

The compulsory license and royalty provision has been under attack in Congress. The problem is that the 1976 Act did not contemplate the changes in FCC rules that have permitted the growth of superstations and increased carriage of distant signals. The result is that an increasing amount of cable programming is coming from distant sources, leaving the program suppliers with less control over geographical distribution of their products. Complaints are also being heard from major sports leagues because, for example, an Atlanta baseball game may be shown on a Boston area cable system at the same time another game is being played in Boston. In 1985 the Atlanta Braves and New York Yankees agreed to pay the other major league teams a special annual fee based on the subscriber base of the superstations that carry their games. The New York Mets and Chicago Cubs, whose games are also carried by superstations, followed suit.

The National Basketball Association tried a different approach to this problem by limiting to twenty the number of games allowed on a local signal received by more than five percent of the cable subscribers located outside the team's local market. Superstation WGN, which had already contracted to carry more than 20 games, successfully sued the NBA, claiming the rule was an unreasonable restraint of trade in violation of antitrust law. Chicago Professional Sports Limited Partnership and WGN Continental Broadcasting v. National Basketball Association, 961 F.2d 667 (7th Cir.), cert. denied 113 S.Ct. 409 (1992).

Broadcasters argued for many years that the compulsory license should be abolished and replaced by a negotiated agreement between the cable system and the originating broadcaster (who, under contract, would need the consent of the copyright owner). The 1992 Cable Act established a limited form of retransmission consent. We will return to this as part of our discussion of the must-carry rules.

A second controversy involves distribution of the royalties collected under the Act. The Copyright Royalty Tribunal, created for the purpose, must allocate the $15 million in cable royalties collected each year. Demands from the various claimants, such as program producers and syndicators, sports leagues, music groups, broadcast licensees themselves and others, greatly exceed 100 percent. In September 1980 the Tribunal allocated the 1978 revenues, giving 75 percent to program producers and syndicators, and 3.25 percent to commercial television broadcasters. This means that total copyright payments to all commercial television for programs carried during 1978 by cable systems amounted to $476,-000.

As a result of the FCC's repeal of the distant signal rules, the Tribunal raised the rates cable operators had to pay for distant signals effective March 15, 1983. Large cable systems became liable for a compulsory license fee of 3.75 percent of their basic revenues for each distant signal added since June 24, 1981. This increase was upheld in National Cable Television Association v. Copyright Royalty Tribunal, 724 F.2d 176, 55 R.R.2d 387 (D.C.Cir.1983). In response, some cable operators dropped distant signals to reduce their copyright liability. Superstations were the major casualty.

Broadcasters maintain that cable's contribution to the fund is tiny when compared with the fact that commercial television broadcasters spend some 35 percent of their budgets on program acquisition. Cable operators claim the current fees, after the 1983 rate hikes, are already prohibitive. Meanwhile, the FCC has asserted that any economic problem for the broadcasters derives from the Copyright Act or the Tribunal's allocation—and relief must come from those sources.

As a result of the FCC's adoption of new syndication exclusivity rules, p. 900, *infra,* the CRT drastically reduced the application of the syndex surcharge. Essentially, it now applies only to retransmission of stations that were covered by the old rules but not the new ones. Broadcasting, July 23, 1990 at 80.

### c.  Must Carry

One of the earliest signal carriage rules was a requirement that cable systems retransmit the signal of any local television station or "significantly viewed" station that requested carriage.  Cable systems were allowed to request a waiver of the rule where it created hardship, but the process was a slow one and few waivers were granted.  The "must-carry" rules imposed a special hardship on the smaller cable systems, which could find most of their channels occupied by must-carry channels.  Due to overlapping, some systems were forced to carry several affiliates of the same network, or similarly duplicative stations, to the exclusion of other non-duplicative services.

As with the other rules, the purpose was to protect local broadcasters, especially UHF stations, whose picture quality was noticeably inferior to that provided by cable.  There was also concern that cable subscribers would remove their television antennas or, at the very least, fail to maintain them, and that this would put broadcasters not carried by the cable system at a great competitive disadvantage.

When the compulsory licensing scheme was enacted in the Copyright Act of 1976, many thought it a trade-off for the must-carry rules.  Although the legislative history on this issue is inconclusive, many cable operators were reluctant to challenge the must-carry rules for fear of losing the compulsory license.

In 1980, however, Turner Broadcasting System petitioned the Commission to institute rulemaking proceedings to delete the must-carry rules.  TBS argued that the rules violated the First Amendment rights of cable operators and that, at the very least, extensive changes in the broadcast and cable industries since the promulgation of the rules required a re-examination of the rules.  The Commission denied the TBS petition.

Meanwhile, Quincy Cable Television Inc., operator of a cable system in Quincy, Wash., was ordered to carry the signals of various Spokane, Wash., television stations and fined $5,000 for failing to do so.  Quincy Cable's appeal of the order and the fine was consolidated with TBS's appeal resulting in what may be one of the most important decisions involving cable television.

In Quincy Cable TV, Inc. v. Federal Communications Commission, 768 F.2d 1434, 58 R.R.2d 977, 12 Med.L.Rptr. 1001 (D.C.Cir.1985), the court concluded that the must-carry rules, as drafted, violated the First Amendment.  In reaching this conclusion the court found it unnecessary to determine what level of First Amendment protection was appropriate because the rules failed even under the O'Brien test.

The court thought that the Commission's rules created "undifferentiated protectionism."  The Commission had failed in its attempt to strike a balance between the competing interests of controlling a new technology that allegedly threatened long-established values, such as serving community needs through a locally-oriented press, and the regulatory throttling of the number and variety of outlets for free expression.

Under pressure from Congress, the Commission drafted a new set of must-carry rules. A First Amendment challenge to the revised rules quickly followed. Century Communications Corporation v. Federal Communications Commission, 835 F.2d 292, 64 R.R.2d 113, (D.C.Cir. 1987).

Along with the new rules the FCC had asserted a new rationale for them. The new rationale was based on an inexpensive piece of equipment called an A–B switch. Using this devise a viewer can switch back and forth between a TV antenna and a cable feed, by merely flipping the switch. The Commission argued that, because of the long history of must carry and the lack of information about A–B switches, it would take five years to for viewers to become acclimated to these devises. The must-carry rules were therefore necessary for this five-year transition period.

The rules themselves were less sweeping than the original ones struck down in *Quincy*.

> . . . [The Commission] set forth limits on how many channels a cable carrier must devote to must-carry: carriers with 20 channels or less were not required to carry any must-carry stations; carriers with between 21 and 26 stations could be required to carry up to 7 channels of must-carry stations; and carriers with 27 or more channels could be required to devote up to 25% of their system to must-carry signals. [ ] It also limited the pool of potential must-carry channels to those satisfying a "viewing standard" generally demonstrating a minimum viewership of the channel in question. . . . The Commission also authorized cable operators to refuse to carry more than one station affiliated with the same commercial network. [ ] Finally, the Commission limited the number of noncommercial stations required to be carried, stating that when the cable system had fewer than 54 channels and an eligible noncommercial station or translator existed, the cable operator must devote at least one channel to a noncommercial station; and that when the cable system had 54 or more stations, it must devote two must-carry channels to such endeavors.

The court of appeals again found it unnecessary to decide which level of First Amendment scrutiny was appropriate because the new rules also failed under the more relaxed *O'Brien* test. The court found that the FCC failed to offer sufficient evidence that absent must-carry rules cable systems would cease to carry large numbers of broadcast stations. Furthermore, even if this were true, there was no evidence to support the assertion that it would take five years for viewers to learn about A–B switches.

At this point the FCC chose not to attempt yet again to draft must-carry rules that would pass constitutional muster. Broadcasters then focused their lobbying efforts on Congress. These efforts were rewarded in the 1992 Cable Act.

The 1992 Act has two separate must-carry provisions. § 614 sets out the must-carry rules for commercial television stations, while § 615 sets out the must-carry rules for noncommercial television stations. Under § 614 cable systems with 300 or fewer subscribers are exempt. Other cable systems with 12 or fewer channels must carry a minimum of three local broadcast signals. Systems with more than 12 channels must carry all local broadcast stations up to a maximum of one third of the total number of the system's channels. If the number of local commercial television stations exceeds the maximum number of must-carry signals, the cable operator is permitted to choose which stations will be carried subject to the following restrictions. First, no low power station can be carried unless all local commercial stations are carried. Second, if a cable operator chooses to carry a broadcast network affiliate, the operator must carry the affiliate of that network that is closest to the principal headend of the cable system.

Notwithstanding these requirements, systems are not required to carry local commercial television stations that substantially duplicate the programming of another local commercial television station carried by the system.

§ 615 sets out the carriage requirements for qualified noncommercial educational television stations. Cable systems with 12 or fewer channels must carry one local noncommercial educational television station. Stations with 13 to 36 channels must carry all local noncommercial educational television stations up to a maximum of three. Systems with more than 36 channels must carry all local noncommercial educational television stations. In the event that there are no local noncommercial educational television stations, a cable system must import one noncommercial educational television station. These must carry requirements do not apply to stations whose signal is considered a distant signal for copyright purposes unless the station pays any increase in copyright costs attributable to the carriage of that station. 47 U.S.C.A. § 535.

As previously noted the 1992 Act created a new alternative to must carry that permits a commercial television station to waive its must-carry right in return for the right to require the station's consent before a cable system can carry its signal. In essence this requires each station to determine the value of its signal to nearby cable systems. The assumption is that the more attractive stations will choose retransmission consent in order to force cable systems to pay for the right to carry them. Lower-rated stations will be likely to opt for must carry. Every three years stations will have the right to change their status. 47 U.S.C.A. § 325.

Not surprisingly, cable groups immediately challenged the new must-carry/retransmission consent provisions. Oral arguments on the must-carry provisions were held before a three-judge district court mandated in the 1992 Act. That decision follows.

### TURNER BROADCASTING SYSTEM, INC. v. FEDERAL COMMUNICATIONS COMMISSION

United States District Court for the District of Columbia, 1993.
819 F.Supp. 32, 72 R.R.2d 366, 21 Med.L.Rptr. 1993.

Before WILLIAMS, CIRCUIT JUDGE, JACKSON and SPORKIN, DISTRICT JUDGES. JACKSON, DISTRICT JUDGE.

Sections 4 and 5 of the Cable Television Consumer Protection and Competition Act of 1992, [    ], ("the 1992 Cable Act" or "the Act") require cable television system operators to carry the video signals of certain commercial and non-commercial educational television broadcast stations requesting that their signals be carried. The plaintiffs in these five consolidated lawsuits contend that these mandatory carriage (or "must-carry") provisions violate their First Amendment rights. Upon consideration of the entire record, the Court holds that sections 4 and 5 of the 1992 Cable Act do not violate the plaintiffs' First Amendment rights.

. . .

Section 4 of the Act requires all cable system operators with more than 12 channels to carry, upon request, the signals of licensed "local" commercial broadcast television stations whose signal is received over-the-air in the same television market as the cable system. The operator need not devote more than one-third of its active usable channels to deliver local broadcast signals, but if there are not enough local broadcast stations to fill the one-third set-aside, the operator must carry the signal of one or two "qualified" low power broadcast stations. Cable systems with 12 or fewer channels must deliver the signals of at least three local commercial broadcast stations unless the cable system has 300 or fewer subscribers, in which case it is not subject to the requirements of section 4 at all. An operator must carry the entire programming schedule of each commercial station it is required to carry, and it may not accept or request payment for doing so. Every commercial broadcast station having a right to mandatory carriage must be carried by the cable operator, at the station's election, on its current over-the-air channel position, at the channel position it occupied on July 19, 1985, or at the channel position it occupied on January 1, 1992.

Section 5 of the Act requires operators of cable systems able to deliver signals on more than 36 channels to carry the signals of every local non-commercial educational broadcast television station requesting carriage, unless the educational station's programming substantially duplicates that of another station carried by the system. Systems with 12 or fewer channels must carry one qualified non-commercial station, and systems having 12 to 36 channels must carry between one and three such stations. Section 5, like section 4, directs cable system operators to carry the entire programming schedule of the broadcast stations they are required to carry, and similarly prohibits operators from accepting payment in exchange for carriage. Each non-commercial station having a mandatory carriage right must be carried, at its election, on its current over-the-air channel position or on its channel position as of July 19, 1985.

Section 6 of the Act, which becomes effective on October 5, 1993, prohibits cable operators from retransmitting the signals of any commercial broadcasting station without obtaining the station's consent. In conjunction with section 4, section 6 provides local broadcasters with an option to request mandatory (but uncompensated) carriage on a system or to negotiate a carriage agreement with the operator. (Presumably, cable operators will want to carry the signals of larger, viewer-popular broadcasters and will pay for the privilege; [6] less popular broadcasters will be able to force their carriage by making a carriage demand under section 4).

[On the day the Act became law, several suits were filed challenging, among others, sections 4, 5, and 6 of the Act, and seeking various forms of relief. Section 23 provided that challenges to sections 4 and 5 be brought to a three-judge district court with appeal directly to the Supreme Court. Other challenges were transferred to a single judge. The controversy over sections 4 and 5 were now before the court on cross-motions for summary judgment and on some motions to dismiss.]

## I.

The plaintiff cable system operators and programmers contend that the must-carry provisions are, on their face, violative of their First Amendment rights to freedom of speech. The primary evil of those provisions, they assert, is that they force cable system operators to devote a portion of their finite signal-carrying capacity to deliver the signals of a privileged class of competing "speakers," i.e., over-the-air broadcasters, thus diminishing the number of channels remaining available to them for other programming they might prefer to carry. Must-carry also violates the First Amendment rights of the operators, they say, because it inhibits the operators' "editorial discretion" to determine what programming messages to provide to their subscribers,[11] compelling them perforce to deliver some programming they might otherwise choose not to carry. And the programmers argue that must-carry exalts broadcasters to preferred status as "speakers" by awarding them favored cable channel positions the programmers covet.

---

**6.** Prior to the 1992 Act, cable operators were free to carry the signals of local broadcasters subject only to the "compulsory license" provisions of the copyright law. See 17 U.S.C. § 111 (1988). Under these provisions, operators may transmit broadcast signals if they pay royalty fees determined pursuant to an administrative schedule.

**11.** The plaintiffs note that the 1992 Act not only requires operators to carry local broadcast stations, it requires operators to carry these stations on a "basic service tier" that must be made available to all subscribers. [§ 543 (b)(7)(A)]

The concept of governmentally ordained mandatory carriage of broadcast signals is not a novel threat to the cable industry. The FCC first began to experiment with must-carry rules in the early 1960s. The perceived need for must-carry today is based on the same premise that gave rise to it then: that local broadcast stations, unable to secure carriage on cable systems serving the same viewer markets, will, over time, lose their audiences and perish. [ ] As the audiences of broadcasting stations decline, so the reasoning goes, their advertising revenues will decrease correspondingly. Local over-the-air broadcasting operations, once they become unprofitable, will expire. Cable carriage of local broadcasting was then and is still now thought by its proponents to be essential not merely to ensure the continuing availability of programming with a "local" flavor to cable system subscribers, but also to preserve the vitality of a free source of over-the-air programming to television viewers unwilling or unable to obtain a cable connection.

Not surprisingly, the parties have expended considerable effort and resources arguing over the level of First Amendment scrutiny to be applied to speech regulation in the cable context. The plaintiffs contend that the must-carry provisions must be subjected to exacting First Amendment scrutiny; if they are not per se unconstitutional, they are assuredly permissible only if found to have been precisely drawn to serve a compelling government interest, and to go no further. [ ] The defendants respond that if the First Amendment is implicated at all in this case, the must-carry provisions need only be judged by the interest-balancing traditionally applied to content-neutral speech regulation or legislation ostensibly unrelated to expression that is discovered to impose incidental burdens on speech. The nature of this inquiry, originating in United States v. O'Brien, 391 U.S. 367 (1968), and refined in Ward v. Rock Against Racism, 491 U.S. 781 (1989), is to uphold such regulation when shown to promote a significant government interest and not to burden substantially more speech than necessary to vindicate that interest. [ ]

## II.

In 1989, Congress began the first in a series of several hearings to assess the video programming distribution landscape in light of the 1984 Cable Act. After an exhaustive factfinding process including hearings held over three years, the 1992 Act was passed. Congress' principal finding was that, for a variety of reasons, concentration of economic power in the cable industry was preventing non-cable programmers from effectively competing for the attention of a television audience. [ ]

Congress specifically found that cable had become the "dominant nationwide video medium." [ ] Almost 56,000,000 households—60 percent of the households with televisions—receive cable television, [ ], and cable service is available to almost 90% of the nation, [ ]. In those homes receiving video signals by cable, cable has all but supplanted over-the-air broadcast television reception. [ ] Congress also found that despite the dominance of cable, there is insufficient competition within the cable industry. First, there is little competition between cable operators. For many reasons "including local franchising requirements and the extraordinary expense of constructing more than one cable television system to serve a particular geographic area," most regions of the country are served by one cable operator only. [ ] [16] Second, the industry has become horizontally concentrated—many operators share common ownership. [ ] [17] Third, the industry is becoming vertically integrated. [ ] Many large entities that operate cable franchises also own and operate programming enterprises. [ ]

Congress determined that geographic monopolization, horizontal concentration and vertical integration have created barriers to entry for non-cable programmers, primarily broadcasters, attempting to obtain carriage on cable. Vertical integration contributes to this cable "bottleneck" by providing cable operators with economic incentive to grant affiliated programmers access to their systems while denying it to others. [ ] Similarly, horizontal concentration and the absence of effective competition among operators have obstructed broadcaster access by creating a climate conducive to another anti-competitive operator practice. Cable operators compete with broadcasters for advertising revenue. [ ] Consequently, operators have an economic incentive to refuse carriage of broadcasters' signals to reduce broadcast viewership, thus attracting advertising dollars that otherwise would go to broadcasters. [ ]

In summary, Congress concluded that the economic forces at work and the market conditions they had already produced had placed free local broadcast television in serious jeopardy. [ ] It determined that mandatory carriage was necessary to remedy unfair trade practices, to preserve local broadcasting for those who do not receive cable television, [ ], as well as those who do, [ ], and to ensure that the public will continue to have access to a wide diversity of sources of video programming, [ ].

This Court is of the opinion that, in enacting the 1992 Cable Act, Congress employed its regulatory powers over the economy to impose order upon a market in dysfunction, but a market in a commercial commodity nevertheless; not a market in "speech." The commodity Congress undertook to regulate is the means of delivery of video signals to individual receivers. It is not the information the video signals may be used to impart. That the video signals can only be used to convey a message is of no particular significance. The same is true of printing presses, or broadcast transmitters; loudspeakers, or movie projectors. Yet no one doubts that Congress could regulate a market in those commodities in danger of chaos or capture without being accused of

16. Evidence received by Congress indicated that less than 1% of the cable operators in the nation face competition from other operators [citing data that of 11,000 communities served by cable, 53 were served by more than one system.]

17. See also Hearings of June 1989, [ ] (testimony of Prof. Bagdikian) (testifying that the operators serving one-third of the cable subscribers in the nation are owned by two cable companies).

attempting to infringe the First Amendment freedoms of those by whom they will be used to express protected "speech." The Cable Act of 1992 is simply industry-specific antitrust and fair trade practice regulatory legislation: to the extent First Amendment speech is affected at all, it is simply a byproduct of the fact that video signals have no other function than to convey information.

In other words, the Court holds that the must-carry provisions are essentially economic regulation designed to create competitive balance in the video industry as a whole, and to redress the effects of cable operators' anti-competitive practices. The regulation is justified by the existing structure of the cable business itself, and by the market peculiarities resulting from the technological differences in the manner in which different video signal distributors deliver their products to their viewers' receivers. So perceived, the Court concludes that the must-carry provisions are, in intent as well as form, unrelated (in all but the most recondite sense) to the content of any messages that these embattled cable operators, broadcasters, and programmers have in contemplation to deliver.

## III.

That the First Amendment is to some extent implicated whenever a government endeavors to regulate a cable industry component, however, is a proposition now too well-established to reconsider. But although many courts have considered the application of the First Amendment to various laws regulating cable, the question of the First Amendment standard to be applied to compulsory signal-carriage requirements has yet to be definitively answered. Despite twice confronting the issue, the D.C. Circuit has avoided its resolution. [citing *Century Communications, supra,* and *Quincy Cable, supra.*]

It appears to this Court that the must-carry provisions of the 1992 Cable Act squarely present this fundamental issue, and these cases demand that it be resolved. The Court today holds that the government need not demonstrate that it has used the least restrictive means to accomplish what is, primarily and essentially, economic regulation of an industry in the business of delivering video signals. The Court concludes that sections 4 and 5 of the 1992 Act will pass constitutional muster if they satisfy the criteria established in *O'Brien* and its progeny.

To be sure, in *Quincy* and *Century*, the D.C. Circuit held FCC rules requiring cable operators to carry the signals of local broadcasters to be unconstitutional. Neither case, however, is controlling here; the court of appeals was careful, in both opinions, to note that must-carry rules are not per se unconstitutional. [ ] The court of appeals simply held, in both cases, that the FCC had failed to make a record demonstrating the existence of a governmental interest of sufficient moment—whether "compelling" or merely "significant"—to warrant such First Amendment burdens as were imposed by its regulations, or to demonstrate that the means it had chosen to employ to its putative end were necessary at all.

The record in support of the 1992 Cable Act, in contrast, was made by Congress. Federal courts do not ordinarily review the adequacy of the record before Congress to support the laws it enacts.

## IV.

All parties agree (at least, the plaintiffs concede) that the must-carry provisions are not viewpoint-based; must-carry rights are conferred upon all full-power local broadcasters, and the obligations upon most cable operators, regardless of any views expressed in the programming of either. The provisions do not compel the carriage of any particular messages nor do they impose any burden on operators or programmers on the basis of the messages they or the broadcasters propose to transmit. Nevertheless, a law need not be viewpoint-based to be subject to strict First Amendment scrutiny. It may, for example, be considered content-based and subjected to strict scrutiny if it purports to restrict a particular type or character of speech, irrespective of the position taken on any issue. Consolidated Edison Co. v. Public Serv. Commission, 447 U.S. 530, 537 (1980) (public policy leaflets accompanying utility bills); Boos v. Barry, 485 U.S. 312, 319 (1988) (placards embarrassing to or disparaging of a foreign government) (plurality opinion).

The plaintiffs contend that strict scrutiny applies because the must-carry provisions compel an operator to utter "speech" not of its choosing; because they alter an operator's editorial decision-making about what to say; and because they favor the speech of broadcasters over that of operators and programmers. But none of the epithets invoked by the plaintiffs—"compelled speech," or "editorial discretion," or "speaker-partiality"—are talismans automatically necessitating strict scrutiny. Strict scrutiny applies only if governmental regulation is overtly content-based or presents an opportunity for official censorship. A compulsory speech requirement, or one imposing upon the discretion of a speaker to say only what he wishes, it appears, is to be strictly scrutinized only if it appears that the government has prescribed the content—either the message or the subject matter—of the speech to be spoken. Examined carefully, all of the compelled speech and editorial discretion cases cited by the plaintiffs can be seen to have involved regulation telling the speaker what to say or at least what to talk about. See Riley v. National Fed'n of the Blind, 487 U.S. 781 (1988) (state law requiring charitable fundraisers to disclose percentage of receipts actually devoted to good works); Pacific Gas & Elec. Co. v. Public Util. Comm'n, 475 U.S. 1, 10–11 & n.7 (1986) (plurality opinion) (state regulation requiring utility to mail fundraising appeals of its rate-making opponents); Wooley v. Maynard, 430 U.S. 705 (1977) (state law requiring motorist to display bellicose state motto on license plates); Miami Herald Publishing Co. v. Tornillo, 418 U.S. 214 (1974) (state law requiring newspaper to carry replies of political candidates it had opposed editorially).

These cases stand in sharp contrast to PruneYard Shopping Center v. Robins, 447 U.S. 74 (1980), in which the Supreme Court upheld a California constitutional provision interpreted to protect speech and petitioning at a privately owned shopping center. Significantly, the speaker's right to speak on the objecting owner's property upheld in *PruneYard* had nothing to do with the content or subject matter of his speech, and there was no danger that, in affording the speaker access to his shopping center, the owner would be affected to any degree in his ability to speak his own piece.

"Speaker-partial" regulations, or those that purportedly favor one group of speakers at the expense of others, similarly are not subject to strict scrutiny unless they are content-based.   . . .

A regulation is deemed to be content-neutral if it is addressed to ends unrelated to the content of expression upon which it may have an effect.  Ward v. Rock Against Racism, [   ]; Texas v. Johnson, 491 U.S. 397, 407 (1989).  As the Court has previously noted, because the record indicates that Congress' primary purpose in enacting must-carry was to restore competitive balance and assure a functional market in the distribution of video signals, whatever might be said with those signals, the must-carry provisions appear to be unrelated to the content of the expression they will affect.

## V.

The plaintiffs argue that the government's asserted interest in "promoting widespread dissemination of information from diverse sources," [   ], betrays a content-based purpose.  That Congress has found it necessary to preserve local broadcast television to promote "diversity," even for those who receive cable television, they contend, indicates that Congress perceives some content difference between the messages of "local" broadcasters and cable programmers.

But if the must-carry provisions are content-related at all, they are only marginally so, to the point of de minimis.  Congress may have presumed, on a very non-specific (and unarticulated) level, that there would be some content differences between the subject matter and/or emphasis of the video signals emitted by local broadcasters and those produced by cable programmers.  It appears to the Court, however, that Congress' solicitousness for local broadcasters' material simply rests on its assumption that they have as much to say of interest or value as the cable programmers who service a given geographic market audience, not on any recognition that there is a discrete "local" subject-matter.  So viewed, the must-carry provisions hardly evince the type of nefarious governmental activity guarded against by the First Amendment generally and the strict scrutiny standard in particular.

Moreover, even if a "local" versus "non-local" dichotomy of message exists, and can be said to be content-related in some abstract way, the cable medium exhibits certain characteristics unique to the way the industry has evolved and is presently structured, and of equally "local" dimensions having nothing whatsoever to do with message.  Cable operators have prevailed upon "local" public authorities to license their use of public rights-of-way over which to string their coaxial cable networks, and there are manifestly limits to the number of such licenses likely to be issued. They vie with broadcasters for "local" advertisers. Cable operators have also historically enjoyed the right to retransmit "local" broadcast programming when and to the extent they wished subject only to administratively set royalty fees. The technology they employ enables a single cable operator to transmit a video signal superior to that of conventional over-the-air transmitters, and to deliver at a "local" television receiver a vastly greater number of channels to watch than all local broadcasters combined. There is, moreover, little competition among "local" cable operators themselves. In short, the term "local" as applied to the cable industry has many implications other than as a synonym for "provincial" as an adjective applied to programming and all were within the contemplation of Congress when it enacted must-carry.

. . .

Absent an indication of a Congressional purpose, whether avowed or covert, to effect a degree of content-control by mandating carriage of "local" broadcasters' signals, the First Amendment should not unduly inhibit Congress in what clearly appears on its face to be an effort to level the economic playing field in the television industry, at large, even if in doing so it may coincidentally inhibit some freedom of choice of the cable operators as to whose signals are to be carried and under what conditions. The Court accordingly concludes that *O'Brien* and *Rock Against Racism* provide the appropriate standard for determining the constitutionality of Congress' mandatory carriage provisions.[25]

## VI.

The inquiry to be made under the *O'Brien–Rock Against Racism* formulation is to ascertain whether the must-carry provisions further a significant government interest, [ ], and whether they are "narrowly tailored" to serve that interest, [ ]. The narrow tailoring requirement is satisfied if the government's regulation will effectively remedy the condition that the government has identified as in need of correction, and if it does not burden substantially more speech than necessary in doing so. [ ] Congress' objective in enacting the mandatory carriage requirements, it has declared, was to promote fair competition among video "speakers" in order to assure the survival of local broadcasting for the benefit of both those who subscribe to a cable service and for those who do not. [ ] Although the D.C. Circuit declined an invitation to rule on whether this is a governmental goal of sufficient significance for

---

**25.** The parties have raised the issue of whether the courts should strictly scrutinize a congressional decision that a particular communications medium warrants special First Amendment treatment. The Court finds that it need not resolve this intriguing question. With respect to the factual findings made by Congress, the Court has provided Congress with the level of deference befitting a co-equal branch of government that is well-equipped to take evidence and make findings. [ ] The Court, however, has viewed as a matter of law, subject to no deference to Congress, the issue of whether the facts present the need for special First Amendment treatment.

*O'Brien* purposes, [   ], other cases establish that the importance of broadcasting generally, and in particular local broadcasting, to the American public is now beyond dispute. [   ]

The plaintiffs submit that even if averting the demise of local broadcasting is deemed an important governmental goal, the factual premise on which the must-carry provisions are based, viz., that local broadcasting is in peril, is incorrect. Citing their own statistics, the plaintiffs contend that broadcasting is alive and well, and has actually grown since the FCC's must-carry rules were struck down in *Quincy*. Oppressive artifices such as must-carry, they say, are unnecessary.

Congress, however, did not agree, and in sharp contrast with the meager record before the FCC when the court of appeals struck down the must-carry provisions in *Quincy* and *Century*, the current must-carry provisions are based on a substantial record assembled by Congress itself. [   ] Congress received evidence demonstrating, to its satisfaction, that cable operators, in significant numbers, are denying carriage to local broadcasters, are attaching onerous conditions to their agreements to carry broadcasters, and are exiling broadcasters being carried to remote channel positions. [   ] Congress also apparently credited evidence indicating that this unfavorable treatment of broadcasters is the result of the cable operators' attempts to obtain a competitive advantage, not a function of consumer demand, [   ].[28] Congress determined that refusal to carry, termination of carriage, and channel repositioning artificially diminish the audiences of local broadcasters, and, in turn, decrease their revenues. [   ] In light of all of the evidence, Congress concluded that local broadcast television is not flourishing; it is in serious jeopardy. [   ]

Furthermore, even if the state of the broadcasting industry is not now as parlous as the defendants contend, the Court finds it to be indisputable on this record that cable operators have attained a position of dominance in the video signal distribution market, and can henceforth exercise the attendant market power. The Court does not find improbable Congress' conclusion that this market power provides cable operators with both incentive and present ability to block non-cable programmers' access to the bulk of any prospective viewing audience; unconstrained, cable holds the future of local broadcasting at its mercy. In light of the considerable body of evidence amassed by Congress, and the deference this Court should accord to the factfinding abilities of the nation's legislature, [   ], the Court must conclude that the danger perceived by Congress is real and substantial.

**28.** The Senate Committee on Commerce, Science, and Transportation, for example, received evidence indicating that "in almost every instance, [broadcast] stations [that have been repositioned] have been replaced by a cable program service in which the system operator is selling advertising or in which the operator has an equity interest or both." [   ] The Committee concluded that channel repositioning of broadcasters is "made solely to enhance the competitive position of the cable operator's programming or its advertising availabilities." [   ]

The plaintiffs also contend that the must-carry provisions are not "narrowly tailored" to accomplish their objective. There seems to be little doubt that the must-carry provisions will be effective in sustaining local broadcasting for the present. Rather than dispute their effectiveness as a means to the end, therefore, the plaintiffs' complaint is that they are overly so; being excessive, they burden speech in instances in which governmental intrusion is unnecessary.

First, they argue that Congress' goal can be achieved by the use of rudimentary technology, (a selector switch, for example), enabling broadcast and cable signals to be equally accessible to cable subscribers who want to watch them; viewer preference will then determine the victor in an idealized "marketplace of ideas." Second, they contend that mandatory cable carriage of all local broadcasters is too much of a good thing; it may require an operator to carry signals of broadcasters it would not otherwise carry in a market in which there is actually a surfeit of "local" programming on cable as well as over-the-air. The Court concludes, however, that the must-carry provisions are sufficiently, if not surgically, tailored to Congress' larger economic market-adjusting objective.

It is, of course, conceivable that there are less restrictive alternatives that Congress could have employed in its attempt to preserve the vitality of local broadcasting. Importantly, however, under *O'Brien*, the government is not required to settle for means that serve its interests less effectively merely because an alternative might be less burdensome. [  ] Congress actually found that input-selector switches were ineffective simply because viewers tended not to use them (a function, perhaps, of viewer inertia as much as viewer preference). [  ] Of more significance, however, is that Congress further found that prophylactic measures were necessary to combat the operators' tendencies toward anticompetitive treatment of broadcasters generally. [  ] Once again, the Court is unwilling to second-guess Congress' determination that the must-carry provisions are necessary to accomplish its objective. Provoking a popularity contest between broadcast and cable programmers was not what it had in mind. [  ]

Finally, the Court concludes that the must-carry provisions do not unnecessarily burden a substantial amount of the plaintiffs' own speech. Operators retain complete discretion over much the greater proportion of the channel spectrum on their systems, and non-broadcast programmers are free to compete for access to those channels not dedicated. . . . Thus, although the must-carry regulations may reduce the overall quantity of cable operator and programmer speech "opportunities," as it were, it leaves open adequate—in fact, plentiful—alternative, intra-medium channels of communication for cable speakers to deliver whatever messages they choose. The Constitution requires no more. [  ]

## Conclusion

The 1992 Cable Act represents a major congressional effort to bring order and stability to an industry that significantly, and often profoundly, touches American lives. It is not the province of this Court to pass judgment upon the wisdom of the policies the national legislature has chosen to pursue in such endeavors. That, of course, is a task our system of government commits to the electoral and political processes, and the Court's power in that regard is not enlarged merely because it is invoked in the name of the First Amendment. Simply put, the governmental intention evinced by the must-carry provisions is economic, not ideologic, and raises no suspicion of the type of ominous government interference with speech against which the First Amendment protects.

[The court rejected a challenge based on freedom of religion in which a cable programmer of religious programs claimed that requiring carriage of local broadcasters, each of whom provided a modest amount of religious programming, would make a channel devoted to religious programming less attractive than it would otherwise be. The court concluded that the must-carry rules did not have a "primary effect" that either advanced or inhibited religion.

The court also refused to extend the must-carry sections to low-power stations. They had claimed that the preference for full-time broadcasters made low-power stations less attractive to cable operators. But there was nothing "irrational about a legislative policy judgment to treat LPTV as a lesser player in the television market, as it has always been, no matter how innovative, imaginative, or deserving the Court might find LPTV to be."]

STANLEY SPORKIN, DISTRICT JUDGE.

I concur. . . . I write separately to emphasize that, because any burden imposed by the 1992 Cable Act on speech is so remote and incidental to the purpose and effect of the 1992 Cable Act, I do not find that the must-carry provisions of the Cable Act of 1992 implicate the First Amendment to the extent to which Plaintiffs claim.

For many years, Congressional policy regarding the telecommunications industry has had a consistent goal: To foster public access to a diverse array of information and views. Congress has found that, to a significant degree because of federal and local governmental decisions in prior years, the cable industry threatens to achieve monopolistic control over the telecommunications market. Thus, a competitive imbalance between the cable and broadcast industries has developed, threatening this important goal.

Congress' finding is based on an exhaustive Congressional record, and deserves the Court's deference. Plaintiffs, under the guise of the First Amendment, would have this Court strike down a statute enacted by Congress in an effort to rein in cable companies' growing economic might and to restore competitive balance in the telecommunications industry. However, this case is not about protecting free speech and the First Amendment. This case is about market domination and control.

I

[Judge Sporkin traced the evolution of the two "young industries."]

Although cable has brought about much good, there have been excesses which, over the years, Congress has felt compelled to alleviate. In particular, Congress has found that certain anticompetitive, monopolistic behavior on the part of cable companies has accompanied their success, behavior which threatens the vitality of broadcast programming and, therefore, the public interest in access to a wide range of information and views.  Thus, while cable has virtually eliminated the problems caused by scarcity on the broadcast spectrum, it has created another scarcity—namely access to the channels on cable systems themselves.

In finding that the must-carry provisions of the Cable Act do not violate the First Amendment, several points merit special emphasis. [Judge Sporkin explored three points.  The first was that "local and federal government regulation played an important role in allowing cable to achieve the position it has today."  The second was that cable companies enjoying "de facto monopolies wield enormous power over programming in the telecommunications market as a whole.  Cable operators can require programmers to provide the operator exclusive carriage rights or a financial interest in the programming as a condition of carriage, and some have done so."  The third was that "as an increasing proportion of the public subscribed to cable (now 60% of American households owning a television set), broadcast stations have become increasingly dependent on cable to reach their television audiences.  As cable has become the primary means for transmission of all broadcast signals in a locality, it has become imperative for broadcasters to obtain retransmission of their signals by the local cable company."]

Congress specifically found that broadcast stations, by being part of the local community, continue to be an important source of local news, public and educational programming and other services critical to an informed electorate.  The cable industry's growing monopolistic hold on the telecommunications industry, Congress reasoned, threatens the viability of its only current competition—local broadcasters.  Congress concluded that, should local broadcasters be forced off the air, the public interest in being able to obtain access to a broad selection of local news and public and educational programming would be endangered.

## II

Sections 4 and 5 of the Cable Act of 1992 are a form of regulation, designed to lessen the monopolistic threat posed by cable to the telecommunications industry.  Contrary to the arguments of Plaintiffs that the 1992 Act limits First Amendment rights on its face, the Act's objective is to enhance the diversity of television voices protected by the First Amendment by neutralizing the adverse effects of cable companies' monopolistic behavior and securing the position of broadcasters' programs.  As an interim measure to accomplish this end, "must-carry" is an integral part of the solution to the problems identified by Congress.[5]

5.  At some point, technological innovation will enable cable systems to accommo-date all broadcasters requesting carriage, thereby rendering "must carry" a problem

Plaintiffs have come before this Court, not because their freedom of speech is seriously threatened, but because their profits are; to dress up their complaint in First Amendment garb demeans the principles for which the First Amendment stands and the protections it was designed to afford.  To the extent to which the First Amendment is implicated, I agree with Judge Jackson that the minimal level of scrutiny outlined in [ *O'Brien* and *Rock against Racism*] is the standard the Court should apply.

Plaintiffs raise two arguments in support of their claim.  First, the cable operators argue that the must-carry provisions are content-based restrictions compelling them to carry the speech of broadcast stations, and as such run afoul of the First Amendment.  Second, the cable programmers argue that the must-carry provisions unfairly prefer the "speech" of broadcasters over their First Amendment rights.  Both of these arguments fail.

A.  Operators' Claim

It is well-established that under the protections afforded by the First Amendment individuals enjoy the right to speak or not to speak.  The government cannot compel an individual to speak.  [  ]  The Supreme Court has extended this principle to apply to newspapers and to privately-owned newsletters in [*Tornillo* and *Pacific Gas*], respectively.

While the plaintiffs would have the Court extend the coverage of [these two cases] to the case at bar, these cases are inapposite to the arguments raised by Plaintiffs [because they involved state penalties for content-based speech].

. . .

Plaintiffs argue that the prohibition outlined in [the two cases] against governmental intrusion into the province of editorial discretion provides an independent basis leading the Court to apply strict First Amendment scrutiny to this case.  In those cases, the clear content-triggered operation of the governmental regulation threatened to alter the mix of information chosen by the newspaper or newsletter at issue.    . . .

While cable operators do exercise some control and judgment about the mix of overall programming they provide, such judgment does not entail the detail-oriented, content-based decisions made by the editors of

of the past.  Indeed, according to a April 6, 1993 article in the Washington Post, Telecommunication's Inc., the nation's largest cable television company, is about to "unveil an ambitious plan to rewire many of its cable systems with 7,000 miles of high-capacity, fiber-optic lines" over the next four years, which eventually will "enable TCI to deliver hundreds of TV channels [and] 'video-on-demand' programming" to its subscribers.

However, while fiber-optic and other technological innovations may be on the verge of a break through which may well cast a different light on Plaintiffs' First Amendment claims, such innovations have not yet realized their potential in the marketplace.  In the context of today's technological landscape, the Cable Act of 1992 must be viewed as regulation designed to alleviate the adverse impact of the cable industries' growing monopolistic hold over the telecommunications industry.

newsletters, newspapers or other published sources of information.    . . .    Requiring cable operators to carry the programs of
broadcasters, whatever the content of those programs may be, simply
does not rise to the level of interference with editorial discretion which
impinges on free speech or threatens to alter the mix of information
available to the public.

B.  Programmers' Claim

Plaintiff programmers challenge the must-carry provisions as impermissibly favoring the speech of broadcaster stations over that of cable
programmers.

"Generally, statutory classifications are valid if they bear a rational
relation to a legitimate governmental purpose.  Statutes are subject to a
higher level of scrutiny if they interfere with the exercise of a fundamental right, such as freedom of speech, or employ a suspect classification."
[ ]  Programmers and broadcasters clearly are not constitutionally
protected groups.  And, having found that must-carry does not violate
the First Amendment, heightened scrutiny is not warranted in this case.[7]
Since I agree with Judge Jackson that the 1992 Cable Act passes muster
under the rational relations standard of review, this argument fails.

Finally, it must be pointed out that the only challenge before this
Court is provided under the First Amendment.  No challenge has been
made under the taking provision of the Fifth Amendment or any other
legal provision.    . . .

III

. . .

Here, the Government has stepped aside to allow the private sector
to perform signal transmission and allocation functions that the Government itself could have reserved for itself, without facing any conceivable
First Amendment challenge by broadcasters or other programmers because of the regulatory method chosen.  To the extent to which cable is
performing a "public utility" function which the Government itself could
perform, Congress certainly has the right to adopt reasonable regulations.

Congress has determined that cable companies' growing anti-competitive behavior and monopolistic power threatens the broadcast industry and the public's access to a wide array of local, public and educational programming.  Congress decided to address this danger by enacting
the Cable Act of 1992.  In so doing, Congress was not motivated by a
desire to stifle the speech of cable operators or programmers—indeed,
ample channels remain open for their use—but by a desire to alleviate
the effects of cable companies' monopolies and to preserve the diversity
of voices represented by local, public and educational broadcasters.

---

7.  Moreover, a requirement that cable
operators carry broadcast programming
cannot be said to compel speech on the part
of cable programmers.  Thus, even if the
First Amendment was implicated in this
case, it is not clear that the programmers
would have standing to assert this claim.

Whether there were other preferable ways of accomplishing Congress' objective is not for the Court to decide. So long as the method adopted by Congress is an appropriate one, it must stand and may not be second guessed by the judiciary. Consequently, I find that the Cable Act of 1992 does not run afoul of the First Amendment.

WILLIAMS, CIRCUIT JUDGE, dissenting.

The must-carry provisions    . . .    require cable operators to set aside just over a third of their channels for local broadcast stations. (The one-third-plus figure comprises both the commercial stations protected under § 4 of the Act and the non-commercial stations protected under § 5.) In addition, each privileged broadcast station has a right to its specific "channel position" on a cable system. [   ]

In considering cable, Congress confronted a very real problem—one for which it has an easy remedy entirely consistent with the First Amendment. The problem is that cable systems control access "bottlenecks" to an important communications medium.    . . .    There are well-developed regulatory responses to this sort of situation. The "bottleneck" holder may be ordered to serve all parties that meet neutral criteria for service.    . . .    These solutions are, of course, imperfect; for example, they pose tricky pricing issues. But mandatory access rules of this sort give no special privilege to one set of access seekers over another.

In fact, in 1984 Congress adopted provision for neutral, compulsory access to cable in § 612, [   ], a solution somewhat refined in § 9 of the 1992 Act. This provision entitles independent programmers to lease access on cable systems, at reasonable prices to be set by the FCC. Although the channels available for lease under § 612 are limited to a specified proportion of each operator's channels (depending on the total number that the operator possesses, [   ], Congress remains free to expand the fraction of channels available. The only programmers excluded from the benefits of § 612 are those affiliated with the cable operator, i.e., the very ones who would be the likely beneficiaries of operator discrimination and who are therefore in no need of the law's intervention.

The must-carry provisions, by contrast, extend the privilege of access only to a special class of unaffiliated programmers—local commercial and non-commercial television stations. Congress rested its decision to promote these stations in part, but quite explicitly, on a finding about their content—that they were "an important source of local news and public affairs programming and other local broadcast services critical to an informed electorate." [   ]   See 1992 Act, § 2(a)(11). Moreover, because of FCC licensing requirements, every such local broadcaster is legally bound to "provide programming responsive to issues of concern to its community." [   ]   In other words, by virtue of provisions of law outside the 1992 Act, the term used by the Act to define the benefitted class automatically entails content requirements.

A number of parties challenge these mandates, among them the cable operators who must carry local broadcast stations in place of their own choice of programming, and, even more significantly, the unaffiliated cable programmers, such as Discovery Network, producer of the Discovery and Learning Channels, whose programming will be supplanted. I shall apply current First Amendment analysis to their claims, but before doing so I think it useful to imagine a few hypothetical cases outside the area of cable. If the answers to those hypotheticals are as clear as I think they are, then—unless there is something terribly special about cable, apart from the bottleneck issue addressed by § 612 of the 1984 Act—the must-carry provisions must fall.

1. The Washington Post develops and patents a special "paper-springer" that enables it to deliver papers at a tiny fraction of others' costs. Assume that paper delivery costs represent a very large share of total costs, so that this technology is a source of overwhelming monopoly power. Congress decrees that The Post must license the paper-springer—but only to publishers of local, neighborhood papers (i.e., not city-wide ones). This cuts out The Washington City Paper, The Washington Informer, and The Washington Times.

2. A state is concerned that large shopping centers represent vital gathering places of citizens and that center owners may not willingly allow the sort of leafletting or soap-box oratory associated with a vibrant democracy. Accordingly it requires owners to allow such leafletting and oratory regardless of the leafletters' or speakers' message. See [*Prune-Yard*] But, finding that local residents are an especially important source of this vibrant debate, it limits the privilege to persons living within four miles of each shopping center. This excludes the proverbial "outside agitator".

These scenarios are in fact less troublesome under the First Amendment than the must-carry rules; the parties selected to benefit from the bottleneck-breaking rules are defined in content-neutral terms. Here, by contrast, the beneficiaries are local stations that are required by government to include specific content that the government has deemed especially worthy.

*Standard of Review.* The standard of review in First Amendment cases usually depends on whether the regulation is content-based, leading to "strict scrutiny", [   ], or content-neutral, leading to more relaxed scrutiny under the formula of [*O'Brien*] as modified in [*Rock Against Racism*]. Here the statute is content-based under controlling precedent. The must-carry provisions mandate speech: they require cablecasters to carry the speech of local broadcast stations. . . .

[After conducting an extensive review of the cases, Judge Williams concluded:

The treatment of First Amendment values as irrelevant cannot be transported to the context of a burden imposed on one set of speakers for the direct and explicit advantage of a limited class of their competitors—a class whose programming must, as a matter of law, include content of a type specified by the government. Accordingly, I conclude that the proper test is strict scrutiny.

In passing he noted "uncontroverted evidence that 2000 cable systems, serving one third of all subscribers, have no excess capacity." He also thought it undisputed that many unaffiliated non-broadcast programmers would lose out because of the preferential treatment of broadcasters.]

*Application of the test.* To survive strict scrutiny, regulation of speech must serve a "compelling" governmental purpose and its "means must be carefully tailored to achieve those ends." Sable Communications v. FCC, 492 U.S. 115, 126 (1989). First we must identify the government's interests, and then assess the fit between each of those interests and the must-carry requirements.

The Senate Report articulated the congressional interests as follows: (1) preserving the benefits of local television service, particularly over-the-air television service; (2) promoting the widespread dissemination of information from diverse sources; and (3) promoting fair competition in the video marketplace. [ ] These purposes are reflected in §§ 2(6)–(15) of the Act. Because this statement of purposes involves some overlap, the analysis will be clearer if we reformulate them as follows: (A) preservation of open access to cable in order to assure diverse programming (see purposes (2) and (3) above); and (B) preservation of local broadcasting (see purposes (1) and (3) above). This second reason involved not only a desire to promote "local news and public affairs programming", see § 2(a)(11) of the Act, but also a wish to assure that local broadcasters could continue to serve those persons who either did not, or could not, subscribe to cable. I address diversity first, then the preservation of local broadcasters.

## Open Access for Diverse Programming

I assume that, at least at some level of abstraction, the interest in promoting diversity of views on cable is compelling. With regard to the broadcast spectrum the Court has characterized programming diversity as an "important governmental objective", Metro Broadcasting, Inc. v. FCC, 497 U.S. 547 (1990). . . .

Here, [as in *Tornillo*], the fit between the interest and the regulation is extremely weak. It is far from clear that giving local broadcasters an entitlement to be carried will increase program diversity at all. Because cablecasters now carry the vast majority of local stations (as explained further below), the must-carry rules may have little effect, but where they have any, it will be only to replace the mix chosen by cablecasters—whose livelihoods depend largely on satisfying audience demand—with a mix derived from congressional dictate.

Moreover, in considering "fit" one must look at the available alternatives. . . . Here, one obvious alternative is expansion of the access provisions of § 612 of the 1984 Act. Those access provisions are far less burdensome—in the critical sense of minimizing government interference in the choice of who will have access to cable. Under § 612, all programmers are eligible for leased access except the ones that don't need it—the affiliates of a cable operator. [   ]

Even neutral remedies such as § 612 are subject to challenge . . . as they replace the cablecaster's speech with that of others. But a number of distinguishing factors argue for upholding the leased access solution. First, a relatively large number of channels is available (ranging from the teens up to 40, 50 and more), so that the scope of the monopolization is greater than in [*Tornillo*]. Second, the channels are discrete, so that viewers will be less likely to attribute all speech on all channels to the cablecaster. And there is no chilling effect on the cablecaster's programming of the remaining channels. Finally, the benefitted group precisely fits the legislative concern—all unaffiliated programmers.

The last is conspicuously missing from must-carry. The difference between the two is the difference between the state rule upheld in [*PruneYard*] and the hypothetical set forth at the start of this opinion—a *PruneYard*-type entitlement limited to a specific class of would-be speakers defined in terms of their location. Indeed, the must-carry requirements are worse than the *PruneYard* hypothetical, for admission to the privileged class requires, as a matter of law, the carrying of specific program content.

It is quite true, of course, that Congress found in 1992 that leased access under § 612 has not been as effective as predicted in 1984, pointing to cumbersome enforcement procedures and undue cablecaster control over prices and other conditions of access. [   ] But the Report went on to "restate[   ]" the Committee's "belief that access requirements establish a form of content-neutral structural regulation 'which will foster the availability of a diversity of viewpoints to the listening audience'." [   ] More important, to the extent that Congress spotted defects in § 612, it set out to correct them. The 1992 Act amends § 612 by clarifying and broadening the FCC's authority to set maximum reasonable rates and other reasonable terms and conditions for access. [   ] Given § 612, and Congress's authority to expand its scope, the must-carry rules do not provide a reasonable fit with the diversity rationale.

Preservation of Local Broadcasting

The second interest that Congress has invoked is the preservation of local broadcasting. Section 2(a)(10) of the Act is explicit: "A primary objective and benefit of our Nation's system of regulation of television broadcasting is the local origination of programming. There is a substantial governmental interest in ensuring its continuation." In part this interest derived from the local content of such broadcasting—"an important source of local news and public affairs programming." 1992 Cable Act § 2(a)(11). But in addition the interest derived from an indirect concern for the households not served by cable—both those unwilling or unable to pay for the service and the 10% for whom such service is physically unavailable.  Here Congress reasoned that if broadcast stations ever lost the advertising revenues attributable to the audiences they reach through cable service, they would be driven from business and thus be unable to provide service for those without cable. There was also special concern that local broadcast stations were exceptionally vulnerable as potential victims of cablecaster bottleneck control, because of their competition with cable for advertising revenue.  [  ]  I will first address the issue of local content, then the preservation of over-the-air service.

*Local content.* It seems extremely doubtful that forcing local affairs content on First Amendment speakers could ever qualify as a compelling interest (at least outside the special preserve of broadcasting itself, to which I return below).  If government "may not select which issues are worth discussing or debating in public facilities", Police Department of Chicago v. Mosley, 408 U.S. 92, 96, (1972), it is hard to see why it may do so on private facilities.

Even if by some stretch an interest in local content were "compelling", far less restrictive means are readily available.  Congress is free to subsidize favored speech if the market is too weak to sustain the quantity that Congress seeks.  [  ]  Given those means, Congress cannot advance specific content by requiring a competing class of First Amendment speakers to carry the favored speech.  "The concept that government may restrict the speech of some elements of our society in order to enhance the relative voice of others is wholly foreign to the First Amendment".  [*Buckley v. Valeo*].

*Preserving over-the-air TV service.*  I assume that as an abstract matter government has a compelling interest in assuring access to TV for those unwilling or unable to subscribe to cable, and especially those beyond cable's physical reach.  The first difficulty with the argument here is that there is no evidence that this access is in jeopardy.  .  .  .

The most plausible evidence would be of local TV stations going under and of licensees turning in their licenses.  Nothing remotely like that is in sight—the facts show quite the opposite.  [Judge Williams cited figures showing that since *Quincy* commercial broadcast stations had increased by 22% and educational stations by 15% and the number of cities receiving television by 16%.]  Whatever risk there may be in the abstract has completely failed to materialize.

Defendants and defendant-intervenors urge in response that this record means little; since *Quincy*, the shadow of possible congressional intervention has fallen across the cable industry, causing operators to be less ruthless than they would be if must-carry were invalidated.  Remove the shadow, they claim, and the operators will show their true monopolist colors.

This argument is incurably flawed.  If the constitutionally fatal aspect of the must-carry rules is the absence of evidence of any visible threat to the over-the-air TV industry, then the rules would become constitutional the minute the industry was visibly threatened. Accordingly, cablecasters would continue to operate under the same shadow of congressional intervention, and over-the-air TV would continue to thrive. Invalidation of must-carry for want of evidence would preserve the supposedly necessary threat.

Supporters of must-carry thus turn to evidence of (1) instances where cablecasters have actually dropped broadcast stations and (2) structural relationships in the industry, which, they say, indicate the threat is real. Indeed, in its findings, Congress noted a "marked shift in market share from broadcast television to cable television", 1992 Act, § 2(a)(13), and also endorsed the structural argument, id. at §§ 2(a)(12) (14–15).

The congressional finding on actual effects is not disputed—nor is it supportive of must-carry. That cable has grown faster than broadcast does not in the slightest suggest that broadcast is in peril.

The record before Congress did, however, include evidence of some cable operators' dropping broadcast channels. Specifically, the Senate Report cites evidence that, of 4303 cable systems disclosing data, 869 had dropped one or more local stations in a total of 1,820 instances. [From this the report extrapolated that there had probably been 3600 instances of denied carriage by a 1700 cable systems. Judge Williams thought these numbers did not show that over-the-air TV was at risk. Some 80 percent of systems had not dropped a single station. It was impossible to know the percentage of total broadcasters dropped or the reasons for the denials. The average cable system in 1990 carried eight local signals, suggesting some 64,000 broadcast signals are being carried. He also cited evidence that in 1988, "98% of all the broadcast stations that would have qualified for mandatory carriage were still being carried despite the absence of such a requirement." The cited one situation in which a Staten Island, New York, cable system was required to carry two stations from Bridgeport, Connecticut: "If many of the stations dropped have as remote a link to the dropping cablecaster's market as do these Bridgeport stations, it would explain why the cable operators' right to drop has coexisted with the broadcast industry's continued growth. Thus we have nothing to connect the limited evidence of cable operators' actual conduct with any inference that a threat to broadcast is imminent or serious."]

The structural argument is that the competition between cable and broadcast for advertising revenue gives cable operators an incentive to drop broadcast stations. See 1992 Act, §§ 2(a)(12), (14–15). (Taken at its best, this theory would lend no support to § 5 of the Act (relating to noncommercial TV), as the educational stations do not advertise.) The evidence cited in the Senate Report consists of a projected 17% growth rate in cable advertising revenues. [ ] Yet rapid growth in advertising seems easily attributable to the growth of cable, and perhaps some branching into advertising-supported programs. In itself, it shows neither a purpose to undermine broadcast TV nor the start of a campaign to do so. Broadcast television evidently still accounts for 92% of all television advertising revenues. [   ]

Further, cable television appears to continue to be dependent on local broadcasters as critical suppliers of programming. Congress explicitly found that "broadcast programming that is carried remains the most popular programming on cable systems, and a substantial portion of the benefits for which consumers pay cable systems is derived from carriage of the signals of network affiliates, independent television stations, and public television stations." 1992 Act, § 2(a)(19). In fact, local broadcaster programming accounts for approximately two-thirds of total cable viewing hours. [   ] Moreover, the ratio of cable subscription fee revenues to advertising revenue is evidently 25:1. [   ] So long as local broadcast programs continue to be so popular, it appears that cable simply cannot afford to drop broadcast channels to any significant degree.

Finally, even if local broadcasters were in perceptible peril, it would not follow that Congress could secure their survival by must-carry provisions. Again, less intrusive alternatives are obvious. First, if evidence of any risk should appear, Congress could get broadcast TV into the homes of cable viewers (and thus preserve the stations' advertising revenues) by expanding leased access under the neutral provisions of § 612 of the 1984 Act. Second, if broadcasters' programs were not popular enough to enable them to pay the leasing fees set by the FCC, Congress could subsidize the difference to the extent necessary. [   ]

In reaching these conclusions, I do not question Congress's power to engage in critical fact-finding. The degree of deference that we owe such findings is hotly disputed between the parties. . . . My view does not turn on any resolution of that dispute, because the legislative findings simply do not support the inferences needed to sustain must-carry. The problems are that (1) there is no finding of any present or imminent harm; (2) the evidence of some dropping of broadcast channels in itself fails to show any widespread problem; (3) the proliferation of local broadcast stations since the end of the FCC's must-carry rules undermines any inference of a problem; (4) the findings as to structure and incentives, taken together with the evidence of cable's dependence on broadcasting, fail to raise the concern beyond the level of speculation; and (5), even if the hazard were perceptible, the record does not address the less intrusive alternatives. If findings as scantily connected to the conclusion as these can justify must-carry, then the door is open—even in the area of First Amendment rights—to exercise of the most naked interest-group preferences. [   ]

Thus I conclude that—unless the analysis of First Amendment issues in the special context of broadcast for some reason supervenes— the must-carry provisions violate the First Amendment.

Proposed Use of Broadcast Analysis

Some defendants urge the court to use the sort of diluted First Amendment analysis applied to broadcasting in [*Red Lion*]. Use of the broadcast standards would be completely inappropriate.

The weakened status of broadcasters under the First Amendment arose from the Supreme Court's conclusion that discretionary government allocation of channels was necessary for the orderly use of the broadcast medium—or at any rate that such allocation was not materially more intrusive on First Amendment values than any visible alternative. In National Broadcasting Co. v. U.S., [  ], the Court upheld the FCC's so-called "Chain Broadcasting" regulations (aimed at preventing monopolization of radio licenses) against a variety of statutory challenges and a First Amendment claim. "Radio inherently is not available to all." [  ] "That is its unique characteristic, and that is why, unlike other modes of expression, it is subject to governmental regulation." [  ] Thus, "The right to free speech does not include . . . the right to use the facilities of radio without a license." [  ]

Although the precise question was not before it, the Court appeared to assume that these factors logically entailed discretionary government allocation of licenses, so that such allocation presented no First Amendment problem so long as the choice was not openly based on the applicants' "political, economic or social views, or upon any other capricious basis." [  ] This of course overlooked content-neutral bases for handling the problems, such as (1) the rule of first possession, which in fact preceded government allocation and tracked the doctrine of prior appropriation, (2) auctions, and (3) lotteries. These content-neutral alternatives evidently went by default, as those raising the First Amendment claims—the incumbent broadcasters—had no incentive to undermine the system under which they held their own quasi-monopoly licenses. *NBC* of course paved the way for *Red Lion*, which upheld, for the broadcast medium, the sort of government-managed right to respond that the Court later struck down for the print media in [*Tornillo*], [  ] Here, of course, not even the defendants or defendant-intervenors suggest that discretionary allocation of channels is necessary or even appropriate to preserve access to cable. In the face of § 612, such a claim would be untenable.

Defendants and defendant-intervenors, however, seeking to deny cable operators full First Amendment protection, point to three special characteristics of cable that in their view justify government management of the channels: (1) the cable operators' need for rights-of-way, along or under city streets, in order to lay their cable; (2) the cable industry's prior enjoyment of special government privileges; and (3) the ability of cable operators to engage in "private censorship" against the speech of broadcasters. Neither alone nor in the aggregate do these justify subjecting cable to diminished First Amendment protection.

*Rights-of-way.* State, city and county governments have property interests in the streets, so that the placement of cable commonly requires government consent. There may also be instances where the federal government holds a proprietary interest essential to the laying of cable. These governments may seek to condition their consents on the operators' waiver or abandonment of their First Amendment rights. If so, courts would presumably assess these efforts under the doctrine of unconstitutional conditions. [ ] We need not speculate on how such cases would work out. Here the federal government is not attaching conditions to the grant of a property interest; it is acting in a purely regulatory role. It cannot lean on proprietary powers that are out of the picture.

*Prior benefits.* Defendants argue that cable's initial growth depended, perhaps essentially, on government assistance in securing the right to retransmit the programs of broadcast channels, free of charge. See 17 U.S.C. § 111, as amended (compulsory copyright access); [ ]. This history seems completely irrelevant. If the Union Pacific Railroad were to own a newspaper, its history as a recipient of government largesse on a grand scale would surely not condemn it to second-class First Amendment protection. Of course current federal government benefits would provide an opportunity for attachment of conditions; but again, just what conditions might prove justifiable in the face of the unconstitutional conditions doctrine is not before us. With the adoption of § 6 of the 1992 Act, Congress gave broadcast stations an unequivocal right to withhold consent to retransmission.

*Cablecasters' power to censor.* Finally, intervenor-defendant NAB argues that cable operators can use their position to censor broadcasters. [ ] This argument amounts to nothing more than a reiteration of the fact that cable operators control a bottleneck. The mere fact that such control might force some programmers to find different ways to reach the public (which all programmers have via § 612, and which broadcasters uniquely have via the airwaves) does not give the government any right to force access on behalf of a preferred class of speakers. . . .

In short, the special character of cable is limited to one feature: bottleneck control of access to an important medium. A straightforward, speech-neutral solution to that problem exists and has already been employed by Congress in § 612 of the 1984 Act, as amended by § 9 of the 1992 Act. I see no constitutional obstacle to the expansion of that solution if Congress should deem it appropriate. Given the availability of that remedy (together with such subsidies as Congress might find suitable), I do not see how Congress can constitutionally deny cable operators the ordinary rights of any First Amendment speaker.

## Conclusion

The must-carry regulations in the 1992 Cable Act clearly burden the protected speech of cable operators, in favor of local broadcasters whose programming content is in material part specified by law. In requiring cable systems to carry a special group of competing speakers, Congress directly, not incidentally, restricts the cable operators' exercise of editorial discretion. None of the interests advanced by Congress supports such a burden. The diversity rationale fits poorly with mandatory carriage of a specific group of programmers, being served with neutrality by § 612's provision for leased access. Although the interest in protecting over-the-air TV for non-cable-subscribers may be compelling in the abstract, the findings in the record neither indicate any real threat nor suggest any flaw in the less burdensome and obvious means for addressing any such threat. For these reasons, I respectfully dissent, and would declare the must-carry provisions to be unconstitutional abridgments of the First Amendment rights of cable operators and unaffiliated programmers.

**Notes and Questions**

1.  Compare each opinion in its treatment of the questions of deference to Congress and in the determination of the level of scrutiny to be applied.

2.  Compare the role of "local" broadcasters and of "local" programming in each of the opinions.

3.  What would you expect to happen if the dissent's focus on § 612 of the 1984 Act were to prevail?

4.  If compression of signals and the era of 500–channel cable systems come into being, what impact will that have on the controversy over the must-carry provision?

5.  In the interim new cable channels continue to be launched. At least 25 new channels project starting service by the end of 1994. Among these new channels are: The Crime Channel, The Game Show Channel, The Golf Channel, two History Networks, The Military Channel, Romance Classics, the Sega Channel, and the Television Food Network. Broadcasting & Cable, June 7, 1993 at 38. What effect will the continuing increase in programming services have on the must-carry controversy?

6.  Cable interests sought to enjoin enforcement of the act pending appeal. Sitting as Circuit Justice, Chief Justice Rehnquist denied such relief. Acts of Congress were presumptively constitutional. An injunction against operation of Congressional legislation was appropriate only if needed in aid of jurisdiction and the merits were "indisputably clear." In this situation the Court would still have full power to rule on the must-carry provisions even if they were to go into effect. On the merits, given the two existing lines of authority of *Tornillo* and *Red Lion*, "it simply is not indisputably clear that applicants have a First Amendment right to be free from government regulation." Turner Broadcasting System, Inc. v. FCC, 113 S.Ct. 1806 (1993) (Rehnquist, C.J. in chambers).

7.  The Supreme Court noted probable jurisdiction. 114 S.Ct. 38 (1993).

8.  In a separate proceeding, a district court found constitutional a number of provisions of the 1992 Cable Act, including retransmission consent, rate regulation and mandatory carriage of PEG channels. Judge Jackson applied the same reasoning he used in *Turner*. Because

the 1992 act was, in his opinion, primarily economic regulation, he held that the *O'Brien* test was the appropriate level of scrutiny. Most of the challenged provisions were, in his view, content-neutral regulations aimed at increasing diversity or, in the case of rate regulation, "to keep rates affordable to the public." Daniel's Cable Vision, Inc. v. United States, 819 F.Supp. 32, 72 R.R.2d 366, 21 Med.L.Rptr. 1993 (D.D.C. 1993).

9. As the deadline approached for television stations to choose between must carry and retransmission consent, both cable MSOs and TV group owners were engaged in public posturing regarding what the MSOs were willing to give and the TV station owners would be willing to accept in return for retransmission consent. For example, Time Warner announced that it would not pay one cent to broadcasters, while Cap Cities/ABC announced that it would be seeking cash compensation. Broadcasting & Cable, June 7, 1993 at 6.

However, less than two months later Cap Cities/ABC and Hearst started signing deals with cable systems whereby, in return for retransmission consent for Capcities/ABC and Hearst TV stations, the cable companies agreed to pay for and carry ESPN2, a new cable channel owned by Capcities/ABC and Hearst. Among the MSOs that agreed to this deal were Continental Cablevision, Jones Intercable, Sammons Communications and Multivision Cable. Broadcasting and Cable, Aug. 9, 1993 at 12.

Fox entered into similar deals trading retransmission consent for its affiliates for carriage of its new cable channel. Fox is charging 25 cents per subscriber for the cable channel. In turn, Fox broadcast affiliates can choose between a seven and one half cent cut or a five cent cut plus an ownership interest in the new cable channel. Broadcasting & Cable, July 12, 1993 at 16.

After months of insisting on cash compensation for retransmission consent, CBS ended up granting retransmission consent for one year without obtaining anything in return. Broadcasting & Cable, Oct. 4, 1993 at 6.

In addition to must carry and retransmission consent broadcasters were given even more authority with regard to cable carriage of their signals. Every station carried under the provisions of § 614, must be carried on either the channel number on which the station is broadcast, "the channel on which it was carried on July 19, 1985, or on the channel on which it was carried on January 1, 1992, at the election of the station." Stations can be carried on other channels only with their consent. The Commission has been given the authority to resolve any channel positioning disputes. 47 U.S.C.A. § 534.

### d. Exclusivity

To protect the local station when it was carrying network programs, the FCC promulgated exclusivity rules (formerly called non-duplication rules) to prevent cable from carrying an imported distant signal that was offering the same network program as the local network affiliate. First, the FCC required the cable system to black out the distant signal if the program was being broadcast on the same day as it was being presented by the local affiliate. Later, the FCC changed the rule to require blackout only if the two showings were at the same hour.

In the mid–1970s the Commission dropped the black-out requirement, permitting the cable system to show the local station's signal (and its commercials) simultaneously on both the local channel and on the channel that normally carries the distant signal, even though the local station might suffer if the local audience stays with the distant station after the program is over.

Another regulation protecting local stations had provided that cable systems in large markets could not carry distant signals showing programs to which a local station had acquired exclusive future local rights. In 1980 the FCC repealed this restriction on the ground that viewers' interest in "time-diversity"—seeing programs when they wanted—was more compelling than the local station's interest in the exclusive programming. Deletion of the old rule would not reduce the supply of programs for television.

In 1988 the Commission announced new syndication exclusivity rules and expanded the network exclusivity rules. The new rules allow stations to enforce exclusivity contracts against cable systems retransmitting distant signals with duplicative programming. Syndicators may also enforce exclusivity in all markets for the first year after their initial sale to a television station. Existing contracts cannot be used to enforce exclusivity unless there is explicit language covering the reimposition of syndication exclusivity.

In addition, stations are allowed to negotiate national exclusivity. This provision, which is particularly valuable for superstations, includes a blanket exemption from the territorial exclusivity rule. Thus, a superstation such as WTBS can obtain national rights to a syndicated program and preclude any other broadcast station in the country from carrying that program.

Cable systems with fewer than 1,000 subscribers are exempted from the new rules as are programs carried on stations generally available off the air.

Network exclusivity was also expanded. The former provision that limited protection to simultaneously aired duplicative network programming has been eliminated. Network affiliates are now allowed to demand protection against all duplicative network programming.

The new rules were upheld on appeal. United Video, Inc. v. Federal Communications Commission, 890 F.2d 1173, 66 R.R.2d 1865 (D.C.Cir. 1989).

### e. Access Channel Requirements

The elimination of the Commission's access channel requirements in *Midwest Video II*, p. 854, *supra*, did not eliminate mandatory access channels. Filling the vacuum were state and municipal requirements. Most cities demanded access channels and studios as a prerequisite for obtaining a cable franchise. Often these demands were more extensive than the FCC's had been.

In the Cable Communications Policy Act of 1984, Congress provided express authorization for access channel requirements. Section 611 states that access channels for public, educational and governmental use ("PEG channels") can be required as part of a franchise proposal or a proposal for renewal. 47 U.S.C.A. § 531. Furthermore, a federal requirement to set aside some channels for commercial use by persons unaffiliated with the operator is imposed on all systems with 36 or more activated channels. The number of channels that must be set aside varies according to the size of the system. 47 U.S.C.A. § 532.

The Court in *Midwest Video II* chose not to address the question of whether mandatory access channels violate the First Amendment. Recall, however, from our discussion of franchising that since then several district courts have addressed this question with inconsistent results. As with other questions involving cable and the First Amendment, the primary problem is determining the appropriate First Amendment standard.

The conflict over access channels has another side—produced by the requirement that the cable operator not censor any access material. More than 1,200 of the nation's 8,000 systems offer some form of public access, and an estimated 40,000 hours of public access programming is produced each week. In cities in which access channels exist, they may be opposed by citizens who are offended by what is presented. Some examples from two channels fully devoted to public access in Austin, Texas, are reported in Schwartz, "Austin Gets an Eyeful: Sacrilege and the Klan," *Channels*, Mar./Apr. 1985, at 42–43: (a) in front of a crucifix "a man in a Charles Manson mask dances and chants incoherently about sex and religion;" (b) a Ku Klux Klan leader interviews a man who had been imprisoned for fire-bombing school buses during Detroit's busing controversy; and (c) a slimy monster comes out of a nearby lake and kills everything in its path in a Halloween program. Some groups wanted to end access, particularly because of the Klan programs.

Apparently, indecency is rarely a problem on the public access channels. "Shows containing nudity are usually more expensive to film and are often shown on other channels, known as leased-access channels, where time is sold for a fee of about $100 a half-hour and commercials are allowed." N.Y. Times, April 13, 1987, at 19. The regulation of indecency is discussed later in this chapter.

Operators of the public access channels are permitted to schedule programs. The Austin channels, for example, extended their hours.

One result was that the group that put the Manson program on was moved from 10:30 p.m. to 1 a.m. In San Francisco, the operators scheduled a Klan program for 3:30 p.m. on Tuesdays and sandwiched it between programs produced by Chinese for Affirmative Action, the Anti–Defamation League, and Jewish Community Relations. S.F. Chron., Dec. 29, 1986, at A6.

Apart from the suits by cable operators seeking to be free of the access requirement, suits are beginning to come from the other direction. In Kansas City, Mo., the Klan failed to get on the access channel. The city had insisted that the franchisee provide an access channel. When the Klan requested access, the operator refused because the show was not locally produced. The Missouri Klan then offered to provide a program featuring interviews with local advocates of white supremacy. The operator agreed to air the show. Before the Klan members could be trained in using the equipment and producing the show, the city council passed legislation converting the channel to a community programming channel under operator control. The operator offered the Klan a guest appearance on a hosted half-hour talk show. The Klan rejected the offer because it had no control over the program. The operator refused to permit the Klan to air its own program.

The ACLU brought suit. One claim was that the city council's action was intended "to suppress the 'racialist' viewpoint" of the Klan. A second argument was that the city, by granting only one cable franchise, had incurred a constitutional obligation to require the operator to provide an access channel. In 1989, the city council reinstated the access channel, and the case was dropped.

### 6. CONTENT REGULATION

#### a. *Political Speech*

Many of the political access rules have also been applied to origination cablecasting. The equal opportunities provision applicable to cable is essentially identical to that which governs broadcasting. There is also an equivalent lowest-unit-rate provision. 47 C.F.R. § 76.205.

The Commission also adopted regulations applying the fairness doctrine, including the personal attack and political editorial rules, to origination cablecasting. 47 C.F.R. § 76.209. In 1983 the Commission instituted proceedings aimed at eliminating the fairness doctrine for cable. As of the end of 1990, no action had been taken in these proceedings.

One political access provision that is not applicable to cable is the reasonable access requirement of § 312(a)(7). In its 1991 political access NPRM, p. 727, *supra*, the FCC proposed extending that requirement to cable. In its final order, p. 727, *supra*, however, the Commission concluded that Congress never intended § 312(a)(7) to apply to cable.

Because the cable operators are not responsible under these rules for secondary transmissions or mandated access channels, and since many of the premium cable channels do not carry any political programming, there have been no real tests of the application of these rules. Also contributing to the lack of cases is the limited size of the audience for many cable programs.

### b. Nonpolitical Speech

Among the restrictions on nonpolitical speech are a prohibition on cablecasting lottery information and a requirement for sponsorship identification. These provisions mirror the broadcasting rules. Also, the ban on cigarette advertising applies to cable.

However, most of the controversy surrounding restrictions on cable programming has involved attempts to ban indecent programs or nudity. For example, in Community Television v. Wilkinson, 611 F.Supp. 1099, 11 Med.L.Rptr. 2217 (D.Utah 1985), the court struck down the Cable Television Programming Decency Act on the grounds that it was unconstitutionally vague and overbroad. The statute authorized the filing of nuisance actions against anyone who continuously and knowingly distributed indecent material over cable television. Material was defined as indecent if it was "presented in a patently offensive way for the time, place and manner, and context in which the material is presented."

The decision was upheld on appeal. The court adopted the lower court's reasoning without adding any of its own. One judge specially concurred to indicate that he felt *Pacifica* should be the standard used in evaluating cable indecency statutes. However, he found the Utah Cable Television Programming Decency Act unconstitutionally vague and overbroad under even the more relaxed *Pacifica* standard. Jones v. Wilkinson, 800 F.2d 989, 61 R.R.2d 1, 13 Med.L.Rptr. 1913 (10th Cir.1986). The Supreme Court summarily affirmed without opinion. 480 U.S. 926 (1987).

The 1984 Cable Act provided that anyone who "transmits over any cable system any matter which is obscene or otherwise unprotected by the Constitution of the United States shall be fined not more than $10,000 or imprisoned not more than two years." 47 U.S.C.A. § 559. Could someone be prosecuted for indecent programming under this statute? As a result of this provision, the Commission eliminated its regulation banning obscene or indecent cable programming. Cable Communications Act Rules, 58 R.R.2d 1 (1985).

The 1992 Act permits cable operators to "enforce prospectively a written and published policy of prohibiting programming that the cable operator reasonably believes describes or depicts sexual or excretory activities or organs in a patently offensive manner as measured by contemporary community standards. Pursuant to the Act, the Commission also promulgated regulations requiring cable operators to place all indecent programming intended for carriage on leased access channels on a single leased access channel. These regulations must also require cable operators to block this channel absent a written request for access from the subscriber. Furthermore, under these regulations, cable programmers will be required to identify indecent programming to cable operators. Finally, the FCC promulgated regulations enabling cable operators to prohibit obscene or sexually explicit material on PEG channels. 47 U.S.C.A. § 532.

In Cable Access Channels (Indecent Programming), 8 F.C.C.Rcd. 998, 71 R.R.2d 1177 (1993), the FCC adopted the required indecency rules for leased access channels. Similarly, in Cable Access Channels (Indecent Programming), 8 F.C.C.Rcd. 2638, 72 R.R.2d 274 (1993), the FCC adopted the required indecency rules for PEG access channels. However, the Court of Appeals struck down both regulations, finding that they violated the First Amendment. Alliance for Community Media v. Federal Communications Commission, 10 F.3d 812 (D.C.Cir.1993) and Action for Childrens Television v. Federal Communications Commission, 11 F.3d 170 (D.C.Cir.1993).

## B. NEW COMMUNICATION TECHNOLOGIES

As we discussed earlier in this chapter, at one time cable was seen as the ultimate communications technology. At the height of the franchising battles, operators were promising that cable would provide everything to everybody. Not only were those promises unfulfilled, but cable is no longer even the "new" technology. A proliferation of new delivery systems such as multi-point distribution service (MDS), direct broadcast satellites (DBS), and satellite master antenna television (SMATV) are fighting for their share of the communications marketplace.

As each of these services has developed, new regulatory questions have arisen. Although a detailed examination of the regulatory framework for each of these services is beyond the scope of this book, we will briefly examine the nature of these services and provide an overview of the regulatory issues raised by their development.

### 1. THE NEW TECHNOLOGIES

*Multipoint Distribution Service.* MDS transmits microwave signals over super high frequencies within a range of about 25 miles. The signal is usually received by master antenna systems or other closed-circuit systems, which convert the signal and show it on a vacant VHF channel. In some urban areas in which cable is not available, MDS has been distributing HBO programming.

In 1983 the FCC reallocated eight of the 28 instructional television fixed service (ITFS) microwave channels to MDS, making multichannel multipoint distribution service (MMDS) available. ITFS (MDS Reallocation), 54 R.R.2d 107 (1983). MMDS operators may also obtain extra channel capacity by leasing an ITFS operator's excess capacity. The maximum number of channels that an MMDS system can currently transmit is 33. However, using digital compression equipment, p. 662, *supra*, expected to be available by late 1994, MMDS systems will be able to offer 300 channels. Broadcasting & Cable, Aug. 2, 1993 at 20.

*Direct Broadcast Satellites.*  DBS is a system of broadcasting directly from studio to home via satellite.  The technology involves the usual transmission to a satellite and the return to earth where the signal is collected by a receiving dish two or three feet in diameter that would be placed on the roof of the home of the subscriber.

The first DBS system began operating in 1983, utilizing medium-powered communications satellites.  United Satellite Communications, Inc. (USCI) began five-channel service to central Indiana.  The consumer response was far less than USCI had envisioned, and the service was discontinued in mid–1985.  The future of DBS is still hard to determine because authorization for high-powered satellites allowing inexpensive receiving equipment was not granted until late 1988.

In 1991 Hughes Aircraft announced that it begin DBS service in 1994.  Hughes, through a newly formed subsidiary, DirecTv, Inc., plans to launch two satellites and use them to transmit hundreds of channels to subscribers.  By mid–1992 no firm program deals had been signed, but the president of DirecTv has indicated that he expects a mix of cable networks, broadcast superstations, sports, movies and narrow interest programming.  Broadcasting, July 27, 1992 at 48.

By July 1993 DirecTv had signed pay-per-view deals with Paramount Pictures, Universal Pay Television and Columbia TriStar International Television.  The 150–channel service is expected to start in early 1994.  Broadcasting & Cable, July 12, 1993 at 34.  Several other companies have announced plans to deliver DBS service, but none of them expect to start before late 1995.  Broadcasting & Cable, Aug. 2, 1993 at 45.

*Satellite Master Antenna Television.*  SMATV involves setting up one or more earth stations on a large building or complex and distributing by wire or cable the various programming received.  Initially, the distinction between SMATV and cable television was that no city streets or rights of way were used.  Subsequently, the FCC decided that SMATV systems serving more than one building would be considered cable systems, even if no public rights of were used.  This definition was upheld in Federal Communications Commission v. Beach Communications, 113 S.Ct. 2096, 21 Med.L.Rptr. 1466 (1993).  The importance of the definition is that cable systems are subject to cable franchising requirements, while SMATV systems are not.  It also limits SMATV systems to large apartments and hotels where sufficient subscribers can be reached.

*Electronic Publishing.*  Electronic Publishing puts pages of information, both text and images, on television sets or other display tubes.  Teletext is a one-way system with signals flowing only from the computer to the screen.  It operates by sending a continuous cycle of information to home television screens during the regular vertical blanking interval of a television signal.  A user chooses the "page" of information he wants from a published index and instructs the receiver terminal to "grab" the page as it goes by.  When the user is finished the page is released from the screen.  Teletext can be delivered by either broadcasting or cable.

Another system, called "videotex," is a two-way system in which the computer holds a much larger data base and the user signals which information he wants to obtain.  The selected pages are then transmitted to the user.  This system requires telephone lines or cable.

*Subsidiary Communications Authorizations.*  In 1983 the Commission authorized radio licensees to use their subcarriers for any purpose they wished.  A subcarrier is a secondary transmission that can be "piggy-backed" on the primary signal.  These subcarriers can only be heard through the use of special receivers.  Under the limited authorization for subcarriers available prior to 1983, broadcasters distributed such services as background music for stores and elevators.  The new expanded authorization allows for such uses as entertainment programming, data transmission and paging.  The Commission also increased the width of the FM baseband from 75 to 99 khz.  This makes two rather than one subcarrier possible for each station.

## 2.  REGULATORY OPTIONS

The FCC does not have complete freedom in developing regulatory frameworks for new technologies.  Rather, the Commission must work within the context of the Communications Act.  Originally, the Act provided two basic models for regulation.  One, the "broadcast" model, we have studied in Chapters XIV–XVII.  The second is the "common-carrier" model to be discussed below.  If a communications technology does not fit either of these models, the authority of the Commission to regulate it is questionable.  This was a major issue in the regulation of cable.  In *Midwest Video I,* p. 854, *supra,* the Commission's jurisdiction over cable was upheld as being ancillary to its jurisdiction over broadcasting.  However, the exact limits of this jurisdiction were never clear, a problem was solved by the Cable Communications Policy Act of 1984.

Common carriers are regulated under Title II of the Communications Act.  The key element of common carrier regulation is that the "content is separated from the conduit."  In other words, unlike broadcasters, common carriers have no editorial discretion.  Instead, they must provide, in a non-discriminatory manner, the facilities for transmission of the customer's message.  National Association of Regulatory Utility Commissioners v. Federal Communications Commission, 525 F.2d 630 (D.C.Cir.1976), cert. denied 425 U.S. 992 (1976).  Telephone and telegraph companies are examples of common carriers.

There are a number of other important distinctions between broadcasters and common carriers.  The federal government has preempted state regulation of broadcasting.  In contrast, common carriers are regulated on both the state and federal levels.  Interstate service is regulated by the Federal Communications Commission, while intrastate service is regulated by state agencies.

Sometimes, however, the Commission will decide to preempt the states and regulate a service on a strictly federal basis, as it did in 1983 with SMATV. When the Commission decides to preempt state regulation it does not necessarily imply that the Commission will choose to regulate to the same extent. Instead, the FCC may choose to "preempt and forbear." This means that the Commission will eliminate the state regulations without substituting any of its own because the Commission believes as a matter of policy that no regulation is the proper regulation for that area.

The regulations most commonly subject to preemption are entry requirements and rate regulation. When a common carrier wishes to provide a service, it is usually required to demonstrate a need for the service. Some states require that, in addition to showing need, an applicant demonstrate that current carriers are either unable to or unwilling to provide the additional needed service. These requirements can effectively bar any new entrants into a given type of service. Such artificial entry barriers present a special problem when the Commission authorizes new technologies to offer services already provided by existing carriers. It was for this reason that in 1984 the Commission preempted entry requirements for SCAs. FM Subsidiary Communications Authorizations, 55 R.R.2d 1607 (1984).

On appeal, the Commission's preemption order was reversed. The court of appeals held that the order went beyond the scope of the Commission's jurisdiction. The mere fact that state regulation might limit entry of FCC licensees was not viewed by the court as sufficient to justify FCC intervention. People of State of California v. Federal Communications Commission, 798 F.2d 1515, 60 R.R.2d 1720 (D.C.Cir. 1986).

Because common carriers often enjoy either a natural or government-created monopoly, they are often subject to rate regulation by either the FCC or appropriate state agencies. Rate regulation is usually eliminated when there is a finding of sufficient effective competition in the services provided.

Traditionally, the Commission assigned services to the two regulatory models based on the method of transmission. Thus, all broadcasting was under the broadcast model while MDS was common carrier. This led to seemingly anomalous results. For example, an STV channel that leased its facilities to a movie service would be subject to different regulations than an MDS channel leasing its facilities to the same movie service. In fact, a third regulatory scheme would obtain when the same movie service was carried over cable. Although many of these anomalies still exist, the Commission has started to take a new approach, imposing regulations based on the service provided as opposed to the method of transmission. In the case of SCAs and DBS, the Commission left the initial choice of regulatory model up to the licensee. In other words, licensees could decide for themselves which regulatory model would be most appropriate for the type of service they wished to offer. That portion of the DBS ruling was struck down, however, on appeal.  The court determined that DBS should be regulated under the broadcast model.  National Association of Broadcasters v. Federal Communications Commission, 740 F.2d 1190, 56 R.R.2d 1105 (D.C.Cir.1984).

In 1987 the Commission changed its regulations to permit MDS operators to choose the regulatory model to be used for them based on the service provided.  47 C.F.R. §§ 21.900–21.908.  The reason for the change was the Commission's recognition that MDS was often being used to deliver broadcast-type services.  This was especially true of MMDS.

Concerned that the decision in *NAB* would apply to other common carrier services, including MMDS, the Commission decided to reexamine its method of classifying STV and other subscription video programming services.  In Subscription Video, 2 F.C.C.Rcd. 1001, 62 R.R.2d 389 (1987), the FCC changed from a content-based approach to service classification, known as the *"Functional Music* test," to an intent-based approach.

The Commission based the change on the language of the Communications Act of 1934.  "The [Act] defines 'broadcasting' as the 'dissemination of radio communications intended to be received by the public, directly or by the intermediary of relay stations.' 47 U.S.C. § 153(*o*). Thus, the words of the statute clearly indicate that broadcast classification turns on the *intent* of the purveyor of radio communications that its service be received by the public."

Arguing that the intent of subscription service purveyors is to limit access to their signals, the Commission concluded that subscription services could not be classified as broadcasting.  The Commission cited the need for special reception equipment and/or decoders to receive the service and the private contractual relationship between purveyors of subscription programming and their audiences as "indicia of an intent that the communications service not be received by the public."

By reclassifying subscription services as non-broadcast services, the Commission removed them from the application of various broadcast rules, including § 315, § 312(a)(7), and the fairness doctrine.

The court of appeals upheld the change, 2–1.  The majority found that the Communication Act definition of "broadcasting" was sufficiently ambiguous as to allow the Commission's interpretation.  It also found that apparent inconsistency between the Commission's decision and *NAB* did not make the decision arbitrary and capricious, because the FCC had conducted a properly noticed rulemaking and supplied a reasoned explanation for the change in its approach.  National Association for Better Broadcasting v. Federal Communications Commission, 849 F.2d 665, 64 R.R.2d 1570 (D.C.Cir.1988).

Chief Judge Wald dissented, arguing that the legislative history of the Act makes it clear that services such as the ones at issue were intended to be treated as "broadcasting."  She quoted former Commissioner Rivera: "It looks like broadcasting, smells like broadcasting, tastes like broadcasting, has all the benefits of broadcasting, but it's not regulated like broadcasting?" Many of her concerns echoed those of the court in *NAB*. For example, the absence of reasonable access and equal opportunities in her view invites unfair political propagandizing.

Meanwhile, a court of appeals' decision involving teletext has given the Commission some flexibility with regard to new technologies regulated under the broadcast model. *TRAC*, p. 646, *supra*. As we discussed in Chapter XVI, the most significant aspect of the decision was the court of appeals' determination that the fairness doctrine was not codified by the 1959 amendments to § 315 of the Communications Act. In addition, the court upheld the Commission's decision not to apply § 312(a)(7) to teletext. However, the court found that the Commission had no authority to exempt teletext from the application of § 315.

Obviously, the flood of new communications technologies has presented the FCC with serious problems as it tries to fit them into the traditional regulatory models. Much of this area is in flux, and it will undoubtedly be some time before the law can catch up with the technology. There is also now the question of the impact of *Preferred Communications* and subsequent cable cases on other communications technologies besides cable. If nothing else, the next few years should prove interesting.

*

# APPENDICES

## Appendix A

# THE CONSTITUTION OF THE UNITED STATES OF AMERICA

We the People of the United States, in Order to form a more perfect Union, establish Justice, insure domestic Tranquility, provide for the common defence, promote the general Welfare, and secure the Blessings of Liberty to ourselves and our Posterity, do ordain and establish this Constitution for the United States of America.

## ARTICLE I.

SECTION 1. All legislative Powers herein granted shall be vested in a Congress of the United States, which shall consist of a Senate and House of Representatives.

SECTION 2. The House of Representatives shall be composed of Members chosen every second Year by the People of the several States, and the Electors in each State shall have the Qualifications requisite for Electors of the most numerous Branch of the State Legislature.

No Person shall be a Representative who shall not have attained to the Age of twenty five Years, and been seven Years a Citizen of the United States, and who shall not, when elected, be an inhabitant of that State in which he shall be chosen.

Representatives and direct Taxes shall be apportioned among the several States which may be included within this Union, according to their respective Numbers, which shall be determined by adding to the whole Number of free Persons, including those bound to Service for a Term of Years, and excluding Indians not taxed, three fifths of all other Persons. The actual Enumeration shall be made within three Years after the first Meeting of the Congress of the United States, and within every subsequent Term of ten Years, in such Manner as they shall by Law direct. The Number of Representatives shall not exceed one for every thirty Thousand, but each State shall have at Least one Representative; and until such enumeration shall be made, the State of New Hampshire shall be entitled to chuse three, Massachusetts eight, Rhode Island and Providence Plantations one, Connecticut five, New York six, New Jersey four, Pennsylvania eight, Delaware one, Maryland six, Virginia ten, North Carolina five, South Carolina five, and Georgia three.

When vacancies happen in the Representation from any State, the Executive Authority thereof shall issue Writs of Election to fill such Vacancies.

The House of Representatives shall chuse their Speaker and other Officers; and shall have the sole Power of Impeachment.

SECTION 3. The Senate of the United States shall be composed of two Senators from each State, chosen by the Legislature thereof, for six Years; and each Senator shall have one Vote.

Immediately after they shall be assembled in Consequence of the first Election, they shall be divided as equally as may be into three Classes. The Seats of the Senators of the first Class shall be vacated at the Expiration of the second Year, of the second Class at the Expiration of the fourth Year, and of the third Class at the Expiration of the sixth Year, so that one third may be chosen every second Year; and if Vacancies happen by Resignation, or otherwise, during the Recess of the Legislature of any State, the Executive thereof may make temporary Appointments until the next Meeting of the Legislature, which shall then fill such Vacancies.

No Person shall be a Senator who shall not have attained to the Age of thirty Years, and been nine Years a Citizen of the United States, and who shall not, when elected, be an Inhabitant of that State for which he shall be chosen.

The Vice President of the United States shall be President of the Senate, but shall have no Vote, unless they be equally divided.

The Senate shall chuse their other Officers, and also a President pro tempore, in the Absence of the Vice President, or when he shall exercise the Office of President of the United States.

The Senate shall have the sole Power to try all Impeachments. When sitting for that Purpose, they shall be on Oath or Affirmation. When the President of the United States is tried the Chief Justice shall preside: And no Person shall be convicted without the Concurrence of two thirds of the Members present.

Judgment in Cases of Impeachment shall not extend further than to removal from Office, and disqualification to hold and enjoy any Office of honor, Trust, or Profit under the United States: but the Party convicted shall nevertheless be liable and subject to Indictment, Trial, Judgment, and Punishment, according to Law.

SECTION 4. The Times, Places and Manner of holding Elections for Senators and Representatives, shall be prescribed in each State by the Legislature thereof; but the Congress may at any time by Law make or alter such Regulations, except as to the Places of chusing Senators.

The Congress shall assemble at least once in every Year, and such Meeting shall be on the first Monday in December, unless they shall by Law appoint a different Day.

SECTION 5.  Each House shall be the Judge of the Elections, Returns, and Qualifications of its own Members, and a Majority of each shall constitute a Quorum to do Business; but a smaller Number may adjourn from day to day, and may be authorized to compel the Attendance of absent Members, in such Manner, and under such Penalties as each House may provide.

Each House may determine the Rules of its Proceedings, punish its Members for disorderly Behaviour, and, with the Concurrence of two thirds, expel a Member.

Each House shall keep a Journal of its Proceedings, and from time to time publish the same, excepting such Parts as may in their Judgment require Secrecy; and the Yeas and Nays of the Members of either House on any question shall, at the Desire of one fifth of those Present, be entered on the Journal.

Neither House, during the Session of Congress, shall, without the Consent of the other, adjourn for more than three days, nor to any other Place than that in which the two Houses shall be sitting.

SECTION 6.  The Senators and Representatives shall receive a Compensation for their Services, to be ascertained by Law, and paid out of the Treasury of the United States.  They shall in all Cases, except Treason, Felony and Breach of the Peace, be privileged from Arrest during their Attendance at the Session of their respective Houses, and in going to and returning from the same; and for any Speech or Debate in either House, they shall not be questioned in any other Place.

No Senator or Representative shall, during the Time for which he was elected, be appointed to any civil Office under the Authority of the United States, which shall have been created, or the Emoluments whereof shall have been encreased during such time; and no Person holding any Office under the United States, shall be a Member of either House during his Continuance in Office.

SECTION 7.  All Bills for raising Revenue shall originate in the House of Representatives; but the Senate may propose or concur with amendments as on other Bills.

Every Bill which shall have passed the House of Representatives and the Senate, shall, before it becomes a Law, be presented to the President of the United States; If he approve he shall sign it, but if not he shall return it, with his Objections to that House in which it shall have originated, who shall enter the Objections at large on their Journal, and proceed to reconsider it.  If after such Reconsideration two thirds of that House shall agree to pass the Bill, it shall be sent, together with the Objections, to the other House, by which it shall likewise be reconsidered, and if approved by two thirds of that House, it shall become a Law.  But in all such Cases the Votes of both Houses shall be determined by Yeas and Nays, and the Names of the Persons voting for and against the Bill shall be entered on the Journal of each House respectively.  If any Bill shall not be returned by the President within ten Days (Sunday excepted) after it shall have been presented to him, the Same shall be a Law, in like Manner as if he had signed it, unless the Congress by their Adjournment prevent its Return, in which Case it shall not be a Law.

Every Order, Resolution, or Vote to which the Concurrence of the Senate and House of Representatives may be necessary (except on a question of Adjournment) shall be presented to the President of the United States; and before the Same shall take Effect, shall be approved by him, or being disapproved by him, shall be repassed by two thirds of the Senate and House of Representatives, according to the Rules and Limitations prescribed in the Case of a Bill.

SECTION 8. The Congress shall have Power To lay and collect Taxes, Duties, Imposts and Excises, to pay the Debts and provide for the common Defence and general Welfare of the United States; but all Duties, Imposts and Excises shall be uniform throughout the United States;

To borrow Money on the credit of the United States;

To regulate Commerce with foreign Nations, and among the several States, and with the Indian Tribes;

To establish an uniform Rule of Naturalization, and uniform Laws on the subject of Bankruptcies throughout the United States;

To coin Money, regulate the Value thereof, and of foreign Coin, and fix the Standard of Weights and Measures;

To provide for the Punishment of counterfeiting the Securities and current Coin of the United States;

To establish Post Offices and post Roads;

To promote the Progress of Science and useful Arts, by securing for limited Times to Authors and Inventors the exclusive Right to their respective Writings and Discoveries;

To constitute Tribunals inferior to the supreme Court;

To define and punish Piracies and Felonies committed on the high Seas, and Offences against the Law of Nations;

To declare War, grant Letters of Marque and Reprisal, and make Rules concerning Captures on Land and Water;

To raise and support Armies, but no Appropriation of Money to that Use shall be for a longer Term than two Years;

To provide and maintain a Navy;

To make Rules for the Government and Regulation of the land and naval Forces;

To provide for calling forth the Militia to execute the Laws of the Union, suppress Insurrections and repel Invasions;

To provide for organizing, arming, and disciplining, the Militia, and for governing such Part of them as may be employed in the Service of the United States, reserving to the States respectively, the Appointment of the Officers, and the Authority of training the Militia according to the discipline prescribed by Congress;

To exercise exclusive Legislation in all Cases whatsoever, over such District (not exceeding ten Miles square) as may, by Cession of particular States, and the Acceptance of Congress, become the Seat of the Government of the United States, and to exercise like Authority over all Places purchased by the Consent of the Legislature of the State in which the Same shall be, for the Erection of Forts, Magazines, Arsenals, dock-Yards, and other needful Buildings;—And

To make all Laws which shall be necessary and proper for carrying into Execution the foregoing Powers, and all other Powers vested by this Constitution in the Government of the United States, or in any Department or Officer thereof.

SECTION 9.   The Migration or Importation of such Persons as any of the States now existing shall think proper to admit, shall not be prohibited by the Congress prior to the Year one thousand eight hundred and eight, but a Tax or duty may be imposed on such Importation, not exceeding ten dollars for each Person.

The Privilege of the Writ of Habeas Corpus shall not be suspended, unless when in Cases of Rebellion or Invasion the public Safety may require it.

No Bill of Attainder or ex post facto Law shall be passed.

No Capitation, or other direct, Tax shall be laid, unless in Proportion to the Census or Enumeration herein before directed to be taken.

No Tax or Duty shall be laid on Articles exported from any State.

No Preference shall be given by any Regulation of Commerce or Revenue to the Ports of one State over those of another; nor shall Vessels bound to, or from, one State, be obliged to enter, clear, or pay Duties in another.

No Money shall be drawn from the Treasury, but in Consequence of Appropriations made by Law; and a regular Statement and Account of the Receipts and Expenditures of all public Money shall be published from time to time.

No Title of Nobility shall be granted by the United States: And no Person holding any Office of Profit or Trust under them, shall, without the Consent of the Congress, accept of any present, Emolument, Office, or Title, of any kind whatever, from any King, Prince or foreign State.

SECTION 10.   No State shall enter into any Treaty, Alliance, or Confederation; grant Letters of Marque and Reprisal; coin Money; emit Bills of Credit; make any Thing but gold and silver Coin a Tender in Payment of Debts; pass any Bill of Attainder, ex post facto Law, or Law impairing the Obligation of Contracts, or grant any Title of Nobility.

No State shall, without the Consent of the Congress, lay any Imposts or Duties on Imports or Exports, except what may be absolutely necessary for executing its inspection Laws: and the net Produce of all

Duties and Imposts, laid by any State on Imports or Exports, shall be for the Use of the Treasury of the United States; and all such Laws shall be subject to the Revision and Controul of the Congress.

No State shall, without the Consent of Congress, lay any Duty of Tonnage, keep Troops, or Ships of War in time of Peace, enter into any Agreement or Compact with another State, or with a foreign Power, or engage in War, unless actually invaded, or in such imminent Danger as will not admit of delay.

## ARTICLE II.

SECTION 1.   The executive Power shall be vested in a President of the United States of America.   He shall hold his Office during the Term of four Years, and, together with the Vice President, chosen for the same Term, be elected, as follows

Each State shall appoint, in such Manner as the Legislature thereof may direct, a Number of Electors, equal to the whole Number of Senators and Representatives to which the State may be entitled in the Congress: but no Senator or Representative, or Person holding an Office of Trust or Profit under the United States, shall be appointed an Elector.

The Electors shall meet in their respective States, and vote by Ballot for two Persons, of whom one at least shall not be an Inhabitant of the same State with themselves.   And they shall make a List of all the Persons voted for, and of the Number of Votes for each; which List they shall sign and certify, and transmit sealed to the Seat of the Government of the United States, directed to the President of the Senate.   The President of the Senate shall, in the Presence of the Senate and House of Representatives, open all the Certificates, and the Votes shall then be counted.   The Person having the greatest Number of Votes shall be the President, if such Number be a Majority of the whole Number of Electors appointed;   and if there be more than one who have such Majority, and have an equal Number of Votes, then the House of Representatives shall immediately chuse by Ballot one of them for President;   and if no Person have a Majority, then from the five highest on the List the said House shall in like Manner chuse the President. But in chusing the President, the Votes shall be taken by States, the Representation from each State having one Vote;   a quorum for this Purpose shall consist of a Member or Members from two thirds of the States, and a Majority of all the States shall be necessary to a Choice.   In every Case, after the Choice of the President, the Person having the greatest Number of Votes of the Electors shall be the Vice President. But if there should remain two or more who have equal Votes, the Senate shall chuse from them by Ballot the Vice President.

The Congress may determine the Time of chusing the Electors, and the Day on which they shall give their Votes;   which Day shall be the same throughout the United States.

No Person except a natural born Citizen, or a Citizen of the United States, at the time of the Adoption of this Constitution, shall be eligible to the Office of President; neither shall any Person be eligible to that Office who shall not have attained to the Age of thirty five Years, and been fourteen Years a Resident within the United States.

In Case of the Removal of the President from Office, or of his Death, Resignation, or Inability to discharge the Powers and Duties of the said Office, the Same shall devolve on the Vice President, and the Congress may by Law provide for the Case of Removal, Death, Resignation or Inability, both of the President and Vice President, declaring what Officer shall then act as President, and such Officer shall act accordingly, until the Disability be removed, or a President shall be elected.

The President shall, at stated Times, receive for his Services, a Compensation, which shall neither be encreased nor diminished during the Period for which he shall have been elected, and he shall not receive within that Period any other Emolument from the United States, or any of them.

Before he enter on the Execution of his Office, he shall take the following Oath or Affirmation:—"I do solemnly swear (or affirm) that I will faithfully execute the Office of President of the United States, and will to the best of my Ability, preserve, protect and defend the Constitution of the United States."

SECTION 2. The President shall be Commander in Chief of the Army and Navy of the United States, and of the Militia of the several States, when called into the actual Service of the United States; he may require the Opinion, in writing, of the principal Officer in each of the executive Departments, upon any Subject relating to the Duties of their respective Offices, and he shall have Power to grant Reprieves and Pardons for Offences against the United States, except in Cases of Impeachment.

He shall have Power, by and with the Advice and Consent of the Senate, to make Treaties, provided two thirds of the Senators present concur; and he shall nominate, and by and with the Advice and Consent of the Senate, shall appoint Ambassadors, other public Ministers and Consuls, Judges of the supreme Court, and all other Officers of the United States, whose Appointments are not herein otherwise provided for, and which shall be established by Law: but the Congress may by Law vest the Appointment of such inferior Officers, as they think proper, in the President alone, in the Courts of Law, or in the Heads of Departments.

The President shall have Power to fill up all Vacancies that may happen during the Recess of the Senate, by granting Commissions which shall expire at the End of their next Session.

SECTION 3. He shall from time to time give to the Congress Information of the State of the Union, and recommend to their Consideration such Measures as he shall judge necessary and expedient; he may, on extraordinary Occasions, convene both Houses, or either of them, and in Case of Disagreement between them, with Respect to the Time of

Adjournment, he may adjourn them to such Time as he shall think proper; he shall receive Ambassadors and other public Ministers; he shall take Care that the Laws be faithfully executed, and shall Commission all the Officers of the United States.

SECTION 4.   The President, Vice President and all civil Officers of the United States, shall be removed from Office on Impeachment for, and Conviction of, Treason, Bribery, or other high Crimes and Misdemeanors.

## ARTICLE III.

SECTION 1.   The judicial Power of the United States, shall be vested in one supreme Court, and in such inferior Courts as the Congress may from time to time ordain and establish.  The Judges, both of the supreme and inferior Courts, shall hold their Offices during good Behaviour, and shall, at stated Times, receive for their Services, a Compensation, which shall not be diminished during their Continuance in Office.

SECTION 2.   The judicial Power shall extend to all Cases, in Law and Equity, arising under this Constitution, the Laws of the United States, and Treaties made, or which shall be made, under their Authority;—to all Cases affecting Ambassadors, other public Ministers and Consuls;—to all Cases of admiralty and maritime Jurisdiction;—to Controversies to which the United States shall be a Party;—to Controversies between two or more States;—between a State and Citizens of another State;—between Citizens of different States;—between Citizens of the same State claiming Lands under Grants of different States, and between a State, or the Citizens thereof, and foreign States, Citizens or Subjects.

In all Cases affecting Ambassadors, other public Ministers and Consuls, and those in which a State shall be Party, the supreme Court shall have original Jurisdiction.  In all the other Cases before mentioned, the supreme Court shall have appellate Jurisdiction, both as to Law and Fact, with such Exceptions, and under such Regulations as the Congress shall make.

The Trial of all Crimes, except in Cases of Impeachment, shall be by Jury; and such Trial shall be held in the State where the said Crimes shall have been committed; but when not committed within any State, the Trial shall be at such Place or Places as the Congress may by Law have directed.

SECTION 3.   Treason against the United States, shall consist only in levying War against them, or in adhering to their Enemies, giving them Aid and Comfort.  No Person shall be convicted of Treason unless on the Testimony of two Witnesses to the same overt Act, or on Confession in open Court.

The Congress shall have Power to declare the Punishment of Treason, but no Attainder of Treason shall work Corruption of Blood, or Forfeiture except during the Life of the Person attainted.

## ARTICLE IV.

SECTION 1.   Full Faith and Credit shall be given in each State to the public Acts, Records, and judicial Proceedings of every other State. And the Congress may by general Laws prescribe the Manner in which such Acts, Records and Proceedings shall be proved, and the Effect thereof.

SECTION 2.   The Citizens of each State shall be entitled to all Privileges and Immunities of Citizens in the several States.

A Person charged in any State with Treason, Felony, or other Crime, who shall flee from Justice, and be found in another State, shall on Demand of the executive Authority of the State from which he fled, be delivered up, to be removed to the State having Jurisdiction of the Crime.

No Person held to Service or Labour in one State, under the Laws thereof, escaping into another, shall, in Consequence of any Law or Regulation therein, be discharged from such Service or Labour, but shall be delivered up on Claim of the Party to whom such Service or Labour may be due.

SECTION 3.   New States may be admitted by the Congress into this Union; but no new State shall be formed or erected within the Jurisdiction of any other State; nor any State be formed by the Junction of two or more States, or Parts of States, without the Consent of the Legislatures of the States concerned as well as of the Congress.

The Congress shall have Power to dispose of and make all needful Rules and Regulations respecting the Territory or other Property belonging to the United States; and nothing in this Constitution shall be so construed as to Prejudice any Claims of the United States, or of any particular State.

SECTION 4.   The United States shall guarantee to every State in this Union a Republican Form of Government, and shall protect each of them against Invasion; and on Application of the Legislature, or of the Executive (when the Legislature cannot be convened) against domestic Violence.

## ARTICLE V.

The Congress, whenever two thirds of both Houses shall deem it necessary, shall propose Amendments to this Constitution, or, on the Application of the Legislature of two thirds of the several States, shall call a Convention for proposing Amendments, which, in either Case, shall be valid to all Intents and Purposes, as Part of this Constitution, when ratified by the Legislatures of three fourths of the several States, or by Conventions in three fourths thereof, as the one or the other Mode of Ratification may be proposed by the Congress; Provided that no Amendment which may be made prior to the Year One thousand eight hundred and eight shall in any Manner affect the first and fourth

Clauses in the Ninth Section of the first Article; and that no State, without its Consent, shall be deprived of its equal Suffrage in the Senate.

## ARTICLE VI.

All Debts contracted and Engagements entered into, before the Adoption of this Constitution, shall be as valid against the United States under this Constitution, as under the Confederation.

This Constitution, and the Laws of the United States which shall be made in Pursuance thereof; and all Treaties made, or which shall be made, under the Authority of the United States, shall be the supreme Law of the Land; and the Judges in every State shall be bound thereby, any Thing in the Constitution or Laws of any State to the Contrary notwithstanding.

The Senators and Representatives before mentioned, and the Members of the several State Legislatures, and all executive and judicial Officers, both of the United States and of the several States, shall be bound by Oath or Affirmation, to support this Constitution; but no religious Test shall ever be required as a Qualification to any Office or public Trust under the United States.

## ARTICLE VII.

The Ratification of the Conventions of nine States, shall be sufficient for the establishment of this Constitution between the States so ratifying the Same.

. . .

## ARTICLES IN ADDITION TO, AND AMENDMENTS OF, THE CONSTITUTION OF THE UNITED STATES OF AMERICA, PROPOSED BY CONGRESS, AND RATIFIED BY THE SEVERAL STATES, PURSUANT TO THE FIFTH ARTICLE OF THE ORIGINAL CONSTITUTION.

### AMENDMENT I [1791]

Congress shall make no law respecting an establishment of religion, or prohibiting the free exercise thereof; or abridging the freedom of speech, or of the press; or the right of the people peaceably to assemble, and to petition the Government for a redress of grievances.

### AMENDMENT II [1791]

A well regulated Militia, being necessary to the security of a free State, the right of the people to keep and bear Arms, shall not be infringed.

### AMENDMENT III [1791]

No Soldier shall, in time of peace be quartered in any house, without the consent of the Owner, nor in time of war, but in a manner to be prescribed by law.

### AMENDMENT IV [1791]

The right of the people to be secure in their persons, houses, papers, and effects, against unreasonable searches and seizures, shall not be violated, and no Warrants shall issue, but upon probable cause, supported by Oath or affirmation, and particularly describing the place to be searched, and the persons or things to be seized.

### AMENDMENT V [1791]

No person shall be held to answer for a capital, or otherwise infamous crime, unless on a presentment or indictment of a Grand Jury, except in cases arising in the land or naval forces, or in the Militia, when in actual service in time of War or public danger; nor shall any person be subject for the same offence to be twice put in jeopardy of life or limb; nor shall be compelled in any criminal case to be a witness against himself, nor be deprived of life, liberty, or property, without due process of law; nor shall private property be taken for public use, without just compensation.

### AMENDMENT VI [1791]

In all criminal prosecutions, the accused shall enjoy the right to a speedy and public trial, by an impartial jury of the State and district wherein the crime shall have been committed, which district shall have been previously ascertained by law, and to be informed of the nature and cause of the accusation; to be confronted with the witnesses against him; to have compulsory process for obtaining Witnesses in his favor, and to have the Assistance of Counsel for his defence.

### AMENDMENT VII [1791]

In Suits at common law, where the value in controversy shall exceed twenty dollars, the right of trial by jury shall be preserved, and no fact tried by a jury be otherwise re-examined in any Court of the United States, than according to the rules of the common law.

### AMENDMENT VIII [1791]

Excessive bail shall not be required, nor excessive fines imposed, nor cruel and unusual punishments inflicted.

### AMENDMENT IX [1791]

The enumeration in the Constitution, of certain rights, shall not be construed to deny or disparage others retained by the people.

### AMENDMENT X [1791]

The powers not delegated to the United States by the Constitution, nor prohibited by it to the States, are reserved to the States respectively, or to the people.

### AMENDMENT XI [1798]

The Judicial power of the United States shall not be construed to extend to any suit in law or equity, commenced or prosecuted against one of the United States by Citizens of another State, or by Citizens or Subjects of any Foreign State.

## AMENDMENT XII [1804]

The Electors shall meet in their respective states and vote by ballot for President and Vice-President, one of whom, at least, shall not be an inhabitant of the same state with themselves; they shall name in their ballots the person voted for as President, and in distinct ballots the person voted for as Vice-President, and they shall make distinct lists of all persons voted for as President, and of all persons voted for as Vice-President, and of the number of votes for each, which lists they shall sign and certify, and transmit sealed to the seat of the government of the United States, directed to the President of the Senate;—The President of the Senate shall, in the presence of the Senate and House of Representatives, open all the certificates and the votes shall then be counted;—The person having the greatest number of votes for President, shall be the President, if such number be a majority of the whole number of Electors appointed; and if no person have such majority, then from the persons having the highest numbers not exceeding three on the list of those voted for as President, the House of Representatives shall choose immediately, by ballot, the President. But in choosing the President, the votes shall be taken by states, the representation from each state having one vote; a quorum for this purpose shall consist of a member or members from two-thirds of the states, and a majority of all the states shall be necessary to a choice. And if the House of Representatives shall not choose a President whenever the right of choice shall devolve upon them, before the fourth day of March next following, then the Vice-President shall act as President, as in the case of the death or other constitutional disability of the President—The person having the greatest number of votes as Vice-President, shall be the Vice-President, if such number be a majority of the whole number of Electors appointed, and if no person have a majority, then from the two highest numbers on the list, the Senate shall choose the Vice-President; a quorum for the purpose shall consist of two-thirds of the whole number of Senators, and a majority of the whole number shall be necessary to a choice. But no person constitutionally ineligible to the office of President shall be eligible to that of Vice-President of the United States.

## AMENDMENT XIII [1865]

SECTION 1. Neither slavery nor involuntary servitude, except as a punishment for crime whereof the party shall have been duly convicted, shall exist within the United States, or any place subject to their jurisdiction.

SECTION 2. Congress shall have power to enforce this article by appropriate legislation.

## AMENDMENT XIV [1868]

SECTION 1. All persons born or naturalized in the United States and subject to the jurisdiction thereof, are citizens of the United States and of the State wherein they reside. No State shall make or enforce any law which shall abridge the privileges or immunities of citizens of the United States; nor shall any State deprive any person of life, liberty, or property, without due process of law; nor deny to any person within its jurisdiction the equal protection of the laws.

SECTION 2. Representatives shall be apportioned among the several States according to their respective numbers, counting the whole number of persons in each State, excluding Indians not taxed. But when the right to vote at any election for the choice of electors for President and Vice President of the United States, Representatives in Congress, the Executive and Judicial officers of a State, or the members of the Legislature thereof, is denied to any of the male inhabitants of such State, being twenty-one years of age, and citizens of the United States, or in any way abridged, except for participation in rebellion, or other crime, the basis of representation therein shall be reduced in the proportion which the number of such male citizens shall bear to the whole number of male citizens twenty-one years of age in such State.

SECTION 3. No person shall be a Senator or Representative in Congress, or elector of President and Vice President, or hold any office, civil or military, under the United States, or under any State, who, having previously taken an oath, as a member of Congress, or as a member of any State legislature, or as an executive or judicial officer of any State, to support the Constitution of the United States, shall have engaged in insurrection or rebellion against the same, or given aid or comfort to the enemies thereof. But Congress may by a vote of two-thirds of each House, remove such disability.

SECTION 4. The validity of the public debt of the United States, authorized by law, including debts incurred for payment of pensions and bounties for services in suppressing insurrection or rebellion, shall not be questioned. But neither the United States nor any State shall assume or pay any debt or obligation incurred in aid of insurrection or rebellion against the United States, or any claim for the loss or emancipation of any slave; but all such debts, obligations and claims shall be held illegal and void.

SECTION 5. The Congress shall have power to enforce, by appropriate legislation, the provisions of this article.

## AMENDMENT XV [1870]

SECTION 1. The right of citizens of the United States to vote shall not be denied or abridged by the United States or by any State on account of race, color, or previous condition of servitude.

SECTION 2. The Congress shall have power to enforce this article by appropriate legislation.

## AMENDMENT XVI [1913]

The Congress shall have power to lay and collect taxes on incomes, from whatever source derived, without apportionment among the several States, and without regard to any census or enumeration.

## AMENDMENT XVII [1913]

The Senate of the United States shall be composed of two Senators from each State, elected by the people thereof, for six years; and each Senator shall have one vote. The electors in each State shall have the qualifications requisite for electors of the most numerous branch of the State legislatures.

When vacancies happen in the representation of any State in the Senate, the executive authority of such State shall issue writs of election to fill such vacancies: *Provided,* That the legislature of any State may empower the executive thereof to make temporary appointments until the people fill the vacancies by election as the legislature may direct.

This amendment shall not be so construed as to affect the election or term of any Senator chosen before it becomes valid as part of the Constitution.

## AMENDMENT XVIII [1919]

SECTION 1.  After one year from the ratification of this article the manufacture, sale, or transportation of intoxicating liquors within, the importation thereof into, or the exportation thereof from the United States and all territory subject to the jurisdiction thereof for beverage purposes is hereby prohibited.

SECTION 2.  The Congress and the several States shall have concurrent power to enforce this article by appropriate legislation.

SECTION 3.  This article shall be inoperative unless it shall have been ratified as an amendment to the Constitution by the legislatures of the several States, as provided in the Constitution, within seven years from the date of the submission hereof to the States by the Congress.

## AMENDMENT XIX [1920]

The right of citizens of the United States to vote shall not be denied or abridged by the United States or by any State on account of sex.

Congress shall have power to enforce this article by appropriate legislation.

## AMENDMENT XX [1933]

SECTION 1.  The terms of the President and Vice President shall end at noon on the 20th day of January, and the terms of Senators and Representatives at noon on the 3d day of January, of the years in which such terms would have ended if this article had not been ratified; and the terms of their successors shall then begin.

SECTION 2.  The Congress shall assemble at least once in every year, and such meeting shall begin at noon on the 3d day of January, unless they shall by law appoint a different day.

SECTION 3.  If, at the time fixed for the beginning of the term of the President, the President elect shall have died, the Vice President elect shall become President.  If a President shall not have been chosen before the time fixed for the beginning of his term, or if the President elect shall have failed to qualify, then the Vice President elect shall act as President until a President shall have qualified; and the Congress may by law provide for the case wherein neither a President elect nor a Vice President elect shall have qualified, declaring who shall then act as President, or the manner in which one who is to act shall be selected, and such person shall act accordingly until a President or Vice President shall have qualified.

SECTION 4.  The Congress may by law provide for the case of the death of any of the persons from whom the House of Representatives may choose a President whenever the right of choice shall have devolved upon them, and for the case of the death of any of the persons from whom the Senate may choose a Vice President whenever the right of choice shall have devolved upon them.

SECTION 5.  Sections 1 and 2 shall take effect on the 15th day of October following the ratification of this article.

SECTION 6.  This article shall be inoperative unless it shall have been ratified as an amendment to the Constitution by the legislatures of three-fourths of the several States within seven years from the date of its submission.

## AMENDMENT XXI [1933]

SECTION 1.  The eighteenth article of amendment to the Constitution of the United States is hereby repealed.

SECTION 2.  The transportation or importation into any State, Territory, or possession of the United States for delivery or use therein of intoxicating liquors, in violation of the laws thereof, is hereby prohibited.

SECTION 3.  This article shall be inoperative unless it shall have been ratified as an amendment to the Constitution by conventions in the several States, as provided in the Constitution, within seven years from the date of the submission hereof to the States by the Congress.

## AMENDMENT XXII [1951]

SECTION 1.  No person shall be elected to the office of the President more than twice, and no person who has held the office of President, or acted as President, for more than two years of a term to which some other person was elected President shall be elected to the office of the President more than once.  But this Article shall not apply to any person holding the office of President when this Article was proposed by the Congress, and shall not prevent any person who may be holding the office of President, or acting as President, during the term within which this Article becomes operative from holding the office of President or acting as President during the remainder of such term.

SECTION 2.  This article shall be inoperative unless it shall have been ratified as an amendment to the Constitution by the legislatures of three-fourths of the several States within seven years from the date of its submission to the States by the Congress.

## AMENDMENT XXIII [1961]

SECTION 1. The District constituting the seat of Government of the United States shall appoint in such manner as the Congress may direct:

A number of electors of President and Vice President equal to the whole number of Senators and Representatives in Congress to which the District would be entitled if it were a State, but in no event more than the least populous State; they shall be in addition to those appointed by the States, but they shall be considered, for the purposes of the election of President and Vice President, to be electors appointed by a State; and they shall meet in the District and perform such duties as provided by the twelfth article of amendment.

SECTION 2. The Congress shall have power to enforce this article by appropriate legislation.

## AMENDMENT XXIV [1964]

SECTION 1. The right of citizens of the United States to vote in any primary or other election for President or Vice President, for electors for President or Vice President, or for Senator or Representative in Congress, shall not be denied or abridged by the United States or any State by reason of failure to pay any poll or other tax.

SECTION 2. The Congress shall have power to enforce this article by appropriate legislation.

## AMENDMENT XXV [1967]

SECTION 1. In case of the removal of the President from office or of his death or resignation, the Vice President shall become President.

SECTION 2. Whenever there is a vacancy in the office of the Vice President, the President shall nominate a Vice President who shall take office upon confirmation by a majority vote of both Houses of Congress.

SECTION 3. Whenever the President transmits to the President pro tempore of the Senate and the Speaker of the House of Representatives his written declaration that he is unable to discharge the powers and duties of his office, and until he transmits to them a written declaration to the contrary, such powers and duties shall be discharged by the Vice President as Acting President.

SECTION 4. Whenever the Vice President and a majority of either the principal officers of the executive department or of such other body as Congress may by law provide, transmit to the President pro tempore of the Senate and the Speaker of the House of Representatives their written declaration that the President is unable to discharge the powers and duties of his office, the Vice President shall immediately assume the powers and duties of the office as Acting President.

Thereafter, when the President transmits to the President pro tempore of the Senate and the Speaker of the House of Representatives his written declaration that no inability exists, he shall resume the powers and duties of his office unless the Vice President and a majority of either the principal officers of the executive department or of such other body as Congress may by law provide, transmit within four days to the President pro tempore of the Senate and the Speaker of the House of Representatives their written declaration that the President is unable to discharge the powers and duties of his office. Thereupon Congress shall decide the issue, assembling within forty-eight hours for that purpose if not in session. If the Congress, within twenty-one days after receipt of the latter written declaration, or, if Congress is not in session, within twenty-one days after Congress is required to assemble, determines by two-thirds vote of both Houses that the President is unable to discharge the powers and duties of his office, the Vice President shall continue to discharge the same as Acting President; otherwise, the President shall resume the powers and duties of his office.

## AMENDMENT XXVI [1971]

SECTION 1. The right of citizens of the United States, who are eighteen years of age or older, to vote shall not be denied or abridged by the United States or by any State on account of age.

SECTION 2. The Congress shall have power to enforce this article by appropriate legislation.

## AMENDMENT XXVII [1992]

No law varying the compensation for the services of the senators and representatives shall take effect until an election of representatives shall have intervened.

# Appendix B

# COMMUNICATIONS ACT OF 1934

48 Stat. 1064 (1934), as amended, 47 U.S.C.A. § 151 et seq.

--------

## TITLE I—GENERAL PROVISIONS
### PURPOSES OF ACT; CREATION OF FEDERAL COMMUNICATIONS COMMISSION

**Sec. 1. [47 U.S.C.A. § 151.]**

For the purpose of regulating interstate and foreign commerce in communication by wire and radio so as to make available, so far as possible, to all the people of the United States a rapid, efficient, Nation-wide, and world-wide wire and radio communication service with adequate facilities at reasonable charges, for the purpose of the national defense, for the purpose of promoting safety of life and property through the use of wire and radio communication, and for the purpose of securing a more effective execution of this policy by centralizing authority heretofore granted by law to several agencies and by granting additional authority with respect to interstate and foreign commerce in wire and radio communication, there is hereby created a commission to be known as the "Federal Communications Commission," which shall be constituted as hereinafter provided, and which shall execute and enforce the provisions of this Act.

. . .

### APPLICATION OF ACT

**Sec. 2. [47 U.S.C.A. § 152.]**

(a) The provisions of this Act shall apply to all interstate and foreign communication by wire or radio and all interstate and foreign transmission of energy by radio, which originates and/or is received within the United States, and to all persons engaged within the United States in such communication or such transmission of energy by radio, and to the licensing and regulating of all radio stations as hereinafter provided. . . . The provisions of this Act shall apply with respect to cable service to all persons engaged within the United States in providing such service, and to the facilities of cable operators which relate to such service as provided in title VI.

. . .

## TITLE III—PROVISIONS RELATING TO RADIO
### LICENSE FOR RADIO COMMUNICATION
### OR TRANSMISSION OF ENERGY
**Sec. 301.  [47 U.S.C.A. § 301.]**

It is the purpose of this Act, among other things, to maintain the control of the United States over all the channels of interstate and foreign radio transmission;  and to provide for the use of such channels, but not the ownership thereof, by persons for limited periods of time, under licenses granted by Federal authority, and no such license shall be construed to create any right, beyond the terms, conditions, and periods of the license.  No person shall use or operate any apparatus for the transmission of energy or communications or signals by radio (a) from one place in any Territory or possession of the United States or in the District of Columbia to another place in the same Territory, possession, or district;  or (b) from any State, Territory, or possession of the United States, or from the District of Columbia to any other State, Territory, or possession of the United States;  or (c) from any place in any State, Territory, or possession of the United States, or in the District of Columbia, to any place in any foreign country or to any vessel;  or (d) within any State when the effects of such use extend beyond the borders of said State, or when interference is caused by such use or operation with the transmission of such energy, communications, or signals from within said State to any place beyond its borders, or from any place beyond its borders to any place within said State, or with the transmission or reception of such energy, communications, or signals from and/or to places beyond the borders of said State;  or (e) upon any vessel or aircraft of the United States;  or (f) upon any other mobile stations within the jurisdiction of the United States, except under and in accordance with this Act and with a license in that behalf granted under the provisions of this Act.

.  .  .

### GENERAL POWERS OF THE COMMISSION
**Sec. 303.  [47 U.S.C.A. § 303.]**

Except as otherwise provided in this Act, the Commission from time to time, as public convenience, interest, or necessity requires shall:

(a) Classify radio stations;

(b) Prescribe the nature of the service to be rendered by each class of licensed stations and each station within any class;

(c) Assign bands of frequencies to the various classes of stations, and assign frequencies for each individual station and determine the power which each station shall use and the time during which it may operate;

(d) Determine the location of classes of stations or individual stations;

(e) Regulate the kind of apparatus to be used with respect to its external effects and the purity and sharpness of the emissions from each station and from the apparatus therein;

(f) Make such regulations not inconsistent with law as it may deem necessary to prevent interference between stations and to carry out the provisions of this Act: *Provided, however,* That changes in the frequencies, authorized power, or in the times of operation of any station, shall not be made without the consent of the station licensee unless, after a public hearing, the Commission shall determine that such changes will promote public convenience or interest or will serve public necessity, or the provisions of this Act will be more fully complied with;

(g) Study new uses for radio, provide for experimental uses of frequencies, and generally encourage the larger and more effective use of radio in the public interest;

(h) Have authority to establish areas or zones to be served by any station;

(i) Have authority to make special regulations applicable to radio stations engaged in chain broadcasting;

(j) Have authority to make general rules and regulations requiring stations to keep such records of programs, transmissions of energy, communications, or signals as it may deem desirable;

. . .

(m)(1) Have authority to suspend the license of any operator upon proof sufficient to satisfy the Commission that the licensee—

(A) has violated any provision of any Act, treaty, or convention binding on the United States, which the Commission is authorized to administer, or any regulation made by the Commission under any such Act, treaty, or convention; or

. . .

(D) has transmitted superfluous radio communications or signals or communications containing profane or obscene words, language, or meaning. . . .

. . .

(r) Make such rules and regulations and prescribe such restrictions and conditions, not inconsistent with law, as may be necessary to carry out the provisions of this Act, or any international radio or wire communications treaty or convention, or regulations annexed thereto, including any treaty or convention insofar as it relates to the use of radio, to which the United States is or may hereafter become a party.

(s) Have authority to require that apparatus designed to receive television pictures broadcast simultaneously with sound be capable of adequately receiving all frequencies allocated by the Commission to television broadcasting when such apparatus is shipped in interstate commerce, or is imported from any foreign country into the United States, for sale or resale to the public.

. . .

## ALLOCATION OF FACILITIES; TERM OF LICENSES
**Sec. 307. [47 U.S.C.A. § 307.]**

(a) The Commission, if public convenience, interest, or necessity will be served thereby, subject to the limitations of this Act, shall grant to any applicant therefor a station license provided for by this Act.

(b) In considering applications for licenses, and modifications and renewals thereof, when and insofar as there is demand for the same, the Commission shall make such distribution of licenses, frequencies, hours of operation, and of power among the several States and communities as to provide a fair, efficient, and equitable distribution of radio service to each of the same.

. . .

(d) No license granted for the operation of a television broadcasting station shall be for a term longer than five years . . . and any license granted may be revoked as hereinafter provided. Each license granted for the operation of a radio broadcasting station shall be for a term of not to exceed seven years. Upon the expiration of any license, upon application therefor, a renewal of such license may be granted from time to time for a term of not to exceed five years in the case of television broadcasting licenses, for a term of not to exceed seven years in the case of radio broadcasting station licenses, and for a term of not to exceed five years in the case of other licenses, if the Commission finds that public interest, convenience, and necessity would be served thereby. . . .

(e) No renewal of an existing station license in the broadcast or the common carrier services shall be granted more than thirty days prior to the expiration of the original license.

## APPLICATIONS FOR LICENSES . . .
**Sec. 308. [47 U.S.C.A. § 308.]**

. . .

(b) All applications for station licenses, or modifications or renewals thereof, shall set forth such facts as the Commission by regulation may prescribe as to the citizenship, character, and financial, technical, and other qualifications of the applicant to operate the station; the ownership and location of the proposed station and of the stations, if any, with which it is proposed to communicate; the frequencies and the power desired to be used; the hours of the day or other periods of time during which it is proposed to operate the station; the purposes for which the station is to be used; and such other information as it may require. . . .

. . .

## ACTION UPON APPLICATIONS; FORM OF AND CONDITIONS ATTACHED TO LICENSES

**Sec. 309.  [47 U.S.C.A. § 309.]**

(a) Subject to the provisions of this section, the Commission shall determine, in the case of each application filed with it to which section 308 applies, whether the public interest, convenience, and necessity will be served by the granting of such application, and, if the Commission, upon examination of such application and upon consideration of such other matters as the Commission may officially notice, shall find that public interest, convenience, and necessity would be served by the granting thereof, it shall grant such application.

. . .

(d)(1) Any party in interest may file with the Commission a petition to deny any application.  . . .

(2) If the Commission finds on the basis of the application, the pleadings filed, or other matters which it may officially notice that there are no substantial and material questions of fact and that a grant of the application would be consistent with subsection (a), it shall make the grant, deny the petition, and issue a concise statement of the reasons for denying the petition, which statement shall dispose of all substantial issues raised by the petition.  If a substantial and material question of fact is presented or if the Commission for any reason is unable to find that grant of the application would be consistent with subsection (a), it shall proceed as provided in subsection (e).

(e) If, in the case of any application to which subsection (a) of this section applies, a substantial and material question of fact is presented or the Commission for any reason is unable to make the finding specified in such subsection, it shall formally designate the application for hearing on the ground or reasons then obtaining and shall forthwith notify the applicant and all other known parties in interest of such action and the grounds and reasons therefor, specifying with particularity the matters and things in issue but not including issues or requirements phrased generally.  . . .

. . .

(h) Such station licenses as the Commission may grant shall be in such general form as it may prescribe, but each license shall contain, in addition to other provisions, a statement of the following conditions to which such license shall be subject:  (1) The station license shall not vest in the licensee any right to operate the station nor any right in the use of the frequencies designated in the license beyond the term thereof nor in any other manner than authorized therein;  (2) neither the license nor the right granted thereunder shall be assigned or otherwise transferred in violation of this Act;  (3) every license issued under this Act shall be subject in terms to the right of use or control conferred by section 606 of this Act.*

. . .

## LIMITATION ON HOLDING AND TRANSFER OF LICENSES
**Sec. 310. [47 U.S.C.A. § 310.]**

(a) The station license required hereby shall not be granted to or held by any foreign government or representative thereof.

(b) No broadcast or common carrier  . . .  license shall be granted to or held by—

(1) Any alien or the representative of any alien;

(2) Any corporation organized under the laws of any foreign government;

. . .

(d) No construction permit or station license, or any rights thereunder, shall be transferred, assigned, or disposed of in any manner, voluntarily or involuntarily, directly or indirectly, or by transfer of control of any corporation holding such permit or license, to any person except upon application to the Commission and upon finding by the Commission that the public interest, convenience, and necessity will be served thereby.  Any such application shall be disposed of as if the proposed transferee or assignee were making application under section 308 for the permit or license in question; but in acting thereon the Commission may not consider whether the public interest, convenience, and necessity might be served by the transfer, assignment, or disposal of the permit or license to a person other than the proposed transferee or assignee.

## SPECIAL REQUIREMENTS WITH RESPECT TO CERTAIN APPLICATIONS IN THE BROADCASTING SERVICE
**Sec. 311. [47 U.S.C.A. § 311.]**

. . .

(c)(1) If there are pending before the Commission two or more applications for a permit for construction of a broadcasting station, only one of which can be granted, it shall be unlawful, without approval of the Commission, for the applicants or any of them to effectuate an agreement whereby one or more of such applicants withdraws his or their application or applications.

(2) The request for Commission approval in any such case shall be made in writing jointly by all the parties to the agreement.  Such request shall contain or be accompanied by full information with respect to the agreement, set forth in such detail, form, and manner as the Commission shall by rule require.

---

* [Section 606 grants substantial powers to the President to utilize communications facilities during wartime or a national emergency.]

(3) The Commission shall approve the agreement only if it determines (A) that the agreement is consistent with the public interest, convenience, or necessity; and (B) no party to the agreement filed its application for the purpose of reaching or carrying out such agreement. If the agreement does not contemplate a merger, but contemplates the making of any direct or indirect payment to any party thereto in consideration of his withdrawal of his application, the Commission may determine the agreement to be consistent with the public interest, convenience, or necessity only if the amount or value of such payment, as determined by the Commission, is not in excess of the aggregate amount determined by the Commission to have been legitimately and prudently expended and to be expended by such applicant in connection with preparing, filing, and advocating the granting of his application.

. . .

## ADMINISTRATIVE SANCTIONS

**Sec. 312. [47 U.S.C.A. § 312.]**

(a) The Commission may revoke any station license or construction permit—

(1) for false statements knowingly made either in the application or in any statement of fact which may be required pursuant to section 308;

(2) because of conditions coming to the attention of the Commission which would warrant it in refusing to grant a license or permit on an original application;

(3) for willful or repeated failure to operate substantially as set forth in the license;

(4) for willful or repeated violation of, or willful or repeated failure to observe any provision of this Act or any rule or regulation of the Commission authorized by this Act or by a treaty ratified by the United States;

(5) for violation of or failure to observe any final cease and desist order issued by the Commission under this section;

(6) for violation of section 1304, 1343, or 1464 of title 18 of the United States Code; * or

* [Relevant provisions read as follows:

§ 1304.  Broadcasting lottery information

Whoever broadcasts by means of any radio station for which a license is required by any law of the United States, or whoever, operating any such station, knowingly permits the broadcasting of, any advertisement of or information concerning any lottery, gift enterprise, or similar scheme, offering prizes dependent in whole or in part upon lot or chance, or any list of the prizes drawn or awarded by means of any such lottery, gift enterprise, or scheme, whether said list contains any part or all of such prizes, shall be fined not more than $1,000 or imprisoned not more than one year, or both.

Each day's broadcasting shall constitute a separate offense.

§ 1343.  Fraud by wire, radio, or television

Whoever, having devised or intending to devise any scheme or artifice to de-

(7) for willful or repeated failure to allow reasonable access to or to permit purchase of reasonable amounts of time for the use of a broadcasting station by a legally qualified candidate for Federal elective office on behalf of his candidacy.

(b) Where any person (1) has failed to operate substantially as set forth in a license, (2) has violated or failed to observe any of the provisions of this Act, or section 1304, 1343, or 1464 of title 18 of the United States Code, or (3) has violated or failed to observe any rule or regulation of the Commission authorized by this Act or by a treaty ratified by the United States, the Commission may order such person to cease and desist from such action.

(c) Before revoking a license or permit pursuant to subsection (a), or issuing a cease and desist order pursuant to subsection (b), the Commission shall serve upon the licensee, permittee, or person involved an order to show cause [at a hearing] why an order of revocation or a cease and desist order should not be issued.   .  .  .

(d) In any case where a hearing is conducted pursuant to the provisions of this section, both the burden of proceeding with the introduction of evidence and the burden of proof shall be upon the Commission.

.  .  .

## APPLICATION OF ANTITRUST LAWS; REFUSAL OF LICENSES AND PERMITS IN CERTAIN CASES
### Sec. 313.   [47 U.S.C.A. § 313.]

(a) All laws of the United States relating to unlawful restraints and monopolies and to combinations, contracts, or agreements in restraint of trade are hereby declared to be applicable to the manufacture and sale of and to trade in radio apparatus and devices entering into or affecting interstate or foreign commerce and to interstate or foreign radio communications. Whenever in any suit, action, or proceeding, civil or criminal, brought under the provisions of any of said laws or in any proceedings brought to enforce or to review findings and orders of the Federal Trade Commission or other governmental agency in respect of any matters as

fraud, or for obtaining money or property by means of false or fraudulent pretenses, representations, or promises, transmits or causes to be transmitted by means of wire, radio, or television communication in interstate or foreign commerce, any writings, signs, signals, pictures, or sounds for the purpose of executing such scheme or artifice, shall be fined not more than $1,000 or imprisoned not more than five years, or both.

§ 1464.   Broadcasting obscene language

Whoever utters any obscene, indecent, or profane language by means of radio communications shall be fined not more than $10,000 or imprisoned not more than two years, or both.

§ 1307.   State-conducted lotteries

(a) The provisions of sections 1301, 1302, 1303, and 1304 shall not apply to an advertisement, list of prizes, or information concerning a lottery conducted by a State acting under the authority of State law—

(1) contained in a newspaper published in that State, or

(2) broadcast by a radio or television station licensed to a location in that State or an adjacent State which conducts such a lottery.   .  .  .]

to which said Commission or other governmental agency is by law authorized to act, any licensee shall be found guilty of the violation of the provisions of such laws or any of them, the court, in addition to the penalties imposed by said laws, may adjudge, order, and/or decree that the license of such licensee shall, as of the date the decree or judgment becomes finally effective or as of such other date as the said decree shall fix, be revoked and that all rights under such license shall thereupon cease: *Provided, however,* That such licensee shall have the same right of appeal or review, as is provided by law in respect of other decrees and judgments of said court.

(b) The Commission is hereby directed to refuse a station license and/or the permit hereinafter required for the construction of a station to any person (or to any person directly or indirectly controlled by such person) whose license has been revoked by a court under this section.

. . .

## FACILITIES FOR CANDIDATES FOR PUBLIC OFFICE
**Sec. 315.  [47 U.S.C.A. § 315.]**

(a) If any licensee shall permit any person who is a legally qualified candidate for any public office to use a broadcasting station, he shall afford equal opportunities to all other such candidates for that office in the use of such broadcasting station: *Provided,* That such licensee shall have no power of censorship over the material broadcast under the provisions of this section.  No obligation is imposed under this subsection upon any licensee to allow the use of its station by any such candidate.  Appearance by a legally qualified candidate on any—

(1) Bona fide newscast,

(2) Bona fide news interview,

(3) Bona fide news documentary (if the appearance of the candidate is incidental to the presentation of the subject or subjects covered by the news documentary), or

(4) On-the-spot coverage of bona fide news events (included but not limited to political conventions and activities incidental thereto), shall not be deemed to be use of a broadcasting station within the meaning of this subsection.  Nothing in the foregoing sentence shall be construed as relieving broadcasters, in connection with the presentation of newscasts, news interviews, news documentaries, and on-the-spot coverage of news events, from the obligation imposed upon them under this Act to operate in the public interest and to afford reasonable opportunity for the discussion of conflicting views on issues of public importance.

(b) The charges made for the use of any broadcast station by any person who is a legally qualified candidate for any public office in connection with his campaign for nomination for election, or election, to such office shall not exceed—

(1) During the 45 days preceding the date of a primary or primary runoff election and during the 60 days preceding the date of a general or special election in which such person is a candidate, the lowest unit charge of the station for the same class and amount of time for the same period; and

(2) At any other time, the charges made for comparable use of such station by other users thereof.

(c) For the purposes of this section:

(1) The term "broadcasting station" includes a community antenna television system.

(2) The terms "licensee" and "station licensee" when used with respect to a community antenna television system, mean the operator of such system.

(d) The Commission shall prescribe appropriate rules and regulations to carry out the provisions of this section.

### MODIFICATION BY COMMISSION OF CONSTRUCTION PERMITS OR LICENSES
**Sec. 316. [47 U.S.C.A. § 316.]**

(a) Any station license or construction permit may be modified by the Commission either for a limited time or for the duration of the term thereof, if in the judgment of the Commission such action will promote the public interest, convenience, and necessity, or the provisions of this Act or of any treaty ratified by the United States will be more fully complied with. No such order of modification shall become final until the holder of the license or permit shall have been notified in writing of the proposed action and the grounds and reasons therefor, and shall have been given reasonable opportunity, in no event less than thirty days, to show cause by public hearing, if requested, why such order of modification should not issue. . . .

(b) In any case where a hearing is conducted pursuant to the provisions of this section, both the burden of proceeding with the introduction of evidence and the burden of proof shall be upon the Commission.

### ANNOUNCEMENT WITH RESPECT TO CERTAIN MATTER BROADCAST
**Sec. 317. [47 U.S.C.A. § 317.]**

(a)(1) All matter broadcast by any radio station for which any money, service or other valuable consideration is directly or indirectly paid, or promised to or charged or accepted by, the station so broadcasting, from any person, shall, at the time the same is so broadcast, be announced as paid for or furnished, as the case may be, by such person: *Provided,* That "service or other valuable consideration" shall not include any service or property furnished without charge or at a nominal charge for use on, or in connection with, a broadcast unless it is so furnished in consideration for an identification in a broadcast of any person, product, service, trademark, or brand name beyond an identification which is reasonably related to the use of such service or property on the broadcast.

. . .

FALSE DISTRESS SIGNALS; REBROADCASTING   . . .

**Sec. 325.   [47 U.S.C.A. § 325.]**

(a) No person within the jurisdiction of the United States shall knowingly utter or transmit, or cause to be uttered or transmitted, any false or fraudulent signal of distress, or communication relating thereto, nor shall any broadcasting station rebroadcast the program or any part thereof of another broadcasting station without the express authority of the originating station.

(b) Consent to retransmission of broadcasting station signals.

(1) Following the date that is one year after October 5, 1992, no cable system or other multichannel video programming distributor shall retransmit the signal of a broadcasting station, or any part thereof, except—

(A) with the express authority of the originating station;  or

(B) pursuant to section 614 of this title, in the case of a station electing, in accordance with this subsection, to assert the right to carriage under such section.

(2) The provisions of this subsection shall not apply to—

(A) retransmission of the signal of a noncommercial broadcasting station;

(B) retransmission directly to a home satellite antenna of the signal of a broadcasting station that is not owned or operated by, or affiliated with, a broadcasting network, if such signal was transmitted by a satellite carrier on May 1, 1991;

(C) retransmission of the signal of a broadcasting station that is owned or operated by, or affiliated with, a broadcasting network directly to a home satellite antenna, if the household receiving the signal is an unserved household;  or

(D) retransmission by a cable operator or other multichannel video programming distributor of the signal of a superstation if such signal was obtained from a satellite carrier and the originating station was a superstation on May 1, 1991.

. . .

(3)(A) Within 45 days after October 5, 1992, the Commission shall commence a rulemaking proceeding to establish regulations to govern the exercise by television broadcast stations of the right to grant retransmission consent under this subsection and of the right to signal carriage under section 614 of this title, and such other regulations as are necessary to administer the limitations contained in paragraph (2). The Commission shall consider in such proceeding the impact that the grant of retransmission consent by television stations may have on the rates for the basic service tier and shall ensure that the regulations prescribed under this subsection do not conflict with the Commission's obligation under section 623(b)(1) of this title to ensure that the rates for the basic service tier are reasonable. Such rulemaking proceeding shall be completed within 180 days after October 5, 1992.

(B) The regulations required by subparagraph (A) shall require that television stations, within one year after October 5, 1992, and every three years thereafter, make an election between the right to grant retransmission under this subsection and the right to signal carriage under section 614 of this title. If there is more than one cable system which services the same geographic area, a station's election shall apply to all such cable systems.

(4) If an originating television station elects under paragraph (3)(B) to exercise its right to grant retransmission consent under this subsection with respect to a cable system, the provisions of section 534 of this title shall not apply to the carriage of the signal of such station by such cable system.

(5) The exercise by a television broadcast station of the right to grant retransmission consent under this subsection shall not interfere with or supersede the rights under section 614 or 615 of this title of any station electing to assert the right to signal carriage under that section.

(6) Nothing in this section shall be construed as modifying the compulsory copyright license established in section 111 of Title 17 or as affecting existing or future video programming licensing agreements between broadcasting stations and video programmers.

. . .

## CENSORSHIP . . .
### Sec. 326. [47 U.S.C.A. § 326.]

Nothing in this Act shall be understood or construed to give the Commission the power of censorship over the radio communications or signals transmitted by any radio station, and no regulation or condition shall be promulgated or fixed by the Commission which shall interfere with the right of free speech by means of radio communication.

## PROHIBITION AGAINST SHIPMENT OF CERTAIN TELEVISION RECEIVERS
### Sec. 330. [47 U.S.C.A. § 330.]

(a) No person shall ship in interstate commerce, or import from any foreign country into the United States, for sale or resale to the public, apparatus described in paragraph (s) of section 303 unless it complies with rules prescribed by the Commission pursuant to the authority granted by that paragraph: *Provided,* That this section shall not apply to carriers transporting such apparatus without trading in it.

.   .   .

## DIRECT BROADCAST SATELLITE SERVICE OBLIGATIONS
**Sec. 335 [47 U.S.C.A. § 335.]**

(a) The Commission shall, within 180 days after October 5, 1992, initiate a rulemaking proceeding to impose, on providers of direct broadcast satellite service, public interest or other requirements for providing video programming. Any regulations prescribed pursuant to such rulemaking shall, at a minimum, apply the access to broadcast time requirement of section 312(a)(7) of this title and the use of facilities requirements of section 315 of this title to providers of direct broadcast satellite service providing video programming. Such proceeding also shall examine the opportunities that the establishment of direct broadcast satellite service provides for the principle of localism under this chapter, and the methods by which such principle may be served through technological and other developments in, or regulation of, such service.

(b)(1) The Commission shall require, as a condition of any provision, initial authorization, or authorization renewal for a provider of direct broadcast satellite service providing video programming, that the provider of such service reserve a portion of its channel capacity, equal to not less than 4 percent nor more than 7 percent, exclusively for noncommercial programming of an educational or informational nature.

(2) A provider of such service may utilize for any purpose any unused channel capacity required to be reserved under this subsection pending the actual use of such channel capacity for noncommercial programming of an educational or informational nature.

(3) A provider of direct broadcast satellite service shall meet the requirements of this subsection by making channel capacity available to national educational programming suppliers, upon reasonable prices, terms, and conditions, as determined by the Commission under paragraph (4). The provider of direct broadcast satellite service shall not exercise any editorial control over any video programming provided pursuant to this subsection.

(4) In determining reasonable prices under paragraph (3)—

(A) the Commission shall take into account the nonprofit character of the programming provider and any Federal funds used to support such programming;

(B) the Commission shall not permit such prices to exceed, for any channel made available under this subsection, 50 percent of the total direct costs of making such channel available; and

(C) in the calculation of total direct costs, the Commission shall exclude—

(i) marketing costs, general administrative costs, and similar overhead costs of the provider of direct broadcast satellite service; and

(ii) the revenue that such provider might have obtained by making such channel available to a commercial provider of video programming.

. . .

## TITLE V—PENAL PROVISIONS—FORFEITURES
### FORFEITURES
**Sec. 503.** [47 U.S.C.A. § 503.]

. . .

(b)(1) Any person who is determined by the Commission, in accordance with paragraph (3) or (4) of this subsection, to have—

(A) willfully or repeatedly failed to comply substantially with the terms and conditions of any license, permit, certificate, or other instrument or authorization issued by the Commission;

(B) willfully or repeatedly failed to comply with any of the provisions of this Act or of any rule, regulation, or order issued by the Commission under this Act or under any treaty convention, or other agreement to which the United States is a party and which is binding upon the United States;

(C) violated any provision of section 317(c) or 509(a) of this Act; or

(D) violated any provision of sections 1304, 1343, or 1464 of Title 18, United States Code;

shall be liable to the United States for a forfeiture penalty. A forfeiture penalty under this subsection shall be in addition to any other penalty provided for by this Act; except that this subsection shall not apply to any conduct which is subject to forfeiture under . . . section 507 of this Act.

(2) The amount of any forfeiture penalty determined under this subsection shall not exceed $25,000 for each violation. Each day of a continuing violation shall constitute a separate offense, but the total forfeiture penalty which may be imposed under this subsection, for acts or omissions described in paragraph (1) of this subsection and set forth in the notice or the notice of apparent liability issued under this subsection, shall not exceed:

(A) $250,000, if the violator is (i) a common carrier subject to the provisions of this Act, (ii) a broadcast station licensee or permittee, or (iii) a cable television operator; or

(B) $5,000, in any case not covered by subparagraph (A).

The amount of such forfeiture penalty shall be assessed by the Commission, or its designee, by written notice. In determining the amount of such a forfeiture penalty, the Commission or its designee shall take into account the nature, circumstances, extent, and gravity of the prohibited acts committed and, with respect to the violator, the degree of culpability, any history of prior offenses, ability to pay, and such other matters as justice may require.

. . .

## PROHIBITED PRACTICES IN CASES OF CONTESTS OF INTELLECTUAL KNOWLEDGE, INTELLECTUAL SKILL OR CHANCE

**Sec. 509. [47 U.S.C.A. § 509.]**

(a) It shall be unlawful for any person, with intent to deceive the listening or viewing public—

(1) To supply to any contestant in a purportedly bona fide contest of intellectual knowledge or intellectual skill any special and secret assistance whereby the outcome of such contest will be in whole or in part prearranged or predetermined.

(2) By means of persuasion, bribery, intimidation, or otherwise, to induce or cause any contestant in a purportedly bona fide contest of intellectual knowledge or intellectual skill to refrain in any manner from using or displaying his knowledge or skill in such contest, whereby the outcome thereof will be in whole or in part prearranged or predetermined.

. . .

## TITLE VI—CABLE COMMUNICATIONS
### PURPOSES

**Sec. 601. [47 U.S.C.A. § 521.]**

The purposes of this title are to

(1) establish a national policy concerning cable communications;

(2) establish franchise procedures and standards which encourage the growth and development of cable systems and which assure that cable systems are responsive to the needs and interests of the local community;

(3) establish guidelines for the exercise of Federal, State, and local authority with respect to the regulation of cable systems;

(4) assure and encourage that cable communications provide and are encouraged to provide the widest possible diversity of information sources and services to the public;

(5) establish an orderly process for franchise renewal which protects cable operators against unfair denials of renewal where the operator's past performance and proposal for future performance meet the standards established by this title; and

(6) promote competition in cable communications and minimize unnecessary regulation that would impose an undue economic burden on cable systems.

. . .

## DEFINITIONS

**Sec. 602.  [47 U.S.C.A. § 522.]**

For purposes of this subchapter—

(1) the term "activated channels" means those channels engineered at the headend of a cable system for the provision of services generally available to residential subscribers of the cable system, regardless of whether such services actually are provided, including any channel designated for public, educational, or governmental use;

(2) the term "affiliate", when used in relation to any person, means another person who owns or controls, is owned or controlled by, or is under common ownership or control with, such person;

(3) the term "basic cable service" means any service tier which includes the retransmission of local television broadcast signals;

(4) the term "cable channel" or "channel" means a portion of the electromagnetic frequency spectrum which is used in a cable system and which is capable of delivering a television channel (as television channel is defined by the Commission by regulation);

(5) the term "cable operator" means any person or group of persons (A) who provides cable service over a cable system and directly or through one or more affiliates owns a significant interest in such cable system, or (B) who otherwise controls or is responsible for, through any arrangement, the management and operation of such a cable system;

(6) the term "cable service" means—

(A) the one-way transmission to subscribers of (i) video programming, or (ii) other programming service, and

(B) subscriber interaction, if any, which is required for the selection of such video programming or other programming service;

(7) the term "cable system" means a facility, consisting of a set of closed transmission paths and associated signal generation, reception, and control equipment that is designed to provide cable service which includes video programming and which is provided to multiple subscribers within a community, but such term does not include (A) a facility that serves only to retransmit the television signals of 1 or more television broadcast stations;  (B) a facility that serves only subscribers in 1 or more multiple unit dwellings under common ownership, control, or management, unless such facility or facilities uses any public right-of-way;  (C) a facility of a common carrier which is subject, in whole or in part, to the provisions of subchapter II of this chapter, except that such facility shall be considered a cable system (other than for purposes of section 621(c) of this title to the extent such facility is used in the

transmission of video programming directly to subscribers; or (D) any facilities of any electric utility solely for operating its electric utility system;

(8) the term "Federal agency" means any agency of the United States, including the Commission;

(9) the term "franchise" means an initial authorization, or renewal thereof (including a renewal of an authorization which has been granted subject to section 626 of this title), issued by a franchising authority, whether such authorization is designated as a franchise, permit, license, resolution, contract, certificate, agreement, or otherwise, which authorizes the construction or operation of a cable system;

(10) the term "franchising authority" means any governmental entity empowered by Federal, State, or local law to grant a franchise;

(11) the term "grade B contour" means the field strength of a television broadcast station computed in accordance with regulations promulgated by the Commission.

(12) the term "multichannel video programming distributor" means a person such as, but not limited to, a cable operator, a multichannel multipoint distribution service, a direct broadcast satellite service, or a television receive-only satellite program distributor, who makes available for purchase, by subscribers or customers, multiple channels of video programming;

(13) the term "other programming service" means information that a cable operator makes available to all subscribers generally;

(14) the term "person" means an individual, partnership, association, joint stock company, trust, corporation, or governmental entity;

(15) the term "public, educational, or governmental access facilities" means—

(A) channel capacity designated for public, educational, or governmental use; and

(B) facilities and equipment for the use of such channel capacity;

(16) the term "service tier" means a category of cable service or other services provided by a cable operator and for which a separate rate is charged by the cable operator;

(17) the term "State" means any State, or political subdivision, or agency thereof;

(18) the term "usable activated channels" means activated channels of a cable system, except those channels whose use for the distribution of broadcast signals would conflict with technical and safety regulations as determined by the Commission; and

(19) the term "video programming" means programming provided by, a television broadcast station.

## CABLE CHANNELS FOR PUBLIC, EDUCATIONAL
## OR GOVERNMENTAL USE

**Sec. 611. [47 U.S.C.A. § 531.]**

(a) A franchising authority may establish requirements in a franchise with respect to the designation or use of channel capacity for public, educational, or governmental use only to the extent provided in this section.

(b) A franchising authority may in its request for proposals require as part of a franchise, and may require as part of a cable operator's proposal for a franchise renewal, subject to section 626, that channel capacity be designated for public, educational, or governmental use, . . .

(c) A franchising authority may enforce any requirement in any franchise regarding the providing or use of such channel capacity. Such enforcement authority includes the authority to enforce any provisions of the franchise for services, facilities, or equipment proposed by the cable operator, which relate to public, educational, or governmental use of channel capacity, whether or not required by the franchising authority pursuant to subsection (b).

. . .

(e) Subject to section 624(d), a cable operator shall not exercise any editorial control over any public, educational, or governmental use of channel capacity provided pursuant to this section.

. . .

## CABLE CHANNELS FOR COMMERCIAL USE

**Sec. 612. [47 U.S.C.A. § 532.]**

(a) The purpose of this section is to assure that the widest possible diversity of information sources are made available to the public from cable systems in a manner consistent with growth and development of cable systems.

(b)(1) A cable operator shall designate channel capacity for commercial use by persons unaffiliated with the operator in accordance with the following requirements:

(A) An operator of any cable system with 36 or more (but not more than 54) activated channels shall designate 10 percent of such channels which are not otherwise required for use (or the use of which is not prohibited) by Federal law or regulation.

(B) An operator of any cable system with 55 or more (but not more than 100) activated channels shall designate 15 percent of such channels which are not otherwise required for use (or the use of which is not prohibited) by Federal law or regulation.

(C) An operator of any cable system with more than 100 activated channels shall designate 15 percent of all such channels.

(D) An operator of any cable system with fewer than 36 activated channels shall not be required to designate channel capacity for commercial use by persons unaffiliated with the operator, unless the cable system is required to provide such channel capacity under the terms of a franchise in effect on the date of the enactment of this title.

. . .

(c)(1) If a person unaffiliated with the cable operator seeks to use channel capacity designated pursuant to subsection (b) for commercial use, the cable operator shall establish, consistent with the purpose of this section, the price, terms, and conditions of such use which are at least sufficient to assure that such use will not adversely affect the operation, financial condition, or market development of the cable system.

(2) A cable operator shall not exercise any editorial control over any video programming provided pursuant to this section, or in any other way consider the content of such programming, except that an operator may consider such content to the minimum extent necessary to establish a reasonable price for the commercial use of designated channel capacity by an unaffiliated person.

. . .

(d) Any person aggrieved by the failure or refusal of a cable operator to make channel capacity available for use pursuant to this section may bring an action in the district court of the United States for the judicial district in which the cable system is located to compel that such capacity be made available. If the court finds that the channel capacity sought by such a person has not been made available in accordance with this section, or finds that the price, terms, or conditions established by the cable operator are unreasonable, the court may order such system to make available to such person the channel capacity sought, and further determine the appropriate price, terms, or conditions for such use consistent with subsection (c), and may award actual damages if it deems such relief appropriate. . . .

(e)(1) Any person aggrieved by the failure or refusal of a cable operator to make channel capacity available pursuant to this section may petition the Commission for relief under this subsection upon a showing of prior adjudicated violations of this section. . . . If the Commission finds that the channel capacity sought by such person has not been made available in accordance with this section, or that the price, terms, or conditions established by such system are unreasonable under subsection (c), the Commission shall, by rule and order, require such operator to make available such channel capacity under price, terms, and conditions consistent with subsection (c).

. . .

(h) Any cable service offered pursuant to this section shall not be provided, or shall be provided subject to conditions, if such cable service in the judgment of the franchising authority is obscene, or is in conflict with community standards in that it is lewd, lascivious, filthy, or indecent or is otherwise unprotected by the Constitution of the United States. This subsection shall permit a cable operator to enforce prospectively a written and published policy of prohibiting programming that the cable operator reasonably believes describes or depicts sexual or excretory activities or organs in a patently offensive manner as measured by contemporary community standards.

(i)(1) Notwithstanding the provisions of subsections (b) and (c) of this section, a cable operator required by this section to designate channel capacity for commercial use may use any such channel capacity for the provision of programming from a qualified minority programming source or from any qualified educational programming source, whether or not such source is affiliated with the cable operator. The channel capacity used to provide programming from a qualified minority programming source or from any qualified educational programming source pursuant to this subsection may not exceed 33 percent of the channel capacity designated pursuant to this section. No programming provided over a cable system on July 1, 1990, may qualify as minority programming or educational programming on that cable system under this subsection.

(2) For purposes of this subsection, the term "qualified minority programming source" means a programming source which devotes substantially all of its programming to coverage of minority viewpoints, or to programming directed at members of minority groups, and which is over 50 percent minority-owned, as the term "minority" is defined in section 309(i)(3)(C)(ii) of this title.

(3) For purposes of this subsection, the term "qualified educational programming source" means a programming source which devotes substantially all of its programming to educational or instructional programming that promotes public understanding of mathematics, the sciences, the humanities, and the arts and has a documented annual expenditure on programming exceeding $15,000,000. . . .

(4) Nothing in this subsection shall substitute for the requirements to carry qualified noncommercial educational television stations as specified under section 615 of this title.

(j)(1) Within 120 days following October 5, 1992, the Commission shall promulgate regulations designed to limit the access of children to indecent programming, as defined by Commission regulations, and which cable operators have not voluntarily prohibited under subsection (h) of this section by—

(A) requiring cable operators to place on a single channel all indecent programs, as identified by program providers, intended for carriage on channels designated for commercial use under this section;

(B) requiring cable operators to block such single channel unless the subscriber requests access to such channel in writing; and

(C) requiring programmers to inform cable operators if the program would be indecent as defined by Commission regulations.

(2) Cable operators shall comply with the regulations promulgated pursuant to paragraph (1).

## OWNERSHIP RESTRICTIONS

**Sec. 613.   [47 U.S.C.A. § 533.]**

(a) It shall be unlawful for any person to be a cable operator if such person, directly or through one or more affiliates, owns or controls, the licensee of a television broadcast station and the predicted grade B contour of such station covers any portion of the community served by such operator's cable system.

(b)(1) It shall be unlawful for any common carrier, subject in whole or in part to Title II of this Act, to provide video programming directly to subscribers in its telephone service area, either directly or indirectly through an affiliate owned by, operated by, controlled by, or under common control with the common carrier.

(2) It shall be unlawful for a cable operator to hold a license for multichannel multipoint distribution service, or to offer satellite master antenna television service separate and apart from any franchised cable service, in any portion of the franchise area served by that cable operator's cable system.   The Commission—

(A) shall waive the requirements of this paragraph for all existing multichannel multipoint distribution services and satellite master antenna television services which are owned by a cable operator on October 5, 1992;  and

(B) may waive the requirements of this paragraph to the extent the Commission determines is necessary to ensure that all significant portions of a franchise area are able to obtain video programming.

(c) The Commission may prescribe rules with respect to the ownership or control of cable systems by persons who own or control other media of mass communications which serve the same community served by a cable system.

(d) Any State or franchising authority may not prohibit the ownership or control of a cable system by any person because of such person's ownership or control of any media of mass communications or other media interests.

(e)(1) Subject to paragraph (2), a State or franchising authority may hold any interest in any cable system.

(2) Any State or franchising authority shall not exercise any editorial control regarding the content of any cable service on a cable system in which such governmental entity holds ownership interest (other than programming on any channel designated for educational or governmental use), unless such control is exercised through an entity separate from the franchising authority.

. . .

## CARRIAGE OF LOCAL COMMERCIAL TELEVISION SIGNALS
**Sec. 614. [47 U.S.C.A. § 534.]**

(a) Each cable operator shall carry, on the cable system of that operator, the signals of local commercial television stations and qualified low power stations as provided by this section. Carriage of additional broadcast television signals on such system shall be at the discretion of such operator, subject to section 325(b) of this title.

(b)(1)(A) A cable operator of a cable system with 12 or fewer usable activated channels shall carry the signals of at least three local commercial television stations, except that if such a system has 300 or fewer subscribers, it shall not be subject to any requirements under this section so long as such system does not delete from carriage by that system any signal of a broadcast television station.

(B) A cable operator of a cable system with more than 12 usable activated channels shall carry the signals of local commercial television stations, up to one-third of the aggregate number of usable activated channels of such system.

(2) Whenever the number of local commercial television stations exceeds the maximum number of signals a cable system is required to carry under paragraph (1), the cable operator shall have discretion in selecting which such stations shall be carried on its cable system, except that—

(A) under no circumstances shall a cable operator carry a qualified low power station in lieu of a local commercial television station; and

(B) if the cable operator elects to carry an affiliate of a broadcast network (as such term is defined by the Commission by regulation), such cable operator shall carry the affiliate of such broadcast network whose city of license reference point . . . is closest to the principal headend of the cable system.

(3)(A) A cable operator shall carry in its entirety, on the cable system of that operator, the primary video, accompanying audio, and line 21 closed caption transmission of each of the local commercial television stations carried on the cable system and, to the extent technically feasible, program-related material in the vertical blanking interval or on subcarriers. Retransmission of other material in the vertical blanking interval or other nonprogram-related material (including teletext and other subscription and advertiser-supported information services) shall be at the discretion of the cable operator. Where appropriate and feasible, operators may delete signal enhancements, such as ghost-canceling, from the broadcast signal and employ such enhancements at the system headend or headends.

(B) The cable operator shall carry the entirety of the program schedule of any television station carried on the cable system unless carriage of specific programming is prohibited, and other programming authorized to be substituted, . . . .

(4)(A) The signals of local commercial television stations that a cable operator carries shall be carried without material degradation. The Commission shall adopt carriage standards to ensure that, to the extent technically feasible, the quality of signal processing and carriage provided by a cable system for the carriage of local commercial television stations will be no less than that provided by the system for carriage of any other type of signal.

(B) At such time as the Commission prescribes modifications of the standards for television broadcast signals, the Commission shall initiate a proceeding to establish any changes in the signal carriage requirements of cable television systems necessary to ensure cable carriage of such broadcast signals of local commercial television stations which have been changed to conform with such modified standards.

Notwithstanding paragraph (1), a cable operator shall not be required to carry the signal of any local commercial television that substantially duplicates the signal of another local commercial television station which is carried on its cable system, or to carry the signals of more than one local commercial television station affiliated with a particular broadcast network (as such term is defined by regulation). If a cable operator elects to carry on its cable system a signal which substantially duplicates the signal of another local commercial television station carried on the cable system, or to carry on its system the signals of more than one local commercial television station affiliated with a particular broadcast network, all such signals shall be counted toward the number of signals the operator is required to carry under paragraph (1).

(6) Each signal carried in fulfillment of the carriage obligations of a cable operator under this section shall be carried on the cable system channel number on which the local commercial television station is broadcast over the air, or on the channel on which it was carried on July 19, 1985, or on the channel on which it was carried on January 1, 1992, at the election of the station, or on such other channel as is mutually agreed upon by the station and the cable operator. Any dispute regarding the positioning of a local commercial television shall be resolved by the Commission.

(7) Signals carried in fulfillment of the requirements of this section shall be provided to every subscriber of a cable system.

Such signals shall be viewable via cable on all television receivers of a subscriber which are connected to a cable system by a cable operator or for which a cable operator provides a connection. If a cable operator authorizes subscribers to install additional receiver connections, but does not provide the subscriber with such connections, or with the equipment and materials for such connections, the operator shall notify such subscribers of all broadcast stations carried on the cable system which cannot be viewed via cable without a converter box, and shall offer to sell or lease such a converter box to such subscribers at rates in accordance with section (b)(3) of this title.

. . .

(10) A cable operator shall not accept or request monetary payment or other valuable consideration in exchange either for carriage of local commercial television stations in fulfillment of the requirements of this section or for the channel positioning rights provided to such stations under this section, except that—

(c)(1) If there are not sufficient signals of full power local commercial television stations to fill the channels set aside under subsection (b) of this section—

(A) a cable operator of a cable system with a capacity of 35 or fewer usable activated channels shall be required to carry one qualified low power station; and

(B) a cable operator of a cable system with a capacity of more than 35 usable activated channels shall be required to carry two qualified low power stations.

(2) A cable operator required to carry more than one signal of a qualified low power station under this subsection may do so, subject to approval by the franchising authority pursuant to section 611 of this title, by placing such additional station on public, educational, or governmental channels not in use for their designated purposes.

. . .

(g)(1) Pending the outcome of the proceeding under paragraph (2), nothing in this chapter shall require a cable operator to carry on any tier, or prohibit a cable operator to carry on any tier, or prohibit a cable operator to carry on any tier, or prohibit a cable operator to carry on any tier, the signal of any commercial television station or video programming service that is predominately utilized for the transmission of sales presentations or program length commercials.

(2) Within 270 days after October 5, 1992, the Commission, notwithstanding prior proceedings to determine whether broadcast television stations that are predominantly utilized for the transmission of sales presentations or program length commercials are serving the public interest, convenience, and necessity, shall complete a proceeding in accordance with this paragraph to determine whether broadcast television stations that are

predominantly utilized for the transmission of sales presentations or program length commercials are serving the public interest, convenience, and necessity. . . . In the event that the Commission concludes that one or more of such stations are serving the public interest, convenience, and necessity, the Commission shall qualify such stations as local commercial television stations for purposes of subsection (a) of this section. In the event that the Commission concludes that one or more of such stations are not serving the public interest, convenience, and necessity, the Commission shall allow the licensees of such stations a reasonable period within which to provide different programming, and shall not deny such stations a renewal expectancy solely because their programming consisted predominately of sales presentations or program length commercials.

. . . .

## CARRIAGE OF NONCOMMERCIAL EDUCATIONAL TELEVISION
**Sec. 615.  [47 U.S.C.A. § 535.]**

(a) In addition to the carriage requirements set forth in section 614 of this title, each cable operator of a cable system shall carry the signals of qualified noncommercial educational television stations in accordance with the provisions of this section.

(b)(1) Subject to paragraphs (2) and (3) and subsection (e) of this section, each cable operator shall carry, on the cable system of that cable operator, any qualified local noncommercial educational television station requesting carriage.

(2)(A) Notwithstanding paragraph (1), a cable operator of a cable system with 12 or fewer usable activated channels shall be required to carry the signal of one qualified local noncommercial educational television station; except that a cable operator of such system shall comply with subsection (c) of this section and may, in its discretion, carry the signals of other qualified noncommercial educational television stations.

(B) In the case of a cable system described in subparagraph (A) which operates beyond the presence of any qualified local noncommercial educational television station—

(i) the cable operator shall import and carry on that system the signal of one qualified noncommercial educational television station;

(ii) the selection for carriage of such a signal shall be at the election of the cable operator;  and

(iii) in order to satisfy the requirements for carriage specified in this subsection, the cable operator of the system shall not be required to remove any other programming service actually provided to subscribers on March 29, 1990;

except that such cable operator shall use the first channel available to satisfy the requirements of this subparagraph.

(3)(A) Subject to subsection (c) of this section, a cable operator of a cable system with 13 to 36 usable activated channels—

(i) shall carry the signal of at least one qualified local noncommercial educational television but shall not be required to carry the signals of more than three such stations, and

(ii) may, in its discretion, carry additional such stations.

(B) In the case of a cable system described in this paragraph which operates beyond the presence of any qualified local noncommercial educational television station, the cable operator shall import and carry on that system the signal of at least one qualified noncommercial educational television station to comply with subparagraph (A)(i).

(C) The cable operator of a cable system described in this paragraph which carries the signal of a qualified local noncommercial educational station affiliated with a State public television network shall not be required to carry the signal of any additional qualified local noncommercial educational television stations affiliated with the same network if the programming of such additional stations is substantially duplicated by the programming of the qualified local noncommercial educational television station receiving coverage.

(D) A cable operator of a system described in this paragraph which increases the usable activated channel capacity of the system to more than 36 channels on after March 29, 1990, shall, in accordance with the other provisions of this section, carry the signal of each qualified local noncommercial educational television station requesting carriage, subject to subsection (e) of this section.

(c) Notwithstanding any other provision of this section, all cable operators shall continue to provide carriage to all qualified local noncommercial educational television stations whose signals were carried on their systems as of March 29, 1990. The requirements of this subsection may be waived with respect to a particular cable operator and a particular such station, upon the written consent of the cable operator and the station.

(d) A cable operator required to add the signals of qualified local noncommercial educational television stations to a cable system under this section may do so, subject to approval by the franchising authority pursuant to section 611 of this title, by placing such additional stations on public, educational, or governmental channels not in use for their designated purposes.

(e) A cable operator of a cable system with a capacity of more than 36 usable activated channels which is required to carry the signals of three qualified local noncommercial educational television stations shall not be required to carry the signals of additional such stations the programming of which substantially duplicates the programming broadcast by another qualified local noncommercial educational television station requesting carriage. Substantial duplication shall be defined by the Commission in a manner that promotes access to distinctive noncommercial educational television services.

. . .

(i)(1) A cable operator shall not accept monetary payment or other valuable consideration in exchange for carriage of the signal of any qualified local noncommercial educational television station carried in fulfillment of the requirements of this section, except that such a station may be required to bear the cost associated with delivering a good quality signal or a baseband video signal to the principal headend of the cable system.

(2) Notwithstanding the provisions of this section, a cable operator shall not be required to add the signal of a qualified local noncommercial educational television station not already carried under the provisions of subsection (c) of this section, where such signal would be considered a distant signal for copyright purposes unless such station indemnifies the cable operator for any increased copyright costs resulting from carriage of such signal.

. . .

## REGULATION OF CARRIAGE AGREEMENTS
**Sec. 616 [47 U.S.C.A. § 536.]**

(a) Within one year after October 5, 1992, the Commission shall establish regulations governing program carriage agreements and related practices between cable operators or other multichannel video programming distributors and video programming vendors. Such regulations shall—

(1) include provisions designed to prevent a cable operator or other multichannel video programming distributor from requiring a financial interest in a program service as a condition for carriage on one or more of such operator's systems;

(2) include provisions designed to prohibit a cable operator or other multichannel video programming distributor from coercing a video programming vendor to provide, and from retaliating against such a vendor for failing to provide, exclusive rights against other multichannel video programming distributors as a condition of carriage on a system;

(3) contain provisions designed to prevent a multichannel video programming distributor from engaging in conduct the effect of which is to unreasonably restrain the ability of an unaffiliated video

programming vendor to compete fairly by discriminating in video programming distribution on the basis of affiliation or nonaffiliation of vendors in the selection, terms, or conditions for carriage of video programming provided by such vendors;

. . .

## SALES OF CABLE SYSTEMS
**Sec. 617 [47 U.S.C.A. § 617.]**

(a) Except as provided in this section, no cable operator may sell or otherwise transfer ownership in a cable system within a 36–month period following either the acquisition or initial construction of such system by such operator.

(b) In the case of a sale of multiple systems, if the terms of the sale require the buyer to subsequently transfer ownership of one or more such systems to one or more third parties, such transfers shall be considered a part of the initial transaction.

. . .

(d) The Commission may, consistent with the public interest, waive the requirement of subsection (a) of this section, except that, if the franchise requires franchise authority approval of a transfer, the Commission shall not waive such requirements unless the franchise authority has approved the transfer. The Commission shall use its authority under this subsection to permit appropriate transfers in the cases of default, foreclosure, or other financial distress.

. . .

## GENERAL FRANCHISE REQUIREMENTS
**Sec. 621. [47 U.S.C.A. § 541.]**

(a)(1) A franchising authority may award, in accordance with the provisions of this title, one or more franchises within its jurisdiction.

. . .

(3) In awarding a franchise or franchises, a franchising authority shall assure that access to cable service is not denied to any group of potential residential cable subscribers because of the income of the residents of the local area in which such group resides.

. . .

(c) Any cable system shall not be subject to regulation as a common carrier or utility by reason of providing any cable service.

. . .

## FRANCHISE FEES
**Sec. 622. [47 U.S.C.A. § 542.]**

(a) Subject to the limitation of subsection (b), any cable operator may be required under the terms of any franchise to pay a franchise fee.

(b) For any 12–month period, the franchise fees paid by a cable operator with respect to any cable system shall not exceed 5 percent of such cable operator's gross revenues derived in such period from the operation of the cable system.

. . .

## REGULATION OF RATES

**Sec. 623.  [47 U.S.C.A. § 543.]**

(a)(1) In general.—No Federal agency or State may regulate the rates for the provision of cable service except to the extent provided under this section and section 612 of this title.  Any franchising authority may regulate the rates for the provision of cable service, or any other communications service provided over a cable system to cable subscribers, but only to the extent provided under this section.  No Federal agency, State, or franchising authority may regulate the rates for cable service of a cable system that is owned or operated by a local government or franchising authority within whose jurisdiction that cable system is located and that is the only cable system located within such jurisdiction.

(2) Preference for competition.—If the Commission finds that a cable system is subject to effective competition, the rates for the provision of cable service by such system shall not be subject to regulation by the Commission or by a State or franchising authority under this section.  If the Commission finds that a cable system is not subject to effective competition—

(b)(1) The Commission shall, by regulation, ensure that the rates for the basic service tier are reasonable.  Such regulations shall be designed to achieve the goal of protecting subscribers of any cable system that is not subject to effective competition from rates for the basic service tier if such cable system were subject to effective competition.

. . .

(7)(A) Each cable operator of a cable system shall provide its subscribers a separately available basic service tier to which subscription is required for access to any other tier of service.  Such basic tier shall, at a minimum, consist of the following:

(i) All signals carried in fulfillment of the requirements of sections 614 and 615 of this title.

(ii) Any public, educational, and governmental access programming required by the franchise of the cable system to be provided to subscribers.

(iii) Any signal of any television broadcast station that is provided by the cable operator to any subscriber, except a signal which is secondarily transmitted by a satellite carrier beyond the local service area of such station.

(B) A cable operator may add additional video programming signals or services to the basic service tier.  Any such additional signals or services provided on the basic service tier shall be provided to subscribers at rates determined under the regulations prescribed by the Commission under this subsection.

(8)(A) A cable operator may not require the subscription to any tier other than the basic service tier required by paragraph (7) as a condition of access to video programming offered on a per channel or per program basis. A cable operator may not discriminate between subscribers to the basic service tier and other subscribers with regard to the rates charged for video programming offered on a per channel or per program basis.

(B) The prohibition in subparagraph (A) shall not apply to a cable system that, by reason of the lack of addressable converter boxes or other technological limitations, does not permit the operator to offer programming on a per channel or per program basis in the same manner required by subparagraph (A). This subparagraph shall not be available to any cable operator after—

(i) the technology utilized by the cable system is modified or improved in a way that eliminates such technological limitation; or

(ii) 10 years after October 5, 1992, subject to subparagraph (C).

(C) If, in any proceeding initiated at the request of any cable operator, the Commission determines that compliance with the requirements of subparagraph (A) would require the cable operator to increase its rates, the Commission may, to the extent consistent with the public interest, grant such cable operator a waiver from such requirements for such specified period as the Commission determines reasonable and appropriate.

(c)(1) Within 180 days after October 5, 1992, the Commission shall, by regulation, establish the following:

(A) criteria prescribed in accordance with paragraph (2) for identifying, in individual cases, rates for cable programming services that are unreasonable;

. . .

(*l*) As used in this section—

(1) The term "effective competition" means that—

(A) fewer than 30 percent of the households in the franchise area subscribe to the cable service of a cable system;

(B) the franchise area is—

(i) served by at least two unaffiliated multichannel video programming distributors each of which offers comparable video programming to at least 50 percent of the households in the franchise area; and

(ii) the number of households subscribing to programming services offered by multichannel video programming distributors other than the largest multichannel video programming distributor exceeds 15 percent of the households in the franchise area; or

(C) a multichannel video programming distributor operated by the franchising authority for that franchise area offers video programming to at least 50 percent of the households in that franchise area.

. . .

(2) require the provision of any service tier provided without charge (disregarding any installation or rental charge for equipment necessary for receipt of such tier); or

(3) regulate rates for the initial installation or the rental of one set of the minimum equipment which is necessary for the subscriber's receipt of basic cable service.

. . .

## REGULATION OF SERVICES, FACILITIES, AND EQUIPMENT
**Sec. 624. [47 U.S.C.A. § 544.]**

(a) Any franchising authority may not regulate the services, facilities, and equipment provided by a cable operator except to the extent consistent with this title.

(b) In the case of any franchise granted after the effective date of this title, the franchising authority, to the extent related to the establishment or operation of a cable system—

(1) in its requests for proposals for a franchise (including requests for renewal proposals, subject to Section 626), may establish requirements for facilities and equipment, but may not establish requirements for video programming or other information services; and

(2) subject to Section 625, may enforce any requirements contained within the franchise—

(A) for facilities and equipment; and

(B) for broad categories of video programming or other services.

(c) In the case of any franchise in effect on the effective date of this title, the franchising authority may, subject to Section 625, enforce requirements contained within the franchise for the provision of services, facilities, and equipment, whether or not related to the establishment or operation of a cable system.

(d)(1) Nothing in this title shall be construed as prohibiting a franchising authority and a cable operator from specifying, in a franchise or renewal thereof, that certain cable services shall not be provided or shall be provided subject to conditions, if such cable services are obscene or are otherwise unprotected by the Constitution of the United States.

(2)(A) In order to restrict the viewing of programming which is obscene or indecent, upon the request of a subscriber, a cable operator shall provide (by sale or lease) a device by which the subscriber can prohibit viewing of a particular cable service during periods selected by that subscriber.

. . .

(e) Within one year after October 5, 1992, the Commission shall prescribe regulations which establish minimum technical standards relating to cable systems' technical operation and signal quality. The Commission shall update such standards periodically to reflect improvements in technology. A franchising authority may require as part of a franchise (including a modification, renewal, or transfer thereof) provisions for the enforcement of the standards prescribed under this subsection. A franchising authority may apply to the Commission for a waiver to impose standards that are more stringent than the standards prescribed by the Commission under this subsection.

(f)(1) Any Federal agency, State, or franchising authority may not impose requirements regarding the provision or content of cable services, except as expressly provided in this title.

. . .

## CONSUMER ELECTRONICS EQUIPMENT COMPATIBILITY
### Sec. 624a. [47 U.S.C.A. § 544a.]

. . .

(b)(1) Within 1 year after October, 1992, the Commission, in consultation with representatives of the cable industry and the consumer electronics industry, shall report to Congress on means of assuring compatibility between televisions and video cassette recorders and cable systems, consistent with the need to prevent theft of cable service, so that cable subscribers will be able to enjoy the full benefit of both the programming available on cable systems and the functions available on their televisions and video cassette recorders. Within 180 days after the date of submission of the report required by this subsection, the Commission shall issue such regulations as are necessary to assure such compatibility.

. . .

## MODIFICATION OF FRANCHISE OBLIGATIONS
### Sec. 625. [47 U.S.C.A. § 545.]

(a)(1) During the period a franchise is in effect, the cable operator may obtain from the franchising authority modifications of the requirements in such franchise—

(A) in the case of any such requirement for facilities or equipment, including public, educational, or governmental access facilities or equipment, if the cable operator demonstrates that (i) it is commercially impracticable for the operator to comply with such requirement, and (ii) the proposal by the cable operator for modification of such requirement is appropriate because of such commercial impracticability; or

(B) in the case of any such requirement for services, if the cable operator demonstrates that the mix, quality, and level of services required by the franchise at the time it was granted will be maintained after such modification.

. . .

## RENEWAL

**Sec. 626. [47 U.S.C.A. § 546.]**

(a)(1) A franchising authority may, on its own initiative during the 6th month period which begins with the 36th month before the franchise expiration, commence a proceeding which affords the public in the franchise area appropriate notice and participation for the purpose of (A) identifying the future cable-related community needs and interests, and (B) reviewing the performance of the cable operator under the franchise during the then current franchise term. If the cable operator submits, during such 6–month period, a written renewal notice requesting the commencement of such a proceeding, the franchising authority shall commence such a proceeding not later than 6 months after the date such notice is submitted.

(2) The cable operator may not invoke the renewal procedures set forth in subsections (b) through (g) of this section unless—

(A) such a proceeding is requested by the cable operator by timely submission of such notice; or

(B) such a proceeding is commenced by the franchising authority on its own initiative.

(b)(1) Upon completion of a proceeding under subsection (a), a cable operator seeking renewal of a franchise may, on its own initiative or at the request of a franchising authority, submit a proposal for renewal.

(2) Subject to section 624, any such proposal shall contain such material as the franchising authority may require, including proposals for an upgrade of the cable system.

(3) The franchising authority may establish a date by which such proposals shall be submitted.

(c)(1) Upon submittal by a cable operator of a proposal to the franchising authority for the renewal of a franchise, the franchising authority shall provide prompt public notice of such proposal and, during the 4–month period which begins on the completion of any proceedings under subsection (a), renew the franchise or, issue a preliminary assessment that the franchise should not be renewed and, at the request of the operator or on its own initiative, commence an administrative proceeding after providing prompt public notice of such proceeding in accordance with paragraph (2) to consider whether—

    (A) the cable operator has substantially complied with the material terms of the existing franchise and with applicable law;

    (B) the quality of the operator's service including signal quality, response to consumer complaints, and billing practices, but without regard to the mix, quality, or level of cable services or other services provided over the system, has been reasonable in light of community needs;

    (C) the operator has the financial, legal, and technical ability to provide the services, facilities, and equipment as set forth in the operator's proposal; and

    (D) the operator's proposal is reasonable to meet the future cable-related community needs and interests, taking into account the cost of meeting such needs and interests.

   . . .

    (3) At the completion of a proceeding under this subsection, the franchising authority shall issue a written decision granting or denying the proposal for renewal based upon the record of such proceeding, and transmit a copy of such decision to the cable operator. Such decision shall state the reasons therefor.

    (d) Any denial of a proposal for renewal shall be based on one or more adverse findings made with respect to the factors described in subparagraphs (A) through (D) of subsection (c)(1). . . .

## DEVELOPMENT OF COMPETITION AND DIVERSITY IN VIDEO PROGRAMMING DISTRIBUTION

**Sec. 628. [47 U.S.C.A. § 548.]**

    (a) The purpose of this section is to promote the public interest, convenience, and necessity by increasing competition and diversity in the multichannel video programming market, to increase the availability of satellite cable programming and satellite broadcast programming to persons in rural and other areas not currently able to receive such programming, and to spur the development of communications technologies.

    (b) It shall be unlawful for a cable operator, a satellite cable programming vendor in which a cable operator has an attributable interest, or a satellite broadcast programming vendor to engage in unfair methods of competition or unfair or deceptive acts or practices, the purpose or effect of which is to hinder significantly or to prevent any multichannel video programming distributor from providing satellite cable programming or satellite broadcast programming to subscribers or consumers.

(c)(1) Within 180 days after October 5, 1992, the Commission shall, in order to promote the public interest, convenience, and necessity by increasing competition and diversity in the multichannel video programming market and the continuing development of communications technologies, prescribe regulations to specify particular conduct that is prohibited by subsection (b) of this section.

(2) The regulations to be promulgated under this section shall—

(A) establish effective safeguards to prevent a cable operator which has an attributable interest in a satellite cable programming vendor or a satellite broadcast programming vendor from unduly or improperly influencing the decision of such vendor to sell, or the prices, terms, and conditions of sale of, satellite cable programming or satellite broadcast programming to any unaffiliated multichannel video programming distributor;

(B) prohibit discrimination by a satellite cable programming vendor in which a cable operator has an attributable interest or by a satellite broadcast programming vendor in the prices, terms, and conditions of sale or delivery of satellite cable programming or satellite broadcast programming among or between cable systems, cable operators, or other multichannel video programming distributors, or their agents or buying groups, . . . .

. . .

(C) prohibit practices, understandings, arrangements, and activities, including exclusive contracts for satellite cable programming or satellite broadcast programming between a cable operator and a satellite cable programming vendor or satellite broadcast programming vendor, that prevent a multichannel video programming vendor in which a cable operator has an attributable interest or any satellite broadcast programming vendor in which a cable operator has an attributable in interest for distribution to persons in areas not served by a cable operator as of October 5, 1992; and

(D) with respect to distribution to persons in areas served by a cable operator, prohibit exclusive contracts for satellite cable programming or satellite broadcast programming between a cable operator and a satellite cable programming vendor in which a cable operator has an attributable interest or a satellite broadcast programming vendor in which a cable operator has an attributable interest, unless the Commission determines (in accordance with paragraph (4)) that such contract is in the public interest.

(3)(A) Nothing in this section shall require any person who is engaged in the national or regional distribution of video programming to make such programming available in any geographic area beyond which such programming has been authorized or licensed for distribution.

(B) Nothing in this section shall apply

(i) to the signal of any broadcast affiliate of a national television network or other television signal that is retransmitted by satellite but that is not satellite broadcast programming, or

(ii) to any internal satellite communication of any broadcast network or cable network that is not satellite broadcast programming.

(4) In determining whether an exclusive contract is in the public interest for purposes of paragraph (2)(D), the Commission shall consider each of the following factors with respect to the effect of such contract on the distribution of video programming in areas that are served by a cable operator:

(A) the effect of such exclusive contract on the development of competition in local and national multichannel video programming distribution markets;

(B) the effect of such exclusive contract on competition from multichannel video programming distribution technologies other than cable;

(C) the effect of such exclusive contract on the attraction of capital investment in the production and distribution of new satellite cable programming;

(D) the effect of such exclusive contract on diversity of programming in the multichannel video programming distribution market; and

(E) the duration of the exclusive contract.

. . .

## CONSUMER PROTECTION AND CUSTOMER SERVICE
**Sec. 632.   [47 U.S.C.A. § 552.]**

(a) A franchising authority may establish and enforce—

(1) customer service requirements of the cable operator;  and

(2) construction schedules and other construction-related requirements, including construction-related performance requirements, of the cable operator.

(b) The Commission shall, within 180 days of enactment of the Cable Consumer Protection and Competition Act of 1992, establish standards by which cable operators may fulfill their customer service requirements.  Such standards shall include, at a minimum, requirements governing—

(1) cable system office hours and telephone availability;

(2) installations, outages, and service calls;  and

(3) communications between the cable operator and the subscriber (including standards governing bills and refunds).

(c)(1) Nothing in this subchapter shall be construed to prohibit any State or any franchising authority from enacting or enforcing any consumer protection law, to the extent not specifically preempted by this subchapter.

(2) Nothing in this section shall be construed to preclude a franchising authority and a cable operator from agreeing to customer service requirements that exceed the standards established by the Commission under subsection (b) of this section.  Nothing in this subchapter shall be construed to prevent the establishment or enforcement of any municipal law or regulation, or any State law, concerning customer service that imposes customer service requirements that exceed the standards set by the Commission under this section, or that addresses matters not addressed by the Commission under this section.

## UNAUTHORIZED RECEPTION OF CABLE SERVICE
**Sec. 633.   [47 U.S.C.A. § 553.]**

(a)(1) No person shall intercept or receive or assist in intercepting or receiving any communications service offered over a cable system, unless specifically authorized to do so by a cable operator or as may otherwise be specifically authorized by law.

(2) For the purpose of this section, the term "assist in intercepting or receiving" shall include the manufacture or distribution of equipment intended by the manufacturer or distributor (as the case may be) for unauthorized reception of any communications service offered over a cable system in violation of subparagraph (1).

.  .  .

## LIMITATION OF FRANCHISING AUTHORITY LIABILITY
**Sec. 635a.   [47 U.S.C.A. § 555a.]**

(a) In any court proceeding pending on or initiated after October 5, 1992, involving any claim against a franchising authority or other governmental entity, or any official, member, employee, or agent of such authority or entity, arising from the regulation of cable service or from a decision of approval or disapproval with respect to a grant, renewal, transfer, or amendment of a franchise, any relief, to the extent such relief is required by any other provision of Federal, State, or local law, shall be limited to injunctive relief and declaratory relief.

(b) The limitation contained in subsection (a) of this section shall not apply to actions that, prior to such violation, have been determined by a final order of a court of binding jurisdiction, no longer subject to appeal, to be in violation of a cable operator's rights.

.  .  .

## CRIMINAL AND CIVIL LIABILITY
**Sec. 638.  [47 U.S.C.A. § 558.]**

Nothing in this title shall be deemed to affect the criminal or civil liability of cable programmers or cable operators pursuant to the Federal, State, or local law of libel, slander, obscenity, incitement, invasions of privacy, false or misleading advertising, or other similar laws, except that cable operators shall not incur any such liability for any program carried on any channel designated for public, educational, governmental use or any other channel obtained under Section 612 or under similar arrangements.

## OBSCENE PROGRAMMING
**Sec. 639.  [47 U.S.C.A. § 559.]**

Whoever transmits over any cable system any matter which is obscene or otherwise unprotected by the Constitution of the United States shall be fined not more than $10,000 or imprisoned not more than two years, or both.

## UNAUTHORIZED PUBLICATION OR USE OF COMMUNICATIONS
**Sec. 705.  [47 U.S.C.A. § 605.]**

(a) Except as authorized by Chapter 119, Title 18, no person receiving, assisting in receiving, transmitting, or assisting in transmitting, any interstate or foreign communication by wire or radio shall divulge or publish the existence, contents, substance, purport, effect, or meaning thereof, except through authorized channels of transmission or reception, (1) to any person other than the addressee, his agent, or attorney, (2) to a person employed or authorized to forward such communication to its destination, (3) to proper accounting or distributing officers of the various communicating centers over which the communication may be passed, (4) to the master of a ship under whom he is serving, (5) in response to a subpoena issued by a court of competent jurisdiction, or (6) on demand of other lawful authority.  No person not being authorized by the sender shall intercept any radio communication and divulge or publish the existence, contents, substance, purport, effect, or meaning of such intercepted communication to any person.  No person not being entitled thereto shall receive or assist in receiving any interstate or foreign communication by radio and use such communication (or any information therein contained) for his own benefit or for the benefit of another not entitled thereto.  No person having received any intercepted radio communication or having become acquainted with the contents, substance, purport, effect, or meaning of such communication (or any part thereof) knowing that such communication was intercepted, shall divulge or publish the existence, contents, substance, purport, effect, or meaning of such communication (or any part thereof) or use such communication (or any information therein contained) for his own benefit or for the benefit of another not entitled thereto.  This section shall not apply to the receiving, divulging, publishing, or utilizing the contents of any radio communication which is transmitted by any station for the use of the general public, which relates to ships, aircraft, vehicles or persons in distress, or which is transmitted by an amateur radio station operator or by a citizens band radio operator.

(b) The provisions of subsection (a) shall not apply to the interception or receipt by any individual, or the assisting (including the manufacture or sale) of such interception or receipt, of any satellite cable programming for private viewing if—

(1) the programming involved is not encrypted; and

(2)(A) a marketing system is not established under which—

(i) an agent or agents have been lawfully designated for the purpose of authorizing private viewing by individuals; and

(ii) such authorization is available to the individual involved from the appropriate agent or agents; or

(B) a marketing system described in subparagraph (A) is established and the individuals receiving such programming have obtained authorization for private viewing under that system.

(c) For purposes of this section—

(1) the term "satellite cable programming" means video programming which is transmitted via satellite and which is primarily intended for the direct receipt by cable operators for their retransmission to cable subscribers;

(2) the term "agent," with respect to any person, includes an employee of such person;

(3) the term "encrypt," when used with respect to satellite cable programming, means to transmit such programming in a form whereby the aural and visual characteristics (or both) are modified or altered for the purpose of preventing the unauthorized receipt of such programming by persons without authorized equipment which is designed to eliminate the effects of such modification or alteration;

(4) the term "private viewing" means the viewing for private use in an individual's dwelling unit by means of equipment, owned or operated by such individual, capable of receiving satellite cable programming directly from a satellite; and

(5) the term "private financial gain" shall not include the gain resulting to any individual for the private use in such individual's dwelling unit of any programming for which the individual has not obtained authorization for that use.

(d)(1) Any person who willfully violates subsection (a) shall be fined not more than $1,000 or imprisoned for not more than 6 months or both.

(2) Any person who violates subsection (a) willfully and for purposes of direct or indirect commercial advantage or private financial gain shall be fined not more than $25,000 or imprisoned for not more than 1 year, or both, for the first such conviction and

shall be fined not more than $50,000 or imprisoned for not more than 2 years, or both, for any subsequent conviction.

(3)(A) Any person aggrieved by any violation of subsection (a) may bring a civil action in a United States district court or in any other court of competent jurisdiction.

(B) The court may—

(i) grant temporary and final injunctions on such terms as it may deem reasonable to prevent or restrain violations of subsection (a);

(ii) award damages as described in subparagraph (C); and

(iii) direct the recovery of full costs, including awarding reasonable attorneys' fees to an aggrieved party who prevails.

(C)(i) Damages awarded by any court under this section shall be computed, at the election of the aggrieved party, in accordance with either of the following subclauses;

(I) the party aggrieved may recover the actual damages suffered by him as a result of the violation and any profits of the violator that are attributable to the violation which are not taken into account in computing the actual damages; in determining the violator's profits, the party aggrieved shall be required to prove only the violator's gross revenue, and the violator shall be required to prove his deductible expenses and the elements of profit attributable to factors other than the violation; or

(II) the party aggrieved may recover an award of statutory damages for each violation involved in the action in a sum of not less than $250 or more than $10,000, as the court considers just.

(ii) In any case in which the court finds that the violation was committed willfully and for purposes of direct or indirect commercial advantage or private financial gain, the court in its discretion may increase the award of damages, whether actual or statutory, by an amount of not more than $50,000.

(iii) In any case where the court finds that the violator was not aware and had no reason to believe that his acts constituted a violation of this section, the court in its discretion may reduce the award of damages to a sum of not less than $100.

(4) The importation, manufacture, sale, or distribution of equipment by any person with the intent of its use to assist in any activity prohibited by subsection (a) shall be subject to penalties and remedies under this subsection to the same extent and in the same manner as a person who has engaged in such prohibited activity.

(5) The penalties under this subsection shall be in addition to those prescribed under any other provision of this title.

(6) Nothing in this subsection shall prevent any State, or political subdivision thereof, from enacting or enforcing any laws with respect to the importation, sale, manufacture, or distribution of equipment by any person with the intent of its use to assist in the interception or receipt of radio communications prohibited by subsection (a).

(e) Nothing in this section shall affect any right, obligation, or liability under Title 17, United States Code, any rule, regulation, or order thereunder, or any other applicable Federal, State, or local law.

# Appendix C

# CODE OF ETHICS

THE SOCIETY OF PROFESSIONAL JOURNALISTS
(FORMERLY SIGMA DELTA CHI)

(Adopted 1973; amended 1984, 1987.)

The Society of Professional Journalists, Sigma Delta Chi, believes the duty of journalists is to serve truth.

We believe the agencies of mass communication are carriers of public discussion and information, acting on their Constitutional mandate and freedom to learn and report their facts.

We believe in public enlightenment as the forerunner of justice, and in our Constitutional role to seek the truth as part of the public's right to know the truth.

We believe those responsibilities carry obligations that require journalists to perform with intelligence, objectivity, accuracy, and fairness.

To these ends, we declare acceptance of the standards of practice here set forth:

RESPONSIBILITY: The public's right to know of events of public importance and interest is the overriding mission of the mass media. The purpose of distributing news and enlightened opinion is to serve the general welfare. Journalists who use their professional status as representatives of the public for selfish or other unworthy motives violate a high trust.

FREEDOM OF THE PRESS: Freedom of the press is to be guarded as an inalienable right of people in a free society. It carries with it the freedom and the responsibility to discuss, question, and challenge actions and utterances of our government and of our public and private institutions. Journalists uphold the right to speak unpopular opinions and the privilege to agree with the majority.

ETHICS: Journalists must be free of obligations to any interest other than the public's right to know.

1. Gifts, favors, free travel, special treatment or privileges can compromise the integrity of journalists and their employers. Nothing of value should be accepted.

2. Secondary employment, political involvement, holding public office, and service in community organizations should be avoided if it compromises the integrity of the journalists and their employers. Journalists and their employers should conduct their personal lives in a

969

manner which protects them from conflict of interest, real or apparent. Their responsibilities to the public are paramount. That is the nature of their profession.

3.   So-called news communications from private sources should not be published or broadcast without substantiation of their claims to news value.

4.   Journalists will seek news that serves the public interest, despite the obstacles. They will make constant efforts to assure that the public's business is conducted in public and that public records are open to public inspection.

5.   Journalists acknowledge the newsman's ethic of protecting confidential sources of information.

6.   Plagiarism is dishonest and unacceptable.

ACCURACY AND OBJECTIVITY: Good faith with the public is the foundation of all worthy journalism.

1.   Truth is our ultimate goal.

2.   Objectivity in reporting the news is another goal which serves as the mark of an experienced professional. It is a standard of performance toward which we strive. We honor those who achieve it.

3.   There is no excuse for inaccuracies or lack of thoroughness.

4.   Newspaper headlines should be fully warranted by the contents of the articles they accompany. Photographs and telecasts should give an accurate picture of an event and not highlight a minor incident out of context.

5.   Sound practice makes clear distinction between news reports and expressions of opinion. News reports should be free of opinion or bias and represent all sides of an issue.

6.   Partisanship in editorial comment which knowingly departs from the truth violates the spirit of American journalism.

7.   Journalists recognize their responsibility for offering informed analysis, comment, and editorial opinion on public events and issues. They accept the obligation to present such material by individuals whose competence, experience, and judgment qualify them for it.

8.   Special articles or presentations devoted to advocacy or the writer's own conclusions and interpretations should be labeled as such.

FAIR PLAY: Journalists at all times will show respect for the dignity, privacy, rights, and well-being of people encountered in the course of gathering and presenting the news.

1.   The news media should not communicate unofficial charges affecting reputation or moral character without giving the accused a chance to reply.

2.   The news media must guard against invading a person's right to privacy.

3.  The media should not pander to morbid curiosity about details of vice and crime.

4.  It is the duty of news media to make prompt and complete correction of their errors.

5.  Journalists should be accountable to the public for their reports and the public should be encouraged to voice its grievances against the media.  Open dialogue with our readers, viewers, and listeners should be fostered.

MUTUAL TRUST:  Adherence to this code is intended to preserve and strengthen the bond of mutual trust and respect between American journalists and the American people.  The Society shall—by programs of education and other means—encourage individual journalists to adhere to the tenets and shall encourage journalistic publications and broadcasters to recognize their responsibility to frame codes of ethics in concert with their employees to serve as guidelines in furthering these goals.

# Appendix D

# FEDERAL COMMUNICATIONS COMMISSION

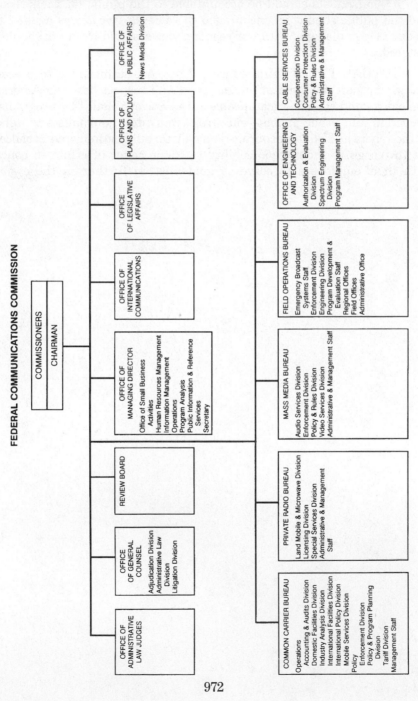

# Appendix E

# JUSTICES OF THE SUPREME COURT
# OF THE UNITED STATES

[Chief Justices are in Italics.]

| Name | Appointed From | Term |
|------|------|------|
| *John Jay* | N.Y. | 1789–1795 |
| John Rutledge | S.C. | 1789–1791 |
| William Cushing | Mass. | 1789–1810 |
| James Wilson | Pa. | 1789–1798 |
| John Blair | Va. | 1789–1796 |
| James Iredell | N.C. | 1790–1799 |
| Thomas Johnson | Md. | 1791–1793 |
| William Paterson | N.J. | 1793–1806 |
| *John Rutledge* | S.C. | 1795 |
| Samuel Chase | Md. | 1796–1811 |
| *Oliver Ellsworth* | Conn. | 1796–1800 |
| Bushrod Washington | Va. | 1798–1829 |
| Alfred Moore | N.C. | 1799–1804 |
| *John Marshall* | Va. | 1801–1834 |
| Harry B. Livingston | N.Y. | 1806–1823 |
| Thomas Todd | Ky. | 1807–1826 |
| Joseph Story | Mass. | 1811–1845 |
| Gabriel Duval | Md. | 1811–1835 |
| Smith Thompson | N.Y. | 1823–1843 |
| Robert Trimble | Ky. | 1826–1828 |
| John McLean | Ohio | 1829–1861 |
| Henry Baldwin | Pa. | 1830–1844 |
| James M. Wayne | Ga. | 1835–1867 |
| *Roger B. Taney* | Md. | 1836–1864 |
| Philip P. Barbour | Va. | 1836–1841 |
| John Catron | Tenn. | 1836–1865 |
| John McKinley | Ala. | 1837–1852 |
| Peter V. Daniel | Va. | 1841–1860 |
| Samuel Nelson | N.Y. | 1845–1872 |
| Levi Woodbury | N.H. | 1845–1851 |
| Robert C. Grier | Pa. | 1846–1870 |
| Benjamin R. Curtis | Mass. | 1851–1857 |
| John A. Campbell | Ala. | 1853–1861 |
| Nathan Clifford | Me. | 1858–1881 |
| Noah H. Swayne | Ohio | 1862–1881 |
| Samuel F. Miller | Iowa | 1862–1890 |
| David Davis | Ill. | 1862–1877 |
| Stephen J. Field | Cal. | 1863–1897 |
| *Salmon P. Chase* | Ohio | 1864–1873 |
| William Strong | Pa. | 1870–1880 |

| Name | Appointed From | Term |
|------|------|------|
| Joseph P. Bradley | N.J. | 1870–1892 |
| Ward Hunt | N.Y. | 1872–1882 |
| *Morrison R. Waite* | Ohio | 1874–1888 |
| John M. Harlan | Ky. | 1877–1911 |
| William B. Woods | Ga. | 1880–1887 |
| Stanley Matthews | Ohio | 1881–1889 |
| Horace Gray | Mass. | 1881–1902 |
| Samuel Blatchford | N.Y. | 1882–1893 |
| Lucius Q.C. Lamar | Mass. | 1888–1893 |
| *Melville W. Fuller* | Ill. | 1888–1910 |
| David J. Brewer | Kan. | 1889–1910 |
| Henry B. Brown | Mich. | 1890–1906 |
| George Shiras, Jr. | Pa. | 1892–1903 |
| Howell E. Jackson | Tenn. | 1893–1895 |
| Edward D. White | La. | 1894–1910 |
| Rufus W. Peckham | N.Y. | 1895–1909 |
| Joseph McKenna | Cal. | 1898–1925 |
| Oliver Wendell Holmes | Mass. | 1902–1932 |
| William R. Day | Ohio | 1903–1922 |
| William H. Moody | Mass. | 1906–1910 |
| Horace H. Lurton | Tenn. | 1909–1914 |
| Charles Evans Hughes | N.Y. | 1910–1916 |
| Willis Van Devanter | Wy. | 1910–1937 |
| Joseph R. Lamar | Ga. | 1910–1916 |
| *Edward D. White* | La. | 1910–1921 |
| Mahlon Pitney | N.J. | 1912–1922 |
| James C. McReynolds | Tenn. | 1914–1941 |
| Louis D. Brandeis | Mass. | 1916–1939 |
| John H. Clarke | Ohio | 1916–1922 |
| *William H. Taft* | Conn. | 1921–1930 |
| George Sutherland | Utah | 1922–1938 |
| Pierce Butler | Minn. | 1922–1939 |
| Edward T. Sanford | Tenn. | 1923–1930 |
| Harlan F. Stone | N.Y. | 1925–1941 |
| *Charles E. Hughes* | N.Y. | 1930–1941 |
| Owen J. Roberts | Pa. | 1930–1945 |
| Benjamin N. Cardozo | N.Y. | 1932–1938 |
| Hugo L. Black | Ala. | 1937–1971 |
| Stanley F. Reed | Ky. | 1938–1957 |
| Felix Frankfurter | Mass. | 1939–1962 |
| William O. Douglas | Conn. | 1939–1975 |
| Frank Murphy | Mich. | 1940–1949 |
| *Harlan F. Stone* | N.Y. | 1941–1946 |
| James F. Byrnes | S.C. | 1941–1942 |
| Robert H. Jackson | N.Y. | 1941–1954 |
| Wiley B. Rutledge | Iowa | 1943–1949 |
| Harold H. Burton | Ohio | 1945–1958 |
| *Fred M. Vinson* | Ky. | 1946–1953 |
| Tom C. Clark | Tex. | 1949–1967 |
| Sherman Minton | Ind. | 1949–1956 |
| *Earl Warren* | Cal. | 1953–1969 |
| John Marshall Harlan | N.Y. | 1955–1971 |

| Name | Appointed From | Term |
|---|---|---|
| William J. Brennan, Jr. | N.J. | 1956–1990 |
| Charles E. Whittaker | Mo. | 1957–1962 |
| Potter Stewart | Ohio | 1958–1981 |
| Byron R. White | Colo. | 1962–1993 |
| Arthur J. Goldberg | Ill. | 1962–1965 |
| Abe Fortas | Tenn. | 1965–1969 |
| Thurgood Marshall | N.Y. | 1967–1991 |
| *Warren E. Burger* | Va. | 1969–1986 |
| Harry A. Blackmun | Minn. | 1970– |
| Lewis F. Powell, Jr. | Va. | 1972–1987 |
| *William H. Rehnquist* | Ariz. | 1972– |
| *(Appointed Chief Justice 1986.)* | | |
| John Paul Stevens | Ill. | 1975– |
| Sandra Day O'Connor | Ariz. | 1981– |
| Antonin Scalia | Va. | 1986– |
| Anthony M. Kennedy | Cal. | 1988– |
| David H. Souter | N.H. | 1990– |
| Clarence Thomas | Va. | 1991– |
| Ruth Bader Ginsburg | D.C. | 1993– |

# Appendix F

# PROPOSED UNIFORM CORRECTION OR CLARIFICATION OF DEFAMATION ACT

[The National Conference of Commissioners on Uniform State Laws in 1993 proposed a "Uniform Correction or Clarification of Defamation Act" to be enacted "in all the states." The American Bar Association approved the draft proposal in February 1994. The intent of the proposed act, according to the Conference, is to provide "strong incentives for individuals promptly to correct or clarify an alleged defamation as an alternative to costly litigation." Further information is available from the Conference, 676 North St. Clair St., Suite 1700, Chicago, Ill. 60611, (312) 915-0195. The proposed act appears below.]

SECTION 1. DEFINITIONS. In this [Act]:

(1) "Defamatory" means tending to harm reputation.

(2) "Economic loss" means special, pecuniary loss caused by a false and defamatory publication.

(3) "Person" means an individual, corporation, business trust, estate, trust, partnership, association, joint venture, or other legal or commercial entity. The term does not include a government or governmental subdivision, agency, or instrumentality.

SECTION 2. SCOPE.

(a) This [Act] applies to any [claim for relief], however characterized, for damages arising out of harm to personal reputation caused by the false content of a publication that is published on or after the effective date of this [Act].

(b) This [Act] applies to all publications, including writings, broadcasts, oral communications, electronic transmissions, or other forms of transmitting information.

SECTION 3. REQUEST FOR CORRECTION OR CLARIFICATION.

(a) A person may maintain an action for defamation only if:

(1) the person has made a timely and adequate request for correction or clarification from the defendant; or

(2) the defendant has made a correction or clarification.

(b) A request for correction or clarification is timely if made within the period of limitation for commencement of an action for defamation. However, a person who, within 90 days after knowledge of the publication, fails to make a good-faith attempt to request a correction or clarification may recover only provable economic loss.

(c) A request for correction of clarification is adequate if it:

(1) is made in writing and reasonably identifies the person making the request;

(2) specifies with particularity the statement alleged to be false and defamatory and, to the extent known, the time and place of publication;

(3) alleges the defamatory meaning of the statement;

(4) specifies the circumstances giving rise to any defamatory meaning of the statement which arises from other than the express language of the publication; and

(5) states that the alleged defamatory meaning of the statement is false.

(d) In the absence of a previous adequate request, service of a [summons and complaint] stating a [claim for relief] for defamation and containing the information required in subsection (c) constitutes an adequate request for correction or clarification.

(e) The period of limitation for commencement of a defamation action is tolled during the period allowed in Section 6(a) for responding to a request for correction or clarification.

SECTION 4. DISCLOSURE OF EVIDENCE OF FALSITY.

(a) A person who has been requested to make a correction or clarification may ask the requester to disclose reasonably available information material to the falsity of the allegedly defamatory statement.

(b) If a correction or clarification is not made, a person who unreasonably fails to disclose the information after a request to do so may recover only provable economic loss.

(c) A correction or clarification is timely if published within 25 days after receipt of information disclosed pursuant to subsection (a) or 45 days after receipt of a request for correction or clarification, whichever is later.

SECTION 5. EFFECT OF CORRECTION OR CLARIFICATION.

If a timely and sufficient correction or clarification is made, a person may recover only provable economic loss, as mitigated by the correction or clarification.

SECTION 6. TIMELY AND SUFFICIENT CORRECTION OR CLARIFICATION.

(a) A correction or clarification is timely if it is published before, or within 45 days after, receipt of a request for correction or clarification, unless the period is extended under Section 4(c).

(b) A correction or clarification is sufficient if it:

(1) is published with a prominence and in a manner and medium reasonably likely to reach substantially the same audience as the publication complained of;

(2) refers to the statement being corrected or clarified and:

(i) corrects the statement;

(ii) in the case of defamatory meaning arising from other than the express language of the publication, disclaims an intent to communicate that meaning or to assert its truth; or

(iii) in the case of a statement attributed to another person, identifies the person and disclaims an intent to assert the truth of the statement; and

(3) is communicated to the person who has made a request for correction or clarification.

(c) A correction or clarification is published in a medium reasonably likely to reach substantially the same audience as the publication complained of if it is published in a later issue, edition, or broadcast of the original publication.

(d) If a later issue, edition, or broadcast of the original publication will not be published within the time limits established for a timely correction or clarification, a correction or clarification is published in a manner and medium reasonably likely to reach substantially the same audience as the publication complained of if:

(1) it is timely published in a reasonably prominent manner;

(i) in another medium likely to reach an audience reasonably equivalent to the original publication; or

(ii) if the parties cannot agree on another medium, in the newspaper with the largest general circulation in the region in which the original publication was distributed;

(2) reasonable steps are taken to correct undistributed copies of the original publication, if any; and

(3) it is published in the next practicable issue, edition, or broadcast, if any, of the original publication.

(e) A correction or clarification is timely and sufficient if the parties agree in writing that it is timely and sufficient.

SECTION 7. CHALLENGES TO CORRECTION OR CLARIFICATION OR TO REQUEST FOR CORRECTION OR CLARIFICATION.

(a) If a defendant in an action governed by this [Act] intends to rely on a timely and sufficient correction or clarification, the defendant's intention to do so, and the correction or clarification relied upon, must be set forth in a notice served on the plaintiff within 60 days after service of the [summons and complaint] or 10 days after the correction or clarification is made, whichever is later. A correction or clarification is deemed to be timely and sufficient unless the plaintiff challenges its timeliness or sufficiency within [20 days] after the notice is served.

(b) If a defendant in an action governed by this [Act] intends to challenge the adequacy or timeliness of a request for correction or clarification, the defendant must set forth the challenge in a motion to declare the request inadequate or untimely served within 60 days after service of the [summons and complaint]. The court shall rule on the motion at the earliest appropriate time before trial.

SECTION 8. OFFER TO CORRECT OR CLARIFY.

(a) If a timely correction or clarification is no longer possible, the publisher of an alleged defamatory statement may offer, at any time before trial, to make a correction or clarification. The offer must be made in writing to the person allegedly defamed by the publication and:

(1) contain the publisher's offer to:

(i) publish, at the person's request, a sufficient correction or clarification; and

(ii) pay the person's reasonable expenses of litigation, including attorney's fees, incurred before publication of the correction or clarification; and

(2) be accompanied by a copy of the proposed correction or clarification and the plan for its publication.

(b) If the person accepts in writing an offer to correct or clarify made pursuant to subsection (a):

(1) the person is barred from commencing an action against the publisher based on the statement; or

(2) if an action has been commenced, the court shall dismiss the action against the defendant with prejudice after the defendant complies with the terms of the offer.

(c) A person who does not accept an offer made in conformance with subsection (a) may recover in an action based on the statement only:

(1) damages for provable economic loss; and

(2) reasonable expenses of litigation, including attorney's fees, incurred before the offer, unless the person failed to make a good-faith attempt to request a correction or clarification in accordance with Section 3(b) or failed to disclose information in accordance with Section 4.

(d) On request of either party, a court shall promptly determine the sufficiency of the offered correction or clarification.

(e) The court shall determine the amount of reasonable expenses of litigation, including attorney's fees, specified in subsections (a)(1)(ii) and (c)(2).

SECTION 9. SCOPE OF PROTECTION. A timely and sufficient correction or clarification made by a person responsible for a publication constitutes a correction or clarification made by all persons responsible for that publication other than a republisher. However, a correction or clarification that is sufficient only because of the operation of Section 6(b)(2)(iii) does not constitute a correction or clarification made by the person to whom the statement is attributed.

SECTION 10. ADMISSIBILITY OF EVIDENCE OF CORRECTION OR CLARIFICATION.

(a) The fact of a request for correction or clarification under this [Act], the contents of the request, and its acceptance or refusal are not admissible in evidence at trial.

(b) The fact that a correction or clarification under this [Act] was made and the contents of the correction or clarification are not admissible in evidence at trial except in mitigation of damages pursuant to Section 5. If the fact that a correction or clarification was made or the contents of the correction or clarification are received in evidence, the fact of the request may also be received.

(c) The fact of an offer of correction or clarification, or the fact of its refusal, and the contents of the offer are not admissible in evidence at trial.

SECTION 11. UNIFORMITY OF APPLICATION AND CONSTRUCTION.

This [Act] shall be applied and construed to effectuate its general purpose to make uniform the law with respect to the subject of this [Act] among States enacting it.

SECTION 12. SHORT TITLE. This [Act] may be cited as the Uniform Correction or Clarification of Defamation Act.

SECTION 13. SEVERABILITY. If any provision of this [Act] or its application to any person or circumstance is held invalid, the invalidity does not affect other provisions or applications of this [Act] which can be given effect without the invalid provision or application, and to this end the provisions of this [Act] are severable.

SECTION 14. EFFECTIVE DATE. This [Act] takes effect. . . .

# GLOSSARY

**absolute privilege**  In libel, an immunity from libel suits granted to government officials and others based on remarks uttered or written as part of their official duties.  Or, an immunity from libel suits granted to broadcast licensees in instances in which they have provided equal opportunities for political candidates under the requirements of Section 315 of the Communications Act.

**absolutism**  A theory of freedom of expression holding that the First Amendment prevents all government interference with expression.

**acquit**  To free or clear from a criminal charge or accusation.

**act**  A written law formally passed by a legislative body (such as the Congress of the United States) and signed by the Executive or passed over his or her veto.

**action**  A lawsuit.

**actionable**  Providing legal basis for a lawsuit.

**actual damages**  The actual loss suffered by the plaintiff.  (In libel, this can include loss of reputation, even though it may be hard to place a dollar value on that loss.)  (Actual damages are one kind of compensatory damages.)

**actual injury damages**  A term created in Gertz v. Robert Welch, Inc., and used only in libel cases for provable monetary loss suffered by the plaintiff.

**actual malice**  In libel, prior knowledge of falsity, reckless disregard of the truth, entertaining serious doubts, or having a high degree of awareness of probable falsity.  (This definition is the one used by the Supreme Court and should not be confused with the common law concept of actual malice—publishing with hatred or ill will.)

*ad hoc* **balancing**  On a case-by-case basis, a judicial balancing of issues in an individual case to determine whether expression may be stopped or subjected to civil or criminal sanctions (in contrast to *definitional balancing*).

**adjudicate**  To decide a matter within the court system.

**administrative agency**  An agency created by Congress, such as the Federal Communications Commission or the Federal Trade Commission, or by a state.

**affidavit**  A written statement that asserts facts, signed and sworn to before a person having authority to administer an oath.

**affirmed**  Signifies that the appellate court agreed with the lower court's result or judgment and has decided to let it stand after review.

*a fortiori*  For a stronger reason;  all the more;  inevitably.

*amicus curiae*  Friend of the court.  (The plural is *amici curiae*.)  One who is not a party in a case but submits briefs on it.

**answer**  A written response to a *complaint*.

**antitrust laws**  Laws designed to prevent businesses from forming monopolies and interfering with free trade among competitors.

**appeal**  An application to a higher court to reverse or modify the judgment of a lower court.

**appellant**  The party appealing a decision or judgment to a higher court.

**appellate court**  A court that hears appeals and reviews lower court decisions.

**appellee**  The party who opposes an appeal.

**appropriation**  In privacy, use of a person's name or likeness or other aspect of personality for advertising purposes without consent.

*a priori*  "From the previous."  Proceeding from a known or assumed cause to a necessarily related effect;  deductive.  Made before or without examination;  not supported by factual study.

*arguendo*  Assume something true solely for the purpose of argument.

**arraignment**  The initial court appearance of a person who is charged with a crime.

**banc**  Bench, or the place where a court sits.  (See *en banc*.)

**beyond a reasonable doubt**  The standard of proof required in criminal cases.

**Bill of Rights**  The first 10 amendments to the U.S. Constitution.

**black letter law**  Legal principles or rules generally accepted by the judiciary.

**brief**  A document prepared by an attorney to support of his or her case for a trial or appeal.  The written legal arguments that are presented to the court by a lawsuit.  A brief is generally partisan.  The brief states the facts and the relevant legal authorities on which a party relies for the result it thinks should obtain.

**burden of proof**  In the law of evidence, the necessity or duty of proving the fact or facts in dispute.  [Questions arise as to which party has the *burden of proof*.  The level to which that proof must rise is different in civil cases ("by a preponderance of evidence") and criminal cases ("beyond a reasonable doubt").  See, for example, *clear and convincing proof*.]

**Canon Law** The law of the Church. During the early Middle Ages, the ecclesiastical or church courts had considerable control over family and other matters in England. The law thus developed influenced the common law.

**cause of action** The particular facts on which an action is based. (A question as to whether one has a *cause of action* is a challenge to whether there is a legal basis for the claim.)

**cease and desist order** A command from an administrative agency to modify or cease specified behavior. (For example, the Federal Trade Commission can issue a *cease and desist order* to stop deceptive or misleading advertising.) An order to cease behavior is similar to an injunction by a court.

**certiorari** "To make sure"; the name of the petition by which a party seeks review of a case by the United States Supreme Court.

*cf.* "Compare." Indicates that a cited source supports a statement in the text but is not precisely analogous.

**change of venire** Bringing in a jury panel from another geographical location.

**change of venue** The transfer of a suit begun in one county or district to another, for trial.

**circuit court** Name given to different types and levels of courts in different states. Named originally because judges "rode circuit" to serve outlying areas.

**citation** A reference to a legal authority that indicates where it may be located.

**civil action** A lawsuit, usually seeking damages, brought to enforce a right or redress a wrong.

**civil law** Law based on codes originating with the Romans. Used in contradistinction to common law.

**clear and convincing proof (or evidence)** A standard of proof in civil litigation more stringent than the normal requirement that the successful party prevail by the preponderance of the evidence.

**code** A compilation or system of laws, arranged into chapters, and promulgated by legislative authority.

**collateral estoppel** Prohibition against making a claim that has already been rejected in a prior case.

**commercial speech** Generally, speech that proposes a commercial transaction. The exact line between commercial and political speech is unclear. (See Chapter IX for extensive discussion.)

**common carrier** A bus line, telephone company or other organization that must do business with all would-be customers. (In communications terms, a medium in which the carrier has no editorial control over the content.)

**common law**   Law that derives its authority solely from usages and customs of immemorial antiquity or from the judgment and decrees of courts (as opposed to that created by statutes passed by legislatures).

**compensatory damages**   Money awarded to compensate the plaintiff for any harm suffered.

**complainant**   The person who brings a lawsuit; plaintiff.

**complaint**   The first pleading on the part of the plaintiff in a civil action.

**concurring opinion**   An opinion in which one judge agrees with the result reached in an opinion of the majority or plurality of the court, but with differing reasoning, emphasis or expression.   (Other judges may join the concurring opinion.)

**contempt of court**   Any act calculated to embarrass, hinder or obstruct a court in the administration of justice, or calculated to lessen its authority or dignity.

**content regulation**   Regulation of expression because of what is said, as opposed to where or when it is said.

**continuance**   The postponement of a trial or hearing.

*contra*   Against.

**contract**   An exchange of oral or written promises between two or more parties to do or not do a particular thing, enforceable by law.

**copyright**   A system for protection of literary or artistic work product. (The currently applicable statute is the Copyright Act of 1976.)

**criminal syndicalism laws**   Laws forbidding individuals to associate for the purpose of advocating violent changes in the form of government.

**damages**   Money awarded by a court to one who has suffered loss, detriment or injury to his person, property or rights due to the tortious acts or negligence of others or to breach of contract.   (The damages may be either to compensate the person harmed or to punish the person causing the harm.)

**decision**   The determination or judgment of the court, as opposed to the reasoning of the court in its opinion.

**declaratory judgment**   A judgment that declares the rights of the parties or expresses the opinion of the court on a question of law, without necessarily ordering anything to be done.

**defamation**   Injuring a person's character or reputation by false and harmful statements.   Includes both *libel* and *slander*.

**defendant**   The party against whom a suit is brought.   In criminal cases, the defendant is the party accused of crime by the state.

**definitional balancing**   Judicial balancing of interests in an entire class of speech to determine whether or how much it is protected by the First Amendment (for example, obscenity) as opposed to a narrow case-by-case analysis. (Contrast to *ad hoc balancing.*)

*de jure*  As a matter of law.

*de minimis*  The law does not concern itself with trifles.

**demurrer**  A legal pleading that says, in effect, "even if, for the sake of argument, the facts presented by the other side are correct, those facts do not give the other side a legal argument that can possibly stand up in court." (A motion to dismiss.)

*de novo* **review**  A new, fresh, more expanded review by an appellate court of both law and facts of a lower court decision—not bound by the lower court's decision.

**deposition**  The testimony of a witness not taken in open court— usually done to find out what possible witnesses know about a case before it comes to trial.

*dictum*  A remark or observation of a judge on unrelated points that are not part of the determination of the court. (The plural is *dicta.*)

**discovery**  A process whereby one party to an action may be informed as to facts known by other parties or witnesses.

**dissenting opinion**  An opinion by one or more judges of an appellate court disagreeing with the disposition of the case.

**disparagement**  An untrue or misleading statement about a competitor's goods that is intended to influence, or tends to influence the public not to buy the goods.

**distinguish**  To point out factual differences between an earlier case and the case being decided or discussed.

**diversity jurisdiction**  The basis for federal court litigation when the persons on one side of a case come from a different state than the persons on the other side. (The case can be tried in federal court even though state law is applied.)

**due process**  Law in its regular course of administration through the courts of justice.

*en banc*; **sitting** *en banc*  A court sitting "en banc" is a session of all the eligible judges together.

**enjoin**  To require a person, by writ or injunction from a court of equity, to perform, or to abstain or desist from, some act.

**equity**  A court's power to "do justice" when specific laws do not cover the situation.

**Espionage Act**  Federal legislation dealing with spying.

**estoppel**  A person's own act, or acceptance of facts, which preclude his later making claims to the contrary.

*ex parte*  By or for one party; done for, in behalf of or on the application of, one party only, without notice to the other.

***ex post facto***   After the fact.  An act or fact occurring after some previous act or fact and relating thereto.  An effort to make something a crime retroactively.

***ex rel.***   A legal proceeding initiated by a district attorney or attorney general on behalf of the government, but at the behest of a party with an interest in the matter.

**fair comment**   The common law right to comment on, or criticize, within limits, the conduct of public officials, entertainers and others whose work subjects them to public view, without being liable for defamation.

**fair trial/free press**   The balancing of First Amendment rights of a free press against Sixth Amendment rights of an accused to a fair trial.  (Also *free press/fair trial*.)

**fairness doctrine**   The rule that, until August 1987, required broadcast licensees to devote a reasonable percentage of time to public issues and to present contrasting points of view on controversial issues of public importance.

**fair use**   A defense to *copyright infringement* found in Section 107 of the Copyright Act.  One may be protected in copying another's copyrighted work where the copying is not likely to hurt the present or potential markets for the work and where copying is likely to be of substantial benefit to the public.

**false light**   In privacy, an untrue—but not necessarily harmful—representation of someone.

**fault**   Negligence;  lack of care;  failure to behave reasonably.

**FCC**   Federal Communications Commission.

**Federal Communications Commission**   The *administrative agency* whose jurisdiction includes broadcasting, cable, other electronic media, telephone companies and other common carriers.

**Federal Open Meetings Law (Government in the Sunshine Act)**   A federal law requiring that certain federal agencies hold their meetings in public.

**Federal Trade Commission**   Federal *administrative agency* whose jurisdiction includes unfair business practices, unfair or deceptive trade practices and anti-competitive practices.

**felony**   A crime of a graver nature than a *misdemeanor*.  Generally, an offense punishable by death or by imprisonment in excess of one year.

**Fourteenth Amendment**   Amendment to the U.S. Constitution extending due process and equal protection to protection from state interference.  Courts have interpreted the due process clause as extending the right of freedom of the press to a protection from state interference.

**free press/fair trial**   See *fair trial/free press*.

**Freedom of Information Act** The federal statute mandating open access to public records.

**gag order** A court order stopping people from speaking or from publishing.

**general damages** In *libel*, damages to reputation that the plaintiff, with or without proof, is presumed to have sustained as a result of the defendant's statement.

**Government in the Sunshine Act** The federal open meetings statute.

**grand jury** A jury whose duty is to receive complaints and accusations in criminal cases, hear the evidence and present bills of *indictment* in cases where they are satisfied that there is probable cause that the accused committed a crime and that a trial ought to be held.

**grandfather** A term that means a party whose conduct was legal prior to a statute is permitted to continue even though the statute would otherwise prohibit it.

*habeas corpus* "You have the body." A writ issued to an officer holding a person in detention or under arrest to bring that person before a court to determine the legality of the detention.

**harmless error** An error committed by a lower court during a trial, found not to be prejudicial and therefore not the basis for a reversal by an appellate court.

**hearing** A court proceeding; a trial-like proceeding that takes place in an administrative agency or other non-court setting.

**holding** That part of the court's opinion that applies the law to the facts of the case. The opposite of *dictum*.

*in camera* In chambers. In private. (For example, when judges examine documents *in camera*, the documents do not become available publicly in the courtroom.)

*in personam* A lawsuit brought to enforce rights against another person.

*in rem* A lawsuit brought to enforce rights in a thing against the whole world.

**indictment** An accusation in writing presented by a *grand jury*, charging that a person has done some criminal act.

**information** An accusation of some offense, in the nature of an *indictment*, but presented by a competent public officer instead of by a *grand jury*.

*infra* Below or under; within; later in this book.

**infringement** A violation, as of a law, regulation or agreement; a breach.

**injunction** A mandatory or prohibitive order issued by a court.

**innocent construction rule**   A libel rule in Illinois providing that, if a statement is capable of a nondefamatory reading, it must be given that reading.

**intrusion**   Entry upon the property or privacy of another.

**invasion of privacy**   The violation of a person's right to be free from outside interference or publicity.

**joint-operating agreement**   An agreement between newspaper owners to combine the business operations of two newspapers.

**journalist's privilege**   The right, sometimes asserted by journalists, to be exempt from requirements to reveal secret sources and other confidences.

**judgment** *non obstante veredicto* **(n.o.v.)**   "Notwithstanding the verdict."   An order by a judge setting aside a jury verdict and deciding the case differently, when the judge concludes that the facts will not support the jury's conclusion.

**judgment of the court**   The legal decision of a court.

**judicial review**   The court's power to declare a statute unconstitutional and to interpret laws.

**jurisdiction**   The court's right and power to decide a case that affects the rights of the parties.

**jury**   A certain number of persons, selected according to law, and sworn to inquire of certain matters of fact and declare the truth upon evidence laid before them.   (See *petit jury* or *grand jury*.)

**legal brief**   (See *brief*.)

**libel**   *Loosely*, a written, printed, or pictorial statement that damages a person by defaming his character or exposing him to ridicule.   (For a better understanding, see Chapter III.   The loose definition fails to include a variety of qualifications.   For example, an otherwise-libelous statement that is *privileged* is not actionably libelous.)

**litigant**   One who is engaged in a lawsuit.

**mandamus, writ of**   A written order issued by a superior court ordering a public official or body or a lower court to perform a specified duty.

*Media Law Reporter* **(Med.L.Rptr.)**   A commercial looseleaf legal service that prints the full text of recent media law cases.

**memorandum order**   A court decision that gives the ruling but no full opinion.

**misappropriation**   In *copyright* law, the systematic taking of another's original work.   In privacy law, using a person's name or likeness or other element of his or her personality for commercial purposes (such as advertising) without permission.

**misdemeanor** An offense of less gravity than a *felony*, for which punishment may be a fine or imprisonment in a local rather than in a state institution.

**mistrial** A trial that is stopped before its normal conclusion because of some legal error or irregularity that destroys the propriety of the trial.

**moot** An issue that need not be decided because the dispute between the parties no longer exists.

**motion to dismiss** See *demurrer*.

**negligence** The failure to do something a reasonable person, guided by ordinary considerations, would do. Or, doing something a reasonable and prudent person would not do.

**neutral reportage** The *privilege*, recognized in some jurisdictions, of news media to report evenhandedly statements made by one public figure or group about another public figure or group.

**Notice of Inquiry (NOI)** Public notice by an *administrative agency*, such as the *Federal Communications Commission*, of its inquiry into a particular subject, so that interested parties may comment.

**Notice of Proposed Rule-Making (NPRM)** Public notice by an *administrative agency*, such as the *Federal Communications Commission*, of a proposed rule, so that the public may comment.

*obiter dictum* An opinion voiced by a judge that has only incidental bearing on the case in question and is therefore not binding. (Same as *dictum*.)

**obscenity** (Although loosely used outside the law as a synonym for indecency, the term *obscenity* has a precise three-part definition under the holdings of the Supreme Court. See Chapter VIII, particularly Miller v. California.)

**opinion** A formal statement by one or more judges or a jury of the legal reasons and principles for the conclusions of the court.

**oral argument** An oral presentation made to a judge or judges in which attorneys for litigants argue the merits of their case.

**ordinance** A city or municipal law.

**original jurisdiction** The power of a court to take a case not yet passed upon by another court, try it and decide it.

**overbreadth** Extent to which a statute, regulation or ordinance attempts to regulate speech protected by the First Amendment. (Depending on the extent of overbreadth, the statute will either be declared unconstitutional on its face or unconstitutional as applied to the protected speech.)

**party** A *plaintiff* or a *defendant* in a lawsuit.

**pandering** In *obscenity* law, commercial exploitation of sexually explicit material.

*per curiam* **opinion**  "By the court"; an *appellate court opinion* written by the court, not identified as the writing of any particular judge.

**peremptory challenge**  The right of parties in criminal or civil cases to dismiss a prospective juror without giving any reason.  (The number of such challenges is limited.)

*per se*  In or by itself; intrinsically.

**petit jury**  The ordinary *jury* of 12 (or fewer) persons for the trial of a civil or criminal case.

**petitioner**  One who makes formal written application requesting a court for a specific judicial action.  (Often used to refer to appellant.)

*Pike & Fischer's Radio Regulation (R.R. or R.R.2d)*  An unofficial service that publishes Federal Communications Commission rule-making actions and case decisions as well as court decisions relating to the electronic media.

**plaintiff**  A person who brings a civil action.  The party who sues or complains.

**pleading**  The process by which the parties in a suit or action alternately present written statements of their contentions, each responsive to that which precedes and each serving to narrow the field of controversy, until there evolves one or more points, affirmed on one side and denied on the other, called the "issue," upon which they then go to trial.

**pleadings**  The consecutive statements, allegations, and counter allegations made in turn by plaintiff and defendant, or prosecutor and accused, to determine whether any fact disputes require trial.

**plurality opinion**  An *opinion* agreed to by several judges, but not enough to constitute a majority.

**political action committee (PAC)**  Organization established by a corporation, union or others to solicit and spend money on behalf of one or more political candidates.

**precedent**  A judicial decision that may be used as a standard in subsequent similar cases.

**preemption**  The dominating right to do anything, as in instances in which federal law preempts state law.

**prejudicial error**  An error that warrants the appellate court's reversal of the judgment before it.  Synonymous with *reversible error*; opposite of *harmless error*.

**preliminary hearing**  The hearing given a person charged with a crime by a magistrate or judge to determine whether the person should be held for trial.  Synonymous with preliminary examination.

**preponderance of evidence**  The greater weight (in terms of quality, not quantity) of evidence, or that evidence which is more believable and convincing.  (This is the normal standard in civil cases.)

**pretrial hearing**  A hearing held before the beginning of a trial (for example, to determine if a confession or some other evidence should be admitted at the trial).

**previous restraint**  An old term for *prior restraint.*

*prima facie*  At first view.  *Prima facie* evidence is proof of one or more facts that create a presumption of the existence of other facts.

**prior restraint**  Any attempt by courts or another branch of government to stop dissemination of expression; censorship.  (*Prior restraint* contrasts with *subsequent punishment*—dealing with problems after dissemination.)

**privilege**  An advantage; a right to preferential treatment; an exemption from a duty others must perform; the right to speak or write defamatory words because the law allows them in certain circumstances.

**public domain**  The status of publications, products and processes that are not protected under patent or copyright.

**public figure**  In libel, a person who possesses widespread fame or notoriety or who has injected himself or herself into a public controversy with the intent of affecting the outcome of that controversy.

**publication (copyright)**  Offering a book or other thing to the public by sale or distribution.

**publication (defamation)**  Communicating to another person.  (One of the essential elements of a defamation case.)

**puffery**  Salesmanship by a seller that is mere general bragging about what is sold, rather than definite promises about it or intentionally misleading information.

**punitive damages**  Money awarded by a court to a person who has been harmed in a particularly malicious or willful way by another person.  This money is not related to the actual cost of the injury or harm suffered.  Its purpose is to keep that sort of act from happening again by serving as a warning.  It is also called "exemplary damages."

**qualified privilege**  In libel law, a privilege good only in the absence of malice—for example, the privilege to express opinions about public officials.

**reply**  The argument of the plaintiff in answer to that of the defendant.  A pleading in response to an answer.

**remand**  To send back (a case) to a lower court with instructions about further proceedings; the act of remanding.

**reporter's privilege**  See *journalist's privilege.*

**respondent**   The person against whom action or relief is prayed.   The party who answers the petition in a case.

***Restatement of Torts***   Book on tort law put out by the unofficial/private American Law Institute explaining its view of what the law is, how it is changing, and what direction this change should take. (Although the *Restatement* has no official or binding effect, it often influences courts in their decisions.)

**restraining order**   See *temporary restraining order*.

**retraction**   Taking something back; for example, taking back a statement and admitting that it was false.

**reverse**   To revoke or annul (a decision or decree).

**reversible error**   An error that warrants the appellate court's reversal of the judgment before it.   Synonymous with *prejudicial error*.

**right to know**   A "right," often asserted by journalists but infrequently recognized by the courts, to information about the government, its records, its meetings and places.

**right of publicity**   The right of people, particularly celebrities, to control how others use their names or pictures.

**rulemaking**   A formal process of making administrative law used by such agencies as the Federal Communications Commission and the Federal Trade Commission.

*scienter*   Knowingly; with guilty knowledge.

**search warrant**   A written order from a judge or magistrate directing an officer to search a specific place for a specific object.

**seditious libel**   The crime of questioning the wisdom of a ruler's policies.

**sequester**   To isolate or hold aside; to sequester a jury is to keep it from having any contacts with the outside world during all or part of a trial.

**sequestration**   Physically isolating jurors during a trial.

**servicemark**   A legally-protected word, name, symbol or device used to identify a service (similar to a *trademark*, which identifies goods).

**shield law**   A statute under which journalists are entitled to some amount of confidentiality.

*sine qua non*   Indispensable.   That without which something cannot be.

**slander**   Oral defamatory statements injurious to the reputation of a person.

**special damages**   In *libel*, specific provable monetary damages.

*stare decisis*   A doctrine that, when a court has once laid down a principle of law as applicable to a certain set of facts, it will adhere to that principle and apply it to future cases where the facts are substantially the same.

**statute** Specific written law passed by a legislature.

**statute of limitations** A *statute* setting a time limit on enforcement of a right in certain cases.

**statutory law** Law passed by legislative bodies.

**strict liability** The legal responsibility for damages or injury even if the defendant is not at fault or negligent.

*sua sponte* On his or her own will; voluntarily.

*sub nom.* Abbreviation for *sub nomine* or "under the name of"; under the title of. (Indicates that the appeal of a case was decided under a different name from the one used in the lower court decision.)

**subpoena** A process to cause a witness to appear and give testimony before a court or magistrate or in pretrial *discovery*.

**subpoena *duces tecum*** A process by which the court commands a witness to produce certain documents or records in a trial.

**subsequent punishment** Fines, punitive damages or jail terms imposed after dissemination of expression. (Contrast with *prior restraint*.)

**substantiation** Establishment of the existence of something or proof of its truth; verification.

**summary judgment** A judge's ruling that, because there are no fact disputes to be resolved, one party to the lawsuit wins without the need to hold a trial.

*supra* Above or over; preceding.

**Supreme Court of the United States** The highest court in the United States. (Note that the term "U. S. Supreme Court," seen frequently in the media, is technically incorrect.)

**temporary restraining order (TRO)** A judge's order to a person to refrain from taking certain action before a hearing can be held on the question.

**third party** A person unconnected with a deal, lawsuit or occurrence, but who may be affected by it.

**time, place and manner regulation** Regulation of where and when expression is made, as opposed to what is said.

**tort** An injury or civil wrong committed, either with or without force, to the person, property, reputation or privacy of another.

**tortfeasor** A person who commits a tort; a wrongdoer.

**trademark** A legally protected "identifying symbol," such as a word, name, symbol or device for goods.

**trespass**  To invade the property, rights, or person of another without consent and with the actual or implied commission of violence; especially, to enter onto another's land without consent.

**trier of fact**  The person or persons charged with determining the facts in a case. The jury or, in a non-jury trial, the judge.

**unfair competition**  Too closely imitating the name, product or advertising of another company in order to take away its business.

***U.S. Law Week (U.S.L.W.)***  A commercial looseleaf legal service that prints the full text of recent Supreme Court opinions.

**vacate**  To make void; countermand; annul.

**vagueness**  Indefiniteness; uncertainty; imprecision.

**veniremen**  Members of a jury.

**venue**  The particular county, city or geographical area in which a court with jurisdiction may hear and determine a case.

**verdict**  The decision reached by a jury (or judge sitting as the *trier of fact*) at the conclusion of a trial.  (The judge renders a *judgment* after the jury returns its verdict.)

***voir dire***  "To speak the truth."  The preliminary examination of potential jurors.

**writ**  An order issuing from a court and requiring the performance of a specified act or giving authority and commission to have it done.

# INDEX

References are to Pages

†